The Mysterious William Shakespeare

ROBERT BROOKE
"Governor of Virginia, 1794 - 1796"

The Mysterious
William Shakespeare
The Myth and the Reality

CHARLTON OGBURN

Dodd, Mead & Company
New York

Library of Congress Cataloging in Publication Data

Ogburn, Charlton, 1911–
    The mysterious William Shakespeare.

    Bibliography: p.
    Includes index.
    1. Shakespeare, William — Authorship —
Oxford theory. 2. Oxford, Edward de Vere, Earl of, 1550–
1604. 3. Dramatist, English — Early modern, 1500–1700 —
Biography. 4. England — Nobility — Biography. I. Title.
PR2947.O90515 1984   822.3 [B]   84-6084
ISBN 0-396-08441-9

822.33

Grateful acknowledgment is made by the author to *Harper's Magazine* for permission to reprint portions of the article, "Shakespeare's Missing Manuscripts," which appeared in the issue of June, 1972. © 1972 by *Harper's Magazine*. All rights reserved.

For Vera — for the best of reasons

He [Kutuzov] knew how ready men are when they desire anything to manipulate all evidence so as to confirm what they desire; and he knew how readily in that case they let everything of an opposite significance pass unheeded.

— Leo Tolstoi, *War and Peace.*

For truth is truth, though never so old, and time cannot make that false which was once true.

— Edward de Vere.

     For truth is truth
To the end of reckoning.

— William Shakespeare, *Measure for Measure.*

Contents

Contents

Book Two "Is Not Oxford Here Another Anchor?" 405

Illustrations

Foreword

It was over dinner in a Washington restaurant nearly twenty years ago that I first heard Charlton Ogburn talk about the mystery of William Shakespeare. We had met to discuss a book on the geology of North America, a book he was to write and I was to edit. At that point I knew him only as the author of several books I had greatly enjoyed — *The Gold of the River Sea, The Winter Beach* — a writer of intelligence and integrity and wonderful feeling for the natural world. Of his interest in Shakespeare I knew nothing.

But once he got started on the subject, I could hardly let him stop, though until then, like most everybody, I'd been perfectly willing to accept the man from Stratford-on-Avon as the author of the plays and sonnets, and while I knew there were those who raised doubts about that, I imagined they were mostly cranks.

He was absolutely spellbinding. The case he made against the man from Stratford-on-Avon seemed to me astonishing, overwhelming, and the more he went on the more impressed I was by both his penetrating mind and his phenomenal grasp of the subject. He seemed to understand Shakespeare better than anyone I had ever met. I kept thinking what a shame his audience wasn't larger.

Now comes *The Mysterious William Shakespeare* and this brilliant, powerful book is a major event for everyone who cares about Shakespeare. The scholarship is surpassing — brave, original, full of surprise — and in the hands of so gifted a writer it fairly lights up the sky. Looking back on that evening years ago, I feel as if I had been witness to the beginnings of a literary landmark. Nothing comparable has ever been published. Anyone who considers the Shakespeare controversy silly or a lot of old stuff is in for a particular surprise. This is scholarly detective work at its most absorbing. More, it is close analysis by a writer with a rare sense of humanity. The strange, difficult, contradictory man who emerges as the real Shakespeare, Edward de Vere, the 17th Earl of Oxford, is not just plausible but fascinating and wholly believable. It is hard to imagine anyone who reads the book with an open mind ever seeing Shakespeare or his works in the same way again.

That Charlton Ogburn persisted and succeeded in so monumental a task, all alone, without institutional backing, without the support or blessing of academia, makes the accomplishment all the more extraordinary.

David McCullough

"With This Acknowledgment . . ."

Few books owe so much as this one to so many.

In the process of bringing it into being I have looked to Vera as to the alpha and omega. It has been her unenviable lot in the beginning, as a trusted wife, to be the first to read each chapter as it limped from the typewriter and to point out what could be better expressed or would be better not expressed at all. At the end, or near it — the very end would be the proof-reading she would be called upon for — she spent hours upon hours with me in libraries running down quotations so that I could cite page numbers that I had lost or had stupidly neglected to record in my absorption in the chase and verifying those I had obtained at second hand. This meant leafing page by page through many tomes, a job of a magnitude indicated by the number of references under "Citations" at the back of the book, which come to more than 1,500. I might add that despite our best efforts, as an indefatigable student may discover, some sources eluded us to the end; these I hope, perhaps with the help of that same student, to make good in the next edition, in the happy event of there being one.

Fully aware as Vera has been — none more so! — of the complexity and risks of the undertaking, she has never, from the time I began this book more than six years ago, given any indication of wavering in her belief in it, no matter how its end continued to recede and the sacrifices it entailed to multiply.

On the professional side, my indebtedness to a wide range of scholars and critics will be apparent, being undisguised throughout. Among them are many who, to say the least, would not have chosen to contribute; since I could scarcely have done without them, however, a measure of thanks is due them. To the others, going back four centuries, who have marked the way for me, especially my parents, Dorothy and Charlton Ogburn, Sr., my gratitude is immeasurable.

Along the way I have had other invaluable help from the field of scholarship.

It is hard to imagine how research for this book would have progressed but for the resources of the Folger Shakespeare Library, made available with singular helpfulness by its staff, beginning with the director, Dr. O. B. Hardison, and with special assistance from the art advisor, Jean Miller. I have seldom been happier while so cold as in the stacks of the Folger, awaiting resuscitation from hypothermia by tea (coffee if you must) with cookies served upstairs between 3:00 and 3:30.

Other librarians who have gone out of their way to assist me have been H. H. Macmichael of Westminster Abbey, Robin Harcourt Williams of Hatfield House, Herts., Laurence A. Gillam of the Central Library of the London Borough of Hackney, Moira Moles, receptionist (rather than librarian, strictly speaking) of Castle Hedingham in Essex and, inexhaustibly solicitous, if less exotic, the staff of Patrick Henry Library in Vienna, Virginia.

All who have made the Library of Congress what it is deserve the awestruck thanks of every quester after knowledge within the reach of its incomparable collection. Certainly they have mine.

To guide my purblind steps in the field of Elizabethan portraiture, I have had the expert advice, graciously given, of Dr. Roy Strong, Director of the Victoria and Albert Museum, of Robin Gibson of the National Portrait Gallery of London — two who also helped me obtain illustrations for the book — and of Helga Kessler of the Costume Institute, The Metropolitan Museum of Art in New York. For guide services of another kind, to sites in Essex important to this book, my wife and I are glad to thank Harold W. Patience of Braintree and Col. Ian S. Keelun of — fortunate man! — Little Dunmow, also in Essex, on whose motorcar we put much mileage.

It was my good fortune to have Herbert A. Kenny take an early interest in the book, making himself its sponsor and godfather. As I sent him the manuscript by instalments he returned a running commentary, bringing to it the experience of a former editorial writer and literary critic of the Boston *Globe,* a poet and versatile writer of his own books. When, as the months and even years passed and it seemed there could be nobody out in the world whom I was addressing, Herb's was always a reassuring voice from the infinite spaces. He has been a treasured asset.

For a further critical reading of the print-outs and for valuable comments, I offer my thanks to a young poet of Washington, D.C., and keen student of the book's subject, Phillip Proulx.

I have saved till here my recognition of my incalulable obligation to other friends. Its magnitude derives both from their unreserved generosity and from the nature of the book. An author who takes issue with the conventional identification of William Shakespeare is categorized by the powers that be with faddists and cranks, to the peril of his livelihood, unless his literary reputation be solidly based on other grounds. He is likely to embarrass his associates, as if he had decided to stake his all on . . . phrenology! Of those who stand by and behind him from a belief in him or in fair-mindedness, his appreciation is immeasurable.

A book such as this one would have had too little chance in the marketplace to warrant my undertaking it had not its thesis been given an intellectual sanction by publication in a leading article in *Harvard Magazine* prominently reprinted in the *Washington Post*. The first of these remarkable developments I owe to the editorial courage of John T. Bethell, and to the moral backing he had from Philip S. Weld, former president of the *Harvard Alumni Bulletin* (predecessor of the *Magazine*), the second to the breadth of mind of the *Post's* managing editor, Howard Simons. To all three, my most grateful duties.

Even as it was, the book must have been stillborn but for Anne and Philip Weld who, to a career as a widely admired publisher of six New England newspapers, has added another as a dauntless seafarer of unsurpassed skill under sail, capping it with *"Moxie,"* an irresistibly engaging book which recounts with mounting excitement all that led up to his victory in the 1980 *Observer's* Single-Handed Trans-Atlantic Race, in which he was the oldest contestant at 65 and the first American to win it.

To four others also I am immensely indebted for the indispensable support they have given the book:

Harmon Hendricks Goldstone, a leading architect of New York, member for six years of the city's Planning Commission and an admirable activist in civic affairs whose friendship I have counted on for fifty years.

Morse Johnson, an eminent attorney of Cincinnati, the founder and for twelve years the president of Playhouse in the Park — a regional repertory theatre — and a highly effective advocate for the case advanced in the pages that follow.

Merrill Windsor, Managing Editor, Special Publications Division, National Geographic Society, and one of its authors who has made the assignments I have had from the Society even pleasanter and more rewarding.

Fielding Ogburn, still to me my young cousin Billy rather than an honored chemist at the National Bureau of Standards, whose family loyalty has never been contingent upon my being able to understand his works.

For continuing encouragement along the way, I am fortunate in being able to thank David Lloyd Kreeger — a source as well of sound advice — whose contributions to the cultural life of the national capital in the fields of music, painting, and the theatre have been a major factor in its rise to artistic eminence; and Rosalee and David McCullough, whose four books (so far) re-investing with life the casts of salient chapters of our country's past have won large and enthusiastic audiences and more awards than I can keep up with, and for good reason.

Two whose cooperation has been of great value and to whom I am correspondingly grateful, are Professor Gordon C. and Helen Cyr of the Shakespeare-Oxford Society, of Baltimore, both experts in this field.

George Stevens, former vice president and editor-in-chief at J. B. Lippincott and editor of the *Saturday Review of Literature,* author of a biography of

"With This Acknowledgment . . ."

John Mason Brown and withal my mother's much younger brother, calls for special mention. Having put my career in writing on the rails to begin with over thirty years ago, he was the first to read this manuscript in its finally-evolved form, and the opinion he voiced of it brought with it a feeling of relief on my part such as he and I almost alone have full reason to appreciate the magnitude thereof.

Because if the book succeeds half way in doing justice to its subject, it will be as worthy of their memories as any platform for the purpose I am likely to achieve, I take the occasion it offers to express my undying gratitude to my late aunt and uncle, Isabel Stevens and Wilfrid McN. Knapp of Savannah, through whose generosity I was spared burdens that must have crushed my family and me and deprived me of the chance to write the book. That I was not irrevocably prevented from doing so, my thanks, as unreserved as may be imagined, must go to Alan Mackintosh and Myron P. Berger, M.D.'s both, and able ones, of Fairfax County, Virginia.

Charlton Ogburn

Beaufort, South Carolina,
October 1983.

"If Thou Read This . . ."

The attribution of the poems and dramas known as William Shakespeare's to the man christened William Shaksper, or Shakspere, at Stratford-upon-Avon rests on certain pointed but ambivalent statements made half-a-dozen years after his death. Before then, readers may be surprised to discover, the only indications we have that such a man was proposed as the author take the form of ridicule of the idea. One particularly curious circumstance may be cited here in justification of the quest for the man who was Shakespeare in which I hope to interest the reader: that is the wholesale, evidently selective disappearance, hardly to be explained as accidental, of records that might be expected to throw light on the object of the quest. It is this circumstance that from the beginning has baffled and frustrated investigation — and given rise to the Shakespeare Problem.

Interest in facts about the author's life seems to have been slight for a century after its end. Samuel Pepys, for example, in the famous diary he kept between 1660 and 1669, records his attendance at thirty-eight performances of Shakespeare's plays and mentions the dramatist's name in connection with only one of them. As curiosity about the dramatist began to grow in the 18th century, so, before long, did doubts about the Stratford man's authorship. These proved persistent and irrepressible — for efforts to repress them have not been lacking. A vigorous and acrimonious controversy over the issue is now in its second century, leaving deposits of scores of millions of printed words. There has been, so far as I know, nothing like it in history. And it has left the disputants as far apart as ever.

Another disquisition on the question of Shakespeare's identity would seem unlikely to be more fruitful than its predecessors. However, I should not have undertaken this book had I not reason to believe that it could lead to a resolution of the issue. I knew a book with that capability would be a large order, for it would have to leave no aspect of the case uncovered, no significant facts unaccounted for; it could take no chances. I did not foresee, though, what a large order it would prove to be.

If I thought the book I planned could succeed where others had failed, it was not, certainly, from any illusion that my powers of intellect gave me an advantage. The reason was that I had been close to the controversy for many years: the roots of this book go back over four decades. I felt I had come to see why earlier treatments of the question had proved ineffective.

"If Thou Read This . . ."

My acquaintance with the orthodox literature was wide. I knew every piece of evidence the Stratfordians could adduce to support their case, and I must have heard every argument. Plainly the evidence was insufficient, the case too weak, to allay the skepticism with which unnumbered thousands devoted to Shakespeare have regarded the credentials of the Stratford man. Among these are formidable figures. Disbelief, in our country, goes back at least to Walt Whitman, John Greenleaf Whittier, Mark Twain, and Henry James, if not to Ralph Waldo Emerson. I could see no resolution of the dispute in favor of the Stratford man without new documentary evidence unequivocally linking him with the authorship, and the facts in the case convinced me that no such evidence would be forthcoming unless it were forged — not that forgery to supplement the meagre remainders of the Stratford man would be anything new; William Henry Ireland at the end of the 18th century and John Payne Collier a generation later were sedulous counterfeiters.

Yet, statements of the case against the Stratford-man theory have lacked what is necessary to overcome the advantages of an established tradition with a body of supporters determined to defend their interest in its perpetuation. Too many statements of the case against the Stratford man have been marred by irrationality. As we may learn from any police department or newspaper city-room, a highly publicized and unsolved crime is certain to bring forth "solutions" urged by unfortunates whose obsessive susceptibilities outpace their reason. (That does not mean, however, that no crime has been committed.) The eccentricities of a minority of anti-Stratfordians have tended to bring discredit upon responsible dissent, or have been used to discredit it. In order to establish the case against the Stratford man, the great need, to begin with, has been to do more than expose the foundations of the Stratford case as unconvincing. A believable alternative had to be offered. The need was met in 1920, as I hope to show, with the publication by a British schoolmaster of the results of a methodical, objective investigation of the field — strangely, the first undertaken. *"Shakespeare" Identified* established a candidate for the poet-dramatist's laurels who appeared to meet the criteria without disqualifications. The book made exciting reading for many. Since then numerous other researchers have enlarged upon the case presented in the — to me — brilliant pioneer study. They have done much to fill the framework and make it, in my view, even more persuasive. Investigation has gone a long way in sixty years.

As I saw it, however, a more compelling presentation of the case could be made than in any of the score of books on the subject. It would, for one thing, have the help of the books that had preceded it and of the journals of two societies concerned with the Shakespeare authorship, one British, one American, that over the years had brought out articles on new and important discoveries. From my own reading I felt I could throw further light on the subject. The opportunity beckoned to present a much greater range and depth of evidence than that contained in any other work.

No less important was the opportunity to repair what I saw as a fatal deficiency of earlier books, including one of which I was part author. All were vulnerable to a demurrer by critics — by those whose backing was essential if a fair hearing of the case was to be had. Of all it could be objected that, "Yes, what you say sounds convincing, but you have argued only one side of a question I am not fully up on. The experts on the subject — the scholars in the universities — have gone over all the evidence thoroughly and have decided against you. They say there is no possible doubt that the Stratford man wrote the works of Shakespeare."

The book I had in mind would allow the critics no such way out. I could not pretend to have made Shakespeare my life work. No one I knew of, however, was as steeped as I in the methods practiced by the academic authorities in meeting challenges to the possession of the high ground they enjoyed by consent of critics, editors, journalists, professors, heads of philanthropic foundations, and, apparently, a determining part of the reading public. One of their weapons was to attack the character and motives, even the sanity, of dissenters. I meant to try not to reply in kind. One of my points would be that *argumentum ad hominem,* while often effective and difficult to combat, does not much advance anyone's understanding of the issues and is the resort, usually, of those unable to defend their case on its merits. What I could do and would do was to put the orthodox academicians on record at every turn and contrast their claims with the facts. I knew the academicians well enough to have little doubt that if their animadversions were matched against those facts they would never again be cited as authorities by anyone with a respect for evidence and reason. It might require considerable illustration to convince reluctant readers, but I had much to draw upon — more than I could find place for.

By putting the leading spokesmen for orthodoxy on the witness stand, I thought, another essential end could be gained. Orthodoxy's first line of defense against dissent is to ignore it. I believed that a book in which the most respected and best-known professionals in the field of Shakespearean letters were held to account for their statements would find its way through any barriers of silence erected against it. Among such savants I include those prominent in the university world, those whose biographies of the conventional Shakespeare are book-club selections, those who appear in magazines and newspapers as august authorities.

Having defeated censorship by disregard — if it had — the book could expect to encounter the second line of defense: counterattack with no weapons barred. If it was to succeed it must be proof against the onslaught.

Obviously it was going to contain mistakes; no book could retail so much information and not slip up here or there on peripheral facts, and such lapses would be pounced on by its adversaries; the reader would have to be relied on for a sense of perspective. On issues that counted, however, the presentation would have to be impregnable. Rebuttals of every significant assault that could be made upon it would have to be built into it. Parenthetically I might add that if past experience was any guide, the book would be misrepresented in its totality in some quarters. That could not be prevented — unless by my confessing to a decision I have been too long in coming to, that the victim of purposed and malignant misrepresentation should forget about standing on his dignity (no one will notice) and take legal action. Finally, the book would have to cover points I might feel could be passed over without loss lest I invite too often that query from hostile critics, "Has the author never heard of such and such?"

In other words, the prescription was for a thorough treatment. The book was not going to be brief, even as it dealt with the Stratford theory alone, quite apart from its exploration of the alternative. The United States government, in support of its suit against IBM for violation of the Sherman Anti-Trust Act, produced about 26 million pages of documents, IBM in its defense about 56 million, and the trial lasted three years. We are not, at any rate, talking of anything on that scale, though the orthodox establishment we are putting on trial has long maintained a monopoly in its field that Standard Oil in its heyday could have saluted. The book will, however, make demands on the reader and try him with rather tedious going in stretches; such is true of some of the most important trials at court. Look at this as a work of detection, not a detective novel in which the author can manipulate the elements for the sake of easy readability, but detective work as it is in real life, entailing much leg-work, the investigation of many documents, and the examination of many witnesses. Recognize at the same time that its aim is not to convict the guilty in some mere mundane infraction of the law but to determine the rightful possessor of the grandest title perhaps ever in dispute — claim to the authorship of our society's greatest written masterpieces — and in doing so solve what is probably the outstanding mystery extant apart from the field of the sciences. We shall be engaged in the greatest manhunt in history and, too, in an intellectual adventure equalled by none I know of.

We shall be establishing, with as near an approach to certainty as the evidence permits, who Shakespeare was, and we shall also be making the more important discovery of what he was. The rewards will not stop with the solution of a mystery. Others await our rereading of Shakespeare's poems and plays in the light of our new knowledge — knowledge I feel will soon be enlarged if some part of the research effort and funds devoted in the past to the investigation of the Stratford man are given a more fruitful application.

To have the curtain lifted, finally, upon the reality of Shakespeare amounts to the discovery in the world of literature of a new continent of inexhaustible wealth. Its exploration will justify any efforts exacted of us and offer each of us the chance to help bring more of the continent within our ken, to help map the terrain — that is, to extend our knowledge of the relationship between the man who was Shakespeare and his works.

A word as to the plan of attack in what follows:

The reader will find that there are actually two books. In *Book One* we confront the blank in the record of Elizabethan times where we should look for Shakespeare the man and the curious nature of the contemporary references his works elicited. We review the grooming of Shakspere of Stratford for the part and then proceed to scrutinize, element by element, the case the orthodox scholars have built up for him. Finding in the process why so many readers have been left dissatisfied, we then examine the qualifications of the other candidates who have been put forward, ending with the one on whom dissent has come chiefly to focus. We turn to the embattled response of orthodoxy to the challenge and, to play fair with the reader, I explain my association with the controversy over the authorship. The balance of the book is given over to deducing from Shakespeare's works what the characteristics of the author must have been and the nature of his experiences; all of this is found consistent with the man who had previously seemed the one convincing candidate and confirms him as uniquely fitting the role of Shakespeare.

In *Book Two* we follow the life of this man as well as it is known, in his relationships with others and against the background of his times. We are rewarded, as we proceed, by accumulating evidence that it was out of these elements that the poems and plays we know as Shakespeare's took form and, incidentally, by discovering some other works not known as such that seem also to have been written by Shakespeare.

Because there is such a great deal of ground to be covered, I have preceded each chapter with a summary of its contents. At the cost, it may be, of conjuring up an uninviting textbookish image, the previews — which the reader may ignore — serve as maps of the terrain ahead and should make it easier to locate any parts to which the reader may wish to revert.

The multiplicity of statements by other writers I have quoted raised the question of how to cite their sources for the interested specialist. Not to put the general reader off with swarms of those little super-lineal, or exponential, numbers at the ends of the quotations, of which there would be, on the average, forty to a chapter, I decided to omit these altogether and rely instead upon a few words descriptive of the quotation, these identifying tags, each preceded by the number of the page on which the quotation occurs, to be set forth serially in the back of the book in the section headed "Citations."

Thus, for example, anyone wishing to know the source of the quotation from Marchette Chute on page 196, that whereas "Meres mentioned a great many playwrights in his book, . . . Shakespeare was the only one he singled out for extended comment," may run down the Citations to 196 and the notation: "Meres's singling out Shakespeare for extended comment: Chute 179." That will tell him that the remark quoted will be found on page 179 of the work cited in the Bibliography under Chute, Marchette, namely, *Shakespeare of London*. New York: Dutton, 1949.

Recalling the dedication of the *Sonnets,* let me wish well the adventurer in setting forth.

Book One

"The Cause and Question Now in Hand"

I

"A Mystery? Ay, Sir, a Mystery"

To begin with: Of Shakespeare's preeminent genius there can be no doubt. We find it commanding an interest among readers and theatregoers that grows only keener with the passage of time, to our own day. We find Shakespeare eliciting tributes surpassing those given any other writer. Yet we find that doubts persist as to who he was. Surely a poet-dramatist of such incomparable powers, whose works enjoyed outstanding popularity during his life and delighted two monarchs, would be a familiar figure to many of his contemporaries. Surely, like other lesser writers, he would be known to us today for the part he played in the literary and intellectual life of his times. But does anyone identified as Shakespeare the writer ever put in an appearance? Does anyone during the years when he is alive ever claim to know him? Why should Shakespeare's name as that of a dramatist never appear in print or even be heard, so far as we can tell, until fifteen or sixteen of the plays we know as his have appeared, when suddenly he is hailed as the best of his nation in both comedy and tragedy? And why should such well-deserved acclaim not be voiced again for a quarter of a century? We shall look into these puzzles and into some notable instances of Shakespeare's nonappearance where we should expect him, and ask ourselves how the dramatist could satirize the Queen's most powerful councillor under an implied claim to royal protection.

Between 1594 and 1598, six plays destined for immortality were printed and sold in London by piratical publishers. They were the plays we know as *Henry the Sixth, Parts One* and *Two, Richard the Third, Titus Andronicus, Romeo and Juliet,* and *Richard the Second.* Doubtless all had also been performed on the stage. In addition, other plays, similarly destined for immortality, which, it was to transpire, were by the same hand, had been performed on the stage without being printed — probably to the number of ten at least. But whether printed or only performed, whether entered in the Stationers' Register (the nearest equivalent to copyright), they appeared with no author's name associated with them. Who had written them? On that point, the record of those years is silent.

But then in 1598 Francis Meres, a Master of Arts of Oxford and Cambridge, published a volume of anecdotes, similes, allusions, and sayings called *Palladis Tamia* in which, in a section comparing English and classical poets, he wrote:

> As Plautus and Seneca are accounted the best for comedy and tragedy among the Latins: so Shakespeare among the English is the most excellent in both kinds for the stage.

In support of this claim he named six comedies of Shakespeare's and six of his tragedies, including four of those cited above. (Unless my reading is at fault, only two other plays by an English playwright were named, both by Dr. Leg. The honor eluded even Marlowe, not to mention Kyd and Lyly.) And so with the first known mention of Shakespeare as a playwright, he has already produced at least fourteen plays — other evidence would raise the number to sixteen — and is being hailed as the best of his nation in both categories of drama. That their author had never previously been named, so far as we know, is the more surprising in that the name "William Shakespeare" was already well known. It had been signed to the dedication to the Earl of Southampton of two long, extremely popular narrative poems published respectively in 1593 and 1594, the only works by "Shakespeare" ever published by himself. Francis Meres paid a tribute to these, too, declaring that "the sweet witty soul of Ovid lives in mellifluous & honey-tongued Shakespeare, witness his *Venus and Adonis,* his *Lucrece,* his sugared *Sonnets* among his private friends, &c." A publisher got hold of two of the sonnets and brought them out in an anthology of poetry in the next year (1599). Thereafter nothing was heard of them until *Shake-speare's Sonnets* to the number of 154 — a deeply emotional and disturbing account of the poet's love for a beautiful young man and an unworthy woman — were published in 1609 with a dedication by the printer indicating that the author was dead. After 1598, when Meres published his *Palladis Tamia,* in which the dramatist for the first time we know of was called "Shakespeare," it was the rule for plays of Shakespeare to appear under his name until thirty-seven or more had been given to the world.

And what plays came from that hand! In words matchless in their magic, the dramatist scaled the heights and plumbed the depths of human experience and could, without too great exaggeration, be said to have first given shape to the human race as we know it in his throng of characters. He shows us people who are gay and debonair, playful and elfin, sharp-tongued and witty; he shows us irresistible — or murderous — womanhood, eloquent as none of our race has been before or since; he shows us people transfigured and transported by love or by jealousy, debilitated by doubt or suiting action to the word with passion that sears the page, consumed by greed and steeped in incomparable villainy. In short, he shows us men and women uncontainably human, who, after nearly four centuries, people the cosmos of educated persons throughout the English-speaking world and beyond. Such was the genius behind these poems and dramas that Thomas De Quincey could assess Shakespeare's "station in literature" as "now irrevocably settled . . . by those who everywhere seek for his works among the primal necessities of life," Thomas Carlyle own to feeling "that there is actually a kind of sacredness in the fact of such a man being sent to this Earth," Heinrich Heine be moved to declare, "Look you, the good God himself naturally has a right to the first place, but the second certainly belongs to Shakespeare," and Algernon Charles Swinburne exclaim of him that:

> There is one book in the world of which it might be affirmed and argued, without fear of derision from any but the supreme and crowning fools among the foolishest of mankind, that it would be better for the world to lose all others and keep this one than to lose this and keep all other treasures bequeathed by human genius to all that we can conceive of eternity — to all that we can imagine of immortality. That book is best known, and best described for all of us, simply by the simple English name of its author. The word Shakespeare connotes more than any other man's name that ever was written or spoken upon earth.

These are extreme-sounding words. Yet it is true that the vitality of Shakespeare's art and the meaning he has for us, matchless among literary works of the past, seem never to diminish. If anything, his appeal grows; certainly our interest in him never flags. The Shakespeare Annotated World Bibliography for 1979 printed in the Folger Library's *Shakespeare Quarterly* lists 2,859 published items — articles and books — reported by a Committee of Correspondents from 25 nations. "Nor," Louis Marder observed in 1963, "should we forget that the plays have now been translated into 68 languages, whose new readers have become as idolatrous as those of the English-speaking world." Other statistics that Professor Marder reports are that the Shakespeare Memorial Library of Birmingham had by 1959 come to include 37,000 volumes, and among the tens of thousands in the Folger Shakespeare Library of Washington, D.C., are 1,300 different complete editions of Shakespeare, 800 editions of *Hamlet,* and 500 of *Macbeth.*

In collections of quotations, Shakespeare has no competitor. The 1980 edition of *Bartlett's Familiar Quotations* contains 85 pages of Shakespeare as against 47½ of the Bible (the work of a congeries of writers), 9 of Milton, 7½ of Tennyson, 7 of Emerson, and between 6 and 6¾ each of Byron, Coleridge, and Wordsworth. In the 1955 edition of the *Oxford Dictionary of Quotations,* with smaller type, there are 66 pages of Shakespeare to 28 of the Bible, 13½ of Tennyson, 13 of Milton, and 11 of Kipling.

In *Paperback Parnassus,* Roger H. Smith reports that only one category of books in this mass market outsells books by or about Shakespeare — manuals to help applicants pass civil service tests. Far from supplanting him, the motion pictures and television have merely given Shakespeare more worlds to conquer. The production by the B.B.C. of all thirty-seven plays in the canon for television beginning in 1979 is probably the greatest Shakespearean event since the first collected edition of the plays was put out in 1623 and of course far surpasses any tribute of the kind so far paid to any other writer. Moreover, it is perhaps especially illustrative of Shakespeare's reach into our souls that he has inspired more music than anyone else who has ever lived, at least in the West. In addition to innumerable musical settings given his works, Berlioz, Mendelssohn, Verdi, Tschaikovsky, and Prokofiev have been among those who have turned his dramas into major musical compositions.

Given the towering place of Shakespeare in our culture, it would be utterly incredible, if we did not know it to be so, that the most fundamental question should arise about him:

Who was he?

The record of the years when he must have been alive has been combed without turning up one reference to him that connects the name with any flesh-and-blood human being. Of course, a number of mentions of William Shakespeare the poet-dramatist appear on the record of those years, but beyond commenting briefly and favorably on his writing, they tell us almost nothing about him and identify him with no recognizable person. Here the reader will, of course, think of the man born and buried in Stratford-on-Avon. There is no suggestion in the record of these years, however, that he was the author. Quite the contrary — as we shall see. Indeed, I know of none before 1623, the year when for the first time the world learned explicitly that he was dead, which tells us anything at all — with one small exception. In 1610 a few lines of verse by John Davies told us that had "Shake-speare . . . not played some kingly parts in sport" he "would have been a companion for a King." A disclosure as important as this seems to be makes us regret all the more that it is unique.

But if there are no other references during those years — the years when he must have been alive — to tell us anything whatever about him as a man, surely the references to William Shakespeare, the disembodied poet-drama-tist, must show that his contemporaries were aware that a great genius was among them. Oddly enough, no. This circumstance is particularly puzzling since we have it later from Ben Jonson, his fellow playwright, that he had delighted the two monarchs reigning during his lifetime — neither of whom is known ever to have spoken the name Shakespeare.

A century ago C. M. Ingleby, LL.D., took it upon himself to spend two years going through the "obsolete or obsolescent literature" of the years 1591 to 1693 in order to "execute a complete catena of extracts relating to one man," as he puts it. The compendium, entitled *Shakespeare's Centurie of Prayse,* was published in 1874. In the "Forespeech" Ingleby wrote: "The draft of his plays was in a manner intelligible, or they would not have been entertaining, to the penny-knaves who pestered the Globe and Blackfriars Theatres. But his profound reach of thought and his unrivaled knowledge of human nature were as far beyond the vulgar ken, as were the higher graces of his poetry. It is to men of sensibility and education that Shakespeare appeals as a man of genius; and it is to the literate class we must look for the impress of that genius." Having looked, Ingleby came to a startling conclusion: "It is plain . . . that the bard of our admiration was unknown to the men of that age." His explanation was that "no one during the 'Centurie' had any suspicion that the genius of Shakespeare was unique, and that he was *sui generis,* that is, the only exemplar of his species."

You do not have to look very far for evidence that Ingleby was led by the shock of his discovery to overstate his case. Indeed, a present-day scholar, Louis Marder of the University of Illinois, working on the same available material, comes to a diametrically opposed conclusion. He bases his judgment in part on the success of Shakespeare's works. He points out that while the author was still alive, *Venus and Adonis* went through seven editions and *The Rape of Lucrece* five and states that fourteen of his plays were published.

Ingleby takes no account of the popularity of the plays, or does so only to write: "If, as Mr. Charles Knight concludes, 'he was *always* in the heart of the people,' that fact speaks more for Shakespeare as a showman than for Shakespeare as a man of genius. Doubtless he knew his men; but assuredly his men did not know him." That was a bit too much even for the editor of the second edition of Dr. Ingleby's work. Invoking "the immense popularity of his dramas in a play-going age," she asserts that "Hamlet, Richard III, Falstaff, and Justice Shallow rapidly attained a personality among the people" as "is amply shown by the allusions."

If that is so, it makes the dearth of commensurate praise of the dramatist all the more peculiar. For I believe very few scholars would go along with Professor Marder when he asserts that "the poet's reputation was as great while he was alive as it is in our own day," if we are to judge by the record. He says that "by the first years of the 17th century Shakespeare had been eulogized in sonnets, alluded to in poetry, praised in prose, commented on in the margins of books, referred to in plays, and anthologized in books of quotations." But if the reader will look up Professor Marder's references I believe he will find, as others have, that they add up to surprisingly paltry recognition of the dramatist. His judgment will be, I have little doubt, that Dr. Ingleby was much nearer the mark than Dr. Marder and that Emerson was not far from it when he remarked on "the absence of all contemporary panegyric."

Absence, that is, until 1623. In that year Ben Jonson delivered a panegyric on Shakespeare that was all Emerson could have looked for. It was an astonishing and dramatic development. Declaring of his "beloved" that he "did so take Eliza[beth] and our James," he hailed Shakespeare in a poem of eighty lines as the soul of the age and Britain's triumph. Probably no other writer in history has received such a tribute from the pen of a fellow.[1]

---

[1] Passages quoted from the First Folio may be found in the first eleven pages of the Folio in either of the two facsimiles cited in the Bibliography.

Here is something extraordinary to take note of, then: Shakespeare the dramatist is ushered in by Meres's calling him his country's best, and ushered out by Jonson's calling him unsurpassed not only by his own countrymen but by "all, that insolent Greece or haughty Rome sent forth" — while no one in between speaks of him in terms in the least comparable. We may ask ourselves, to begin with, which represented the estimate in which Shakespeare was held by his contemporaries — the superlatives of Meres and Jonson or the reserve of others in between? It is the question that divides Dr. Ingleby and Dr. Marder, though neither seems to have considered it, as we have formulated it.

I think we have to recognize that Jonson would never have lauded Shakespeare as he did had he not felt safe in doing so. He must have been confident that he would not be making himself ridiculous, that the exalted opinion of the dramatist he was expressing was shared by others. And how could it help being so? A genius that is obvious to us could hardly have been wholly hidden from the cultivated persons who made the Elizabethan age synonymous with an outpouring of poetry, drama, and music and with a passionate response to life and the world around. It is scarcely conceivable that they could have failed to appreciate in Shakespeare the supreme voice of their generation — the soul of their age.

If such be the case — and I do not see how it could be otherwise — how did it happen that recognition of the greatness of the plays was so inadequately voiced except upon the dramatist's entrance upon the scene and upon his final departure from it? Obviously the question takes us deep into the mystery of William Shakespeare.

If only one might go back for half a day to Elizabethan London and ask such writers-about-town as Gabriel Harvey, Thomas Nashe, and, above all, Ben Jonson for light upon the mystery! As it is, we must make do with the sparse, fragmentary, and elusive testimony of those who chose to put pen to paper and whose words have not been lost. If, seeking an answer to the question we have raised, we examine the early allusions to Shakespeare, we find two odd references that may barely have made it into the record and yet may tell us much. One consists of two entries inscribed by a diarist who could have had no idea of the importance his casual jottings might have someday. The other was a versifier who knew well the importance of what he was saying; he was addressing himself directly to the mystery and must have hesitated long before doing so and thus coming close to violating a taboo as he evidently considered it.

John Manningham, the diarist, was a barrister-at-law of the Middle Temple. In his diary for 13 March 1602, he made a reference to Shakespeare that is highly exceptional in that it relates an anecdote about him, the only one, in fact, that has come down to us from his lifetime. The anecdote is, however, merely a joke and almost certainly fictitious, and it does not imply that Shakespeare was a writer or anything else — though it does recall to us the Shakespeare who played kingly parts in sport. Manningham wrote:[2]

> Upon a time when Burbage played Richard III there was a citizen grew so far in liking with him that before she went from the play she appointed him to come that night unto her by the name of Richard the Third. Shakespeare, overhearing their conclusion, went before, was entertained, and at his game ere Burbage came. The message being brought that Richard the Third was at the door, Shakespeare caused return to be made that William the Conqueror was before Richard the Third. Shakespeare's name William.

Two points about the entry are of interest. The first is that, at a time when Shakespeare's plays were in the full tide of their success, Manningham had to remind himself, so that the point of the story would not be lost, that Shakespeare's first name was William. He did not have to remind himself that Burbage's was Richard. More striking still, it clearly did not occur to him that a play he had seen at a feast and described in his diary for February 2nd, *Twelfth Night,* was by Shakespeare. And Manningham was a perceptive playgoer with a literary bent. Likening *Twelfth Night* to *A Comedy of Errors,* but making no mention of Shakespeare in connection with either, he derived the latter, quite correctly, from the *Manaechmi* of Plautus, then observed that *Twelfth Night* was "most like and near to that in Italian called *Inganni.*"

If Manningham's diary is any indication, audiences were seeing Shakespeare's plays without taking in whose they were and his name was simply not widely known as that of a playwright. Necessarily, however, the small literary minority who bought printed plays would at least have been better informed. If they were backward in rendering his genius the tributes that were its due, the second reference to Shakespeare of which I spoke above would suggest that the cause was not any lack of appreciation of what they were hearing or reading but an inhibition about expressing that appreciation. *Wits Recreation* of 1640 contained an anonymous epigram reading:

> *To Mr. William Shake-spear*
> Shake-speare, we must be silent in thy praise,
> 'Cause our encomions will but blast thy bays
> Which envy could not, that thou didst so well;
> Let thine own histories prove thy Chronicle.

It is difficult to divine the writer's meaning. Why should praise destroy Shakespeare's fame where envy of his having done so well could not? What a pity the logic of the warning is so elusive! The last line of the quatrain seems clear enough, and is of great value if we wish to learn more of Shakespeare: his life story is to be learned from his plays. And the nature of the injunction laid down in the first line is also plain: when it came to praising Shakespeare his admirers had reason to be silent. Whatever the

---

[2] I shall make it a practice to modernize the spelling of Elizabethan texts throughout except for proper names and titles and in special circumstances.

reason, it evidently carried weight. Praise, on the whole, was muted. And it may be worth noting that of the 104 entries in the *Centurie of Prayse* up to 1623 that Ingleby includes as allusions to Shakespeare, only twenty-six mention his name, though several others use his initials.

If there ever was an occasion in Elizabethan times when the authorship of a play should have attracted attention and the author's name been heard resoundingly, it was in February 1601, just a year before Manningham saw *Twelfth Night*. On that occasion a play entered upon the stage of state affairs after it had entered many times upon the stage of the theatre, and the play was one of Shakespeare's. On the eighth of the month the Earl of Essex sought to rouse the populace in his cause against the aging Queen and regain his lost position at Court. To prepare the public mind the plotters paid the Lord Chamberlain's men, whose distinction it was to present Shakespeare's plays, to perform the tragedy of *Richard the Second,* which tells of the deposition of a predecessor of Elizabeth on the afternoon preceding the fateful evening (though evidently the play was not given). The populace failed to rise and the rebellious Earl at length surrendered and was condemned to death. An investigation into the scheduling of the play was held, however. Sir Gelly Meyricke, testifying as one of the plotters, spoke of *Richard the Second*. Representing the Lord Chamberlain's men, Augustine Phillips stated that he and his fellows had not wished to play *Richard the Second,* which was an old play and would attract "small or no company," but they had acquiesced on receiving 40 shillings more than ordinary. Francis Bacon recapitulated the testimony as prosecutor for the Crown, again speaking of *Richard the Second*. But none of them made any mention of an author. None spoke of Shakespeare.

Nor did Elizabeth in commenting bitterly on the play six months afterwards. The Queen was receiving from William Lambarde, Keeper of the Records of the Tower, his "Pandecta" of her documents. Lambarde wrote that in going over the rolls "her Majesty fell upon the reign of King Richard II, saying 'I am Richard II, know ye not that?'" Lambarde replied: "Such a wicked imagination was determined and attempted by a most unkind Gent. the most adorned creature that ever your Majesty made." Lambarde was presumably referring to the Earl of Essex, but Elizabeth, at least, was evidently thinking about the play and its author. "He that will forget God," she exclaimed, "will also forget his benefactors; this tragedy was played 40^{tie} times in open streets and houses" — an offense hardly chargeable against Essex, who was certainly, moreover, never accused of having forgotten God.

If Elizabeth deemed herself portrayed as Richard II, she might well complain that a play about that unhappy monarch's fate had been performed forty times before the public (which, by the way, attests to the popularity of Shakespeare's plays). But why had she stood for it? Tudor monarchs were anything but powerless to determine the theatrical fare of their subjects. The jail awaited any playwright or actor who gave offense. Thomas Nashe was incarcerated for his *Isle of the Dogs* and the play obliterated. Here we are with further mystery. The Lord Chamberlain's men remained in the Queen's good graces — they were playing at Court in the month after the aborted rebellion — and the author, it seems, escaped any attention whatever. What are we to make of it? To present the deposition of a British monarch in a play was a criminal offense. For that matter, portraying a contemporary figure as a character on the stage was also enough to bring the playwright before the Star Chamber. Yet, as few would deny, not just *a* person, but William Cecil, Lord Burghley, Elizabeth's high and mighty Lord Treasurer, was lampooned as Polonius in *Hamlet.* And the play was not seized and destroyed, the author not taken into custody. Burghley was, it is true, dead when *Hamlet* was printed, but his son, Robert Cecil, Elizabeth's secretary, himself portrayed in part as Laertes, was anything but powerless. Far from coming under court edict, *Hamlet* was printed in quarto with the royal coat-of-arms on the first page.

Writing a hundred years ago of the allusions to Shakespeare collected by Ingleby, Frederick G. Fleay observed, "They consist almost entirely of slight references to his published works, and have no bearing of importance on his career. Nor, indeed, have we extended material of any kind to aid us in this investigation; one source of information, *which is abundant for most of his contemporaries,* being in his case entirely absent. [My italics.] Neither as addressed to him by others, nor by him to others, do any commendatory verses exist in connection with any of his or other men's works published in his lifetime — a notable fact, in whatever way it may be explained."

Shakespeare proved to be the exception again when he died without the tribute paid him of the elegiac verses that poets at the time habitually indited upon the passing of one of their fellows. So far as the record shows, the death of the greatest of them all went unremarked, by them or anyone else. Shakespeare's departure from the scene was as silent and mysterious as his arrival upon it had been. He was like a ship that approaches out of the fog, gradually taking shape, is for a while dimly to be perceived, and then, even as one is looking, has vanished. But in his passage, he had left the world such creations of language as had never before and perhaps never would again come from one human mind.

"It is a great comfort, to my way of thinking, that so little is known concerning the poet," Charles Dickens wrote. "The life of Shakespeare is a fine mystery and I tremble every day lest something should turn up."

Not everyone can entertain so benign an indifference to, and not feel the urge to resolve, if possible, the unique mystery enveloping the literary genius whose works, in Emerson's estimate, come "only just within the possibility of authorship."

2

"Cry Out Thus upon No Trail"

What is the origin of the belief that the immortal William Shakespeare was the man christened William Shakspere in Stratford-on-Avon in 1564? We find it in two or three remarks dropped in the prefatory verses of the first published collection of Shakespeare's plays, the First Folio of 1623. The question then arises as to how biographers of Shakespeare get from those slender beginnings to the book-length accounts of today. As we see in this chapter, two generations after the First Folio is given to the world, a gossipy fellow named John Aubrey scribbled a sketch of the Stratfordian "Shakespeare," to be followed a generation later still by a short "life" appended by Nicholas Rowe to an edition of Shakespeare's plays he is bringing out; and we take due note of what they say. This lode of information leads us to the crux of the matter: how is it that the more we learn of the Stratfordian the greater grow the apparent discrepancies between him and the dramatist as we should deduce him to have been? To bring these to a head we have the first biographical notes recorded about "Shakespeare" — those set down by a rector of the church at Stratford twenty years before Aubrey took the subject in hand — which offer a hint as to where the solution to the mystery is to be sought. The problem is set forth succinctly for us by a lawyer. To finesse it by subterfuge is, we find, of the essence in the Stratford theory.

The full greatness of what Shakespeare had wrought was for the first time revealed to the world in 1623, in our civilization's outstanding literary event. In that year there burst upon the world, published in folio, *Mr. William Shakespeares Comedies Histories & Tragedies,* containing thirty-six plays, all but one (*Pericles*) of those customarily attributed to Shakespeare, twenty of them never before printed, including three that had apparently never even been heard of before (*Timon of Athens, Coriolanus,* and *All's Well That Ends Well*). The First Folio, as it has come to be called (three others were to follow), was dedicated *To the most noble and Incomparable Paire of Brethren, William Earle of Pembroke, &c. Lord Chamberlaine to the Kings most Excellent Majesty. and Philip Earle of Montgomery, &c. Gentlemen of his Majesties Bed-Chamber. Both Knights of the most Noble Order of the Garter, and our singular good Lords.* Presumably it was the two Earls who had defrayed the very heavy costs of the publication.

The dedicatory epistle and a further letter *To the great Variety of Readers* are signed by two of the former Lord Chamberlain's players, John Heminge and Henry Condell. Then come four poems lauding the author. Much the longest of these is by Ben Jonson, being the ringing acclamation I have spoken of, hailing Shakespeare as the soul of the age and Britain's triumph and calling forth the greatest dramatists of antiquity for comparison and to do him honor. I confess I cannot remain unmoved when I come to the invocation near the end:

> But stay, I see thee in the hemisphere
> Advanced, and made a constellation there!
> Shine forth, thou star of poets. . . .

Two ingredients of the First Folio make it unprecedented, apart from the plays it brings us. One is, of course, the first overt adequate estimate of Shakespeare's achievement. The second is the ostensible evidence as to who Shakespeare was. The information supplied is so slight as to make one wonder why the contributors, with all the wordage they gave us, were so peculiarly niggardly with it; but such as it is, and taken at face value, it would seem to be unmistakable.

First, Heminge and Condell call Shakespeare "so worthy a friend & fellow," and because they were actors and shareholders in two theatres, it would appear that Shakespeare was also an actor or a theatrical shareholder, or both. This status would accord, moveover, with his inclusion among "The Names of Principal Actors in these Plays," which the editors vouchsafe us; indeed, "William Shakespeare" leads all the rest. Second, Leonard Digges, in a poetical address to the *Author Master W. Shakespeare,* refers to "thy Stratford monument." The purchaser of the First Folio would have no doubt that the monument's location was in the town of Stratford just northeast of London, had the reference stood alone. Three pages earlier, however, Ben Jonson had apostrophized the author as "Sweet Swan of Avon!" A reader who related the two remarks and who also was acquainted with Warwickshire would have been led to connect Shakespeare with the village of Stratford on the river of that name. And then there was Ben Jonson's postulation in his eulogy, "And though thou hadst small Latin, and less Greek. . . ." If the passage was taken to mean that Shakespeare actually *had* small Latin and less Greek (the reader is warned that Jonson is going to prove to be a very cagey witness), the conception of the dramatist as the product of a provincial small town was reinforced.

A visitor to Stratford-on-Avon following the publication of the First Folio would have found confirmation of what he had read in it in a monument to "Shakspeare" (first heard of in a reference to it in the Folio) containing a bust of the subject, in the wall of the chancel in Holy Trinity Church at the edge of the village on the river. (See page 210.) The inscription, which Americans may read on the life-size replica of the monument in the Folger Library in Washington, is:

IUDICIO PYLIUM, GENIO SOCRATEM, ARTE MARONEM:
TERRA TEGIT, POPVLVS MAERET, OLYMPUS HABET.[1]

STAY PASSENGER, WHY GOEST THOV BY SO FAST?
READ IF THOV CANST, WHOM ENVIOVS DEATH HATH PLAST
WITH IN THIS MONVMENT SHAKSPEARE: WITH WHOME,
QUICK NATVRE DIDE: WHOSE NAME DOTH DECK Y[s] TOMBE.
FAR MORE THAN COST: SIEH ALL, Y[t] HE HATH WRITT,
LEAVES LIVING ART, BVT PAGE, TO SERVE HIS WITT.

Unquestionably the First Folio and the monument taken together invited the curious to identify William Shakespeare with a man who, as future generations were to learn, was baptized in Stratford-on-Avon on 26 April 1564, as William Shaksper or Shakspere; who married at eighteen and had three children; who lived in London at least in the later 1590s and sometime in 1603 and 1604; who evidently was a shareholder in the Globe and Blackfriars theatres and is said to have been an actor; and who in the prime of life returned, quite wealthy, to the village he had once departed presumably penniless, to die in 1616.

Publication of the First Folio seems to have brought no celebrity to Shakspere's birthplace.[2] In a Folger Library booklet James G. McManaway writes that "Within a few years of his death Shakespeare was bringing fame to Stratford." The facts, as far as we know them, are quite different. The "notoriety . . . which the memory of William Shakespeare has brought to Stratford," says the *Encyclopaedia Britannica* (11th edition) "sprang into strong growth only towards the end of the 18th century." Our information is that during the two generations following the death of "Will. Shakspere gent," as the burial register had it, four or five persons finding themselves in Stratford were led to connect the town with the writer, probably each of them because of finding there "a neat monument," as one of them, a Lieutenant Hammond, put it in 1634, "to that famous English poet, Mr. William Shakespeare." Hammond also found in the church a tomb of "Mr. Combe, upon whose name the said poet did merrily fan up some witty and facetious verses, which time would not give us leave to sack up." The verses, evidently cited by the townsfolk as an example of the local poet's work, are, in one version, as follows:

Ten in the Hundred the Devil allows
But Combes will have twelve, he swears & vows:

[1] A Nestor in wisdom, a Socrates in intellect, a Virgil in art: The earth encloses, the people mourn, Olympus holds.

[2] When referring to the Stratfordian I shall follow the convention of calling him Shakspere, for the spelling of the family name in Stratford clearly called for a short *a* in the first syllable. Where the reference is specifically to the author I shall use Shakespeare, because that was the standard rendering of the name, with or without a hyphen between the syllables, by his contemporaries.

If any one asks who lies in this Tombe:
Hoh! quoth the Devil 'Tis my John o' Combe

That is how they were recorded, also ascribed to Shakespeare, by John
Aubrey, the first person we know of who went, or who seems to have gone,
to Stratford because of the Shakespeare connection. The time of his visit
would have been about 1681, some sixty-five years after Shakspere's death.
Described as an antiquary, Aubrey had undertaken to collect information on
important lives for Anthony à Wood, who was compiling his *Athenae Oxonienses,* a history of the bishops and writers educated at Oxford. "Minutes
of Lives," Aubrey called his garnerings. In one of them he wrote:

> Mr. William Shakespear was born at Stratford upon Avon, in the County of
> Warwick; his father was a butcher, & I have been told heretofore by some of
> the neighbours, that when he was a boy he exercised his father's trade, but when
> he kill'd a calf, he would do it in *high style,* & make a speech. . . . This Wm.
> being inclined naturally to poetry and acting, came to London I guess about 18.
> and was an actor at one of the play-houses and did act exceedingly well. . . . He
> began early to make essays at dramatic poetry, which at that time was very low;
> and his plays took well: He was a handsome well shap't man: very good
> company, and of a very ready and pleasant smooth wit. . . . He was wont to go
> to his native country [i.e., county] once a year. . . .

Aubrey went on to quote Sir William Davenant, a theatrical manager and
playwright born in 1606, as having said that "he had a most prodigious wit"
and: "That he never blotted out a line in his life: said Ben Jonson, I wish he
had blotted out a thousand." Aubrey concludes: "Though as Ben Jonson
says of him, that he had but little Latin and less Greek, he understood Latin
pretty well: for he had been in his younger years a schoolmaster in the
country." In another note he indicates that Sir William told him that "Shakespeare" used to lie over at the Davenants' tavern in Oxford on the way to
Warwickshire and that Sir William "seemed contentended [*sic*] enough to be
thought his son." That bit of gossip was rejected by Wood.

Aubrey made a note to himself: "W. Shakespeare — quaere Mr. Beeston,
who knows most of him from Mr. Lacy." That was William Beeston, whose
father had been with the Lord Chamberlain's players in 1598. The only
indication that Aubrey ever actually saw Beeston, however, is a marginal
note "From Beeston" beside the report of his subject's having been a schoolmaster, and Mr. Lacy's competence is altogether problematical.

In 1709, Nicholas Rowe, a successful playwright and friend of Alexander
Pope's, published a collected edition of Shakespeare's plays prefaced with
the first serious attempt at a biography of the author. In it he credits most
of the facts it sets forth on Shakespeare's life to the actor Thomas Betterton,
who had made "a journey into Warwickshire, on purpose to gather up what
remains he could of a name for which he had so great a value." Rowe tells

us that Shakespeare's father was a considerable dealer in wool but had so large a family

> that tho' he was his eldest son, he could give him no better education than his own employment. He had bred him, 'tis true, for some time at a Free-School, where 'tis probable he acquir'd that little Latin he was master of: but the narrowness of his circumstances, and the want of his assistance at home, forc'd his father to withdraw him from thence. . . . In order to settle in the world after a family manner, he thought fit to marry while he was yet very young. His wife was the daughter of one Hathaway, said to have been a substantial yeoman in the neighborhood of Stratford.

However,

> He had, by a misfortune common enough to young fellows, fallen into ill company; and amongst them, some that made a frequent practice of deer-stealing, engag'd him with them more than once in robbing a park that belong'd to Sir Thomas Lucy of Cherlecot, near Stratford. For this he was prosecuted by that gentleman, as he thought, somewhat too severely; and in order to revenge that ill usage, he made a ballad upon him. And tho' this, probably the first essay of his poetry, be lost, yet it is said to have been so very bitter, that it redoubled the prosecution against him to that degree, that he was obliged to leave his business and family in Warwickshire, for some time, and shelter himself in London.

Evidently it did not trouble the biographer that the greatest of all poets should have made "the first essay of his poetry" only shortly before leaving for London in his mid-twenties, and then only upon provocation of excessive prosecution for deer-stealing. Rowe continues:

> It is at this time, and upon this accident, that he is said to have made his first acquaintance in the playhouse. He was receiv'd into the company then in being, at first in a very mean rank; but his admirable wit, with the natural turn of it to the stage, soon distinguished him, if not as an extraordinary actor, yet as an excellent writer.

As we shall find attested again and again, wit seems to have been the one attribute of mind for which the Stratford man would be remembered. Rowe reports "Shakespeare" possessed of such agreeable qualities that

> he made himself acquainted with the best conversations of those times. Queen Elizabeth had several of his plays acted before her, and without doubt gave him many gracious marks of her favor. . . . [Moreover,] he had the honour to meet with many great and uncommon marks of favour from the Earl of Southampton. . . . [However,] what particular habitude or friendships he contracted with private men, I have not been able to learn, more than that every one who had a true taste of merit, and could distinguish men, had generally a just value and esteem for him.

Thus Rowe, a century after the event. He has Edmund Spenser speak of him in his *Teares of the Muses* and attributes to him an acquaintance with Ben Jonson beginning when "Shakespeare" reads a play that the company had turned down and finds he likes it "so well" as to "recommend Mr. Jonson and his writings to the public." After some discussion of Shakespeare's own plays, Rowe tells us that the latter part of his subject's life was spent

> in ease, retirement, and the conversation of friends. He had the good fortune to gather an estate equal to his occasion, and . . . is said to have spent some years before his death at his native Stratford.

Beginning with Edmund Malone, the Irish scholar, research into the life of William Shakspere of Stratford and into the works attributed to him became a literary undertaking of unexampled proportions. (Malone, who had written a two-volume supplement to an edition of Shakespeare's plays by Samuel Johnson and George Steevens (1778), spent seven years on an edition of his own. When he died in 1812, he left it to James Boswell the younger — whose father Malone had assisted in his biography of Samuel Johnson — to complete his work on a new edition and bring it out, in 1821, as the famous twenty-one-volume Variorum.) The trouble was that the more that was learned of Will Shakspere on the one hand and the works of William Shakespeare on the other, the greater, in the minds of many, grew the evident disparity between them and the grounds for doubt that the former had had anything to do with the latter. Specifically, it has come to appear that the celebrated Stratfordian

§ Was in character, background, education (or lack of it), apparent interests, and range of experience that might have been his, very nearly the antithesis of the kind of person the works lead us to picture as the author;

§ Was never in his lifetime, as far as we can find it suggested in the record, regarded as an author of any kind, and was never credited by his fellow Stratfordians for generations after his death with the composition of any verse but the four lines of doggerel Aubrey quoted and — of comparable quality — the famous curse on his tombstone;

§ Was never, except in respect of his wealth, regarded as of any special consequence by anyone who knew him in Stratford or by his relatives and descendants as far as they gave any known sign of it;

§ Evidently took no interest in the fate of the incomparable works said to have been his; and,

§ Could hardly, within the bounds of the possible, have been the author considering what his contemporaries said about Shakespeare.

I shall set forth in subsequent chapters the facts that lead to those conclusions as well as to another: that the author of the plays indicated that "William Shakespeare" was a pseudonym and that the name was widely recognized as such at the time.

Dissatisfaction with the attribution of Shakespeare's works to the Stratfordian naturally led the dissenters back to the texts on which it had originally been based. Those who have reread the introductory material of the First Folio and the inscription on the Stratford monument with the attention they deserve have found that they seem to say one thing and in fact say quite another. I shall reserve this reading for another chapter, anticipating that when we come to it readers will see for themselves that the two memorials, which are conventionally taken as prime supports of Shakespearean orthodoxy, are, rather, embarrassments to it.

That will leave us with those writers who took the two materials at face value and gave the Stratford legend its initial impetus, notably Aubrey and Rowe. Something may be said of them here.

Of Aubrey, with whom we see the first lineaments of the conventional Shakespeare, we read that "As a hanger-on in great houses he had little time for systematic work, and he wrote the 'Lives' in the early morning while his hosts were sleeping off the effects of the dissipation of the night before. . . . He made some distinction between hearsay and authentic information, but had no pretence to accuracy." Wood, his employer, called him "a shiftless person, roving and magotie-headed, and sometimes little better than crazed"; he "thought little, believed much, and confused everything."

Nicholas Rowe was quite a different order of biographer. He made mistakes and he told some truths, but as to where the division occurs between the two there is no consensus. He was, after all, as I have said, writing a century and more after the fact. Much of what he put in his *Life* strikes me as credible *if* we take it that he was writing about two persons combined as one: the Stratford Shakspere and the dramatist Shakespeare. Partisans of the Stratford man will, of course, hear of no such thing. They will, moreover, point out that in treating of the early fashioners of the conventional Shakespeare I have neglected an important witness, John Ward, and what he wrote.

The Reverend Dr. Ward became vicar of Stratford-on-Avon in 1662. I have not forgotten him. Rather, I have saved him till now precisely because of his importance. His jottings will, I think, be found to contain the key to the Shakespeare mystery. If, as James McManaway of the Folger Library avows, his testimony is "unimpeachable," then it deals the Stratford case a fatal blow; we may see this immediately. (Clearly Dr. McManaway was not aware of what he was endorsing. We shall find repeated instances of the failure of orthodox scholars to read the simple English of crucial documents.)

In his notebook of 1661 to 1663, Dr. Ward set down a few sentences about "Shakespeare." These begin with a report that he had "2 daughters, one whereof M[r.] Hall, the physician, married and by her had one daughter, to wit, the Lady Bernard of Abbingdon"; and they include a reminder to himself "to peruse Shakespears plays and be versed in them, that I may not be ignorant in that matter." Despite this resolution and despite the priceless opportunity to acquire and record information about the immortal dramatist ostensibly afforded by the availability of Shakspere's granddaughter, Dr. Ward dropped the subject like a hot — or cold — potato. No further word is heard of Shakespeare in his notebooks (of which there are sixteen), though he remained vicar of Stratford for nineteen years. The inference certainly suggests itself that he had found nothing was to be learned of the dramatist in Stratford.

Between the two entries from Dr. Ward's diary that I have quoted, however, are sixty-four words that if I am right put us on the track of a solution to the Shakespeare mystery.

First, Dr. Ward wrote that "I have heard that Mr. Shakespeare was a natural wit, without any art at all. . . ." This was very likely true of Will Shakspere, whose wit, as I say, is repeatedly vouched for. It was also monstrously untrue of the poet-dramatist, the supreme artist in words of our language, acclaimed on the monument in Dr. Ward's church as a Virgil in art.

Second, Dr. Ward wrote that "he frequented plays all his younger time . . . [he] supplied the stage with 2 plays every year, and for that had an allowance so large that he spent at the rate of £1000 a year, as I have heard." Now young Will Shakspere, in the village of Stratford, hardly had a chance to frequent plays all his younger time. Most certainly he never had £1,000 a year to spend, let alone having come by such an income in the form of an allowance; no Shakespearean scholar has ever subscribed to such an absurdity. But Dr. Ward tells us that what was monstrously untrue of the Stratford man was true of Shakespeare. If Dr. Ward's testimony is unimpeachable, as Dr. McManaway avers, then it is clear that, as one might surmise from Nicholas Rowe's biography, the Shakespeare who has come down to us is a combination of two very different men. One would have been the villager of an artless, natural wit, the other a poet-dramatist of probably privileged youth who certainly attained high rank and importance; an annual grant of £1,000 would be one of the largest made by the throne — the only possible source. It would be the equivalent today of more than twice the salary paid the Prime Minister.

For the sake of completeness, let us take note that in 1663, the year after Ward came to Stratford, Thomas Fuller published his *Worthies of England*, in which, in the section on Warwickshire, he included a few brief paragraphs about Shakespeare. These interest us by showing that not a scrap of information was available to him about the poet-dramatist as a person, and none about the Stratford man, either, beyond the salient characteristic that had come to Ward's ears. Reporting that "his learning was very little," he went on to say that "nature it self was all the art which was used upon him." That he believed he was characterizing the preeminent master of the language, in whose fine-filed phrase Meres had justifiably said the Muses would speak if they spoke English, demonstrates the height of mindlessness to which literary criticism can mount on the wings of the Stratford legend. Fuller's effort concludes with its best-known passage:

> Many were the wits-combats betwixt him [Shakespeare] and Ben Johnson, which two I behold like a Spanish great galleon and an English man of war; Master Johnson (like the former) was built far higher in learning; solid, but slow in his performances. Shake-spear, with the English-man of war, lesser in bulk, but lighter in sailing, could turn with all tides, tack about and take advantage of all winds, by the quickness of his wit and invention.

Chambers comments on this passage that it "reads like fancy, not tradition." We may agree that it does.

Morse Johnson, an attorney of Cincinnati, has put his finger on the nub of the problem about the authorship as well as anyone, I think, in writing as follows:

> Beyond a similarity (*not* identity) of names, I have never been shown one shred — and I mean a single shred — of probative evidence (I do not consider the fact that the Stratford man did have some connection with the theatre as probative evidence for this purpose) which in any way connected the Stratford man with the immortal works during his lifetime. Clearly the works were well known and applauded while he lived and less than ten years after his death the First Folio sold out in which Ben Jonson acclaimed the author as "Star of poets," etc. It is certain, therefore, that whoever wrote the works must have been known both personally and by reputation to a number of his contemporaries. Why, then, is there no reference during his lifetime by a friend or relative or a neighbor or a theatre colleague or a business associate connecting the works with the man?
>
> There has to be some rational explanation for this undeniable fact and unique mystery. The only one that makes possible sense to me is that, whoever wrote the works, every effort was for some reason made to conceal his authorship.

"In no case has it been possible to produce a shred of evidence that anyone in Shakespeare's day questioned his authorship," McManaway writes as curator of the Folger Library. And, of course, no one questions it today. What people have questioned and do question is whether "William Shakespeare" was the man christened Gulielmus Shaksper, or Shakspere, or was a pseudonym adopted by a writer possessed of the qualifications for the authorship that the Stratford man would seem to have lacked. Many writers have published works under a name not their own, and with less reason than a nobleman would have had in writing for the stage in Tudor England. We know François Marie Arouet as Voltaire, Marian Evans as George Eliot, Amandine Aurore Dupin, baronne Dudevant as George Sand, Charles Ludwidge Dodgson as Lewis Carroll, William Sidney Porter as O. Henry, Jacques Anatole Thibault as Anatole France.

It is a principle of the orthodox case that references to William Shakespeare *ipso facto* and of necessity are references to Shakspere of Stratford; and, of course, if we take this as an assumption it is very easy to arrive at it as a conclusion. A distinguished orthodox scholar, Giles E. Dawson, a colleague of Dr. McManaway's at the Folger Library, had occasion to defend this principle in 1949 when his deposition was being taken in a lawsuit brought by Charles W. Barrell on the grounds that his integrity had been impugned by the Folger curator in connection with investigations he had made of the Library's "Ashbourne" portrait, which had led to its identification (albeit mistakenly) as one of "Shakespeare." (The case was settled with a disclaimer by Dr. Dawson of any such intent.) While taking Dr. Dawson's testimony, the interrogating attorney — my father, as it happened — reminded him of his having stated that Shakespeare's authorship was attested by "a mass of perfectly clear evidence." Question and answer proceeded as follows:

> Q. What evidence have you got that Shaksper of Stratford wrote the plays?
> A. Well, that evidence is not the sort of thing that I could nail down in two minutes.
> Q. But you say a mass of perfectly clear evidence.
> A. In the aggregate I think it is perfectly clear.
> Q. Can you mention one item of evidence that Shaksper of Stratford wrote the plays? Omit altogether things after his death.
> A. One bit of perfectly clear evidence. In my opinion Ben Jonson clearly accepted the fact without any hesitation.
> Q. Well, quote that. That is highly important. If you can say that Ben Jonson ever accepted William Shaksper of Stratford as the author, then you have contributed something.
> A. Well, of course you will not agree that his verses facing the title-page of the First Folio were any such evidence. I think they were.
> Q. Well, they were written seven years after his death.
> A. Yes, but he knew Shakespeare during his life.
> Q. And there is nothing in those verses that refers to Shaksper of Stratford except the expression Sweet Swan of Avon.
> A. Well, there is certainly nothing that specifically connects the author with Stratford, that does —
> Q. Couldn't someone else have had a place on the Avon?
> Dr. Dawson acknowledged that there was another, thought by many to have been Shakespeare, who, he believed, did have such a place.

At that time, in short, Dr. Dawson, while under oath, was unable to cite a single item of evidence during Shakspere's lifetime linking him with the authorship of the plays. Yet we find him later assuring an audience that "Of some fifty printed or written references set down during his [Shakespeare's] lifetime," none "expressed even the faintest hint of doubt as to the authorship of the plays." He did not add that none expressed even the faintest hint of belief that the author was the Stratford man.

The orthodox academicians have been at pains to create the impression that Shakspere of Stratford was fully accepted as the author during his lifetime and that skepticism on that score came long afterward. The facts are otherwise. The first indications we have that the authorship was being fixed on the Stratford man are two references that mock the proposition that the author was an unlearned man such as Shakspere was, with gifts deriving from nature rather than education. (These, as we shall see in Chapter 7, come in a play put on about 1602 by students at Cambridge and in a poetical letter of around 1615 to Ben Jonson by "F.B.," presumably Francis Beaumont, the playwright.) In other words, our evidence of disbelief in the Stratford man's authorship antedates any evidence of belief in it.

With nothing to identify the author during his life, it is also impossible to know now what picture of him was entertained by educated readers through the balance of the 17th century. "Sweetest Shakespeare, fancy's child," as John Milton called him, was a description oblivious of five-sixths of what Shakespeare wrote and of what he must have been himself. Until the 18th century, those who purchased and read successive editions of Shakespeare's works apparently had little curiosity about the author, incredible as we may find their indifference to the human being who could produce such words, whom their contemporary, John Dryden, was recognizing (in 1668) as "the man who of all modern, and perhaps ancient, poets had the largest and most comprehensive soul" and hailing him as "Divine." The century was well along before any great public interest in the poet himself began to be shown. In 1741 Shakespeare achieved a place at last in the national hagiography comparable to that of lesser poets when a statue of him, idealizing the gross features of the Stratford bust, was erected in Westminster Abbey. Five years later, a theatrical manager and actor, John Ward, put on a benefit performance of *Othello* in the Old Town Hall at Stratford to raise the money needed to refurbish the monument in Trinity Church. It was in 1769 that Stratford came into its own — or, as many would say, into some more deserving town's own — with a three-day jubilee staged there by David Garrick to make a suitable occasion of his presentation to the town of a cast of the Westminster statue. A century and a half after his death, Will Shakspere had finally and fully arrived.

In the following two centuries a veritable industry has been built upon the Stratfordian. His quadricentennial, in 1964, was celebrated throughout the English-speaking world, with the United States issuing a special commemorative stamp and the Ford Foundation contributing $250,000 to make the occasion in the land of his birth a memorable one. On April 23rd, "one hundred and thirteen nations were represented at the Stratford festivities. There were conferences, festivals, a thousand new productions in the United States, a hundred in Russia, and two hundred in Germany" — although, as Professor J. Isaacs of London University goes on to remark, "Nobody knows when Shakespeare was born."

It behooves us, then, to see what has actually been discovered about the object of this adulation.

3

"Such a Deadly Life"

Orthodox writers assert that much is known about the man they conceive to be Shake-speare, more, indeed, than about all but one of his fellow playwrights. In two centuries, legions of scholar-sleuths (one of whom alone combed a collection of three million uncatalogued documents) have in fact, in a literary dragnet of unparalleled scope, come up with an extensive assortment of facts about the Stratfordian. We find it enlightening to review these to see what activities are indicated for the purported master poet and playwright and what kinds are notably missing, and to see what items are listed and what kinds not listed in the inventory of his life's effects recorded in his will.

In April 1973, the curator of manuscripts at the Folger Shakespeare Library discovered that on 12 June 1593, Richard Stonley, a London businessman, had recorded in his diary his purchasing a copy of *Venus and Adonis.* The work had been licensed for printing two months earlier, but this was the first record of a copy of the work being purchased, the first of Shakespeare's to be published. Hence considerable interest attended the discovery. James G. McManaway, consultant emeritus and former assistant director at the Folger Library, described it as "sensational."

That was rather strong. Someone had to be the first on record to purchase a work of Shakespeare's, and, in fact, Stonley's having done so had been reported back in the 18th century. But Dr. McManaway, as quoted in the *Washington Post,* went on to declare that the find "provides . . . clues about the shadowy, early days of Shakespeare's writing career." It does nothing of the sort. We see in Dr. McManaway's claim the eagerness of orthodox scholars to turn up something that will associate the Stratford man with literary activity.

"We know more about him than about any other dramatist of the time, with the exception of Ben Jonson, who lived rather later and had a longer life," says the flag-bearer of the Stratford academicians, Alfred Leslie Rowse of Oxford University. Dr. McManaway himself, in his Folger booklet, asserts that "For a playwright of his time, Shakespeare's life is well documented." He goes on to cite gaps in the biographical data on Edmund Spenser, John Milton, and Sir Walter Raleigh to have us believe that these gaps are as significant as the gaps in Shakespeare's record. It is conventional among orthodox writers to contend that we know as much about the Stratford man as we could legitimately expect to know about Shakespeare, if not more than that. If they were being aboveboard with us their point would be an important one. If not, that also should tell us much. The facts will make clear the truth of the matter.

A considerable amount, certainly, is known about Shakspere of Stratford. After all, there has been let loose upon him a century-and-a-half-long investigation of an intensity, scope, and thoroughness unexampled in the history of literary research. Of its results, however, skeptics would say that never in the field of biography have so many labored so diligently and so long for so little, certainly so little of what they were seeking. "Of the person of Shakespeare," Walt Whitman declared, with warrant, "the record is almost a blank — it has no substance whatever." Writing on *Shakespeare After 400 Years*, J. Isaacs, professor emeritus of English literature at Queen Mary College, London, observes that "The last time anything of importance about Shakespeare personally turned up was in 1910, when Professor C. W. Wallace of Nebraska, who has never had much credit for it, looked through some three million uncatalogued documents in the basement of the Public Records Office and came up with a lawsuit in which Shakespeare was a witness, and showed him as a lodger in the house of a Huguenot wig-maker off Cheapside, helping in the romance of his landlord's daughter with a young apprentice." As Hugh R. Trevor-Roper, formerly Regius Professor of History at Oxford University, remarks, "One hundredth of the effort devoted to one of Shakespeare's obscure contemporaries would have produced a respectable biography." We come now to the biography of the famous Stratfordian, whom I have proposed we call William Shakspere (without an *e* after the *k*), which is consistent with the variety of spellings of the family name in and around Stratford and that of the man's own so-called signatures. This spelling shows that the first syllable of the name was pronounced with a short *a*.

He was christened on 26 April 1564, as "Gulielmus filius Johannes Shakspere," the final *e* being perhaps a Gothic flourish. Though the date of his birth is celebrated as April 23, we do not know when it occurred. We also do not know exactly where he was born — an uncertainty worth remarking only because of the assiduity of the Shakespeare Birthplace Trust in directing the throngs of pilgrims to the house that the Trust asserts categorically was the birthplace. It is amusing, by the way, that when the Shakespeare Action Committee under Francis Carr applied for a summons against the Trust in 1968 under the Trade Description Act, contending that there was no evidence to show that Shakspere was born in the house on Henley Street, the Trust won a dismissal of the application by the town magistrates; the dismissal was granted on the grounds not that there was such evidence but that the trustees were not carrying on a trade or business as defined by the Act! Bernard Levin, well-known British literary columnist, writes: "Stratford per-

mits — indeed encourages — one of the biggest frauds in England to rage
unchecked. . . . I mean those two monumental frauds 'Shakespeare's Birthplace' and 'Anne Hathaway's Cottage.'"

The father, presumably the John Shakspere of nearby Snitterfield, first
appears in Stratford, in 1552, as having been fined a shilling for having a
dunghill in front of his house. Evidently on the strength of his looking after
his father Richard's lands, John Shakspere was described as a husbandman
and yeoman. His father had held part of these lands as a tenant of Robert
Arden of Wilmcote, and John had married Arden's daughter Mary. Orthodox
scholars and critics, while accusing anti-Stratfordians of an unholy bias in
favor of high birth ("An innate snobbishness is responsible for the recurring
suspicion that the plays attributed to Shakespeare were actually written by
someone else, preferably a nobleman," Richard Watts, Jr., assures us in the
New York Post), like to link Robert Arden with the aristocratic Ardens of
Park Hill. ("The Ardens were superior folk, probably related to the Arden
gentry of Park Hill in north Warwickshire," A. L. Rowse avers.) And Ivor
Brown tells us that "The Ardens of the senior succession were lordly people
indeed, pre-Conquest notables, accepted by William the Conqueror," and so
on. William Shakspere himself, along with his partisans, seems to have been
guilty of just that predilection for aristocratic lineage of which those who
question his credentials are accused. Having, as soon as his fortunes permitted, obtained a coat-of-arms in his father's name (by dubious means, as we
shall later see), he sought to impale the arms of the Park Hill Ardens with
those he had recently acquired — only, however, to be overruled by the
Heralds' College.

John Shakspere's business in Stratford was apparently that of glover and
wool-dealer. He had bought two houses in Henley Street in 1556 and two
others within twenty years. Clearly these were years of some prosperity for
him. By 1568, he had risen from chamberlain to burgess to alderman and
bailiff. By 1577, however, his success, whatever its origin, was over. We find
him proceeding against one of the Quineys — a family close to his own —
for a debt of £50 and, upon his failing to meet a debt of his own, having a
warrant outstanding for his arrest. He stopped attending meetings of the
town council: "Mr. Shaxpere doth not come to the halls." Accordingly he
was replaced by a new alderman. He failed to pay off a mortgage of £40 on
his wife's property when due. Misbehavior seems to have been added to
misfortune, for, in 1580, he was bound over at court to give security against
a breach of the peace and fined the heavy sum of £40, half of it in default
of payment by a partner in the offense, a Nottingham hatmaker. He became
involved in the decline of his brother Henry, who died heavily in debt in
1596. In 1592, he was cited as one of those who "it is said . . . come not to
church for fear of process for debt."

The first records of William Shakspere following his christening come when he was eighteen. A license for his marriage to Anne Whately of Temple Grafton was issued in Worcester on November 27, 1582. The next day, a bond given by two sureties to protect the Bishop of Worcester from any untoward consequence from the insufficient posting of the banns (there had been only one asking in place of the prescribed three) names as bride Anne Hathwey of Stratford. The groom is called Shaxpere on one document, Shagspere on the other. Particularly because the next record of our subject refers to the christening of his daughter Susanna six months later, we are tempted to visualize a prospective marriage to the first Anne aborted by an irate father demanding that the bridegroom do right by the second, whom he had got with child. The orthodox biographers assure us that "Anne Whately of Temple Grafton" was a scribal error for "Anne Hathwey of Stratford." Although the slip could hardly be described as a natural one, let us not argue and merely take note of Joseph Hunter's report of "the entry in the parish register of Stratford, of the marriage of one Anne Hathaway of Shottery to William Wilson on Jan. 17, 1579." Whoever she was, Anne Shakspere was eight years her husband's senior, as we know from the inscription on her grave.

The marriage was only six months old when a daughter, Susanna, was baptized. In 1585, the baptism of "Hamnet and Judeth, son and daughter to William Shakspere," was recorded. Plainly the twins were named for a neighboring couple, Hamnet and Judith Sadler.

In 1589, William and his father were named in legal proceedings aimed at recovering the property of Mary Arden on which John had failed to lift the mortgage.

That is all we know about our subject until his thirtieth or thirty-second year. Of the playwrights other than Shakespeare by whom the age is known, most very inferior — Marlowe, Kyd, Lyly, Greene, Heywood, Nashe, Webster, and Jonson — only John Webster (whose genius went unrecognized until Charles Lamb discovered it) confronts us with such a blank. Even Webster left us the kind of testament we look for in vain from the conventional "Shakespeare": an epistle to one of his dramas, of 1612, in which he speaks in complimentary terms of seven of his fellow playwrights, including "M[aster] Shake-speare," who is one of three praised for their "right happy and copious industry" with the hope that "What I write may be read by their light." We have a richer acquaintance with the first three decades of the Venerable Bede, who died in 735 in the depths of the Dark Ages, than we have of Shakspere's.

What was Will doing in the years before his appearance in London? Various stories have filtered into the vacuum, the best known involving deer poaching, but they are without substantiation or even plausibility. He "may or may not have travelled in Europe, either as a touring actor or in the company of a noble patron," Ivor Brown theorizes. Louis P. Bénézet of Dartmouth College has garnered a fine crop of postulations, all designed to endow young Will in some measure with the range of knowledge and experience clearly possessed by the author of the dramas. Among the conjecturers are: the *Encyclopaedia Britannica* (1894 edition), which suggests that Shakspere must have spent much time in the "forest of Arden, . . . picking up his remarkable knowledge of forest law"; J. Dover Wilson, who has him acting from 1581 to 1599, except when he was tutoring the Earl of Southampton ("in a country school") and taking a trip to Italy with the Earl and John Florio, a writer and teacher at Magdalen College; Joseph Quincy Adams, who also believes that he was teaching in a country school and in addition had been hunting to hounds and practicing falconry; Edgar I. Fripp, who is convinced that he was studying law till 1587; Karl Elze, who believes that he was travelling in Italy; Edward Garnett and Edmund Gosse, who favor his travelling and fighting in the Low Countries; Caroline F. E. Spurgeon, who sees him spending his time in deer-hunting, horseback-riding, hawking, bowling, tennis-playing, and engaging in other sports; Churton Collins, who is sure that he was working in an attorney's office; William Allen Neilsen, who is sure he filled his waking hours with the devouring of books. To these, Samuel Schoenbaum adds Arthur Gray of Jesus College, according to whom the young Stratfordian was a page to Sir Henry Goodere of Polesworth Hall and there acquired his knowledge of Latin and of polite society; Frances Yates, who has him teaching in a secret Catholic institution, and others more eccentric.

Sir Edmund K. Chambers, in his monumental and definitive biography, is more noncommittal. "Who shall say," he asks, "what adventures, material or spiritual, six or eight crowded Elizabethan years may have brought him." Or who — if I may bring us back to the record, taking account of his having the financial burden of a wife and three children, no known business or profession to put money in his pocket, no advantageous connections that have ever come to light, and a father pursued by creditors — shall say what drab employment filled his days in those years? "It is," says Chambers, "no use guessing."

Guessing, however, is what his biographers resort to when they come to tell us when he went to London. They postulate the late 1580s but have no evidence to back them up. ("One fine day in the later 1580s," A. L. Rowse informs us, "He took the road to London.") They stake their case on the publication in 1592, when Will Shakspere was twenty-eight, of *Greenes Groats-worth of Wyt,* in which the author warned certain playwrights of an actor, an "upstart Crow" and "Johannes Factotum" who esteemed himself the only "Shake-scene" in the country. They identify this actor as Shakspere but their faith in this, we shall see in Chapter 5, rests upon a characteristic failure to read the plain English of the text upon which it rests.

Two years passed after the *Groats-worth* appeared, during which *Venus and Adonis* was published with a gracious and courtly dedication to the Earl of Southampton signed by William Shakespeare — the first we hear of such a writer. Then, in December 1594, according to an entry added much later to an account of the following March, "Will Kempe, Will Shakespeare & Richard Burbage servants to the Lord Chambleyne" were paid £20 for two comedies or interludes acted before the Queen. This is a peculiar record and suspect, as again we shall see.

In August 1596, "Hamnet, filius William Shakspere" was buried in Stratford.

In October 1596, a grant of a coat-of-arms seems to have been made to John Shakspere, doubtless at his son's instigation, though the grant may not have finally been made until 1599. The arms feature a spear in the diagonal of the shield and a falcon as the crest. In the upper left-hand corner of the draft of 1596 appear the words *Non, Sanz Droict* ("No, Without Right"), this being evidently the Heralds' judgment on the merits of the application. The words are crossed out but are again inscribed, just above the original notation. Then, in a larger hand and in upper-case letters the words *NON SANZ DROICT* are written across the top. Someone, it would seem, had taken the dismissal and by dropping the comma turned it into an endorsement: "Not Without Right." This became the motto for his arms, albeit rather a defensive one. William Dethick, Garter principal king of Arms, who authorized the grant and was already in bad odor for his greed, was in 1602 accused by Ralph Brooke, York Herald, of having made grants to base persons, among whom "Shakespeare" was named. Dethick's defense of his actions must have been successful, for he continued to hold his office and was even knighted in the following year, but shortly thereafter his transgressions led to his dismissal. In 1599, when Shakspere sought an "exemplification" of his coat of arms,[1] Ben Jonson in his *Every Man Out of His Humor* has a rustic character called Sogliardo who is ridiculed as one "so enamoured of the name of a gentleman, that he will have it though he buys it." For Sogliardo's coat-of-arms another character suggests, "Let the word be, *Not Without Mustard*."

In late 1596, it was recorded on the rolls of the Court of the Queen's

---

[1] By an exemplification the Heralds accepted an applicant's claim of a right to bear arms without ruling on it. It was on this occasion that Shakspere sought to have his arms impaled with those of the Ardens of Park Hill on the basis of his mother's descent, but this joining was disallowed and a less aristocratic Arden coat substituted. So far as is known, however, Shakspere never quartered any Arden arms with his own, perhaps advisedly, for it has never been established that his mother was entitled to arms of any kind.

Bench in London that William Wayte craved sureties of the peace against "William Shakspare" and three others "for fear of death and so forth." We are assured by Stratfordians that there was nothing invidious in being so cited.

In May 1597, "Willielmum Shakespeare" bought the 260-year-old house known as New Place — the second largest in Stratford — from William Underhill, evidently for £60. The price would be about equal to the amount an author would receive for ten plays and presumably does not represent the total cost of the house.

In November 1597, the tax collectors for the Ward of Bishopsgate, London, listed "William Shackspere" among those owing a tax that could not be collected because of their having died or left the ward.

In January 1598, Abraham Sturley of Stratford wrote to Richard Quiney that "our countriman [i.e., of the same county], Mr. Shaksper" may be moved "to deal in the matter of our tithes."

In February 1598, "Wm. Shackespere" of Chapple Street Ward, Stratford, was listed as holding "x quarters" (80 bushels) of grain. Three wet seasons had produced a great dearth of grain, and the "engrossers" who held large amounts, like Shakspere, despite orders from the Privy Council to sell the excesses, were termed by the council "wicked people . . . like to wolves or cormorants." As E. K. Chambers writes, "There was wild hope [among the people] of leading them in a halter and, 'if God send my Lord of Essex down shortly, to see them hanged on gibbets at their own doors.'"

In October 1598, "William Shakespeare" was again listed as a tax delinquent, in the parish of St. Helens, London, the collectors having once more been unable to bring him to book.

Also in October 1598, Richard Quiney wrote "To my loving good friend & countryman Mr. Wm. Shackespere," asking him for £30 to help "me out of all the debts I owe in London." (The letter, the only one we know of ever to have been addressed to Shakspere, was evidently not delivered, for it was found in Quiney's papers.) A few days later Richard Quiney's father, Adrian, wrote to him that "If you bargain with Mr. Sha. or receive money therefor, bring your money home if you may. . . ." A few days after that, Abraham Sturley wrote to Richard Quiney referring to a letter from the latter indicating "that our countryman Mr. Wm. Shak. would procure us money," remarking that this "I will like of as I shall hear when, and where, and how. . . ." When it came to getting money from William Shakspere it was apparently a matter of seeing is believing.

Also in 1598, the Chamber Account of Stratford for Christmas records ten pence paid to Mr. Shaxpere for one load of stone.

In February 1599, according to testimony given twenty years later by John Heminge and Henry Condell, "William Shakespere" was a shareholder in the Globe, erected in that year. He was one of those who held a 10 per cent interest, as against 50 per cent held by the Burbages. Thirty-six years later, in 1635, Cuthbert Burbage testified that in building the Globe, "to our selves were joined those deserving men, Shakspere, Heminges, Condell, Philips and other partners."

In May 1599, an inventory of the property of Thomas Brend, father of Nicholas Brend, lessor of the land on which the Globe was built, listed a house newly built in the parish of St. Saviour "in occupacione Willielmi Shakespeare et aliorum."

In October 1599, "Willelmus Shakspeare" was listed as a tax delinquent from the parish of St. Helen who had moved to Sussex.

In October 1600, the tax owed by "Willelmus Shakspeare" was referred for collection to the Bishop of Winchester. Later the Bishop accounted on his rolls for a lump sum received from persons referred to him by the sheriff.

In May 1602, William Shakespeare paid William Combe and John Combe £320 for 107 acres of land north of Stratford, the deed "Sealed and delivered to Gilbert Shakespere," William's brother. William was described as "of Stratford upon Avon."

In September 1602, "Shackespere," referred to also as "Shakespere," purchased a cottage on "Walkers Street alias Dead Lane" on the chapel side across from New Place for an undisclosed amount.

In late 1602, in another legal action respecting New Place, "Willielmum Shakespeare" was described for the first time as "generosus," gentleman.

Circa 1603 to 1616, a lease of property east of New Place said that "The barn on the west side bounds by Mr. William Shaxpeare."

In May 1603, it was recorded on the patent rolls that King James "do licence and authorize these our Servants lawrence ffletcher Willm Shakespeare Richard Burbage Augustyne Phillippes Iohn hemings henrie Condell Willm Sly Robt Armyn Richard Cowly and the rest of their associates freely to use and exercise the art and faculty of playing comedies tragedies," etc. "for the recreation of our loving subjects as for our solace and pleasure."

In March 1604, the accounts of the Master of the Great Wardrobe recorded the grant to "diverse persons" of four yards of red cloth each in preparation for his Majesty's progress through the City of London. All those persons licensed in the foregoing item as members of the King's Company are listed as recipients of the cloth, "William Shakespeare" heading the list.

At some time during 1604, our subject was lodging with the family of Christopher Mountjoy, a French Huguenot maker of women's headdresses, in Cripplegate Ward. This we know because a deposition was taken of "William Shakespeare of Stratford upon Avon" in connection with a suit brought by Mountjoy's son-in-law, Stephen Belott, charging that Mountjoy had broken promises with respect to his daughter's dowry. The deposition is signed "Willn Shakp," the first of the six signatures ascribed to the famous Stratfordian known to exist. Willn Shakp's inability to recall circumstances crucial to the case suggests to E. K. Chambers that he was perhaps then, at the age of forty-eight, "of failing memory."

In July 1604, "Willielmus Shexpere" brought a legal action to collect a debt in the amount of £1 15s 10d from an apothecary of Stratford, Philip Rogers, for malt with which he had supplied the debtor beginning in the preceding March.

In May 1605, Augustine Phillipps made a will in which he bequeathed "unto and amongst the hired men of the Company which I am of . . . the sum of five pounds . . . to be equally distributed amongst them." First of those to be named was "my fellow William Shakespeare."

In July 1605, "William Shakespear" purchased for £440 half the corn and hay tithes of three hamlets in Stratford parish — Old Stratford, Welcombe, and Bishopton. (Following abolition of the monasteries under Henry VIII, the tithes formerly paid by the tenants on the vast monastery lands were made over to civil authorities and were leased out for collection.) Shakspere agreed to pay £5 a year to a creditor of the former leaser of the tithes and £17 to the Stratford Corporation. In 1611, his interest in the tithes was valued at £60 annually.

In June 1607, there appeared in the marriage register of Stratford the entry: "John Hall gentleman & Susanna Shaxpere." Hall, a physician whose case-book was to be translated from the Latin and published in 1657 by the surgeon James Cooke, brought the Shakesperes their first recorded intellectual distinction.

In August 1608, according to testimony given in 1619 by John Heminge and Henry Condell (referred to above), Blackfriars Theatre was leased by seven men, among them the two Burbages, John Heminge, William "Shakespeare," and Henry Condell. In testimony given in 1635 (also referred to above), Cuthbert Burbage speaks of having "purchased the lease remaining from Evans with our money, and placed men Players, which were Heminge, Condall, Shakspeare, &c."

Between December 1608 and June 1609, William "Shackspeare" was proceeding against John Addenbrooke, whom he had had arrested, to collect £6 that Addenbrooke owed him, plus £1, 5s costs. After having a fellow townsman stand surety for him, Addenbrooke left Stratford and Shakspere "avenged himself," as the orthodox biographer Sir Sidney Lee put it, by proceeding against the unfortunate surety.

In 1610, William "Shakespere" was involved in a further legal action with respect to New Place, evidently seeking additional assurance of title and possibly buying an additional twenty acres.

In 1611(?), "William Shackspeare, of Stratford upon Avon" and two other leaseholders of the tithes submitted a bill of complaint in the Court of Chancery in Stratford seeking relief from having to make good the nonpayment of rents by fellow leaseholders. There are two documents, the second sworn to in February 1611.

In September 1611, seventy-one citizens of Stratford were listed as contributing to a fund for "prosecuting the bill in parliament for the better repair of the highways." In the margin is added "Mr William Shackspere."

In January 1613, John Combe of Stratford drew up a will in which he gave "to Mr William Shackspere five pounds." Combe was evidently a money-lender who at one time held the Stratford Corporation's plate in pawn.

(In March 1613, the Earl of Rutland's steward paid "to Mr. Shakspeare in gold about my Lord's impreso, xliiij^s" [44 shillings]. Because the same entry records payment of an equal amount to Richard Burbage "for painting and making it," Stratfordians consider the reference to be to their man. It is not clear, however, what a well-to-do businessman, even if he was also a famous dramatist, would be doing "about" a painted shield to be used in the tilt. Burbage, who was again paid three years later "for my Lord's Shield" [£14, 18s] was a skilled painter. Charlotte C. Stopes suggests, reasonably, that the payment was to John Shakespeare, maker of horses' bits for the King.)

On 10 March 1613, "William Shakespeare of Stratford upon Avon . . . gentleman" bought a house in Blackfriars near Blackfriars Theatre (both once part of a large Dominican priory) for £140, obviously as an investment, since he never occupied it. The next day he mortgaged the property back to its previous owner for £60. The device barred inheritance of any part of the property by his wife, who would otherwise have been entitled to her dower right of a third of its value. The deed for the property is signed "William Shakspē," the indenture "Wm Shakspē." Neither of the cosigners of the two documents, William Johnson and John Jackson, had any difficulty signing his surname in full.

In 1614, the account of the Chamberlains of Stratford listed: "Item for one quart of sack and one quart of claret wine given to a preacher at new place. xx^d."

Beginning in the fall of 1614, certain landowners, including William Combe (son of John Combe the money-lender), attempted to enclose for their own benefit the common lands of Welcombe belonging to the Stratford Corporation. Opposition from the Corporation and local citizens was intense. Shakspeare or Shackeseare, as he is called in documents bearing on the case, was involved both as owner of 106 acres in the area and as part owner with Thomas Greene of the tithes from neighboring lands. Thomas Greene, the Town Clerk, wrote in his diary for November 17 that "Shakspeare . . . told me that they assured him they meant to inclose no further than to gospel bush" and quoted from further observations of his on the intentions of the enclosers. This quotation, together with a memorandum of Greene's of "Shakspeares telling J Greene that J Greene was not able to bear the enclosing of Welcombe" is all that Shakspere ever said that has come down to us. Shakspere joined with Greene in obtaining a deed from Combe indemnifying both against any injury they might suffer from the enclosure. For the rest, the orthodox biographers today characterize Shakspere's part in the complicated and long-drawn-out proceedings as peripheral. Unfortunately, the Town Council's correspondence with Shakspere, like so much else of possible incompatibility with the role in which he has been cast, has disappeared. Sir Sidney Lee, whose practice was to give Shakspere the benefit of every doubt, declares that "having thus secured himself against all possible loss, Shakespeare threw his influence into Combe's scale." Later commentators are at pains to show how this was not so; but at best Shakspere was neutral in the dispute, and evidently he remained on good terms with the Combes.

In May 1615, "William Shakespere" is named in a suit aimed at clearing up the record of ownership of Blackfriars properties.

On 10 February, 1616, we quote again from Professor J. Isaacs in *The Listener,* this time basing his statements on new "startling information,"

> Shakespeare finally got his thirty-one-year-old daughter, Judith, off his hands, married to a rather shifty person, Thomas Quiney. . . . He was twenty-six. The marriage took place within the period of prohibition when a special licence was required. They were married without a licence. The Bishop of Worcester summoned them to appear before the Consistory Court, they didn't turn up, and they were excommunicated. In January 1616 Shakespeare drafted his will, on March 25 he made a new one, crossing out his son-in-law's name. What caused Shakespeare to lose confidence in Thomas Quiney? The mystery is now solved. On March 25, 1616, Thomas Quiney is called before the ecclesiastical court and presented for incontinence with a certain Margaret Wheeler. He appeared and confessed that he had had carnal intercourse with the said Wheeler, and was sentenced to appear three Sundays in a penitential sheet in Stratford Church. But even more startling is an entry in the Stratford Burial Registers a month after the marriage, and ten days before Shakespeare altered his will. On March 15, 1616, the burial entry reads, "Margaret Wheeler and her child."

On 25 March 1616, "W^{mj} Shackspeare" made his will, evidently a revision of one done in January. A bequest to his "son in L" is crossed out (see above) and evidence of displeasure with Judith seems to be indicated. The instrument, three pages long and most revealing, is minutely detailed in its bequests and in its planning for various contingencies of inheritance. Clearly the testator was looking forward to a dynasty through the line of Susanna and her husband, John Hall. Monetary provision is made for Judith, to be increased if she resigns her right in the testator's Rowington copyhold, but for the rest, all real property goes to Susanna — the freehold and dwelling, with appurtenances, called the New Place, "wherein I now dwell," the freeholds and dwellings, with appurtenances, in Henley Street, and "all my barns stablers Orchards gardens lands tenements & hereditaments" situated in the towns or grounds of Stratford-on-Avon, Old Stratford, Bishopton, and Welcombe, together with the freehold and dwelling in Blackfriars. After bequeathing his broad, silver gilt bowl to Judith, he leaves "all the rest of my goods chattels Leases plate Jewels and household stuffs whatsoever . . . to my Son in Law John Hall gent & my daughter Susanna his wife." He gives 26 shillings 8 pence to four friends, two of them to buy themselves rings, and 20 shillings to his godson. Following this comes an interlineation by which also 26 shillings 8 pence each for the purchase of rings are given "to my fellows John Hemynge Richard Burbage & Henry Cundell." Evidently it had come to the testator as an afterthought (supposing that the thought was his) that, after all, the closest associates of his life were — were they not? — in the theatre!

Stratfordians are sensitive about the will on several counts. One is the famous interlineation near the end just before Judith comes in for the silver gilt bowl, "Item I give unto my wife my second best bed with the furniture." The lone and slighting reference to his helpmeet and mother of his children has, Professor Gerald Eades Bentley of Princeton complains, "given rise to many romantic or lurid tales." Chambers declares that "A good deal of sheer nonsense has been written about this." Stratfordians argue, with Chambers, that "Mrs. Shakespeare would have been entitled by common law to her dower of a life interest in one-third of any of the testator's heritable estates on which dower had not, as in the case of the Blackfriars property, been legally barred; and to residence in the principal mansion house." It is unkind of Sir Edmund to recall how Shakspere exerted himself to bar his wife's dower rights in the Blackfriars house. In any case a man well disposed towards his wife would surely not have made a point of bequeathing every scrap of real property over her head to the children, even her home itself, in which she would now be a mere tenant, for whom a place was required by law; it would have been as easy to give her lifetime possession of that at least. Far from being singled out to receive some object of special value, Anne was not even permitted to dispose of her husband's clothes; they, too, were willed away. Further, as Marchette Chute writes, "Most of the wills of this period are personal and affectionate" — and she cites as examples those of actors with whom Shakspere is associated — but "Shakespeare was one member of the company whose will does not show a flicker of personal feeling."

No mention appears in the will of shares in the Globe and in Blackfriars. Chambers thinks these would have been comprehended in "leases." But shares that he estimates would have brought in about £200 a year — enough today to meet the mortgage payments on a very expensive house — would, one supposes, hardly be dealt with so casually. (Under the will, Judith received only £150 plus the yearly interest on another £150.) And, as Chambers concedes, the shares never turn up in the records of Shakspere's heirs. One wonders if the William Shakespeare who held shares in the two theatres was the Stratfordian after all.

Louis P. Bénézet writes:

> The wills of Heminge, who died in 1630, aged 75, and of Condell, who was deceased in 1627, in literary style and clearness are so far above the rambling, unpunctuated scrawl that is today worshipped as the final literary composition of the world's greatest author-genius as to suggest that they belonged to a monde at least two strata above him. Heminge speaks of his books, specifies that five pounds shall be spent in purchasing volumes for the education of his grand-child, and writes again and again of his income from the Globe and Blackfriars playhouses and its disposal. Condell wills to his son his yearly dividend from the "Blackfriars" and the "Bankside."

No reference appears in Shakspere's will to books or manuscripts. The books, we are told, would have been lumped under "goods . . . & household stuff." Goods and household stuff — the beloved library on which the impoverished villager would have soared to the highest literary pinnacle! Ben Jonson was liberal in his gift of books. Had Shakspere no companions of shared interests to whom he might have willed some jointly treasured volumes, as he willed his sword to Thomas Combe, his wearing apparel to his sister Joan? "It does seem odd to us nowadays that objects of such affection as some of Shakespeare's books must have been to their owner were not specified but left to go in with the rest of his personal belongings," says Ivor Brown. Very odd indeed. T. W. Baldwin, whose two-tome study of Shakspere's education is considered the ultimate on the subject, writes, "It is easy enough to find books once owned by Ben Jonson. Had Shakspere [as he calls both author and Stratfordian] purchased books as ardently as he did certain other forms of real property, we should certainly have more trace of his activities in that way." As it is, "we have no absolutely conclusive external proof, so far as I know, that he ever owned a book of any kind."

What about the manuscripts of his plays, which he had never shown any interest in having printed? They were "the property of the [theatrical] company," Gerald E. Bentley of Princeton tells us. Even if this statement were warranted — and we shall see in due course why it is not — the manuscript copies the writer might be assumed to have had would be left out of account. Professor Bentley will allow him only "early drafts or 'foul papers,'" and these, he asserts, would have been embraced in — yes — those "goods . . . & household stuff." As for why these and other papers a literary man would accumulate, or any books we may believe to have been his, have never turned up, neither he nor any other orthodox academician has anything to say. Did the alleged dramatist own no copies of his own works?

We are talking, let us recall, not of some harassed scribe living hand-to-mouth in a succession of London lodgings, but of a very substantial property owner dwelling during the last years of his life in one of the finest houses in the community. He is survived for seven years by his wife (the burial register for 8 August 1623 recording simply, "Mrs. Shakspeare"), and by the time she dies, publication of the First Folio edition of Shakespeare's plays has ensured the author's immortality. Shakspere's daughters live until 1649 and 1662 respectively, his granddaughter Elizabeth Hall, who marries John (later Sir John) Bernard, until 1670. By then, so popular and respected had Shakespeare's works remained, so clearly destined to live, that a third folio had been called for. Few persons in England had cause for as great pride of descent as Elizabeth Hall, who still retained New Place, as did her husband until his death in 1674. Circumstances could hardly have been more favorable to the preservation of the great writer's papers, if Shakspere were he. Yet Stratford has never produced a scrap of them, or anything in its illustrious son's hand but the three signatures on the will. Marchette Chute quotes from charming, affectionate letters written by the actor Edward Alleyn, Shakspere's contemporary, to his wife while on tour, but if Shakspere, who lived away from his family for far longer times (if what we are told of his London years is true) ever wrote a letter to his wife or daughters — or to anyone else, for that matter — we have nothing to show it. Papers bearing the signatures or marks of the men with whom Shakspere did business in Stratford have survived, but none to which his hand was affixed. It is another case of important documentary evidence disappearing, and one wonders if the vanished papers showed the reputed literary genius signing them with a mark. The quality of the signatures on the will makes this possibility seem likely. These also have been an embarrassment to orthodoxy. Inasmuch as the signatory was only a month from his death when the will was executed, it is sometimes proposed that the palpable difficulty he had inscribing his name was attributable to a fatal malady, I believe by some of the very pleaders who would have us take seriously, as applying to their man, the Reverend Dr. Ward's report of a half-century later that he had died of a drinking bout with Ben Jonson and Michael Drayton. But the allegation of debilitating affliction, somewhat gainsaid by the testator's solemn avowal to being "in perfect health," runs squarely afoul of the last sentence in the will, which includes the declaration "I have herunto put my Seal," with "Seal" crossed out and "hand" substituted. Are we to believe that the solicitor, being unaccustomed to having Mr. Shakspere sign papers, prepares the will for his seal, then, upon discovering him to be too ill to control his hand, elects to have him sign the three pages of the will after all? Or that Mr. Shakspere himself decides to reverse his practice now that signing has become almost impossible?

The signatures on the will are so damning that McManaway prudently omits them from the photograph of the subject's signatures in the Folger Booklet *The Authorship of Shakespeare,* though there is ample room for all six. In Chapter 8, I shall cite the latest and most expert testimony so far on the signatures.

The burial registers of Trinity Church in Stratford for 1616 contain this record:

Aprill 25 Will. Shakspere gent.

After Shakspere's son-in-law died, the burial register read:

Johannes Hall, medicus peritissimus.

Professor Bentley writes, "The parish clerk's unusual designation of 'medicus peritissimus,' most skillful physician, suggests a great respect for Dr. Hall in the town." He does not say what he believes the designation of Will. Shakspere simply as "gent" suggests.

4
"A Case of Lives"

Having duly examined all that Shakspere left of himself in the records of his time, we turn to the observances with which the world signalized its loss upon his passing, and we address ourselves to what his life seems to add up to, as it stands revealed in the documents that unexampled scholastic industry has brought to light. We turn then to the claims of his partisans that our information about him exceeds that which we have about almost all his fellow writers. This contention prompts us to ask, "Yes, but what kind of information?" Putting the authorities to the test, we review the knowledge we have of the lives, especially the literary lives, of two of those other writers — John Lyly (who would hardly be known to us were it not that orthodoxy has assigned him a formative influence upon Shakespeare) and Edmund Spenser. What we learn about Shakspere by comparing his kind of life with that of his two contemporaries is matched by what we learn about the orthodox authorities by comparing their assurances with our own discoveries. We then inquire what difference there may have been between the kind of notice taken of Shakspere's death and that accorded much lesser writers of the time upon theirs, and the results are equally revealing.

As far as the record shows, no notice was taken of Shakspere's death apart from the burial record of Holy Trinity Church. If any of his contemporaries in Stratford thought the master of New Place of any importance other than as a man of property, we have nothing to show it. Dr. John Hall, Susanna's husband, whose casebooks were to be translated from Latin and published after his death, evidently never found occasion to mention his father-in-law in his writings, though he recorded personal details of many patients, including Michael Drayton, whom he called "an excellent poet." Nothing indicates that he or his wife and her sister or any of their fellow townsmen considered that their lives had been touched by greatness when in 1623 Shakespeare was proclaimed the soul of the age to whom "all scenes of Europe homage owed." (B. Jonson) Yes, some time before his death, the monument to "Shakspeare" (page 211) was installed in the wall of Holy Trinity Church, but almost certainly, as we shall see, it was the work of outsiders, and though it makes extravagant claims for him, it does not identify him as poet, dramatist, or actor.

Shakspere's gravestone in the chancel of the church bears no name. This omission seems not to trouble his partisans, though others may be pardoned for finding it odd that the town would leave unidentified the tomb of the man who should have towered over all others in its pride. As far as I know, it is recognized as Shakspere's only through hearsay and because of its position between that of "Anne Shakespeare" and Susanna's. The inscription bespeaks a corpse of scant distinction. A leaflet prepared for visitors to the church passes its crudity off lightly. It enjoins them to "Read the immortal lines he rather mischievously wrote to ensure his grave would remain undisturbed." They do not sound very mischievous to me. Least of all do they sound like the work of a poet. Inelegantly rendered as is the present epitaph, its predecessor was even cruder — for it would appear that the original slab was replaced by one somewhat more in keeping, probably in the late 1700s. Our source for the earlier version is the renowned Shakespearean editor George Steevens, who in 1785 wrote that the "epitaph [is] expressed in the following uncouth mixture of small and capital letters:

Good Friend for Iefus SAKE forbeare
To diGG ⊤E Duft Encloafed HERe
Blefe be ⊤E Man ^Y_T fpares ⊤Hs Stones
And curft be He ^Y_T moves my bones."

A Mr. Dowdall, visiting Stratford in 1693, wrote in a letter that the epitaph was "made by himself a little before his death." In 1694, William Hall, B.A. of Queens' College as of that year, also cited the verses in a letter and wrote:

> The little learning these verses contain, would be a very strong argument for the want of it in the author; did not they carry something in them which stands in need of a comment. There is in this Church a place which they call the bone-house, a repository for all bones they dig up; which are so many that they would load a great number of waggons. The poet being willing to preserve his bones unmoved, lays a curse upon him that moves them: and having to do with clarks and sextons, for the most part a very [i]gnorant sort of people, he descends to the meanest of their capacities; and disrobes himself of that art, which none of his co-temporaries wore in greater perfection.

The orthodox scholars seem to go along with this notion. The epitaph, says Giles E. Dawson, former curator of books and manuscripts at the Folger Library,

> has been attributed to Shakespeare himself, and rude doggerel though it be, there is no serious bar to our accepting the attribution. The obvious purpose of the epitaph is to frighten off anyone planning to disturb the grave, and it is not difficult to conceive that Shakespeare, who always knew how to suit poetic style to his auditory and his purpose, would here pitch his verse to the level of gravediggers and the like.

Quite apart from my difficulty in recalling any play or poem of Shakespeare's that was written down to an audience, I find the argument unaccountable. Are we to suppose that the Englishman whose epitaph above all others, whether written by himself or another, could have been expected to be distinguished at the least by dignity and high-mindedness, is the one Englishman to have had his tomb debased by "rude doggerel" addressed to gravediggers?[1] And if Shakspere were the great Shakespeare, what sense would it make for him to have composed such an epitaph? We are talking of the renowned writer whose consciousness of his achievement led him to boast in the *Sonnets* that his verse would outlive the marble monuments of princes. Would such a one have imagined his fellow townsmen's permitting his mortal remains to be carted off to the charnel-house when in fact those remains could have been expected to make a shrine of Stratford? If they were going to be moved at all, it would have been to Westminster Abbey. Indeed, had he been the poet-dramatist, Shakspere would have had every reason to expect interment in the Abbey. In the first comment we have on Shakespeare's passing, probably of 1622, an Oxford student, William Basse, called for a place to be prepared for him there:

> Renowned Spencer, lie a thought more nigh
> To learned Chaucer, and rare Beaumont lie
> A little nearer Spenser to make room
> For Shakespeare in your threefold fourfold tomb.

From what we know of Shakspere, can we imagine his not exulting in the prospect of resting in the pantheon of England's great or his taking any action to bar such an apotheosis? Surely it would not have been out of sentimental attachment to his native heath: a conspicuous feature of his affluent years in Stratford, as Marchette Chute points out, is that he took no part in the affairs of the town and contributed nothing to it.

I am torn between two views of the crude verse on the gravestone. Was it devised by Shakspere himself and representative of his intellectual level and legitimate fear of ending in the bone-house? Or was it, like the monument in the wall not far away, the work of outsiders who, appalled at the possibility of the corpse's being installed in the Abbey, were making sure that it would stay where it was? Ben Jonson, in his eulogy of Shakespeare in the First Folio, goes out of his way to reject the proposal made by young Basse:

> My Shakespeare, rise; I will not lodge thee by
> Chaucer or Spenser, or bid Beaumont lie
> A little further, to make thee a room. . . .

And why will Jonson not do so? Because

---

[1] This statement may not be quite true. A baker dying around 1630 is reported to have had almost the same epitaph as Shakspere.

Thou art a monument, without a tomb. . . .

Never mind that the Stratford man had a tomb as plain as day.

And art alive still, while thy book doth live,
And we have wits to read and praise to give.

In other words, Shakespeare cannot be buried in Westminster Abbey because (unlike the Stratford man) he is incorporeal, a monument consisting of his immortal works and hence still living.

Because my sojourns in the realm of Shakespearean orthodoxy are accompanied by a sense of insuperable bafflement at what I find to be believed, I remind myself that there is a *prima facie* case for the orthodox view. Fairness demands that I acknowledge it here. If such a *prima facie* case were not at hand the conviction that the Stratford Shakspere and the poet-dramatist William Shakespeare were the same would never have taken root.

The names of the two are similar, and after the Stratfordian had been to London his name was sometimes rendered not *Shak*spere (or Shaksper, or Shagspere, or Shaxpere) but *Shake*speare, like the dramatist's, though not by the Stratfordian in his signatures or on the monument, and never was it hyphenated as the dramatist's name often was. Shakspere was associated with the theatre and there is evidence that he was an actor of sorts. The period during which the works we know as Shakespeare's were becoming familiar to London audiences (for the first time, according to orthodoxy) or were being printed for the first time (with one exception) — between 1591 and 1623 — is consistent, if we do not look too closely into the matter, with Shakspere's having written them. The inscription on the Stratford monument and the introductory material to the First Folio — if, again, we follow the example of the Stratfordians and read them but cursorily — seem to point to Shakspere as the author. Without these two posthumous memorials, the singular and fascinating character of which we shall later explore, it is scarcely conceivable that anyone would ever have thought of the Stratford Shakspere as the writer.

Why do I say that? If we strip from Shakspere's biography all such records as would be paralleled for thousands of Elizabethans — undistinguished records of christenings, marriages, deaths, business transactions, court actions, tax collections, wills, and the like — what have we left to mark Shakspere as in any way out of the ordinary? Well, we have his successful pursuit of armorial bearings, but these were granted for his antecedents' attainments, not his, and in any case could be duplicated for scores or hundreds of other Elizabethans having no connection with the arts. Let us then scratch those references, too. We end up with several records associating him with actors and several others identifying him (if indeed it be he) as a shareholder in two theatres. And that is all. Curiously, in all but one of the six or seven records of any significance, he is mentioned as one of a group of men, never singly, and even in the one exception — the inventory of Thomas Brend's property — the mention is of "William Shakespeare and others."

What, on the other hand, is missing from the record? No mention is found of the subject's ever having had a day's schooling. Nothing associates him with literary or intellectual interests of any kind. Never, so far as we know, did he speak of having written anything, and during his lifetime no one we know of ever suggested that he had written anything, let alone that he had any connection with the works attributed to "William Shakespeare" or "Shake-speare" that appeared during his lifetime. Nothing he ever said was recorded except a few remarks in relation to the enclosure of common lands neighboring his own. Not only is no letter of his preserved, but no indication that he ever wrote one — or, for that matter, that he ever received one. Apart from the evidence that he was an actor, which, we shall see, is outweighed by the evidence that he was not, nothing in the record is inconsistent with his having been nearly illiterate, and the character of his surviving signatures reinforces rather than contradicts the impression that he was.

As Mark Twain wrote:

> Isn't it odd, when you think of it, that you may list all the celebrated English-men, Irishmen, and Scotchmen of modern times, clear back to the first Tudors — a list containing five hundred names, shall we say? — and you can go to the histories, biographies, and cyclopedias and learn the particulars of the lives of every one of them. Every one of them except one — the most famous, the most renowned — by far the most illustrious of them all — Shakespeare! . . . About him you can find *nothing*. Nothing of even the slightest importance. Nothing worth the trouble of storing away in your memory. Nothing that even remotely indicates that he was ever anything more than a distinctly commonplace person.

The "small village" to which he was native, the Missourian goes on to comment, "did not regard him as a person of any consequence, and had all but forgotten all about him before he was fairly cold in his grave."

"I suppose," Sir Ralph Richardson observes, "there is no author who is as widely read and performed today as William Shakespeare, and yet we know next to nothing about him." And why are we so ignorant of the Stratfordian's life-history? Mark Twain's answer is, *"He hadn't any history to record.* There is no way of getting around that deadly fact."

We have, however, A. L. Rowse's assurance that we know more about Shakespeare than about any other dramatist of the time except Ben Jonson, "who lived rather later," and Dr. McManaway tells us that "For a playwright of the time, Shakespeare's life is well documented." As I have observed, it is a fundamental tenet of the Stratfordian biographers, vigorously brought forward, that we know as much about "Shakespeare" as we could expect. "Shakespeare is not alone in his obscurity," says Gerald Eades Bentley. And, anticipating Rowse, he declares that we have "more records of the activities of the dramatist . . . , in fact, than we have for any other playwright of the times except Ben Jonson." As director of the Folger Library, Louis B. Wright has asserted that "We know even less about the lives of many writers and some men of affairs than we know about Shakespeare." He assures us that "Much more is on the record about Shakespeare than about many other Elizabethan men of letters." Marchette Chute's contribution is that "It is extremely fortunate that the greatest of Elizabethan playwrights should also have been the best documented." The height of fantasy is reached by Bergen Evans of Northwestern University, writing in the *Saturday Review*: "We know more about him than we do about any of the other claimants [*sic*] except Bacon. He was, apparently, one of the best-known citizens of his day."

Is it, then, that we are so in the dark about Shakespeare's literary contemporaries? Let us consider an Elizabethan playwright and novelist who was born ten years before Shakspere, whom probably few have read for pleasure for two centuries or more, and whose life has received a micro-fraction of the attention that research scholars have devoted to Shakespeare's. I select him because I have inherited his *Complete Works,* with an introductory *Life,* by R. Warwick Bond.

John Lyly was recorded as matriculating at Magdalen College, Oxford, on 8 October 1571, at the age of seventeen, some two years after actually entering the university. He obtained his bachelor's degree in 1573 and a master's in 1575 and was incorporated a Master of Arts of Cambridge in 1579. In May 1574, he had written a letter in Latin to Lord Burleigh begging, apparently without success, for a fellowship at Magdalen and alluding to past favors shown him by the great Lord Treasurer. He wrote of himself that Oxford "before she brought me forth . . . played the nice mother in sending me into the country to nurse, where I tired at a dry breast for three years." Gabriel Harvey, a contemporary of Lyly's prominent at both Oxford and Cambridge, exclaimed of him that "They were much deceived of him at Oxford . . . that took him only for a dapper and deft companion" and spoke of his "horning, gaming, fooling and knaving."

Harvey knew Lyly when the latter was engaged on his first work, *Euphues,* in 1578, "in the Savoy," where needy scholars and writers found lodging. Lyly's were evidently paid for by the Earl of Oxford. The "Fiddlestick of Oxford," Harvey called Lyly, ostensibly referring to the University, but probably expecting to be taken as meaning the Earl. Lyly resented this appellation, according to the playwright Thomas Nashe, who wrote that "With a black sant he means shortly to be at his chamber window." Years later Lyly was to write a brochure attacking Harvey, which has disappeared. In *Euphues* he made a thinly disguised attack on his alma mater and in a second edition sought to lessen the effect in an address "To my verie good friends, the Gentlemen Scholars of Oxford."

From a letter of Lyly's of 1582 and from Harvey we know that Lyly was engaged as a private secretary to the Earl of Oxford, who had two companies of actors and was himself highly praised as a writer of comic dramas. From this information we may infer with Lyly's biographer, R. Warwick Bond, that "Suggestion, encouragement and apparatus thus lay ready to Lyly's hand." (*Euphues and His England,* when it appeared in 1580, was dedicated "To the Right Honourable my very good Lorde and Maister Edward de Vere, Earle of Oxenforde.") Also in 1582, in a letter to Thomas Watson, who had dedicated a collection of love sonnets to the Earl, Lyly alludes to an affair of the heart he had once had. In that year, too, he wrote a long letter to Lord Burleigh defending himself against some unspecified charge. In 1580, he had got into trouble with Harvey. The latter had written a poetical satire on an Italianate Englishman that undoubtedly was directed at Oxford, who at twenty-six had returned from an Italian tour to some extent Italianized in dress and tastes — in fact, bringing the Italian Renaissance to England. Harvey wound up before the Privy Council on a charge of libel, and though he got off with an apology, he blamed Lyly for seeking to excite the Earl against him, while also reporting that the Earl, with "Jovial" good nature, had shrugged the matter off.

In 1579, when another candidate was appointed Master of the Revels, Lyly was "entertained" Queen Elizabeth's "servant by her own gracious favor" and, it seems, encouraged to aim at the post himself in the future. Of this ambition he reminded the Queen in a petition addressed to her, evidently in 1595, recalling the hopes he had been given and lamenting that for ten years he had waited in vain. If her Majesty thought him unworthy, she should, he suggested, waft him into the country where, in "a tha'tch't cottage," he might "write prayers; instead of plays." Apparently in 1585, however, he had obtained a post supervising part of the functions of the Revels. By then he had become vice-master of the St. Paul's choir school, which provided one of the children's companies of actors that were a feature of the Elizabethan theatre, somewhat puzzling to the modern mind. The company was known as "Oxford's Boys" until 1586, and in 1583 Oxford transferred to Lyly the lease of a room in Blackfriars where the boys were rehearsed for appearances at Court. In 1597, Lyly was writing to the Queen's Secretary, Sir Robert Cecil, that "I find it folly that, one foot being in the grave, I should have the other on the stage" and referring to the "P'roguing of her maties promises" — "her maties" being an abbreviation of "her Majesty's" that falls on our ears today with a startling air of familiarity. In a second, despairing petition, apparently of 1598, he reproached the Queen that he has now been "Thirteen years your Highness' servant; but yet nothing."

Meanwhile, the two parts of the novel *Euphues* and six comedies attributed to him, all acted before the Queen, had made him famous and successful. He was elected to Parliament in 1589 from Hindon, from Aylesbury in 1593 and again in 1601, and from Appleby in 1597. In 1598, he wrote a tract, *Pappe with an hatchet,* for the High Church party in a battle with opponents of episcopal authority known as the Martin Marprelate controversy. Lyly was involved in this slugging-match of pamphleteers in league with Thomas Nashe, from whom, incidentally, we learn that Lyly was a smoker and had taught him to admire the sermons of Dr. Lancelot Andrews. If, as Harvey implies, Lyly had by 1589 obtained work as a reader of new books for the Bishop of London before they received the official imprimatur, that office could have led to his enlistment in the religious controversy.

Supposing that Lyly is represented in the character of Fastidious Brisk in Ben Jonson's *Every Man Out of His Humour* (the play in which Shakspere's pretensions to gentility are mocked in the oafish Sogliardo), as by general consent he is, we have an illuminating picture of him as "a neat, spruce, affecting courtier, one that wears clothes well, and in fashion," who practises deportment before a mirror, uses quotations well though addicted to the lowly viol and to tobacco, is prone to seek a lady's favor and a great man's familiarity, and is adept at obtaining from his merchant the credit on which he lives.

The 1590s brought the plays of Shakespeare to the boards, "works which threw the best that Lyly ever had, or could have, produced, utterly in the shade," R. Warwick Bond writes in his *Life of John Lyly,* and after 1595 "we have practically no new work from Lyly's pen." Ending his days in poverty and neglect, he was buried in St. Bartholomew the Less on 30 November 1606, having composed his own rueful estimate of his writing: "I have ever thought so superstitiously [i.e., with unreasoning awe] of wit, that I fear I have committed Idolatry against wisdom." He was soon virtually forgotten and remained so until rediscovered by 19th-century scholarship, the *Euphues* having been out of print for 150 years. "He owed his revival in the first instance to the increasing interest and thoroughness of the study of Shakespeare," Bond observes.

It will not be lost on the reader that the information brought to light about the forgotten minor writer, John Lyly, as a mere by-product of the interest in the ever-celebrated Shakespeare, is of the sort that has eluded Shakspere's investigators for all their thoroughness. For we find in Lyly's biography that which is conspicuously lacking in Shakespeare's. We see Lyly receiving his education, and at the two universities. We find him writing letters — which we can read today — to important persons and to other literary figures. We observe him involved with other men of letters and can read what they wrote about him, among those men being his play-writing contemporary, Oxford, whose confidence as one-time secretary he enjoyed. We have him in public positions both in the theatrical world and the world of affairs. We see him taking part in a public controversy that was to lead to the Puritan rebellion. We hear him speaking of his writing and even appraising it. Writing of the Stratford "Shakespeare," Professor Stephen Orgal of Johns Hopkins University recently reaffirmed the dictum that "we know more about him than about any other Elizabethan playwright," but in fact we know less about him as a playwright or likely playwright than about any Elizabethan playwright who is remembered at all.

If we find in Lyly's record what we seek in vain in Shakespeare's, we find it even more in Edmund Spenser's. And Spenser, the reader may recall, was named by Dr. McManaway with Raleigh and Milton as comparable with Shakespeare in the amount we do not know of him. At the risk of imposing too far on the reader, I think it will be worthwhile to review what we *do* know of Spenser. Doing so will further advance our knowledge of how far the orthodox scholars are to be trusted.

Spenser was born in London, he indicates, about twelve years before the celebrated nativity at Stratford. He wrote of descending from "a house of ancient fame" — the Spencers of Althorpe in Northampton. John Spenser, identified as his father, is said to have been a gentleman by birth. He was, however, only a "free journeyman" in the "art or mystery of clothmaking." The early circumstances of Edmund and the young Shakspere must have been similar, but their paths soon diverged. With help from a charity set up by Robert Nowell, a Londoner of Lancashire (like John Spenser), Edmund and his brother were enrolled as "poor scholars" in the Merchant Taylors school. E. de Selincourt writes:

> The poet was fortunate in his school. Mulcaster, its first head master, was a keen scholar with a generous conception of the aims of education. . . . [He] grounded his pupils in Hebrew, Greek, and Latin, he trained them daily in music both vocal and instrumental, and was a convinced advocate of the study of the mother tongue, and of the educational value of acting. He presented plays yearly before the court, in which his boys were the actors. . . . At School, too, Spenser acquired some knowledge of French, and made his first experiments as a poet.

The reference is to translation of poems by du Bellay and Petrarch that were published in *Theatre for Worldlings* in 1569 and later included in a volume of Spenser's poems and were certainly his; "It is natural," the *Encyclopaedia Britannica* tells us, "that a poet so steeped in poetry should show his faculty at a very early age" — a point it forgets when it comes to Shakespeare.

In that same year — 1569 — on 20 May, again with help from the Nowell charity, Edmund was admitted to Pembroke Hall at Cambridge as a sizar, one who receives an allowance from the college. His health at the University was not good, but he took his bachelor's degree in June 1572 and his master's in 1576. His later offer to teach Greek to a friend in Ireland indicates that he had acquired a proficiency in the language.

One of the Fellows at Pembroke was Gabriel Harvey, who favored Spenser with a different side of himself from the prickly belligerence he showed Lyly and others. Harvey (about whom, by the way, much more of significance is known than about the conventional "Shakespeare") was vain and pedantical, but, as de Selincourt writes, he "was a scholar of eminence, deeply versed in all that was accounted learning in his day," in most respects "a sound and judicious counsellor," whom years later Spenser "delighted to refer to . . . as his 'entire friend.'"

A quarrel with the master of a society to which Spenser belonged at Cambridge "respecting some preferment unjustly conferred upon a rival," a commentator of the past century wrote, destroyed his hopes of further advancement at the university. He departed northward to join his kinsfolk in Lancashire. There he fell in love with the "widow's daughter of the glen," whom he celebrated as Rosalind in his poems. Though he never divulged her identity, she appears to have been "of good family and high spirits." Edmund won the respect of the country maiden — according to Harvey, "gentle Mistress Rosalind once reported him to have all the intelligence at commandment, and another time christened him Signor Pegaso" — but her love was given to another, the Menalcas of his poem the *Shepheardes Calender,* which came out in 1578.

By then, on the advice of Harvey, Spenser had moved to London. There, through his mentor, he gained the friendship of Philip Sidney, who introduced him to his uncle, the powerful Earl of Leicester, the Queen's favorite and, as it had appeared likely, future husband. Spenser became a member of the Earl's household and was employed, as he says in one of his letters, in preparing an account of the Earl's genealogy. To de Selincourt

> It seems highly probable that Leicester employed him as a private messenger to friends at a distance, and that in this capacity he paid his first visit, in 1577, to Ireland, where Leicester's father-in-law, Sir Henry Sidney, was then Governor-General. But the greater part of his time seems to have been divided between the houses of Sidney and Leicester at Penshurst and in London.

Of this period we read elsewhere:

> His letters to Harvey and Harvey's letters to him furnish hints for a very engaging fancy picture of Spenser at this stage of his life — looking at the world through rose-coloured spectacles, high in favour with Sidney and Leicester, dating his letters from Leicester House, gaily and energetically discussing the technicalities of his art, . . . gcing to court in the train of Leicester, growing pointed beard and mustachios of fashionable shape, and frightening his ever-vigilant friend and mentor Harvey by the light courtier-like tone of his references to women.

Harvey, indeed, was soon warning him of the allure of another "Rosalin-dula." If, however, Spenser made highly placed friends at this time, one of the Eclogues of the *Shepheardes Calender* that alluded unflatteringly to Arch-bishop Grindall angered a man whose enmity could count for more in the long run than anyone else's sentiments but the Queen's. This was William Cecil, Lord Burghley, and he was to be further antagonized when Spenser wrote a biting attack in the form of a fable upon the proposed marriage of Elizabeth and the Duke of Alençon, which the Lord Treasurer favored, and had a fox, as Tucker Brooke says, symbolize "Burghley's imperiousness, avarice, and nepotism." The victim was not to be placated by an adulatory sonnet the unhappy poet later addressed to him.

Spenser was active in 1579 and 1580 in the literary group meeting at Leicester House, which Spenser called the Areopagus, its principal other members being Sidney and Sir Edward Dyer. Mediating between the literary theories of this group and those of Harvey, he was also busy writing poetry that would be published later. His experience at Court, however, had brought him around to the view reigning there, that poetry did not afford a profession for a gentleman: a gentleman did not publish his verse, for a reason Spenser put in a nutshell, lest he "seem rather for gain and commodity to do it." His primary object now became the improvement of his fortunes. He wrote Harvey: "While the iron is hot, it is good striking, and the minds of nobles vary as their estates."

He struck it with some result, and the mind of Leicester was swayed to have him appointed secretary to Arthur Lord Grey de Wilton, newly desig-nated Lord Deputy of Ireland, in August 1580. This post he held for two years, while his superior, a fanatic and deeply religious Protestant, undertook the "pacification" of the isle with a severity that made him its scourge and brought about his recall. Spenser would portray Lord Grey de Wilton in heroic guise in his *Faerie Queene* and years later defend his character and aims in a long paper entitled *Veue of the Present state of Ireland*. In this work he put forth a plan for dealing with the restless island by measures he acknowledged to be "bloody and cruel," but which he argued were essential to maintaining English power and the Protestant faith, both then menaced by mighty Spain.

De Selincourt tells us that:

> After Grey's departure Spenser remained in Ireland executing subordinate but not unlucrative duties as a civil servant. Already, in the previous year, he had been appointed Clerk of Decrees and Recognizances in the Irish Court of Chancery, and had obtained the lease of the Abbey and Manor of Enniscorthy, in Wexford County. But . . . in December 1581, he had relinquished it . . . and in the following month was granted for six years a house in Dublin, valued at five pounds. Later in 1582 the House of Friars, called New Abbey, County Kildare, was granted to him to be held on a twenty-one years' lease at a rent of three

pounds. In May 1583 "Edmund Spenser of New Abbey" is nominated with some others "to be a commissioner of musters in the County of Kildare, its crosses and marches. . . . In 1586 he dates a sonnet to Harvey from Dublin; in 1589 he succeeds his friend Ludovick Bryskett as Clerk of the Council of Munster . . . [which] was actively engaged in "planting" Munster with English colonists, dividing the province into different seigniories to be assigned to different gentlemen undertakers whom the crown was anxious to enrich. . . . Prominent among these was Sir Walter Ralegh, who obtained various grants, amounting in all to some forty thousand acres. Spenser himself received the more modest grant of the manor and castle of Kilcolman in the county of Cork. It consisted of 3,028 acres, with six English householders settled under him as cultivators of the land.

The reader not under the spell of Spenser's verse must by now be fully ready to cry "Hold! Enough!" However, that cannot be if we are to lay once and for all the myth concocted by orthodoxy of the comparative richness of Stratfordian biography, but I shall be as brief as necessity permits.

Spenser's years in Ireland were anything but poetically fallow, and his life on the forfeited estates of the Earls of Desmond, where he had evidently settled in 1589, must have been very pleasant, with the commodious castle of Kilcolman overlooking a fine lake and his friend Raleigh's vast property only thirty miles distant. The local society of expatriate English in Dublin held him in high regard. We owe his friend Bryskett a grave, mellisonant account of Spenser's response when Bryskett asked him to satisfy the company by "declaring unto us the great benefits which men obtain by the knowledge of Moral Philosophy, and in making us know what the same is." The poet begged that "I shall be excused at this time," for

> I have already undertaken a work tending to the same effect, which is in heroical verse under the title of a *Faerie Queene* to represent all moral virtues, assigning to every virtue a knight to be the patron and defender of the same, in whose actions and feats of arms and chivalry the operations of that virtue whereof he is the protector, are to be expressed, and the vices and unruly appetites that oppose themselves against the same, to be beaten down and overcome.

Such was Spenser's exegesis of the work by which posterity would chiefly know him.

He had completed three books of his *Faerie Queene* when Raleigh visited him in autumn 1589. In *Colin Clout's Come Home,* he would describe his meeting with the poet-navigator, whom he identifies as "The Shepherd of the Ocean." This work he was to dedicate to Raleigh, acknowledging "myself bounden unto you, for your singular favors and sundry good turns showed to me. . . ."

Meanwhile, if Spenser, as is likely, fanned the flames of the passion for poetry in Raleigh, it is clear that the ambitious courtier fanned those for worldly eminence in the poet. At Raleigh's urging, Spenser returned with him to London, taking with him the first installment of his masterwork, which was entered in the Stationers' Register before the end of the year and published soon thereafter.

The *Faerie Queene* was given to the world preceded by a long explanatory letter to Sir Walter Raleigh, who, with three other poets, including Harvey, contributed commendatory verses at the head of the volume, Raleigh's being a notably polished sonnet. In response Spenser addressed to Raleigh one of seventeen dedicatory sonnets he wrote to powerful and noble personages. In it, he deprecated his own "rhymes" as "unsavory and sour" compared to the verse of "the summer's Nightingale," as he called Sir Walter.

Sir Philip Sidney having met his immortal end on the field at Zutphen, Raleigh had become Spenser's patron, and with no reason to regret it. The *Faerie Queene* was an immense success and put its author "on easy terms with all lovers of the arts," while "among the ladies of the court he had many friends." Some of these he cultivated with dedications of poems, notably the Countess of Pembroke and the Marquesse of Northampton. Through the good offices of Raleigh he was received by the Queen and granted by her a pension of £50. When added to the former estates of the Earls of Desmond, this stipend, sufficient in itself to feed and decently house an individual today, would seem to us rather generous acknowledgement of a poet's claims. Spenser was looking for higher office, however, and for his ill success in that respect blamed Burghley's continuing enmity. Although he had maintained his prolific output in London and during a stay in Alton in Hampshire, he decided, no doubt correctly, that the atmosphere of the Court, poisoned by intrigue for high stakes, was far less salubrious for poetry-making than the beauties of Kilcolman, which he had learned to love, and to these, and the duties of his clerkship, he returned in 1591.

Here, we know that he was involved in a dispute over boundaries with a neighbor, Lord Roche, and, more happily, was married on 11 June 1594 to Elizabeth Boyle after a year's courtship, an event that inspired one of his loveliest poems, the *Epithalamion*. Very likely as part of the marriage settlement, he turned over his clerkship to the Council of Munster to his bride's father, Sir Robert Boyle.

Within eighteen months of the wedding, Spenser was in London again, this time to register a second installment of the *Faerie Queene* with the company of Stationers and to pursue his unflagging hopes of preferment, those now centering — disappointingly — upon the Earl of Essex. *Fowre Hymnes* was dated "Greenwich, the first of September 1596" and was followed by poems dedicated to the Countesses of Cumberland and Warwick and work on his prescription for Ireland. Treading very uneasy ground, this harsh recommendation was entered on the Register only in 1598, and then with the proviso that further authority be obtained for its printing.

The year before, Spenser had returned to Kilcolman, to be followed in

September 1598 by a recommendation from Elizabeth that he be made Sheriff of Cork as "a gentleman dwelling in the county of Cork, who is so well known unto you for all his good and commendable parts, being a man endowed with good knowledge in learning, and not unskilful or without experience in the war." The office must have been welcome, for the poet now had four children to feed. He was not, however, to enjoy it for long. As he would have seen it, laxness had bred its inevitable offspring. The Earl of Tyrone, having routed an English army, roused the countryside of Munster. Kilcolman was burned to the ground, consuming in its flames, some have believed, the last part of the *Faerie Queene*. De Selincourt writes:

> Spenser escaped with his family to Cork, and there was entrusted by Sir John Norreys, the President of the province, with despatches to be delivered to the home government. He left Cork on the 9th of December and before the 24th he was in London. With the despatch of Sir John Norreys he presented to the queen a statement drawn up by himself written mostly before his departure, containing "certain points to be considered in the recovery of the Realm of Ireland."

Spenser's health gave way, as his spirit must have faltered earlier, and on 16 January 1599 he was dead. Ben Jonson's report of many years later that he had returned "20 pieces" the Earl of Essex had sent him on hearing of his need, replying that he "had no time to spend them," is almost certainly not to be taken, as Jonson asserted, as meaning that he died for lack of bread.

. . . .

Such is our bibliographic information about Edmund Spenser. Dr. Mc-Manaway, as a recognized scholar of the Elizabethan age and an assistant director of the Folger Library, must have been conversant with it. In his *The Shakespeare Authorship,* however, all he concedes as being known about the poet is as follows:

> London was "his most kindly nurse."
> His mother's name is known only because the poet's praise of his second (or perhaps third) wife, Elizabeth Boyle, mentions the fact that the Queen, mother, and wife shared the one name. There is no absolute certainty about the identity of Spenser's first wife.
> In Ireland, to which he seems to have been rusticated, he acquired property and became Clerk of the Council of Munster; but in 1581 he is also, mysteriously, prebendary of Effin. [The source of that bit of information is mysterious, anyhow.]
> As clerk [*sic*] to Lord Grey, and in other official capacities, Spenser wrote many letters and documents, at least fifty-nine of which have been identified. They are written in three distinct hands: two for English (secretary and italic) and one for Latin.

That is all. Everything else we have read here about Spenser's life is consigned to limbo as irreconcilable with McManaway's purpose. On top of that, the Folger curator has invented an earlier wife (if not two earlier wives) of uncertain identity, evidently in order to enlarge the years in the poet's life of which he claims we are ignorant. What significance he attaches to the several hands in which the official papers are written, I cannot say, but in fact it surely signifies that Spenser was not a clerk, as McManaway says, but, as we know, Lord Grey's secretary, who would have had clerks under him. When he goes on to add that "No personal letter to or from him has come to light and not one line of poetry in his handwriting" I am in no doubt as to his object. That is plain from the facts he pointedly does not tell us: first, that part of Spenser's correspondence with Harvey has not only come to light but was published by Harvey himself and may be read in any edition of Spenser's complete works; second, that if no line of poetry in his handwriting has been found, it is just possible that the fire which totally destroyed his home three months before his death, about which McManaway is mute, may have had something to do with it.

The ethics that distinguish Shakespearean orthodoxy, or the lack of them, are revealed by reviewing what McManaway does not tell us. He refrains from acknowledging that a variety of Spenser's holographs may be found in his own library in Greg's *English Literary Autographs* (Z42. G82, if the Folger would like to verify this source), including letters, which he denies exist. He conceals from us that Spenser enjoyed a long, intimate, and fruitful relationship with Gabriel Harvey, and that it was in a responsible position that he accompanied Lord Grey to Ireland ("to which he seems to have been rusticated," indeed!). He also does not let us know anything about Spenser's education; about his residing in the house of the most powerful nobleman in England; about his having had as literary patrons two of the most prominent and active men of affairs in England, both poet-knights; about the great estates in Ireland he was granted; about his literary triumph in London; about his extensive acquaintanceships in the Court; about his exchange of poetical compliments with Sir Walter Raleigh; about his reception and pensioning by the Queen; about what he writes of himself and his work; or about the admiring regard in which he was held by the English society of Dublin.

In suppressing all that and more, McManaway counts upon our ignorance to enable him to get away with it. He practices upon our trust when he cites Spenser's known biography (and Raleigh's and Milton's, of which he would have to suppress just as much) as grounds on which to expect nothing more from Shakespeare's than a string of mostly humdrum, or even sordid, and irrelevant episodes in which not a person of intellectual, literary, or social note appears. He would have us know no more about Spenser's death than about his life. The contrast with Shakspere's would be too deadly. The facts withheld in *The Authorship of Shakespeare* we may come by elsewhere, however, learning that Spenser was buried in the abbey, near the tomb of Chaucer, with a splendid funeral, at the expense of the Earl of Essex. The pall was borne by poets; and with a true poetic feeling, tributory verses by the most illustrious of his contemporaries [Shakespeare excepted], with the pens that wrote them, were thrown into his grave. [His fellows] vied with each other in Elegiac tributes to his memory.

Though the Red Queen in *Through the Looking-Glass* had practiced believing impossible things for half an hour every day and had sometimes accomplished as many as six before breakfast, I imagine that even she would have found her credulity taxed by the proposition that those who had paid such respect to Spenser upon his passing would have allowed Shakspere's death to go unremarked had they thought him the genius whom Ben Jonson, then the reigning voice of the theatre, would seven years later proclaim the soul of the age, Britain's triumph, the star of poets.

Upon Spenser's death, the Queen ordered a monument erected at his tomb, but either her notorious parsimony caused her to think better of it or pressure from other affairs and about Essex put it out of her mind. Such concrete demonstration of the nation's regard for the poet had to wait for thirty years. The monument that the Countess of Dorset had placed in the Abbey in 1620 was defaced by the Puritans in the Civil War but we may still read its inscription eulogizing at length the "Anglicorum Poetarum," for it was preserved by the annalist William Camden.

Yes, "Shakespeare," too, achieved a place in the national shrine at Westminster. Recognition came with the standing figure leaning on an elbow, sculpted by Scheemakers, erected in 1740, a century and a quarter after the man ostensibly represented by it had died, when his misty figure was at last beginning to solidify as the great poet-dramatist's.

We have seen that the apologists for the orthodox "Shakespeare," who make a point of how much we know about him in comparison with his literary contemporaries, are deceiving us. As to any connection with literary activities or with literary figures of his time or any associated with literature, the Stratfordian's record is a blank, in striking contrast with that of lesser or vastly lesser writers.

I have not meant to attribute unique culpability to Dr. McManaway. The complicity of the orthodox Shakespeare establishment is entire, whether active or passive, in the cozenage of the public — for I feel sure that not one voice in good standing with that establishment has ever been raised to question the cynical way in which facts are treated in *The Authorship of Shakespeare,* which the Folger Library reprinted as recently as 1978.

Thomas Hardy, in 1916, the tercentenary of Shakspere's death, wrote that when its now famous son's "life of commonplace" was over at his "last breath, with mindless note / The borough clocks as usual tongued the hour, / . . . With other native men's accorded a like knell." The poem continues:

> And at the strokes some townsman (met maybe,
> And thereon queried by some squire's good dame
> Driving in shopward) may have given thy name,
> With "Yes, a worthy man and well to do;
>   Though as for me,
> I knew him but by just a neighbor's nod, 'tis true.
>   I' faith, few knew him much here, save by word,
>   He having elsewhere led his busier life;
>   Though to be sure he left us his wife.
>   Ah, one of the tradesmen's sons, I now recall. . . .
>   Witty, I've heard. . . .
> We did not know him. . . . Well, good-day, Death comes to all."

Henry James takes it from there in his story, "The Birthplace." As Leon Edel expresses it in his greatly acclaimed biography of the novelist:

> Lady Trevelyan had told him of a man and his wife who had been placed in charge of the Shakespeare house. They were "rather strenuous and superior people" from Newcastle. They embraced the job eagerly, only to find at the end of six months that they could not stand the "humbug."

Such is the experience of the newly appointed keeper in James's story.

> He would have liked to stick to hard facts, but the visitors impose upon him their desire for homely detail. He finds, in a visiting American couple, kindred spirits. And to them he confides that "there *is* no author. . . . There are all the immortal people *in* the work; but there's nobody else." And then, when he realizes that he may lose his job, he is able to yield to his own reconstructing imagination. He starts to embroider the legend; he becomes a creator himself.

He supplies the "homely detail." He

> creates a fanciful fabric. He is now a success. The directors vote to double his pay. The resourceful imagination triumphs over the mundane.

That, as the reader will realize, is about how we come out where we have in the matter of the Stratford legend.

5

"The Baseless Fabric"

Biographers of the Stratford man as Shakespeare, unable to find anything else in the record of the years when he was alive that can be cited as warrant for styling him an author and an actor known to the Elizabethan stage, greatly stress two seeming exceptions to the record's unhelpfulness. One is a publication of 1592 offered as the deathbed testament of the writer Robert Greene, in which the author upbraids an actor, an "upstart Crow" who is "in his own conceit the only Shake-scene in a country," and which is followed by a published expression of regret by Henry Chettle for having brought it out. The other is an entry in the accounts of the Treasurer of the Chamber recording a payment to the two best-known players of the Lord Chamberlain's company and to Shakespeare for two comedies shown before the Queen in December 1594. Without these props, biographies of Shakspere as the poet-dramatist of undying fame would be scarcely possible. Accordingly, they call for, and receive, our scrutiny. Our findings repay our trouble. Not the least way in which our examination of Chettle's offerings to the literary public advances us in our investigation into the question of the Shakespeare authorship is by raising the question of whether the orthodox scholars are unable or unwilling to read English. We detect little sign of their being put out of countenance by published evidence of their failure to do so in this context or by the discovery through recent computer analyses that they have mistaken the authorship of Greene's alleged swan song.

"Biographies of Shakespeare," a reviewer observes in *Publishers Weekly*, "invariably impress upon one how little is really known about his life." Biographers of the conventional "Shakespeare" have in truth an unenviable task. They have to persuade us of the validity of a figure who must be unique among the famous beings of history in never once making an appearance on the stage of his times in the character for which he is famous. No occasion is known to us on which a man identified as Shakespeare the writer was present. We know of no communication, oral or written, which anyone ever had from or made to a man so described. We have to wait until he had, presumably, been dead for years before anyone to our knowledge implied, even briefly and uninformatively, that he had ever seen such a one. Throughout his life, Shakespeare the poet-dramatist was the man who was not there. For all that the record of those years tells us, the poems and plays that bear his name could very nearly have materialized out of nowhere.

Invisible as a writer, Shakespeare was scarcely less so as an actor. A. L. Rowse of Oxford, his twice-over biographer, tells us that "Several tributes were paid to Burbage, though nothing like so many as his friend received." Rowse does not confide in us that the tributes to Shakespeare were tributes to a name only, and to an author's, not an actor's, name. In one of the tributes to Burbage that Rowse quotes, the speaker exclaims, "Oft have I seen him leap into the grave," and "Oft have I seen him play this part in jest." No one that we have heard of ever said that he had seen Shakespeare doing anything on a stage, oft or even once.

In the void that confronts them, Stratfordian biographers heedlessly embrace a document that might seem to provide a foundation for the edifice they erect. With it we come to the crux of the Stratfordian case. Accordingly it is worth the effort to get the facts about it sorted clearly in our minds.

The document in question, to which I have previously referred, is a famous one. It purports to be the testimony of a dying playwright, poet, and pamphleteer, Robert Greene. The Stratfordian scholars pledge their fortunes and their sacred honor, if not their lives, upon its proving that in 1592 Will Shakspere of Stratford-on-Avon was recognized as both an actor and a writer of plays. "We have no certainty [read, "no evidence whatever"] of Shakespeare's presence in London before 1592, when a scoffing notice by Robert Greene shows that he was an actor and a writer of plays," E. K. Chambers states flatly. They all state flatly that is what the "scoffing notice" shows. "The most important thing about Greene's attack," Marchette Chute says, "is that it established the fact that Shakespeare was a successful actor before he became a playwright. This, in turn, explains what he had been doing in the intervening years, since the birth of his twins in Stratford in 1585." But the testimony on which these claims are based, on which Stratfordian biography rests, like a pyramid inverted upon its apex, collapses when we read what it actually says.

Robert Greene's last month was spent in the home of a poor shoemaker near Dowgate, London, in poverty and degradation, if we are to believe the report by his bitter enemy, Gabriel Harvey. The end came on 3 September 1592, and on 20 September *Greenes Groats-worth of Wyt, Bought with a Million of Repentence* was entered on the Stationers' Register.

The *Groats-worth* is in form a barely fictionalized confession of the purported writer's misspent life. The part destined for a stellar place in English letters, however, is more directly spoken. It is the part, too, which is responsible for poor Greene's being held in obloquy — quite unwarrantably. It begins: *"To those Gentlemen his Quondam acquaintance, that spend their wits in making plays, R.G. wisheth a better exercise, and wisdom to prevent his extremities. . . ."* From there it launches into the famous attack on actors:

> Base-minded men all three of you, if by my misery you be not warned: for unto none of you (like me) sought those burs to cleave: those puppets (I mean) that spake from our mouths, those anticks garnisht in our colours. Is it not

strange, that I, to whom they all have been beholden: is it not like that you, to whom they all have been beholden, shall (were ye in that case as I am now) be both at once of them forsaken? Yes trust them not: for there is an upstart Crow, beautified with our feathers, that with his *tigers hart wrapt in a players hide,* supposes he is as well able to bombast out a blank verse as the best of you: and being an absolute *Iohannes fac totum,* is in his own conceit the only Shake-scene in a country. O that I might entreat your rare wits to be employed in more profitable courses: & let those apes imitate your past excellence, and never more acquaint them with your admired inventions. . . . Whilst you may, seek you better Masters; for it is pity men of such rare wits, should be subject to the pleasure of such rude grooms.

In other words, "R.G." is telling his three fellow playwrights: "Be warned by my fate, for in the hour of my extremity I have been forsaken by the actors who are beholden to me for the words I have put in their mouths, and so shall you be. In particular, mistrust a merciless upstart, beautified through our agency, who, being a jack-of-all-trades, believes himself as well able to fill out a blank verse as the best of you and esteems himself the only actor of power in the country. Let the actors perform the plays with which you have already supplied them and give them no more." Notice that "R.G." has paraphrased a line from the play *Henry the Sixth, Part Three*: "O tiger's heart wrapped in a woman's hide." This line is read as giving special significance to the term "Shake-scene." It is easy to assume that "R.G." had Shakespeare in his thoughts, though as far as we know the name had never yet been heard as that of anyone with literary or theatrical associations.

To the Stratfordians it is as plain as pudding. The "upstart Crow" was "Shakespeare" as certainly as if "R.G." had called him that — though not until the latter part of the 18th century did anyone suggest it. "Greene's letter in itself is sufficient to show that by September 1592 Shakespeare was both a player and a maker of plays," Chambers declares. "The first London reference to Shakespeare appropriately combines his acting and his writing functions," Gerald E. Bentley asserts no less baldly, "and the context of Greene's allusion makes it plain that Shakespeare's success as a playwright was already sufficient to make him a serious rival to the University Wits."

I leave it up to the Stratfordians to explain what it was about their man to have caused a dying penitent, facing eternity, and in the presence of his Maker, to castigate him as an arrogant upstart with a tiger's heart — *a tiger's heart,* mind you. Even if professional rivalry alone could account for such a savage characterization — which we may well doubt — Greene would surely have passed beyond such considerations: *he* was not going to write any more for the stage. But when the Stratfordians tell us that Greene identified the upstart crow as a playwright, we have to draw the line. He did no such thing. "R.G." was inveighing against *actors,* one in particular who was "beautified with our feathers" — that is, we playwrights' feathers — not his own. The upstart crow's plumes were borrowed plumes — borrowed from the playwrights. "R.G.," in charging that the upstart believed himself able to fill out a blank verse — *a* blank verse — "as well . . . as the best of you [playwrights]," was surely attributing to him the kind of transgression against which Hamlet warned the traveling stage company when he said, "let those that play your clowns speak no more than is set down for them." There is no basis for Chambers's assertion that Greene, in speaking of the actors who have deserted him, meant that "they will desert his friends likewise, since they now have a writer of their own." "R.G." said nothing of the kind. He did say practically the opposite. He warned that the actors would desert his friends (the playwrights whom he was addressing) *though beholden to them for the words they speak.* And he urged his *friends* to desert the *actors,* letting them go on producing his friends' old plays but providing them with no new ones. The implication surely is that the actors would then be left in the lurch. No suggestion appears in what "R.G." said that the actors have one of their own who would supply them with plays. Quite the contrary.

Having misconstrued *Greenes Groats-worth* to make Will Shakspere a playwright, the Stratfordians misconstrue the next publication in the case to make him an honored one. The *Groats-worth* having evidently caused something of a furor, the man who had supplied the printer with the manuscript of the work offered an explanation of sorts in *Kind-Harts Dreame,* which appeared before the year was out. This was Henry Chettle, a writer of plays and miscellanies. As he tells us, he was accused of having written the *Groats-worth* himself. Judge of his distress:

> About three months since died M. Robert Greene, leaving many papers in sundry book sellers hands, among other his Groatsworth of wit, in which a letter written to divers playmakers, is offensively by one or two of them taken: and because on the dead they cannot be avenged, they wilfully forge in their conceits a living author: and after tossing it to and fro, no remedy, but it must light on me. . . . With neither of them that take offense was I acquainted, and with one of them I care not if I never be: The other, whom at that time I did not so much spare, as since I wish I had, . . . I am as sorry as if the original fault had been my fault, because my self have seen his demeanor no less civil than he excellent in the quality he professes: Besides, divers of worship [worthship] have reported his uprightness of dealing, which argues his honesty, and his facetious [urbane, polished] grace in writing, that approves his art.

The Stratfordians embrace this passage with the same eagerness that they do the *Groats-worth.* Having made the upstart crow Shakespeare, they now do the same for the playwright whom Chettle was sorry not to have spared, of whom persons of high standing had spoken well. He, too, is Shakespeare. Of Chettle's expression of regret, Samuel Schoenbaum, called by the Folger Library "the foremost living Shakespearean scholar," says: "It is a glowing tribute to Shakespeare, this first glimpse we get of him as a man. . . . The reference to testimonials from 'divers of worship' — did Shakespeare bear them in hand when he visited Chettle or were they sent along to him afterwards? . . ." The airy reconstructions that the Stratfordians go in for are sometimes of ludicrous effect, as of Shakespeare's seeking out Chettle with a sheaf of written testimonials in his clutch. Rowse also has Shakespeare calling upon Chettle — though without written testimonials. He calls Chettle's subsequent tribute to the unnamed playwright "the most handsome apology that I know of in the Elizabethan age. They all read Latin and would know that 'facetious' was the compliment Cicero paid to Plautus."

But wait a minute. How is this?

Chettle wrote that the playwright who had taken offense and whom he was sorry not to have spared *was one of the three playwrights addressed by Greene.* If the offended playwright was Shakespeare and the actor denounced by Greene as the upstart crow was also Shakespeare, then Greene in warning the playwright about the actor was warning Shakespeare about himself!

Let us be clear about this misreading, for it brings us to the indispensable foundation of Stratfordian biography and shows the foundation to be a palpable misconstruction. If we accept the orthodox scholars' reading, we have Greene saying: "Base-minded men all three of you — you, Shakespeare, and you two other playwrights — if you be not warned by what I am going to tell you of that actor Shakespeare." Obviously the upstart actor and the offended playwright were and had to be different persons. That they were different, Chettle incidentally makes doubly plain by leaving us in no doubt that it was *not* the actor, the victim of "R.G.'s" attack, who protested, but one of the playwrights addressed by "R.G." (It can only be that the latter had a protective feeling toward the former.) When a man has been mortally insulted you do not say that he "took offense," as Chettle said one or two of the playwrights did; people *take* offense when offense would not necessarily seem to have been given. Least of all do you say that a mortally insulted man was *one of those* who took offense, as if he had no more cause to than the others. So far as the record shows, the insulted actor remained mute.

For those who cannot swallow the double-barreled misreading of Chettle and the absurdity of "R.G.'s" warning Shakespeare the playwright about Shakespeare the actor, orthodox biography collapses. Take away the misreading of *Groats-worth* and *Kind-Harts Dreame* and nothing during Shakspere's life remains to suggest even remotely that he was a writer — and little enough that he was an actor.

Is the misreading one that has escaped detection heretofore? Far from it! It has been pointed out continually at least since 1890. As long ago as that, Frederick G. Fleay — a Stratfordian — wrote that "Shakespeare was not one of those who took offense: they are expressly stated to have been two of the three authors addressed by Greene." Also in the past century, E. T.

Castle, Queen's Counsel, recognized the discrepancy. He said, "A whole succession of writers, Malone, Steevens, Dyce, Collier, Halliwell, Knight and a host of minor authors, are so blinded by their admiration for Shakespeare [i.e., Shakspere], that they cannot read a simple document correctly, or are such simple followers of Malone [who gave the misreading currency in the 18th century] that they have adopted his mistakes and made no inquiry for themselves."

It is illuminating to see how the Stratfordian biographers maneuver around the facts in the case. Marchette Chute in her bestselling *Shakespeare of London* (which receives the endorsement of the Folger Library), withholds any mention of Chettle's statement that Greene's letter was "offensively taken by one or two of the divers play-makers," which leaves her free to state that Shakespeare objected to Greene's attack. In *Shakespeare the Man,* after coolly telling us that Greene launched an "attack on Shakespeare openly," Rowse discreetly fails to mention Chettle's having said that the offended playwright was one of those addressed by Greene. That leaves *him* free to state that "The dying Greene proceeded to warn his friends the writers — Marlowe, Peele, Nashe — against the players. . . ." He breezes on: "There was a rumpus, for both Marlowe and Shakespeare protested."

"This means," says McManaway of the Greene-Chettle episode, "that Shakespeare was thus early a good actor ('the quality he professes') and a successful writer, that he conducted himself like a gentleman. . . ." How it rolls off the presses! Louis B. Wright announces that "By 1592, he [Shakespeare] was so well established and popular that he incurred the envy of the dramatist and pamphleteer Robert Greene, who referred to him as an 'upstart crow' . . . in his own conceit the only Shake-scene in a country." And, "Shortly after the publication of Greene's ill-natured comment, Chettle published an apology . . . in which he says, referring to Shakespeare, 'I am as sorry as if the original fault had been my fault. . . .'" It is all put before us as simply matters of fact. The innocent reader would suppose that both Greene and Chettle had referred to Shakespeare by name. This chicanery is evidently what Wright means by the method of "the historical scholar," who, he informs us, "is trained to analyze evidence, not to win cases."[1]

---

[1] In this statement, Wright was contrasting historical scholars with "lawyers [who] have shown a special tendency to plead cases against William Shakespeare [*sic*]." Did he mean that lawyers, of whom so many have been disbelievers of Shakspere of Stratford, are not "trained to analyze evidence?" Well, not quite. "A distinguished Washington jurist," said Wright, "recently shook his head sadly and commented: 'Of course lawyers are not interested in evidence; they are trained to win cases tried before other lawyers who know the rules of courtroom procedure.'" Wright's reproof did not pass unnoticed by the bar. W. Barton Leach, Story Professor of Law at Harvard, wrote to the *American Bar Association Journal*: "The identity of the saddened 'distinguished Washington jurist' whom Dr. Wright quotes directly is an interesting subject of speculation. Perhaps Dr. Wright, if requested, might reveal it so that a confirmation, and possibly elaboration, of the quote could be obtained." Instead of responding to this invitation, Dr. Wright dropped the distinguished jurist

Chapter 5: The Baseless Fabric

On page 50 of his *Shakespeare's Lives,* Professor Schoenbaum introduces us to Greene's "letter to three of his 'fellow scholars about this city': Marlowe and (probably) Nashe and Peele." It seems to be generally agreed among orthodox scholars that the three playwrights addressed by "R.G." were Marlowe, Nashe, and Peele — though Schoenbaum calls them "fellow scholars," not playwrights. He then goes on to omit the heading of "R.G.'s" letter: *To those Gentlemen his Quondam acquaintance, that spend their wits making plaies. . . .* On page 51, he writes, "Chettle confesses that Greene's 'letter written to diverse play-makers' has been 'offensively by one or two of them taken.' The grieved parties were, the context makes clear, Marlowe and Shakespeare." It would take an alert reader to stop the shell-game here to object: "Wait! You've just said that Greene's letter was offensively taken by one or two of the play-makers to whom it was addressed, whom on the preceding page you identified as Marlowe, Nashe, and Peele. How can one of them suddenly be Shakespeare?"

In the rewriting of *Groats-worth* and Chettle, Wright and McManaway are worth special attention because they speak for the Folger Library, which the public supports generously and trustingly, Schoenbaum because of the prominence he has been given, the grants he has received from the Guggenheim Foundation, the National Foundation for the Humanities, and the Huntington and Newberry Libraries, and the positions of influence and honor he occupies in the Shakespeare establishment, including, as of 1972, membership on the board of trustees of the Folger Library, which describes his books in its catalogue as "masterpieces." Schoenbaum invites particular attention, too, because of his claim to have read voluminously in anti-Stratfordian literature. Or, as he puts it, he has been under "the necessity of having to make his way through thousands of pages of rubbish, some of it lunatic rubbish." Passing over the tautology in "the necessity of having to," let us realize that in those thousands of pages he was certain to have read repeatedly why the interpretation of Chettle he asserts in *Shakespeare's Lives* rests on an absurdity. He certainly had it explained, and twice over, in *Shakespeare: The Man Behind the Name.* This book he dismissed as a "stew," but since he ascribed my part in its authorship to my father, the extent of his acquaintance with it is conjectural.

E. K. Chambers, to do him justice, in 1930 recognized and acknowledged what Chettle had actually written — the only Stratfordian I know of to have

---

altogether in a subsequent reversion to the subject, contenting himself with the proposition that "lawyers are trained to do the best they can for their clients regardless of the weight of evidence against them." Anticipating the objection that this case has no clients, he surmised that "The game probably appeals to their sporting instincts to see what they can do with a doubtful case." If Wright has other instances at hand of this singular perversity in the legal profession, he has not vouchsafed them to us.

done so in the present century. Like his fellows, he identified the one or two offended playwrights as Marlowe and Shakespeare, but he admitted that "Greene's letter was obviously not written to Shakespeare." How to get around this fatal difficulty? Easy. There was "some looseness in Chettle's language." Chettle had stated plainly that the one or two offended playwrights were among those addressed by Greene, but Chettle was confused, it seems, and Chambers straightens him out. Chambers, three and a half centuries later, knows better than Chettle what Chettle meant.

Amusing at the time, Chambers's self-assurance became ludicrous in 1969, when it was shown that *Greenes Groats-worth of Wit* was written not by Greene but by Chettle himself! (It was against the suspicion this was so that Chettle had defended himself in *Kind-Harts Dreame*.) The man to whom we are indebted for the discovery is Warren B. Austin of Stephen F. Austin State College of Texas.

Postulating that an author exhibits stylistic preferences in his writing which are "largely unconscious" and which will betray his authorship regardless of subject matter and date of composition, Professor Austin went to work with an IBM 7094 computer on five of Greene's works and three of Chettle's. He spent about three years on the task, and his report of his findings, entitled *A Computer-Aided Technique for Stylistic Discrimination — The Authorship of Greene's Groatsworth of Wit,* and published by the office of Education of the U.S. Department of Health, Education, and Welfare, from which financing for the project came, is as large as the Manhattan telephone directory.[2] It shows that by virtually every criterion used in the testing, Chettle is the author of *Groats-worth*.

Describing Professor Austin's work at length in his *Shakespeare Newsletter* for December 1970, Professor Louis Marder of the University of Illinois at Chicago Circle called it "what may turn out to be one of the three most significant contributions to Shakespearean scholarship in this century."[3] It could have been expected to change drastically the treatment of the events of 1592 by Stratfordian scholars. In fact it has had virtually no effect — perhaps not so surprisingly after all, for it invalidates an essential premise of Stratfordian biography. In April 1973, more than three years after announcement of Professor Austin's discovery, McManaway, interviewed by Jean M. White of the *Washington Post,* was quoted as saying that "By the summer of 1592 Shakespeare had begun to make his name as an actor and had written some successful plays that had drawn barbs from the jealous Uni-

---

[2] The report is summarized by R. L. Miller in Looney, 3rd rev. ed., II, 346–350.

[3] The other two he cited were the discovery by Charles W. Wallace and his wife of the deposition in the Belott-Mountjoy case signed Willn Shaksp, and William J. Neidig's proof that quartos of Shakespeare's plays published by Thomas Pavier, though some were dated as early as 1600, were printed in 1619.

versity Wits. One of these, Robert Greene, savagely attacked his rival in the famous denunciation of the 'upstart Crow,' the actor who presumed to write plays and considered himself 'the only Shake-scene' in the country." Not only did McManaway repeat the oft-exposed nonsense and ignore Professor Austin's discovery; he even expanded the fantasy, making Greene only one of those from whom Shakespeare "had drawn barbs." In the next year the director of the Folger Library, O. B. Hardison, Jr., replying in the *Washington Post* to the *Post's* abridged reprint of an article of mine in *Harvard Magazine,* was assuring his readers that "The first reference to Shakespeare after the 'lost years' is in 1592. It is an indignant warning by Robert Greene to his fellow dramatists to beware of a playwright," et cetera: the same old goods.

What do Stratfordians say when the facts of the *Groats-worth* affair as they have been presented in this chapter are forced upon their notice? Well, I presented them in my article in *Harvard Magazine,* including Austin's findings. (This part was omitted in the *Post's* reprint.) G. B. Evans and Harry Levin, the two Harvard professors who undertook to rebut the article, had this and this only to say on the subject: "Mr. Ogburn seems baffled by the earliest allusion to him [Shakespeare] in Robert Greene's *Groatsworth of Wit,* which is clearly a protest against a mere actor who has presumed to become a dramatist." That was it. All disposed of in a sentence, and as if reason had never been voiced or Professor Austin been born. This was routine. In his introduction to the *Riverside Shakespeare,* "which displays all that is best in Harvard literary scholarship today," Professor Levin omits all mention of Professor Austin's three-year labors, along with all that has been written to elucidate what actually was said in *Groats-worth* and Chettle's defense.[4]

It may be said to his credit that Schoenbaum, "distinguished prof. English, U. City of N.Y., 1975–76," and "distinguished prof. Renaissance studies U. Md. 1976–" (I quote from *Who's Who*) in his *William Shakespeare: A Documentary Life,* does take cognizance of Austin. He does so, however, only after eight pages on the *Groats-worth* affair treating Greene's authorship as a matter of unquestioned fact. And his bow to Austin sends him off the stage. "Austin has quarried five selections from Greene and three from Chettle: a sample not statistically overwhelming," Schoenbaum writes, neglecting quite to tell us that the selections from Greene totaled more than 100,000 words, those from Chettle more than 43,000. Calling Austin's exhaustive findings an "hypothesis," he delivers the judgment of the court:

[4] Professor Levin presents the standard fiction: "The earliest critical recognition of his career had been a truculent outburst from Robert Greene hack-writing upon his very deathbed in 1592 and denouncing Shakespeare as a young upstart for his presumption in vying with those already established playwrights whom we call the University Wits." Well, not quite standard: Levin has discovered that "Shakespeare" was denounced not only as an upstart but as a *young* upstart.

"Austin has not proved his case." Watch it, and you will see Austin fade away. "In the absence of conclusive proof to the contrary [Austin having presumably offered merely proof], Greene must continue to bear responsibility for his death-bed diatribe [being "his," the diatribe could not of course have been anyone else's], and we may accept, with some traces of unease, Chettle's apologia." Thus Austin's painstaking labor of years vanishes before our eyes, leaving only "some traces of unease" behind it. If that: "the *Groatsworth of Witte*," Schoenbaum asserts, "contains — no question — a desperate shaft directed at Shakespeare."

But the case against the professors, I am afraid, goes even beyond their disregard of Austin and misreading of *Groats-worth* and Chettle. They should not have been taken in by *Groats-worth* to begin with.

"Gentlemen," that pamphlet begins. "The Swan sings melodiously before death, that in all his life useth but a jarring sound. *Greene* though able enough to write, yet deeplier searched with sickness than ever heretofore, sends you his swan-like song, for that he fears he shall never again carol to you wonted love lays, never again discover to you youth's pleasures." And so it goes for pages upon pages, voluble, literary, allegorical. It is not, surely, the way a man writes with death staring him in the face. Compare it with Greene's *bona fide* last communication, his terse, agonized letter to his wife, or with his valedictory *Repentence*, an intense, straightforward, bitter self-accusation in such contrast with the fancy, leisured prolixity of the *Groats-worth* as to make you wonder all the more how scholarship could have been so long taken in by Chettle's artifice. "Cursed be the day wherein I was born, and hapless be the breasts that gave me suck": such is the tone of the *Repentence*.

Chettle's artifice was entered in the Stationers' Register as "a book intitled GREENES *Groatsworth of Wyt bought with a million of Repentence*" and with a caveat suggesting that the publisher had smelled a rat: "upon the peril of Henrye Chettle." That Chettle was from the start suspected of having written *Groats-worth* himself we have seen. So was Thomas Nashe, a poet, playwright, pioneer novelist, and pamphleteer; and Nashe in replying pronounced it in effect a forgery. "Other news I am advertised of," he wrote, "that a scald trivial lying pamphlet, called *Greens groats-worth of wit,* is given out to be of my doing. God never have care of my soul, but utterly renounce me, if the least word or syllable of it proceeded from my pen. . . ." Nashe, his friend and defender, would surely have known if Greene had written *Groats-worth*, and in calling it a scurvy, lying pamphlet he was unmistakably declaring that Greene had not.

The extreme terms in which Nashe abjured complicity in *Groats-worth* argue that the playwright who took offense at it was someone important — a great deal more important than a johnny-come-lately from the provinces;

and if Shakspere had ever even been in London by 1592, he had left no discoverable trace of himself there. Who could the playwright have been? The Stratfordians have long stated as a fact that here is where we pick up Shakespeare's trail, and I think they are right — except that the trail is not of Will Shakspere but of the man who *was* Shakespeare. This is a matter we shall come to in due course.

If the misconstruction of the Greene-Chettle episode provides the indispensable basis of the case for Shakspere as Shakespeare, the orthodox seize upon an occurrence of two years later to buttress the argument. Or, as Ivor Brown puts it, "It is late in December, 1594, that we reach the vitally important information left in the Accounts of the Treasurer of the Chamber." He refers to a recorded payment of £20 to "Will Kempe Will Shakespeare & Richard Burbage servants to the Lord Chamb[er]lain . . . for two several comedies or interludes shewed by them before her Ma[jesty] . . . upon St. Stephens day & Innocents day." If we take the "Shakespeare" named to be the Stratford man it is an astonishing entry, for it would show that, as far as any intervening records go, Shakspere had in a bound gone from his native village to a position on the stage that Burbage and Kemp had taken years of work to achieve. The proposition is indeed vital to the Stratford case, second only to the misreading of the *Groats-worth* papers as a foundation for conventional biographies. On the strength of it, Shakspere is made a leading member of the Lord Chamberlain's Company from 1594 on. We read in Marchette Chute, for example, as if we were reading matters of plain fact, that "His company put on about fifteen new plays a year and Shakespeare, as a regular acting member of the company, must have appeared in most of them" and that "Shakespeare visited this district [Dover] more than once with his company." Professor G. B. Harrison, in his *Introducing Shakespeare,* calls a chapter "Shakespeare's Company." Giles E. Dawson of the Folger Library writes, "In 1594 the Lord Chamberlain's company was formed, and there is ample evidence of Shakespeare's connection with it from that year onward. . . ." In fact, of all the records from the reign of Elizabeth, only this one associates a "Shakespeare" with the Lord Chamberlain's company, or with acting at all.

Only this one: and it, like *Groats-worth,* will not bear examination. On Innocents' Day — December 28 — 1594 contemporary records show the Admiral's company, not the Lord Chamberlain's, playing before the Queen at Greenwich and the Lord Chamberlain's putting on *A Comedy of Errors* at Gray's Inn in London. It is by no means on that account alone, however, that the record is suspect. The official responsible for making payments for theatrical performances at Court was Sir Thomas Heneage, Treasurer of the Chamber; but, as Charlotte C. Stopes discovered, "The person who rendered the Bills from 29th September 1592 till 16th December 1595 was Mary

Countess of Southampton." The Countess, long a widow, had married Heneage, but only in May 1594. Quite clearly, when she came "to lose her
affectionate husband on 17th October 1595" she found the records of payments lacking all the way back to 29 September 1592. As Mrs. Stopes
observes: "She was . . . to have sad worries over his accounts, receiving an
unpleasant letter even from the Queen herself about the deficit." The Queen
wrote: "At the decease of your late husband, Sir Thomas Heneage, he had
£1314, 15, 4 in hand as Treasurer of the Chamber. . . . You, as Executrix,
have paid up £401, 6, 10, and £394, 9, 11, to the guard and others. . . . We
require immediate payment of the balance £528, 18, 7, to the Treasury of
the Chamber." The widow's problem would thus have been to come up with
vouchers accounting for the expenditure of as much as possible in order to
reduce the amount by which she would be out of pocket. Such were the
circumstances in which she recorded the payment of £20 to Kemp, Shakespeare, and Burbage. "For the *first* and *last* time," Mrs. Stopes writes (the
italics being hers), "'William Shakespeare' was among the players, and among
those that received the payments." The regular payee for performances by
the Lord Chamberlain's company was John Heminge.

Thus we have payees to whom no other payment is known to have been
made. We have the suspicious circumstances in which the payment was
reported. We have the payment made for a performance that was not given
on the date specified. And the report would have us believe that Shakspere
had become an actor on a par with Kempe and Burbage (respectively, as
Gerald Eades Bentley observes, "the most popular comedian in London" and
"the greatest English actor of the time") without leaving any other trace of
himself as an actor in the records of Elizabeth's reign.[5] (Ben Jonson, it is
true, places him in the cast of a play of his in 1598, but he had this
afterthought twenty-five years later and, as we shall see, was almost certainly
having us on.) As a pedestal on which to erect a career on the Elizabethan
stage for Shakspere, the little record entered by Sir Thomas Heneage's har-
rassed widow is required to bear a prodigious load indeed.

How, then, did the Countess come to name "Will Shakespeare" in her
perhaps rather desperate contrivance? Though we have no way of knowing,
I incline to attribute it to two circumstances. First, the Countess is one person
who presumably would have known the poet-dramatist who called himself
William Shakespeare, for he had dedicated to her son, the 3rd Earl of
Southampton, the only works of his that he himself ever had published as
Shakespeare's, *Venus and Adonis* (1593) and *The Rape of Lucrece* (1594).
Second, if this man was who I and many others believe him to have been,
there are good reasons for identifying his as the directing hand within the

---

[5] I am reminded of a cartoon many years ago showing Robinson Crusoe bent over a single footprint
in the sand with the legend, "He must have flown the rest of the way."

Lord Chamberlain's company, the chosen agency by which Shakespeare's plays were introduced to the public. With a similar title he would seem much more likely to have been responsible for the success of the company — as we shall see when we come to the year 1594 in "Book Two" — than the men who in turn held the post of Lord Chamberlain in the years when the company bore that name.

R. R. Newton of the Applied Physics Laboratory of Johns Hopkins University writes in *The Crime of Claudius Ptolemy* (1977):

> We need to be extremely skeptical about what we read in science, in history, and in all other areas. We must always remember that what we are reading may be fraud. We must also remember that what we are reading may be a collection of clichés that have been passed down uncritically from one generation of writers to another, with no one bothering to examine the veracity of what was written.

6

"How Much Art Thou Shrunk!"

Stuck as they are with the Stratford man's record as conspicuously one of commercial interests unmarked by any concern for the fate of the Shakespearean dramas or even of the Sonnets — *upon which, because they are pure poetry, he would have depended, according to our instructors, for his future literary standing — we look on fascinated, not to say appalled, as the leading and most popular orthodox biographers tailor the character of our greatest genius to the qualities of an ordinary man of practical affairs. We marvel as they joyfully represent him as governed by mean and shallow purposes that the most obvious characteristics of his dramas (as — so some might say — the merest common sense) tell us cannot have been his, and we survey the evidence the detractors have had to ignore, including explicit statements in the First Folio and insights from assorted qualified witnesses speaking with a saving unawareness about the implications their testimony has for the question of the Shakespeare authorship.*

Failure of Conventional Biography

Reviewing in the *New York Times* a book by the late Alfred Harbage of Harvard, whom he called "the foremost American Shakespeare scholar," Oscar James Campbell of Columbia made a telling point. "Harbage rejects any direct relationship between the poet's work and his life, including the interpretation of the chronological succession of the plays as the reflection of the poet's inner life, or his changing moods." He "believes, for example, that it detracts from the beauty and artistic significance of the sonnets to read them as a record of the dramatist's wayward love life. In thus eliminating all that is personal from the poet's art, Harbage risks reducing Shakespeare's image to that of a no man."

Given no relationship between the poet's work and Shakspere's life, a no-man is what we inevitably find in conventional biographies. Emrys Jones says in his *The Origins of Shakespeare*, "Biographies of Shakespeare all suffer from one serious defect. They are all lives which leave 'Shakespeare' out. What is always missing is what matters most, his mind. These lives have a void at the center which leaves the reader finally more perplexed than enlightened." I was struck by this feature in Stratfordian biography particularly in reading Marchette Chute's highly successful contribution to the field, which the popular lecturer and drama critic John Mason Brown lavishly praised. And Ms. Chute deserves praise. She brings admirably to life, in rich detail, the theatrical world that Shakespeare would have known. But her success in this makes only more conspicuous the "void at the center" where Shakespeare should be. The subject of the biography is a puppet, obedient to the strings but without life of its own. Her *Shakespeare of London* could better have been called *London of Shakespeare*.

In 1980, the Folger Library sent forth upon a prolonged tour around the country a much-applauded exhibition of Elizabethiana under the title "Shakespeare: The Globe and the World." Accompanied by a catalogue with text by Samuel Schoenbaum, also highly publicized, it was paid for by grants from the National Endowment for the Humanities, the Exxon Corporation, the Corporation for Public Broadcasting — all of which disdain discordant voices on the authorship — and Metropolitan Life. And what did the exhibition tell us about Shakespeare? That he ranks, John Russell puts it in the *New York Times,*

> just a notch or two below Homer . . . among the big men who got clear away. It was so at the time when people first began to wonder what he was like. Several hundred years later, the position has not changed at all. . . .
>
> At the time of the quatercentenary of Shakespeare's birth in 1964, all this was almost painfully evident. Fat biographies were thrust upon us, but they told us only what we knew already — that beyond three or four facts that were beaten into us in school, all is surmise. Behind the standard grammatical formulas — he "could have," he "might have," he "must have" and he "probably did" — a huge emptiness lurks.

George B. Harrison of the University of Michigan, himself a biographer of Shakespeare, addresses the problem with unexpected frankness. He writes: "Readers often complain that there is no good biography of Shakespeare. There never can be. . . . There are the plays in which again and again Shakespeare used his experiences but nothing to show where and how he came by them. 'Biographies' of Shakespeare are therefore of two kinds: collections of facts and records" that "are usually dull reading, for a scholar is bound by his code to give evidence for his statements," and "attempts to fill out the records by guess and surmise" by "popular biographers [who] are free to use, misuse, and ignore the evidence, and to guess without scruple." What do Professor Harrison and his colleagues tell themselves when the thought crosses their minds, as it must, that perhaps there is nothing to show where and how Shakspere came by the experiences that are used again and again in the plays because he never had them? Do they ever seriously ask themselves why "Shakespeare" should cause his biographers greater problems than any other writer back to Homer, lost in what are called the mists of antiquity? Do they not find it odd, the Oxford historian Hugh R. Trevor-Roper remarks, that "Of all the immortal geniuses of literature, none is personally so elusive as William Shakespeare"? Professor Trever-Roper himself recognizes how extraordinary this vacuum is:

> It is exasperating and almost incredible that he should be so. After all, he lived in the full daylight of the English Renaissance, in the well-documented reigns of Queen Elizabeth and King James I. . . . Since his death, and particularly in the last century, he has been subjected to the greatest battery of organized research that has ever been directed upon a single person. Armies of scholars, formidably equipped, have examined all the documents which could possibly contain at least a mention of Shakespeare's name. One hundredth of this labor applied to one of his insignificant contemporaries would be sufficient to produce a substantial biography. And yet the greatest of all Englishmen, after this tremendous inquisition, still remains so close to a mystery that even his identity can still be doubted.

Henry Hallam expresses himself to similar effect:

> Of William Shakespeare whom, through the mouths of those whom he has inspired to body forth the modifications of his immense mind, we seem to know better than any human writer, it may be truly said that we scarcely know anything. . . . We as little feel the power of identifying the young man who came up from Stratford, was afterward an indifferent player at a London theatre [probably not even that, as we shall find], and retired to his native place in middle life, with the author of *Macbeth* and *Lear,* as we can give a distinct historic personality to Homer. All that insatiable curiosity and unwearied diligence have hitherto detected about Shakespeare, serves rather to disappoint and perplex us than to furnish the slightest illustration of his character. It is not the register of his baptism, or the draught of his will, or the orthography of his name that we seek. No letter of his writing, no record of his conversation, no character drawn of him with any fulness by a contemporary can be produced.

Or, Trevor-Roper goes on to say:

> During his lifetime nobody claimed to know him. Not a single tribute was paid to him at his death. As far as the records go, he was uneducated, had no literary friends, possessed at his death no books, and could not write. It is true, six of his signatures have been found, all spelt differently; but they are so ill-formed that some graphologists suppose the hand to have been guided. Except for these signatures, no syllable of writing by Shakespeare has been identified. Seven years after his death, when his works were collected and published, and other poets claimed to have known him [actually — we shall see — only one: Ben Jonson], a portrait of him was painted. The unskilful artist has presented the blank face of a country oaf.

It is not so much that too little is known to us of Shakspere of Stratford as that what is known makes up a trivial and sordid record, and with this his biographers are stuck. Calling Shakespeare "the most complex and passionate personality in the world, whether of life or letters," Frank Harris protested, back in 1911, that "Without a single exception the commentators have missed the man and the story; they have turned the poet into a tradesman, and the unimaginable tragedy of his life into the commonplace record of a successful tradesman's career." Harris, a British-born American writer of short stories and biographies and a prominent London editor, who in my view wrote of Shakespeare the man with an insight unique among Stratfordians, was quite right, I think, in describing Shakespeare's life as a profound tragedy; but the truth is that Shakspere's career *was* that of a successful tradesman. Professor Edward Quinn of New York University put his finger on it when he wrote that "The more one looks at the facts of his life, the more one becomes convinced that they have very little to do with his plays." Certainly it is true that the facts of Shakspere's life have very little to do with Shakespeare's plays.

Faced with the mundane, wholly uninspiring record of the Stratford man's life, what recourse have the orthodox biographers? They can Professor G. B. Harrison says, "fill out the record by guess and surmise," being "free to use, misuse, and ignore the evidence, and to guess without scruple." Hear, for example, A. L. Rowse:

> William Shakespeare in the end was a complete man of the theatre: player, dramatist, producer, part-owner, sharer of profits. . . . The stage and the players are commented on from almost every angle (except that of business, which he kept to himself). He was a good actor, we know from John Aubrey, and he had the appearance and personality for it — "a handsome, well-shaped man, very good company, and of a very ready and pleasant smooth wit." There were the mobile, flexible features we know so well, the sexy nose and sensuous lips, the large, luminous eyes and dome of a cranium. The tradition is that he played "kingly" parts, and old Adam in *As You Like it.*

What a "sexy nose" is I do not pretend to know, but the rest of this characterization of Rowse's subject is nine-tenths unsupported by any evidence worthy of the name — and that we have to wait for half a century after his death to hear that Shakspere was a good actor (and from Aubrey, that paragon of unreliability) is the most revealing item in Rowse's portrait. But a biographer who can tell from an engraved wooden face and a sculpted wooden face that the subject had "mobile, flexible features" is not one to be circumscribed by the record. In invoking a "tradition that he played 'kingly' parts," Rowse is simply dissembling with the reader, as we shall see when we come to the source of the statement.

Or take Oscar James Campbell of Columbia University, writing in *Harper's:*

> He [Shakspere] had already become interested in new developments taking place in the vigorous young drama of the 1580s, and the leisure he could steal from his duties as a pedagogue he devoted to writing plays. When he had finished two dramas to his satisfaction, a comedy in imitation of Plautus and a bloody tragedy in the approved Senecan manner, he took them up to London in the hope of selling them to one of the companies playing there. The actors, finding them to their liking, bought and produced both works. Indeed, they were so favorably impressed with these first heirs of his dramatic invention that they attached Shakespeare to their company. He became an assistant to their "book-

keeper," an official who combined the duties of librarian, prompter and producer.

This — pure, imaginative conjecture, every word of it — Professor Campbell asks the reader to accept as straight, solid history. Indeed, it was written specifically to confute the anti-Stratfordians with what he called the facts.

When in "Shakespearean biographies . . . conjecture has been lifted up as fact," says Henrietta Buckmaster in a book review in the *Chicago Tribune,* anti-Stratfordians are "of course" provided with the "food" on which they "feed so voluptuously." I had not thought that taking issue with travesties of truth afforded particularly vampire-like satisfactions, but something must be allowed the sensitivities of an author such as Ms. Buckmaster, who had sent forth into the world a novel about "Shakespeare" that would be found to suffer, as one reviewer said, from "the inevitable drawbacks." I can see how the orthodox biographers would take out on the dissidents their frustrations with the material they have to work with. "Smiling villains," Ms. Buckmaster calls the skeptics.

I have not read Ms. Buckmaster's book, but I *have* read *You, My Brother: A Novel Based on the Lives of Edmund and William Shakespeare,* by Philip Burton. Mr. Burton is a scholar of the theatre and a teacher of actors, and his third book, like Marchette Chute's biography, has much of interest in it, and fails only where the poet-dramatist himself enters into it. As I wrote in reviewing it in the *Washington Post,* his Shakespeare, "a man of 'quiet command and gentle dignity,' devoid of temperament, reminds one of the doctor in a television serial." It was hardly surprising that Ned, the brother, should have "'wondered what went on in Will's soul that could produce the torment of Hamlet.'" And what, for that matter, went on in the soul of that "relaxed and happy man" (Marchette Chute), "this busy, prudent, discreet man, . . . with his good nature and good business sense" (A. L. Rowse) to have produced the anguish in *Othello,* the terror and agony in *King Lear?*

With all the latitude they allow themselves, whether in novels or in biographies that are scarcely less fictional, those who chronicle the Stratford Shakspere are never able to produce a Shakespeare in whom the reader can detect the sources of the poems and dramas. On this score there seems to be no limit to the absurdity that a widely respected "Shakespearean" biographer is capable of hatching or a widely venerated journal of retailing in the name of the Stratford legend. This we see in Ivor Brown and the *New York Times Book Review* respectively: "There he [Shakespeare] was, memorizing parts, going to rehearsal, attending to the sharers' managerial responsibilities — and knocking off an 'Othello' or 'Macbeth'"! "How did he reach the wit, the humour and the assured mastery of verse exhibited in a delightful early comedy like *Love's Labour's Lost?*" George Sampson asks in *The Concise Cambridge History of English Literature.* "These are some of the questions to which we desire an answer; but answer there is none." Calling *Hamlet* "the first great tragedy Europe had produced in two thousand years," Frank Kermode of University College, London, says in the new *Riverside Shakespeare,* "How Shakespeare came to write it is, of course, a mystery on which it is useless to speculate."

Is it, indeed? Do we know of another writer with whom there is any such great mystery in how he came to write his masterwork? In Shakespeare's case, we are told, it is a mystery about which it is useless even to speculate; and not only that, but *of course* useless even to speculate. Orthodoxy throws up its hands helplessly over the most important and elementary questions to be asked about Shakespeare. At the same time it slams the door angrily on those who offer, in place of their Shakespeare, one with whom the answers to those questions come readily and *Hamlet* and *Love's Labour's Lost* are natural outgrowths. To Gwynne Blakemore Evans of Harvard, chief architect of the *Riverside Shakespeare,* those who presume to do so constitute a "small . . . band of zealots," to Professor Sampson of the *Cambridge History* "a succession of cranks representing the extreme of ignorant credulity and morbid ingenuity."

If authorities from the two Cambridges are at a lost to answer crucial questions about the authorship, it should come as less of a surprise to learn, extraordinary as it still may seem, that Levi Fox, director of the Shakespeare Birthplace Trust, refused to be interviewed on the subject by the British Broadcasting Company and the press. Queried about this disinclination, Professor Louis Marder said, "My opinion of Mr. Fox is that he is so sure of his position, and knows so well that proper evidence is available that he does not trouble himself to answer." Others may come to a different conclusion.

When Emerson remarked on the wide contrast between the Shakespeare of the Shakespeare Societies and Shakespeare's thought and said he could not marry the one to the other, he was expressing the difficulty the orthodox biographers encounter — and not the biographers alone. Thomas Gainsborough was evidently defeated by the same problem. Having done a full-length portrait of David Garrick, he was asked by the actor to paint an ideal portrait of Shakespeare to grace the celebration at Stratford that Garrick was to stage-manage in 1769. Gainsborough seems to have responded with alacrity. He would do a portrait that "should take the form from his pictures and statues, just enough to preserve his likeness, . . . and supply a soul from his works." But this appears to have been just what he was unable to do. He wrote to Garrick that "I have been several days rubbing in and rubbing out my design of Shakespeare." He went on to say, "Shakespeare's bust is a silly, smiling thing; and I have not sense enough to make him more sensible in the picture, and so I tell ye, you shall not see it." In another letter, he wrote that

"Shakespeare shall come forthwith." But no evidence tells that he ever finished the work or let anyone see what he had done. Even Gainsborough could not bring it off.

Denigration of Shakespeare

Not too much should be made, I suppose, of Shakspere's unprepossessing character. The conduct of great artists has often, no doubt, left something to be desired. Hag-ridden by the dæmon of creativity, they are likely to be a trial to others. But it is Shakspere's distinction, in the ranks to which he has been elevated, never during his lifetime to have had a redeeming trait attributed to him by anyone acquainted with him, as far as we have heard. He was mercenary and grasping. He hoarded grain in time of dearth and at the least stood benevolently by while associates of his sought to enclose the village common lands. When a debtor of his escaped from Stratford, he proceeded against the unfortunate individual who had stood surety for the loan; he was, Sir George Greenwood observes, "as rigorous as Shylock in strictly enforcing the conditions of the bond." His pursuit of the trappings of gentility has been deemed by his partisans to call for an apologia. "As his fame increased," Joseph Quincy Adams of Cornell explains, "it was natural for him to seek to lift himself in the social ranking of the day. In such a light we must view his efforts to secure a coat of arms. A dignity of this sort was the more necessary in his case because he belonged to the then despised tribe of actors." Professor Adams forgets that two pages earlier he had beguiled us with the supposition that "He must have been welcome to the society of those gallants of the law Inns and young noblemen of the Court who haunted the theatres and eagerly sought the acquaintance of actors and playwrights" — not so despised after all. He also passes over the evidence that, after being turned down in his application, Shakspere obtained the grant of arms by bribery.

In a famous scene in *Every Man Out of His Humour*, Ben Jonson, G. B. Harrison says, "made an unkind cut at Shakespeare's [i.e., Shakspere's] gentility." He has the character recognizable as Shakspere — Sogliardo — complain of the "Harrots" — Heralds — that "they speak i' the strangest language, and give a man the hardest terms for his money, that ever you knew." But, "I can write myself Gentleman now, here's my Patent, it cost me thirty pound by this breath." The knight Puntarvolo asks what the crest is, and Sogliardo replies, "Marry, sir, it is your Boar without a head Rampant." At this, another character interjects, "Ramping to gentility." As A. L. Rowse puts it, "For motto he [Puntarvolo] suggests 'Not without mustard,' and for the crest 'a frying pan had had no fellow.' We remember that William

Shakespeare's [i.e., Shakspere's] was, alliteratively, a falcon and his motto, somewhat boastfully, 'not without right,' in French." To Rowse, who omits the exchanges ridiculing Sogliardo-Shakspere, it is all "making fun of taking out coats-of-arms and crests. And very good fun it is, at the expense of the Herald's office, and people putting down good money so that they can write themselves Gentlemen." Sogliardo is described by Jonson as "an essential clown" who "comes up every term to learn to take tobacco and see new motions." It "is not," E. K. Chambers assures us, "a 'portrait' of Shakespeare." Not a *portrait,* exactly.

Shakspere, on the word of his partisans, spent four-fifths of his adult life in London, though "we do not know that he ever let go altogether of Stratford," Chambers says. "Unlike the other actors in his company," Marchette Chute tells us, "he had no wife and family in London and for nearly twenty years he lived there in hired lodgings." In other words, he preferred to have his wife and children a hundred miles away. "The family man, a responsible member of society," Rowse calls him; and again: "Shakespeare, normal family man." Then surely the normal family man and responsible member of society, even if he chose to spend his active years apart from his dependents, saw to it that they did not want? The only mention of Anne Shakspere "between her marriage in 1582 and her husband's death in 1616," Sir Sidney Lee relates, "is as the borrower . . . of forty shillings from Thomas Whittington, who had formerly been her father's shepherd. The money was unpaid when Whittington died in 1601, and he directed his executors to recover the sum from the poet, and distribute it" — a cynical comment, surely, on the likelihood of its being recovered — "among the poor of Stratford." Whittington referred in his will to "Shaxpere" and "it need hardly be mentioned, says nothing about 'the poet,'" George Greenwood points out, and adds: "It is sad to think that the man who in 1597 was so rich that he was able to purchase the largest house in Stratford, known as New Place, left his wife so badly provided for that she was constrained to borrow from her father's shepherd and to find that the debt remained unpaid at the death of the lender in 1601." Such callousness toward her is in accord with his cutting her off with the second-best bed in his cold-blooded will.

Sir Hugh Clopton built a bridge over the Avon for the convenience of his fellow Stratfordians, but William Shakspere in his prosperous retirement did nothing for the town, served it in no office. His idea of civic purpose was to dun the Corporation for the cost of a half-gallon of wine he served a visiting preacher. We need not wonder that Stratford, so far as we can tell, withheld any token of regard for him. (The monument was quite evidently the work of outsiders, with their own purposes.) A biography of Shakspere confined to the kind of knowledge we have about him would present him as the most unattractive man occupying a prominent place in English letters. When biographers go beyond that and try to amalgamate his figure with that of the creator of Shakespeare's verse and dramas, the effect is of combining opposites, an acid and a base, a negative and a positive quantity. The sum is zero. It is the nullity, the no-man of conventional Shakespearean biography. Such is the fate we visit upon the genius who stands at the zenith of achievement among English-speaking peoples.

Shakespeare as a Mercenary Writer

There is worse. We have it thrust upon us that Shakespeare's "sole aim" — this is from the great biographer J. O. Halliwell-Phillipps — "was to please an audience most of whom were not only illiterate but unable either to read or write." We must submit to being told in the *Times Literary Supplement* that "Shakespeare, envying Marlowe his gentility as much as his genius, was more concerned to acquire heraldic proof that he was a gentleman than to ensure the preservation for posterity of his incomparable contribution to English drama." We have to endure slurs by Anthony Burgess, for whom "Shakespeare's main aim was, I think, to make money, not to bequeath deathless plays to posterity. . . . Making money was a means of becoming a gentleman with a fine cloak, and a coat of arms was a means of twofold redemption — a bad marriage and an improvident father. . . ."

Is that what we are to believe of him? — of the Shakespeare about whom Emerson wrote:

> What point of morals, of manners, of economy, of philosophy, of religion, of taste, of the conduct of life, has he not settled? What mystery has he not signified his knowledge of? What office or function, or district of man's work, has he not remembered? What king has he not taught state, as Talma taught Napoleon? What maiden has not found him finer than her delicacy? What lover has he not outloved? What sage has he not outseen? What gentleman has he not instructed in the rudeness of his behavior?

"An ordinary man," Anthony Burgess calls him, "with an irrelevant talent — a talent he didn't really care a damn about. That's what I've always liked about him — the way he took the money and ran." As for his own case, Mr. Burgess writes: "If my concern were only subsistence I would practice a far easier trade than confecting fiction for the discerning reader. Writing is excruciatingly hard, and the more you write the harder it gets." The difference is, we are to believe, that Mr. Burgess is a creative artist but Shakespeare was a manufacturer of potboilers for the undiscerning.

Swinburne had a word for that point of view — though he could never have met it in so virulent a form. It was "vulgar." He wrote:

> Of all vulgar errors the most wanton, the most wilful, and the most resolutely tenacious of life, is that belief bequeathed from the days of Pope, when it was

pardonable, . . . that he [Shakespeare] wrote 'for gain, not glory,' or that, having written *Hamlet,* he thought it nothing very wonderful to have written. . . . That he was in the fullest degree conscious of its wonderful positive worth to all men for all time we have the best evidence possible — his own; and that not by word of mouth, but by actual stroke of hand. . . . Scene by scene, line for line, stroke upon stroke, and touch after touch, he went over all the old laboured ground again; and not to ensure success in his own day, and fill his pockets with contemporary pence, but merely and wholly to make it worthy of himself and his future students. . . .

Such reworking was, I think, true above all for *Hamlet,* which must have been written and rewritten over years. We find evidence of that in the chief character's aging during the play. Appearing as a college youth in the first act, Hamlet by the fifth, after a supposed lapse of only a few months, is thirty and at the end sounds on the eve of middle age; the author has wrought his own development into his protagonist. Other plays clearly embody work bridging years. *All's Well That Ends Well* and *Cymbeline* (which, despite its unpracticed artifices of plot, scholars unreasonably assign to the dramatist's last period) would seem to be early plays that the mature Shakespeare took up again to improve. But to resort to such courtroom evidence of Shakespeare's care for his work is beneath the dramatist and beneath us. It is necessary only to read the plays to gauge the immense labor that went into them, the inexhaustible fidelity to artistic purpose. No amount of genius — "nothing else," Frederick the Great called it, "than a great aptitude for patience" — could have rendered the demands imposed by that exalted achievement other than barely supportable. One has only to read the plays to know that.

Even the most prolific among the grand masters of English literature, Anthony Trollope, testifies that "There is no way of writing well and also of writing easily." Only a lifetime's grueling application could have produced the greatest works by the pen of man. We should recognize that, had those works been assigned to any other writer than Shakespeare. Why do we not concede it to him? If we do so, can we for a moment suppose him to have been indifferent to the fate of the vessels into which he poured himself, once he had been paid for them? I do not know how to reason with anyone who could imagine anything so far outside human nature and comprehension. Let the reader imagine that he himself had written a stanza or two of verse, nothing more, and ask himself if it would not afford him comfort and satisfaction to know that his creation would be appearing over his name in anthologies a century hence. Then let him conceive what his feelings on the score would be if the fruits of his literary toil were beyond the genius of any other writer. Would any human being turn his back on immortal renown? Or did Shakespeare so underrate his work as not to credit the possibility of its survival?

Far from it! No writer ever asserted the claims of his verse to undying life more unequivocally than Shakespeare:

> So long as man can breathe, or eyes can see,
> So long lives this. . . .

> Not marble, nor the gilded monuments
> Of princes, shall outlive this powerful rime.

> When all the breathers of this world are dead,
>   You still shall live, — such virtue hath my pen.

These boasts, taken from the *Sonnets,* attest only to Shakespeare's belief that his rhymed verse was immortal, the Stratfordians assert. His plays, they contend, were a different matter — of no lasting consequence or concern to their author. They would have us believe that Shakespeare placed his poetry in two categories, one labeled "verse," the other "drama," and that the former held all his pride while the latter, to which his genius and his labors were given in vastly greater measure and which is of vastly greater worth, he shrugged off, uninterested in what happened to it. This extraordinary dictum collapses at once in the absence of any reason to doubt that the *Sonnets* themselves, which were to outlive marble and the gilded monuments of princes, would have passed unpublished into oblivion had it been left to Shakspere. Let us, however, go along with the argument so far as to see how it is defended. We are told that plays in Elizabethan times were held in low regard. Marchette Chute, speaking about the dedication of *Venus and Adonis,* says that Shakespeare "called the poem 'the first heir of my invention' because it would not have occurred to the young playwright-turned-poet that his stage plays were worth mentioning, as from Southampton's point of view they certainly were not." She neglects to mention that Southampton was so addicted to stage plays as to be criticized for allowing them to keep him from court.

To satisfy the voracious London public, scores of playwrights had to turn out hundreds of plays. The bulk of them could obviously have been only hackwork, like most television dramas today. But that is not to say that the highly cultivated minority of Elizabethan theatre-goers would not have recognized genius on the boards, or that the theatre itself did not have a high standing. "The English drama was born to the purple," the *Times Literary Supplement* reminds us. "Inspired and disciplined by royal and aristocratic patronage, poets became skilled and daring dramatists," producing "entertainments that delighted the monarch and the court." Rowse reports that "by 1600 foreign visitors regarded the London theatre as a chief glory of the nation." McManaway writes under the Folger imprint that "Plays written for the public stage were not considered literature" and quotes from the title page of one play quarto, "We know these things to be nothing." He cannot, however, ignore Francis Meres's testimony on the first introduction of Shakespeare's name as that of a playwright. After giving Shakespeare high rank among the poets of the day, Meres (the reader will recall) compared him with the Roman dramatists Plautus and Seneca as being preeminent in the nation for comedy and tragedy alike, then declared "As Epius Stolo said, that the Muses would speak with Plautus' tongue, if they would speak Latin: so I say that the Muses would speak with Shakespeare's fine filed phrase, if they would speak English." In other words, Shakespeare's plays were regarded as literature of the highest order and McManaway stood flatly contradicted. What was he to do? Simple: he reduces the statement of Meres's I have quoted to read only "The Muses would speak with Shakespeare's fine filed phrase, if they would speak English," then has it follow directly upon what Meres wrote of Shakespeare as a poet. The comparison with Plautus and Seneca the Folger curator removes from its original place and puts last, so that it is no longer as the English equivalent of the outstanding Roman dramatists that Shakespeare teaches the Muses to speak in his fine-filed phrase. If the reader, like me, knows no more of the rougher side of life than what may be learned in five summers as a hired hand on a farm and in the infantry during four and a half years in the wartime Army, he will find himself a babe-in-the-woods when it comes to academe.

How Shakespeare's plays were accounted by his contemporaries is demonstrated, as we have seen, by their collecting and publishing them in the enormously expensive First Folio with exalted praise for them comparing the dramatist with the greatest of Greece and Rome, and in the edition's sale of some one thousand copies at a price equivalent to that for a suit of clothes today.

That a writer whose work was so highly prized by others would have utterly disvalued it himself is a proposition that no one who has ever had to deal with authors will entertain. No creative writer will either, if he is honest about it and not committed at all costs to the Stratford legend; he well knows that only a belief in the importance of what he is doing will sustain one of his calling in the trials to which he subjects himself, even if its importance consists only of the fame he hopes it will bring him.

Swinburne wrote:

> Of poetry pure and simple, imaginative and sublime, there is no master who has left us more: of humour there is no master who has left us as much of so high a quality and so deep an insight: of women as of men there is no poet who has created so many so surely endowed with everlasting life. All that can be known of manhood, of womanhood, and of childhood, he knew better than any other man ever born. It is not only the crowning glory of England, it is the crowning glory of mankind, that such a man should ever have been born as William Shakespeare.

To that we may add the appraisal by George Steiner, of Churchill College, Cambridge, and of *The New Yorker*'s book-review pages: "No other writer will surpass Shakespeare. . . . Shakespeare is not only the greatest writer who has ever lived, but will ever live."

Are we really to imagine that such a writer, of all writers, wrote only from venal motives and had no regard for his achievement apart from what worldly advantages it would bring? Again, to counter so monstrous a charge, it should not be necessary to bring out mundane, circumstantial evidence. Since apparently it is, let us have at it. Let us realize that if money were Shakespeare's object he would not have taken up play-writing as a means of gaining it. There was no money in that business. Twenty years after he had started writing for the stage, Ben Jonson said that he had never made even a couple of hundred pounds from the plays. "Shakespeare," says Marchette Chute, "could not have made a living from writing plays." She is right. A play brought six or seven pounds. The dramatist would have had to write three a year to equal the emoluments (including lodging) of the schoolmaster back in Stratford-on-Avon, whose status was lower than the parson's. Did Shakspere have any more lucrative calling open to him? Quite evidently. The sum he put out in just one of his investments — £440 for a moiety of the tithes from three villages back home — was almost double the amount the thirty-seven plays would have made for him. Even by 1597, he had struck it rich enough to buy one of the two finest houses in Stratford. How he came by all this money is an interesting question but one that need not detain us here. The Stratfordians have their Shakespeare furiously writing plays to make money while actually acquiring his wealth otherwise. Then, when he has made his pile and is being amply provided for, they have him plugging away at more plays — for a pittance — while casting away the opportunity to write the kind of verse that alone (they say) would have brought him the respect he sought by obtaining a coat-of-arms, not to mention the promise of immortality, which it is human nature to long for.

Why do reputable scholars argue anything so irrational? Because, if they are to maintain Shakspere's authorship, they have no choice. They may wince, but they are without comeback when Anthony Burgess tells the world that Shakespeare, having a talent he really didn't care a damn about, took the money and ran. Literary critics voice no outrage. They accept it placidly when Mr. Burgess writes and proclaims on public television in the United States that the dark lady of the *Sonnets,* to the poet's "dear doting heart" the "fairest and most precious jewel," was Lucy Negro, a black woman from a brothel in Clerkenwell. (Not that Burgess was the first with that libel.) We see how far we may trust Shakespeare's reputation to the literati.

If Shakspere were Shakespeare, then it is true, as Samuel Johnson wrote:

> So careless was this great poet of future fame, that, though he retired to ease
> and plenty, while he was yet little *declined into the vale of years,* before he could
> be disgusted with fatigue, or disabled by infirmity, he made no collection of his
> works, nor desired to rescue those that had already been published from the
> depravations that obscured them, or secure to the rest a better destiny, by giving
> them to the world in their genuine state.

In other words, the conventional Shakespeare — whom evidently Johnson
accepted without its having occurred to him that there was any alternative
— cared nothing for the survival of his life's work, matchless in the literature
of his civilization. Stratfordians have to believe that. They have to abjure
common sense. That this does not come easily to all we have an indication
from the Cambridge professor and literary essayist George Steiner, whose
opinon as to the unattainability, ever again, of Shakespeare's achievement
we heard quoted on the preceding page. Questioned by Bill Moyers in an
interview on WNET, Channel Thirteen, New York, of 22 May 1981 as to
his view of Shakespeare's identity, Dr. Steiner replied:

> I believe there was one Shakespeare. I believe he is the man of Stratford, but
> I refuse to dismiss one haunting problem which is this. We know through his
> will . . . that he dies checking everything that belongs to him, and he does not
> mention sixteen major, gigantic plays [actually 20 in all] not yet printed at his
> death in any form. Hence, if existing at all, on the floor of the theatre, somewhere
> in London, in rough papers and rough actors' parts. And that psychological
> riddle, that a man would make no reference to that; I have no answer for, and
> I find it haunting.

For George Steiner and his fellows, however, the choice is inescapable:
they must either abandon their belief in Shakspere as Shakespeare or accept
Ivor Brown's dictum that "the dramatist . . . did not bother to preserve his
texts." Anyone who can go along with Mr. Brown in that should have little
difficulty with the further revelation he provides, as literary critic for the
Observer of London. "If he had been told that this play [*The Merchant of
Venice*] would never leave the stage and would be revived in London three
times in two months with many leading actors some 357 years later, he
would either have fainted or laughed his head off." Those of us not bound
to the Stratford man will recognize that surely an author of plays so surpassing in quality as Shakespeare's would have been fully aware of their
merit and have received Mr. Brown's tidings with a sense that his confidence
in his genius had been vindicated, even though to a degree he could hardly
have anticipated. "Not marble, nor the gilded monuments of princes. . . ."
We may believe that he was not as silly as Mr. Brown. When Cassius reflects

> How many ages hence
> Shall this our lofty scene be acted o'er
> In states unborn and accents yet unknown!

we may surely allow with Harry Levin of Harvard that "Shakespeare showed prophetic insight into his own future. " It is not a characteristic of literary geniuses to undervalue their powers or the durability of their art.

Let us recall again that the Stratfordians have to have Shakespeare sloughing off even the *Sonnets,* quite ready to forget them. They had lain around in manuscript for years, and when they were published Shakspere had nothing to do with it; we have no reason to believe he even had a copy of them. Yet even to orthodox scholars, the *Sonnets* were "literature," unsullied by connection with the stage; and in them the poet had written self-revealingly of all that was of supreme importance to him. He had done so, moreover, intending that "eyes not yet created shall o'er read" them. He meant for them to be known "So long as men can breathe," "even in the eyes of all posterity." Standing supreme in his nondramatic poetry, "the *Sonnets* in poetic worth immeasurably surpass the *Venus and Adonis* and the *Lucrece,*" says Edward Dowden, "nor can the author have been unaware of this fact." Why, then, did the author publish the two long narrative poems and leave the survival of the *Sonnets* to chance? Why — setting aside as unworthy of consideration the Stratfordian doctrine that he was indifferent to the fate of the work that would make him immortal — did he also fail to provide for the survival of his plays?

Incredibly, almost, the answer has proclaimed itself to us for three and a half centuries. Those in a position to know tell us that if Shakespeare did not arrange to have his plays published, it was because the opportunity to do so was denied him. Authorities whose word the Stratfordians take as gospel in other contexts, the editors of the First Folio of 1623, make that plain in the dedication to the Earls of Pembroke and Montgomery and in the address "To the Great Variety of Readers," both signed by the actors John Heminge and Henry Condell. In the first, they refer to the plays' "outliving" the author and "he not having the fate, common with some, to be executor to his own writings." In the second they are more explicit: "It had been a thing, we confess, worthy to have been wished, that the author himself had lived to have set forth, and overseen his writings. But since it hath been ordained otherwise, and he by death departed from that right, we pray you do not envy his friends the office of their care, and pain, to have collected and published them." If Shakespeare did not see to the preservation of his works it was not because he was unconcerned for their future. It was because he did not live to do so, because he was deprived of the right to do so by death. The editors of the First Folio were not, could not have been, talking about Shakspere of Stratford, who spent his last years in affluent leisure, evincing not the slightest concern for the plays.

Midway through the past century, John Payne Collier was troubled on this score.[1] "It is one of the problems in the life of our great dramatist that will never be solved," he wrote, "how it happened that he, who could write such plays, could be so indifferent to their appearance in print." Yet the answer to that problem has stared scholars in the face from the beginning. If Shakspere showed no care for the publication or survival of Shakespeare's works the reason was, and had to be, that he was not their author.

Shakespeare as a Playwright for the Commercial Theatre

The proposition that Shakespeare's object as a playwright was to make money has a corollary no less vehemently urged upon us. Not only did Shakespeare have "no time to attend to the printing of his plays, even if he had been interested in doing so," says Rowse; but: "There is no sign that he was — the play was the thing: the play on the stage." We are to conceive of Shakespeare above all as a workaday playwright turning out his wares to meet an acting company's needs, tailoring his work to the predilections of his audience and the requirements of the stage — a man totally of the theatre. This view consorts well with a down-to-earth Stratfordian Shakespeare. It has an air of shrewd appraisal about it — of sophistication. "Now Shakespeare was a working dramatist, most concerned with the immediate success of his plays on the stage": so we have it from G. B. Harrison. To G. E. Bentley of Princeton it is self-evident: "If Shakespeare's proper context is not the London commercial theatres and the professional troupes, then evidence has no meaning."

On the other hand, if evidence — on which law and science are based — has a meaning, then Shakespeare's context was not what Professor Bentley says it was. "Shakespeare's plays were *not* composed for the gawkish groundlings of the Globe, but for theatres and audiences far more worthy of them," says Richard Levin of the State University of New York. Writing in the *Times Literary Supplement,* Professor Levin goes on to name eighteen of Shakespeare's plays that were written for presentation at Court, the Inns of Court, or the Universities. Shakespeare himself may be assumed to have shared Hamlet's view of the "groundlings," that they "for the most part" were "capable of nothing but inexplicable dumb-shows and noise."

"He was a man of the theatre, first and foremost," says Louis Auchincloss, whose study of Shakespeare, less well known than his novels, is worthy of thoughtful attention. But to Mr. Auchincloss, I oppose Mr. Swinburne, to whom it was an

---

[1] Collier not only misread crucial Shakespearean documents, like his fellow scholars, but miswrote them; he was an addicted forger. All the same, he contributed to our knowledge about the dramatist.

indisputable certainty that Shakespeare never wrote merely for the stage, but always with an eye on the future and studious reader, who would be competent and careful to appreciate what his audience and his fellow actors could not. The perfect *Hamlet* was so far beyond their apprehension that the lying rascals who published the first edition of its author's collected plays did not fear to strike out from the already published text the very finest and most important passage in the poem [the soliloquy beginning "How all occasions do inform against me"]: whence we may infer to what a process of mutilation plays first issued under their most inauspicious auspices must only too surely have been subjected.

To the passage of his I have previously quoted on Shakespeare's going "over all the laboured ground again" in *Hamlet,* Swinburne added, "Every change in *Hamlet* has impaired its fitness for the stage, and increased its value for the closet in exact and perfect proportion." And citing again the dropping of "the supreme soliloquy of Hamlet," he commented that "Even in Shakespeare's time the actors threw out his additions; they throw out those very same additions in our own."

Shakespeare knew they would throw them out and knew they had to. When Maurice Evans, in 1938, did the unheard-of and put on his uncut *Hamlet,* the play ran to five hours. That was twice what the Elizabethan public theatre could accommodate, owing to the short winter days. According to Professor Alfred Hart, plays began at two o'clock and were over between four and five. The chorus in *Romeo and Juliet* speaks of "the two hours' traffic of our stage," and Marchette Chute, setting the "normal playing time" at "two hours," observes that "many of his [Shakespeare's] finished scripts needed an acting time of more than three hours and could not have been brought to an end during the brief daylight hours of a winter afternoon."

There are 3,965 lines in *Hamlet. Richard the Third* has almost 3,600, *Troilus and Cressida* almost 3,500, *Henry the Fourth, Part Two,* and *Coriolanus* more than 3,400, *Cymbeline, Lear,* and *Othello* more than 3,300. Ben Jonson's plays also ran long, averaging around 3,500 lines, according to Professor Hart, but most of them are prose, making comparison difficult; *Sejanus,* entirely in verse, has 3,156 lines. By contrast, there are 2,510 lines in John Webster's *The Duchess of Malfi*; 2,557 in John Fletcher's *Faithful Shepherdess*; and 2,260 in Christopher Marlowe's *The Jew of Malta.* The average was about 2,500, according to Professor Hart. How badly *Hamlet* has suffered in production over the centuries by being brought down to such a length is suggested by John Mason Brown's review of the uncut version:

> Those five hours race by at the St. James. . . . One leaves them not fatigued but filled with uncommon exhilaration. . . . A great play so greatly done that all its innumerable greatnesses are made incessantly communicative. . . . It emerges as a thrilling entity, a work of art in which the supreme artist who fathered it has his unimpeded sway. No hacks have dared to prune his script pretending they knew his business better than he did. . . . The so-called subsidiary characters

. . . now explain themselves to theatre-goers as in the past they have done only
to readers.

That Shakespeare was looking beyond his theatre audiences to his future
readers, I think *Hamlet* makes it impossible to doubt. But not in their length
alone do Shakespeare's plays impel us to this conclusion. Samuel Taylor
Coleridge wrote: "I believe Shakespeare was not a whit more intelligible in
his own day than he is now to an educated man, except for a few local
allusions of no consequence." My suspicion is that a great many topical
allusions in Shakespeare clear to his more knowing contemporaries, escape
us today, but for the rest I see no grounds on which to dispute Coleridge. If
some words used in an Elizabethan sense puzzle us, these are probably
balanced by those, familiar to us, which Shakespeare coined and sprang on
an unready audience. Shakespeare's first audiences therefore may well have
missed much that is in the plays, even in such parts as were presented, just
as we do on a first hearing.

The greater the economy with which a writer can express himself, the
sharper the effect on his reader, and Shakespeare was a master at compression. The requirements of compactness and of blank verse often led him into
involved constructions, so that he reminds one of a packer fitting objects of
assorted shapes, as many as possible, into tidy compartments. His thought
was rich and subtle, his imagery original and unexpected. On the stage,
unless you already know the text, a speech is likely to be left behind before
you have half sorted it out. Many, many passages in Shakespeare, with the
text before me, I have had to work over to fathom and some I cannot be
sure I have understood. To grasp the full meaning of these passages when
first heard on the tripping tongue of an actor would be out of the question.
Shakespeare requires close reading if his "good wit" is, as Touchstone says,
to be "seconded with the forward child Understanding." It is characteristic
of him that the more you read him the more you get out of him. To suppose
his verse, which challenges all that the most thoughtful can bring to it, was
written to be gulped by a predominantly illiterate theatre audience seems to
me to abdicate judgment.

It is also in the nature of his plays to make us feel the inadequacies that
constrict the stage. We may or may not agree with Frank Harris that "Shakespeare . . . was nearly always an indifferent playwright, careless of the
architectural construction of his pieces, contemptuous of stage-craft." But
Anthony and Cleopatra, one of Shakespeare's great tragedies, seems hardly
to have been written for the stage at all. Edward Dowden informs us, "We
do not know of a performance before 1759, when an abridged and altered
version . . . was produced. . . . Its run was short. . . . From 1678 onwards

for a century and a half Dryden's rival tragedy [*All for Love, or the World Well Lost*] displaced a work incomparably greater yet one less fitted for success upon the boards." He concludes, "It cannot be denied . . . that Shakespeare's tragedy fills the imagination better than the stage." Shakespeare himself could not have intended it for the stage he knew. We are unworthy of him and of ourselves if we imagine him creating the infinitely subtle, complex, maddeningly feminine, nearly forty-year-old Serpent of the Nile only to have her enacted by a prepuberal male no more acquainted with passion than a puppy. To do justice to Shakespeare's masterpiece in his gallery of women is scarcely within the compass of a mature actress of the greatest talent. The dramatist's fatal Egyptian Queen herself clasps the asp to her bosom rather than have "some squeaking Cleopatra boy my greatness."

Or consider *Richard the Third.* In 1700, Colley Cibber took the play in hand and recast it, retaining less than a fourth of the original and replacing the deletions with passages from the other historical plays and with a thousand lines of his own. Vulgar as the revision was, "it cannot be denied," Dowden admits, that it "was theatrically effective; it held the stage, to the exclusion of Shakespeare's tragedy, for more than a century." George Bernard Shaw calls it a "thing of shreds and patches" but "more effective on the stage than Shakespeare's arrangement."

In other plays we can hardly be unaware of how Shakespeare strives to burst the confines of the theatre. "O!" cries the chorus in *Henry the Fifth* "for . . . a kingdom for a stage, princes to act, monarchs to behold the swelling scene." He asks "pardon, gentles all," for those who have dared "on this unworthy scaffold to bring forth / So great an object: can this cockpit hold / The vasty fields of France? or may we cram / Within this wooden O the very casques / That did affright the air at Agincourt? . . . Let us," he pleads, "On your imaginary forces work." And again, "Piece out our imperfections with your thoughts: . . . Think when we talk of horses that you see them / Printing their proud hoofs i' the receiving earth." In the wartime motion picture *Henry the Fifth*, starring Laurence Olivier, who also produced and directed it, we actually see the magnificent steeds doing just that. We behold "the warlike Harry, like himself / Assumes the port of Mars" in "the vasty fields of France," even if they were in Ireland.

Olivier's *Henry the Fifth* "liberates Shakespeare's poem," *Time* said, calling it one of the screen's "rare and great works of art." John Mason Brown, having seen two parts of *Henry the Fourth* on the stage, confessed that, even with the benefit of such superlative performers as Laurence Olivier and Ralph Richardson

> Whenever the restless script wandered out of doors, especially when it jumped to Gadshill, the battlefield at Shrewsbury, or the streets of London, I discovered

that I was fretting at the theatre's inadequacies not less than at the formlessness of the chronicle-history plays.

It was not until I saw Mr. Olivier play Henry in his motion picture production of *Henry the Fifth* . . . that I realized what I was missing. Though as a loyal lover of the stage it hurts me to say this, I am unable to keep it in. I was missing what the screen can do with these materials that the theatre cannot dream of matching. I was missing those qualities of physical freedom, of the chronicle-history uncaged and sent soaring skyward, which make *Henry the Fifth* by all odds the finest movie I have ever seen, and one of the most enthralling and stirring Shakespearean performances I ever hope to see.

That Shakespeare fretted no less than Mr. Brown over the limitations inflicted on him by the stage seems evident. The chronicle-histories, formless on "this unworthy scaffold," are not formless when the camera supplies all that cannot be brought within the "wooden O." It would be easy to conceive that Shakespeare was writing with the motion picture in mind. In fact, he was writing, surely, for a medium that excels even the camera in mobility and in capacity for conjuring up the possible and the impossible. He had in mind not primarily the theatre but our "imaginary forces." Though he cast his work in dramatic form, he disregarded the dramatic unities, displeasing traditionalists, and let his action stray over months and hundreds of miles while, like life itself, it combined and juxtaposed tragedy and farce, the elegantly playful and the brutally violent. Though he gave us marvellous theatre, I think we must recognize that he was above all a novelist, and a novelist above all other novelists. Later we shall consider evidence that the novel form itself had its genesis with the man we know as Shakespeare.

Henry the Fifth, with its scenic sweep, lent itself peculiarly well to realization of its potential on the screen. But in other plays, Shakespeare's characters, his greatest characters, seem beyond the portrayable dimensions of actual human beings, in whatever medium. Charles Lamb wrote of *King Lear* that "the contemptible machinery by which they mimic the storm which he goes out in, is not more inadequate to represent the horrors of the real elements, than any actor can be to represent Lear: they might more easily propose to personate the Satan of Milton upon a stage, or one of Michael Angelo's terrible figures." Lamb declared, "I cannot help being of the opinion that the plays of Shakespeare are less calculated for performance on a stage, than those of almost any other dramatist whatever." William Hazlitt said of Shakespeare: "We do not like to see our author's plays acted, and least of all, *Hamlet.* There is no play that suffers so much in being transferred to the stage. Hamlet himself seems hardly capable of being acted." Further on he explained his view more fully:

The *Midsummer Night's Dream,* when acted, is converted from a delightful fiction into a dull pantomime. All that is finest in the play is lost in the representation. The spectacle was grand; but the spirit was evaporated, the genius was fled. — Poetry and the stage do not agree well together. . . . The *ideal* can have no place upon the stage, which is a picture without perspective; everything there is in the foreground. That which was merely an airy shape, a dream, a passing thought, immediately becomes an unmanageable reality. Where all is left to the imagination (as is the case in reading), every circumstance, near or remote, has an equal chance of being kept in mind, and tells accordingly to the mixed impression of all that has been suggested.

Some, certainly, would rather have Shakespeare on the stage than read him, as T. S. Eliot said he would. I think that either they do not mind missing a great deal of the play or, like Eliot, they know the play well enough not to miss much of it and gain added pleasure from an inspired performance. (A good British actor, as the Hollywood film producer Milton Sperling said to me, can grip you with the line "The Bismarck is a thin-skinned vessel.") Sir Laurence Olivier greatly enhanced, for me, the appeal and charm of the boyish King Harry; but inescapably he made Hamlet more finite and circumscribed, and the play was the loser.

Having been justified, surely, in rejecting the notion that Shakespeare wrote primarily to make money, we may safely, I think, now reject this other foundation of orthodoxy: the canard that he was "most concerned with the immediate success of his plays on the stage."

Shakespeare in His True Dimensions

"All men," said Emerson, "are impressed in proportion to their own advancement in thought, by the genius of Shakespeare, and the greatest minds value him the most." Unfortunately we have left Shakespeare too much to those who, by Emerson's test, are of small mind. Where the Coleridges, Swinburnes, Macaulays, and Carlyles — and Emersons — show how great were their minds in their perception of the poet-dramatist, scholars and critics seek often, it seems, to diminish him. Perhaps it is a matter of gaining stature for themselves by climbing on top of him. "Shakespeare," says Edmund Wilson in a review in *The New Yorker,* "was not a scholar, or self-consciously a spokesman for his age, as Dante and Goethe were; he was not even an 'intellectual.' . . . He began by feeding the market with potboilers and patching up other people's plays, and he returned to these trades at the end." It would be difficult to find more misinformation, and more derogatory misinformation, about Shakespeare in briefer space. These disparagements from the ranks of the professionals recall Harold J. Laski's reflections on "expertise." "It too often fails to see round its subject," he wrote. "Too often, also, it lacks humility; and this breeds in its possessors a failure in proportion which makes them fail to see the obvious which is before their very noses." Mr. Laski, incidentally, has a further cautionary word for those who might hope that the academicians could be brought to reexamine the authorship question. "It [expertise] breeds an inability to accept new views from the very depths of its preoccupation with its own conclusions."[2]

To counterbalance Edmund Wilson and the professors, I propose to bring forward Hermann Sinsheimer. I do not know who Mr. Sinsheimer is, or was: he died some twenty years ago. At least I know only that he fled Germany in the late 1930s for Britain and the United States and that, in 1947, Gollancz in London published a small book he wrote on Shylock. But from the quotation from that book which follows, I think the reader will find that its author understood the phenomenon of Shakespeare in his times as no orthodox biographer has, whatever his scholarly qualifications. Notice that he did not, by the way, fail to perceive in Shakespeare the androgynous quality that is likely to characterize creative artists. How he reconciled his conception of Shakespeare with his acceptance of the Stratford man, I do not know. Perhaps he never thought about it. He did, however, observe wonderingly that the Stratfordian's views on money seemed more those of Shylock than of Shylock's debtor, Antonio. He wrote:

> At a distance of four centuries, Elizabeth Tudor and William Shakespeare look like brother and sister. He too had a unique receptivity. . . . He assembled a thousand years around his throne. He is, as it were, a woman-man just as his sister Elizabeth is a man-woman. . . . To us, William's work is embedded in Elizabeth's role and William's poetry is redolent of Elizabeth's work. He is *the* Elizabethan poet, . . . she is *the* Shakespearean Queen. Shakespeare the Spear-shaker! . . .
>
> The plays are Elizabethan conquests, extensions of territory, expansions of privilege and power, additions of wealth to a nation that is experiencing a whole world in itself before it lays hands upon it. . . .
>
> Long flights this eagle of the European stage made in search of food. Back into antiquity, on into history, out into mythology, to the Continent, above all to Italy, the cradle of humanity, where antiquity, history and mythology lay bound together. . . . There was not room enough for him in the island of Britain. He had to roam far and wide in order to keep his genius supplied with raw material. Like Drake and Raleigh, he discovered and held as booty the material which set his imagination on fire. By so doing he gained space and time for the British nation. The fact that, except for *The Merry Wives of Windsor,* he did not set any contemporary plays on English soil finds its ultimate explanation in the mission of a national poet to enrich from outside sources from every corner of space and time, a nation that is struggling into her proper, uninsular shape. Between the lines and between the characters one may read the legend: Our island is too small; our kingdom is the world! Shakespeare was, in the realm of poetry, one of the founders of British "Imperialism."

---

[2] According to the columnist Jack Anderson, a sign on the wall of an office in the Department of the Navy recalls the statement made during World War II by Admiral William Leahy, Chief of Naval Operations: "The A-bomb is the biggest fool thing we have ever done. . . . The bomb will never go off, and I speak as an expert on Explosives."

"Marlborough, you recollect," Carlyle reminds us, "said he knew no English history but what he had learned from Shakespeare." And he quotes August Wilhelm von Schlegel, poet and translator of Shakespeare, as calling the historical plays "a kind of National Epic." They are that, certainly, a National Epic from the 13th-century reign of John to the eve of Elizabeth. They gave Englishmen a vivid and vital awareness of the national past and a national consciousness when England stood between insularity and world greatness. If Edmund Wilson and his fellows have believed that Shakespeare made that gift to his country — "this land of such dear souls, this dear, dear land" — without knowledge of what he was doing, then I think they have shut themselves off from one of the great stories in our past.

He whom Ben Jonson hailed as "soul of the age" was not consciously a spokesman for his age, as Dante and Goethe were? "Shakespeare," says Swinburne, "could have taken up Homer in his right hand and Dante in his left." I think that Mr. Wilson's and Professor Bentley's successors will find that, like Elizabeth herself, and abetted by her, he was knowingly a creator of that age, just as he was the creator, more than any other dozen writers, of the language we speak. Upon the passing of the Shakespearean Queen and the Elizabethan poet — within fifteen months of each other, if I am right as to who Shakespeare was — their contemporaries might well have been put in mind of Octavius Caesar's valedictory to Antony and Cleopatra in Shakespeare's tragedy:

> No grave upon the earth shall clip in it
> A pair so famous.

7

"And Thereupon These Errors Are Arose"

Beyond citing what Greene and Chettle were supposed to have said on the subject and did not, orthodox writers tell us that William Shakspere of Stratford must have been the author William Shakespeare because: (1) his name and the author's were the same; (2) he was a professional actor and thus qualified and disposed to write for the stage; (3) he was identified as the author in a play brought out by the young men at Cambridge in 1602 and called The Return from Parnassus; *(4) Francis Beaumont, his fellow playwright, writing of Shakespeare in a letter to Ben Jonson around 1615, left no doubt that the dramatist was he; and, (5) his contemporaries clearly regarded him as the dramatist. Examining these contentions in turn, we find that in each the facts are other than they have been construed, beginning with the pointed evidence that the name the dramatist wrote under was a pseudonym. As for Shakspere's striking failure to protest or take action when plays of Shakespeare's were pirated one after another in corrupt editions, we find little reason to accept orthodoxy's argument that an author in those days had no legal rights in his product, and good reason to reject it.*

If this book succeeds in its purpose, it will have no future except as an historical curiosity. Readers, having found that the Stratford theory does not stand up, will wonder why I continued to belabor it in these pages. If it failed by two or three decisive tests, what need was there to go on showing how it failed by others? I can only plead that at the time I was writing the sentiment in favor of the Stratford man was so strong and the orthodox establishment so nearly unassailable that, if the case were to be brought to a conclusive judgment, I seemed to have no choice but to hold all orthodoxy's tenets up to the light.

The question of the Shakespeare authorship did, interestingly, come up for judicial review in 1964, in England. A Miss Hopkins had died leaving a third of her estate to the Francis Bacon Society for the purpose of searching for the manuscripts of the plays attributed to Shakespeare. Her heirs, having, as heirs sometimes will have, less regard for the testator's wishes than for the sum about to elude them — £6,500 — sought to have this provision in the will set aside on the grounds that the search would be "a wild goose chase." They had no difficulty marshalling professional testimony on their side. Professor Kenneth Muir argued that he was at a loss to imagine where any useful search could now be made, all probable places having long since been examined — a matter of some dispute. Having heard both parties, Mr. Justice Wilberforce, stating that the court could not go beyond the evidence presented to it, found that although "a number of alternative authors have been suggested, none has been accepted by scholars and little solid fact has been found to support any of them" (no one having been there to present the case for anyone but Bacon) but that (1) "the evidence in favor of Shakespeare's authorship is quantitatively slight"; that (2) "there is a number of difficulties in the way of the traditional ascription"; and (3) that "as Professor Trevor-Roper of Oxford points out, so far from these difficulties tending to diminish with time, the intensive search of the Nineteenth Century has widened the evidentiary gulf between William Shakespeare the man, and the author of the plays." It was reported that Professor Trevor-Roper, "while keeping his own position firmly in the ranks of the orthodox and stating that he definitely does not believe that the works of 'Shakespeare' could have been written by Francis Bacon," said that "he also considers that the case for William Shakespeare rests on a narrow balance of evidence and that new material could upset it, that though almost all professional scholars accept 'Shakespeare's' authorship, a settled scholarly tradition can inhibit free thought, that heretics are not necessarily wrong." Mr. Justice Wilberforce concluded that "the question of the authorship cannot be considered as closed."[1] The court sustained the bequest.

The Name "Shakespeare" as a Pseudonym

Had I been at the Hopkins trial I should have entered the strongest objection to references to the Stratford man as Shakespeare. In their biographies the orthodox writers always give the name of the Stratford family as Shakespeare, but that is just a license they assume, to create a presumption that their subject was the same man as the dramatist. The name was demonstrably not Shakespeare. However unanimously the biographers write of the father as John Shakespeare, John was never called Shakespeare by his fellow Stratfordians, as far as we know, and neither was his brother Henry of Snitterfield. In the Stratford Register of christenings, marriages, and burials, the rendering of the name as Shakspere is "fairly uniform," according to Chambers. In

---

[1] Gwynne Evans and Harry Levin of Harvard have denounced my inclusion of Professor Trevor-Roper in the ranks of the heretics on the authorship question as "an unwarranted slur against Trevor-Roper's professional reputation." He himself made no objection, however, to the article in which the listing occurred. As early as 1962 an article of Trevor-Roper's in *Réalités* was subtitled "The paradox of Shakespeare, an undisputed genius whose identity is still in doubt." Today, Lord Dacre of Glanton, as he is now, describes himself as an agnostic on the issue inclining, on the present balance of evidence, toward orthodoxy.

only one of the thirty entries he reproduces is the name given as Shakespeare; that is the record of the christening, in 1583, of Will's daughter Susanna — who, twenty years later, is married as Susanna Shaxpere. John's name was nearly always rendered Shakspeyr by one town official, while another tended to Shaxpeare, Chambers tells us; they never wrote it Shakespeare. Walter Roche, ex-master of the Stratford grammar school, whose authority I think we may grant, spelled it Shaxbere. It was Shaxpere on one of Will's marriage documents, Shagspere on the other.

Admittedly, as the orthodox writers reiterate, Elizabethan spelling was erratic and a name was often spelled in varied ways. But I think we may assume that frequent users of a name would give it a constant pronunciation, following the lead set by the bearer of the name. We can hardly believe that the noted householders of Henley Street would sound their name Shaxpere one day and Shakespeare the next or that their neighbors would do so. The Stratford name was spelled with a very high rate of consistency — twenty-nine times out of thirty in the Town Register — so as to require a short *a* in the first syllable, the dramatist's name with a very high rate of consistency as Shakespeare or Shake-speare, requiring a long *a* in the first syllable. That was the way the dramatist himself spelled his name in the dedications of *Venus and Adonis* and *Lucrece,* and that was the way it was habitually spelled, with the few variants to be regarded as mistakes; when it appeared as Shak-speare on an early quarto of *Othello,* it was corrected to Shake-speare in the next printing. There is nothing in a name pronounced Shaxpere to suggest the shaking of a spear. But this action is inevitably called up mentally by a name pronounced Shake-spear — as Ben Jonson recognized when, in writing about the dramatist's "true-filed lines," he exclaimed, "In each of which, he seems to shake a lance, / As brandish'd in the eyes of ignorance."

As the name Shakespeare became famous, William of Stratford may have come to fancy it. (I am assuming that he was competent to discriminate.) The first indication of such a preference was in his application for a coat-of-arms in the name of John Shakespeare. Or it may be that others, increasingly familiar with the name, wrote it as Shakespeare without his having anything to do with it. This choice seems more likely since in all six of his alleged signatures the spelling calls for the short *a* in the first syllable. Orthodox scholars evidently do not feel they have to explain this fact while insisting that his name was Shakespeare.

The first recorded occurrence of the name William Shakespeare as that of the author came with publication of *Venus and Adonis* in 1593, and the way in which it was introduced indicates that it was a pseudonym and meant to be recognized as such. To begin with, it appeared not on the title page but only as the subscription to the dedication, as it did also for the poet's next published work, *The Rape of Lucrece,* which followed a year later. In other words, in the only two works we attribute to Shakespeare that the author himself published, he kept his name from the place where the author's name is conventionally placed. The title page reads:

> Venus and Adonis *Vilia miretur vulgus: mihi flavus Apollo Pocula Castalia plena ministret aqua.* LONDON. Imprinted by Richard Field, and are to be sold at the signe of the white Greyhound in Paules Churchyard, 1593.

Orthodox writers make much over Field's origin as son of a tanner of Stratford-on-Avon, which could have led to Will Shakspere's seeking him out. As we shall see, however, there was equally good reason for Field to have been given the job by the man who, on the best evidence (in my view), we may believe to have been Shakespeare.

G. George Greenwood translates the quotation from Ovid's *Amores* that follows the title as: "Let the common herd admire common things, so long as to *me* Apollo's self hands goblets brimming with the waters of Castaly." And he adds ironically, "Of a truth the young Player, at his first literary venture, was not troubled with any superfluous modesty!"

One would have to look far in Elizabethan literature to find prose of simpler clarity and more effortless graciousness than the famous dedication of *Venus and Adonis.* It reads:

TO THE RIGHT HONOURABLE
HENRY WRIOTHESLEY,

EARL OF SOUTHAMPTON, AND BARON OF TICHFIELD.

RIGHT HONOURABLE,

I know not how I shall offend in dedicating my unpolished lines to your lordship, nor how the world will censure me for choosing so strong a prop to support so weak a burthen; only, if your honour seem but pleased, I account myself highly praised, and vow to take advantage of all idle hours, till I have honoured you with some graver labour. But if the first heir of my invention prove deformed, I shall be sorry it had so noble a godfather, and never after ear [till] so barren a land, for fear it yield still so bad a harvest. I leave it to your honourable survey, and your honour to your heart's content; which I wish may always answer your own wish and the world's hopeful expectation.

Your honour's in all duty,
WILLIAM SHAKESPEARE.

The dedication, A. L. Rowse declares, was composed by the author "in his grand gentlemanly manner." Grand and gentlemanly it is, though one may be puzzled to understand how in Tudor England such a manner came to invest a provincial glover's son not long versed in speaking English intelligible to Londoners and striving to make a way in a class of "rogues and vagabonds," as actors were then accounted. But let that pass for the moment. The crucial clause is that "first heir of my invention." Construing this expression to mean "the first product of my inventive faculty," orthodox writers have to explain why Shakespeare's plays, of which between three and five had already appeared even by their reckoning, were not regarded by him as products of that faculty. Here they fall back on the argument that plays were not considered worthy of regard in such a connection. Again I am not impressed. In 1592, Thomas Nashe had written of a play that, he said, "would have joyed brave Talbot (terror of the French)." Acknowledged to have been *Henry the Sixth, Part One*, it had, Nashe said, moved to "tears . . . ten thousand spectators (at several times)." I cannot believe that a supposedly budding writer who had had so great a success would have deemed his powers of invention so far fruitless, least of all in commending himself to a lord who shared his addiction to the theatre.

But even if we accept the orthodox alibi on that issue, what about the author's earlier verse? *Venus and Adonis* is far from the top rank of Shakespeare's works, but it is a finished and sophisticated major performance of 1,194 lines, of sufficient merit as to have achieved immediate popularity and to have gone through edition after edition. Surely it was preceded by other respectable poems? Why were they not products of its author's invention? Well, we are told, they were not *published*.

The case grows weaker and weaker, and the more so when we ask the Stratfordians what the purpose of the dedication was. Their answer is that the actor-playwright was seeking a patron. "I feel that Shakespeare was . . . shy of involvement in the world," says Anthony Burgess, "But he rushes at the world with his sword when he wants money and advancement. Hence the fervent embracing of the golden chance of securing the Earl of Southampton as his patron." If that is what Stratfordians like to believe of their candidate, that is their privilege; but they must recognize that seeking a patron in the past was like seeking a grant from a philanthropical foundation today: the last way to recommend yourself — as we who have been constrained to hit the foundation trail well know — would be to plead your lack of accomplishment. It goes without saying that you would not have the prospective donor, however modestly you might commend yourself, receive the impression that you had never done anything. Especially would this apply if you were no longer very young. A poet who had produced nothing worthy of consideration by age thirty would seem to offer an indifferent investment.

All difficulties with "the first heir of my invention" disappear if we take it that the author, as was his practice, was using words in accordance with their meaning. A poem cannot inherit an inventive faculty; it is the product, not the heir of such a faculty. On the other hand, if "my invention" is an invented name, the poem that appears under it can very well be said to have inherited it. A name is above all what an offspring does inherit.

"William Shakespeare" was evidently recognized at once as a pseudonym.

As J. Q. Adams writes, "When the poem [*Venus and Adonis*] was still all the rage, there was entered in the Stationers' Register, on May 17, 1594, a close imitation by one 'T.H.,' with the same theme of unrequited love, approximately the same plot, the same setting, the same richly ornate style, and with the title *Oenone and Paris,* parallel to the title *Venus and Adonis.* As *Venus and Adonis* was from Ovid's *Metamorphoses, Oenone and Paris* was from his *Heroides.*" The Folger Director adds, "Throughout the text, verbal plagiarism of Shakespeare's poem is everywhere conspicuous." In the dedication of *Oenone and Paris* to "Curteous Readers," T.H. parodies the dedication of *Venus and Adonis*:

> Here you have the first fruits of my endeavours and maidenhead of my pen; which, how rude and unpolished it may seem in your eagle-sighted eyes, I can not conceive, and therefore, fearing the worst, I have sought in some sort to prevent it. Apelles having framed any work of worth, would set it openly to the view of all, hiding himself closely in a corner of the work-house, to the end, that if some curious and gaping fellow came to find any fault, he might amend it against the next market. In the publishing of this little poem, I have imitated the painter, giving you this poor pamphlet to peruse, lurking in the meanwhile obscurely till that, hearing how you please to censure [judge] of my simple work, I may in some other *Opere magis elaborato* apply my vein to your humours. . . .

Having pretended that the poem was his first and in the same words making fun of the pretence, "T.H." says he is offering the poem under concealed authorship in imitation of the Greek painter Apelles so that he may see how the dedicatees like it, in anticipation of his offering to their "humors" a more ambitious work — just as the author of *Venus and Adonis* promised to "honour" the dedicatee with "some graver labor." It mimics Shakespeare's dedication from start to finish, though it misconstrues the purpose of his pseudonymity.

That "Shakespeare" was widely seen to be a made-up name is shown by the frequency with which those who referred to it hyphenated it. When we encounter in fiction names consisting of a descriptive word or pair of words — Mistress Quickly and Doll Tearsheet in Shakespeare, Sir Martin Marplot in William Cavendish, Lydia Languish and Mrs. Malaprop in Sheridan, Doctors Rerechild and Fillgrave and the lawyer Bideawhile in Trollope — we know we are not expected to accept these as *bona fide* names of human beings; we recognize that the author is whimsically labeling a character with his or her predominant trait or activity. Similarly, when a writer assumes a pseudonym that he expects to be recognized as such he is apt to select such a name, especially one describing an action. Martin Marprelate (the unknown anticlerical pamphleteer) and Cuthbert Curryknave (a pen name of Thomas Nashe's) are examples from Shakespeare's day, Mark Twain one from our own. Of course a real person may bear a name describing an action: Drink-water or Lovejoy — or, for that matter, Shakespeare, a not too uncommon family name. But when we encounter a publication signed Robert Drink-water or Mildred Love-joy we may be sure that these are pseudonyms — doubly sure if the names are appropriate to the message, if Mr. Drink-water is urging abstinence from alcohol and Miss Love-joy advertising a dance studio.

And so it is with the name William Shake-speare. We could be sure even if the action described were not particularly appropriate to a dramatist. But it is appropriate. Indeed, the coincidence would be startling if the leading dramatist of our civilization had actually been born with the name Shake-speare. *Hasti-vibrans,* the Spear-shaker, was the sobriquet of Pallas Athena, who was said to have sprung from the brow of Zeus fully armed and brandishing a spear. And Pallas Athena was the patron goddess of Athens, home of the theatre, while in Rome the guild of poets and dramatists met in the Temple of Pallas. "The spear of Pallas shake," says a verse in a collection of Shakespeare's poems of 1640.

E. K. Chambers lists eighty-three versions and variants of the name Shake-speare occurring as family names in Britain and of course in none is the name hyphenated. "Shake-speare" is clearly in the category of those whom Mistress Overdone's tapster names in *Measure for Measure* as being in jail (Mistress Overdone herself being in the category): "Young master Deep-vow, and Master Copper-spur, and Master Starve-lackey, the rapier and dagger man, and young Drop-heir that killed Lusty Pudding, and Master Forthlight, the tilter, and brave Master Shoe-tie the great traveler, and wild Half-can that stabbed Pots." This is to say, it is a symbolic, not an actual name. Only two kinds of names are hyphenated in English usage: Family names that combine two names each of which is itself a family name, as Burne-Jones, Trevor-Roper, or, the subject of one of Ben Jonson's *Epigrammes,* Brayne-Hardie — and in such cases both names are capitalized. "Shake-speare" is manifestly not of this order. The other kind is the name manufactured to denote an action — "Master Starve-lackey" — and is unfeignedly fictitious, and it is only to this category that "Shake-speare" can belong.

What have the Stratfordians to say to this contention? As a rule, nothing. Louis Marder, who is unique among orthodox scholars in inviting and replying to points raised by dissenters, handles this one by a fallacious premise followed by a *non sequitur.* "The hyphenation," he declares, "means — once and for all — absolutely nothing. And the reason that it means nothing is that it is absolute and irrevocable evidence that *Shakespeare* was *not* constant! Moreover, analysis of this problem gives absolute and irrevocable evidence that Shakspere was Shakespeare. If Shake-speare is a pseudonym it should be constant." One can understand the emotion behind Professor Marder's extremity of language but hardly his reasoning. No one claims that the hyphenated "Shake-speare" was chosen by the author as his pseudonym;

it was not on the two recorded occasions on which he used the name by which we know him. In signing the dedications of the two long narrative poems he did not hyphenate it. It was used by others who, in hyphenating the name can only have been showing that they recognized *Shakespeare* as a pseudonym — and the fact that not all did so is irrelevant. They would have had no reason to hyphenate the name other than to identify Shakespeare as a pseudonym — and if Professor Marder thinks they would have had some other reason perhaps he will tell us what it was. Even if Professor Marder were right in his premises, his vehement argument would be without merit. Had Thomas Nashe varied the spelling of his pseudonym with "Curry-knave" he would simply have been making the fictitious character of the name even more apparent. He would not have been offering "absolute and irrevocable evidence" that Curryknave was the real name of the author, as Professor Marder would insist on our believing.

Because I cited the hyphenation of the name in *Harvard Magazine,* Professors Evans and Levin, in replying to the article, evidently felt they had to take cognizance of it. They accused me of "draw[ing] far-reaching implications [meaning inferences] from occasionally misplaced hyphens." But they did not explain why the dramatist's name should alone of all simple English names have been hyphenated at all. And what we are talking about is something much more than hyphens "occasionally misplaced." Of thirty-two editions of Shakespeare's plays published before the First Folio of 1623 in which the author was named at all, the name was hyphenated in fifteen — almost half. It was hyphenated in the *Sonnets,* in *A Lover's Complaint,* and in the collection of Shakespeare's poems published in 1640. It was hyphenated by John Davies of Hereford in his crucial poem addressing the dramatist as "Our English Terence," by Shakespeare's fellow dramatist, John Webster, in his appraisal of contemporary playwrights, in two of the four dedicatory poems in the First Folio, and by the epigrammatist of 1639 who wrote, "*Shake-speare,* we must be silent in thy praise. . . ." We see that the hyphenation was frequent, not occasional, and clearly conscious and purposed, not "misplaced."

I think we have every right to ask that the Stratfordians either acknowledge that Shakespeare's contemporaries were signalling the name as a *nom de plume* or produce another case of an English name so treated. To me, the hyphenation is so clearly inexplicable except as designating the name as fictitious that I do not see how there can ever have been any question about it.

Incidentally, the first six of Shakespeare's plays to be published [before Francis Meres sprang upon the world the name Shakespeare as that of England's foremost playwright] appeared with no author named. Professors Evans and Levin charged me with error in making that statement. "Due recourse to bibliographical facts," as they patronizingly put it, showed "*Love's Labour's Lost* with Shakespeare's name on the title page." The professors in their recourse to facts, however, stopped short of taking the facts in. *Love's Labour's Lost* was either the seventh, or more probably the eighth, play of Shakespeare's to be published.[2]

Facing all the evidence irreconcilable with the Stratford man's authorship of Shakespeare's works, his supporters produce what they consider a trump card. He was, they claim, a successful actor and thus had keen insight into the drama. "Shakespeare shows the actor's capacity for entering the minds of his vast and highly differentiated cast of characters," say Professors Evans and Levin. They mistake the ability to enact a character on the stage with ability to create one on paper. If the principle they lay down were valid, actors would rank prominently among playwrights and novelists. But I cannot think of anyone who starred in both roles before Jean Baptiste Poquelin (who chose Molière as his *nom de théâtre*) or anyone after him until we come to Noel Coward. Considering that actors and playwrights share each other's world and could each be expected to try his hand at the other's craft, it can only be that the qualities making for success in the two fields respectively are very different. In any event, Shakspere could have been an actor ten times over and not on that account have been the incomparable poet-dramatist. But was he, in fact, an actor at all?

Shakspere's Alleged Career on the Stage

The most detailed theatrical records of the times, those kept by Philip Henslowe, proprietor of several London theatres, and those kept by his son-in-law, a leading actor-producer and founder of Dulwich College, Edward Alleyn, make no reference to Shakespeare. Louis P. Bénézet of Dartmouth College writes:

> In the diary Henslowe records the plays that he put on the boards; he gives the exact gate or intake for every night's performance; he enters the sums that he is obligated to pay authors for "books." He names the actors whom he hires and to whom he is constantly lending or advancing money. In dozens of instances authors have signed in the book, receipts for sums he has paid them. Groups of actors sign to serve Henslowe or acknowledge that they have received money from him.

[2] G. E. Bentley, in his *Shakespeare: A Biographical Handbook*, lists seven plays preceding it, all with no author named: *The Most Lamentable Romaine Tragedie of Titus Andronicus* (1594); *The First part of the contention betwixt the two famous Houses of Yorke and Lancaster* (a bad quarto of *Henry VI Part 2*) (1594); *A Pleasant Conceited Historie called The taming of a Shrew* (which, Bentley comments, only a minority of scholars regard as the Shakespeare play) (1594); *The true Tragedie of Richard Duke of Yorke* (a bad quarto of *Henry VI Part 3*) (1595); *The Tragedie of King Richard the second* (1597); *The Tragedy of King Richard the third* (1597); *An Excellent conceited Tragedie of Romeo and Juliet* (1597); and, *The History of Henrie the Fourth* (1598).

99

860258

8/85

But not Shakespeare; he is not mentioned. Professors Evans and Levin observe sarcastically that "Mr. Ogburn . . . has searched for him vainly in the records of Philip Henslowe and the memoirs of Edward Alleyn — the manager and leading actor of the rival company to the troupe at the Globe." Dr. McManaway writes in much the same vein: "Since after 1594 Shakespeare acted and wrote only for the company of which he had become a sharer [the Lord Chamberlain's], his name could not appear in Henslowe's records, any more than the president of General Motors could be named on the payrolls of Chrysler or Ford."

As Dr. McManaway is fully aware, we are not talking about presidents (though I trust the former Folger curator suffered the embarrassment that was his due when Lido Anthony [Lee] Iacocca during 1978 was named on the payrolls of both Ford and Chrysler as the president of each). It is not a question of whether the manager of one acting troupe would appear on the payroll of another. Actors have always been mobile. As the Folger curator must have known, the two most prominent members of the Lord Chamberlain's company, among others, had formerly been in Henslowe's employ. According to his biographers, Shakspere had arrived in London by 1588 and, as McManaway argues, "must shortly have become an actor and a playwright." He had been acting, then, let us say, for five years before the Lord Chamberlain's company was formed — ten before the Globe opened. And the Lord Chamberlain's company — "Shakespeare's" company — was formed from Lord Strange's company upon the death of its patron (who had become the 5th Earl of Derby) in April 1594. "This splendid Strange organization," Joseph Quincy Adams, former director of the Folger Library (where McManaway was his assistant), writes, "with such expert actors as Alleyn, Burbage and Kemp, performed at the Rose" — Henslowe's theatre — "until June 22, 1592, when . . . theatres were closed by the order of the Privy Council. On December 29, the plague having subsided, they reopened the Rose and continued to act there until February 1593." And Professor Adams adds, "On, or before, June 3, 1594, the Chamberlain's Men arrived in London, and reported to *their former manager Henslowe*." (Italics mine.) And Sir Sidney Lee writes, "the Rose Theatre" — Henslowe's theatre — "was doubtless the earliest scene of Shakespeare's pronounced successes alike as actor and dramatist."

There is, I might add, no question but that Henslowe put on Shakespeare's plays — eight or nine of them, historical plays repeatedly — for they are entered in his books. We may be forgiven for thinking it odd that an actor credited with writing them should not have appeared in any — and odder still that while producing Shakespeare's plays Henslowe never once mentioned his name. The names of all other prominent playwrights of the time, however, find a place in his diary along with the names of famous actors and others who would be unknown but for his records — and if Professors Evans and Levin and Dr. McManaway could have cited another case of an actor of Shakspere's alleged prominence not mentioned by Henslowe or Alleyn it is a fair assumption that they would have done so.

Having found little merit in the efforts of Shakspere's supporters to explain it away, let us, then, recognize that the absence of his name from the most comprehensive rolls of the players in his day is strong indication that his alleged career on the stage is illusory. It is notable, too, that no record has ever been found of a payment to an author for a play by Shakespeare. And we should expect to find none if the author were a nobleman writing under a pseudonym. Proponents of the Stratford man who claim that he wrote plays for gain have yet to show that he made a farthing from them.

Here I might digress a little to recall, as illustrating the claims made to link Shakspere with the stage, how Dr. McManaway tells us that it was "Sir William Davenant (1606–1668) . . . who instructed Betterton in how Shakespeare had taught Burbage to play Prince Hamlet." The origin of this nugget is a report of 1708 by John Downes, a former prompter in London theatres. Mr. Downes wrote:

> The Tragedy of *Hamlet; Hamlet* being perform'd by Mr. Betterton, Sir William [Davenant] (having seen Mr. *Taylor* of the *Black-Fryars* Company act it, who being instructed by the author Mr. *Shakespeur*) taught Mr. Betterton in every particle of it.

Downes says nothing of Burbage. That is Dr. McManaway's invention — and how Dr. McManaway could imagine that Davenant knew how Shakespeare taught Burbage to play Hamlet when Davenant was only thirteen when Burbage died, ten when Shakspere died, is beyond me. As for Mr. Taylor's being taught by Shakespeare, as Downes states, E. K. Chambers observes that is hardly likely since he joined the company only in 1619 — three years after the Stratfordian's death.

There is no record of a part ever assigned to a Shakespeare. Faced with this blank, Shakspere's biographers are thrown back upon a story circulated in the mid-18th century that Will's younger brother, having in his old age (more than a hundred years before) been questioned about his famous kinsman in his "dramatic character," said all he could recollect of Will "in that station was . . . once having seen him act a part in one of his own comedies, wherein being to personate a decrepit old man, he wore a long beard, and appeared so weak and drooping and unable to walk, that he was forced to be supported and carried by another person"; the part has been identified as that of the minor one of Adam in *As You Like It*. Much more illuminating is a report by Nicholas Rowe in the *Life* he attached to his *Works of Shakespeare* (1709), from which I have already quoted. Being curious as to "what sort of Part" his subject "used to play," he wrote that "tho' I have inquir'ed I could never meet with any further account of him this way, than that the top of his performance was the Ghost in his own Hamlet."

Scholars accept this report respectfully and in all sobriety. But if the *best* that Shakspere achieved on the stage was as a character with but two speaking appearances, one of six lines, in a five-act play, this does not say much for his standing as a player. I do not believe, however, that the remark Rowe quoted had anything to do with Shakspere's alleged acting. Surely it was a waggish tip-off that the height of his performance was as the Shade in his own Hamlet — the stand-in for the author in the village of Stratford! Granted that I am predisposed to interpret the remark in that sense, I must confess I find it delightful to think that some knowing wit was sly enough to get his subversive message into Rowe's biography, as a nimble little wasp will lay an egg beside a grub to hatch out an offspring that will wholly consume the host.

Not only is there no record of a part ever assigned to a Shakespeare, but no record has come down to us from the time when the Stratfordian was alive listing a Shakespeare in the cast of any play. The records of seventy municipalities in which acting companies played have been searched without disclosing a mention of his name — a gap about which Stratfordians, including Professors Evans and Levin, seem to have nothing to say. None of this lack is very surprising in view of the evidence suggesting that Shakspere had difficulty writing. A lack of proficiency with the written word would not consort with a ready ability to learn parts.

For generations no citizen of Stratford of whom we have heard ever suggested that Shakspere was an actor, any more than that he was an author. I have always been tickled by the discretion on the subject shown by a clerk of the Stratford church who was quoted by a visitor to the town in 1693, a Mr. Dowdall. "The clarke that shew'd me this Church," Mr. Dowdall wrote, "is above 80 years old; he says that this Shakespear was formerly in this town bound apprentice to a butcher; but that he run from his master to London, and there was received into the playhouse as a serviture, and by this means had an opportunity to be what he afterwards prov'd" — whatever that may have been. About Will Shakspere's early training, John Aubrey had written in 1681 — for what it may be worth — that "his father was a butcher, & I have been told heretofore by some of the neighbors, that when he was a boy he exercised his father's trade, but when he kill'd a calf he would do it in a *high style,* & make a speech." Evidently the neighbors had nothing else to report that bore upon the supposed career of their immortal townsman. Nothing. This is a point worth emphasizing. No one in Stratford who could have known Shakspere, or his daughters, or his granddaughter, or even whose parents could have known the last of Shakspere's descendants, has ever been quoted as saying anything indicating a belief that Will was either a writer or an actor. In 1773 the Reverend Dr. Richard Graves (1715–1804) published a book called *The Spiritual Quixote,* which became very popular. Describing the peregrinations and mild adventures of several friends, doubtless based on the author's own rambles about England, it introduces, as it enters Warwickshire, a waiter who exclaims:

> Oh, I know Stratford-on-Avon well; it's the place where Shakespeare the *great Jester* was born. — Grand-father's father lived a servant with the jester himself; and there is a mulberry tree growing there now, which he helped Mr. Shakespeare to plant, when he was a boy.

Lest readers dismiss the episode as altogether in keeping with the book's subtitle, *A comic romance,* the Reverend Dr. Graves resorts to a footnote to tell us, "All the idea which the country people have of that great genius is that he excelled in smart repartee and selling of bargains, as they call it."

What do orthodox writers say about Shakspere's comprehensively blank record on the stage? Well, it is naturally not one of their favorite topics. More or less forced to acknowledge it by having undertaken to reply to an article in which I had raised the issue, Professors Evans and Levin charged that "Mr. Ogburn . . . sets no store by the actors lists in the First Folio and in Jonson's wherein Shakespeare is prominently named." They mean by "Jonson's [lists]" this: Jonson, in preparing his collected works for publication, recorded the casts that he said had played his *Every Man Out of His Humour* in 1598 and his *Sejanus* in 1603, putting Shakespeare at the head in one case, Shake-Speare in the other. Since these records stand so conspicuously by themselves and were set down so many years after the event — in 1616, the year of Shakspere's death — I do not, in truth, set much store by them as endowing Shakspere with a stage career. That "honest Ben" was telling us fairly that a Shakespeare — not the Stratford man — acted in his plays is possible, and I shall come to that in a moment. But Jonson was evidently the chief means by which the idea that Shakespeare was the Stratfordian was floated, and I should suppose he had that purpose in mind in recalling so long *ex post facto* that Shakespeare had acted in two of his plays. And, as the probable impresario of the First Folio, he would have been responsible for listing in that historic compendium "The Names of the Principal Actors in all these Plays" (to which Professors Evans and Levin refer) headed by William Shakespeare.[3] Such a list would hardly be expected in a

---

[3] I say these things not in disparagement of Jonson. It is true that if his role in the First Folio was what it seems to have been, then his contribution was indispensable to the subsequent belief that Shakspere was Shakespeare. But, as we shall see, the recognition as such that he seemed to bestow upon the Stratford man with one hand he decisively, for the open-eyed reader, took away with the other.

collection of plays. I should guess that it was incorporated — like the casts of his plays in Jonson's collected works — with the aim of putting it across that Shakespeare was a noted actor in his day, scant as any previous indication of it had been. But as even the most ardent Stratfordolators (as Mark Twain called them) will acknowledge, honesty was jettisoned in listing Shakespeare first among the principal actors in his plays, ahead of such truly prominent professionals as Burbage, Kempe, Heminge, and Augustine Phillips. This placement was quite unjustified — unless the primacy given him was based on rank of birth.

Rank of birth? Yes, that would presumably have been justified by the one record of substance and body in which we see a Shakespeare on the stage. It is a poem by John Davies of Hereford from which I have already quoted. Entered in the Stationers' Register in 1610, it reads:

> To our English Terence, M[aste]r Will. Shake-speare.
>
> Some say (good *Will*), which I, in sport, do sing,
> Hadst thou not played some Kingly parts in sport,
> Thou hadst been a companion for a *King*;
> And been a King among the meaner sort.
> Some others rail; but, rail as they think fit,
> Thou hast no railing, but, a reigning Wit:
>> And honesty thou sowst, which they do reap;
>> So, to increase their stock which they do keep.

This is, as I say, the only truly informative reference to Shakespeare as an actor that has come down to us, and I cannot see any interpretation but one to put upon it: "Shake-speare" was a nobleman who lost caste by appearing on the stage, though he took kingly parts and played them only in sport. It is true that Davies said he himself was relating this identification "in sport," but to have made such a disclosure even in sport would, we may surmise, have taken daring. Moreover, those he was quoting were *not* speaking in sport. They were serious. And Davies himself is warrant for Shakespeare's having, with his reigning wit (i.e., intellectual powers) sown honesty (from the Latin "*honestus*, respectable, honourable, honoured": Eric Partridge in *Origins*) from which others have benefitted. The implication, I take it, is that, while sacrificing his own standing, Shakespeare lent respectability to the stage.

Is there any suggestion as to the rank he had? From Eric Partridge we learn that the title "count" derives from the "Latin *comes*, a companion, originally on the march," *comes* having become "a companion to the Emperor." The English equivalent of count is earl, translated *comes* in Latin, there being no count in the English peerage, though the wife of an earl is a countess. An earl would be a companion to the sovereign, "a companion for a *King*."

Chapter 7: And Thereupon These Errors Are Arose

We can account for John Davies's poem in two ways. One is to accept what he appears to be telling us, that "Shake-speare" was indeed a man of high birth, probably an earl, who lowered himself by taking parts on the stage, albeit under a pseudonym. The other is to argue that Davies, for reasons difficult to imagine, contrived and published a falsehood to that effect.

How do Stratfordians accommodate Davies's poem to their theory? They do not. They are at a loss. "The bit about 'companion for a King' is cryptic," E. K. Chambers says, advancing a theory to account for it that he immediately rejects. Some Stratfordians toy with the idea that "a *King*" was a man named King. But they have no candidate for the role and cannot reconcile a Shake-speare who played some kingly parts, or any others, in sport with their evocation of a busy professional actor making a livelihood from the stage. A. L. Rowse, in *Shakespeare the Man*, sneakily attributes to hearsay the concrete statement by Davies, a well-known poet of the day. He says simply, as we have seen, "The tradition is that he played 'kingly' parts" and skips on, divulging nothing of Shakespeare's having played only "some" kingly parts and those in sport, nothing of his having sacrificed the opportunity to be a companion to a monarch. Professors Evans and Levin are equally evasive. In replying to my article, they dismissed the subject with a reference to "the poem quoted and misquoted from Davies of Hereford," neither acknowledging what the poem said nor attempting to show that I had misquoted it — merely slinging a bit of mud in passing.

In two other short poetical passages about actors by John Davies, of 1603 and 1605 respectively, the initials W.S.R.B. appear in the margin. In one we read:

> And though the stage doth stain pure gentle blood,
> Yet generous ye are in mind and mood.

In the other:

> Yet some she [Fortune] guerdoned not, to their deserts. . . .

Another John Davies, later *Sir* John, wrote a long allegorical poem entered in the Stationers' Register in 1594 in which, in the concluding five stanzas, he eulogizes, without naming, poets recognizable as Homer, Virgil, Spenser, Samuel Daniel, and Philip Sidney, and two others, perhaps the same, of more masked identity. Of one he exclaims:

> O, could I, sweet Companion, sing like you,
> Which, of a shadow, under a shadow, sing: . . .

That "Companion" again: *comes,* count, earl . . . of a shadow, under a shadow singing.

Mockery of a Shakspere-like Shakespeare by Contemporaries

The epigram "To our English Terence, Mr. Will. Shake-speare" is one of only three contemporary references to Shakespeare the dramatist that suggest an actual person behind the name. Of the remaining two, I had space in *Harvard Magazine* (as I explained in the article) to quote only one. The two professors accused me of having "conveniently ignored" the other, "the important reference from the *Parnassus Plays* (1598–1602), where Shakespeare is specifically saluted in both roles [as actor and dramatist] (and as a poet, too)." Let me now conveniently include this reference, and let us see what it actually says.

The three *Parnassus* plays were put on at St. John's College, Cambridge, probably in successive Christmas seasons. They seem to have been somewhat analogous to the plays produced annually by members of the Hasty Pudding Club at Harvard. In the third, *The Return from Parnassus, Part Two,* a character called Kempe, speaking to one called Burbage, delivers himself as follows:

> Few of the university men pen plays well; they smell too much of the writer Ovid and that writer Metamorphosis, and talk too much of Proserpina and Jupiter. Why, here's our fellow Shakespeare puts them all down, I [ay] and Ben Jonson too. O that Ben Jonson is a pestilent fellow; he brought up Horace giving the poets a pill, but our fellow Shakespeare hath given him a purge that made him bewray his credit.[4]

The first thing to be remarked about this passage is that Kempe is represented as being so ignorant as to suppose Ovid's *Metamorphoses* to be a writer called Metamorphosis; we are justifed in surmising that a special point is being made of his ignorance. (Burbage and Kempe, says J. B. Leishman of Oxford, most recent editor of the *Parnassus* plays, are represented as an "illiterate pair.") Will Kempe the actor played clowns' parts. In the first *Parnassus* play, *The Pilgrimage to Parnassus,* a character comes on stage "dragging a clown in with a rope," exclaiming, "Why what an ass art thou! dost thou not know a play cannot be without a clown? Clowns have been thrust into plays by head and shoulders ever since Kempe could make a scurvy face."

The second point that strikes us is that it is Shakespeare himself who, of all writers, is redolent of Ovid; *every* scholar agrees about that. Until 1598, the year in which the first of the *Parnassus* plays was performed, the only works publicly attributed to Shakespeare were *Venus and Adonis* and *Lu-*

---

[4] Jonson gave the poets a pill in *The Poetaster.* If it were known wherein Shakespeare gave him a purge that made him disfigure his reputation, it might, along with jealousy, explain the animus Jonson sometimes seemed to bear his greater contemporary.

crece; and as Edward Dowden writes of the former, "There can be no question that Shakespeare's chief debt was to the *Metamorphoses* of Ovid (Book X)," and of the latter, "It may be said with assurance that his chief sources were the *Fasti* of Ovid and the history of Livy." In the first public references to Shakespeare as a playwright, in 1598, Francis Meres wrote, "the sweet witty soul of Ovid lives in mellifluous & honey-tongued Shakespeare, witness his *Venus* and *Adonis,* his *Lucrece,* his sugared Sonnets among his private friends, &c." Schoenbaum is unequivocal on the point: "Ovid, especially *The Metamorphoses,* would remain Shakespeare's favorite classical poet, to be drawn upon over and over again." What do Dowden, Schoenbaum, and their fellows think the authors of *Parnassus* meant by having "Kempe" charge that it was the university men who smelled too much of Ovid and "Metamorphosis"?

As for the university men talking too much of Proserpina and Jupiter, as "Kempe" says, let us note that Shakespeare in his plays refers to Jupiter 30 times — and to Juno 19 times, to Venus (exclusive of the planet) 17 times, to Diana 50 times, to Neptune 23 times, to Mercury 15 times, to Mars 36 times, to Phoebus Apollo 42 times. Proserpine, daughter of Ceres (to whom Shakespeare refers six times) has never been invoked in lovelier imagery than in *The Winter's Tale* (which evidently had been written by 1594) when Perdita cries:

> O Proserpina!
> For the flowers now that frighted thou let'st fall
> From Dis's waggon! daffodils,
> That come before the swallow dares, and take
> The winds of March with beauty; violets dim,
> But sweeter than the lids of Juno's eyes
> Or Cytherea's breath; pale prime-roses,
> That die unmarried, ere they can behold
> Bright Phoebus in his strength. . . .

There, by the way, are five classical references in nine lines.

We are being told in the satirical passage from *The Return from Parnassus,* surely, that by the criteria Kempe sets up — redolence of Ovid and incidence of classical allusion — Shakespeare is preeminently a university man, and that only an ignoramus would be able to believe that Shakespeare was a fellow of such as Kempe the clown. If the passage is not mocking the attribution of Shakespeare's works to an ill-educated fellow of two actors, then I should like to have the Stratfordians explain why Kempe is made to speak as he does.

In the same *Return from Parnassus,* Kempe boasts: "Be merry, my lads, you have happened upon the most excellent vocation in the world for money; they come North and South to bring it to our playhouse; and for honours, who of more report than Dick Burbage and Will Kempe? He is not accounted a gentleman that knows not Dick Burbage and Will Kempe. There's not a country wench that can dance Sellengers Round but can talk of Dick Burbage and Will Kempe." Burbage and Kempe were leading members of the Lord Chamberlain's company — "Shakespeare's company" — and it would have been natural for Kempe to include that other supposed luminary of the company, Shakespeare himself, with those actors of unsurpassed "report"; but no mention is made of him.

Actors are spoken of with contempt in the play:

> And must the basest trade yield us relief?
> Must we be practis'd to those leaden spouts,
> That nought do vent but what they do receive?

Hardly true of Shakespeare if he was an actor. He is, indeed, spoken of in *Part One* of *The Return* with marked respect. Gullio asks Ingenioso to compose some verses for his mistress and upon being asked in what vein he would have them, replies, "in Chaucer's, Gower's and Spencer's and Mr. Shakspeare's." Notice that Shakespeare is the only one to have the honorific "M[aste]r" bestowed on him. A point is made of this repeatedly. "O sweet Mr. Shakspeare," Gullio goes on, "I'll have his picture in my study at the Court." He quotes from Shakespeare and Ingenioso exclaims "Sweet Mr. Shakspeare!" (These references are among the very few in which the dramatist's name is written with the first syllable *Shak*.) Gullio goes on: "Let me hear Mr. Shakspeare's vein," and on being indulged with a quotation, again differentiates between Shakespeare and other poets: "Let this duncified world esteem of Spencer and Chaucer, I'll worship sweet Mr. Shakspeare and to honour him will lay his Venus and Adonis under my pillow."

The Cambridge students who wrote the *Parnassus* plays of 1598–1602 were clearly taking no stock in any notion that Shakespeare was of that "basest trade," one of those "leaden spouts" — an actor.

Kempe's speech in *The Return from Parnassus* is the first intimation we have that the Stratfordian was being spoken of as the poet-dramatist, and it is one of the only two such intimations we have before the 1620s. That the absence of a plausible alternative requires us to read it as satirizing that identification is, of course, hard on Shakespearean orthodoxy. Even harder on it, and delivering the *coup de grâce,* if one were needed, is the second reference. Of this it would seem that there could be even less doubt — none at all — that it is intended to poke fun at the notion of Shakspere *qua* Shakespeare. It occurs in a poetical letter of about 1615 to Ben Jonson from "F.B." Of the signatory, E. K. Chambers says, "I see no reason why it should not be Francis Beaumont, who wrote another well-known verse epistle to Jonson, and to whom the theatrical allusions . . . would be natural." Certainly it is from a friend of Jonson's.

Chapter 7: And Thereupon These Errors Are Arose

The epistle has been known for more than half a century and been continually quoted approvingly by orthodox Shakespeareans, evidently without their taking in what it says. They interpret the key passage *as if* it read in its entirety:

> Here I would let slip
> (If I had any in me) scholarship,
> And from all learning keep these lines as clear
> as Shakespeare's are, which to our heirs will show,
> how far sometimes a mortal man may go
> by the dim light of Nature.

The Stratfordians hail the passage as supporting their man's authorship, as indeed it would if the text I have quoted were the whole of it. "A priceless document," Milward W. Martin exclaims of it in his *Was Shakespeare Shakespeare?* a book highly praised by Professor Leslie Hotson, Professor Louis Marder (who contributed an introduction to it), and John Wain, English novelist and widely published literary critic.

> Here we see one contemporary playwright writing to another contemporary playwright a personal letter, not for publication. Both of them, Beaumont and Jonson, knew their own contemporary playwright Shakespeare, whoever he was; and here, in simple language not intended either for the public eye or for posterity, one of them tells the other of the profound admiration he has for Shakespeare. And in telling him he refers to Shakespeare as having gone far without "schollershippe" but "by the dimme light of Nature."

But that is not what F.B. said, though Mr. Martin (general counsel for the Pepsi-Cola Company and mayor of Locust Valley, New York), Professors Hotson and Marder, and Mr. Wain all evidently thought it was. What he *did* say was this:

> And from all learning keep these lines as clear as Shakespeare's *best* are

Which he would not have written without reason, the only plausible reason being that he meant to imply, with tongue in cheek, that Shakespeare's *other* lines are far from clear of all learning. He goes on:

> as Shakespeare's best are, which our heirs shall *hear*
> *Preachers apt to their auditors to show*
> how far sometimes a mortal man may go
> by the dim light of Nature. . . .

In other words, it is not that Shakespeare shows how far a man without learning may go by the dim light of nature. Beaumont would have had no reason to insert the line I have italicized if it were. He was saying that this is something posterity is going to *hear* from preachers apt ("suited, fitted, adapted") to their audiences. And how right he was! That is what posterity has heard and is still hearing, and from preachers well suited to their auditors, their gullibility being equal to though far less excusable than the public's.

Evidently after his book had been set in type but before it had gone to press, Milward W. Martin came upon a booklet in which I had called attention to the actual wording of F.B.'s letter and what it clearly means, as I have above. The bearer of bad news cannot expect to fare well, least of all when he is one of those "self-deluded lotus-eaters" who have "thrown off all restraint and discipline" to seek "Lionization at cocktail parties" — Mr. Martin's characterization of his opponents. The news, that F.B., as it seemed, "was on to the plan to have it appear that Shakespeare was an uneducated man," was calculated to undermine the whole basis of *Was Shakespeare Shakespeare?* In an addendum to the book, Mr. Martin begins, "As we have seen *supra,* Beaumont, in his letter to Ben Jonson in 1615, said what appeared to mean that Shakespeare went far 'by the dimme light of Nature.'" He has been sufficiently shaken and is sufficiently true to his profession as a lawyer, to speak now of "what *appeared* to mean." Then he lashes out: "But see what Mr. Charlton Ogburn, Jr., does to those words." Of what I had written, he said, "we see strained interpretation blossoming into its fullest flower." Moreover, "Such strained interpretations" — with "never, never, so much as one scintilla of evidence to support [them]" — "are the stock-in-trade of every anti-Stratfordian. Indeed, without them they would be unable to keep themselves in the public eye." But though there was more in this vein, he never attempted to tell us wherein my reading of F.B. was in error and what other reading was possible. As for Professors Evans and Levin, they prudently avoided mentioning the subject: best not to remind the reader of the fatal letter from F.B.

Rejection of Shakspere as Shakespeare

"We are told," say Evans and Levin, quoting me, "that 'Shakespeare's contemporaries made it quite plain that they did not consider the Stratford man the author.' Plain? Where? Such cavalier misstatements can only be supported by far-from-plain misreadings out of context, and even these ambiguous contortions yield merely the darkest of hints."

Let us remind the two professors of the facts. In doing so we shall be clarifying the issue of the authorship for those who believe (with a reviewer for the London *Times Literary Supplement*) that "Shakespeare's contemporaries had no shadow of doubt about his being the author of the plays and poems and . . . we too need have none," or (with an editorial-page columnist of the *New York Times*) that "For half a century Shakespeare's contemporaries and intimates, men who rehearsed and acted the plays with him, refer to them as his. No doubts arose for another century and more." It is extraordinary how much confusion there is on this score, how many writers who

make pronouncements on the subject have not ascertained what the controversy over the authorship is about. When the plays were ascribed to anyone
at all, of course they were produced, printed, and referred to as by William
Shakespeare. No one has ever disputed that. The question is, who was meant
by "William Shakespeare"? Not the Stratford man, if we may judge by the
record recapitulated herewith.

§ No one, to our knowledge, in the years when he was alive, ever suggested
that Shakspere of Stratford was William Shakespeare the poet-dramatist.
Those who, in two instances, addressed themselves to the proposition that
the poet-dramatist was an unlettered man did so only to ridicule it.

§ No one we know of outside Stratford ever paid any attention to Shakspere except for (1) tax collectors, who, at the height of his supposed fame,
did not know where to find him, (2) the signatory of a petition to keep the
peace brought against him "for fear of death," and (3) Augustine Phillips of
the Lord Chamberlain's men, who died in 1605 leaving a bequest to his
"fellow" William Shakespeare among others — whatever construction may
be put upon that. (I exclude the specious record of a payment made to
Shakespeare, Kempe, and Burbage in 1594.) That he was listed among the
shareholders in two theatrical properties, among those licensed in 1603 to
perform on the stage and the next year (at a time when he was suing a
neighbor in Stratford) among actors granted cloth to march in a procession
honoring the new king — always as one among others — does not suggest
a man of individual distinction and certainly does not imply that anyone
regarded him as an illustrious author.

§ "The greatest of intellects," Thomas Carlyle called Shakespeare. Unless
we are to imagine that no other Elizabethans of intellectual powers had any
interest in making the acquaintance of this supreme mind during the twenty
years we are told Shakspere lived in London or he in entering into communication with them, we must believe that Shakspere was not regarded as the
man of whom Carlyle was speaking.

§ The literary figures of Shakespeare's time — all but Ben Jonson, writing
years later — testified to their view of "Shakespeare's" corporeal existence
by their utter silence respecting it, and among these are many to whom the
Shakespeare of conventional biography would have been a familiar figure.
Eight years after the last indication can be found of Shakspere's residing in
London, John Webster and Thomas Heywood made passing references to
Shakespeare as a writer but not as a recognizable human being, and three
years later Francis Beaumont spoke of him in a way to undermine the
conventional biographee altogether. Of their fellow playwrights, however —
Robert Greene, Thomas Nashe, John Lyly, George Peele, Christopher Mar-
lowe, Henry Chettle, Thomas Dekker, George Chapman, Thomas Middleton

— none, so far as we know, ever uttered the name Shakespeare. Among the scores of other contemporary writers, the half dozen or so who did mention it, to our knowledge, attributed no human identity to it. Those literary men and patrons of the theatre who would have known the stock figure of Shakespearean orthodoxy either put no credence in it if they had heard of it at all, or were at marvellous pains to dissemble with us.

§ The wide practice of hyphenating "Shakespeare" denoted the name as a pseudonym and set the author apart from anyone born with the name.

§ "His death evoked no great outpouring of homage," Professor Schoenbaum writes. In fact (to repeat), apart from the entry in the burial register, Shakspere's death as far as the record shows went entirely unremarked; Thomas Fuller, in his *Worthies* of 1663, had to date the event as simply "16—." This emptiness was in an age when the passing of noted poets called forth copious elegies from their fellows, such as (as we saw) had accompanied Spenser to his tomb. Francis Beaumont had been mourned with a similar shower on his death in the month before Shakspere's. When Bacon died in 1626, thirty-two elegies, in Latin, were published honoring him, and Ben Jonson's death was mourned within six months in a whole book of verses by the leading poets of the day. Michael Drayton, upon his passing in 1631, was honored by a "funeral procession to Westminster escorted by gentlemen of the Inns of Court and others of note." In the year following his burial in the Abbey a monument to his memory was erected by the Duchess of Dorset and verses attributed to Ben Jonson and others were contributed. Drummond wrote a letter expressing his grief. When Richard Burbage died in 1619, the playwright Thomas Middleton declared, "in London is not one eye dry" and complained, "When he expires, lo! all lament the man, / But where's the grief should follow good Queen Anne?" — who had died eleven days earlier. Charlotte C. Stopes writes that "The city and the Stage were clothed in gloom" and reproduces five epitaphs to the deceased actor, one of eighty-seven lines. If no public regret was shed when Shakspere died, no public word of praise or regret uttered, the only reason I can think of is that he was not regarded as Shakespeare. Can the professors suggest another?

§ William Camden (1551–1623), historian, antiquary, and headmaster of Westminster School, named William Shakespeare in his *Remaines* among the poets he called the "most pregnant wits of these our times, whom succeeding ages may justly admire." Yet in his *Britannia,* brought out two years later in 1607, he ascribes all Stratford-on-Avon's dignity to an Archbishop of Canterbury who built the church and to Hugh Clopton, Lord Mayor of London, who built the bridge. He goes on about the latter's genealogy and about his descendants, and one would think he might have had a word for the supposedly illustrious Shakespeare's connection with the town, particularly in view of the extreme praise he gives Chaucer and Spenser in discussing those buried in Westminster. But there is nothing, though Camden knew Stratford as Shakspere's home from having been Clarencieux King-of-Arms when his father was granted bearings. It remained for Edmund Gibson in an English translation of the *Britannia* of 1695 to add in a supplement about Warwickshire a further note under Stratford that "in the Chancel lies William Shakespeare, a native of this place, who has given proof of his genius and great ability in the forty-eight [*sic*] plays he has left behind him." Even an edition of 1637, fourteen years after publication of the First Folio, makes no mention of him. Camden, the historian of Elizabeth's and James's reigns, observed Richard Burbage's passing ("On Master Burbidge the Tragedian: Exit Burbidge") and recorded its date (9 March 1618 / 19) but had nothing to say of Shakspere's three years earlier.

§ So far as anyone has been able to ascertain, not one Stratfordian in the two centuries after Shakspere's death ever attributed to him either authorship or acting. (See Chambers, II, 186–298 for all the reports and bits of hearsay discoverable about "Shakespeare.")[5] If Will Shakspere impressed his fellow townsmen as in any particular worthy of fame, we have never heard of it from any of them or from their descendants to the sixth generation. Even John Aubrey, though certainly not one to pass by a good story, seems to have found in Stratford, as we have seen, no further testimony to the man's supposed genius than that as a boy when "he kill'd a calf, he would do it in a *high style,* & make a speech." And even in exhibiting this degree of promise young Will was not alone. "There was at that time," Aubrey tells us, "another butcher's son in the town, that was held not at all inferior to him for a natural wit, his acquaintance & coetanean, but died young." The burghers of Stratford did not find that Shakspere even merited having his name on his tomb.

§ In 1635, Richard Burbage's brother Cuthbert, in petitioning the Earls of Pembroke and Montgomery for help, pleading the heavy expenses incurred in connection with the Globe, referred to the men who had joined him and his brother in building the theatre as "those deserving men Shakspere, Hemings, Condal, Philips and others." Is it really credible that, in putting his case before, of all persons, one of the "incomparable pair of brethren" to whom the First Folio had been dedicated, Burbage would have casually lumped Shakspere in with the other shareholders, as no more than one of the deserving men, had he been speaking about the dramatist apostrophized in the

---

[5] True, Chambers tells us about the report by Malone, quoting "a person then above eighty years of age, whose father might have been contemporary with Shakespeare," that, upon being asked by a drunken blacksmith with a carbuncled face what the difference was between a youth and a young man, Shakespeare "immediately replied, 'Thou son of fire, with *thy face like a maple,* The same difference as between a scalded and a coddled apple.'" He must, indeed, have been a natural wit, quick in repartee.

First Folio as the equal of all that Greece and Rome could show, the soul of the age, the star of poets? As a dedicatee of the collected plays and one who, with his brother, had undoubtedly defrayed the huge cost of publication, the Earl would have been nettled indeed by such obtuseness.

That, half a dozen years after his death, limited and self-contradictory steps were taken, chiefly through Ben Jonson, and using the names of actors Heminge and Condell, to turn curiosity about authorship of the plays toward the Stratford man is undeniable. But for the rest, if Shakspere's contemporaries believed him to be the dramatist, their concealment of their belief must be accounted a marvel of collective human behavior for which a motive would not be easy to find. If the professors can point to a single reference to Shakspere of Stratford during his lifetime that links him with authorship of Shakespeare's works or to a single reference in those years to the poet-dramatist that suggests he was the Stratford man — or, for that matter, identifies him with any actual person — they will do what no one else has been able to do.

Shakspere's Lack of Commercial Interest in the Plays

During Shakspere's life, sixteen of Shakespeare's plays were printed, evidently without the author's sanction: we read in the First Folio of the "stolen and surreptitious copies, maimed, and deformed by the frauds and stealths of injurious impostors" with which the public had been "abus'd." Yet Shakspere, resolute as he was in pursuing a debt, apparently never lifted a finger to protect the author's rights in these valuable properties. (A nobleman whose authorship of the plays had to be concealed would of course have been forced to stand by helplessly while the pirates appropriated his work.) But did an author in Elizabethan times have any rights in his literary products?

Apologists of the Stratford man insist on this point: that there was then no copyright law as we know it. Of course they are right. But the simple statement leaves much unsaid. Publication was by no means *ad liberum*. It was rigidly controlled. Sir George Greenwood points out:

> By decree of the Star Chamber, dated June 23, 1586, it was ordered that "no person shall imprint or cause to be imprinted . . . any book work copy matter or thing whatsoever except the same book, etc., hath been heretofore allowed or hereafter shall be allowed before the printing thereof, according to the order appointed by the Queen's Majesty's Injunctions, and been first seen and perused by the Archbishop of Canterbury and Bishop of London for the time being, or any one of them." No printing presses were to be permitted except in London and the two Universities. Under the system so established an author would, as it seems, sell his manuscript "out and out" to a member of the Stationers' Company, who, having duly obtained a license to print the work, and having

entered the title on the register of the company, would thenceforth be the owner of the "copy," or copyright.

Parenthetically we might quote Greenwood as observing that

> Copyright in the . . . sense of . . . the exclusive right of multiplying copies . . . had its origin, not in any enlightened desire to protect authors, but in the desire of "authority," as represented by the sovereign, and especially by the Star Chamber, to prohibit the publications of all works not especially licensed for that purpose. One of the means by which this was accomplished was by granting a monopoly to the Stationers' Company.

As·for the author's position, Greenwood states that

> The law is thus stated in Mr. Coninger's well-known work on the subject (Third edition, p. 7): "Every man has the right at common law to the first publication of his own manuscript. . . . He has, in fact, supreme control of his own productions, and may either exclude others from their enjoyment or may dispose of them as he pleases." . . . In the celebrated case of Millar v. Taylor, which was decided at the time of Lord Mansfield, the law on this point was thus stated by Mr. Justice Yates. "Most certainly the sole proprietor of any copy may determine whether he will print it or not. If any person takes it to the press without his consent, he is certainly a trespasser." . . . This, therefore, being part of the common law, had, according to these learned judges, always been the law of the land.

Greenwood concedes that there is no record of an author's having in Star Chamber times successfully appealed to the courts for vindication of his common-law right to prevent publication of his works, but he reports the statement by the Justice in Millar v. Taylor, that "Most of the judicial proceedings of the Star Chamber are lost or destroyed." He continues:

> I think we may confidently assert that English law would never have sanctioned a proceeding so entirely iniquitous as that [by] which a publisher might, without let or hindrance, publish a stolen manuscript if only he had obtained the licence of the Stationers' Company for such publication. The judgments of Millar v. Taylor are direct authority to the effect that our law never tolerated any such inequitable proceedings and show that the right in question was recognized as a common-law right in the early part of the seventeenth century. . . . [However,] the offending publisher would, of course, be a member of the powerful Stationers' Company, and the poor author might consequently find that it was better to "take it lying down" than endeavor to obtain justice by litigation.

The Stratfordian was nothing if not a ready litigant, and to Greenwood

> it seems tolerably clear that if Shakespeare acquiesced in the unauthorized publication of any of his manuscripts, the right to which he had not disposed of, whether of dramas or other works, . . . it was not because there was . . . no law of copyright at all to which he might have appealed. On the contrary, we must conclude that for some reason or other he preferred to put up with the injustice done to him rather than to appeal to the law for protection. . . . Good, easygoing man!

If the Stratfordians have ever cited another Elizabethan writer whose works were pirated on such a scale as Shakespeare's were, I have not seen the citation. Ben Jonson, as Greenwood remarks, did not have to put up with piracy. And as Alfred W. Pollard points out in *Shakespeare's Fight with the Pirates,* professional writers who depended on their pens for livelihood were not molested by unscrupulous publishers. Literary piracy, he says, primarily dealt "with the works of dead authors, or of men whose rank would have forbidden them to receive payment for their books." In this judgment I think Professor Pollard — that "distinguished student" of Shakespeare and "great bibliographer," as Schoenbaum calls him — has spoken the decisive word.

We come in the next chapter to what must be considered the crowning disqualification of the Stratford man for the place in letters accorded him.

8

"Are They Not Lamely Writ?"

A professional writer, whatever his other deficiencies, could be expected to wield a practiced pen. With this assumption before us, we appraise the tokens of facility with the instrument Shakspere left behind and — perhaps of even greater significance — failed to leave behind. In this investigation, we look into the assertion by some orthodox scholars that in addition to the six signatures that have generally been taken as comprising all that we have in his hand, a scene in the manuscript for the aborted play Sir Thomas More *was penned by him.*

Surely it is a supreme irony that the outstanding works in the English language should be attributed to a man whose record contains nothing to counter the inference to be drawn from it that he was of limited literacy at best.

Shakspere's parents, his candid biographer Halliwell-Phillipps concedes, were "absolutely illiterate."[1] His wife was illiterate. Of his two daughters, Judith was illiterate and Susanna, so far as is known, could do no more than sign her name.[2] "Judith," says A. L. Rowse, "evidently took after her mother — she couldn't write"; one would think it was a matter of inheritance, like a large nose. No indication remains that any aunt or uncle of hers could write, either. What a matrix this would be in which to find the ultimate

[1] Determined Stratfordians would make out that John Shakspere was one of those two or three eccentrics who have turned up over the length and breadth of Britain who, though able to write, signed a paper with a mark. Sir Sidney Lee was one who pressed that view, prompting Greenwood to write, "It is . . . indisputable that John Shakspere used a mark, not only 'when attesting documents' [as Lee acknowledged], but also when attesting deeds. If, then, we are to credit Mr. Lee, we have this very remarkable fact, viz., that one who 'could write with facility' nevertheless deliberately chose to appear as a marksman when executing a deed, the most solemn of all documents; that, too, in an age when to be able to write one's name was something to be proud of, at any rate in the class to which the Shakspere family belonged." Professor Louis Marder honestly acknowledges, "Although there is evidence that other 'marksmen' could write, I believe that John would have written his name if he could have."

[2] "There is no evidence that Judith could write," says Professor Marder. "But Susanna could and if Susanna went to school, she probably took Hamnet [Judith's twin brother who died at eleven] too." And he adds, "If Judith's illiteracy proves anything then Susanna's literacy cancels it." Passing over this elusive logic, it is difficult to accept literacy in a woman with illiterate parents and sister on the strength of a signature when she could not recognize her husband's handwriting; and this even though his writing was particularly consistent and distinctive, as Greenwood points out. When, in 1642, the surgeon James Cooke came to New Place to examine the books Dr. Hall had left behind him, the doctor's widow refused to believe that the case-book her husband had maintained was his own, in his own hand, though Dr. Cooke, who knew Dr. Hall's writing, assured her that it was.

master of the written word — amid three generations of illiterates! If his failure to have had even one daughter taught to read and write strikes the professors of English as in any way odd they do not confess it. Of no literary figure are we asked to believe that he would so disvalue the medium of his expression, except for the greatest of all.

John Aubrey wrote an interesting memorandum on Shakespeare, of which a photographic reproduction in E. K. Chambers, facing II, 252, reads:

> The more to be admired q[uia] he was not a company keeper lived in Shore-ditch, wouldn't be debauched, & if invited to writ:he was in paine.

Scholars of the Stratford camp characteristically change the punctuation of the note — among them Schoenbaum, in his *Shakespeare's Lives* — by slipping a comma in after "to" in order to have the sentence read: "wouldn't be debauched. And if invited to, writ: he was in paine." Ivor Brown adds a comma after "and" as well as one after "to." McManaway revises it more liberally, though retaining the quotation marks to disavow any alteration between them. He writes that "About 1681 Christopher Beeston told John Aubrey, among other things, that Shakespeare had been a schoolmaster." (Having just told us that "Christopher was a fellow member of Shakespeare's company in 1598," McManaway would have Aubrey's informant a good hundred years old.) "He was also Aubrey's authority for the statement that Shakespeare '. . . wouldn't be debauched. And if invited to, wrote [that] he was in pain.'" (The bracketed "that" is Dr. McManaway's.)[3]

The academicians are having the note tell us that Shakespeare would receive invitations to be debauched and — recovering, one must suppose, from his astonishment, though this perhaps diminished with repetition — would write declining on the grounds that he was in pain. The picture thus conjured up, of carousal so formalized as to call for written responses to invitations to take part, presumably also written, would require revisions in one's idea of tavern life in Elizabethan London. But Aubrey's note as penned — viz., without the comma — appears actually to say that when invited to write, "Shakespeare" claimed to be in pain as a reason for begging off. And it does seem that whereas one might well sometimes plead a previous engagement or press of work as a reason for foregoing an orgy, a pain in the hand or arm would be the one grounds on which a refusal to demonstrate one's penmanship could well be based.

I should be hesitant to accept even the proposition that "Shakespeare" had two legs on the strength of John Aubrey's unsupported statement. Yet the Stratfordian's purported six signatures — and we have nothing else to

---

[3] Schoenbaum, in his *William Shakespeare: A Documentary Life*, reproduces Aubrey's memorandum on page 205, just below the author's own rendition, which has the comma added!

judge by — are of such character as to make it seem very likely that their author was not eager to take quill in hand before others. Three are incomplete and the others, on his will, appear executed with painful difficulty. As I reported earlier, McManaway omits the latter altogether from the page he gives to Shakspere's signatures in the Folger booklet on the authorship. It is difficult to imagine what his motive could be other than fear of the reader's drawing the logical conclusions.

Professors Evans and Levin write: "Mr. Ogburn speaks of him as 'a near illiterate.' [That is what I said Shakspere was "on the record."] He goes on to reveal his own ignorance of the secretary hand by speaking of 'incomplete' signatures, not recognizing abbreviated forms which are standard in that hand." It is some consolation to me to know that Sir Edmund K. Chambers, "the most eminent of modern Shakespeareans," whose "achievement . . . exceeds one's reasonable expectations of what may be accomplished in several lifetimes," the man by whose "single massive presence" almost all other contributors "to biographical scholarship . . . are overshadowed" (Schoenbaum says), was evidently as ignorant as I of what is standard in the secretary hand. The signatures on both the Blackfriars conveyance and mortgage are parchment strips, and Chambers quotes the speculation that "Shakespeare . . . signed the strips before they were inserted in the deed, and that, in trimming them to fit the slits, the scrivener mutilated the ends of the signatures." But he finds that "This does not sound plausible as legal procedure. Moreover, there was plenty of room for trimming on the left-hand side of the strips." He leaves unexplained why on three legal documents calling for the signatory's most serious performance Shakspere should not have managed to complete his name. "Shaksp," "Shakspē," and "Shakspē" is as far as he got, according to Chambers's reading.

Chambers deciphers the three signatures on the will as "William Shakspere" (judging by old facsimiles, most of this signature having disappeared as the paper on which it is written deteriorated), "Willm Shakspere," and "William Shakspeare." Of the last, he reports the opinion of the paleographer Sir E. Maunde Thompson that the signature originally ended with a contraction and that the last three letters were then added. In all six signatures the first syllable is "Shak," which would be pronounced with a short *a*.

The reader can hardly fail to be struck, too, by how crudely the signatory wrote. Dr. Wilson R. Harrison, M.Sc., Ph.D., one of Scotland Yard's foremost document-examiners, who exhaustively examined the signatures in the first half of 1979, recognizing "the poor quality of the handwriting," speculates that "When Shakespeare left London for Stratford to spend his last years in retirement . . . he may well have been a man in decline in both mental and physical powers." The vagaries in the signatures on the will he appears

Belott-Mountjoy Affidavit, 1612.   Public Records Office.

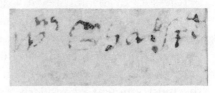

Blackfriars Mortgage, 1613. British Library.

Blackfriars Conveyance, 1613. Guildhall
Library

From the three pages of the will.   Public Records Office.
25 March 1616.

William Shakspere's Signatures

Courtesy of the Shakespeare-Oxford Society

definitely to attribute to the penman's illness, believing that he signed the last page first, for "compared with the main signature, the additional effort on page 2 is very poor indeed." He declares:

> It is quite easy to think of the signatory summoning up sufficient strength to write "William" in a most satisfactory manner and finding the effort too much to further undertake the much more difficult task of writing the surname. This being accomplished after a fashion, one can well imagine the sick man once again bending his failing energies to signing yet two more pages so as to complete the will to the satisfaction of his legal adviser.

But why was his writing of the family name so inferior to that of the first name in the earlier signatures? Dr. Harrison's answer is:

> If Shakespeare was suffering some complaint in 1612 — at about the time he apparently gave up his literary work — which affected the nervous control of his fingers, this would explain why he found it so much easier to write the one rather than the other.

Dr. Harrison had been commissioned by the Shakespeare-Oxford Society of the United States to study the Shakspere signatures. It is a pity that he had no writing of the Stratfordian's to analyze but five signatures executed "near to or just after he ceased to write," when, judging by their quality, he was suffering impaired physical powers. Incidentally, Dr. Harrison volunteered that "I also dipped into Shakespearean scholarship — and was disgusted. I expected to find that contemporary documents had been treated in the same scientific manner as the Mozart manuscripts and that some reliance could be placed on some of the theories which have grown up around the life of W.S. As far as I can tell, the vaguest suppositions of one writer are quoted by those who come after as fact, and that his 'life story' as generally received consists of fables." He said he "could quite understand . . . why some people have doubted whether all the signatures were written by one man" — which, however, he concluded they were.

Joseph M. English, an American documents-examiner from the Forensic Science Laboratory of Washington, D.C., and Lecturer in Law at Georgetown University, had also examined the Shakspere signatures for the Shakespeare-Oxford Society. Stressing that his conclusions must be regarded as provisional only since he had only halftone reproductions to work with (where Dr. Harrison was able to gain access to the originals), he had offered as his opinion that the shortcomings in the signatures could not be explained by their having been simplifications; that they were, rather, those of a man simply not familiar with writing his own name, in particular lacking familiarity with the latter part of his family name, which in the two legible signatures on the will he was more or less guessing at. After delivering his report, Mr. English was heard to murmur that if he were told that these were the signatures of a man supposed to be a writer, politeness would compel him to keep silent.

I should point out that neither examiner of the document knew what position the Society held on the authorship of Shakespeare's works, or Mr. English that there had ever been any question about it.

Professors Evans and Levin, challenging the assertion that six signatures are all we know that Shakspere wrote, declare that "an intensive study of Shakespeare's handwriting would identify his holograph in a scene from the *Sir Thomas More* manuscript, which has been accepted into the canon of two recent editions" — one by none other than the two professors themselves.

The manuscript of the play *Sir Thomas More* was originally written in a hand that has been identified as Anthony Munday's. In this manuscript, however, portions were deleted and substitutions made in five other hands. Scholars have proposed identifications for these contributors. One designated D, author of a single scene, was proclaimed in 1871 to have been Shakespeare. The case rests partly on the hand in which the contribution is written and partly on its literary qualities. Sir E. Maunde Thompson, Director of the British Museum, found similarities between Shakspere's handwriting and that of D convincing him that they were the same. Another specialist, S. A. Tannenbaum, questioned the validity of some of his points and called attention to dissimilarities between the two hands. Chambers, declaring that the play must have been written a good many years before the first of the Shakspere signatures (which dates from 1612) and that these signatures contain only eleven of the twenty-six letters of the alphabet and only three capitals, finds "the basis for comparison" of the handwritings "slight." Dr. Wilson R. Harrison, who observes that "When looked at as a group, there is no doubt that all the [six Shakspere] signatures have a family look about them," discovered no such look embracing other writings proposed as Shakspere's by Schoenbaum, including "D's" hand in *Sir Thomas More*. If drawings of these on one sheet of paper are made, he wrote, "I have no doubt there will be found a complete absence of any impression of a family resemblance." As for the long-spurred *a* in Shakspere's signature on the Blackfriars mortgage, about which much has been made in linking his writing with "D's" in *Sir Thomas More*, Dr. Harrison comments: "It is simply one of the variant methods of writing 'a' in the Secretary hand, and in Schoenbaum's illustration of the Secretary hand (p. xix) it can be seen along with other equally bizarre formations. As evidence of common authorship, it is light-weight indeed."

English Literary Autographs, 1550–1650, by Walter Wilson Greg, contains facsimiles of the holographs of thirty-five dramatists (including Rowley, Chettle, Drayton, Dekker, Munday, Chapman, Massinger, Kyd, Peele, Lyly, Marston, Lodge, Nashe, Daniel, Heywood, de Vere and Jonson), thirty-six prose writers and forty-two poets — but none of "Shakespeare."

My favorite rebuttal to the evidence that the Stratford man was of very doubtful competence with a pen was put forth in the *Saturday Review* by Bergen Evans, professor of English of Northwestern University, an academician of national reputation. (The etymological program, "The Last Word," launched by Dr. Evans on CBS in 1957, had a coast-to-coast following.) He wrote:

> As for the man himself, it cannot be denied that his report cards have not been preserved, but surely the writing of the plays ought to render them unnecessary as proof of his literacy.

So much for *that*.

Of Shakspere's six purported signatures, all derive from the last four years of his life, none from the years of his alleged literary activity, none arising in a literary connection. Nothing in his hand other than the signatures on his will has been found in Stratford. His having (as we read) dwelt for two decades in London while maintaining a family and conducting business in Stratford would have necessitated much correspondence between the two centers. As we have seen, New Place remained in the hands of his descendants for more than half a century after his death, by which time three folio editions of Shakespeare's collected plays had been published and his immortality been ensured. Would not a note or two in Shakspere's hand have been saved had any ever existed, and were he the dramatist? Papers bearing the signatures or marks of those with whom he did business *have* survived.

The suspicion voices itself that the papers on which Shakspere had set his hand in Stratford were made to disappear because they showed the great writer signing with a mark — just as the records of the Stratford Grammar School of his early years would have disappeared because they showed he did not attend it, just as "the volumes of the Lord Chamberlain's Warrants," which "supply much information concerning plays and players," Charlotte C. Stopes writes, are "unfortunately missing for the most important years of Shakespearean history," because they would have showed how little consequential a figure Shakspere cut in the company. Charles W. Barrell reports that the official books of Edmund Lylney and Sir George Buck, Masters of the Revels under Elizabeth and James respectively, "(together with all office records of the Lord Chamberlain who supervised the Masters of the Revels in those times) have hopelessly vanished. With them have disappeared the voluminous and detailed correspondence and memoranda covering the origin, selection, licensing, casting, mounting, costuming, rehearsal and finished production of literally scores of plays, including Shakespeare's." It is, as he sums it up, "a great mystery."

"It is a thousand pities," A. L. Rowse declares, "that the Burbages' papers have not survived as Henslowe's have done" — and Edward Alleyn's, he could have added. "If only they had we should have known much more about the performances of Shakespeare's plays, their takings and receipts." And no doubt much more, too, about Shakespeare. But the papers have disappeared.

As will be brought out in the next chapter, it appears that Shakspere might well never have been heard of had he been able to write with any facility.

9

"Look Here, upon This Picture, and on This"

Interest in the kind of man Shakespeare was appears to have been minimal in the 17th century. We learn that it develops in the next and that as it does so, Stratford comes in for notice as the purported Birthplace. At the same time, irreverent voices begin to suggest, allegorically and whimsically, that the man born there was not the author of the plays. Serious skepticism is first publicly expressed in 1837 in the unlikely medium of a novel by a future British Prime Minister. But if Shakspere did not write the plays, who did? Among the many Elizabethans who are brought forward, an effort is made in what follows to assess fairly the case for each of three who appear to deserve being taken seriously. These are Sir Francis Bacon, Christopher Marlowe, and the 6th Earl of Derby. If the premise in the present book is sound, however, the crucial event in the search for the man who was Shakespeare comes in 1920, when a British schoolmaster, having pursued the quest methodically without preconception or preference as to where it might lead, publishes the results in "Shakespeare" Identified. We regard the reception given it and summarize its consequence. Taking the curious Stratfordian dictum that the plurality of candidates for Shakespeare's honors is an argument for Shakspere's author-ship, we apply the principle to the plurality of Shakesperes put forward by Stratfordians to account for Shakespeare's many facets. In conclusion we consider whether Shake-speare's identity is important.

In the very year of David Garrick's Stratford jubilee — 1769 — firmly establishing William Shakspere as his nation's greatest writer, a book was published with an innuendo that all was not above-board in the matter of his authorship. This was a rather tedious allegorical narrative, supposedly by Garrick's friend, the physician Herbert Lawrence, in which a character called Common Sense, born in Athens, the son of Truth and Wit, relates his picaresque adventures. Well along in the story he tells how his father, Wit, joined by Genius and Humour, "made a trip to London, where upon their arrival they made an acquaintance with a person belonging to the playhouse; this man was a profligate in his youth, and, as some say, had been a deer-stealer; . . . he certainly was a thief." This character was demonstrated when he robbed the travelers "of everything he could lay his hands on," among other things a book containing the means "to express all different sentiments of the human mind," a glass "by which he could penetrate into the deep recesses of the soul of man," and "a mask of curious workmanship" through which the wearer's every utterance came out "extremely pleasant and enter-taining." "With these materials, and with good parts of his own, he com-menced play-writer, and how he succeeded is needless to say, when I tell the reader that his name was Shakespear." The victims of his thievery refrain from betraying him because "we could not distress this man without depriv-ing his country of its greatest ornament." Whether, in implying that "Shake-spear's" success came about from the purloined gifts of others, the *Life and Adventures of Common Sense* reflects a suspicion about the Stratfordian's *bona fides* that had existed all along, it certainly foreshadows later doubts about it.

So also, it would seem, does *The Story of the Learned Pig*, appearing in 1786. Another historical allegory, this one was by "An Officer of the Royal Navy." The hero-narrator, who signs himself TRANSMIGRATUS, has been reincarnated in innumerable forms going back at least to Romulus, occupying the bodies of insects and higher animals, including a cat belonging to the widow of an officer killed at Bosworth field, who is done to death as a witch. Among his exceptional human appearances, he was

> initiated in the profession of horse-holder to those who came to visit the play-house, where I was well-known by the name of "Pimping Billy." My sprightly genius soon distinguished me from the common herd. . . . I soon after contracted a friendship with the great man and first of geniuses, the "Immortal Shake-speare."

It seems that "Shakespeare" had to flee Stratford because he had written a ballad about his intimacy with the wife of a country Justice. It was not true that he had

> to run his country for deer-stealing. . . . With equal falsehood has he been fathered with many spurious dramatic pieces. "Hamlet, Othello, As you like it, the Tempest, and Midsummer's Night Dream," for five; of all of which I confess myself to be the author.

But such is the "great countenance" shown "Shakespeare" by "all people of taste and quality" that spleen puts an end to Billy's existence. There is little logic in it, yet indisputably it singles out Shakespeare as an author not who he seemed to be. As for who the author was, "Learned Pig" may be meant to suggest Bacon.

Sir Francis Bacon was the explicit choice of Dr. James Wilmot, who may be said to have begun the modern period of critical dissent from the Stratford attribution in about the same year as *The Learned Pig* was published. A fellow of Trinity College, Oxford, and friend of Samuel Johnson's and Laur-ence Stern's, Wilmot had retired around 1781 to his native Warwickshire, to become rector in a village near Stratford. Evidently he hoped to take advantage of his situation to learn more about Shakespeare's life. The full results of his researches, which led him by about 1785 to conclude that the

Stratfordian was not the author of the plays, were, alas, never to be known to the world; for he gave instructions that upon his death a local schoolmaster and his housekeeper were to "burn on the platform before the house all the bags and boxes" that they could "discover, in the cabinets in my bedroom," and these instructions were scrupulously carried out. We should not know of Wilmot's investigations at all had he not, in about his eightieth year, confided their gist to a visitor, one James Corton Cowell. Cowell, a member of the Ipswich Philosophical Society, had undertaken to obtain information for a paper he was to read before the Society in 1805 on the life of Shakespeare.

His audience was in for a shock. Cowell reported that he had come to a "strange pass." He confessed himself "a Pervert, nay a Renegade to the Faith I have proclaimed and avowed before you all." So serious was his fall from grace that he expressed himself "prepared to hear from you as I unfold my strange and surprising story cries of disapproval and even of execration." What had happened was that he had failed to find any adequate information on Shakespeare's life either in books or through personal inquiries at Stratford. "Everywhere," he declared, "was I met by a strange and perplexing silence." The darkness surrounding the dramatist, which left him puzzled and defeated, was, however, to be dissipated by a "new light." He hastened to confess further

> that the author of this New Light was not myself but an ingenious gentleman of the neighborhood of Stratford on Avon. . . . I have not his permission to make public his name since as he rightly pointed out the townsfolk of Stratford on Avon have of late years taken such a vast pride in the connexion of the poet with their town that they would bitterly resent any attempt to belittle the poet.[1]

For Stratford's dearth of reminders of the poet, Cowell went on:

> My friend has an explanation that is so startling that it is easy to understand his timidity in putting it forth boldly and I share his reticence. He goes so far as to suggest that the reason for the non-existence of the manuscripts is that they were the work of some other person who had good reason for concealing his connection with them. . . . My friend has a theory which he supports with much ingenuity that the real author of the plays attributed to Shakespeare was Sir Francis Bacon.

Evidently having incurred the excoriation he expected, Cowell reappeared before the Society two months later to exculpate himself. Swearing the Society's members to secrecy, he divulged the identity of the friend he had quoted and retailed some of his reasoning. He recalled that on his first visit

---

[1] In *The Life and Adventures of Common Sense* we were told that to expose the conventional Shakespeare for what he was would amount to "depriving the country of its greatest ornament," and here again we meet this befuddled view, which will be heard up to the present: to disbelieve in that Shakespeare is to belittle the beloved poet-dramatist.

to Wilmot various country folk had been present but that when "these bucolic guests had departed . . . the Doctor and I were able to approach the subject of our colloquy." Dr. Wilmot, "does not venture so far as to say definitively that Sir Francis Bacon was the author, but through his great knowledge of the works of that writer he is able to prepare a cap that fits him amazingly." Among the reasons for the belief he had come to was the knowledge Shakespeare possessed beyond the Stratfordian's likely reach, such as an awareness about the circulation of the blood before Harvey had announced it, and Shakespeare's failure to make use in his plays of odd characters and legends extant in Stratford in his day. Thinking that Shakespeare's books "would have soon passed for money from his poor and illiterate next of kin into the hands of the local gentry who alone purchased books," Wilmot said "he had covered himself with the dust of every bookcase for 50 miles round" without discovering a single volume that might once have belonged to the poet.

So faithfully did the members of the Ipswich Philosophical Society honor their vow that Cowell's papers became known to the public only when the University of London fell heir to a collection of books in which they were included and Professor Allardyce Nicoll reported on them in the *Times Literary Supplement* for 25 February 1932.

What is interesting in all this is not only that Wilmot had found the Shakespeare record a blank at Stratford and had come to conceive the kind of doubts that would assail legions of readers in the future. It is also that Cowell spoke as if Shakespearean orthodoxy were an embattled religion. In departing from it he called himself a "Pervert" and "a Renegade to the Faith." He made plain, moreover, that he had earlier had occasion to *proclaim and avow a Faith* in orthodoxy. Why was it a matter of Faith? We may be sure that he had never felt it necessary to proclaim and avow a Faith that Ben Jonson was who he seemed to be, or Marlowe, or Chaucer. The Stratford attribution, which in the historical record is being mocked even before it surfaces, was clearly in trouble in 1805. I suspect it had never been out of trouble. Not only was it apparently on the defensive in Cowell's day, but a critic who challenged it could expect *execration*. One asks oneself if the authors of *Common Sense* and the *Learned Pig* were serious disbelievers in the approved Shakespeare who felt it unsafe to express their misgivings except in the most far-fetched allegory. And if that be so, as seems probable from Cowell's experience, one wonders if our curiosity will ever be fully satisfied as to why it was dangerous two centuries ago to take issue with Shakespearean convention.

One further item of interest is afforded by Cowell. It had been only "in late years" — nearly two centuries late — that Stratford had come to take great pride in the original of that bust in the church.

Owing to the suppression of James Wilmot's theories, the distinction of being the first to make a serious public statement of explicit disbelief in the accepted Shakespeare belongs to no less a figure than Benjamin Disraeli, Lord Beaconsfield, who voiced it through the hero in one of his novels, *Venetia,* published in 1837. Lord Cadurcis exclaims: "And who is Shakespeare? We know of him as much as we do of Homer. Did he write half the plays attributed to him? Did he ever write a single whole play? I doubt it. He appears to me to have been an inspired adapter for the theatres, which were then not as good as barns. I take him to have been a botcher up of old plays." Cadurcis is said to have been modeled on Lord Byron, whose opinion of the Shakespeare authorship was quite likely to be known to Disraeli, a stellar adjunct of literary circles in young manhood. One wishes we could know whether Cadurcis in this particular recapitulated the model!

A botcher up of plays written by others is just the opinion of Shakespeare expressed by Joseph C. Hart, a New York lawyer and writer and colonel in the National Guard, in an unlikely vehicle, a book on his sailing experiences. *The Romance of Yachting,* published in 1848, is conventionally credited with marking the earliest dissent from the Stratford attribution. Hart was side-tracked into an extended discussion of Shakespeare by being reminded of the landing on "the desarts of Bohemia" in *The Winter's Tale.* He writes:

> After "the bard" had been dead for one hundred years and utterly forgotten, a player and a writer of the succeeding century, turning over the old lumber of a theatrical "property-room," find bushels of neglected plays, and the idea of a "speculation" occurs to them. Thus "I want an author for this selection of plays," said Rowe. "I have it!" said Betterton; "call them Shakespeare's!" . . . This is about the sum and substance of the manner of setting up Shakespeare.

The Stratfordian, Hart charges, "grew up in ignorance and viciousness and became a common poacher. And the latter title, in literary matters, he carried to his grave. . . . It is a fraud upon the world to thrust his surreptitious fame upon us." (Hart was not the first to characterize Shakspere as a thief in his profession. More than a hundred years earlier, in 1738, Louis Riccoboni wrote of "Shakspear" in a book on European Theatres: "Having consumed his patrimony, he entered upon the profession of a thief.") His early-Victorianism offended by the bawdry in Shakespeare, Hart blamed it on the Stratfordian, who, with an eye to the box office, introduced "Impurities" in the scripts he had appropriated, and he was able to quote the 18th-century Shakespearean commentator, George Steevens, as having said that Shakespeare's "offensive metaphors and allusions are undoubtedly more frequent than those of all his predecessors and contemporaries." One by one, Hart went through thirty-three of Shakespeare's plays aiming to show that they were derived from other plays. Like Cowell, he indicates that others, too, had questions about Shakespeare, citing a critic of the day who remarked that "A singular and unaccountable mystery is attached to Shakespeare's private life; and by some strange fatality, almost every document concerning him has either been destroyed or still remains in obscurity." It was an astute observation.

In the year after Hart's publication, the disturbing gulf between the character and interests of the reputed author and the qualities of the plays and poems was openly recognized by a fellow countryman whose opinion carried great weight. Ralph Waldo Emerson wrote in *Representative Men*: "The Egyptian verdict of the Shakespeare Societies comes to mind, that he was a jovial actor and manager. I cannot marry this fact to his verse. Other admirable men had led lives in some sort of keeping with their thought; but this man, in wide contrast."

The discrepancy led to a 3,200-word anonymous article entitled "Who Wrote Shakspeare?" in a journal published in Edinburgh, in an issue of 1852. The astute, ironic inquiry is surprising in showing that the kind of doubts about the reputed authorship of Shakespeare that trouble readers by the thousands in our times were being heard 130 years ago and, one judges, were nothing novel even then.

> Who wrote Shakspeare? a question, we humbly think, which might be made the theme for as much critical sagacity, pertinacity, and pugnacity, as the almost equally interesting question of who wrote Homer. . . . Take Ben Jonson, or Kit Marlowe, or Geoffrey Chaucer, and each and all of them have external marks by which we could assign the authorship, even if the production had been published anonymously. Try Shakspeare's plays by the same test, and suppose *Hamlet, Macbeth,* &c, had been successively published after the fashion of Junius [pseudonym of a contributor to a London newspaper], and what critic of any age would ever had ascribed them to William Shakspeare? . . .
>
> Had Shakspeare, like Homer, been wholly unknown, and every record of him lost; we should then, as in the case of Homer, have judged exclusively from the internal evidence of the works themselves, and formed a brilliant ideal picture of what the astonishing author must have been in his daily walk, correspondence, and conversation. But, unfortunately, enthusiasm worked up to its pitch, sweeping the clouds for a bird's-eye view of the high pinnacle of human greatness commensurate with the "local habitation and the name" of such a genius, is at once "cabined, cribbed, confined" by the authenthic recorded whatabouts, whenabouts, and whereabouts of William Shakspeare. . . . On the one hand, research has traced his life from the cradle to the grave, and by means of tradition, legal documents, records, and inscriptions, formed a very accurate skeleton biography; while on the other hand, with the single exception of Ben Jonson, to be noticed hereafter, records and even tradition are silent upon his walk and conversation; and though his signature has been several times disinterred, his whole correspondence, if he ever wrote a letter, has sunk like lead beneath the dark waters of oblivion. . . .

Acknowledging "the dedication of the *Venus* and the *Lucrece*" to Southampton by "Shakspeare," the anonymous author asks,

> But if Southampton really knew him to be the author of the dramas, how comes it that Raleigh, Spenser, and even Bacon — all with genius so thoroughly kindred to the author of *Hamlet* — have all ignored his acquaintance? Raleigh

and Bacon seem not to have known of his existence; while Spenser, if he alludes to the works, takes care to avoid the name. In short, Heywood, Suckling, Hales, and all the others who are recorded to have spoken of Shakspeare "with great admiration," confine themselves to the works, and seem personally to avoid the man — always excepting "*Rare Ben Jonson.*" . . .

Why this one exception? Because Jonson was

bound by the strongest ties to keep his secret, if secret there were.

It is almost maddening. The writer is right on track . . . only to be thrown off by a false double assumption, one into which orthodoxy has always led the unwary, to the infinite confusion of the issue. The assumption is that the Stratfordian's name and that of the dramatist were the same and that any reference to Shakespeare must be a reference to the Stratfordian. For a way out of the dilemma he has created, the Edinburgh journalist asks, rather whimsically,

May not William Shakspeare — the cautious, calculating man, careless of fame, and intent only on money-making — have found . . . some pale, wasted student, with a brow as ample and lofty as his own, who had written the *Wars of the Roses* and who, with eyes of genius gleaming through despair, was about, like Chatterton, to spend his last copper coin upon some cheap and speedy means of death? What was to hinder William Shakspeare from . . . purchasing these dramas, and thereafter keeping his poet . . . ?

. . . .

Well, reader, how like you our hypothesis? We confess we do not like it ourselves; but we humbly think it is at least as plausible as most of what is contained in the many bulky volumes written to connect the man, William Shakspeare, with the poet of *Hamlet*.

The year 1856 was portentous in bringing the first open proposals for a concrete alternative to Shakspere as the author. With encouragement from Emerson, to whom she had appealed, and an introduction supplied by Nathaniel Hawthorne, Delia Bacon had written her exegesis of Shakespeare, which would be published in the next year in London. In 1856, with Emerson's backing, some parts of it were printed in *Putnam's Monthly* in New York. In that same year, a Londoner named William Henry Smith sent a pamphlet to the Shakespeare Society proposing Francis Bacon as the author, and this he published in more extended form the next year.

Delia S. Bacon, a Midwestern American, sister of a leading Congregationalist minister, Leonard Bacon, had achieved something of a name for herself as a writer and lecturer before her imagination was seized by the philosophical implications of Shakespeare. Conventionally regarded as the pioneer Baconian, she in fact held that the plays were jointly created by Sir Walter Raleigh as poet and Sir Francis Bacon (to whom she was not related) as philosopher, with contributions by other poets and dramatists, especially Edmund Spenser. "There were men in England who knew well enough what kind of instrumentality the drama had been," she wrote. "And there were men in England, in the age of Elizabeth, who had mastered the Greek and Roman history . . . and who knew precisely what kind of crisis in human history they were born to occupy." Her idea was that these men came together with the object of promoting "the culture and instruction of the masses" in defiance of a repressive Court: "Elizabethan England rejected the Elizabethan man." The question about the authorship of the plays was to Miss Bacon merely incidental to that of their purport, but she protested that their meaning could not be understood if we were "condemned to refer the origin of those works to the illiterate man who kept the theatre, compelled to regard them as merely the result of an extraordinary talent for pecuniary speculation. . . . Thus blinded we shall not perhaps distinguish that magnificent whole . . . in which we shall one day see, not the burning Illium, not the old Danish court or the tenth century, but the yet living, illustrious Elizabethan age, with all its momentous interests still at stake." Many today would applaud that perception.

"No man or woman has ever thought or written more sincerely," Hawthorne declared of Delia Bacon. "It is for the public to say whether my countrywoman has proved her theory. In the worst event, if she has failed, her failure will be more honorable than most people's triumphs." Nevertheless, it was her fate to be the first to furnish Stratfordians with the weapon of ridicule in their assault upon dissent. Her overwrought, torrential style was the vehicle for an ardent, impetuous vision, not for objective analysis, and her hours-long attendance one night in Trinity Church by Shakspere's tomb, a shovel in her hands, seems a prelude to the loss of her mind and commitment to an institution not long after publication of her book. These aberrations enabled such a writer as Schoenbaum to speak of "the nightmare scaffolding of Delia's paranoia" and to regale the reader with her pitiful expressions of increasing mental disorder.

The collaborative authorship in which she believed is not on its face, however, out of the question. She has had many followers in her belief, to whom Shakespeare has seemed to touch convincingly more facets of experience than one man could have known. Many Elizabethan plays were the work of two or more hands, and some credited to Shakespeare are still being analyzed to determine which parts are actually his. Those for whom it is laughable to suppose a committee capable of functioning as a literary organism must find themselves having to explain the King James Bible. On the other hand, the genius that elevates Shakespeare's plays so far above any others in our language is so consistent with itself and so peerless in imagination and expression that to imagine it jointly wielded is all but unthinkable; take away the parts that bear the unmistakable impress of that unique mind and what remains would be quickly forgotten.

Sir Francis Bacon as Shakespeare

William Henry Smith, Whose *Bacon and Shakespeare* was published in the same year as Miss Bacon's book — 1856 — pointed out that

> not one single manuscript has ever been found to identify Shakespeare [i.e., Shakspere] as the author of these productions; nor is there, among all the records and traditions handed down to us, any statement that he was ever seen writing or producing a manuscript; nor that he ever claimed as his own, or repudiated (as unworthy of him) any of the worthless productions presented to the public in his name.

Smith observes, quite justifiably, about Ben Jonson's long poem in the First Folio, which is indispensable to the Stratford case, that "The lines are in many parts incomprehensible, and throughout exhibit a mysterious vagueness quite at variance with the general character of Ben Jonson's laudatory verses." He adds that in his *Discoveries* Jonson speaks of Bacon's having "performed that in our tongue, which may be compared and preferred to insolent Greece and haughty Rome" — the very comparison he had drawn with Shakespeare. He claims that Bacon not only had the requisite learning and experience to qualify as Shakespeare, but also that "his wit and poetic faculty were exactly of the peculiar character which we find exhibited in these plays."

As to that, not everyone, surely, would agree. But certainly Smith performed a valuable service in revealing, as his predecessors had done, that in his day, too, the Stratford attribution was under suspicion. In 1856, he tells us, the editor of the *Athenaeum* wrote: "We believe that a very plausible case could be made against the assumed authorship of William Shakespeare by anyone with knowledge of the times. There is, for example, the one great fact to begin with . . . Shakespeare never claimed the plays as his own." The editor went on to speak of allusions in Shakespeare to passing events, which "it is natural to infer . . . came from some one higher in station than a poor player." He found it striking, too, that Bacon, while commenting freely on other notable contemporaries, failed "ever to refer to Shakespeare."

In launching the Baconian theory, William Henry Smith gave rise to a very considerable literature. To anyone rejecting the Stratfordian as the author, Francis Bacon offered the most conspicuous eligible alternative. A philosopher, statesman, and essayist, he receives two more pages in the great eleventh edition of the *Encyclopaedia Britannica* than Shakespeare, not counting the special section on Shakespeare's portraits. Born in 1561, the son of Sir Nicholas Bacon, he was educated at Cambridge and studied law at Gray's Inn. His efforts at self-advancement, while proceeding but poorly under Elizabeth, carried him far under James, though, failing of his patrimony, he was in debt all his life. He became successively Attorney General, Lord Keeper, and Lord Chancellor, and, having been knighted in 1603, was created Baron Verulam of Verulam in 1618 and Viscount St. Albans in 1621.

Bacon's intellect, says the *Encyclopaedia Britannica,* "was far-seeing and acute, quick yet cautious, meditative, methodical and free from prejudice." His legal training and experience could account for the deep and easy familiarity with the law that experts have found in Shakespeare. He was a voluminous and highly accomplished writer. Of his fifty-eight celebrated *Essays,* Emerson wrote that "Few books ever written contain so much wisdom and will bear to be read so many times. . . . They are clothed in a style of such splendor that imaginative persons find sufficient delight in the beauty of expression." He translated the psalms into English verse. He is said to have delighted in the theatre and wrote masques for Gray's Inn. He had a close relationship with Ben Jonson, who said that "He seemed to me ever, by his work, one of the greatest men, and most worthy of admiration, that had been in many ages."

The case for Bacon is strengthened by the similarities between apothegms in his notebook and lines in Shakespeare's plays. If the parallels are mere coincidences, they are remarkable ones. Ruling out the unlikely possibility that Shakespeare cribbed from Bacon's private writings, they certainly afford grounds for attributing to Bacon at least a hand in Shakespeare's plays — unless those plays were written before the orthodox scholars say they were, and, I interject here, as strong evidence says they were: that would make Bacon the borrower. Another argument in Bacon's favor is that the texts of plays in the First Folio of 1623 show revisions made in them after Shakspere's death; Bacon lived till 1626. The famous manuscript discovered in Northumberland House, from which it takes its name, has also weighed in the scales for Bacon. Among the crowded jottings it exhibits, "Mr. ffrauncis Bacon" (with "your soveraign" upside down between the two names) is closely associated with "Rychard the second" and "Rychard the third" and "William Shakespeare," which is repeated numerous times, including fragmentary renderings. Some allusions to Bacon, especially after his death, make it conceivable that even before the mid-1600s curiosity as to who Shakespeare could have been found an answer in that master intellect. That could possibly have accounted for the Northumberland manuscript, but Gwynneth Bowen argues persuasively that the manuscript was merely connected with writings "gathered for unauthorized printing," which included an edition of Bacon's *Essays.*

The Baconian theory has been supported by highly intelligent, educated persons down to the present. Some of its champions, however, did it a lasting disservice and put another instrument for ridicule in the Stratfordians' hands in their claims to have found ciphers in Shakespeare's works revealing Bacon's authorship. A well-known pioneer among them was Ignatius Donnelly, a three-term U.S. Representative from Minnesota, a brilliant and erudite man and successful writer. In 1888, Donnelly ably analyzed the problem of the Shakespeare authorship marring his work by interjecting his purported discovery in the plays of a cipher that gave the title to his book, *The Great Cryptogram.* Donnelly was one of two Baconians contributing to a "tribunal" on the Shakespeare authorship that ran for about a year, beginning in mid-1892, in an intellectual magazine published in Boston called *Arena.* From our perspective at a later date it is quite extraordinary that a magazine of *Arena's* calibre would accord a hearing to dissenters from Shakespearean orthodoxy. (To Schoenbaum, it is a matter of "solemn" editors having indulged in "sensational exploitation.") The experiment would be repeated but once, and then under safeguards, in the next eighty years. The Stratfordian position had four champions including Frederick J. Furnivall, biographer of Shakespeare and founder of the New Shakspere Society of London, and Professor R. E. Shelling. The Baconians had two: Donnelly and Edwin Reed, author of *Bacon Versus Shakespeare.* Both were greatly compromised, the one by his announced discovery of those unconvincing ciphers in Shakespeare, the other by his amazingly switching sides as he ended his presentation — to the disgust of Donnelly, understandably, and even of one among the Stratfordian contributors, who complained of having patiently gone through the four installments in Reed's presentation only to have them cancelled in the end.

When the contestants had had their say, a jury of twenty-five was heard from. Of these, one voted for Bacon, twenty for "the defendant," including Edmund Gosse, Sir Henry Irving, and Alfred Russell Wallace, who was particularly aggressive in his opinion. Two favored composite authorship and two — A. E. Dolbear and Mrs. Mary A. Livermore — believed that "the defendant" had not written the plays but were not convinced that Bacon had. That only two were in the last category seems to me remarkable. If the Stratfordians elaborated with devastating effect the striking incompatibility between Bacon's genius and Shakespeare's, the arguments marshalled against the Stratford man — those to be made familiar in the future — were in my view no less deadly. It is 'no wonder that Professor Shelling treated his adversaries with that scathing rudeness of a troubled polemicist that the future was also to make familiar. Indeed, one juror, A. B. Brown, was able to cling to his orthodoxy only by reaching out beyond the known world for a source of the plays. "It would seem not unreasonable," he wrote, "to claim him [Shakespeare] as one of those subjects whom the esoteric forces of the universe so often use to present great and marvellous truths to the external world." I should say that the two sides knocked each other fairly out of the ring. Accordingly it seems to me almost incredible that no juror came out and asked why it had to be either Bacon or the Stratfordian.

Professor Dolbear did so tacitly, however, in his verdict. He began by observing that Shakspere's signatures "show, as plainly as need be, that the hand which wrote those had no facility with a pen." He went on to say:

Until lately commentators have found in the works evidence of great and varied accomplishments: knowledge of ancient and modern languages, of history, of law, of science and philosophy. Attainments in these fields imply much more than genius: they imply opportunities. Genius can dispense with learning in music, in mathematics, in mechanism; but there is no such thing as innate knowledge of language or law or history or science. It is a necessary presumption that whoever possesses any of them in any degree has acquired so much, and eminence implies great and persistent efforts. There is no evidence that Shakspere had either opportunity or inclination to concern himself with such matters. On the contrary his known tastes were a long remove from them. Fancy, if one can, Bacon retiring from London as a money-lender and beer brewer.

Dr. [W. J.] Rolfe [one of the Stratfordians] says, "It is amazing that any Shakespearean scholar should have ever conceived that there is evidence of learning in the plays." Nevertheless he is well aware that the most eminent of them have found abundance of it there. . . . It was found there until it became apparent that it damaged Shakspere's claim.

He concluded:

As the defense seems to acquiesce in the statements of the Baconians concerning what is really known of Wm. Shakspere and draws its inferences from a hypothetical Shakespeare rather than the one we know something about, it appears from the evidence presented that it is highly improbable that Wm. Shakspere either did [write] or could have written what has been attributed to him.

I cannot help exclaiming: if only the force of Professor Dolbear's reasoning could have been conceded at the time!

"That Bacon wrote it," Dolbear finished, "does not seem so certain."

Very far indeed from certain, one would surely say. Shakespeare was a poet through and through; as Henry James says, "the plays and the sonnets were never written but by a Personal Poet, a Poet, and Nothing Else, a Poet, who being Nothing Else, could never be a Bacon." He was a poet, one might add, in whom every human emotion found expression in poetry, whose song is music in words. He can hold us in thrall with the witchery of his verse:

In such a night
Stood Dido with a willow in her hand
Upon the wild sea-banks, and waft her love
To come again to Carthage.

I cannot imagine the author of *Novum Organum* capable of such verse. Bacon's virtues were at the other pole from Shakespeare's, those of a brilliant rationalist; his was a mind to which prose was the native vehicle, and it is science and philosophy that is indebted to him; in anything to which he put his name, the creative arts are indebted to him not at all. Writing about Shakespeare, Thomas Carlyle said, "It is truly a lordly spectacle how this great soul takes in all kinds of men and objects. . . . *Novum Organum,* and all the intellect you find in Bacon, is of a quite secondary order: earth material, poor in comparison."

It is hardly conceivable that a man who wrote the language's greatest poetry under a pseudonym should never have managed to write any under his own; the one selection from Bacon's efforts, *The Fate of Man,* in the *Oxford Book of Sixteenth Century Verse,* has meter and rhyme but is not poetry and could scarcely be less like Shakespeare's. It is hardly likely that the author of *King Richard the Third* could have taken as detached a view of that monarch as Bacon did when he wrote, "Although he were a Prince in militar virtue approved, jealous of the honour of the English nation and likewise a good lawmaker for the ease and solace of the common people: Yet his cruelties and parricides in the opinion of all men weighed down his virtues and merits." It is far more unlikely that the First Folio would have been published without the author's participation had he been alive, as Bacon was. Certainly he had no hand in it. He was, as the Danish scholar Georg Brandes observes, "scrupulously careful as to the form in which his works appeared . . . and corrected them so carefully that scarcely a single error of the press is to be found in his books." He asks: "Can he have been responsible for the publication of these thirty-six plays, which swarm with misreadings and contain about twenty thousand errors of the press?"[2]

I do not believe those who edited the First Folio would have stated categorically that the dramatist was dead had he been still alive. I find it unimaginable that Bacon, who, trying the Earl of Essex for treason, conducted the prosecution with a viciousness that would blacken his own reputation forever, was the Shakespeare who adored the Earl of Southampton — the same young Earl who had sided with his friend Essex in the rebellion and stood to lose his head with Essex's, thanks to Bacon's relentlessness. I cannot conceive that the man possessed of the great and humane soul that illumines Shakespeare's dramas could have condoned and even recommended torture to extract confession, as Bacon did. Apart from all other considerations, it must be plain to us that Shakespeare's plays, two narrative poems totaling nearly 3,000 lines, and the sequence of 154 sonnets make up a life's work, and one that surely could not have been fitted into Bacon's otherwise busy career. Finally, I cannot believe that Bacon would have gone to his grave without claiming credit for the outstanding literary masterpieces of our language had he written them. That nobody, so far as our information goes, ever claimed credit for them — and that goes for Shakspere of Stratford as well as for anyone else — is certainly one of the most arresting aspects of our mystery, as it is one for which a reasonable explanation must be offered for any man we are willing to accept as Shakespeare.

[2] Dr. Brandes, writing in 1895, was deeply disturbed that a *Bibliography of the Bacon-Shakespeare Controversy* published in 1884 reported that of 255 publications on the authorship up to then "73 were decidedly opposed to Shakespeare's [*sic*] authorship, while 65 left the question undetermined." Shockingly, "out of 161 books, only 23 were in favour of Shakespeare."

Christopher Marlowe as Shakespeare

Although Bacon as an alternative to Shakspere had a larger following than any other through the first two decades of the present century, he was by no means the only alternative put forward. *It Was Marlowe: A Story of the Secret of Three Centuries,* a novel by a San Francisco attorney, William G. Ziegler, published in 1895, presupposed that Christopher Marlowe was not murdered in 1593, as believed, and had him live on to write the works ascribed to Shakespeare with assistance by Sir Walter Raleigh and the Earl of Rutland. The book made scant impression and little would have been heard of Marlowe as Shakespeare had not Calvin Hoffman, an American poet, writer, Elizabethan specialist, and university lecturer, revived the idea in more serious form sixty years later. The proposal, however, is appealing on several grounds.

Born in 1564, the grandson, reportedly, of a prosperous tanner in Canterbury and of the rector of St. Peter's, Canterbury, Christopher Marlowe was one among a number of distinguished pupils of King's School, Canterbury, and one of Archbishop Parker's scholars at Cambridge, where he obtained the bachelor's and master's degree. He was an intimate of Sir Francis Walsingham's kinsmen and a friend of Sir Walter Raleigh's. He "is said to have met in free converse" with Raleigh, "the poetical Earl of Oxford," two leading mathematicians of the time, and Thomas Harriott, "the notable astronomer." The author of four plays described as great and of highly praised lyrical verse, he is one dramatist who at his best could turn out verse worthy of Shakespeare. "The place and value of Christopher Marlowe as a leader among English poets it would be almost impossible for historical criticism to over-estimate," Algernon Charles Swinburne wrote.

> He first, and he alone, guided Shakespeare into the right way of work: his music, in which there is no echo of any man's before him, found its own echo in the more prolonged but hardly more exalted harmony of Milton's. He is the greatest discoverer, the most daring and inspired pioneer, in all our poetic literature. Before him there was neither genuine blank verse nor a genuine tragedy in our language. After his arrival the way was prepared, the paths were made straight, for Shakespeare.

Not bad for a writer who, though only two months older than the Shakespeare of orthodoxy, died just as the latter was beginning to become known.

It is certainly striking that six months after Marlowe is silenced, William Shakespeare, whose name has not been heard before, comes out with his skilled and polished *Venus and Adonis,* which he describes as "the first heir of my invention," and then proceeds to write plays for which "the paths were made straight" by Marlowe. More striking still are the similarities between passages in Marlowe and passages in Shakespeare. When we have

Marlowe's Jew of Malta crying "O, my girl, my fortune, my felicity" we certainly hear Shylock's "My daughter! O my ducats! O my daughter!" and consider, also from the *Jew of Malta*:

> But stay! What star shines yonder in the East. . . .
> The lodestar of my life, if Abigail.

while from *Romeo and Juliet*:

> But soft! What light through yonder window breaks?
> It is the east, and Juliet is the sun.

Instances of such parallels could be multiplied. They cannot be airily dismissed as simply "accounted for by the acknowledged influence of Marlowe on Shakespeare," in Schoenbaum's words. They go beyond mere influence.

The immediate obstacle to the Marlovian theory is of course that its principal was reported to have died in 1593. In *The Murder of the Man Who Was Shakespeare* (1955), Calvin Hoffman argues that he did not die then.

Marlowe at the time stood charged with atheism and, clearly with warrant, with homosexuality. He had been implicated in heretical activities by Thomas Kyd, his fellow playwright, while the latter was under torture by orders of the Privy Council seeking his confession to authorship of "lewd and mutinous libels." Marlowe was arrested and interrogated, and though released on bail, he was a marked man. A few days later he was reported dead of the plague. Then it was said that he had been "stabbed to death by a certain bawdy Serving-man," in Deptford. In 1820, parish records in Deptford were found to show burial on "1st June 1593 Christopher Marlowe, slain by Francis Archer." Then, in 1925, the original record of the coroner's inquest was discovered, and it named Ingram Frizer as the killer on the strength of sixteen witnesses' testimony. The report had it that in a quarrel Marlowe seized Frizer's dagger and stabbed its owner twice in the head, whereupon Frizer wrested it away and with it in turn struck Marlowe in the head, giving him a cut two inches deep and one wide and killing him instantly. Frizer was pardoned as having acted in self-defense.

Hoffman finds some peculiarities in the events, which in his view turn upon Marlowe's having had an erotic relationship with Thomas Walsingham, a wealthy patron of the arts whose cousin was Sir Francis Walsingham, head of the Queen's secret service. He found that Frizer was a notorious swindler employed by the former and that, of two companions of his at the scene of the quarrel, one was a "robber" and "cut-purse" who had been an accomplice of Frizer's in a nefarious undertaking for Thomas Walsingham and the other, at least equally unsavory, had on the day of the stabbing returned from espionage work abroad. The inquest report was incredible to Hoffman because it had these two sitting passively by while Marlowe attacked Frizer, even blocking their buddy's escape, and because neurosurgeons, whom he quotes without naming, said that Marlowe's immediate death from the wound described was medically impossible. Richard Bentley, writing on the problem of the Shakespeare authorship in the *American Bar Association Journal,* which he edited, said he had corroboration of this finding from Dr. Frederic Schreiber of Detroit, a leading neurosurgeon with wide experience in head injuries.

Hoffman's idea is that the fatal affray was a put-up job in which the victim was a drunken sailor picked up by the four participants and was part of a plan by Thomas Walsingham, assisted by his cousin, Sir Francis, to save Marlowe from death at the stake as a heretic, the fate suffered by Francis Kett four years earlier. While given out as dead, Marlowe, in this interpretation, is spirited abroad in disguise and continues his literary work, sending his manuscripts to Walsingham, his erstwhile paramour, who, to avoid recognition of his writing, has them copied before passing them on to the acting company and the printer — and Hoffman cites an unusual bequest to a scrivener in Walsingham's will. A poor actor is bribed to allow his name to be used as the author's.

It is an ingenious and defensible reconstruction. Its most obvious weakness is that though the evidence as to Marlowe's murder may be unsatisfactory and suspicious, there is none at all that he survived except insofar as one may see a continuity between his work and Shakespeare's. As for that, we have Ben Jonson telling us how by far Shakespeare

> . . . didst our Lily out-shine,
> Or sporting Kid, or Marlowe's mighty line.

So far as we know, it was never even rumored that Marlowe survived.

That the strong religious convictions entertained by Sir Francis Walsingham would have permitted him to look with favor upon the rescue of an atheist is difficult to believe. To anyone familiar with the Queen's prime sleuth's dedication to his office, it is all but inconceivable that he would have risked his career, not to mention his neck, in snatching such a one from the authority of the Privy Council — and his collaboration in the scheme would have been essential. Least of all can he be imagined putting his survival hostage to the discretion and loyalty of the three scoundrels who would have carried out the plot. Then there is the matter of *Venus and Adonis* and *Lucrece,* the former entered upon the Stationers' Register in the month before Marlowe's reported death and published five months after it. For Marlowe to have dedicated it to the prominent Earl of Southampton as William Shakespeare and *Lucrece* the next year in words revealing a much advanced degree of intimacy between the two would have been gratuitous folly on Marlowe's part and certainly in the eyes of the Walsinghams and of the Earl, even if the facts disclosed by the dedications could be squared with Hoffman's hypothesis.

Marlowe's education was greatly superior to any that Shakspere of Stratford could have enjoyed. The Cambridge Master of Arts was able to translate Ovid's *Elegies* and a book of Lucan. He lacked, however, the opportunity to acquire Shakespeare's evident knowledge of the law. He would not have had the nobleman's instincts and consistently aristocratic point of view we shall find conspicuous in Shakespeare. He would, surely, not continually have turned to the court for the setting and *dramatis personae* of his dramas or have, as a playwright, moved in its highest circles with the sure touch of second nature, which we shall again find in Shakespeare. Even less than in Bacon's case do we find a correspondence between Marlowe's background and the experience we may attribute to him and those which (on grounds I expect to establish) we shall deduce to have been Shakespeare's from his plays and poems. In other words, the reasons for dissatisfaction with Shakspere as a candidate apply with only somewhat less force to Marlowe. Alfred Hart observes that a distinctive characteristic of "Shakespeare's early work is the large number of allusions to insects, birds, reptiles, animals, fish, etc.," whereas "Marlowe's fauna is scanty and narrow in its range." He remarks also that Marlowe's vocabulary was limited compared to Shakespeare's and, curiously, became smaller as his plays grew longer. Moreover, Marlowe would seem to bear an additional heavy disqualification. Shakespeare's heroines are portrayed with such loving feeling and are so easy to love that to think of their creator as a homosexual is very difficult, though I recognize that the practice of casting boys in the female roles in his day could be used as an argument on the other side. In any event, Marlowe would hardly have had so obsessive an affair with the dark lady of the *Sonnets* — and that she could actually have been a male I cannot believe. The *Sonnets* pose another obstacle to his candidacy. When they were being written the author was avowedly in his declining years. Marlowe was in his early thirties, Shakspere likewise, and Bacon was only three years older than they.

If we find, as I believe we shall, that the writing of Shakespeare's early plays goes back to a time before Shakspere could have managed it, then the case for Marlowe must fail on these grounds too. Here I may say that if Shakespeare and Marlowe were different persons, as I am satisfied they were, it is much easier for me to believe that the lesser writer took from the greater than the other way around. In short, I believe that Shakespeare was an older man and came first. If so, then of course Swinburne's eulogy of Marlowe as the innovator should go to him. As the percipient Coleridge declared, Shakespeare's "language is entirely his own, and the younger dramatists imitated him." His "blank verse is an absolutely new creation." Samuel Johnson is equally emphatic on Shakespeare's priority:

> He found the English stage in a state of utmost rudeness; no essays either in
> tragedy or comedy had appeared, from which it could be discovered to what

degree of delight either one or the other might be carried. Neither character nor dialogue were yet understood. Shakespeare may be truly said to have introduced them both among us.

William Stanley, Earl of Derby, as Shakespeare

Dating the plays earlier would also eliminate the one remaining candidate for the authorship of Shakespeare's works among those who in my judgment have deserved to be taken seriously yet do not meet the requirements. William Stanley, 6th Earl of Derby, was born in 1561, the same year as Bacon, and lived long enough to have been responsible for the revisions in the plays made after Shakspere's death. Indeed, as the close relative by marriage of the man I am satisfied *was* Shakespeare, he did, I suspect, make them, in accordance with what was in the author's papers. But to have been the author himself, he lived too long — past 1623, when the editors of the First Folio stated that the author was dead, and until 1642. I find it impossible to believe of Derby as of Shakspere that the author of supreme literary treasures would at the height and in the full exercise of his powers have thrown down his pen never to take it up again in the ensuing years for so much as a line of literary endeavor. History affords no example of such an abandonment of a talent that would have been admired and envied by every cultivated person it touched.[3]

The idea of Derby as Shakespeare was one of those that come in a flash. It sprang from a report of 30 June 1599 by a Jesuit agent in England to two of his correspondents on the Continent that the Earl was unlikely to be available to take part in a plot against the Queen, being "busy in penning comedies for the common players." The letters were intercepted by agents of the Privy Council, whence they made their way into state papers. There they were discovered by a British archivist, James Greenstreet, who wrote a series of articles in *The Genealogist* in 1891 and 1892 proposing Derby as Shakespeare. The case was of course based not just on the Earl's reported play-writing activities; Derby was, as many have felt that the man who was Shakespeare had to be, a nobleman trained in the law — at the Inns of Court — practiced in the aristocratic sports, widely traveled on the continent, and having a close connection with the theatre: his older brother, the 5th Earl, was Lord Strange, eulogized by Edmund Spenser as Amyntas, whose company of players was at one time among the best known in England. Greenstreet died soon after the articles were published. Though his theory was revived in 1915 by Robert Frazer, an American, in *The Silent Shakespeare*,

---

[3] Critics may point out that Arthur Rimbaud, early in his wildly assorted existences, wrote a volume of original and sensational poetry — at fifteen, indeed, in 1871 — and never wrote anything after nineteen, but the case is hardly parallel.

and later was supported in three books by the Dean of the Faculty of Science at the University of Liverpool, A. W. Titherley, the major literature it has inspired has been European. French, Swiss, Belgian, and Dutch writers have contributed to it. The most eminent was Abel Lefranc of the Collège de France, one of forty members of the Académie des Inscriptions et Belles Lettres and his country's foremost scholar on the French Renaissance and Rabelais.

Born in 1863, Professor Lefranc had his attention drawn to the Shakespeare problem in boyhood by a schoolmaster. His literary researches led him to the view, according to a colleague, Professor Georges Lambin, that "no literary work can be rightly and fully appreciated unless the greatest attention be paid to its human surroundings: social, political, geographical"; and that "These create indissoluble links between a writer and his production." He found, however, that "between the works of William Shakespeare, the dramatist, and the life of William Shakespeare, the actor, no such links could be detected." His quest for an author who *was* linked to the works by their human surroundings led him to Derby. Beginning with *Sous le masque de Shakespeare* in 1918, he advocated and defended Derby's title to them in four massive volumes, the last two in 1946 and 1950. Although by far the majority of non-Stratfordians today believe he was on the wrong track, though not by much, they would also credit him with a most valuable contribution in establishing Shakespeare's detailed knowledge of things French, with which Derby was exceptionally well acquainted. It was his conversance with continental languages, cultures, and customs, corresponding with what seemed to be Shakespeare's, that made him a favorite of Europeans.

Lefranc's work was capped by Georges Lambin's *Voyages de Shakespeare en France et en Italie,* dedicated to Lefranc, of which I am indebted for my knowledge to John Russell of the Shakespeare Authorship Society. Sir John writes of the book that in it is

> overwhelming evidence that the Plays were written by a man who knew his Italy, his France, and the intimacies and intricacies of French politics personally and well. This claim is not based on a few, a dozen, or a hundred statements of fact, but upon a myriad, all pointing away from the Man of Stratford to a cultured, travelled gentleman, almost certainly of the highest grade in the aristocracy.

Among the myriad examples, take one from *All's Well That Ends Well*:

> This rather unpleasant play is, of course, set largely in France, Roussillon, Paris, Marseilles, with a visit to Florence. It has always been assumed that Roussillon must be that province at the foot of the Pyrenees. Insoluble problems of geography and history could only be solved by siting Roussillon in another Erewhon. Our author fortuitously and fortunately found the real Roussillon, a little Château in the valley of the Rhone, near Tournon, and dear to the Kings of France. This Roussillon makes sense of an entirely gratuitous and unnecessary

passage in Act V iii. 130 in which Helena is said to have come from Marseilles to Roussillon "in four or five moves." Nonsense if Roussillon was by the Pyrenees, but, oddly enough, correct in fact, for from Marseilles to Roussillon there were in fact four stages — Lançon, Avignon, Montelimar, Valence.

In the 1570s (the time with which we are going to deal), the château was occupied by the Dowager Countess of Roussillon, mother of Hélène of Tournon, who died tragically for love of a young nobleman in 1577; one thinks of Helena of Roussillon in *All's Well*.

Then there is *Measure for Measure*. Though it is laid by Shakespeare in Vienna, the historical background is straight from real life in Paris, according to Mr. Lambin, who points out that of the persons involved in the actual events, Claude Tonard became Claudio in the play, Angenoust became Angelo, de Vaux became Varrius, Saint-Luc Lucio, Bernardio Bernadine, and so on.

Professor Lefranc's eminence as a literary scholar did not preserve him from the obloquy habitually visited upon dissenters from Shakespearean orthodoxy. "An eminent critic, writing in a well-known English newspaper," his colleague recalls, "felt no shame in proclaiming, as an irrefutable argument, that Lefranc's astounding results were no more than 'an old man's dotage'" — and not much care for facts, either, since those results were thirty-two years in the accumulation. Criticism took a more concrete form, too: "A wealthy but extravagant Stratfordian devotee went so far as to buy as many copies as could still be procured of Lefranc's Shakespearean statements and had them burnt up as heretical!"

He would probably have done better, had it not been too late, to buy up and destroy all the copies he could lay hands on of a 523-page critique of the Stratford case that had appeared in 1908, ten years before Professor Lefranc had entered the lists. This was *The Shakespeare Problem Restated*, the first of Sir George Greenwood's works on the authorship.

Greenwood was born in 1850. He had gone to Eton and to Trinity College, where he took his degree with first-class honors in classical "tripos." Called to the Bar by the Middle Temple three years later, he was elected to Parliament in 1906 and would serve there until forced by rheumatism to retire in 1918. In his obituary in 1928, the *Sunday Times* would recall "his enthusiasm in the constant controversy over the authorship of the Shakespeare plays." His contribution won praise by the press for what the *Nation* called "a wide and close study, a critical temper, and a general mastery of the subject." Of *The Shakespeare Problem Restated*, it said that "we doubt whether the case has ever been stated more persuasively or with greater force." To *The Academy* "it is a pretty strong case of course; it always was." The reviewer for the *Daily News* confessed, "Let the biographers begin by confuting Mr. Greenwood. I cannot," while *The Bookman* admitted that "having entered the book in a spirit of sanctimonious orthodoxy, we have emerged from it sick and sore at heart, our deepest convictions bleeding and battered."

Greenwood never said who he thought had written as Shakespeare, but we shall see that it is pretty clear where he came out in the end on the question.

The Last and Most Convincing Shakespeare

The Earl of Derby was not the only Elizabethan nobleman who had made the Continent his province after mastering the law at one of the Inns of Court. He had married the daughter of another only eleven years his senior who shared his addiction to the theatre. That the latter has been widely recognized as Shakespeare was the work initially of a master in an elementary school in County Durham, John Thomas Looney. (An "unfortunate name," it was called in an article on the authorship in *Life,* but an honorable one on the Isle of Man, where it is pronounced "Loney.") Born in 1870, Looney was to make a wholly new contest of the Shakespearean controversy. He is described by a friend, Professor V. A. Demant, Canon of Christ Church, Oxford, as a person of broad philosophical, religious, and literary interests, well read in the whole range of English poetry, drawn to writers like Carlyle, Emerson, John Stuart Mill, and Herbert Spencer, at home with Homer and Dante. "I would describe Looney as a sage," the Reverend Dr. Demant writes.

> You would never know from his general conversation that he was producing a shattering contribution to the authorship question. . . . He had dropped hints to me towards the end of the 1914–18 war, that the Stratfordian authorship was impossible to hold, and that he was setting about deliberately to find, if possible, the true author. This was all the result of a conviction borne upon his mind after years of teaching Shakespearean plays to schoolboys, some of them over and over again.[4]

Looney did what no one had done before. He approached the quest for the author systematically, and with a completely open mind. "We must," he wrote, "free the problem from illogical intanglements and miraculous assumptions, and look for scientific relationship between cause and effect." As far as the evidence allowed, he proceeded as a police inspector would in tackling a mysterious crime. "The common-sense method," he wrote, "is simply to examine closely the work itself, to draw from the examination as definite a conception as possible of the man who did it, to form some idea of where he would be likely to be found, and then to go and look for a man who answers to the supposed description." He deduced seventeen character-

[4] A far more extensive account of Mr. Looney, much of it in his own words, may be found in "Discoverer of the True Shakespeare Passes," *Shake. Fellow. Quar.,* Vol. V, no. 2 (April 1944), 17–23, another not quite so full by R. L. Miller in Looney, 3rd ed., I, 648–654.

istics of the author and then set out to comb through the annals of the Elizabethan age to see who would come closest to possessing them. That any one man would meet with all the specifications — which I shall detail later — might have seemed unlikely. Yet if Shakespeare's characteristics had been correctly identified, then one man should exhibit them without exception. The possibility will occur to the reader that although one man should possess all these characteristics, too little might be known about him for them to be recognized in him. Looney deduced, however, from the convincing way in which "kings and queens, earls and countesses, knights and ladies move on and off his stage 'as to the manner born'" that the man who was Shakespeare would have "high social rank, and even a close proximity to royalty itself," and further that "the greatness of his powers" could not have remained undetected by others, though the obscurity cloaking their exercise would have given him the appearance of "wasted genius." In other words, the characteristics of the unknown individual made it inevitable that he would be of some prominence.

The quest succeeded. The man Looney found met all seventeen requirements. In 1920, the schoolmaster made his report in a book entitled *"Shakespeare" Identified*. Inside the cover the title was given in full: *"Shakespeare Identified as Edward de Vere, the Seventeenth Earl of Oxford*. Gelett Burgess, novelist and short-story writer, said what I think no one could dispute: "Once having read this book, I doubt if anyone, friend or foe, will ever forget it." John Galsworthy, lawyer as well as novelist, called it "the best detective story I have ever read" and gave many copies to friends. Sigmund Freud was deeply impressed. "The man of Stratford . . . seems to have nothing at all to justify his claim, whereas Oxford has almost everything," he declared, and wrote to the author of the "remarkable book . . . confessing myself to be a follower of yours." Writing in *The Bookman*, to which the leading literary figures of the day contributed, Edwin Björkman took as his point of departure in a five-page review that

> generations of scholars have striven stubbornly to fit the works [of Shakespeare] into the Procrustean bed furnished by the miserable store of available biographical and chronological facts.

By contrast, he wrote,

> It is impossible in an article like this to do justice to the wealth of evidence collected by Mr. Looney or to the ingenuity displayed by him in its coordination. Perhaps the most remarkable aspect of his labors is that they affect not only the central problem of William Shakespeare's relation to the work named after him, but a whole series of literary enigmas that have puzzled every painstaking student of the period for nearly two hundred years. The peculiar thing is that all these problems seem to fall into place and form a consistent picture the moment you accept the theory of Oxford's connection with the Shakespearean plays.

When an American edition was published after the plates were destroyed in the bombing of London, the *Library Journal,* defying academia, announced that because "many small libraries did not purchase in 1920" and "circulating and many reference copies have long since worn out" it was "particularly fortunate" to have this "great contribution to Shakespearean authorship . . . restored to the active lists." In the introduction to the new edition, William McFee, the Anglo-American novelist and essayist, wrote:

> There is nothing sensational in Looney's methods of presentation, nothing smacking of the Sunday supplement. It resembles in general tenor *The Origin of Species.* In my opinion, after several readings, *"Shakespeare" Identified* is destined to occupy in modern Shakespeare studies the place Darwin's great work occupies in evolutionary theory. . . . All modern discussion of the plays and poems will stem from it, and owe the author an inestimable debt.

In *The New Yorker* for 8 April 1950, Hamilton Basso, reviewing Stratfordian biographies of "Shakespeare" by William Bliss, Ivor Brown, Marchette Chute, Duff Cooper, and Hesketh Pearson, wrote:

> The one thing they have in common — besides their preoccupation with the same subject — is the making of bricks without much straw. . . . As a brickmaker, Pearson seems to come out ahead of anybody else. . . . Bliss sensibly points out the facts about his subject can be written on a half sheet of notepaper. . . . Brown has drawn too many sweeping conclusions from too little evidence. . . . Let us take Miss Chute at her foreword. . . . She has based her book entirely, she says, "on contemporary documents. . . . The confusion that surrounds Shakespeare's life has not been caused by any lack of information." Having [been] made so large a promise, . . . we can only wait for Miss Chute to stand and deliver, . . . but she doesn't. She, too, is hamstrung by a paucity of source materials. . . . She has two ways of overcoming the difficulty, by making one flat unproved statement after another, and by using "if" and "probable." . . .
>
> At this point I think we had better let Mr. Looney take the stand. . . . His contention, put forward in nearly five hundred sober, modest, heavily documented pages is . . . that Shakespeare was not the Shakespeare that Mr. Bliss, Mr. Cooper, Mr. Brown, Mr. Pearson, and Miss Chute take for granted. . . . Mr. Looney is no crank. He is an earnest level-headed man who has spent years trying to solve the world's most baffling literary mystery. . . . If the case were brought to court, it is hard to see how Mr. Looney could lose. . . . The various mysteries that surround Shakespeare . . . are mysteries no longer if the man we know as Shakespeare was really Edward de Vere.

"Shakespeare" Identified and the impression it made led to formation of the Shakespeare Fellowship, later the Shakespeare Authorship Society, in London in 1922 and the Shakespeare Fellowship in New York in 1939 to encourage and publish the results of research in the field that had been opened up. The English society was delighted to welcome as members two of the most distinguished anti-Stratfordians, Sir George Greenwood, who became its first president, and Professor Abel Lefranc (an exchange professor at Harvard and the University of Chicago during the Society's early years).

The portrait of Edward de Vere that took form in *"Shakespeare" Identified* was immensely enhanced by the work of Captain (in the British Army) Bernard M. Ward, who, in quest of information on the subject, spent five years searching documents in the British Museum, the Public Records Office, and the Bodleian Library, together with the collection of manuscripts at Hatfield House and the Lansdowne, Harleian, Rawlinson, and other private repositories. The fruit of this labor was published in 1928 in *The Seventeenth Earl of Oxford,* a biography of 400 pages, including appendices. Others whose scholarly work advanced and expanded on Looney's discoveries in those early years were Canon Gerald H. Rendall and Percy Allen in England[5] and, in the United States, Louis P. Bénézet of Dartmouth College, Charles Wisner Barrell, and Eva Turner Clark, whose *Hidden Allusions in Shakespeare's Plays* strengthened the case for Oxford with abundant evidence that the plays had been written well before the dates assigned by Stratfordian scholars.[6]

Although Calvin Hoffman's book stirred considerable public interest in Marlowe as Shakespeare in 1955, Looney's investigations and those of his followers have narrowed the field of the controversy to two primary candidates for Shakespeare's honors. Both, I might add, had homes on the River Avon. When, in 1959, the *American Bar Association Journal* ran the article by Richard Bentley from which I have quoted, entitled *Elizabethan Whodunit: Who Was "William Shakespeare?"* the dubiety Mr. Bentley expressed about Marlowe and Bacon, as well as Shakspere, quickly brought very competent replies from their supporters, and these also were printed. Altogether ten articles *pro* and *contra* Oxford (whom Mr. Bentley clearly favored), Shakspere, Marlowe, and Bacon were published in the magazine and later collected in a book, which by 1978 had sold about 9,000 copies without appearing in a bookshop or being advertised outside the *Journal.* An article in *Life* for 23 April 1964, entitled "History's Biggest Literary Whodunit," by Dora Jane Hamblin, gives principal attention to the four candidates considered in the *A.B.A. Journal* but makes passing mention also of the 6th Earl of Derby, the 5th Earl of Rutland, the 2nd Earl of Essex, and Sir Walter Raleigh. I believe it fair to say, however, that the contest is now mainly between supporters of Shakspere and those of Oxford, who, as the most

[5] Sadly, after contributing greatly to the field, Percy Allen suffered the mental debility that sometimes comes with advanced old age and wrote about séances in which the spirits of those purportedly involved in the authorship had speaking parts. Samuel Schoenbaum seized upon these vagaries with glee in his *Shakespeare's Lives,* having nothing to say about the years of valuable work Allen had done.

[6] I am glad to say that Looney's *"Shakespeare" Identified,* expanded with additional material in two lavishly illustrated volumes, and Clark's *Hidden Allusions,* both edited by Ruth Loyd Miller, were republished in 1974–75 by the Kennikat Press of Port Washington, N.Y. It is encouraging, too, that Greenwood's *The Shakespeare Problem Restated,* has also been republished, by Greenwood Press of Westport, Conn.

recent edition of the *Encyclopaedia Britannica* (1975), says, "became, in the 20th century, the strongest candidate proposed (next to Shakespeare [*sic*] himself) for the authorship of Shakespeare's plays." I have in mind the numbers in each camp and the amount of their research and of their publications.

Others proposed are heard of today most often in writings by Stratfordians, who make an important point about the variety of candidates who at one time or another have been put forward, especially of those exceedingly unlikely ones who have attracted eccentrics. Thus McManaway in his Folger booklet tells us that those who believe "the plays must have been written by a learned man, an intimate of the court, who had traveled extensively" have asked themselves "Who had these qualifications?" and proposed various persons "until twenty or more rivals were in the field, including Queen Elizabeth I and Anne Hathaway." And we should certainly have to agree with McManaway that anyone who considered Anne Hathaway a learned man, an intimate of the Court, who had traveled extensively, would be an odd sort of person, not to be taken very seriously, though not much odder than one who thought the Queen an extensively-travelled man. Gwynne Evans and Harry Levin of Harvard present the argument habitually urged by orthodox academicians in declaring: "The fact that the anti-Stratfordians seldom agree on a rival candidate is itself an argument in favor of the incumbent." ("Seldom agree? Does that mean that they sometimes agree on a rival candidate?) This is like saying that disagreement among scientists on the origin of the universe is an argument favoring the tradition that it sprang into being by divine *fiat* in 4000-odd B.C.

The truth is certainly that a number of possible Shakespeares have been put forward by persons each persuaded that his choice had the superior qualifications, among them Shakspere of Stratford. Equally, to account for Shakespeare's apparent first-hand acquaintance with various spheres of knowledge, a number of Shaksperes have been put forward by Stratfordians, each living a different life during the so-called lost years of Shakspere's young manhood. One young Will is a schoolmaster, another is engaged in the home of a great lord, a third travels to Italy in a nobleman's retinue, a fourth is employed in an attorney's office, a fifth sails before the mast with Raleigh, a sixth enlists in a regiment bound for combat in the Low Countries. We might make a sounder application of the Evans-Levin principle: That the Stratfordians cannot agree on one Shakspere to account for Shakespeare's range of knowledge is itself an argument for rejecting all the different and irreconcilable Shaksperes.

On one point every participant in the controversy is of a single mind and heart: it is of the greatest importance who Shakespeare was. Let the objection be repeated no matter how often that his identity is immaterial, or, as the

Wall Street Journal put it, "We think it really doesn't matter if de Vere or Shakespeare [*sic*] wrote those works. The short and the long of it is that someone wrote them and they are here, chronicles in immortal language to ease the winter of our discontent, to make more pleasant this existence swift as a shadow, short as any dream though it may be." Our answer is that those to whom the identity of the author doesn't matter are those to whom the works don't matter — very much. Ivor Brown, the noted orthodox biographer, spoke for all when he found

> the assertion made by neutrals [that] the author's identity is of no importance . . . an astonishing attitude. The man who wrote the greatest poetry in the English language and the plays which many think the finest in the history of the world's theatre deserves more than a shoulder-shrugging indifference about his name. Furthermore, a detective story has its own excitement and, if there is indeed a Shakespeare Mystery, one must be singularly lacking in curiosity to remain thus aloof and unconcerned at its presence.

He might have added that if it makes no difference who Shakespeare was, all literary biography is pointless.

The controversy over the authorship, Dora Jane Hamblin wrote for *Life*'s seven million subscribers,

> sends each new generation back to Shakespeare to try to find, like any other whodunit reader, the truth within those wonderful words. It also refutes the stupid question, "What does it matter who wrote Shakespeare?" It matters a lot. Whoever wrote the finest words in the English language should be revered in the pantheon of humanity.

It matters, too, if we would know what the plays tell us and what we might learn from them about the nature and process of artistic creation.

10

"To Defend the City from the Rebels"

Readers brought up in accordance with academic proprieties may be in for some surprises. First is the extent of scholarly and popular disbelief in Shakspere of Stratford as Shakespeare indicated by statistics. Next is the eminence of many outspoken dissenters, who include three of the most highly regarded American writers. Finally, we face the vindictiveness of the orthodox Shakespearean establishment's response to anyone questioning the conventional Shakespeare's credentials, which is likely to take any reader aback who is not already acquainted with academia's reaction when its dogma is challenged. As we see, however, not only the academicians have an investment in the Shakespearean status quo, professional and psychological in their case. Most interested writers and critics, and both liberals and conservatives, we observe, have an ideological investment in it, while the Shakespeare industry brings the town of Stratford millions of pounds a year. On the other hand, those who believe that the determining voice in the Shakespeare controversy, as in any other, should be that of evidence and logic may be encouraged to know how these finally prevailed in the quite parallel fifty-year scientific controversy over whether the continents are fixed or moving, to open new and exciting reaches in the study of the earth and a new comprehension of the planet's vitality.

In the 1940s, according to Samuel Schoenbaum, Joseph S. Galland of Northwestern University compiled a bibliography of dissent from the conventional attribution of Shakespeare's works. It came to six volumes in typescript and included 4,509 items, many of them hundreds of pages long — and that was thirty years ago; how greatly the list would be extended if brought up to date is anybody's guess.

The figures attest the extraordinary proportions of the objection to Shakespearean orthodoxy. It is a matter not only of quantity, moreover, but also of quality. Among the eminent men who have regarded the Stratford man with skepticism, at the least, have been: Lord Palmerston, Prime Minister during the American Civil War (who included among the three things he "rejoiced to have lived to see . . . the explosion of the Shakespearean illusion"); Walt Whitman ("I am firm against Shaksper — I mean the Avon man, the actor"); John Greenleaf Whittier ("Whether Bacon wrote the wonderful plays or not, I am quite sure the man Shakspere neither did nor could"); Henry James ("I am 'sort of' haunted by the conviction that the divine William is the biggest and most successful fraud ever practised on a patient world"); W. H. Furness, eminent American scholar and father of the editor of the *Variorum* ("I am one of the many who have never been able to bring the life of William Shakespeare [i.e., Shakspere] and the plays of Shakespeare within planetary space of each other"); Prince Otto von Bismarck (sēe page 260); Mark Twain ("I am the Brontosaurian" who "doesn't really know which of them did it [wrote Shakespeare's works], but is quite composedly and contendedly sure that Shakespeare [i.e., Shakspere] *didn't*"); John Bright, British statesman and Lord Rector of the University of Glasgow ("Any man who believes that William Shakespeare of Stratford wrote *Hamlet* or *Lear* is a fool"); John Galsworthy and Sigmund Freud, as we have seen; Charles Chaplin ("I'm not concerned with who wrote the works of Shakespeare, . . . but I hardly think it was the Stratford boy"); John Buchan, Lord Tweedsmuir, historian, poet and novelist, lawyer, M.P. for the Scottish Universities and Chancellor of Edinburgh University; Peter Sammartino, Chancellor of Fairleigh Dickinson University and Director of the New York City Cultural Center; W. Barton Leach, Story Professor of Law at Harvard; J. Enoch Powell, Craven Scholar, First Chancellor's Classical Medalist, Porson Prizeman, and Browne Medalist at Trinity College, Cambridge, Fellow of Trinity College, author of works on Herodotus, and currently Member of Parliament; and, it would seem, Benjamin Disraeli and Charles de Gaulle.

The disaffection from the approved assignment of Shakespeare's works, in its extent and vigor, stands altogether alone in the history of the arts. There have, to be sure, been disputed attributions of other artistic masterpieces, but never directed at the total corpus of a man's work of such transcendent importance, about the origin of which it seems that there should be so little reason for uncertainty. You would think that where so many responsible persons have been opposed to a conventional view, the old adage "Where there is smoke there must be fire" would be accepted as applying; only consider what huge persistent billows have arisen from this conflagration! You would think, in other words, that the dissenters from Shakespearean orthodoxy would be given the benefit of an acknowledgement that there must be *some* grounds for their misgivings, even if insufficient grounds. But no. If orthodox Shakespearean authorities have ever conceded that there could be any basis, however slight, for the least uneasiness about their attribution of Shakespeare's works, I have yet to hear of it.

Speaking about the 4,509 anti-Stratfordian articles and books listed by Professor Galland, Schoenbaum, then also of Northwestern University, said, "The voluminousness of output is matched only by its intrinsic worthlessness." Devoting 100 pages of his *Shakespeare's Lives* (1970) to denigration of this literature (by methods of which I shall have something to say later), Schoenbaum could not find in it one point having the slightest validity. He can only "lament on the necessity of having to make his way through thousands of pages of rubbish, some of it lunatic rubbish." What assurance of one's rectitude it must take to dismiss as intrinsically worthless, if not lunatic rubbish, the literary judgments of three of the leading American writers of all time!

Now, the insistence of the Stratfordian academics that the dissenters' views are devoid of the least merit or justification, unworthy of the smallest consideration, is bound to be met with raised eyebrows by anyone aware of the number and respectability of the dissenters. This would therefore appear to be a risky line for them to take, for an argument that cannot bear scrutiny is likely to recoil upon the polemicist, arousing the very suspicions it was intended to allay. Sound cases do not require unsound defenses or benefit from them. The Stratfordian academics are not stupid, for the most part; Samuel Schoenbaum is uncommonly smart. Yet they cleave to a policy of total denunciation of dissent and dissenters. Why? I stand to be corrected, but the only answer I can give is that they assess the risks of any other course to be greater. In this view, they feel, consciously or unconsciously, that their case depends absolutely upon absolute acceptance: give admittance to the tiniest doubt, and doubt, proceeding from one element of incongruity and implausibility in the structure to another and growing by what it feeds on, must speedily consume the whole. Only on this premise — that in their hearts they fear that the Stratford faith must be unblinkingly swallowed whole if it is to be swallowed at all — can I explain to myself the contumely heaped upon those who hesitate over the dish.

We may recall how as far back as 1802, James Cowell was repudiated as an apostate when confessing to doubts about the Faith, as he put it. In 1895, the illustrious Danish critic Georg Brandes declared that the "great name" of Shakespeare had been "besmirched by American and European imbecility." Of "the theory that Shakespeare did not write the plays," he thundered that "we cannot but find it unrivalled in its ineptitude," the product of "a troop of less than half-educated people." "Literary criticism," which, he protested, "must be handled carefully and only by those who have a vocation for it," had "fallen into the hands of raw Americans and fanatical women." In 1901, Sir Sidney Lee of the University of London, Chairman of the Shakespeare Birthplace Trust and the most noted Shakespearean biographer of his time, called the Baconian theory a "foolish craze," "morbid psychology," and "madhouse chatter," its proponents victims of "epidemic disease" who were "unworthy of serious attention from any but professed students of intellectual aberration." From then on such excoriations were to be routine.

Sir George Greenwood, who quotes Lee's fulminations (and asks "Why so warm, Sir Fretful?") cites also the case of Bellyse Baildon, who in the Arden Edition of Shakespeare observes:

I have never seen it remarked, though the fact seems obvious enough, that the skepticism with regard to Shakespeare's authorship . . . is part of that general skeptical movement or wave which has landed us first in the so-called "Higher Criticism" in matters of Religion and finally in Agnosticism itself. . . . Surely the world might by this time accept Kant's great proof of the futility of Pure Reason! . . . The position of the man who declines to believe that the Stratford Shakespeare wrote the works attributed to him is precisely the same as that of Hume on "Miracles."

It is no part of my purpose to second David Hume in his skeptical regard for miracles; let who will, accept them. The anti-Stratfordians hold only that an explanation for a phenomenon that relies on the miraculous ought to be rejected where a rational explanation is available. This is what puts them at odds with orthodoxy, as represented by the Folger Library, under whose imprimatur we are assured that Shakespeare did not need to have been in foreign lands of which he writes familiarly because "The truth of the matter is that poetic genius overleaps both space and time." Shakspere, we are to believe — and Shakspere alone of all mortals, it would seem — had this magic power. Maybe so. But if the content and character of Shakespeare's works can be accounted for without resort to the supernatural, by identifying as Shakespeare an author whose experience in all respects fitted him for the role, one might be forgiven for favoring this alternative.

But not by orthodoxy. Those who look elsewhere than to Stratford for the author, Louis B. Wright declared as Director of the Folger Library, are "disciples of cults" that "have all the fervor of religion," prey to "emotion that sweeps aside the intellectual appraisal of facts, chronology and the laws of evidence." They are "fanatic sectarians" who "rail on disbelievers and condemn other cultists as fools and knaves," and "who welcome a new convert to their beliefs with the enthusiasm accorded a repentant sinner at a Holy Rollers' revival," while "a fog of gloom envelops them." They have developed a "neurosis . . . that may account for an unhappy truculence that sometimes makes them unwelcome in polite company." Indeed, "one gets the impression that they would gladly restore the faggot and the stake for infidels from their particular orthodoxy."

I thought when I read Dr. Wright's animadversions that they were unlikely to be excelled for forcefulness. I believe, however, that William M. Murphy of Union College may have gone Dr. Wright one better. Disbelievers in the conventional Shakespeare, Professor Murphy writes in the college quarterly, are "the Jack Rubys of literary history," who, "translated from the world of biography into the world of politics, . . . become the John Birchers of our day." They engage in an "outpouring of verbal vitriol" characterized by a "richness of dementia." They may be known by their "unconscious self-identification . . . with the heroic or the divine" and their "intense hatred of other heretics and their false gods." In their "inability to keep their aberrations within bounds" they are "like those unfortunate beings in mental institutions who think they are Napoleon or Jesus Christ," except that this "paranoid" type, "with instinctive shrewdness, knows he will be carted off to the booby-hatch if he claims to be George Washington or the Angel Gabriel." Professor Murphy, like Dr. Wright, does not cite examples of his adversaries' intemperate behavior so that we might know who the offenders are. We owe to the professor, I might add, the information that "anti-Stratfordians hate Shakespeare" and the injunction to "Imagine the damage they might cause if they were involved in real life."

Instructive in itself, Professor Murphy's exegesis had an even more enlightening aftermath. Its author having, to strengthen his case, resorted to glaring misquotations of a prominent book dissenting from Shakespearean orthodoxy (to which I shall revert), these were called to the attention of the Union College authorities along with the article's slanderous character as a whole and, I may say, vigorously protested — by me. In his reply, the Provost and Dean of the Faculty of Union College, Theodore D. Lockwood (since 1968 President of Trinity College, Hartford), wrote that "We do not share the view implicit in much of your comment that the College should cast itself in the role of determiner of 'right' and 'wrong' or 'truth' and 'error.'"

The public that supports the educational establishment on the most generous scale must find it surprising that an institution of higher learning, on the word of the dean at a respected college established in 1795, is not in the business of discriminating between right and wrong, truth and error. The public has been under the impression that making such discriminations, rather than promoting and standing by demonstrable falsehood, is just what education is supposed to do. It must be further enlightening that Dr. Lockwood (author of *Our Mutual Concern: The Role of the Independent College*), puts "right" and "wrong" and "truth" and "error" in quotation marks, as if these were arbitrary conceptions to which the College is superior. This is a point of view to bear in mind as we consider pronouncements by academia on the Shakespeare authorship.[1] Parenthetically, it would seem that "the

---

[1] President Lockwood tells me that "What my remarks were meant to convey, as I think you realized, is the widely held position that a college does not determine the truth *per se* and officially enshrine it. . . . I was clearly using the quotation marks around right and wrong, truth and error, to lend them emphasis, not to suggest that they are arbitrary conceptions to which the college is superior." He adds that "one of the functions of a college" — a position of which "I think you are totally aware" — "is to encourage inquiry into the truth without presuming in advance that it knows the truth in every instance and thus close down the search for better explanations." I was reminded of this exemplary statement less than a month later by a dispatch in the *Washington Post* of 25 May 1981 reporting that when Jeane Kirkpatrick, the United States Ambassador to the United Nations,

> spoke to students at the University of Pittsburgh last month, 45 students turned their backs to her in protest of Reagan administration policy in El Salvador and South Africa. On April 16 the ambassador withdrew her acceptance of an invitation to address graduates at Trinity College here after similar opposition was voiced by students and faculty.

One hopes that President Lockwood may make his faculty as totally aware of the college's position as he is sure I am.

College" does not set itself up as a discriminator between "sense" and "nonsense," either. Professor Murphy puts in the mouths of his opponents the argument that the Stratfordian could not have written the plays of Shakespeare because his character as he reveals it in the autobiographical *Sonnets* is too debased.[2] That the Stratfordian, if he did not write the plays, did not write the *Sonnets* either was not a consideration that bothered the professor, the editor of *Symposium*, or the dean of the college. In defending academic dogma from heresy — and now we have come to what the College *does* set itself up to do — you do not scruple over-nicely in the choice of weapons.

"One is invariably impressed," Day Thorpe wrote as literary editor of the *Washington Star* "that the anti-Stratfordians always arouse the establishment to blind, hysterical fury." It may occur to the reader that such a response to challenge hardly connotes great confidence in one's position. However that may be, the thought will introduce a question that must have been in the reader's mind from the start: how, unless the case for the Stratford man is a solid one, is it to be explained that he seems so generally accepted as the author? That question is to me almost as fascinating as the question of who Shakespeare was. Let me see what answer I can make to it.

That it could possibly be believed that "anyone has a vested interest in William Shakespeare [i.e., Shakspere] is," to Louis B. Wright "a mystery that passeth understanding. Aside from a few curio vendors at Stratford-upon-Avon, who might have to alter their stock a bit, nobody has any vested interest in maintaining Shakespeare's superiority simply out of deference to William." Of course no one questions Shakespeare's superiority; the question is who Shakespeare was. But let that pass. Let us simply recognize that Stratford-on-Avon is the biggest tourist attraction in Britain after London. According to the *Daily Mirror* in 1969, foreign visitors to the town alone amounted to 400,000 a year and they left almost £3,500,000 — then about $10,000,000 — in the hands of those "few curio vendors." British visitors, surely outnumbering the foreign, must have added at least another $10,000,000 — and the figures cannot have been much less in 1964, when Dr. Wright's *Shakespeare for Everyman* was published.[3] Presumably Dr. Wright would consider an investment producing $20,000,000 per annum not negligible; but then he believes, or would have us believe, that it would

---

[2] Murphy says: "He reveals in the *Sonnets* — which are autobiographical, of course — that he had latent homosexual tendencies and that he carried on a protracted and degrading adulterous affair with a repulsive dark-skinned lady who probably gave him a loathsome disease. In short, Shakespeare didn't write the plays because we don't know enough about him — or because we know too much. The layman takes his choice."

[3] According to the Heart of England Tourist Board, "Stratford attracted around 1.5 million visitors in 1975. Total spending by tourists in Stratford during 1975 is estimated to be in the order of £10 million."

not be imperiled by unseating the Stratford Shakspere from Shakespeare's place. As an attraction for "Britons and Americans, who both appreciate a skilful hoax," says Dr. Wright, "Stratford's business might even improve with notoriety."

Let us move from Dr. Wright to a candid assessment of Stratford's situation by Tyrone Guthrie, the distinguished theatrical producer who has put on many of Shakespeare's plays in Stratford. Writing in the *New York Times,* Sir Tyrone asks

> What if it turns out, as it just possibly might, that William Shakespeare [i.e., Shakspere] was not the author of the plays ascribed to him? There is a theory, advanced by reputable scholars seriously and, in my opinion, plausibly, that Shakespeare merely lent his name as a cover for the literary activities of another person, perhaps the Earl of Oxford. If, by some terrible chance, this theory should be proved, then . . . the Birthplace, Anne Hathaway's Cottage and New Place, where Shakespeare died in 1616, would be discredited; the Theatre would go broke and become the Jam Factory, which it already resembles; Hotels, great and small, would be going, going gone. Once more the beautiful, gray church, with its Impostor's Tomb, would dominate Birmingham's quietest dormitory.

As Doris Dawson, daughter of the proprietress of the Windmill Pub in Stratford put it, "if it's found that Shakespeare didn't write the plays everyone would flock to where the other bloke was born and we'd be finished."

To prevent the unthinkable must be a primary concern of the Shakespeare Birthplace Trust, in which Louis B. Wright was given lifetime membership, which certainly he had earned by his services to Stratford as Director of the Folger. To this end, the Trust is able to draw on an annual budget of £200,000, according to the *Daily Telegraph.* How significant a factor in the hardihood of the Stratford "Shakespeare" these hundreds of thousands of pounds, these tens of millions of dollars may be, I cannot say. I should, though, rather have that kind of money for me than against me. That goes, too, for the hundreds of thousands of dollars each that the National Endowment for the Humanities, the Andrew W. Mellon Foundation, and the Ford Foundation, and the lesser thousands that the John Simon Guggenheim and Rockefeller Foundations have contributed to agencies of the orthodox Shakespeare establishment — philanthropy for which dissidents need not apply.

Of much greater importance, I feel sure, is the professional, economic, and psychological investment in Shakespearean orthodoxy by academicians on both sides of the ocean — all those, and the critics and other literary figures, too, who have committed themselves publicly to the Stratford man. Two diabolical elements in the case make it exceedingly difficult for such authorities to divest themselves of their ties to him. First, it has always been part of orthodoxy to pour scorn on dissenters, this having seemed the most feasible way of dealing with them, and that makes it awkward to concede that they were right. Second, it is characteristic of the Stratford case that when you do not believe in it you find it not simply unlikely but preposterous. Take away the attribution of Shakespeare's works to Shakspere and nothing about him suggests the kind of man who would have written them. Indeed, without the works to his credit, his record is that of a near illiterate. It is these considerations, of which they are aware, that I think cause the Stratfordians to respond to challenge with such singular venom. Even with no such element, Joseph Alsop writes:

> In academic debates, as long experience proves, almost anything goes once both sides are deeply committed. For the side that sees its position being shot to hell by new evidence, also sees prestige, careers, position and all else being shot to hell.
>
> Here think of Heinrich Schliemann digging up Mycenae when the whole European academic world was deeply committed to the view that there was no indigenous Greek civilization in the Bronze Age. Mycenae plainly proved the very opposite. Yet the German and English professoriate bullied poor Schliemann so unmercifully that he finally agreed that Mycenae, the true citadel of Agamemnon and his forebears, was nothing but a Phoenician trading post!
>
> Where the professoriate is deeply but wrongfully committed, in other words, factual evidence of an inconvenient kind is frequently handled with total ruthlessness.

John Dos Passos was speaking from the experience of many when he wrote that "No man can meddle with the established conformities of an institution of learning and come out with a whole skin." Or, as Bernard Weisberger put it, "I am a professor myself, and I know of few groups more insular and conceited." One need only heed testimony of those who know in order to appreciate how far unwelcome facts are likely to carry in the universities where the faculties have made up their minds. Hear, especially, Andrew M. Greeley, a sociologist with the National Opinion Research Center at the University of Chicago and professor of higher education at the University of Illinois, on "academics" — a term, he explains, that "is not used to represent all, or even a majority of, college professors but rather the influential minority that sets the tone and style and the fashion of the academy at a given time." And it is the fashion that rules. Citing recent cases in which responsible thinkers have fallen afoul of the academy and tasted its intolerance to show "how little room there is in the academy for dissent," Professor Greeley goes on to observe:

> The typical academic suffers from an excess of what can only be called religious zeal. . . . [He] is serenely confident of his own judgment and thus assumes that those who dare to disagree with him are not only wrong but are either stupid or in bad faith or, quite conceivably, both. . . .
>
> The faults and failings of the Grand Inquisitor are railed against in the literature courses, but they have not by any means been exorcised from the academy. . . .
>
> For the past five years [from 1970] the academy has sat on its hands while young fascist toughs have disrupted other people's right of freedom of speech and freedom of assembly.

President Kingman Brewster of Yale drew the same comparison with those professors and students who refused to accord a visiting lecturer a hearing and hooted him from the platform: "Storm troopers," he called them.[4]

The denunciation by academicians of any deviation from orthodoxy in the attempt to account for Shakespeare's works reminds me of the scorn heaped on Alfred Wegener, the German geologist who sought to explain surface features of the earth by what he called "continental drift." It was Wegener's theory, announced in 1912, that the continents had at one time been joined, as the "fit" between South America and Africa suggested, and had split apart and migrated to their present positions. For half a century, most geologists treated proponents of the theory with ridicule or contempt, when they did not simply ignore them. An anthology of geological papers published in 1955, *The Crust of the Earth* (which was given to my daughter to study in school in 1970), does not even mention Wegener or the theory of continental movement. Instead, a contributor tells us that "Whatever the difficulties, contraction of the earth in cooling remains by far the most obvious and most likely cause of both vertical and horizontal movements of the crust. . . ." And, in language reminiscent of what we are given in authorized Shakespearean texts, we are assured that while "there are mysteries and things difficult to understand" in geology, as in other sciences, "fortunately these need not concern us greatly because most of the important facts are easily understood."

All along, however, Nigel Calder, a British physicist, tells us in *The Restless Earth,* a few geologists knew Wegener must be right. Some of the most arresting geological phenomena, such as the upthrust of great folded-mountain belts, like the Appalachians, Andes, Alps, and Himalayas, and the distribution of plants and animals could be explained only if the continents had periodically collided and separated. Finally, the evidence that they had done so had by the 1960s become so overwhelming as to breach academic resistance and win general acceptance. Yet in the United States, Calder reports, "even in the early 1960s, reputable scientists were openly laughed at for uttering what is now standard doctrine." Writing in 1972, he recalls that "as one geologist remarked to me: 'Ten years ago, you couldn't become professor at a U.S. university if you believed in continental drift.'" Lest it be thought that academic open-mindedness has been the gainer, he added wryly, "now the opposite's true."

How is it that a conception with such revolutionary consequences for geology was first clearly enunciated by a German explorer who was not even a professional geologist? Calder writes:

> Wegener was a generalist, one of those rare men who do not fear to learn and use branches of knowledge in which they are not formally trained, in order to

[4] I must point out that I wrote Dr. Brewster for confirmation of this newspaper report but never received a reply on the stamped and addressed post-card I enclosed for one.

arrive at a greater synthesis: conversely, over-specialization among Wegener's opponents blinkered their imagination.

If conformity is the rule in academia, it is met with, too, in the "Fourth Estate." Self-censorship is to be expected from a daily press that is "extremely centralized, and most of it owned by wealthy men who have every motive to be dishonest on certain topics," George Orwell wrote in a preface to *Animal Farm*. (Rejected by the publisher as if to demonstrate the validity of Orwell's thesis, the preface was finally published a few years ago in the *Times Literary Supplement* as "The Freedom of the Press" and cited by Bernard Rossiter in the *Washington Post*.) "But the awful fact is," Orwell went on, that

> the same kind of veiled censorship also operates in books and periodicals. . . . Anyone who challenges the prevailing orthodoxy finds himself silenced with surprising effectiveness. A genuinely unfashionable opinion is almost never given a fair hearing. . . . If liberty means anything at all it means the right to tell people what they do not want to hear. . . . It is the liberals who fear liberty and the intellectuals who want to do dirt on the intellect.

In his anatomy of academic intolerance, Andrew M. Greeley says that "One must certainly include the allies of the academy in the mass media who tend to feel guilty vis-à-vis the full-fledged academic who presumably knows more and is morally purer than the huckster in the media." The effectiveness the alliance has in the field of the Shakespeare authorship may be judged by its results. I know of no instance between 1937 and 1974 when a dissenter from orthodoxy was permitted to expound his case in a general-interest American periodical — magazine or newspaper. Editors, confronted with a statement on the anti-Stratford case, seem with few but notable exceptions to take the view that, however compelling the case may appear to be, the matter has been thoroughly looked into by the authorities in the universities and they appear to be of one mind that the Stratford man was the author. That settles it for them.

Finally, Shakespearean conventionalism has benefitted by the social bias in our culture. Our world is in principle a democratic one. Our popular heroes are likely to be men and women who have combatted privilege — the hereditary power of kings and aristocrats to begin with, more recently the acquired power of wealthy upper classes and economic interests. Rank does not sit well with most of us, who do not possess it. Most of us start without the advantages bestowed by means or position; and those who, armed with talent alone against heavy odds, would win the contest for recognition as wordsmiths — educators, writers, journalists, critics, editors — naturally feel sympathy for and affinity with that figure of tradition who, a poor trades- man's son, left the Warwickshire village of his nativity for London and on the strength of sheer native genius triumphed among Tudor England's no- bility, becoming the greatest wordsmith of all. That the Shakespeare of convention was a kind of theatrical journeyman, an actor who dashed off his masterpieces on order for the commercial stage, for the money they brought, and was unconcerned for their survival, only adds to his appeal to those I am speaking of; for in these attributes he represents a thumb to the nose at all superiority. The wordsmiths as a group are particularly prone to set themselves apart from the privileged interests and to deem it their function to expose and discomfit the powerful few in the cause of greater social equity; and those educators, writers, journalists, who themselves acquire the privileges, often considerable, that go with success in their field are under compulsion to stand no less firmly with the "have-nots" as against the "haves" lest it appear that they have been corrupted. It is asking a great deal of these, our intellectual arbiters, to consider the possibility that while their hearts are indubitably in the right place their minds may be in the wrong about Shakespeare and should be opened to the evidence that the deathless poems and dramas were produced not by an obscurely born, untutored provincial but by a scion of one of the noblest houses in England, albeit one who betrayed his birth under the goad of his genius and paid in heartache for its privileges. The proposition is repugnant to their conception of life. To make it more so there is the drumfire of assurances from academia that those who put it forward, the anti-Stratfordians, are motivated by snobbishness, and not only that but that they are naïve as well. This assertion comes from no less an authority than the Folger Library. "Most anti-Shakespeareans [*sic*] are naïve and betray an obvious snobbery," Louis B. Wright stated as its director; they imply that "obviously so great a writer must have had a title or some equally significant evidence of exalted social background." Most journalists, certainly, would rather be charged with embezzlement than with naïveté or snobbery.

Defense of the Shakespearean status quo brings together unaccustomed allies. Liberals, identifying themselves with the cause of the unprivileged, naturally disfavor transferring Shakespeare's title from a commoner to a lord. Conservatives do so no less because it would undermine an established verity; if the conventional identification of Shakespeare is to be questioned, what hitherto fixed reference points will be safe?

There is, and long has been, in short, an extremely potent combination ready and able to smother any dissent from Shakespearean conventionalism. Anyone who has sought to challenge it will have soon discovered how very potent it is.

How such a tacit censorship can operate so successfully in a supposedly free and intellectually tolerant society is not up to me to explain. I pretend to no expertness in these matters. All I can say is that my experience in this field and others confirms Orwell's pronouncement, that "Anyone who challenges the prevailing orthodoxy finds himself silenced with surprising effectiveness."

There would seem, however, to be no mystery in the maintenance of academic uniformity. No young instructor in a Department of English, even if his early educational conditioning does not preclude his examining objectively that which he has been taught to scoff at as the badge of his professionalism, will find his career advanced if he threatens to expose the tenets of his elders as nonsense. He will, if I may adapt a line of Kipling's *Mandalay,* be learnin' 'ere in London — and everywhere else — what the tenure soldier tells. . . . Once he has his professorship he is hardly likely to repudiate the steps by which he attained it and certainly he is not going to read himself out of his profession and bring down on his head the obloquy of his fellows, vicious as we have seen such can be.

"I don't like to have my myths tampered with," Sir Winston Churchill is said to have replied when it was proposed that he read J. Thomas Looney's *"Shakespeare" Identified.* Who, for that matter, does like to part with myths? But some myths are better sacrificed to reason for the rewards that accrue. In this case, it is a matter not only of having honor rendered where boundless honor is due in Shakespeare's works, but of having new riches revealed in those works and with them the human story behind them, which must bring them closer to us than they have ever been.

The analogy with the discoveries of Alfred Wegener holds here too. Reconsidered in the light of continental movement, geology has become a new and far more exciting and satisfying science. The necessity of accounting for the moving crustal plates now known to form the earth's surface has required postulating a force adequate to produce it, and this force — convection currents in the earth's plastic mantle resulting from the heat generated by radioactivity — is seen to give the planet life, a prodigious vitality. Just as geology itself has come into a new life as it unfolds the dramatic forces creating the earth-forms around us, so also do Shakespearean studies when, behind the masterpieces, a vital, fully human, and credible author is substituted for the vacuous Stratford "Shakespeare," whom no one has ever been able to render recognizable as a human being.

"For the first time we can now write a three-dimensional biography of William Shakespeare," Alfred Leslie Rowse of Oxford University told us in his *Shakespeare the Man* (He had persuaded himself, but few others, that he had identified the Dark Lady of the *Sonnets*) with "consequences" that were "immense," among them that he had "triumphantly vindicated" his "method." As for whether he had done any better than his predecessors, I should think most readers would agree with *Publishers Weekly:* "No flesh-and-blood figure stalks out of these rather tired pages." Rowse was on firmer ground in stating that "Shakespeare scholarship" — of the orthodox kind — "has long reached a dead end." As Calder writes of "the old geology": it "had become curiously dispirited."

II

"I Will Hereupon Confess"

Here, at the cost of putting himself unbecomingly front and center, the author thinks it well to lay his cards on the table. He explains how, while starting as an unquestioning Stratfordian, he is won over to the Oxford side by J. Thomas Looney's "Shakespeare" Identified, as are his parents and others among his friends and acquaintances and many more. He recalls his parents' ensuing experiences as participants — writers — in the controversy over the authorship and his own. He dwells in particular on the consequences following the courageous publication by the country's leading university alumni magazine of an article of his on the authorship that forces orthodox scholarship to come out of its sanctuary and show what it can do in a point-by-point response to the case for dissent beyond simply inveighing against it — though there is plenty of invective too in its reaction. (An account of what happens when the author is struck by a persuasive idea about the disposition that may have been made of the vanished Shakespearean manuscripts — an idea later set forth in Harper's Magazine — *and of academia's response to the possibility of uncovering the priceless treasure, originally incorporated in the chapter, has been relegated to an appendix as tangential to the main subject.)*

I had better explain my connection with the Shakespeare controversy.

Admittedly I am a partisan in the dispute, and the reader will naturally bear that in mind in judging what I have to say. I may, however, point out that I began, as have most others, with no doubts about the Stratford man's authorship. I recall my father's suggesting rather whimsically in my boyhood that the plays were written by Francis Bacon, but he was given to making provocative statements in a humorous spirit. When, a few months after my fifteenth birthday I joined my parents in Europe, to which business had taken my father, and my mother and I visited Stratford-on-Avon, it was with no question in our minds but that we were paying homage at the veritable shrine. When, nearly a dozen years later, my views changed, it was not because I had an axe to grind or some form of self-promotion in mind; and when, much later still, having taken up writing as a means of livelihood, I decided to collaborate in a book taking issue with orthodoxy, I had my literary agent's warning in my ears that I was choosing one of the surest roads to ruin. Louis B. Wright had asserted two years previously, in 1959, that "one of the fastest growing industries is the anti-Shakespeare [meaning anti-Stratford] business," offering opportunities "which a canny publisher may not wish to overlook." But he cannot have supposed there was any truth in this. I know of no writer whose time invested in the anti-Stratford case has ever begun to be compensated by the earnings from it. As for publishers, those more interested in showing profits than in bucking the academic-literary establishment have always placed their bets where the ready-made market is. It is the conventional Shakespearean biographer with his popular thesis and the sanction of his peers who, abetted by a book-club selection, reaps the golden harvest: Marchette Chute, A. L. Rowse, Samuel Schoenbaum.

To account for my neglecting my agent's advice I must go back a long way. I have before me a copy of *The Saturday Review of Literature* of May 1, 1937, across the cover of which my mother has written: "P. 11. This started the whole thing." "This" is a three-page article entitled *Elizabethan Mystery Man*, by Charles Wisner Barrell, a film specialist whom enthusiasm for Looney's book turned into a prime researcher in the field. For Bernard DeVoto, then editor of *The Saturday Review*, to publish it took unusual fair-mindedness and courage, as I came to understand. He took care to cover himself, however. In a prefatory note explaining that belief in Oxford's authorship of Shakespeare's plays had gained enough momentum to interest the magazine's subscribers, he said that Professor Elmer Edgar Stoll would reply to the article in the next issue. (In my lifetime, no editor publishing an argument of the Stratford case has *ever* been willing to follow it with a reply by a dissenter.) Mr. Barrell began:

> At Gateshead-on-Tyne, England, lives a retired schoolmaster who is looked upon by many keen students of Elizabethan literature as the greatest of literary detectives.
>
> This modest, sixty-seven-year-old pedagogue bears the provocative name of J. Thomas Looney. He is the "onlie begetter" of the theory that the plays and poems credited to "Mr. William Shakespeare" were really written by Edward de Vere, 17th Earl of Oxford.
>
> Mr. Looney's discoveries, leading to this conclusion, were first published some seventeen years ago in a volume entitled *"Shakespeare" Identified*. Smart aleck detractors and reviewers who didn't bother to read his book, seized upon the Looney cognomen for purposes of ridicule.
>
> But the documentary facts and hundreds of "co-incidences" connecting the mysterious Earl of Oxford with the plays and poems which the author of *"Shakespeare" Identified* presents in his dossier are not to be laughed off so easily.

Looney's work, Mr. Barrell wrote, went back to increasing difficulties he had with the Stratford attribution and to a decision to seek a rational explanation for the origins of Shakespeare's plays and poems.

> Ultimately the trail led to the previously disregarded and half-obliterated foot-prints of Edward de Vere, Queen Elizabeth's wayward and unhappy Lord Great Chamberlain and one-time lover — a poet, Court dramatist, and patron of players of outstanding contemporary fame, but a man whose consuming passion

for art and scholarship made him a prey to designing machinations of politicians
and courtiers, to escape whose blighting influence he turned to the companionship of common poets, dramatists, musicians and actors; one who fell afoul of
the taboos of his own caste and "lost his good name" as a result; a nobleman,
bearing the second oldest title in the realm, who "wasted his substance" and
"squandered his patrimony on men of letters, whose bohemian mode of life
seems to have attracted him."

Noting that historians had treated de Vere "with considerably less than
justice," Mr. Barrell recalled that

> on the other hand, Dr. A. B. Grosart, one of the great pioneers in Elizabethan
> research, commented in 1872 on the force and beauty of Lord Oxford's early
> verse and lamented their seemingly unfilled promise in these words: "An unlifted
> shadow lies across his memory."
> This shadow has now been lifted to disclose a personality that seems to
> anticipate on a grander and more tragic scale the strange career of Lord Byron.

For this, said Mr. Barrell, we could thank not only Looney but also Bernard
M. Ward, whose biography of de Vere, published in 1928,

> directly connects this remarkable man with the literary renaissance that came to
> full flower in the last years of Elizabeth. The collated facts of his life, his letters
> and writings, match up with so many situations, plots, characterizations, tech-
> nical tricks of composition, and, in fact, whole passages of poetry that reappear
> in the work published under the name of William Shakespeare that Oxford's
> identification with the plays and poems is unmistakable.

The article, which went on to illustrate the parallels between Oxford and
Shakespeare, made my parents and me immediately aware of our profound,
if heretofore mostly unconscious, dissatisfaction with the conventional Shakespeare. We were no less quickly stirred by the force and persuasiveness in
the alternative Mr. Barrell offered. *At last* and *Of course* expressed our
reaction. Even so we were hardly prepared for the excitement with which
we would read J. Thomas Looney's book itself. At about this same time, I
took up a book on historic lost and buried treasures and found my sense of
adventure aroused to such a pitch that I had to put the book down unfinished.
It was this way with *"Shakespeare" Identified,* except that, gripped by the
unfolding parallels between Oxford and Shakespeare, I did not put it down,
at least for long. That this thrilling work of ratiocination, this landmark in
English literary history, as many view it, has largely disappeared from ken,[1]
smothered by the hostility or silence of our literary mentors, is to me as
reprehensible an act of bibliocide as any public book-burning. It is all the
more inexcusable considering the recognition that *"Shakespeare" Identified*
had from Hamilton Basso in *The New Yorker* in 1950, which I have already
quoted.

---

[1] though reprinted in a small edition in the United States in 1948 and in another by Kennikat
Press, Port Washington, N.Y., in 1975.

I do not know how many others whom Charles W. Barrell's article sent to its source felt as we did about Looney's achievement. My uncle, William F. Ogburn, head of the Department of Sociology at the University of Chicago, was one. So too was his colleague and former student, Professor and later Senator Paul H. Douglas. So too was my close friend Louis J. Halle, who later went from the Policy Planning Council of the Department of State to the faculty of the École de Hautes Études Internationales in Geneva and whose numerous distinguished books on society and foreign affairs culminated in the cosmic epic of evolution, *Out of Chaos*. So too was my later friend Philip S. Weld, who, a few years after we first met in a troopship in World War II, borrowed money to buy the *Gloucester Times*, then one by one acquired and made a success of five other New England newspapers — having meanwhile been a director of the *Boston Globe* and president and publisher of the International Edition of the *New York Herald Tribune*. So too was Richard Bentley, president of the Chicago Bar Association and editor of the *American Bar Association Journal*. So too was Peter Sammartino, who as its president built Fairleigh Dickinson from an obscure little college into a major university. So too was David Lloyd Kreeger, today a central figure in the cultural life of Washington, D.C., and, devoting to good works a fortune he made from scratch, one of its two leading philanthropists. So too was another notable philanthropist, Sol Feinstone, an impoverished immigrant's son whose introduction to Shakespeare was in the Yiddish theatre of New York's lower East Side and whose subsequently acquired wealth was devoted to public ends, including acquisition for the public of the largest collection of memorabilia of the American Revolution outside the Library of Congress. These are just men I have known personally who were enthralled by Looney's book and were persuaded by it, with Sigmund Freud, that "the man of Stratford . . . seems to have nothing at all to justify his claim, whereas Oxford has almost everything." Among others I have not known, Cyrus Durgin, former drama critic of the *Boston Globe,* and the actor Leslie Howard would certainly have high place. So too would Daniel Frohman. Of the latter, Forrest Rutherford writes that at a dinner attended also by Alma Gluck, Efrem Zimbalist, Fannie Hurst, and others, Mr. Frohman, "then Dean of American stage producers and a wise old authority on plays and theatrical history, enchanted us with the story of J. Thomas Looney's great discovery as given in his '*Shakespeare' Identified*. 'Read it', said Uncle Dan, 'and you will never again believe the old Stratford legend. Shakespeare was Edward de Vere, the 17th Earl of Oxford.'"

My parents' lives were destined to be altogether changed by it. Especially was this true of my mother, Dorothy Ogburn, a writer of very literate mystery novels and one of the early enthusiasts and collectors of D. H. Lawrence. It was, however, my father, Charlton Ogburn, a corporation counsel in New York, who first broke into print on the subject of their new studies with his *The Renaissance Man of England,* a booklet on Oxford as Shakespeare that, though privately published, went through five printings. That was in 1947, the year in which he was representing Mr. Barrell in his suit for libel against Giles E. Dawson of the Folger Library. In 1952, there was published by Coward, McCann the fruit of my parents' many years of joint research in *This Star of England,* a 1,300-page biography of Oxford and study of his self-revelation in Shakespeare's plays and poems, much the greater part by my mother. (My father had to give his business hours to his law office.) To me it was a great achievement. I find the story of Oxford as Shakespeare the most fascinating in literary annals, and I think they told it well. Certainly it attracted many enthusiastic adherents. Professor William Y. Elliott of Harvard called it "one of the great books of our time" and the reviewer for the *American Bar Association Journal* "an outstanding exemplification of research, scholarship, and exposition." Withal, however, the effect on the academic-literary establishment was very little. That, I suppose, was predictable. Any establishment, faced with a violation of its canon, will probably, to the extent feasible, ignore it and for the rest abuse it. But the malevolence of the abuse, as from Professor Oscar James Campbell of Columbia University in the *New York Times,* stunned my parents.[2] So too, twelve years later, did the diatribe against dissenters by William M. Murphy of Union College, of which I have already spoken and which was aimed particularly at them. Instances in which he deliberately misquoted them are worth citing, I think, for readers hardly able to believe that unabashed dishonesty would be stooped to in a college of high standing and condoned by the administration. A passage in *This Star of England* about William Shakspere read in part:

> We are told that his interest in the literary age he crowned was so slight that after dashing off the plays he returned to the grain business in Stratford and for a period of years paid no further heed to literature, . . . was never referred to, while living, as a writer. . . .

Professor Murphy decided to make the statement absurd by inserting "Shakespeare" in it, within the quotation marks, as follows:

[2] Writing in the *Book Review* section of 8 February 1953, Professor Campbell found it "tempting to dismiss this fascinating exhibition of mental gymnastics and perverted ingenuity with ridicule. But," he said, "that would ignore some questions of great human interest." Having raised these questions, he provided the answer in the "inducement the Oxfordians offer to their neophytes" in "the delight in becoming members of an esoteric cult. . . . Theirs is a religion in which the more unreasonable the faith the more ardently it is held." Professor Campbell, whom we met in Chapter 6 presenting his personal imaginings about Shakespeare as facts with which to refute apostasy, shared with many scholars a simple view on the issue of the authorship. Since the works were offered as by William Shakespeare, that settled any doubt as to their having been by William Shakspere of Stratford. The *Times* declined to publish replies.

> "Shakespeare was never referred to, while living, as a writer," we are told: so Francis Meres and Thomas Thorpe, Gabriel Harvey and Sir John Davies and all the rest, are categorically disposed of.

There are, incidentally, in the index of *This Star* five references to Meres, three to Thorpe, thirty-seven to Harvey, and two to John Davies of Hereford and what each said on the subject; whatever Professor Murphy may believe, *Sir* John Davies, so far as is known, never mentioned the name Shakespeare. Professor Murphy wrote:

> Sir Philip Sidney, even though he had demonstrated some poetical ability by writing one of the world's great sonnet sequences, could not have composed the poetry of Shakespeare because, the Ogburns sniff, he was not knighted "until three years before his death."

Whether Sidney could have written the poetry of Shakespeare was a proposition the Ogburns of course never considered. What they wrote was:

> Philip Sidney (who was not, by the way, knighted until three years before his death) was beyond all doubt an estimable young man, courtly and brave. . . . As a poet, however, he was merely facile.

The February 1959 issue of the *American Bar Association Journal* carried an article by Richard Bentley, the editor, entitled "Elizabethan Whodunit: Who was 'William Shake-speare'?" In it, Shakspere of Stratford came off quite badly. The article aroused so much interest and controversy that Mr. Bentley opened the magazine to contributors with conflicting points of view to express. (What can editors of academic journals like the *Shakespeare Quarterly* have made of such a concession to intellectual freedom and fairness?) Of the nine articles that followed, two were by my parents. All ten, with several pages of letters about them, were published in 1961 in book form as *Shakespeare Cross-Examination,* to which I have already referred. In a brief foreword, Tappan Gregory as Editor-in-Chief wrote:

> The Shakespeare works display such polish and cultivation that many have found it hard to attribute them to their reputed author, the man who is buried in Stratford-upon-Avon. The problem is not merely a literary one; the question of the identity of the author of the plays is also one of evidence, and therefore within the province of lawyers.

The original article had been followed in the Spring (1959) issue of the *Virginia Quarterly Review* by "The Anti-Shakespeare Industry and the Growth of Cults," by Louis B. Wright. This was an attack on dissenters of a nature indicated by the imprecations I quoted from it in the preceding chapter. Those who stood to suffer both from its slanders and impudent treatment of fact were, needless to say, permitted no reply in the *Review*.[3]

---

[3] That he had been unable to bring himself to name my parents' book as an object of his obloquy must have rankled with Wright, for he later got around his inhibition by resort to the underhand. I recognized his voice at once in an editorial in the *Washington Post* of 27 May 1962, which began:

Wright's article in the *Virginia Quarterly* came out just as my first full-length book (unrelated to Shakespeare) was enjoying a gratifying success. Its reception presented advantages that I thought I might use to try to redress the malice visited upon my parents and others of like mind and gain a fair hearing for a view of the authorship that I, no less than they, believed warranted one. I felt that the way to resolve the controversy was by an approximation of a trial at law in which, under a qualified judge to ensure fair play, each side would be allowed to present its case fully and have the right of rebuttal and counter-rebuttal. I laid these views before the editor at the publishing house — Harper & Brothers — that had brought out the book I mentioned, proposing that the trial also take the form of a book. He was keen about the idea.

How was a spokesman from the orthodox camp to be enlisted? We could not solve the problem, and I have never since been able to do so for any kind of debate on the authorship — with one exception. In 1968, on his retirement from the directorship of the Folger Library, Dr. Wright, speaking of his "annoyance" with dissenters from Shakespearean orthodoxy in an interview with the *National Observer,* said, "From time to time I have had to rise up and smite a bore, because these people are tiresome beyond belief. They come at you with a thesis rather than a body of fact, and their case is often based on sheer snobbery." When two months later, however, Joseph Borkin, a prominent lawyer of Washington, D.C., asked Dr. Wright if he would be willing to meet me on a forum at the National Press Club to discuss the Shakespeare controversy, he declined the invitation. Moreover, he could "think of no serious scholar willing to waste time on so fruitless a task as the discussion of the so-called 'Shakespeare controversy.'"

As the difficulties in achieving my hope for a trial in book form became apparent, time began to be pressing. My father, then nearing eighty, had suffered a painful affliction of the spine and, confined to bed in a nursing home, was failing. I thought that even without a spokesman for the opposing side, the kind of presentation of the case I had in mind would be effective

---

We have disconcerting news for a group of solemn lawyers who have lately generated and argued a case for the Earl of Oxford as the author of the works of William Shakespeare of Stratford. A new star now shines in the firmament, but instead of being a star of England it belongs to Arabia. Dr. Safa Al-Khulusi, a research scholar from the University of London . . . has discovered that William Shakespeare was not an Englishman at all but an Arab named Sheikh Zubair.

Thus it went on for sixty lines, with references to Oxford as "a crashing bore" whose "advocates have magnified his tediousness" and to "Oxfordians" as "long-winded and grim" in that tone of jocularity forced through set teeth that I should know as Wright's if I were reading from an Egyptian papyrus. The Folger Director's slyness in getting an editorial in the *Post* in which an assault on Oxfordians would be seen by the knowing as aimed at the authors of *This Star of England* would have won the kudos of his fellows, but James Russell Wiggins, the editor, did not appear amused by the trick when I remarked upon it.

and was eager to have it appear while he was alive. We went ahead with it, and, with my mother supplying most of the information, got the book finished in that year. To our great gratification, my editor called it "magnificent" — though I have to confess that he was an Oxfordian to begin with. A week later he telephoned to say that Harper's college department had put its foot down with respect to the book and, with much regret, he was having to return it. The college department's fear of reprisals by the universities against a publisher who brought out such a book was doubtless sound, and we had the consolation of knowing that the book had not in any way been found wanting; simply, its point of view was unacceptable. We were fully consoled when William Morrow & Co., which seemed to be interested in having me as an author, embraced the manuscript. The decision came in time for my father to hear it, though he died before *Shake-speare: The Man Behind the Name* came out in 1962.

At the last minute I thought I saw a way to make up for the lack of a Stratfordian antagonist in the book. The Folger Library had been feeling the heat of dissenting opinion. As the foremost guardian of the Stratford interest in this country, it felt itself behooved to put out a brief in defense of that interest. This publication took the form of the Folger Booklet *The Authorship of Shakespeare,* by Dr. McManaway. Of necessity, its treatment of the facts was cavalier. How misleading it was from start to finish I undertook to show in a point-by-point critique, which ran to nineteen single-spaced typewritten pages. This rebuttal Morrow had mimeographed and distributed with copies of the book to about twenty reviewers along with copies of the McManaway booklet in which I had numbered in red ink the seventy-nine statements it contained that were challenged, by number, in my indictment. I cannot say that much was accomplished by this effort. Reviewers doubtless felt, understandably, that they were paid little enough for the time they spent on a book without having to master two and adjudicate between them for the price of one.

Day Thorpe, literary editor of the *Washington Star,* was an exception. He read book, booklet, and critique and on that basis wrote an article on the controversy for the Sunday *Star Magazine* that was quite extraordinary in its fair-mindedness. In the same spirit of impartiality, Mr. Thorpe had sought McManaway's opinion of the book and the critique (of which I had sent a copy to the chairman of the Folger trustees two months earlier). McManaway had read neither and did not feel that they would be worth his while, since "these people are like religious zealots."

It was true, as an informative review of *Shake-speare: The Man Behind the Name* in the *American Bar Association Journal* pointed out, that "A few critics and reviewers have affected a lofty and intolerant attitude, notably in *The New York Times,* toward the Ogburns and indeed toward any author with temerity enough to question the Stratford tradition." On the other hand, it was pleasant to find that so many found the book "fascinating" even while they were not going to go out on a limb about it. *Life* welcomed it in an editorial in which it stated that the Oxford case had one "great advantage. Unlike Shaksper's, Oxford's known life is that of a man who could easily have written the plays." What especially encouraged me was the evidence that a book bitterly offensive to academia may yet be presented fairly to the nation's librarians. "A fascinating addition to a perennial mystery," the *Library Journal* called it in a review by a Yale University librarian. "Recommended for all large literature collections"; and in a later issue: "a well written and fully documented book . . . for all high school literature collections and young adult collections."

The *New York Herald Tribune* sent the book for review to G. B. Harrison of the University of Michigan, with results that help clarify the status of the Shakespeare controversy. The theory evidently was that Professor Harrison would judge the book fairly and, if he found it meritorious, willingly write off all his own works on Shakespeare and with them his whole career. Since he was not going to do either, he saved the time it would have taken to read the book and merely dipped into it for one or two quotations he could use. Owing to the circumstances in which it had been written, against time, with my mother distracted by my father's steady decline and my knowledge of the subject limited, a number of factual errors appeared in the first printing. These would admirably have served Professor Harrison's purpose, but he caught none of them. The Ogburns, Harrison declared, "vent their indignation on the orthodox." There was nothing of the kind in the book. There was not a word in it or in any other source the professor was able to cite to warrant his complaint that "even the mildest scholar becomes irritated when he finds himself or his colleagues mocked as fools or denounced as knaves." He was pleased to put it exactly backwards. Crane Brinton, the noted professor of history at Harvard, did read *The Man Behind the Name* and said "it seems to me a fair-minded, balanced, and very well written treatment of a subject which has very rarely indeed been so treated." And he added, "The Ogburns have been successful in persuading me that the conventional attribution of the writings of 'Shakespeare' deserves at best the old Scots verdict of 'not proven.'"

In the matter of Shakespeare's evident familiarity with court life, Professor Harrison asserted in his review "The recorded sayings of Queen Elizabeth are closer to the vocabulary of Doll Tearsheet than that of Gertrude and Hermione." Well, a glance at the *Oxford Dictionary of Quotations* (1955) would have yielded a sample of her recorded sayings, which a knowledge of her life would have told him were characteristic:

> I am your anointed Queen. I will never be by violence constrained to do anything. I thank God I am endued with such qualities that if I were turned out of the Realm in my petticoat I were able to live in any place in Christome.

> As for me, I see no such great cause why I should either be fond to live or fear to die. I have had good experience of this world, and I know what it is to be a subject and what to be a sovereign. Good neighbors I have had, and I have met with bad; and in trust I have found treason.
>
> Though God hath raised me high, yet this I count the glory of my crown, that I have reigned with your loves.

Some Doll Tearsheet.

"The fact is," said Harrison, "that the Oxfordite claim can only be established or rejected if all interested parties are willing and able to examine the arguments objectively, without emotion or prejudice." A reviewer for the Wilton, Connecticut, *Bulletin* picked up the pronouncement and remarked that "the Oxfordians we know would be pleased to accept his challenge." They would indeed.

The object of any honest book on the Shakespeare authorship must be to bring about just that objective examination of the arguments without emotion or prejudice which Professor Harrison professed to desire. Only our leading literary figures can insist successfully that the examination take place. Whether any book could move them to do so, when they are so comfortable with the Stratford theory, I do not know; but insofar as *Shake-speare: The Man Behind the Name* did not so move them it must be accounted a failure. Its shortcomings are plain to me. Aiming to present the case simply and in high relief, I treated far too briefly all that forty and more years of research had brought out — a store of information that the years since its publication have added to. Furthermore, I lacked the background that would have enabled me to put the orthodox academicians on record in their treatment of evidence and methods of dealing with dissenters — and a knowledge of those practices will, I think, assist in a fair-minded judgment as to where the merits lie in the controversy over the authorship and whether Shakespeare should be left so exclusively in the Stratfordians' hands. Since then I have acquired that background and had much first-hand acquaintance with those practices. What I am relating here of my experiences with the academicians is both too little and too much. It omits a great deal but at the same time is keeping us too long away from our investigation into the facts of authorship. I am, however, leading up to what serves us well in that investigation. It is the nearest thing yet to a debate on the issues in the controversy. It began with the publication in *Harvard Magazine* of a statement to which I have several times referred, of the essential case against the Stratford man and that for the Earl of Oxford. For once the academic establishment was put on the spot to address the issues. The reply, by two members of the Department of Comparative Literature at Harvard, from which I have also been quoting, represents the best by way of a counter-attack in defense of orthodoxy that two Stratfordian authorities could design. By examining the claims on which it rests as we come to them in pursuing the facts, we have a better idea than would otherwise be possible of where the truth is likely to reside. We can even learn a little from the professors' choice of weapons. If I give something about the background of the initial development, the reader will understand how exceptional it was and why such a howl went up when the initial presentation came out.

The obstacle to reaching a large audience with a book disputing the conventional view of the Shakespeare authorship had long been apparent to me: you were likely to attract only those readers whose thinking was already sufficiently unorthodox to incline them to take up the book. A magazine or newspaper would carry the argument to a broader public.

Over the years I have contributed articles on varied subjects to a number of magazines that might be expected to take an interest in the authorship of Shakespeare. Accordingly, it seemed not too much to expect that I could win one of them over to an article on the case against the conventional Shakespeare, the case being so strong. So, I kept trying, though with no encouragement from editors.

One of my first efforts was directed at the *New York Times Magazine,* in July 1963. The reply was that "If you care to submit 2,500 words on speculation giving the case against Shakespeare being the author of the plays, we will be happy to consider it." Disposing of the Stratford man and establishing Oxford in his place within such compass proved to be a devilish job. To support the argument in the eyes of the editors who would pass on it, I accompanied the article with a 7,500-word elaboration and explained my purpose in doing so in a letter. The article was turned down in just ten words by a new editor and on two counts. The second was that it "was not sufficiently news oriented" — an odd criterion to be sprung on me considering that the journalist world was then cranking up to celebrate the Stratford man's quadricentennial in an outpouring of tributes. But the first was the clincher: the article was "too long." The editor, it appeared, had not apprised himself of the contents of the packet he was returning.

All was not lost, however. An expansion of the 7,500-word version was very nicely printed by the Shakespeare-Oxford Society in 1964 as a booklet and has done good service, I think. In 1974, hoping that it might do more, I wrote to O. B. Hardison, Jr., Louis B. Wright's successor as director of the Folger Library, pointing out that the two Folger booklets on the authorship were "strictly Party-line publications" and that "a reader depending on these two booklets for his knowledge of the Shakespeare authorship would be left seriously uninformed." I might have pointed out that the "Suggested Reading" with which both close excludes all non-conformist publications from mention, whereas in one (*The Authorship of Shakespeare*), Dr. Wright's slanderous and unscrupulous article on "The Anti-Shakespeare Industry and the Growth of Cults" is recommended as "a spirited attack upon faddist speculation." I recalled that he had received from me the "20-page critique I wrote of the McManaway booklet showing how continually it misled the reader" and I proposed that, with the object of a fair and honest presentation to the public, my *Shakespeare and the Man of Stratford* be offered for sale in the Library bookshop alongside the two Folger booklets, which it matched in format. A reprinting being in order, I said that "If you find any mistakes or significant omissions in it I should be glad to make the necessary changes, subject to limitations of length." The Folger Library did not reply to this suggestion. Four years later, when I repeated it, I was told that if I wished to reprint the pamphlet it could be given "to the Kiosk Committee for consideration." I was not tempted.

Two years earlier I had proposed to the Folger Library that it publish a contribution of mine on the authorship in the *Shakespeare Quarterly,* a scholarly journal it had recently taken over. To show what I had in mind I sent along a copy of an essay I had just written on *The Man Who Shakespeare Was Not.* I was told that the *Quarterly* had a "three-year backlog." I protested that "If the case for Shakspere of Stratford is as weak as it would appear from the analyses I have presented, then surely an article demonstrating those weaknesses would be more important than any I can imagine that the *Quarterly* has in its hands." I recalled in my letter that for years Louis B. Wright had vilified dissenters from the sanctuary of the Folger while refusing to be drawn into a public debate in which they could answer back. I pointed out that Dr. Wright's paperback books on Shakespeare, bearing the cachet of the Folger Library, in which public ignorance of essential facts of the Shakespeare authorship is abused and dissenters misrepresented and sneered at, were on sale at the Folger. It seemed to me, I said, that the Folger had something to make up for. I pointed out that an editor who had the authority to accept or reject articles certainly could determine the order in which they were printed.

The editor, Richard Schoeck, replied: "I do not argue that an article accepted for publication must wait its turn: I state it as a firm principle of editorship. The question is not what problems or issues have priorities. . . ."

The correspondence allowed no grounds for belief that an article of the kind the Shakespeare controversy called for would be published in three years or thirty years. It made plain only when it would *not* be published. If an institution owing its existence to public support were going to serve a special interest in opposition to the public's on an issue inseparable from its purpose, I felt that at least its doing so should be known. I imparted this view to the literary editor of the *Washington Star,* Day Thorpe. He took up the cudgels in an article of 3 December 1972, under the heading "Does the Folger Want the Truth About Shakespeare?" Recalling the old regime, he wrote that "When a man suggests that the Shaksper of Stratford-on-Avon was not the same man as the poet Shakespeare of London, the Folger attacks the heretic with invective and contempt hardly imaginable among civilized scholars" and proceeded to give examples. Referring to the Folger's position that the *Quarterly* was booked up for three years, Mr. Thorpe proposed ironically that if the Folger could not afford a special issue of the magazine to accommodate an article enlarging on the case against the Stratford man it sell one of its seventy-nine copies of the First Folio to raise the needed funds; they would do more good anyway if distributed around where they could be seen.

Dr. Hardison's reply was published in the *Star* on 17 December. Ignoring most of Mr. Thorpe's article, it asserted that "Ogburn's essay . . . has never been submitted"; the writer was uninformed. "Like most scholarly journals today the *Quarterly* has a substantial backlog — currently about three years," it said, then stated that "the editor does not engage in favoritism by arbitrarily publishing articles out of sequence."

Ten months later, in the Folger's October 1973 *Newsletter,* forgetting that "firm principle," the editor was soliciting contributions to the *Shakespeare Quarterly* on Shakespeare in the classroom for publication in the next spring issue.

At the same time there have been revolutionary changes at the Folger Library. Later in the 1970s, *Shake-speare: The Man Behind the Name* appeared on display at the Folger bookshop, to my stupefaction, and there remained until half a dozen copies had been sold. Of course no dissenter would yet be permitted in the *Quarterly* or in the Folger's lecture program. No dissident work is included in the Folger's *Educational Catalogue* to balance Samuel Schoenbaum's "masterpieces" and other canonical literature. The public's confidence is still abused with publications bearing the Folger's seal of approval that the Soviet Writers' Union would find exemplary in ideological zeal. Any administration at 201 South Capitol Street that moved far toward objectivity in such matters would doubtless fall afoul of the authorities of Amherst College and never be heard from again. What Wright's successor, O. B. Hardison, Jr., did, to begin with, was to put the Folger Library in the cultural mainstream of the nation's capital. This was done primarily by turning the replica of the Globe the Library houses into a living theatre and putting on its boards plays both Shakespearean and contemporary. To help launch the innovation, Dr. Hardison had the assistance of Richmond Crinkley, a man very much of the theatre whom he had brought with him. (Unfortunately, Richmond was to leave before long for higher realms in his field, taking with him his lively company and sympathy with a dissenting view of the authorship.) The theatrical program has been an exciting success.

Dr. Hardison resembles his predecessor about as one portrait Hamlet holds up to his mother resembles the other. For the Library's marvellous collection of books, however, he tells me that an immense debt is owed Dr. Wright. Praise be given where praise is due. More than I could ever give is due Dr. Hardison himself. A program of rehabilitation and construction that required closing the reading-room and stacks from early in 1979 to April 1981 transformed the building. A new climate-control plant resembling the bowels of an ocean liner will ensure preservation of the irreplaceable collection. The underground deck containing the stacks has been enlarged to the length of a city block. In fact, the capacity of the vaults and stacks has been more than doubled. A beautifully paneled exhibition room will help prospective donors appreciate the great worthiness of the Library.

To pay for the long-overdue improvements, $8 million has been required. It took all the persuasiveness of thorough knowledge that is Dr. Hardison's and all his gifts of personality to come near it — all the graciousness for which my wife and I have had occasion to be grateful. My contention with the institution has not prevented me from becoming a Friend of the Folger or from urging others to do likewise. My obligation to and enthusiasm for the Library, its resources, its helpful, capable, friendly staff, its hospitality to the researcher and congenial atmosphere, are great; I could never have done without it.

Another matter to put in perspective: I had not meant in the preceding part of this chapter to assume any mantle of unique knowledge regarding the case for Oxford. If I do not here name others — not a few — whom I know to be as well informed as I on the subject it is only because I do not wish to risk leaving out any unfairly through inadvertence. A number have written worthy books in the field, and that these have remained unpublished or required private financing for their publication testifies to the continuing barrier to non-conformist views of Shakespeare.

This *de facto* censorship has been so stringent that I might have given up hope of ever breaking through it but for John Fischer and Robert Schnayerson at *Harper's,* which published an article of mine on "Shakespeare's Missing Manuscripts" (see Appendix) and the literary editors of Washington's two newspapers, Day Thorpe of the *Star* and William McPherson of the *Post* (winner of a Pulitzer Prize in 1977), who, seeming to feel that some balance was due in the treatment of books on Shakespeare, sent me a few by Strat-fordians to review.

Then, in 1974, came the break I had been hoping for. Early in that year I received a solicitation for a subscription from the business manager of the new *Harvard Magazine,* formerly the *Harvard Alumni Bulletin,* which claimed that the magazine was not afraid of controversy. In a somewhat ironic spirit, I responded with a counter-proposal: would she be willing to read a manuscript on the Shakespeare authorship from which I thought an important and compelling and certainly controversial article could be taken? To my surprise the editor, John Bethell, wrote back inviting me to send it in: "Our magazine is willing and eager to touch the untouchable." I immediately proffered the cup, fully aware of how far it was to the lip, and how much courage would be needed to take it there. With the moral backing of Philip S. Weld, former president and publisher of the *Bulletin,* of whom I have already spoken, Mr. Bethell had that courage. The article was scheduled for the November issue under the title I had given it: *The Man Who Shakespeare Was Not (and Who He Was)*; for this was basically the same manuscript I had sent the Folger Library, with some added pages on Oxford as Shakespeare. The entire manuscript would be printed with two portraits of Oxford in color and other black-and-white illustrations and it would be the cover story in the issue of November 1974. Having the highest regard for *Harvard Magazine,* I was elated. I was also in terrible suspense, for I knew that when the Harvard English faculty got wind of the planned enormity, the professors would stop at nothing to get the article killed. Would the pressure be too fierce even for Mr. Bethell to resist? Miraculously, word of the article never got around until the magazine hit the stands. The storm then was all I had anticipated.

"I haven't read the offending article and doubt that I would waste time reading it if I had a copy," Professor Gwynne Evans declared. That did not prevent his being "deeply disappointed to learn that such an article had appeared in a Harvard publication" or his knowing it to be "half-baked guff." (As editor of the expensive, strictly orthodox *Riverside* edition of Shakespeare's works newly published by Houghton Mifflin, Professor Evans had particularly impelling reason to condemn, sight unseen, an attack upon the Stratford case.) But really he had "nothing to add to what Mr. Kaiser says so trenchantly."

Professor Walter Kaiser had asked if future articles would appear in the magazine asserting "that the earth is flat" and that "Queen Victoria was in fact a Peruvian transvestite." He had accused the editor of "irresponsible journalism," of giving "idiocies a Harvard cachet," and of doing "a very real disservice to a community dedicated to *veritas.*" He and his colleagues, he wrote, could have told the editor "(1) how fatuous the article is, (2) what the real facts are, (3) why its publication is such a travesty of the standards of scholarship this university professes." Forgetting *veritas,* he added as (4) "that this particular crank has, I understand, been trying to peddle this article for years."

Professor Harry Levin, author of the Introduction to the *Riverside Shakespeare,* put his finger on the heart of the offense when, in a letter to the president of the university and the dean of the faculty of arts and sciences,

he attacked the editor for having "opened up a Pandora's box for all of us."
Writing, as he said, "more in sorrow than in anger," he declared that it had
come "as a sudden and crucial blow to see the University's public image so
lightly and so widely associated with a notoriously long-exploded aberration." Professor Levin, it developed, thought I was my father. That is to say,
he knew nothing about me whatever. He knew, however, that I was a
"crackpot" and one "who had been at this game for years." He recalled that
"long ago" when "he" (not I, as he thought, but my parents) had sent the
manuscript of a book on the Shakespeare authorship to Macmillan, the
publishers had sent it to him, Levin. They were aware, he said, of "its utter
fallaciousness" but wished to back up their rejection of it with an expert
opinion. (That Macmillan would send the manuscript to a reader compelled
by vital self-interest to excoriate it out of hand gives an idea of what the
anti-Stratfordians have been up against.) Professor Levin having supplied the
required opinion, he assumed that the manuscript must have fared similarly
at other publishing houses "since Ogburn and his collaborator finally had to
have the thing privately printed." The fact is that *This Star of England* was
to have been published by Simon & Schuster. Why that fell through, I am
not sure. It may have been because the firm decided to put its money instead
on a conventional work on Shakespeare or because it held out for substantial
cuts in the manuscript, which my parents would not agree to. Lincoln Schuster had definitely planned to publish it. He had written its authors: "Let me
congratulate you on a truly dazzling achievement. Your vast erudition and
your indefatigible and pioneering researches are matched at many points by
the truly Renaissance splendor of your writing" — and more in that vein.
Mr. Schuster joined the Shakespeare-Oxford Society and remained a member
until his death twenty years later. *This Star of England* was published commercially by Coward, McCann in 1952. Professional Stratfordians know
little if anything about the writings of their opponents and Levin had never
heard of *Shake-speare: The Man Behind The Name* (William Morrow, 1962),
of which I *was* part author. When finally he got it straight about the Ogburns,
his scorn was withering: "Academic pieties could scarcely vie with such
devout familial commitments."

That was in the reply that Professors Levin and Evans wrote to my article.
Mr. Bethell had said that he counted on a rejoinder, one that "would point
out specifically where Mr. Ogburn's historical facts are askew, if indeed they
are." It was to appear in the issue of February 1975.

Within a fortnight of publication of *Harvard Magazine* with my offending
article, the offense to orthodoxy was greatly compounded in a way tending
to vindicate Mr. Bethell's editorial judgment and giving me abundant additional cause for satisfaction. The article was reprinted, somewhat abridged,
with a very effective layout, in the leading place in the Sunday editorial
section — *Outlook* — of the *Washington Post.* Thanks for this stunning

demonstration of intellectual openness by a leading newspaper were owing to the managing editor, Howard Simons. As was doubtless inevitable, I suppose, Dr. Hardison was quick to appeal to that right of rejoinder in the cause of fairness which the Folger rigidly denies anyone who would object to the misrepresentation, slander, and nonsense disseminated to the public under its aegis. The reply that he sent the editor was duly printed in *Outlook*. It presented the familiar Stratfordian case and did not so much rebut the *Harvard Magazine* article as disregard it.

Denunciations continued to come in to *Harvard Magazine* and were aired in the letters columns. Edward Fisher, an award-winning writer and artist of Washington, D.C., author of three books on Shakespeare, wrote, like Professor Levin, "more in sadness than in anger." He was "amazed, shocked and disgusted that THE magazine of the world's greatest university should actually publish more of the stale old spinach of the Oxford lunacy by that non-Shakespearean scholar, Charlton Ogburn. . . . What is your answer?" he finished. "It had better be good. If no Harvard authority on Shakespeare blasts you with a thorough refutation of this perennial Looney moonshine, I shall do it myself. I hate to have to take the time from useful labors, but somebody ought to give you the works." (After the Evans-Levin reply had appeared, the president of the Shakespeare-Oxford Society telephoned Major Fisher to inquire if he found it adequate and, upon learning that he did not, offered him the vehicle of the Society's newsletter for a reply of his own, but he declined to avail himself of the opportunity.) Another of the first to take pen in hand had graduated from Harvard forty-five years after Major Fisher, but no generation gap was in evidence. "Charlton Ogburn," Peter Wirth weighed in, "is a fool and a snob." Altogether, "the Shakespeare identity crisis," as another correspondent wittily called it, provoked more letters than any other issue ever raised by an article in the magazine or its predecessor. Both sides were well represented in the more than thirty letters published in six issues before the editor announced that he was having to ring down the curtain on the correspondence.

The Evans-Levin reply appeared midway in the fracas. In one of the letters to the editor it inspired, Charles C. Dickinson, III, of the Union Theological Seminary in Richmond, Virginia, wrote:

> Professors Evans and Levin characterize Mr. Ogburn and all his tribe as "obfuscating" and "paranoid" "zealots" who have the upstart temerity to inject their "dubious" "animosity" and "heresy" into your sheet "at the cost of no little strain on Harvard's Latin Motto [*Veritas*]." . . .
>
> But whether they are right or wrong, if ever I have read a "paranoid," shrill, even hysterical defense by the "orthodox" of sacred territory encroached upon by infidels, it is that of Professors Evans and Levin.

It would be asking too much to expect the two professors to be able to see themselves in that light. In their hearts, however, I think they must have recognized the warrant in a comment on their reply made in another letter to the magazine by Profesor Harold C. Hinton of the Department of Political Science and International Affairs at the George Washington University: "If this is the best the Stratfordians can do, no wonder doubts have persisted for three and a half centuries."

Despite the examples of forbearance that had been set me, I am afraid I read the Evans-Levin reply more in anger than in sorrow. In a letter that Mr. Bethell showed great courage for a second time in printing, I said that the two professors had relied on "slanders, misquotations, evasions and misstatements of fact." I suggested that inasmuch as they had departed from their role as educators in favor of adversary proceedings, "let us have a trial, . . . each side to have a chance to present a full brief for its case, one not confined to the compass of a magazine article, and full opportunity for rebuttal. Let a representative of the Harvard Law School preside to ensure fairness." In a letter following mine, Philip S. Weld offered to pay the costs of the trial, including those of "a court reporter, box lunches and sherry for the opposing players, rental of a fair-sized hall, and a suitable award for the judge with guts enough to sit on the case." And he suggested that "If no one at Harvard wishes to argue the case for the Stratfordian, perhaps you could engage someone from the Yale English department."

No one, it appeared, did wish to argue the case for the Stratfordian — no one at Harvard or at Yale or at any other institution. At the same time, the professors' wrath over publication of my letter apparently exceeded even their ire when the original article appeared. Mr. Bethell asked me for a brief memorandum, if it would not be "inconvenient," enumerating the points in the Evans-Levin reply that I contended did violence to the facts, and I dashed off a partial listing of thirty-one of them in six pages single-spaced. The professors, I heard, called the published letter false and libelous, spoke of legal action (as if a trial were not just what I wanted), and demanded that the magazine dissociate itself from the letter. In the end, in an editorial note closing out the correspondence, John Bethell recognized that some of the letters had been "strongly stated" and went so far as but no further than to remark that "Needless to say, the sentiments expressed in letters to this magazine are the responsibility of the writers, and do not reflect editorial opinions. The same is true of signed articles."

The low blows struck by the professors still rankled with me, and I allowed my resentment to spill over in a letter to Professor Levin. I wrote: "Any scholar in your and Professor Evans's position with self-respect and confidence in his case would have demanded that I either retract and apologize for my charges or substantiate them. But not you two. Had you done so the result would have been that the defense of my charges, which naturally I should not have withdrawn, would have gone before disinterested third parties for, in effect, adjudication." And that, I said, "is precisely what you must at all costs avoid." But Levin would not be baited. Evans, who had described my article to a correspondent as "a tissue of distortions, half truths, misinterpretations, jugglings, and errors of fact," was as little disposed to fair adjudication.

One specific point of dispute between the two professors and me I feel is sufficiently revealing to be worth mentioning before we move on. In my article I had quoted Henry James's remark in a letter to Violet Hunt that "I am 'sort of' haunted by the conviction that the divine William is the biggest and most successful fraud ever practised on a patient world." The professors in their reply charged that I had done an "injustice" to Henry James "by a truncated quotation which misses out on his irony." The rest of what James said, with such irony as may be detected in it, was, "The more I turn him round and round the more he so affects me. But that is all — I am not pretending to treat the question or carry it any farther. It bristles with difficulties, and I can only express my general sense by saying that I find it *almost* as impossible to conceive that Bacon wrote the plays as to conceive that the man from Stratford, as we know the man from Stratford, did." It might have been added that Leon Edel quotes James as feeling that the "facts of Stratford did not 'square' with the plays of the genius" and as speaking of "the lout from Stratford."

Professor Gordon C. Cyr quoted the foregoing in a partial rebuttal of the Evans-Levin reply in the Shakespeare-Oxford Society *Newsletter,* of which a copy was sent to the two professors. In a subsequent *Newsletter,* Professor Cyr reported having found a reference in a later letter of James's to Mrs. Hunt to the work of Sir George Greenwood, that devastating critic of the Stratford case. James wrote that *The Shakespeare Problem Restated* by "a fellow called Greenwood" best expressed his views on the authorship question, being "an extremely erudite, fair, and discriminating piece of work." And he lent Mrs. Hunt a copy. (What Greenwood thought, in a word, was that "The idea that those works were written by the player who came to London as a 'Stratford rustic' in 1587, is surely one of the most foolish delusions that have ever obsessed and deceived the credulous mind of man." Professor Cyr sent a copy of this report to Professor Evans, from whom he received the following response:

> Thank you for the off-print of your reply. I am afraid I find your arguments no more cogent or acceptable than those of Charlton Ogburn.

12

"My Name Be Buried Where My Body Is"

Those who hold that it would take a conspiracy of impossible extent to conceal the origin of Shakespeare's plays if Oxford were their author clearly mistake the facts. No conspiracy would be required under an autocratic government with the means of enforcing its will in such a matter, and England has such a government under Queen Elizabeth and William Cecil Lord Burghley, who for forty years manipulates that power, ruthlessly as he deems it desirable. Moreover, whoever the author is, whether Shakspere or someone more resembling our picture of him, the fact is, as we see, that the record from the years while he was alive is expunged of all that would connect him with the plays, leaving a void where we should expect to find him. Bearing in mind that Oxford is the ranking Earl of the realm at a time when a connection between a nobleman and the public theatre is unthinkable, that he is Burghley's son-in-law, formerly his ward, and one of the inner Court circle, we find the reasons for keeping it secret if he were the dramatist to be singularly compelling, especially if he is suspected in his playwriting of holding, as 'twere, the mirror up to his illustrious associates. We endeavor to deduce what Oxford's feelings must be at being deprived of the credit for having written the imperishable masterpieces, if they are his. We review the evidence as to when the decision to embody the authorship in "Shakespeare" is made and the reasons why, to keep the pseudonym from being exposed, William Shakspere is selected for the role and how he is set up as an out-of-sight stand-in for the author. We then turn briefly to the rationale behind the case for Oxford as the author, observing the means by which his connection with the plays could be kept secret and why the Cecils — Burghley and his son and successor — would be especially eager to keep it secret; and we consider some contemporary clues to the authorship, assiduously glossed over by orthodoxy, which fit the case for Oxford.

Some years ago, *Life* magazine's editorialist, John K. Jessup, writing under the heading "Fresh Troops Join the Battle of the Bard," observed that the case for Oxford "has increasingly responsible support." He went on to say, however, that "it involves an assumed conspiracy to perpetuate his pseudonymity." And he added that scholars find this conspiracy "hard . . . to take." He went on to say, as I have reported, that "Against this need to assume a conspiracy, the Oxford case has one great offsetting advantage," the advantage being that "unlike Shaksper's, Oxford's known life is that of a man who could easily have written the plays."

Mr. Jessup's editorial was that rarity, a commentary on the Shakespeare controversy by a journalist who is, on the whole, informed and fair in his appraisal. But it gave further currency to a widely held misconception central to the problem of the authorship. The case for Oxford (as for any other pseudonymous author) does not "assume a conspiracy." It takes cognizance of a fact. The fact is that every contemporary document that might have related authorship of Shakespeare's plays and poems to an identifiable human being subsequently disappeared. Every last scrap of paper that would have told who Shakespeare was — whether the Stratford man or any other — simply vanished; like the papers that would have shown whether Shakspere went to school; like the papers that would have told what his activities in the theatre were, if any; like the papers to which he set his hand in his business dealings in Stratford: all vanished. Whatever view of the authorship one may take, orthodox or otherwise, one must accept the absence of all contemporary documentation establishing Shakespeare's identity and explain why it should have disappeared. This is not to assume anything but to acknowledge the actuality and build upon it. And I think we cannot simply attribute the blank record to accident. For a body of work as superior as Shakespeare's, it is simply not conceivable that every reference during the author's life, and evidently for some years thereafter, which linked the work to a flesh-and-blood author, including everything in the author's own words, written or quoted, should have passed into limbo by chance. Chance is not so purposeful. Elizabethan writers of far less stature than the author of Shakespeare's works have been found unmistakably associated with their products by concrete references that have not had to be unearthed through the exhaustive searches over years by legions of investigators.

To me there can be but one explanation for the empty-handedness of generations of scholars after lifelong quests. Someone saw to it that those quests would be fruitless. A conspiracy was not necessary. Autocratic societies are run not by conspiracies but under central direction. And Elizabethan society was autocratic. Even less than on the other side of the iron curtain today, where typewriters and copying machines are available even to *samizdat* publishers, was proscribed information likely to get on the record. Sir Walter Raleigh wrote in his *History*:

> I know it will be said by many that I might have been more pleasing to the reader if I had written the story of my own times, having been permitted to draw water as near the well-head as another. To this I answer that whosoever, in writing a modern history, shall follow truth too near the heels it may haply strike out his teeth.

The expression of opinion, orally or in print, was rigidly controlled. No presses were tolerated except in London and at the two universities, and permission by the Archbishop of Canterbury was required for publication. Atheism was punishable by death. John Stubbs could get his right hand cut off for inditing a pamphlet that, while voicing his devotion to the Queen, opposed her marriage to a French prince. Official surveillance was carried out by a small army of spies, and traps were laid for those suspected of treason. No document was automatically safe. Torture was regularly employed to extract confessions from suspects and incriminate others.

But surely, it will be argued, there must have been persons acquainted with the identity of the man behind the name Shakespeare who risked confiding their knowledge to personal letters or private papers — why then have these not come to light? The question should, of course, be put to Stratfordians as well as to their opponents. Speaking for myself, I can say only that I hope, not without optimism, that such documents will be turned up among the masses of Elizabethan manuscripts that have been inadequately combed by investigators knowing what to look for, if combed at all. Indeed, my guess is that an enormous opportunity beckons young scholars. But let me say this, too. If a literary sophisticate like John Manningham could witness a performance of *Twelfth Night* without being aware that its author was William Shakespeare (see page 9), I judge that the majority of even educated theatregoers may well not have associated an author's name with the dramas. Of course "William Shakespeare" was widely known as the name signed to the dedication of the two long narrative poems. Certainly it was known, too, by those acquainted with printed versions of plays brought out after 1598 as his, and I suspect that most of such persons, if they were interested, recognized it as a pseudonym. But how many were aware whose pseudonym it was? My guess is: two small sets, though more may have been. One was a tight circle at Court, whose class interest required silence on the matter. The other would have been a group of writers, with perhaps a few actors. These had good reason to be chary of putting anything on paper that would offend the ruling power if it came to light; some had been before the Star Chamber and thence to jail, and their example would not have been lost on others. When *The Isle of Dogs* was staged in 1597 and found to contain "slanderous and seditious matter," Thomas Nashe, its part-author, was sent to the Fleet prison, the theatre closed at which it was shown, and evidently every copy of it was destroyed. In 1604, Marston and Chapman were arrested simply because one or two passages in *Eastward Ho* were deemed insulting to the Scots. What would be the point of noising information about when doing so could lead to trouble and could accomplish nothing? The Star Chamber took a severe view of loose speech. John Stow writes in his *Annales,* apparently for the year 1601:

> The last of June Atkinson a Customer of Hull, was set on the Pillory in Cheape, and with him three other [*sic*], to wit, Wilkinson, Alson, & Cowley brought thither on horseback, with their faces towards the horse tails and paper on their heads. They were there whipped on the Pillory, and lost their ears, by

judgement given in the Star Chamber, for slanderous words by them spoken &
written against the Lord Treasurer, and others of the council.

An earlier Lord Treasurer and a later, his son, are to play leading parts in
our unfolding story, as they did in the England of their day. They are William
and Robert Cecil.

Born in 1521, the grandson of an innkeeper, though he claimed more
illustrious remoter ancestors, William Cecil studied at Cambridge, then at
Gray's Inn. He took service under the Protector Somerset, uncle of the boy
king, Edward VI, and managed to come almost unscathed through that
nobleman's fall. He served next under Somerset's supplanter, Northumberland; then, foreseeing trouble ahead for the detested Duke, became an in-
triguer against him and thus survived again when the second Protector went
to the block. Nevertheless, it was a near thing, for under Northumberland's
instruction, Cecil had a large hand in King Edward's "devise," by which the
succession would go to neither of the King's sisters, Mary and Elizabeth,
King Henry VIII's other offspring, but to Northumberland's daughter-in-law,
the studious young Lady Jane Grey. It was this, in 1553, which proved fatal
to both the Duke and the tragic, irreproachable girl, whose head also fell. It
had been by going to Mary with timely disclosures about the Duke's machinations that Cecil won immunity for himself. Foreseeing the end of Queen
Mary's five-year reign, he took the opportunity to display his wiliness once
more. Albert F. Pollard writes:

> He was in secret communication with Elizabeth before Mary died, and from
> the first the new queen relied on Cecil as she relied on no one else. Her confidence
> was not misplaced; Cecil was exactly the kind of minister England then required.
> Personal experience had ripened his rare natural gift for avoiding dangers. . . .
> He was an eminently safe man, not an original thinker, but a counsellor of
> unrivaled wisdom. . . . From 1558 for forty years the biography of Cecil is
> almost indistinguishable from that of Elizabeth and from the history of England.

Elizabeth came to the throne in a weak country riven within living memory
by the bloody War of the Roses and newly riven by deep religious schism, a
country that under her predecessor had been a virtual apanage of a monstrously powerful Roman Catholic Spain, whose ruler through Elizabeth's
life was to strive for her and England's subordination and the destruction of
its Protestant allies on the Continent. She left it secure at home and invincible
upon the seas, its native church indestructible, the bases laid for a British
Empire that would soon rival and then eclipse Spain's own. And for this, at
least among civil officers, William Cecil, her First Minister, deserves credit
probably second only to Elizabeth herself.

That is how historians see Cecil, as royal advisor, sage and steadfast. But
there was also Cecil the person, and this Cecil is known to a larger audience
being mildly caricatured in the figure of Polonius in *Hamlet,* as has long

been widely recognized. Only one person I know of would have had the audacity and recklessness, the intimate knowledge of his subject, and the play-writing background to skewer so formidable a personage on the stage and also have enjoyed sufficient favor with the Queen to get away with it. That was Edward de Vere.

"In January 1561, he [Cecil] was given the lucrative office of master of the court of wards," Professor Pollard relates, "and he did something to reform that instrument of tyranny and abuse." (Something, but not everything.) In the next year, following the death of the 16th Earl of Oxford, his father, the twelve-year-old Edward became a royal ward in Cecil House. In December 1571, at age twenty-one, he was wed to Cecil's fifteen-year-old daughter Anne. Thus in real life Hamlet married Ophelia. The alliance had been made suitable when Cecil, earlier in that year, was elevated to the peerage as Baron Burghley of Burghley. The match Burghley had promoted was a brilliant one for his lineage, but the cost was to be heavy in unhappiness for all three principals. After Anne's death, the couple's children also became wards of her father. It was a lifetime linkage between two potent personalities that were profoundly antithetical.

Burghley was "a politician of the rising middle class of small gentry, a pestilent heretic," G. M. Trevelyan writes. He was shrewd, calculating, worldly, avaricious, and probably humorless. The Earl of Oxford came of a family established half a millennium earlier by a Norman knight, descendant of the Vikings, whom the British called Danes. Alberic Veer, or Aubrey Vere, fought at Hastings under William but had already held land in England under Edward the Confessor. For four hundred years, the family had held the Earldom of Oxford. De Vere was thus among the oldest of the old nobility to whom the rising middle class were upstarts and to whom the Roman church was apt to appeal as part of the structure in the feudal order. Doubtless he regarded politicians with the contempt that Shakespeare visits on them. He was rash, headstrong, improvident, a brilliantly accomplished courtier and probably somewhat derisive of himself as such, a prankster, and a fighter hungry for military exploits. But he was a poet-fighter, as Villon, Cyrano, and Byron were, and if he thirsted for the military honors his antecedents had won, he thirsted for foreign travel with acquisitive intellect and imagination as an offspring of the Renaissance. Of his promise as a poet, Sir E. K. Chambers, commenting on how curiously barren the first half of Elizabeth's reign proved to be in worthy successors to Wyatt and Surrey, said, "The most hopeful of them was Edward de Vere, Earl of Oxford, a real courtier, but an ill-conditioned youth, who also became mute in late life." (Who only then achieved his full stature, albeit under another name, many of us would say.) As a playwright, again in his youth, he was called by Anthony à Wood "the best for comedy in his time." He was a friend and generous promoter and patron of writers and even, it would seem, an habitué of their demi-monde as Prince Hal was of the Boar's Head Tavern (the reader not forgetting that the Oxford crest was a boar). I have but little doubt that in Prince Hal and his taste for the low but impudent and vital company of the likes of Poins, Bardolph, Nym, and Pistol, we have a picture of the young de Vere, and that in the Prince's later justification for his unseemly carryings-on we have the Earl's:

> And we understand him well,
> How he comes o'er us with our wilder days,
> Not measuring what use we made of them.

The "he" who came o'er Oxford with his wilder days was assuredly Lord Burghley, who we know complained of his son-in-law's companions, calling them "lewd" in the early sense in which Shakespeare used the word when he had Petruchio, ragging his Kate, call the hat made for her a "velvet dish: . . . 'tis lewd and filthy" — that is, misbegotten, vulgar.

Francis Edwards, S.J., writes:

> It was Edward de Vere's misfortune or distinction to live with Sir William [Cecil] without becoming subservient or even submissive to him. Most of the time their relationship could be explained in terms of an older man with a near monopoly of money, influence and power, doing his best to thwart every effort toward independence in his high-spirited junior. In much de Vere resembled Robert Devereux, Earl of Essex [another of Cecil's wards]: able, dashing, impetuous, extravagant, in full sympathy with the literary flowering of the age, and, in Oxford's case, a distinguished contributor. Small wonder he failed to appreciate the other side of Burghley, his earthly outlook and grasping acquisitiveness for all its mask of external piety and endless expressions of selfless service to the state.

The method of science, as rationality in general, is to accept the simplest explanation for a phenomenon that most readily accommodates all the facts and to hold with that explanation unless and until other facts are brought to light that conflict with it. The Stratford theory is, to me, to be rejected because at every turn it requires us to accept that which is at odds with human experience and with what is reasonable and believable; the facts are not assimilable to it. The theory of the Shakespeare authorship to be offered here does, as I see it, accommodate the facts without strain, both those we have discussed and those we have yet to come to. It is based on four postulates.

Postulate Number One: Shakespeare a Nobleman

My initial proposition is that the plays and poems we know as Shakespeare's were the work of a nobleman, hence necessarily one employing a pseudonym. I see no reason why a titled aristocrat cannot as well as a commoner be born with potential literary genius or necessarily lack incentive to develop it. Brooks Atkinson, drama critic of the *New York Times,* quotes approvingly an argument of Edward Hubler's that is also heard from other Stratfordians: "The simple truth is that in England the peaks of literary greatness have been bourgeois from the beginning. Chaucer, Spenser, Shakespeare, Milton and so on down through the years were all middle class." We have here, by the way, a notable example of Stratfordian reliance on circular reasoning: Shakespeare, Mr. Hubler tells us, could not have been of the nobility because Shakespeare, among other great English writers, was of the middle class. To give himself a case, Mr. Hubler confines his examples to England, thus conveniently eliminating a writer considered by many the greatest of all novelists: Count Leo Tolstoy. Thus he also eliminates the French Renaissance figure Pierre de Ronsard, known to his generation as the "prince of poets," descendant of Baudouin de Ronsard and the noble family of de Chaudrier. Joseph Conrad, a scion of the Polish landed gentry with an aristocrat's code of behavior, also goes by the boards; though a leading English novelist he was of foreign birth. Lord Byron, however, whom Mark Van Doren calls one of the nine poets of all time who have spoken with "the noble voice of Calliope," is also omitted, though surely he would have been surprised to have been considered as either non-English or middle class. So too is James Boswell, writer of the biography generally regarded as the greatest in English and now thought by some to have written the greatest autobiography as well; he was very proud of being the son of Lord Auchinleck, whose mother was the daughter of the 2nd Earl of Kincardine. Another who fails to make the grade is Sir Walter Scott, who claimed descent from various chiefs of Border clans — but then, of course, he was from the wrong side of the Tweed. (Of Scott it is said that "pride of family . . . tempted him into courses that ended in commercial ruin; but throughout his life it was a constant spur to exertion." Much the same thing could probably be said of Oxford.) Robert Burns was also Scottish but still is an embarrassment to the class view of literary genius. The son of a farmer, forced early into permanently damaging labor, Burns was of well below middle-class origin. D. H. Lawrence was the son of a coal-miner. But the chief point to be made is that even if great literary genius were twenty times as likely to appear in the uppermost class as in a lower, there would still be a thousand times as many such geniuses in the ranks of the people as in those of the nobility. This is a matter of sixth-grade arithmetic: there are twenty thousand (or however many) times more commoners than peers. To say that a nobleman who wrote great literary works would be an extraordinary departure from the norm is no argument at all. Of course he would be. The odds against a great author's appearing in any given family are millions to one.

Postulate Number Two: The Inadmissibility of a Nobleman's Authorship

My second proposition is that a nobleman in Shakespeare's time who wrote literary works for publication would have felt under obligation and been under strong social pressure to conceal his authorship. The Stratfordians do not dispute this fact. If Sir Walter Scott, early in the 19th century, felt constrained to publish the Waverly novels anonymously for thirteen years because he considered the writing of novels beneath the dignity of his position, we may imagine how unthinkable it would have been for an Earl in Tudor England to have his name on a published poem like *Venus and Adonis* or, most monstrous of all, acknowledged his authorship of plays appearing on the public stage. No one, I believe, would argue otherwise. R. C. Churchill, in his scourge of apostasy entitled *Shakespeare and His Betters,* writes: "I believe it is as well for the officials of the Shakespeare Fellowship that the Earl of Oxford is safely dead, for they would be in some danger of being run through if they insulted the Earl in person by suggesting he had written Shakespeare's plays. For a courtier brought up on Castiglione, a greater insult could hardly be imagined." Yes, but suppose that the Earl *had* written those plays, driven by a dæmon that early in life had made of him a poet and playwright of comedies. Suppose the earl-dramatist is having his protagonists speak for himself when the ebullient Bastard Faulconbridge exclaims:

> And so am I, . . .
> > to deliver
> Sweet, sweet poison for the age's tooth. . . .

that he is speaking for himself again when the melancholy Jaques says:

> Invest me in my motley; give me leave
> To speak my mind, and I will through and through
> Cleanse the foul body of th' infected world,
> If they do patiently receive my medicine. . . .

that once more he is speaking for himself in Hamlet's disheartened recognition that:

> The time is out of joint. O cursèd spite
> That ever I was born to set it right.

Suppose, in brief, that the earl-dramatist felt he had a mission to expose what was rotten in the state of England. Suppose the plays, if correctly attributed to a courtier close to the throne, would be seen as commentaries on affairs at Court by an insider, as sardonic and mischievous portrayals of highly placed figures and as intimate revelations about the author himself unheard of on the part of a nobleman — and this a nobleman with the proudest name! — and hence as intolerably unbecoming in the eyes of his peers. Powerful interests would thus have a stake in keeping the author's identity hushed up — if they could not shut him up to begin with: "Art made tongue-tied by authority," the poet bitterly remarks in the *Sonnets.* Not least among the censorious would be the Queen's First Minister and Lord Treasurer, the author's guardian, his father-in-law and guardian of his children, whose watchword was respectability, who had little use for the arts, condemned all that smacked of bohemianism, would suffer no scandal to touch his house if he could help it, and was determined to establish that house as a lasting power in the realm — and so far succeeded that even four centuries later a Cecil, the 3rd Marquess of Salisbury, would become his nation's Prime Minister. We must remember, too, that if his contemporary, John Davies, is to be believed — and I do not know why he should not be — the author of the plays sacrificed high position to appear on the stage himself. Even if surreptitious, this was insufferable behavior in a nobleman.

Here the question must arise as to what the author's own feeling would have been about his necessary anonymity. When he cried in the *Sonnets,* "My name be buried where my body is," was he voluntarily renouncing the fame that could have been his or was he, sick at heart, acquiescing in a fate pronounced by others?

Two things are certain. One is that de Vere was conscious of his noble birth and what it required of him and proud of the de Vere name. An early poem signed E.O. — perhaps wrung from him by the shock of having the legitimacy of his birth challenged when he was thirteen — came as a cry from the heart "To wail this loss of my good name." When, at age twenty-one, he wrote a preface to a translation of Castiglione's *The Courtier* by his former tutor, he spoke out from his full rank:

> Edward Vere, Earl of Oxford, Lord Great Chamberlain of England, Viscount Bulbeck and Baron Scales and Badlesmere, to the Reader — Greeting.

He sought honor in the lists of the tournament and won it. As Shakespeare (if he was) he was preoccupied with honor, as any reader must be aware; the word recurs in the plays no less than 690 times. "If it be a sin to covet honour, / I am the most offending soul alive," says Henry V, clearly the dramatist's favorite monarch. Even Othello, after murdering his guiltless wife, can plead, transparently with the playwright's approval, "Nor ought I did in hate, but all in honour." Frank Harris remarks on "Shakespeare's love of good blood, and belief in its wondrous efficacy; it is one of his permanent and most characteristic traits." He says, "Shakespeare loved a lord with a passionate admiration, and when he paints himself it is usually as a duke or prince." He accuses the dramatist of an "almost inconceivable snobbishness." The charge would be warranted had Shakespeare been the man Harris took it for granted he was. Consider the response by the Earl of Suffolk in *Henry the Sixth, Part Two,* when the pirate who holds him captive demands "now will ye stoop?"

> . . . No, rather let my head
> Stoop to the block than these knees bow to any
> Save to the God of heaven, and to my king;
> And sooner dance upon a bloody pole
> Than stand uncovered to a vulgar groom.
> True nobility is exempt from fear.

This intense partisanship toward the virtues of noble birth that runs through Shakespeare could, if displayed by the son of a failed small-town glover, most reasonably be explained as sycophancy. It would be his play for the favor of the powerful. In a de Vere it would be natural expression of an ingrained habit of mind. But a de Vere who, driven by a passion and a genius for poetry and the drama, wrote plays for the common theatre, consorted with writers like Nashe and Greene, Kyd and Marlowe, and sneaked incognito into stage-parts himself, would have been intensely conscious of having betrayed his class and dishonored the names of sixteen precedent earls and the de Vere escutcheon, which his heirs would bear. He might well have seen it as his sacred obligation as a de Vere to yield to pressure and veil these enormities and spare his "good name" the disgrace they would otherwise bring upon it. I can imagine that this pressure amounted to a command from the highest quarters.

But — and here is my second certainty — the desire for recognition is a force in human nature second in persistence only to the instinct for survival, of which it is but another expression. A child of four will bring you his crayon drawing for praise and be distraught if you discard it. No writer ever lived but who yearned to have his words, and he with them, admired by posterity: *there* is immortality for even the convinced disbeliever in any other kind. How must this human longing work in one whose literary creations are the greatest ever? What must be the cost to him of renouncing their authorship?

My picture of the author of Shakespeare's works in his later years is of a man on the rack, pulled in opposing directions by well-nigh irresistible forces in respect to the acknowledgment of the fruits of his genius. I think this was in part the source of the despair and anguish we read in him, of the emotional instability I seem to see in Oxford and Shakespeare alike. If they were the same, as I believe, we have a human being who did well not to lose his mind. The old question as to whether Hamlet was insane or only feigning insanity may come down to his awareness of its incipience in himself. "Let me not be mad," Lear cries, "not mad, sweet heaven, . . . I would not be mad!"

The psychiatrist Eliot Slater has written of Shakespeare that "if we ever ascertain them, the facts of his life must throw light on his work." And he believes E. K. Chambers is right in supposing Shakespeare to have had a nervous breakdown. "Chambers is right also," he goes on, "in seeing the effects of this experience in *Hamlet, Lear* and *Timon*." Of *Lear*, Dr. Slater writes: "This tremendous work was never written by a man in a state of mental illness, but its utter nihilism was, I believe, the vision of horror of a man who has passed through mental illness and has to tell mankind what he has seen."

Did de Vere finally intend for Shakespeare's masterpieces never to be known as his, if they were? It is difficult to know, "he not having the fate, common with some, to be executor to his own writings," as we are told in the First Folio was true of the author. De Vere was evidently carried off suddenly, by the plague, at age fifty-four, leaving no known will. (It would have been characteristic of him to have neglected to make one but also not surprising if his will had vanished in the general disappearance of documents bearing on Shakespeare's identity.)[1] He would, however, have been either more or less than human not to have dropped some hints in the plays as to how things were. Thus, when we return to the subject in the last chapter, I believe we shall find to our satisfaction that he did — hints enough to confirm what we may deduce William Shakspere's part in the proceedings to have been.

That brings me to my third proposition.

Postulate Number Three: The Need for a Stand-in for the Author

If the authorship of the plays was to be concealed, it would not be enough for them to be offered under a pseudonym. It would be all very well for them to be put out as by William Shakespeare, but the question was bound to arise: Who is William Shakespeare? Unless there were someone to point to, a stand-in for the author, the pseudonym was bound to be penetrated. There had to be a William Shakespeare in the flesh, somewhere.

Well, there was one, of sorts. Sometime between 1588 and 1596 there had arrived in London a William Shakspere (or Shaksper, or Shaxpere, or Shag-

---

[1] In quoting the Reverend Dr. John Ward's jottings about Shakespeare of 1662 on page 19, I omitted one sentence, viz., "Shakespear, Drayton and Ben Jhonson [*sic*], had a merry meeting, and it seems drank too hard, for Shakespear died of a fever there contracted. . . ." I find it not difficult to believe that de Vere, then living outside London in Hackney, had injudiciously indulged with two fellow poets (as Robert Greene had done in his company at that fatal banquet) before being stricken by the fever that marked the plague—and does not follow any amount of drinking. That Drayton and Jonson would have made a three-day journey to Stratford to bend an elbow with Will Shakspere years after his departure from London seems to me highly unlikely.

spere) who had become a hanger-on of the theatre; it was later reported that he had held horses there and, as we have seen, that he was a "servitur." Was his presence on the scene a remarkable coincidence? Not necessarily. In the 1583 and 1584 season, a troupe of players in Lord Oxford's livery performed in Stratford, and they may have put on plays said to be by a mysterious lord who called himself William Shakespeare. Or Shakspere perhaps heard of the mysterious Shakespeare from word sent back to his native town by Richard Field, who printed *Venus and Adonis*. He may have taken to the road with the idea of capitalizing on the similarity of names. Did he then, in London, endeavor to palm himself off as the unknown poet and dramatist, knowing that he was safe from denunciations by the lord masked behind the name? There is evidence in the poem *On Poet-Ape* that he may have operated in such a fashion. The diatribe is by Ben Jonson, to whom or from whom we find almost all roads leading when we come upon dissimulation of the authorship. It deals with a "poor Poet-ape" — one who mimics a poet — "that would be thought our chief" — would be thought to be Shakespeare? — "Whose works are e'en the frippery of wit": "frippery" comes from a word for "rag" and a *fripperer* came into the language in 1584 meaning a dealer in cast-off clothing. The Poet-ape

> From brokage is become so bold a thief,
>   As we, the robb'd leave rage and pity it.

At first he would "buy the reversion of old plays," but

> now grown
> To a little wealth and credit in the scene,
>   He takes up all, makes each man's wit his own,
> And told of this, he slights it, Tut, such crimes
>   The sluggish, gaping author devours.

Some Stratfordian commentators have believed that Poet-ape to have been Shakspere, partly because it is difficult to know who else he could have been: Ivor Brown writes that "It was a permissible jest to hint that Shakespeare was a poet-ape and play-broker." But the Poet-ape certainly could not have been the dramatist. If Jonson had the Stratford man in mind, we may take it that Shakspere became a play-broker, then an outright thief, stealing the work of others — notably Shakespeare's, one would suppose — and marketing it as his own. And the reader may recall that early in the 18th century Shakspere was said by a French writer to have undertaken the profession of thief. (Plays were generally stolen in those days by pirates who would bribe actors to recite their lines and those of other characters as well as they remembered them.) Let us leave it that Shakspere may or may not have been in the business of purloining plays and get on to what has been explicitly reported.

Nicholas Rowe, in his life of Shakespeare of 1709, wrote that "my Lord Southampton, at one time, gave him a thousand pounds, to enable him to go through with a purchase which he heard he had a mind to." E. K. Chambers expresses the orthodox view when he says: "The sum named is quite incredible. . . . Probably a cipher has been added to the figures during the transition of the story; and some such amount as £100 Shakespeare may have spent on acquiring a share in the Lord Chamberlain's Company when it was formed during 1594." Certainly £1,000 would be an enormous amount. Rowe was aware of that. "A bounty very great, and rare at any time," he called it. That is a good reason for accepting Rowe's otherwise unsupported hearsay. Perhaps another is that the report is so implausible on its face as hardly likely to have been hatched without basis. And while Chambers says that "the aggregate of Shakespeare's known purchases throughout his life does not reach £1,000," if you add those purchases, including the theatrical shares, and the cost of comfortable living, you quite easily come to such a figure. The income from thirty-seven plays would barely have enabled the author to make ends meet over a twenty-year period, and certainly Shakspere did not make sufficient mark as an actor to have prospered in that capacity. The renowned Richard Burbage at his death held property worth £300, in addition to personal possessions. Shakspere put down £440 in one investment, to purchase tithes. This was after supposedly acquiring shares in the Globe, which made him, according to Gerald E. Bentley, "among the 300 and more authors who contributed to the great achievement called the Elizabethan drama, . . . the only one who is known to have been, over a long period of years, a theater owner." It was also after having, even earlier, in 1597, bought New Place with a payment of £60, probably representing only part of the cost. Queen Henrietta Maria, traveling across England in 1643, put up for two nights at New Place, leading Professor Bentley to observe, without intended irony, that "A house which was thought fit for the entertainment of the Queen was a most unusual possession for a dramatist and actor to pass on to his children." Most unusual indeed, especially when the "dramatist and actor," when he bought it, had been only nine years at his alleged calling, by the most generous estimate.

Everything falls into place, Oxfordians have long pointed out, if we take it that in 1597 the persons in whose hands the matter rested decided that the authorship of the plays we know as the world's greatest would be lastingly concealed; that they would be openly and authoritatively credited to the William Shakespeare who had dedicated *Venus and Adonis* and *Lucrece* to the Earl of Southampton; and that the idea would be floated that William Shakespeare was the peace-threatener, tax-evader, theatrical functionary, and possible play-broker Will Shakspere. This tactic necessitated getting Shakspere out of sight so that his glaring disqualifications for the role of the dramatist would not queer the game. Southampton was made the agent for paying him £1,000 to return to Stratford and there maintain a noncommittal reserve about his London activities. This he did, and in Stratford, except for perhaps an occasional visit to London and a brief sojourn in the city in 1604, he appears to have remained in affluent obscurity.[2] Of his business activities there from 1598 on, the record leaves no doubt, whatever interests he may have retained in London, such as the 10 per cent share in the Globe that William Shakespeare was recorded, twenty years later, as having held.

It was in 1598, more or less coincident with the shift of Shakspere's locus of activity back to Stratford, that "William Shakespeare" was unveiled as the author of immortal dramas hitherto anonymous in origin. As we have several times had occasion to notice, the instrument of the unveiling was Francis Meres, a Master of Arts of both universities widely acquainted with literary men. It is worth repeating how in his *Palladis Tamia,* under the heading "A comparative discourse of our English Poets with the Greek, Latin, and Italian Poets," he wrote that "As Plautus and Seneca are accounted the best for comedy and tragedy among the Latins: so Shakespeare among the English is the most excellent in both kinds for the stage," then named six of Shakespeare's comedies and six of his tragedies. It will be recalled that he also wrote that "the sweet witty soul of Ovid lives in mellifluous & honey-tongued Shakespeare, witness his *Venus* and *Adonis,* his *Lucrece,* his sugared Sonnets among his private friends, &c," and that "the Muses would speak with Shakespeare's fine filed phrase, if they would speak English." Shakespeare is also included by Meres among those by whom "the English tongue is mightily enriched," among the best lyric poets, and among "the most passionate among us to bewail and bemoan the perplexities of love."

Meres, in listing "The best for comedy amongst us," starts with "Edward Earle of Oxforde" (as social form would require) and includes Shakespeare among the sixteen others who follow. Orthodox academicians seize upon the conjunction of the two names. Oscar James Campbell of Columbia declares: "If the list proves that Oxford was a successful writer of comedies it proves just as clearly that Shakespeare was too and it establishes the separate identity of the two dramatists." Presumably it would come as a surprise to the professors to learn that Willard Huntington Wright and S. S. Van Dine, though named separately in publishers' lists, were the same man, that the

---

[2] Professors Evans and Levin quote this statement, but in doing so misquote what preceded it and then leave out the part about the visits to London so that they can imply that I am ignorant or suppressing information. "As a matter of fact," they write, "he is mentioned among the cast of Jonson's *Sejanus* in 1603, and there is legal evidence for his presence in London on several occasions during his later years." As I have already pointed out, the listing of "William Shake-Speare" in the cast of *Sejanus* took place thirteen years later, and it stands suspiciously all by itself. Shakspere was presumably in London in 1612 and 1613, perhaps for not more than a day or two each time, when truncated forms of his name were signed to legal documents.

same was true of Ray Stannard Baker and David Grayson, and that William Sharp and Fiona Macleod had separate biographies in *Who's Who* in the 1890s, though they also were the same person. Joseph Shearing, Marjorie Bowen, George R. Preedy, John Winch, and Robert Payne have all been listed individually in publishers' catalogues, three of them having each had entries in *Who's Who,* and Professor Campbell and his colleagues would take this as proof positive that they were different persons. Yet all five were Mrs. Margaret Vere Campbell Long, who also wrote as Margaret Campbell and was the author of more than a hundred books. The editors of *Who's Who* did not learn of her multiple identity until she informed them of it.

It is difficult for me to understand how generations of scholars should have made nothing of Shakespeare's extraordinary advent upon the scene as a playwright, of his having been suddenly sprung upon the world as the author of six comedies and six tragedies, the best of their kind in English in both categories. It is noteworthy, too, Marchette Chute says, that whereas "Meres mentioned a great many playwrights in his book . . . Shakespeare was the only one he singled out for extended comment." (Incidentally, could one single out more than one?) Indeed, we may remind ourselves that he named no other plays but two of Dr. Leg's. There must be a reason for all this, and the only realistic one I can find is that the decision had been reached that the author of the hitherto unattributed dramatic masterpieces was to be "Shakespeare" and Meres had been selected to launch the artifice unobtrusively. This may well have been the sole purpose behind the "comparative discourse" inserted into *Palladis Tamia.* "Clearly," says Samuel Schoenbaum, "Meres did not believe that the Earl [of Oxford] wrote *Comedy of Errors, Romeo and Juliet,* and the rest"; but the professor has no way of knowing, any more than I have, what Meres believed. If Meres was in on the concealment of Oxford's hand in "Shakespeare's" authorship, which he may not have been, he was certainly not going to blow the Earl's cover and defeat the purpose for which he was writing. Meres would have performed an invaluable service for literary history if he had given the names of the plays — presumably entertainments for the Court — for which Oxford was known, and no doubt too well known for Meres to omit his name from those "best for Comedy." Alas, no word of them has come down to us, though I am satisfied that they are well known to us in later form as Shakespeare's.

What was the public's response to the disclosure that Shakespeare was among them, the greatest of the nation's playwrights? Muted. Guarded, I should put it. As we saw in Chapter 1, it was to be just a quarter-century before the superlative acclaim Shakespeare received in *Palladis Tamia* was to be seconded — by Ben Jonson. In between, it was, as the epigrammatist later divulged in *Wits Recreation,* a matter of "Shakespeare, we must be silent in our praise."

Will Shakspere was fitted not only by name to serve as the author's surrogate: he had the further essential qualification of being barely literate. That means he would not be writing letters or other mementos in language hopelessly unworthy of a great author. As far as it went, that expectation was sound. But alas! The Stratfordian proved unable to refrain altogether from having a go at verse — doubtless orally conveyed. Future idolators would gaze with troubled eyes on the crude exhortation on his tombstone, supposedly expressing the poet's last message to the living world. They would wince at the doggerel of which his fellow townsmen spoke to a Lieutenant Hammond in 1634, as something he had composed (page 14).[3] Only those able to take much on faith would be able to believe that the village rhymester remembered for a quatrain to which no Longfellow, no Robert Frost, no Ogden Nash would stoop, was the poet whose unforced pen flowed with the sublime music he so often invoked:

> How sweet the moonlight sleeps upon this bank!
> Here will we sit and let the sounds of music
> Creep in our ears; soft stillness and the night
> Become the touches of sweet harmony.

Even in his later years in Stratford, it would seem that Shakspere was not forgotten by those who had made his return to his native town worth his while. Before she died in 1612, Lady Oxford, the Earl's second wife, bequeathed an unspecified number of pounds to be paid quarterly "to my dombe man," one would guess to ensure his remaining dumb. (Professor Evans and Levin had no comment on the singular provision.) This gift was followed by Shakspere's purchase of the Blackfriars gatehouse in London as an investment. Whatever de Vere's intentions may have been respecting the ultimate attribution of Shakespeare's works, it is evident that his widow did not mean to have the authorship divested of the pseudonym. The wife of the poet who wrote the *Sonnets* could hardly be expected to have relished seeing his identity revealed.

Up to now our postulates have been:

One. The author was a nobleman. Innumerable readers have been convinced of this fact by evidence such as I shall present in Chapter 14.

Two. There was reason for the author's identity to be concealed. I think no one familiar with Elizabethan mores will deny that the second postulate follows from the first.

---

[3] An early version of the doggerel reads:

Ten in the hundred must lie in his grave,
But a hundred to ten whether God will him have?
Who then must be interr'd in this tomb?
Oh (quoth the Devil) my John a Combe.

Three. If the author's identity were to remain concealed another man would have to be established as the author in his place. This seems to me axiomatic. The writer of thirty-seven plays, many highly popular on the public stage, had to have been *some*body.

But now we come to a fourth postulate of quite a different order of credibility.

Postulate Number Four: Eradication of the Author's Traces

This final postulate is highly implausible, and because of the misunderstanding we saw illustrated in the *Life* editorial, which found a "conspiracy" to conceal the authorship difficult to credit, its implausibility is what has chiefly blocked a more general acceptance of "Shakespeare" as having been a pseudonym.

If the conditions in the third postulate were to be satisfied — if, that is, the surrogate author were to be accepted by posterity — all testimony as to the actual authorship and all testimony as to the surrogate's ineligibility would have to be forestalled and where it was committed to paper the incriminating documents would have to be gathered up and destroyed. It sounds impossible; no wonder theories of the authorship that seem to differ from the conventional in resting on this contingency have met with widespread skepticism. But as we saw early in this chapter, what sounds impossible is in fact what happened. The question of plausibility does not arise. Plausible or not, a nearly clean sweep was made of contemporary documentation touching on the authorship. Included in the path of the vacuum cleaner, it would seem, were the "lost years" of Will Shakspere, of which every trace vanished. These facts are an obstacle primarily to the Stratfordians. The far-reaching effort required to sanitize the record was called for only if the truth of the authorship, were it generally known, would cause embarrassment in high places. It would have made no sense if the author had been the Stratford man.

A few bits did get by Operation Clean Sweep: John Davies's poem on the playwright's acting kingly parts in sport; the *Parnassus* plays poking fun at the idea of an untutored Shakespeare in whom the public (as we learn from the plays for the first time) was being asked to believe; two copies of "F.B.'s" letter to Ben Jonson also poking fun at it; and the six damning signatures doing duty as Shakespeare's. One highly awkward circumstance was unavoidable. If Shakespeare was fitted for his role by his near illiteracy, which would forestall (almost) his leaving unseemly compositions behind him, it followed that he would also not leave behind him any holographs or literary memorabilia such as an author *would* leave. But that drawback could be counterbalanced when it came to getting out Shakespeare's collected plays. These would be presented in the First Folio with a certain implication that they were Shakspere's. Thanks to the man chosen as editor (it appears) to convey this impression — Ben Jonson — it would be more conclusively implied that they were not his. It may have been forgotten, however, that he was called honest Ben Jonson. And probably his slyness went generally unnoticed. This we shall come to in the next chapter.

Anyone trying to satisfy himself, and others, as to the authorship of Shakespeare's plays must be just as glad that he does not have to account for the means by which history was rendered so nearly silent in the matter but need only observe that it was so. Nevertheless, we who ascribe the plays to Edward de Vere are as curious as anyone must be as to what those means were. And our inquiries give us more reason to believe that de Vere was the man.

To begin with, the task was probably less formidable than we may picture it. When handwriting and hand-printing were the only methods of putting words on paper, documentation by our standards was meagre indeed. Moreover, I think that expressing oneself on the Shakespeare authorship, orally or in writing, where the indiscretion might come to be known, was simply not done. We can read nearly the whole of Victorian literature and gain no inkling of the activity that enables the human race to perpetuate itself and is a major preoccupation of mankind's; writers simply steered clear of the matter. In Elizabethan England, if I may repeat, behavior was governed not merely by social convention but by lively awareness of the ever-present agencies of a jealous central authority. With regard to the Shakespeare authorship, those who had the greatest interest in keeping it quiet — if de Vere was the author — were those in the best position to achieve that purpose.

Power of the Cecils over the Records

For more than 370 years, the Cecils have had a family seat in Hatfield House — for they remain, of course, one of the great families of England. A Jacobean palace, originally Elizabethan in architecture, of red brick trimmed in limestone, the splendid edifice is set in a spacious park 21 miles north of London. I had the rich experience of touring it in 1978. Its treasures are awesome. William Cecil Lord Burghley is there, painted in magnificent black and red robes, grey-bearded like Polonius, but with a smooth face and rather glowing complexion. So too is his sharper-featured, paler, and more sombrely clad son Robert Cecil, a hunchback of whom it was said that no one could remember him as young. Sir Robert was elevated above his father to become the Earl of Salisbury, and there is a famous portrait by Sir Joshua Reynolds of the dashing 1st Marchioness of Salisbury to remind the visitor that the family was further ennobled by George II. The 3rd Marquess, thrice Prime Minister between 1855 and 1902, looks down with quite moving compassion in a full-length portrait showing him in the gold-brocaded robe of a Chancellor of the University of Oxford. Queen Elizabeth I, in two regal portraits, is inscrutable, the artist having perhaps been very uncertain as to what, in safety, he might have scrutiny reveal. Among the displays are a hat, gloves, and silk stockings — said to be the first in England — worn by the Queen.

Hatfield House gave me an idea of the splendor in which a powerful nobleman set about to domicile himself in the year of England's achieving its first permanent foothold in the New World. Imposing as the palace is, however, it is greatly overmatched by Burghley House, some 80 miles north of London in Stamford, certainly as the latter has stood since it was remodeled and landscaped by Lancelot, "Capability," Brown in the 18th century. Even this, however, was not the most pretentious of Burghley's three homes. That was Theobalds, his country seat on the northern outskirts of London, of which next to nothing now remains. Burghley built Theobalds for his son Robert (Burghley House being destined for his elder son, Thomas), but when James came to the throne he much fancied it, and Sir Robert had little choice but to accept the King's proposal and exchange it for the original century-old Hatfield Palace.

Here, as a girl, Elizabeth had lived and endured her strict schooling, and here she had been a virtual prisoner during her sister Mary's reign. She was twenty-five, in 1558, when Queen Mary died. Lord Cecil recalls: "Seated under an oak tree which still survives in the park, Elizabeth was reading when the news of her accession was brought to her. 'It is the Lord's doing,' she said; 'and it is marvellous in our eyes.' Her first act was to send for Lord Burghley" — Cecil, as he then was. Half a century later, ten years after Burghley's death, Robert tore down three sides of the quadrangular old Castle and began construction of Hatfield House. Looking at the remaining side, I wondered if Edward de Vere had ever entered it.

Whether or no, a part of him was present in Hatfield House itself. From the Palace's famous archives, the librarian, R. H. Harcourt Williams, put himself to the trouble of extracting a volume containing an original letter of de Vere's. This I took in my hand with, I confess, a sense of touching the greatness of history at the quick and with the belief that it would in time have a place of honor in the glass-topped document-case upstairs. (In this is now exhibited the order for the decapitation of Mary Queen of Scots, which even Elizabeth, for all the stony-heartedness she could command in herself, could not bring herself to execute and left to Lord Burghley, who drafted it with many untypical crossings-out and interlineations.) The letter was addressed by the twenty-five-year-old de Vere from Siena to his father-in-law,

Burghley. It is like him in that the forward-sloping handwriting, with its long vertical strokes, is much easier to read than that of most of his contemporaries, in that the expression is exceptionally clear for the times (1575), when the language as we know it was just taking shape, and in that its subject was the young writer's financial straits. I can read the copy Mr. Harcourt Williams sent me with little difficulty.

> My Lord I am sorry to hear how hard my fortune is in England as I perceive by your Lordship's letters, but knowing how vain a thing it is to linger a necessary mischief (to know the worst of myself, & to let your Lord. understand wherein I would use your honorable friendship), in short I have thus determined, that whereas I understand the greatness of my debt, & greediness of creditors grows so dishonorable to me, and troublesome unto your Lordship that that land of mine wh[?] is in Cornwall I have appointed to be sold. . . .

I have just noticed that the prose is like de Vere's, too, in having a Shakespearean overtone. The harmonic here struck is with a peculiarly touching sonnet, number 90:

> Give not a windy night a rainy morrow,
> *To linger out a purposed overthrow*
> . . . .
> But in the onset come, so shall I taste
> *At first the very worst of fortune's might.*

If we insert two monosyllables, as Shakespeare would have done for the sake of the meter, a line from the letter could almost stand beside the foregoing, could it not?

> how vain a thing it is
> *To linger [out] a necessary mischief:*
> *To know the worst of my [own] self. . . .*

England under Burghley's forty-year ministry has been called *Regnum Cecilianum*. Speaking of the historical records of the time, his biographer M. A. S. Hume wrote eighty years ago, "Everything passed through his hands." Camden states in his *Annales* that Lord Burghley "willed" him to write a history of Elizabeth's reign, having "opened up" to him the "memorials" from which to compile it. Referring to gross slander of de Vere that found a place in the record (the author of the slander was a peer whose treasonous connection with Spain de Vere had exposed), Father Francis Edwards writes:

> The whole episode reminds us usefully of a basic fact which must be taken increasingly into account by Jacobean historians of the future: for at least 50 crucial years — until 1612, in fact, England was virtually ruled, and with remarkable consistency and effectiveness, by Sir William Cecil and Sir Robert, his son. As principal secretaries, they had all the power necessary to preserve or destroy for posterity the materials of future history that lay in public hands. As Masters of the Court of Wards, they had similar opportunities to deal, sooner

Remaining Section of Old Hatfield
Palace

Courtesy of the Marquess of Salisbury.

or later, with the private records of a great many leading families. No one who
has attempted research on important figures who collided or disagreed with the
regime at any point can fail to notice the curious lop-sidedness of the records.

As Burghley himself wrote, "Princes have many eyes and ears, and very
long arms." Burghley and his adjunct, Sir Francis Walsingham, were above
all others those eyes, ears, and arms.

I do not know how much malice the Cecils may have borne de Vere,
though surely they resented and disapproved of him. When *Hamlet* appeared
with its satirical portrayal of the chief counsellor to the throne, there must
have been a great to-do, for the name given to the pompous old man who
cited maxims so like Burghley's *Preceptes* was Corambis — *Cor ambis,* "two-

hearted," a palpable swipe at Burghley's motto, *Cor unum, via una,* "one heart, one way." Clearly, only a dramatist with royal protection could have got away with it. But the record is silent on any reaction, though Cecil power was sufficient to have Corambis changed to Polonius after the first printing. Both from internal evidence and Nashe's reference to it in 1589, we may judge *Hamlet* to have been written by that year, but it may be that the prolix old counsellor was made recognizably Burghley only after his death in 1598, five years before the play was first printed.

If there was lasting rancor against de Vere, the correspondence does not show it — as doubtless it would not after passing through Cecils' hands. Ostensibly, relations between the two sides were amicable to the end. They almost had to be. Neither could well afford to come to an open break with the other. But when such opposites as William Cecil and Edward de Vere, each strong where the other was weak, are yoked together by bonds of circumstance, each is certain to be sorely tried by the other, and was in this case.

In framing the historical record as it involved de Vere, I judge that the Cecils had several objectives. The self-righteous Lord Burghley would seek to have the record show all he had suffered at the hands of his son-in-law, and with what magnanimity, and be silent on the provocations the latter had endured. Themselves new members of the nobility, the Cecils would be protective of its prestige. As patriots, they would also believe that its prestige should be cherished as essential to a strong England and not be compromised, as public knowledge of theatrical activities of a de Vere would have compromised it. Those plays which fired the spirit of English nationalism they would have seen the value of and might on their account have been willing to forgive their author a great deal. Burghley could have felt that in producing such powerful stimulants to national unity under the guns of Spain, the author was rendering England even more important service than any de Vere had on the battlefield. The Queen must surely have thought so and, the facts indicate, generously encouraged their author in writing them. But on no account would the Cecils have wished to have de Vere seen as the author of Shakespeare's plays — ever. They did not mean to have the public pricking up its ears to what the plays might be giving away — such as the real-life model for Polonius — if their origin were known. Burghley had a keen sense of family; Burghley House was a reconstruction of the family seat. A collector of books, his special hobby was genealogy and heraldry. His concern for the record is attested by the tens of thousands of documents covering the period down to his death that he preserved for posterity. He would have exerted his far-reaching power to safeguard himself and his heirs from any breath of scandal. Oxford was father to his grand-daughters and Sir Robert's nieces. But the Cecils could well have felt that they were serving Oxford's true interests as well as their own in expunging all traces of his connection with the stage — except that they seem almost to have effaced Oxford himself from the record. Even so admiring a biographer as Conyers Read in writing of Burghley's last work for publication — in which he finds some facts "deliberately misrepresentations" — acknowledges that it "like all the rest of them was definitely propagandistic." As he says, "it is a pity that it was so" for "he might have told the inside story." We may be sure that the same propagandistic aims governed his treatment of all records under his far-reaching control.

Some readers may still find themselves unable to believe that so wide-ranging a suppression of information as I have ascribed to the Cecils could have been carried out. If the nearly blank contemporary record on the authorship of Shakespeare's works does not convince them that it could be done, and was, nothing I can add is likely to do so. Still, I may cite a striking case of controlled information in our own far freer and more blabber-prone society.

It was in 1944 that I had my first contact with information that was to be kept so successfully from public knowledge. As a first lieutenant I had come from overseas to report for duty to the Director of Intelligence, G-2, War Department. Upon being sworn to safeguard what was about to be imparted to me, I was let in on the astonishing achievement by British and American cryptanalysts in decoding the most vital radio communications of our enemies. "This source of intelligence is classified Ultra Top Secret." I was told. "Is the term itself classified?" I asked. "The term is itself classified Ultra Top Secret," was the reply. "No reference is to be made to the term or to any material so classified outside certain offices which will be identified to you."

Until the war's end I was one of those who worked with Ultra, the incredible flow of messages from the highest German and Japanese commands that were decoded and translated into English. There were hundreds of us, from enlisted clerks — men and women — on up through the ranks in a dozen headquarters around the world. Bales of documents bore the Ultra Top Secret stamp. The break-throughs achieved by our cryptanalysts must have shortened the war by many months. Without their success it is possible that Britain would have succumbed to Admiral Doenitz's wolf-packs or Fortress Europe have proved impregnable and the outcome of the greatest war of all time have been other than it was. In short, this was one of the great stories of World War II, of history. Yet for more than thirty years no word of it was spoken in public. Had not the British authorities consented to its release (in 1974), there is no reason to believe that the truth need ever have come out.

In reverting a few pages back to the few revealing references to the Shakespeare authorship that have survived, I omitted one. This is the daring preface to the first edition of *Troilus and Cressida* of 1609, which, having been printed and distributed, could not very well be quashed. It was, however, dropped from the second edition in that year. Under the heading "A never writer, to an ever reader. Newes," it begins: "Eternal reader, you have here a new play, never staled with the stage, never clapper-clawed with the palms of the vulgar." It goes on to give high praise to the author, while managing never to speak of Shakespeare. Were the names of comedies changed to those of commodities, it says, "you should see all those grand censors that now style them such vanities, flock to them for the main grace of their gravities: especially this author's comedies, that are so framed to the life, that they serve for the most common commentaries of all the actions of our lives, showing such a dexterity, and power of wit, that th[os]e most displeased with plays are pleased with his comedies." These come in for more encomiums, the writer finding that they seem "to be born in that sea that brought forth Venus." At the end comes the following:

> And believe this, that when he is gone, and his comedies out of sale, you will scramble for them, and set up a new English Inquisition. Take this for a warning, and at the peril of your pleasure's loss, for not being sullied with the smoky breath of the multitude; but thank fortune for the scape it hath made amongst you. Since by the grand possessors' wills I believe you should have prayed for them rather than been prayed.

I do not know what Stratfordians make of the assurance that the play had never been "clapper-clawed with the palms of the vulgar" or "sullied with the smoky breath of the multitude"; it is hardly the way one would speak of a product by a playwright of the people who turned out plays for money to meet the demands of performers on the commercial stage. By "grand possessors" the Stratfordians are constrained to maintain that an acting company is meant, though it would surely never have occurred to an Elizabethan to associate grandeur with a troupe of players.

What the preface appears to be telling the reader is that the dramatist's plays are held by members of the nobility and that *Troilus and Cressida* was somehow sprung from their control. For this the reader had better thank fortune, since, if those who held the plays had their way, he would be praying to have the plays instead of being prayed not to hold it against this comedy that it had never been performed. The reader is warned that the time is coming when he will have to scramble for the dramatist's comedies and set up a new English Inquisition to get them.

The fact certainly is that after 1609, none of Shakespeare's twenty hitherto unpublished plays was printed until the collection was brought out in the First Folio in 1623, apart from one that a printer got his hands on in the year before. Indeed, except for *Troilus and Cressida* and two others that made a "scape" in 1608 and 1609, along with the *Sonnets,* none of the twenty-three plays yet unpublished in 1603, the year before de Vere's death, was printed for the next nineteen years. The preface speaks of the reader's having to scramble for the dramatist's plays "when he is gone, and his comedies out of sale." But this situation has already come to pass; one does not in any case in referring to a living writer coolly speak of how things will be with his works when he is dead, even if one could foresee how they would be. That the dramatist was dead by 1609, when the Stratford man had seven more years to live, there is other evidence. William Barkstead, in a poem of 1607 addressed to his muse exclaimed, "His song was worthy merit (Shakespeare he). . . . Laurel is due him": not his song *is,* but his song *was.* In 1609, "Shake-speare's" *Sonnets* were published with the author apostrophized in the dedication as "our ever-living poet," and "ever-living" is a term never applied to a person who is in fact alive. Can one imagine introducing the writer of a sonnet sequence to an audience as "our ever-living poet"? The listeners would be baffled: "Obviously he's living. But what does 'ever' mean? That he isn't sometimes dead?" The Reverend Dr. W. A. Ferguson reports that a search of the leading English dictionaries, from Dr. Johnson's to the great Oxford and the Century, besides the glossaries of seven major poets from Milton to Shelley, has disclosed twenty-three occurrences of "ever-living," not one applied to a person who was still alive. Another plain indication that the author was dead was the title under which the *Sonnets* were registered and published; that is, as "*Shake-speares Sonnets*" (cf. the posthumous *Greenes Groats-worth of Wit*) rather than as "*Sonnets* by William Shakespeare," in the "more urbane collocation of words," as Sidney Lee says, "invariably" expected "by living authors." The Stratford theory must have more lives than a dozen cats to trip fatally on so many facts and yet still greet us at our doorstep whenever we look.

That the author was not identified as "Shakespeare" in the preface to *Troilus and Cressida* does not mean, I think, that he was not named. Look back at the curious heading, "A never writer to an ever reader. Newes." Oxfordians have held all along that the author was named twice in that. The heading may be taken as meaning both "A writer who never was to a constant reader" (the "eternal reader" addressed in the preface) and "An E. Ver writer to an E. Ver reader." Whichever way you take it — and I know of no third choice — it is bad business for the Stratfordians. So too is the preface as a whole. The Stratfordians do not like it. Marchette Chute and A. L. Rowse in his *Shakespeare the Man* omit most of it, including both the heading and the "grand possessors." Gerald E. Bentley, in *Shakespeare: A Biographical Handbook,* says only: "One of the two issues of *Troilus and Cressida* printed in 1609 has an epistle to the reader, but it was written not by the author, as Jonson's and Heyward's were [We may be very sure it was not written by the author], but by the publisher as a device to sell his book." Of the preface itself Professor Bentley quotes not a word. This is after charging that the anti-Stratfordian writer "simply denies any recorded facts that do not fit his own picture of the author of the plays." Professor Bentley does not cite any recorded facts that the anti-Stratfordian writer denies, and it would be too much to expect him to do so. But I may point out that in addition to omitting the preface to *Troilus and Cressida,* the Princeton professor leaves out of his *Handbook* any reference to the John Davies poem and the letter from "F.B.," and when he comes to quoting the brief remarks entered in his diary by John Ward upon becoming vicar of the Stratford church in 1662, he omits the most informative, viz., that "I have heard that Mr. Shakespeare was a natural wit, without any art at all," that "he frequented the plays all his younger time," and that "he supplied the stage with two plays every year, and for that had an allowance so large, that he spent at the rate of £1,000 a year, as I have heard." One can easily see how it occurred to the Princeton professor to charge his opponents (whose works, I suspect, are *terra incognita* to him) with denying facts that do not fit their picture of the dramatist.

13

"A Very Ancient and Fish-Like Smell"

Having waited half a dozen years after the stand-in's death, the authorities, we see, undertake concrete steps, minimal and ambiguous, to attach the authorship of Shakespeare's works to Shakspere. We look first at the monument in the Stratford church and perceive how it is conceived (1) to allow visitors in the future to take it as commemorating the dramatist Shakespeare while conveying no such message to the locals, who, knowing Shakspere, would doubtless have received it with incredulous amazement, and (2) to invite the observer's skepticism in proportion as it implies that the man commemorated was the illustrious writer. The question of who is responsible for the monument directs us to the Herbert brothers — the Earls of Pembroke and Montgomery (with their connections with Oxford), to whom the First Folio will be dedicated — and to their capture of the offices controlling the public drama. We find that, evidently as a consequence, the further printing of hitherto unpublished Shakespearean plays is largely arrested from the time of Oxford's death until 1623, when the collected edition, the First Folio, is brought out. We are led to reject the Stratfordians' contention that the epochal publication is the work of the actors Heminge and Condell, as it purports to be, and read the signs to indicate that Ben Jonson, as agent of the Herberts, is impresario of the volume. We examine Jonson's ambivalent attitude toward Shakespeare, then give our attention to the great Folio. We remark the clearly contrived grotesqueries of the Droeshout portrait and a give-away line in it, then scrutinize what follows: Jonson's poem facing the portrait, the two dedicatory addresses (evidently both of Jonson's authorship), and the famous panegyric to Shakespeare in which Jonson, carrying out his apparent instructions to pull the wool over posterity's eyes, risks all to tell it not to be fooled, not anticipating that its mentors will refuse to read what he writes. Throughout we find that the sanction the artificer of the Folio seems to accord to a Stratfordian Shakespeare with one hand, he unmistakably takes away with the other.

In the last two chapters we have dealt with the mainly successful undertaking to pass on to posterity a record that would be mute as to the origin of Shakespeare's plays. We have seen that whatever our view of their origin, we have to recognize that a most remarkable disappearance of documents took place, leaving blanks in the Stratford man's history, yawning gaps in the theatrical records of the day, and a near void wherever we should look for the author of Shakespeare's works. So much was accomplished in a negative way. But if the author's identity was to remain protected, positive steps had to be taken to vest the authorship in the Stratford man. Most surprising is that so little was done in this direction and that when a significant effort was finally made, it was so very limited and so ambivalent. We can only infer that those on whom it depended to groom the Stratford man for the part of Shakespeare had no heart for the business. I believe they would have been dumbfounded to know that the gossamer mantle of authorship they draped on him would go for centuries without being generally seen through.

To begin with, there seems to have been an intention to endow Shakspere with a shadow of a stage career. That, I take it, is the meaning of Jonson's having included Shakespeare in the casts of two of his plays, as enacted in 1598 and 1603 respectively, when he brought out his collected works in 1616. This tactic, together with the veritable Shakespeare's having played some parts on the stage (and Jonson called him "Shake-Speare" in the cast of *Sejanus*), plus Shakspere's having ostensibly been a shareholder in the Globe, are what, I think, have led to the common view of the Stratford man as an actor. Orthodox writers make much of Shakspere's bequest of money for the purchase of rings to Heminge, Burbage, and Condell — an afterthought on someone's part interlined in the will. Maybe Shakspere had remembered his bargain and did his bit by putting himself in the company of actors. Maybe he had a genuine regard for the three as fellow shareholders in the Globe. Maybe it was done after his death; an overseer of his will was related to Leonard Digges, who was brought in as a contributor to that great work of engineering, the First Folio.

A few seeming connectives between Shakspere and the stage would have been quite insufficient to give him the place in history he has come to have. For the instruments of that transubstantiation we have to wait for as much as ten years after Robert Cecil's death, six after Shakspere's. The delay suggests that the persons concerned were uncertain how to proceed.

Action had to be taken if survival was to be ensured for Shakespeare's plays. Even with the flurry of publications in 1608 and 1609, only eighteen had been printed, none altogether as the author had written them, and some in appallingly corrupt texts. It was unthinkable to leave it to the vagaries of the theatrical marketplace as to whether improved editions of the debased texts and the twenty hitherto unpublished plays would be brought out. Those who we may suppose were determined upon publishing the plays we may also deduce faced a problem. Enjoined from publishing the plays under their author's name and constrained to go along with and further the impression that had been given the public that they were the work of "William Shakespeare" of Stratford-upon-Avon, they found difficulties in doing what they were expected to do.

One was that many persons in London still remembered Shakspere, while

The Bust of "Shakspeare" in the
Stratford monument as it is today.

Photograph by Jarrold, Norwich, England.

most of the inhabitants of Stratford did so. The explicit, formal attribution
of the plays to a man of his character, who could not even write with facility,
might have caused such an explosion of ridicule as to be beyond containment.
There were also those who had known and esteemed the actual author and
who would have been revolted by the conclusive crediting of his masterpieces
to the man Ben Jonson had lampooned as the crude, clownish Sogliardo.
The problem was how to seem to establish Shakspere as the author without
leaving oneself open to the charge of having done so. It would appear
insoluble. Yet the clever persons we are talking about were equal to it.

Engraving of the Original
Monument to "Shakspeare" in the
Stratford church by Sir William
Dugdale of 1656.

By permission of the Folger Shakespeare
Library.

The Stratford Monument

To prepare for publishing the collected plays, which they had decided on,
the image of the Stratford man as the author would be given a foundation
in the form of a monument. The monument would escape the derision of
Londoners by being placed in Stratford. It would be safeguarded from the

derision of the Stratfordians by stopping short of making claims for Shakspere that would, in their eyes, be warranted only for a great poet-dramatist like Shakespeare. At the same time, future visitors to Stratford, expecting to find the great poet-dramatist commemorated in his supposed home town, would find the monument not irreconcilable with their expectations. The claims made for their subject would certainly have to be extreme for Shakspere and minimal for Shakespeare, but still they might be got away with; people generally see what they expect to see, not what they *are* seeing. The designers' calculations were to be borne out.

The monument (page 210) is said to have been the work of Gerard Johnson, son of Gheerart Janssen, a Dutch immigrant whose workshop was in London. Another son of Janssen's had designed the tomb of the 5th Earl of Rutland, which, erected in 1619, clearly served as a model for the artifact to be installed in the wall of the Stratford church. Where Rutland's memorial stone gives an extensive record of his life, however, the Stratford monument, though wordy, cites no biographical fact about the deceased whatever except, in very small letters, the date of his death — April 23, 1616 — and his age at death: fifty-three; presumably no one remembered the date of his birth.

A square block topped by a jawless death's-head — a curious bit of symbolism — and bearing Shakspere's coat-of-arms tops the memorial, flanked by Cupid-like figures. The most prominent feature is of course the bust. Commenting on the wooden appearance and blank expression of the effigy, Professor J. Dover Wilson speaks of its "general air of stupid and self-complacent prosperity." And he adds, "All this might suit well enough with an affluent and retired butcher, but does gross wrong to the dead poet." But then who can say that it is supposed to represent a poet?

The first known depiction of the monument is an engraving in Sir William Dugdale's *Antiquities of Warwickshire*, published in 1656 (page 211). It portrays a figure quite different from the one we know. Rather sour-looking with a tapering face and down-drooping moustaches, the subject clutches a sack, probably to be taken as full of grain. In the present bust he has a pen in one hand and a sheet of paper under the other, both resting on a cushion. To Sir George Greenwood, as to many others, "it seems absolutely certain that the Stratford bust . . . is in reality not the original bust at all." It is difficult to see how it could be. Taking the monument to represent the poet, Dugdale could hardly have failed to notice the pen and sheet of paper — symbols of literary composition — had they been present. Even if the plume had been broken off, the hand would still be in the position for holding a pen, the sheet of paper still present. Moreover, while I can understand how a cushion might have been substituted for the bulging sack in a replacement, *faute de mieux*, to convert a grain-dealer into an author, I cannot comprehend having a cushion as a writing surface to begin with.

The conclusion that the present bust is a substitute for the original is to

Louis Marder, as a spokesman for orthodoxy, an "argument that ought to be embalmed as a curiosity of criticism. There is superabundant evidence that Dugdale worked too quickly, misrepresented grossly, and accepted shoddy work. The Clopton monument and the Carew monument, both in Holy Trinity in Stratford, are hopelessly misrepresented and out of proportion." He speaks of "the numerous errors [in Dugdale] pointed out by Thomas and other writers." But "in 1730 Dr. Thomas, a Warwickshire man residing near Stratford, brought out a second edition of Dugdale's work which was revised, corrected and expanded," Francis Carr, the Baconian, writes. "Yet we find that the representation of the original monument is from the same unaltered block which Dugdale himself used." He adds that "where inaccuracies occur in Dugdale's books, the drawings were supplied by the families concerned, and were *not* drawn by Dugdale himself."

It is also true, as Carr points out, that Nicholas Rowe, in his edition of Shakespeare's works in 1709, includes an engraving of the monument substantially as depicted by Dugdale. As may be seen on page 214, the subject's visage has been redrawn to render it less sour- and more alert-looking and been given more hair, but there is little other change *and* the figure is still clutching the distended sack. Rowe had the advantage of information he says was brought back from Warwickshire by Thomas Betterton. A leading actor much favored by the public and highly esteemed by Charles II, Betterton was still alive and acting in 1710, and it is hardly conceivable to me that, had the subject of the monument been writing on a sheet of paper (unaccountably on that pillow), Betterton would have let go unchallenged so misleading a representation as Dugdale's, and Rowe's, would have been.

In response to Professor Marder's assertion that "the alterations made [in the monument] in 1748 were carefully controlled" to ensure its being changed as little as possible, Mr. Carr maintains that the restorer, the theatrical manager John Hall, "had a free hand." I, at any rate, can see scant room for doubt that the man honored in the original monument was portrayed not as a literary figure but as a dealer in bagged commodities.

Turning from the bust to the inscription (see page 14), we find that the most extravagant tributes to the subject are in the preliminary Latin, in which the townsfolk would not be well versed. More recondite learning still would be required to recognize that IVDICIO PYLIVM meant "A Nestor in respect of wisdom" and ARTE MARONEM "A Virgil in respect of art." Probably no one in Stratford could have done so except the parson and the schoolmaster, and they could have been set to rights by a few words from the builder: "This is how the authorities want it, and without a lot of talk." What the townsfolk could understand of the Latin, they would probably accept as obituary license. After all, their neighbor had made a lot of money in London and rich strangers thought well enough of him to have the monument erected.

It is noteworthy, too, that Nestor, Socrates, and Virgil are not at all the

Engraving of the monument to
"Shakspeare" in Nicholas Rowe's
Life of 1709.

By permission of the Folger Shakespeare
Library.

classical figures that would suggest themselves as comparisons for Shakespeare. Shakespeare had much less in common with Virgil than with Ovid;
Rowse says, "People spoke of his poetry as that of an English Ovid." Socrates
is so inappropriate for comparison that commentators, beginning with
George Steevens two centuries ago, have conjectured that Sophocles was
intended. The theory that the stone-chiseler made a mistake was pretty well

laid to rest, however, by a recent writer's observation that an artisan ignorant enough to render SITH as SIEH was hardly apt to have had Alexander the Great's tutor so much in his thoughts as to have substituted his name absent-mindedly for the Athenian dramatist's. If the inscription had likened the subject to Sophocles and Ovid, his identification with the great Shakespeare would have been unequivocal; and that, as I take it, was just what the perpetrators of the monument did not intend.

Consider now the English inscription. As homage to an immortal Shakespeare, a pupil in the local Grammar School could have done better. Nothing is said to indicate that the man honored was a poet or dramatist (or actor, either). However — and this is important — the possibility is not entirely excluded. We read: ALL YT HE HATH WRIT LEAVES LIVING ART, BVT PAGE, TO SERVE HIS WITT. "His *wit*?" says the future visitor. "Surely that's a lame characterization of the genius that gave us that lyric poetry and *Hamlet* and *Lear*. But probably the relative who wrote it wasn't much with words." "*His* wit? Shakspere's?" says the townsman who knew Susanna's and Judith's father. "Well, we always did account him a wit, and he must have made a rare show of it in London. Or maybe he ordered the monument himself and paid for it. It would be like him — the way he got that coat-of-arms." His widow and daughters were certainly not responsible for the memorial. They would not have approved an inscription that put the body in the monument when they had buried it years before under the floor. Moreover, to the immediate family a member's first name is of particular importance, since the last name is common to all. And no "William" appears on the monument.

I do not see how the inscription can be read except as an invitation to skepticism about its seeming import. STAY PASSENGER, WHY GOEST THOV BY SO FAST? Why should it be assumed that the visitor will hurry by too fast to take in what he is seeing? If there is any monument in the English-speaking world which should arrest the visitor's attention, which should bring visitors from afar to see it, it would surely be one to William Shakespeare. Why, if it was feared that the passer-by would not take in whose monument this was, did not the designer set forth boldly upon it the name WILLIAM SHAKESPEARE? Why was the most elementary and obvious convention of memorial sculpture set aside and the name of the deceased — the last name only, and without an *e* after the *Shak* — buried in the inscription? READ IF THOV CANST, WHOM ENVIOVS DEATH HATH PLAST, WITH IN THIS MONVMENT SHAKSPEARE: Why is the passer-by enjoined to read *if he can* what the inscription is telling him when, if he cannot read, he will not know that he is being directed to read and cannot read what he is directed to read even if he would? Why is he told that envious (malicious) death hath placed "Shakspeare" within the monument when it is obvious to him that the monument is too small to contain Shakespeare's body or anyone else's and when the body supposedly referred to is interred elsewhere, in the floor beneath the stone bearing the well-known curse?

That these questions arise makes it, to me, impossible to accept the monument for what we are told it represents; and I cannot put the peculiar inscription down to its being "just poetry," as I have been told to. On the face of it, its injunctions are inexplicable. If, however, the reading of it which occurred to me some years ago, which I have referred to earlier and set forth in the Appendix, is sound, then the inscription, having in fact been passed by unread all these years, makes excellent sense and the monument is even more ingenious than it would otherwise have seemed.

In any case, the monument was most shrewdly conceived to serve the essential purpose. Visitors disposed to regard the Stratford Shakspere as Shakespeare would find in it confirmation of that view, while to those who knew the local figure it affirmed no such thing. On top of that, it fairly cried out to the observant to smell a rat.

Engineers of the Crucial Artifacts

Who was responsible for the monument? There is no way of knowing. Perhaps it was those who were also responsible for the First Folio. These, it would appear, were primarily the "Incomparable Paire of Brethren" to whom the First Folio was dedicated. The brothers were William and Philip Herbert, sons of the 2nd Earl of Pembroke and of Mary Sidney. Mary, the famous Countess of Pembroke, was the devoted sister of Philip Sidney. She was his collaborator in one of his poetrical works, his literary executor, and patroness of the poets her brother had taken under his wing, including Spenser. William, who became the 3rd Earl of Pembroke in 1601, inherited his mother's literary leanings. A writer of verse himself, he surrounded himself with poets and scholars. John Donne was one of his closest friends and Ben Jonson a protégé. He was called "the greatest Maecenas of learning of any peer of his time or since." He was also described as the Hamlet of the English Court. Pembroke College at Oxford was named for him. In 1597, when he was seventeen, his parents had sought for him the hand of de Vere's thirteen-year-old daughter, Lady Bridget Vere. While the father favored the match, it fell through. In 1605, however, the younger brother, Philip Herbert, married Oxford's youngest daughter, Susan Vere. In that same year he was created Earl of Montgomery. We read that he "was for some years the chief favorite of James I, owing this position to his comely person and his passion for hunting and for field sports generally." Like his older brother before him, Philip became Chancellor of Oxford University. In succession, also, the two became Lord Chamberlain of England.

"The Lord Chamberlain, then as now, was the supreme authority in the world of the theatre," we are reminded by Gwynneth Bowen, from whom I am taking most of what follows. "He supervised Court entertainments and controlled the public stages — insofar as they were controllable." Details of administration were, however, left to his subordinate, the Master of the Revels. When James I came to the throne there was competition for the reversion of that office — that is, the right to succeed to it when the incumbent should relinquish it. In 1603, this right was granted temporarily to a resident of Castle Hedingham, the Earls of Oxford's ancestral seat. Later in the year the reversion was given to George Buck, a friend and admirer of Edward de Vere's. In 1607, while serving as acting Master, Sir George (as he had become) moved the Revels office to an old house near Blackfriars, which, in 1590, had been partially let to de Vere and his protégés. The Earl of Pembroke, whose London home was nearby in historic Baynard Castle, became Lord Chamberlain in 1615 after having worked hard for several years to obtain the office. His object was not preferment, which he was too wealthy to need. He wanted that specific office in his hands. Though repeatedly offered higher positions, he as often rejected them. He would not consider parting with the Lord Chamberlainship except on the condition that his brother Philip succeed him in it. The arrangement was made, but the succession did not take place until 1626, when we may believe that Pembroke had achieved the purpose for which he had striven for the office and clung to it. Three years earlier, following the death of Sir George Buck, a young kinsman of Pembroke's, Sir Henry Herbert, had bought a lease on the office of the Master of the Revels. The public theatre was now hedged about with three Herberts.

Between 1594 and 1603, fifteen of Shakespeare's plays had been published, some several times, none with the author's participation. ("Not one was printed just as he had written it," says Gerald E. Bentley. "It is obvious that he did nothing about seeing them through the press.") But from the time that Sir George obtained the reversion of the Master's office in 1603, less than a year before de Vere's death, no hitherto-unprinted play of Shakespeare's was published for nineteen years — except, as we have seen, the three that came out in 1608 and 1609, of which, we may recall, one — *Troilus and Cressida* — was said in the preface to have made a "scape" from certain "grand possessors."[1] Although for a time after 1603, new editions of previously published Shakespearean plays continued to appear, these, too,

---

[1] What caused a rupture at that time in the controls that had obviously been imposed, no one can say. It has been speculated that when, in 1608, Lady Oxford left the house in which her husband had spent the last years of his life — King's Place in Hackney in London's northern suburbs — an intruder took advantage of the confusion incident to moving to gain possession of copies of the three plays and the *Sonnets*. However, there is no indication that this was so, beyond the rather striking coincidence.

ceased after Pembroke became Lord Chancellor — apart from the Pavier quartos (see page 62), which were printed in 1619 *but falsely dated as of the early 1600s*. Pembroke stepped outside the law to forbid the Company of Stationers to publish any plays of the King's Men — formerly the Lord Chamberlain's, who had customarily presented Shakespeare's plays — without special consent.

The design must be apparent to us: Pembroke, with Buck's cooperation, was clamping down on the traffic in Shakespeare's plays anticipating publication of an authorized edition with the whole collection. This was to come out, of course, as the First Folio in 1623, printed on William Jaggard's press. Most suprisingly, however, in October 1621, *Othello* was entered in the Stationers' Register "under the handes of Sir George Buck and Master Swinhowe warden"; it was published in 1622. At the same time, work on the First Folio at Jaggard's was suspended and was not to resume for a year.

How was Sir George's lapse to be accounted for, and was the temporary shelving of the First Folio related to it? Poor Sir George, it developed, was losing his mind. This must have been evident to Pembroke, for on 5 October 1621, the very day before *Othello* was licensed, the reversion of the Master's office was obtained for Pembroke's protégé, Ben Jonson. From the suspension of work on the First Folio, Gwynneth Bowen draws the "reasonable inference" that Buck as Master of the Revels had been the "chief agent" of the Earls of Pembroke and Montgomery in their plans for the Folio "and perhaps editor." In April 1622, Buck was officially declared insane. He died at the end of October. Jonson did not get to succeed him after all. The Herberts evidently considered it necessary to have the office in reliable hands, however, and it was in the following July that Sir Henry Herbert obtained it by lease at £150 a year. As we have had occasion to notice, the books of the office disappeared. Sir Herbert said they had been burnt. It would not be surprising to learn that the books would have told how the First Folio came into being and perhaps other things as well.

The Stratfordians have their own version of the great Folio edition's genesis and it takes no account of the foregoing circumstances. "Shakespeare," they say, had sold all his plays to "his" company and thus washed his hands of them. "Posterity," Gerald E. Bentley confesses, "has often found this neglect incredible." Well — yes. Speaking of the plays published during Shakspere's life. Professor Bentley writes, "Whether he ever looked at them or collected copies of them no one knows," though four of them were "so distorted" that if he did he must have found them "ludicrous or horrifying." (In the remarkable world the Stratfordians inhabit an author may have no curiosity about his published works.) That we have better versions of these and that twenty of the plays did not pass into oblivion, the Stratfordians tell us is owing entirely to circumstances that John Heminge and Henry Condell took it upon themselves to round up the plays and have them published. But the explanation leaves major questions unanswered — even apart from its imputation to Shakespeare of an inexplicable indifference to the fate of his soaring masterpieces. It does not tell us why the King's Men would let two of their members appropriate so valuable a property and dispose of it on their own — for there is no suggestion that the company itself had any hand in publishing the plays. It does not tell us how two actors would have raised the small fortune such a publishing venture would have called for or why anyone putting up the funds would have left the immensely important task of editing the thirty-six plays and preparing them for the printer to two undistinguished stage-players with no experience to fit them for the work, one of them to turn grocer. If we seek answers to the crucial questions the First Folio raises, I think we shall be forced to accept the indications that those primarily responsible for the publication were the Herbert brothers, that they took the first steps toward this end as early as 1604, the year of Oxford's death, and that, following the incapacitation of their ally in the office of the Revels — Sir George Buck — they engaged Ben Jonson to nurse the great planned work into being.

Ben Jonson and Shakespeare

Jonson was the logical choice for the mammoth undertaking as the leading and most honored playwright of the time, one who in fact was offered a knighthood. (So much for the notion that plays were then held to be of no worth.) How Jonson may have felt about the assignment we can only guess. Outside the First Folio, he made only two known references to Shakespeare the author, both carping.

The first came in 1618, when, as Samuel Johnson was to do a century and a half later, he made a journey through Scotland, his native country, on foot. In the course of it he paid a visit to the scholarly poet William Drummond of Hawthornden and regaled his host with an account of himself and his career with reminiscences of distinguished men he had known. In the record Drummond made of these divulgences, called the *Conversations*, are the following two entries:

> His censure of English poets was this . . .
>   That Shaksperr wanted art.
> Sheakspear in a play brought in a number of
>   men saying they had suffered shipwreck
>   in Bohemia, where there is no sea near by
>   some 100 miles.

It should be observed that "Shaksperr" was by no means singled out for "censure." A dozen poets took a drubbing, including Sidney, Spenser, Daniel,

Drayton, and Donne, who, Ben allowed, "for not keeping of accent, deserved hanging." As for himself, he "was better versed, and knew more Greek and Latin, than all the poets in England." No wonder his host said of him, "He is a great lover and praiser of himself, a contemner and scorner of others," to which he added, "jealous of every word and action of those about him." Jonson was full of garrulous reminiscences: how he, Chapman, and Marston had been imprisoned for *Eastward Ho* and were going to have "had their ears cut and noses" and "after their delivery, he banqueted all his friends, . . . Camden, Selden, and others," and in "the midst of the feast his old mother drank to him," etc., etc.; how he had many quarrels with Marston, beat him, and took his pistol," etc.; how he was "in his youth given to venery" and "thought the use of a maid nothing in comparison with the wantonness of a wife," ETC.; how "S. W. Raulighe sent him governor with his son, anno 1613, to France" and the "youth being knavishly inclined" was given to such "pastimes as the setting of the favour of damsels on a codpiece," etc., etc. In three sentences he could have told more about Shakespeare the man than can be found in Halliwell-Phillipps's four-volume *Life* and in the ton of his followers' biographies, but all we have to thank him for are two bilious, uninformative remarks, of which the second brings out not Shakespeare's ignorance of Bohemia but Jonson's own. He declared that "Chapman and Fletcher were loved of him" — of Jonson himself — but of the man he would protest five years later that he had loved "this side idolatry" and would rank at the top of the playwrights of two millennia he had nothing to say.

Obviously there is something peculiar in all this. In his *Epigrammes*, dedicated to the Earl of Pembroke, which he had published two years earlier, in the year Shakspere had died without a word of commemoration from the near-idolatrous lover of Shakespeare, Jonson addressed verses to his noted acquaintances, including Sidney, Beaumont, and Donne, but not to the "star of poets." He did, however, salute "ONE THAT DESIRED ME NOT TO NAME HIM." It is as a writer acutely jealous of others, as Drummond described him "(especially after drink)," that Jonson appears in his one extended commentary on Shakespeare outside the Folio. Captioned *De Shakespeare nostrati*, this was taken from one of his notebooks and was evidently written after 1623, when his earlier notebooks were destroyed by fire. Published posthumously, it reads:

> I remember, the Players have often mentioned it as an honour to Shakespeare, that in his writing, (whatsoever he penned) he never blotted out a line. My answer hath been, would he had blotted a thousand. Which they thought a malevolent speech. I had not told posterity this, but for their ignorance, who choose that circumstance to commend their friend by, wherein he most faulted. And to justify mine own candor, (for I loved the man, and do honour his memory (on this side Idolatry) as much as any.) He was (indeed) honest, and of an open,

and free nature: had an excellent Fantasy; brave notions, and gentle expressions; wherein he flowed with that facility, that sometimes it was necessary he should be stopped: *Sufflaminandus erat*; as Augustus said of Haterius. His wit was in his own power; would the rule of it had been so too. Many times he fell into those things, could not escape laughter; as when he said in the person of Caesar, one speaking to him; *Caesar thou dost me wrong*. He replied: *Caesar did never wrong, but with just cause* and such like: which were ridiculous. But he redeemed his vices, with his virtues. There was ever more in him to be praised, than to be pardoned.

The lines from *Julius Caesar* as they have come down to us are:

> Know, Caesar doth not wrong, nor without cause
> Will he be satisfied.

Jonson's version makes perfectly good sense, however, as Ingleby long ago pointed out.

That the hard-laboring Jonson, loading his plays with solid chunks of learning, was jealous of the iridescent genius of Shakespeare, whom learning served as Ariel did Prospero, and resented the success of Shakespeare's plays, which his own could never equal, is easy to believe. "Ben," says Nicholas Rowe, "could not but look with an evil eye upon anyone that seem'd to stand in competition with him." What may have eaten at Jonson more than envy of his great predecessor, however, was the prospect that the plays which so outshone his own would be credited to a man vastly below him, whom he had held up to scorn on the stage as the bumpkin Sogliardo. That would indeed have stung and have caused him to lash out at "Shakespeare."

On the other side, as a fellow craftsman, and one who above all took satisfaction from his cognomen "honest," he cannot have failed to appreciate Shakespeare's transcendent accomplishment, as his eulogy in the First Folio shows he did. The editorship of the Folio would offer him the chance to stand forth for all time as the one who gave the world the first adequate appraisal of that genius. If it would compel him to float the fiction of Shakspere's authorship, it would also enable him to torpedo it for those who could and would read — few as they have proven to be. In any case, he was beholden to the Earl of Pembroke for generous favors and, Ruth Loyd Miller brings out, was long closely associated with the Herbert brothers as well as with Oxford's daughters, of whom one, Susan, as we saw, became the wife of Philip Herbert and another, Elizabeth, the wife of the 6th Earl of Derby. Jonson addressed one of his *Epigrammes* to Susan as Countess of Montgomery. Among those who took part in a masque by Jonson presented at Whitehall in 1605 were Susan and Elizabeth and their husbands — the Earls of Montgomery and Derby — and William, Earl of Pembroke, while of the twenty-nine ladies of the court who appeared in the four masques by Jonson given between 1605 and 1610, Susan was one of the only three who took part in all four, according to Mrs. Miller, the other two being the Queen and Elizabeth's mother-in-law, the dowager Countess of Derby.

In 1621, the year Jonson was put in line to succeed Buck at the Revels, his annual pension from the crown was temporarily increased from £100 to £200. Pembroke is credited with having arranged for the original pension, granted in 1616, and for the increase.

The First Folio

That "there is something fishy" about the First Folio was remarked by James Boswell the younger, who, in 1821, brought out in twenty-one volumes the Variorum edition of *The Plays and Poems of William Shakespeare* begun by Edmund Malone. The fishiness was proclaimed — purposely, we must believe — in the supposed representation of Shakespeare that challenges us from the frontispiece in the great Folio. This engraving is, at least to me, all but impossible to explain other than as intended to warn the reader of trickery ahead, which it does in quite droll fashion. I am tempted to believe that London was combed for an artist mature enough to execute it yet young enough never to have known the subject, but all we can say for sure is that such a person was found in Martin Droeshout, the grandson of Flemish immigrants, born in 1601.

Droeshout's is the standard portrait of "Shakespeare," the one by far the most frequently reproduced; little is seen of the even more repugnant effigy in the monument, supposedly approved by Shakspere's wife and daughters. Stratfordians, who have no case if they do not take the First Folio at face value, must grant it the claim of authenticity. It goes hard with some or most of them, who would find it difficult to dispute the judgment of the painter Gainsborough respecting the engraving: "Damn the original portrait. I never saw a stupider face. It is impossible that such a mind and such a rare talent should shine with such a face and such a pair of eyes." Thus Ivor Brown wails, "It is as bad as the effigy in the church," which he calls "that of a 'puddin'-headed' William who could never have written anything except a note of hand to buy malt." J. Dover Wilson laments that the engraving, "which J. C. Squire has called 'the pudding-faced effigy of Droeshout,' [should] stand between us and the true Shakespeare," being "so obviously false" to "the greatest poet of all time that the world turns from [it] in disgust and thinks it is turning from Shakespeare himself."

Samuel Schoenbaum writes of the Folio engraving: "The portrait has not gone entirely without admirers. 'What a powerful impression it gives,' enthuses Dr. Rowse: 'that searching look of the eyes understanding everything, what a forehead, what a brain!' But the engraver has depicted not the brain,

Frontispiece of the First Folio of
1623 with engraving by Martin
Droeshout

By permission of the Folger Shakespeare
Library.

only the forehead, described by another as that 'horrible hydrocephalus development.'" The deformity does not disturb "Shakespeare's" latest biographer. To Robert Payne it is "the soaring forehead of a man who thinks too much for his own comfort. . . . We have only to look at the Droeshout portrait to know that he has fine manners and is fastidious to a fault." But to return to Professor Schoenbaum: "Droeshout's deficiencies are, alas, only too gross. The huge head on the plate of ruff surmounts a disproportionately small tunic. One eye is lower and larger than the other, the hair does not balance at the sides, light comes from several directions."

Professor Schoenbaum is amusing, but let us not be beguiled. The fact is that the portrait owes its singular character not to any deficiencies on the engraver's part, as he would have us believe — it is quite skillfully executed — but, clearly, to design. As the *Observer* has recalled, Lord Brain, head of the Royal College of Physicians, commented in 1945 that the subject had been given two right eyes (the outside corner of the eye on our right should manifestly be the inside corner), while *Gentlemen's Tailor*, as long ago as 1911, had commented that the tunic "is so strangely illustrated that the right-hand side of the forepart is obviously the left-hand side of the back part and so gives a harlequin appearance to the figure which it is not unnatural to suppose was intentional, and done with *express object and purpose*." (Italics mine.) It could hardly have been otherwise. Then there is the line curving down from the unreal ear to the chin, paralleling the line of the cheek. It corresponds to no lineament of the human face and would have been lost in shadow had the engraver not high-lighted it on either side; if the "light comes from several directions," it does so evidently not through inadvertence. What does the line represent? I can think of nothing but the edge of a mask, just as the mere tab of an ear jutting out unnaturally to the side suggests the makeshift aural appendage of a mask. If we take it as such we shall find Droeshout's handiwork altogether consistent with the letters signed Heminge and Condell that follow it. We shall find it revealing indeed. No one I know of has offered to explain that line as other than the edge of a mask.

In a poem facing the engraving, Ben Jonson writes:

> This Figure, that thou here seest put,
>   It was for gentle Shakespeare cut; . . .

It is not a *portrait of* Shakespeare that Jonson offers us but a *figure* that was cut *for* him — "figure," of the same root as "feign," having a derogatory flavor as used here: a mere figure, as in a figure of speech. Jonson goes on:

> Wherein the Graver had a strife
>   with Nature, to out-do the life: . . .

This is taken from *Venus and Adonis*, lines 189 and 191, in which the same rhyme is employed. But there the poet is speaking of a painter of a horse who tries to improve on nature. Why the "Graver" should seek to improve on Shakespeare we may leave it to the Stratfordians to tell us. We may leave it to them to tell us, too, whether "Shakespeare" looked so exactly like the "constipated dullard" of the engraving as Jonson seems to say he did in what follows or whether honest Ben is having us on.

> O, could he but have drawn his wit
>   As well in brass, as he hath hit
> His face; the print would then surpass
>   All, that was ever writ in brass.
> But, since he cannot, Reader, look
>   Not on his picture, but his book.

In current slang, the bottom line is indeed the bottom line: Don't look at the picture; read the plays. Sound advice.

Inasmuch as Jonson started rather a fashion in his reference to "gentle Shakespeare," we might pause to ask ourselves what he meant. If there was ever an author who, in what he wrote, went to the opposite extreme from "soft and tender" and must have had in his make-up the potentiality of the violence he evoked with such gusto and realism, it was Shakespeare. We might recall how he was wont to use the adjective himself — one of which he was exceptionally fond — as in Mark Antony's address to "You gentle Romans" and in the historical plays. For example:

> *Edward:* Where is the Duke of Norfolk, gentle Warwick?
> *Warwick* [shortly afterward]: And he that throws not up
>   his cap for joy
>   Shall for the fault make forfeit of his head.
>   . . . .
> *Norfolk:* We'll all assist you; he that flies shall die.
> *York:* Thanks, gentle Norfolk.
>   . . . .
> *Northumberland:* The next news is: I have to London sent
>   The heads of Salisbury, Spencer, Blunt
>   and Kent.
> *Bolinbroke:* We thank thee, gentle Percy, for thy pains.

The Romans, the Duke of Norfolk and the Earls of Warwick and Northumberland, were gentle in that they were of superior birth, certainly in no other sense.

The frontispiece of the First Folio is followed, as we saw in Chapter 1, by two letters signed by John Heminge and Henry Condell. The first is addressed *To the Most Noble and Incomparable Pair of Brethren, William, Earl of Pembroke, &c, Lord Chamberlain to the King's Most Excellent Majesty, and Philip, Earl of Montgomery, &c., Gentleman of His Majesty's Bed-Chamber. Both Knights of the most Noble Order of the Garter, and our singular good Lords.* The second is *To the great Variety of Readers.* They are alike in being repellent, the first in its sycophancy, the second in its crude commercialism. Ben Jonson, I judge, conceived of their spirit as appropriate to lowly actors, and Stratfordians presumably also consider it quite natural to them.

"When we value the places your H. H. sustain" — your Highnesses, no less, — the first letter says, "we cannot but know their dignity greater, than to descend to the reading of these trifles." Three times the plays are termed "trifles." But the signatories dare "hope that . . . you will use the like indulgence toward them, you have done unto their parent. . . . For, so much were your L. L. [Lordships] likings of the several parts, when they were acted, as before they were published, the volume asked to be yours. We have but collected them," they said, "only to keep the memory of so worthy a friend, & fellow alive, as was our SHAKESPEARE, by humble offer of his plays, to your most noble patronage." Their Lordships, they had observed, were not approached "but with a kind of religious address." They had heard that with nations "that had not gums and incense . . . it was no fault to approach their Gods, by what means they could: And the most, though meanest, of things are made more precious, when they are dedicated to Temples. In that name therefore, we most humbly consecrate to your H. H. these remains of your servant Shakespeare. . . ." Gods and Temples: Heminge and Condell must have squirmed when they read these words of adulation, which they were supposed to have indited.

That the two actors had anything more to do with the Folio than to receive the intelligence that they were to be named as shepherds of the collection is very much to be doubted. Sir George Greenwood concluded that the dedication "To the Incomparable Pair," drawing as it does on Pliny and Horace, may reasonably be supposed to have been written by Jonson, while two centuries ago Edmund Malone, by setting forth in parallel columns extracts from the address "To the great variety of Readers" and from Jonson's works, showed that Jonson had written at least the first half of the address. E. K. Chambers, recalling that Malone's predecessor, George Steevens, "called attention to some parallels between the epistle to the readers and the works of Ben Jonson," inclines himself to favor "Jonson's claim."

This portion is written as an unblushing sales-pitch, directed, condescendingly enough, "From the most able, to him that can but spell: There," it says, "you are numbered." Perhaps it should be regarded as humorously meant. Some significance doubtless attaches to the exclamation "Well! it is now public," however, with its implication of *at last*. It goes on: "& you will stand for your privileges we know: to read, and censure [judge]. Do so, but buy it first. That dost best commend a book, the Stationer says." And again, "But whatever you do, Buy. Censure will not drive a trade, or make the jack[ass] go." Heminge and Condell, presumably being not without dignity, must have winced again. They must have been puzzled, too. "The great variety of Readers" addressed in this slangy preface could not possibly afford the costly volume.

The second and longer paragraph strikes a more serious note. It makes the famous claim, "as where (before) you were abused with diverse stolen, and surreptitious copies, maimed, and deformed by the frauds and stealths of injurious impostors, that exposed [printed] them: even those, are now offered to your view cured, and perfect of their limbs; and all the rest, absolute in their numbers, as he conceived them." This is an amplification of the claim made on the title page: "Published according to the True Original Copies." Stratfordians, who rest their case on the reliability of Heminge and Condell as editors of the Folio, do not face the question of why, having made false statements about it, they should be trusted in any other claims they made. For everyone knows that the plays in the Folio were not published according to the true original copies or as the author conceived them. The sheets of the Folio as they were first pulled from Jaggard's presses abounded in errors, which were corrected as the printing proceeded in accordance with the printer's ideas of what was right, so that probably no two copies of the more than one thousand printed were alike. What remained, however, was an edition in which in some places the names of actors are printed instead of those of characters, poetry is sometimes rendered as prose, and luminous passages in the quartos are passed over. According to A. W. Pollard, "the Folio prints about three times as many errors in *Richard II* as in the First Quarto." The soliloquy beginning "How all occasions do inform against me," which Swinburne considered "the very finest and most important passage in the poem," was omitted in the Folio, along with all but nine of the sixty-six lines of Act IV, Scene 4, leading Swinburne to call its editors "lying rascals." In other words, far from giving us the plays of Shakespeare "perfect in their limbs" and "absolute in their numbers, as he conceived them," the Folio in numerous instances does not even come up to the earlier quartos.

What were the sources of the Folio versions? Sir Walter Greg, the great textual expert, says that eleven of the plays in the Folio were taken from the quartos, with some consultation with the playhouse manuscripts by unknown editors. Charles Tyler Prouty, in the Yale facsimile edition, adds that "For the remaining 25 plays of the Folio, manuscripts were used as the compositor's copy, but the nature of the manuscripts in many instances is far from certain. The author's foul papers, the fair copy, the promptbook, and transcripts of the latter two all appear to have been used, but our lack of exact knowledge as to the nature of such documents often renders a categorical statement impossible." They were "a very mixed bag indeed." Sir Sidney Lee, who brought out a facsimile edition half a century earlier, evidently doubted that any of the author's manuscripts were available to the editors; he speaks of "the inevitable absence of his autograph MSS."

From boasting about the authenticity of the edition, the letter to the Readers goes on to commend the "Author" (whom it does not name), saying that "what he thought, he uttered with that easiness, that we have scarce received from him a blot in his papers. But it is not our province, who only gather his works, and give them you, to praise him. It is yours that read him." And it adds: "his wit could no more lie hid, than it could be lost" — lying hid evidently being a fate that threatened it. "Read him, therefore; and again, and again: And if then you do not like him, surely you are in some manifest danger, not to understand him." One is put in mind of Touchstone's observation in *As You Like It*, that "When a man's verses cannot be understood, nor a man's good wit seconded with the forward child Understanding, it strikes a man more dead than a great reckoning in a little room." It has long been noticed that the last six words are peculiarly descriptive of the murder of Christopher Marlowe. Touchstone's speech, addressed to "a country wench" who could not possibly understand it, is irrelevant to the dialogue and the action, and like other extraneous elements in Shakespeare — as no doubt in other writers — may probably be taken as telling us about the author himself, consciously in this case, as it may be unconscious in others. Touchstone, "the fool that hath been a courtier," would seem to be one of the many characters in which the dramatist appears before us as himself. In the speech I have quoted he seems to be telling us that unless readers bring understanding to his verse, in which he reveals himself, he will be obliterated more thoroughly even than Marlowe was by his assassins; and I believe it is of this danger that we are warned in the prefatory letter of the First Folio. If there is another explanation of Touchstone's interjection, I am open to it.

The claim by "Heminge" and "Condell" that "our Shakespeare" was "so worthy a friend and fellow" is put forward by Stratfordians as Proof Number One that the dramatist was Shakspere. In this they ignore Jonson's denunciation of the two supposed signatories' presumption in what follows. They also ignore the statements in the letters that would rule out Shakspere's authorship, as we have seen. The letters refer to the author as "not having the fate, common with some, to be executor to his own writings" and call it a thing "worthy to have been wished, that the author himself had lived to have set forth and overseen his own writings" while reporting that "it has been ordained otherwise, and he by death departed from that right." Shakspere above all writers would have had the opportunity the author was denied, for death did not carry him off until he had — as no writer of stature ever has in the intellectual prime of life — gone for years producing nothing, his affluent leisure uninterrupted by the least literary effort.

Jonson's Eulogy of Shakespeare

From the prefatory letters in the Folio, the reader turns the page to experience one of the great dramatic moments in the history of literature. It comes in Ben Jonson's poem of forty couplets *To the memory of my beloved, The Author Mr. William Shakespeare: And what he hath left us.* In this the denigration of the dramatist that has preceded it is dismissed and the plays for the first time are acclaimed for what they truly are.

Among the *Verses to the Author of the Faerie Queene* forming a preface to Edmund Spenser's prodigious allegory, the last, signed Ignoto, which we shall find reason to believe concealed de Vere's authorship, concludes with the following stanza:

> Thus then to show my judgment to be such
> As can discern of colours black and white,
> As alls to free my mind from envy's touch,
> That never gives to any man his right;
>   I here pronounce this workmanship is such
>   As that no pen can set it forth too much.

In the opening of his poem, Jonson borrows from this as he borrowed from *Venus and Adonis* (of the same stanza form) in his poem on the engraving:

> To draw no envy (Shakespeare) on thy name,
> Am I thus ample to thy book, and fame;

(To bring no harm upon your name, I shall be liberal, unstinting, to your plays and your fame.)

> While I confess thy writings to be such,
>   As neither man, nor muse, can praise too much.
>   'Tis true, and all men's suffrage. . . .

(As all men assent to be so. [Suddenly, after all these years of seeming gross under-valuation of Shakespeare's plays, it appears that they are universally held to be beyond praise by man or even muse!])

>   . . . But these ways
> Were not the paths I meant unto thy praise:

(But the ways taken in what precedes this were not the paths I meant to take in praising you.)

> For seeliest ignorance on these may light,
>   Which, when it sounds at best, but echo's right;

(For blindest ignorance may fasten upon the testimonials we have heard and tell us that which, even at its most plausible, merely echoes what is right.)

> Or blind affection, which doth ne're advance
>   The truth, but gropes, and urgeth all by chance.

(Or a blind predilection might do so, which never advances the truth but gropes its way and urges us to accept what it comes upon by chance.)

> Or crafty malice, might pretend this praise,
>   And think to ruin, where it seemed to raise.

(Or those whom we have heard might pretend to praise the author out of malice, intending to ruin him by seeming to elevate him [i.e., by implying that he is of such low standing that he must be made worthy by being dedicated and consecrated to two lords].)

> These are, as some infamous bawd, or whore
>   Should praise a matron. What could hurt her more?

(So much for the two actors who were represented in praising you in the prefatory letter and calling you friend and fellow. Nothing could hurt you more than having them do so. [If Heminge and Condell really were the editors of the Folio and let it stand that they were comparable to street-walkers, they were unlike any editors I have known.])

> But thou art proof against them, and indeed
>   Above th'ill fortune of them, or the need.

(But you are proof against the two, who had complained of the "ill fortune" they were fallen upon in undertaking a rash enterprise when they were fearful of its success and had spoken of the "pain" that had been theirs in the necessity they were under to collect and publish the plays. You are above them.)

A more logical interpretation of Jonson's lines may be possible, showing the foregoing to be in error. I have, however, not seen one, or indeed any other explanation at all of his meaning, and unless one is forthcoming I think we must conclude that Jonson has characterized the testimony offered over the names of Heminge and Condell as originating in malice and intended to ruin his beloved, the author, and to mislead the reader.

Let us pause here and think about what we are being told. Why should anyone, it is surely fair to ask, seek maliciously to ruin Shakspere of Stratford, seven years after his death? And who? And how would praise by two supposed fellow actors hurt him? The orthodox critics, seeming not to have read the lines that give rise to these questions, do not recognize that any questions are raised requiring answers. Even after I had called attention to Jonson's revealing utterances in *Harvard Magazine*, Professors Evans and Levin in their ostensible reply to the article would have none of it. They passed the subject by in silence.

Thus, even if the Stratfordians close their eyes to the plain import, we see Jonson in the opening lines of his poem dismissing as ignorant and malicious what has come before — that is, the treatment of the author in the prefatory addresses: those were not the ways *he* meant unto Shakespeare's praise. Let me, he says, having *myself* undertaken to work no mischief on your name (Shakespeare), make a new start:

> I, therefore, will begin. . . .

I cannot help being thrilled by what follows, in which nothing more will be heard of the plays as "trifles" of which a "humble offer" must be made, nothing more of their fate depending on "your purses": no, by God!

> I, therefore, will begin. Soul of the age!
>   The applause! delight! the wonder of our stage!
> My *Shakespeare*, rise. . . .

It is as if, after decades during which the author labored unseen and his plays were shown to the muted response of his contemporaries, years after he has passed from the scene, the curtain was at last being raised upon the greatest of all literary geniuses. "Well! it is now public"! Does the story of man's creative triumphs anywhere take a more stirring turn than this?

> I will not lodge thee by
> *Chaucer*, or *Spenser*, or bid *Beaumont* lie
> A little further, to make thee a room:

Here Jonson is quoting the proposal made by William Basse that Shakespeare be buried in Westminster Abbey beside his fellow poets. (See page 40.) He rejects it because

> Thou art a monument, without a tomb,
> And art alive still, while thy book doth live,
>   And we have wits to read, and praise to give.

Of course immortality is a reason for, not against, interment in the Abbey. But perish the thought that Shakspere of Stratford should receive that honor! Jonson, putting the quietus on that possibility, is saying that Shakespeare *is* his monument, his works. And being only a name and hence incorporeal, he is. As such he can have no tomb, unlike Shakspere, whose tomb is there for all to see.

> . . . if I thought my judgement were of years,
>   I should commit thee surely with thy peers,
> And tell, how far thou didst our *Lily* out-shine,
>   Or sporting *Kid*, or *Marlowe*'s mighty line.

In years, de Vere was the peer (i.e., the equal or companion) of Lyly, Kyd, and Marlowe, his writing contemporaries, whose work was finished almost before Shakspere's alleged career began.

We come now to a line that has probably been more productive of mischief than any other sentence in English. It is one of the two most famous lines in Jonson's eulogy, and the only one to which a derogatory intent may be imputed. Such an intent continually *is* imputed to it by those who misquote it. From John Aubrey to Samuel Schoenbaum and Professors Evans and Levin, negligent readers have told us that "Ben Jonson said that Shakespeare had 'little Latin and less Greek.'" Samuel Johnson, who should have known better, fell into the misreading. He tells us why he feels he has to believe it, his thinking growing muddled: "Jonson, his [Shakespeare's] friend, affirms, that *he had small Latin and no Greek* [corrected in a later edition to *less Greek*]: who, besides that he had no imaginable temptation to falsehood, wrote at a time when the character and acquisitions of Shakespeare were known to multitudes." Here is what Jonson said, with what follows:

> And though thou hadst small Latin, and less Greek,
>   From thence to honour thee, I would not seek
> For names; but call forth thund'ring *Æschilus*,
>   *Euripedes*, and *Sophocles* to us,
> *Pacuvius, Accius*, him of Cordova [Seneca] dead,
>   To life again, to hear thy buskin tread,
> And shake a Stage. . . .

"Though" is a conjunction that means not only "notwithstanding" and "in spite of the fact that"; it means also "even if" or "even supposing that." (*Oxford Universal Dictionary*.) In writing "And though thou hadst small Latin and less Greek," Jonson could have meant that Shakespeare *had* small Latin and less Greek. In that case, however, syntax would have called for "I shall not seek for names, . . ." expressing mere futurity. By employing the conditional mood of "shall" — "should" or "would" — he gives the statement the reverse meaning of that attributed to it. This is what *Webster's Collegiate Dictionary* calls "The conditional mood . . . in the conclusion of sentences of rejected condition," as in "If he were here, he *would* tell us." But he is *not* here. What Ben Jonson is saying is "even if you had small Latin and less Greek — which is not the case — I would not seek for names. . . ." Similarly, when Paul says, "Though I speak with the tongues of men and of angels . . . ," he does not mean he does speak with their tongues; he means even if he did. When Kipling writes, "Though all the Dead were all forgot . . ." and "Tho' I walks with fifty 'ousemaids outer Chelsea to the Strand . . ." he does not mean that the dead *are* all forgot, or that the cockney soldier *does* walk fifty housemaids over the course; if he did walk all fifty and walked them back, too, the total would come to more than 300 housemaid-miles, even at only one round trip per female.

One hundred years ago, C. M. Ingleby in his *Shakespeare's Centurie of Prayse* pointed out that "Ben does not assert that Shakespeare had 'little Latin and less Greek.'" The "hadst," he pointed out, "is the subjunctive. The passage may thus be paraphrased:

> Even if thou hadst little scholarship, I would not seek to honour thee by calling thee, as others have done, Ovid, Plautus, Terence, &c., *i.e.*, by the names of the

classical poets, but would rather invite them to witness how far thou dost outshine them.

Ingleby has been echoed repeatedly down to the present by those skeptical of the Stratford case, yet the orthodox writers — even those who testify to Shakespeare's extensive reading in the classics, including works not yet translated — persist in ignoring what Ingleby and others have pointed out. They assert, we recall, the familiarity with the dramatist claimed by Heminge and Condell as Proof Number One that Shakespeare was the Stratford man — but as we have seen, the actors' ostensible testimony was almost certainly the contribution of Jonson and is repudiated by him with contumely. As Proof Number Two the orthodox writers attribute to Jonson a derogation of Shakespeare's knowledge of the classics based on a misreading of what Jonson says.

Obviously Jonson was permitting the reader to take his statement as the Stratfordians have done, and do; otherwise he would not have made it. May we not recognize that he was playing both sides of the street, as he was doing in framing the actors' two letters and then denouncing them? If we can hardly view the Stratford monument as other than designed to convey different things to different spectators, we can hardly explain the introductory material in the First Folio except as intended to have one meaning for the superficial reader, the opposite for the observant. All the wordage in the two letters and five poems gives us almost no biographical facts about the author. This can scarcely be an oversight. In what little we are told, it erects as the author a figure just barely identifiable as the Stratfordian's but only, as we see if we pay attention, to pull the rug out from under it. Jonson performed as, I judge, he was expected to and lent himself to the proposition that Shakespeare was such as to have been an ill-schooled friend and fellow of Heminge and Condell; and, revolted, he took his revenge. He did all that a brave man could have been expected to do in the circumstances to sabotage his own endeavor and tip posterity off to the sham — and it was not his fault if posterity would require even plainer speaking than he dared risk. That the Herberts were aware of what he was up to, I think we must assume.

Jonson's poem is all laudation. As Shakespeare in his "buskin tread" is to the greatest tragedians of antiquity, so when his "socks were on" he caused "tart Aristophanes, neat Terence and witty Plautus" to be forgotten and could alone compare with

> . . . all, that insolent Greece, or haughty Rome
> sent forth, or since did from their ashes come.

Hear him!

> Triumph, my Britain, thou hast one to show,
> To whom all scenes of Europe homage owe.
> He was not of an age, but for all time!

In telling us

> And all the Muses still were in their prime,
> When like Apollo he came forth to warm
> Our ears, or like a Mercury to charm!

Jonson is reminding us again that Shakespeare, unlike the Shakespeare of orthodoxy, came early to the English stage. Though

> Nature herself was proud of his designs,
> And joyed to wear the dressing of his lines:

and though classic writers of comedy were by comparison

> . . . not of Nature's family,
> Yet must I not give Nature all: Thy Art,
> My gentle Shakespeare, must enjoy a part.

For though Nature provides the poet's material, it is his art that fashions it:

> And, that he,
> Who casts to write a living line, must sweat,
> (such as thine are) and strike the second heat
> Upon the Muses' anvil: turn the same,
> (And himself with it) that he thinks to frame;
> Or for the laurel, he may gain a scorn,
> For a good poet's made, as well as born.
> And such wert thou.

Here Jonson is dealing with an essential premise in the Stratford attribution. He is burying (or thought he was) the picture of Shakespeare — to which he himself had contributed in a less worthy moment — as a poet deficient in art who owed his excellence to untutored gifts and to Nature. It was the notion that "F.B.," presumably Francis Beaumont, had ridiculed in writing to Ben Jonson himself. Jonson is also attacking the corollary fancy we met with in the second prefatory letter, that Shakespeare wrote easily and without second thought.

Who would create living lines such as Shakespeare's were, Jonson tells us, must sweat and take them back to the Muses' anvil to reshape them. He must turn his work again, and himself with it — turn himself this way and that for his own inspection, one might say. A good poet such as Shakespeare was is not only born; he has to make a poet of himself, improving on native talent, if he would reap the laurel and not scorn.

> Look how the father's face
> Lives in his issue, even so, the race
> Of Shakespeare's mind, and manners brightly shines
> In his well-turned and true filed lines:
> In each of which, he seems to shake a lance,
> As brandished in the eyes of ignorance.

In an image that seems to speak for the author's breeding, Jonson again emphasizes how his lines were re-turned and honed. The antithesis of Gilbert

Highet's "comparatively ill-educated man," Shakespeare is a writer whose every line is a reproach to ignorance, as Jonson declares in a play on his name consistent with its having been made up to connote an action — shaking a spear.

Now comes the famous invocation:

> Sweet Swan of Avon!

This, of course, is cited as Proof Number Three of Shakspere's title to the works of Shakespeare. I fear, however, that it too must be considered annulled. On its way to Stratford, the Avon passes through Rugby, where Edward de Vere had a home — Bilton.

> . . . what a sight it were
> To see thee in our waters yet appear,
> And make those flights upon the banks of Thames,
> That so did take Eliza, and our James!

Shakespeare — "now it is public" — was the delight of two monarchs: What must the readers of the First Folio have thought to find the hitherto unsaid, and so presumably unsayable, so openly proclaimed? We have seen the leading literary figure of his time, out of the blue, pay Shakespeare such tributes as no other writer in English has ever received. And there are still to come the lines I think I have confessed I can never, after a lifetime's experience of Shakespeare's enshrinement, read without a constriction of the throat:

> But stay, I see thee in the hemisphere
> Advanced, and made a constellation there:
> Shine forth, thou star of poets. . . .

Other Introductory Material of the Folio

Three other eulogies follow that of Jonson's. One of fourteen lines by Hugh Holland, whose patroness, Lady Hotton, was a first cousin of de Vere's daughters, speaks of Shakespeare's plays as having "made the Globe of heav'n and earth to ring" and of those "bays" — laurels — "which crowned him Poet first, then Poet's King." A longer verse is by Leonard Digges, who had dedicated his translation of a Spanish novel to the Earls of Pembroke and Montgomery and whose father was a mathematician admired and patronized by Lord Burghley. Ringing the changes on the theme of Shakespeare's immortality, it begins:

> Shake-speare, at length, thy pious fellows give
> The world thy works: thy works, by which, out-live
> Thy tomb, thy name must when that stone is rent,
> And time dissolves thy Stratford monument,
> Here we alive shall view thee still.

Digges, we are told, supplies Proof Number Four of the Folio editors' intention to identify Shakspere as Shakespeare. But the proof, like all the others, is double-edged. Digges speaks of the Stratford monument only to anticipate its dissolution. Moreover, as I observed earlier, most purchasers of the Folio, on reading Digges's poem would think of the Stratford that was then northeast of London,[2] in which it is now merged; and that Stratford was the town nearest Hackney, where Edward de Vere was buried, doubtless beneath the conventional monument, now lost — dissolved by time, I suppose one could say.

The Fifth alleged Proof we had occasion to mention in Chapter 9. Following Digges's poem and one of eight lines *To the Memorie* of M. W. *Shakespeare* by "I.M.," is a list, *The Names of the Principal Actors in all these Plays*, headed by William Shakespeare. "A most unusual feature," Gerald E. Bentley calls it, "one never found before in an English collection and seldom since." In other words, it was dragged in. And I may repeat that even those who claim the most for Shakespeare's career on the stage cannot argue that he deserved first listing, above even Richard Burbage. After all, they cannot produce even rumors of any parts he played till generations later, when on dubious authority he was placed in minor roles. But de Vere, if he was the "M. Will. Shake-speare" who played kingly parts in sport would be listed first, as in Meres's catalogue of those "best for comedy," on the strength of his rank.

In its presentation of Shakespeare's plays, I think the First Folio may be termed a masterpiece of equivocation and Ben Jonson be given top marks for skill. That it was seen as such by alert readers, I can hardly doubt. The compiler of the next collection of Shakespeare's works certainly recognized it for what it was, or seems to be, for he parodied it.

The Revealing 1640 Edition of "Shake-speare's Poems"

Poems Written By Wil. Shake-speare, Gent., appeared in 1640 with a title-page stating that copies were "Printed by Thos. Cotes, and are to be sold by John Benson, dwelling in St. Dunstan's Churchyard." The fact that John Benson is a metathesis of Ben Jonson is a striking coincidence, to say the least; and when we find that the introduction to the volume, headed "To the Reader," is signed I.B., just as Ben Jonson's introductory verse, "To the Reader," in the First Folio is signed B.I., we may fairly suspect that we are in on some mockery.

Our suspicions are progressively substantiated. The frontispiece, opposite,

---

[2] Stow speaks of the time in 1512 when "the carts of Stratford came laden with bread to the City."

This Shadowe is renowned Shakeſpear's: Soule of th'age
The applauſe? delight? the wonder of the Stage.
Nature her ſelfe, was proud of his deſignes
And joy'd to weare the dreſſing of his lines,
The learned will Conſeſs, his works are ſuch,
As neither man, nor Muſe, can prayſe to much.
For ever live thy fame, the world to tell,
Thy like, no age, ſhall ever paralell.
W. M. ſculpſit.

Frontispiece of *Poems Written by
Wil. Shake-speare, Gent.* of 1640.

By permission of the Folger Shakespeare
Library.

is the Droeshout engraving rather redrawn and reversed as in a mirror image, matching the Ben Jonson / John Benson inversion. In addition, a courtier's cape has been draped over the subject's right shoulder and the portrait extended downward to permit inclusion of the subject's left arm and hand, the latter gauntleted and clutching a spray of foliage. The leaves and drupe are recognizable as those of the olive tree. Such sprays symbolized victory in the classical world and adorned "the crown of the Roman conqueror at ovation." I believe the portraitist has added it to Droeshout to remind us about the origin of the poet's name. The olive in Greek mythology was the gift of Pallas Athena, who caused it to spring from the barren rock of Attica, in gratitude wherefor the people who sheltered below the Acropolis and were to create dramas matchless until "like Apollo" Shakespeare "came forth," named their town after the goddess — the Spear-shaker. "And in thy hand the Spear of Pallas shake," we read in one of the poems assembled in the volume.

The cream of the jibe is in the verse beneath the portrait. Most of the eight lines are from Ben Jonson's eulogy. But the first two are transformed by the use of what I can see only as interrogation marks. If that is what they are — and the reader may judge for himself — we have the following extraordinary expressions:

> This shadow is renowned Shakespeare's? Soul of th'age
> The applause? delight? the wonder of the stage.

The writer may well express incredulity. But quite apart from his punctuation marks, there is the fact that the image characterized as a mere "figure" in the First Folio is at his hands not even that. It is now only a "shadow." That is very nearly enough in itself to expose the introduction to Shakespeare's plays in the Folio for what it is.[3] But read the last two lines of the poem. They deliver a thunderclap comparable to the unexampled acclaim given Shakespeare by Ben Jonson:

> For ever live thy fame, the world to tell,
> Thy like, no age shall ever parallel.

Shakespeare is not only unequaled in the past and present, but he will remain forever without peer. That is about as far as homage can go, and it brings home to us again a feature as odd as any in the strange case of William Shakespeare. We have on the one hand the paucity of praise, apart from Meres, given his works when they were being written and the apparent absence of any mention of his name by any of the leading contemporary poets or by any of the contemporary playwrights in the years when the plays were being written (even by orthodox reckoning) and scant mention of it by any of them even thereafter, except by Jonson. On the other hand, in the first edition of his collected plays and the first of his collected poems we have him hailed respectively as the greatest dramatist that ever was and the greatest poet that ever will be.

Curious Shortcomings of the Folio

The First Folio "is the greatest secular book in the English language, perhaps in any language," Dr. McManaway asserts with ample warrant. Why are the

---

[3] The foregoing discussion of the 1640 volume follows closely the treatment of the subject in *Shake-speare: The Man Behind the Name*, by Dorothy Ogburn and the present author.

imperfections of so great a book so many and some so gross? It is perhaps possible that the author left his manuscripts in a state of almost insuperable confusion; the hypothesis would accord with the disclosure that he was deprived by death of the chance to put his writings in order. To me, the signs are that few if any of his manuscripts were available to the compilers. If so, what, then, had happened to them? It poses a pretty mystery. One possibility is that they were destroyed, most if not all before the compilers of the First Folio could lay hands on them. But can we believe that anyone could bring himself to do away with Shakespeare's originals before printed versions had been made of them? To believe that we must, I think, believe that they were dangerous indeed to a person or persons in a position to get hold of them or already in possession of them. The alternative is that they were hidden by such a person or persons. In the latter case, it is possible that they still exist somewhere and that we may yet turn them up and discover for the first time what the dramatist actually wrote: and what a tantalizing possibility that is! What seems to me self-evident is this: that either the manuscripts were deliberately destroyed to remove incriminating evidence or they were deliberately concealed, one or the other with consummate thoroughness. All things considered, it seems to me hardly credible that Shakespeare's manuscripts, many if not all unduplicated by the printer, could have disappeared by accident down to the very last scrap. I cling to the hope set forth in the Appendix.

A second reason for the textual failings of the Folio must be that however long the collection had been planned the actual production was rushed. A much better job could have been done with the materials available. Were the compilers fearful that the longer the work of assembling and printing took the greater the danger would be of provoking a reaction at the highest level of the realm and of a bar to the publication? A guess as to the cause of haste, relying on our present information, can be only a shot in the dark.

14

"Most Like a Noble Lord"

We find that if we read Shakespeare for what he tells us of himself, we cannot mistake the nobleman within the dramatist. We find that continually, sometimes apparently even despite himself, his aristocrat's hauteur is betrayed in his patronizing treatment of the lower classes and even of the middle class and that he is manifestly most at home in the highest reaches of society, from which, with few exceptions, he recruits those characters he accords three-dimensional treatment and important roles. We are struck by his idealization and envy of the simple life led by the lower orders, which clearly he has not had to endure, and his empathetic and convincing evocation of the ordeals and anguish that go with royal place. We remark, too, his expert's knowledge of the nobility's sports, especially falconry and hunting to hounds. If we ask how the Stratfordian authorities deal with the problem the dramatist's social background, as attested by the plays, raises for them, we find that some simply pooh-pooh the attestation while others endow the Stratfordian tradesman's son with noble and even royal associations that he cannot be shown to have, and would not have, enjoyed. To the assurances we have on good authority that Shakespeare early in his dramatic career displayed an insider's knowledge of the arena of power, we find they have no answer, any more than they have an explanation for the contrast between his contemptuous attitude toward money and Shakspere's avarice. As well as by his feudal outlook we are impressed by Shakespeare's acute sensory refinement and by his sympathy and fellow feeling for hunted animals — in his day both, surely, the product of delicate and privileged upbringing.

If you read through Shakespeare's works, you marvel at his prodigal invention, his magic with words, his insight into human nature, his understanding of life. That goes without saying. But what comes through with a force perhaps second only to that of his art is the perspective from which he regards society, which is that of a thoroughgoing nobleman. It is to me perfectly extraordinary that Shakespeare should appeal so much more to our age and seem so much more relevant to it than he has to most intervening generations when the social and political convictions he expresses and that shape his works are anathema today as never before. Especially are they unspeakable in academia, where egalitarianism is gospel (except, one hears, as it might impinge on academic privileges). The similarities between our age and the Elizabethan, both being times of crumbling bench-marks and expanding horizons, have been adduced as a basis of the immediacy Shakespeare has for us, and no doubt with warrant. But the paradox of Shakespeare's irreproachable standing in the universities, where as a visiting lecturer he would be hooted from the platform, remains. It is to be explained, I think, only by a convention among the orthodox to minimize or wholly gloss over that "almost religious sense of the inviolability of the crown," as Louis Auchincloss calls it, that "love of good blood, and belief in its wondrous efficacy," in Frank Harris's words, and that disdain of the lower orders, all so characteristic of Shakespeare. This may be one reason why professors of English cling to the picture of the dramatist as a commercial-minded tradesman's son. When he is resolutely conceived of as such, it simply cannot *be* that he stood for those things which his works tell us that he so unblushingly did stand for.

To avoid recognition of Shakespeare's partiality for high station, the blemish is transferred to those readers who take Shakespeare at his word and deduce therefrom the kind of man he must have been. "Social snobbery is an unspoken shibboleth among the anti-Stratfordians," say Gwynne Evans and Harry Levin. Only one orthodox academician of whom I know fairly confronts Shakespeare's archconservatism, and that, because he seems to share it. The maverick Dr. Rowse, speaking of *Troilus and Cressida*, declares that "it gives them [the people] what they most need to be told — the evidence is in the break-up of society all around us: the absolute necessity of social order, authority and obedience, of people knowing their place and doing their duty." Further: "Coriolanus knows what idiots they [the people] always are, and is filled with contempt for them." One can sympathize with the Stratfordians that these anti-democratic sentiments were voiced by the leading publicist for their side and not by one of their opponents whose alleged snobbishness has yet to surface in a single discoverable utterance.

In *Troilus and Cressida* Professor Rowse has in mind a famous speech by Ulysses amounting to a lecture interjected into that disillusioned drama of human unworthiness. The Greek hero spells out what is clearly the author's conception of the proper form of human society:

> The heavens themselves, the planets, and this centre
> Observe degree, priority, and place,
> Insisture, course, proportion, season, form,
> Office and custom, in all line of order:
> And therefore is the glorious planet Sol
> In noble eminence enthron'd and sphere'd
> Amidst the other.

The sun rules as King,

> But when the planets
> In evil mixture to disorder wander,
> What plagues, and what portents, what mutiny,
> What raging of the sea, shaking of earth,
> Commotion in the winds, frights, changes, horrors
> Divert and crack, rend and deracinate

The unity and married calm of states
Quite from their fixture! O! when degree is shak'd,
Which is the ladder to all high designs,
The enterprise is sick. . . .

    . . . .

    Take but degree away, untune that string,
And hark! what discord follows. . . .

    . . . .

    Force should be right; or rather, right and wrong

    . . . .

    Should lose their names, and so should justice too.

    . . . .

    And appetite, a universal wolf,
So doubly seconded with will and power,
Must make perforce a universal prey,
And last eat up itself.[1]

Belarius in *Cymbeline* leaves no doubt of Shakespeare's belief in class distinctions:

Though mean and mighty rotting
Together, have one dust, yet reverence —
That angel of the world — doth make distinction
Of place 'tween high and low.

That which creates social distinctions is the *angel of the world*. It is natural to Shakespeare that after the battle of Agincourt (which you would never know from Shakespeare was won by the anonymous English long-bowmen) the French herald should ask license

To sort our nobles from our common men;
For many of our princes — woe the while! —
Lie drowned and soaked in mercenary blood;
So do our vulgar drench their peasant limbs
In blood of princes.

Even death was not to be permitted to close the gulf between classes.

The fastidious patrician in Shakespeare speaks from the Duke's lips in *Measure for Measure:*

    I love the people,
But do not like to stage me to their eyes.
Though it do well, I do not relish well
Their loud applause and Aves vehement,
Nor do I think the man of safe discretion
That does affect it.

Continually there crops out in Shakespeare a contempt for the populace, collectively and individually, that would scandalize us if we acknowledged

---

[1] "Deracinate" is one of the many words Shakespeare coined from Latin roots. "Insisture" is another, but it failed to catch on.

it. In *Love's Labour's Lost* the young aristocrats' patronizing and callous treatment of their social inferiors who are trying to entertain them with a play is embarrassing, even if we make allowances for the upbringing of a nobly born Shakespeare. The play is an early one, but the lowly amateur actors in the later *Midsummer-Night's Dream* fare little better at the author's hands. They are described by the Master of the Revels as

> Hard-handed men, that work in Athens here,
> Which never labored in their minds till now,

and by Puck as

> A crew of patches, rude mechanicals,
> That work for bread upon Athenian stalls,

with their principal member, Bottom,

> The shallowest thick-skin of that barren sort.

Autolycus, a thoroughly sympathetic character in *The Winter's Tale*, exclaims "Let me have no lying; it becomes none but tradesmen." That is Shakespeare's opinion of the class to which Shakspere's father belonged. Shakspere appears to have been unattractive enough in his own right. As Shakespeare he would have been a monster — as would Christopher Marlowe, too. Frank Harris's stricture would have been justified, that the "native snobbishness in him was heightened to flunkeyism."

We see in Shakespeare the attitude of hereditary privilege toward the employee class in every age and clime when Orlando addresses Adam in *As You Like It.*

> O good old man! how well in thee appears
> The constant service of the antique world,
> When service sweat for duty, not for meed!
> Thou art not for the fashion of these times,
> When none will sweat but for promotion
> And having that, do choke their service up.

That essential medium of popular government, the politician, is held up to scorn in Shakespeare. Lear says:

> Get thee glass eyes;
> And, like a scurvy politician, seem
> To see things thou dost not.

Hamlet is equally scathing when the gravedigger turns up a skull:

> This might be the pate of a politician, which
> this ass o'er offices, one that would circumvent
> God, might it not?

To base government on the people's will would in Shakespeare be the road to ruin.

> A habitation giddy and unsure
> Hath he that buildeth on the vulgar heart

states the Archbishop of York in *Henry the Sixth, Part Two*. One reason is set forth by Julius Caesar:

> This common body
> Like to a vagabond flag upon the stream,
> Goes to and back, lackeying the varying tide,
> To rot itself with motion.

The fickleness of the populace is a recurrent theme in Shakespeare. In *Henry the Sixth, Part Two*, Jack Cade's rebel army is swayed to cry now "God save the King," now "We'll follow Cade!" until the popular leader himself exclaims, "Was ever feather so lightly blown to and fro as this multitude?"

The historic John Cade and his followers had legitimate grievances: extravagance and favoritism at Court and the breakdown in administration of justice reflected on a regime already discredited by loss of royal lands in France. But one would never know it from Shakespeare: in the play it is "The rascal people, thirsting after prey" who "join with the traitor." In Shakespeare's view, Cade's success would mean the triumph of what we should call Communism, and what Shakespeare thought of *that* may be judged by the words he has Cade speak:

> There shall be in England seven halfpenny loaves sold for a penny; the three-hooped pot shall have ten hoops; and I will make it a felony to drink small beer. All the realm shall be in common, and in Cheapside shall my palfrey go to grass. And when I am king — as king I will be . . . there shall be no money; all shall eat and drink on my score; and I will apparel them all in one livery, that they may agree like brothers, and worship me their lord.

Cade later promises that

> The proudest peer in the realm shall not wear a head on his shoulders, unless he pay me tribute; there shall not a maid be married, but she shall pay to me her maidenhead, ere they have it; men shall hold of me in capite [i.e., as from the sovereign].

We are to understand that a popular leader would institute a regime like the crude tyrant Papa Doc Duvalier's in Haiti.

When Henry V is making the rounds of the camp in disguise on the night before the battle of Agincourt, he engages three soldiers in conversation. *Time*, in reviewing Olivier's film of the play, said: "In appearance and most of what they say, the three soldiers . . . might just as well be soldiers of World War II. No film of that war has yet said what they say so honestly or so well." They voice the kind of doubts about the King's cause and trustworthiness that men in the ranks anywhere might entertain of authority. And that makes the scene unique in Shakespeare. At least if anywhere else he has ordinary men stand up to their liege lord with dignity and with his at least passing sympathy, I cannot recall it; and even here they do not know who their lord is. If we wait for any member of a lower order of society, anyone of Shakspere's class, to take the stage in Shakespeare and inform us of the hardships and sufferings that went with his lot in life, we wait in vain. But the dramatist enters readily enough into the minds of kings to make real for us their weighty burdens. Directly after his conversation with the soldiers around the campfire, Henvy V (whom Louis Auchincloss, finding it unthinkable that Shakespeare could have had "the smallest acquaintance with royal circles," deems a mere "pageant monarch") contrasts his lot enviously with theirs:

> What infinite heart's ease
> Must kings neglect that private men enjoy!
> And what have kings that privates have not too,
> Save ceremony, save general ceremony?
> And what art thou, thou idle ceremony?
>   . . . .
>   The throne he sits on, nor the tide of pomp
> That beats upon the high shore of his world,
> No, not all these, thrice-gorgeous ceremony,
> Not all these, laid in bed majestical,
> Can sleep so soundly as the wretched slave,
> Who with a body fill'd and vacant mind
> Gets him to rest, cramm'd with distressful bread; . . .

And he goes on, idealizing the life of the "lackey" in comparison with that of the monarch. To put himself in a king's place evidently came easily to Shakespeare. Henry IV, founder of the Lancastrian line, which the Earls of Oxford supported against the Yorkists, yearns for "sleep! O gentle sleep!" with even keener poignancy than his son and successor was to do:

> Wilt thou upon the high and giddy mast
> Seel up the ship-boy's eyes, and rock his brains
> In cradle of the rude imperious surge . . . ?
>   . . . .
>   Canst thou, O partial sleep! give thy repose
> To the wet sea-boy in an hour so rude,
> And in the calmest and most stillest night,
> With all appliances and means to boot,
> Deny it to a king? Then, happy low, lie down!
> Uneasy lies the head that wears a crown.

Envy of the "happy low" goes further in Henry VI, who cries

> O God! Methinks it were a happy life,
> To be no better than a homely swain;
> To sit upon a hill, as I do now. . . .

He dwells at length upon the attractions of a simple, regular routine, crying again:

Ah! What a life were this! how sweet! how lovely!
Gives not the hawthorn bush a sweeter shade
To shepherds, looking on their silly sheep,
Than doth a rich embroidered canopy
To kings, that fear their subjects' treachery?
Oh, yes! it doth; a thousand-fold it doth.
And to conclude, the shepherd's homely curds,
His cold thin drink out of his leather bottle,
His wonted sleep under a fresh tree's shade,
All which secure and sweetly he enjoys,
Is far beyond a prince's delicates,
His viands sparkling in a golden cup,
His body couched in a curious bed,
When care, mistrust and treason wait on him.

Romanticizing a life close to nature is almost exclusively a reaction against the evils of a too-replete civilization, with which only the highly privileged could be afflicted before the industrial revolution. It is most express in *As You Like It*. Shakespeare "has written no happier play," as Edward Dowden says, than this of a love that "moves through the sun-dappled spaces and over the dewy sward beneath the oaks of Arden. Arcady and England meet in this forest of France." Duke Senior speaks to his "brothers in exile":

Hath not old custom made this life more sweet
Than that of painted pomp? Are not these woods
More free from peril than the envious court?
Here we but feel the penalty of Adam,
The season's difference; as, the icy fang
And churlish chiding of the winter's wind,
Which, when it blows and bites upon the body,
Even till I shrink with cold, I smile and say
"This is no flattery: these are counsellors
That feelingly persuade me what I am."
    . . . .
 And this our life exempt from public haunt,
Finds tongues in trees, books in the running brooks,
Sermons in stones, and good in everything.

Amiens, one of the lords addressed by the Duke, sings:

Under the greenwood tree
Who loves to lie with me,
And tune his merry note
Unto the sweet bird's throat,
Come hither, come hither, come hither;
 Here shall we see
  No enemy
But winter and rough weather.

Are we not in these passages hearing a poet more accustomed to the trials of life at Court than to dependence on the mercies of the land, one who from sallies afield, well-clad, in inclement weather, had a good meal in a warm abode to return to? To an ordinary Elizabethan, to whom adequate covering was hard come by and whose house was frigid and draughty, it would scarcely have occurred to speak of no "penalty" but "the icy fang . . . of the winter's wind," "no enemy but winter and rough weather." *But?*

Shakespeare was the first in English literature to find solace and rewards in nature as we conceive them in our over-civilized times. As a poet of nature he has never been excelled. But though he discovered for us nature's restorative benison, he knew what it was to be deprived of cultivated society even in the Arcady of Arden; de Vere had suffered exile from the Court. Touchstone, asked how he liked "this shepherd's life," replies just as one of us might who had fled the pressures of Manhattan to the simplicity of backwoods Vermont:

> Truly, shepherd, in respect of itself, it is a good life. . . . In respect that it is solitary, I like it very well; but in respect that it is private [i.e., isolated], it is a very vile life. Now, in respect it is in the fields, it pleaseth me well; but in respect it is not in the Court, it is tedious. As it is a spare life, look you, it fits my humour well; but as there is no more plenty in it, it goes much against my stomach.

He has not forgotten that he "hath been a courtier." "Why," he says to his interrogator:

> if thou wast never at Court, thou never sawest good manners; if you never sawest good manners, then thy manners must be wicked; and wickedness is a sin, and sin is damnation.

To Touchstone, named for the mineral by which the worth of an object is known, you learned good manners at Court and nowhere else, and without them were damned.

In Shakespeare there is one law for the higher orders, another for the lower, and what may be forgiven the former is intolerable in the latter. The high-principled Isabella in *Measure for Measure* explains that

> Great men may jest with saints; 'tis wit in them,
> But, in the less, foul profanation.
>   . . . .
> That in the captain's but a choleric word,
> Which in the soldier is flat blasphemy.

R.H.I.P. is a bit of shorthand with which today one is greeted upon initiation into officerhood in the hierarchical military services: Rank Has Its Privileges. It is matched by R.H.I.R.: Rank Has Its Responsibilities. Both are bedrock in Shakespeare. In the many wars of which he wrote, military chiefs — earls, dukes, princes, and even kings — did not command from the rear. They led, fighting sword in hand in the front rank. Richard III was the last

English monarch to die in combat, and the battle of Bosworth Field in 1485, in which he was cut down, was the last military action of which Shakespeare was interested in writing. Courage to the bitter end was taken for granted in Shakespeare's feudal lords, whether high-minded like Henry V or villainous like Richard III. Much besides in the way of personal character was expected of a true nobleman. The Earl of Worcester sets forth what may not be allowed him in reprimanding Henry Hotspur, son of the Duke of Northumberland, for having been "too wilful-blame" — meaning deliberately incurring blame — in his treatment of the Welsh chieftain Owen Glendower. And of this fault the Earl says:

> Yet oftentimes it doth present harsh rage,
> Defect of manners, want of government,
> Pride, haughtiness, opinion, and disdain:
> The least of which haunting a nobleman
> Loseth men's hearts and leaves behind a stain
> Upon the beauty of all parts besides,
> Beguiling them of commendation.

It is interesting, indeed amusing, to hear the dramatist pronouncing pride incompatible with true nobility when it lurks barely below the surface in all the noble characters he creates.

> Tell the Dauphin I will keep my state,
> Be like a king and show my sail of greatness
> When I do rouse me in my throne of France —

So Henry V delivers himself to the luckless ambassador of France, who has brought a gift mocking the King for his "wilder days."

> I will rise there with so full a glory
> That I will dazzle all the eyes of France,
> Yea, strike the Dauphin blind to look on us.

Talk of pride!

In Coriolanus, Shakespeare undertook to present a Caesar-like figure of pride raised to impossible heights. The results tell us much. A warrior whom we see red with the gore of the enemy, a conqueror who has added to Rome's greatness, Caius Marcius, surnamed Coriolanus after his capture of Coroli, capital of the Volsces, is a man of such indomitable passion and towering pride that when the patricians put him up for consul he cannot descend to ordinary civility to the citizenry; to him the prescribed solicitation of their favor would be fawning. When, outraged by his contemptuous arrogance, the tribunes pronounce his banishment and the citizens take up the cry, "It shall be so, — it shall be so," Coriolanus replies

> You common cry of curs! whose breath I hate
> As reek o' the rotton fens, whose loves I prize
> As the dead carcasses of unburied men
> That do corrupt my air, I banish you . . . !

One is reminded of Cleopatra's warning to her attendant Iras of the consequences of their capture by the Romans:

> Mechanic slaves
> With greasy aprons, rules and hammers, shall
> Uplift us to the view; in their thick breaths,
> Rank of gross diet, shall we be enclouded,
> And forc'd to drink their vapour.

Coriolanus is unique in that in it Shakespeare concedes that the people can bear legitimate grievances against their overlord — that they can have a case. Within limits they enjoy his sympathy. Conventionally, I believe, the play is regarded as the drama of a man destroyed by pride. Edward Dowden expresses probably the prevailing view when he writes: "The passions and pride of Coriolanus are in truth the mob in his own nature. . . . And his ruin is wrought . . . by the violence and haughty egoism which makes him the foe to his country and for a while the scorner of his friends."

It is quite likely that is how Shakespeare initially conceived the story. If so, he found himself unable to let the matter rest with that. Banished, Coriolanus makes common cause with Aufidius, the Volscian general, and at the head of the Volscian army marches on Rome. A Roman general reports:

> He is their god: he leads them like a thing
> Made by some other deity than Nature,
> That shapes man better; and they follow him,
> Against us brats, with no less confidence
> Than boys pursuing summer butterflies,
> Or butchers killing flies.

The feudal lord in Shakespeare has become fascinated by the super-warrior — or, rather, I believe it is the military hero Shakespeare felt he ought to have been who has been caught up by the dramatist's own creation.

First Citizen declares: "I ever said we were i' the wrong when we banished him," and Second Citizen rejoins fervently, "So did we all." Once again in Shakespeare the populace oscillates between extremes.

But surely the mighty conqueror has grown great past all bearing? Meninius, his devoted, father-like friend, speaks hopelessly of the change in him:

> When he walks, he moves like an engine, and the ground shrinks before his treading: he is able to pierce a corselet with his eye. . . . He wants nothing of a god but eternity and a heaven to throne in. . . . There is no more mercy in him than there is milk in a male tiger.

But he says — and here we come to the crux of the play —

> The gods will not be good to us. When we banished him, we respected not them; and he, returning to break our necks, they respect not us.

Early in the play Meninius had warned the people's tribunes of their debt to the Senators of Rome, the patricians:

> No public benefit which you receive
> But it proceeds or comes from them to you,
> And no way from yourselves.

He had raked them over the coals, calling them "a brace of unmeriting, proud, violent, testy magistrates — alias fools." And how have they brought this fire down upon their heads? Because they "must be saying Marcius [Coriolanus] is proud"!

If Rome is not to be sacked it must depend on the pleas of Coriolanus' mother, wife, and boy-child. They implore his mercy with Shakespeare's wonted eloquence, but only at long last does the victor relent. For the first time, in the lines in which he yields, he touches us with a revelation of his humanity and the play is suddenly deeply moving.

> O, mother, mother!
> What have you done? Behold! the heavens do ope,
> The gods look down, and this unnatural scene
> They laugh at. O my mother! mother! O!
> You have won a happy victory to Rome;
> But for your son, believe it, O! believe it,
> Most dangerously you have with him prevail'd.
> If not most mortal to him. But let it come.

First the citizens of Rome had lost the gods' favor by opposing Coriolanus, and now Coriolanus has lost it by allowing pity to come between him and his obligations to his partner in heroic exploit. We must believe that it was Shakespeare's conviction that the stature of the ruler must be maintained, come what may, and the people suffer him however overweening his demeanor. At least he believed that was what the gods willed. In *Julius Caesar*, Brutus even by Antony's estimate was the noblest Roman of them all; yet when he gave countenance to the plot against the supreme figure of the state he was doomed; "The heavens themselves . . . observe degree, priority, and place." He could not win even over a dead Caesar: "Caesar, thou art mighty still," he concedes at the end — and thus is the play called *Julius Caesar* and not *Marcus Brutus*.

In agreeing to spare Rome, Coriolanus has done the Volsces out of their triumph and plunder. He turns to Aufidius apologetically, even humbly:

> Sir, it is no little thing to make
> Mine eyes to sweat compassion. . . .

And it is compassion, not pride after all, that brings Caius Marcius down. Aufidius to himself observes:

> I am glad thou has set thy mercy and thy honour
> At difference in thee: out of that I'll work
> Myself a former fortune.

When Coriolanus presents himself in Corioli, Aufidius and three co-conspirators slay the conqueror, now abdicated of his invincibility. But in the end the honors rest with Coriolanus, who in life had stood above them all. The First Lord of the Volscian capital himself orders:

> Bear from hence his body;
> And mourn you for him! Let him be regarded
> As the most noble corse that ever herald
> Did follow to his urn.

Nothing is heard now of excessive pride; and his very murderer, Aufidius, who delivers the eulogy, puts aside even the slaughter of his own people at the Roman's hands:

> My rage is gone,
> And I am struck with sorrow. Take him up: . . .
> Beat thou the drum, that it speak mournfully;
> Trail your steel pikes. Though in this city he
> Hath widow'd and unchilded many a one,
> Which to his hour bewail the injury,
> Yet he shall have a noble memory.

The reader may recall what we observed about the length of Shakespeare's plays and what it told us of his supposed dedication to the commercial theatre, in which plays could run only two or at most two and a half hours. When Coriolanus was put on by the Royal Shakespeare Company in London in 1978, *Time*'s reviewer wrote that "Terry Hands' hot-spirited direction makes 3½ hours pass like one."

The reviewer quoted the self-justification with which Coriolanus counters his mother's counsel, that he show the plebeians more respect:

> Why did you wish me milder? Would you have me
> False to my nature? Rather say I play
> The man I am.

In her retort,

> You might have been enough the man you are
> With striving less to be so

Shakespeare shows he understood well enough the flaw in his hero's makeup. Still, we might take Coriolanus's self-avowal as Shakespeare's reply to us today if we reproach him with his contempt for the political principles we make a virtue of and for asking us to remember the insufferably arrogant Coriolanus for his "nobility" — Shakespeare's highest accolade. In treating social relationships as would a feudal lord, Shakespeare, we may suppose, played the man he was.

Hugh R. Trevor-Roper writes:

> Whatever his own social circumstances, in his outlook Shakespeare was an unquestioning aristocrat. To him the established order is a mystical harmony, kings rule by divine right, and any challenge to that harmony, that right, is unforgivable. It was its usurpation of the throne which, in the historical plays,

was the hereditary tragedy of the house of Lancaster. On the other hand, popular leaders — whether Roman Empire tribunes or English rebels — are to him merely vulgar demagogues. The people, indeed, are quite unfit for public affairs. Kings may make war for trifles, nations may be sacrificed to chivalric honour, but the duty of the people is to admire and obey.

The Human de Vere Within the Dramatist

I recognize that the more the reader sees Shakespeare as the man he evidently was, the more antagonism he is likely to feel for the star of my story. Readers who had overlooked in the conventional Shakespeare the views we have seen characteristic of the dramatist, not really perceiving in the plays anything so unlikely to have issued from the Stratford man, may well be incensed by them as coming from an Earl and be turned against Edward de Vere and, somewhat paradoxically, against the case for his having been the author. There are two things I may say about that, other than that we have seen the worst and that more congenial characteristics of the poet-dramatist will be appearing as we proceed.

The first is that de Vere when writing as himself was by no means so unperceiving about the plight of the disadventured as he seems when addressing the world and posterity, with all due weight, as I am confident he was doing when Shakespeare took the stage. In his youthful *Labour and Its Reward* he saw that

> The labouring man that tills the fertile soil,
>   And reaps the harvest fruit, hath not indeed
> The gain but pain; and if for all his toil
>   He gets the straw, the lord will have the seed.

He knew that

> The mason poor that builds the lordly halls
>   Dwells not in them: they are for high degree; . . .

And that

> The idle drone that labours not at all,
>   Sucks up the sweet of honey from the bee; . . .

And prophetically, having perhaps already had a taste of the fate that was to be his, he added,

> So he that takes the pain to pen the book
>   Reaps not the gifts of goodly golden muse; . . .

Second, de Vere undoubtedly felt that with the loosening of feudal bonds and the rise of a new trading class with mercenary standards, perhaps in the emergence of new continents across the sea, he was witnessing the passing of the structured world that the *noblesse oblige* of the de Veres and their kind had held together. A. L. Rowse speaks of "the breakup of society all around us." Shakespeare was so far ahead of his time in his understanding of so much, so modern in what he can tell us of ourselves, we may forget how backward-looking he was in the settings he chose for his plays. In this, his rejection of contemporary England was very nearly complete. A man like de Vere would have seen an alien future in birth. In an image of such compact power as only Shakespeare can be counted on to give us (it follows Ulysses' speech on the heavenly order), he would have seen

> The baby figure of the giant mass
> Of things to come at large.

Shakespeare, like Coriolanus, had his breaking-point. In *King Lear*, finally and for the first time, compassion for the poor, the ill-clothed, the powerless, wells up and spills over in a protagonist of Shakespeare's — and what brought the author to this access of fellow feeling for the wretched we shall try to discover as we get on with our story.

Controversy over Shakespeare's Social Position

The fair-minded reader may protest that I have been taking views that Shakespeare's noble characters would naturally express and attributing them to Shakespeare himself. What would I have, that medieval kings be made to speak up for democracy in order that the plays stand warrant for the author's enlightenment? The point is that every character in Shakespeare through whom the author could be imagined as speaking on social and political issues *is* of noble birth or privileged station and asserts the outlook of his class with uncommon, sometimes even gratuitous vigor and intensity. In the whole history of Western literature no writer ever wrote more consistently from a nobleman's point of view than Shakespeare, and the characters that he considered worthy of his genius are almost without exception of the nobility.

How would those statements, which I made in *Harvard Magazine*, go down with the English Departments? Gwynne Evans and Harry Levin reply: "Even if his ideological leanings were such as are attributed to him here" — which the professors would have us believe they are denying while knowing better than actually to do so — "could he stand comparison in this respect with — to mention just one name — Castiglione?" Had the professors been able to mention any other name, or a better example, we may hazard a guess that they would have done so. Baldassare Castiglione (1478–1529) is the only writer they have to propose whose point of view was as consistently that of a nobleman as Shakespeare's, and Castiglione was not a writer at all in the sense in which we are speaking. He was a diplomat known to literature for a small body of elegant verse, his letters, and one book. *Il Cortegiano* has the form of an imagined discussion in the drawing-room of the Duchess of Urbino on the qualities making up a perfect courtier. The professors would hardly have brought up the Italian, even out of desperation, had they expected the reader to know (even if they knew themselves) that *The Courtier* was published in English in 1572 with a long and graceful preface by the young Edward de Vere, who had doubtless been a prime mover in its translation.

To the second statement, about the nobility of Shakespeare's characters, the professors object that "Such overwhelming exceptions as Shylock and Falstaff spring to mind at once, together with a host of lesser figures — tapsters, whores, foot-soldiers, sailors, pedlars, rustics who do not seem unworthy of his genius." It was, of course, Shylock I had in mind in writing "almost without exception."[2] Falstaff, though he had been a page to the Duke of Norfolk, is only a knight, but he is treated as one of the company of noblemen. The Duke of Lancaster, the King's son and general of the King's forces, greets him familiarly: "Now, Falstaff, where have you been all this while?" and Lord Bardolph, enumerating the losses on the field of Shrewsbury, includes "Harry Monmouth's brawn, the hulk Sir John" among only seven he names, the others being a prince and earls. Falstaff speaks up to King Henry IV as if he *were* an earl. And I think he was. When the dramatist changed his name from Oldcastle, as he was called in the original version of the *Henry the Fourth* plays, to Falstaff, I think it was because he meant the character to be a bitter-comic caricature of himself in later years, the Shakespear who had become a Fall-staff. (While I have no wish to challenge Professor Rowse's and Anthony Burgess's titles as the most prurient commentators on Shakespeare, I think we may read an indelicate innuendo in the name.) As for the Harvard professors' "tapsters, whores, foot-soldiers, sailors, pedlars, rustics," these are treated summarily and never developed three-dimensionally; compare them with their equivalents in Dickens. Moreover, they enter the plays only as they come within the purlieus of the noble principals.

Shakespeare "was an aristocrat born . . . and felt in himself a kinship for the courtesies, chivalries, and generousness of aristocratic life," Frank Harris observes. "Everybody has noticed the predilection with which he lends such characters [as Bassanio, Benedick, and Mercutio] his own poetic spirit and charm. His lower orders are all food for comedy or farce; he will not treat them seriously." That it apparently never occurred to Harris to question Shakespeare's identification as the Stratford man is astonishing.

It has certainly occurred to Hugh R. Trevor-Roper, who has referred to

---

[2] Hermann Sinsheimer makes the point in his study of Shylock that in *The Merchant of Venice* Shakespeare "took sides unequivocally with the oppressed and injured — again a unique feature in the work of this poet of rulers and noblemen."

Shakespeare as "whoever he was." We have already heard him enlarge upon Shakespeare's aristocratic outlook. He goes on:

> The independent, sub-noble world of artisans and craftsmen, if it exists for Shakespeare, exists only as his butt. Bottom, Quince, Snug, Dogberry and Verges, Dull — these poor imbeciles are used only to amuse the nobility by their clumsiness. Even the middle classes are scarcely better treated.

A century ago, Walt Whitman made the same point, coming to a rather quaint conclusion about it. He remarked that Shakespeare's

> low characters, mechanics, even the loyal henchman — all in themselves nothing — serve as capital foils to the aristocracy. The comedies (exquisite as they certainly are) bringing in admirably portray'd common characters, have the unmistakable hue of plays, portraits, made for the divertissement only of the élite of the castle, and from its point of view. The comedies are altogether non-acceptable to America and Democracy.

In this connection, Louis P. Bénézet draws an interesting contrast between Shakespeare and Jonson:

> As one reads the plays of these two greatest dramatists of the Elizabethan-Jacobean era one is immediately struck by a great contrast between them. One is aristocratic, the other bourgeois. The noblemen of one author are natural, at ease, convincing. They talk the language of their class, both in matter and manner. They are aristocrats to the core. On the other hand in portraying the lower classes Shakespeare is unconvincing. He makes them clods or dolts or clowns, and has them amuse us by their gaucheries. He gives them undignified names: Wart, Bullcalf, Mouldy, Bottom, Dogberry, Snout, etc. Only occasionally does Shakespeare hold up a gentleman to ridicule, as he does with Slender and Aguecheek, said by Professor Dowden to represent the same person, a sentiment strongly seconded by certain Oxfordians, who see Philip Sidney as the original.
>
> On the other hand, Jonson's bourgeois characters are natural, while his nobles are caricatures. They bear the same kind of names that Shakespeare gives to his commoners: Sir Paul Eitherside, Sir Amorous La-Foole, Sir Epicure Mammon, Lady Haughty, Sir Diaphanous Silkworm, etc.
>
> There is always a strong tendency on the part of the English writers from the upper middle class to be resentful of the attitude assumed toward them by the titled nobility. It is characteristic of Ben Jonson. He has no sympathy with aristocrat aloofness and superiority.
>
> On the other hand, Shakespeare is the natural aristocrat. He never has to think to make his characters of gentle blood act their parts. They do so as naturally as they breathe.

Margaret L. Knapp remarks, "The untaught genius may score a success by writing about what he knows, or like Marlowe in *Tamburlaine*, about what the rest of the world does not know, but when he deals with things near at home he had better know his subject by heart." When Shakespeare set out to call up a royal court in all its grace of manners and lurid clash of passionate ambitions before the habitués of such a court, the results, I think, warrant our believing that he did so in no trepidation but with the sound expectation of riveting his audience's attention to the mirror he held up to their world — the world in which he moved as confidently as Hamlet in Elsinore.

"It is not my purpose," says Louis Auchincloss in *Motiveless Malignity* "to waste any time on attempted rebuttals of crackpot theories about the authorship of Shakespeare's plays." He does, however, take time to state that there "is one argument . . . that strikes me as peculiarly idiotic, and that is that Shakespeare's plays must have been written by a person born close to the crown because of the intimate familiarity they show with court life." Mr. Auchincloss thereupon undertakes to mock the dramatist as revealing "himself a bit of a hick" in his portrayals of medieval royalty. The deportment of Margaret, daughter of the King of Naples whom Henry VI takes to wife, he finds particularly "unregal." (Curiously, Shakespeare's Margaret condemns King Henry for that selfsame fault, in a speech of an imperial pitch that the novelist in Mr. Auchincloss might find it not easy to surpass. "Is this the government of Britain's isle," she scornfully inquires, "And this the royalty of Albion's king?") Queen Margaret instances her unregality in Mr. Auchincloss's view when, taking it rather amiss that the Duchess of Gloucester schemes to supplant her on the throne, she pretends to mistake her Grace for a servant and gives her a box on the ear. Unregal it may have been when Queen Elizabeth fetched the Countess of Essex just such a clout, but, alas, she did so — as she later landed a stinging one on the Earl of Essex's own face. The novelist also finds it unqueenly of Margaret to be other than herself when she is presented with the severed head of the Earl of Suffolk, her lover and her "soul's treasure." He sets a high standard of royal sangfroid. The dramatist is given further failing grades in this department by Mr. Auchincloss: in the historical plays he "showed little first-hand knowledge of life at court" — that is to say, less knowledge than Mr. Auchincloss possesses. But — it seems that "In *King Lear* and in *Antony and Cleopatra* he created a king and a queen who, had he written nothing else, and written them anonymously, might almost seem to justify the supposition that the author was an intimate of royalty." Almost. "Surely Lear, as he says of himself, is every inch a king, and Cleopatra is royal to the tips of her fingers." How is this to be explained? "The man who created them had seen persons of great style at close quarters." I think it likely.

Because the treatment given this subject by Professors Evans and Levin is significant, I quote here the passage in the *Harvard Magazine* article that provoked them. It follows my observation that the world in which Shakespeare laid his dramas was foreclosed to Shakspere, whose knowledge of it would have been second-hand at best. I wrote:

> Literature affords no parallel for what we are asked to believe of Shaksper. That three successive monarchs delighted in his plays merely tends to confirm,

surely, what we recognize for ourselves, that the world of which Shakespeare wrote was the world he knew. So also, I think, does Charles Chaplin, from the other side, when he writes: "I dislike Shakespearean themes involving kings, queens, august people and their honor. Perhaps it is something psychological within me, possibly my peculiar solipsism. In my pursuit of bread and cheese, honor was seldom trafficked in. I cannot identify myself with a prince's problems." And that, we may well believe, would have been the feeling of Shaksper.

Recalling his visit to the dramatist's alleged birthplace, Chaplin declares: "That such a mind ever dwelt or had its beginnings there seems incredible. . . . In the work of the greatest of geniuses humble beginnings will reveal themselves somewhere — but one cannot trace the slightest sign of them in Shakespeare."

This theory evidently gave the two professors trouble. They decided it could best be handled by ignoring Mr. Chaplin altogether and changing the meaning of what I had said. They wrote: "'Literature affords no parallel for what we are asked to believe of Shaksper [*sic*],' Mr. Ogburn declares: that a country-born commoner could write plays that delighted monarchs." Addressing themselves to the absurdity they had put in my mouth, they went on: "Mr. Ogburn should be informed that Terence, an African slave, charmed the high Roman circle of Scipios with the refinements of his style and wit."

The facts are that the famous Latin playwright, while brought as a slave to Rome from Roman Carthage (he was that kind of African), "was educated like a free man in the house of Terentius Lucanus, a senator, by whom he was soon emancipated; whereupon he took his master's nomen Terentius," Ernest Harrison and William Y. Sellar tell us. "He was admitted into the intimacy of young men of the best families, such as Scipio, Laelius and Furius Philus; and he enjoyed the favor of older men of literary distinction and official position." A slave, in short, given remarkable advantages. That is not all of interest in Terentius. Terence was accused in his own day of being a front for the actual playwrights, Scipio and Laelius. Quoting again from Harrison and Sellar: "He meets the charge of receiving assistance in the composition of his plays by claiming as a great honour the favour which he enjoyed with those who were the favourites of the Roman people. But the gossip, not discouraged by Terence, lived and throve; it crops up in Cicero [who named Laelius as the author] and Quintilian." Roger Ascham, who grew up under Henry VIII to become a leading classical scholar and tutor to the young Elizabeth, attributed to Scipio comedies assigned to Terence in which, he said, "doth sound in mine ear the pure fine talk of . . . the flower of the worthiest nobility that ever Rome bred." It seems to me very likely that John Davies had in mind the persistent belief that the Carthaginian was only a mask for a high-born actual playwright when he addressed "Shakespeare" as "our English Terence."

Stratfordians have seen the necessity for according Shakspere some, at least, of the advantages enjoyed by Terence. Louis B. Wright, it is true, scoffs at the weakness of his fellows. If the plays apparently "show an intimate acquaintance with kings and nobles" it is because, he says, "the author took his material from popular works of history, took it wholesale, in huge chunks," as "the skeptics" would know "if they took the trouble to investigate." His predecessor as director of the Folger Library and former Cornell professor, Joseph Q. Adams, however, had "no doubt" that "Shakespeare often was a guest at tavern entertainments given by Southampton, or Rutland, or Pembroke, or Sir Walter Raleigh, or Sir John Salisbury." Southampton, Rutland, and Pembroke were earls, Salisbury, who had royal blood, was the husband of the illegitimate daughter of another earl and, like Raleigh, was a favorite of the Queen's.

Robert Payne tells us that the subject of his biography, *By Me, William Shakespeare*, "met kings and queens, and was at ease with them, and he was on terms of intimacy with many members of the nobility and felt equal to them. Knowing that he was himself descended from ancient Saxon kings, he felt no need to humble himself before anyone." One can only stand open-mouthed before the dream-stuff purveyed to the public as fact.

According to William Lyon Phelps, popular and famous professor of English literature at Yale in the years before World War II:

> Whatever social position Shakespeare may have had in Stratford or during the earliest years in London, it is certain to my mind that he very soon had for his intimate friends social aristocrats and that he made visits in spendid homes. For example, in the famous song on winter in *Love's Labour's Lost*, the tone is patrician; the affectionate intimacy in the attitude towards servants is the true patrician attitude.

Because it is, as he says, "snobbish nonsense" to think that only "some earl or other" could have written Shakespeare's plays, A. L. Rowse reasonably asks, "Then how did he know so much about the life of the Court and upper-class life?" He has an answer ready. "Quite simply, from performing so frequently at Court — that gave him a close-up view of people and happenings there." Louis Auchincloss resorts to those Court appearances also, which gave Shakspere "now frequent opportunities to see the old Queen in person" and "to talk with many of the courtiers." So, too, Professors Evans and Levin: "Shakespeare's troupe was under the patronage of Elizabeth's Lord Chamberlain and later King James himself. Court performance is regularly recorded, as well as participation in one other royal occasion."

There must be some kind of record in this for building much upon little. Largely upon the listing of a payment to Shakespeare for two performances before her Majesty, cooked up by a Court Treasurer's widow evidently to expand an expense account (see pages 65–6) is constructed a regularity in such performances and frequent opportunities to see the Queen. Upon this in turn is built an entrée to the society of the nobility, and upon this, in turn, Shakespeare's intimate grasp of the inner workings of royal courts, the stamp he bears of one to the manner born, and the outlook of a feudal aristocrat he exhibits through thirty-six dramas. To contribute to this metamorphosis there was of course that "one other royal occasion" Professor Evans and Levin bring up: a William Shakespeare, we may recall, was listed among nine members of the King's company due to be issued red cloth to take part in a procession through the streets of London upon James's accession to the throne.

"Then, too, his association and friendship with his younger patron, the Earl of Southampton, was a tremendous advantage in opening a world of greater refinement and culture to the actor," says Rowse, who refers elsewhere offhandedly to "his fellow townsmen — regarding him respectfully as Master Shakespeare, and knowing his grand London associations." It is certain that the Earl of Southampton and the poet we know as Shakespeare were on intimate terms, but Charlotte G. Stopes, Southampton's pioneer biographer, spent seven years or more combing the records of the Earl and his family without turning up a single indication that the fashionable young lord had ever had any contact with a Shakespeare, and for that reason deemed the great work of her life a failure. Two subsequent biographers, Rowse being one, have done no better.

As for those grand London associations the Stratfordians conjure up, there is of course not a smidgin of evidence of them — of Shakspere's having ever exchanged two words with or been in the company of any courtier. Is it really to be imagined that of the noblemen with whom Shakspere was supposed to have consorted not one would have dropped a hint where we would hear of it that he had ever met him, had any done so, believing him the dramatist proclaimed by the leading literary figure of the time the soul of the age and the star of poets? I think we might allow that John Dryden (1631–1700) is to be trusted when, speaking of playwrights, he said, "I cannot find that any of them had been conversant in courts, except Ben Jonson; and his genius lay not so much that way as to make an improvement by it. Greatness was not then so easy of access, nor conversation so free, as it is now."[3]

---

[3] Ben Jonson did have connections with the nobility and these are known. When he had been jailed for his part in *Eastward Ho*, the Earl of Salisbury had him freed. He was employed by the Court to design masques in collaboration with Inigo Jones, and royalty and nobility took parts in them. He traveled in France as a kind of tutor to Sir Walter Raleigh's son. In addition to the Earl of Pembroke, his noble patrons and patronesses included the Earl, later the Duke, of Newcastle and the Countess of Rutland and her cousin Lady Worth, and we may read that, in 1619, his visits to the country seats of the nobility were varied by a sojourn at Oxford, where he was granted a master's degree. Two years later he was offered a knighthood. He was pensioned by King James and received a gift of £100 from King Charles. It is of such attentions that Shakspere's record is totally devoid.

Some Cogent Testimony on the Subject

Walt Whitman would have been surprised to learn from Gwynne Evans and Harry Levin that "social snobbery is an unspoken shibboleth" with him. I mention Whitman because of what he wrote in his *November Boughs*:

> We all know how much *mythus* there is in the Shakespeare question as it stands today. Beneath a few foundations of proved facts are certainly engulf'd far more dim and elusive ones of deepest importance — tantalizing and half suspected — suggesting explanations that one dare not put into plain statement. But coming at once to the point, the English historical plays are to me not only the most eminent as dramatic performances . . . but form, as we get it all, the chief in a complexity of puzzles. Conceiv'd out of the fullest heat and pulse of European feudalism — personifying in unparallel'd ways the medieval aristocracy, its towering spirit of ruthless and gigantic caste, its own peculiar air and arrogance (no mere imitation) — only one of the "wolfish earls" so plenteous in the plays themselves, or some born descendent and knower, might seem to be the true author of those amazing works — works in some respects greater than anything else in recorded history.

Charles Chaplin, in whom also social snobbery would not have been suspected, said in an extension of the remarks already quoted:

> It is easy to imagine a farmer's boy emigrating to London and becoming a successful actor and theatre owner; but for him to have become the great poet and dramatist, and to have had such intimate knowledge of foreign courts, cardinals and kings, is inconceivable to me. I am not concerned with who wrote the works of Shakespeare, . . . but I can hardly think it was the Stratford boy. Whoever wrote them had an aristocratic attitude.

Where Louis B. Wright charges that Shakespeare would "use sloppy grammar and syntax" ("And make as many gaffes as any other thirsty writer trying to finish a scene in time to get to the tavern for a drink with the boys"), and infers a lack of "profound book learning," Chaplin shows himself far sager. He observes that "his utter disregard for grammar could only have been the attitude of a princely, gifted mind." "Utter disregard" is a little strong, I think; but we shall find Thomas Nashe, addressing a man surely Lord Oxford, referring to his hostility to a grammarian. As George Stuart Gordon says in *Shakespeare's English*, "Shakespeare was to do what he liked with English grammar, and drew beauty and power from its imperfections. In the rankness and wildness of the language he found his opportunity, and exploited it royally, sometimes tyrannically."

Prince Otto von Bismarck, who may speak with some authority, supports Whitman's and Chaplin's opinion and the urging (if I may say so) of common sense. He says:

> I could not understand how it were possible that a man, however gifted with the intuition of genius, could have written what was attributed to Shakespeare, unless he had been in touch with the great affairs of state, behind the scenes of

political life, and also intimate with all the social courtesies, and refinements of thought, which in Shakespeare's time were only to be met with in the highest circles.

He finds it

incredible that a man who had written the greatest dramas in the world's literature, could of his own free will, whilst in the prime of life, have retired to such a place as Stratford-on-Avon, and lived for years cut off from the intellectual society and out of touch with the world.

So, too, Henry James, who, Leon Edel tells us,

could under no circumstances swallow the legend that Shakespeare wrote *The Tempest* and then gave up writing. This was not the way of a genius with so much abundance in him. *How*, James asked, "did the faculty so radiant here contrive, in such perfection, the arrest of its divine flight? By what inscrutable process was the extinguisher applied and, when once applied, kept in its place to the end?"

The extinguisher, we may be confident, was death, and no other, following closely upon the final scene the dramatist was to write.

Even by orthodox reckoning, the Stratfordian lived for three or four years after the appearance of the last play credited to him in his forty-ninth year, but Shakespeare, like other great writers struck down at the intellectual prime of life, must have died virtually with pen in hand.

When we encounter appraisals of Shakespeare by men who know his dramas and have also led real and potent lives in the real and potent world — the world that Shakespeare wrote about — we realize how mistaken we have been to leave the great Elizabethan to scholars in university libraries whose claim to competence in judging him we have measured solely against criteria they and their fellows have set.

Another student of Shakespeare with experience in the world of affairs, a long-time member of the House of Commons, is J. Enoch Powell. Recalling how in 1964 he had been asked to contribute a chapter on Shakespeare and politics to a volume on the dramatist put out by the BBC, he observes:

Reading the historical plays again, as an ex-Cabinet minister after nearly twenty years of life in politics, I was struck by the early date of the plays which showed the keenest insight. I see I described *Richard III* as "that compendium of politics," and that it was with quotations from the first part of *Henry VI* that I illustrated the observation: "The relish and verve with which Shakespeare's characters speak the language of ambition, intrigue and policy is not synthetic or theoretical — it could only be drawn from experience of the political struggle.

Mr. Powell goes on to say that the nine historical plays

contain a penetrating and sustained representation of statecraft and political ambition. They span the entire diapason of political emotions and exhibit the human personality in the coveting, the enjoyment and the loss of supreme power. The appetites, the hatreds and the exhilarations of the most absorbing of human pursuits are depicted with the immediacy of a participant. In the council scene in *Richard III* in Westminster Hall, the writer reveals the authentic knowledge of how men behave and feel at and around the political summit.

Even the orthodox scholars concede that *Richard the Third* had been written by 1592–1593 and *Henry the Sixth, Part One*, a year earlier. That was twelve or thirteen years before "William Shakespeare" received the cloth for marching in that procession which, the Harvard professors tell us, deepened the authentic understanding the dramas display of the passions and intrigues that swirl about the throne.

Frank Harris emphasizes an attitude in the plays that the reader must also have discovered and must recognize as putting the dramatist poles apart from the Stratford man as he appears in the record and from the "Shakespeare" of Stratfordian biographers. He says:

> The same prodigality and contempt of money are to be found in nearly all of Shakespeare's plays and curiously enough the persons who show this disdain are usually the masks of Shakespeare himself. A philosophic soliloquy is hardly more characteristic of Shakespeare than a sneer at money. This peculiarity is not a trait of his youth chiefly, as it is with most men who are free-handed. It seems to be a reasoned attitude toward life and it undoubtedly becomes more and more marked as Shakespeare grows older.

How orthodox writers square this undoubted idiosyncrasy of Shakespeare's with the Stratford man's business preoccupations, parvenu prosperity, grain-hoarding, and hounding of debtors, I could never comprehend. In his pride, even Iago, consummate villain, is above the squalor of money: who stole his purse stole trash. King Henry IV muses bitterly:

> How quickly nature falls into revolt
> When gold becomes her object!
> . . . .
> The cankered heaps of strange-achieved gold, . . .

In his youthful high spirits, impudent good humor, and martial zeal, the Bastard Faulconbridge in *King John* is a representative early Shakespearean protagonist and one of the twenty aristocratic Shakespearean characters in whom Harris finds the author's likeness. "Mad world! mad kings!" he cries, then lays with mettlesome cynicism into "Commodity" — the power cupidity holds over us —

> that same purpose-changer, that sly devil,
> That broker, that still breaks the pate of faith,
> That daily break-vow, he that wins of all,
> Of kings, of beggars, old men, young men, maids,
> Who having no external thing to lose
> But the word "maid," cheats the poor maid of that,
> That smooth-fac'd gentleman, tickling Commodity,
> Commodity, the bias of the world.
> . . . .

> And why rail I on this Commodity?
> But for because he hath not woo'd me yet.
> Not that I have the power to clutch my hand
> When his fair angels [coins] would salute my palm;
> But for my hand, as unattempted yet,
> Like a poor beggar, raileth on the rich.
> Well, whiles I am a beggar, I will rail
> And say there is no sin but to be rich;
> And being rich, my virtue then shall be
> To say there is no vice but beggary.

He concludes:

> Since kings break faith upon Commodity,
> Gain, be my lord, for I will worship thee!

But in fact he never comes to that.

Is there any aristocratic attribute that we do not find innate in Shakespeare, or, conversely, any quality of Shakespeare's that is out of keeping with nobility? His bawdry, which from as far back as I can remember has been held up to censors, along with the Bible, as an irrefutable argument against their designs on literature, may seem at odds with an ancient name and refinement of breeding. Perhaps it is. Yet I rather fancy that it sprang from that same princely mind's disdain for the conventions inhibiting lesser mortals that we can see behind Shakespeare's use of double negatives when it suited his whim and metrical euphony, and of redundant comparatives ("less happier lands") and superlatives ("most stillest"). It is not difficult to believe, too, that he delighted in showing how much he could get away with in offending the Puritans, who were always striving to shut down the theatres.

Shakespeare's Proficiency in the Sports of the Nobility

Shakespeare's England, a two-volume symposium that some forty contributors required eleven years to prepare, devotes 150 pages to "Sports and Pastimes" in Elizabethan and Jacobean times. Hunting, falconry, coursing with greyhounds, archery, fencing and duelling, horsemanship, dancing, and games are treated in detail and illumined with quotations from Shakespeare that show his precise and comprehensive knowledge of the subject. A portrait of the dramatist is limned as a man of leisure able to have indulged freely in the nobility's active diversions and make himself proficient in them. If he was ever guilty of a slip in treating them he has not been caught in it. Concluding the section on hunting, the Honorable J. W. Fortescue comments that probably "in all ages good sportsmen, like good men, are rarer than bad; but good there must have been in all times, and among the best of the sixteenth century we must certainly rank William Shakespeare."

It would suit my thesis to cover the ground as thoroughly as *Shakespeare's England* does, but I shall have to be narrowly selective.

"Shakespeare's earlier writings have a perfect fixation on hunting the deer," Rowse observes "— numerous descriptions of deer and hounds, too, all by one who knew the fine points of the chase." True enough — and those who hunted with hounds were the upper classes.

> My love shall hear the music of my hounds
> Uncouple in the western valley; let them go. . . .
> And mark the musical confusion
> Of hounds and echo in conjunction.
>
> . . . .
>
> Besides the groves,
> The skies, the fountains, every region near
> Seem'd all one mutual cry. I never hear
> So musical a discord, such sweet thunder.

The author of *A Midsummer-Night's Dream* was writing about what he knew well. So he was, too, in the Induction to *The Taming of the Shrew*:

> *Lord*: Huntsman, I charge thee, tender well my hounds:
>   Trash Merriman, the poor cur is emboss'd
>   And couple Clowder with the deep-mouth'd brach.
>   Saw'st thou not, boy, how Silver made it good
>   At the hedge-corner, in the coldest fault?
>   I would not lose the dog for twenty pound.
> *First Huntsman*: Why, Bellman is as good as he, my lord;
>   He cried upon it at the merest loss,
>   And twice today pick'd out the dullest scent:
>   Trust me, I take him for the better dog.
> *Lord*: Thou art a fool; if Echo were as fleet,
>   I would esteem him worth a dozen such.
>   But sup them well, and look unto them all:
>   Tomorrow I intend to hunt again.

It takes Mr. Fortescue (who believes "Trash" an incorrect rendering) a paragraph to elucidate the foregoing. To me the passage suggests that the author knew what it was to be a lord so sure of his knowledge of hounds that he was given even to disputing his huntsman's professional opinions.

In the quoted dialogue Shakespeare is showing what kind of lord he is talking about. In doing so he must demonstrate his proficiency in the lord's sport. That makes the passage unusual in Shakespeare. Ordinarily his familiarity with a special field of human activity — hunting, or seafaring, or whatever — comes out incidentally when he is talking about something else. That is what William Allan Neilson and Ashley Horace Thorndike overlook in seeking to impeach testimony by specialists who have affirmed Shakespeare's competence in their fields. The two professors (whose *Facts About Shakespeare* is known to a generation or more of college students) charge that they "are apt to forget how much a man of acute mind and keen observation can pick up of a technical matter that interests him for the time, and how intelligently he can use it. The cross-examination of an expert witness by an able lawyer is an everyday illustration."

Well, Ben Jonson was one who could "bone up" in that fashion. Mr. Fortescue quotes a twenty-line passage from his *Sad Shepherd* full of the technical knowledge about hunting that Professors Neilson and Thorndike are talking about. "Are we then to infer that Ben Jonson knew more of hunting than did Shakespeare?" he asks. "Just the contrary," he replies, and proceeds to show how the passage is "the result of book-learning." He then quotes from Antony's apostrophising the corpse of Caesar:

> Here wast thou bay'd, brave hart.
> Here didst thou fall; and here thy hunters stand,
> Sign'd in thy spoil, and crimson'd in thy lethe.

And he comments, "Here speaks the man who has seen a large field, stained, as was the custom, with the blood of the hunted stag, not the man of books, Jonson."

Stratfordians like the pair I have just quoted — Professors Neilson and Thorndike — fail to distinguish between knowledge that is sought for a special purpose and paraded and knowledge that reflects a man's life and habits or has been acquired along the way by a man of ranging intellect. It is manifold knowledge of the latter kind that comes out in images called up to sharpen and heighten the effect when Shakespeare is writing on quite unrelated subjects. Dr. Max Huhner, a surgeon with a lifelong, devoted interest in the dramatist, sees the distinction plainly. Like the professors, he points out that Shakespeare with his "observant genius" could have accumulated a store of information on a variety of subjects and thus might have obtained the knowledge to write convincingly on angling. "When, however," he goes on, "we find a dramatist like Shakespeare, in so many passages *subconsciously* introducing metaphors taken from fishing we must conclude that such a writer must have been an angler, for no one would read up a treatise on fishing simply to employ it for metaphorical purposes." He concludes from the examples he cites that Shakespeare's "expressions and references throughout the plays . . . must have come from a mind which has long since been filled with the pleasures of angling." Without seeking to detract from Dr. Huhner's excellent point, I venture to guess that the surgeon is himself an angler, for the evidence is that angling had a lesser hold on Shakespeare than other sports. Undoubtedly he had fished. A. Forbes Sieveking brings out in *Shakespeare's England* that the dramatist knew that pike feed on dace and that carp are wary, gudgeon eager biters, but he does not find him "much interested in the sport."

Shakespeare's plays are replete with metaphors revealing the dramatist's habituation to the pursuits of a nobleman afield. Fortescue observes, "There were untrue hunters, who would leave the sweet scent of a hare, and speak to the rank scent of a fox," then regarded as a pest to be done to death without ceremony.

> Sowter will cry out upon 't, for all this, though it be as rank as a fox.
> (Twelfth Night)

> But the crime of all crimes was to hunt counter . . . : a fault which
> might set the whole pack wrong in working out the doubles of a
> hare.

> How cheerfully on the false trail they cry!
> O! this is counter, you false Danish dogs!

> says the Queen in *Hamlet*, when she hears that the rabble acclaims
> Laertes king.

Rosencrantz reports the players' approach earlier in the play with the line

> We coted them on the way; and hither they are coming to offer you service.

A greyhound "cotes" the hare, Mr. Sieveking explains, when it outstrips the quarry and turns it from its intended course. "The chief technicalities of the sport are abundantly represented in Shakespeare," he says.

No doubt because the birds of prey hold a special place in an enthusiasm I have for birds in general, I am particularly struck by the dramatist's feeling for them. Hunting with these coursers of the air for sport and for the larder had been popular for centuries by Elizabethan times. As an expert tells us, however, "stringent laws and enactments" governed the practice from the reign of William the Conqueror to that of Elizabeth and "falcons and hawks were allotted to degrees and orders of men according to rank and station — for instance, to the emperor the eagle and vulture [the eagle-like lammergeier], to royalty the jerfalcons [the great arctic species], to an earl the peregrine, to a yeoman the goshawk, to a priest the sparrow-hawk, and to knave or servant the useless kestrel." The goshawk and (European) sparrow-hawk are not falcons at all and, though deadly sprinters, afford less sport than the high-mounting falcons and have been regarded as lacking class; Page's "fine hawk for the bush" in *Merry Wives* can only be one of these. I recall no mention of either in Shakespeare except in that uniquely middle-class comedy, in which Mrs. Ford appropriately addresses the bright little page Robin with "How now, my eyas-musket!" A musket is the small male sparrow-hawk, an eyas a bird that has been taken in infancy from the nest. An eyas hawk or falcon seldom acquires the power and dash of a haggard — a bird that has grown to maturity in the wild and been trapped. Viola in *Twelfth Night* observes that the Clown must be wise and not,

> . . . like the haggard, check at every feather
> That comes before his eye.

A falcon "checks" when it flies at other than the intended quarry.

In Shakespeare it is "the falcon, towering in her pride of place," unmistakably the noble peregrine — *the* falcon and mainstay of the sport — that repeatedly comes in as an object for reference and comparison.

> O! for a falconer's voice,
> To lure this tassel-gentle back again,

Juliet repines. The falcon gentle — "gentle" again connoting a finer grain — is the peregrine, a tassel or tiercel being the male, so called apparently because it runs a third smaller than its mate.

Thomas Heywood in one of his plays has a scene with country squires out with a "falconer" (a trainer) and their birds, one at least a merlin, a small falcon usually assigned to ladies; and here again we find a contrast with Shakespeare. The scene is very impressive, as it is meant to be, in showing what the dramatist could do in splattering his rendition of the hunt with technical terms. I can think of only one such scene of falconry in Shakespeare, and it is brief enough to recapitulate in whole. It is from *Henry the Sixth, Part Two*:

> *Queen Margaret*: Believe me, lords, for flying at the brook
>   I saw not better sport these seven years' day:
>   Yet, by your leave, the wind was very high,
>   And, ten to one, old Joan had not gone out.
> *King Henry*: But what a point, my lord, your falcon made,
>   And what a pitch she flew above the rest!
>   To see how God in all his creatures works!
>   Yea, man and birds are fain to climbing high.
> *Suffolk*: No marvel, an it like your majesty,
>   My Lord Protector's hawks do tower so well;
>   They know their master loves to be aloft,
>   And bears his thoughts above his falcon's pitch.

The scene differs from Heywood's in being unlabored and brought in as a parable: the dramatist is talking not about falconry but the Lord Protector's ambition, for which the falcon at her pitch above the rest is a metaphor.

Shakespeare does not tell us about falconry, except incidentally. His falconry, however, tells us about Shakespeare. So imbued with it is he that time after time we find it supplying him with images to make more telling for us what is in his mind. We have a keener understanding of Othello and a stimulant to the imagination when the vengeful Moor exclaims:

> If I do prove her haggard,
> Though her jesses were my dear heart-strings,
> I'd whistle her off and let her down the wind,
> To prey at fortune.

All Othello is saying is that if his suspicion of Desdemona's infidelity proves warranted he'll abandon her to her own devices, devoted to her as he may be. But compare the two ways of expressing it! Jesses are the leather thongs affixed to a falcon's tarsi. Affixed to the jesses are bells. Boasts the Earl of Warwick in *Henry the Sixth, Part Three*:

> Neither the king, nor he that loves him best,
> The proudest he that holds up Lancaster
> Dares stir a wing if Warwick shake his bells.

What a picture of great lords cowering if the warlike Earl make but a menacing move!

In the young Shakespeare the bird-of-prey metaphor may be called up with such evocative power as to overwhelm the object it is supposed to serve:

> Even as an empty eagle, sharp by fast,
> Tires with her beak on feathers, flesh and bone,
> Shaking her wings, devouring all in haste,
> Till either gorge be stuff'd or prey be gone.

As description that could hardly be improved on. But as an analogy for voracious kissing — Venus's — it is in danger of provoking a smile. I think it tells us that the young poet was still more at home in the field than in the toils of woman's desire — as was Adonis himself.

Petruchio would subdue his Katherine, the Shrew, as he would his falcon that

> . . . now is sharp and passing empty,
> And till she stoop she must not be full-gorg'd.
> For then she never looks upon her lure.
> Another way I have to man my haggard,
> To make her come and know her keeper's call;
> That is, to watch her, as we watch those kites
> That bate and beat and will not be obedient.

One of the ways to "man" a haggard was to "seel" its eyes — pull up the threads that were drawn through each lower lid and tie them above its head. (The barbarous practice was long ago altogether replaced by hooding the bird.) We have read how sleep will "seel up the ship-boy's eyes." Likewise Desdemona might "seel her father's eyes up close as oak" and "The wise gods seel our eyes," Antony says.

One practice of falconers is so tangential and so lightly touched on in *Richard the Second* as to be likely to go unremarked even by the avian-minded:

> If then we shall shake off our slavish yoke,
> Imp out our drooping country's broken wing. . . .

When a falcon's flight feather was broken a new terminal portion was "imped" on by inserting a splint halfway into the shaft of the latter and halfway into that of the remaining stub. Anyone in whose thoughts such a parallel for restoring a nation's powers would crop up must have been steeped in the sport, could not have been a mere observer.

When Hamlet says, "We'll e'en to 't like French falconers, fly at anything we see," it is — I am satisfied — the author recalling what he had observed.

"Sweet Mercy Is Nobility's True Badge"

Shakespeare lost his taste for hunting early in manhood, I believe, as his sympathy went out to the victim of the chase —

> the poor frighted deer, that stands at gaze,
> Wildly determining which way to fly,

as does Lucrece. In *Venus and Adonis* the action is altogether stopped while we watch the "purblind hare" and

> Mark the poor wretch, to overshoot his troubles
> How he outruns the winds, and with what care
> He cranks and crosses with a thousand doubles.

For five stanzas, I think the most moving of the poem, in a digression on the flimsiest excuse, we follow the tiring quarry's desperate evasions as feelingly and circumstantially set forth as if the poet had been in its place. Fortescue comments: "There is little more to say about hare-hunting" — a favorite of the nobility or squirearchy — "than is contained in these stanzas."

"Come, shall we go and kill us venison?" asks the Duke in *As You Like It*, then reflects:

> And yet it irks me, the poor dappled fools,
> Being native burghers of this desert city,
> Should in their confines with forked heads
> Have their round haunches gor'd.

He is not alone in his distress. "The melancholy Jaques grieves at that," too, we are told. He has been espied under an oak by a brook,

> To the which place a poor sequester'd stag,
> That from the hunters' aim had ta'en a hurt,
> Did come to languish,

and Jaques is heard to inveigh against "a careless herd, full of pasture," that passes their stricken fellow by, and against

> The body of the country, city, court,
> And of this our life, swearing that we
> Are mere usurpers, tyrants, and what's worse
> To fright the animals and kill them up
> In their assign'd and native dwelling-place.

This plea for animals as having a rightful place in the earthly scheme that man is a usurper and a tyrant to deny them is one that will scarcely be heard again for hundreds of years after Shakespeare, indeed until nearly our own day. Even naturalists as late as those on whom I was brought up would still be writing from an anthropocentric point of view. A tender-hearted sympathy for four-footed victims of man's cruelty, surely a rarity in Tudor times, combined with total mistrust of popular rule and abhorrence of the vulgar crowd is the mark of a man of privileged birth and upbringing. A feeling for our fellow creatures as such is a refinement not to be looked for among those whose experience is of the brutal necessities at the margin of existence in a primitive society.

The Fastidious Aristocrat

In her book *Shakespeare's Imagery*, the staunchly Stratfordian Caroline Spurgeon finds the dramatist a "competent rider who loved horses, as he did most animals," a man "with a deep understanding and quick sympathy for all living things," His first interest, she says, is falconry, and the games he knows best are "bowls, football and tennis, but his images from bowls, which he clearly knew and liked best, are about three times as many as from any other game" — this at a time when public bowling-alleys were proscribed by repeated acts of Parliament and only a gentleman whose land brought him at least £100 yearly was licensed to play on his own green. "If he is abnormally sensitive," says Miss Spurgeon, "he is also unusually courageous, mentally and spiritually." She speaks of Shakespeare's fastidiousness in eating and his "sensitive digestion" and of his "horror of bad smells." This would have been an odd legacy of Stratford-upon-Avon, where, Halliwell-Phillipps writes, "house-slops were recklessly thrown into ill-kept channels that lined the sides of unmetalled roads, . . . while here and there small middens were ever in the course of accumulation, the receptacles of offal and of every species of nastiness." ("How delightfully it must have smelt!" Rowse is captivated by the "wax, honey and other things in the apple-chamber" of the dwelling only one door removed from John Shakspere's dunghill in a village of "small houses bowered in trees and birdsong.") Miss Spurgeon is led to wonder how, with his susceptibility to things offensive to the senses, Shakespeare, "ever managed to survive the dirt and smells of Elizabethan England."

Professor Trevor-Roper writes:

> Now this delicacy of perception, combined with his zest for natural life, gives Shakespeare's early works their marvellous freshness, their glancing, sparkling luminosity. But the same sensitivity had also its obverse side. Shakespeare, we often feel, had a skin too few: whatever he saw he felt, and he felt it far more

intensely than most of his contemporaries. This too we can see in his love of nature. . . . His sympathies are always with "the poor hunted deer," the trapped bird, the over-driven horse, the baited bear. . . . How did this sensitive creature, this delicate, aristocratic character so acutely aware of the pleasures and pains, the comedy and tragedy of life, himself survive the rough-and-tumble of the Elizabethan age? The answer is, I think, that he did not survive it intact. . . . The exquisite poet of Arcadia became the greatest tragic poet of the modern world.

15

Myriad-Minded Man of the Renaissance — 1

Of the knowledge revealed in Shakespeare's works, we have specialists in various fields to support the impression we must form of its breadth. How do the Stratfordians meet the problem with which this vast knowledge confronts them? Recognizing the necessarily narrow limitations of the Stratford grammar school and reacting to the argument that Shakespeare must have had a far better education than it could have provided even if young Will Shakspere attended it (which seems highly unlikely), we find the orthodox scholars belittling the evidence and seeking to persuade us that a straitened existence in a small medieval town better prepared a young man to write of "life" than the varied, stimulating, and broadening influences of a university. On the other hand, when facing up to Shakespeare's demonstrable scope of learning we find them bestowing upon the Stratford school a curriculum that would turn small boys into classical scholars of awesome attainments and dreaming up other educational opportunities for Shakspere, all in defiance of the record. What comes out in his writings and is vouched for even by Stratfordian scholars, is Shakespeare's wide reading in Latin and even Greek originals, his familiarity with French and Italian — and quite likely Spanish — writers in their own language and with England's literature and his uncommon knowledge of the Bible. On top of that, we find him employing the widest range of rhetorical figures and enriching the vocabulary of his mother tongue as no other writer ever has.

No writer, I think it safe to say, has ever so far surpassed his contemporaries in breadth of frame of reference as Shakespeare.[1] That he wrote with intimate knowledge about extraordinarily diverse subjects we have specialists in those subjects to tell us. That is by no means to say that the Stratfordians altogether accept their testimony. In two fields particularly — the classics and the law — debate has been sharp. The issues are fairly joined. How much knowledge did Shakespeare possess and how did he come by it? To pursue the inquiry merely in order to pile up more evidence against the Stratford theory would hardly seem to justify the time, but to learn all we can about the man who possessed the greatest creative intelligence in Western literature is surely

[1] While Professors Evans and Levin have no retort to that estimate, they maintain that "His text reveals no 'polymath on the order of Leonardo da Vinci' [as I had said], but it does bespeak the 'myriad-mindedness' (Coleridge's phrase) of a Renaissance man." I am not sure that I see any great distinction between myriad-mindedness, such as that man of the Renaissance da Vinci assuredly had, and a mind that has equipped itself in varied fields — a polymath. But in giving a title to this chapter I am quite content to follow the professors' formulation. What counts, as always, are the facts.

worth our while, even apart from the help the knowledge will give us in deciding who he was. The inquiry will also further extend our acquaintance with the competence and *mores* of academia — a not unimportant matter, I should think.

The Astonishing Stratford School and the Miracle of "Genius"

One would hardly look to the controversy over Shakespeare's attainment for laughs, but it does seem to have an amusing side. Orthodox scholarship, strenuously minimizing Shakespeare's store of knowledge and maximizing the capacity of the Stratford grammar school to provide it, reminds one of a bather who, caught in the partial buff, tries to pull down a brief upper garment and pull up a brief lower to cover the intervening nudity. On the comic side, too, is the derogation by educators of the vestment that would do much to bridge the gap: a higher education. One would hardly have expected to hear the professors play down the importance of the ivied halls. Shakespeare's "was the university of life — more exacting, more deeply informative," in Rowse's considered opinion. Louis B. Wright is of the same view. A college or university class? To be a successful writer "an experience of life is a much better school, as the literary geniuses of the world demonstrate." By last count, in 1968, Louis B. Wright had received twenty-six honorary degrees. In 1976, he was given a national Phi Beta Kappa award.

Thus, for an aspirant writer, if we are to believe our mentors, a higher education is not only useless but positively to be shunned — in favor of "life." The excitement and anguish of college, the stimulus to one's potentials from varied young and vital personalities, not to mention the intellectual demands, all that one thought was life is apparently not life at all. As for those drinking parties and that "wenching" with which the undergraduate body at Oxford and Cambridge in Shakespeare's day was accused of leavening the formalistic curriculum rather too liberally, they were not life, either. The truly enriching life, in Rowse's and Wright's books, is to be bound to the day-long drudgery that would have been a son's lot in a debtor's home in Elizabethan times. It is to be further pressed to the narrow necessity for unremitting labor by the acquisition of a wife at eighteen and three children by age twenty-one. It is to be confined to a town like Stratford-upon-Avon till one's mid-twenties at least.

And what kind of town was that? "An important center of trade, the business metropolis of a large and fertile area." *Metropolis*? So Oscar James Campbell of Columbia University says. In fact in 1590, the town comprised 217 houses. Calculating from recorded births and burials, Knight estimates its population in the year of William Shakspere's birth at 1,400. It does not even exist for the *Historical Atlas* by William R. Shepherd (also of Columbia) assigned me at Harvard, which recognizes only the Stratford near London. "Exclusive of Bibles, Church Services, Psalters and educational manuals, there were certainly not more than two or three dozen books, if so many, in the whole town," according to Halliwell-Phillipps, that indiscreet but thorough Stratfordian biographer. Ivor Brown objects: "The idea of a 'bookless neighborhood' as Tudor Stratford has been described can be dissipated easily." How? Overlooking the faulty English, we find that "The parson who baptized William Shakespeare [as Shaksper or Shakspere], John Bretchgirdle, had a large library. . . ." Yes, and he died in the year after Will Shakspere was born, and his library, probably consisting mostly of just the kind of books Halliwell-Phillipps mentioned, was scattered under his will "among the young hopefuls of Stratford," according to the specialist Professor T. W. Baldwin. "The Stratford that John Shakespeare knew was . . . in spirit," Marchette Chute writes, "a tight, narrow little medieval community." An inhabitant was fined if he played cards "or any other unlawful games," or if his children were not at home by eight o'clock in the summertime. "If he wanted to bring an outsider into his house he had to have a special license from the High Bailiff, and if from a sense of compassion he gave shelter in his house to 'any stranger woman' who was pregnant he was heavily fined." This was the town in which Shakspere spent the first half of his life, becoming, as we are told, the myriad-minded man of the Renaissance, and this the town to which he was content to return in his forties, there to spend the last part.

But young Will had a privileged upbringing as son of an alderman and bailiff, did he not? Much is made of the dignities and status accruing to John Shakspere from these offices. In a passage quoted from Edgar I. Fripp by Samuel Schoenbaum and lifted almost verbatim, without acknowledgement, by Rowse, we see the bailiff and his deputy "escorted from their houses to the Gild Hall by the serjeants bearing their maces before them. They were waited on by the buff-uniformed officers once a week to receive instructions, and accompanied by them through the market on Thursdays, through the fair on fair-days, about the parish bounds at Rogation, and to and from church on Sundays," and so on. One almost pictures the Lord Mayor of London. The regard in which the municipal offices were actually held may be learned from Mark Eccles. In 1571, Thomas Dixon was sued in Chancery for refusing the office of alderman and paid a fine in 1585 rather than act as bailiff. Perrott was bailiff in 1588 but later refused to serve and made a vow never to be of the corporation. George Badger, chosen as alderman in 1594, was removed in 1598 for refusing to attend and serve as bailiff. John Sadler, bailiff in 1570, declined the office in 1582, when John Shakspere voted for him. Alex Aspinall, elected bailiff in 1606, paid a fine rather than serve and paid another in 1614 for permission to resign as alderman. Of nineteen alderman and burgesses, Charles Knight points out, only six could write their names. It is sad to think of the thirteen illiterates, Sir George Greenwood comments drily, when there "was such an education in their midst, to be had for nothing."

The reference, of course, is to the Stratford Grammar School and the excellences attributed to it. The high-water mark of claims for the school — the heftiest upward yank of the nether garment — must have been made by John McCabe of the Department of Dramatic Art at New York University. In an interview with *The New Yorker*, Professor McCabe declared that the Stratford school's "sixteenth-century syllabus, which I've examined, contains a lot of Latin, Greek, and history. Kids who got through that school had a training equivalent to that of a lot of college graduates here." The assertion by a university professor that the education to be had from many American colleges today is no better than that given by a provincial grammar school of four centuries ago may be received in respectful silence. As for the claim preceding it, one trusts that Professor McCabe blinked his "honest brown eyes," as *The New Yorker* called them, when he made it, for no syllabus of the Stratford school has survived. In a friendly response to an inquiry of mine he readily admitted to having erred in his facts. It was, he said, a syllabus from a comparable school he had seen. Even there his imagination had certainly assisted his memory.[2]

Had Will Shakspere attended school, what actually would he have found there? "The discipline was severe and the hours long," says Ivor Brown. How severe he finds indicated in *The Grammar Schoole*. Its author, John Brinsley, held children "to be the natural prey of Satan, and the way to deal with that was to whip the devil out of them. Brinsley believed the cane and the birch were sanctified by God for the salvation of young souls. . . . The rod, which he blatantly called 'God's instrument' was to be applied to all 'stubborn or unbroken' boys" and "if one resisted this form of spiritual cure 'three or four scholars known to be honest and strong were to hold him fast

---

[2] Professor McCabe's elucidation was given in rebuttal to an interview in *The New Yorker* with a prominent Oxfordian, the New York lawyer Francis Carmody. The rest of it was on a par with what we have just heard. "The contemporary references to Shakespeare" that "are clear and unmistakable," such as "'By William Shakespeare' in the folio of his scripts that John Heminge and Henry Condell, two of the actors in his company, got out in 1623" and "the eulogies at the beginning of the book — including the great one by Ben Jonson — on Shakespeare's ability as a playwright" settled the matter of the authorship for Professor McCabe. As for others for whom they did not, he said that "they don't know what they're talking about." When anti-Stratfordians claimed that Shakespeare "had traveled extensively on the continent," he said, fudging the question of whether the dramatist had traveled there at all, why, "all this is the big lie, and the boys don't know they are lying." There the matter rested as far as *The New Yorker* cared. If Mr. Carmody had quite wrongly been made to look foolish and its readers deceived as to the facts, there was nothing the editors could do about it. And so it usually goes.

over some form' while the master carried out God's work." Roger Ascham (see page 257) wrote that

> when the schoolmaster is angry with some other matter, then will he soonest fall to beat the scholar; and though he himself be punished for his folly, yet must he beat some scholar for his pleasure. . . . Over many such be found everywhere.

Ascham wrote of "the master many times being as ignorant as the child." In 1571, he called the teaching in English schools "mere babblement and motions." Henry Peacham, a Master of Arts of Trinity College, Cambridge, wrote in 1622 that poor teaching "is a general plague and complaint of the whole land; for one discreet [i.e., discerning, sagacious] and able teacher, you shall find twenty ignorant and careless." These judgments may have been a bit harsh, but it is well to remember that qualified observers gave voice to them when we read of all that grammar school did for Shakspere, by his thirteenth year.

But the Stratford school was exceptional, was it not? It was "one of the best in England," says Oscar James Campbell. The Folger Library under Dr. Wright officially informed the public of the "facts" that Shakspere "had a very good education acquired in the Stratford Grammar School, one of the best of the day." The fact is that nothing whatever is known about the quality of instruction at the Stratford school, comparative or otherwise, and that there has never been a shred of evidence that young Will ever spent a day in it. What is known about the school? That successive masters held university degrees. Although such degrees were normally required of grammar school masters, great stress is attached to this by orthodox writers, even while we are being assured that university education at the time was so dreary that Shakspere was lucky to have escaped it. We also know the names of the masters in Shakspere's day and that they were paid £20 annually. This salary is the basis of the preeminence accorded the Stratford school by its boosters. It was "twice as large as that usual in similar posts elsewhere," says Ivor Brown; and Louis Marder: "Eton was paying £10." But as Schoenbaum tells us, out of his £20 the Stratford master had to pay his usher £4, defray the cost of repairs to the school, and buy his meals, unlike his counterpart at Eton. If the Stratford Council did pay more than the going rate for schoolmasters, I should venture the guess that it had to, if such a post were to be filled. That the mastership at Stratford was no plum is indicated by the rapid turnover in incumbents; between 1565 and 1575, there were five masters.

What reason do the orthodox scholars give for supposing that Will Shakspere even went to school at all? "The Stratford Grammar School was a good one," say Evans and Levin, echoing the familiar refrain, "and it was free for inhabitants of the town. What was he doing from seven to 13, at a time when his father was a leading citizen, if not going to school?" I do not know what he was doing: probably more or less what other boys his age were doing, which was not going to school. Two-thirds of the leading citizens (by the professor's definition), including his father, could not even sign their names, as we have seen. "The English nation, in the time of Shakespeare," Samuel Johnson wrote, "was yet struggling to emerge from barbarity. . . . Literature was yet confined to professed scholars or to men and women of high rank. The public was gross and dark; and to be able to read and write, was an accomplishment still valued for its rarity." Edwin Goadby observes that "The common people were densely ignorant. They had to pick up their mother tongue as best they could. The first English grammar was not published until 1586. It is evident that much schooling was impossible, for the necessary books did not exist. The horn-book for teaching the alphabet would almost exhaust the resources of any common day-schools that might exist in the towns and villages. The art of writing was a great accomplishment." With a handle like that of a hand mirror, a horn-book was a board on which, framed in wood, was affixed a sheet displaying the alphabet in capitals and small letters and the Lord's Prayer, covered by a thin sheet of transparent horn. Undeniably Stratford was not lacking in literate folk. They were exceptional, however. Even much later, in 1598, Ben Jonson, after killing an actor in a duel, was able to escape the gallows and cut short his imprisonment by benefit of clergy; his ability to read and write made him a potential cleric. Charles Knight says that there was a feeling of its being not quite safe to write. "Twelve years before [1564] the Bible had had to be hidden in dark corners. It was come out again, but who could tell what might again happen? It was safer not to read. It was much less troublesome not to write."

Even to get into school a boy had to know his letters. St. Paul's and Shrewsbury (which Philip Sidney attended) demanded ability to read and write both English and Latin. "William Shakspere should have learned from someone, at present unguessable, to read English, and about the age of seven, in the course of 1571 have entered the grammar school," T. M. Baldwin speculates. Maybe he should have; but did he? and from whom? Not his parents!

Professor Baldwin is one of two scholars to whom Evans and Levin refer readers for "careful assessments of the curriculum and the extent of his learning." He calls his work *Shakspere's Small Latine and Lesse Greeke* (referring to both Stratfordian and dramatist as Shakspere), and this is not meant ironically. He speaks of "the small Latine and lesse Greeke" with which Ben Jonson endowed him," and, having taken his mould from a misreading of Jonson, proceeds to cram his subject into it. "He had indeed but small Latin and less Greek, and even that small was no great fault of his own." No wonder the Harvard professors do not quote the upshot of that "careful assessment." Other Stratfordians would likewise have none of it. They all quote Jonson, incorrectly, to counter the dissenters' reasoning that Shakespeare was a far better educated man than Shakspere could have been, but they do not care to have the misquoted appraisal rubbed in. They do not believe what they say Jonson said. As Rowse has it, "Grammar-school education was almost entirely in Latin," in fact, "the boys were supposed to converse in Latin." For thirty-six or more weeks a year for six years, young Will is alleged to have spent the hours from six in the morning to seven in the evening with time out for meals being educated in Latin: it was "Latin, more Latin and still more Latin," Marchette Chute says. Is it to be argued that all he got out of it was "small Latin"? Gerald E. Bentley tells us that "the boys would have read Terence, Cicero, Virgil, Ovid, Horace, Juvenal, Martial, and Seneca." Believers in the Stratfordian have a devil of a job getting their story straight. "It is without controversy," Nicholas Rowe confidently asserts, "that he had no knowledge of the writings of the ancient poets."

Professor Baldwin himself pulls out all the stops in favor of the education available to young Will. As names of classical authors jostle one another in his curriculum, the mind reels from the course of study through which he puts the children in the idealized Elizabethan grammar school of his postulation, preparing them for a doctorate before their voices changed. From William Lyly's *Brevissima Institutio* (I think) they would learn the rules of accidence, which would equip the seven-year-olds for construing various Latin texts, including a Latin version of Aesop's fables. The English Bible would supply passages for translation into Latin, while the *Linguae Latinae* of Vives would prepare them for conducting all conversation in Latin, including that at play. One wonders if the professor has ever met a seven-year-old. The *Dialogi sacri* of Castalia and colloquies of Erasmus, including his *De Copia Verborum*, would lead to Terence, Plautus, and perhaps a Latin translation of Lucian, and to the study of poetry beginning with the Italian Renaissance poets Mantuan and Palingenius. Thereafter the classic preceptors come thick and fast: Cicero, Quintilian, Susenbrotus (whoever he was), Horace, Ovid, Virgil, Lucan, Juvenal — I do not know who all: there are hundreds of pages of this. With the aid of Latin-English dictionaries of Withals, Baret, and Cooper, logic and rhetoric were assimilated, Latin speech and styles mastered, themes written, Latin prose rendered into poetry, orations given. All this, six years of total immersion, produced "small Latin," remember; Professor Baldwin seems hopelessly at odds with himself. Maybe the New Testament was read in Greek, too, he says.

"At the Stratford school," Oscar J. Campbell assures us, "the boys read much more Latin than even the best classical students in an American college of today." *Much more*, mind you, than the *best*. If the result of such indoctrination as the professors speak of was only small Latin, one wonders what considerable Latin would have been and what reading and instruction would have been required to produce it. Surely Professor Campbell at least does not hold with that small Latin? But wait. At this very point he chooses to remind us with satisfaction that "Ben Jonson . . . spoke of his friend's 'small Latin and less Greek.'" What can he be thinking of? The explanation is that he is combatting the case for de Vere. Read his next sentence, which I have italicized: *"The phrase could not have been applied to the Earl of Oxford."*

And so now we have it. When it comes to equipping the Stratford stripling to write the plays of Shakespeare, the best is none too good. He is given by age thirteen an education that would be the wonder of future ages. On the other hand, he has still got to be John Aubrey's butcher's apprentice making a speech as he slaughters a calf, or a young deer-poacher, or something of the sort. The suspicion must not arise that Shakespeare was one who might be expected to have had the best education the times afforded — a young lord. Thus, Will's learning has to have been really very limited: small Latin. "Not a scholar," says Edmund Wilson.

Had Shakspere gone to the university, we may suspect that we should be hearing of all he had learned there; much of the burden would be lifted from the Stratford curriculum. As such was not the case, Baldwin informs us that the Stratford school was so fully adequate to Shakespeare's needs that college would have been superfluous. "If William Shakspere had the grammar school education of his day — or its equivalent — he had as good a formal literary training as any of his contemporaries." Indeed, to listen to Wright the university would have been positively baneful to his budding talent. Says the *beau idéal* of academia: "If Shakespeare had gone to either Oxford or Cambridge, he might have turned out to be a parson." Of course Wright is not so mentally deficient as to believe that; it is just that he thinks we may be. Or most of us. He is aware that some are incorrigible and will go on believing that Shakespeare possessed the most cultivated mind of his times, and, believing this, will believe by the same token that he must have been exceptionally well educated and that it would help account for his exceptional education if he had gone on beyond grammar school to the university. Wright is ready for them. "They think," he says, "that the author of these great plays should have had a diploma to hang on his wall, a diploma just like their dentist's."

Wright, as we have seen, does not think education has much to offer an aspirant writer. "Even learned Ben Jonson, who could spout Latin and Greek at the drop of his pint pot, got all his schooling at Westminster, supplemented by a spell of bricklaying, his stepfather's trade." His stepfather was, it is true, a master bricklayer, but "he provided his stepson with the foundations of a good education," we read. Young Ben went first to a private school in

St. Martin's Lane and later at Westminster studied under one of the foremost Elizabethan scholars, William Camden, of whom he wrote:

> Camden, most revered head, to whom I owe
> All that I am in arts, all that I know.

Wright does admit in passing that "some of Shakespeare's contemporaries went to the universities." Who were among them, for example? Christopher Marlowe studied for some five years at Cambridge. Edmund Spenser was also a Cambridge man, as was Gabriel Harvey (who became a fellow of Pembroke Hall), Thomas Nashe, who was there for nearly seven years, and John Fletcher. Thomas Lodge took a B.A. and an M.A. at Oxford and went on to Lincoln's Inn. Robert Greene also took both degrees at Oxford, where Philip Sidney and George Chapman studied, too; also Thomas Heywood, who became a fellow of Peterhouse, and Francis Beaumont, who matriculated at age twelve. Thomas Kyd did not make it to the university, but he attended Merchant Taylors school in London, where he and Edmund Spenser studied under Richard Mulcaster, whose work *Elementarie* (1582), testified to his "robust faith in the artistic capacities of English," and where Lodge, who went there too, may also have been a schoolmate of his. Contrast the known facts about these writers' education with the absolute blank respecting Shakspere's, whose life's record is supposed to be so much better known to us than theirs.

Whether Wright would consider Shakespeare's fellow writers fools for having gone to the university, I cannot say. Presumably he would, for he says that if the "anti-Shakespeareans," as he likes to call the anti-Stratfordians, "don't want to stand in the corner wearing a dunce cap themselves, they ought to learn a little . . . about the sterility of much university education." That much university education in Elizabethan times (as conceivably in our own) was sterile has never been in question. What the Stratfordian Ph.D.s never let on to is what else there was of the universities besides "logic-chopping theological discussions," as Wright describes it.

We may learn of that from Mark H. Curtis, who tells us that "Formal lectures and academic exercises comprised only a part of the instruction available." Probably already by the 16th century, "the work of the college tutors" was "the most important influence on a scholar's education." He goes on to say that "The good will of the tutors and the interest of the scholars were all that were needed to introduce the study of modern as well as classical history, modern languages as well as Latin and Greek, geography, cosmography, and navigation as well as astronomy, the study of practical politics [Gabriel Harvey was studying Machiavelli at Cambridge in 1571] as well as moral philosophy, and the cultivation of manners, courtesy, and other social graces." To this, Wallace Notestein adds that "As always there were, especially at Cambridge, young men of literary ambitions, who discussed poetry and plays, and were trying their hand at writing them." Indeed, as early as 1537, the scholars of Christ College, Cambridge, put on a play, Muriel C. Bradbrook reports — one that scandalized their chancellor by depicting the Pope as Anti-Christ. It was the students of St. John's College, Cambridge, who produced the *Parnassus* plays at the turn of the century. In one, a future parson contrasts what lies ahead for him with what he knew at the university:

> 'Mongst russet coats and mossy idiots,
> Ne'er shall I hear the Muses sing again,
> Whose music was like nectar to my soul.

Notestein recalls that "It was the poets he had read while at the university that Marlowe remembered," and he makes the sapient observation that "The graduates had something done to them that was more than intellectual. A change came over a boy from a 'mean' background as he lived in college with others of another kind, and fell under the influence of men of breeding. . . . The son of a weaver learned what availed him much, whether he was to stand before kings or in some country pulpit."

It was from all such advantages that a boy cut himself off when he called it quits with grammar school. Anyone for whom the things of the mind mattered most set his sights on the university as a matter of course. Lack of means was not necessarily a bar to his hopes. What Wallace Notestein writes of the period from 1603 to 1630 was probably scarcely less true of the last decades in the century before:

> The progress of a talented boy to the university was facilitated. . . . Colleges at both universities awarded scholarships to youths from [certain] schools. In some boroughs the mayor or councilors or aldermen might vote three or four pounds a year to boys from the local school toward their university expense. If no other methods of sending a bright boy to the university could be found, the teacher, or more often a clergyman, might persuade a prosperous citizen to act as benefactor. The annals of the early seventeenth century are full of delightful stories of how boys of talent were given their chance.

Christopher Marlowe was one who received an allowance from the University. It is difficult to believe that a youth on the way to becoming, in Carlyle's words, "the greatest intellect who, in our recorded world, has left record of himself in the way of literature," would not have found a way to get there too.

We come to the nub of T. W. Baldwin's *Shakspere's Small Latin and Lesse Greek* on page 663 of volume two: "No miracles are required to account for such knowledge and techniques from the classics as he exhibits. Stratford grammar school will furnish all that is required." Having made this bold pronouncement, the professor punches a hole in it big enough to drive through with a four-in-hand: "The miracle lies elsewhere; it is in the world-old miracle of genius."

The miracle of genius! There is always that escape-hatch for Stratfordians, and they are always resorting to it. James McManaway, we may recall, found it necessary to endow Shakespeare with that "poetic genius" which "over-leaps both time and space." The explanation offered by the respected British Shakespearean scholar Allardyce Nicoll of Shakspere's having managed to encompass all that he and we find in Shakespeare's work is that "In the wonder of his genius he was able to grasp in lightning speed what could be attained only after dull years of work by ordinary minds."

These are remarkable statements. In them we find the scholars employing the device that gets them over all the humps: assume at the start that which is to be demonstrated, thus obviating the need to support the proposition with evidence. The unspoken assumption, for example, is that disbelievers in the Stratford "Shakespeare" can only be snobs. Thus their snobbishness may be confidently asserted as fact. No evidence is required and none has ever been produced. If we take as given to begin with and not open to question that genius is such as to have provided Shakspere with all the store of Shakespeare's mind, then it follows that everything we find in the dramatist is explained by his genius. To be dissatisfied with the demonstration is to be too stupid or too perverse to grasp the nature of genius. The principle is at the heart of the orthodox case. It requires no citation of parallels for such "a world-old miracle of genius" as accounts for Shakespeare. It does not matter that no one other than "Shakespeare" ever had the power mentally to overleap both time and space, to grasp at *lightning speed* — in seconds? — what ordinary minds can attain only *after years* of work.

Genius, Arnold Wilson, professor of philosophy at the University of Cincinnati, observes sagely, "explains nothing because it explains everything." Samuel Johnson said what should surely be obvious: "Nature gives no man knowledge, and when images are collected by study and experience, can only assist in combining or applying them. Shakespeare, however favoured by nature, could impart only what he had learned." The actual process of the poet-dramatist's mind and being were, to me, never better expounded than by Coleridge when he wrote:

> Shakespeare, no mere child of nature: no automaton of genius; no passive vehicle of inspiration possessed by the spirit, not possessing it; first studied patiently, meditated deeply, understood minutely, till knowledge, become habitual and intuitive, wedded itself to his habitual feelings, and at length gave birth to that stupendous power by which he stands alone, with no equal or second in his own class.

Those who are willing to do so may believe that the laws of nature were suspended for Shakspere's benefit and for his alone and that unlike other mortals he did not have to acquire knowledge by learning. Others may be forgiven for thinking otherwise when there is available a Shakespeare whose acquisitions of mind may be accounted for without recourse to the supernatural, to the suspension of the rules of cause and effect.

Even some orthodox scholars — in fact two of their deans — have difficulty in swallowing what orthodoxy requires. Joseph Quincy Adams, former director of the Folger Library, confesses that "if we are forced to think of him [Shakspere] as early snatched from school, working all day in a butcher's shop, growing up in a home devoid of books and of literary atmosphere, and finally driven from his native town through a wild escapade with village lads [a reference to the legend of his having poached deer], we find it hard to understand how he suddenly blossomed out as one of England's greatest men of letters with every mark of literary culture." J. Dover Wilson, editor of the *Cambridge New Shakespeare* and imaginative biographer of the dramatist, is even more troubled. "It is certain that Shakespeare had picked up as good an education in life and the world's concerns as any man before or since," he writes. "It is also clear that, if the author of *Merry Wives* knew his middle class, the author of *Love's Labour's Lost* had made himself equally familiar with the life, manner and conversation of ladies and gentlemen of the land. To credit that amazing piece of virtuosity to a butcher boy who left school at 13 or even to one whose education was nothing more than what a grammar school and residence in a little provincial borough could provide is to invite one either to believe in miracles or to disbelieve in the man of Stratford." That is indeed plain speaking from a leading contributor to the canonical writings.

"How did he reach the wit, the humor and the assured mastery of verse exhibited in a delightful early comedy like *Love's Labour's Lost*?" asks George Sampson in the *Concise Cambridge History of English Literature*. "These are some of the questions to which we desire an answer; but answer is there none." This confession of helplessness comes directly after an attack (previously quoted) on those who have sought an answer by looking elsewhere than to the Stratfordian for the authorship: they represent, says Professor Sampson, "the extremes of ignorant credulity and morbid ingenuity."

From the cruel dilemma they have outlined, Professors Adams and Wilson, at least, have allowed themselves an answer of sorts: *teaching*. Shakspere became a teacher. One had supposed that by acquiring an education one becomes qualified to teach, but it seems that it can work the other way, and that by becoming a teacher one acquires an education. "We may," as Adams gives us leave to do, "imagine Shakespeare as for some five years teaching a country school, and thus mastering the elements of grammar and composition, acquiring a thorough grounding in the best of Latin culture — Ovid, Cicero, Horace, Virgil, Terence, Plautus, Seneca — and by these means securing the training that was necessary to prepare him for his sudden emergence as the chief poet of the English Renaissance." Wilson has young Will receive his education "as a singing boy in the services of some great Catholic nobleman," which "would help to explain how he became an actor," the transition taking place, as he says, "almost inevitably." He has Shakspere on the London stage at seventeen, the year before he got his future wife with child, then when the plague closed the theatres (1592 to 1594) teaching the young 3rd Earl of Southampton at the family seat at Tichfield and travelling in Italy with Southampton and his recognized tutor, John Florio; that would explain his "intimate knowledge" of Venice and other Italian cities. To say that there is no evidence for this scenario would be a gross understatement. Suffice it to state that Wilson has found no takers for the proposition that the nineteen-year-old Earl, a Master of Arts of St. John's College, Cambridge, would for an instructor subpoena from the London stage a journeyman actor who had never seen the inside of a university.

Both Adams and Wilson rest heavily, as do Stratfordians generally, on the report that Shakespeare "had been in his younger years a schoolmaster in the country." This they like to dignify as a "tradition." It is a "tradition" to O. J. Campbell. Schoenbaum writes that "Baldwin regards as plausible the tradition that Shakespeare taught school for a while in the country." Evans and Levin state that "There is a fairly well authenticated tradition that he was briefly employed as a schoolmaster." This is to dupe the reader. There is no such tradition, let alone one that is fairly well authenticated. The manuscript of John Aubrey's *Brief Lives* of 1681 is the sole source of the report, beside which, in the margin, is written "from Mr. ——— Beeston," identified as William Beeston, whose father had been a player in the Lord Chamberlain's company eighty years earlier; Beeston, we heard Aubrey report in Chapter II, knew most of Shakespeare "from Mr. Lacy," whoever he may have been. Aubrey had collected the material for his *Brief Lives* for the *Athenae Oxonienses* of Anthony à Wood, who, we may recall, described Aubrey as "a shiftless person, roving and magotie-headed," who "thought little, believed much and confused everything."[3]

---

[3] Evans and Levin reply to my quotation of Wood's characterization of his agent by stating: "We cannot but express a certain admiration when a writer in Mr. Ogburn's position" — whatever that may mean — "is courageous enough to echo such phrases as these." They go on: "At all events Wood, who relied on Aubrey for biographical field work" — and learned of his mistake when sued for slander after having accepted a report of Aubrey's on the Earl of Clarendon — "has weathered less well than his research assistant." This extraordinary judgment was apparently coined by the professors for lack of any better rejoinder. Halliwell-Phillipps called Aubrey "unfortunately . . . one of those foolish and detestable gossips who record everything they have heard or misinterpreted." Much more recently, writing for the *Washington Post*, Professor Richard Freedman of Simmons College, called *Brief Lives* "funny, dirty and wildly inaccurate." Professors Evans's and Levin's standard of reliability may be gauged from Aubrey's report that Ben Jonson "killed Mr. Marlowe, the poet, on Bunhill, coming from the Green Curtain play-house."

The orthodox writers would of course not build so much on a few words in a book like *Brief Lives* were their needs less great. Aubrey's report may be rejected on two grounds. First, for Shakspere to have obtained a post as schoolmaster when he had himself been to school, even by his champions' reckoning, only until thirteen years of age, is highly unlikely if not all but impossible. Second, any school in which the future Shakespeare taught would never have allowed the world to remain oblivious of that fact or to forget it. And after all, when the dramatist was hailed as the greatest ever in 1623, some of his supposed pupils would still have been less than fifty years old. But no village or town has ever claimed Shakespeare as a schoolmaster.

. . . .

Let us take leave of Will Shakspere as he sets about the preliminaries for his nuptials. It would be pleasant for his biographers to record that he took with him to serve as bondsmen on this solemn occasion two elder intellectual exemplars steeped like him in love of books, with whom he had often compared readings of Ovid, "the love of his life among Latin poets," as Rowse says. But, Joseph Hunter writes, "Two more unseemly persons to attend at a poet's bridal can hardly be conceived . . . two husbandmen who were unable to write their names and whose marks are so singularly rude that they betray a more than common degree of rusticity."

Shakespeare as an Educated Man

Like Chaucer, says Lincoln Barnett, Shakespeare was a man of "enormous erudition." A leading classical scholar of our day, J. Enoch Powell, observes that "So far from 'knowing' that Shakespeare had 'small Latin and less Greek,' we more likely have Jonson's testimony that Shakespeare, whoever he was, was an accomplished Grecian and Latinist."

"No scholar today would see Shakespeare as a mere 'child of nature,'" says Professor Trevor-Roper, now Lord Dacre of Glanton. He might have been answering Professors Evans and Levin, to whom the dramatist was simply a *lusus naturae*, a natural phenomenon. (I can hardly believe that the Harvard professors would have been as eager as we have seen them to stand warrant for Trevor-Roper's orthodoxy were they better acquainted with his views.) More than a century and a half ago, Coleridge spoke with disgust of those "few pedants," who "took it upon them, as a happy medium and refuge, to talk of Shakespeare as a sort of beautiful *lusus naturae*, a delightful monster" and gave us "the wild, the irregular genius of our daily criticism! What!" he exploded, "are we to have miracles in sport? Or, I speak reverently, does God choose idiots by whom to convey divine truths to man?" Shakespeare a mere child of nature? "On the contrary," Trevor-Roper goes on, "we realize that he was highly educated, even erudite. It is true he does not parade his learning. He wears no carapace of classical or Biblical or philosophical scholarship, like Dante or Milton. But he is clearly familiar, in an easy, assured manner, with the wide learning of his time."

He does not parade his learning. No, and this is what throws educators off. They tend to equate learning with the parade of it. What is the purpose of it if you don't get credit for it? When the young Shakespeare's learning rises to the surface, it "is ostentatiously paraded before us," Allardyce Nicoll asserts of the following:

> I'll play the orator as well as Nestor,
> Deceive more slyly, than Ulysses could
> And, like a Simon, take another Troy. . . .
>   And thus he goes,
> As did the youthful Paris once to Greece,
> And hope to find the like event in love,
> But prosper better than the Trojan did.

"It is all a parade of learning," Professor Nicoll repeats. When one of Shakespeare's early characters drops a French oath or a Latin maxim, the professor "can almost hear the [author's] purr of preening self-esteem." Even the learning Shakespeare is accused of parading does not bespeak its genuine possession, apparently. Like "anyone who has written even a routine piece of fiction," says Alfred Harbage, Shakespeare "was aware of the necessity of faking . . . bits of technical knowledge." That, we are to understand, is what it all comes down to. Evidently it is possible to spend a lifetime studying the greatest of writers and believe he was an intellectual con-man, one with a "more than routine skill in deception." Yet, elsewhere, apparently forgetting himself, Professor Harbage acknowledges that the "surprising items of information — legal, medical, linguistic — subtending the imagery of the plays" with which "we are constantly struck," are "not of the kind that would be 'looked up' for the particular occasion; since the occasion is often inappropriate." For the truth of the matter we may turn to James J. Dwyer, who writes that "Shakespeare's scholarship is of that high order which represents complete assimilation of source material and its transmutation into the idiom of [his] own currency. Classicism has merely undergone a sea-change."

To that, Shakespeare-shrinking scholasticism must close its mind. A parader and faker of learning where his learning cannot be overlooked, the dramatist was a mere *lusus naturae* in that he does not hit us over the head with his learning: such is their message. Ben Jonson is of course in their view another matter. They recognize his classical learning; he *does* parade it and hit us over the head with it. Edmund Wilson writes of him, "His reading of Greek and Latin, for all the boasting he does about it, has served him very insufficiently for the refinement and ordering of his work, and usually appears in his plays as either an alien and obtrusive element or, when more skillfully managed, as a padding to give the effect of a dignity and weight which he cannot supply himself."

Shakespeare's Knowledge of the Classics

Orthodox scholarship, however, has found itself having to grant Shakespeare something at least of his due. In his *Studies of Shakespeare* of 1904, the eminent classicist John Churton Collins treats at length Shakespeare's evident familiarity with Ovid's *Metamorphoses, Fasti, Heroides, and Tristia,* and Plautus's *Menachmi, Amphitruo, Mostellaria,* and *Trinimus* (mostly acquired, it seems, at the Stratford school), and an acquaintance with Virgil's *Aeneid, Georgics,* and *Eclogues,* comedies of Terence, and "portions of Caesar, Sallust, Cicero, and Livy" (such acquaintances also acquired at that singular institution — and heaven help me when I think of my literary progress from seven to thirteen). These, plus Horace's *Odes* (of which reminiscences "appear to abound" in the plays), Seneca, Lucretius, and Juvenal are reflected in passages Collins cites, which, he says, "are typical," adding that "the impression which they and scores of other passages make is, that Shakespeare was writing not with any direct or perhaps conscious intention of imitating or even with the original before him, but with reminiscences of it floating vividly in his memory." Sir George Greenwood comments that "If this be so then Shakespeare must have been saturated with classical learning, so far as the Latin authors are concerned."

"So much, then, as to Latin. What of Greek?" Greenwood asks. "Here Mr. Collins seems to be struggling between a reluctance to proclaim a theory so startling to Stratfordian minds as that Shakespeare was able to read the Greek classic authors in the original, and an inward conviction that so it must have been." Professor Collins stoutly maintains, however, that it was his knowledge of Latin (we have forgotten the small Latin) that "gave him access to the Greek classics, nearly all of which had been popularized through Latin versions." He quotes many passages as illustrations of "Shakespeare's probable obligations to the Greek dramatists." He finds that between the Elizabethan's works and the epigrams of the Greek Anthology, popular among scholars of the 16th century, "parallels swarm; and, even if we resolve two-thirds of them into mere coincidences, are collectively too remarkable to be the result of accident." He goes on: "Nor must we forget the many curious parallels between his play on words, his studied use of paronomasia, of asyndeton, of onomatopoeia, of elaborate antithesis, of compound epithets, of subtle periphrasis, and above all his metaphors — with those peculiarly characteristic of the Attic dramas." No less "remarkable" than other parallels "is the perfect correspondence between the attitude of Shakespeare and that of the Greek dramatists, though we must except Aeschylus, towards the great problems of death and of man's future beyond it." And, "if he is Greek in his metaphysic he is equally Greek in his ethic, though in important respects his ethic is tempered with Christian ideals."

Could anything less than the short tether anchoring him to Stratford prevent acknowledgement of Shakespeare's familiarity with the far fields of Greek as well as Latin? Professor Collins resists as best he can. "It is not likely that Shakespeare could read Greek with facility, but if he possessed enough of it to follow the original in the Latin version, as he probably did, he would not only be able to enrich his diction with its idioms and phraseology, but would acquire that timbre in style of which in the last installment of this essay I gave illustrations." George Steevens, 18th-century editor of Shakespeare, says of the lines from Act I, Scene 1 of *Titus Andronicus*,

> The Greeks upon advice did bury Ajax
> That slew himself; and wise Laertes' son
> Did graciously plead for his funerals,

that "This passage alone would sufficiently convince me that the play before us was the work of one who was conversant with the Greek tragedies in their original language. We have here a plain allusion to the *Ajax* of Sophocles, of which no translation was extant in the time of Shakespeare." Professor Collins is equally confident: "If Shakespeare had not read the *Ajax* and been influentially impressed by it, there is an end to all evidence founded on reference and parallelism. Reminiscences of it seem to haunt his dramas."

"We can be sure," says Gilbert Highet of Columbia University, well-known classical scholar, "that he had not read Aeschylus. Yet what can we say when we find some of Aeschylus' thoughts appearing in Shakespeare's plays?" What indeed? "The only explanation is that great poets in times and countries distant from each other often have similar thoughts and express them similarly." It is clear to Professor Highet that "Shakespeare did not know much of the Latin language" and "knew virtually no Greek." (All the same, he was, "directly and indirectly, a classically educated poet who loved the classics"; and — what is this? — "he has rendered better than anyone else, even better than the sources which he used, the essence of the Roman republic and its aristocracy"!)

In *Henry the Sixth, Part One*, the Dauphin extols Joan la Pucelle for the expedition with which she "hath performed her word" in rescuing Orleans from the English and, turning to her, exclaims:

> Thy promises are like Adonis' garden
> That one day bloom'd and fruitful were the next.

Scholars had always been puzzled as to the source of the reference. Only after many years was it discovered in Plato's *Phaedrus*.[4]

Shakespeare's Knowledge of Modern Languages and Literature

Charles T. Prouty of the University of Missouri has no doubt that Shakespeare "read both Italian and French and was familiar with both Bandello and Bellefont." He draws the two main lines of descent of *Much Ado About Nothing*, one from Ariosto's *Ariodante and Genevra*, the other from Bandello's *Timbreo and Fencia*, embroidered by Belleforest. Of French, William Allan Neilson and Ashley Horace Thorndike in their standard *Facts About Shakespeare*, find it "fairly certain that Shakespeare had a working knowledge," and certainly he knew Montaigne, Rabelais, and Ronsard, "the three greatest French writers of his century, and French may well have been the medium through which he reached authors in other languages." They continue: "The class of Italian literature with which Shakespeare shows the most acquaintance is that of the novelle," as composed by "Boccaccio, Bandello, Cinthio, Ariosto, Giovanni Fiorentino, Straparola." Andrew S. Cairncross finds the Italian epic *Orlando Furioso* the source of the bedroom-window scene in *Much Ado*, the trial by combat in *Lear* between Edgar and Edmund and the ocular "proof" scenes in *Othello*, all of which, he says, are treated very differently in the English translation by Harrington or omitted altogether. He concludes that Shakespeare's "knowledge and use of Italian" is "established." It would not have occurred to Shakespeare, I believe, to have Hamlet remark "His name's Gonzago; the story is extant, and writ in very choice Italian" had he not himself been able to recognize Italian that was very choice. James J. Dwyer (a partisan of de Vere's) has cited echoes of Dante in Shakespeare and challenged Paget Toynbee, the great Dante scholar, on his dismissal of such echoes with cogency.

"When we approach the romances we catch curious glimpses of extended explorations into source material," says Allardyce Nicoll. All the same, let us of course be very careful in what we concede. "Sometimes, we may suppose, the peculiar parallels between the plays and works by others may be due to coincidence, to the intermediary of writings now lost or to that of

---

[4] Shakespeare has in mind Socrates' asking whether a husbandman would plant his seeds "in some garden of Adonis, that he may rejoice when he sees them in eight days appearing in beauty." The dramatist is engaging in subtle irony that only the most thorough student of the classics would grasp. The point of the question is that "a husbandman who is a man of sense" would not do so if "he wishes [his seeds] to bear fruit" but "sows in fitting soil" and "is satisfied if in eight month the seeds . . . arrive at perfection." In other words, Joan's promises will be fruitful only to ephemeral effect.

conversations with friends, but" — *but* — "even when allowance has been made for all such possibilities," Nicoll writes, "enough remains to warrant the assumption [by which is meant conclusion] that he was easily familiar with Latin, French and Italian, that he read widely in these as in English, and that he frequently took the trouble to examine several renderings of a story before he himself sat down to write."

That Shakespeare is denied what would be allowed to other writers is the consistent pattern. *Diana Enamorada*, a Spanish romance by the Portuguese writer Jorge de Montemayor, is generally recognized as a source of *Two Gentlemen of Verona*, "and there can be little question as to the correctness of this," says Edward Dowden. No English translation of the work was published until 1598, however, well after the Shakespeare play had appeared. But "Shakespeare may have seen one of the manuscript copies" of the translation, "or a French version of the Spanish romance."

Then there is Shakespeare's reading in English. "We are coming more and more to believe that he took far greater pains with his preparatory planning than had hitherto been supposed," Allardyce Nicoll acknowledges. "Quite clearly, he read much more than Holinshed's *Chronicles* when he was writing the history plays." Professors Neilson and Thorndike consider the *Chronicles* "the most useful book in all his reading," though finding that "no single author was so important in providing materials for the plays as the Greek Plutarch, the translation of Sir Thomas North being the direct source." Along with "Holinshed's *Chronicles* he used the work by Hall on *The Union of Lancaster and York,* the *Chronicles* of Grafton and of Fabyan, and the *Annals* of John Stowe. Also the *Book of Martyrs,* of John Foxe." He had "read books like Eden's *History of Travayle in the West and East Indies*, Raleigh's *Discoveries of Guiana*, and such pamphlets as were used in the vast compilation of Richard Hakluyt." The scientific knowledge implied in the plays derived in part from Pliny and *Batman uppon Bartholome His Booke De Proprietatibus.* "We find allusions to the Arthurian romances, to *Guy of Warwick, Bevis of Hampton, The Squire of Low Degree, Roland and Oliver,* and to *Huon of Bordeaux.*" His acquaintance with "more formal letters" included Chaucer, Caxton, Gower, and Henryson. Several books had appeared on the supernatural, and "one of these at least Shakespeare read, Harsnett's *Declaration of Egregious Popish Impostures.*" "To deal adequately with Shakespeare's reading in the plays of his time would be to write a history of Elizabethan drama." Professors Neilson and Thorndike go on: "Finally, Shakespeare knew his Bible. Several volumes have been written to exhibit the extent of this knowledge, and it has been shown by Anders that he knew both the Genevan and the Great Bible, as well as the Prayer Book." Indeed, Charles Wordsworth, Bishop of St. Andrews, a scholar well versed in both Latin and Greek, writes: "Take the entire range of English literature;

put together our best authors, who have written upon subjects not professedly religious or theological; and we shall not find, I believe, in them *all united*, so much evidence of the Bible having been read and used, as we have found in Shakespeare alone."

After concluding their "summary account" of the "amount of literature" of which there are "evidences in the plays and poems," Professors Neilson and Thorndike acknowledge "that only a fraction of what any author reads leaves a mark that can be identified in what he writes."

How do orthodox scholars assimilate this vast reading to the life of the Stratfordian "Shakespeare," who arrived in London from the literary desert of a provincial town, presumably without means, speaking the crude War-wickshire dialect, harassed to support himself and three dependents at home, the craft of acting to learn, including duelling (before experts) and dancing, parts to memorize by the dozen, who during his first ten years there wrote sixteen dramas, two long narrative poems, and probably most of the sequence of 153 sonnets, and in addition fraternized with the nobility, acquiring an unfaltering familiarity with their modes, manners, and sports, while also living all the "life" that we are told better prepared him for writing than learning would have? Says Professor Rowse, "We have seen what an avid, if rapid reader he was" — of course we have seen no such thing — "very much a reading man, and he read quickly." He would have had to, all right. He would indeed have had to be "able to grasp at lightning speed what could be attained only after dull years of work by ordinary minds." That, we may suppose, would have left him time to master French and Italian just to fill up the empty hours, not to mention all the knowledge and experience we have not yet come to.

Shakespeare's Verbal Resources

If there were any doubt that Shakespeare was one of the best-read, best-educated men of his time, certainly supreme in literary background, it is dispelled by his "verbal riches," Alfred Hart calls them, "compelling the employment of superlatives in describing them." The philologist Max Müller writes that "a well educated person in England . . . seldom uses more than about 3,000 or 4,000 words in actual conversation." He adds that "the Hebrew Testament says all it has to say with 5,642," while "Milton's works are built up with 8,000," but "Shakespeare, who displayed a greater variety of expression than probably any writer in any language," employed "about 15,000." That figure would surely be found conservative, as would even Alfred Hart's count, which gives Shakespeare a vocabulary of 17,677 words, twice the size of Milton's and more than two and a half times Marlowe's.

Louis Marder points out, "Shakespeare was so facile in employing words that he was able to use over 7,200 of them — more than occur in the whole King James version of the Bible — only once and never again."

Evans and Levin have no reply to these statistics, of which they are wise enough not to remind their readers. Instead they invoke the authority of the "scholarly . . . Milton . . . who appraised him early" as "a genius who owed more to nature than to art." Wisely again they do not quote what Milton in his colossal impudence or colossal ignorance actually said: he invited us to hear — heaven help us! — "sweetest Shakespeare, fancy's child, / Warble his native wood-notes wild."

Never has such verbal prodigality as Shakespeare's been approached. "Shakespeare's unmistakable sign-manual in a play," Professor Hart writes, "is the presence of plenty of words peculiar to it alone." And he cites six plays in each of which more than eight percent of the vocabulary consists of words not found in any other play, a much larger proportion than Marlowe introduced, he says. The *Oxford English Dictionary* credits Shakespeare with being the first to use about 3,200 words and the list would doubtless be longer had the compilers been aware that the plays were (as seems clear) written well before the Stratfordian calendar allows. Lewis Theobald was saying the least when in a preface to his *Works of Shakespeare* he spoke of the dramatist's "surprising effusion of Latin words made into English, far more than in any one English author I have ever seen." At the other extreme, Max Müller reports that Shakespeare several times used the possessive pronoun "its," which he says Ben Jonson refused to accept in his grammar, and since the *Oxford Universal Dictionary* gives "*c* 1600" as the date for the word's formation, I have little doubt that Shakespeare will be found to have coined it.

Mark Van Doren of Columbia University wrote in 1948: "Perhaps nobody any more supposes that Shakespeare warbled words without knowing what he did or how he did it [nobody but Evans and Levin]; but not until now have we modern readers been told how immense a thing rhetoric was in the Renaissance — how immense in scope, and how endlessly detailed in its numerous parts. Nor has it been apparent how thoroughly Shakespeare was master of this rhetoric." What had made the difference was publication by the Columbia University Press of *Shakespeare's Use of the Arts of Language* by Sister Miriam Joseph, C.S.C. In this remarkable book she devotes nearly 400 pages to showing, "how Shakespeare used the whole body of logical-rhetorical knowledge of his time" — rhetoric being "the art of using language to influence or persuade others." According to Sister Miriam, "A concordance of the Tudor figures [of speech] approximates two hundred," and few of the names given to these will be known to many modern readers: prosthesis, proparalepsis, aphaeresis, syncope, synaloepha, agocope, antisthecon, hyperbaton, anastrophe, tmesis, etc., etc. Early in the book she explains that the entire "essential general theory of composition and of reading current in Shakespeare's England . . . , with few negligible exceptions, is illustrated from Shakespeare's plays and poems in the following pages." And they are, satisfying her and us that Shakespeare "utilized every resource of thought and language known to his time" and "that his genius, outrunning precept even while conforming to it, transcends that of his contemporaries and belongs to all time." Although, as she says, he can "good-humoredly satirize the pedant," as he does Holofernes in *Love's Labour's Lost*, "Shakespeare excels all his contemporaries in his skillful use of the topics of logic and the flowers of rhetoric, whether for comic or serious purposes." The author takes us through those figures of rhetoric in Shakespeare which "proclaim his conscious and sophisticated approach to art." And she disposes, one trusts for good, of all the Gwynne Evanses and Harry Levins who divorce nature and art in order to deny Shakespeare — of all artists! — the latter. She quotes the speech in *The Winter's Tale* in which King Polixenes observes that "that art which you say adds to nature . . . which does mend nature — change it rather . . . itself is nature." And she adds, bowing to Shakespeare, "only one gifted by nature can use art supremely."

"Of Shakespeare it may be said without fear of exaggeration," Professor Ernest Weekley asserts, "that his contribution to our phraseology is ten times greater than that of any writer to any language in the history of the world." That he set about open-eyed and deliberately to develop in the English language the incomparable richness it has had since he wrote seems to me hardly to be questioned. Surely it was, at the least, James J. Dwyer says, one of his "purposes to make the English language suffice for the ideas gathered from multitudinous sources and served up for the edification of his fellow-countrymen." My mind harks back to Hermann Sinsheimer and his perception that "The plays are Elizabethan conquests of territory" (page 89). The greatness that Hawkins, Drake, Frobisher, and other sea-dogs were winning for England off distant shores, along with Spanish bullion ships, Shakespeare was reaping for her language from the treasures of classical antiquity, re-fashioned by his venturesome imagination, turning it into what "may be the greatest symbol system the world has ever devised," as Professor Richard Mitchell, father of the *Underground Grammarian*, called it in an interview in *Time*. In our fixation upon the Stratford man we have closed our eyes to the outstanding story in our cultural history.

The Crux of the Matter

When the problem is to persuade us that Shakespeare was Shakspere, a small-town recruit to the commercial theatre with limited opportunities for self-improvement, that he need *not* have been an outstandingly well-educated, well-read man of leisure — a privileged aristocrat — the Stratfordians pronounce Elizabethan schooling valueless if not positively baneful beyond six years of grammar school and proclaim the dramatist a man of small Latin and shallow knowledge of other fields, of which he betrays his ignorance by blunders, but with a commonplace ability to bone up a subject to impress an audience.

When, on the other hand, it comes to accounting for the exceptional learning and rich intellectual experience that are unmistakable in Shakespeare's plays, Shakspere acquires an extraordinary proficiency in Latin and classical literature, a knowledge of French and Italian writings, and a comprehensive reading in English texts, plus a familiarity with manners, modes, and objects well beyond his social and geographical sphere through the unexampled, wonder-working capabilities of the Stratford grammar school and a "genius" that gave him immediate command of that which all other human beings have to labor long and experience at first hand to achieve.

The further we look into the subject, whether back at the realities of the Stratford man or ahead into the further attainments of Shakespeare, the greater grows the gulf that "genius" has to bridge, the more miraculous powers we have to concede it, the further from us we have to put rationality.

16

Myriad-Minded Man of the Renaissance — 2

By way of prelude we remark that the two-score authors who contributed to a capacious, two-volume survey of the life and manners of Shakespeare's England (as it is entitled) are able to illustrate their subject's various aspects with swarms of quotations from the poet-dramatist himself, adding to our appreciation of the astonishing compass of his frame of reference. We proceed to hear what other well-qualified persons have to say about, and to see exampled in his writings, Shakespeare's professional knowledge of the law, his evidently first-hand acquaintance with Italy, his grasp of medicine, the abundant information he draws on in his enthusiasm for flowers and his observant awareness of nature as a whole, his continually attested love of and proficiency in music, his background in military matters and the sea. We observe in passing how the evidence of Shakespeare's attainments is dissimulated by some prominent Stratfordians. In conclusion we see that Oxford had, uniquely, the opportunity to acquire the varied knowledge and experience the plays tell us their author possessed.

It was not only in his assimilation of classical literature and of works in Italian and French, in addition to the literature of his own country, that Shakespeare stands out among creative writers of his time. Beyond that, the multi-faceted richness we find in his background helps us further to liberate him from the strait-jacket of orthodoxy and to discover him as he must have been.

We might begin with a glance at a two-volume work to which we referred for what it told us of the author as a sportsman. This is *Shakespeare's England: An Account of the Life & Manners of His Age.* Published in 1916 under an ode to Shakespeare by the Poet Laureate, Robert Bridges, the work covers its subject in thirty chapters, each of which takes up a different feature of the Elizabethan Age with particular reference to the treatment it receives in Shakespeare. The two-score contributors are all Shakespearean conformists — conformity doubtless having been required for admission — and are at pains to show how circumstances could be stretched to allow the Stratford man to gain the knowledge about their specialties that crops out in the plays. The cumulative effect, however, undoes their best efforts. Shakespeare's prodigious frame of reference comes out in the number of quotations from his works selected by the contributors to show how the dramatist uses a knowledge of their fields. By my reckoning, based on a special index, these quotations total no fewer than 2,275.

Shakespeare's Knowledge of the Law

The chapter on law is by Arthur Underhill, who tells us that "Shakespeare" purchased New Place from one of his ancestors. That would no doubt help explain the extremity of Stratfordism inspiring his first sentence, viz.:

> Despite Shakespeare's frequent use of legal phrases and allusions his knowledge of law was neither profound nor accurate.

There follows a dissertation in which, despite the author, very extensive knowledge of the law on Shakespeare's part comes through, and without inaccuracies. Meanwhile, we are told on page one, in partial explanation of that knowledge, that

> the dramatist and his father, like most of their contemporaries, were prone to litigation, and not infrequently figured in suits in the local Court of Record at Stratford-upon-Avon. The dramatist's purchases of houses and land in his later life must also have brought him into professional contact with lawyers and legal procedure.

But what is this? We find (much later) that "the common method of conveying land to a purchaser" is "frequently referred to in popular Elizabethan literature," and citations are made to Spenser and the dramatist Webster. "Shakespeare himself, however, never mentions the subject, although he was not only a considerable purchaser of real estate, but seems to have been involved in litigation in relation to it." (I cannot help adding here that poor Edward de Vere had scant experience in purchasing land; he was always having to sell portions of what he had.)

I am certainly not equipped to pass judgment on Shakespeare's knowledge of the law (or of the classics either, for that matter). But competence in others is, I think, not impossible for the uninformed to recognize, and I think we may fairly recognize competence in the matter at issue in Sir George Greenwood, barrister-at-law and Member of Parliament, who has probably looked further into Shakespeare's legal attainments and written more on the subject than anyone else. In *The Shakespeare Problem Restated* he expressed his conclusions and those of others with more than ordinary competence. His forty-seven-page chapter on the subject begins:

> The *Plays* and *Poems* of Shakespeare supply ample evidence that their author not only had a very extensive and accurate knowledge of law, but also that he was well acquainted with the manners and customs of members of the Inns of Court and with legal life generally.
>
> "While novelists and dramatists are constantly making mistakes as to the laws

of marriage, of wills and inheritance, to Shakespeare's law, lavishly as he expounds it, there can neither be demurrer, nor bill of exceptions, nor writ of error." Such was the testimony borne by one of the most distinguished lawyers of the 19th century who was raised to the high office of Lord Chief Justice in 1850, and subsequently became Lord Chancellor. Its weight will, doubtless, be more appreciated by lawyers than by laymen, for only lawyers know how impossible it is for those who have not served an apprenticeship to the law to avoid displaying their ignorance if they venture to employ legal terms and to discuss legal doctrines. "There is nothing so dangerous," wrote Lord Campbell, "as for one not of the craft to tamper with our free-masonry."

And what does the same high authority say about Shakespeare? He had a "deep technical knowledge of the law," and an easy familiarity with "some of the most abstruse proceedings in English jurisprudence." And again: "Whenever he indulges in this propensity he uniformly lays down good law." Of *Henry IV, Part 2*, he says: "If Lord Eldon could be supposed to have written the play, I do not see how he could be chargeable with having forgotten any of his law while writing it." . . . Malone, himself a lawyer, wrote: "His knowledge of legal terms is not merely such as might be acquired by the casual observation of even his all-comprehending mind; it has the appearance of technical skill." Another lawyer and well-known Shakespearean, Richard Grant White, says: "No dramatist of that time, not even Beaumont, who was the younger son of a judge of the Common Pleas, and who after studying in the Inns of Court abandoned law for the drama, used legal phrases with Shakespeare's readiness and exactness. . . . Legal phrases flow from his pen as part of his vocabulary, and parcel of his thought. Take the word 'purchase' for instance, which, in ordinary use, means to acquire by giving value, but applies in law to all legal modes of obtaining property except by inheritance or descent, and in this peculiar sense the word occurs five times in Shakespeare's thirty-four plays, and only in one single instance in the fifty-four plays of Beaumont and Fletcher. It has been suggested that it was in attendance upon the courts in London that he picked up his legal vocabulary. But this supposition not only fails to account for Shakespeare's peculiar freedom and exactness in the use of that phraseology, it does not even place him in the way of learning those terms his use of which is most remarkable, which are not such as he would have heard at ordinary proceedings *nisi prius*, but such as refer to the tenure or transfer of real property, 'fine and recovery,' 'statutes merchant,' 'purchase,' 'indenture,' 'tenure,' 'double voucher,' 'fee simple,' 'fee farm,' 'remainder,' 'reversion,' 'forfeiture,' etc. This conveyancer's jargon could not have been picked up by hanging round the courts of law in London two hundred and fifty years ago, when suits as to the title of real property were comparatively rare. And besides, Shakespeare uses his law just as freely in his first plays, written in his first London years, as in those produced at a later period. Just as exactly, too. . . ."

To all this testimony (and there is more which I have not cited) may now be added that of a great lawyer of our own times, viz., Sir James Plaisted Wilde, Queen's Counsel, 1855, created a Baron of the Exchequer in 1860, promoted to the post of Judge-Ordinary and Judge of the Courts of Probate and Divorce in 1863 and better known to the world as Lord Penzance, to which dignity he was raised in 1869. Lord Penzance, as all lawyers know, . . . was one of the first legal authorities of his day. . . .

Lord Penzance speaks of Shakespeare's "perfect familiarity with not only the principles, axioms, and maxims, but the technicalities of English law, a knowledge so perfect and intimate that he was never incorrect and never at fault. . . . The mode in which this knowledge was pressed into service on all occasions to express his meaning and illustrate his thought, was quite unexampled. He seems to have had a special pleasure in his complete and ready mastership of it in all its branches. . . . At every turn and point at which the author required a metaphor, simile, or illustration, his mind ever turned first to the law. He seems almost to have thought in legal phrases, the commonest of legal expressions were ever at the end of his pen in description or illustration. That he should have descanted in lawyer fashion when he had a forensic subject in hand, such as Shylock's bond, was to be expected, but the knowledge of law in 'Shakespeare' was exhibited in a far different manner: it protruded on all occasions, appropriate or inappropriate, and mingled itself with strains of thought widely divergent from forensic subjects."

Five years after George Greenwood's work was published there appeared *The Baconian Heresy — A Confutation* by his friend J. M. Robertson. This, Greenwood noted, was "directed . . . in large measure against my humble self," though, he added, "for my part, I have never subscribed to the 'Baconian Heresy'!" Forty-five years later, Greenwood's friendly assailant was invoked by another confuter of heresy, the English writer R. C. Churchill, in a book introduced by Ivor Brown. "Robertson," said Churchill, "proved by quotation, and at great length, that lawyers have in fact held widely different views upon this matter. His book was published as long ago as 1913, but his argument still holds." Mr. Churchill does not tell us, but Mr. Robertson's attempt to confute Greenwood was effectively countered by Greenwood three years later in his *Is There a Shakespeare Problem?*[1] One crossed swords with Sir George at one's peril. Even Schoenbaum treats him, dead as he has long

---

[1] You have to watch Mr. Churchill. Notice, for example, how he finds proof of Shakspere's authorship of the plays in the trial of the conspirators in the Essex rebellion of 1601. Following the disclosure that they had paid to have *Richard the Second* performed, presumably so that Richard's deposition would inspire the London populace to condone rebellion against Elizabeth, Mr. Churchill's script has it that when the "secret police under Walsingham and Cecil — their leader was a man called Topcliffe" — conducted an investigation into the authorship of the play, "they must have found evidence of Shakespeare's [i.e., Shakspere's] authorship so convincing that there was no need even to take the author to the Tower and torture him" to get "the name of his noble author out of him" as they would have done had they believed him a mere "figurehead." One trouble with this proof of the Stratford man's authorship is that there is not a bit of evidence that such an investigation was ever made or any reason why it should have been. The authorship of the play was immaterial. It was already, in 1601, an "old play," having indeed been printed as early as 1597. What mattered was the motive of those who paid the players to perform it. Had the author of *Richard the Second* been going to get in trouble for the contents of the play, he would have got in trouble when it appeared in 1595 and 1596. Incidentally, we must regret that Mr. Churchill does not tell us whether he thinks his investigation would have taken place if Robert Cecil, who with Walsingham controlled the secret police, had known that his brother-in-law, the Earl of Oxford, was the author, or whether Topcliffe would have clarioned the information had he discovered for himself that the culprit was the father of the boss's nieces.

"Fair-minded," says Ivor Brown of Mr. Churchill. Louis B. Wright goes him one better. "Mr. Churchill is scrupulously fair." Evidently he found this quality noteworthy among scourgers of the dissidents.

been, with circumspection as a "talented attorney" whose "onslaughts against the orthdox citadel" were made "with a curious mixture of suavity and abuse." I have never detected the latter, but it is true that "Serpents of cultivated malice lurk in the fine print of footnotes."[2]

The question of Shakespeare's attainments in the law came up in a series of articles in the *American Bar Association Journal* in 1959. In one of these, William H. Clary, a prominent attorney in Los Angeles, observed that "genius . . . has a way of cropping out in men whose parents were illiterate and who grew up in 'bookless neighborhoods,' as in the case of our own Abraham Lincoln." Stratfordians often bring up Lincoln as a parallel to Shakspere, and so perhaps the point is worth a brief digression here. Mr. Clary continues: "We do not know, and we never will know, how Lincoln acquired the ability to write the beautiful and poetic line, 'The Father of Waters goes unvexed to the sea,' when he wished to dramatize the fact that, after the capture of Vicksburg, the Mississippi was open to steamboat traffic."

I should say that we could give a guess as to whence that ability in part derived. Lincoln employed his leisure hours, which he did not altogether lack, by saturating himself in Shakespeare and the King James Bible. These were not available to Shakspere, if he had access to any books at all before he went to London — and if he had any leisure even then. It is not true that Lincoln's parents were illiterate, though his father could not read until after his marriage. His mother, said to have been superior in intellect and character to others of her neighborhood and background, herself taught young Abe to read and his stepmother urged him to study. Burns's poetry and *Pilgrim's Progress* were among the youthful Lincoln's other favorite works. We are apt to forget that when the young Shakespeare would have been striving to find what could be done with words, there was little English literature to demonstrate the forms that expression could take. Malory's *Morte Darthur*, *Piers the Plowman*, Chaucer, and a scattering of other poets of less than enduring stature were about all that qualified, unless we further except Wyatt and Surrey. Subsequent writers were to be given an immense head start, above all by Shakespeare. (Among them were those who gave the world the

---

[2] Greenwood it was, we may recall, who Henry James said best expressed his view of the authorship. Schoenbaum, moreover, has seen Mark Twain's copy of Greenwood's *The Shakespeare Problem Restated*, "heavily and approvingly annotated" and with the notation on the title-page "this book reduces him [Shakspere] to a skeleton & scrapes the bones." I recommend to the reader Professor Schoenbaum's professorial condescension to Twain on the score of his "frontier invective" on the subject and the footnote to his reproof, which is even more to be savored:

A brief, cogent psychological analysis of Twain's anti-Stratfordianism is to be found in Alfred Harbage's *Conceptions of Shakespeare* (1966). In the transplanted waifs of *Pudd'n'head Wilson* and *The Prince and the Pauper*, Harbage [of Harvard] discerns Twain's "sublimination of his own 'cloudy sense of having been a prince.'"

I can hardly see how self-satire, even if deliberate, could go much further.

King James Bible. Charles Wordsworth, the bishop of St. Andrews whom I have previously quoted, an accomplished classical scholar, shows close correspondences between its language and Shakespeare's, observing phraseology derived from Greek and Latin, and concluding that "It is probable that the translators of 1611 owed as much or more to Shakespeare than he owed to them." Shakespeare's pen having assuredly been laid down before 1611, the debt was all on one side.) Lincoln's prose stemmed from a discriminating intellect and sensitive humanity. It had wonderful clarity, economy, and effect, even a quality of poetry, but its range was minor compared with Shakespeare's. So too was Lincoln's frame of reference, I should suppose, and what posterity has found memorable in his works, apart from the Gettysburg Address, is very little beside the store with which Shakespeare has enriched the common consciousness.

In another article in the *A.B.A. Journal*, Charlton Ogburn, Sr., then a forty-year member of the New York bar, cited examples of Shakespeare's informed use of the law from fifteen plays. He wound up with Hamlet's musing over Yorick's skull and with the gravediggers' argument over Ophelia's corpse, which make clear the author's familiarity with Plowden's Report of the case of Hales v. Petit, tried in the reign of Mary Tudor. In a subsequent issue, John N. Hauser, a young member of the California bar, undertook to reply. He pointed out that Ben Jonson (long afterward) also used the phrase "tripartite indentures," which Shakespeare "seems" to have taken from Holinshed. He quoted a passage from Jonson full of law terms, which he rightly called "legal mumbo jumbo." And he cited a study published in Baltimore in 1942 by two lawyers in which, "after they had read and indexed all the plays of Shakespeare and seventeen of the best known other dramatists," they concluded that "Not only do half the playwrights employ legalisms more freely than Shakespeare, but most of them also exceed him in the detail and complexity of their legal problems and allusions, and with few exceptions display a degree of accuracy at least no lower than his."

The editor of the *Journal*, Richard Bentley, past president of the Chicago Bar Association, in a following issue observed gently that what was called for was not simply analysis of the use of legal terms "(such as Mr. Hauser's examples from Ben Jonson) merely on a quantitative basis" since in many other instances as well "the use of such terms consisted in no more than the mere rattling off of a string of legal terms in gibberish mockery of lawyers." What required evaluation "was the degree of legal knowledge required to use legal terms with pertinence as well as accuracy." He implied that the authors of the Baltimore study might be less well qualified in the field than Lord Campbell, Edmund Malone, George Greenwood, and "most other leading Shakespeare scholars" who agree about the "remarkable legal attain-

ments of the author." Rather pointedly, Mr. Bentley also recalled that inasmuch as Lord Campbell's testimony as to Shakespeare's knowledge of the
law

> seemed impossible to reconcile . . . with what is known of Shaksper of Stratford,
> doubt as to the authorship was confirmed. To the rescue came Charles G. Allen,
> a Boston lawyer, who wrote a chapter entitled "Bad Law in Shakespeare,"
> contending that Shakespeare made many errors in his legal allusions. To this
> replied Sir George Greenwood, . . . expert in Elizabethan law. Sir George showed
> with conclusiveness that the "bad law" is in Allen's book, and not in Shake-
> speare's works."

As Greenwood asserted long ago, "It is not to the purpose to compile
more lists of legal terms and expressions from the pages of other Elizabethan
writers. The question is, whether Shakespeare, when we consider his works
as a whole, does not exhibit such a sound and accurate knowledge of law,
such a familiarity with legal life and customs, as could not possibly have
been acquired (or 'picked up') by the Stratford player; whether it be not the
fact, as Richard Grant White puts it, that 'legal phrases flow from his pen
as part of his vocabulary, and parcel of his thought'?" Sir George's answer
was a well-supported Yes.

The distinction is one with which we have met before. Any intelligent
writer can acquire knowledge of a subject and serve it up as required. Ben
Jonson does it with hunting, Latin and Greek, and the law. It is something
else to have been so immersed in a subject and to have assimilated it so
thoroughly that it has become part of one's nature, shaping one's view of
the world, coming forward spontaneously to prompt or complete a thought,
supply an image or analogy. Ivor Brown says, "I agree with [Edgar I.] Fripp's
conclusion that law is part of him [Shakespeare] and 'slips from him una-
wares.'" In Fripp's view "The facts . . . demand professional experience in
an attorney's office, and without doubt at Stratford, in or about the years
1579–87." But as Lord Campbell replied when asked about the possibility
of his having been a clerk in such an office, "it might reasonably be expected
that there would have been deeds or wills witnessed by him still extant, and
after a very diligent search none such can be discovered." Lord Penzance
agreed: "It cannot be doubted but that Lord Campbell was right in this. No
young man could have been at work in an attorney's office without being
called upon continually to act as a witness, and in many other ways leaving
traces of his work and name." Shakspere left none.

Moreover, there were all those other activities in which Shakspere was
having to busy himself if he was to acquire something of the background
exhibited in the plays and poems. (Among these, curiously, orthodoxy seems
not to have him doing any writing.) There was, especially, his familiarity
with Italy to be accounted for.

Shakespeare's Knowledge of Italy

> Much research has been devoted to a conjecture that he spent part of this period [1592–1594] in northern Italy. It is certainly true that when the plague was over he began a series of plays with Italian settings, which was something of a new departure in English drama; that to a modern imagination, itself steeped in Italian sentiment, he seems to have been remarkably successful in giving a local colouring and atmosphere to these and even that he shows familiarity with some minute points of local topography.

That is the ultimate orthodox authority, Sir Edmund K. Chambers, speaking — one supposes with reluctance. But the two or three years he assigns to those possible travels were the very ones during which Shakespeare was supposed to have been writing the long and demanding narrative poems, *Venus and Adonis* and *Lucrece*. Moreover, by Chambers's own reckoning, the years 1592 to 1595 were those in which four Italian plays came out — *Comedy of Errors, Taming of the Shrew, Two Gentlemen of Verona,* and *Romeo and Juliet* — along with *Richard the Third, Titus Andronicus,* and *Love's Labour's Lost*: busy years. Of course nothing in Shakspere's record suggests that he had ever traveled anywhere except between Stratford and London.

An iron-clad orthodoxist, Gilbert Highet recalls that "As soon as I reached the northern provinces of Italy I was constantly being reminded of Shakespeare."

Hugh R. Trevor-Roper writes that Shakespeare's "knowledge of Italy was extraordinary. An English scholar who lived in Venice has found his visual topographic exactitude in *The Merchant of Venice* incredible in one who had never been there." Dr. Ernesto Grillo in his *Shakespeare and Italy* supports that opinion. He says of *The Merchant* that "the topography is so precise and accurate that it must convince even the most superficial reader that the poet visited the country." To this, Pietro Rebora in his *L'Italia nella Dramma Inglese* adds that Shakespeare "possessed a profound knowledge of Italian language and culture, of which he made an amazing use in the plays."

George Greenwood asks, "And what are we to say of his accurate knowledge of the towns of northern Italy — of Padua, Verona, Milan, Mantua and especially of Venice? On this subject the reader should by all means consult Professor [Karl] Elze's essay on 'The Supposed Travels of Shakespeare.' . . . The argument here is cumulative to show that Shakespeare must have had personal knowledge of some of the towns of which he presents us with such vivid and accurate portraiture." Sir George quotes from the German scholar:

> As to Venice, it would be difficult to say which play transfers us more completely to the city of the lagunes, the *Merchant of Venice* or *Othello*, although it is only the first act of the latter that is acted at Venice.

Seconding Dr. Johnson, Professor Elze observes that

> The poetic imagination may be ever so lively and creative, and the power of intuition ever so highly developed, but one thing cannot be disputed, namely, that it bestows upon no one a knowledge of facts, but that such knowledge can only be acquired either by experience or be imparted by others.

He leaves no doubt as to how he thinks Shakespeare acquired his knowledge of Venice.

One element in Dr. Elze's case for the dramatist's having traveled in Italy is the description of Belmont in *The Merchant of Venice*, which he says

> has its prototype unquestionably in one of those splendid summer residences, surrounded with well-kept gardens and adorned with treasures of art, which the merchant princes of Venice possessed even in Shakespeare's day. . . . From the context it appears with certainty that Shakespeare possessed a perfectly accurate knowledge of the locality.

In the play Portia sends her servant to fetch Bellario's "notes and garments" with the words as originally rendered:

> Bring them, I pray thee, with imagined speed,
> Unto the tranect, to the common ferry
> Which trades to Venice

Elze comments:

> The nonsensical word "tranect," which is found in all the quartos and folios, and has been retained even by the Cambridge editors, proves that copyists and compositors possessed no knowledge of this word, and still less of the thing itself. Even the word "tragect," which Theobald has correctly restored, is not a genuine English word, otherwise the poet would not have added the apposition "to the common ferry," which he surely did only to make the meaning clear to his readers and hearers. What visitor to Venice does not here directly recognize the Venetian traghetto (tragetto)? The ferry takes us across the "laguna morta," and up the great canal to the city, where we in spirit land at the Rialto. Shakespeare displays a no less accurate knowledge of this locality than that of the villas along the Brenta, as he does not confound the Isola de Rialto with the Ponte di Rialto. He knows that the exchange "where merchants do most congregate" is upon the former; nay he appears to have been better acquainted with the Isola de Rialto than Coryat, fifteen years afterward, for the name of Gobbo, which he has bestowed on the clown, reminds us vividly of the Gobbo di Rialto, a stone figure which serves as a supporter to the granite pillar of about a man's height, from which the laws of the Republic were proclaimed. . . .

"By gentle hints and indications," Elze observes, Shakespeare

> transfers us, without our being aware of it, into an Italian atmosphere, and in the fifth act makes us enjoy the charms of an Italian night as they could scarcely be felt more lively on the spot itself. The moonlight scene at Belmont is indeed a masterpiece which defies all rivalry, and is far above any that has proceeded from an Italian pen.

In a contrast drawn by Elze we find once more the difference between knowledge flowing naturally from experience and that achieved from reading. Compare, he says,

> the "Merchant of Venice" and B. Jonson's "Volpone," the scene of which is likewise laid in Venice. Jonson not only exhibits a profound knowledge of the Italian language, but shows himself conversant with Venetian institutions, customs, and localities; he, so to say, lays the local coloring on inches thick; but it is everywhere the work of a book-worm whose object it is to display with self-sufficiency his own learning compiled *ad hoc* from other books.

With the foregoing in mind, turn to *The Merchant of Venice*, V. i, for the mood of a southern night conveyed by Lorenzo in his cajoling of Jessica. There is no study in it: it is as casual and as brief as if the young lover were speaking in real life of what was actually before him.

> The moon shines bright: in such a night as this,
> When the sweet wind did gently kiss the trees
> And they did make no noise. . . .
>   . . . .
> How sweet the moonlight sleeps upon this bank!
>   . . . .
>   look, how the floor of heaven
> Is thick inlaid with patines of bright gold.

No Southerner, no one who has come under the spell of the tropics, can read those lines in a northern clime without having his heart lean toward them.

An empathy for Shakespeare's feeling for Italy that is quite startling to come upon unexpectedly in the *Times* of London is voiced there by Stewart Perowne in an article entitled "Shakespeare's Italy":

> This is the first attraction of Shakespeare's Italy — it was something that the English longed for but had not yet achieved. [By that is meant] all the things the English have always loved most, quiet pleasures, music, the company of friends, gardening, hunting and fine clothes. And all this, which England was not to know for another century had been there for more time than that. . . . Shakespeare's England has gone. . . . Shakespeare's Italy, on the other hand, is still flourishing. Look at the pictures of Giorgione: those same landscapes, haunted by unheard melodies, still glow in the Italian spring. The Venetian gossip of Carpaccio still buzzes on the unchanged Piazza. More, the very people of Veronese and Titian, of Tintoretto and Lotto, still move in the same way. . . . In the villas the same large life is led [— villas] of which Portia's Belmont is the Shakespearean image.

Shakespeare and Art

In an essay in which he "reflects on the 1964 anniversary," Professor Emeritus J. Isaacs of the University of London informs us that Shakespeare "knew nothing about art." Had the poet sought to impress future professors he might have gone on with the imagery with which Sonnet 24 begins:

> Mine eye hath play'd the painter and hath stell'd
> Thy beauty's form in table of my heart. . . .

In *Shakespeare's England*, Lionel Cust quotes these lines and for the benefit of us who are not as expert in art as Professor Isaacs explains that "stell'd" and "table" are technical terms meaning, respectively, "portrayed" and the "board or other flat surface on which a picture was painted." The two lines have the distinction of being quoted twice in the *Oxford Universal Dictionary*, once under "stell," once under "table." Mr. Cust goes on to cite two brief descriptions of paintings in the Induction to *The Taming of the Shrew* and judges that "these allusions are evidently to mythological pictures of the Italian school, and suggest famous pictures by Correggio, Giulio Romano, and other painters." Proceeding, he writes, "In the poem of *Lucrece*, a 'piece of skilful painting' of the siege of Troy is described in detail and at considerable length (11. 1366–1456). At Mantua [reader please take note] the painter Giulio Romano (in addition to his renowned paintings in the Palazzo del Te) executed in the castle, between 1532 and 1536, a famous series of paintings of the Trojan War." (Is Mr. Cust allowing Shakspere a tour of Mantua? Not at all. Or not *necessarily*. The "wonders" of these paintings, he says, "may have been described to the young Shakespeare and may have impressed him.")

But to return to Professor Isaacs. "He knew nothing about art, and in *The Winter's Tale* when he speaks of a sculptor being 'that rare Italian master Julio Romano,' he did not know that Julio Romano was not a sculptor. . . ." Other Stratfordians have also made this charge. But more than sixty years before the professor's article, Elze remarked that in the first edition (1550) of Giorgio Vasari's classic *Lives of Seventy of the Most Eminent Painters, Sculptors and Architects*, two Latin epitaphs of Romano are given which evidently were inscribed on his tombstone in the church of San Barnaba in Mantua, which Dr. Elze says, "has completely disappeared since the renovation of the church." The second reads in part:

> *Videbat Jupiter corpora sculpta pictaque*
> *Spirare, aedes mortalium aequarier coelo*
> *Julii virtute Romani. . . .*

"Tres artes! Corpora Sculpta!" Elze exclaims. "Shakespeare is right; he had made no blunder. . . . And more than this, his praise of Romano wonderfully agrees with the second epitaph, in which truth to nature and life is likewise praised as being Julio's chief excellence (if he could put breath into his work, — videbat Jupiter corpora spirare)."

In *Winter's Tale* we are told that the statue of Hermione is

> now newly perform'd by that rare Italian master, Julio Romano, who, had he himself eternity and could put breath into his work, would beguile Nature of her custom, so perfectly is he her ape.

"How and where he [Shakespeare] came across that name [Julio Romano] Lord only knows," says Professor Isaacs. I am sorry, but I cannot help remembering at this juncture Gilbert K. Chesterton's "Dream of Bottom the Weaver:"

> Once, when an honest weaver slept
>   And Puck passed by, a kindly traitor,
> And on his shoulders placed the head
>   Of a Shakespearean commentator. . . .

But I am over-hasty. There is, of course, the question probably only the Lord *could* answer. "We stand," as Elze says, "before the dilemma, either Shakespeare must have studied Vasari, or he had been in Mantua and had there seen Romano's works and read his epitaphs." One experience or the other — and Vasari was not translated into English until 1850 — must have brought Giulio to mind when he wanted a "rare Italian master," not one of the famous sculptors, excelling in lifelike work. Incidentally, no work of sculpture is claimed for Giulio in the play. The statue of Hermione that "Third Gentleman" attributes to "that rare Italian master" is of course not a statue at all, but Hermione herself.

Shakespeare's "Blunders"

Stratfordians are much given to citing errors in Shakespeare in belittling the dramatist's erudition. Most of these are anachronisms. Wittenberg, Hamlet's university, was not in existence when the historic Amleth lived. Aristotle, cited in *Troilus and Cressida*, came long after the siege of Troy. Artillery is used in *King John*, a century or two in advance of its times. A clock strikes the hour in *Julius Caesar*.

Those who make an issue of such discrepancies seem unaware that in Shakespeare's day historical consistency in details like those was still a fetish of the future. No one would have seen anything wrong in Malory's furnishing King Arthur's post-Roman Britain with the modes, manners, and trappings of eight centuries later; we do it today in treating the Arthurian cycle. In Henry Peacham's illustration of *Titus Andronicus*, reproduced by E. K. Chambers, while Titus is shown in an approximation of Roman garb, the soldiers are in thoroughly Elizabethan dress and carry halberds. That would have bothered an Elizabethan audience as little as Rembrandt's contemporaries of the next century were bothered by his depiction of Aristotle contemplating the bust of Homer dressed as a 17th-century Dutch burgher or the goddess Diana as a matron of Amsterdam. When Titus Andronicus says "With horn and hound we'll give your grace bon jour," it is not to be imagined that Shakespeare or those he wrote for supposed that the Romans knew French or that the language existed then. But if you were going to practice the supreme anachronism of having the Romans speak English instead of Latin, why not have them toss off French expressions and garb the soldiery in Elizabethan dress?

What we must also bear in mind is that Shakespeare's plays were akin to shot silk, which is one color or another depending upon the position from which you view it. Looked at from one angle, the plays were of other times and places while from another, I think it will be found, they were of contemporary England and of persons and kinds of persons known to the author. When Cleopatra warns Iras of the fate in store for them if they fall into Octavius' hands, the playwright makes a slight bow in the direction of time and place.

> Saucy lictors
> Will catch at us, like strumpets, . . .

But immediately he shifts to the treatment that the highly placed could expect if brought low by scandal in 16th-century London, quite indifferent, we may be sure, to its inapplicability to Rome:

> . . . and scald rimers
> Ballad us out o' tune: the quick comedians
> Extemporally will stage us, and present
> Our Alexandrian revels. Antony
> Shall be brought drunken forth, and I shall see
> Some squeaking Cleopatra boy my greatness
> I' the posture of a whore.

That Shakespeare's Cleopatra was a reflection of Queen Elizabeth, I am far from the first to suspect.

The most famous error alleged in Shakespeare is the attribution of a sea-coast to Bohemia. From Ben Jonson to Louis B. Wright, critics have ridiculed Shakespeare for that, not troubling to inform themselves that the Kingdom of Bohemia under King Premyal Ottaker II (1253–1278) stretched to the Adriatic, and in 1526, upon the accession of the first Hapsburg to the throne of Bohemia, the realm of the King of Bohemia comprised the Archduchy of Austria, which bordered the Adriatic between territories of the Venetian Republic. Again, however, I think Shakespeare's attention to such detail of a faraway land as whether Bohemia had a sea-coast would have been measurable in a thimble. So too it would have been, I think, had the dramatist been charged with the one real boner — not a mere anachronism — I know of in his works; or he might just have laughed. In the opening scene of *Two*

Gentlemen of Verona, Valentine is said to have "parted hence, to embark for Milan," being, it seems "shipp'd already." Milan is, of course, inland of Verona, itself an inland city. I had once thought, as others have, that to speak of shipping from one to the other could be justified if the traveler were setting forth by canal-boat, but this explanation is clearly precluded by Proteus' speech to Valentine's servant at the end of the scene:

> Go, go, be gone, to save your ship from wrack;
> Which cannot perish, having thee aboard,
> Being destin'd to a drier death on shore.

Indisputably the dramatist was thinking of a sea voyage. Was he so ignorant as to believe that one was necessary between the two Italian towns, as Louis B. Wright charges? Of course not. Later in the play he has his young lovers set forth from Milan for Verona in the acceptable way, overland — to be captured by outlaws in the forest. My hunch is that Valentine's being shipped from Verona harks back to the dramatist's own embarkation from one Italian port to another, perhaps to an original conception of the play, before Verona was decided on. The outrageous, easily avoidable howler is just the kind that a studied Ben Jonson or a playwright from a Warwickshire village, sensitive about the cultural poverty of his background, would have been at pains not to fall into. It took that "princely mind" not to give a hang. How little of a hang the dramatist gave is shown in *The Winter's Tale*, in which he has a 16th-century Italian artist — the same Giulio Romano — invoked in pre-Christian Bohemia. Louis B. Wright, we may be sure, would have known better. The explanation, I suppose, is that the play was written in two stages, in an earlier version and then added to in a later, which the author could not be bothered to reconcile.

"Real-life doctors, lawyers and soldiers, indeed just about real-life anything, usually laugh at their fictional counterparts," Joel Swerdlow observes in a book-review in the *Washington Post*. True; and one of the striking properties of Shakespeare's intellect is that readers who find a character of Shakespeare's drawing upon a special interest of theirs for a metaphor or illustration do not laugh at the way he uses it. On the contrary: there is nothing else in the world's literature comparable to the attention that specialists in many fields have been led to give to the insights into their field displayed in Shakespeare. We have seen what sportsmen, statesmen-politicians, classicists, lawyers, and Italianists have had to say about Shakespeare as one of them. More unexpected is what we hear from physicians.

Shakespeare's Acquaintance with the Sciences

Tributes to the dramatist's medical knowledge go back well over a century. Writing in 1895, Georg Brandes observed:

In 1860 a Doctor Bucknill devoted a whole book to the subject, in which he goes so far as to attribute to the poet the most advanced knowledge of our own time, or, at any rate, of the 'sixties, in this department. Shakespeare's representations of madness surpass all those of other poets. Alienists are full of admiration for the accuracy of the symptoms in Lear and Ophelia. Nay, more, Shakespeare appears to have divined the more intelligent modern treatment of the insane, as opposed to the cruelty prevalent in his own time.

According to Dr. Samuel M. Dodek of the George Washington University School of Medicine, writing in the *Journal of the District of Columbia Medical Society,* Shakespeare "had enough knowledge of medicine to rate hanging out his shingle as an Elizabethan M.D." While Sir William Harvey is credited with discovering the circulation of the blood, which he described in 1619, he was anticipated by Shakespeare in *Hamlet* (I, v, 65).[3] Before the discoveries of the early 19th century, doctors had referred to the process of metabolism "with vague theories of 'innate heat' and 'vital spirits.'" If they had looked at *Coriolanus* I, i, 134, Dr. Dodek says, they would have found "startling, significant [statements] . . . regarding digestion and nutrition."

Dr. Frank N. Miller, Jr., of the same faculty, who conducts a seminar on Shakespeare for medical students, has written a paper in which he speaks of "a dazzling array of over fourteen hundred medical references in Shakespeare's dramas and poems." He continues:

> As with almost every other aspect of Elizabethan life, Shakespeare had a remarkably thorough knowledge of Renaissance medicine. . . . The physician Cerimon is one of the proofs that Shakespeare wrote at least the last three acts of *Pericles, Prince of Tyre*. It is unlikely that such a learned and articulate character could have been created by any of Shakespeare's contemporaries. . . . Medical images . . . heighten the atmosphere of the plays, especially the tragedies. *Hamlet, Troilus and Cressida, Othello, King Lear, Timon of Athens, Macbeth* and *Coriolanus* are suffused with pathology. The references to disease, whether they are related to studies of disturbed states of mind or disordered political conditions, are vivid and telling.

Dr. Walter E. Vest of Huntington, West Virginia, speaking at the International Gerontological Society's second congress on the problems of aging, said that Shakespeare understood full well both the physiological and pathological characteristics of senescence and quoted abundantly from his works to make his point. He considered that Shakespeare's knowledge of physiology was greater than that of the physicians of his day.

"Shakespeare was the greatest analyst of all," according to Dr. Daniel E. Schneider, author of *The Psychoanalyst and the Artist* and one of five psychologists lecturing on Shakespeare at Columbia University. As for who Shakespeare was, he judged that "the so-called authentic Shakespeare could not possibly have written the plays. It seems to me that he was a front-man for somebody else."

[3] Michael Servetus (the Spaniard Miguel Serveto) had discovered that some of the blood circulates through the lungs and had published his discovery in 1546.

There is a plentiful literature on medical knowledge in Shakespeare. The poet-dramatist's scientific insights were not confined to physiology and pathology, however.

As late as the middle of the 19th century, the leading American geologists, one the founder of the Rensselaer Institute, the other the first president of the American Association for the Advancement of Science, were still bound by the biblical version of the definitive creation of the earth. Shakespeare, 350 years earlier, was conceiving in modern terms of geological processes that could change the face of the planet:

> O God! that one might read the book of fate,
> And see the revolution of the times
> Make mountains level, and the continent
> Weary of solid firmness, melt itself
> Into the sea!

A century before Sir Isaac Newton was formulating the law of gravitation, locating the point of mutual attraction between bodies at their center, Shakespeare was tossing off a reference to the same principle:

> Time, force, and death,
> Do to this body what extremes you can,
> But the strong base and building of my love
> Is as the very center of the earth,
> Drawing all things to it.

Even to Georg Brandes we have "proof that several of the men whose society Shakespeare frequented were among the most highly-developed intellects of the period," while his "general understanding of these questions bears witness to his high culture."[4]

Shakespeare and Nature

A special interest of mine is the world of nature, particularly birds. In that world, flowers probably came first with Shakespeare. No one who knows him at all can have missed his love for them. Passages in which they move him to exquisite lyricism, however, beginning with "I know a bank where on the wild thyme grows," are so well known that the point need not be proved. "A devoted gardener," Trevor-Roper calls him: "only Francis Bacon compares with him." Schoenbaum writes that "the brilliantly colored garden" in Shakespeare's works, "in which flowers, wild and cultivated, flourish

---

[4] Dr. Brandes, to whom any question of the Stratford man's authorship is "unrivalled in its ineptitude," does accuse Shakespeare of having "never got beyond the Ptolemaic system," but the very passage in *Troilus and Cressida* (I, iii, 90–94) on which he bases the charge clearly proves the contrary. While referring to the "glorious" sun as a planet, probably for the sake of the meter, Shakespeare, manifestly a Copernican, sees it at the center of the solar system, "enthron'd . . . amid the other," to which it issues "the commandment of a king."

side by side, . . . comprises over 150 varieties, according to one tabulation." Several books have been written on his flora.[5]

James E. Harting, an ornithologist of the past century, was able to write a book on *The Birds of Shakespeare*, in which he cited references to about sixty kinds. Many are to birds as they appear in legend and literature, but some show that his observation of those in the field was, Trevor-Roper observes, "intimate and minute" — such as in his "ouzel-cock [male black-bird], so black of hue, With orange-tawny bill," and Hamlet's: "This lapwing runs away with the shell on his head." Anyone who has noticed that evidence of young lapwings' activity almost from the moment of hatching, or thinks to have Hero say in *Much Ado*

> For look where Beatrice, like a lapwing, runs
> Close by the ground, to hear our confidence. . . .

must have been one who missed little in the countryside.

The Fool epitomizes King Lear's plight in the lines:

> The hedge-sparrow fed the cuckoo so long
> That it had its head bitten off by its young.

The cuckoo lays its eggs in the nests of many species, but its favorite victim is the hedge-sparrow.

It would be hard to improve on Shakespeare's "ribbald crows" or his lines:

> As wild geese that the creeping fowler eye,
> Or russet-pated choughs, many in sort,
> Rising and cawing at gun's report,
> Sever themselves and madly sweep the sky.

(I grant that I am a little unclear, however, as to what the poet had in mind by "russet-pated," choughs being black.)

Shakespeare's observations of nature could take notice of details, as in "the cold brook, candied with ice," and Queen Gertrude's mention of the willow "that shows his hoar leaves in the glassy stream," which reminds us that it is the greyish underside of the leaves that would be reflected from below. He could also be evocative of nature on a grand scale, as when Horatio exclaims,

> But, look, the morn in russet mantle clad,
> Walks o'er the dew of yon high eastern hill,

and we are reminded of how in *Richard the Second* the sun

> . . . fires the proud tops of the eastern pines

---

[5] In *Shakespeare's Flowers* by Jessica Kerr (New York: Crowell, 1969), the subjects are beautifully rendered in color by Anne Ophelia Dowden, more than compensating for the author's Stratfordian interpretations. *The Shakespeare Garden* (New York: Century, 1922) by Esther Singleton, one of the first American Oxfordians, contains a much more extensive text and is illustrated with period prints.

and then of Antonio's symbol of futility in *The Merchant*:

> You may as well forbid the mountain pines
> To wag their high tops, and to make no noise
> When they are fretted with the gusts of heaven,

(one of Shakespeare's double negatives). Trees appear on mountain-tops in several of the plays, strengthening belief that Shakespeare had seen eminences higher than the Cotswolds, even

> . . . far off mountains turnèd into clouds.

Indeed he tells us, speaking in the *Sonnets* as himself,

> Full many a glorious morning have I seen
> Flatter the mountain-tops with sovereign eye.

"His love and understanding of the country are extraordinary; far deeper than that of any other poet, even in England," Trevor-Roper says. But it goes beyond that: "Indeed, Shakespeare sees mankind almost as part of nature: sometimes basking in a delightful, smiling Nature; sometimes caught up in a fierce, cruel, inexorable, insatiable Nature."

To Gilbert Highet it is "quite obvious" that the plays of Shakespeare — "a comparatively ill-educated man" — were the work of "someone . . . without the power of organized, abstract thinking." (One can imagine how widely read the dramatist would be today had he devoted his powers to abstract thinking.) More perceptively, Samuel Johnson found that from the works of Shakespeare "may be collected a system of civil and economical prudence." The dramatist could also epitomize a conception of nature's wholeness that mankind would be a dozen generations in catching up with. We have heard Jaques in *As You Like It* defend the rights of animals as tenants of their "native dwelling place," in which men when they "kill them up" are "mere usurpers, tyrants and what's worse." Not until the middle of the 20th century would the progress of scientific understanding bring society to the point of comprehending, which is certainly not to say accepting, an idea so enlightened and to grasping the ecological verities of Friar Laurence's soliloquy in *Romeo and Juliet*:

> O' mickle is the powerful grace that lies
> In herbs, plants, stones, and their true qualities:
> For nought so vile that on the earth doth live
> But to the earth some special good doth give,
> Nor aught so good but strain'd from that fair use
> Revolts from true birth, stumbling on abuse.[6]

[6] The beginning of this remarkable poem, I cannot help mentioning, could serve as the opening stanza of Edward Fitzgerald's *Rubaiyat of Omar Khayyám*:

> The grey-ey'd morn smiles on the frowning night,
> Chequering the eastern clouds with streaks of light,
> And flecked darkness like a drunkard reels
> From forth day's path and Titan's fiery wheels.

Shakespeare and Music

As much as anything, I think Shakespeare loved and understood music. Lorenzo in *The Merchant* surely speaks the author's mind:

> the poet
> Did feign that Orpheus drew trees, stones, and floods;
> Since naught so stockish, hard, and full of rage,
> But music for the time doth change his nature.
> The man that hath no music in himself,
> Nor is not mov'd with concord of sweet sounds,
> Is fit for treasons, stratagems, and spoils;
> The motions of his spirit are dull as night . . .
> Let no such man be trusted.

That the poet-dramatist was so moved himself is well attested in what he wrote. "Shakespeare's plays have some 500 passages dealing with music," Harold C. Schonberg, music critic, remarks in the *New York Times*: "Hundreds of studies about Shakespeare and music have been written." He is said to have employed 100 musical terms. As in other categories of knowledge, Shakespeare's music is so much a part of him that its imagery stands ready to prompt him. Thus Hamlet says bitingly to Guildenstern, "You would seem to know my stops: . . . you would sound me from my lowest note to the top of my compass." So also Iago reveals to us his fell designs upon Othello in a musical term:

> O! you are well tun'd now,
> But I'll set down the pegs that make this music,
> As honest as I am.

It is unlikely that Iago, whose affections, if anyone's ever were, were dark as Erebus, played an instrument — or that the dramatist did not.

Shakespeare's Experience of War and the Sea

We might wonder if the dramatist had not known the heady stimulant of a military campaign, romanticized in retrospect, when the stricken Othello puts his command forever behind him:

> Farewell the plumed troop and the big wars
> That make ambition virtue! O, farewell!
> Farewell the neighing steed, and the shrill trump,
> The spirit-stirring drum, the ear-piercing fife,
> The royal banner, and all quality,
> Pride, pomp, and circumstance of glorious war!
> And, O you mortal engines, whose rude throats
> The immortal Jove's dread clamours counterfeit,
> Farewell!

One reason for our suspicion is that Othello, commissioned by the Republic of Venice, would not have fought under a "royal banner"; the author would have. We should be more apt to credit Shakespeare with military experience when he lets escape him such a simile as

> Like powder in a skilless soldier's flask,
> To set a-fire thine own ignorance.

It may be germane to quote what Ernest Hemingway wrote in bringing out the anthology *Men at War* in 1942 to help men bear the shock of combat. He was recalling a time when he had been severely wounded in action.

> I was very ignorant at nineteen and had read little and I remember the sudden happiness and feeling of having a permanent protecting talisman which a young British officer I met when in the hospital first wrote out for me, so that I could remember them, these lines:
> "By my troth, I care not: a man can die but once; we owe God a death . . . and let it go which way it will, he that dies this year is quit for the next."
> That is probably the best thing that is written in this book and, with nothing else, a man can get along all right on that.

If Hemingway, with his knowledge of war, thought that those lines by a simple youngster being pressed into military service in *Henry the Fourth, Part Two*, were the best ever spoken to strengthen a soldier's nerve, so too Joseph Conrad felt that the ultimate characterization for that remorseless element with which he contested through his many years before the mast was in Shakespeare's apostrophization of Iago, as "more fell than anguish, hunger or the sea." Lieutenant-Commander A. F. Falconer, V.R.D., M.A., R.N.R., in his *Shakespeare and the Sea*, says "that Shakespeare, on coming to London to take up his new career as a dramatist, brought with him knowledge of the sea and the Navy can be seen from his earliest plays." Reviewing the book, which he praises for its "objectivity, and sensibility," Vice Admiral Sir Ian L. M. McGeoch, K.C.B., D.S.O., D.S.C., writes:

> How illuminating, for example, is commentary such as that which Professor Falconer makes on Sonnet 16:
>> It is the star to every wandering bark,
>> Whose worth's unknown, although his height be ta'en.
>
> He reminds us that the Pole Star enables the navigator to determine his latitude or "height" as well as to check his course. . . .
> Professor Falconer points out that whereas many educated Elizabethans understood the art of navigation . . . only those who actually served at sea could acquire a profound knowledge of the practice of seamanship and the correct meaning and use of the terms proper to the working of ships. That Shakespeare possessed such a profound knowledge is instanced many times. An example which interested me particularly, as showing inspired accuracy of allusion, seasoned with wit, is quoted by Professor Falconer from *King John* IV.2.23:
>> And like a shifted wind unto a sail,
>> It makes the course of thoughts to fetch about.

> Tacking is to bring a ship's head to lie the other way. True. And "to fetch about" is synonymous with "to tack"; but subtler still is the reference to "course," which is not only the direction in which a ship is heading, but also the name given to the principal sail on any mast of a square-rigged ship.

Exposed to the sea, a receptive imagination, especially one responsive to echoes of the infinite, is bound to take a deep impress; and that Shakespeare's was haunted by the sea became evident to me as I reread his works. It is of "the wet sea-boy" that the sleepless Henry IV thinks: even to him "upon the high and giddy mast" repose is given. To bring insecurity home, Richard III calls up

> a drunken sailor on a mast;
> Ready with every nod to tumble down
> Into the fatal bowels of the deep

For him were

> . . . the clouds that lour'd upon our house
> In the deep bosom of the ocean buried.

The ocean's disquieting depths had an evidently fixed hold upon Shakespeare's mind. Florizel in *A Winter's Tale* will not break his oath for all

> . . . the profound sea hides
> In unknown fathoms.

Providence

> Knows almost every grain of Plutus' gold,
> Finds bottom in the uncomprehensive deeps.

A campaign in France, Henry V is told, will

> . . . make your chronicle as rich with praise
> As is the owse and bottom of the sea
> With sunken wrack and sumless treasuries.

Hotspur would even

> . . . dive into the bottom of the deep,
> Where fathom-line could never touch the ground,
> And pluck up drowned honour by the locks.

At the end, Ariel is singing of the eerie sea-changes in a corpse where at

> Full fathom five thy father lies.

"Fathom" occurs sixteen times in the plays.

To Shakespeare, to be insatiable was to be "as hungry as the sea," as "the never-surfeited sea." Madness was "as the sea and wind, when both contend which is the mightier," and he knew "it boots not to resist both wind and tide." To be desiccated (Jacques says it of Touchstone's brain) is to be "as dry as the remainder biscuit / After a voyage." What clinches it for me, coming on top of everything else, is having Cleopatra say of Antony:

> His delights
> Were dolphin-like, they showed his back above
> The elements they liv'd in.

I could understand how a writer telling us of an ocean voyage would bring in dolphins for verisimilitude even if he had never been afloat, but should be much surprised if he happened to think of dolphins in a connection as remote from the sea as a lover's delights unless after watching them from shipboard and being taken by their playfulness.

Orthodoxy on the Hook

"Shakespeare's marine contacts are strange and worth investigation," Ivor Brown acknowledges, then seizes the nettle: "My own conviction is that Shakespeare certainly did have voyages." Other Stratfordians receive his embarrassing deposition in silence.

The late Alfred B. Harbage, Harvard's contribution to latter-day Shakespearean studies, has a double-barrelled solution to the problem in the dramatist's evident wide and intimate familiarity with matters outside the Stratfordian's range. With one discharge, which we have already recorded, he gives us a Shakespeare who tricks us with a more than routine skill at faking knowledge. With the other, we have an *elevatio ad absurdum* (if I may call it that) of specialists' testimony as to the knowledge Shakespeare possessed. By means of this chicane, Professor Harbage is able to ignore what those specialists have actually brought out. Thus, "The enthusiastic naturalist has . . . created a god in his own image. So with the various musicians, sailors, soldiers, doctors, and others, especially lawyers, who have . . . fostered the idea that Shakespeare not only knew and loved music, as he truly did, but could take down and reassemble a spinet (if he did not invent the instrument), as well as navigate a ship, command an army, and perform a frontal lobotomy, while his exhaustive knowledge of the law might have disrupted even the capacious brain of the Lord Chief Justice." Physicians who have attested to Shakespeare's remarkable insights respecting pathology and human physiology and psychology are, says Harbage, to be "praised for their restraint, never having claimed that their revered Renaissance predecessor, Dr. William Harvey, was the true author of the plays even though the characters seem to have circulating blood." Having thus, with professorial wit, disposed of the medical witnesses for a second time, the professor rather strangely allows candor to get the better of him, as we saw him do before. He quotes the "impressive" physician who understood the ailing Lear's needs:

> Our foster nurse of nature is repose,
> The which he lacks. That to provoke in him
> Are many simples operative, whose power
> Will close the eyes of anguish.

"He prescribed," says Harbage, "nothing further than a sedative, fresh garments, music, and, wisest remedy of all, the attendance of Cordelia at his side. The treatment deserved its success." He contrasts this enlightened, quite modern professional approach with medicine as typically practiced in Shakespeare's day, drawing upon the case-book of Shakspere's son-in-law. A seventy-year-old whom Dr. Hall treated was "oppressed with Melancholy, and a Feaver with extraordinary heat." The doctor applied "Radishes sliced besprinkled with Vinegar and Salt" to the soles of the patient's feet" to draw back the "Vapours," which caused "starting and fear." "This," says Professor Harbage, "was his mildest prescription. Leeches were applied, and enemas, physics, and emetics administered, all composed of frightening ingredients," one being an "Emetick Infusion" containing "oxymel of Squils."

To observe how Dr. McManaway disposes of the evidence of Shakespeare's breadth of experience is to be sufficiently instructed in the standards of orthodox Shakespearean scholarship. The late Folger curator concedes that "Several of Shakespeare's plays . . . appear to suggest firsthand observation of foreign places and customs," Thus "Bacon or the Earl of Derby might be proposed as the authors of *Love's Labour's Lost*," which "shows more than casual familiarity with French names, . . . because of their travels in France." Similarly, there are "those who would assign *Hamlet*," in which "some knowledge of Elsinore is supposed to be revealed," to the "Earl of Rutland [who] had an embassage to Denmark." Also "a reputed journey to Italy by the Earl of Southampton encourages some writers to think he wrote *The Two Gentlemen of Verona*," which "has unusual geographic details." He proceeds: "Plays have been attributed on similar grounds to the Earl of Essex, Sir Walter Raleigh and others." However, says Dr. McManaway, if "evidence could be found to support any or all of these various ascriptions, the results would be chaotic, for it would be necessary to believe that a coterie composed of these and perhaps other [other than the "others" already mentioned?] people wrote the plays."

We need not ask why evidence to support *one* of these ascriptions would require a *coterie* of authors; in writing this paragraph, Dr. McManaway was doubtless a bit rattled over its duplicity. Why Southampton as the proposed author of *Two Gentlemen*? There is no evidence of his ever having been away from England apart from a brief flight to Dieppe, before it was enacted in December 1594, when he was only twenty-one — Dr. McManaway having endowed him with that previous trip to Italy as he endowed the poet Spenser with one or two extra wives — and no one I have ever heard of has been so irrational as to suggest that he had written it. But, as Dr. McManaway is well aware, Edward de Vere had traveled in Italy.

The case for de Vere as Shakespeare poses *the* great threat to orthodoxy, however, and Dr. McManaway cannot risk mentioning him. Honesty is a slippery slope, and the dissembler who steps on it may not be able to scramble back to safety. De Vere would have been acquainted with those "geographical details" of Verona and with "French names" and would have had "some knowledge of Elsinore." If these facts were not known at the Folger Library when it published Dr. McManaway's *The Authorship of Shakespeare* in 1962, they were known directly afterward when the many sleights-of-hand practiced in the booklet were called to the attention of the trustees of the Library. But the Library continued to sell the booklet, unaltered, and, as of the time this book went to press, still was selling it.

As Shakespeare, de Vere requires no "coterie" to have written the plays and poems, no concatenation of miracles, ascribed to "genius," to explain their contents, no wilful disregard of the point of view from which they are written. So far as I know, no one, whatever his beliefs as to the authorship, has been able to deny that de Vere's origins, background, training, opportunities, and experience were just what we have deduced the dramatist's to have been. That does not of course — even if we accept all the inferences we have drawn from Shakespeare's works as correct — make de Vere the dramatist. It goes without saying that there are other criteria that anyone put forward as the author must satisfy. But by those we have established so far, de Vere is the only one of the candidates still in the running, and he is impressively so. If he should turn out to be disqualified on some count we should have to find another Elizabethan heretofore unmentioned — and I do not believe or know anyone else who believes that a person so obscure as to have escaped all scrutiny could have been the author — or go back over our criteria to find where we may have gone astray; that, I should construe to be an unpromising enterprise. I know of no bar to de Vere's authorship lying in wait for us, and I am acquainted with the farthest-reaching efforts of its opponents to erect one; if I did know of one I should not be writing this book.

17

"As the Very True Sonnet Is. . . ."

In his series of 154 sonnets, Shakespeare has written a first-person account of his relations over an unstated period of years with at least two persons. One of these is a young man of beauty and fair complexion, his "better angel," whom he loves to the point of self-abnegation and tries at the outset to persuade to take a wife in order to perpetuate himself. The other is his "worser spirit a woman colour'd ill," which is to say dark, whom he is helplessly infatuated with and helplessly watches lure the youth away from him. On so much and on little else is there general agreement. To some students of Shakespeare the implications of the Sonnets are so distressing and so difficult to reconcile with their picture of the dramatist that they pronounce the collection a mere literary exercise. We see, however, why few persons of human understanding will doubt that the poems are genuinely self-revelatory. As such, and as the dramatist's only explicitly autobiographical writing, they call, surely, for our best efforts to decipher the situation and the story of which they drop continual hints and of which our predecessors have adduced almost as many versions as they themselves have numbered. Why is there such an ardent interest on the poet's part in having the youth beget progeny? Why does he address him in terms normally reserved to a man's devotion to a woman? What in fact is their relationship? What kind of young man is he? Who is he? How is the strong evidence of his identity to be squared with the printer's dedication of the Sonnets to "Mr. W. H."? When were the Sonnets written? How is it that the poet combines idolatry of the young man with harsh censure of his weaknesses? What do we learn of the poet's age? station? who he is? Why should he anticipate oblivion as his lot? Looking for answers in what the author discloses, one of us has as much chance as another to find the right ones.

We come now to the most tantalizing and provocative, most hauntingly beautiful, most eloquent, most disquieting confession in English poetry or by a master of English literature in any form. It is a testament as unnervingly outspoken as it is consistently enigmatic: "The greatest puzzle in the history of English literature," A. L. Rowse calls it. "This is 'Shake-speares Sonnets,' to give it the name under which it was published."

Nothing else in Shakespeare, except the comprehensive question of the poet's identity, has given rise to such conflict of views and interpretations as his *Sonnets*. The collection is a forest of secret passages that generations of literary explorers have undertaken to chart for elucidation of its mysteries, only to emerge from its shadowy mazes sometimes years later — if, really, at all — with a look of confusion about the eyes belying the confidence in the reports, scarcely two of which are alike. "In this field," Louis Auchincloss says, "nobody, let alone angels, fears to tread." And, he asks, "Who can blame them? Here are 154 Sonnets of the greatest English poet, possibly the greatest literary figure in history, and they constitute the only hint or fragment of an autobiography that we have. . . . I think that the man who does not try to probe the sonnets for traces of the poet's heart or personality is a critic austere to the point of inhumanity." One would think, indeed, that if this is the poet's only explicit autobiography, as it is, one would look to it not alone for traces of his heart and personality but for something of his life's story — as indeed Mr. Auchincloss does, unconcerned for the dire perils lying in wait in those woods for Stratfordians.

There are, however, others in the orthodox camp who, having had a glimpse of the shapes within, declare that the forest contains nothing — nothing, that is, that *counts* — and confine themselves to its exterior glories. As Samuel Schoenbaum reports, "Bolton Corney expressed a popular view when, in a privately printed pamphlet on *The Sonnets of William Shakespeare* (1862), he concluded that 'they are, with very slight exceptions, mere *poetical* exercises.'" At this stage, however, it was not the threat to the conventional view of the authorship that caused the *Sonnets* to be characterized as artifices; that view was not yet so much on the defensive. It was the disturbing tendencies that, when taken as genuine confession, the *Sonnets* seem to expose in the author. But any reason for denying them standing as self-revelation collided with a question put by Edward Dowden: "Why did not Shakespeare publish them, if they were a mere work of art, as he had published his narrative poems? It would have been easy, in a few words of prose or verse, to have explained that the story was not real but imagined, if such was indeed the case." Though Stratfordians tell us, however, that it was on his poetry (in which the *Sonnets* stand incomparably supreme) that he staked his claim to lasting fame, he did not publish them.

Dr. Dowden could also have observed that a poet telling a fictitious story of love in a sonnet sequence would surely write of more conventional or acceptable affections and not of self-abasement to passionate attachments that would embarrass most of posterity. As intelligent and reasonable a critic as Henry Hallam (whose son's premature death Tennyson mourned in *In Memoriam A. H. H.*) could write of the *Sonnets*, "It is impossible not to wish that Shakespeare had never written them."

The effort to escape from the *Sonnets'* apparent implications by assigning them to pure invention runs into one obstacle above all. Transparently they are real, heartfelt in every line, sincere to the point of desperation and exaltation. Literary critics who cannot hear that sincerity in the poet's voice are surely in the wrong business. Wordsworth was saying no more than what must be evident when he wrote: "Scorn not the sonnet. . . . With this same key Shakespeare unlocked his heart" — which is not to deny that Browning may have had a point in commenting, "If so, the less Shakespeare he." Or, for that matter, that Swinburne may have had one in his rejoinder to that: "No whit the less Shakespeare but undoubtedly the less like Robert Browning." Whichever we agree with, we can hardly dispute Carlyle's judgment in *The Hero as Poet*: "Doubt it not, he had his own sorrows: those Sonnets of his will testify expressly in what deep waters he had waded, and swum struggling for his life." Unquestionably Stratfordian though he was, Sir Walter Raleigh (the one who died in 1922) put the matter decisively:

> To say that they do not "express his own feelings in his own person" is as much as to say that they are not sincere. And every lover of poetry who has once read the *Sonnets* knows this to be untrue. It is not chiefly their skill that takes us captive, but the intensity of their quiet personal appeal. . . . These are not self-contained poems, like Daniel's sonnet on Sleep or Sidney's sonnet on the Moon; they are a commentary on certain implied events. . . . The greater poets — Sidney, Spenser, Drayton — reflect in their sonnets the events of their own history. Shakespeare's sonnets are more intense than these; and less explicable, if they be deprived of all background and occasion in fact. . . . The situations shadowed are unlike the conventional situations described by the tribe of sonneteers, as the hard-fought issues of a law-court are unlike the formal debates of the Courts of Love. Some of them are strange, wild, and sordid in their nature, themes not chosen by poetry, but choosing it, and making their mark on it by the force of their reality.

Yet Sir Sidney Lee and Joseph Quincy Adams could describe the *Sonnets* as, in the main, literary exercises and still be taken as supreme Shakespearean authorities on their respective sides of the ocean![1] Today's equivalent view is urged by George Sampson, who in *The Concise Cambridge History of English Literature* (1961), shows how far defense of doctrine can go:

> That Shakespeare (like other men) had disturbing emotional experiences which he projected into poems and plays may be taken as possible: that the sonnets describe details of these experiences can be dismissed as impossible. And, upon any interpretation, the story comes to very little and tells us next to nothing.

Similarly, Marchette Chute finds that "Very little can actually be said about the Sonnets," and in her so-called biography of Shakespeare relegates consideration of them to the appendix! Gerald Eades Bentley, in his *Shakespeare: A Biographical Handbook*, has it that "Some of the sonnets appear to refer to events that may be either real or fictitious, and many accounts have been published, usually wildly imaginative, in attempts to fit these events into the life of Shakespeare," and can make no deductions from them about the author: none whatever.

---

[1] To the former "the autobiographic element" in the *Sonnets*, "although it may not be dismissed altogether," is of "slender proportions," while the latter sees the *Sonnets* as representing essentially "a trial of skill with his [Shakespeare's] fellow poets" conforming to "certain conventions" and "well-worn stock themes."

Shakespeare's *Sonnets* first come to our attention in a reference by Francis Meres in 1598 to "his sugared Sonnets among his private friends." A year later W. Jaggard, having somehow got hold of two of the most intimately self-revelatory (numbers 138 and 144), used them in the leading place in a collection of poems he attributed to "W. Shakespeare" and called *The Passionate Pilgrim*. No further exposure of the *Sonnets* was recorded for ten years. Then, in 1609, the entire collection as we know it was brought out by Thomas Thorpe, who, Sir Sidney Lee tells us, had "through thirty years' experience of the book trade held his own with difficulty in its humblest ranks." How he obtained a copy, nobody knows. As G. E. Bentley observes, "Shakespeare evidently had nothing to do with the printing of Thorpe's volume, for he wrote no dedication, as he had for his two previous nondramatic publications, and the book has many misprints so obvious that not even a competent proofreader, much less the author, could have missed them all." That the author had no hand in it is hardly to be wondered at since, as we saw in Chapter 12, the dedication assuredly tells us that he is dead; and in that it was supplied by the publisher, not by the author, it gives us further reason for believing so.

Probably no other feature of the *Sonnets* has given rise to so much conjecture and controversy as the identity of the dedicatee, whose initials alone we are vouchsafed. The dedication is as shown in the facsimile of the original on the opposite page.

For a brief description of the poetical sequence that follows I cannot improve on Edward Dowden's:

> The *Sonnets* consist in the main of two series. If we accept the original order of the poems . . . the first series, addressed to a young man of great beauty and apparently of high station, includes the Sonnets from 1 to 125, and closes with an envoy, 126, consisting of six couplets. . . . The second series, the order of which seems somewhat confused, runs from 127 to 152; the poems are either addressed to a woman or suggested by the relations of the writer with her. The entire collection closes with two sonnets — 153 and 154 — which deal with the same theme, the fire of Cupid's brand, and it was noticed by Hertzberg that these are variations on a Greek epigram by Marianus, found in the *Palatine Anthology*, which had been translated into Latin.

The poet himself gives us the argument of the entire sequence in number 144, which also conveys the unpleasant taste recurrent in the sequence, the extravagance of naked emotion to which the poet's twin but opposing obsessions at times drive him, and the frequent obscurity of what he is expressing:

> Two loves I have of comfort and despair,   144
> Which like two spirits do suggest me still;
> The better angel is a man right fair,
> The worser spirit a woman colour'd ill.

TO.THE.ONLIE.BEGETTER.OF.
THESE.INSVING.SONNETS.
M^r. W. H. ALL.HAPPINESSE.
AND.THAT.ETERNITIE.
PROMISED.

BY.

OVR.EVER-LIVING.POET.

WISHETH.

THE.WELL-WISHING.
ADVENTVRER.IN.
SETTING.
FORTH.

T. T.

Dedication page of "Shake-speares Sonnets"

To win me soon to hell, my female evil
Tempteth by better angel from my side,
And would corrupt my saint to be a devil,
Wooing his purity with her foul pride.
And whether that my angel be turn'd fiend,
Suspect I may, yet not directly tell,
But being both from me, both to each friend,
I guess one angel in another's hell:
    Yet this shall I ne'er know, but live in doubt,
    Till my bad angel fire my good one out.

Louis Auchincloss, in his *Motiveless Malignity*, entitles his chapter on the subject "The Sonnets — A Thousandth Theory." I shall not emulate Schéhérazade and formulate a one thousand and first. Rather I shall confine myself to what seems to be evident and others have discerned and will help us define the author.

Of the first 125 sonnets, all concerned with the "better angel," the "Man right fair," comprising almost five-sixths of the whole, more than a hundred are addressed to him directly, in the second person. The first seventeen have all one burden. They urge him to marry that he may have issue and

> Make thee another self, . . .   10
> . . . .
> That beauty still may live in thine or thee.

If he fails in this

> The world will be thy widow and still weep   9
> That thou no form of thee hast left behind.

All seventeen ring the changes upon the theme of his taking a wife. This, by the way, would seem to erect an obstacle at the start to those who, finding much justification for their view in the language in which the poet addresses his better angel, maintain that his interest in the young man was an unnatural one, as it used to be called. But along with the poet's concern that he beget his likeness, other themes are sounded in this initial series that will be developed in what is to come. We learn of the youth's extraordinary attractiveness:

> If I could write the beauty of your eyes   17
> And in fresh numbers number all your graces,
> The age to come would say 'This poet lies:
> Such heavenly touches ne'er touch'd earthly faces.'

Already in those lines we learn of the poet's confidence that his verse will be read in the long future. In another pair we discover that the young man's conquests are wide and that he is inclined to selfishness:

> Grant, if thou wilt, thou are belov'd of many,   10
> But that thou none lov'st is most evident.

Already, too, the knell of the sequence's underlying theme is heard — what Mark Van Doren calls "The great single subject of the sonnets": "Time, swift-footed, terrible Time that writes death on faces, roots out the work of masonry, fades roses, brings winter after spring, and makes in general the music to which all the world marches groaning to its end."

> But wherefore do not you a mightier way   16
> Make way upon this bloody tyrant Time?
> And fortify yourself in your decay
> With means more blessed than my barren rime?

After Sonnet 17, nothing more is heard of the youth's marrying and immortalizing his beauty in an heir. And whereas, as we just saw, the poet in Sonnet 16 urges the youth to defeat Time by reproducing himself, from now on it is the poet's verse — what he has just called his "barren rime" and will now speak of as his "eternal lines" — that is going to immortalize that beauty. This is announced immediately upon abandonment of his marriage-theme, in Sonnet 18 (the famous one beginning "Shall I compare thee to a summer's day?"):

> But thy eternal summer shall not fade,   18
> . . . .
>   So long as men can breathe or eyes can see,
> So long lives this, and this gives life to thee.

What follows through 126 is a reflection in the poet's thoughts and in his address to the fair youth of the ups and downs of their relationship, of his exaltation and heartache, or mutual reproaches, or separation and reunion, of a "hell" jointly suffered, of the threat to their bond from the rivalry for the youth's favor from another poet and, much more dangerously, from a woman of wiles who, it seems, prevails with the "sweet boy." Here I should say that there are keen students of Shakespeare on both sides of the authorship controversy who believe that more than one young man is involved in the *Sonnets* — for example, Louis Auchincloss among Stratfordians, Louis P. Bénézet, evidently with Mr. Looney as a convert, among Oxfordians. Though fully aware of my presumption, I must say I cannot see it. The manner in which the recipient of the poet's love is invoked seems to me consistent throughout, as I believe it does to the majority of readers, who also, I think, would find it hard to understand how the author could profess such dedication to, not to say infatuation with, two youths — both, incidentally, of surpassing beauty, both widely courted, both to be known through the poet's verse in an age or ages to come.

Edward Dowden says, "The Sonnets shadow forth a story, real or imaginary, a parallel for which has not been found in the whole range of English sonnet-literature" — and certainly not sonnet-literature alone. In none of my other reading does one man speak of another in such terms. In Sonnet 10 — if I may fill out in italics a line I quoted above with an ellipsis — the youth is entreated to

> Make thee another self *for love of me.*   10

Proceeding, we hear the youth cautioned:

> Presume not on thy heart when mine is slain,   22
> Thou gav'st me thine not to give back again.

All through the sequence the unity of poet and young friend is stressed:

> Then happy I, that love and am belov'd,   25
> Where I may not remove nor be remov'd.

> . . . Thou art all the better part of me . . .   39

> . . . Here's the joy; my friend and I are one.   42

My spirit is thine, the better part of me.   74

. . . Thou, being mine, mine is thy good report   96

As easy might I from myself depart   109
As from my soul, which in thy breast doth lie:
That is my home of love . . .

                              . . . Thou mine, I thine.   108

His love of the youth hardly stops short of worship and self-effacement:

Be thou the tenth Muse, ten times more in worth   38
Than those old nine which rimers invocate.

Whilst I, my sovereign, watch the clock for you.   57

Lord of my love, to whom in vassalage   26
Thy merit hath my duty strongly knit.

Being your slave, what should I do but tend   57
Upon the hours and times of your desire?

There is almost no limit to the credit he gives his "sovereign":

                              . . . That which I compile.   78
                              . . . is thine, and born of thee.   78

To enhance the tribute of praise there is a kind of self-deprecation that,
coming from myriad-minded Shakespeare, makes us rub our eyes indeed:

But thou art all my art, and dost advance   78
As high as learning my rude ignorance.

The attachment, it seems, is not all on one side, for the poet proves capable
of neglecting his better angel and the latter of resenting it:

Accuse me thus: that I have scanted all   117
Wherein I should your great deserts repay.

He has

                    . . . hoisted sail to all the winds
Which should transport me farthest from your sight.

But he asks that the youth

Bring me within the level of your frown,
But shoot not at me in your waken'd hate;
   Since my appeal says I did strive to prove
   The constancy and virtue of your love.

The excuse does not sound very convincing. The reality of the poet's suffering
can hardly be mistaken, however, when two sonnets later, he finds himself
losing what he had thought to win and reflects on

What wretched errors hath my heart committed   119
Whilst it hath thought itself so blessed never!

He cries

> What potions have I drunk of Siren tears,   119
> Distill'd from limbecks foul as hell within.
>   . . . .
> How have mine eyes out of their spheres been fitted,
> In the distraction of this maddening fever!

But as a "benefit of ill" he is enabled to "find true" that

> . . . ruined love, when it is built anew,
> Grows fairer than at first, more strong, far greater.

The intensity of emotion between the two makes searing ordeals of their fallings-out, for one as for the other — if, indeed, it is the young man who figures in these two sonnets.

> For if you were by my unkindness shaken,   120
> As I by yours, you've passed a hell of time.
>   . . . .
> O! that our night of woe might have remember'd
> My deepest sense, how hard true sorrow hits.

I am reminded of the characterization of the poet-dramatist in the publicity for the Time Inc. "Reading Program." Promoting Ivor Brown's *Shakespeare*, the Programmers announce that "Here is Shakespeare for the millions who quote him but do not know what kind of a man he was — the affable, sociable, fastidious, thrifty man whose name is a household word but whose character is obscure." The author of the *Sonnets*, and of *Hamlet* and *King Lear*: affable, sociable, thrifty! A perfect *maître d'hôtel*.

If the poet-dramatist's character is obscure, the nature of his feelings for the young man who so enthralled him should throw some light upon it. And if we knew the identity of the young man we might have more to go on in assessing those feelings, as well as further evidence of the author's own identity.

As to that, the *Sonnets* are chary of hints. The word "beauty" is repeatedly applied to the youth. He is described as "fair." His mental attainments, we are to believe, do him credit:

> Thou art fair in knowledge as in hue.   82

We are told three times in quick succession that he is "fair, kind and true."

> "Fair, kind and true" is all my argument,   105

Even if we may believe he was all those things, we are not helped much. He was certainly vain, Peter Quennell remarks, and spoiled. When the poet admits he has not written enough in his praise, excusing himself on the grounds that the young man's merits are beyond his reach, the youth evidently agrees that they are, for he has sought out other poets to celebrate him. He has been not only Shakespeare's inspiration, we read, but theirs, teaching "the dumb on high to sing" (78). Indeed, "every alien pen . . . under thee their poetry disperse" (78). Doubtless jealousy exaggerates the extent of the youth's influence. One other poet in particular, however — variously identified, from the allusions to him, as Marlowe or Chapman — appears as a formidable rival. We learn that

> . . . a better spirit doth use your name,   80
> And in the praise thereof spends all his might,
> To make me tongue-tied, speaking of your fame!
> But since your worth — wide as the ocean is, —
> The humble as the proudest sail doth bear,
> My saucy bark, inferior far to his,
> On your broad main doth wilfully appear.

We need not take this disvaluation of his verse very seriously. In the very next sonnet Shakespeare is proclaiming of it that

> Your name from hence immortal life shall have.   81

In Elizabethan days only a nobleman would have had so much made over him by poets. The youthful son of anyone not highly placed would hardly have had a portrait done of him. ("Your painted counterfeit" — 16.) And that the fair youth was noble of birth we have additional evidence when we are told that "All tongues — the voices of souls — give thee [thy] due." (69) and that

> . . . many maiden gardens yet unset,   16
> With virtuous wish would bear you living flowers.

These are the kinds of things that would be said to a prince of the realm.

Speaking of the *Sonnets'* "central mystery," Lawrence Durrell says, "The clues seem to be abundant. The little volume is covered thick in fingerprints." Manifold as they appear to be, they are general and imprecise. They do not tell us who the fair youth was. If, however, we put what they tell us beside what we know from another source, it would seem to me as to many others that they point to our man.

When *Venus and Adonis* came out in 1593, it bore a dedication, which I have quoted, to Henry Wriothesley, the 3rd Earl of Southampton, then not quite twenty years of age. In this the signatory vowed "to take advantage of idle hours, till I have honoured you with some graver labour." In the following year *Lucrece* was published, dedicated to the same young lord in the following words:

> The love I dedicate to your lordship is without end; whereof this pamphlet, without beginning, is but a superfluous moiety. The warrant I have of your honourable disposition, not the worth of my untutored lines, makes it assured of acceptance. What I have done is yours; what I have to do is yours; being part

in all I have, devoted yours. Were my worth greater, my duty would show greater; meantime, as it is, it is bound to your lordship, to whom I wish long life, still lengthened with happiness.

Your lordship's in all duty,

WILLIAM SHAKESPEARE.

Two things about the dedication strike us immediately. A. L. Rowse says of one of them, "Everyone has noticed the warmth — and we may add, the confidence — with which Shakespeare expresses his devotion. I know of no Elizabethan dedication that gives one more sense of intimacy." Professor Rowse also speaks of the poet's "courteous, stately language" and adds "indeed there is a certain lordliness." Indeed there is. As Canon Gerald H. Rendall declares of the dedication, "addressed by a prentice player to the Earl of Southampton, it becomes a rank impertinence which would have stopped all chances of further intercourse."

(Observing that the printing of *Venus and Adonis* — which for explicit eroticism can be exceeded by few literary works openly published and sold in the English-speaking world for the next 350 years — was personally authorized by the Archbishop of Canterbury, George Philip V. Akrigg comments, "We have lost a good story concerning Archbishop Whitgift's license." To see that that story not be lost — the story of a poet who could sail through archiepiscopal sanctions with Venus' candid invitations and address the Earl of Southampton in lordly language [vastly different in its "dignity and restrained expression," Professor Rowse acknowledges, from Nashe's, Markham's, and Florio's servilely effusive dedications to the same young peer] — is why we are engaged in our present efforts.)

What secondly we must notice about the dedication to *Lucrece* is how closely its terms parallel those in which the poet of the *Sonnets* addresses the noble youth. Considering how singular those terms are in the speech of one man to another, we naturally conceive that the object of address in the two cases is the same, unless there be some bar to this conclusion.

I see none. Nothing about Southampton is at odds with the description of the young nobleman. Born in October 1573, young Henry Wriothesley had full opportunity to acquire the "knowledge" in which the *Sonnets* have him excel: attending St. John's College, Cambridge, like Edward de Vere (who was twenty-three years his senior), he graduated, like de Vere, in his fifteenth year and went on to receive an M.A. and to enter the law school of Gray's Inn, in both respects again like de Vere. Before going off to college he had become a royal ward in Lord Burghley's household, as had both de Vere and Robert Devereux, the Earl of Essex, in whose later rebellion Southampton was to be implicated, to his near destruction. He was to acquire an absorbing interest in the drama and to become a munificent patron of poetry, in both again like de Vere.

Henry Wriothesley, 3rd Earl of Southampton

Portrait by an unknown artist, Welbeck
Abbey.

By permission of Lady Anne Bentinck for
the estate of the Duke of Portland.
Photograph from the National Portrait
Gallery, London.

Chapter 17: As the Very True Sonnet Is. . . .

According to Akrigg, in his *Shakespeare and the Earl of Southampton*, the young Wriothesley "lacked stability," was "slapdash and careless . . . hot-tempered and sudden in quarrel" and "could be intolerably stiff-necked," Such was his "prodigality" that "within four years of attaining his majority he had so dissipated his fortune as to have to sell land, turn over the administration of his debt-encumbered estate to the family's old men of business, and retreat to the Continent." He and de Vere would have had much in common.

But with "all the follies of the young earl," Professor Akrigg says,

> he attracted people . . . and bound them to himself and his fortunes. Even as a young boy he must have had something singularly attractive about him. When Southampton was only fifteen, his brother-in-law, writing to Burghley, noted that "your lordship doth love him" and added, for himself, "My love and care of this young Earl enticeth me." William Camden, who as master of Westminster School had learned to appraise boys and young men, seems to have had a decided liking for young Southampton. Mountjoy, the conqueror of Ireland, trying to get for him the governorship of Connaught, wrote, "I can name no man that I love better than the Earl of Southampton." . . . Sir Charles Danvers, after the Essex rebellion, could declare that his chief motive for joining it had been "the great obligation of love and duty" that bound him to Southampton.

He was, Professor Akrigg goes on, "passionately loyal to his friends." If "he could be selfish and unkind, seducing Elizabeth Vernon and then leaving her amid her tears, . . . he did finally marry her" when "every consideration of Elizabethan common sense demanded that he repair his ruined fortunes by taking some rich heiress, not penniless Elizabeth, for his countess." The "young Southampton was an exceptionally handsome man . . . with a particular brilliance of the eyes," which two poets extolled in sonnets addressed to him. ("If I could write the beauty of your eyes," Shakespeare says in Sonnet 16.)

Professor Akrigg observes that "Southampton sought to realize in his own person the Renaissance ideal epitomized by Sir Philip Sidney." Sidney died eleven days after Southampton's thirteenth birthday. I should be greatly surprised if the youth's chief model had not been the incomparably more gifted, myriad-minded man of the Renaissance who honored him with the two long narrative poems and with whom the *Sonnets* evidently tell us he had an intimate and emotional relationship.

All three of Southampton's biographers — Constance C. Stopes, Akrigg, and Rowse — are satisfied that their subject was the fair youth of the Sonnets.[2] So too, probably, are most scholars. Doubtless opinion would be

---

[2] Stratfordians all, they are not disturbed that, as Akrigg concedes, "We have no evidence as to when, where, or under what circumstances William Shakespeare first met the Earl of Southampton," or, if the truth be told, that Shakspere ever met him at all. But what the record will not supply, fancy will. Charlotte Stopes writes:

unanimous on the score were it not for the *Sonnets* being dedicated to that bothersome "Mr. W. H."

In dedicating the *Sonnets* to "Mr. [i.e., Master] W. H.," the signatory calls him their "only begetter." This would seem to allow of no other interpretation than that he inspired them. It has, however, been argued that "Mr. W. H." is someone who managed to get his hands on the manuscript of the *Sonnets* and turned it over to Thorpe. A certain William Hall, a rather disreputable figure, is favored for the role, partly because the "H" is followed by "all," though the separation is greater than that between other words in the dedication. But, Edward Dowden says, "No example in English literature of 'begetter' in the sense of procurer has been discovered," and "to an Elizabethan as to a reader of the present day, it would, I believe, have seemed absurd to speak of begetting a manuscript or begetting a poem, unless the begetter had been either the author or the inspirer." Equally, I cannot see the publisher of the *Sonnets* dedicating that masterpiece of literature to the likes of William Hall, or deeming a mere surreptitious manuscript-procurer worthy of the immortality that the poet had bestowed on his better angel — even if he was about to be married, as we are told that Hall was. Moreover, it is clear that in wishing Mr. W. H. "eternity," Thorpe is simply wishing him that which had already been promised him by "our ever-living poet."

Among many critics to whom all this has been evident, there has been much casting about for an alternative to Southampton as the fair youth who had the initials W. H. Only one candidate has been brought forward — by John Dover Wilson, among others — who can be taken seriously: William Herbert the Earl of Pembroke, who was to be one of the dedicatees of the First Folio and evidently a chief engineer in preparing the way for it. But he does not fit. As Charles Wisner Barrell has it:

It seems most likely that Southampton introduced himself, willing the player to come to him, because he wanted, while thanking him for a good representation, to find fault with him on some minor points, perhaps his accent, his gesture, his posing, or in the play itself.

Speculation quickly yields to unequivocal statement as of fact:

He felt he must have a private talk with this "man from Stratford," and took him home with him to supper. And this was not once or even twice. . . . Southampton tried to stimulate his ambition to higher walks of literature than the dramatic was then esteemed. He would show his visitor some books he read and give bright analyses of their contents. . . .

Vertigo overcomes one at picturing the all-seeing observer, the storehouse of reading, the matchless master of words, taking instruction from a boy of nineteen.

Then, being tired of indoor air, he would swear Shakespeare his servant for the day, mount him, and lead him off to Hampstead Heights, by the Wych Elm grove (old then, but not extinct even yet), up past the Well to the crest of the Horse Shoe hill.

Mind you, this is offered not as fiction but as history. "Twenty-eight years in the making, this is still," in Samuel Schoenbaum's words, "the fullest life of the Earl." It is full, all right. No wonder the impression gets about that we know a lot about "Shakespeare."

Chapter 17: As the Very True Sonnet Is. . . .

> Far from being an Adonis with incandescent eyes and long blond locks that curled into "buds of marjorum" that made Southampton the outstanding male beauty of his day, Herbert is described as stout and swarthy. And although he developed into one of the great personalities of his age, of stronger character-fibre than Southampton, he was the reverse of beautiful. There is no record of anyone writing sonnets to celebrate the glory of his person.

Thus we are brought back to the problem of Mr. W. H. Perhaps I should take it more seriously than I do. The view I subscribe to is that if the dedication had been to "Mr. H. W." it might just as well have said in letters a foot high HENRY WRIOTHESLEY, THE THIRD EARL OF SOUTHAMPTON, and since the purpose must have been to avoid clearly identifying the only begetter — otherwise we should not be arguing about it 370 years later — the initials were simply reversed, as we might write Wriothesley, Henry. (J. T. Looney observes that in *England's Helicon*, an important anthology of verse published in 1600, the editor appears as L. N., almost certainly the transposed initials of Nicholas Ling.)

The poet, I take it, intended the *Sonnets* to be dedicated by name to the fair youth, as the two narrative poems had been dedicated by name to Southampton — otherwise how could it be that "your name from hence immortal life shall have"? — and the person or persons responsible for bringing out the volume came as close to carrying out his desire as discretion would seem to have allowed.

The dedication of *Venus and Adonis* indicates that the poet had come to have a special regard for Southampton by 1593. By 1594, when *Lucrece* appeared, their bond was certainly a close one. We should not go far wrong, I think, if we take it that these years mark the beginning of the period when the *Sonnets* were being addressed to their "only begetter" — and we might notice that the drafter of the dedication went out of his way to make clear that there was only one begetter, not two young men to share the honor. Stratfordians and Oxfordians alike tend to believe that the first seventeen were composed in order to encourage Southampton to go through with a marriage to Elizabeth Vere, Oxford's daughter, then being fostered by their joint guardian, Lord Burghley. One group supposes that Shakspere was prevailed upon to lend his pen to this objective, the other that Oxford as the poet was trying to bring about the union of two youngsters whom he loved.

The facts would seem to be against this theory. It was in 1590 to 1592 that the Southampton-Vere match was being promoted, and this was before the relationship between Shakespeare and Southampton had led even to the rather formal first dedication. (By 1592, Southampton's — and perhaps Elizabeth's — resistance had caused Burghley to look to Northumberland as a husband for his granddaughter. The lady ended by marrying the 6th Earl of Derby.) Obviously, too, the poet was not trying to push the youth into a particular marriage. He was interested not in the girl but in the young man and in perpetuating his qualities, "truth and beauty," as he several times calls them. Any of a number of young women would serve the purpose

> For where is she so fair whose unear'd womb   3
> Disdains the tillage of thy husbandry?

And, as we have seen,

> . . . many maiden gardens yet unset,   16
> With virtuous wish could bear you living flowers . . .

Moreover, Southampton when the pressure was on him to marry Elizabeth was only seventeen to eighteen and would surely have laughed at being urged to "let not the winter's ragged hand deface in thee thy summer" (9) and being told "that thou consum'st thyself in single life" (9) and must "make thee another self" (10) in order to "fortify yourself in your decay" (16). Granted that men aged faster in those days than in ours, it is difficult enough to believe that even an Elizabethan youth of twenty-one could have been expected to heed such considerations.

When we try to ascertain how long the writing of the *Sonnets* continued, we come to a stumbling block. From number 104 we learn that

> Three winters cold   104
> Have from the forests shook three summers' pride,
> Three beauteous springs to yellow autumn turn'd
> In process of the seasons have I seen,
> Three April perfumes in three hot Junes, burn'd,
> Since first I saw you fresh that yet are green.

That would be almost four years, from, say, December 1592, to the autumn of 1596, at the very latest from winter 1593–94 to autumn 1597. Yet in number 107, only three sonnets later, we come to the only one of all 154 that appears to refer unmistakably to outside events, which events appear unmistakably to be of the year 1603. Here are the first ten lines:

> Not mine own fears, nor the prophetic soul   107
> Of the wide world dreaming on things to come,
> Can yet the lease of my true love control,
> Suppos'd as forfeit to a confin'd doom.
> The mortal moon hath her eclipse endur'd.
> And the sad augurs mock their own presage;
> Incertainties now crown themselves assur'd,
> And peace proclaims olives of endless age.
> Now with the drops of this most balmy time
> My love looks fresh, and Death to me subscribes.

To a reader of Elizabethan verse, the moon as an allegorical representation can mean only the Queen. "The mortal moon hath her eclipse endur'd": Elizabeth has died. The prophets of troubles to follow her passing make fun of their own predictions: "The sad augurs mock their own presage." The succession to the throne has taken place tranquilly: "Incertainties now crown themselves assur'd." After decades of strife, the prospect of lasting peace with Spain has come in with James: "Peace proclaims olives of endless age." With Southampton having been indefinitely imprisoned in the Tower for his part in the Essex rebellion, the poet had been deprived of his love: "The lease of my true love, . . . / Suppos'd as forfeit to a confin'd doom." But by James's order Southampton has happily been set free: "Now with . . . this balmy time / My love looks fresh." The poet's own days, are, however, numbered: "Death to me subscribes." De Vere would die in the following year.[3]

If Sonnet 107 followed on the heels of 104, then Shakespeare first saw the fair youth in 1599. But Meres spoke of Shakespeare's "sugared Sonnets" in 1598 and Jaggard published two of them in 1599, including number 144, which indicates that the relationship between the poet and his young friend was already well along. I think we may take it that the *Sonnets* were not printed in the order in which they were written. There is no particular reason to believe they were. Louis Auchincloss says:

> The sonnets to the dark mistress, 126 *et seq.*, although late in Thorpe's chronology, have so many similarities to *Love's Labour's Lost* that I would date them early in the series, and I suspect that those which deal with her seduction of the young man, 133 through 140, refer to the same incident covered in sonnets 40 through 42. . . . Sonnet 145, in octosyllabic lines, seems to me utterly out of place in the whole series and possibly not by Shakespeare at all. Sonnet 145, dealing with the poet's soul, seems to be Shakespeare's, but not to belong in the series at all. It is very interesting as the only instance in his poetry that gives any hint of personal religiosity.

---

[3] Rowse, who ends the *Sonnets* in 1595, cannot, of course, accept the foregoing dating of 107. His friend Louis Auchincloss I think disposes of his argument, however.

Pretty well every serious critic has agreed that the mortal moon is Queen Elizabeth herself, and Rowse maintains that her eclipse was the conspiracy by her physician, Dr. Lopez, and others, to assassinate her and that the peace was the victory in France of Henry of Navarre and consequent end of the religious wars. But try as I may, I cannot see why a conspiracy should "eclipse" a monarch. While nobody knew of it, the Queen could hardly be said to be in the darkness, and with its discovery and prevention, the darkness was avoided. Where then was the eclipse? As to the victory of Henry of Navarre, one has only to read *The Elizabethan Journals* by G. B. Harrison to see that this was not followed by any immediate cessation of hostilities. The fighting in France continued for years.

Shakespeare used the word "endured" in the sense of "suffered" in *King Lear*, and in *Antony and Cleopatra*. Antony's reference to the eclipse of the "terrene moon" (Cleopatra) refers not to her temporary disappearance behind another celestial body, but to her end.

Mr. Auchincloss's reasons for assigning the sonnet to 1603 included those I have cited. We may notice that Thomas Cecil wrote in a letter to his brother Robert in 1595 that "I left the moon in the wane at my last being at the court; I hear now it is a half moon again, yet I think it will never be at the full, though I hope it will never be eclipsed, you know whom I mean."

I agree with all that, and with D. S. Ogburn's marginal comment on the last sentence: "Yes — near the end." It is hardly conceivable to me that the poet meant number 151, with its startlingly explicit description of his physical response to his mistress, to be the next to last in the sequence. (Numbers 153 and 154, having nothing to do with the *dramatis personae* of the preceding, are simply tacked on.) The unequivocal treatment of a very carnal phenomenon in 151 cannot have been meant to follow the lofty finality of 146, which Mr. Auchincloss mentions. In the latter the poet sorrowfully exclaims:

> Poor soul, the centre of my sinful earth,   146
> Fool'd by these rebel powers that thee array,
> Why dost thou pine within and suffer dearth,
> Painting thy outward walls so costly gay?
> Why so large cost, having so short a lease,
> Dost thou upon thy fading mansion spend?
>   · · · ·
>   Is this thy body's end?
> Then, soul, live thou upon thy servant's loss,   146
>
>   · · · ·
>
> Buy terms divine in selling hours of dross. . . .   146

If he is here looking toward the Everlasting, as Hamlet called it, he comes back in the final couplet to the bitter irony in the face of a dark, even macabre reality with which I suspect he ultimately viewed life — and the lines may have been the last, psychologically if not literally, that Shakespeare wrote:

> So shalt thou feed on Death, that feeds on men,   146
> And Death once dead, there's no more dying then.

Number 107, with its initial lines looking indecipherably into the future, as we saw a few pages back, comes properly, I suspect, soon or immediately before 146. Unless we can be persuaded otherwise, I think we may take it that the *Sonnets* were mostly written over a period beginning in 1593 with those to the young friend, possibly 1592, and ending in 1603, possibly 1604, probably most in the first few years of the period, though some may have been written considerably earlier. Number 107 may well have been moved forward to avoid focusing attention upon the poet's having been near his end in 1603. If the reader were to accept that, the sequence might as well have been signed Edward de Vere. And why should he not accept it? Why should he believe the poet to have been mistaken in anticipating his early death in 1603 and then to have let stand an error that would make him look foolish? Bacon lived until 1626 and Derby until 1642, while the case for Marlowe, or what may be imagined remaining of it, crashes upon the patent impossibility of his having, while supposedly dead and living in deepest hiding, conducted an intimate relationship for a decade with a public figure like Southampton. As for Shakspere, at the time the poet was writing of his imminent death, he was supposedly being licensed to perform with nine players of the former Lord Chamberlain's company, receiving cloth to march in a procession, suing a debtor in Stratford, buying half the tithes of three villages in his biggest investment, and having thirteen more years of life to look forward to.

It is now that we are finally brought to view the orthodox attribution of Shakespeare's works with something like fright, as perhaps we should have much sooner. It shows how ideology, or doctrine as it used to be called, can blind highly intelligent men and women to facts and reason. What the poet tells us of himself in the *Sonnets* is patently irreconcilable with what we know of the Stratford man. That he was near death in 1603 is only the last disclosure at wide variance with Shakspere's biography. Writing when the Stratfordian was around thirty and would have been just getting started on the literary career engrafted upon him, the poet was outspokenly in his declining years — "middle-aging," Rowse puts it, to say the least. He was a man who could write feelingly of "the bloody tyrant, Time" (16) and of "the wrackful siege of battering days" (65). He could weep "for precious friends hid in death's dateless night" (30), "all those friends I thought buried" (31), and for "my lovers gone" (31). This was a man looking backward upon life, not forward at the outset of his career. He was "beated and chopp'd with tann'd antiquity, . . . with Time's injurious hand crush'd and o'erworn" (62). He could say in number 73

> That time of year thou mayst in me behold   73
> When yellow leaves, or none, or few, do hang
> Upon those boughs which shake against the cold,
> Bare ruin'd choirs, where late the sweet birds sang.

Leslie Hotson, who actually assigns the *Sonnets* to the years 1587 to 1589, when Shakspere was twenty-three and twenty-five, argues that it was merely a convention for a young sonneteer to feign advanced years. How Professor Hotson explains that Shakespeare's *Sonnets* show a much greater maturity in the poet and in his genius than the narrative poems of 1593 and 1594 — "The *Sonnets* in poetic worth immeasurably surpass the *Venus and Adonis* and the *Lucrece*," says Edward Dowden — how any Stratfordians explain the difference, I do not know. (To Oxfordians it is simply further evidence that the two narrative poems were relatively youthful works written many years before they were brought forth and perhaps given a little more polish to be presented to the Earl of Southampton as being the kind of thing a boy of about twenty would appreciate.) Surely only unthinking subservience to doctrine could ascribe to pretence the dirgeful tone that haunts the *Sonnets*, the knell of Time — "swift-footed, terrible Time," to quote Mark Van Doren again: "The death of days and seasons, the springing and withering of plants (and of men as plants), ravaged faces and ravaged shores, the chronicle of wasted time, the poet's own decline and death, the loss of precious friends, woe, loneliness and doom."

In Sonnet 138, reflecting on his mistress, the poet sadly accuses himself of

> . . . vainly thinking that she thinks me young,   138
> Although she knows my days are past the best.

"On both sides," he acknowledges, "is simple truth supprest." His mistress admits "not she is unjust" ("though I know she lies") and the poet admits "not that I am old" and each pretends to accept the other's self-deception, for

> . . . age in love loves not t'have years told;   138
> Therefore I lie with her, and she with me,
> And in our faults by lies we flatter'd be.

The Stratfordians find it easier to ignore than explain the poet's continual reversion to his aging, only too unmistakably genuine in its pain. Rowse, however, has a wonderful way of dealing with it. "It is time," he declares, "to register a protest against Shakespeare's writing himself down as old"!

The *Sonnets* leave no doubt that the poet was well along in years in the mid-1590s. They add confirmation to his having been a nobleman. Infatuated as he is with the youth he is addressing, he does not hold back from up-braiding him where he feels it is called for:

> But why thy odour matcheth not thy show,   69
> The soil is this, that thou dost common grow.

> You to your beauteous blessings add a curse,   84
> Being fond on praise, which makes your praises worse.

> How sweet and lovely dost thou make the shame   95
> Which, like a canker in the fragrant rose,
> Doth spot the beauty of thy budding name!
> O! in what sweets dost thou thy sins enclose!
>   . . . .
> O! what a mansion have those vices got   95
> Which for their habitation chose out thee.

Says Rowse in *Shakespeare's Sonnets*, "Here is a bit of straight talk of a tutorial kind from an older man [one of twenty-nine, as Rowse has it] to a younger, however grand," and "Here is the tutorial attitude toward the young man with a vengeance." The Oxford don tells us that he has been uniquely able to solve all problems of the *Sonnets* because "this is the first time an historian of Shakespeare's own age has addressed himself to them." But as any such historian knows, it would have been utterly unthinkable in Tudor

England for the son of a provincial wool-merchant, a lowly player, to have told a proud, sought-after young earl like Southampton that he was growing common and was a mansion of concealed vices. The transgressor would have been fortunate indeed if no worse befell him than instant and permanent severance of his access to the insulted nobleman. To remind us of the vast gulf traditionally separating a man of Shakspere's station from the English nobility, we have Sir Kenneth Clark's description in his autobiography of the snubs at the hands of the young aristocrats at a public school to which he and other sons of "tradesmen," even of Britain's leading men of commerce, were subject — and this is the democratic 20th century.

Rowse takes refuge in the claim that the *Sonnets* "were not written for publication at all," but even if this were the case, Southampton would certainly never have tolerated them. And plainly it was not the case. The poet states emphatically — it is a recurrent theme — "That in black ink my love may still shine bright" (65), that

> So long as men can breathe, or eyes can see,   18
> So long lives this, and this gives life to thee.

And

>   Your praise shall still find room   55
> Even in the eyes of all posterity.

Only a man of rank at least equal to Southampton's — and the Wriothesleys were ennobled only a few years before Oxford's birth — could have taken the young Earl to task as the poet does. There is other evidence as well that the poet was a nobleman. When he says

> Thy love is better than high birth to me,   91
> Richer than wealth, prouder than garments' cost,
> Of more delight than hawks or horses be,

he is saying of more delight *not* than hawks or horses *would* be but than they *are*, and so I think we must believe of the other appurtenances of a nobleman he cites; the comparison has meaning only as the poet has enjoyed those appurtenances.

Sonnet 125 is particularly illuminating:

> Were't aught to me I bore the canopy,
> With my extern the outward honouring,
> Or laid great bases for eternity,
> Which proves more short than waste or ruining?
> Have I not seen dwellers on form and favour
> Lose all, and more, by paying too much rent,
> For compound sweet forgoing simple savour,
> Pitiful thrivers, in their gazing spent?

The poet's rhetorical question calls up the picture of the Court and those pitiful hangers-on of greatness who give up simple satisfactions they could have had to seek richer favors: it is what an experienced courtier might tell us. But the clincher is the first line. The best that Rowse can do to divert us from its significance is to translate it as "Were it anything to me that I bore the canopy over you." But Southampton would not have had a canopy borne over him. It was the monarch who had that honor, and one of those entitled to bear the canopy over Elizabeth was the Earl of Oxford, as Lord Great Chamberlain. Who but a privileged peer could be speaking in the foregoing lines? No wonder the poet wrote in Sonnet 76:

> That every word doth almost tell my name, 76
> Showing their birth, and whence they did proceed.

The *Sonnets* tell us other things about the author. He was a loser in life, unlike Shakspere, whose material success exceeded anything he could have anticipated. He writes in Sonnet 25:

> Let those who are in favor with their stars 25
> Of public honour and proud titles boast,
> Whilst I, whom fortune of such triumph bars. . . .

It is difficult to see what would have prevented Shakspere from receiving the public honor attaching to the authorship of Shakespeare's works if he had written them. That he should have felt out of favor with his stars and ill used by fortune in that he lacked a proud title would certainly not have occurred to him. Proud titles were, however, what de Vere saw being bestowed on favorites of the Queen — unworthily he must have felt in some cases — for offices he doubtless felt he could have performed as well had these not been withheld from him. He went to his grave with only those titles he had been born to and with those tarnished by the accusations made against him. At Castle Hedingham, where the de Veres had their seat, I was told in 1978 that he had been the black sheep of the family.

Frank Harris finds the poet giving in to self-pity in the *Sonnets*, and the charge seems warranted by number 29, at least:

> When in disgrace with Fortune and men's eyes 29
> I all alone beweep my outcast state. . . .

Yet what writer could escape such feelings had he performed the greatest literary service ever rendered his nation and been rewarded by denial of recognition for that service, by dishonor and deprivation? What kind of despair might other great artists have given way to, what kind of reputations have left behind, had they been judged solely on their behavior by those ignorant of all they had created? The poet associates the adversity he suffers with the guilt and shame that are his. "Fortune" is to him

> The guilty goddess of my harmful deeds. 111

He warns the young man:

> O! lest the world should task you to recite   72
> What merit lived in me, that you should love
> After my death — dear love, forget me quite,
> For you in me can nothing worthy prove.
> I may not ever more acknowledge thee,   36
>   Lest my bewailed guilt should do thee same,
> Nor thou with public kindness honour me,
> Unless thou take that honour from thy name.

In what respect the poet might or might not acknowledge young Southampton must give us food for speculation.

That the poet has, in his own eyes, been dishonored by his theatrical activities seems clear:

> Alas! 'tis true I have gone here and there,   110
> And made myself a motley to the view;

And,

> Thence comes it that my name receives a brand,   111
> And almost thence my nature is subdu'd
> To what it works in, like the dyer's hand.

Rather than that the young man "for love speak well of me" that which is "untrue," let

> My name be buried where my body is,   72
> And live no more to shame nor me nor you.
>   For I am sham'd by that which I bring forth,
>   And so should you, to love things nothing worth.

We are reminded of the powerful attraction the theatre is known to have had for Southampton.

When we ask ourselves how it could have been within Shakspere's province to acknowledge or not acknowledge a young earl and how he could have been shamed by bringing forth dramas that are the glory of our language, we realize how far we have put the Stratfordian behind us. The distance between him and the poet of the *Sonnets* is made even plainer when the latter exclaims that

> . . . I, once gone, to all the world must die.   81

How it can ever have been imagined that the author of Shakespeare's works could anticipate such oblivion unless he were being denied credit for them is difficult to understand.

If we saw in the preceding chapters that the further an open-eyed reading of Shakespeare's plays takes us from Shakspere, the nearer it brings us to someone on the pattern of de Vere, we find the same to be true of the

341

Sonnets. Everything I can see that the *Sonnets* tell us of their author is consistent with what we know of de Vere and with our knowledge of no one else. He alone would seem to pass the test of the poetical autobiography.

No one has ever found, however, that a resolution to his satisfaction of the poet's identity and that of the young friend in the *Sonnets* has brought him much nearer an answer to the question I raised earlier: what was the relationship between the two? That it was intense is plain enough, but what was its nature? Was it — and this has always been the main issue — homosexual? The notorious Sonnet 20 has the closest bearing on the matter:

> A woman's face with Nature's own hand painted   20
> Hast thou, the master-mistress of my passion;
> A woman's gentle heart, but not acquainted
> With shifting change, as is false women's fashion;
>   . . . .
> And for a woman wert thou first created;
> Till Nature, as she wrought thee, fell a-doting,
> And by addition me of thee defeated,
> By adding one thing to my purpose nothing.
>   But since she prick'd thee out for women's pleasure
>   Mine be thy love, and thy love's use their treasure.

What the sonnet seems to say is that the poet's regard for the youth is inherently amorous with a potentially sexual element but is diverted from a sexual purpose by the youth's physical equipment as a male, which would not divert a homosexual. ("Passion," by the way, did not have the meaning of sexual desire or impulse until the next century.) That is not, let it be admitted, a wholly satisfactory answer to the question. What about the known proclivities of the two principals, or those I conceive to be they?

Akrigg writes, "Nothing would be less surprising than to learn that during periods of his early life Southampton passed through homosexual phases but, until better evidence is found, only a fool will declare that he did." A charge of homosexuality was leveled at de Vere in his thirty-second year, replete with lurid details of an alleged episode (quoted verbatim with relish by Rowse in the London *Times*), but his accuser, who charged him with every other sin as well ("all kinds of vice and shameful treacheries, without one care of God, of honour or of nature") was a man whose treason de Vere had exposed and who was fighting for his life. If de Vere ever had homosexual interests, they were surely subordinate. He had two wives and four children by them and probably a number of liaisons, and the sexual obsession of his life seems to have been with Anne Vavasor, who bore him a son.

In the plays, the dramatist is plainly disgusted by Achilles' sexual relationship with Patroclus in *Troilus and Cressida* and for the rest shows no interest in the subject of perversion. True, he is fond of having his heroines don male attire for disguise, but it must be remembered that they were in fact males, and there must have been something comic in having boys play young women pretending to be young men. The practice of putting comely boys in girls' parts and costumes, however, in which they were reportedly as fetching as the real thing, was acknowledged to perturb men associated with the Elizabethan stage and some ambivalence may have been common at the time.

Be all that as it may, the two principals in the *Sonnets* are explicitly men of heterosexual desires and activities, and in the sequence both have an affair with a woman — unhappily the same one. Edward Hubler, an Elizabethan scholar at Princeton, judges that "The charge of homosexuality can neither be proved nor disproved on the available evidence, but the balance of probabilities discredits it." Robert S. Hillyer of Harvard observes that

> any enthusiasm sufficiently powerful will evoke terms at least as strong as those of sexual passion and frequently similar to them in tone. No pornographic imagination can transform the lovers' hymns of the Middle Ages addressed to Christ or the Virgin Mary into mating songs, however perfervid may be their expression.

Rowse, who is an astute reader of Shakespeare as far as his preconceptions allow — and much as his reading is at the mercy of his tendency to "absurd claims" and "slipshod methods," as Bernard Levin calls them — makes a point unlikely to escape an attentive reader of the poems: "All through these Sonnets there is a quasi-parental element, an anxious sense of responsibility for the fatherless youth, so apt to be misguided, almost as if Shakespeare was *in loco parentis* — to use a university term." Indeed, in number 37, the poet declares:

> As a decrepit father takes delight   37
> To see his active child do deeds of youth,
> So I, made lame by Fortune's dearest spite,
> Take all my comfort of thy worth and truth.

If the poet were the youth's father, much of the *Sonnets'* tenor that is otherwise all but inexplicable would be explained and an added significance be given the lines in number 3, which already tell us much:

> Thou art thy mother's glass, and she in thee   3
> Calls back the lovely April of her prime

— when the poet must have known her. Pose the hypothesis: the poet, in his forties ("When forty winters shall besiege thy brow" — 2), author of imperishable dramas never to be known as his, discovers that he has a son in this beauteous seventeen-year-old. Might not he see himself renewed in the youngster, who would have for him all the charm of his own vanished youth, now perceived in regretful retrospect? Might he not see himself justified, redeemed of his past misdeeds, in this, "my lovely boy" (126)? Would he not be inspired to pour his near idolatry into verse that should be immortal and thus convey immortality upon his son, to whom, to gain his favor, he would boast of what he had done, which no other poet had it in him to equal? Given the young man's popularity, the competition for his regard by rival poets, would he not be jealous and possessive, desperate and frantic at the possibility of losing the youth's love? Would he not be deeply upset by his weaknesses and transgressions? Would he not especially, if he had no son about whom he could feel as a proud father would (as perhaps de Vere could not about the illegitimate son he had by the scandalous Anne Vavasor), urge the youth to marry and

> Make thee another self for love of me,   10
> That beauty still may live in thine or thee

— that beauty which was his mother's in "the lovely April of her prime"? Urge him with warnings of Time's ravages lying in wait for him, even though these warnings would risk his laughter?

Well, perhaps. But if so why would the "dynastic sonnets" stop abruptly with the seventeenth? If one looks for an answer to that question one can find it. In 1593, de Vere had a legitimate son, destined to become the Earl of Oxford, *whom he named Henry*, though Henry was not one of the names that recurred among the de Veres or the Trenthams, either, his new wife's family. Continuation of the line ensured through a respectable maternity, he might have been just as content not to have Southampton rush into matrimony.

Even if we are willing provisionally to suspend disbelief as far as this, do we not find the postulation of a father-and-son relationship come crashing upon Sonnet 20? Surely no man would ever say of his son that "for a woman were thou first created" but that "Nature . . . by addition me of thee defeated!" *Exactly*. He would not. Then why . . . ? The reader will be justified in deeming my answer too ingenious by half. Still, here it is.

Let us grant that Shakespeare was a man of some intelligence and understanding of human nature. It could not have escaped him that to readers who thought about the matter, the love he expressed in the *Sonnets* could have only one of two bases. No man ever experiences such intense devotion to one of his own sex unless the other arouses in him the feelings ordinarily kindled in a man by a woman with whom he is in love or unless the feelings are paternal. (I omit the kind given to a charismatic leader.) Certainly he could not have borne to have it thought that his love of the youth was homosexual. The problem was that if he explicitly ruled out that alternative, only the other would be left. And for some reason he was not in a position to have it publicly known that the youth was his son: "I may not ever more acknowledge thee." The solution to the problem he hit upon was shrewd and, as far as I can see, the only one possible. He would make it clear that his love for the youth could not be that of a man for a woman because of that addition making the youth a male; that ruled out a homosexual attachment. At the same time, by implying that he would love the youth as he would a woman but for that addition, he would exclude the possibility of the youth's being his son. At one stroke he would eliminate both kinds of heartfelt devotion an older man might feel for a younger. This he accomplished in the otherwise quite gratuitous Sonnet 20. And he bequeathed the world a paradox on which it has been gnawing pretty much ever since.

If, following Rowse's lead, we have seen that the poet's extraordinary love for the young man *could* be explained as a father's love, we are left to account for the other extraordinary element in his profession of feeling for the youth: a respect near to reverence. While he reproves the youth stingingly, as a father might, he also pays him the honor, or something like the honor, due from a subject in a feudal society:

> Lord of my love, to whom in vassalage   26
> Thy merit hath my duty strongly knit, . . .

Here is further paradox. For a suggestion as to how it might be resolved, we may turn to a fellow scholar of Rowse's. Before I quote Leslie Hotson on the subject, however, let me say of the hypothesis I am developing that I take no position on it, either of belief or disbelief.

Professor Hotson finds the poet continually addressing the young man in a fashion then appropriate to princes. He compares the youth to the sun, a god, the ocean or sea — all terms used by Elizabethans to denote a monarch. "Crowned" appears in several references to him, as do "succession," "heir," and "issue." The poet admits that he cannot tell "princes' fortunes" by consulting the heavens and calls the youth "my sovereign." He writes, "And take thou my oblation," which is offered only to kings. "To thee I send the written ambassage," he says and speaks of an "embassy of love to thee" and of the youth's bounty and largesse, which Shakespeare elsewhere identifies with kings. He uses "king" and "kingdom" in connection with him and continually attributes grace to him and also glory. Such is Hotson's argument.[4]

That Southampton was by birth both de Vere's son and, in his eyes, his prince by virtue of his descent from his mother is a proposition on which,

---

[4] His theory is that with Queen Elizabeth on the throne and jealous of her prerogatives, it was not possible for any Englishman to be called a prince with the exception of those young men of princely manner chosen to preside over the Christmas revels at academic institutions. Having decided that the *Sonnets* were written in 1587 to 1589, Professor Hotson was led to William Hatcliffe, a handsome young man who reigned as Prince of Purpoole over the revels at Gray's Inn in the winter of 1587–1588, and identified him as the Mr. W. H. and the fair youth of the *Sonnets*. "Hotson's Sonnet Theories Astound Scholars," Louis Marder captioned a notice of the book, *Mr. W. H.*, in his *Shakespeare Newsletter*.

as I say, I take no stand.[5] I have introduced it because I think the reader is entitled to hear the one theory so far propounded that would account for the tone and burden of the 126 "fair-youth" *Sonnets*. My hope is that, perceiving how greatly our understanding of the author is at stake in our fathoming of the *Sonnets*, the reader will go back to them and, free from the constraints of the Stratford attribution, see if he can extract from them what has hitherto eluded us. The *Sonnets* tell us so much of our greatest writer — if only we could be sure what all of it is!

Some years ago I had a letter from a Mr. P. E. Gilbank of Hamilton, Ontario, proposing that the *Sonnets* were addressed not to actual persons but the Theatre in the guise of such. Certainly it is an appealing idea that at least the dark lady, so called, might be a symbolic representation of the stage — and a not implausible idea considering that one or two of Shakespeare's female characters do seem for him to have stood for his plays. Sonnet 130 readily lends itself to this interpretation with its mocking and rather nasty derogation of the poet's mistress — how "black wires grow on her head" and "the breath that from my mistress reeks." I am persuaded by Mr. Willson Disher, however, that what we have here is a "literary frolic" making fun of Spenser's excesses in praise of lady-loves.[6] Having reread numbers 127 to 152 with Mr. Gilbank's theory in mind, I am afraid we must take it that Shakespeare means these sonnets literally, however disturbingly he may be revealed in them, in the grip of violently antagonistic emotions about a woman he cannot escape though well aware that her favors are accessible to others than himself. In a single sonnet he confesses

> For well thou know'st to my dear doting heart   131
> Thou art the fairest and most precious jewel

And

> In nothing art thou black save in thy deeds.[7]

We have seen how, in the poet's ravaged outlook

> To win me soon to hell, my female evil   144
> Tempteth my better angel from my side,
> And would corrupt my saint to be a devil,
> Wooing his purity with her foul pride.

---

[5] It was put forward some years before A. L. Rowse and Leslie Hotson addressed themselves to the *Sonnets*, by Dorothy Ogburn and Percy Allen, who arrived at it independently.

[6] Especially her of the "ruddy cheeks, goodly bosom, nipples (like young blossomed Jessemynes)" in *Amoretti* IX and LXIV.

[7] Incidentally, the last line raises some doubt about the actual complexion of the wanton whom we call the dark lady. Though applying "black" several times to his mistress, Shakespeare is capable of using the adjective invidiously to denote a quality of disposition. In *Two Gentlemen of Verona*, Julia is explicitly described as fair but in Act IV speaks of having become black simply through losing her lord's favor and suffering exposure to the sun.

346

He cries

> Is't not enough to torture me alone,   133
> But slave to slavery my sweet'st friend must be?

Evidently so; the wanton proves irresistible:

> So, now I have confess'd that he is thine,   134
> And I myself am mortgaged to thy will.

It is an appalling state of things. He offers to give himself up — "myself I shall forfeit" — to save "my next self"

>   so that other mine   134
> Thou wilt restore, to be my comfort still:
> But thou wilt not, . . .

Two sonnets follow (numbers 135 and 136) that are most famous of all for baffling the understanding, the "Will" sonnets, in which the author plays continually and puzzlingly upon the name and word. They begin:

> Whoever hath her wish, thou hast thy *Will*,   135
> And *Will* to boot, and Will in over-plus; . . .
> More than enough am I that vex'd thee still,
> To thy sweet will making addition thus.

To Edward Dowden, "By no strained, unnatural interpretation can the conclusion be escaped that the friend who had wronged the poet was named, like the poet himself, 'William.'" It is not so inescapably evident to me. If by making addition to her sweet will (a word which, by the way, had the meaning of amorous desire for the Elizabethans) the poet means he has rendered his young friend up to his mistress, endowing her with Will to boot and Will in over-plus, he is certainly treating the matter in a very different spirit from that which it elsewhere evokes. For the remainder of the two sonnets Will is in the singular — in fact it nowhere appears in the plural. The pair ends:

> Make but my name thy love, and love that still,   136
> And then thou lovest me, for my name is *Will*.

Incessantly punning and reading somewhat like Valentine's Day offerings, the two sonnets are so out of keeping with the rest as to raise a doubt that they were intended for inclusion with them.[8]

---

[8] A. L. Rowse achieved a widely publicized "clarification" of the two sonnets by discovering that "will" in Elizabethan usage meant a sexual organ — a discovery on which I am not competent to pass judgment — and where "Will" is capitalized and italicized ten times in the original printing to indicate a name (the convention I have followed in the quotations above), by uncapitalizing and unitalicizing it in all but two places to convert it from the name Will to the word will. By these devices he renders the two sonnets not so much "very naughty," as he says, but blatantly obscene and evades any implication that the young man was called Will like the poet.

If the young friend was called Will, as Dr. Dowden among others insists that Sonnet 135 tells us, and Southampton was the young man, I suspect that it was in the theatrical world that he was referred to as such. He would have had the example of the poet himself, who, in the clandestine part of his double life, left his rank behind him to mingle freely with actors and other playwrights as Master William Shakespeare (even if the masquerade was transparent and *pro forma* only), the name under which he dedicated the two long poems to his young friend and presumably intended to dedicate the *Sonnets* also. This raises the possibility that the young man, engrossed in the theatre to the point of alarming the poet, as the *Sonnets* suggest he was and as Charlotte C. Stopes indicates Southampton may well have been, presumed upon his relationship with the redoubtable William Shakespeare to offer himself as the heir apparent, as it were — a young Will. His doing so could well have aroused resentment; Southampton was, says Mrs. Stopes, "in the habit of giving good advice about their business to all the players" — this at age nineteen. One might infer from the exercise of such authority that he followed Shakespeare's example and in his "Will"-identity surreptitiously took part in plays himself. If he did, we may wonder if Henry Chettle did not perceive in the conduct of the spoiled, aristocratic youthful protégé of the personage known as William Shakespeare an opportunity to create a scandal and profit himself and did so by fabricating *Greenes Groatsworth of Wit*, which holds up to scorn a *Johannes factotum*, a know-it-all, who esteemed himself in his conceit the only Shake-scene in the country.

To speculate upon what we can never know is very likely to be futile. What we can also probably never know about the *Sonnets* is what ultimate impression the poet intended them to make. We should, we may suppose, have no difficulty about this if we knew in what order he would have arranged them and if we had any that may be missing — supposing, that is, that he thought of them as a unitary sequence telling a story, which is far from certain. Given such information, we should presumably know what final impression he would have had the *Sonnets* leave with us. If, however, we cannot tell what meaning above all the poet intended them to convey, we do know — at least I feel I know — what meaning above all they do convey. It is the triumph of art — as it has never elsewhere been so ringingly proclaimed.

The young man whom the poet loves with distracted devotion, compounding truth and beauty as in an angel, is yet a mansion that vices have sought out. The woman on whom he dotes is black in her faults. The poet himself is shamed by sinful deeds and nameless guilt and is ground down by humiliation at the hands of his "two loves" who jointly and in collusion betray him. But out of this flawed triumvirate, doomed by ravaging Time, to which youth, loves, lives, seasons, years, the ocean's shores, and the most enduring materials with which man builds all yield, rises the poetry of the *Sonnets*, imperishable, bestowing immortality on the poet's beloved in its superiority to Time itself. Truly the poet has swum struggling for his life, as Carlyle says, but before the waters close over him as they must over us all, he defies the universal fate with a claim upon eternity for what he has wrought. His exultant cry resounds for us still, in the pride of the unquenchable spirit of art:

> Not marble, nor the gilded monuments   55
> Of princes, shall outlive this powerful rhyme. . . .

18

"Have Writ Your Annals True"

Compelled by the exigencies of their theory of the origin of Shakespeare's dramas, Stratfordians tell us that a writer's personality, background, and acquaintance with life and other persons need have little if anything to do with the character and content of his works. Some, it is true, strain to detect a few bits of Shakspere's supposed experience in the plays but, as we see, unconvincingly. We observe that in general they make it a positive virtue on "Shakespeare's" part to have kept himself out of his works, though they must make him unique in doing so. We find, however, that among commentators whose judgments command respect, the verdict is unanimous as to the self-revealing, even autobiographical character, broadly speaking, of works of the imagination, even scientists rejecting the imputation of pure objectivity to their fellows. They tell us that the characters a writer creates not only reflect the men and women he has known but in the final analysis each is an embodiment of some part of his own nature. With this warrant we turn to Shakespeare's plays for a self-portrait of the author. Being led inevitably and at once to Hamlet, we find our suspicion that the dramatist's qualities are most fully realized in the Prince evidently confirmed when in reviewing other plays we see Hamlet's traits cropping up again and again in other characters, even inappropriately. Exploring, therefore, the world's most famous play for the light we may expect it to throw upon the dramatist's personality and circumstances, we reap rich and illuminating rewards and are left with little doubt as to the kind of man Shakespeare was and as to the world in which he moved.

In the *Sonnets*, most of us are satisfied, we look into the poet's heart and soul. The view they offer, however, is such as we might have by peering at a distance in the darkness through a small window into an illuminated interior. It has a poignant depth but little breadth. Much lies outside its scope. If the *Sonnets* told us all we were to know of the author, we should have but a narrowly restricted knowledge of his life-story. But they are his sole autobiographical writings in a formal sense only. Beyond these, there is everything else he wrote.

One writer after another has told us that what writers write about is themselves. Joseph Conrad, for corroboration of his own view, quotes Anatole France as declaring that "failing the resolution to hold our peace, we can only talk of ourselves." "Every man's work whether it be literature or music or pictures or architecture or anything else is always a portrait of himself," Samuel Butler declared, "and the more he tries to conceal himself, the more clearly will his character appear." A man's "work is autobiographical in spite of every subterfuge," the poet Wallace Stevens wrote, adding, "it cannot be otherwise." Said Havelock Ellis: "Every artist writes his own autobiography," and the playwright Edward Albee, "Your source material is the people you know, not those you don't know." Ultimately, however, "every character is an extension of the author's own personality."

The foregoing paragraph is quoted, slightly amplified, from my *Harvard Magazine* article, in which it was followed by the remark that "what Shakespeare tells us of himself in his plays and *Sonnets*, of his background, interests and character is altogether different from Shaksper as he appears on the record." The testimony of creative artists as to the sources of their art is of course hardly welcome to Shakespearean orthodoxy. Professors Evans and Levin charge that the authors I quoted are all "modern figures writing in a subjective vein. Albee is the only dramatist among them, and subjectivity may be his weakness. Drama is traditionally as objective as a literary form can be. . . ."

Having the principle of the drama's objectivity enunciated reminds me of the courtroom scene in *Alice in Wonderland*, in which the King of Hearts announces "Rule Forty-two. All persons more than a mile high to leave the court," and Alice replies, "That's not a regular rule; you invented it just now."

The principle the two professors brought forth to fit the needs of the argument has little to be said for it. When Richard L. Coe, drama critic of the *Washington Post*, asserted that "George Bernard Shaw was astute enough to put himself, sometimes a little, sometimes a lot, into every character he wrote," he was crediting to the playwright's intention that which the *New York Times's* drama critic perceived he could not help: to Brooks Atkinson, "In the final analysis, all characters represent at least some aspect of the author, for no one can write about anything that is totally outside his experience."

Writing also in the *New York Times*, Barbara Gelb observed:

> Eugene O'Neill, America's greatest playwright . . . ended his career with the writing of a starkly autobiographical play. *Long Day's Journey into Night* is the story of the four O'Neills — called the Tyrones in the play — at a moment of anguished crisis in the summer of 1912. The play's names and events are so thinly disguised that there is no disputing the literal nature of its revelations. [While it] is the final, naked revelation of O'Neill's "truth" about his family, it is by no means O'Neill's only significantly autobiographical play. But it was not until the publication of the play in 1956, three years after O'Neill's death, and the recognition of its autobiographical content, that it became possible to discern how very autobiographical many of his earlier plays had been. . . .

Do Shaw and O'Neill incline us to believe that drama is as objective as a literary form can be? Does Anton Chekhov support the professors' position, that drama tells us little or nothing of the author's life?

In his *Chekhov: Observer Without Illusion*, Daniel Gillès finds the playwright's characters "already almost all present" in his "first play, . . . borrowed from that provincial Russian society bogged down in boredom and resigned inanity but uneasy over its fate" — the same society Chekhov had come to know early in life. "*Platanov* is like the wings from which all those Chekhov 'types' will go on the stage in *Ivanov, The Three Sisters* and *The Cherry Orchard*." Of *The Sea Gull*, Mr. Gillès writes:

> Its nostalgic, emotional heroine, Nina, seduced and then deserted by a writer, Trigorin, was certainly like Lika and her unfortunate love, both in its betrayal by Potapenko and, perhaps secondarily, in its rejection by Chekhov. He had had the couple under observation before, during and after their own drama, and once more, as in the case of Levitan's love affair, he had been unable to resist that too frequent temptation of the writer: taking the inspiration from the lives of his intimates.

Nothing is new in this. A writer whose characters we feel to be real people in a real world, be he a novelist or a dramatist, would have been lost had he not had his own experiences and surroundings to draw upon. The mere faculty of memory may play a vital role in his art. I suspect that the more we may learn of a writer's life, the more important we shall find memory to have been with him — assisted by notebooks, which we may judge that Shakespeare kept from his advising the fair youth of the *Sonnets* to do so. (When Hamlet, observing in his state of near derangement after his first encounter with the Ghost that "one may smile, and smile, and be a villain," I think it is the self-mockery of a writer, by whom all is turned into words, that causes him to exclaim, "My tables! Meet it is I set it down.") In reading the novels of Aleksandr I. Solzhenitsyn, I became increasingly impressed by the evident role that an astonishing memory played in them. Then I came across a passage — I do not now remember where — in which he spoke of his indebtedness to a memory that was all-retentive.

The Harvard professors object that the writers I quote on the relationship between an author and his works are all modern. That is so. It is because none I can find addressed himself to the subject earlier than François René, Vicomte de Châteaubriand (1768–1848), who said:

> We are convinced that the great writers have put their history in their works. One paints only one's own heart in attributing it to another, and the better part of genius is composed of memories.

The better part of genius is composed of memories. Châteaubriand put explicitly the point I would have made, that the modern writers whose testimony I cite are speaking of creative writing itself, not merely of its current forms; he was referring to *all* "great writers." So too was Friedrich Nietzsche when, speaking of Shakespeare, he said that "he conceived the type of Caesar. Such things a man cannot guess — he either is the thing or he is not."

To speculate on why one person encompasses more of the span of human nature than another, why he is, or can be, more different human beings, I must leave to others. But it is interesting to read what Edmund Wilson writes of Ben Jonson:

> Though he attempts a variety of characters, they all boil down to a few motivations, recognizable as the motivations of Jonson himself and rarely transformed into artistic creations. . . . Jonson merely splits himself up and sets the pieces — he is to this extent a dramatist — in conflict with one another; but we have merely to put these pieces together to get Jonson, with little left over.

Continuing the statement I have quoted from *Ecce Homo*, Nietzsche declares that "The great poet draws only from his own experience — to such an extent that later he can no longer endure his own work."

That Paul Gallico is hardly in the front rank of his calling does not detract from the validity of his insight in observing:

> For there is no creative product that so exposes the past life, the background, the adjustment or lack of adjustment to life, the fears and foibles, the failings and strivings of the human being behind it as does writing. . . . The writer appears in many guises throughout his stories, and each of them has a meaning and a reason, some valid relation to his character or person or the kind of human being he is.

Of his first effort at novel-writing, Louis Auchincloss says, hardly recognizing the obstacle he was setting up to his view of Shakespeare's identity:

> I learned then and there that all a novelist's characters are himself. There may be a character who is the author dressed up to look like John Jones or Mary Smith, but it is still basically the author.

James Lord, in a review of Henri Troyat's *Tolstoy*, observes of "the greatest creative personalities" that

> their lives become interpenetrated by the art through which they attempt to give life to life, and such a profound interdependence is generated between what they are and what they do that ultimately the two achieve a common character.

I recognize that in stressing an author's self-revelation in his works I am belaboring the point. It is, however, at the heart of the question of Shakespeare's identity, as well as crucial to an understanding of artistic creation. With the reader's indulgence, therefore, and at the risk of boring him, I shall pursue the subject a little further. I think I may find a special license in doing so in Sir Victor S. Pritchett's assurance that even Hans Christian Andersen's fairy tales "were transfigurations of his own life."

All the testimony we have heard as to an author's experience being reflected in his work must be swept aside by orthodoxy, as Evans and Levin sweep it aside. Peter Quennell, an inflexible Stratfordian, has conceded that "An artist's work and the circumstances of his life are inextricably bound up together," but the concession must have slipped by in an unguarded moment, with Shakespeare's authorship far from his thoughts. Certainly John Wain, a staunch defender of orthodoxy, will have none of any such idea. He complains that

> Leafing through some recent books on Shakespeare, I was saddened to find so many people playing the dreary game of deducing the writer's biography from his works. Any writer whose life-story *could* be so deduced, it seems to me, would by definition be a second-rate artist.

Of the novelists writing in Britain during John Wain's lifetime, I suppose that by the critics' consensus the three greatest would be Joseph Conrad, D. H. Lawrence, and James Joyce. Mr. Wain would have to be wilfully obtuse not to be able to deduce from their works the kind of lives they had led, even in considerable detail.[1]

The Canadian Professor Northrop Frye tells us that Shakespeare had

> a capacity for subduing his nature to what it works in unrivaled in the history of culture, a career which leaves him not only without a private life but almost without a private personality.

What he is saying, of course, is that the nature, private life, and private personality of the Stratford man are undetectable in the works of Shakespeare. It would be astonishing if they were detectable. To imagine Shakspere as having been the author of those works would indeed make him unrivaled in the history of culture for eliminating himself from what he wrote. It would make him unique in nature. And it does not take me to point out that the phenomenon that is unique in nature does not exist.

Here, not for the first time or the last, Frank Harris seems to me far ahead of the generality of Stratfordian commentators in perception and candor. He declares that:

> It is the life-work of the artist to show himself to us, and the completeness with which he reveals his own individuality is perhaps the best measure of his genius. . . . Sincerity is the birthmark of genius, and we can be sure that Shakespeare has depicted himself for us with singular fidelity.

Edward Albee expressed himself to similar effect in response to my inquiry as to whether he was speaking not for himself alone (as the Harvard professors would have us think) when he wrote that "Your source material is the people you know," but that ultimately "every character is an extension of the author's own personality." He said, "*All* good writers take from themselves, from people they know & (via the unconscious) from people they don't know they know."

It is a new idea to me, linking merit in a writer with self-divulgence. But I believe I see the rationale. The novelist or playwright obeys an external or internal bidding, or he obeys one to a larger extent than the other. He

---

[1] Since first writing the foregoing I find that Mr. Wain in reviewing a biography of James Joyce declared that "So far from being the high priest of a cool impersonality, he is as self-revelatory as Byron; his work is autobiographical both on the grand scale and on the minute."

expresses the collective consciousness of his kind and is comparatively absent from his works, as Stratfordians must believe Shakespeare is, or he creates a world in the light of an inner, personal vision, giving of himself — and continually giving himself away. With a greater or lesser degree of ingenuity, those who take their guidance from without mirror the literary fashions of the time, its conventions and ways of looking at life, above all following the lead of what has been or is being written. It is they whom John Wain could justifiably call the second-raters. For the writers of originality, the pioneers in understanding human nature and human life — and they are those from whose ranks arise the writers whom posterity judges to be great and keeps alive — the alternative and the only alternative is to look within themselves and to transmute into language the substance of what they are and have grown into by exposure to life and to others. It is a matter of genuine versus artificial. Truly, as Pamela Hansford Johnson (the late widow of C. P. Snow) says, "No novelist should attempt to write his full autobiography — he has written himself and his life into his novels, no matter how much both are disguised." W. Somerset Maugham made the same point. But what distinguishes the genius, I think, is that he perceives himself and his life and his fellows not as others would perceive them, in habitual modes — his work would still be autobiographical if he did — but with the freshness of a child's vision. ("*Shakespeare,*" says Samuel Johnson, "whether life or nature be his subject, shews plainly, that he has seen with his own eyes; he gives the image which he receives, not weakened or distorted by the intervention of any other mind.") The more gifted the writer, the less does he follow in the grooves of others' apprehensions and the more does he cut his own, in the light of his own nature. His work, being so individually his own, must be especially revealing of himself. The more gifted, the more we feel we know him. We are far better acquainted with Henry James than with Edgar Rice Burroughs, with Mark Twain than with Zane Grey — granted there was more to be acquainted with. Blindfolded in a company of writers, we could probably recognize James and Twain in a fifth the time it would take us to recognize the author of *Tarzan* and *The Riders of the Purple Sage,* however well we know their works.

To those who argue that we do not know Shakespeare the man because drama is "objective" or because of his "impersonality" or his "chameleonic empathy" — the terms are the Harvard professors' — we may exclaim with the 19th-century French critic H. A. Taine, "Do you not see Shakespeare behind the crowd of his creatures? They had made him known; they have all exhibited something of him."

As Robert Beverly Hale, the renowned art teacher, says, "The artist doesn't see things as they are, he sees things as he is." And having seen them as he is, the true master leads the rest of us to see them in that way, too. We do not doubt that this is the way they *are* and have been all along. But that is not so. More than we comprehend, I think, Shakespeare invented men and women as we see them and the kinds of human nature they manifest. We assume that mankind as we know it was there to begin with, for Shakespeare to observe with uncanny astuteness and report with unrivaled felicity of language, and I suppose we cannot deny that that is so. Yet paradoxically it is equally true, I believe, that Shakespeare did not simply discover us to ourselves but brought into being what was not there before. He gave us emotions to feel, a race of men and women to perceive, and a world of nature to be in, richer than we should otherwise have known, which he evoked with Prospero's magic. We have been bemused by the academicians who tell us that he kept himself out of his plays, unaware of the absurdity in the preachment — that he had simply "an actor's capacity for entering the minds of his vast and highly differentiated cast of characters," as Evans and Levin inform us. As to the origin of those characters, our preceptors are vague. Perhaps, like Baby in a coy ditty popular in my childhood, they came from "Out of the Nowhere into the Here" — independent of human agency.

Militant orthodoxy has not only misled us as to the authorship of Shakespeare's works. It has also, in order that we might swallow its version of their derivation, talked us out of understanding the creative process. That is a crime against the chief glory of our species. Its perpetrators should be required to read and digest two statements bearing on the subject that I am going to quote, both made by respected spokesmen of the world of science in the joint presentation by BBC and Time Television of Jacob Bronowski's *The Ascent of Man*.

Here is Bruce Mazlish, professor of history and head of the Humanities Department at the Massachusetts Institute of Technology, contrasting Darwin and Wallace:

> Many people have the idea of science as something abstract, detached from men, certainly from men and women who in fact make the great discoveries, as if scientific laws were something "Out there" to be discovered. But I don't think it's at all like that. I think that the actual discoverer leaves his imprint upon the discovery. There's a style, a way of approaching it and a way, in fact, of delivering it, and that was very different for Wallace and for Darwin.

The other is Gerald Holton of the Jefferson Physics Laboratory at Harvard, and he too is drawing a contrast between scientists: Newton and Einstein. He says:

> Their work itself in some way showed how closely interpenetrating are the personality factors in both these cases. Their childhood history, for example, and the final work which they ended up by doing. One often thinks that the work of scientists is somehow disembodied from the humanity that they have; but on the contrary, it seems to those who study both the science and the biography that the science itself is a reflection of their whole personality, and therefore the formation of this personality in a sense prepared them for the kind of physics which they ended up by doing.

If the discoverer of a scientific law leaves his imprint upon the discovery, if the work of a mathematician is a reflection of his personality, how much more must this be true of the work of the artist!

I cannot recall any effort by the orthodox to show how the works of Shakespeare bear the imprint or reflection of the commercial-minded Stratfordian's personality. As for their bearing the marks of his background, Professors Evans and Levin come up with two instances of the relationship. One is "the deer-stealing incident, which may well have been reflected in the plays." The elevating report that "Shakespeare" was "much given to all unluckiness in stealing venison & rabbits particularly from Sir Lucy who had him oft whipped & sometimes imprisoned. . . ." is first heard from a clergyman who was not even born until seventy-two years after Shakspere's death. The best that Gerald E. Bentley can say of it is that "there are no sufficient grounds for denying the legend entirely." How it "may well have been reflected in the plays," the professors do not tell us.

As for the other instances of such a reflection, they write that "Caroline Spurgeon's study of Shakespeare's imagery has shown how such poetic sensibilities could have been nourished by the Warwickshire countryside" — as they could equally well have been nourished by the countryside in any of a dozen English counties — "matching the very eddies under Clopton Bridge with those that swirl in *The Rape of Lucrece.*" Here is how the latter swirl:

> As through an arch the violent roaring tide   1667+
> Outruns the eye that doth behold his haste,
> Yet in the eddy boundeth in his pride
> Back to the strait that forced him on so fast
> In rage sent out, recalled in rage, being past . . .

What we have in those lines is a description of the eddies that form on the downstream side of any broad bridge-piers in flowing water, such as the poet could doubtless have witnessed at bridges scattered all across Britain, those of masonry all necessarily arched. How they are peculiarly apposite to the "quiet, slow-gliding waters" — as Levi Fox, director of the Shakespeare Birthplace Trust of Stratford calls them — of the Avon at Clopton Bridge is not clear.

So here we have it. Those are the two most striking examples the Harvard professors can cite of the stamp of Shakspere's background on the poems and plays by William Shakespeare.

The Author Revealed in Shakespeare's Works

In the preceding four chapters, we have seen what the plays would actually appear to owe to the author's background. In brief, they suggest that his milieu was that of a highly cultivated nobleman. We have been admitted through the *Sonnets* to the poet's heart and given further evidence that his background was what we had deduced, and we have had his word for it in them that he was near death in 1603.

In the present chapter we have found that the consensus among the best-informed is that in all creative effort the creator creates in his own image. In narrative literature telling human stories — the short story, the novel, and the drama — we might expect self-revelation to be particularly close to the surface, and I think those whose opinions should carry greatest weight would agree that this is so. The narrator who conjures up real-seeming men and women to move in a convincing likeness of the actual world — as does Shakespeare with more memorable effect than any other — may be expected to delineate his experience in theirs.[2] Within measure we should be able to tell what kind of person the narrator was and what kind of life he was familiar with in what kind of surroundings. Certainly we should be able to do so for a genius, who will be outstanding in awareness and in compulsion to "bear true testimony" (Joseph Conrad's phrase) to the impression he has received of life.

In the chapters to come, we shall test the congruity of Shakespeare's experience, as we should deduce it from his writings, with the life-story (insofar as we know it) of the one man who apparently could have been Shakespeare judging from the evidence we have examined and is not eliminated by criteria that appear to be valid. As part of this undertaking, we shall also be determining as well as we can whether he exhibited qualities consistent with Shakespeare's genius. Before doing so, however, let us consider a crucial question.

We take it that the story-writer's — novelist's, dramatist's — works are ultimately autobiographical. We believe this to mean that his *dramatis personae* all have traits of men and women who have entered his life — as Edward Albee says, he does not write of people he has never known — and not only that, but that these traits are those which strike a responsive chord in him, are traits that he would be capable of exhibiting himself, or would were there not stronger inhibiting traits. In other words, insofar as his characters are real and not mere derivatives of his reading, they are characters that he has within himself.

Proceeding a step further, we may reasonably adduce — and our knowl-

---

[2] Two centuries ago Samuel Johnson wrote:

It will not easily be imagined how much *Shakespeare* excels in accommodating his sentiments to real life, but by comparing him with other authors. . . . The theatre, when it is under any other direction, is peopled by such characters as were never heard, upon topics which will never arise in the commerce of mankind. But the dialogue of this author is often so evidently determined by the incident which produces it, and is pursued with so much ease and simplicity, that it seems scarcely to claim the merit of fiction, but to have been gleaned by diligent selection out of common conversation, and common occurrences.

edge of literature justifies our doing so — that some of a writer's characters will be more fully himself than others. Almost certainly, the more profound and explicit the character's complexity and the more fully the character is achieved — the more a rounded, living person we find him or her — then the more the character will be found to be a self-portrait of the author. And to this it might be added that the more a character is all these things, the greater the talent that will have gone into his or her creation.

Given the foregoing, the question is: in which of Shakespeare's characters are we likeliest to find the dramatist most fully and faithfully revealed?

There can, I think, be but one answer to that question. If the purpose of stage-playing is, as Hamlet says, "to hold, as 'twere, the mirror up to nature," can there be any doubt that Shakespeare held the mirror up to his own nature in the character of Hamlet? The Prince is surely the most fully achieved human being of all creations in fiction, and it is this which enables us all to see something of him in ourselves, of ourselves in him. To no other character does recognition go out so unreservedly. "You are, Prince Hamlet, of all times and of all countries," Anatole France exclaimed. "You have not aged an hour in three centuries. Your soul is of the age of our souls. We live together (*ensemble*) and you are what we are, a man in the midst of a universal sickness (*au milieu du mal universel*)."

A contrived character can be fully comprehended because the author knows what elements are being compounded in him, but no living human being can be so. Because Hamlet was the one person his creator could put on paper true to life without fully comprehending him — that person being himself — he is real, with a real human being's many-faceted nature, contradictions, loose ends, and ultimate unfathomability. He is the greatest character in fiction because he mirrors his creator, who was the greatest genius in literature. He "is an enigma because he is real," says Mark Van Doren. "We do not know why he was created or what he means," he goes on, his eyes closed to the implications in what he is acknowledging. "We simply and amply perceive that he exists." Then he adds that which should have told him that Hamlet was the living embodiment of the dramatist: "He is that unique thing in literature, a credible genius."

Let us see how a character with a life of his own — his creator's life — acts in a way that a contrived character would not. Hamlet is intensely exercised by the report that his father's ghost has appeared on the castle's battlements. "For God's sake, let me hear," he cries to Horatio and the two soldiers who have beheld the apparition. He plies them with questions. He resolves "I'll speak to it, though hell itself should gape / And bid me hold my peace." That night Hamlet and Horatio join Marcellus in his watch. A character manipulated by the author would behave as reason would have him behave and be in a state of single-minded anticipation, gripped by suspense. But not Hamlet. The sounds of kettle-drum and trumpet, advertising the king's wassail, set him off on a philosophic disquisition on the injury to the nation's good name by its reputed drunkenness, whence he proceeds to the broader theme of how men may "in the general censure [judgment] take corruption" from "the stamp of one defect." It is evident that the reason for his being on the parapets is quite out of mind. He is still holding forth, absorbed in his subject — and seeing nothing inappropriate in this because the dramatist, being Hamlet, is being himself — when the ghost appears, and his attention has to be called to it.

It could be argued, of course, that the dramatist is in this purposely demonstrating the character of Hamlet's mind. There are two reasons for doubting this, however. First, no attention is called to this kind of aberration on Hamlet's part and his illogical abstraction from the scene on the battlements might therefore be expected to escape notice — has in fact, so far as I know, escaped comment. Secondly, others of Shakespeare's protagonists are apt to slip out of character into "Hamlet's peculiar habit of talking to himself," Frank Harris points out, and into Hamlet's way of thought and expression.

Harris, the versatile Anglo-American literary man, is capable of going far adrift when seized with misinformation about Shakespeare derived from the Stratford theory, but for the rest, the acuteness of *The Man Shakespeare and His Tragic Life-Story* (1911) shows to peculiarly glaring effect, for me, how shallow, feeble, and unseeing is the portraiture of Shakespeare in other orthodox works — how altogether far afield. Harris is especially shrewd, I think, in the matter of autobiographical give-aways in the dramas. He writes:

> Even if it be admitted that Hamlet is the most complex and profound of Shakespeare's creations, and therefore probably the character in which Shakespeare revealed most of himself, the question of degree still remains to be determined. . . . If one could show that wherever Shakespeare fell out of a character he unconsciously dropped into the Hamlet vein, one's suspicion as to the identity of Hamlet and the part would be enormously strengthened. . . . Suppose that Shakespeare in painting another character did nothing but paint Hamlet over and over again trait by trait, virtue by virtue, fault by fault — our assurance would be almost complete; for a dramatist only makes this mistake when he is speaking unconsciously in his proper person. But if both these proofs were forthcoming, not once but a dozen times, then surely our conviction as to the essential identity of Hamlet and Shakespeare would amount to a practical certitude.

At length and in detail, in character after character, Harris shows how both these proofs *are* forthcoming. Hamlet is "bookish and irresolute, a lover of thought and not of action, of melancholy temper, too, and prone to unpack his heart with words." This, as he says, calls up Romeo, whom Hazlitt called "Hamlet in love." Rather, says Harris, he "is a younger brother of Hamlet." His "last speech . . . is characteristic of Hamlet: on the very threshold of death he generalizes. . . . There is in Romeo, too, that peculiar mixture of pensive sadness and loving sympathy which is the very vestiture of Hamlet's soul."

I must say I am struck by how repeatedly Hamlet takes over Romeo's character. It is the mature, world-weary Prince, filled with foreboding in Act V of *Hamlet*, hardly the youthful, ardent lover Romeo is supposed to be, who speaks in Act I of *Romeo and Juliet*:

> my mind misgives
> Some consequence yet hanging in the stars
> Shall bitterly begin his fearful date
> With this night's revels, and expire the term
> Of a despis'd life clos'd in my breast.

When Romeo declares "This is not Romeo, he's some other where," he is expressing the same thought Hamlet will voice. Though it is Romeo speaking, Hamlet could well cry, and with better cause than Romeo, "O! teach me how I should forget to think," and:

> Not mad, but bound more than a madman is:
> Shut up in prison . . .

From Romeo Harris moves on to Jaques in *As You Like It*, in whom, by the way, Edward Dowden finds all the qualities of Hamlet detected by critics. Says Harris: "Jaques is only sketched in with light strokes, but all his traits are peculiarly Hamlet's traits. For Jaques is a melancholy student of life, as Hamlet is, with lightning-quick intelligence and heavy heart. . . . If we combine the characters of Romeo, the poet-lover, and of Jaques, the pensive-sad philosopher, we have almost the complete Hamlet."

Of *Richard the Second*, Harris observes that Shakespeare had intended to present the king as a vile and cruel Richard of tradition (a monarch who established "an unveiled despotism," Winston Churchill writes, and moved upon a course of murder "in cold hatred rarely surpassed among men"), then midway in the play veers around and lays stress on his weakness by suffering. (Here I might interject that Edward de Vere would certainly not have been unaware that Richard doted on his ancestor, the 9th Earl of Oxford, who went to deserved ruin in the king's cause.) "From the time Richard appoints York as Regent, Shakespeare begins to think of himself as Richard." Then the Hamlet traits begin to come out. "Who is not reminded of Hamlet's great monologue when he reads: 'For within the hollow crown . . .'?"

Harris overdoes it, I think, when he speaks of Macbeth as "merely our gentle, irresolute, humanist philosopher masquerading in galligaskins as a Scottish thane." Yet he can find a basis for his claim that in this other regicide Shakespeare "had painted" a "second Hamlet unconsciously." Macbeth, he says, acts and speaks at first appearance just as Hamlet would, perceiving instantly with Hamlet's nimble-quick intelligence the implications of the witches' prophecy, which escape Banquo. He points to Macbeth's inappropriate soliloquy when hailed Thane of Cawdor, in which he finds arguments against action. Lady Macbeth fears his nature, which is "too full of the milk of human kindness." In words "which come from the inmost of Hamlet's heart," he soliloquizes:

> I have no spur
> To prick the sides of my intent, but only
> Vaulting ambition, which o'erleaps itself,
> And falls on the other.

Again and again Macbeth succumbs to thought and reverie. "No wonder Lady Macbeth exclaims 'These deeds must not be thought / After these ways: so, it will make us mad.' But nothing can restrain Macbeth: he gives rein to his poetic imagination, and breaks into an exquisite lyric, a lyric which has hardly any closer relation to the circumstances than its truth to Shakespeare's nature: 'Methought I heard a voice say. . . .'"

Samuel Schoenbaum comments on Harris's observations that "To some readers it may come as a surprise that Macbeth, Bellona's bridegroom and dead butcher, is bracketed with Hamlet as a kindly aesthete." Harris does not, of course, represent Macbeth as a kindly aesthete, any more than Shakespeare represents him, simply, as a butcher. (And why "dead" butcher? Was *Hamlet* written about a dead prince?) The difference between Frank Harris and Professor Schoenbaum, one feels, is that where the former was passionately concerned with Shakespeare, to the latter the dramatist appears merely a subject for scholarship and very clever writing.[3]

To anyone who will trouble to read the play, it is evident that Macbeth, though he coveted the crown, would have balked at murder to gain it had he not been goaded by Lady Macbeth. In a long, wrenching soliloquy he declares that Duncan's virtues

> Will plead like angels trumpet-tongued against
> The deep damnation of his taking-off.

They plead successfully with Macbeth himself, and the decision he announces to his lady is that "We will proceed no further in this business."

The facts about the historic Macbeth were available to the dramatist in Holinshed, who called him "a valiant gentleman, and one that if he had been somewhat cruel of nature, might have been thought most worthy the government of a realm." He was a "most diligent punisher of all injustice and wrongs" and was to make "many wholesome laws and statutes for the public

---

[3] If, on the evidence, Harris has read Shakespeare far more thoughtfully than Schoenbaum, it is not that the latter lacks the mental equipment. Far from it. Schoenbaum is too astute to hazard the deep waters beneath the surface of the plays.

weal." Holinshed said, however, "in his aspiration to the crown, the words of the three weird sisters [had] greatly encouraged him, but specially his wife lay sore upon him to attempt the thing, as she was very ambitious, burning in unquenchable desire to bear the name of a queen." Shakespeare's Macbeth is from the start appalled to contemplate what his achievement of the crown promised by the weird sisters and dreamed of before his encounter with them must entail. The

> horrid image doth unfix my hair
> And make my seated heart knock at my ribs.

Repeatedly in the early part of the play, Harris shows, Macbeth speaks with Hamlet's poetic voice and with Hamlet's introspection, compassion, and high-mindedness. But once he has given in to Lady Macbeth and followed her plan for Duncan's murder, he is led inevitably in self-protection to one crime after another. Hamlet was himself ambitious. He tells us as much, and one of his initial charges against King Claudius is that the usurper has come between him and the succession. *Macbeth* could well have been written by Hamlet to rationalize his inherent disinclination to take on leadership of events. "See," he might have been saying to himself, "this is how a decent, brave, reflective nobleman is turned into a monster and led to his destruction by an agency of the supernatural inciting him to displace the occupant of the throne."

It comes as no surprise that Schoenbaum, the current Laureate of American Stratfordians, excoriates Frank Harris. "Liar, libertine and blackmailer," he calls him: in short, "a scoundrel." In *The Man Shakespeare* he finds "the rhinestones and tinsel alloy of a second-rate mind," revealing "the man Harris as a literary charlatan." He does report that Arnold Bennett said of it that "A masterpiece on Shakespeare has at last been written," one that "has destroyed nearly all previous Shakespearean criticism." His scorn remains complete, however. The internationally renowned 19th-century Danish scholar, Georg Brandes, comes in for it, too, and for similar reasons. Brandes "repudiated the notion of Shakespeare's impersonality and discovered the artist's 'whole individuality' in his writings." *That* put him beyond the pale. The dramatist, Brandes found, was, in Schoenbaum's words, "a fellow aristocrat" with a "royalist view of history" and contempt "for the common herd." Horrors! Worse still, betraying an understanding of literary creation, Brandes concluded that "He had lived through Hamlet's experience — all."

It must be said that there are two grave weaknesses in Harris's *The Man Shakespeare*, and these Schoenbaum did not overlook. Moreover, he finds both in Brandes's *William Shakespeare* as well — not surprisingly; it is difficult to see how a Stratfordian attempting to bring a credible Shakespeare to life could escape either. First, endeavoring to erect a biography of Shakespeare on the facts of Shakspere's life, Harris is led into fantasies. Secondly, he falls into a very human proclivity. From grasping most readily in another person those traits he shares with us, we find it but a short step to magnifying those traits in our characterization of him, perhaps out of all proportion. Biography, though less, of course, than narrative fiction, tends to self-portraiture. In Shakespeare, Harris would find more of Harris than the rest of us would. In Schoenbaum's probably correct view, that would account for his seeing so prominently in Shakespeare a sensuous, retreative neuropath. The author of *Shakespeare's Lives* is as struck as I by Harris's refusal to allow Shakespeare the ability to create a truly manly character; persuaded that the dramatist lacked within himself the model for such a character, he ascribes the manly traits of Hotspur, Henvy V, and the Bastard Faulconbridge in *King John* to borrowings from earlier playwrights. In this, too, however, Harris was somewhat carried astray by misinformation, namely, the view of scholars in his day that early versions of Shakespeare's historical plays were by writers other than Shakespeare.

What makes Harris virtually unique among orthodox writers is that he interprets Shakespeare from an understanding of the creative imagination, showing how in character after character a consistent personality seeps through, appropriately or not, which can only be the dramatist's own. Other Stratfordian biographers appear by contrast far afield and trivial, or, like Marchette Chute, stunning.

Addressing herself to the familiar proposition that Shakespeare cast himself as the magician Prospero in *The Tempest*, she sets us to rights with acerbity: "He was an objective artist and not in the habit of suddenly inserting pieces of autobiography into his plays." So much for that. We have already observed that she relegates the *Sonnets* to the appendix of her book. The poet's one and extended confession, addressed to posterity, she finds of no interest to the biographer because "no single theory can safely be formed about it." So away with it. Turning to the most profound and enigmatically real and most universal character in literature, its "one credible genius," she discovers for us that Hamlet

> was born in part of the young men who had been glooming about the universities and Inns of Court in the *fin de siècle* atmosphere of the late 1590s and passing remarks on the hollowness of life, the futility of heroic action and the degrading nature of sexual intercourse, but he was also the product of a more specialized group that was interesting the doctors of the period, [who] would have diagnosed Hamlet as a melancholic and put much of his "internal darkness" down to physical causes.

The author of these opinions is recommended by the Folger Library. Schoenbaum writes of her, "Within her self-imposed limits she has produced an admirably sane book."

The point is not that Ms. Chute has no comprehension of the subject of her biography, *Shakespeare of London,* or of literary creation, and that the Folger Library, John Mason Brown (who extols her book), and Professor Schoenbaum cannot recognize these disqualifications. Everyone has his shortcomings. I bring up the two cases because in placing Ms. Chute's and Schoenbaum's works at the top of their fields, we — editors, critics, readers — have shown how far we have failed to read perceptively the writer to whom we owe more than to any other, ever. What he has written we have not "seconded with the forward child Understanding," and that "strikes a man more dead than a great reckoning in a little room." Dead indeed is the Shakespeare of orthodox biographies.

Hamlet as the Dramatist Himself

To resume our quest for self-revelation in Shakespeare's works, let me quote from Louis J. Halle, who in *Hamlet and the World* takes us with uncommon depth of perception and empathy, I think, into the Prince's mind and heart. An acutely observant and thoughtful writer of wide interests and professor at the Institut Universitaire de Hautes Études Internationales in Geneva, Halle turns in his Chapter 3 "to the picture of the author that forms in my mind as I read the poems and plays." He finds them consistently written "from the standpoint of one who was a member of the higher nobility" to whom "all the life that is seen intimately is the life of courts," who "knows poignantly . . . what it is to be a great lord, weighed down with the obligations of living up to his station" and with a "longing for the simple and uncorrupted life that the common people are thought to lead." He goes on:

> There is no doubt in my own mind that Hamlet is Shakespeare himself. What does it mean, however, to say this? There must be something of Shakespeare in Othello, too, but this does not mean that Shakespeare was a Moor. Neither was he, to adopt the *reductio ad absurdum,* the son of the King of Denmark.
>
> In the first instance, we have to distinguish character from topical circumstances. Hamlet is Shakespeare in terms of character. I have no doubt that, just like Hamlet, Shakespeare was introspective; that he was given to musing about life rather than taking action; that he felt a revulsion against the existential world that made the thought of death attractive to him; that he was given to variations of mood from sportive gaiety to profound melancholy; that he found his greatest release from the frustrations of life in words, whether in the poignancy of poetic utterance or in simply unpacking his heart: that he knew self-contempt and such pangs of conscience as made him feel, on occasion, that it were better his mother had not borne him; that he knew both sexual desire and a revulsion from sexual relations (see sonnet CXXIX); and that he found his most abiding refuge from all his inner torments in the philosophical detachment that comes from contemplating the infinite spaces of the cosmos, the immeasurable magnitude of eternity, the shortness of human life, and the fact that death levels all. Indeed, all these items of character are found more or less prominently in the sonnets, which might have been written by Hamlet as he grew older.

After reviewing the circumstances of the Stratford man's background and familiar sphere, which were evidently far removed from those of the dramatist's, Professor Halle proceeds:

> Surely Hamlet is Shakespeare in more than the elements of his character. There are circumstances other than those I have already mentioned that support the identification. A nobleman by birth, Hamlet is something like a playwright by vocation. Confronted with a frustrating problem, his first move is to write a play about it. He is repeatedly improvising rhymes. He is unhappy in the society of the court, but at his happiest and most relaxed in the company of actors, to whom he still stands, however, in the relation of a high patron.
>
> On the internal evidence of the plays and poems as a whole, and of *Hamlet* in particular, I should then arrive at the conclusion that they had been written by someone who was so high of birth as to be a member of the royal entourage; a man profoundly maladjusted and in rebellion against the requirements of his birth and station, as Edward VIII was maladjusted and in rebellion; a man who consequently had sought, on occasion, the kind of escape that Prince Hal found in the company of Eastcheap, who found his greatest relief in the composition of the poems and plays, and who consorted with acting companies in connection with the double life he led. (Indeed, in the sonnets Shakespeare is explicit about his high station, his dishonoring of it, and the public disguise under which he maintains his authorship. . . .) Moreover, leading such a double life, he would feel the need to disguise the illicit half of it. . . .
>
> When one has concluded that the author of the plays must have been a member of the highest nobility at Queen Elizabeth's court, however, one is left with the problem of specific identification. There is one member of the court who fits the picture I have deduced from the plays and poems. Edward de Vere, Earl of Oxford, is Hamlet in his essential character and circumstances alike. . . .

We can take it as almost axiomatic, I believe, that the more fully a writer represents himself as the protagonist in his story, the more the circumstances in which the story evolves will approximate those with which he is familiar. We find it difficult to act naturally, to be ourselves, in situations of which we have had no experience. When a writer puts himself in a part, he will automatically contrive the kind of setting and "business" in which the character who is himself can *be* himself. Another way of expressing it would be to say that the character himself will pull the script into consistency with his experience. This is another reason why I believe we may take it that Shakespeare was as familiar with and as much at odds with Elizabeth's court as Hamlet with the court at Elsinore.

Another feature of closely autobiographical fiction is that it will have an unplanned air. It will move as life moves, one thing seeming to lead to another in itself, albeit with an inner consistency, such as our lives have. It will not be as a constructed story in which every part fits. This characteristic of *Hamlet* was observantly remarked upon by William Hazlitt:

> There is no attempt to force an interest; everything is left for time and circumstance to unfold. The attention is excited without effort, the incidents

succeed each other as matters of course, the characters think and speak and act just as they might do, if left entirely to themselves. There is no set purpose, no straining at a point.

Hazlitt need have mentioned but one further feature of *Hamlet* to be saying that the dramatist was writing about life as he had lived it. That is the presence of elements that make no sense in terms of the play for which one might expect to find an explanation in the reality from which the play is taken. Three of these come to mind.

The first is Hamlet's having presented himself to Ophelia after hearing the Ghost's horrifying report in a condition far more shaken, according to her account, than when we saw him directly after the encounter. He had, she then relates, fallen

> to such perusal of my face
> As he would draw it. Long stay'd he so;
> At last, a little shaking of mine arm,
> And thrice his head thus waving up and down,
> He rais'd a sigh so piteous and profound
> That it did seem to shatter all his bulk
> And end his being.

Nothing he had heard from the Ghost would justify such behavior or cause him to scrutinize Ophelia's face for what he evidently found there. The episode seems, however, to take us straight into a shattering event the real-life Hamlet — de Vere — had been through when rumors reached him in France that the real-life Ophelia — his wife, Anne Cecil — had been unfaithful to him.

Another seemingly irrational turn is given the play when Hamlet, having killed Polonius by mistake, treats the slaying lightly, even jocularly. The sensitive, humane prince we have known would have been overwhelmed by remorse at the deed. Here again it looks to me like an instance of reality intruding. The real-life Hamlet did not kill the real-life Polonius — Lord Burghley. He did not skewer the venerable counselor with his sword but — let us, as Dorothy Ogburn suggests, transpose the "s" — he did so with his words. That was what he had done in writing the play *Hamlet*: he had lampooned Anne Cecil's father. The intent was malicious, but it was not homicidal.

My third instance is of a similar kind. It is where in the last act Hamlet appeals to Laertes:

> Give me your pardon, sir; I've done you wrong;
> But pardon't, as you are a gentleman.

That is how one might ask forgiveness of a man whom one has maligned, not of one whose father one has slaughtered and whose sister one has driven to loss of sanity and suicide. But we may suspect that the terms were appropriate as between the real-life Hamlet and the real-life Laertes, who was Burghley's son. Sir E. K. Chambers points out that it was to the younger son, Robert Cecil, that Burghley addressed his *Certaine Preceptes, or Directions*, which are imitated in Polonius' advice to Laertes; "but," Chambers goes on to say, "Laertes is less like Robert Cecil than Burghley's elder son Thomas."

To add to these three, a fourth instance might be cited of the dramatist's stepping out of his Hamlet guise and out of the play back into his real-life self. That is when the prince gives his famous instructions to the traveling players. In the play he has only proposed to insert a speech of a dozen or sixteen lines in *The Murder of Gonzago*, which he has arranged to have presented so that King Claudius will betray his guilt when he sees enacted a murder such as he has been accused by the Ghost of having perpetrated. The precise manner in which these lines might be spoken, indeed the quality of the acting throughout, which was sure to be competent — these were professional actors, remember — would have affected the upshot not a tittle. And upon the upshot hinged Hamlet's whole future and whether he had any, as well as that of Denmark. Would Claudius' guilt be proclaimed, and would Hamlet thereupon slay his uncle where he stood? Would the king's faction — as surely there would have been one — have fallen upon him the instant he raised his sword? The prince faced the deadliest crisis in his life. The suspense he was in would have been all but unendurable. His last thought would have been for the niceties of the interpolated lines' delivery. But hear him:

> Speak the speech, I pray you, as I pronounced it to you, trippingly on the tongue; but if you mouth it, as many of your players do, I had as lief the town-crier spoke my lines.

The man who was Hamlet has stepped back into his own life and the play's driving imperatives are forgotten as he pursues the subject of absorbing interest to him: the art of acting. "Use all gently," he urges,

> for in the very torrent, tempest, and — as I may say — whirlwind of passion, you must acquire and beget a temperance. . . .

and so on. But

> Be not too tame neither, but let your own discretion be your tutor: suit the action to the word, the word to the action; with this special observance, that you o'erstep not the modesty of nature; for anything so overdone is [far] from the purpose of playing, whose end, both at the first and now, was and is, to hold, as 'twere, the mirror up to nature; to show virtue her own feature, scorn her own image, and the very age and body of the time his form and pressure.

On he goes, holding us intent on what he is saying. But what has it to do with the desperate matter at hand? Nothing whatever. It does, however, call up the picture of the real-life Hamlet instructing the cast he has assembled on how he wishes his play done, addressing them not as an ill-paid play-wright or common share-holder would address such giants of the theatre as Burbage and Kempe but as one who speaks with an authority even they would respect. Thus, in the midst of *Hamlet* he finds the opportunity irresistible to interrupt the play to formulate his ideas about the craft of acting. Well, these have probably not been excelled in four centuries. But no audience would swallow such behavior, irrational and inconsistent with the situation as it is, except that Hamlet is so fascinating a character and the play written with such convincing conviction of its reality that whatever it tells us we are persuaded to accept as having been the case.

The late Elizabeth Taylor, whose novels do not suffer in comparison with Jane Austen's, has one of her characters remark that she "can never understand why Polonius has to look so ancient . . . with those youngish children" and another explain that "He has to look like Lord Burghley, you see. I've no doubt he was made up to be the spit image at the first performance, and the idea has gone on ever since." That the tradition is at one with the author's intention can hardly be doubted — though this is a fact from which the Stratfordians have to tiptoe quietly away, quite unable to explain how a mere actor-playwright would dare lampoon the man who for forty years was nearest the Queen in power and whose son was coming to fill his shoes and how, if he had so challenged authority, he could conceivably have got away with it. (Let alone can they account for the appearance of the royal coat-of-arms on the first page of the play containing this enormity as it was printed, evidently with fidelity to the author's manuscript upon Oxford's death in 1604.) Yet there it is — the unquestionable travesty of Burghley in Polonius.

Burghley was fifty when Oxford married his fourteen-year-old daughter, and the Earl at twenty-six, as we know from a letter he wrote him at the time, considered his father-in-law already aged; probably the Lord Treasurer even then had the white beard in which, alone, we know him. Corambis, as Polonius was called in the first quarto of *Hamlet*, is palpably a play on Burghley's motto, "*Cor unum* . . . ," as we have seen. Another verbal play establishing the same link comes when Hamlet, having dispatched Polonius, tells the King:

> A certain convocation of *politic worms* are e'en at him.
> Your worm is your only *emperor* for *diet*. [Italics added.]

Burghley was given to recalling that he was born during the Diet of Worms, which Emperor Charles V had opened and at which Martin Luther had defended his doctrines. When Hamlet calls Polonius "a fishmonger" he is referring to Burghley's having put a bill through Parliament making Wednesday a meatless day in addition to Friday to encourage the fisheries; the Catholics called it "Cecil's Fast." Then there are those maxims Polonius recites for his son's guidance, which we have heard Sir E. K. Chambers acknowledge parallel those which Burghley wrote for his son's, which had not been printed when *Hamlet* was written; "Conceivably," Chambers says with notable lack of conviction, "Shakespeare knew a pocket manuscript." Some of Burghley's *Certaine Preceptes* are, beginning with the best known:

> And that gentleman who sells an acre of land, sells an ounce of credit. For gentility is nothing but ancient riches.
> Let thy hospitality be moderate; & according to the means of thy estate; rather plentiful than sparing, but not costly.
> Beware of surety for thy best friends. He that payeth another man's debt, seeketh his own decay.
> Be sure to keep some great man thy friend, but trouble him not for trifles.

In the *Harvard Magazine* article (to which I have to keep reverting because it put the highest orthodox authorities on the spot to answer to the evidence) I had only small space to give to autobiography in Shakespeare's plays. After quoting Queen Elizabeth's angry remark, "I am Richard the Second; know ye not that?" I said that "actually, she seems much more fully to have been Queen Gertrude in *Hamlet*, and the Earl of Leicester — as near to a husband as Elizabeth ever had — to have been King Claudius." I then quoted from a characterization of *Hamlet* in a book by Brigid Brophy, Michael Levey, and Charles Osborne: "The prototype of western literature's most deplorable and most formless form, autobiographical fiction." Pointing out that the dramatist "left us his speaking self-portrait as the most memorable character in English letters," I had room left for only the following:

> His relations to Burghley's daughter Anne, whom he married, were very much those of Hamlet's to Polonius's daughter Ophelia. His mother seems to have married just a few months after her husband's death, as Queen Gertrude, Hamlet's mother did. Leicester, widely believed to have murdered his wife, Amy Robsart, to clear the way to his marriage to Elizabeth, was given possession of the bulk of the estates belonging to the future dramatist [the real-life Hamlet], then a boy — just as Claudius, who also cleared the way to his marriage to Gertrude and the throne by murder, acquired the kingdom to which Hamlet was heir by the favor of Gertrude.

The Harvard professors replied that:

> It is true that the Earl [of Oxford] had a stepfather, Leicester; but the analogy can be carried further only by straining and twisting; and Mr. Ogburn cannot make up his mind whether Oxford's mother or Queen Elizabeth should be cast as Gertrude.

The first part of that sentence, as we have earlier remarked, reveals the extent of the professor's ignorance of Oxford, if not of Elizabethan history. As for what the rest reveals — well, it was the editor's idea, not the professors' that they undertake to reply to the article. I have not the least difficulty in making up my mind as to the prototype for Gertrude. In the dramatist's mind, I am fairly confident, she stood for Elizabeth, to whom de Vere's attitude would probably have been ambivalent. He would, I think, have seen her partly from the point of view of a son, in the sense in which the Queen identified herself in her prayers as the "mother" of the "children," her subjects; writing of her to Robert Cecil upon her death, de Vere would use the phrase "under whom both you and myself in our greenest years ["green in judgment," as Cleopatra says] have in a manner been brought up." Partly, I judge, he would have seen her as would one who, in youth, may well have been her lover, or close to it, though seventeen years her junior. (Modern stage-directors have been astute, by these tokens, in bringing out an "inces-tuous" element in Hamlet's regard for Gertrude, following John Barrymore's innovation. At the same time I can well believe that young de Vere's resent-ment of his widowed mother's over-hasty remarriage, which cropped up in Hamlet's resentment of his mother's similar precipitancy, presumably was the inspiration for the dramatist's having Gertrude's remarriage follow so hard upon her husband's death.

To Evans and Levin the discovery in the writer's own life of characters and situations in his works is a game of "far-fetched charades" from which "nothing is gained and everything is diminished." What is gained in this case is light on the identity of the author, which would account for the professors' harsh view of the procedure. As for the general proposition they have for-mulated, we may suspect it of being another case of a King of Hearts' rule, just invented. It would condemn just about every literary biography, a prime purpose of nearly all being to relate the author's life and his works. "Hamlet, after all," they say, "is not a topical skit." Probably that is why no one has ever called it one. Curiously, however, it was in *Hamlet* itself, in the last passage I quoted from it, that the protagonist stresses that one of the ends of stage-playing is "to show . . . the very age and body of the time his form and pressure." It is Hamlet, too, who calls the players "the abstracts and brief chronicles of the time": and in both cases it seems clear that the dramatist would have us understand that he is speaking of what the players play. Acting can hardly show the age and body of the time his form and pressure — it is the playwright who has the power to do that — and where players could be reporters and chroniclers, only the plays themselves could be abstracts and chronicles.

Professor Evans, having incorporated in the *Riverside Shakespeare* a confession of the bankruptcy of orthodoxy to account for *Hamlet* ("How Shakespeare came to write it is, of course, a mystery on which it is useless to speculate"), he and Professor Levin in *Harvard Magazine* retire from the field in a manner irresistibly suggestive of an octopus's covering its escape by ejecting a cloud of ink: *Hamlet*, they tell us, "is the refined end-product of a long sequence of sources, and its powerful resonances of conflict and passion have a mythical origin." *Any*way, "Whoever wrote the play did not envisage it as a self-serving letter in code to a puzzled posterity."

The characteristic style of that last utterance also reminded me of something, I knew, and in Kipling's *Just So Stories* I ran it down: "This is the way Bi-Coloured-Python-Rock-Snakes always talk." But let me not be distracted. The professors raise the question of how the dramatist *did* envisage *Hamlet*. The view of many, including me, is that it was his ultimate accounting of himself and witness of his encounter with the world. In specifying what the dramatist did not intend the play to be, the professors failed to travesty the Oxfordians' position as much as they doubtless meant to. Remove the pejorative verbiage from their statement and we have remaining a not altogether incorrect description of what the dramatist did in part, I believe, have in mind: a letter to a puzzled posterity.

I think we should take into account the poet's confession in the *Sonnets* of his unspoken shame and guilt and with it the discredit Edward de Vere brought upon his name in the eyes of many, including historians, unwitting of his true story (as we conceive it), when we hear Hamlet's dying plea to his trusted friend, in whom we may see de Vere's cousin Horace, often known as Horatio (as he is to the *Dictionary of National Biography*). "Report me and my cause aright," Hamlet entreats him.

Was it Horace Vere who, in discharging this commission, upon Oxford's death, provided for Nicholas Ling to publish the 1604 quarto of *Hamlet*, "Newly imprinted and enlarged to almost as much againe as it was, according to the true and perfect Coppie," and for a second edition to be stamped with the royal arms, as befitting a prince's final exit? Chambers believes the text "may very possibly be from the author's manuscript," with the proviso "that this was not very legible." Horatio could have provided it — and what would one not give to know! If he did, he enabled his cousin himself to report his cause aright, and not so much "to the unsatisfied" as to a forever enthralled posterity. His failure to do more, perhaps because he was "made tongue-tied by authority," it remains for us now to endeavor to make good.

19

"See, Where Oxford Comes!"

Time's glory is to calm contending kings,
To unmask falsehood and bring truth to light.
— *Lucrece*

After some introductory generalizations about the case for the Earl of Oxford as Shakespeare, we hear what some eminent Stratfordian professors have to say about it by way of obfuscating its logic and misrepresenting and slandering its originator, J. Thomas Looney, and go on to further examples of their apparent lack of scruples. We then turn to Looney himself and to the methods he applies in his quest for the man who was Shakespeare — the characteristics he infers would be those of the unknown author and the deductions from Shakespeare's evidently early verse that lead him at the start toward Oxford, in whom, despite how curiously little the historians have to say about the Earl, he subsequently finds satisfied, one by one, the criteria he has established. We take up next the reasons the Stratfordians advance why Oxford could not have been the dramatist. The first is that he died before some of the greatest of Shakespeare's plays were written; the second, that his poetry is much inferior to Shakespeare's; the third, that his character is to be strongly disapproved of. We find these objections untenable. First, the plays could well have been written before Oxford's death and evidently began to appear before the Stratford man could have written them, and by recognizing their earlier dates of composition, we redeem Shakespeare from the irrational charge of having plagiarized inferior writers. Second, Oxford's verse, apparently youthful, is quite like some of Shakespeare's, if not indistinguishable from it, while in demonstrated talent, any gap between Oxford and the early Shakespeare is far less than that between the early and the mature Shakespeare. Third, artistic geniuses, prey to a creative urge that relentlessly gnaws at them for expression, are quite likely not to conform to social forms — in which respect Oxford comes off probably rather better than most, certainly when seen as he was rather than in the hostile reports of pro-Cecilian historians.

The case for Edward de Vere as Shakespeare is not as overwhelmingly strong as the case against Shakspere; proving who did something is generally harder than proving who did not. Its persuasiveness lies in this: that nothing we know about de Vere or about Shakespeare is incompatible with their having been the same; that the positive indications that they were the same are plentiful and striking and accumulate with investigation; that the facts are found to eliminate all other candidates, leaving de Vere the only one who could have been Shakespeare. Reasons why he could not have been, urged by his opponents, fail upon examination, as we shall see.

A Word from Mr. Looney

J. Thomas Looney, the Durham County Schoolmaster whose quest for the man known to us as the one sought, responded to the question of why the problem had gone so long without being systematically addressed by observing:

> It must not be forgotten . . . that "Shakespeare" had to wait until the Nineteenth Century for his full literary appreciation; and this was essential to the mere raising of the problem. "Not until two centuries had passed after his death," says Emerson, "did any criticism which we think adequate begin to appear."

Once the problem had been raised, he saw the solution as inevitable, the result of converging currents. The first of these was "the tendency to put aside the old conception of a writer creating everything by the vigour of his imagination, and to regard the writing as reflecting the personality and experience of the author." The second current he saw as bringing "from obscurity, into our knowledge of Elizabethan literature and drama, the name and figure of one still quite unknown to the vast mass of his countrymen."

His search for Shakespeare having led to this figure, Mr. Looney in November 1918 deposited with the Librarian of the British Museum a sealed envelope containing the result of his years of investigation. In thus establishing priority for his discovery, he was following Charles Darwin's example. I mention Darwin in part because a comparison between Looney's *"Shakespeare" Identified* and *On the Origin of Species* (which William McFee drew) may not be as far-fetched as it must seem. It is no small thing in itself to discover the person behind the West's supreme literature; but beyond that, where Darwin had laid to rest the notion about spontaneous generation of life-forms and showed that they evolved from earlier forms, so Looney laid to rest the notion, based on the Stratford attribution, that works of art could come about by spontaneous generation and cleared the way for us to understand that in fact they evolve, in Mr. Looney's words, from their creator's personality and experience.

In 1920, *"Shakespeare" Identified* was published. We saw in Chapter 9 what the consequences were.

The Attack upon Mr. Looney

Disparaging Mr. Looney, insofar as he could not be ignored, has of course been a necessity for Stratfordian scholars, and they have not been squeamish about weapons. Taking off from my statement in *Harvard Magazine* that "What Looney did was to identify the characteristics we should expect in the man who was Shakespeare, then comb the records of the period to see who met the requirements," Professors Evans and Levin call this "a fair description of an irrational procedure." They do not, however, offer a better. (I should probably explain yet again that in repeatedly putting these two professors on the stand I am not pursuing a personal vendetta but taking advantage of an unusual case of Stratfordian scholars having been compelled to come forth and address themselves to specifics.) Mr. Looney himself, raising the question "what then is the usual common-sense method of searching for an unknown man who has performed some particular piece of work?" answers: "It is simply to examine closely the work itself, to draw from the examination as definite a conception as possible of the man who did it, to form some idea of where he would be likely to be found, and then to go and look for a man who answers to the supposed description."

The method appears sensible enough. The professors' objection is that "It begins by demanding acceptance for one man's arbitrary reading of an author uniquely notable for the volume and diversity of the critical interpretations — not to say the controversies — that his works have evoked. It follows the exploded assumption that Shakespeare's plays, most of them based on pre-existing narratives and adapted to the conventions of the theatrical medium, can be treated as chapters of an autobiography."

When he comes to them a few pages hence, the reader may judge for himself how arbitrary Mr. Looney's criteria are. If the professors have more reasonable ones to propose, they are at liberty to do so. That "diversity of critical interpretations" they speak of, has little or nothing to do, as far as orthodox scholarship is concerned, with the plays as keys to the kind of man the author was, which is what we are talking about. And no one, of course, has ever suggested that *A Comedy of Errors, Richard the Third, Cymbeline,* and the rest may be "treated as chapters of an autobiography"; how, then, such an "assumption" can have been "exploded" is a little difficult to see, particularly as we are not told who the exploder was and when the explosion took place. Having explicitly rejected testimony by all the qualified witnesses we heard in the preceding chapter, that great creative artists reveal themselves in their work, the two professors still cannot quite bring themselves to say that Shakespeare does not put himself sufficiently in his work for us to tell what kind of person he was, but that seems to be what they are trying to convey by innuendo. In doing so, they dismiss the adjuration by the epigrammatist of 1640, who, addressing "Shake-speare," wrote that, because "we must be silent in our praise," you must "let thine own histories prove thy chronicle" — in other words, "let your plays tell your life story." ("Mr. Ogburn," they complain, "confounds the biographical with the theatrical meaning of the key words, 'histories' and 'chronicle'" — whatever they mean by that.) It would be interesting to hear the professors account for the long succession of correspondences Mr. Looney and his followers have found between the content of Shakespeare's plays and Edward de Vere's life.

The author of *"Shakespeare" Identified* made one judgment that surely was a serious mistake. He concluded that *The Tempest*, which, from faulty information, he believed, on the whole, to have been written after de Vere's death, was not the work of "Shakespeare." I suppose no Oxfordian today would agree with him, if any ever did, but I must say that he makes an able case for his point of view. Orthodox scholars believe some of Shakespeare's later plays were produced by collaboration; and it is quite possible that de Vere left some plays only partially written, with hiatuses sketched in, and that another or others completed them. One other hand might well have been that of his son-in-law, the Earl of Derby, whom the Jesuit agent reported to have been "busy in penning comedies for the common players."

Samuel Schoenbaum in his *Shakespeare's Lives* makes the most of the opportunity Mr. Looney's lapse affords for his mocking sarcasm. A few examples will tell us all we need know of his treatment of the English schoolmaster. He writes: "It is difficult to escape the conclusion that snobbery led Looney, a gentle retiring soul, to seek a Shakespeare with blue blood in his veins. His own family, the pedagogue boasted, was descended from the Earls of Derby, once kings of the Isle of Man, whence came Looney's immediate forebears." What Mr. Looney actually said on the subject is in a letter to Charles W. Barrell:

> Publishers and friends foresaw the handle my name would provide for the critics, and wished me to adopt a nom-de-plume. I declined and lost one of the foremost English publishers in consequence, thus risking a premature disclosure of my discovery. It was, indeed, this fact which led me to deposit with the British Museum Librarian the sealed document referred to in the preface to *"Shakespeare" Identified*.

("Covetous of priority," says Schoenbaum, "he resorted to the device of the sealed letter with its overtones of mysterious significance so congenial to the anti-Stratfordian mentality.")

Mr. Looney went on to say that one reason for "refusing to make the concession was that people for whom I write are not the kind of people to whom the mere name of a writer would make any difference," another "the great respect I felt for others who have borne the name, & for whom I had no reason to be ashamed." He went on:

> In passing, it may interest you to know that the name is Manx, that my immediate forefathers came from the Isle of Man and the family is descended, as I have been informed, from the Earls of Derby, once Kings of Man. I have no vanity about things of this kind; but they do help to make up the sum of those subtle influences by which a man's surname establishes links of sentiment with the distant past and thus come to have for him a kind of sacred claim

which makes him resent a disrespectful use of it. It is this probably which has always dictated to people of good feeling the rule of treating the surnames of others with some respect. . . .

(Of the name Looney, Schoenbaum quotes as "apt" the assertion that it "could only have the effect of adding risibility to derision.")

Here we have seen how "the pedagogue boasted" of his descent and betrayed to Schoenbaum a "snobbery" that led him "to seek a Shakespeare with blue blood in his veins." But that was not the end. Mark this passage from *"Shakespeare" Identified*:

> "Of the incidents of his [Shakspere's] life in London," Professor Sir Walter Raleigh tells us, "nothing is known." He lodged at the time in Bishopsgate and, later on, in Southwark. We know this, not because lords and ladies in their coaches drove up to the door of the famous man, not because of anything else which could be called a personal incident, but because he was a defaultant taxpayer . . . for whom the authorities were searching in 1598, ignorant of the fact that he had moved, some years before, from Bishopsgate to Southwark.

To Schoenbaum, it is another dead give-away. Mr. Looney, he reports, "in an unconsciously revealing passage implies that a great writer must have lords and ladies in coaches driving up to his door."

Of the English schoolmaster's method of proceeding in his investigation of the authorship, Schoenbaum says, "Sober literary history is metamorphosed into a game of detection, in much the same manner as the American lady in the Lake Country transformed *Macbeth* into a Hercule Poirot thriller ('Oh, Macduff did it all right,' said the murder specialist.)" He deems it unnecessary to point out that the American woman was fictitious, a product of James Thurber's beguiling fancy in whom the author's indulgent satire is directed not at detective fiction but at an addict who knows no other reading. Detective work, on which self-governing societies have learned to rely to bring the guilty to book and clear the innocent, would hardly have met with Thurber's scorn as a subject of fiction. Authoritarian governments, perceiving the threat represented by its espousal of the objective pursuit of truth, are notoriously hostile to detective fiction. Stratfordians who, to discredit Looney, belittle detective techniques in contrast to those of the historian and scholar, as Schoenbaum does, may be reminded that the techniques are indistinguishable, consisting as they do of the patient and thorough search for relevant evidence and derivation from it of reasonable inferences. An investigator in any field who makes an important discovery is conventionally and rightly congratulated on his brilliant detective work.

The hundred-page section in *Shakespeare's Lives* devoted to dissenters from Shakespearean orthodoxy begins, "During the palmy days of mid-century bardolatry a rough beast slouched towards Stratford to be born." The rest lives up to that opening sentence. The assault on the reputation of

Joseph C. Hart, whose digression on the Shakespeare authorship in his book on *The Romance of Yachting* (see page 129) made him in 1848 the anti-Stratfordians' "first indisputable . . . standard-bearer," establishes Professor Schoenbaum's standards of morality. Hart, a man of intelligence and integrity, "a New York lawyer, an officer in the National Guard, and United States consul at Santa Cruz," as Schoenbaum acknowledges, had, the professor informs us, "an untutored and volatile mind." His "principal contribution" was "the ferocious application of snob values to the authorship question." Shakespeare "reduces Hart to a state of apoplexy," his "obscenities . . . kindle Hart's fury." These epithets must greatly surprise anyone who is familiar with Hart's book but not with the devices of academic character-assassination. Schoenbaum does not scruple to insinuate that his respected and defenseless victim suffered a mental derangement: "Strange thoughts can come to possess a man in the isolation of Santa Cruz, surrounded by the Sulu Sea" — the Sulu Sea having the happy connotation of the Wild Man of Borneo.

Well, I do not know what effect the Sulu Sea would have on one's mental processes, but I do know that (1) while there are five Santa Cruzes in the Asian-Pacific region, all in the Philippines, none is on the Sulu Sea, let alone surrounded by it, (2) the United States has never had a consulate in any of them, (3) the Santa Cruz in which Colonel Hart was United States Consul is in the Canary Islands, and (4) when he was appointed to that pleasant sinecure in recognition of his services to American letters he had already written *The Romance of Yachting*.

"Fascinating, chastening," says Benjamin DeMott, prince of academia, of Professor Schoenbaum's book: "superbly informed, elegantly composed, intensely readable." And Professor DeMott of Amherst University (Guardian of the Folger Library) and half a dozen other universities, Fulbright professor, twice Guggenheim Fellow, of the staffs of *Harper's, Saturday Review,* and *Atlantic Monthly,* of the Carnegie Foundation, Rockefeller Foundation, Guggenheim Foundation, National Foundation for the Arts, National Foundation for the Humanities, and various elect education commissions, is moved by his fellow two-time Guggenheim Fellow, Samuel Schoenbaum, to some elegant composition himself. "Consider," he explains, "the endless succession of snobbery-ridden nonbelievers in Shakespeare — Baconians, Oxfordians and the like — a crew that isn't limited to chuckle-making names like Looney, Schmucker and Mrs. Gallup, but includes men as great as Freud" — "searchers after True Life," whose record is "one of fatuity, madness, meanness."

Mr. Looney's Tracking Down of Oxford

In setting out to uncover the man who wrote as William Shakespeare, Looney made, as he writes, "some legitimate surmises as to what we might expect to be the conditions of his life, and the relationship of his contemporaries towards him." In essence, these were:

1. *Of recognized genius, and mysterious.* It is hardly likely that he would have been able to conceal the greatness of his powers wholly from his associates, while at the same time the productive use he made of those powers must have escaped their notice. The record of wasted genius is, therefore, what we might reasonably look for.

2. *Apparent eccentricity.* His impressionability, his powers of entering into and reflecting vividly the varied moods, fierce passions, and subtle movements of man's mind and heart, all in all his poetic temperament and exuberance of poetic fancy mark him as a man much more akin to Byron or Shelley than to the placid Shakespeare suggested by Stratfordian legend. He is likely to have been found by his contemporaries not merely eccentric but guilty of pronounced vagaries.

3. *A man apart, and unconventional.* Because possession of abnormal powers and a highly strung temperament interposes a barrier between a man and his social environment, he is likely to have been aloof and have provoked hostility in smaller men, toward whom he would assume a mask; and penetration of this mask might require a reversal of former judgment of him.

4. *Apparent inadequacy.* The work in question being the highest literary production of the age, the author, whoever he may have been, must when discovered seem unequal to its production, which again will call for a radical correction of the "judgment of three hundred years' standing."

5. *Of pronounced and known literary tastes.* The work's character compels us to believe that the author will have had dominating literary tastes and an absorbing interest in classical and Italian literatures and the history of England during the period of Lancastrians and Yorkists and that he will have been swept by force of genius into the strong literary current of his times.

6. *Enthusiasm for the drama.* The author's intense interest in this literary force, attested by his having devoted his genius largely to working in it and also by his frequent use of "stage" as a simile, warrants our believing that he appeared to his contemporaries as a man fascinated by the theatre.

7. *A lyric poet of recognized talent.* Although his contemporaries may not have known that he was producing masterpieces of drama, his foremost place among the lyric poets of the times makes it likely that his production of lyric verse was not as completely concealed, that some of it would be known and appreciated, and that he would have left us some published under his own name.

8. *Of superior education and an associate of educated men.* That the author was one whose education was of the best that the times could offer would be the unanimous judgment by any jury of the most mixed backgrounds in the absence of a countervailing prepossession. It is equally evident

that, while in contact at every point with life itself, he was in habitual intercourse with men of intellectual interests wide and varied like his own.

In addition to the foregoing "general features" that might be deduced to have set the author apart, Mr. Looney defined what would appear to have been "special characteristics" of his. Since these must be apparent to any thoughtful reader of Shakespeare, and because we have already explored most of them at length, I shall forgo his discussion and only list them, in his words. They are:

1. A man with feudal connections.
2. A member of the higher aristocracy.
3. Connected with Lancastrian supporters.
4. An enthusiast for Italy.
5. A follower of sport (including falconry).
6. A lover of music.
7. Loose and improvident in money matters.
8. Doubtful and somewhat conflicting in his attitude to women.
9. Of probably Catholic leanings, but touched with skepticism.

Along with his manifest intelligence and thoughtfulness, one thing that inspires confidence in Looney from the start is that he began with no preferred candidate who might have exerted a gravitational pull on his judgment. Far from favoring Edward de Vere, he barely knew of him. What put him on the Earl's trail was *Venus and Adonis.* He turned to the first heir of the author's invention because "it seemed to stand just where his anonymous works begin" and was to be suspected of "being an early work, kept in manuscript for some years." Because "the facility with which he uses the particular form of stanza employed in this poem pointed to his having probably used it freely in shorter lyrics," Looney turned to an anthology of 16th-century poetry. This contained surprisingly few examples of what he was looking for, and of these only two seemed in style and matter parallel with Shakespeare's work. One of these was anonymous. The other was on *Woman's Changeableness* and attributed to Edward de Vere. "Its distinctive qualities were, on the one hand," Looney recalls, "enhanced by the force of contrast with other work of the same period, and on the other hand empha-sized by a sense of its harmony with Shakespeare's work." He says, "I give this poem in full because of its importance to the history of English literature if the chief contention of this treatise can be established." I follow his example:

> If women could be fair and yet not fond,
>   Or that their love were firm not fickle, still,
> I would not marvel that they made men bond,
>   By service long to purchase their good will,
> But when I see how frail those creatures are,
> I muse that men forget themselves so far.

Chapter 19: See, Where Oxford Comes!

To mark the choice they make, and how they change
  How oft from Phœbus do they flee to Pan,
Unsettled still like haggards wild they range,
  These gentle birds that fly from man to man,
Who would not scorn and shake them from the fist
And let them fly, fair fools, which way they list?

Yet for disport, we fawn and flatter both,
  To pass the time when nothing else can please,
And train them to our lure with subtle oath,
  Till, weary of their wiles, ourselves we ease;
And then we say, when we their fancy try,
To play with fools, Oh what a fool was I.

The line "How oft from Phœbus do they flee to Pan" of course recalls Queen Gertrude's flight from "Hyperion to a satyr." Equally the likening of women to "haggards" that "fly from man to man," so that one would "shake them from the fist / And let them fly . . . which way they list," is almost too close for mere coincidence to Othello's threat that "If I do prove her haggard / . . . I'd whistle her off and let her down the wind, / To prey at fortune." It is also rather striking to find de Vere using as a metaphor the lure, a device for training falcons, in speaking of training women just as Petruchio does in speaking of training his Kate: "For then she never looks upon her lure."

Looney was the first but not the last "Oxfordian" to be struck by the obscurity cloaking Edward de Vere — an obscurity one becomes convinced was unnatural in his position as Elizabeth's Lord Great Chamberlain and England's premier Earl and, as Looney was to learn, the notable reputation as a poet-dramatist he had gained as a young man; he had, Thomas Babington Macaulay writes, "shone at the court of Elizabeth, and had won for himself an honourable place among the early masters of English poetry." The literary sections in several English histories were "all silent as the grave in reference to the Earl of Oxford. . . . Beesley's *Queen Elizabeth* barely mentions his name in a footnote of quite insignificant import." What, then, must have been unexpected was how fruitful was the article on the de Veres in the *Dictionary of National Biography*, contributed, ironically, by Sir Sidney Lee, leading Stratfordian biographer of the day.[1] His excitement may be imagined on his reading the following in the *Dictionary*:

> Oxford, despite his violent and perverse temper, his eccentric taste in dress, and his reckless waste of his substance, evinced a genuine taste in music and wrote verses of much lyric beauty. . . .
> Puttenham and Meres reckon him among the best for comedy in his day; but though he was a patron of players no specimens of his dramatic productions survive.

---

[1] Looney makes an unstinting acknowledgement of indebtedness to Lee for the material his sketch of Edward de Vere and biography of Shakspere furnished for the argument of *"Shakespeare" Identified*.

> A sufficient number of his poems is extant to corroborate Webbe's comment, that he was the best of the courtier poets in the early days of Queen Elizabeth, and that "In the rare devices of poetry he may challenge to himself the title of the most excellent among the rest."

Altogether, the portrait of the 17th Earl of Oxford showed that he satisfied thirteen of Looney's criteria and that he satisfied the remainder was not to remain long in doubt.

The 350 pages of *"Shakespeare" Identified* that follow his first picking up the scent set forth what its author discovered about the "fit" between de Vere's life and Shakespeare's works and about the foreshadowing in de Vere's acknowledged poetry of the poetry by "Shakespeare." In the remainder of the present book, recounting de Vere's life story, we will recapitulate what seem to me the most significant of Looney's discoveries and those of subsequent investigators; for the past sixty years have seen Looney's explorations greatly extended and his inevitable mistakes corrected. Before we proceed, however, the reader has a right to know what the case *against* de Vere as Shakespeare consists of.

Orthodoxy's Objections to de Vere's Authorship

The orthodox scholars would disqualify de Vere on three grounds: (1) his dates are too early; (2) his known verse is too inferior to Shakespeare's; and, (3) his character is not the sort we should expect — or prefer — in Shakespeare. Let us examine these objections in turn.

1. The Question of de Vere's Dates

Specifically, de Vere's opponents charge that his death in 1604 rules him out. As Gwynne Evans and Harry Levin phrase it, "Given the general consensus on dating, this would not account for a dozen of Shakespeare's best plays." But the consensus is that of Stratfordians, who naturally assume that the dates of the plays must conform to Shakspere's. And when Schoenbaum, as grounds for rejecting de Vere, names ten plays of Shakespeare's that "appeared on the stage" after his burial, he is giving grounds for rejecting Shakspere as well because he had been buried before seven of the plays were given their first known performance, had, indeed been dead seven years before three of them were even heard of.

The truth is, proof is wholly lacking that any of Shakespeare's plays were written after 1604 — when as we saw in Chapter 6, an abrupt interruption in the publication of hitherto unprinted Shakespearean plays took place. Reasonable inferences from the facts bear out Looney's judgment that if we look at them "with the eyes of common sense, we shall be inclined rather to view the outpouring of dramas from the year 1590 onwards as the work of a more matured man [than Shakspere], . . . who was elaborating, finishing off and letting loose a flood of dramas that he had been accumulating and working at during the preceding years."

Here we ought to recall that the beginning of more adequate theatrical records in the 1590s gives purely fortuitous support to the conventional dating of Shakespeare's plays. Earlier performances are much less likely to be heard of. F. P. Wilson points out,

> Few of the plays acted in the fifteen-eighties have survived. So serious are the losses that the historian of the Elizabethan drama — especially of this period, before the practice of printing plays to be read became popular — often finds himself to be in the position of a man fitting together a jigsaw puzzle, most of the pieces of which are missing.

Showings at Court, recorded by the office of the Revels, were "for the most part," S. J. Sisson writes, "taken from among those tried and proved by public performance," which could well have been in "the inn-yard theatres," of which records were not kept. Sisson observes, moreover, "it was the fashion for the nobility to present plays for the amusement of their guests in their own houses" and that "it is a matter of great interest to consider how far plays were actually written for such occasions." The dates cited by orthodoxy for the first appearance of Shakespeare's plays have next to nothing to do with when they may have been written. When Marchette Chute, looking "well into the next reign after Elizabeth's," writes that, "It was only the old-fashioned dramatists like William Shakespeare who still wrote the kind of plays that had once been popular with everyone," what she is inadvertently saying, surely, is that the plays had been written much earlier. So it is, clearly, with A. L. Rowse, too. "From the first Shakespeare was a magpie," he writes, "picking up pieces from everywhere." He was "mimetic and imitative," "an inveterate borrower . . . the most generous borrower of them all."

Such denigration of Shakespeare — though not usually proclaimed with such gusto — has been constitutional with Stratfordianism. No one who comprehends Shakespeare's genius could go along with it — or need do so. The alternative is that Shakespeare came before those whom he is supposed to have borrowed from or been influenced by — Lyly, Marlowe, Lodge, Greene, Peele, Kyd, and the authors of half a dozen anonymous plays he is said to have cribbed — and that it was he who scattered the pieces that lesser playwrights gleaned and was himself author of the anonymous plays; "Shakespeare," said Dryden, "was the Homer, or father of our dramatic poets." One would think that lovers of Shakespeare would welcome and proclaim this evidence that he was, as he must have been, the originator, the fountain from which the others imbibed.

Welcome or not, the evidence is there. Conventional scholarship has long held that Shakespeare, as Edward Dowden says, "based his *King John* upon an older dramatic treatment of the reign in two parts, which had been printed in 1591 as *The Troublesome Raigne of King John of England*," the authorship of which "is a matter of conjecture." E. K. Chambers says of Shakespeare's *King John*, "The writing itself is all new, but Shakespeare must have kept the old book before him." Yes, these outstanding scholars actually consider Shakespeare so failing in inventiveness and imagination as to have required for a prop an inferior existing drama to lean upon — the game-poacher of Stratfordian legend become a play-poacher. And so too with Shakespeare's early plays *King Henry the Sixth, Parts Two* and *Three*. These "are undoubtedly, in my view," Dr. Dowden writes, "recasts of the earlier dramas" *The Contention Betwixt the Two Famous Houses of Yorke and Lancaster* and *The True Tragedy of Richard Duke of Yorke*. But even respected Stratfordian scholars have been coming to accept the "older" plays as in fact corrupt, pirated versions of the Shakespeare plays, which therefore preceded them, just as Samuel Johnson maintained two centuries ago.

As for *Henry the Fifth*, Dr. Dowden was again presenting the prevailing conviction when he declared that "The sources from which Shakespeare drew materials or suggestions for his play were two — Holinshed's *Chronicle*, and the old play, which had been of some service to him in writing *Henry IV* — *The Famous Victories of Henry the Fift: containing the Honourable Battell of Agin-court.*" In opposition to that view, the noted Stratfordian scholar Andrew S. Cairncross writes of *The Famous Victories*, "It is now recognized that this play is a piracy of the loose type already examined in *The Troublesome Raigne*. It covers the same ground as *1* and *2 Henry IV* and *Henry V*." And of these three plays of Shakespeare's, conventionally assigned to the years 1597 to 1599, he adds that "a reinterpretation of existing evidence will then make it clear that they belong not later than 1588" — the year after Shakspere's partisans say he arrived in London. In Chapter 20 the reader will find important evidence that *The Famous Victories* was in fact written in the 1570s, by Oxford.

In his book *Marlowe and the Early Shakespeare*, F. P. Wilson says,

> My conclusion is, though I am frightened at my own temerity in saying so, that for all we know there were no popular plays on English history before the Armada and that Shakespeare may have been the first to write one. [Moreover,] if we have to believe that *King John* was written by 1590, then we shall have completely to revise our ideas about Shakespeare's relationship with Marlowe and other contemporaries.

That must come very hard for Stratfordians.

In *King Lear*, dated 1605 in orthodoxy, Shakespeare is supposed to have made "fairly obvious use," E. K. Chambers states, of an old play entitled

The True Chronicle History of Kinge Leir. A. S. Cairncross writes, "It now seems certain, however, that the relation of the two plays has been inverted; that in reality *Lear* was written first . . . and that *Leir* represents an attempt to reproduce the main plot." Since, as he says, "it is generally conceded that *Leir* was written earlier than May 14, 1594, on which date it was entered on the Stationers' Register," that would mean Shakespeare's *King Lear* was written more than ten years earlier than orthodoxy has held and was the one entered in the Stationers' Register as *King Leare* in April 1594 and mentioned two days later in Henslowe's diary. The orthodox scholar Peter Alexander writes: "The notion that Shakespeare was in the habit of revising old plays by other men is seen to be unsupported by any concrete evidence. . . . Shakespeare's *Lear* may be like his *Hamlet* his revision of one of his own earlier pieces" — i.e., "the *King Leare* of which Henslowe records a performance at Easter in 1594."[2]

In her *Hidden Allusions in Shakespeare's Plays,* Eva Turner Clark brings out many topical references in them dating them earlier than orthodoxy can allow. She makes the point, too, that Shakespeare would not have made so much of euphuism as he does in his early comic drama if this had meant reviving the artificial form of address years after it had passed from fashion. The heyday for euphuism was the late 1570s and early 1580s, and *Love's Labour's Lost,* in which it is satirized, would have been whipping a dead horse if written in 1594, as E. K. Chambers has it. Dr. Dowden comes a little closer to reality, as we must conceive it, when he seems to accept "1589

---

[2] It was long ago noticed that the names of the devils that possessed "Poor Tom" in *King Lear* appeared in Samuel Harsnett's *A Declaration of Egregious Popish Impostures.* Kenneth Muir has found more extensive parallels and, observing that the *Declaration* was entered in the Stationers' Register in March 1603, has declared that "we can be certain that it [*King Lear*] was not written until after that date." And Peter Alexander, while prepared to concede the existence of a first draft of Shakespeare's play as early as 1594, stipulates that the version we know cannot predate Harsnett. Gwynneth Bowen reports, however, that Harsnett in his preface says that he has used "the expresse words eyther of some part of the Miracle book, penned by the priests, and filed upon Record, where it is publique to be seen, or else a clause of theyr confessions who were fellow actors in this impious dissimulation." Miss Bowen explains that the "booke of Miracles" seems to have been a kind of diary or case book kept by the priests at the time of the exorcisms and found in the possession of a Roman Catholic recusant. These exorcisms were of "parties supposed to be possessed," Harsnett says, and the "play of sacred miracles was performed in sundry houses," among them "the house of Lord Vaux at Hackney," the time being "the yeeres [15]85 and 86." Miss Bowen writes that "a comparison between Professor Muir's page-references to Harsnett and Harsnett's own page-references to the book of *Miracles* has convinced me that wherever the author of *King Lear* appears to be indubitably echoing Harsnett, Harsnett is himself either quoting the book of *Miracles* . . . or, less formally, echoing it." She points out that Edward de Vere was living in Stoke Newington, adjacent to Hackney, where Lord Vaux had his house, in the early 1590s. Almost certainly the two were acquainted, for after Lady Oxford bought King's Place in Hackney in 1595 Lady Vaux shared it with her and her husband. (Probably it was a matter of continuing to live in a house that Lord Vaux had owned.) Hence Oxford could very well have seen the book of *Miracles* in ample time to have drawn upon it before *Lear* appeared in 1594.

or 1590 as a probable date for the original play." But he then says of two of its characters that "Don Adriano and Holofernes have much more in common with the generalized types of the braggart and the pedant in Italian comedy then with any individuals who trod the soil of England." Apparently he finds it quite credible that the raw recruit from a Warwickshire village should have based his first play on a familiarity with Italian comedy or have written one of which Walter Pater would say with the approval of Dr. Dowden, who quotes it: "It is this foppery of delicate language, this fashionable plaything of his time, with which Shakespeare is occupied in *Love's Labour's Lost*."

Karl Elze says that "[Charles] Knight is perfectly right when he 'advisedly' says that there is absolutely no proof that Shakespeare had not written the *Two Gentlemen of Verona*, the *Comedy of Errors*, *Love's Labour's Lost*, the *Taming of the Shrew*, and *All's Well That Ends Well* before 1590." That is before E. K. Chambers — presumably aware of what would be possible for the Stratford man — has any of Shakespeare's plays written.

Although we are told that *Twelfth Night* appeared at the end of the century, topical allusions in the play cited by E. T. Clark would put its original composition twenty years earlier and identify it with a composition that Francis Peck called "a pleasant conceit of Vere, Earl of Oxford, discontented at the rising of a mean gentleman in the English court, circa 1580." It was just at that time that that mean — i.e., ordinary — gentleman, Christopher Hatton, whose identification with Malvolio in *Twelfth Night* seems indisputable, was rising at the court of Elizabeth. Professor Cairncross believes that "the new map with the augmentation of the Indies" referred to in *Twelfth Night* is the Molineux map or globe of 1592, now standing in Middle Temple, where John Manningham saw the play performed in 1601." He believes it was probably written (*revised*, I should say) for a performance on 6 January 1593, seven years ahead of its supposed first appearance.

The Merchant of Venice, conventionally assigned to 1596 to 1597, seems very likely to have been in its original version a play called *The Jew* described by Stephen Gosson in the *School of Abuse* of 1579 as representing "the greediness of worldly choosers and the bloody minds of usurers." Certainly it seems so in the light of Edmund Spenser's having in that same year signed a letter to Gabriel Harvey, "He that is fast bound unto thee in more obligations than any marchant in Italy to any Jew there."

The Winter's Tale is referred to 1610 or 1611 by E. K. Chambers, but the listing in the accounts of the Revels in 1611 of *The Winter's Night's Tale* leaves little doubt that it was Shakespeare's play that was entered in the Stationers' Register by a pirate-publisher in 1594 as "a Wynters nightes pastime."

King Henry the Eighth is put even later than the foregoing by Chambers. Yet in a list of costumes by Edward Alleyn dating from the early part of

"Shakespeare's" career, John Collier says, we find a "Harry the VIII gown" and a "Cardinall's gown," and the presumption is that they were used in Shakespeare's play.

Hamlet is, I think, of special interest. It, too, is said by orthodoxy to have been based on an old play, "whether by Kyd it seems to me impossible to say," Chambers observes: yes, even *Hamlet*. Sometimes called the *Ur-Hamlet* and considered lost, the old play is alleged to have been the *Hamlet* that was staged by Henslowe in June 1594. Shakespeare is also reputed to have been influenced by *The Spanish Tragedy*, which according to Ben Jonson appeared in the later 1580s and has been attributed to Thomas Kyd on the strength of an off-hand remark by Thomas Nashe. What is the truth of the matter?

In his Epistle to Robert Greene's *Menaphon* of 1589, eleven years before orthodoxy has *Hamlet* written, Nashe says, "Yet English Seneca read by candlelight yields many good sentences . . . : and if you entreat him fair in a frosty morning, he will afford you whole *Hamlets* of tragical speeches." The passage, Cairncross finds, is "quite clearly directed against Kyd, among others," who would have been lifting from Shakespeare rather than the other way around. As between the *Hamlet* of the First Quarto, entered in the Stationers' Register in 1602, and *The Spanish Tragedy*, he goes on, "the similarity of the plays is itself suspicious; so is the similarity of parallel phrases." But the similarities are "not signs of Kyd's authorship, not remains of the supposed *Ur-hamlet*, but instances of the tricks played by the association of ideas and phrases in the memory of the actor who played Lorenzo in *The Spanish Tragedy*" and who was a source for the First Quarto of *Hamlet*, which "is an acting version, a prompt copy, . . . a cut version and a reproduction made from memory." Professor Cairncross goes on to say that "It may be assumed, until a new case can be shown to the contrary, that Shakespeare's *Hamlet* and no other is the play mentioned by Nashe in 1589 and Henslowe in 1594." He shows that by the latter date *Hamlet* had become familiar. The ridicule of euphuism in the play, as in the character Osric, he maintains, dates it shortly before or after 1590. He then narrows the date on the basis of the play's contents to the summer or autumn of 1588. In that year "interest was centered in the Armada. Shakespeare, in some way not known to us, was interested in the sea and in naval enterprise; and acquainted, beyond the limits of a landsman, with naval terms. It is not unlikely, then, that the naval preparations of 1588 find a reflection in the lines from Hamlet:

> Why such impress of shipwrights, whose sore task
> Does not divide the Sunday from the week.
> Why this same strict and most observant watch
> So nightly toils the subject of the land;
> And why such daily cast of brazen cannon,
> And foreign mart for implements of war. . . ."

Cairncross further says that a reference to Tarlton in the First Quarto was deleted, the actor having died in 1588; that the conversation between Hamlet and Rosencranz about an "ayrie of children, little eyases," refers to a theatrical "war" of 1588 and 1589, pitting the Queen's company and Paul's Boys, with whom Lyly (de Vere's secretary) was associated; that *Hamlet* was evidently produced in Germany in 1591, giving rise to a German version, *Tragödia der Bestrafte Brudersmord*, with a preface clearly of English origin, though dropped from the English play.

The play on which Stratfordians bank absolutely to refute the case for Oxford is *The Tempest*. E. K. Chambers writes, "that it cannot have been written much earlier than 1611 is clear from the use made of the narratives describing the wreck of Sir George Somers at the Bermudas during a voyage to Virginia on 25 July 1609." He argues, as do other Stratfordians, that Shakespeare's main source of information about the wreck was a report by William Strachey to the London Council of Virginia of 1610, which, since it was not printed before 1625, "it seems that he can only have seen in manuscript." Not a scintilla of evidence exists, however, that Shakspere was in London between 1604 and his visit in 1612, six months after a performance of *The Tempest*, when he was described as "of Stratford upon Aven," or any reason to believe he would have seen a manuscript report to the council if he had been.[3]

Had Shakespeare needed an historical model of a shipwreck on the island of Bermuda he could have found it in that of Henry May in 1593, but the only connection *The Tempest* has with the island is that it is from "the still-vexed Bermoothes" that Ariel has once been summoned by Prospero. Insofar as it is anywhere, the island in the play is in the Mediterranean, as is made quite clear. (Professor George Lyman Kittredge of Harvard used to be irked with those who failed to grasp this.) If any landing on an island in the New World inspired Shakespeare it would seem more likely to have been the one put forward for the honor by J. Donald Adams, editor of the *New York Times Book Review*.

---

[3] George Lyman Kittredge, while holding "That Shakespeare owes something to narratives of Somers's adventures is certain," goes on to say that "These three narratives, however, are in no sense to be regarded as sources of *The Tempest*. At most they furnished Shakespeare with a few items of information or with miscellaneous suggestions which he has followed after his own fashion. Strachey's account of the wreck, for instance, is in striking contrast to what we find in *The Tempest*. The *Sea Adventure* has sprung a leak and is in imminent danger of foundering. Crew and passengers, exhausted by four days' desperate toil at the pumps, are in raptures when they sight Bermuda, which, by good fortune, is on their weather. They lay their course for the shore, run the ship aground, and make a safe landing — a hundred and fifty of them — in their boats. The situation in *The Tempest* is utterly different. There is, in fact, no wreck at all. The sailors make every effort to weather Prospero's island, which is on their lee, for they can defy the storm if they have 'room enough.' They do not succeed, but by the help of Ariel the ship is not dashed to pieces upon the rocks, but makes her way into a 'deep nook' or cove, where she rides in safety. Shakespeare's handling of the vessel shows an accurate knowledge of seamanship which he cannot have learned from the Bermuda narratives."

Mr. Adams proposes that we go back to an address by Edward Everett Hale in 1902 entitled "Miranda [heroine of *The Tempest*] was a Massachusetts Girl." No, this is not a joke. Hale pointed out that there is not a single tropical allusion in *The Tempest*, not a palm-tree (though there is in *As You Like It*), and theorizes that the play had its inception in the landing of Bartholomew Gosnold in 1602 on Cuttyhunk, in the Elizabeth Islands, due south of Falmouth. When one reads that the expedition was sent out by the Earl of Southampton, one pricks up one's ears. It was in Southampton's house, Dr. Hale supposed, that the playwright met and talked with the gentlemen adventurers and the seamen who made up the expedition. Mr. Adams writes:

> His island tallies with the descriptions contained in the reports of the gentlemen adventurers. It was small and heavily wooded, with little fresh water brooks. As in the reports, his castaways divide into two parties — the sailors and the adventurers.
> The parallels are numerous and specific. Brereton's report mentions "Meadows very large and full of green grass," and we have Shakespeare's "How lush and lusty the grass looks, how green." Gosnold speaks of "Stearnes, geese and divers other birds which did breed upon the cliffs," and Caliban says, "I'll get thee young sea-mews [scamels] from the rock." Gosnold's "herbs and roots and ground nuts . . . mussel shells" are reflected in Prospero's words to Ferdinand: "Thy food shall be fresh brook mussels — roots and herbs," and in Caliban's "Dig thee pig nuts with my long nails." Also, the only trees mentioned in *The Tempest* are oak, pine and cedar. The reports mention crabs and so does Caliban. And so it goes. There is a profusion of such similarities.

The reports of Gosnold's expedition would seem much more likely to have contributed to a play written in 1603, when they were fresh, than one written nine years later, when they would have been long out of mind. If lines in *The Tempest* reflect Strachey's report of 1610 — and Chambers speaks of numerous verbal parallels, without citing any — I should guess that they were put in by Derby (who could well have seen a manuscript copy of the report) in filling out a play left unfinished at the author's death in June 1604. Here it is worth recalling in a remark by Ivor Brown that "the plays were, in some cases, . . . revised for later appearances. Hence a possible allusion to a[n] historical event proves nothing much. . . . It may, for example, have been put in for topical effect during a revival."

Of the time of *The Tempest's* composition, Karl Elze states that "all external arguments and indications are in favor of the year 1604." One of his points is that Jonson paraphrases and satirizes the play in *Volpone* of 1605. Chambers acknowledges the similarities to *The Tempest* of *Die Schöne Sidea* by Jacob Ayrer of Nürenberg, who died in 1605: "Here, too, are a prince and magician, with a familiar spirit, a fair daughter, and an enemy's son, whose sword is held in thrall by the magician's art, who must bear logs for the lady, and who wins release through her love." But Chambers is hardly going to admit that it was suggested by Shakespeare's play. "Use of a common source is a more plausible explanation," he says. "But it has not been found."

A. S. Cairncross's study of the evidence led to the conclusion in *The Problem of Hamlet* that "Shakespeare wrote his plays . . . much earlier than has hitherto been surmised." In his chronology he lists *Pericles* ("a composite work") first without suggesting a date. The first general category is "Histories," written as early as 1587. This is followed by "Latin adaptations and themes" (*Comedy of Errors, Titus Andronicus,* and *Julius Caesar*) up to 1589, then by "Senecan tragedy" (*Hamlet, Othello, Macbeth,* and *King Lear*) by 1591 and the Italian "translations" (*Taming of the Shrew, Romeo and Juliet* 1591(?), *Merchant of Venice,* and *Twelfth Night*) 1593. Last comes *The Tempest,* 1603.

Cairncross deserves great credit for his perspicuity and independence of mind. But the latter never extended to his questioning the orthodox view of the authorship, at least openly. This meant that he could not push composition of the plays back before the late 1580s. To find that Shakespeare wrote his plays much earlier than had been surmised, he also had to find that he had to write them "in much more rapid succession."

To imagine the provincial villager writing *Hamlet* at twenty-four, within a year of his purported arrival in London and four years before the relatively youthful *Venus and Adonis,* would surely be to defy common sense. No wonder that *The Problem of Hamlet* is to Louis Marder "a very controversial book." I know of no evidence to prove it wrong in bringing the dates of Shakespeare's plays into conformity with those of Edward de Vere's life. This having been done, acceptance of de Vere's authorship clears the way to recognizing the plays' beginnings in the 1570s and to avoiding Cairncross's compression of their composition into seventeen years.

2. The Quality of de Vere's Verse

The second argument raised against the case for Oxford is that his signed verse is not in a class with Shakespeare's. Gwynne Evans and Harry Levin say, "It is very wise of Mr. Ogburn not to quote from Oxford's extant poetry. The little that we have gives no indication of either an especially large vocabulary or of any way with language above the conventional range of court wit. His sonnet in Shakespearean form is markedly inferior to almost any of Shakespeare's" — not any, but almost any.

Let us, to begin with, concede that the last sentence is quite warranted. Here are the last six lines of the sonnet by de Vere, who was one of the first to write a sonnet of the kind later to be known as Shakespearean — and notice that they form the stanza identical to that employed in *Venus and Adonis,* composed of a quatrain and couplet with the rhyme-scheme a b a b c c:

Chapter 19: See, Where Oxford Comes!

> In constant truth to bide so firm and sure,
> To scorn the world regarding but thy friends?
> With patient mind each passion to endure,
> In one desire to settle to the end?
> Love then thy choice where such choice thou bind,
> As nought but death shall ever change thy mind.

Were those lines inserted in the Shakespearean Sonnet sequence I am not at all sure they would jar on Professors Evans and Levin as out of place. We may concede, however, that they are inferior to the following, for example, from that sequence:

> What merit do I in myself respect,
> That is so proud thy service to despise,
> When all my best doth worship thy defect,
> Commanded by the motion of thine eyes:
> But love hate on, for now I know my mind;
> Those that can see thou lov'st, and I am blind.

But it would be surprising if a sonnet a man wrote in his twenties were not markedly inferior to those he wrote in his forties. At the same time, I doubt that anyone would cite that unintentionally rather ludicrous line "Commanded by the motion of thine eyes" as an instance of "Shakespeare's" superiority.

As for de Vere's poetry exhibiting "no especially large vocabulary," "the little that we have" — these are the two professors' words — does not permit a judgment. What his prose writing might indicate was outside the professors' compass.

What the professors are saying is that de Vere had not, in the poems accepted as his, probably almost all written by the time he was twenty-six, shown the capacity to write Shakespeare's works. That is a defensible position to take. But it is not one allowed Stratfordians, whose own "Shakespeare" had not by age twenty-six shown the capacity to write verse of any kind, as far as we know — certainly, it would seem, any worth saving.

Had de Vere, after writing poetry and prose of such skill and evincing such an attachment to literature as he had by twenty-six suddenly ceased writing anything at all except letters and written nothing but letters during the latter half of his life, he would be incomprehensible and, as far as I know, unique. Were the Stratford man Shakespeare and had he demonstrated no ability as a writer during the first half of his fifty-two-year life he would also, as far as I know, have been unique, the most retarded poet of consequence on record — a fact to which the Harvard professors offer no rejoinder.

If we scarcely see the future Shakespeare in the young de Vere's poetry, we scarcely see him in Shakespeare's early work, either. Much of this — for instance, *Pericles* and three parts of *Henry the Sixth* — falls so far short of his later drama that orthodoxy is compelled by Shakspere's chronology to attribute it to lesser playwrights.

Consider *Love's Labour's Lost*, an exercise in artificiality (and aristocratic superciliousness) lacking "except perhaps in the one instance of Berowne," says Dr. Dowden, "any full study of presentation of character." And *The Comedy of Errors*, with its dependence on the most preposterously implausible coincidences in literature and, Mark Van Doren says, rhymes that "rattle like bleached bones," the "long speeches" that "are stiff and prim," and the initial fooling between Antipholus of Syracuse and his Dromio, which is "among the dullest things of its kind in Shakespeare." Consider also *The Merry Wives of Windsor*, which in its preponderant prose parts, burdened by labored punning, is for page after page pedestrian and boring.[4] "After *The Comedy of Errors* it is Shakespeare's most heartless farce," says Mark Van Doren, to whom *The Taming of the Shrew* is a third in that category. Rather than recognize in the *Shrew's* inferior parts the youthful Shakespeare's still-unsure hand, displayed as well in the other three comedies we have been talking about, orthodoxy asserts that the *Shrew* represents, as Dowden puts it, "a hasty revision by Shakespeare of an older play, with certain additions which are characteristically his own." E. K. Chambers even gives him "the assistance of a collaborator," whose "work, although not incompetent, is much less vigorous than Shakespeare's" and "has many awkward lines." And so once again we have Shakespeare debased to a "cobbler" of second-hand plays and collaborator with inferior playwrights. Yes, he reworked old plays — his own; and he had an awkward collaborator — his youthful self: can we doubt that that was how it was?

I come now to my point. Take from *Love's Labour's Lost*, the *Errors*, the *Wives*, and the *Shrew* the mature dramatist's contributions (amounting to

---

[4] Orthodoxy, making the writing of the *Wives* contemporary with that of *Hamlet* — and apparently scholars are really capable of believing that — is stumped to account for its embarrassing lameness. Dr. Dowden tells us to forget Shakespeare's qualities and "view the play . . . as genially as we are able." The legend is always cited that, Nicholas Rowe reports, Elizabeth "was so well pleased with the admirable character of Falstaff, in the two parts of Henry the Fourth, that she commanded him [the dramatist] to continue it for one more play, to show him in love. This is said to be the occasion of his writing the *Merry Wives of Windsor*." The play, however, does not show Falstaff in love — or Falstaff at all (quite apart from his having been dead over a century and a half when the *Merry Wives* takes place). We are asked to believe that having created in the Falstaff of *Henry the Fourth* the greatest comic character in literature, irrepressible and irresistible in circumstances that would crush with shame a mortal unable to draw unblushingly on limitless resources of wit, Shakespeare would descend to the Falstaff of the *Wives*, a fatuous and continually humiliated dupe of transparent japes. If we are to make sense of the matter, I think we must believe that the *Wives* was originally written by a Shakespeare still far from finding his talent, probably before 1580, that in it he had a character who foreshadowed the later Falstaff in being fat and chronically the butt of fate (as Slender in the *Wives* is clearly a precursor of Sir Andrew Aguecheek in *Twelfth Night*), and that he took up the play again much later and added to it, especially the character of the Host, who blows in like a gust of high-spirited glibness and *is* Falstaffian, and the parts in blank verse, notably the scene with the Fairies. Maybe the legend is correct insofar as he did this to satisfy the Queen's whim, doing it without enthusiasm and resignedly bestowing the name Falstaff on the victim of Mistress Page's and Mistress Ford's trickery.

one or two passages in *Labour's* and, on Chambers's word, three-fifths of the *Shrew*); and take from all four the name Shakespeare. Then imagine we had nothing else of Shakespeare's until we come to *Hamlet, Macbeth, Antony and Cleopatra*, and *King Lear*. Surely in that case the proposition that the author of the four comedies was also author of the four great tragedies would be hooted out of court.

In contrast with the wide gulf between the youthful Shakespeare and the mature dramatist, there would seem to be a clear consanguinity between the youthful de Vere's poetry and the youthful Shakespeare's (and even some of the older's). Take *Verses Made by the Earl of Oxforde* and *A Lover's Complaint* by "William Shake-speare." I think I should find it easier to believe that they had a common authorship rather than a different. Indeed, coming to them in ignorance I am not sure I should be able to pronounce with absolute certainty which was Oxford's, which "Shake-speare's," except that the former's is in iambic heptameter. Here are the opening lines of each — and notice that one ends and the other begins with an invocation of an echo:

> Sitting alone upon my thoughts in melancholy mood,
> In sight of sea, and at my back an ancient hoary wood,
> I saw a fair young lady come, her secret fears to wail,
> Clad all in colour of a nun, and covered with a veil;
> Yet (for the day was calm and clear) I might discern her face,
> As one might see a damask rose hid under crystal glass.
> Three times with her soft hand, full hard on her left side she knocks,
> And sigh'd so sore as might have mov'd some pity in the rocks;
> From sighs and shedding amber tears into sweet song she brake,
> When thus the echo answered her to every word she spake. . . .
> . . . .

> From off a hill whose concave womb re-worded
> A plaintful story from a sistering vale,
> My spirits to attend this double voice accorded,
> And down I laid to list the sad-tun'd tale;
> Ere long espied a fickle maid full pale,
> Tearing of papers, breaking rings a-twain,
> Storming her world with sorrow's wind and rain.

> Upon her head a platted hive of straw,
> Which fortified her visage from the sun,
> Whereon the thought might think sometime it saw
> The carcass of a beauty spent and done. . . .

The reader who does not see signs of a common origin in the two sets of verses might test his ability to discriminate between the styles of Oxford and "Shake-speare" on a pot-pourri made up by Louis P. Bénézet of Dartmouth. Acknowledging that "Of course I got my idea from reading Mr. Looney's scholarly comparison of the poetry of Edward de Vere with the *Sonnets* and poems," Professor Bénézet writes:

This mixture contains seventy lines; there are six passages from the works of one author, seven from the other; no passage is longer than eight lines; none shorter than four.

It has been most interesting to see the Shakespeare scholars tackle this problem. I handed the book to a former college instructor in Elizabethan literature, now an editor for a well known publishing firm. He picked it up with an air which said: "This is going to be easy. Just watch me detect the true Shakespeare lines." I had given him the number of lines in each selection, so it should have been doubly easy. He not only failed to pick the Shakespeare passages among the first forty lines; *he exactly reversed them*, attributing de Vere's stanzas to Shakespeare and Shakespeare's to de Vere.

He did a little better on the next part, for he recognized lines from two of the Sonnets, but closed his answer as he began, attributing the last six lines to the wrong author.

An old friend of mine, who has been teaching English for forty years, took my booklet home and made an honest attempt, after careful reading and study, to pick out the Shakespeare passages. I met him afterwards, and he confessed that he had missed three of the first eight and was not sure enough to go on to the end.

But the most surprising test was an interview which I had, four years ago, with a famous professor of literature from one of the nation's oldest and greatest universities, a man whose name is synonymous with literary knowledge and who is quoted from coast to coast [William Lyon Phelps of Yale].

I read him the pot-pourri. "What do you think of it?" I asked.

"It is beautiful," he replied.

"Where do you place it?" I asked.

"Oh, it is Elizabethan," was his answer.

"Did one man write all of it?" I persisted.

"Oh, unquestionably," said he.

"I think so," said I, and I proceeded to tell him the story of the dual authorship.

He was aghast. "What does Kittredge say to this?" he demanded. "Kittredge won't listen to it," I answered. "A friend of mine tried to obtain an interview with him, but when he learned what it was about, he refused."

A prominent literary figure, a committed Stratfordian, to whom I submitted the test, would have nothing to do with it, calling it "dirty pool" and "a cheap lawyer's trick." Here it is:

If care or skill could conquer vain desire,
Or reason's reins my strong affections stay:
There should my sighs to quiet breast retire,
And shun such sights as secret thoughts betray;
Uncomely love, which now lurks in my breast
Should cease, my grief by wisdom's power oppressed.
My reason, the physician to my love,
Angry that his prescriptions are not kept,
Hath left me, and I desperate now approve
Desire is death, which physic did except.
Past cure I am, now reason is past care,
And frantic mad with evermore unrest.
Fain would I sing but fury makes me fret,
And rage hath sworn to seek revenge of wrong;

My mazed mind in malice is so set,
As death shall daunt my deadly dolours long;
Patience perforce is such a pinching pain,
As die I will or suffer wrong again.
For if I should despair, I should go mad,
And in my madness might speak ill of thee:
Now this ill-wresting world is grown so bad,
Mad slanderers by mad ears believed be.
Love is a discord and a strange divorce
Betwixt our sense and rest, by whose power,
As mad with reason, we admit that force
Which wit or labour never may endower.
My thoughts and my discourse as madmen's are,
As random from the truth vainly express'd;
For I have sworn thee fair and thought thee bright
Who art as black as hell and dark as night.
Why should my heart think that a several plot
Which my heart knows the wide world's common place?
Or mine eyes seeing this, say this is not,
To put fair truth upon so foul a face?
Who taught thee first to sigh, alas, my heart?
Who taught thy tongue the woeful words of plaint?
Who filled your eyes with tears of bitter smart?
Who gave thee grief and made thy joys to faint?
Who first did paint with colours pale thy face?
Who first did break thy sleeps of quiet rest?
Above the rest in court who gave thee grace?
Who made thee strive in honour to be best?
Who taught thee how to make me love thee more
The more I hear and see just cause of hate?
O, though I love what others do abhor,
With others thou shouldst not abhor my state:
What worldly wight can hope for heavenly hire,
When only signs must make his secret moan:
A silent suit doth seld to grace aspire,
My hapless hap doth roll the restless stone.
Yet Phoebe fair disdained the heavens above,
To 'joy on earth her poor Endymion's love.
And shall I live on earth to be her thrall?
And shall I live and serve her all in vain?
And shall I kiss the steps that she lets fall?
And shall I pray the gods to keep the pain
From her that is so cruel still?
No, no, on her work all your will.
And let her feel the power of all your might,
And let her have her most desire with speed,
And let her pine away both day and night,
And let her moan and none lament her need;
And let all those that shall her see,
Despise her state and pity me.
Let him have time to tear his curled hair,
Let him have time against himself to rave

Let him have time of Time's help to despair,
Let him have time a beggar's orts to crave,
And time to see one that by alms doth live
Disdain to him disdained scraps to give.

In concluding this section I must in fairness report that Steven W. May, in a review of Oxford's poetry published in 1980 by the University of North Carolina Press, questions or denies the legitimacy of the attribution to the Earl of certain poems by printers during his lifetime and others by Alexander Grosart a century ago. Professor May accepts sixteen known poems as by Oxford. The "Echo Verses," which we have just read, and *Woman's Change-ableness*, which first put Looney on the trail of Oxford as the man he was seeking, are two of four he names as only "possibly" by Oxford. He brands as "Poems Wrongly Attributed to Oxford" six included in Looney's *Poems of Edward de Vere* and announces with unconcealed satisfaction that two poems claimed by Looney as by de Vere and as of key importance in his identification as Shakespeare were of other authorship.

Professor May's judgments are based on records of publication or attribution or both. Prior assignment to another of poems attributed later to Oxford he seems to accept as conclusive. In this, not everyone would go along with him. Moreover, the gusto with which he takes out after Oxford is not very reassuring as to his objectivity. He is unconcerned with stylistic criteria. Apparent stylistic affinities he does not attempt to interpret or explain, except on the general grounds that Elizabethan poets often sounded alike. His study thus invites much further investigation and analysis, with doubtful prospect of reaching indisputable conclusions, even with such aid as computers may give.

Even if we accept all Professor May's judgments, the consequences for determining Oxford's place in literature would be only peripheral. Professor May himself tacitly recognizes that this might be so. He writes of Oxford's role in Elizabeth's reign: "He is her first truly prestigious courtier poet, and while we cannot know to what extent his example spurred on those who followed, his precedent did at least confer genuine respectability upon the later efforts of such poets as Sidney, Greville, and Ralegh." He then speaks of how much "the work of these poets overshadows Oxford's." Yet he has earlier recognized that "Both Webbe (1586) and Puttenham (1589) rank him [Oxford] first among the courtier poets, an eminence he probably would not have been granted, despite his reputation as a patron, by virtue of a mere handful of lyrics." In fact, Gabriel Harvey makes clear, as we believe Thomas Nashe does, that the verse attributed to Oxford today can amount to but a small fraction of his output. Thus Webbe and Puttenham, on the strength of a much broader basis of comparison than that available to May, as May acknowledges, rank Oxford ahead of all other courtier poets, including those

May places ahead of him.[5] Here I have again been anticipating myself, as I shall be doing further in suggesting that all that vanished verse of Oxford's has not vanished at all but is well known to us — only not as his.

Our examination of two of the three principal objections to the case for de Vere urged by Stratfordians seems to me to leave the case unimpaired if not to a large extent actually strengthened. What about the third?

3. De Vere's Character

We are told that the Earl's behavior was deplorable. And so it may have been in some respects. But the specific iniquities charged against him are by no means at odds with his having been Shakespeare. On the contrary. He is castigated for having acted abominably toward his wife, the hapless Anne Cecil — but we need only reflect upon Hamlet's contribution to Ophelia's insanity and suicide, Othello's jealous murder of Desdemona, Angelo's treacherous repudiation of Marianna in *Measure for Measure*, Bertram's callous rejection of Helen in *All's Well*, Leontes's cruel condemnation of Hermione in *The Winter's Tale*, and Postumus's faithless casting off of Imogen in *Cymbeline* to perceive how likely it was that the dramatist had a conscience tormented by self-accusations of just such wrong-doing and was expiating in play after play. All six heartlessly abused heroines had points in common with the first Countess de Vere, and four came to grief because of an alleged fall from virtue, just as the Countess did.

Further, de Vere is denounced for having been a vexation — "a frightful headache," A. L. Rowse puts it — to his father-in-law, Lord Burghley, who, to blacken the Earl's character the more, is endowed by anti-Oxfordians with a worthiness and magnanimity that assuredly would have surprised the smooth old fox's associates. Yes, de Vere was a trial to Burghley as Burghley to him, as Hamlet was a trial to Polonius and Polonius to him — and at least Lord Oxford did not run the Queen's verbose counselor through with a sword as Lord Hamlet did.

To instance what Burghley had to bear at his ward's and son-in-law's hands, de Vere is accused of heedless extravagance. Again the Earl's advocates must enter a plea of guilty — with another reminder of the contempt for money and for acquisitors that comes out in Shakespeare. And also with a question: are we being asked to believe that prodigality and impracticality in money-matters have been found to be incompatible with artistic genius?

---

[5] May's exposition takes unexpected turns. It comes as a stunning and welcome surprise to find an orthodox professor writing of "the Oxfordian movement" that "its leaders are educated men and women" whose "arguments for de Vere are entertained as at least plausible by hosts of intellectually respectable persons." This, however, is followed by a venomously slanted brief biography of Oxford — which in turn leads into an emphatic tribute to the miscreant Earl as the outstanding literary patron of his time.

In sum, I think it is fair to say that the chief culpabilities found in de Vere by ill-wishers are such as we should not be surprised to detect in Shakespeare. But, though satisfied on that point, I yet have to confess that as I have looked further into de Vere as he stands in the record, I have come to anticipate that a verdict of *not likable* is one that many if not most readers will be apt to pass upon him. Divorce him from Shakespeare's work and what remains is a man ostensibly unprepossessing — arrogant, unstable and erratic, self-centered, given to wild schemes for making money, a poor father and worse husband, high-handed and reckless in antagonizing those deserving of respectful treatment.

At the same time I think we must recognize that most great creative geniuses in the arts, if denied the products of their genius, would probably come out but little if at all better. Few can have been anything but difficult to get along with even when their genius has been recognized — though Oxford's fellow writers were evidently devoted to him. "An artist is a creature driven by demons," William Faulkner declared. "He is completely amoral in that he will rob, beg, borrow or steal from anybody and everybody to get the work done. . . . He has no peace till then. Everything goes by the board: honor, pride, decency, security, happiness, all, to get the book written." Of course, admirable and engaging qualities also come out in de Vere on the record, such as are consistent with those we should have surmised him to have had from the protagonists of his dramas, if they were his; and I am thinking especially of his early dramas, which would show him to have had impulsive high spirits and playfulness, lightning wit, an ardent appreciation of woman as an equal, impudence, ready generosity, heedless courage. Combine Benedick in *Much Ado* and the Bastard Faulconbridge in *King John* and you have that side of him as a young man.[6] Characters whom we have seen in Chapter 18 as probably most representative of the author would show him also to have been shot through with melancholy, increasingly acquainted

---

[6] In 1929, having eight years earlier explained how she had been transformed from a bristling defender of the Stratford man into a believer in Oxford as Shakespeare by the Looney work, Esther Singleton published a book of stories entitled *Shakespeare Fantasias*, in which, as we may read in the *Shakespeare Fellowship Quarterly* (Vol. VII, no. 1, Jan. 1946),

the merry mad-cap Earl of Oxford [is] introduced as the Berowne of *Love's Labour's Lost*, the melancholy Jacques of *As You Like It* and the Benedick of *Much Ado About Nothing*. . . .

and on solid grounds, in my view. Moreover,

Mr. Henry Clay Folger of the Folger Shakespeare Library found them so much to his taste that he purchased twenty or more copies of the book to present to his friends.

Not only that, but he undertook to have the Library obtain the manuscript. Thus it would appear that to the subsequent custodians of the Library, its creator, who put so magnificent a roof over their heads, stands condemned by inference as "naive," "ignorant," guilty of "an obvious snobbism," and worse.

with black nihilism and despair, and capable of a savage appraisal of his fellow men and women. Such characters, I should judge too, have him turn contemptuously upon those below him in caliber and in station with whom he consorted and especially upon the flatterers drawn by his largesse. We may deduce, I believe, that it took the experience of abnegation that anguish brings to wring out of him a too careless and disdainful pride and open his heart to the humanity that came to Lear.

That the great Elizabethan poet-dramatist was a deeply flawed human being, he tells us in the *Sonnets*. They reveal him stricken with remorse, the sense of his guilt and shame and degradation, and, rather than having his beloved young friend reproached by their mutual love after his death, he declares it would be better that his name be buried where his body is. If we cannot bear our Shakespeare so blemished, then we had better close our eyes and shut our ears and re-embrace the bland, affable, impersonal businessman of the Stratford story. If we want the truth, we must recognize what Shakespeare was — Bertram, Benedick and Romeo, Hamlet, Othello, Antony and Lear, King Claudius, Macbeth, Richard III and Iago, yes, and Rosalind, Portia, Lady Macbeth and Goneril, at once Prospero and Caliban, and a score of others as stormy with life and demanding to be given their hour upon the stage, at whatever cost in turmoil to the beleaguered soul that encompassed them. No one ever spoke more understandingly of him than Margaret Cavendish, Marchioness (later Duchess) of Newcastle when, in 1664, she wrote:

> So well hath he expressed in his plays all sorts of persons, as one would think he had been transformed into every one of those persons he hath ascribed; and as sometimes one would think he was really himself the clown or jester. He reigns, so one would think, he was also the king and privy counsellor; also as one would think he were really the coward he feigns, so one would think he were the most valiant and experienced soldier. Who would not think he had been such a man as his Sir John Falstaff; and who would not think he had been Harry the Fifth?

And one who thought it would not be wrong. He *was* Falstaff and Prince Hal especially; but he was all the others who would give him no peace. The wonder was, as with Wagner, not that he could be inconsiderate, egotistical, and indifferent to whom he hurt, not that he was immoderate and incontinent in speech, but that the multifarious beings that his creative impulse aroused in him did not tear him apart altogether.

If allowances must be made for those of consuming creative gifts — the price being small enough compared with our rewards — in de Vere's case a special allowance is called for if we are to judge him by the record. We must be very cautious in that. Reading his correspondence a suspicion amounting to certainty dawns upon us that the Cecils saw to it that the letters that survived would be those which sought their help in the writer's times of need and would put them, father and son, in a generous and forbearing light; those of contrary effect would disappear. They had the motive, the natures, and the power to bring this about. That, on the evidence, they did so has a close bearing on a thrust sometimes made at Oxford, for example by Oscar James Campbell. After attributing various obnoxious limitations to the Earl, the late Columbia University professor asserts, "Most serious of all, he never shows anywhere in his letters or in the twenty-four lyric poems the slightest sense of humor."

First, about the letters. Apart from one written in French at age thirteen and another about purchasing a ship, none of Oxford's is known to survive except those he wrote the Cecils, father and son. Let the reader ask himself — Professor Campbell not being available — how much humor he would put in letters to two humorless, chronically disapproving in-laws. Copies of letters written to Oxford by his wife were carefully preserved in the Cecil files, but every one he wrote to her has disappeared. Surely the fate of Oxford's correspondence, bespeaking a literary crime of major proportions, is a significant circumstance and one that asks to be related to the clean sweep of contemporary records eliminating any that tied Shakespeare to an actual person.

As for the deficiency in humor of Oxford's lyric poetry, I cannot recall any either in the lyric poems that have come down to us as Shakespeare's; lyric poetry is by definition not a vehicle for humor. Professor Campbell, for that matter, should have been asked to point out the gags in Shakespeare's 154 *Sonnets* — and explain how a man without "the slightest sense of humor" could have been accounted among the best of his time for comedy.

Regarding the reprehensible character given Oxford in conventional portraiture, we should above all bear in mind how, as we shall discover, it has been colored by charges levelled at him by a pair of highly placed plotters whose treasonable activities he had exposed and who were desperate to impugn his testimony.

Certainly had Oxford at all resembled the picture etched by his detractors it is inconceivable that it could have been said of him, as it was when he was twenty-one, that the Queen delighted more in his personage than in any other's. Moreover, as we shall see, those with whom he shared the field of letters paid him glowing tributes. He received evidently heartfelt praise for his generosity to indigent scholars and writers — a Mæcenas, Robert Greene called him; and the term was echoed by Thomas Nashe. In 1980, as the reader may have remarked, Professor Steven W. May called him the most open-handed patron of literature of his day.[7]

Oxford was praised no less for his own literary attainments. Commentators

---

[7] "Oxford's character," Cyril Connolly assures us, "lacked the large charity and benevolence of the dramatist's." He finds the requisite large charity and benevolence in Shakspere's hounding of debtors, jailing of a surety for one of them, and profiteering in grain amidst hunger.

— Gabriel Harvey, William Webbe, Henry Peacham — left no doubt, as I have said, that he wrote far more, and of outstanding quality, than has heretofore been credited to him; he was first among those courtly poets who would be seen to "have written excellently well," Puttenham wrote, "if their doings could be found out and made public with the rest." He was most favored of the Muses, on the word of Edmund Spenser, who proclaimed in one of the sonnets preceding *The Fairie Queene*

> the love which thou dost bear
> To th' Heliconian Imps and they to thee,
> They unto thee, and thou to them most dear.

In a play published in 1613 but considered probably written much earlier, the poet George Chapman, whose translation of Homer so moved John Keats, has a character report how

> I overtook, coming from Italy,
> In Germany, a great and famous Earl
> Of England; the most goodly fashion'd man
> I ever saw: from head to foot in form
> Rare and most absolute; he had a face
> Like one of the most ancient honour'd Romans
> From whence his noblest family was deriv'd;
> He was beside of spirit passing great
> Valiant and learn'd, and liberal as the sun,
> Spoke and writ sweetly, or of learned subjects,
> Or of the discipline of public weals:
> And 'twas the Earl of Oxford.

Such was de Vere at twenty-six, in the eyes of one who was in all probability the rival poet of the *Sonnets*.

While in all this I am getting still further ahead of myself, I shall not resist the temptation to extend the chapter with a few lines of verse that seem to me especially significant. They are from *Scourge of Villanie*, printed anonymously in 1598, by John Marston, whose first published work, earlier in that year, had been an erotic poem in the meter of *Venus and Adonis*. Son of a barrister of the Temple, a B.A. of Oxford, Marston was a satirist and dramatist to whom Henslowe once advanced 40 shillings, who engaged in a celebrated quarrel with Ben Jonson and later collaborated with him in a play that sent them both to jail. In a book of fulminations against human iniquity he breaks into a poem with lines that have virtually nothing to do with the rest of it and are totally out of keeping with the book as a whole, exclaiming:

> Far fly thy fame,
> Most, most of me beloved, whose silent name
> One letter bounds. Thy true judicial style
> I ever honour, and if my love beguile
> Not much my hopes, then thy unvalu'd worth
> Shall mount fair place when Apes are turned forth.

Who had a "silent name" that "one letter bounds"? Who but Edward de VerE? If it is de Vere who is addressed — and who else could it be, and have the invocation make sense? — is not Marston foreseeing the time (unless his love is giving too much rein to his hopes) when de Vere, his worth now unvalued, shall achieve his deserved and honored place and his fame fly far, all this when pretenders — Apes — have been sent packing?

It seems to me evident that Marston epitomized our case for us and gives us leave to anticipate — if our love of *Twelfth Night* and *The Tempest*, *Hamlet*, and *Lear* beguile not too much our hopes — that the time cannot be much longer delayed when the man who was Shakespeare will gain his rightful place and his fame fly far "as men can breathe, or eyes can see."

Recalling the Reverend Dr. John Ward's report of having heard that Shakespeare, for producing two plays a year, had an allowance so large that he spent at the rate of £1,000 a year, some readers may also recall the proposition I hazarded that if a candidate for Shakespeare's honors qualified on other scores had received an annual allowance, unaccounted for, of that astonishing magnitude — about what 140 to 150 plays would have brought their authors on the commercial market — we should have our man; and they may wish to know without further delay: how about Oxford? The answer is that he was granted just such an allowance, in mysterious circumstances.

Where We Stand

In the nineteen chapters now behind us, we have, I think, eliminated Shakspere of Stratford from further consideration as the Shakespeare of the plays and poems. We have seen how the contemporary record was "sanitized" of any links between the authorship and a living human being and how, in order to keep the authorship concealed, it was doctored to create a Stratfordian "Shakespeare." In the quest for the man who was in fact Shakespeare, we have found all possibilities evidently disqualified but one and that one — Edward de Vere, 17th Earl of Oxford — the man whom methodical, unbiased literary detective work has identified as the believeable Shakespeare we have sought. In his case we discover that the persons with the most compelling reasons for keeping the authorship from being recognized were the very ones in a unique position to make sure that it would not be. We have discerned in Shakespeare's works the nature of the author's background, education, kind of experiences, and intellectual attainments, and these, we see, are just such as Oxford had or would have had or — with respect to those intellectual attainments — would notably have had the opportunity to demonstrate. The reasons orthodox scholars assert for rejecting Oxford's authorship we have discovered, upon examination of the facts, to provide additional reasons for accepting it. These are reinforced, we have observed in conclusion, by contemporary tributes to Oxford.

In the eighteen chapters yet to come, we shall trace Oxford's life story as well as it is known and explore its relationship with works of Shakespeare. In this, I trust, we shall be performing the service that Wyndham Lewis finds of compelling need in a penetrating observation:

> Anyone who defines in the body of Shakespeare's work a personality and traces of passion and opinion is rescuing him for us from the abstract in which he might eventually disappear where less important men would survive.

We are encouraged by a remark by T. S. Eliot:

> "Who has a first-hand opinion of Shakespeare? Yet I have no doubt that much could be learned by a serious study of that semi-mythical figure."

Book Two

"Is Not Oxford Here Another Anchor?"

20

"What's Past Is Prologue"

Queen Elizabeth's visit to Castle Hedingham, seat of the de Veres, during Edward de Vere's boyhood. — A visit today to the Castle and other nearby de Vere memorials, beginning at Cunobelinus's (Cymbeline's) capital of Colchester. — Tributes to the illustrious record of the family. — Young Edward at Hedingham, as he may be visualized; his two poetical uncles; his father's players. — Origin of the de Veres; Aubrey's participation in the Norman invasion and the great rewards that came to him. — Designation of the second Aubrey as Lord Great Chamberlain and the third as Earl of Oxford. — The 2nd Earl's command under King John and the parallel in Shakespeare's play between John's situation and Elizabeth's. — Military service rendered the first three King Edwards by the 6th Earl. — The 7th's contribution to the English victories at Crécy and at Poitiers. — The close and mutually destructive companionship of the scandalous 9th Earl and Richard II and the conspicuous omission of the Earl from the Court noblemen in the Shakespearean play. — Participation by the 11th Earl in the battle of Agincourt and exaggeration of his role in the battle and as adviser to the King in The Famous Victories of King Henry the Fift, *a skimpy and amateurish play clearly the precursor of the Shakespearean play and attributable to Edward de Vere in his twenties. — Prominence of the 13th Earl under Henry VI; the repeated enthusiastic acclaim he receives in Shakespeare's account of the reign; the Earl's leading role at the Battle of Bosworth, where Richard III is slain. — Economic near ruin visited upon the 13th Earl by his beneficiary, the grasping Henry VII, and passing over of Henry's reign in the sequence of Shakespeare's historical plays. — The 15th Earl at Henry VIII's historic meeting with Francis I at the Field of the Cloth of Gold. — A tribute to the "warlike" 16th Earl's intrepidity in the hunt and the posthumous challenge to the validity of his second marriage and hence to his son Edward's legitimacy, and a parallel with the Bastard Faulconbridge in* King John. *— Edward's early education, his father's death, his mother's apparently quick remarriage, and some parallels with* Hamlet.*

Elizabeth I was in her third year on the throne when she came with her retinue to visit the 16th Earl of Oxford at Castle Hedingham, in Essex, ancient seat of the de Veres. The four days of her stay, from August 14 to 19, 1561, must have been electrifying for the scion of the house, eleven-year-old Edward de Vere. The entourage had at its head one of the most fascinating women who ever ruled a nation, surely second to none in ability, and one with "a capacity for inspiring devotion," Winston Churchill writes, "that is perhaps unparalleled among British sovereigns." Elizabeth was then nearing her twenty-ninth birthday, handsome, vital and vivacious, intellectual and shrewd, temperamental as Edward himself was to prove to be. She had

407

learned to speak French, Italian, and Spanish as fluently as English besides acquiring proficiency in Latin and Greek, not to mention Welsh. This was even before her education was taken over in her early twenties by the renowned scholar Roger Ascham, who said of her that her mind seemed to be free of female weakness and her power of application like a man's; he had never seen a quicker apprehension or a more retentive memory. Among her studies, she had become well versed in Italian scholarship and statecraft under Italian instructors and had been taught by Castiglioni[1] a handwriting "so beautiful," says Elizabeth Jenkins, "that the sight of letters written in its prime gives a pang of aesthetic pleasure." It would be ironical if Edward de Vere acquired, at this time, a first yearning for Italy from the Queen who was later to stand in the way of his gratifying it.

Elizabeth would have brought with her the refulgence of the new dawn that had cast its awakening light across England with her accession to the throne. This had taken place when, in November 1558, her unhappy half-sister, the Catholic Queen Mary, wife of the future King Philip II of Spain, had closed her dismal reign by dying amid general rejoicing. "A paragon of the New Learning [the religious reform movement led by Dean Colet and Erasmus]," as Churchill calls Elizabeth, around whom "had gathered some of the ablest Protestant minds," she boasted of being "mere English" — as no sovereign since Harold had a better right to do — and no claim she could have made would have endeared her more to her subjects. John de Vere, 16th Earl of Oxford, whose adherence to the new Anglican Church established under Henry VIII had forced him to seek obscurity at Castle Hedingham when Mary strove to restore the sway of Rome, was one of the noblemen chosen to conduct Elizabeth from her own seclusion at Hatfield House to the coronation, while the Countess of Oxford was named a Maid of Honor to the new Queen. Soon thereafter, we find in an Elizabethan chronicle, the "second son to Gustabus King of Sweden was sent to treat a marriage for his elder brother Ericus with the Queen's Majesty of England" and when "he arrived in Harwich in Essex" he "was there honorably received and entertained by the E. of Oxford, which said Earle, and the Lord Robert Dudley, with a goodly band of gentlemen and yeomen, conveyed him to London." During Elizabeth's stay at Castle Hedingham it must have been in the royal visitor's mind as in her host's how far both had come since the Court spelled not honors and triumph but deadly danger for each.

Elizabeth was not only every inch a queen — with lapses — but in most inches a daughter of the king her father, Henry VIII, whose gusto for life would reverberate down to the age of television. A champion at tennis, in

---

[1] Not to be confused with Baldassare Castiglione, author of *The Courtier*, a mistake made in the *Encyclopaedia Britannica*, 11th edition.

Queen Elizabeth I

As drawn from life by Federigo Zuccaro,
1575.

By permission of the British Museum.

the lists, and with the bow, he was an indefatigable huntsman; and if a
passion for field sports was less marked in his daughter, probably only the
constraints of her sex made it so. We may be sure that much of her stay
with the 16th Earl of Oxford, himself a great sportsman, was spent on the
bowling green, in the archery butts, and in hunting, falconry, and riding,
which she loved. In these pursuits her small future favorite would have been
in constant attendance, already displaying a horsemanship that not long

hence would be highly praised. Late in the day would have come music; for in this taste too Elizabeth recalled a father accomplished on every instrument, in whose court music flourished, as did poetry; Henry is represented in the *Oxford Book of Sixteenth Century Verse* by three selections, Elizabeth by two. In these enthusiasms, too, Elizabeth would have had a wide-eyed partner in her host's son (whose initials, E. of O. appear, interestingly enough, as the signature of an ancient manuscript *Miscellany* containing the first of the two poems attributed to Elizabeth in the Oxford anthology). And when in the evening the Earl's troupe of actors would have performed for the assemblage, he would surely have been not far from her side, and we may allow imagination to wonder in which one, Elizabeth or Edward, a delight in the masques and plays would have been the most infectious to the other. Was the basis for their future intimacy laid now? Those late-summer scenes must have been the subject of shared recollection, fond and doubtless amusing, when, for a few years, the young 17th Earl as courtier, dancer, poet, playwright of comedies, and musician was to throw others in the shadow at Elizabeth's Court.

You may visit Castle Hedingham today, or what remains of it. It is only fifty miles north-east of the heart of London by highway through Chelmsford and Braintree. Or, better, you may go by the Great Eastern Railway on through Braintree to Colchester. Here was the capital of Cunobelinus, whom the Queen's young companion in those August days in 1561 was to make better known (in an obviously early play later improved) as Cymbeline. Here, too — as, much later, Robert Graves and the B.B.C. were to make widely known — the Emperor Claudius was deified after conquering the town shortly after Cunobelinus' death, to make it the center of the Roman occupation. (Colchester and its inhabitants were wiped out by the warrior-queen Boadicea [Budicca] at the head of an army of vengeful Britons but the town was rebuilt, and today a marvelous collection of antiquities recalls its Roman past.) Renting a car at Colchester, you should back-track, taking Route A604 westward through Halstead, passing on the way through Earls Colne. This, like Colchester, takes its name from the Colne River, at the mouth of which is Wivenhoe, where Edward de Vere was living at twenty-three; this part of Essex and adjacent Suffolk is all de Vere country. At Earls Colne a great priory was established by Aubrey de Vere in 1105, and the church once housed the tombs and monumental effigies of twelve of the Earls of Oxford and their families. Harold W. Patience of nearby Braintree (an authority on de Vere history and the Oxford case) suggests that "it is possible that Colmekill, ancient burial place of the Scottish kings, was dragged into *Macbeth* because of the similarity of name. We read that Duncan was

> Carried to Colmekill;
> The sacred storehouse of his predecessors
> And guardian of their bones."

When the monasteries were dissolved under Henry VIII, Colne Priory was returned to the family of the donor, in the person of the 15th Earl. Within half a century, in obscure circumstances, it had become a ruin. As such, apparently, it passed into the possession of our Earl, the 17th, and out of it again as part of one of the estates he was forever selling. Nothing remains of the Priory church but two blocks of crumbling masonry, less than a man's height, in a brushy pasture to which we were taken by Mr. Patience. The effigies that survived — only three, of the 5th Earl, the 7th, and the 11th and his Countess — were removed just before World War II by the owner of the property, Colonel W. G. Carwardine Probert, to his family estate four miles to the north at Bures, where he installed them in the little hilltop chapel of St. Stephens, built in the early 1200s and lately restored, with thatched roof.

The Keep at Castle Hedingham

Photograph by the author.

At Halstead, 4 miles on from Earls Colne, you could turn northeast and in 13 miles be in Lavenham and at the great church built by the 13th Earl of Oxford — the most illustrious of the line down to the 17th — and a wealthy wool merchant of the town. Edward de Vere would have been well acquainted with Lavenham as a center of weaving and with the troubles there, shortly before his time, of which Queen Katherine, seconded by the Duke of Norfolk, informs the King in the play *Henry the Eighth*: how, "upon these taxations, . . . the spinners, carders, fullers, weavers . . . are all in uproar."

Driving on up the River Colne you come within 4 miles of Halstead to the delightful village of Castle Hedingham. Turning right into St. James's Street, you pass a partially half-timbered, stucco house of gabled ends facing forward, the whole quaintly askew. Called Moot House, it goes back to the 15th century. The small village preserves much of the charm that has long been England's, and one wishes that the inhabitants could be brought to recognize in time to control it the commercialism that will threaten it if, and I should say *when*, it comes to be accepted as the birthplace of the man who was Shakespeare. The former seat of the de Veres had been in the Majendie family since the 18th century, but on the death of the last of the line it passed in 1981 to the Honorable Thomas Lindsay, younger son of the 28th Earl of Crawford and great grandson of the 10th Duke of St. Albans, of the family of de Vere Beauclerc; and so the Castle, such as remains of it — "One of the mightiest castles of East Anglia and still standing high above the old trees as a reminder of Norman power," Nicholson's Guide to Great Britain has it — is again in the possession of a descendant of its builder.

The village's verdant setting reminds one of the Virginia Piedmont in a season of adequate rain. One can understand how the painter Thomas Gainsborough, who was reared in nearby Sudbury, could ascribe his first love of art to the beauty he saw around him.

On a visit to Castle Hedingham in 1978, my wife and I made the village church our first place of call. This is said to have been built by the 15th Earl of Oxford. Of cobble-like exterior trimmed with brick and with a stocky brick clock-tower, it is entered past two windows each set with a medallion of stained glass. A circular one shows an ox fording a stream. The other is the shield with the molet argent — the silver, five-pointed star — of the de Veres in its second quarter, the likeness of which may be seen in Washington among the sixteen banners bearing devices associated with Shakespeare hung from the lofty ceiling of the main hall of the Folger Library. (The star, repeated every few feet, forms part of the balustrade of the church at Lavenham.) By the altar is the 15th Earl's splendid black marble tomb. Earlier on that day we had been taken by Colonel G. O. C. Probert from his treasure-filled Elizabethan manor-house at Bures to the lonely little chapel of St.

Stephen in which his father had installed the three de Vere tombs from Earls Colne. And so we had seen four of the five surviving tombs of seventeen generations of the Earls of Oxford. (That of the 3rd Earl is at Hatfield Broad Oak in Essex.) "These, then," Robert Innes-Smith writes, "are the only sad remnants of what was possibly the most complete set of monumental effigies set up to any English family."

The grounds by then being open, we ascended to the grassy summit of a partly wooded hill above the village from which arises an 85-foot building, cubical but for being a quarter again as high as broad, topped by two 15-foot rectangular towers cater-corner to each other. Scantily pierced by very narrow windows, it recalls one of the concrete structures one sees from miles away standing alone above the grain-fields of the American plains. It was

The keep at Castle Hedingham

An interior view.

Photograph by the author.

413

built not for aesthetic effect or the amenities but as a fortress to withstand siege. It is the keep of Castle Hedingham and all that is left of the buildings, including the dwelling-quarters, erected in the reign of King Stephen by the first of the de Veres holding the Earldom of Oxford. We are disheartened to have the receptionist within, a very personable young woman, repeat the story circulated in 1796 by Lewis Majendie that the other buildings were torn down by the 17th Earl, "the black sheep of the family," to spite Lord Burghley, to whom he was making over the property. Nothing is less likely (if Moira Moles, the receptionist, will forgive my saying so). In 1592, when the transfer took place, Lord Oxford not only had no cause for resentment of Burghley but was seeking to augment his over-strained resources by obtaining one of the trading monopolies from the Queen and needed all the support he could get from her Lord Treasurer. Edward de Vere may be reproached for having sold the estate comprising Colne Priory (also in 1592) to meet expenses — divested of the authorship of Shakespeare's works he must indeed appear a black sheep — but hardly for having destroyed the buildings at Castle Hedingham for revenge.

I was still in the mood induced by reminders of the de Veres' vanished tombs and of the lack of so much as a plaque anywhere to honor the 17th Earl when we had mounted the stone steps to the entrance of the great keep, past the ruins of the tower that had once stood beside it. The floors and roof were consumed by fire in 1918 but have been replaced. From the first level, on which the garrison was quartered in time of siege, we ascended a spiral staircase (constructed from left to right, Musette Majendie's guide-pamphlet explains, so that a defender has his sword arm free while an assailant, taking what shelter he can from the spiral wall, must use his left for attack.) This led us to the armory or banqueting hall, the chief features of which were an arch spanning it, pronounced by a qualified antiquarian "the finest of its kind in the world," and a cavernous fireplace on the opposite side flanked by windows set back at the end of corridors 11 feet long — such being the thickness of the walls. The great hall was a void, vacated, one felt, even by memory.

> I heard a great peer of this realm and a learned say, when he lived, there was no King in Christendom had such a subject as Oxford.

So spoke Lord Chief Justice Randolph Crewe in an "exordium" in 1626 that Lord Macaulay called "among the finest specimens of the ancient English eloquence." Recalling the grant to "Oxford" — he used the name collectively — of the title of Great Chamberlain of England and the Earldom, the Chief Justice pursued:

> This great honour, this high and noble dignity hath continued ever since in the remarkable sirname of de Vere, by so many ages, descents and generations,

as no other kingdom can produce such a peer in one and the self same name and title.

. . . .

I suppose there is no man that hath any apprehension of gentry or nobleness, but his affections stand to the continuance of so noble a name, and a house, . . . and yet time hath his revolution, there must be a period and an end of all temporal things, finis rerum, an end of names and dignities, and whatsoever is terrene, and why not of de Vere?

For where is Bohun? Where's Mowbray? Where's Mortimer? &c. Nay, which is more and most of all, Where is Plantagenet? They are intombed in the urns and sepulchres of mortality.

And yet let the name and dignity of de Vere stand so long as it pleaseth God.

In the minuteness of our comprehension it little behooves us to speculate upon the nature of God or the sources of his pleasures. Yet my observation of life emboldens me to attribute to the Arbiter of Destinies a weakness for the ironic twist. If it pleaseth God to have the name and dignity of de Vere stand immortal, I shall not be surprised if they are rendered so above all by the de Vere who, alone of the lustrous tribe, made himself "a motley to the view" and earned an "outcast state," the de Vere whom respectable scholarship singles out to be clucked over with dismay and disapproval but whom it pleased God to endow with the supreme power of art.

Such in some sort was the tenor of my thoughts as we looked down on the banquet hall from the balcony to which a further spiral staircase had taken us, as it had the minstrels who once performed there. I tried to imagine the character of the first acquaintance, germinating here, of the great Shakespearean Queen and the future great Elizabethan dramatist. All that could safely be surmised, I felt, was that, as the precocious young Edward could not fail to have been stirred and excited by the glamorous, magnificent, and magnetic personage of red-gold hair to whom it was his hereditary duty to excel in service, so Elizabeth must have been taken with the stripling Bulbeck and his lively and informed intelligence.

Even before his ninth birthday the boy had so far progressed in scholarship as to have been admitted as an "impubes" fellow-commoner (the category conventionally of the sons of wealthy families for whom a payment of 30 shillings was made) at Queen's College, Cambridge. Literary as well as sporting and martial interests came to him through family environment. A sister of his father's, Lady Frances de Vere, herself a versifier, was married to Henry Howard, the Earl of Surrey, whose ten poems near the beginning of the *Oxford Book of Sixteenth Century Verse* include three sonnets that, like seven others of the fifteen or sixteen ascribed to him, are of the form later known as Shakespearean. With some by his friend Sir Thomas Wyatt, they represent the first of their kind. In his translation of the *Æneid*, Surrey employed the first blank verse in English; in this, too, Edward de Vere's uncle prepared the way for Shakespeare. "Through Wyatt and Surrey," Tucker

Brooke of Yale writes, "stationed like Pillars of Hercules at the head of the Elizabethan sea, flowed the inspiration." Professor Brooke speaks of the "grace and tenderness of feeling" that "beautify Surrey's work" and of his use of his "observation of natural beauty" and says: "He had a good many of the qualities of Lord Byron and like Byron became a romantic figure." He had little time to make his mark on his age, losing his head to one of Henry VIII's rages at age thirty. "Surrey circulated much verse in manuscript during his lifetime," we learn. "But" — in observance of the taboo — "it was not published till 1557, ten years after his death." Another poetical uncle of Edward de Vere's, Edmund Baron Sheffield, the husband of the 16th Earl of Oxford's sister Lady Anne, had even less time, being killed at twenty-eight in helping to suppress a rebellion. H. A. Taine, in his classic *History of English Literature*, includes Sheffield with Surrey as being responsible for "the prolongation of chivalric poetry." It was reported of him: "Great his skill in music, who wrote a book of sonnets in the Italian fashion" — entirely lost.

That the poetical achievements of these two uncles both influenced and inspired the boy Edward seems certain. But of at least equal importance in steering his tastes and arousing a lifelong enthusiasm must have been the troupe of players his father maintained. Doing so was a family tradition. We read in M. C. Bradbrook's authoritative *The Rise of the Common Player* how even "before 1509, Henry VII had rewarded . . . the men [i.e., the players] of the Lords of Oxford, Northumberland and Buckingham," and that after Henry VIII succeeded him in that year "the most magnificent court entertainments," which "came from the Gentlemen and Children of the Chapel Royal," were "rivalled by the performers of [the Lord Chancellor, Cardinal] Wolsey's Chapel, perhaps by Lord Oxford's."[2] The Earl's players, as was the custom of acting companies in the 16th century, toured the country during the summer but were available at Castle Hedingham during the rest of the year, to restore spirits flagging from administration and anxious amid the ominous uncertainties of the times — especially when inclement weather barred field sports. (Anticipating such enforced inactivity, a great Jacobean house like Robert Cecil's at Hatfield would provide a "long gallery" for — take note — jogging!) We may remember how the Reverend Dr. John Ward a hundred years later got wind of the report that "Mr. Shakespeare . . . frequented the plays all his younger time." We may picture Edward looking on absorbed and with growing critical judgment, beginning to acquire the discrimination that Hamlet was to put in words. More explicitly, Hamlet may hark back to these days in a later speech, when he takes the skull from the grave-digger:

---

[2] E. K. Chambers tells us that "A company belonging to the 16th Earl caused a scandal by playing in Southwark when a dirge was being sung for Henry VIII at St. Saviour's on 6 February 1547."

> Alas, poor Yorick! I knew him, Horatio: a fellow of infinite jest, of most
> excellent fancy: he hath borne me on his back a thousand times. . . . Here hung
> those lips that I have kissed I know not how oft. Where be your gibes now?
> your gambols? your songs? your flashes of merriment, that were wont to set the
> table on a roar?

It is an evocation of scenes with an intimate familiarity persuading us that
the author had experienced them with just such a jester. For a moment it
does bring the banquet-hall at Castle Hedingham to life with its animated
company — a small boy beside himself — on which the warm light flickered
from blazing logs in the now long-darkened fireplace. The character of the
fool in his motley was continually to beckon de Vere the playwright.

At such a table as Hamlet remembered, Edward must have heard more
than the minstrelsy from above, the speeches of the players, the gibes of the
jester, talk of the day's events. Gervase Markham, poet, captain under Essex
in England, reputed importer of the first Arab stallion into Britain, and
voluminous writer on varied topics, declared in 1624:

> And what is the most memorablest and glorious Sun which ever gave light or
> shine to Nobility? Our Veres, from the first hour of Caesar to this present day
> of King James (which is above a thousand seven hundred years ago) never let
> their feet slip from the path of nobility, never knew a true eclipse of glory, never
> found declination from virtue, never forsook their country being wounded, or
> their lawful King distressed, never were attainted, never blemished, but in the
> purity of their garments . . . lived, governed, and died, leaving the memory
> thereof on their monuments, and in the people's hearts; and the imitation to all
> the Princes of the World, that either would be accounted good men or would
> have good men to speak good things of their actions.

Good things of the actions of his forebears would hardly have been omitted
from discourses in the family circle aimed at fitting the boy for the Earldom.
To the heir of the bountiful glory Markham extols, if we may judge by the
results, that glory must have been both inspiring and ever-reproachful. It had
been accumulating a long time. While descent from Julius Caesar must (we
need not grieve) be disallowed, though it may have been accepted by the
family, there seems to be good reason to believe that Alberic, or Aubrey, de
Vere, who established the family in England, was the issue of a de Vere of
Veer, in Zeeland, and of a daughter of the Count of Flanders, whose family
came down in direct line from Charlemagne. However that may be, the de
Veres must in origin have been Vikings — Danes to the Anglo-Saxon English,
who suffered so horribly from Danish raiders — for Alberic clearly held an
important command in the Norman invasion of England, to account for the
rich rewards that came to him. It may have been with special glee that a
later de Vere, writing a play about Henry V, would have the royalty of France
bitterly declare of the counter-invading English army, in which another de
Vere held a command, "Our scions, put in wild and savage stock": "Normans, but bastard Normans, Norman bastards!" That same Edward, when

in after years he came upon the story of *"Amleth, qui, depuis, fut Roy de Daunemarch,"* in Belleforest's *Histoires Tragiques* of 1570, would perhaps remember that he was of Danish extraction; to have cast himself as a prince would have given him not the slighest trouble.

Among the great estates granted to Alberic, or Aubrey, de Vere was that of Cheneston, now Kensington. Aubrey House and Aubrey Walk on Camden Hill preserve the de Vere connection with Kensington, while no present-day Oxfordian who visits London fails to take tea, at least, at the quite fine De Vere Hotel on Kensington Road, facing Kensington Gardens. Well do my wife and I know the coign of medieval serenity preserved by the Church of St. Mary Abbots at the turbulent intersection of Kensington High Street and Kensington Church Street, off which were our bed-and-breakfast lodgings; the original church was given by Aubrey. Generation after generation, the de Veres gave churches — which may account for Hamlet's bitter rejoinder upon being reminded by Ophelia that his father has been dead not just two hours but twice two months: "Then there's hope a great man's memory may outlive his life half a year: but, by'r lady, he must build churches then." Lands in Essex were among the many granted to Aubrey, who died as a monk in the Priory he built at Colne.

To the second Aubrey was accorded by the king the office of Lord Great Chamberlain. This made him financial officer to the King's household, but the tedious function was from the start relegated to subordinates and the office — not to be confused with that of the Lord Chamberlain — has always been largely ceremonial. To this day, as the *Encyclopaedia Britannica* informs us, the Lord Great Chamberlain

> At the opening or closing of the session of parliament by the sovereign in person . . . disposes of the sword of state to be carried by any peer he may select and walks himself in the procession on the right of the sword of state, a little before it and next to the sovereign. . . . At coronations he emerges into special importance; he still asserts before the court of claims his archaic right to bring the king his "shirt, stockings and drawers" and to dress him on coronation day and to receive his ancient fees, which include the king's bed and "night robe." He also claims in error to serve the function of the "ewry," a distinct office held by the Earls of Oxford. At the actual ceremony he takes an active part in investing the king with the royal insignia.

It was the second Aubrey who built Castle Hedingham and a third who was created an earl; evidently given the choice of several earldoms by the sovereign, he selected Oxford. Both these Aubreys were crusaders. Of the first crusade, in which the earlier fought in 1098, it was written about the contest with the Admiral of the Sultan of Persia:

> The night coming on in the chase of this battle, and waxing dark, the Christians being four miles from Antioch, God willing the safety of the Christians showed a white star or molette of five points on the Christian host, which to every man's sight did light and arrest upon the standard of Albry, there shining excessively.

Thus it came about that the *molette* — literally the rowel of a spur — or molet became emblazoned in the arms of the de Veres. And thus in turn it may have followed that stars would be so frequently drawn upon for symbols and imagery in the dramas of Shakespeare — more than 100 times, no less. If for good reason we take the author to identify himself with Prince Hal, later Henry V (and Edward Dowden, describing the Prince, actually asks archly if there was "a young fellow from Stratford . . . of whom such things were true"!), then his proclaiming Henry "this star of England" could have a double significance, as could Ben Jonson's hailing of the dramatist as "star of poets." But all that is as may be.

To return to fact: in 1194, the third Aubrey died and was interred in Colne Priory under the inscription:

> *Hic jacet Albericus de Vere filius Alberici de Vere, Comes de Quisney et primus Comes Oxoniae, Magnus Camerarius Angliae.*

Percy Allen adds:

> He is described, in the same inscription, as "Grymme Aubrey," a double reference — first to the ferocious temperament of the Earl himself, and secondly to his kinship in fierceness with the Verres, or blue boar, a beast which the de Veres — who right down to Shakespeare himself seem ever to have loved a pun — chose as a Rebus, or pictorial representation of their name.

The de Veres properly enter our story with the accession of John to the English throne in 1199; it is with his reign that Shakespeare's historical plays begin. In him, Winston Churchill writes, "the restless energy of the Plantagenet race was raised to a furious pitch of instability." The consequences were disastrous for the realm, the continental parts of which he succeeded in losing to the French King, Philip Augustus. Aubrey, the 2nd Earl of Oxford, stood by him. He commanded King John's forces in Ireland, where the rebellious barons and assorted kinglets were brought into line — after which the King found it expedient to withdraw before the ire that it was his nature to arouse. When, Holinshed says, the Pope absolved the English people of fidelity to John (1211), one of those "that did take his part" was "Alberike de Veere erle of Oxford." Robert, who succeeded him shortly afterward as the 3rd Earl, was, however, among the barons goaded into rebellion by the King's erratic mischief-making and tyrannies. At Runnymede in 1215 the barons forced his acceptance of the ancestor of human-rights proclamations, the Great Charter. Oxford soon found himself a target for the King's revenge. John, once excommunicated himself for defying the Papacy, obtained the Pope's sanction for annulling the *Magna Carta* and the excommunication of the "troublers of the king and kingdom" and commenced raising a mercenary army for their subjugation. The barons offered the crown of a despairing England to Prince Louis of France, husband of John's niece, and invited in a French force. John counter-attacked by ravaging southern England "like a captain of banditti." In Holinshed's *Chronicles* for 1216, we read that "the

French who held the castle of Colchester delivered it up to King John. After this the castle of Hidingham was won, which belonged unto earle Robert de Vere." Resistance, though fierce, did not avail, and Oxford regained his estates only when John withdrew before the invading force of Prince Louis, to die shortly thereafter.

The tangled events of John's reign are of interest here primarily because of the treatment they were to receive in the Shakespearean play. The striking omission of any mention of the Great Charter is habitually brought to notice. It need not surprise us, however. In the 1580s, with the Spanish at the door, the dramatist was not going to publicize the fragmentation of the central power — that of the Throne — at the hands of rebellious barons. All his historical plays would be written with an eye to the present, and the parallels between John's situation and Elizabeth's would cry out to him as to his audiences. The two monarchs were alike threatened by the Papacy, which they had defied and which would gladly have encompassed their ruin. King John's speech in Shakespeare's play spurning the Pope's authority — a dramatization of the historic event that gave occasion for Aubrey, or Alberic, de Vere to "take his part" — would have sent the blood pounding in English veins from the Queen and her court down to the groundlings pressing forward to catch every word:

> Tell him this tale, and from the mouth of England
> Add thus much more, that no Italian priest
> Shall tithe or toll in our dominions. . . .

Neither John nor Elizabeth held an unquestionable title to the crown. As John's hold on the throne was imperilled by the claims of Arthur, third son of Henry II, so too was Elizabeth's by those pressed on behalf of Mary, Queen of Scots, granddaughter of Henry VIII's sister. Both claimants had powerful and dangerous backing on the continent. Neither English monarch would be safe as long as the claimant lived, and both encompassed the claimant's death. Such are the parallels that Shakespeare made the most of, at the cost of some liberties with the earlier history. John was already a symbol of English anti-papism; Shakespeare made his story a vehicle of English patriotism at a time — if the chronology of his plays is what I believe it to be — when England faced invasion by Philip II as it had under John by Philip Augustus of France.

Edward de Vere would have been disturbed, I imagine, that an Earl of Oxford would have sought the deposition of his king and invasion by a French prince. In *Henry the Sixth*, generally accepted as the first of the Shakespearean historical dramas, he would have celebrated an Oxford's role to the point of jeopardizing his anonymity. In taking up *The Life and Death of King John* he could well afford to forget the role of Robert de Vere, the

3rd Earl, and cast himself as a loyal supporter of the Throne, like the second Earl. This he would do recognizably, I think, in the character of Philip Faulconbridge, bastard nephew of the King's, the youthful, ardent, impudent, quick-witted *beau idéal* of Shakespearean heroes, as Coleridge calls him. De Vere, both in his own life and in Shakespearean protagonists, would be given rather light-heartedly to fantasies of himself as a great soldier, and Faulconbridge would become a leading military lieutenant of the King's, loyal to the end despite all; in the Shakespearean canon, a subject owes his monarch, however blameworthy, unswerving fidelity.

The 5th Earl of Oxford, another Robert, was of a party of noblemen who, with the King's brother-in-law, Simon de Montfort, Earl of Leicester, the guiding spirit, also rebelled against their sovereign; but, embracing "the wisest and most patriotic section of the baronage," they had as their object not the King's replacement but his reform, and they sought no foreign help. Earl Simon "was esteemed the natural exponent of all the wrongs of the realm," and when the rebels met and defeated a much larger royal force at Lewes in 1264, the upper hand seemed theirs. In the next year, however, the King's son and successor, Prince Edward, raised an army that defeated a force under Simon the Younger and Earl Robert of Oxford, then annihilated that of Earl Simon under sheer weight of numbers. Robert's lands were confiscated but later returned under an amnesty.

The next Robert and next Earl, the 6th, called Robert the Good for his outstanding virtues, amply repaid the clemency shown his father. He fought with valor and prowess under three successive Edwards — the highly capable Edwards I and III and the contemptible II, whose ignominious weaknesses and final assassination would be dramatized for the stage in *Edward the Second*, a play ascribed to Christopher Marlowe, though one in which "Shakespeare's" hand is more than a little evident.

In the martial career of the 6th Earl, young Edward could have found much to inspire the zeal he would later show to distinguish himself in arms. And, beginning with the Hundred Years War in France, there was more to come to arouse that zeal and instill the Shakespearean plays with war and combat. The 7th Earl, John, was one of Edward III's leading captains. He fought in the first battalion beside Prince Edward in 1346 at Crécy, where the French chivalry with a four-to-one advantage charged the English fourteen times, only to be mown down under such a hail of arrows "that it seemed as if it snowed." In Laurence Olivier's *Henry the Fifth*, motion picture audiences six centuries later would hear a French king shudderingly remember that day

> When Cressy battle fatally was struck
> And all our princes captived by the hand
> Of that black name, Edward, Black Prince of Wales:

Whiles that his mountain sire, on mountain standing,
Up in the air, crowned with the golden sun,
Saw his heroical seed, and smiled to see him. . . .

Ten years later, Earl John of Oxford led the English archers at Poitiers. There the odds against the English were even heavier than at Crécy and the most overwhelming and astonishing victory in the whole war was won by the Black Prince, with whom Earl John was later retained to "abide for life." Young Edward would have been poor in spirit had his patriotism not been stirred by tales of the battle in which his ancestor had played a leading part and the cream of the French nobility been killed or captured, their king with them. He would hardly have been an offspring of his forebears had the feudal ideal not been reaffirmed in his mind by the Black Prince's chivalry in seating his royal prisoner in his own chair with all ceremony due him and serving him the best viands procurable. When the 7th Earl died before the walls of Rheims and was buried in Colne church, the estates he left stretched over parts of ten counties.

The first Earl of Oxford to achieve a separate entry in the *Encyclopaedia Britannica* stood as the nadir of the line. This was the 9th, another Robert, from youth an intimate of the young Richard II, with whom his friendship, we read, "was to prove fatal to both" — as it was later to enrich English literature. Unprecedented honors, in addition to castles and lands, were bestowed upon Robert by his royal companion. Under the year 1386, Holinshed reports that "The Lord Robert Véer earle of Oxenforde, whom the king in the last parliament had made marquesse of Dublin, was now, in this parliament created Duke of Ireland: the other lords sore envying so high preferment in a man that so little deserved, as they took it." The addiction to luxury that King Richard encouraged in Earl — now Duke — Robert, the latter encouraged in the King, whose exactions upon his subjects were accordingly laid in part at his door. Revolt brewed. "The lords," remarks Holinshed, "said, that they assembled their forces together, for the profit of both king and realm, and specially to take away from him such traitors as remained continually about him; to wit Robert de Véer duke of Ireland, Alexander NeVill archbishop of York," and others.

The time came when the king had to call upon Duke Robert to raise an army and come to his support. The Duke assembled 5,000 men but in marching on London found the hostile noblemen had destroyed the bridge over the Thames near Chipping Norton and were blocking the valley with their forces. Forsaken by elements of his army, he "began to wax faint-hearted," and, telling the remainder that they would be safe should he "withdraw myself," proceeded to do so. But "enclosed with his enemies on the one side, and the river of Thames on the other, he thought to put all in adventure; and casting away his gauntlets, and sword, . . . gave his horse the spurs, and leapt into the river; but missing the ford, and not able to land with his horse on the further side, he forsook him, and swimming over as well he might, got to the bank, and so escaped." Thought drowned, he reappeared on the continent. His sovereign's infatuation with him survived even in this dénouement, and several years after Robert had been killed by a boar during a hunt in Brabant in 1392, Holinshed tells us that

> King Richard . . . caused his corpse, being embalmed, to be conveyed into England, and so to the priory of Colnie in Essex, appointing him to be laid in a coffin of cypress, and to be adorned with princely garments, having a chain of gold about his neck, and rich rings on his fingers. And to show what love and affection he bare unto him in his lifetime, the king caused the coffin to be opened, that he might behold his face bared, and touch him with his hands: he honored his funeral exequies with his presence. . . .

A dramatization of the reign faithful to history would hardly neglect this singular and consequential relationship, but not a word is breathed of any Earl of Oxford or Duke of Ireland while thirteen other noblemen tread the boards in *The Tragedy of King Richard the Second.* What the conscious mind censors, the unconscious may betray, and it was perhaps a Freudian give-away that Oxford, the town, is named six times, twice as often as in all the other Shakespearean plays combined. It does seem likely that, recognizing in his ancestor, Robert de Vere, something of the King's *alter ego,* the dramatist midway in the play — if Frank Harris is right — came to see himself in the part of Richard, who, from a reckless tyrant, becomes a poetic and reflective victim of adversity.

No battle was to be made better known by "Shakespeare" than that of Agincourt. Here Henry V, in 1415, meeting even heavier odds against him than his predecessors had had to face at Crécy and Poitiers, turned the tide of war by skillful use of his long-bowmen. What spectator of Olivier's cinematic triumph will ever forget the English archers waiting with drawn bowstrings as the mounted nobility of France lowers lances for the charge? The victory, and the victor, would have made a strong appeal to young Edward de Vere. As B. M. Ward maintained in 1928, the anonymous play *The Famous Victories of Henry the Fift* probably was de Vere's first attempt to dramatize the life of the monarch, who, in later and much expanded and improved versions, would disport with the high spirits of youth as Prince Hal in the two parts of *King Henry the Fourth* and with manly majesty wear the crown in *King Henry the Fifth.* I think there can be little doubt of this. One can scarcely read *The Famous Victories* and not see in the skimpy little prose-play an early, comparatively amateurish exercise on the themes that would later come to magnificent flower in the Shakespearean dramas. The point is a most important one, as we shall see. Consider, for example, the reception by the newly crowned Henry V of the belittling gift of tennis balls from the French Dauphin. Here is his response in *The Famous Victories:*

> My Lord Prince Dolphin is very pleasant with me! But tell him instead of balls of leather we will toss him balls of brass and iron — yea, such balls as never were tossed in France. The proudest tennis court shall rue it. . . . For I vow by heaven and earth that the proudest Frenchman in all France shall rue the time that ever these tennis balls were sent into England. . . .

Here, in small part, is how he masterfully conveys the message in *Henry the Fifth*:

> We are glad the Dauphin is so pleasant with us;
> His present and your pains we thank you for:
> When we have match'd our rackets to these balls,
> We will, in France, by God's grace, play a set
> Shall strike his father's crown into the hazard.
> Tell him he hath made a match with such a wrangler
> That all the courts of France will be disturb'd
> With chaces. . . .
> And tell the pleasant prince that this mock of his
> Hath turned his balls to gun-stones; and his soul
> Shall stand sore charged for the wasteful vengeance
> That shall fly with them.

Unless we are among those who can believe that Shakespeare's soaring genius required the crutch of plagiarism (and plagiarism of such plays!) we must perceive in the second quotation the mature dramatist that the apprentice of the first had become. But now observe what follows from the perception.

Ward brought out that the historic role of the 11th Earl of Oxford at Agincourt was elaborated in *The Famous Victories*. It is more than that. Apart from Henry IV, his son (later Henry V) and the two Dukes who are his brothers, Oxford is the only nobleman on the English side in the play! He brings Prince Hal to his royal father and after his coronation is continually at his side. The new King solicits his opinion of his right to the crown of France: "What say you, my good Lord of Oxford?" On the eve of Agincourt, when the Duke of York has made the dolorous report to the King that "many of your men [are] sick and diseased, and many of them die for want of victuals," Oxford steps forth heroically to "beseech our Grace to grant me a boon," which is "That your Grace would give me the vanguard in battle." (The King cannot, having "already given it to my uncle, the Duke of York," but thanks "my Lord of Oxford" — making sure the audience will know who it was who asked this noble boon — "for your good will.") When the King wishes to know "What company is there of the Frenchmen?" it is Oxford who has the information: "about threescore thousand horseman and forty thousand footmen." Then, upon the King's ordering stakes driven into the ground that the French may "gore themselves upon them" and be counter-attacked, it is Oxford who offers to "take that in charge, if your

Grace be therewith content" — which the King is: "With all my heart, my good Lord Oxford."[3]

Seymour M. Pitcher, Professor of English in the New York State University system, in his *The Case for Shakespeare's Authorship of "The Famous Victories"* (from which my quotations from the play are taken) cannot help recognizing the extraordinary prominence the play gives Oxford, departing in this from historical sources. His explanation is that the twenty-two-year-old Stratfordian had adopted "the device of elaborating the role of the medieval Oxford to serve the cause of Edward de Vere" and "as complimentary" to him! If the 11th Earl is brought center stage in *The Famous Victories* well beyond historical warrant, the fact is that he did have an important command at Agincourt. This makes it all the more striking that when the dramatist would come again to tell the story of his favorite monarch in the two-part *King Henry the Fourth* and in *King Henry the Fifth* the Earl of Oxford would be entirely dropped, not even appearing in the *dramatis personae*. Where a speech of his from *The Famous Victories* had to be given, as when he reports that

> If it please your Majesty, there are of the French army slain above ten thousand twenty-six hundred, whereof are princes and nobles bearing banners. . . .

the lines in the later play would be given to the King himself:

> This note doth tell me of ten thousand French
> That in the field lie slain: of princes, in this number,
> And nobles bearing banners, there lie dead
> One hundred twenty-six. . . .

In the initial inflation and later eradication of Oxford's part (as a Soviet official may be air-brushed out of a group photograph) we are unmistakably on to something telltale and important. What it is should be evident to us. By the time Edward de Vere would come to cover the life of Henry V again, his anonymity would be jeopardized if he continued to bring an Earl of Oxford forward — for, after writing *The Famous Victories*, he would have gone on to paean another Oxford in the trilogy of *King Henry the Sixth* and also to a lesser extent in *King Richard the Third*. It would not do to have a performance of one of his plays at Court greeted with ill-suppressed knowing chuckles. The Queen herself may have put her foot down.

The three-part drama of *King Henry the Sixth* concerns the events, almost all harrowing and calamitous for England until the very end, of the reign of that hapless monarch and his successor, in which England's continental

---

[3] Among other reasons, it is because of the unique prominence given Lord Oxford that I cannot accept A. S. Cairncross's opinion that *The Famous Victories* is a pirated version of the three Shakespeare plays covering the same ground.

possessions were finally lost and the nation ravaged by the War of the Roses from 1453 to 1485. (In *Henry the Fifth* the pretty French princess Katherine is charming in her broken English, and her robust wooing by the victor of Agincourt has delighted a dozen generations of readers and the millions who saw Olivier as the suitor. Unfortunately, however, the offspring of the union who inherited the thrones of both England and France within a fortnight before his second birthday and was later crowned Henry VI, took after his mother's line, not his warrior father's. Pious and almost simple-minded, he eventually fell heir to the insanity of his maternal grandfather, Charles VI.) This protracted dynastic war of massacres and beheadings pitted the Lancastrians, under the red rose, supporters of Henry VI (grandson of Henry of Lancaster, who had become Henry IV) against the Yorkists, under the white rose, supporters of Richard, Duke of York, and his son, who defeated the Lancastrians in 1461 and ascended the throne as Edward IV. The usurper laid waste his enemies, driving Henry VI to take refuge in Scotland.

Among those put to death by Edward was the 12th Earl of Oxford and his heir. The 17th Earl would not forget when he came to write *Henry the Sixth, Part Three*. Entreated by the Earl of Warwick, the King-maker, to "leave Henry and call Edward king," the eighteen-year-old John de Vere, now the 13th Earl, replies with defiant eloquence:

> Call him my king, by whose injurious doom
> My elder brother, the Lord Aubrey Vere,
> Was done to death? and more than so, my father,
> Even in the down fall of his mellow'd years,
> When nature brought him to the door of death?
> No, Warwick, no; while life upholds this arm,
> This arm upholds the house of Lancaster.

Warwick having switched sides, Oxford joined him in 1470 in a successful campaign to restore Henry to the throne. In the play the Earl is repeatedly acclaimed:

> *Warwick*: And thou, brave Oxford, wondrous well belov'd. . . .
> *King Henry*: Sweet Oxford. . . .
> *Warwick*: Oh cheerful colors! See, where Oxford comes!
> *Oxford*: Oxford, Oxford for Lancaster!
> *Queen Margaret*: Why, is not Oxford here another anchor?
> *Queen Margaret*: . . . sweet Oxford, thanks.

For all John de Vere, the 13th Earl's, valor and ability — and these made him the second of the line to win an entry of his own in the *Encyclopaedia Britannica* — ill betided the Lancastrians. Edward, who had escaped to Holland, returned in the next year, rallied his followers, and slashed through to London. Two days later he was met by Warwick and Oxford at Barnet and would probably have been defeated but for a singular mischance. Oxford, having successfully charged the Yorkist left, sought to strengthen Warwick's position, but the day was misty and Warwick's force, mistaking the de Vere star of Oxford's followers for the sun displayed by the Yorkists, let loose a swarm of arrows on them. Poor visibility compounded the confusion, and before the situation could be straightened out the battle was lost. The play makes the Duke of Clarence's defection responsible — and the fact is that Clarence, having deserted King Edward in favor of King Henry, had switched colors back again. With the words "Fly, lords, and save yourselves; for Warwick bids you all farewell, to meet in heaven," Warwick dies — as he did in real life — and Oxford cries: "Away, away, to meet the queen's great power!" But Queen Margaret's force is given inadequate time to prepare and at Tewksbury the Lancastrians suffer decisive defeat. King Edward proclaims:

> Away with Oxford to Hames Castle straight:
> For Somerset, off with his guilty head.
> Go, bear them hence; I will not hear them speak.

And Oxford rejoins:

> For my part, I'll not trouble thee with words.

Actually, four years elapsed between the defeat and death of Warwick and Oxford's imprisonment. The Earl had escaped from Barnet to France, where, in 1473, — Henry VI having meanwhile been murdered in the Tower — "he organized a Lancastrian expedition which, after an attempted landing in Essex, sailed west and seized St. Michael's Mount in Cornwall. It was only after a four-months' siege that Oxford was forced to surrender. . . . He was sent to Hammes near Calais." There he would be held until escaping after Edward IV had died and his younger brother, Richard Duke of Gloucester, had had himself crowned king, in 1483. It was Richard's misfortune to be dramatized by an unforgiving Lancastrian and a de Vere and be made to revel in a villainy unmatched in literature.

When Duke Richard in the play takes advantage of Edward IV's transient anger toward their brother the Duke of Clarence to have Clarence murdered (his body afterward stuffed in the famous butt of Malmsey) to remove him from his own way to the succession, the dying king, appalled, recalls of his dead brother how

> in the field by Tewksbury,
> When Oxford had me down, he rescued me. . . .

It is a forgivable bit of fiction on the dramatist's part.

"Richard was no monster born," G. M. Trevelyan says, "nor, prior to his usurpation of the throne, was his record as treacherous as that of his brother Clarence or as bloody as that of his brother Edward." While the charge that he murdered the two little princes in the Tower may be disputed, however, still, the nation suffered enough under his exactions and scandalous behavior.

Churchill writes, "All hopes in England were now turned towards [Henry Tudor, Earl of] Richmond, and it was apparent that the marriage which had been projected between him and Edward IV's eldest daughter Elizabeth offered a prospect of ending for ever the cruel dynastic strife of which the land was unutterably weary. . . . In France, Richmond was joined by the Earl of Oxford, leading survivor of the Lancastrian party, who had escaped from ten years' incarceration and plunged once again into the old struggle." Other Lancastrians and Yorkists joined forces with Richmond, who with his followers landed in Milford Haven in 1485 and marched inland, to be met by Richard III at Market Bosworth. The King's army was far superior in numbers, but as Oxford (who held a high command under the challenger) was to proclaim in the play:

> Every man's conscience is a thousand swords,
> To fight against that bloody homicide.

And so it was to prove. Defections from the King's standard were to decide the day. Richard "hurled himself into the thickest of the fray in the desperate purpose of striking Richmond down with his own hand." But, "the tides of conflict swept the principals asunder. Richmond was preserved, and the King, refusing to fly, was borne down," Churchill says, "and slaughtered as he deserved." Whereupon, "Richard's crown, which he wore to the last, was picked out of a bush and placed upon the victor's head." In *Richard the Third*, Richmond declares that

> as we have ta'en the sacrament,
> We will unite the white rose and the red.
> . . . .
> O, now let Richmond and Elizabeth,
> The true successors of each royal house,
> By God's fair ordinance conjoin together.

Edward de Vere could be confident that with the crucial two lines he gave his forebear in the play before the battle, his Queen, when she saw it performed, would be reminded of how John de Vere, falling heir to the championship of the Lancastrian cause as he fell heir to the Earldom of Oxford in 1462, had been the great stand-by of the red rose twenty-three years later and a leading hand in placing her grandfather, Henry VII, on the throne and establishing the Tudor line.

The new King restored all the titles, offices, and lands of the 13th Earl of Oxford, created him the first Knight of the Garter, and had him stand as one of the godfathers to his son, the future Henry VIII. But the Earl had gone on to earn further royal gratitude. At Stoke, in 1486, he "led the van of the royal army. In 1492 he was in command in the expedition to Flanders, and in 1497 he was foremost in the defeat of the Cornish rebels on Blackheath." And in the next year he was almost ruined by his sovereign, who had turned out to be as crafty as he was tireless in finding replenishment for his treasury. The eventuality came to pass during a visit by the King to Castle Hedingham. As told by the Duchess of Cleveland,

> the entertainment was so sumptuously arranged that [the king] was astounded by the magnificence displayed. On his departure he said to the Earl, "My lord, I have heard much of your hospitality, but I see it is greater than the speech. These handsome gentlemen and yeomen which I see on both sides of me, are surely your menial servants?" The Earl smiled, and said, "It may please your Grace, they are not for mine ease; they are most of them my retainers, that are come to do me service at such a time as this; and chiefly to see your Grace." The King started a little, and rejoined, "By my faith, my lord, I thank you for your good cheer, but I may not endure to have my laws broken in my sight; my attorney must speak with you." The attorney spoke, and to some purpose; for the graceless guest positively caused his hospitable entertainer to be mulcted of £10,000, for having, in his desire to do honor to his Sovereign, ventured to exceed the number of retainers prescribed to him.

(We may remember how Lear is stripped of his retainers — his hundred knights.)

Eva Turner Clark points out that the fine, to be reckoned in the millions of dollars today, has "by many been thought to have been the beginning of the financial disintegration of the ancient house of de Vere." But the house of de Vere was to have a revenge that Henry VII could scarcely have anticipated. In the immortal Shakespearean dramas in which the royalty of England would be restored to grandeur from the accession of Richard II to the death of Henry in 1547, the reign of Henry VII alone would be passed over.

When the renowned 13th Earl died in 1512, he was succeeded by another of the same name, called "Little John of Camps," his usual residence being at Castle Camps in Cambridgeshire. (The name may recur in *Cymbeline* when Imogen, disguised as a man, introduces herself as "Richard du Champs.") In 1520, at twenty-one, the Earl accompanied the King, whose ward he had been, to the Field of the Cloth of Gold, near Calais, where amid scenes of rich ornament, pomp, and medieval chivalry that impressed all Europe — the temporary palace erected for the English Court covered nearly two and a half acres and was supplemented by 2,800 tents — Henry VIII and Francis I of France pledged amity and mutual support. The 14th Earl of Oxford's retinue is said to have consisted of three chaplains, six gentlemen, 33 servants, and 20 horses. "In 36 Henry VIII," he "was at the siege of Boullogne, having command in the rear of the King's army." At his death in 1526, the title passed to a descendant of an uncle of the 13th Earl. The 15th Earl, the fourth successive John, carried the crown at the coronation of Anne Boleyn, mother of the future Queen Elizabeth. At the dinner following the ceremony, "on the right side of her chair stood the Countess of Oxford," according to Stow's Annals, while "in the middest, between the Archbishop [of Canterbury] and the Countess of Oxford, stood the Earl of Oxford, with a white staff all dinner time." Some idea of the 15th Earl's character, showing that he would have been at home in the country scenes of Henry Fielding or Anthony Trollope, may be had from a letter written in 1531 by a schoolboy, Gregory Crumwell, to his father:

> Father, I beseach you when you meet the Right Honorable Lord of Oxford, to give thanks unto his Lordship, for when he came to a town called Yeldam, to the persons thereof to hunt the fox, he sent for me and my cousins, and made us good cheer; and let us see such game and pleasure as I never saw in my life.

When Earl John died in 1540, the eldest of his four sons who succeeded to the title as the 16th Earl was another of the same name. The youngest son, Geoffrey, was the father of Francis and Horace, or Horatio, Vere, two of Queen Elizabeth's most illustrious military captains, as may be surmised from the magnificent tomb in which they are interred in Westminster Abbey. Of the Earl's four daughters, one married Henry Howard, Earl of Surrey, another Edmund Lord Sheffield — poets both, as we have seen.

The 16th Earl was "known in the county as a good landlord and a keen sportsman," sharing the tastes of his huntsman father. We see this and catch an illuminating glimpse of his character in an account by Gervase Markham of his daring in a boar-hunt in France, in which he had been invited to take part because of his "warlike disposition." (This was in 1544, three years before the accession of Mary led to his retirement to Castle Hedingham.) Markham explains that this is "a sport mixed with much danger and deserving the best man's care for his preservation and safety" and hence "the Frenchmen, when they hunt this beast, are ever . . . mounted on horseback, and having chasing staves like lances in their hands." The Earl of Oxford, however, had armed himself for the hunt with "only a dancing rapier." But . . .

> Anon the boar is put on foot (which is a beast both huge and fierce), and the chase is eagerly pursued, many affrights are given, and many dangers escaped. At last the Earl, weary of the toil or else urged by some other necessity, alights from his horse and walks alone by himself on foot; when suddenly down the path in which the Earl walked came the enraged beast, with his mouth all foamy, his teeth whetted, his bristles up, and all other signs of fury and anger. The gallants of France cry unto the Earl to run aside and save himself; everyone hallooed out that he was lost, and . . . none there was that durst bring him succor. But the Earl (who was as careless of their clamours as they were careful to exclaim) alters not his pace, not goes an hair's breadth out of his path; and finding that the boar and he must struggle for passage, draws out his rapier and at the first encounter slew the boar. Which, when the French nobility perceived, they came galloping in unto him and made the wonder in their distracted amazements, some twelve times greater than Hercules twelve labors. . . .

We read, however, that the Earl made light of his performance.

He was not so dextrous in his marital affairs. After his first wife's death, he evidently contracted a liaison with "a gentlewoman," a certain "Mistress

Dorothy," who waited upon his younger daughter Catherine. Things had proceeded so far that the banns had been called two of the three times required if marriage was to be entered upon. But the Earl was evidently deterred from the step by his brother-in-law. On 1 August 1548, he was wed to Margaret Golding of nearby Belchamp St. Paul's. She bore him two children, Mary and Edward, named presumably after the two elder offspring of Henry VIII. Edward was born in 1550, on April 11 old style, April 22 new, so that if we celebrate his birthday as Shakespeare's we shall have to move the occasion only one day from the date on which posterity decided to have William Shakspere born: the 23rd.

B. M. Ward quotes the parish register of the marriage of Edward's parents, and this official record is important. The 3rd Baron Windsor, husband of Lord Oxford's first daughter, Catherine, would challenge the validity of the marriage, evidently in the belief that the affair with Mistress Dorothy had led to an earlier one, and declare Catherine the Earl's only legitimate issue. The charge was brought after the Earl's death in Edward's fourteenth year. It gave the boy an early taste of being "in disgrace with fortune and men's eyes." If a poem signed E. O. was written by him at this time he took it very hard. Entitled *Loss of Good Name* ("He that filches from me my good name, . . ." Iago was to protest), it sounds very youthful. Here is the third and final stanza:

> Help Gods, help saints, help sprites and powers that in the heaven do
>   dwell,
> Help ye that are aye wont to wail, ye howling hounds of hell;
> Help man, help beasts, help birds and worms, that on the earth do
>   toil,
> Help fish, help fowl, that flock and feed upon the salt sea soil,
> Help echo that in air doth flee, shrill voices to resound,
> To wail this loss of my good name, as of these griefs the ground.

Whatever his response to the allegation of illegitimacy may have been at thirteen, he had evidently learned to take it with impudent lightness and turn it upon his accuser when he came to write *King John*. Faulconbridge exults in the bastardy with which his brother Robert — half-brother, actually — charges him in order to deny him an inheritance; his illegitimacy makes him a natural son of Richard Coeur de Lion instead of a "three-farthings" off-shoot of Robert's pusillanimous father. "Now blessed be the hour, by day or night," he cries, "When I was got. . . ." And so Edward de Vere, legitimate or not, was undeniably the son of the "warlike" 16th Earl of Oxford, where his half-brother-in-law, who was seeking to deny him his inheritance, was merely the son of a 2nd Baron Windsor. In any event, the shadow of doubtful claim to the title may have followed him through life, as it did Queen Elizabeth, for in 1660 the 7th Baron Windsor renewed the charge — unsuccessfully — in a petition to the Crown to gain the office of Lord Great Chamberlain for himself as Catherine de Vere's great-grandson.

Elizabeth's accession had brought the 16th Earl out of retirement.

> In September 1559 he was appointed, with Lord Robert Dudley, to attend the King of Sweden's second son John, Duke of Friesland, when the duke came to England to offer Elizabeth marriage in behalf of his elder brother, Prince Eric. He met the Duke on his landing at Horwich, and showed him "great sport" in the valley of the Stour. . . . He held through life many posts of honour. . . . [He was] popularly known as "the good earl."

From Stow we learn that the priory of Torington's house in Candlewick Street had been granted to his father, the 15th Earl, and that he "kept great state here. . . . The great house [was] called London Stone or Oxford House." The manner of the Earl's travel from Hedingham to London must have deeply impressed his young son and scarcely have inclined him toward frugality when he should have come into the title. Stow wrote in 1598 that

> The late Earl of Oxford . . . hath been noted within these forty years, to have ridden into this City, and so to his house by London Stone, with 80 Gentlemen in a livery of Reading Tawny, and chains of gold about their necks before him, and 100 tall yeomen in the like livery to follow him without chains, but all having his cognizance of the blue Boar embroidered on their left shoulder.

Oxford House, according to Ward, would in time be Edward's principal London dwelling, until he should have sold it in 1589. Its site is recognized today. Oxford Court is on an alleyway leading off the Strand close to where a fragment of London Stone is still preserved, set behind a grating in the wall of a bank. Believed part of the Roman defense-works of the city, the Stone has had an importance that comes out in *Henry the Sixth, Part Two*, when Jack Cade, a demagogic laborer encouraged by the Duke of York to take the name of John Mortimer, whom he resembles, leads his rabble into London and, striking the ancient rock with his sword, proclaims, "Now is Mortimer lord of this city."

We know little of Edward de Vere's childhood beyond what may be inferred from his position and subsequent attainments. These vouch for his having ridden beside his father in the chase ("The game's afoot! Follow your spirits. . . !") and been proficient in arms as far as his years allowed. At the same time his matriculation at St. John's College before his ninth birthday indicates how early his bookish tastes (against which he was later to be warned) manifested themselves. One of his tutors was Sir Thomas Smith, a fellow of Queen's College, Cambridge, later Vice Chancellor of the University, and one of the great classical scholars of his time. Later, too, one of Queen Elizabeth's most trusted Protestant counsellors, he, like the de Veres, had to lie low in Queen Mary's reign. Edward must have taken it all in as Sir Thomas talked of his student days in Italy and France, to which he was to return as an ambassador. Another whom the standard reference books credit with a part in the boy's education, doubtless with warrant, is Arthur Golding, his mother's half-brother and an eminent translator from Latin and French, especially of religious texts. Golding's firmly espoused Puritanism would have tended to put his nephew off, but his prodigal sacrifice of the lands he inherited (his family was an ancient one locally) in pursuit of intellectual interests would suggest a temperamental affinity between the two and there are later signs of a mutual affection. Certainly the association was to be auspicious for literature.

Edward was only twelve when the 16th Earl died. At that age especially a boy is apt to look up to his father as to the embodiment of manhood, unless the facts hopelessly belie it, as in the Earl's case they must have stood in striking confirmation. That Edward would have been stricken by his father's death seems very likely. Then within a few months, it would seem, his mother married again. Shock and revulsion would have been his natural reaction. Surely we hear his anguish years later when Hamlet, wishing his own death in equivalent circumstances, contrasts his dead father with his mother's new lord as being "Hyperion to a satyr" and cries "O God! a beast that wants a discourse of reason / Would have mourned longer."

If we recognize in de Vere the author of Shakespeare's plays, doors are opened to us as never before on the working of a supreme creative mind in transmuting personal experiences into the stuff of fiction.[4] In what it tells us, *Hamlet* is unmistakably in the forefront of the plays. It is true that the man who replaced Edward's father in his mother's bed did not murder to get there, as Claudius did to displace Hamlet's father. He bore, however, the name of a murderer who to the boy would have been as vile as any in English history — Tyrrell, whom Richard III in the play suborned to kill the little princes in the Tower to clear his way to the throne. (When James Tyrrell was brought to trial, the 13th Earl of Oxford was one of his judges.) To Edward it would have seemed that his new step-father, Charles Tyrrell, having the odor of murder in his name, had murdered his father's memory. As I wrote some chapters back, it would appear that in Queen Gertrude and her new consort, Claudius, the dramatist had in mind Queen Elizabeth and Robert Dudley, Earl of Leicester, who came closer than anyone else to being her husband. If Leicester did not murder an earlier mate of Elizabeth's, he was widely thought to have arranged the murder of his wife, Amy Robsart, to free himself to marry the Queen and make himself King of England. Claudius in murdering his way to the throne had come between Hamlet and the succession, as the Prince does not fail to remark, and it had always

---

[4] In writing "if" I do so for the last time in this connection. It is not that I consider myself any one to say with finality that de Vere was Shakespeare — though to me the facts leave no doubt of it — but that as a practical matter I cannot pitch all that follows in the conditional tense.

seemed that here the parallel with Leicester and de Vere broke down. But at this time let us turn the podium over to one of the ablest of Shakespearean researchers, Gwynneth Bowen:

> Oxfordians have always maintained that *Hamlet* is very largely autobiographical — with Oxford in the title-role. . . . The "o'er hasty marriage" of Oxford's mother — a point which greatly impressed Freud — has been given due weight, but Lady Oxford never quite filled up the role of Gertrude, and Tyrrell did not loom large enough for Claudius. The transition from Lady Oxford to Queen Elizabeth as the prototype of Gertrude was logical, since Oxford became her ward and Cecil (Polonius) was her chief minister. To that extent, anyway, the Danish Court reflected the English Court, but Claudius remained an enigma. The idea that the character was based on Leicester is not entirely new and has been maintained, among Oxfordians, by Dorothy and Charlton Ogburn [Sr.]. Vis-à-vis the Queen, Leicester (or his contemporary image [as probably the murderer of his wife]) fits admirably, but for most Oxfordians, if they thought of it at all, the difficulty was to fit him into the *family group*. No one by the wildest flight of fancy supposed that he had "usurped" the lands of the Earl of Oxford.

But that was before Ms. Bowen had pored over the records and made a most significant discovery in connection with the demise of the Earl's father.

> Briefly: Lord Robert Dudley [Leicester] was granted "all . . . the lands . . . and all the singular there appertaining in the counties of Essex, Suffolk, and Cambridgeshire, late in the inheritance of the Right Hon. John de Vere Earl of Oxford," and since nearly all the lands of the Earl of Oxford were in these three counties, we should not be far wrong in saying Dudley got the lot!

Dudley's possession was not permanent, of course, but neither did it end with Edward's attainment of his majority. As Gwynneth Bowen learned, Earls Colne Priory did not revert to him until he was thirty-eight! She continues:

> So it was not Cecil; not Charles Tyrrell; but Robert Dudley who succeeded Edward's father (for the time being) as Lord of the Manors of Castle Hedingham, Earls Colne, etc. The spoils were divided: Tyrrell married the late Earl's widow; Cecil obtained custody of his son; but Dudley got the lands.

That was not quite all that could cause Edward de Vere to dip his pen in gall and cast Leicester as Claudius. Leicester's grandfather, Edmund Dudley, served as one of Henry VII's two principal extortioners, having at the same time "amassed a great amount of wealth for himself." We may wonder if it was not he who collected the ruinous fine imposed by his royal master upon the 13th Earl of Oxford. One thing further: Leicester, as we shall find, would be rumored to have fatally poisoned the noble Earl of Sussex, to whom Edward de Vere in his twenties is quite likely to have stood in a somewhat filial relationship.

21

"Learning and Ingenious Studies"

1562 to 1569: The death of the 16th Earl of Oxford and the departure of the twelve-year-old Edward from Hedingham and from the Countess his mother to take up life as a royal ward (in a scene to be duplicated in All's Well*) in the household of Sir William Cecil, the Queen's First minister. — Edward's opportunity to acquire the grasp of ambition and intrigue at the center of power displayed in Shakespeare's early historical plays and, from Cecil's famous horticulturist, the feeling for and knowledge of flowers characteristic of Shakespeare. — The grueling schedule of Edward's schooling; his distinguished tutor; his rapid progress in his studies; his achievement of a bachelor's degree from Cambridge at fourteen and of a master's from Oxford at sixteen. — The tribute to Edward's intellectual interests we might expect to the young Shakespeare by his maternal uncle, the scholar-translator Arthur Golding; the close association of the two preceding publication of Golding's translation of Ovid's* Metamorphoses *(a book scholars agree was a favorite of Shakespeare's) and the likelihood that the racy work, totally unlike anything else the Calvinist Golding ever set his name to, was the product of Edward's pen under his uncle's direction. — Golding's dedication to his nephew of two learned works that would have an evident influence on Shakespeare's. — The publication in Edward's thirteenth year of the childish narrative poem* Romeus and Juliet*, an undisputed source of the Shakespearean play, and the reasons for believing it of Edward's composition. — The extravagant habits the young lord acquires for which he will later be reproached by Cecil, under whose guardianship he acquires them. — His matriculation at Gray's Inn, where he would be able to master Shakespeare's knowledge of the law and to take a hand in "masques" and "revels."*

At the funeral procession of the 16th Earl of Oxford, we read,

> were three Heralds of Arms, Master Garter, Master Lancaster, Master Richmond, with a standard and a great banner of arms, and eight banner rolls, crest, target, sword and coat armour, and a hearse with velvet and a pall of velvet, and a dozen of escutcheons, and with many mourners in black; and a great moan [was] made for him.

The Earl had left bequests to Sir Nicholas Bacon, the father of Francis, and to Sir Nicholas's long-time and close friend, Sir William Cecil, later Lord Burghley. It is interesting that the Earl described Cecil, who was to play so large a role in his son's life, as "my trusty and loving friend." Ward speculates that during Queen Elizabeth's visit to Castle Hedingham in the preceding year the Earl had discussed plans with her for having young Edward made

William Cecil Lord Burghley

In the portrait attributed to Marcus
Gheeraedts

By permission of the National Portrait
Gallery, London.

a royal ward in Cecil's household in the event of his early death. Cecil, as we have seen, had the year before, in 1561, been "given the lucrative office of master of the court of wards," and had "done something to reform that instrument of tyranny and oppression." The description gives an idea of what Edward was headed for. Cecil had but two wards of his own, so far as we know, but he had guardianship of the royal wards, of which eight were to be of the noblest families in England. The senior, in 1562, was the fourteen-year-old Earl of Rutland. The next in order, who "played an important part in Burghley's life for years to come," Conyers Read observes in his two-volume history of William Cecil and Queen Elizabeth, was Edward de Vere.

The boy Earl of Oxford's departure from Castle Hedingham would give rise to the exchange that opens *All's Well That Ends Well,* in which the dramatist's appearance in the guise of Bertram represents a much more youthful view of himself than he was to entertain when he wrote *Hamlet:*

> *Countess*: In delivering my son from me, I bury a second husband.
> *Bertram*: And I, in going, madam, weep o'er my father's death anew:
> but I must attend his majesty's command, to whom I am now in
> ward, evermore in subjection.

Probably he left with regret and foreboding but also with anticipation of new scenes and the stir of London, its pulse that of the Court, of commerce, of crowds. A contemporary diarist records that

> On the 3rd day of September came riding out of Essex from the funeral of the Earl of Oxford his father [actually three days after it], the young Earl of Oxford, with seven score horse all in black, through London and Chepe and Ludgate, and so to Temple Bar . . . between 5 and 6 of the afternoon.

The report that the twelve-year-old was accompanied by 140 horses of any color is one I think we might treat with reserve.

According to contemporary accounts, Cecil House, in Westminster (not then part of London) had been built in the reign of Edward VI

> of brick and timber, very large and spacious; but of later time it hath been far more beautifully increased by the late Sir William Cecil, baron of Burghley. . . . Standing on the north side of the Strand [across from the site of the present Cecil Hotel], a very fair house raised with bricks. . . .

Burghley, an anonymous biographer wrote, "greatly delighted in making gardens, fountains and walks." The grounds of Cecil House were probably acres in extent, though they were to be dwarfed by those of the great mansion of Theobalds he was later to build. The embellishment of the latter by the statues of twelve Roman emperors among others suggests that he favored show as well as flowers. Beginning at Cecil House, however, he employed for twenty years the most noted English horticulturalist of the time, John Gerard, who dedicated to him his well-known *Herball, or General History of Plants*, of 1597. The reader will of course think at once of the prominence of flowers in Shakespeare. In this connection *Horticulture* magazine, in its issue of November 1977, remarks, with a bow to Oxfordians, on the similarity observed by J. S. Lever between the last song in *Love's Labour's Lost* and a passage in Gerard's *Herball*. The song reads:

> When daisies pied, and violets blue,
> And lady-smocks all silver-white
> And cuckoo-buds of yellow hue
> Do paint the meadows with delight,
> The cuckoo then on every tree
> Mocks married men; for thus sings he "Cuckoo;
> Cuckoo, cuckoo."

"Compare this," says *Horticulture*, "to a description by Gerard of 'Cardinine lactea (milk white Ladie smocks)' that appears on the same page with the statement that 'these flower for the most part in April and Maie, when the cuckoo doth begin to sing her pleasant notes without stammering.'"

Coming under Sir William Cecil's guardianship, Edward had been transplanted from the fields and woods of rural Essex to the hearth of a man at the nexus of the nation's power-structure, as we should call it today, and of the never-ending struggle for place centering upon the throne. Churchill writes: "Of Sixteenth-century English statesmen Cecil was undoubtedly the greatest. He possessed a consuming thirst for information about the affairs of the realm, and was to display immense industry in the business of office. Cautious good judgment marked all his actions. Elizabeth, with sure instinct [had] summoned him to her service. . . . It was a tremendous burden which the young Queen imposed upon her First Minister, then aged thirty-eight. Their close and daily collaboration was to last, in spite of shocks and jars, until Cecil's death, forty years later." Thus from an early age Edward had the best of opportunities to acquire that familiarity with "the language of ambition, intrigue and policy" which, the reader may remember, a prominent Member of Parliament of our day, Enoch Powell, finds in Shakespeare, especially in the early plays, and which, he maintains, "could only be drawn from experience." There is much to testify to de Vere's respect for Cecil. It is significant that even when he came to work off the frustrations of a quarter-century's dealings with the First Minister by caricaturing him as Polonius, the maxims he had the pompous counsellor recite to his departing son Laertes, inspired by the *Certaine Preceptes, or Directions*, that Cecil wrote as guidance for his son Robert, are such as to strike us, four centuries later, as shrewd and sound advice. It does seem likely, though, that the most famous of them, "This above all, to thine own self be true . . . ," has not quite the

Coat-of-Arms of the de Veres

With the legend "Nothing Truer than
Truth" or "Nothing Truer than Vere."

high-minded intent we read into it but rather the connotation "To thine own interests be true."

How the young Edward took the transition there is no knowing or perhaps even imagining. It is not easy for an offspring of twentieth-century egalitarianism to put himself in Tudor England in the place of a young de Vere who by virtue of his inheritance was entitled to picture himself as virtually a prince of the realm — as, indeed, he was to do in play after play. We have Shakespeare's works, however, to testify to their author's susceptibility to nature and to the supremacy he accords to nature as a ruling force, in which he was so far ahead of his times as to speak for ours. "O thou goddess!" Belarius, the nobleman exiled to the wilds, exclaims in *Cymbeline*, "Thou divine Nature. . . ." And King Polixenes explains perceptively in *The Winter's Tale*:

> Yet nature is made better by no mean
> But nature makes that mean; so, over that art,
> Which you say adds to nature, is an art,
> That nature makes.

There is the longing, too, expressed in his early plays, written after the author's brilliant success at Court and later disillusionment, for the simple, wholesome life close to nature. All this calls up for me a picture of one who had learned in boyhood — a privileged boyhood — to delight in the enchantments of the country out-of-doors, for a standard by which all else is measured is likely to be acquired, if at all, early in life. And so I should guess that nostalgia for those Essex meadows and beech groves was part of Edward's portion in Cecil House. And it could well have been intensified by the curriculum contrived to prepare him for the role of a de Vere. The "Orders for the Earl of Oxford's Exercises," which have come down to us, thanks to his guardian's concern for the documentary record, read as follows

7:00–7:30 — Dancing	10:00–10:30 — Writing and drawing
7:30–8:00 — Breakfast	1:00–2:00 — Cosmography
8:00–9:00 — French	2:00–3:00 — Latin
9:00–10:00 — Latin	3:00–4:00 — French
	4:00–4:30 — Exercises with his pen.

The common prayers and so to dinner

On holidays such studies were suspended to make time for the pupil to "read before dinner the Epistle and Gospel in his own tongue, and in the other tongue ["Greek?" Conyers Read interjects] after dinner. All the rest of the day to be spent in riding, shooting, dancing, walking, and other commendable exercises, saving the time for prayer."

If Edward missed the life at Hedingham, those rides and walks would have taken him perhaps once a week into a countryside probably much like Essex, which in those days must have impinged closely on Westminster. For companionship he may have had Edward Manners, the two-year-older Earl of Rutland; one would like to know how the boys got along. Brachs at the horses' hooves, tiercel gentles on fists, a falconer somewhat to the rear for professional advice: one can see the mounted party, and, if one has beheld a peregrine in its breathtaking display of power and speed, recapture a little of the excitement as worthy game was sighted — a crafty "crow that makes wing to the rooky wood" or a pigeon that could "faster than Venus' pigeons fly" (or at least as fast) and pursuit was let slip.

There were compensations at Cecil House, too. Sir William valued mental attainments and his second wife, Mildred, was accounted by Roger Ascham one of the two most learned women in the country. (Mildred's sister was the wife of Sir Nicholas Bacon and thus the mother of Francis.) The atmosphere must have been an intellectual one and in that respect congenial to the boy de Vere, though evidently he got along ill with the reputedly difficult Lady Cecil. The omnivorous mind we know as Shakespeare's doubtless already active, he probably took to his studies with alacrity; after all they had been his fare at Hedingham, too. "There can be little doubt that Oxford was a diligent student," the Burghley-oriented Conyers Read concedes, and more: "Oxford distinguished himself as a classical scholar, showed considerable talent as a poet, took a great interest in the drama, and has since been put forth seriously as the author of Shakespeare's plays." The tutor engaged for him, Lawrence Nowell, Dean of Litchfield, wrote a letter in Latin to Sir William in June 1563 stating that "I clearly see that my work for the Earl of Oxford cannot be much longer required." Certainly it says something that a "scholar of distinction," as Read calls him, the brother of Alexander Nowell, who was master and prebendary of Westminster School and for forty-two years Dean of St. Paul's, should find that a boy newly turned thirteen would not much longer gain from his instruction! A letter that Edward wrote two months later in French, in a hand close to that of his mature years, reproduced below, shows how far he had gone in that language.

Letter by the Earl of Oxford at
Thirteen

BOOK TWO: Is Not Oxford Here Another Anchor?

In August 1564, during the Queen's Progress to Cambridge, Edward, then fourteen and four months, and young Manners received degrees from the University; Cecil himself was given a degree of Master of Arts. Though de Vere had evidently taken up lodgings for a time at St. John's College — Cecil's own — Manners had never attended the University, and it is likely that both degrees were awarded in recognition of achievements demonstrated by the two boys in Cecil's household. (Manners was a good scholar and "later distinguished himself at the bar and came within an ace of being Lord Chancellor," Read points out.) John Brooke, himself a graduate of Trinity College, recalled the award in "committing" a work to Oxford's "defence of learning" and "honourable patronage" in 1577, writing that he understood

> right well that your honour hath continually, even from your tender years, bestowed your time and travail towards the attaining of [learning], as also the University of Cambridge hath acknowledged in granting and giving unto you commendation and praise thereof, as verily by right was due unto your excellent virtue and rare learning.

Of the Queen at the exercises that included the awarding of the degrees to her First Minister and his two wards, Elizabeth Jenkins writes:

> All her powers were engaged in listening, noticing and responding, and she never perhaps appeared more stikingly as a product of the Renaissance than on this visit, with her intelligent participation in a long programme of speeches, debates and plays in Latin, while at the same time she was entrancing the onlookers by her state and elegance, her cordial charm and her agility of mind.

The scenario for the occasion, we might add, had been minutely planned by Cecil, who specified even the accommodations the royal and noble visitors were to have, the entertainments to be presented to compliment Her Majesty's learning, and the measures to ensure decorum in the student body.

In 1566, the two young earls journeyed together to Oxford in another royal progress and were alike accorded the degree of Master of Arts, as was, again, their guardian. The proceedings duplicated those at Cambridge two years before, only Cecil had not been in on the planning and perhaps in consequence the undergraduates, unrestrained, crowded so enthusiastically into a performance of *Palamon and Arcite* that a wall fell and a staircase collapsed under them, injuring three fatally. The Queen had her doctor do all he could, and the next day the play was resumed.

How much time, if any, Edward actually put in at Oxford is not known; but if the surmises we may make as to his pursuits up to that time are warranted, the degree was fully deserved. What we may infer brings us to a matter of outstanding significance in the career of Oxford as Shakespeare.

In May 1564, Edward's uncle, the scholar and translator Arthur Golding, had dedicated *Th' Abridgement of the histories of Trogus Pompeius* to the boy, declaring that:

> It is not unknown to others, and I have had experience thereof myself, how earnest a desire your honour hath naturally graffed in you to read, peruse, and communicate with others as well the histories of ancient times, and things done long ago, as also the present estate of things in our days, and that not without a certain pregnancy of wit and ripeness of understanding.

Thus in his fourteenth year Edward had already shown an earnest desire not only to learn about the events of the past and the state of things in the present but to *communicate them to others*: just what he would do in the great dramas. It is not remarkable that Golding should have entertained

> a great hope and expectation of such wisdom and experience in you in times to come as is meet and beseeming for so noble a race.

This dedication and another at the end of 1564 were dated from Cecil House, indicating that Golding was living there. It could hardly be otherwise than that he was taking a hand in his nephew's education, replacing Nowell. To his descendant and biographer, Louis Thorn Golding, it "would appear reasonable" that he was Edward's tutor. How long he was domiciled under Cecil's roof is not known. Probably when not in residence he was a visitor, for Cecil had appointed him "receiver" for Edward and his sister Mary. As such, he was evidently recipient of revenues from bailiffs of the youngsters' estates. We find that a dedication he wrote in April 1567 was dated from one of the de Vere estates in Essex.

That dedication introduces a work famous to this day, the only one for which Golding is remembered. The title-page reads: THE XV BOOKES OF P. OUIDIUS NASO, ENTYTLUED *Metamorphosis, translated oute of Latin into English meeter, by Arthur Golding Gentleman. A worke very pleasaunt and delectable.* Two years earlier, the same printer had brought out Golding's translation of the first four books of the *Metamorphoses*, similarly presented.

Now, if there is anything that all Shakespearean commentators are agreed upon, it is the strong influence of Publius Ovidius Naso upon the poet. "People," says A. L. Rowse, referring to Shakespeare's contemporaries, "spoke of his poetry as that of an English Ovid." In a valuable introduction to a reprinting of the Golding translation by Macmillan in 1965, John Frederick Nims, of the University of Illinois at Chicago, writes:

> L. P. Wilkinson, in the best book we have on Ovid, reminds us that Shakespeare echoes him about four times as often as he echoes Vergil, that he draws on every book of the *Metamorphoses*, and that there is scarcely a play untouched by his influence. Golding's translation, through the many editions published during Shakespeare's lifetime, was the standard Ovid in English. If Shakespeare read Ovid so, he read Golding.

He goes on, however, to cite informed opinion that Shakespeare used the Latin original as well as the translation.

Of the "collaboration" between Ovid and Golding — "between the sophisticated darling of a dissolute society, the author of a scandalous book of seduction, and the respectable country gentleman and convinced Puritan who spent much of his life translating the sermons and commentaries of John Calvin" — Professor Nims finds it "odd"; "hardly less striking than the metamorphoses the work dealt with," which transform men and women into four-footed animals, plants, rocks, and celestial bodies. "Strange," the *Encyclopaedia Britannica* calls it; Golding's only original work, it declares, "is a prose *Discourse* on the earthquake of 1580, in which he saw a judgment of God on the wickedness of his time." Actually, he did write another original, short prose work, *A brief discourse of the late murther of master George Sanders* to instruct the reader in "the avoiding of misconduct and also the use of the example for the amendment of thy life." He also produced one poem outside those in the *Metamorphoses*. This was an introduction in thirteen seven-line stanzas to a work by Barrets, which he commends to the reader as having been composed "for thy welfare." The prefatory verses in the two separate parts of the *Metamorphoses* may be assumed to be of his conception. Their purpose is to show through exhaustive example how, by taking Ovid allegorically, we may arrive at a Christian interpretation of the scandalous episodes, no matter how far-fetched. Golding's moral disapproval of the characters is unsparing of Jove himself

> . . . whom heathen folk do arme with triple fyre
> In shape of Eagle, bull or swan to winne his foul desyre.

If we find it odd and strange that the staunch and sober Puritan should have gone to the immense and surely uncongenial labor of rendering into English iambic heptameter couplets the 12,000-line Latin work — longer than *Paradise Lost* — of a poet whose salacity contributed to his exile from Rome (no less!), we shall, if we read much of the English version, find it much odder and stranger still that such a man as Golding could have produced it. That a translator whose evidently sole literary interest was in the moral improvement of mankind would have been drawn to Ovid to begin with would be next to incomprehensible. Professor Nims compares the wordiness, ostentatious parade of adjectives, and outlandish inversions of language in the translation with a passage in the straight-forward "patterns of English speech" of Golding's *Discourses* — and the contrast could hardly be greater. The Illinois professor can only marvel at it. Should we feed the language of the two into a computer set up to discriminate styles and ask if the works had the same author, the electronic reply could only be, "Are you kidding?"

If the faults in the translation are most unrepresentative of Golding, so too are its merits. And these it has, even if Ezra Pound was stretching them in calling it "the most beautiful book in the language," adding: "my opinion and I suspect it was Shakespeare's." Professor Nims considers it "still more enjoyable, more plain fun to read, than any other 'Metamorphoses' in English." Where a professional Latinist and translator like Golding would surely have aimed at fidelity to the original, the author of the translation breezily dismisses all that. He has, says Professor Nims, "something very engaging of his own to give us. He begins by metamorphosing Ovid: by turning the sophisticated Roman into a ruddy country gentleman with tremendous gusto, a sharp eye on the life around him, an ear for racy speech, and a gift for energetic doggerel." He goes on to show how the author infallibly "Englishes" the stories, "modernizes military equipment, frankly turning an ancient siege engine into a gun," often gives "even proper names . . . their English equivalent" (the Aegean Sea becomes "Goat Sea," Partenium Nemus "Maiden Wood"), and "when he doesn't translate names, he declassicizes them with jaunty Elizabethan abbreviations. Pentheus, Theseus, Orpheus . . . are called 'Penthey,' 'Thesey,' and 'Orphey,'" He "is at his best in describing places and people," says Professor Nims, citing his setting of the scene "of the great Calydonian boar hunt." In this we are shown a hollow

> To which the watershots of raine from all high grounds drew

and where

> great store of Osiers grew:
> And swallows lithe, and flackring Flags, and moorish Rushes eke,
> And lazie Reedes on little shankes, and other baggage like.

"The whole boar hunt is well done in Golding, whose rough-and-tumble verses," Professor Nims continues, "often do well with scenes of hubbub and uproar, into which he throws himself with the zest of a sportscaster."

This, *Golding*? The insatiable translator of grim works like *Abraham's Sacrifice* and Calvin's sermons on Job, which in Golding's rendering, according to Louis Thorn Golding, occupied 751 royal folio pages and ran to 1,200,000 words?[1]

Professor Nims finds "Golding" close to his best "where Ceres is searching the world-around for her daughter Proserpina." At one point in the quest the goddess is served an unappetizing-sounding "Hotchpotch" and

> While Ceres was eating this, before hir gazing stood
> A hard-faced boy, a shrewde pert wag, that could no manners good:

---

[1] In his biography, *An Elizabethan Puritan*, Mr. L. T. Golding recognizes that "It has been a surprise to many that so stern a puritan as Golding later showed himself to be, should have translated the *Metamorphoses* of Ovid." He acknowledges that "To such a man, the morals or lack of morals in the *Metamorphoses* must have come as a shock." He finds it "easy, however, to see that the new spirit of life in the country and in the castle [Hedingham], coupled with the opportunity to observe, and probably to associate with the great, possible with royalty itself, would stir interest and imagination and make him drink in eagerly the Roman poet's tales." How such association would cause an unbending puritan to drink in immorality with eagerness is not quite clear to me. Moreover, if the imagination fired within him by the new spirit enlivened any other part of Golding's life or any breath of the deep draughts he had drunk of heady Roman paganism is wafted from the stern puritan's other works — and he plied his pen busily for another forty years — his biographer fails to bring it out.

He laughed at hir and in scorne did call hir "Greedie gut."
The Goddesse being wroth therewith, did on the Hotchpotch put
The liquor ere that all was eate, and in his face it threw. . . .

In the scene of Philemon and Baucis we see the old country couple vividly, Professor Nims remarks, "the old lady 'busie as a Bee' stirring about with her skillet and her coleworts and her hoarded bacon and her 'jolly lump of butter' to bring everything 'pyping from the fyre.'"

The translator liberally made up words, which he explained in footnotes on the first several occurrences. Professor Nims writes: "Sometimes with Golding's weird and piquant vocabulary, we feel we are in Lewis Carroll country, in a land where corsies whewl, where orpid buggs sty awkly in the queach, where froshes yesk, and flackering pookes ensue. None of this may be quite 'beautiful,' but it would be hard to deny it is rich in delights of its own." Are we to ascribe this impudence with language to the humorless reformer who insisted upon "sound orthography" and "due construction both of words and sense"?

That Golding, having written nothing remotely like it before, would have given Elizabethan England a *Metamorphoses* still notable for "its racy verve, its quirks and oddities, its rugged English gusto," and written nothing remotely like it thereafter, and having produced no verse we know of he would turn to, compose a poem 400 pages long, and leave us no other to have kept his name alive: this to me is simply not credible, and I do not believe it. My explanation will already be obvious to the reader: it was by no coincidence that the aberration, the *XV Books*, was the product of just that period when Golding and Edward de Vere were in proximity. That "racy and vivid language . . . so often cramped and attenuated . . . to the meter" would have been as alien to the didactic moralist as it would be native to a teen-aged Berowne, Benedick, or Mercutio still serving his awkward apprenticeship as a poet. I agree with D. S. Ogburn that in the circumstances it would have come only from the hand of the boy "Shakespeare," and that, having converted it by the prefaces to object-lessons for Christian instruction, Arthur Golding was prevailed upon to have it published as his because publishing it as by the 17th Earl of Oxford would have been unthinkable.

It is not straining at plausibility, I think, to picture Edward and his uncle seated shoulder to shoulder over the taper-lighted Latin text, the elder elucidating the more difficult bits, the younger chewing the tip of his quill as he considered how to fit them to his rhymed fourteeners. That he took to the task, the spirit of execution seems to assure us. As for the uncle, I assume license to imagine him pondering with brows knit how elevating precepts could be drawn from the recalcitrant "Paynim" — pagan — material and enlightening his secretly amused nephew with his findings.

Golding must, to say the least, have been doubtful about the enterprise, despite the exemplary end to which it was being turned. Moreover, he would not have been the man he was not to be troubled in general about his nephew, whom Conyers Read sees as "something of a maverick" in Cecil's household. That he was concerned for his soul would come out in the dedication to the young Earl four years later, in 1571, of his translation of *John Calvin's version of the Psalms of David.* In this he admonishes him that it is in "true Religion, true Godliness, true Virtue . . . that your Lordship may do God, your Prince, and your Country best service" and that "The greater gifts of Nature, the more graces of mind, the more worldly benefits that God hath bestowed upon you, the more are you bound to be thankful unto him," which "you cannot be without the true knowledge of him . . . by his word." He warned that "The devil hath more shapes than Proteus" — as L. T. Golding says, "very vigorous language to use towards one of the greatest and wealthiest nobles of England."

If Golding hoped his nephew could be led to seek God's word where he himself found it he was to be disappointed. Yet Edward did not altogether balk at walking through the doors his relative opened. As Shakespeare he would fully demonstrate the value to a writer of a piece of advice I once heard from an Irish novelist — the best for its length I ever have: "Let nothing be wasted upon you." Richard Noble writes in his *Shakespeare's Biblical Knowledge* (1935): "From first to last there is not a play in the Folio entirely free from a suggestion of a use of the *Psalms.* In two plays, *2 Henry IV* and *Henry VIII,* the allusions to the Psalms run into double figures. Even the *Sonnets* are not devoid of quotations from the *Psalms.*" Of his knowledge of the Bible generally, Mr. Noble also finds it "beyond all shadow of doubt that on occasions Shakespeare used the Genevan, just as on others he used the Bishops; and on others again, a rendering found in the Prayer Book, . . . but the evidence is in favor of Shakespeare's possession of a Genevan Old Testament." To this may be juxtaposed an item from an account-book in Cecil's papers recording a payment "on behalf of the Earl of Oxford." then nineteen,

> To William Seres, stationer [who had printed the translation of the *Metamorphoses*], for a Geneva Bible, gilt, a Chaucer, Plutarch's works in French, with other books and papers.

It is hardly necessary to add that Plutarch was a prime source for plays of Shakespeare's and a tale of Chaucer's for *Troilus and Cressida.*

Edward de Vere evidently read Golding's own early translations with profit, for, as Charles W. Barrell has shown, these are echoed in numerous instances in early Shakespearean plays. (Both translations were done during the association of the two.) For example:

§ In the *Histories of Trogus Pompeius*, translated by Golding and dedicated to his nephew in 1564 (as I have brought out), Tomyris, whom Cyrus by one account met his death attacking, is referred to as a Scythian queen where

Herodotus and others speak of her as Queen of the Massagetae. And in *Henry the Sixth, Part One,* the Countess of Auvergne exclaims:

> The plot is laid; if all things fall out right,
> I shall be as famous by this exploit
> As Scythian Tomyris by Cyrus' death.

§ In Golding's *Histories* we are told of Semiramis, the mythical Queen of Assyria, and her criminal exploits with her son. This is recalled in *Titus Andronicus* when the blood-thirsty Tamora, Queen of the Goths (here evidently representing the Spain of Philip II, says Mr. Barrell), is compared with "this Semiramis, this nymph, this siren," and in the induction to *The Taming of the Shrew* in which we read of "the lustful bed trimmed up for Semiramis."

§ Golding's *Histories* reports of Alexander's death that "when his friends saw him dying, they asked him 'whom he would appoint as his successor to this throne.' He replied, 'The most worthy.'" In *The Winter's Tale,* Paulina reassures the King in his seemingly childless widowerhood with the words:

> Care not for issue:
> The crown will find an heir: great Alexander
> Left his to th' worthiest; so his successor
> Was like to be the best.

§ The *Histories* also recalls that Alexander murdered his confidential friend Cleitus during a drinking bout. In *Henry the Fifth* the Welsh captain Fluellen speaks of how "Alexander . . . did, in his ales and his angers, look you, kill his pest friend, Cleitus."

§ In Golding's translation of Caesar's *Commentaries,* dedicated to Sir William Cecil in 1565, we have Caesar remarking, "Of all the inhabitants of this isle, the civilest are the Kentish-folke." In *Henry the Sixth, Part Two,* Lord Say remarks that

> Kent, in the Commentaries Caesar writ,
> Is term'd the civill'st place of all this isle.

Mr. Barrell also cites instances in the plays in which an uncle is spoken of in a father's role, which he suggests reflect the relationship of Golding and his nephew: (1) "When my uncle told me so, he wept, / And hugged me to his arm." (*Henry the Sixth, Part Two.*) (2) "And thy uncle will / As dear be to thee as thy father was." (*King John.*) (3) "An old religious uncle of mine taught me to speak," and "This boy . . . hath been tutor'd in the rudiments of many desperate studies by his uncle." (*As You Like It.*)

De Vere seems also to have drawn on his uncle's translation, in 1578, of Seneca's work on *Benefiting.* Dr. Lily B. Campbell in her *Shakespeare's Tragic Heroes* uses the Golding text to show how the basic theme of *King Lear* was developed in accordance with Seneca's observations on the good and evil results of wise or foolish benefactions, pointing out that in the play the law of benefiting is not observed by either party, for the King never ceases to recount the good he has done and the gratitude that is owed him, while his undutiful daughters forget altogether the benefits they have received and fail to be grateful for them.

And she might have added from *As You Like It* the song:

Freeze, freeze, thou bitter sky,
Thou dost not bite so nigh
As benefits forgot.

In crediting the adolescent Edward with the English versification of the *Metamorphoses*, I have taken a good deal on myself — enough, one would think, certainly. But three chapters back I let myself in for taking on more. Since the issue arises in 1562, it must now be faced.

In that year, Edward's thirteenth, there came off the press a poem called *The Tragicall Historye of Romeus and Juliet* by one Arthur Brooke. Clearly it had its roots in an Italian romance that had evolved into two versions published in the previous decade, and no less clearly it was to give rise to Shakespeare's play. It was, says E. K. Chambers, "substantially his source," and A. L. Rowse calls it an example of "the borrowing characteristic of Shakespeare" and "the basis of *Romeo and Juliet.*" Now, I have rejected the contention of Stratfordians, insulting to the peerless dramatist and unreasonable on its face, that Shakespeare stooped to cribbing the grossly inferior work of others. Thus I must either climb down from that position or again follow D. S. Ogburn in attributing the 1562 poem to Edward de Vere. If the latter alternative seems to be reaching very far, it is nonetheless my choice. In its defense let me quote Marchette Chute:

It is no easy thing to read Brooke's version seriously, for his style is strongly reminiscent of Bottom's immortal production of Pyramus and Thisbe. [Examples of the style follow.] Shakespeare could read this sort of thing and believe in the story wholeheartedly without being affected in the least by the childish narrator. Brooke's stupidity as a poet did not irritate him in the least, as it might very well irritate a lesser man. Shakespeare's spirit accepted the whole of Brooke's with the same steady patient courtesy that made it possible for him, as an actor, to appear in so many bad plays in the course of his life without ever becoming discouraged with this profession.

Setting aside Ms. Chute's fantasies about human nature and Shakespeare's character and career, we have a residuum of sound observation. If the narrator of *Romeus and Juliet* seems childish, he does so, I submit, for the best possible reason: he was little more than a child. If "Shakespeare" was not put off by its childish clumsiness, which other commentators than Ms. Chute have derided, and if he would accept a story wholeheartedly from such a source and overlook its stupidity, the only reasonable explanation I can think of is that he had written it himself in his boyhood and, probably touched by it, regarded it with parental indulgence. If this is the explanation, I can see that in his place I should have felt that, in turning the awkward effort into the undying drama of the star-crossed lovers as we know it, I was repaying a debt to the earnest, striving boy I had been.

But what about Arthur Brooke? Apart from his writing the poem, the only thing he seems to have done in life is die. George Turberville, in 1567, wrote *An epitaph on the death of Master Arthur Brooke drounde in passing to New Haven.* It is the only report we have of him. The reason, I suggest, is that he had never existed. I think that, having served his purpose, he was disposed of as an unwanted kitten may be, as a favor to de Vere by Turberville, a poetical disciple of de Vere's uncle, the Earl of Surrey. It is, however, what the epitaphist says in his brief valedictory to Brooke that strikes the reader, for it seems to clinch the impression one has of the author of *Romeus and Juliet* as a boy poet:

> . . . for sure his virtues were
> As many as his years in number few.
> The Muses him in learned laps did bear
> And Pallas' dug this dainty Bab did chew.

Could a dainty babe be more than a child? As for how the name was chosen, if the reader will permit and will bear in mind Shakespeare's addiction to puns in an age of punning, I may point out that the sound of the first two letters in *Arthur* may be transposed to give us *Rother* (the *o* as in *bother*), "an animal of the ox kind," which makes Rother Brooke a play on both de Vere's titles, Earl of Oxford (ox-ford, "ford" being a "tract of shallow water," i.e., "brook") and Viscount Bulbeck (bull-beck, "beck" being "a brook or stream"). What we should have is an ingenious double pun.

Rowse — interestingly — contrasts a set of "Brooke's lumbering fourteeners," viz.,

> The proverb saith unminded oft are they that are unseen.
> And as out of a plank a nail doth drive,
> So novel love out of the mind the ancient love doth rive,

with their reappearance in Shakespeare:

> Even as one heat another heat expels,
> Or as one nail by strength drives out another,
> So the remembrance of my former love
> Is by a new object quite forgotten.

Such, I submit, is the difference between the poet at twelve and the poet at thirty-one.

"For such verse [as that quoted above] Brooke should have been drowned," says Rowse, who, in common humanity, we must hope will escape the retribution for *his* transgressions that such a remark invites. We owe him thanks, incidentally, for having found in Brooke's poem not only the source of *Romeo and Juliet* but, significantly, of "various motifs and incidents [that] appear in *Two Gentlemen of Verona.*"

Rowse's denigration of Brooke's "lumbering fourteeners" recalls C. S. Lewis's execration of "ugly fourteeners" in the "Golding" translation of the *Metamorphoses.* Come to think of it, why not see what the poet does with a quatrain of the latter, from Book 14, viz.,

> Even so have places oftentimes exchanged their estate.
> For I have seen it sea which was substantial ground alate,
> Again where sea was, I have seen the same become dry land,
> And shells and scales of seafish far have lyen from any strand,

When he reverts to them in maturity, in Sonnet 64, they become:

> When I have seen the hungry ocean gain
> Advantage of the kingdom of the shore,
> And the firm soil win of the watery main,
> Increasing store with loss, and loss with store. . . .

Such, if I am right, is the difference three decades make. Long before then, of course, the poet had got over his addiction to fourteeners, which, the reader will recall, were employed in the *Echo* verses by the Earl of Oxford quoted in Chapter 19.

"Brooke" himself recognized the shortcomings of his art — which are not so short for a twelve-year-old. Introducing his poem with a kind of apology more likely to come from a diffident boy expecting to do better in the future than from an adult standing on the merits of the offering, he wrote, "I saw the same argument lately set forth on stage with more commendation than I can look for: (being there much better set forth than I have or can do.)" No earlier play on the theme has been heard of, incidentally. Perhaps there had been some kind of presentation of "the same argument," derived from Italian sources, on the stage at Castle Hedingham; and it would be pleasant to think that it might have been arranged for Queen Elizabeth during her visit as a compliment to her fluency in Italian. We should not forget that Edward's tutor at this time had been a student in Italy.

This has been a good deal of time to give "Arthur Brooke," not to mention the Golding connection, but time is well spent if it helps fill out the sparse details we have on the early years of the genius whom the future would set above all other writers in our language. And, if warranted, the picture of the boy Edward moved to try his wings under Melpomene's inspiration at twelve, already impelled by the born writer's urge to get his product into print, carries our understanding of our subject a long step forward.

If in all this I seem to be claiming remarkable precocity for a stripling, I may cite the author who years later addressed Oxford with the avowal that his "infancy from the beginning was ever sacred to the Muses." He must have meant something by so unusual an apostrophe.

Cecil's account-books show that at nineteen Edward was buying not only the Geneva Bible, Chaucer, Plutarch's works in French, and other books, coming in all to two pounds, seven and ten, but subsequently "two Italian books" and later "Tully's and Plato's works in folio, with other books, paper and nibs" in the amount of four pounds, six and four — then a great deal of money. (His purchase of the works of Plato reminds us of how, after centuries of puzzlement, the source of Shakespeare's reference to "Adonis' gardens" was found in Plato's *Phaedrus*.)

While clearly the keen student and reader we should expect the young Shakespeare to have been, he was, however, no book-bound drudge. "Small have continual plodders ever won," says Berowne in *Love's Labour's Lost*, "save base authority from others' books."[2] For the first four years of his wardship "the apparel, with rapiers and daggers, for my Lord of Oxenford, his person," cost more than £627. That equals tens of thousands of 1980s dollars. B. M. Ward may well remark that when "in later years we shall find Lord Burghley continually upbraiding Lord Oxford for his extravagance, . . . it will be well for us to remember these bills — vouched for by Burghley himself — which were incurred by Oxford when he was between the ages of 12 and 16 . . . : it is hardly reasonable for him to complain that when he [Oxford] grew up he had developed extravagant habits." I think we may go further. Bearing in mind the reports circulating in Burghley's day that the basis of his great fortune was the money he made from "the lucrative office of master of the court of wards," we may guess that Edward was encouraged in his spendthrift ways and that a substantial percentage of that £627 was skimmed off before it left Cecil House. Those heavy expenditures went right on, moreover. For a mere three-month period when Oxford was nineteen the "Summa Totalis" was nearly £146. *Some*one must have been taking a cut when "for potions, pills and other drugs, for my Lord's diet in time of his sickness" my Lord was nicked for nearly £16 and, in the same quarter, "during his being sick at Windsor, for rewards to his physician, and others, for servants' wages . . . and for the charges of keeping in the stable and shoeing of four geldings for my Lord's service," over £36 — more than a third of Cecil's annual salary as Principal Secretary of State.

The expense accounts exhibit other points of interest. Noticing that Edward was "sick at Windsor," we recall that Windsor was the setting of a play that I think must in its original form have been one of his early efforts: *The Merry Wives*. The youth liked his comforts: an upholsterer is paid for "one fine wood bed bolster, and pillows of down." If we hear Cecil's voice in Polonius's advice, "Costly thy habit as thy purse can buy," then we see

---

[2] James G. McManaway of the Folger Library, who quotes these lines to prove that Shakespeare was "not bookish," fails to quote the King's reply to them: "How well he's read to reason against reading."

the results in the accounts; and very likely by age nineteen the young lord needed little abetting in his sartorial tastes. John Spark is paid "for fine black [cloth] for a cape and riding cloak," Myles Spilsby "for one doublet of cambric, one of fine canvas, and one of black satin, and the furniture of a riding cloak," John Martin "for one pair of velvet hose black," John Maria "for a rapier, dagger and girdle," Chester Herald "for six sheets of fine holland, six handkerchiefs and six others of cambric, and for four yards of velvet, and four others of satin, for to guard and border a Spanish cape," and Brown, "my Lord's servant, for ten pairs of Spanish leather shoes, and three pairs of Moyles [slippers]." And all this in only three months. In the next quarter the payment that brings the young lord before us as the dandy he doubtless was: to William Tavy "for one velvet hat, and one taffeta hat: two velvet caps, a scarf, two pairs of garters with silver at the ends, a plume of feathers for a hat, and another hat band."

We have overleaped two years with these accounts. At seventeen, in 1567, Edward was admitted to Gray's Inn, there to acquire the legal knowledge that would impress so many in the plays. Gray's is one of the Inns of Court, the others being Lincoln's Inn, Inner Temple, and Middle Temple. The Inns came into being about the end of the 13th century as the earliest settled places for students of the law and are still carrying on their original functions. Members of an Inn of Court comprise the benchers (its supervisors), practicing barristers, and students. A young man entering upon his legal studies divests himself at the door of distinction of rank, be it ever so high, and so it would have been with Edward.

The appearance of the Inns today is that of academic campuses. In the heart of London, they are oases of the past and of greensward and flowerbeds that invite the stroller. The gardens of Middle Temple, sloping down to the Thames embankment, like those of the adjacent Inner Temple, are planted with roses where, in 1455, Yorkists and Lancastrians — in Shakespeare if not in history — launched their bloody feud as each plucked a Temple rose to signify his stand. The reader will remember the scene as it unfolds in *Henry the Sixth, Part One*, with Richard Plantagenet, later Duke of York, asking that "him that is a true-born gentleman . . . / From off this briar pluck a white rose with me," and the Earl, later Duke, of Somerset, inviting those of "the party of the truth" to "Pluck a red rose from this thorn with me." To the tourist a kind of electric current seems to come up from the ground at the spot.

From the Temple, Gray's Inn lies back from the river, across the Strand, up Chancery Lane, past Lincoln's Inn, then across High Holborn. William Cecil studied at Gray's Inn, and Francis Bacon, its treasurer, had chambers in the Inn from 1576 until his death in 1626. *A Comedy of Errors* was performed in the Hall of Gray's (destroyed in World War II) in 1594. It was probably in Middle Temple Hall, then a comparatively new building of stone and small Elizabethan brick, that John Manningham, himself of Middle Temple, saw a performance of *Twelfth Night* in 1601. Shrines of the law may seem unlikely places for enacting comedies or plays of any kind; but British history has had a way of bringing the diverse together in odd combinations not readily given up by the British people. We read that

> the students of the Inns of Court learned to dance, sing and play instrumental music; and those accomplishments found expression in the "masques" and "revels" for which the societies formerly distinguished themselves, especially the Inner Temple and Gray's Inn. . . . The plays and masques performed were sometimes repeated elsewhere than in the hall of the inn, especially before the sovereign at court. A master of revels was appointed, commonly designated Lord of Misrule.

One play given at Gray's Inn in 1567 was George Gascoigne's *Supposes*, a translation of Ariosto's *I Suppositi*, which is accepted as a source of the story told in *The Taming of the Shrew*. The performance would appear to have taken place five weeks before de Vere entered Gray's but since the Inn was only half a mile from his home at Cecil House, we may believe he would have elected to be there for it.

Although the chapel of Gray's Inn was severely damaged in World War II, there is still an original panel of the stained-glass windows of three knights standing side by side. On this, it is provocative to conceive, Edward's eyes must sometimes have rested — with what thoughts one would give much to know. With his known proficiency in music and the dance and his love of the stage combined with his avidity for knowledge he would have been in his element at Gray's Inn. If we know our man, he lent a hand in the writing and production of those masques and acted in them, taking the first steps to making himself "a motley to the view." But about the details of his life at the Inn we know nothing. That is, alas, only too typical. His life comes down to us almost without continuity, not, as it were, as a motion picture but as a scattering of still-shots snipped from the reel. One or two are all we have to tell us about whole chapters in his life and aspects of his character, like flashlight photographs taken in the darkness. One such, in his eighteenth year, reveals the young Earl with rapier in hand and a mortally wounded man at his feet. In July 1567 his guardian wrote in his diary: "About this time Thomas Bricknell, an under-cook, was hurt by the Earl of Oxford at Cecil House in the Strand whereof he died, and by a verdict found *felo-de-se*,[3] with running upon a point of a fence sword of the said Earl's." At a later time, when, Conyers Read says, "Burghley was far less kindly disposed towards Oxford . . . he recorded a different version of the affair." He wrote:

---

[3] One who "deliberately puts an end to his own existence, or commits any unlawful malicious act, the consequence of which is his own death" (Blackstone). *O.U.D.*

"I did my best to have the jury find the death of a poor man whom he [Oxford] killed in my house to be found *se defendendo.*" The episode, certainly shocking enough in itself, stands alone in the record, without antecedents or aftermath.

As we shall find time and again, history is mute as to de Vere's side of things: not for nothing did the records pass through the hands of William Cecil and of his son Robert. That in his guardian's view the killing did not reflect seriously on the youth's moral character is evident from his having a few years hence consented to a marriage between the youth and his daughter — and nobody has ever found Cecil lacking as a father. What stands out in his account of the episode, which would be unlike Cecil if it were not self-serving, is the lack of any mention of Edward's provocation. Even the quickest-tempered and most impetuous youth does not slay without cause. Had Cecil had the least regard for him or for fairness, had his intent not been malevolent, he would, in speaking of "the death of a poor man whom he killed," have put in some word as to why he had done so. Or he would have unless the reason were discreditable to himself. I suspect it was. Here, as so often, I think, we have to look to the plays for de Vere's version of events. The thought leads immediately, of course, to Hamlet's slaying of Polonius when a cry from behind the arras betrays the presence of the spy; and that spying was Polonius' practice comes out in his dispatching Reynoldo to make clandestine inquiries as to his son's habits in France; Cecil maintained "a small army of spies and informers. . . . A vile band." Especially if Edward's behavior with the eleven-year-old and perhaps idolatrous Anne Cecil was under surveillance (as it was Hamlet's with Ophelia that the royal counsellor first secreted himself to observe), I can understand how the hot-blooded young lord might have run Burghley's agent through in the heedless, infuriated instant of discovery.

Edward's mother, the Countess Margaret, died in December 1569, a year and a half later, and her husband, Charles Tyrrell, a year and a half after that, bequeathing "unto the Earl of Oxford one great horse that his lordship gave me." If Edward resented his mother's "overhasty" marriage to a man he would probably have held much inferior to his father, as many have speculated, his relations with his mother may have been lastingly chilled. In the year following the boy's departure from Castle Hedingham, the Countess had written Cecil apologizing for her responsibility for a delay in processing "my Lord's late will," explaining that things "committed" to her had been "kept secret from me" and that "the doubtful declaration of my Lord's debts hath so uncertainly fallen out." It sounds as if the estate were seriously encumbered. Beyond that, no message of affection is sent to the boy, which, as Ward observes, "seems to indicate that the widowed countess handed him over to Cecil . . . without a pang." She referred to him only to say that "I mean the honour or gain (if any there be) might come wholly to my son, who is under your charge." If her conduct had outraged the boy she may have been too timid to address him from the heart and to seek to make amends. Yet she does not even inquire about him. J. T. Looney contrasts this coolness with the Countess of Southampton's solicitude for her son, who became a royal ward in Cecil's household in his ninth year, a generation after Oxford had done so. "In his case . . . his mother remained near him, looking after his interests and not remarrying until he had reached his maturity." In fact within ten days of her husband's death she was seeking the Earl of Leicester's intercession with the Queen for the welfare of her children. Looney believes that the warm figure of the Countess in *All's Well*, Bertram's mother, is likely to have been modeled on the Countess of Southampton, the Countess of Oxford having died long before her son reached manhood. It is possible that Edward in adolescence was without family warmth except as his uncle may have supplied it. If so, the lack might have made him more responsive to the favor showed him by the Queen and more wounded by her fickleness, more discouraged by the limitations he came up against in his wife after he had taken her to his heart, the readier to capitulate to the fascinating dark seductress of the *Sonnets* — the three women who were to occasion upheavals in his life.

22

"Amongst the Infinite Doings of the World"

1569 to 1571: The Court with which de Vere has become familiar in boyhood: the excitement, after the other-worldliness of the Middle Ages, of the here-and-now; the opulence and splendor with which Elizabeth surrounds herself; the delight in sensory satisfactions; the cultivation of music and poetry; Elizabeth's enthusiasm for the drama; the opening up of the world for exploration, maritime and intellectual, which Shakespeare hails. — Contrasting insecurity and barbarity of life at the time. — Relationship of contemporary events to the Shakespearean plays and the dramatist's intimated purpose. — Religious division of England and of the Continent; Elizabeth's policy; ambitions linking Mary Queen of Scots and the Catholic powers; plot to marry Mary to Thomas Howard, 4th Duke of Norfolk and de Vere's cousin, with the northern earls to rise in her support and, backed by a Spanish army, to replace Elizabeth with her on the throne. — Parallel between defeat of the Northern Rebellion of 1569 and that of 1403 as treated in Henry the Fourth, Part One. *— De Vere's military service on the northern frontier under the high-minded Earl of Sussex. — Denigration of the young de Vere by historians and contradictory contemporary testimonials to his attractiveness, mental attainments, and keen literary interests. — Pressure for Elizabeth to marry and produce a successor and her coyness for reasons of temperament and policy. — De Vere's assumption of his seat in the House of Lords. — Surprising results of his entry in a great tournament and brilliance of his position at Court. — Striking similarity of a tribute to his horsemanship and one to Prince Hal's in* Henry the Fourth, Part One. *— Magnificence of Cecil's new seat of Theobalds as his triumph, like his ward's, is for a time, and for the last time, unalloyed.*

"Oxford became a prominent figure at Elizabeth's court during his boyhood," we read. One tries to picture him in the great rooms opening one upon another and upon gardens and riverside through doors swung wide during the long summer days and twilights, chill beyond the reach of blazing fires when the low winter sun set in midafternoon and the torches gave an intimate or conspiratorial community to the gentlemen and their ladies drawn to the source of warm and shifting light from the farther gloom. One imagines that the youngster, alert in apprehensions, soon had the strands that made up palace life sorted out and was not long in holding his own in the verbal exchange, parry and riposte, Elizabeth delighted and excelled in.

That he held his own sartorially with at least such youthful contemporaries as shared the aura of the Queen's presence we have those bills to persuade us. The age was one of splendid attire, of velvet, brocade, gold, and jewels, attaining its most resplendent in Elizabeth, whose strings of pearls comported with the translucent pallor of her complexion and the fire kindled in her rubies with the passions to which she could be aroused. A poet — the young de Vere, it seems likely for reasons we shall come to — wrote:

> Her hair of gold, her front of ivory,
> (A bloody heart within so white a breast)
> Her teeth of pearl, lips ruby, crystal eye,
> Needs must I honour her above the rest:
> Since she is formèd of none other mould,
> But ruby, crystal, ivory, pearl and gold.

The raiment of monarch, courtiers, and ladies emblazoned the kingdom's improving fortunes as it discovered the true sources of wealth — production and trade — in an almost unprecedented spell of peace, or suspension of war, which the Queen made it her object with shrewd and wary wits to preserve. It proclaimed the pursuit by an intensely vital people of the rewards to be had in a brief time on earth. The great monasteries in which the world was renounced, at least in principle, for the admonishment of mankind and an example had been dissolved, their holdings disposed of for the ever-needy State. From the medieval preoccupation with the eternal kingdom of God, the privileged few, the adventurous, the ambitious, the talented were rousing to the beckonings of the here-and-now. The mettlesome reached out beyond the sphere that had confined their forebears to expand human experience and knowledge. Some set their sights on lands where monuments of classical antiquity measure the heights of achievement men once had scaled, others on perilous shores of storied wealth beyond seas scarce acquainted with Western keels.

Panthino says in *Two Gentlemen of Verona*:

> Some to the wars, to try their fortune there;
> Some to discover islands far away;
> Some to the studious universities.

Their unleashed, questing intellects tracked the nature of things and, keen to life's savor, they sought sensuous satisfactions that appetites had hungered for or been unacquainted with: the wealthy had their oranges and were discovering perfumes; Elizabeth, in 1560, was given a pair of woven silk stockings and thereafter was happy with nothing else, as in time, no woman the world around would be satisfied without her nylons.

Edmund Bohun in his *Queen Elizabeth* (1693) wrote, "In the furniture of her palaces she ever affected magnificence and an extraordinary splendor. She adorned the galleries with pictures by the best artists; the walls she covered with rich tapestries. She was a true lover of jewels, pearls, all sorts of precious stones, gold and silver plate, rich beds, fine couches and chariots,

458

Persian and Indian carpets, statues, medals, &c which she would purchase at great prices." At the same time, Lucy Aikin maintained in her *Memoirs of the Court of Queen Elizabeth* (1819), "Europe had assuredly never beheld a court so decent, so learned, or so accomplished as hers," though assertions of its morality must certainly be taken in a relative sense.

In their pride the Elizabethans built opulently for temporal delight on a scale to match both the somber fortresses in which preceding generations had taken shelter from the malignant forces of this world and the great cathedrals that had embodied their aspirations toward a better. But no more fertile fields of exploration lured them than those of the imagination, which nurtured the divine faculty of creation. Their spirit spoke to the Elizabethans as did Tranio to Lucentio in *The Taming of the Shrew*:

> . . . Practise rhetoric in your common talk;
> Music and poesy use to quicken you;
> The mathematics and the metaphysics
> Fall to them as you find your stomach serves you.
> No profit grows where is no pleasure ta'en:
> In brief, sir, study what you most affect.

From their affecting architecture began to rise the great dwellings set in gardens of matching magnificence that a dozen generations later would awe the returning heirs of the venturesome Elizabethans who had settled the far coasts of the North Atlantic. With Shakespeare's Claudio the Elizabethans cried, "Now, music, sound and sing. . . ." The younger ones, according to Bohun, applied themselves to their "lutes, citharnes, pricksong and all kinds of music." With the organist-composer William Byrd as its first luminary and Henry Purcell in the next century its culmination, English music entered upon a heyday not to be equalled for two more centuries. But of all the arts, it was in a way with words that the British genius then and after best expressed itself.

Many noblemen wrote verse, circulating their efforts in manuscripts that in time would number "Shakespeare's sugared Sonnets among his friends," as Meres would write. To have had their poems printed during their lifetime would have been *infra dignitatem*; even Philip Sidney, well known a poet as he was and never more than knight, was not published until after his death. De Vere, in whom the writer contested with the nobleman, was not above infringing the taboo, but his doing so was highly exceptional, and from the considerable volume of verse we have reason to believe he wrote, quite apart from "Shakespeare's," only two dozen examples have come down to us identified as his. It was on the strength of this sampling, however, that Macaulay would write of him: "The seventeenth earl shone at the court of Elizabeth, and had won for himself an honourable place among the early masters of English poetry." Anthony à Wood, the 17th-century antiquary, compiler of the biographies that made up the two folio volumes of *Athenae Oxonienses*, would report that "This most noble Earl of Oxford . . . was, in his younger days, an excellent poet and comedian, as several of his compositions that were made public showed, which I presume are now lost and worn out."

At the time Edward came to London as a royal ward, plays were becoming a favorite fare of the Court. Edmund Bohun recalls that "There were then acted comedies and tragedies with much cost and splendor; from whence proceeded in after-times an unrestrainable desire of frequenting these divertissements; so that there was afterwards a greater concourse at the theatre than at the sermon. When these things had once been entertained, the Courtiers were never more to be reclaimed from them; and they could not be satiated, or wearied with them." Even before the time of which Bohun is speaking, one reads that when the new and attractive Spanish ambassador, de Silva, was received by Elizabeth in 1563 in the noble house she was visiting, she insisted upon his staying to watch a comedy, which she translated for him, followed by a masque put on by the gentlemen of the Court. It was the next year, in Cambridge, on the occasion of Edward's receiving his bachelor's degree, that the Queen sat up till midnight watching a play given on a stage erected across the nave of King's College Chapel, torches held by her guardsmen serving for illumination. Two years later, it will be remembered, when the Queen journeyed to Oxford for ceremonies that included the award to Edward of a master's degree, another play was given: *Palamon and Arcite* (these being the two noble kinsmen in the later play of that name in which Shakespeare's voice is scarcely mistakable.) "The stage-manager had arranged a cry of hounds for Theseus," says Elizabeth Jenkins, "and the artless lads who were new to plays thought it a real hunt and started hallooing from the windows." (Not in ignorance but in high spirits, would be my guess. In any case, these same students someday seeing *A Midsummer-Night's Dream* would hear Theseus extol, "the music of my hounds" and exclaim, "A cry more tuneable / Was never holla'd to." Young Shakespeare would from the beginning surely have taken a hand in any theatricals in which he had a chance to.) Elizabeth was one of the greatest strokes of luck ever to befall the English-speaking world, not least in providing enthusiasm for verse and drama at the pinnacle of Court and Realm just when Edward de Vere was growing up. Until now the Kingdom had produced but two writers of immortal stature, Chaucer and Malory; beginning with Elizabeth's stripling courtier, who would set his nation's literary star at the zenith of the firmament, no generation in Britain would fail to do so.

There was, however, a hectic flush to the brilliance of the age. If the Elizabethans were making up for past deprivations they were probably doing so in a spirit of grasping at life's prizes while the offer held good. All that they possessed they held precariously. Existence was at best little likely to be long; a man was old at fifty. Death was commonplace and not hidden away as with us but displayed on every side; the veriest children had seen men hanged, drawn, and quartered. The plague was recurrent; that of 1563 and 1564 carried off a thousand a week in London out of a population of fewer than 100,000 and that of 1592 was worse. Religious faith was strong, atheism punishable by death, and the ironical consequence was that a human life had no such claim to inviolability as it was later to acquire. A misstep could well precipitate an offender into the next world, dispatched by executioners comfortable in the assurance of his receiving his due at divine hands from an omniscience far beyond their aspiring to and, if God saw fit, a mercy more than making up for lost benefits below that at best were transient. Elizabeth's ready threat to have a miscreant shortened by a head was by no means to be heard lightly. While one crime the Queen committed, which we shall come to, was on a scale far beyond condoning, it must be said of her that few of her subjects stood for so long in such chronic jeopardy of life as she. If the Star Chamber was harsh in its judgments and the rack frequently resorted to — and Cecil placed much reliance on it — there was a reason: treason and incipient rebellion were ever biding their time. Elizabeth's mother had died under the axe (actually a sword), and for at least the first fifty years of her life the Queen stood in very real danger of such an end. The Wars of the Roses had been over for forty-eight years when Elizabeth was born, but she and her contemporaries knew of the anguish it had brought from the children of those over whom the tides of that unending and bloody struggle had poured. (I was born fifty four years after Appomattox, in the city from which Sherman began his incendiary march to the sea, and I can testify how vividly the war lived in memory.) None knew but that a repetition was in store.

The references and parallels to contemporary events in Shakespeare's plays have been explored to illuminating and valuable effect by Eva Turner Clark in *Hidden Allusions in Shakespeare's Plays* (1931). The volume runs to 680 pages, and while taking advantage of Ms. Clark's findings, I am obviously not going to recapitulate them — would not, even if I accepted them all — or try to anticipate future scholarship. Still, we do learn from Arthur Golding of how "earnest a desire" de Vere already had at thirteen to acquaint himself and "communicate with others . . . the present estate of things," as we hear from Hamlet himself that the players deliver "the abstracts and brief chronicles of the time." Accordingly, if we are to understand what the dramatist was about, we must recognize that he did, very much, take account of current events and of his surroundings, especially of persons prominent in them, in his writing. We have to bear in mind what was going on in his world. I may as well confess at the start, however, to a conclusion that I was a long time in coming to that the plays do not have as much topical content as their author intended them to have as he conceived them. (And this, I think, betrayed Eva Turner Clark into perhaps discovering in them a greater wealth of topical allusions than exists.) I do believe that de Vere felt that the times were out of joint and that a cursed spite had laid on him, as a de Vere and as a prince of the realm like Hamlet, an obligation to set them right. As I may recall again, Jaques, in whom the author also appears on stage, cries

> Invest me in my motley: give me leave
> To speak my mind, and I will through and through
> Cleanse the foul body of the infected world. . . .

There is something touching in this. De Vere initially, I believe, sought to play a direct role as a shaper of history, but, like Hamlet, he found that his temperament was against it — as well as his sovereign. Thus he undertook to do what Hamlet did when he set about to trap the conscience of the King and make the drama an instrument of practical effect. In a playwright's motley he would cleanse the foul body of the world. And he did not lose sight of these aims. But here again — thank heaven — his temperament was to carry the day and his art to transcend any harness. His powers of observation and understanding, his creative genius, gradually developing, were to plumb the depths and scale the heights of the universal and timeless in the human response to life. But the personal experience of the dramatist and character of his world would necessarily and recognizably remain his source.

In the 16th century, England was divided on lines threatening even deadlier mischief than the contest over the succession that bred the Wars of the Roses. The independence of the English church from that of Rome, asserted by Henry VIII and retracted under Mary (who had 300 Protestants burned at the stake), had been reinstituted under Elizabeth, who herself was to be excommunicated by Rome just as de Vere came of age and thus exposed to much greater danger. Apparently almost half the population of the country remained Roman Catholic. The older nobility tended to retain at least strong ties of sentiment with Rome, and this soon proved to be true of de Vere. Naturally conservative, the aristocracy saw in the traditional religious forms and affiliations a part of the framework, sanctified by time, sustaining the established feudal order. The partiality was reinforced by resentment of the growing influence wielded by the new mercantile class, which was predominantly Protestant. Elizabeth had no counselors on whom she so relied as Sir William Cecil and Sir Francis Walsingham, and both were products of this class, as was Sir Nicholas Bacon, Lord Keeper of the Great Seal. "A new type of Privy Councillor," says G. M. Trevelyan of these three, "aspiring to be numbered among the country gentlemen, but connected with the trading community." As affinities with the old Church were strong in the House of Lords, those of the Commons were staunchly with the new. Some of the old nobility remained unswervingly in the Roman fold.

In respect of these religious differences, as in almost every other way, Elizabeth was the ideal monarch for the time. Her view of them was worldly and pragmatic. She had no objection to freedom of conscience until it imperiled national unity or led to treason. So long as the outward forms of the state religion were observed, she closed her eyes to Masses in private and even to the practice of Judaism — for, although officially banned from the Realm, a colony of Jews throve in London, passing as Lombards, Genoese, or Venetians, and were outwardly conforming while thoroughly orthodox behind their own doors; one was to be a confidential steward of de Vere's. Elizabeth's tolerant policy toward her Roman Catholic subjects was, however, to be tried too far. That a split should occur was perhaps inevitable, for those who retained the old allegiance were subject to divided loyalties. In adhering to Rome they were put under great strain not to adhere, too, to the Continental rulers who served Rome's cause against the heresy that held sway in England. There was always the question of which way the Roman Catholics in England would go in the event a champion of their faith took the field to bring down Elizabeth and the Protestant power in their country.

For the first thirty years of Elizabeth's reign, the focus of the chronic plotting to destroy her and bring England to heel was the Roman Catholic Queen of Scots, Mary Stuart. Elizabeth was the child of Henry VII's son Henry VIII, Mary only the grandchild of Henry VII's daughter, but in the eyes of the Roman Catholic church, Elizabeth was more immediately the offspring of a royal whore, Anne Boleyn, whereas the legitimacy of her first-cousin-once-removed was incontestable. In addition, Mary was not only a scion of the royal house of Scotland (the Stuarts) on her father's side but on her mother's that of France (the Guises), not to mention having herself been crowned Queen of France at seventeen, in the year after Elizabeth's coronation. Her husband, Frances II, himself not yet eighteen, died in the following year, 1560, however, and the first of Catherine de' Medici's sons came to the throne as Charles IX. The power of her Guise uncles thus being eclipsed, Mary had returned to Scotland and to the throne in the castle high above Edinburgh. She had no intention of being confined to it, however, though to leaven the comparatively bleak cast of her far northern capital in the interim she brought in some of her cultivated retainers from the Court in Paris. She was bent upon making good her claim to the Crown of England, relying in this ambition upon support from her co-religionists everywhere and prepared to sacrifice Elizabeth's life to its achievement. The fear of the English Court was that a French army would land in Scotland to carry Mary's cause south across the Cheviots on its pikes, which would be almost certain to bring in a Spanish army to forestall France's aggrandizement by so rich a fiefdom — for then, as now, a common ideology could not be counted on to override nationalist rivalries. Once again, in that case, England would be fought over, but this time by foreign ravagers.

More feminine than Elizabeth, Mary was an artful creature with a romantic appeal and charm that bewitched many and, as a persisting legend, still does. But Elizabeth Jenkins writes, "She combined a lust for power with the utmost incapacity for ruling." S. T. Bindhoff writes in his *Tudor England* that "she played at being queen as she played at nearly everything. Even her steadfastness in her faith" — tested by the strength of John Knox's Presbyterian establishment — "appears to those who do not share it as but the obverse of her political ineptitude. But it was men who were Mary's undoing." Her cousin Lord Darnley, whom she married within a few years of her return to her native country, "had nothing to commend him save his looks, his lineage [as another great-grandchild of Henry VII's], and his ability to get her with child." The marriage only added to her difficulties with the Scottish feudal powers. Darnley was an arrogant fop whom she soon came to despise, but he was capable of sufficient jealous rage to murder her favorite, David Rizzio, one of the imports from the French Court who had become her closest advisor. Apparently the deed was done before her eyes.

In June 1566, Mary bore a son. Queen Elizabeth heard the news with the sad comment, "The Queen of Scots is lighter of a fair son, and I am but barren stock." (It was a curious comment for a reputed virgin to make.) She must have foreseen that if she persisted in single blessedness the boy would be very likely to succeed her. (This indeed he was to do, as James I, and as his mother's one success.) Shortly after her delivery Mary contracted another disastrous liaison, this time with a warlike border lord who seemed to possess the strength that Darnley lacked, the Earl of Bothwell. That the wretched Darnley must be got rid of as her spouse, her council of nobles had resolved. Ill, Darnley was removed outside Edinburgh's walls to Kirk O'Field, which during the night was blown to pieces. Bothwell was universally deemed the agent of his dispatching. When Mary refused to investigate the homicide, which she had evidently known was planned, and then, scandalizing her cousin and fellow queen, Elizabeth, married Bothwell (who already had a wife), it was too much. The nobility, not proposing to suffer an adultress implicated in murder to rule incompetently over them with a grasping buccaneer as her consort, revolted. The force assembled by Bothwell dissolved before the enemy, and while its commander withdrew, Mary was yielded up. Later escaping, she crossed the border in May 1568, never to see Scotland again. In England, as Elizabeth had foreseen, she was to prove an enormous embarrassment and even more dangerous than before. As a deposed fellow monarch, Mary called for Elizabeth's succor as a matter of inviolable principle. As an incorrigible claimant to Elizabeth's crown, she was a mortal foe. She was allowed to retain a small court of ladies and gentlemen and servants but was confined, comfortably enough, in Tutbury Castle, in Stratfordshire, under the charge of the lenient Earl of Shrewsbury. There from the beginning, as expected, she proved a center of Roman Catholic plots — which in time would be of consequence for the young Earl of Oxford.

Events were set in motion in 1568 by the arrival of a new and aggressive Spanish ambassador. De Spes brought with him a plan for reclaiming England for Rome. A marriage was then being bruited between Mary and Thomas Howard, 4th Duke of Norfolk, head of the powerful Howard clan, sole duke of the realm, and, as son of the 16th Earl of Oxford's sister, Frances Vere, and the Earl of Surrey, de Vere's first cousin. The marriage would be promoted, the northern Earls of Northumberland and Westmorland, both adherents of the old Church, would rise, as would also their fellow Roman Catholics as they marched southward, while in their support the Duke of Alva, then embattled in the Low Countries, would throw an army across the Channel. Thus would Elizabeth and Cecil be disposed of and Mary and her councillors be established in their place. Mary herself wrote to de Spes to "tell your master that if he will help me, I shall be Queen of England in three months and mass shall be said all over my kingdom."

The Duke of Norfolk, who had already buried three wives by age thirty-two, was an unlucky man and out of his depth from the beginning. Likable, of some estimable qualities but not those to take the possessor through life's shoals, he was befuddled by the prospect of marriage to the woman who stood next in the succession to Elizabeth — the prospect of being King of England. Mary spun her always fatal web of fantasy about them both. Norfolk was firmly Protestant but probably thought he could restrain Mary in acts governing religion in the nation. The Rev. Francis Edwards, S.J., observes, "Mary appeared outwardly at least as a 'politique' in her adherence to Catholicism during her rule in Scotland. Years were to pass before she would acquire the aura of a martyr suffering for the faith as much as, if not more than, for politics." Norfolk made the stupid mistake of lying to the Queen when she asked point-blank if he intended to wed her cousin. And naturally he was found out. On 6 October 1569 Cecil appealed to the Queen "only to enquire of the fact and circumstance," which he was confident would not "appear manifest within the compass of treason." Nevertheless, Norfolk was clapped into the Tower three days later. His fatal troubles, which his young cousin was to take hard, had begun.

Meanwhile Norfolk had told the Earls of Northumberland and Westmorland that the uprising must be postponed. They had, however, gone ahead and, alarmed by Norfolk's arrest, had with 4,000 retainers seized Durham, held a mass there, and set forth southward to free Mary and meet the Duke of Alva's condition of sending aid. Elizabeth and Cecil had, however, been forehanded. Thomas Radcliffe, 3rd Earl of Sussex, whose campaigns in Ireland had shown him to be one of Elizabeth's ablest commanders, had been made Lord President of the North, and on October 25th Mary was

Thomas Radcliffe, 3rd Earl of Sussex

From *Thane's British Autography* by John Thane.

Courtesy of Virginia State Library.

spirited from Tutbury to Coventry. Sussex was too weak in cavalry initially to meet the rebel earls. These, however, left in the lurch by their confederates, the Duke of Norfolk and the Earl of Derby, and by the failure of their co-religionists in the Midlands to rise, and with their own followers melting away, fled ignominiously across the border into Scotland, Sussex in pursuit.

Cecil had sent his elder son and his oldest royal ward, the Earl of Rutland, to the north, but the nineteen-year-old Oxford had been laid up ill. On November 24th he wrote his guardian:

> Sir, Although my hap hath been so hard that it hath visited me of late with sickness, yet, thanks be to God, . . . I find my health restored, and I find myself doubly beholden unto you both for that and many good turns which I have received before of your part. . . . I am bold to desire your favour and friendship that you will suffer me to be employed by your means and help, in this service that is now at hand.

He has always, he says, desired to see "the wars and services in strange and foreign parts" and asks that he be accorded "so much honour as that, by your purchase of my license, I may be called to the services of my Prince and country, as, at this present troublous time, a number are."

It was to be the end of March before Cecil, quite possibly at the behest of the Queen, saw his way to comply with the plea — which was a forecast of the similar frustration that Oxford's zeal for service and travel was to encounter in the future. But the impression made on the youth by the northern rebellion was such that when he came to write the first of the two *Henry the Fourth* plays he made a similar rebellion against that monarch by an earlier Earl of Northumberland, with the Earl of Worcester his coadjutor, the crowning feature of the play. In the uprising against Elizabeth, Northumberland and Westmorland were doomed by the failure of Norfolk and Derby to support them. In the play, Northumberland's son Hotspur and Worcester are doomed by the failure of Northumberland himself and the Welsh leader, Owen Glendower, to bring up their strengths before battle is forced on them at Shrewsbury, as was actually the case; but the dramatist puts Northumberland *hors de combat* by illness, as Norfolk was by detention, though historically he was coming up with his adherents as fast as he could. The parallel between the northern rebellion of 1403 in the play and the northern rebellion of 1569 would have given *Henry the Fourth, Part One*, an impact upon its early audiences that we are likely to be unaware of today. Such parallels between past and present developed by the dramatist must have given immediacy equally to other Shakespearean historical plays, of which *King John*, as we saw in an earlier chapter, would have been a notable example. It of course suited his purpose to choose themes that could be treated for topical significance. He was also drawn to characters with whom he could identify himself, as he transparently did with the wayward Prince Hal. Seizing upon the redoubtable Hotspur's death in combat at Shrewsbury, Oxford makes Prince Hal his slayer — having to make Hotspur a generation younger than he was that he might better serve as a foil for the young Prince. Well, Oxford would not be the last writer to perform stellar roles in his make-believe that eluded him in life.

Early in January 1570, Elizabeth set aside the advice of the Earl of Sussex and ordered barbarous reprisals against his rebel captives. Directing that the lives of those "that hath freeholds or noted wealthy" be spared in anticipation of stripping them of their holdings, she issued reiterated commands for the death of the rank-and-file — and 800 were hanged. "Nothing in Elizabeth's life is more dreadful than the callous savagery which she permitted and more than permitted, in this slaughter and pillage of the northern rebellion," says the *Dictionary of National Biography*. More than permitted indeed. "She heard of it all and did as her father would have done in the fury of his wrath." Such reprisals were those of a monarch who had had a very great fright and was lashing out in insurance against a repetition. They must be judged, though certainly not condoned, in the light of Elizabeth's expectations, sharpened by memories of her narrow escape from the block in childhood, that the objects of her vengeance would have served her and her adherents no more mercifully had their rebellion succeeded. We must remind ourselves again that the medieval view of earthly existence as a mere momentary prelude to a life in which previous unmerited sufferings would be richly made up for, had by no means been entirely superseded.

The pillage of which the *Dictionary* speaks was wholesale indeed. It followed the invasion of Scotland by Elizabeth's captains in pursuit of the rebels who had been raiding from across the border. Sussex on April 10th, having returned to the theatre of operations from a stay in London, wrote to Cecil that he expected "before the light of this moon be past to leave a memory in Scotland whereof they and their children shall be afraid to offer war to England." A week later he crossed the border with his small army. Before he and the other English columns had done, 90 fortified castles and other buildings together with 300 villages had been razed. Edward must have arrived for the beginning of it and seen some of the sharp fighting that accompanied it, for on 30 March 1570 Cecil had written the chief disbursing officer:

> . . . As the Queen's Majesty sendeth at this present the Earl of Oxford into the north parts to remain with my Lord of Sussex, and to be employed there in Her Majesty's services; these are to require you to deliver unto the said Earl . . . the sum of £400. . . ."

Probably the chief action Edward would have witnessed was Sussex's siege of Hume Castle, which he had enveloped after an over-night march. A bombardment was followed by Lord Hume's suit for a parley, to which Sussex, whose powder was running low, agreed, with the result that the defenders were permitted to retire upon abandoning their weapons. One wonders if the scene recurred to the dramatist as he visualized Henry V's army laying siege to Harfleur and the parley that raised it. He must have taken some pride from the commendation his commanding officer received from the Queen. Addressing him "Right trusty and well-beloved cousin, we greet you well," the monarch wrote that "you have deserved both praise and thanks. For indeed we have not known in our time, nor heard of any former, that such entries into Scotland, with such acts of avenge have been so attempted and achieved with so small numbers, and so much to our honour, and the small loss or hurt of any of our subjects."

No word would remain in Cecil's copious files of his ward's performance in Scotland, from which I think we may infer that it was creditable. I doubt that it could have been otherwise since afterward Sussex gave Oxford disinterested support when it counted for most. And his having done so says more about Oxford's worth than all the detraction by far-from-disinterested schemers that was to be served up to history. It is the universal verdict, I believe, that no finer man than Sussex came within the purlieus of the Queen. He had stood loyally, and at enormous risk to himself, by the panic-stricken girl Elizabeth had been when her half-sister Mary sent her to the Tower, and he served her ever after with the same incorruptible high-mindedness, not the least in standing out against that most unworthy object of her infatuation, Robert Dudley, Earl of Leicester. "The Earl of Sussex was one of the great nobles of the Elizabethan period," says the *Encyclopaedia Britannica.* "Though his loyalty was questioned by his enemies, it was as unwavering as his patriotism. He shone as a courtier: he excelled in diplomacy; he was a man of cultivation and even of scholarship, a patron of literature and the drama on the eve of its blossoming into the glory it became soon after his death [in 1583]." Sussex's first wife was the daughter of the 1st Earl of Southampton, which made him the uncle of the Southampton with whom "Shakespeare" was so close. From the time of the Scottish campaign, B. M. Ward declares, Oxford "was the staunchest supporter Sussex possessed at Court. He was to Sussex what Philip Sidney was to the Earl of Leicester." As "Sidney was devoted to the Earl of Leicester, the magnificent uncle who was so very kind to him," Elizabeth Jenkins represents it, "Oxford, with a sense and good feeling conspicuously absent in many of his relationships, had attached himself to the Earl of Sussex." By "many" of his other "relationships" Ms. Jenkins can mean only his associations with other writers, of which it seems she is as disapproving as was her revered Sir William Cecil.

What kind of young man was our protagonist becoming? Writing of him two years hence, Elizabeth Jenkins says in her *Elizabeth the Great* that he "dazzled the Queen and absorbed the attention of her leisure moments. Edward de Vere, 17th Earl of Oxford, was a young man of high birth, arresting presence and exceptionally disagreeable temper. A pathological selfishness did not deprive him of attraction, and though very poor, he attained for a short time the peak of fashionable celebrity; spoiled and ruthless as he was, the Maids of Honour were wild about him." My! How the historians do take out after de Vere! He must even be made "very poor" — propertyless but for that "great house" at London Stone and all those estates he is to be reproached for selling. "A young, unwhipped cub," Conyers Read calls him in his *Lord Burghley and Queen Elizabeth*, provoked because of his having a few years later "dared to write" as he did "to the chief minister of the Queen." A portrait called the Welbeck, said to be one painted of de Vere in Paris at age twenty-five by an unknown artist, reveals to Professor Read "a face [that] is hard, cold, calculating, supercilious" — and not only that but *"with a mere shadow of a moustache and scarcely any eyebrows"*! (I feel that the gravity of the charge justifies my italics.) Not everyone's impression of the young Oxford in the Welbeck portrait, opposite, is like that formed by Read, who I doubt had ever seen other than a half-tone reproduction of it or was aware that the Welbeck is itself only a copy of a lost original. David J. Hanson found that the rather unfavorable impression made upon him by reproductions was dispelled by the "magnificent" painting itself — which I have not seen — in Montacute House, where the viewer looks up at the "hawking eye" given to Bertram in *All's Well* and sees a "youthful champion" of "great physical prowess."

Of the other two portraits labeled as of the 17th Earl of Oxford, one, attributed to Marcus Gheeraedts the elder, is of an older man than the Welbeck and endows him (for what it may be worth) with substantial eyebrows. The third, a miniature by Nicholas Hilliard, gives the subject's age as thirty while being dated 1588, when Oxford was thirty-eight, and has been pronounced not of the Earl by an expert in the field, Dr. Roy Strong, Director of the Victoria and Albert Museum.

The presumed Gheeraedts portrait (page 600) is unquestionably an original where the Welbeck is a copy of a lost original. Dr. Strong and Robin Gibson of the National Portrait Gallery, however, declare the subject's costume in the former to be of a period fifteen to thirty years before it could have been painted if of the 17th Earl, taking the subject's age to be about forty. Although portraits shown me by the Costume Institute of the Metropolitan Museum of Art of a later date than that seemed to my untutored eye of similar costume, I should not, of course, doubt the judgment of those two authorities in such matters. Moreover, one would hardly, on first impression, take the portraits as representing the same sitter. Yet the boar figurine hung about the neck of the older would seem to identify him as a de Vere, while until recently purchased by American Oxfordians the presumed Gheeraedts belonged to the 13th Earl of St. Albans, himself a de Vere, to whom it had come from his forebears. And as Ruth Loyd Miller, who has lived with it, observes, inspection reveals similarities of features in the two subjects making it easy to believe them the same, painted fifteen years apart. (Under different lighting, too.) Edward de Vere, she recalls, was known as "a singular passing odd man," independent in dress. I can well conceive of his selecting a doublet more in keeping with the old nobility than with current fashion in an *arriviste* Court. I say this being struck by the older sitter's resemblance to the 18th Earl of Oxford in the portraits by Daniel Myrtens (belonging to Lord Wakehurst) and by an unknown artist numbered 950 in the National Portrait Gallery (page 756).

To return to Professor Read's opinion: a Ph.D. from Harvard, B.L. from Oxford and professor of history at Princeton, Chicago, and Pennsylvania

---

[1] The assertion by some modern commentators that he was below medium height is based upon a palpable misconstruction of the evidence adduced in its support. Only a notable physique could have enabled the young Earl to achieve his successes in the tilt.

Welbeck portrait of the 17th Earl of Oxford

Copy of a lost original by an unknown artist, believed painted in Paris in March 1575.

By permission of Lady Anne Bentinck for the estate of the Duke of Portland. Photograph from the National Portrait Gallery, London.

who managed also to be president of a textile-manufacturing company, Read does acknowledge that "George Chapman later described Oxford as 'the most goodly fashioned man I ever saw.'" The impression made on Chapman by Oxford at first hand is discounted by Read. "The encomiums of impecunious playwrights must be taken with many reservations," he cautions. George Chapman by the consensus of scholars was the poet whom the *Sonnets* disclose to have been Shakespeare's rival and was hardly likely to have been beholden to their writer. Apart from that, the insinuation that Chapman (though described by his first biographer as "religious and temperate") would have inserted into a play an insincere twelve-line eulogy of Oxford in the expectation of pecuniary gain is somewhat blunted by Chapman's having been one writer who never addressed a dedication to Oxford or acknowledged a favor from him. But no matter. King Henri III of France at the time the Welbeck portrait is said to have been painted, learning that Lord Oxford "had a fair lady," rejoined, "*Il y a donc ce un beau couple.*" Maybe the king was impecunious too.

If de Vere's behavior to his wife was as shameful as it appears on the record — and, though one gets a different view of it in *Hamlet*, the dramatist condemns himself for it in play after play — there is reason for the disapproval of historians. But their evident malice goes beyond such warrant. One obvious source is awe and admiration of William Cecil Lord Burghley. This is based in part on Cecil's indubitably masterful statesmanship during his forty years as a royal counselor, in part on their taking their history from Cecil's own hands. Where the Great Man and his wilful son-in-law were at cross-purposes, the fault must have been altogether the latter's. It goes without saying that the stream of tributes paid to Oxford by the other writers of the day, the generous encouragement and support they received from him, the extraordinary witness the Queen gave of her high regard for him, which King James seconded, are ignored by orthodox historians. Ms. Jenkins, being perhaps as a woman more whole-souled than a man, even manages to devote ten pages to Oxford's doings — mostly of indignant censure — without so much as a hint that he was a poet, let alone a highly praised one, and a playwright among "the best for comedy."

A further cause of the historians' animus toward Oxford is not hard to find. He has been put forward on the basis of impressive evidence as Shakespeare. There is in this a threat to throw altogether out of kilter the Elizabethan age the historians have lived with and depicted — and, as O. B. Hardison observes in his absorbing analysis of modern man's predicament (*Entering the Maze*), scholars tend "to become a political constituency" and "to resist changes . . . because change threatens to make their skills obsolescent." Better for Elizabethan specialists to swallow hard and hurry by the question of how two of the greatest of all English careers could have been carried on within the radius of a mile or two and never have touched. Forget how especially astonishing it would be with one the career of the nation's greatest dramatist, the other that of a monarch particularly addicted to the theatre.[2] Ms. Jenkins and Professor Read write at length and in detail of Elizabeth's reign without finding reason so much as to mention Shakespeare in the index.

From the conventional detraction it is a long vault back to de Vere himself — insofar as we can reconstruct him. The record, skimpy as it is, reveals such contrary dispositions we hardly know how to visualize the youth; we should, I suppose, expect to find Shakespeare a contradictory character. A brilliant courtier, captivating the Queen by his company and dancing (a diversion she dearly loved), turning the heads of the Maids of Honour (". . . in the sportive court," as Helen says to Bertram, "where thou / Wast shot at with fair eyes. . . .") he would appear to have been given over to the pursuits of a socially accomplished golden boy. Yet we find writers warning him against bookish tastes. The first was Thomas Underdowne who in 1569 dedicated to him his translation from the Greek of *An Aethiopian Historie* by Heliodorus. Underdowne complimented him on "such virtues" as are in "your honour, so haughty courage ["of exalted courage": O.U.D.] joined with great skill, such sufficiency of learning." But, contrasting the Greeks, who "in all manner of knowledge and learning did far surmount the Romans," with the "Romans [who] in administering their state, in warlike facts and in common sense were much their superiors," he goes on to say "I do not deny but that in many matters, I mean matters of learning, a nobleman ought to have a sight: to be too much addicted that way, I think it is not good." The message was clear: a de Vere ought to be less like an Athenian and more like a *nobile* of the Tiber.

His intellectual interests are well attested. In 1572, dedicating to him his translation of *John Calvin's version of the Psalms of David* with the express hope of turning him toward "true religion, true Godliness," Arthur Golding acknowledged that "the disposition of your years" would be inclined more to "some history of the conquests and affairs of mighty princes, some treatise of the government of common weals, some description of the plat of the whole earth or some discourse of chivalry and feats of arms." Thomas Twyne sounded the same theme a year later in dedicating to de Vere his translation from the Latin of a *Breviary of Britain.* He considered his lordship though

---

[2] The play-writing career of Richard Edwards lasted all of two years and produced exactly two plays, yet we read that after the showing of one of these at Oxford the Queen thanked the dramatist and stood for a while exchanging witticisms with him, one of which is recorded. And this was back in 1566, thirty years before the much more fully documented period of Shakespeare's greatest glory. Yet no word has come down to us of any contact between Elizabeth and the historians' Shakespeare — the dramatist who alone wrote play after play of English kings and queens.

yet but of "tender age" a "very fit person for it" who when "at leisure to look" would bestow on it "such regard as you are accustomed to do on books of geography, histories, and other good learning, wherein I am privy your honour taketh singular delight."

This brings us back to a curious episode of de Vere's eighteenth year and to Thomas Churchyard, a well-educated, prosperous farmer's son, four years employed as a youth in the household of the Earl of Surrey and his Countess, Elizabeth de Vere. Combining, in the best Elizabethan form, a career as a writer and a prominent, far-ranging soldier-of-fortune, he first appears briefly in our story when Philip II of Spain was launching his lifelong drive to extirpate heresy in the Low Countries. After serving the Protestant champion, Prince William of Orange, Churchyard had returned and entered the employ of Edward de Vere. In 1567, he reports in a *Discourse*, he was sent back by de Vere to join William. B. M. Ward says that it was probably Cecil who sent him, in order to be informed of events in the great struggle then beginning, "though he would not be unwilling that the expense should be borne by his ward." Still, that the young Edward should have been as much involved in the intelligence mission as he must have argues a remarkably precocious interest in events abroad. In 1580, Churchyard would propose dedicating two works to "the most worthiest (and towards noble man), the Erle of Oxford," Steven W. May reports.

It must have been an active mind and curiosity that also put Edward in touch with John Dee, another Elizabethan hardly imaginable in any other age. A mathematician and astronomer who had studied at Cambridge, Louvain, and Rheims, where he had become a celebrated lecturer on Euclid, Dee was also an astrologer who was retained by Lord Robert Dudley to set a propitious date for Elizabeth's coronation (propitious for himself, too, no doubt, since he and Elizabeth were born on the same day at the same hour). Thereafter the Queen "took lessons in the mystical interpretation of his writings." His delvings into the supernatural, however, leading to necromancy, got him in trouble, and it was in his defense against charges of sorcery that the de Vere connection comes out. Citing his association with the nobility, he invoked "the honourable the Earl of Oxford, his favourable letters, anno 1570." Writing of Oxford in later years, a poet asked, "For who marketh better than he / The seven turning flames of the sky?" A familiarity with such supposed planetary influences on Oxford's part is probably attributable to acquaintance with Dee, as is likewise the knowledge of astronomy claimed by the poet of the *Sonnets*. We shall meet Dee again in the flesh when Oxford had reason to be fed up with him and also, it seems, in the character of Owen Glendower in *Henry the Fourth, Part One*. The tales of magic powers that somehow accreted to that formidable fighter and Welsh national hero evidently joined in the dramatist's mind with the claims made by Dee that he could raise spirits by incantation; in the latter 1580s he was going around Poland and Bohemia professing to do so.

Thus we may probably picture de Vere as he came of age relishing and augmenting the glamor of the Court, treading his measures, and charming and agitating the fair sex, notably Diana herself. (We may imagine how long our historians' cold, supercilious, ruthless, unwhipped cub of exceptionally disagreeable temper would have lasted with Elizabeth.) Probably he was already Berowne of *Love's Labour's Lost,* "the merry madcap lord" whose

> . . . eye begets occasion for his wit;
> For every object that the one doth catch
> The other turns into a mirth-moving jest.

Yet de Vere remained the keen reader he had been, and he attracted the attention of serious students as worthy of their works. He must at the same time have been setting his hand to the poems and comedies for which he would soon come to be known. Excelling, as he seems to have, in these varied departments of cultivation not often combined in a youth, he might be thought to have lacked in masculinity, to have been something of a hothouse plant. Because Benedick in *Much Ado* (whom we have previously known as Berowne) will not kill his friend Claudio, who has grievously injured her cousin, Beatrice flays him with the taunt that "manhood is melted into curtsies, valour into compliment, and men are only turned into tongue, and trim ones too." The reproach was as wide of the mark with Benedick as it would have been with his original, de Vere. Thomas Bedingfield (son of Sir Henry Bedingfield, whose unwelcome task it had been to keep the girl Elizabeth in confinement when Queen Mary had accused her of plotting her death) spoke of "arms being your Lordship's chief profession and mine also." The occasion was his presenting de Vere with a manuscript copy of his translation of *Cardanus Comfort.* In his letter he also says: "A needless thing I know it is to comfort you, whom nature and fortune hath not only inured but rather upon whom they have bountifully bestowed their grace: notwithstanding sith you delight to see others acquitted by [of] their cares." That was written on 1 January 1571, evidently New Style, which would make the addressee not yet twenty-one. By then it was evidently already his habit to share his bounty with other writers. He must, in addition to all the rest, have been an outdoorsman at the peak of physical condition, hardened by training in weapons, to account for the feat of arms with which he was to astonish London within ten days of turning twenty-one; and, to account for the praise his horsemanship elicited, he must have sat his saddle like a circus-rider. Michael Tolaydo, who played the title-role in the Folger Library's production of *Hamlet* in 1978, observed that the Prince was that rare thing, a brilliant man who was also a superb athlete.

How singular it was that the Renaissance ideal should have been realized most fully in England in a man who could never cease looking back with regret, as A. L. Rowse recognized, upon the feudal past.[3]

The Queen had borrowed heavily to defray the costs of the military campaigns on both sides of the border. In anticipation of a reckoning, at the time Edward was coming of age, she was put to the necessity of convening Parliament to authorize the requisite taxation. It was the first time she had done so in five years, the expedient being one she heartily disliked. She resorted to it now in apprehension of being pressed by Lords and Commons alike to marry and beget a successor.

William Camden had said that Parliament "besought her to be joined by the sacred bond of marriage with whom she would, in what place she liked and as soon as she pleased, to the end to have children for help to the kingdom," for if she died childless, "England that breathed by her spirit, would expire with her." It was a legitimate fear; a monarchy's nightmare is a disputed succession. Whether she ever intended to yield to the urging that came from every side, including William Cecil, is problematical. She was to give unequivocal indication of her purpose to accept the Duke of Alençon, brother of Henri III of France, but honesty was not one of Elizabeth's weaknesses. She would lie without shame. Morality to Elizabeth meant the good of her country. Probably she could never have brought herself to share power. Robert Dudley, Earl of Leicester, was her favorite over the years, her unsanctified husband, it might not be too much to call him. But even with him there were limits. That came out when once he presumed too far and was put down with an oath: "God's death, my lord, there will be but one mistress here and no master." S. T. Bindhoff writes: "The time was not yet when the consort of an English queen could, like Victoria's, be rendered politically negligible. . . . Queen Elizabeth's husband would have expected — and have been expected — to be more than Queen Elizabeth's husband. What such expectations might mean both Queen and country knew only too well. For Elizabeth, her sister's example [Mary having married the future Philip II] was probably decisive; she would not commit her own happiness and her country's welfare to any foreigner. But it did not pay her to say so; on the contrary, to keep the possibility open would greatly strengthen her hand with the Continental dynasties. So for twenty-one years she toyed with these foreigners in turn." Specifically, Churchill puts it, she used "her potential value as a match to divide a European combination against her."

At the time of the Parliament of April 1571 she was holding herself out to the Duke of Anjou, the second of Catherine de' Medici's sons, the future

---

[3] This characteristic of the dramatist's did not escape a poet who would have preferred its antithesis. For all that Shakespeare "stands for so much in modern literature," Walt Whitman wrote, "he stands entirely for the mighty æsthetic sceptres of the past, not for the spiritual and democratic, the sceptres of the future."

Henri III. Catherine, says Elizabeth Jenkins, "hankered to see the Crown of England fall to one or another of her goblin brood; she tried to get it for three of her sons in turn and she began by proposing Charles IX as a husband for the English Queen," the boy being then seventeen and Elizabeth thirty-two. Anjou's turn came when a scheme was hatched to have him marry Mary Queen of Scots. It was to kill this that Elizabeth gave it out that she was eligible, and the prospect of the much greater catch was sufficient to extinguish Catherine's interest in Mary. It took Anjou only three months to conclude that Elizabeth was not serious, but by then the Scots match was dead.

The manoeuvres for the Queen's hand were to be reflected in Shakespeare's plays. So too was the issue that proved actually to be the chief concern of the Parliament of 1571: the forms of divine worship. The English State and its Church were beset on opposite fronts by aggressive faiths alike in asserting their independence of the secular authorities: Roman Catholicism and Calvinism. While the Duke of Alva was pressing hard to reclaim the Low Countries for the former, the Puritans at home had made great headway in the Commons. Their goals were freedom of organization for themselves and more militant support for the beleaguered Protestants across the Channel. On the first score, the kind of theocratic authoritarianism they set up in their communities was a direct challenge to the Crown. On the latter, Elizabeth meant not to be drawn into war at any price unless England's independence were threatened. As Churchill sees it:

> A crack was opening in the surface of English society, a crack which would widen into a gulf. The Lutheran church fitted well enough into monarchy, even with absolutism, but Calvinism, as it spread out over Europe, was a dissolving agency, a violent interruption of historic continuity, and with the return and resurgence of the exiles who had fled from Mary Tudor an explosive element was lodged in the English Church and State which ultimately was to shatter both.

De Vere would have had but a low regard for the Puritans. One suspects that when, writing *The Tempest*, he came to name the brutish creature who sought to capture control of Prospero's enchanted isle he thought of the Puritans who sought to extinguish the enchanted world of the theatre, which I think the island represented to him, and "Calvin" entered into "Caliban."

For the first time in the Parliament of April 1571 de Vere and Cecil took seats in the House of Lords. The former attained his majority in that very month and the latter had in February been created Baron Burghley of Stamford Burghley. Oxford carried the Queen's train in the procession from the service at Westminster Abbey. As Lord Great Chamberlain and by virtue of the antiquity of his title he took precedence over the other earls. On his side, Burghley, now Lord Treasurer, yielded place only to the Vice Regent and Lord Chancellor Sir Nicholas Bacon.

During the first three days of May a tournament was held before the Queen at Westminster in which Oxford was one of the challengers. It was the second of what seem to have been five great tournaments held during Elizabeth's reign in addition to the Annual Accession Day tournaments, each on some special occasion. No other being apparent for the second, the occasion may have been Oxford's coming of age, to give him a chance to earn his spurs. An account of the procedure in such a contest of arms by Sir William Segar, afterward Garter King at Arms, will, I think, remind the reader of the formalities in the lists at Coventry in *Richard the Second*, when Bolingbroke and Mowbray are to do battle:

> "The King's pleasure being signified unto the Constable and Marshal, they caused Lists, or rails, to be made; and set up in length three score paces, and in breadth 40 paces. . . . At either end of the Lists was made a gate . . . with a strong bar to keep out the people. . . . One gate opened towards the east, and the other toward the west, being strongly barred with a rail of seven foot long, and of such height as no horse could pass under or over the same."

> Before the tournament began the pledges, or hostages, of the Challengers and Defendants were brought in and placed below the royal box, where they remained until redeemed by the valour of their champion.

> "The Challenger did commonly come to the east gate of the Lists. . . . Beholding the Challenger there, the Constable said: 'For what cause art thou come hither thus armed? And what is thy name?' Unto whom the Challenger answered thus: 'My name is A. B. and I am hither come armed and mounted to perform my challenge against C. D., and acquit my pledges.' . . . Then the Constable did open the visor of his headpiece to see his face, and thereby to know that man to be he that makes the challenge."

> The same ceremony took place at the west gate when the Defendent appeared; after which the Constable measured their lances, and administered the first oath:

> "The Constable, having caused his clerk to read the Challenger's bill . . . said: 'Dost thou conceive the effect of this bill? Here is also thine own gauntlet of defiance. Thou shalt swear by the Holy Evangelists that all things therein contained be true; and that thou maintain it so to be upon the person of thine adversary, as God shall help thee and the Holy Evangelists.'"

> When both the Challenger and Defendent had taken the first oath, the Constable administered the second oath, which was to the effect that they had not brought into the Lists any illegal "weapon . . . engine, instrument, herb, charm or enchantment"; and that neither of them should put "trust in any other thing than God."

> The Heralds then cleared the Lists, and warned the crowd against uttering "any speech, word, voice, or countenance, whereby either the Challenger or Defendent may take advantage. The Constable then did pronounce with a loud voice, 'Let them go, let them go, let them go.'"

One imagines the armored knights on their chargers thundering toward each other.

The challengers at the tournament of May 1571 were, in addition to Oxford, Charles Howard, Sir Henry Lee, and Christopher Hatton, Esq., Oxford's chief foe at Court. The defendants were Lord Stafford, Thomas

Cecil (Burghley's older son), Robert Colsell, Thomas Coningsby, Oxford's friend Thomas Bedingfield, and Thomas Knyvet, who in a few years was to play Thibault to Oxford's Romeo-Mercutio.

The grand prize would be awarded to the contestant who "breaketh most spears, as they ought to be broken," delivers blows of the prescribed kind or "beareth a man down with the stroke of a spear." (That, at least, is a summary of the refined scoring procedure.) Segar writes;

> This Triumph continued three days. The first at Tilt; the second at Tournay; and the third at Barriers. On every of the Challengers Her Majesty bestowed a prize, for the receiving whereof they were particularly led, armed, by two ladies into the Presence Chamber.

Stow reports that "The challengers . . . all did very valiantly, but the chief honour was given to the Earl of Oxford." His prize was "a tablet of diamonds."

Sir Edmund K. Chambers says that "A 'cheque' or scoring sheet [of the tournament] is extant which shows that [Sir Henry] Lee [the Queen's champion] ran over 51 courses in the tilt against seven defendants and broke 32 lances. The Earl of Oxford, however, did better still, for he broke as many lances, and also scored three 'attaints,' or direct hits on head or breast." Conyers Read openly wonders at it: "Considering that Oxford was just 21, and that the other contestants were much more experienced, it was an amazing performance — as one commentator put it, 'far above the expectation of the world!'" Virtually the creator of the tilts, Sir Henry Lee was ten years older and in his prime: "that flower of chivalry," Dr. Roy Strong calls him.

Of Oxford's horsemanship we read a rousing account by Giles Fletcher, an Eton boy and graduate and fellow of King's College, Cambridge, and future diplomat. Translated from the Latin verses, it reads:

> But if at any time with fiery energy he should call up a mimicry of war, he controls his foaming steed with a light rein, and armed with a long spear rides to the encounter. Fearlessly he settles himself in the saddle, gracefully bending his body this way and that. Now he circles round; now with spurred heels he rouses his charger. The gallant animal with fiery energy collects himself together, and flying quicker than the wind beats the ground with his hoofs, and again is pulled up short as the reins control him.
>
> Bravo, valiant youth! 'Tis thus that martial spirits pass through their apprenticeship in war. Thus do yearling bulls try the feel of each other's horns. Thus too do goats not yet expert in fighting begin to butt one against the other, and soon venture to draw blood with their horns.
>
> The country sees in thee both a leader pre-eminent in war, and a skilful man-at-arms. Thy valour puts forth leaves, and begins to bear early fruit, and glory already ripens in thy earliest deeds.

It is interesting to compare this tribute (in which, by the way, I rather think that Fletcher was trying to nudge the young Earl into activities appropriate to a de Vere) with Sir Richard Vernon's reply in *Henry the Fourth, Part One*, when Hotspur asks contemptuously about his enemy Prince Hal, "The nimble-footed madcap Prince of Wales, / And his comrades." After describing their resplendence, Vernon goes on:

> As full of spirit as the month of May,
> And gorgeous as the sun at midsummer;
> Wanton as youthful goats, wild as young bulls.
> I saw young Harry, with his beaver on,
> His cuisses on his thighs, gallantly arm'd,
> Rise from the ground like feathered Mercury,
> And vaulted with such ease into his seat,
> As if an angel dropp'd down from the clouds,
> To turn and wind a fiery Pegasus,
> And witch the world with noble horsemanship.

Observing the unlikely invocation of young goats and young bulls in connection with horsemanship in both passages and bearing in mind the dramatist's association of himself with Prince Hal — a "madcap Prince" as Berowne was a "madcap lord" — we may well doubt that the similarity of the pictures called up in the two passages is merely coincidental. The goats-and-bulls reference in the Shakespearean play could even have been a broad wink at Master Giles Fletcher, with whom de Vere had been an undergraduate at Cambridge and at King's College at the time of the Queen's famous visit, when the *Aulularia* of Plautus was performed on a stage in the College Chapel.

One of the defendants in the tournament of 1571, George Delves, wrote to de Vere's fellow ward, the Earl of Rutland, that "The Earl of Oxford's livery was crimson velvet, very costly [*that* we may believe]; he himself, and the furniture, was in some more colors, yet he was the Red Knight." It was Delves who wrote that "Lord Oxford has performed his challenge at tilt, tournay, and barriers, far above expectation of the world," to which he added: "There is no man of life and agility in every respect in the Court but the Earl of Oxford."

Since Conyers Read could hardly be accused of over-favoring the young lord, we might let him sum up for us:

> Oxford, in short, when be became of age seemed to have everything. His family, the Veres, was one of the oldest and most distinguished in England. He was in person rather sturdy than tall[?], with hazel eyes and curly hair — a good dancer, a competent musician, . . . a first-rate scholar, a fine horseman and now, as it appeared, already a master at the foremost of all courtly exercises. No wonder that he speedily won for himself a high place in the royal favor.

"But," the writer recognizes, "he never played the courtier's game enthusiastically."

De Vere was not alone in achieving the heights at this time. The new Lord

Burghley's chickens were coming home to roost, as peacocks. Professor Read writes:

> The beginning of the year [1570] found William Cecil, in his fiftieth year, secure in his office, secure in his royal confidence, secure in the leadership of Elizabeth's Council. As he had grown in political stature he had grown also in affluence. From the revenues and perquisites of the Court of Wards he was becoming rich.

The more estates de Vere was forced to surrender to meet his obligations the more estates came into the possession of the Master of the Court of Wards, who also

> was rapidly transforming his family seat at Stamford Burghley into one of the most imposing of Elizabethan country mansions. And he had already begun an even more imposing structure at Theobalds in Hertfordshire.

We go on to read that this estate had its beginnings in a moated manor house which Cecil acquired in 1564, and which I think we shall meet in "Marianna of the moated grange" in *Measure for Measure*. It was to take twenty-one years to complete. Construction was in full swing by 1571, with annual expenditures climbing to £2,700. The next year Elizabeth was to pay the first of her ten visits to Burghley at his new seat, each of which, "according to his anonymous biographer, . . . cost him between £2000 and £3000. . . . This is doubtless an exaggeration, but certainly royal entertainments bit deep into his purse." The Queen was a great one for traveling about, both in obedience to her restless disposition and to shift to others the cost of her upkeep.

The road from London, where it came to be called Theobalds Road (pronounced Tibbals), ran straight to the estate. The mansion, built of brick trimmed with stone, stood in a park three miles long and was approached by a mile-long avenue of cedars. While nothing remains of it today but a few stones, full plans survive, and these have convinced a specialist in the field that, with two possible exceptions, it was "the most important architectural adventure of Elizabethan times" and certainly "the most influential of all." It was built about two principal quadrangles, respectively 86 and 110 feet on a side, and among its many apartments was a gallery 113 feet long, "wainscoted with oak," according to Parliament's Commissioners; "and paintings over the same of divers cities, rarely painted and set forth." On the south side stood a large open cloister "well painted with the kings and queens of England and the pedigree of the old lord Burghley and divers other ancient families: with paintings of many castles and battles." Gardens were laid out on three sides of the mansion by the horticulturalist John Gerard, and with the "fountains and walks," the anonymous biographer wrote, "were perfected and most costly, beautifully and pleasantly." Trees and shrubs seen rarely if at all in Britain were imported from abroad. The gardens were widely known in Europe. One was "encompassed with a moat full of water, large enough," a German visitor recounted, "for me to have pleasure of going in a boat and rowing between shrubs" among "a great variety of trees and plants." With the summerhouse, in which, standing in a semi-circle, stood the twelve Roman emperors in white marble — statuary was brought from as far as Venice — it presented forceful evidence that the counselor, whom a Spanish diplomat described in 1572 as in effect the King of England, had arrived.

If his ward seemed to have everything as the '70s opened, so too did Burghley. Yet each was about to receive at the other's hands the great misfortune of his life.

23

"And Summon Him to Marriage"

1571: Unexpected betrothal of Oxford and Cecil's fourteen-year-old daughter Anne. — Cecil's tempered gratification in the brilliance of the match for his daughter. — Condemnation of Oxford for the ill success of the marriage by pro-Cecilian historians and the contradiction in their indictment. — The question of how the engagement came about and what could have led the young lord into it, given Anne's evidently modest endowments. — Contradictory testimony as to the origins of the match to be read in The Merry Wives of Windsor *and* All's Well That Ends Well *and the close parallels to the situation in both plays. — Plausible suggestion in* All's Well *that Cecil was created Baron Burghley at this time to give Anne sufficient rank to marry an earl of ancient title. — The Ridolfi plot and exposure and arrest of the befuddled Norfolk in a renewal of the plan for his marriage to Mary as a step toward her displacement of Elizabeth on the throne. — Oxford's rumored purpose to spirit his cousin Norfolk out of England. — Marriage of the young couple in Westminster Abbey before the Queen, in a gala day for Burghley.*

On 28 July 1571 Lord St. John wrote to the Earl of Rutland:

> The Earl of Oxford hath gotten him a wife — or at least a wife hath caught him; this is Mistress Anne Cecil; whereunto the Queen hath given her consent, and the which hath caused greet weeping, wailing, and sorrowful cheer of those that had hoped to have that golden day. Thus may you see whilst that some triumph with olive branches, others follow the chariot with willow garlands.

Eighteen days later Burghley confirmed the news, also in a letter to Rutland:

> I think it doth seem strange to your Lordship to hear of a purposed determination in my Lord of Oxford to marry with my daughter; and so before his Lordship moved it to me I might have thought it, if any other had moved it to me himself. For at his own motion I could not well imagine what to think, considering I never meant to seek it nor hoped of it. And yet reason moved me to think well of my Lord, and to acknowledge myself greatly beholden to him, as indeed I do. Truly, my Lord, after I was acquainted of the former intention of a marriage with Master Philip Sidney, whom always I loved and esteemed, I was fully determined to have of myself moved no marriage for my daughter until she should have been near sixteen, that with moving I might also conclude. And yet I thought it not inconvenient in the meantime, being free to harken to any motion made by others as I should have cause to like. Truly, my Lord, my goodwill serves me to have moved such a matter as this in another direction than this is, but having more occasion to doubt of the issue of the matter, I did forbear, and in mine own conceit I could have as well liked there as in any other

place in England. Percase your Lordship may guess where I mean, and so shall I, or I will name nobody. Now that the matter is determined betwixt my Lord of Oxford and me, I confess to your Lordship I do honour him from my heart as I do my own son, and in any case that may touch him for his honour and weal, I shall think him mine own interest therein. And surely, my Lord, by dealing with him I find that which I often heard of your Lordship, that there is much more in him of understanding than any stranger to him would think. And for my own part I find that whereof I take comfort in his wit and knowledge grown by good observation.

(Bronson Feldman points out that the same appraisal was to be made of Hamlet when King Claudius observes, "There's more in him than shallow eyes can see" and in Polonius' exclamation, "How pregnant sometimes his replies are.")

What are we to make of it all?

Burghley would doubtless have preferred the seventeen-year-old Sidney, as a person, to the intractable Oxford. "The darling Philip," he called him and said he loved him as he would a son. We read that

> Henry [Sidney] took practical advantage of the affection which his son inspired in the great statesman by proposing that a marriage should be arranged between Philip and Cecil's older daughter, Anne. . . . Cecil politely hinted in reply that his daughter . . . must seek a richer suitor. [However,] Leicester, who heartily approved the match undertook to provide Philip with an income of 266*l*, 13s, 4d on the day of his marriage [and] with a reversion to a fixed income of 840*l*, 4s, 2d. . . . Cecil agreed to pay down 500*l*, and leave his daughter an annuity of 66*l*, 13s, 4d.

(The relevance of these figures we shall come to.) Perhaps it was Philip's disinclination to the match that doomed it; the girl's preference would hardly have counted with her father. At any rate, the plans came to nothing.

Burghley might also have preferred Rutland to Oxford as a son-in-law. Rutland was certainly supposed to read such a preference between the lines of the letter, though in that respect the letter may have simply been politic. But with Oxford as his daughter's husband, Burghley could reasonably expect to have a grandson who would be a de Vere and the 18th Earl of Oxford, and for a commoner-born who, try as he might, could not in honesty trace his lineage back beyond Henry VII, that was coming a long way. Reason had moved him "to acknowledge myself greatly beholden" to the young man of many estates who put him in the way of this honor. The marriage was one he had not "hoped of." That he welcomed it is evident and important to have understood. For the rocky times ahead for the marriage the historians put the blame entirely on the husband. They find his conduct unspeakable, his father-in-law's by contrast almost saintly. But they can hardly have it both ways. The blacker they paint de Vere, the wickeder Cecil must become for having married his daughter to him. Ignorance of de Vere's character cannot be pled in extenuation; the Cecils had seen it develop at the closest

484

quarters, day by day, from the time the boy was thirteen, had, indeed, had his training in their hands. Nor can it be argued that Anne's passion for the youth with whom her childhood was shared — and did she not know him either? — was too great for her father to oppose. Commenting on the letter to Rutland, Conyers Read says, "It reveals, as all of Burghley's letters do on the subject of the marriage of his children, that their views about the matter never appear as a factor in his arrangements." After the proposed match with Philip Sidney fell through, *he* had not thought of moving the matter of his daughter's marriage before she was sixteen. The marriage with Oxford is determined upon because *he* has thought well of my Lord. There is no nonsense about his not wishing to stand in the way of young love, or any mention of love at all. If de Vere was selfish and ruthless, how selfish and ruthless must a father have been who, knowing this better than anyone, would yet turn his tender child-daughter over to the keeping of such a reprobate, under no dictates but those of ambition?

If Burghley's motives in forwarding the match present no mystery, the same cannot be said of Oxford's. Knowing how ill-advised it was to prove, one wonders what led him into it. Was it indeed the girl who "caught him"? If so, how? How could little Anne at fourteen (just Juliet's age at her marriage) have worsted in competition the more experienced and sophisticated young ladies at Court, who in some cases at least must have excelled her in beauty and wit, for neither of which was Anne known? With a brilliant career his almost for the asking, what was Edward's rush about tying himself down at twenty-one with a wife, and a child-wife, anyway? A romantic attachment seems unlikely for a young man toward a girl with whom for seven years he would have been on a brother's terms of familiarity with a little sister.

For indications of what impelled Oxford to the marriage we naturally turn to the plays. Two of them plainly deal with the matter, but in somewhat conflicting fashions. One is *The Merry Wives of Windsor*, which I take to be the earliest of the plays known to us as Shakespeare's though the version we have clearly incorporates much later revisions and additions.[1] Instilled, Edward Dowden recognized, with "the local colour of the Windsor scene," which Oxford knew so well in his youth, it bring us two middle-class couples, the Fords and the Pages, and the daughter of the latter, Anne, whose hand

---

[1] My reasons for this view I have set forth in an earlier footnote. A prevailingly tedious comedy-farce relying for its humor mostly on slapstick, strained puns, and Welsh and French accents, it cannot conceivably have been written at the height of the dramatist's powers in 1598, as even intelligent orthodox writers have it. The final touches must have given the play in 1592 or very shortly thereafter. In that year Count Mümpelgart, the prospective Duke of Württemberg, came to London, and the event lent itself to a comic interpolation about "cosen-germans" and "garmombles" that depended for its punch on the author's being up-to-the-minute, like a stand-up comedian today; dragged in years later it would have fallen flat.

is sought by, or for, three suitors. The play is written altogether in prose, which alone would make it of very early composition, except for parts of the latter half, chiefly those involving Fenton. Fenton is a youth of noble birth and he speaks in blank verse and inspires blank verse in others. We are told of him that "He capers, he dances, he has the eyes of youth, he writes verses, he speaks holiday, he smells April and May." If we are up on our early Shakespearean comedies, we know who *he* is. And with his first speech we find Oxford evidently raising the curtain on his courtship of Anne Cecil. Not even the girl's given name is changed. Here is how it goes:

> *Fenton*: I see I cannot get thy father's love;
> Therefore no more turn me to him, sweet Nan.
>   *Anne*: Alas! how then?
>   *Fenton*:   Why, thou must be thyself. He
> Doth object, I am too great of birth,
> And that my state being gall'd with my expense,
> I seek to heal it only by his wealth.
> Besides these, other bars he lays before me,
> My riots past, my wild societies;
> And tells me 'tis a thing impossible
> I should love thee but as a property.

(J. Thomas Looney observes that, if the phrases characterizing Fenton "had been submitted in combination to any courtier between 1570 and 1580, he would have pointed at once to the Earl of Oxford as the prototype.")

>   *Anne*: May be he tells you true.
>   *Fenton*: No, heaven so speed me in my time to come!
> Albeit I will confess thy father's wealth
> Was the first motive that I woo'd thee, Anne;
> Yet, wooing thee, I found thee of more value
> Than stamps in gold or sums in sealed bags;
> And 'tis the very riches of thyself
> That now I aim at.
>   *Anne*:   Gentle Master Fenton,
> Yet seek my father's love; still seek it, sir.

They are interrupted by the entrance of Justice Shallow and his young cousin Slender, who has been put forward as another of Anne's suitors. The youth is a mildly entertaining comic character, a kind of plaintive milksop of whom Dowden cogently remarks that "when he has grown some years older, [he] may walk arm-in-arm with Sir Andrew Aguecheek." Both — and they are manifestly one — are recognizable as caricatures of Philip Sidney, whom in a famous quarrel Oxford was to call a puppy.

After some exchanges, most inane on Slender's part, Anne remarks aside to Fenton:

> This is my father's choice.
> O, what a world of vile ill-favour'd faults
> Looks handsome in three hundred pounds a year!

Chapter 23: And Summon Him to Marriage

(It will be remembered that Leicester had promised to provide Philip Sidney with more than £661 a year upon his marriage to Anne Cecil. But that is not the only monetary tie-in with actuality in this explicit play. In the first scene it is brought out that Anne Page is to receive "700 pounds" willed to her by her grandsire "when she is able to overtake 17 years old" — and by that same proposed marriage settlement with Leicester, Anne Cecil was to receive £500 down from her father (old enough to have been her grandsire) and an annuity of more than £66 upon his death. According to Looney, the "fit" is even closer. By combing the records, he found that Sidney "already has £80 a year, so that . . . his total immediate income would be something over *300 pounds a year*" and that, under the marriage arrangement with Sidney, Anne Cecil would "have, in reversion, after the death of her father and mother, £200 lands, and also a dwelling-house . . . of £500 lands." Not only would her inheritance come to "exactly *700 pounds*," but Looney adduces evidence to show how it would have come to her from "her grandsire on his death's bed."

With Slender chiming in fatuously, Shallow argues the youth's suit, provoking Anne to suggest that he woo for himself. But Slender, misunderstanding, still requires prompting:

> *Anne*: I mean, Master Slender, what would you with me?
> *Slender*: Truly, for mine own part, I would little or nothing with you. Your father and mine uncle have made motions; if it be my luck, so; if not, happy man be his dole! They can tell you how things go better than I can.

So Oxford would have us understand that the match between Anne Cecil and Philip Sidney had been entirely in Burghley's and Leicester's hands, with Philip too callow and Anne having no stomach for it. We may notice that Slender speaks of the two elders having "made motions," employing Burghley's own term for proposing a marriage. . . . It occurs to me here to wonder if an attraction of the match for Oxford lay in the temptation it held out to gain what Philip had let get by — Anne's "father's wealth" — and to pay Lord Burghley back for the preference he had shown for an anemic adolescent. If so, later self-recrimination would have further poisoned his feeling about the marriage.

Page-Burghley protests to Fenton-Oxford:

> You wrong me, sir, thus still to haunt my house;
> I told you, sir, my daughter is dispos'd of.

Mistress Page tells Anne, "I seek you a better husband." Her choice is Dr. Caius; Lady Burghley would of course prefer a learned savant.[2] Anne's reply

---

[2] "Caius," the name of the French physician, can hardly have had another source than Dr. John Caius, who, holder of a degree in physics from Padua, was second founder of a college of Cambridge University of which he was master while Edward de Vere was earning his degree there. That he died in 1573 is another indication of the early composition of *Merry Wives*.

is in that slangy Shakespearean hyperbole that could be the idiom of our own day. She would "rather be," she says, "bowl'd to death with turnips."

In the upshot, Fenton characteristically solves his problem by means of the drama: he arranges a masque in which all his adversaries are fooled and foiled and he and Anne irrevocably plight their troth. To the reproaches of her parents, the young man replies:

> You would have married her most shamefully,
> Where there was no proportion held in love.

She cannot be accused of disobedience since she has escaped

> A thousand irreligious cursed hours,
> Which forced marriage would have brought upon her.

The disappointed elders take it philosophically.

In *The Merry Wives*, Oxford would seem to have been paying his wife a reassuring compliment and placating her parents with a statement of his case. His choice of the name Fenton for the character representing himself would perhaps have been a whimsical part of the compliment, for in 1575 a book entitled *Golden Epistles* was dedicated "To the right honorable and virtuous Lady Anne Countesse of Oxenford" by its author, Geoffrey Fenton, who wrote that "learning and judgment shone" in her, "as doth the pearl in gold." In *All's Well That Ends Well* we see the facts from another side. I think that the one was written before the dramatist's Continental travels, the other after and, like the former, revised years later. (That some of Shakespeare's plays represent efforts bridging a long period, as much as two decades, is evident. But Stratfordian chronology cannot encompass any such thing or orthodox scholars therefore consider it. To account for broad discrepancies in manner and quality they must bring in other writers as having had a hand in these plays. For *All's Well*, Edward Dowden has to acknowledge, however, that "while portions of the comedy are written in a manner which we hardly find in Shakespeare before the production of *Hamlet*, other portions, and especially the numerous passages in rhymed verse, remind us of the early comedies.") The basic plot of the play is taken from *Novella IX* of the *Third Day* of Boccaccio's *Decameron*, which tells of Beltramo, Conte di Rossiglione, "a fine youth," who has been brought up from childhood with a physician's orphan called Giletta, she having "had an infinite esteem and love (more than was common at such an age) for him; whilst he, on account of his father's death" is "left to the king's care." One suspects that in Giletta's precocious regard for the king's ward, Beltramo, Oxford saw the child-girl Anne's for the royal ward who was himself.

The story as it unwinds is an unpleasant one and critics have long wondered why the dramatist should have undertaken to "struggle" with such "obstinate material" (Dowden) or to "pad a dry skeleton with living flesh"

(Mark Van Doren). The reason is, we may surmise, that the story offered such parallels with his own (the most astonishing of which will have to be put over to a later chapter). It is these, and the self-revelation it contains, that make the play fascinating to Oxford's biographers. The parallels begin with the very opening of the play, if I may repeat an earlier quotation. The newly widowed Countess is sending her son off to royal wardship, and his farewell is virtually word-for-word what Edward de Vere's could have been in identical circumstances:

> . . . I, in going, madam, weep o'er my father's death anew; but I must attend his majesty's command, to whom I am evermore in subjection.

Bertram (Beltramo) does little in the play to win our sympathy or respect. He is as self-centered and unfeeling as the historians say Oxford was. Louis Auchincloss writes, "There has always been concern among some commentators over the flawed characters of some of Shakespeare's comedy heroes. . . . But from Dr. Johnson's day to our own, it is Bertram . . . who receives the crown for caddishness." Mr. Auchincloss goes on to say, however, "Bertram has beauty, breeding and physical courage and is shown as very young. . . . Is it so unusual for young soldiers to be selfish, proud, stubborn and lustful?" Whether or no, the unmistakable trademark of the dramatist as a young lord is stamped upon Bertram by the Clown, the special combination of temperamental melancholy with gayety and a readiness to part with estates:

> I take my young Lord to be a very melancholy man. . . . Why, he will look upon his boot and sing; mend the ruff and sing; ask questions and sing; pick his teeth and sing. I know a man had this trick of melancholy sold a goodly manor for a song.

He will later be Romeo-Mercutio, later still, Jaques-Touchstone, and the Clown's description would be equally apt of Berowne or Benedick.

The physician's daughter, Helena (Boccaccio's Giletta), has put many readers off by engaging early in the play, seemingly quite out of character, in brazen banter about virginity with Bertram's ignoble side-kick, Captain Parolles. Reminded of how a bawdy vein comes out in Ophelia when loss of sanity relieves her of inhibitions, one wonders if there were such a vein in Anne Cecil.

We are put in mind of Ophelia at the outset when Helena exclaims:

> That I should love a bright particular star
> And think to wed it, he is so above me.

Hamlet "is a prince out of thy star," Polonius warns his daughter, as Page warns his that Fenton "is too high of birth," as Burghley would thus seem to have warned Anne of Edward. Burghley would seem unmistakably to appear in *All's Well*, too, as Lafeu, an elderly counselor to the monarch standing somewhat *in loco parentis* to Helena; the common identity of the two lords must have been in the minds of those responsible for the 1980 BBC production of *All's Well*, for they laid their introduction to the play, called "Perspective," in Burghley House — and, more interesting still, brought in the Earl of Oxford very suggestively (which I shall come to later). As the dramatist's compliment to Burghley, Lafeu is allowed to put down Parolles, who, theatrical in deportment and long on words (hence his name) as he is short on honor, evidently stands for Oxford's disreputable writer- and actor-companions as his father-in-law saw them.

The change of Giletta's name to Helena calls attention to the links revealed in *All's Well* between Oxford and the authorship of the plays. The reader may remember from an early chapter that Georges Lanvin, who found that the names of military officers mentioned in *All's Well* correspond to actual 16th-century Frenchmen, also discovered that the Rousillon of the play is not Boccaccio's Rossiglione, the Province of Rousillon in southern France, but the Castle of Rousillon in Dauphiny, 20 miles from Tournon, of which only a traveler in the area would be likely to have heard. As Ruth Waine-wright brings out, at the time Oxford was in France the Castle was occupied by the dowager Countess of Rousillon and Baroness of Tournon, the mother of Hélène of Tournon, whose tragic story appears in the memoirs of Mar-guerite of Valois, published for the first time in 1628. Hélène died in 1577, as Ms. Wainewright says, but in the preceding year she was living with her mother at Rousillon, which Oxford, who was in near-by Lyons in the spring of 1576, may have visited to see the noted Countess.

Bertram, over his strong objections, is required to marry Helena because the King, in gratitude for having been cured of a fatal ailment by a potion of her father's that she had brought him, has offered her the pick of his courtiers for a husband and her choice has lighted upon the young lord with whom she grew up. The play follows the novella in this, but with two interesting differences. Where in the original the King suffers a nameless "swelling in his breast," in the play he is given a fistula (a long, narrow ulcer) to identify him with Queen Elizabeth, who was afflicted with one. Again in departing from Boccaccio, *All's Well* has the monarch over-ruling the husband-elect's rejection of the bride appointed for him with the rejoin-der, " 'Tis only title thou disdain'st in her, the which I can build up." But this makes no sense in the play; Helena has no father through whom the honor could come — and in fact nothing further is heard of it. It fits Oxford's circumstances perfectly, however. Anne Cecil by no means suffered Helena's deficiency in parentage. She very much had a father. And it is far from inconceivable that the Queen, indebted to that father as the King in the novella is indebted to Giletta's, agreed to ennoble him and thus "build up" what was lacking for a match between Anne and the apple of her Maids of Honor's eyes; Cecil was created Lord Burghley just a few months before it

became publicly known that "The Earl of Oxford hath gotten him a wife —
or at least a wife hath got him." Could we be hearing his cry in Bertram's
on being informed of his fate?

> My wife, my liege! I shall beseach your highness
> In such a business give me leave to use
> The help of mine own eyes.

Moreover, not alone a desire to reward her Lord Treasurer may have moved
Elizabeth in the matter. "In a long letter to the Queen Mother, December
the 22nd, 1571," according to Eva M. Tenison, "the French Ambassador
alleged that *'le Comte d'Oxford'* was *'ung peu broiller ez affaires du Duc de
Norfolc,'* and therefore it had been deemed advisable to marry him to a
family so securely tied to the Crown as that of Burghley." If any such
suspicion rankled in the young Earl's mind, the marriage was off to a very
doubtful start indeed.

Immediately after the enforced marriage with Helena, Bertram flees the
Court without consummating it. Oxford waited two and a half years before
making a break for it and then barely got across the Channel before the
Queen had him fetched back.

Or did he wait? On September 21st, five weeks after Burghley's letter to
Rutland about the engagement, Hugh Fitz-Williams wrote to the Countess
of Shrewsbury that "They say the Queen will be at my Lord of Burghley's
house beside Waltham [Theobalds] on Sunday next, where my Lord of
Oxford shall marry Mistress Anne Cecil his daughter." (One notices the use
of the imperative "shall.") The Queen and her Court arrived at Theobalds
on the 22nd. But there was no wedding. Did Oxford, like Bertram, flee from
his nuptials? It is just possible that a wedding planned for September had to
be postponed because the groom had disappeared. Escape from the altar,
however, need not have been his purpose, or at any rate his only purpose. If
he slipped across the channel clandestinely just before the date reported set
for the wedding by Fitz-Williams, as is conceivable, his action could have
been part of a gallant but foolhardy plan to help his cousin escape a much
worse fate than any marriage.

We left Thomas Howard, 4th Duke of Norfolk, as the gates of the Tower
swung to behind him in October 1569. He had unwisely proposed to marry
Mary Queen of Scots and compounded his unwisdom by denying the intention when asked about it by Elizabeth. Released to house arrest in the next
year, he had gone from unwisdom to consummate folly by allowing himself
to be used by the Queen's mortal enemies. The machinations that undid him
are known to history as the Ridolfi plot.

Roberto di Ridolfi was of a family famous in Florence, a banker who had
come to London fifteen years before and gained such importance that he
consorted with William Cecil and other persons of consequence. The plot

that bears his name was hatched out of familiar ingredients. It grew from the discovery on 10 May 1570 of a document nailed to the gates of the Bishop of London's palace that proved to be a Bull issued in February by Pope Pius V excommunicating Queen Elizabeth and absolving her subjects of any oaths they might have taken to her. Ridolfi determined to see the Jezebel deposed and England brought back into the Roman Catholic fold. The elements of his plan had all seen prior service in the promotion of the Northern Rebellion, which boded ill for his hopes. He had no trouble rekindling in Norfolk and Mary Queen of Scots an ardor for their union, but meeting in Brussels with the Duke of Alva and in Madrid with the King of Spain he found both with their hands full militarily and extremely uneager to spare the troops for an invasion of England. Philip told him to come back when Elizabeth and her councilors had been dispatched. The English Catholics, moreover, were in no mood to revolt against a ruler who had brought new security and prosperity to the land and allowed them their masses. Burghley and Walsingham, besides, were not easily to be duped. Ridolfi's messenger was apprehended at Dover in April bearing enciphered documents that turned out, it was said, to expose the conspiracy. Burghley had three sessions with him, threatening him not only with the rack but also with death and disfigurement. The messenger implicated Queen Mary's ambassador to the English Court — the Bishop of Ross — and three functionaries of Norfolk's. All were faced with torture; in Tudor times the rack was as ready at hand as the polygraph today and the information obtained given as much credence, at least when it served the administrator's purpose. Norfolk's involvement was pronounced in August, even as the Queen was visiting him. Coming at such a time, the disclosure made her the angrier. The Duke was confined to his room by his warder and in early September was recommitted to the Tower. There he confessed to corresponding with Mary and to having sent her £600 in gold but refused to say more except to Burghley, to whom he promised to reveal everything. But Burghley would not see him. An enciphered letter from Mary to Ross had been discovered under some tiles at Howard House and was said to reveal Norfolk's close connection with Ridolfi's plans.

Sir William Dugdale, the 17th-century antiquarian and historian (who left us the first representation of the Stratford monument), wrote of Oxford that he was "an entire friend" of Norfolk's. As such he would assuredly have been greatly agitated over the danger in which his relative stood. Later testimony had it that he "railed" at Norfolk for his tame submission. The charge was another made by Charles Arundel when he was seeking to destroy Oxford to save his own skin, but probably it contained some truth. That Oxford was willing to run grave risks for the Duke seems indicated by what followed. On 10 December 1571, the French ambassador to the English Court, de la Mothe Fénelon (who may have given his name to Moth in *Love's Labour's Lost*) sent the Sieur de Sabran to Paris with a dispatch including the report that

> The good affection that the nobility of this realm bear towards the King [of France] will be shown in a letter that one of them, Sr. [Ralph] Lane, wrote to me in Italian, the contents of which, as well as certain other matters Sr. Lane confided in me, will be explained to the King by de Sabran; and he will also tell him of a certain proposal recently made by the Earl of Oxford to some of his friends, and what came of it.

Of this proposal, too sensitive to be put in writing, nothing further is heard. (More is heard of Ralph Lane, on the other hand; in 1585 he was sent out to be governor of the first English colony in the New World, on Roanoke Island.) Its burden, however, would seem to be revealed in a petition submitted three years later to the Privy Council under the heading "A poor woman's complaint."

> Certain conspiracies that of force I have been acquainted, touching Your Majesty. . . . At the time that the late Duke of Norfolk was removed out of the Tower to the Charter House, my husband being prisoner in the Fleet, the Earl of Oxford provided a ship called "The Grace of God," and £10 was earnest thereupon, and £500 more was to be paid to me, my husband's liberty granted, and the ship to be given him with £2,000 in ready money, the one half to be paid here, the other to be delivered to him at the arrival of the Duke in Spain. My husband opened these dealings to me, and offered me £900 of the first payment. . . . But I utterly refused such gain to receive; I had a care of the duty I owe to your Majesty, as also I feared it would be the utter destruction of my husband. . . . And so that enterprise was dashed.

Of course the good woman's self-serving petition stood to ensure her husband's destruction, not to mention that of the commander of the Fleet prison for having released the husband on his treasonable mission, as well as to have cost Oxford his head; one would like much to know how the Privy Council disposed of the poor petitioner's allegations, which are not without a certain persuasive circumstantiality. If Oxford had truly planned to spirit Norfolk out of the country it is possible that he managed to cross the Channel in secrecy and that he even met Alva. But nothing is known of this, and if plan there was it was aborted. Maybe Norfolk refused to go through with it. Whether or not, it is here that one begins to feel that Oxford has an ill fortune in practical affairs. It is also here, with his having been apparently unscathed by the "poor woman's complaint," that one begins to feel that none other of her subjects was accorded such latitude by the Queen — which would show once again that no one knew better than she where her and her country's true interests lay.

Edward at twenty-one and Anne at fifteen were married just before Christmas with the Queen in attendance, the party afterward repairing to Cecil House for a great feast.

24

"Of Courts, of Princes, of the Tricks. . . ."

1572: The trial of Norfolk and, despite his disavowal of treasonable intent, his con-
demnation to death in a success by and for Burghley. — The Queen's months-long
vacillation over execution of the sentence and the possibility that Oxford's pleas are
partly responsible. — Historians' credence of a report on Oxford's determination to
make his new father-in-law pay for Norfolk's death and its palpable falsity, despite his
good reasons for bitterness, including signs that Norfolk was the victim of entrapment
by Burghley and his aide, Sir Francis Walsingham. — Oxford's contribution of a pre-
face in Latin to his former Cambridge tutor's translation of Castiglione's The Courtier,
in which he praises qualities to be found best exemplified in Shakespeare, and the
judgment of a modern critic that the qualities prescribed for the courtier by Castiglione
are notably exemplified in Hamlet. — Exemplification in Robert Dudley, the Queen's
perennial favorite and later Earl of Leicester, of the qualities prescribed for the Prince
by Castiglione's contemporary fellow countryman and foil, Machiavelli, synonym in
Shakespeare for evil; the probability that Dudley was her lover; his suspected complic-
ity in the death of his wife, who stood in the way of his ambitions. — Rise of Christo-
pher Hatton in Elizabeth's affections and his recognition of the threat to his hopes in
her attachment to Oxford. — Famous royal entertainment at Warwick Castle and Ox-
ford's leading part in a realistic mock battle. — Massacre of the Huguenots in France
beginning in Paris on St. Bartholomew's Day. — Warm affirmation of his fidelity by
Oxford in a letter to his father-in-law, a pillar of Protestantism, seeming in expression
to foreshadow Shakespeare, and his vain plea for the Lord Treasurer's help in obtaining
sea duty for him. — Necessity of continued alliance with France in the face of the
common danger from Spain and the beginning of the Duke of Alençon's courtship of
Elizabeth, to be long protracted by her apparently reciprocating his ardor for her. —
Oxford's reference to machinations by third parties to turn his father-in-law against
him in a letter to the latter urging him not to be misled.

The marriage of Edward de Vere and Anne Cecil did not bring joy in all quarters. The Spanish ambassador, de Spes, whose recall from England was shortly to be demanded because of his complicity in the Ridolfi plot, wrote to Philip:

> Lord Burghley is celebrating with great festivity at the palace the marriage of his daughter with the Earl of Oxford. The son of the Earl of Worcester is married also to the sister of the Earl of Huntingdon, which means taking two families away from the Catholics.

Oxford was heretofore evidently accounted at least potentially of the Old Faith. This was probably inferred from his championship of Norfolk, who was shortly to be removed from the running.

The Duke was brought to trial within a month of the wedding, on 16 January 1572, with results that must have cast a heavy shadow on such hymeneal joys as may have been the bridegroom's. The trial took place in Westminster Abbey before a court of twenty-six peers. Of these, only Burghley took an active part. Norfolk's "life was inevitably forfeit," Elizabeth Jenkins writes. "The jury of his peers demanded it. Burghley demanded it." The prisoner was not a man to make an effective defense. His plea was that while he had known of the conspiracy he had had no hand in it. He declared truthfully that he had not sought to organize his formidable popular following in the cause of rebellion. In his trial he demanded, "Is it likely that I would have brought in a foreign power, or joined with them to the overthrow of religion? These witnesses themselves admit that I could not be recovered from my religion. I would not be changed from my religion — I had rather be torn with wild horses." And it is true that in the face of eternity he held steadfast to the Protestant faith. The verdict of treason was never in any doubt, however, and the sentence was death.

Now, however, events took an unexpected turn. The Queen, who, on learning of the Duke's hand in the northern rebellion two years before, vowed that she would send him to the block on her personal authority, had obtained legal sanction for doing just that, and she would not, seemingly could not, act. She put off signing the warrant for execution of the sentence, and when she did sign it, rescinded it. This went on day after day, week after week, even month after month. Her health broke under the strain. Succumbing to colic and fever, she lay seemingly in peril of her life. Her councilors were terrified. Putting aside their mutual hostility, Burghley and Leicester sat up at her bedside for three nights. Walsingham, when he got the news in Paris, was reported "in a marvellous agony."

Historians speculate as to the cause of her self-destructive vacillation. Burghley had written Walsingham that "The Queen's Majesty hath always been a merciful lady," then perhaps had hurried on, remembering the 800 hanged on the Border. But, he said, "I cannot write you what is the inward cause of the stay of the Duke of Norfolk's death. . . ." I should be surprised if the inward cause were not Edward de Vere, beseeching the Queen's mercy for his cousin, arguing his innocence of treasonable intent, pleading his rank in the nobility. When, in Burghley's words, we hear how Elizabeth "speaketh of the nearness of blood, of his superiority of honour, etc.," the voice of her ardent young courtier can with little strain be detected.

Apparently to spare the Queen and relieve her as much as possible of the burden of decision, the convening of Parliament was urged and her consent obtained. On May 8th it assembled. It lost no time in calling for Norfolk's head — only not for his alone. There was that "person in this land whom no law can touch," who was the fountainhead of treason. But Elizabeth refused unshakably to give in on Mary Queen of Scots; and that perhaps made it easier for her to yield up Norfolk. With the forbearing and gentle dignity he had displayed all along he went to his end on June 2nd.

Ten weeks earlier a report had been sent to Burghley from one of his agents, in Antwerp, relating that in the matter of Norfolk's impending decapitation the Papists in the Low Countries

> be fully persuaded that the Queen dare not proceed further therein, and also affirm that the Duke has secret friends and those of the best, and such may do very much with the Queen; and that the Earl of Oxford (who has been a most humble suitor for him) hath conceived some great displeasure against you for the same, whereupon he hath, as they say here, put away from him the Countess his wife.

Conyers Read remarks, "There is certainly nothing but idle gossip of Catholic refugees to indicate that at this junction Oxford 'had put his wife from him.' In any case, Oxford and his father-in-law appear to have been on the best of terms less than a year later." Burghley himself would certainly have recorded any rejection of his daughter by Oxford and did not. But in the next century William Dugdale picked up the story and embroidered it, asserting that the Earl,

> being an entire friend to Thomas Duke of Norfolk, when he discerned his life in danger . . . earnestly interceded with the lord treasurer Burghley . . . for the preserving him from destruction; but not prevailing, grew so highly incensed against Burghley, knowing it was in his power to save him, that, in great indignation, he said, "he would do all he could to ruin his daughter"; & accordingly, not only forsook her bed, but sold and consumed that great inheritance once descended to him. . . .

The allegation is proved baseless by the two affectionate letters Oxford wrote Burghley in autumn of that year — 1572 — and also by B. M. Ward's investigations of his sales of his estates, which show "that out of 56 sales only two occurred before 1576, the earliest taking place in 1573." But historians who take an odd satisfaction in blackening Oxford's character, perhaps angered by the suggestion that he was Shakespeare, do not bother to consult his biography. "Oxford was capable of generous feeling," Elizabeth Jenkins tells us, "but he had a vicious temper. His marriage was only a few months old, but in return for Burghley's refusal to save his cousin, he swore 'that he would ruin the Lord Treasurer's daughter.'"

If Oxford was not bitter against his father-in-law, it was not for lack of cause. Disregarding the advice of a fellow Council member, Burghley had refused to hear Norfolk's account of events. He had been first in determination to bring Norfolk to the block. And in order to do so he could be suspected of entrapment. At about the time of Norfolk's first detention, on the eve of the Northern Rebellion in autumn 1569, Ridolfi had been arrested on grounds of receiving large sums of money from the Low Countries and disbursing them to ministers of the Scottish Queen and servants of Norfolk's. He was placed in the custody of Sir Francis Walsingham. Admitting the transactions, he explained them away as incidental to his banking business. Historians say that he hoodwinked both Burghley and Walsingham. One who surely would not have believed that was one who knew Burghley best. To Oxford, I imagine, what the two spy masters had done was let a complacent Ridolfi loose to lure the ambitious stars of the scheme into action so that, reaching out for the grand prize, they could be caught red-handed and scooped up — which was just as it fell out. The consequences would be far-reaching. "The destruction of the Duke was the triumph of Burghley and the new men over the old feudal nobility," Alan Gordon Smith writes. "But for Burghley personally it meant something more: the strengthening of his hold upon the Queen. . . . Henceforth she knew she was committed to Burghley utterly."

It was now, perhaps, that the epithet "politician" began to be one of opprobrium to Oxford. The fascinated horror with which the dramatist would look on the bloody doings of the highly placed contenders for power whose ruthlessness he brought to life again in the historical plays must have owed something to the image of the noble Norfolk's severed head held high by the executioner for the mob's gratification. And so must his contemptuous treatment of popular leaders and people's tribunes have drawn upon the memory of the Commons clamoring for the butchery of his kinsman and of an anointed Queen. Of the intrigues among the hungerers-after-place that would increasingly turn him against the milieu of the Court, he would soon, too, have further and more personal acquaintance.

Two weeks after joining his life to Anne Cecil's and less than that before Norfolk's trial, perhaps for a respite from doubly occasioned tensions, Oxford took a long step toward his later dedication to literature. He contributed a preface in Latin to a work of translation. With this and with a prefatory letter and poem (no less) he contributed to another such work in the next year, he broke with his class traditions and put himself forward openly as a writer, in print. The translator of the first, into Latin, was his former tutor at Cambridge, Bartholomew Clerke, and the book Clerke had translated was Baldassare Castiglione's *Il Cortegiano. The Courtier* purported to be a discussion with participants of both sexes at the Court of the Duke of Urbino, "confessedly the purest and most elevated in Italy," on the question of what constituted the perfect courtier. Written by the Genoese diplomatist and man of letters in 1514, it was published in 1528, the year before his death. As if to emphasize the significance of the step he was taking, Oxford presented the work boldly under the full panoply of his titles:

BOOK TWO: Is Not Oxford Here Another Anchor?

Edward Vere, Earl of Oxford, Lord Great Chamberlain of England, Viscount Bulbeck and Baron Scales and Badlesmere, to the Reader — Greeting.

The English reader had never before been addressed in even terms by such a lord, and the subscription to the preface could well have been intended to make doubly plain the standing the lord was claiming for letters:

Given at the Royal Court on the 5th of January 1571.

(That was 1572 new style.) Between heading and ending the 1,100-word preface was a remarkably finished piece of work for a twenty-one-year-old writing in a classical language; Gabriel Harvey was to call it more polished than the writings of Castiglione himself. As translated by B. M. Ward it reads:

> A frequent and earnest consideration of the translation of Castiglione's Italian work, which has now for a long time been undertaken and finally carried out by my friend Clerke, has caused me to waver between two opinions: debating in my mind whether I should preface it by some writing and letter of my own, or whether I should do no more than study it with a mind full of gratitude. The first course seemed to demand greater skill and art than I can lay claim to, the second to be a work of no less good-will and application. To do both, however, seemed to combine a task of delightful industry with an indication of special good-will.

After more on the reasons for his decision, the writer argues most revealingly that "praises of every kind" may appropriately be given to a "work descriptive of a Courtier" —

> For what more difficult, more noble, or more magnificent task has anyone ever undertaken than our author Castiglione, who has drawn for us the figure and model of a courtier, a work to which nothing can be added, in which there is no redundant word, a portrait which we shall recognize as that of the highest and most perfect type of man. And so, although nature herself has made nothing perfect in every detail, yet the manners of men exceed in dignity that with which nature has endowed them; and he who surpasses others has here surpassed himself, and has even outdone nature which by no one has ever been surpassed.

There I think we see foreshadowed the lines I have already quoted from *The Winter's Tale,* ending with ". . . that art, / Which you say adds to nature, is an art / That nature makes." The prefacer says that the author

> . . . has been able to lay down principles for the guidance of the very Monarch himself.
>
> Again, Castiglione has vividly depicted more and even greater things than these. For who has spoken of Princes with greater gravity? Who has discoursed of illustrious women with a more ample dignity? No one has written of military affairs more eloquently, more aptly about horse-racing, and more clearly and admirably about encounters under arms on the field of battle. I will say nothing of the fitness and excellence with which he has depicted the beauty of chivalry in the noblest persons. . . . Whatever is heard in the mouths of men in casual talk and in society, whether apt and candid, or villainous and shameful, that he has set down in so natural a manner that it seems to be acted before our very eyes.

And so we have Oxford extolling in Castiglione the qualities we shall find given their highest expression in Shakespeare.

After praising the translator's restoration of Latin, the language of Roman eloquence, to its former polish and dignity, the writer declares:

> All this my good friend Clerke has done. . . . He deserves all the more honour, because that to great subjects — and they are indeed great — he has applied the greatest lights and ornaments.
>
> For who is clearer in his use of words? . . . Or who can conform to the variety of circumstances with greater art? If weighty matters are under consideration, he unfolds his theme in a solemn and majestic rhythm; if the subject is familiar and facetious, he makes use of words that are witty and amusing. When therefore he writes with precise and well-chosen words, with skillfully constructed and crystal-clear sentences, and with every art of dignified rhetoric, it cannot be but that some noble quality should be felt to proceed from his work.

Again the writer has celebrated those literary attainments which will be his above anyone else's as Shakespeare.

> To me indeed it seems, when I read this courtly Latin, that I am listening to Crassus, Antonius, and Hortensius, discoursing on this very theme.

A bit of one-upmanship, perhaps, but then Oxford was only as old as a junior in college today.

Commending Clerke for having dedicated his work to the Queen, "in whom all courtly graces are personified" and having obtained "the protection of that authority" — which only Oxford himself could have gained for him — the preface eulogizes Elizabeth in phrases that must have widened her eyes with gratification and acclaims her as one "to whom alone is due all the praise of all the Muses and all the glory of literature."

The glory of literature: It tells us much about Oxford, I believe, that he would so express it.

In an introductory note to the Everyman edition of *The Courtier,* Drayton Henderson goes so far as to

> venture to say, if a trifle hyperbolically, that without Castiglione we should not have Hamlet. The ideal of the courtier, scholar, soldier developed first in Italy, and perfected in the narrative of Il Cortegiano, was Castiglione's gift to the world. . . . Hamlet is the high exemplar of it in our literature.

Hamlet, Mr. Henderson goes on to say, was "the Courtier, he was *the* Prince." He shows, one by one, how Hamlet fulfilled Castiglione's qualifications, concluding with that

> "certain recklessness" or nonchalance which is Castiglione's hallmark of gentility. But it is not only Shakespeare's Hamlet that seems to follow Castiglione. Shakespeare himself does.

And for the best of reasons, Mr. Henderson might have observed: Shakespeare and Hamlet were the same person.

While Castiglione was writing *The Courtier,* a disagreeable and cynical but brilliant, out-of-favor Florentine statesman, Niccolò Machiavelli, was writing its antithesis, *The Prince*. Where the one was exalting the aristocratic ideal of cultivation of mind and manners, of high principles and *noblesse oblige,* the other, observing omens of doom for the medieval frame of life that gave rise to that ideal, took a view of human nature that we should call "realistic." Developing techniques for managing affairs based on that appraisal which would be of advantage to the state, he bequeathed the science of politics to our century. In the Shakespearean plays Machiavelli is a font of evil. The most villainous character in them, Richard of Gloucester, scheming for the crown, vows "to set the murderous Machiavel to school." (That Machiavelli was no more than fourteen at the time, the dramatist was far too cavalier in such matters to care at all.)

Oxford would not have found Machiavellianism wanting in his surroundings. For a diligent exemplar of the Florentine's approach he would have had to look no farther than his father-in-law. If Burghley toiled to strengthen his country, such no less was Machiavelli's goal. That may not, however, have been the dominant consideration of some whom Oxford found around him. Among these the Queen's perennial favorite was the dark Robert Dudley — dark in complexion, dark in certain of his ways. His grandfather, for

Robert Dudley, Earl of Leicester

In a portrait by an unknown artist.

By permission of the National Portrait Gallery, London.

excessive zeal as Henry VII's extortioner, had lost his head to Henry VIII's busy executioner. His father, the Duke of Northumberland, lost his to Queen Mary's for plotting to make Lady Jane Grey successor to Edward VI with his elder son enthroned beside her. Robert, the younger son, had been himself sentenced to death but had been pardoned and even made Master of the Ordnance. Perhaps the male magnetism of the tall, handsome sensualist worked on Mary as it was certainly to work on her sister. On coming to the throne, Elizabeth quickly made Dudley her Master of Horse as well as of the Ordnance. The appointment was a natural one. Her choice for the post was a master of horsemanship, which would greatly have commended him to so keen and dashing an equestrienne as Elizabeth. The two were continually in each other's company, behaving with a mutual warmth and license that led to the common belief that they were lovers. With him as with other men who took her fancy in years to come, Elizabeth's conduct would scarcely leave room for any other interpretation. Biographers in the past, however, have found it more congenial to explain away the occasions of shameless conduct on her part than to face up to them. Her scant reluctance to exhibit the charms of her person to an intimate does not disturb Ms. Jenkins. "The distinction was quite clear in her own mind, that to be unchaste meant to commit the sexual act; to display her naked beauty to the gaze of an adoring man did not deserve this term." (The biographer's confidence in this information is as complete as its source is mysterious.) A physical impediment to the consummation of desire in the form of a "membrana" was attributed to her by Ben Jonson, upon which the comment by my physician friend Myron P. Berger is that "when there's a will there's a way." The trauma of her past is also alleged as a deterrent: when passions were aroused she would back off from the brink, the theory is. If nothing else, however, our generation should be able to view more skeptically the likelihood of such squeamishness in a woman powerfully susceptible to vital, good-looking males, particularly as we have it on Henry Kissinger's authority that power is an aphrodisiac; and since one of those males in the Queen's circle was Edward de Vere, her propensities are relevant to our story. When Elizabeth came to the throne a ballad had it that "His daughter doth him so revive / As if the father were alive." The notion that a female in whom Henry VIII was revived would shy at the sight of a bed is one I think we may dismiss, as probably most of Elizabeth's contemporaries dismissed it. A more likely question in their minds was whether their Queen was Dudley's wife by a secret marriage or intended to be by an open one. At an early age Robert had been wed to Sir John Robsart's daughter Amy. After his locus was transferred to the Court upon Elizabeth's accession, they lived mostly apart. In the prevailing circumstances, it came to be in the air that Amy's removal would lift the bar to her husband's marriage to the Queen. A plot to accomplish this end with poison was being rumored when in September 1560 word came of the lady's death in mysterious circumstances. This was followed by the report that she had fallen down the stairs and broken her neck. The verdict of history seems to be that Dudley was guiltless, but many at the time would not have believed it. Perhaps few would have. Some were dubious even about the Queen's innocence in the death. The scandal was international. Elizabeth, however, only showed her suitor more favor, bestowing on him the castle of Kenilworth and valuable estates and in 1564 making him Earl of Leicester.

In that same year, however, the Queen's eye was caught by a participant in a masque at Court who in a few years would come abreast of the new Earl of Leicester in her regard. This was Christopher Hatton, another fine figure of a man, equally handsome, and one of exceptional physical grace; he would be said by the Queen's half-brother to have danced his way into her favor in a galliard. Hatton was nine years younger than Leicester and seven than Elizabeth. Of no special descent, he lacked Leicester's bearing of remote, aristocratic pride and did not cast the shadows that fell athwart some in the Earl's background. He was altogether a tamer playfellow. Where Leicester was "the Gypsy" to his enemies, Elizabeth called Hatton her *mouton* — and Oxford her "Turk." She installed Hatton at Court as one of her fifty Gentlemen Pensioners, the select ceremonial bodyguard for which height and appearance were among the qualifications. By 1572, when he enters our story, he had become its captain. Meanwhile, in 1571 — having in the preceding three years received more benefactions at the Queen's hands than her established favorite — he had entered the House of Commons, in which he was destined in time to be the Queen's spokesman. Elizabeth Jenkins writes that in that year one of her subjects was had up for declaring that "Mr. Hatton had more recourse to Her Majesty in her Privy Chamber than reason would suffer if she were so virtuous and well-inclined as some noiseth," while in the next year the agitated Archbishop of Canterbury wrote to Burghley of another examined by the Mayor of Dover who had been "uttering the most shameful words against her, as that the Earl of Leicester and Mr. Hatton should be such to her" — Such as what? The Mayor would not write down the words because "the matter is so horrible."

At that time Leicester cannot have been deeply concerned to monopolize the Queen's attention. He had been seized by a consuming appetite for Lady Sheffield. (Later, upon the young woman's being suddenly widowed — her husband, some said, having been sped on his way by Leicester's poisoner — the Earl would go through the motions of a private marriage with her four days before she was brought to bed of a son by him.) But as Hatton recognized to his alarm, Leicester's abstraction did not leave the field clear for him with the Queen. There was now Oxford's attraction for her to contend with. Oxford "dazzled the Queen and absorbed the attention to her leisure

Sir Christopher Hatton

From *Thane's British Autography,* by John Thane.

Courtesy of Virginia State Library.

moments," Elizabeth Jenkins says. Eager to advance his cause against the versatile young Lord, Hatton turned for advice to Edward Dyer, a highly regarded poet and ornament of the Court (in Harvey's estimate) whom Leicester, his patron, once thought of putting forward to undercut Hatton himself with the Queen. The strategy Dyer proposed in a letter to the supplicant was perhaps the one he would have used against Hatton himself:

> First of all, you must consider with whom you have to deal, and what we be towards her; who though she do descend very much in her sex as a woman, yet we may not forget her place, and the nature of it as our Sovereign. . . .
>
> The best and soundest way in my opinion is . . . to use your suits towards Her Majesty in words, behaviour, and deeds; to acknowledge your duty, declaring your reverence which in heart you bear, and never seem to condemn her frailties, but rather joyfully to commend such things as should be in her, as though they were in her indeed: hating my Lord of Crm in the Queen's understanding for affections sake, and blaming him openly for seeking the Queen's favor. . . . Marry, thus much would I advise you to remember, that you use no words of disgrace or reproach towards him to any; that he, being the less provoked, may sleep, thinking all safe, while you do awake and attend to your advantages.

No "Crm" or "Ctm" is identifiable. It is generally taken that Hatton's secretary in transcribing the letter for the copybook (whence comes our only text) misread either "Lord of Oxon" or "Lord Chm (Chamberlain)." Ralph Sargent, who interprets the abbreviation "Oxen," remarks in his biography of Dyer that "Oxford, a genuine scion of the Norman nobility, was a particular object of opprobrium to the whole Leicestrian faction." That it was Oxford against whom Dyer was arming the Captain of the Queen's Body-Guard seems certain in the circumstances. In the next year, 1573, while convalescing in Spa, near Liège, Hatton would write to the Queen in the extravagant style he favored in conveying his ardor to her, in this case evidently in response to a tender of her affection:

> God bless you for ever; the branch of the sweetest bush I will wear and bear to my life's end: God witness I feign not. It is a gracious favour most dear and welcome unto me: reserve it to the Sheep, he hath no tooth to bite, where the Boar's tusk may both raze and tear.

Elizabeth would recognize "the Sheep" as her *mouton* — the writer himself — and "the Boar" as an invidious reference to the Earl whose crest it was. Whatever injury he saw a figurative tusk capable of inflicting, the Boar's wicked pen was going to give him cause to regret ever having "made a match with such a wrangler."

In August 1572, before Hatton's enmity comes to the surface, Oxford took a leading part in a famous royal entertainment, and the opportunity for at least a simulation of the military action he sought must have helped distract his mind a little from Norfolk's recent grisly end. The scene was Warwick Castle, to which one of the Queen's progresses had taken her Court, comprising Lord Burghley, the chief Earls and their Countesses, "and many other lords, bishops and ladies."

The Queen remained in the vicinity for a week, with a two-day interlude that she and Leicester spent at Kenilworth Castle, a few miles north of Warwick. On her return

> it pleased her to have the country people resorting to see her dance in the Court of the Castle, . . . which thing, as it pleased well the country people, so it seemed Her Majesty was much delighted, and made very merry.[1]

---

[1] Writing of festivities at Kenilworth, even grander ones, three years later, A. L. Rowse finds "no reason why Shakespeare's father, then an alderman of Stratford, should not have brought along his clever boy of 11, with the wide-open eyes to take it all in. Nor — with our better knowledge of the way in which contemporary events were absorbed into his experience to reappear in his work — is there any reason why there should not be a reminiscence in Cupid['s] aiming his shaft

At a fair vestal, thronèd by the west . . .

and missing; for

the imperial votress passed on,
In maiden meditation fancy-free."

Professor Rowse suggests that the reference is to the Queen's foregoing "Leicester's last bid to capture her in marriage." His failure was presumably part of all that was being taken in by the clever boy of eleven.

Chapter 24: Of Courts, of Princes, of the Tricks. . . .

The main event during the Queen's stay was held that evening. Two forts had been built of "slender timber covered with canvas." Of one "was governor the Earl of Oxford, a lusty gentleman, with a lusty band of gentlemen." Artillery pieces brought by the Earl of Warwick from the Tower of London were fired by powder trains

> and so made a great noise, as though it had been a sore assault. . . . [Whereupon] the Earl of Oxford and his soldiers, to the number of two hundred, with calivers and arquebusses, likewise gave divers assaults; they in the fort shooting again, and casting out divers fires, terrible to those that have not been in like experiences. . . . The wild fire falling into the River Avon would for a time lie still, and then rise and fly abroad, casting forth many flashes and flames, whereat the Queen's Majesty took great pleasure. . . .

Realism got somewhat out of hand. Fireballs sailed over the Castle and fell in the town, so that four houses were burning at one time. In a house at the end of the bridge over the Avon on which a ball of fire fell, a man and his wife were asleep. Only with difficulty were they rescued by Oxford and Fulke Greville, who appears to have been his opponent in the mock battle as, being the ardent friend of Philip Sidney, he was in actuality. Ward says it is comforting to read that a purse was made up by the Queen and her courtiers to recompense the householders.

The embers of the staged sanguinary strife at Warwick Castle had scarcely cooled before rumors reached England of the real thing in its most despicable form in Paris. Even before the Court had returned to London any doubt about the dreadful happenings had been removed. On August 22nd an attempt had been made on the life of Admiral Coligny, the outstanding French Huguenot. It was an ill omen for the Protestant leaders. Their assemblage in Paris for the marriage of Henry of Navarre and Marguerite of Valois was seen by Catherine de' Medici as a heaven-sent opportunity. At her instigation, on the morning of Sunday the 24th — St. Bartholomew's Day — a massacre of the Protestants began.[2] By the time it had spread out from Paris and run its course, 50,000 are estimated to have been slaughtered.

The effect in England may help account for the savagery meted out to the Jesuits in that country. Certainly it must have brought home to Oxford how the fire Norfolk had been playing with could mount into a conflagration capable of sweeping France and maybe more. Fanned by Pope Gregory XIII, who had bonfires lighted and a medal struck commemorating the cleansing of France of heresy, it might leap the Channel. Oxford may even have reconsidered his view of his father-in-law's course respecting Norfolk's transgressions. Of his shock and dismay over the news from France, a letter he wrote Burghley as it came in leaves no doubt. A preliminary portion

[2] For which deed, Catherine was in July 1981 voted by the faculty of Catholic University in Washington, D.C., one of the ten monsters of all time.

hardly suggests there had been any estrangement at all between the two. It deals with the management of the young man's estates, of which he says that "both in this as in all other things I am to be governed and commanded at your Lordship's good devotion." The body of the letter I have not been able to resist breaking up into segments to bring out the first intimation we have, as it seems to me, of the tone of a Shakespearean historical drama, even of the future accents of *Henry the Fifth*. It follows:

> I would to God your Lordship would let me understand some of the
>   news
> Which here doth ring dolefully in the ears of every man
> Of the murder of the Admiral of France,
> And a number of noblemen and worthy gentlemen,
> And such as greatly have in their lifetime
> Honoured the Queen's Majesty our Mistress; on whose tragedies
> We have a number of French Æneases in this city
> That tell of their own overthrows with tears falling from their eyes,
> A piteous thing to hear, but a cruel and far more grievous thing
> We must deem it then to see. . . .
> And I think if the Admiral in France
> Was an eyesore or beam in the eyes of the papists,
> That the Lord Treasurer of England is a block and crossbar in their
>   way,
> Whose remove they will never stick to attempt,
> Seeing they have prevailed so well in others.
> This estate hath depended on you a great while, as all the world doth
>   judge,
> And now all men's eyes not being occupied any more on these lost
>   lords,
> Are, as it were on a sudden bent and fixed on you,
> As a singular hope and pillar, where to the religion hath to lean.
> And blame me not, though I am bolder with your Lordship than my
>   custom is,
> For I am one that count myself as a follower of yours now in all
>   fortunes;
> And what shall hap to you I count it hap to myself: . . .
> Thus, my Lord, I humbly desire your Lordship
> To pardon my youth, but to take in good part
> My zeal and affection toward you,
> As one on whom I have builded my foundation either to stand or
>   fall.
> And, good my Lord, think I do not this presumptuously
> As to advise you that am but to take advice of your Lordship,
> But to admonish you, as one with whom I would spend my blood
>   and life
> So much you have made me yours.

It is hard to imagine what more the Lord Treasurer could have asked in the way of filial affection, concern, and duty. Never, so far as we know, did he respond in kind to his son-in-law. I should judge from that letter and the next that if Edward's attitude to him in the future distressed him the fault cannot have been altogether Edward's. The other letter was written in the same month. Evidently the Countess had just left for the Earl's estate at Wivenhoe, at the mouth of the Colne in Essex, with her husband expecting to follow directly. The letter is addressed "To my singular good Lord the Lord Burghley, and Lord Treasurer of England, give this at the Court."

> My Lord, I received your letters when I rather looked to have seen yourself here than to have heard from you; sith it is so that your Lordship is otherwise affaired with the business of the Commonwealth than to be disposed to recreate yourself, and repose you among your own, yet we do hope after this — you having had so great a care of the Queen's Majesty's service — you will begin to have some respect for your own health, and take a pleasure to dwell where you have pains to build. My wife, whom I thought should have taken her leave of you if your Lordship had come, till you would have otherwise commanded, is departed unto the country this day: [and my]self as fast as I can get me out of town to follow. If there were any service to be done abroad, I had rather serve there than at home, where yet some honour is to be got. If there be any setting forth to sea, to which service I bear most affection, I shall desire your Lordship to give me and get me that favour and credit that I might make one. Which, if there be no such intention then I shall be most willing to be employed on the sea coasts to be in a readiness with my countrymen against any invasion. Thus remembering myself to your good Lordship, I commit you to God; from London this 22nd of September, by your Lordship to command.
>
> Edward Oxenford.

No such assignment was to be sanctioned. Oxford was to be held back for two women's sake — by Burghley for Anne's and by the Queen for her own. Or so it would appear. "Our gentry," says one of the lords in *All's Well,* "are sick for breathing and exploit." In March 1573 Burghley wrote Walsingham that "noblemen and gentlemen of ancient and great livelihoods" had offered to equip an army at their own expense to send to southwestern France, where the Huguenots, falling back upon the coast, were under siege at La Rochelle. But the Queen put her foot down. Not for the first time or the last in international affairs, moral considerations were to give way to sterner. The Treaty of Blois between England and France, newly concluded when the anti-Huguenot outrages sorely strained it, was to stand. With Spain, enriched by the spoils of the New World, upon their thresholds, neither nation could afford to do without the other. Politics make strange bedfellows, and while there is no certainty it came to that between Elizabeth and the Duke of Alençon, it at least came close. Stunted and disfigured by smallpox, the French Duke was a strange enough fellow, in bed or out. He was the third son of Catherine de' Medici, who had rushed him forward as a candidate for Elizabeth's hand the moment the proposed marriage between the

Queen and her second son, now Henri III, had fallen through as had that which she had planned for her first. The match was now revived. Altogether, it was to hang fire for a decade. Alençon himself conceived an odd passion for the much older woman. While privately asking rhetorically if she "could marry a man as young as the Earl of Oxford" — an interesting analogy to have suggested itself — Elizabeth was to come closer to accepting him than any other foreign prince. Unless, however, she had a perverse taste it is hard to see how she could have contemplated matrimony with such a creature.

Apart from the difference in ages, Oxford would quite likely, during the years when she was thwarting his desire for foreign adventure, have been Elizabeth's first choice among possible mates, if choose she had to. I say this in the belief that he probably satisfied more sides of the Queen's nature than any other courtier ever did, troublesome as he must have been to her. Her attachment to him at this time was signalized by her visiting him at one of his estates. Of this we should know nothing but for Morant's *History of Essex,* which, speaking of Havering-in-the-Bowerie, says, "When Queen Elizabeth was here in 1572 it was the property of the Lord High Chamberlain, Edward de Vere. . . . The park contained 1000 acres."

Christopher Hatton would have been aware of the visit along with other marks of the Queen's affection for his talented junior. These can only have bitten into his flesh. His efforts to undermine his rival's position at Court, doubtless sharpened by Dyer's calculating advice, evidently began to make trouble for Oxford in a secondary quarter. That reports of a nature to poison his father-in-law's mind against him were being circulated comes out in a letter he addressed before the end of the year (1572) to "The right honourable my singular good Lord, the Lord Treasurer."

> My Lord, Your last letters, which be the first I have received of your Lordship's good opinion conceived towards me, which God grant so long to continue as I would be both desirous and diligent to seek the same, have not a little, after so many storms passed of your heavy grace towards me, lightened and disburdened my careful mind. And, sith I have been so little beholden to sinister reports, I hope now, with your Lordship in different judgment, to be more plausible unto you heretofore; through my careful deeds to please you, which hardly, either through my youth, or rather my misfortune, hitherto I have done. But yet lest those, I cannot tell how to term them but as backfriends unto me, shall take place again to undo your Lordship's beginning of well meaning of me, I shall most earnestly desire your Lordship to forbear to believe too fast, lest I, growing so slowly into your good opinion, may be undeservedly of my part voted out of your favour. . . . Though perhaps by reason of my youth, your graver and severer years will not judge the same. Thus therefore hoping the best in your Lordship, and fearing the worst in myself, I take my leave, lest my letters may become loathsome and tedious unto you, to whom I wish to be most grateful. Written this 31st day of October by your loving son-in-law from Wivenhoe.
>
> Edward Oxenford.

However the older man's severity had been provoked, much had obviously gone amiss between the two, though not beyond the younger's hope of a more relenting demeanor on the other's part. As for those "sinister reports," which must in part have accounted for Burghley's "heavy grace," Christopher Hatton, whether or not first among the "backfriends," was soon — unless I am mistaken — to feel the victim's sting.

¶A Hundreth sun-
drie Flowres bounde
vp in one small Poesie

Gathered partely (by translation) in the fyne outlandish Gardins
of Euripides, Ouid, Petrarke, Ariosto,
and others: and partly by inuention,
out of our owne fruitefull Or-
chardes in Englande:

Yelding sundrie svveete sauours of Tragical, Comical, and Morall Discourses, bothe pleasaunt and profitable to the
well smellyng noses of lear-
ned Readers.

Meritum petere, graue.

AT LONDON,
Imprinted for Richarde Smith.

Title page of *A Hundreth Sundrie Flowres*

25

"Entertainment to My Princely Queen"

1573 et seq.: Indications that Elizabeth and Oxford were lovers, especially as suggested in verses by Oxford and "Shakespeare" and one poem attributed both to Oxford and to Elizabeth. — A poem evidently descriptive of Elizabeth most logically to be attributed to Oxford in A Hundreth Sundry Flowres *and the complicated puzzle of that important anthology. — The significance of* The Adventures of Master F. I., *with which* Flowres *begins, a prose narrative interspersed with verse, which may be considered the embryonic beginning of the English novel; the likelihood that it is intended to be recognized by the cognoscenti as a pretended disguised confession by Christopher Hatton of a love affair with Elizabeth; how it may most reasonably be explained as a jape by Oxford to embarrass his rival. — The question of who wrote the hundred poems composing the rest of* Flowres, *apart from a minority attributed slightingly to George Gascoigne; reasons for suspecting them, also, to be of Oxford's hand and mostly to concern his relations with Elizabeth. — Uncertain, veiled suggestions in the* Sonnets *and in a few Shakespearean plays that Elizabeth had a son by Oxford and the theoretical possibility of the boy's having been Henry Wriothesley.*

It is easy to see why Elizabeth would have been drawn to Oxford. With a title proud enough to bridge any difference between him and a Tudor monarch, he was the equal in arms of her own champion at the tourney and mounted for the chase could match the impetuosity with which she rode, to the consternation of her Master of Horse. To judge by heroes in his early comedies, he had a light-hearted gayety, a gift for banter, and a view of women as intellectual equals and worthy partners in verbal jousting, such as one would hardly again find on the stage until the advent of Bernard Shaw and Noel Coward. A merry, madcap Lord, he was probably given to turns as a court jester for her private amusement, parodying her solemn councilors, as he was to parody Burghley's repetitious, humorless style of address in Polonius. He had, it is evident, that carelessness of consequence which to Castiglione marked the courtier, or, as we would say, the instinctive aristocrat. With it must have gone a brooding depth of temperament setting him apart in the Court and, to her discerning eye, an emerging genius for which almost anything was to be forgiven him.

In May 1573, Gilbert Talbot, a member of Parliament, though only twenty, wrote to his father:

> My Lord of Oxford is lately grown into great credit, for the Queen's Majesty delighteth more in his personage and his dancing and valiantness than any other. I think Sussex doth back him all he can. If it were not for his fickle head he would pass any of them shortly. My Lady Burghley, unwisely, has declared herself, as it were, jealous, which is come to the Queen's ear, whereat she has been not a little offended with her, but now she is reconciled again. At all these love matters my Lord Treasurer winketh and will not meddle in any way.

The letter draws the curtain back a crack on a possibly crucial chapter of Oxford's life, and the biographer suffers maddening frustration at being so tantalized and so little satisfied by the record's other meagre offerings. If Talbot's letter is to make good sense we have to take it that "My Lady Burghley" was a slip-up for "My Lady Oxford" or possibly that the writer was using "jealous" as we do in speaking of being jealous of one's reputation. In either sense the imputation seems plain: the Queen is pursuing an amorous affair with Anne's husband and the politic Burghley, loyally serving both his sovereign in her extracurricular needs and himself in his pursuit of influence, has shut his eyes to it.

Not only in the somewhat public palaces of London were the Queen and her young courtier together. We have already heard how Elizabeth visited Havering — "Havering utte Bower," it is called in Morant's *Essex* — in 1572 when it belonged to Oxford. John Nichols reports that "Havering appears to have been from an early period a favorite residence of our Saxon monarchs and their descendants, probably from the uncommon beauty and variety of its prospects." Of the palace there even in his day he could write (1823), "Not a vestige remains." After Oxford had accompanied Elizabeth on a visit to the Archbishop of Canterbury in March, 1574, Nichols remarks that "In the latter end of May, as appears by . . . letters from Lord Talbot to his father, the Earl of Shrewsbury, the Queen passed six days in retirement at Havering," which, he also says, "was frequently visited by Queen Elizabeth, in her different progresses."

Undeniably Edward was for a time, perhaps even for several years, her favorite. To me, given the Queen's ardent nature and the *carte blanche* that goes with the crown, that means he was her lover. I simply do not believe, as I have intimated, that a queen who allowed herself such liberties with men, who notoriously did "descend very much in her sex as a woman," would have chosen or been able to deny herself the consummation of her passions. For evidence that that was how it went with Edward, however, we have only a few allusive pointers to go by.

The most concrete of these is in Sonnet 66, in which the poet counts off the experiences that have embittered him and made him long "for restful death." If the Sonnet means what I think it does — and certainly I may be wrong — he was subjected to sexual demands as an adolescent at Court that came as a disagreeable shock. Among fate's buffets he recalls "maiden virtue rudely strumpeted." No one I can well imagine was in a position to strumpet young Edward's virtue but Elizabeth, a sovereign who could hardly be gainsaid. Here, of course, one thinks at once of *Venus and Adonis*, in which a skittish, still unawakened youth is subjected to and repelled by heated advances of an experienced Queen of Love, only to be slain, like the 9th Earl of Oxford, by a boar, the de Vere symbol. The long poem, as it reads, is an early one set aside for a dozen years, more or less, and improved in spots before being published in 1593 as appropriate for dedication to the nineteen-year-old Earl of Southampton. The germ of the story would have come from the Tenth Book of Ovid's *Metamorphoses*, which tells how Venus (in the "Golding" translation) "lov'd Adonis more / Than heaven. To him she clingèd ay, and bare him companye." Most of the episode in Ovid, however, deals with Venus' warning to the youth of being "too bold" with "savage beasts," among them "cruell Boares." The effect upon the goddess of the "beawty of the lad" is dealt with in a few words, more attention being given to her grief at his death. Of Adonis' response to her infatuation, one way or another, Ovid says nothing.

Frank Harris, in alleging that the poet "used the sonnets" to reveal "his feminine qualities—passionate self-abandonment" and "self-pity"—was overstating the case, as I see it. I do think, however, that artists, being particularly self-aware, are prone to dramatize themselves and that Oxford both as himself in his poems and letters and as Shakespeare in the *Sonnets* put heavy stress on his misfortunes and sufferings; it was one of the contradictions in his character. The possibility is to be borne in mind in reading the toll of his grievances in Sonnet 66. When it comes to his "maiden virtue" having been "rudely strumpeted," we may feel that he was perhaps overdoing it. It is not a complaint one often hears from men.

If his initiation to sex came on Elizabeth's doing and as a jolt, the trauma passed. Consider the following sonnet in the Shakespearean form, entitled *Love Thy Choice* and signed "Earle of Oxenforde," in which the poet puts a series of questions to himself:

> Who taught thee first to sigh, alas, my heart:
> Who taught thy tongue the woeful words of plaint?
> Who filled your eyes with tears of bitter smart:
> Who gave thee grief and made thy joys to faint?
> Who first did paint with colours pale thy face?
> Who first did break thy sleeps of quiet rest?
> Above the rest in Court who gave thee grace?
> Who made thee strive in honour to be best?
> In constant truth to bide so firm and sure,
> To scorn the world regarding but thy friends?
> With patient mind each passion to endure,
> In one desire to settle to the end?
>   Love then thy choice wherein such choice thou bind,
>   As nought but death shall ever change thy mind.

Who in Elizabeth's Court could have given the 17th Earl of Oxford grace
— or who would he have said had done so? I can hardly imagine anyone
but Elizabeth. What other lady of the Court would have made him strive in
honor to be best?

The sonnet, with its pledge of undying love, is probably not out of line
with the eulogy to which the Queen was accustomed, but it goes beyond
generalized flattery to specifics and, I think, beyond contrivance to expression
of genuine feeling. Elizabeth, if I mistake not, could reasonably be surmised
to have been practiced in the arts of love, and however other-minded Adonis
may have been at the start, answering chords could hardly fail to have been
struck in him. (Was it possibly not Adonis himself but his innocence, his
"maiden virtue," that the boar of passion slew?) No one doubts that Elizabeth was a fascinating woman. If one wishes to know how both bewitching
and maddening in her young courtier's eyes, and how potent in her glamour
("if e'er thou looks't on majesty"!), one is at liberty to recall the Shakespearean queen whom age could not wither and whose infinite variety custom
could not stale. Eva Turner Clark has drawn upon historians' descriptions
of Elizabeth and Cleopatra to bring out their striking similarities. The years
had not withered Elizabeth for the young poet, I venture to believe; when
he was twenty-one she was just Cleopatra's age at Actium: thirty-eight.

In the Rawlinson manuscript collection is a poem attributed to Queen
Elizabeth which in another manuscript miscellany is signed "E. of Ox." One
of the two with which Elizabeth is credited in *The Oxford Book of Sixteenth
Century Verse*, it tells how

> When I was fair and young then favour gracèd me;
> Of many was I sought their mistress for to be.
> But I did scorn them all, and answered them therefore,
> Go, go, go, seek some otherwhere,
>   Importune me no more.

"Fair Venus' son," however, takes her in hand and

>   . . . such change grew in my breast
> That neither night nor day I could take any rest.
> Then lo! I did repent, that I had said before
> Go, go, go, seek some otherwhere,
>   Importune me no more.

That both Elizabeth and Oxford are associated with authorship of these
verses on a haughty dame's conquest by Cupid is most interesting. The refrain
of all four stanzas is worth remarking, especially as it appears in the first,
for it is very similar to a line spoken in *The Two Gentlemen of Verona* by
a lady who seems to have represented Elizabeth to the dramatist:

> Therefore be gone, solicit me no more.

A poem signed *Meritum petere, grave,* appearing in the first anthology of
Elizabethan verse begins:

When first I thee beheld in colors black and white,
Thy face in form well framed with favour blooming still:
My burning breast in care did choose his chief delight,
With pen to paint thy praise, contrary to my skill,
Whose worthiness compared with this my rude devise,
I blush and am abash'd, this work to enterprise.

The poem could hardly have been addressed to anyone other than Elizabeth, for "black and white" were the heraldic colors of virginity and called "my colors" by the Queen. The line following the first stanza speaks of "thy sundry gifts of grace," while another poem in the anthology also refers to "her gifts of grace," recalling Oxford's "Above the rest in Court, who gave thee grace?" A third from which I have already quoted as being recognizably descriptive of Elizabeth, with "Her hair of gold, her front of ivory" (Chapter 22) is the more so for the poet's declaring that

ev'ry word she speaks
A jewel seem in judgment of the wise.

That all are by Oxford, I think, can be shown to be most probable.

The anthology into which I have dipped is entitled *A Hundreth Sundrie Flowres,* called by Tucker Brooke of Yale "the richest collection of early Elizabethan poetry." Prefaced by a letter of concealed authorship subscribed "From my lodging near the Strand" — the location of Vere House — "the 20 January 1572 (1573 new style)," it was published later in that year. It has confronted scholars with a first-class puzzle. Writing of the collection more than a century ago, William Hazlitt said that its "great curiosity and literary value . . . seem to have been entirely overlooked." So they remained until 1926. In that year Bernard M. Ward performed the signal service of having *Flowres* reprinted with an illuminating introduction.[1]

Who are the authors of the hundred flowers? One is George Gascoigne, of whom the anthologist explains disdainfully that "he hath never been dainty of his doings, and therefore I conceal not his name." As for the rest, accounting for the bulk of the contents, the reader is left to guess. The question of the authorship could be of the greatest import. Certainly it would be if its resolution should turn up, as I believe it does, a hundred pages of verse composed by Shakespeare in his early twenties offering clues to crucial experiences of his. What professor of English or literary critic would not give almost anything he possesses to discover such a trove? Well, one thing he

---

[1] Captain Ward's edition, which cut the prose parts of *The Adventures of Master F. I.* to the bone, was limited to 400 signed copies. That it is readily available today, thanks are owing to Ruth Loyd Miller, who brought it out in a new edition, much augmented with related documentation, in 1975. (Kennikat Press, Port Jefferson, N.Y.) Meanwhile, Charles Tyler Prouty had edited a new edition of the complete *Flowres,* with an introduction offering his own interpretation of the book and its successor. This was published by the University of Missouri Press in 1942 and reprinted in 1970.

would not give up is his preconceptions — and a six-year-old in Stratford could hardly have contributed to the anthology. Orthodoxy's position is that *A Hundreth Sundrie Flowres* is in its entirety the product of George Gascoigne.

What are the facts? I have delved for them in the book itself and in the several commentaries, but those I have come up with, as I have synthesized them, make too formidable and compressed a loaf, I am told, for general digestion. Reluctantly, because I hope that the complicated, uncertain story of *Flowres* — how it came to be and what it says — might provoke others as it has me, I have dropped the account from the book hoping to bring it out later. The decision has been the harder to come to because Ward, though making an invaluable contribution, fell into unfortunate blunders, in my opinion, while orthodox doctrine on the authorship of *Flowres* as argued by its chief proponent, Charles Tyler Prouty, seems to require only the exposure of its contradictions to cause it, in military jargon, to self-destruct. Here I shall confine myself to my conclusions.

The initial and major part of *Flowres* is a 25,000-word narrative in prose interspersed with fourteen poems, *The Adventures of Master F. I.* Called the first original prose narrative in English (by the *Encyclopaedia Britannica*) and sometimes the first English novel, this depicts "the emotions and day-by-day lives of a group of idle gentlefolk in a great house in northern England" as Professor Brooke puts it, with "the air of being drawn from life." The story is of the clandestine, amorous adventures of F. I., and a Mistress Elinor. Sixteen poems follow signed *Si fortunatus infoelix,* which of course links up with F. I. From Gabriel Harvey we learn that *Fortunatus Infoelix* was "lately the posie of Sir Christopher Hatton." So we find Hatton returning in October 1573 from a five-month convalescence on the Continent, to which we may recall that he was sent by the Queen, to be greeted by a publication containing a supposed detailed and highly indiscreet confession, by a versifier who would be taken to be himself, of a sultry love-affair with a lady whom everyone at Court would identify as Elizabeth. The confession, the reader is told, was lent by the author in strict confidence to a friend who, composing the prose story of the affair in explanation of the verses — his inside information making plain that he was both versifier and narrator — had unscrupulously passed it on to a printer. It is no surprise that, according to the writer on whom the authorship was later foisted, "sundry well-disposed minds should have taken offense . . . at *The Adventures of Master F. I.*" and "presumed to think that the same was indeed written to the scandalizing of some worthy personages." To Hatton's horrible embarrassment would have been added fury at the perpetrator of the volume, who, it would seem, could have been but one person. If the indications may be trusted, the Earl of Oxford had got back at him with deadly sportiveness.

Nearly three years later, when Oxford in his turn had left for the Continent, Hatton would reverse the field: *Flowres* would be reissued, much altered and bowdlerized, as *The Posies of George Gascoigne* and the authorship of the entire contents be claimed as Gascoigne's. ("The effect," Tucker Brooke writes, "was to close a door which had for the nonce been very invitingly opened.") *The Adventures of Master F. I.* would be rendered innocuous by being transformed into a translation from the Italian of a *Fable of Ferdinando Ieronimi and the Lady Elinora de Valasco*. (But meanwhile Hatton would have been made "a common recreation," as was said of Malvolio in *Twelfth Night,* in whom Oxford would some years later caricature Hatton to make sport of him again. (See Chapter 32.) Both the Captain of the Queen's Body-Guard and Malvolio, Countess Olivia's steward, were hoist by the petard of a hoax employing faked authorship of an amorous confession, one that exploited their ambitious profession of a tender passion for a lady high above them in station.) Moreover, the revenge Oxford took in *Twelfth Night* was not all. He had already turned the tables on Hatton as Hatton had turned them upon him, if the signs are what they appear to be: he had pulled this off just as Hatton had done, on returning from the Continent. It took him four months, but these were months when he had more pressing matters on his mind. In August 1576, according to Ward, the Queen's ministers called in all unsold copies of *The Posies of George Gascoigne,* putting an end to its future distribution. This would be but further evidence against the ortho-dox stand that the *Posies* was the authentic version and that Gascoigne was the author of the whole of *Flowres*. To Sir Sidney Lee, "There is little doubt that Gascoigne is responsible for the whole," and Prouty would scotch even that residue of doubt. Clearly, if Ward has his facts right — and Prouty does not challenge him on this point as he does on others — in the view of the authorities, the *Posies* was the impostor.

Oxford may be said to have had, and, by virtue of the immortal character of Malvolio, still to be having the last word as far as Hatton is concerned. It must, however, have gone hard with him to anticipate that the only name ever to be associated with the hundred sundry poems in *Flowres* over which he had labored — if indeed they were his — would be that of another man and one for whom he had scant respect.

If Oxford embarked on *Flowres* with the idea of an anthology serving the simple purpose of a receptacle for a composition that would pay Christopher Hatton back, he went far beyond it. It happened as in play after play, which he evidently began with a topical theme in mind; his imagination, it would seem, became more and more aroused to the vehicle as a medium for the portrayal of life and human nature set to the language of poetry; inevitably he came to give the anthology his best and, forgetting Hatton, put himself increasingly into it. We have seen how, in the plays, the dramatist would often lend his villains an eloquence worthy of demigods (like the superlatively gracious English of the fratricide Claudius's opening speech beginning "Though yet of Hamlet our dear brother's death. . . .") and instil such unlikely characters as Richard II and Macbeth with his own sensitive, philosophic, poetic nature. No great poetry marks *Flowres* but such a quantity of the kind there is should tell us much about the writer, if we are astute enough. That is why I hope that "learned minds," as the anthologist of *Flowres* calls them — minds more qualified than mine — will apply themselves to its assessment.

What kind of poetry will they find? Other than that by Gascoigne it is remarkably uniform in tone and subject. In nearly all the one hundred selections we read of the ups and downs of the fortunes of love. In them the lover is paired with a gentlewoman explicitly or implicitly of high degree. There is nothing I can see in most of them to differentiate her from one poem to the next. In two, as I have said, it seems evident that she is Elizabeth, one being that in which "the lover declareth his affection" for the lady "in colours black and white" — avowedly Elizabeth's. In a third, the longest of all, there would appear to be scant other possibility. We read:

> Me thinks I see the states, which sue to her for grace,
> Me thinks I see one look of hers repulse them all apace.

Apart from the verse intended to put Hatton on the spot and, of course, Gascoigne's, I'd settle for most of its being addressed by Oxford to Elizabeth. One is written to a "Gentlewoman" for whom the poet has been unable to show his affection since both are "attended" by "jealous looks" — true enough, probably, of Oxford's situation initially vis-à-vis the Queen. It begins:

> Thou with thy looks on whom I look full oft,
> And find therein great cause of deep delight. . . .

Some are composed as the lady's reply, such as one *Written by a Gentlewoman in court who . . . seemed to disdain him.* Another, by *A Loving Lady being wounded in the spring time* who "doth therefore thus bewail" contains the suggestive lines:

> The lustie *Ver* which whilom might exchange
> My grief to joy, and then my joys increase,
> Springs now elsewhere. . . .

and:

> What plant can spring that feels no force of *Ver?*

Notice that "ver," a Middle English word for "spring," is here capitalized and italicized to mark it as a proper name.

Other verses reflect bitterly on the poet's treatment at the hands of his lady. *To a gentlewoman who blamed him for writing his friendly advice in verse unto another lover of hers* sounds as if Elizabeth might have reprimanded Oxford for amicably advising Hatton to crawl back under a rock. This follows one about *the lover being disdainfully abjected by a dame of high calling who had chosen (in his place) a play fellow of baser condition*, which suggests the same triangle. It begins:

> Thy birth, thy beauty, nor thy brave attire,
> (Disdainful Dame, which does me double wrong)
> Thy high estate, which sets thy heart on fire,
> Or new found choice, which cannot serve thee long. . . .

It is not impossible for me to imagine the author of those lines twenty years later writing Shakespeare's *Sonnets*. (Thirteen of the poems signed F. I. or *Si fortunatus infoelix* are sonnets in the Shakespearean form. Other verse forms continually recurring in *Flowres* are the six-line stanza of *Venus and Adonis* and iambic couplets of alternating fourteen- and twelve-syllable lines, which Oxford's uncle, the Earl of Surrey, had made popular.)

The foregoing verses are followed in turn by *The lover disdainfully rejected contrary to former promise, thus complaineth*, which sounds a theme recurrent in Shakespeare's treatment of women, as in the last stanza:

> But yet for thee I must protest,
> That sure the fault is none of thine,
> Thou art as true as in the best,
> That ever came of Cressede's line:
> For constant yet was never none,
> But in inconstancy alone.

"When I see how frail those creatures are," Oxford would muse, ". . . that fly from man to man." And Hamlet would second it: "Frailty thy name is woman."

The poet of *Flowres* comes back to Cressida again and again. "Cresside's name," he says, is "written wide on every wall," and "thou mightst be she, / Cressyde for inconstancy"; and, "Troylus fum'd / When Cressyde dwelt with Diomed." He speaks of the longing lust which Priam's son — Troilus — "Had for to see his Cressyde," and in *An uncourteous farewell to an unconstant Dame* exclaims:

> For Cryssyde fair did Troylus never love,
> More deare than I esteem'd your framèd cheare.

At least three other times he reverts to them.

George Lyman Kittredge writes that "the medieval tale of Troilus had interested Shakespeare long before he dramatized it." The Harvard professor goes on to quote the lines in *Lucrece* descriptive in detail of the "skilful painting" depicting a scene from the tale and cites references to Troilus or Cressida or both by six characters in as many Shakespearean plays. (Oxford at age twenty, it may be remembered, bought a volume of Chaucer, whose rendering of the two Trojan lovers was then the best known.) Edward Dowden asks, "Did Shakespeare write *Troilus and Cressida* to unburden his heart of some bitterness by an indictment of the illusions of romance, which had misled him?" It is a good question. Declaring that, "When Shakespeare wrote *Troilus and Cressida* a passion of bitterness possessed him," Frank Harris displays his often sound intuition, I think, in observing that "The same model evidently served for both women" — Cressida and Cleopatra. Does Shakespeare's Cressida partake of Elizabeth, an Elizabeth who brought to the character an anticipation of Cleopatra's wanton wiles and fatal chameleon femininity? Cressida moves the youthful and idealistic Troilus to the supreme expression in English (in my view) of love's urgency only to betray him, voicing misgivings about herself, to the experienced, licentious Diomedes — "sweet honey Greek," she calls him; one thinks of the Gypsy, the Earl of Leicester. "O Cressid!" Troilus cries. "O false Cressid! false, false, false!" Even among orthodox critics *Troilus and Cressida* is recognized as an early play taken up again in the dramatist's maturer years. Mark Van Doren, who rails against it, lumps it with *All's Well* and *Measure for Measure* to censure the three as the comedies that "are in any final sense unsuccessful." But the dramatist was not primarily concerned with their theatrical success. He was surely obeying the motive every writer knows, to give external form to a gnawing experience that he may come to terms with it.

The emotional apogee between Oxford and Elizabeth probably was reached sometime in 1572 or 1573. During this period a boy was conceived who would be given the name of Henry Wriothesley and later the title of 3rd Earl of Southampton. Was there a causal relationship? Some have been led to believe so as the only way of accounting for the tenor of the *Sonnets*. My inability to think of any other is balanced by my inability to regard such a theory of Southampton's parentage as other than far-fetched — which is not, however, to say impossible. As I stipulated in bringing up the theory before, I take no position on it. On its face it is so unlikely that perhaps fairness requires pointing out a few points in its favor, beyond the chief ones already brought out in Chapter 17.

The poet of the *Sonnets* insists that "truth and beauty . . . thrive" in the young man who forms their chief subject; "both truth and beauty . . . depends" upon him. The de Vere name and motto would suggest "truth" as symbolizing Oxford, while "beauty" is an adjective with which Oxford might seem perhaps to identify Elizabeth both in *Flowres* and as Cressida. A single line in Sonnet 76 — "Why write I still all one, ever the same" — has been taken as identifying Southampton, Elizabeth and Oxford himself as the principals of the sequence. "All one" suggests Southampton's motto, "Ung par tout, tout par ung." "Ever the same" is Elizabeth's "Semper eadem." (In correspondence with Leicester she signed herself "Ever the same.") The three words also yield Oxford: "E. Ver the same" In this sonnet, too, we are told "That every word doth almost tell my name. . . ." Then there is Sonnet 33, in reading which we might bear in mind that "region," with its similarity in sound to "regina," is of the same root. After observing how he has seen many a glorious morning sun permit the basest clouds to hide its celestial face from the forlorn world, the poet declares:

> Even so my sun one early morn did shine,
> With all-triumphant splendor on my brow;
> But out! alack! he was but one hour mine,
> The region cloud hath mask'd him from me now,
>   Yet him for this my love no whit disdaineth;
> Suns of the world may stain when heaven's sun staineth.

Given the cryptic nature of the lines whatever they may mean, it is possible that what the poet is saying is that he basked in his son's radiance but briefly before the Queen hid him from his view and that he will not disdain his son for his guilt (in having remained out his sight?), for the sons of this world can hardly be blamed when the sun of heaven — the Queen — is blameworthy. As Launcelot says in *The Merchant of Venice,* like an actor departing from his lines to make a point beyond the significance of the scene, "truth will come to light; murder cannot be hid long; a man's son may, but in the end, truth will out." In *A Midsummer-Night's Dream* the refusal of Queen Titania to give up her "little changeling boy" to her somewhat estranged king, Oberon, sets the action of the play in motion — an idea that seems unlikely to have put itself forward out of the blue and one that never recurs in the play except in a fleeting reference toward the end.

The passages I have touched on could certainly have other connotations than those I may be accused of having forced on them. But there is one that seems to point almost blatantly in the direction in which we have been looking. It is an exchange in *The Two Gentlemen of Verona.* One of the participants is the trusting, open-hearted Valentine, who in the play's opening lines associates himself with the young Oxford's preoccupation, protesting that "Home-keeping youth have ever homely wits" and declaring that he will "see the wonders of the world abroad" rather than "living dully sluggardized at home."[2] In Act II, Scene 1, his servant, Speed, is twitting him about his love of Silvia, the Duke of Milan's daughter. In the course of the verbal engagement, Speed catches up his master on his assertion that Silvia is "Not so fair, boy, as well-favored."

---

[2] Mark Van Doren rightly says of this speech that "Valentine has caught the tone which will be heard henceforth in the golden world of gentlemen where Shakespeare's comedy will occur. It is a world whose free and graceful movement finds a symbol for itself in the travel of young men . . . awaited somewhere by ladies of fine and disciplined feeling . . . accustomed to compliment" who "in their grace understand the arts both of bestowing and of receiving praise." That Professor Van Doren could soberly construe that golden world as an outgrowth of the meagre, ill-favored, toilsome, uncouth existence that would have been Will Shakspere's until his mid-twenties at least gives an idea of the strength of convention.

Speed: . . . she is not so fair as, of you, well-favored.
Valentine: I mean that her beauty is exquisite, but her favor infinite.
Speed: That's because the one is painted and the other out of all
    count.
Valentine: How painted? and how out of count?
Speed: Marry, sir, so painted to make her fair, that no man counts on
    her beauty.
Valentine: How esteemest thou me? I account of her beauty.
Speed: You never saw her since she was deformed.
Valentine: How long since she has been deformed?
Speed: Ever since you loved her.
Valentine: I have loved her ever since I saw her, and still I see her
    beautiful.
Speed: If you love her you cannot see her.
Valentine: Why?
Speed: Because love is blind. O! that you had mine eyes.
Valentine: What should I see then?
Speed: Your own present folly and her passing deformity.

Now, I may be exercising too much or too little imagination, but there is only one way I can think of in which a woman suffers a passing deformity upon a man's first loving her and only one interpretation I can put upon Speed's gibes (and I am following several other writers in this): Valentine has made big with child a woman who, to make her fair, is so painted that no man can assess her beauty. And the Elizabethan lady notorious for the make-up to which she resorted increasingly with the years, until it came to cover her face like a mask, was the Queen, with whom Silvia has already been linked in the play by the point made of the gloves she has had from Valentine: this was just the gift Oxford brought back from Italy for Elizabeth, making an impression on the Court and on history. It is not only that a painted face and the possession of gloves given by a suitor were attributes of Elizabeth but that unless Oxford had meant for them to bring Elizabeth to mind he would at all costs have mentioned neither in connection with Silvia.

One assumes that this wedge of apparent reality, totally at variance with the treatment Silvia otherwise receives, had not been thrust into any version of the play the Queen knew. Elizabeth would have been flattered by the song beginning "Who is Silvia?" with its riposte

> Holy, fair and wise is she;
>   The heaven such grace doth lend her,
> That she might admired be.
>   . . . .
>
>   She excels each mortal thing
>   Upon the dull earth dwelling.

She would, I dare say, have deduced that the title, *The Two Gentlemen of Verona*, was to be translated as "The two gentlemen of one Vere"; by this token one side of the dramatist was the noble, virtuous Valentine, the other Proteus (named for the sea-god who could change his shape at will), whom

Silvia calls a "subtle, perjured, false, disloyal man." "I knew him as myself," Valentine says of Proteus, "from our infancy"; they have grown up inseparable. To take the two as a single, composite person is the only way to make sense of the last scene, which has baffled and exasperated commentators. Here it may be interjected that Oxford is not the only human being to have been bemused and even despairing at finding diametrically opposed characters in himself, or, I suppose, the only youth who, from being a prudish Adonis with an older seductress, has soon passed to the discovery in himself of a potential Tarquin to a beautiful and helpless Lucrece.

In the scene Proteus threatens Silvia, Valentine's betrothed, to

> . . . woo you like a soldier, at arms' end.
> And love you 'gainst the nature of love, — force ye.

Valentine arrives in the nick of time to save the young lady and reflects:

> Who should be trusted now, when one's right hand
> Is perjur'd to the bosom?

In four lines Proteus acknowledges his guilt and asks forgiveness. That is enough for Valentine, who cries

> Then I am paid;
> And once again do I receive thee honest.

Professor Van Doren says it is a "reconciliation which no one believes." As one between different persons nobody could believe it. But forgiveness of oneself comes easily. Only if addressing an aspect of himself could Valentine speak his next lines to Proteus:

> And, that my love may appear plain and free,
> All that was mine in Silvia I give thee.

"The lines," says Edward Dowden, "have been a stumbling-block to many critics." I should think so, if the critics try to believe that a high-minded young man, having just saved his beloved from sexual assault at the hands of his treacherous best friend, magnanimously, to show his good will, turns the young lady over to the still-panting intended rapist. To Professor Dowden it also "seems strange and undramatic that Silvia herself at this moment should utter no word." In fact, after crying "O heaven!" when threatened with a fate worse than death, Silvia speaks not another syllable in the play. The dramatist, I judge, had not the foggiest notion what the young noblewoman would say during or after these ostensibly outrageous proceedings; and to him, in any case, the transactions between the two young men amounted to an interior dialogue within a single protagonist, inaudible to their object. To Silvia's father, who has bitterly opposed Valentine's suit, the suitor is now revealed as of "unrivall'd merit" and one that "hast deserv'd her." The Duke holds him, indeed, *worthy of an empress' love.*

Two Gentlemen was mentioned by Meres in 1598 as one of Shakespeare's plays; very likely it had been shown for the select circle of the Court. But for the rest nothing is heard of it or that other revealing early comedy, *All's Well*, until they crop up in 1623 in the First Folio, when the events evidently mirrored in them were long and safely passed.

Elizabeth is held by a school of opinion to have been incapable of having children. One of her physicians, however, assured a French embassy that if she married Charles IV, "I will answer for her having ten children." She was, in fact, reported persistently at the time to have had one or two offspring — two by Dudley, according to some rumors. As far as we know, Elizabeth could well have had a child by Oxford. From Adonis' blood "that on the ground lay spill'd," in the poem dedicated to Henry Wriothesley, "A purple flower sprung up," and Venus, comparing its fragrance "to her Adonis' breath," tells it "This was thy father's guise, / Sweet issue of a more sweet-smelling sire." "Here was thy father's bed, here in my breast," she pursues; "Thou art the next of blood, and 'tis thy right, / Lo, in this hollow cradle take thy rest." And "weary of the world," she hies in her light chariot to Paphos, where she had been born of the foam and now "means to immure herself and not be seen."

From admitting the possibility of a son begotten of Elizabeth and Oxford it is still a far cry from having him planted with the 2nd Earl and Countess of Southampton. Could it conceivably have happened? Could he conceivably have been a "little changeling boy"? D. S. Ogburn and Percy Allen, at least, have thought so. There are few absolute impossibilities in human affairs. Southampton had been imprisoned in the Tower because of "his well wishes toward the marriage of the Duke of Norfolk and Mary Queen of Scots, to whom and to whose religion he stood not a little affected." Whether he was visited there by his wife I have not learned. On 1 May 1573 he was released to the more comfortable confinement of a private home and in July permitted to move to his father-in-law's house. From there he wrote on October 6th of "the sudden seizing of my wife today" and went on to say that "this present morning at three o'clock, my wife was delivered of a goodly boy (God bless him)." Charlotte C. Stopes, the authority on the family, adds, "Thus was the only son of the Earl of Southampton born" at "the house of his mother's people." To this she appends a footnote that "It has always been said he was 'the second son,' but there is no authority for that." Naturally one wonders if what "has always been said" may not be right and that the son born on 6 October 1573 died and was replaced by a little changeling. "It is strange," Mrs. Stopes goes on to say, "that there has been preserved no record of his baptism." Moreover, "there appears to be no later allusion to the godparents of the young Lord." Curiouser and curiouser. Not to have had godparents in those days is singular enough but it is doubly so for the son of an Earl who at his own christening had the King and Queen as sponsors. In about 1577 the Earl became estranged from his wife. To overcome the bar he erected to communications from her, the distraught Countess had something unspecified intended for him which, she wrote her father, "I sent him by my little boy." That was the last she saw of the boy until her husband died four years later. Marriage had been made so distasteful for her, as Mrs. Stopes put it, that she did not venture upon it again for thirteen years.

If there is nothing in the theoretical possibility we have been considering, the case for Oxford as Shakespeare is in nowise impaired. If, on the other hand, the possibility were the actuality the reasons for denying Oxford the authorship of the poems and plays, potent enough in any case, would have warranted any efforts to that end lest from those poems and plays the story be deduced.

Those are the last words I shall say on the subject, or, for that matter, have any occasion to say. Increasingly, Oxford's interests were in travel, in writing, and in a third woman in his life.

26

"To Me It Is a Prison"

1573–1574: Oxford's contribution, in a second violation of the nobleman's code, of a letter to the Reader and a poem (perhaps inspired by having had the credit for A Hundreth Sundry Flowres *given to another author) as an introduction to Bedingfield's translation of Girolamo Cardano's* De Consolatione; *novel usages found both in Oxford's letter and in Shakespeare; the well-established influence of the book,* Cardanus Comfort, *on Shakespeare's thought, especially in* Hamlet, *and the two-century-old proposition that it is the book the Prince is discovered reading during the play. — The hold-up staged by Oxford's men of messengers on the highway between Rochester and Gravesend, which will reappear as the hold-up in* The Famous Victories of Henry the Fift *on the same highway and the same day of May and later in* Henry the Fourth, Part One, *still in the same location and with the same characters. — The strange implication of Oxford in a pro-Spanish plot, in which he is apparently acting either in a pet at being kept in England or as Burghley's "private eye." — His longing for foreign travel and its frustration by Burghley and the Queen, echoed by Bertram, his double, in* All's Well. — *Bertram's resolution to "steal away," and Oxford's doing just that, to the Continent; the Court's fear that he intends to proceed to Brussels and make common cause with the escaped leaders of the northern rebellion; the dispatch of Bedingfield by the Queen to fetch him back; the relief that he did not join her enemies and his restoration to royal favor. — The likelihood that it was at this time that he wrote* The Famous Victories, *with its brazen build-up of an earlier Oxford's eminence. — The wildly extravagant tale he is charged by an indignant enemy with having fabricated of his leading the Duke of Alva's army in a victorious advance while on the Continent.*

Though *The Posies of George Gascoigne* had been suppressed, the outcome nevertheless was that the major contributor had sowed for another to reap. It must have gone hard with Oxford, if it was he, that he was powerless ever to reclaim his purloined verse. With his decision to make literature the focus of his life, which we may guess was made in about 1573, he must have realized that his rank and position would stand in the way of his acknowledging his work. The gall of this awareness may have infected him when he sat down to compose a poem that year entitled

The Earl of Oxford to the Reader of Bedingfield's
"Cardanus Comfort"

The poem has no apparent connection with the book; its relevance is more to the poet's own prospects. The first and last (sixth) stanza read:

The labouring man that tills the fertile soil,
    And reaps the harvest fruit, hath not indeed
The gain, but pain; but if for all his toil
    He gets the straw, the lord will have the seed.

So he that takes the pain to pen the book
    Reaps not the gifts of golden goodly muse;
But those gain that, who on the work shall look
    And from the sour the sweet by skill shall look,
For he that beats the bush the bird not gets,
But who sits still and holdeth fast the nets.

Thomas Bedingfield, it may be remembered, had sent Oxford a manuscript copy of his translations from the Latin of the book he called *Cardanus Comfort* with a letter apologizing for having "busied" himself in philosophy rather than "in some discourse of arms (your Lordship's chief profession and mine also)." (Page 475) Oxford, perhaps as part of a growing preoccupation with letters, had decided that it should be presented to the public and undoubtedly paid the costs of publication himself.

De Consolatione had been brought out in Venice in 1542, the work of Girolamo Castellione Cardano of Milan, known to most English writers as Jerome Cardan, a mathematician, philosopher, and poet. The author explained that he had written it out of the experience of many disappointments to help him bear those the future might bring. In a further confession he summed up for us a lifetime of instruction in the perceptions of a noble and humane soul. "This work," he said, "was at first called *The Book of the Accuser,* because it contended against the vain passions and false persuasions of mankind: afterward it was changed to Consolation, because it appeared that there was a far greater number of unfortunate men needing consolation, than of fortunate ones in need of blame." In quoting the passage, Charles W. Barrell adds that this "human sympathy . . . is also typical of Shakespeare, who rarely fails to give even his deepest-dyed villains opportunity to air their grievances against fate" and uses "*comfort, consolation* and their derivatives . . . 237 times."

The title-page of Bedingfield's work reads:

CARDANUS
Comforte, translated
And Published
by commaundement of the right
Honourable the Earle of
Oxenforde.

Readers who had rubbed their eyes at the auspices under which *The Courtier* was brought out now had occasion to rub them again. The favor shown the book by Oxford on the title-page was more than seconded in the prefatory letter that followed. It began:

> To my loving Friend Thomas Bedingfield, Esquire,
> one of Her Majesty's Gentlemen Pensioners.
>
> After I had perused your letters, good Master Bedingfield, finding in them your request far differing from the desert of your labour, I could not choose but greatly doubt whether it were better for me to yield to your desire, or execute mine own intentions towards the publishing of your book. For I do confess the affections that I have always borne towards you could move me not a little. But when I had thoroughly considered in my mind, of sundry and diverse arguments, whether it were best to obey mine affections, or the merits of your studies; at the length I determined it were better to deny your unlawful request than to grant or condescend to the concealment of so worthy a work. Whereby as you have been profited in the translating, so many may reap knowledge by the reading of the same that shall comfort the afflicted, confirm the doubtful, encourage the coward, and lift up the base-minded man to achieve to any true sum or grade of virtue, whereto ought only the noble thoughts of men to be inclined.

There, I should say, is the young idealist whose inevitable disillusionment would produce the pessimism and resignation of the later Shakespeare. It certainly conforms but little with the picture of Oxford the historians have given us. The letter, some 770 words long, ends:

> Again we see, if our friends be dead we cannot show or declare our affection more than by erecting them of tombs, when they be dead indeed, yet make we them live as it were again through their monument. But with me behold it happeneth far better; for in your lifetime I shall erect you such a monument that, as I say, in your lifetime you shall see how noble a shadow of your virtuous life shall hereafter remain when you are dead and gone. . . .
>
> Thus earnestly desiring you in this one request of mine (as I would yield to you in a great many) not to repugn the setting forth of your own proper studies, I bid you farewell. From my new country Muses of Wivenhoe, wishing you as you have begun, to proceed in these virtuous actions. For when all things shall else forsake us, virtue will ever abide with us, and when our bodies fall into the bowels of the earth, yet that shall mount with our minds into the highest heavens.
> From your loving and assured friend,
> E. Oxenford.

Percy Allen and Gwynneth Bowen have written on parallels between the letter to Bedingfield and the *Sonnets* and Mr. Barrell at some length on parallels with the plays. A few examples of the latter are particularly noteworthy. The *Oxford Universal Dictionary* in defining "persuade" in the sense of "to commend to adoption" cites as its first use Shakespeare's "Your king . . . Sends me a paper to persuade me patience." Yet here in the letter is Oxford saying that "nothing doth persuade me the same more than philosophy." ("The same" are the ideals expressed in its first paragraph.) Again the *Dictionary* gives Shakespeare's "Macbeth hath murdered sleep" as the first use of the verb in such a figurative sense, while in the letter Oxford declares that, by neglecting Bedingfield's manuscript he would have committed "the unpardonable error to have murdered the same." The *Dictionary* cites "Base, fearful and despairing" in *Henry the Sixth, Part Three,* as the first use of "base" as a quality of character; but in the letter we read of "base-minded men" (as in *King John* we shall read of "a base mind").

Mr. Barrell brings out that the detection by scholars of similarities between *Cardanus Comforte* and *Hamlet* goes back at least 140 years. In 1845 Joseph Hunter said that "It seems to be the book which Shakespeare placed in the hands of Hamlet." His reason for believing so stems from a passage in *Comforte* headed "Old men's company unpleasant," in which Cardan remarks of senile bores that "Their senses serve not their bodies, their bodies obey not their minds. . . . How many old men have been, for whom it had been better to have died in youth. . . ." ; that could well be what Hamlet had before him when Polonius asks him what he is reading and he replies:

> Slanders, sir: for the satirical rogue says here that old men have grey beards, that their faces are wrinkled, their eyes purging thick amber and plumtree gum, and that they have a plentiful lack of wit, together with most weak hams."

Dr. Lily B. Campbell agrees. In her highly regarded *Shakespeare's Tragic Heroes* she writes:

> It is easily seen that this book of Cardan has long been associated with *Hamlet.* I should like to believe that Hamlet was actually reading it or pretending to read it as he carried on his baiting of Polonius.

Dr. Campbell shows that *Comforte* was a book from which Shakespeare's thought repeatedly took stimulation, and the noted orthodox scholar, the late Hardin Craig, finds the Prince's mind so steeped in it that in an essay on the subject he calls *Comforte* "Hamlet's book" (an essay that, needless to say, he contrived to write without any mention of Lord Oxford). To understand what he means we need only compare Hamlet's great soliloquy with this passage from Cardan:

> What should we account of death to be resembled to anything better than sleep. . . . Most assured it is that such sleeps be most sweet as be most sound, for those are best wherein like unto dead men we dream nothing. The broken sleeps, the slumber, the dreams full of visions, are commonly in them that have weak and sickly bodies. . . . But if thou compare death to long travel . . . there is nothing that doth better or more truly prophecy the end of life, than when a man dreameth that he doth travel and wander into far countries . . . and that he traveleth in countries unknown without hope of return. . . . We are assured not only to sleep, but also to die. . . . Only honesty and virtue of mind doth make a man happy, and only a cowardly and corrupt conscience do cause thine unhappiness.

Not only in literature, it would seem, Oxford at twenty-three sought relief from the niceties and stultification of life at Court. In May 1573, two of the Earl's former employees write Lord Burghley accusing their "late good Lord and master" of a "raging demeanor" and three of his men (one being "Deny the Frenchman," of whom we shall hear more) of lying in wait for them in a ditch "by the highway from Gravesend to Rochester" and firing "calivers charged with bullets" at them, barely missing them, "whereupon they mounted on horseback and fled towards London." Their "late Lord and master," they ask pardon for stating, "is to be thought as the procurer of that which is done." Indeed, he must have been one of the party, to have exhibited that "raging demeanor." One can see him, as part of the prank, leading the mock assault like a wildman.

Readers of Shakespeare know the episode from Act II, Scene 2, of *Henry the Fourth, Part One,* in which Falstaff and three of Prince Hal's other companions of the Boar's-Head Tavern hold up and rob some travelers bearing "money of the king's . . . on the way to the king's exchequer" on the highway near Gad's Hill, which is the same highway between Rochester and Gravesend on which the outrage cited in the letter to Burghley took place. The episode had previously appeared in the play's precursor, *The Famous Victories of Henry the Fift,* probably Oxford's first venture in historical drama. There it is stated that the robbery of the king's "receivers" by Prince Hal's followers took place on "the 20th day of May last in the fourteenth year of the reign of our sovereign lord King Henry the Fourth." Oxford did not even change the month of the actual occurrence. In the fourteenth year of Henry IV's reign, however, there was no May; the reign ended two months short of it;[1] but it was in the fourteenth year of Elizabeth's reign that the actual robbery took place. (We can imagine the elation of the Stratfordians if they were able to come up with as dramatic a correlation between Shakspere's life and one of the plays as proof of his authorship.) We have already taken note of Oxford's extraordinary boldness in letting his connection with *The Famous Victories* be surmised — and the date of the robbery is not repeated in the later play. In both plays Prince Hal is present for his amusement at the scene, as Oxford must have been too. Prince Hal returned "with advantage" the money taken and we may assume that Oxford did likewise.

The "fickle head" that Gilbert Talbot spoke of as preventing Oxford from passing everyone else at Court was probably the symptom of high spirits bursting the seams of restraint. Ralph Lane found a similar epithet for the young lord's head in a letter to Burghley of 17 January 1574 touching upon his ostensible involvement in a far more serious escapade. The affair was one it is difficult to make head or tail of, but according to Lane (who had previously reported Oxford's secret moves on Norfolk's behalf) Antonio de Guaras, a Spanish agent in England, was to be supplied with 1,200 men and

---

[1] Henry Bolingbroke was crowned Henry IV upon the abdication of Richard II on 30 September 1399 and died after reigning thirteen years, five months and 20 days on 20 March 1413.

six ships (for the use of the Duke of Alva in the Low Countries, it is inferred) and "my Lord E." was of the opinion that £3,000 borrowed of Guaras on the pawn of land should be sufficient for the purpose. Lane says he "hopes nothing can escape his [Burghley's] intelligence, touching any [of] the said lord's dealings" to "cut off not only this, but any other advantages that foreign factions may seek to take of his young unstaid mind."

Burghley's endorsement on Lane's letter agrees in identifying "My Lord E." as his son-in-law and as the chief spokesman for recruiting the expeditionary force. Burghley himself, however, had been dealing with de Guaras for months, for while he was endeavoring to strengthen the Dutch against Alva he was also striving to extract trade advantages from the Spanish for England in the Low Countries. Could Oxford with his encouragement have been keeping open a channel of communication with de Guaras, promisingly baited? We have a strong indication from Gabriel Harvey seven years later that Oxford served as the eyes of the Crown on his travels when he wrote in *Speculum Tuscanismi,* "Not the like Lynx to spy out secrets and privities of States." Conyers Read, to whom "the whole matter is puzzling," takes a contrary view in holding that "the most charitable interpretation to place upon his [Oxford's] behavior is that he was bored to death with Court life and casting about desperately for action."

There can be little question but that the young nobleman felt pent up and frustrated. Ward writes:

> Towards the end of the year [1573] Oxford's old longing to see "strange and foreign parts" broke out afresh. We cannot say actually how near he was to going; but we know that Sir William Cordell, the Master of the Rolls, was told to settle the necessary financial arrangements, which he did on September 2nd. The biggest problem was the question of the Earl's debts. "To determine what my debts are certainly," Lord Oxford replied to one of Cordell's interrogations, "it is not possible, and because I have not yet the right of them all; but my debts to the Queen's Majesty are these which I have gathered together considered. I have just cause to think that the sum of my debts will be £6,000 at the least." For the payment of this sum he agrees to set aside between £400 and £500 a year. He then goes on to outline his family arrangements. "For my wife to live on during my absence I have assigned £300; and for her jointure £669 6s. 8d, . . . and for my sister £100."

Nothing, however, came of this project and he continued at Court for the remainder of the year, both the Queen and Lord Burghley being, as we know, very much opposed to the idea of foreign travel.

Oxford may not have been beyond conniving with the Spanish as leverage upon the Queen. (I think that the Spanish, feudal to their fingertips, pristine champions of the Old Religion, votaries of pride, honor, and punctilio, made a romantic appeal to him.) He was still on good terms with Elizabeth, it appears, however, for in March 1574, two months after Lane's warning to Burghley, he accompanied her on that visit to the Archbishop of Canterbury. But his spirit was probably that of Bertram in *All's Well* when the king speeds the other young lords to Italy "Not to woo honour, but to wed it" and the young Count, kept at Court, cries:

> I am commanded here and kept a coil with —
> "Too young," and "The next year," and "'Tis too early."
>   . . . .
>   I shall stay here the forehorse to a smock,
> Creaking my shoes on the plain masonry,
> Till honour be brought up, and no sword worn
> But one to dance with.

On New Year's Day, 1580, Philip Sidney "presented the Queen with a cambric smock, the sleeves and collar wrought in black and edged in gold and silver lace." Thus we would appear to have Oxford here voicing his resentment at playing a decked-out processional lead-nag before the Queen's Majesty. The complaint would have been recognizable for what it was to the *cognoscenti,* who would have seen, too, that it was double-edged; for Sidney had been given the benison of the Crown to go traveling on the Continent at seventeen to learn foreign languages.

Bertram vows at the end of the foregoing speech,

> By heaven, I'll steal away.

That Oxford two years earlier had stolen away to arrange a refuge for the Duke of Norfolk and escape matrimony, like Bertram, is only a bare possibility, but steal away he unquestionably did in mid-1574. We know little about the episode; nothing Oxford wrote about it survived in the records. But young courtiers did not take it upon themselves to quit the country without royal sanction, as Oxford had done. What made it far worse was his destination, if the report of the English ambassador in Edinburgh is to be credited. He wrote on July 18th, a fortnight after the event, that "My Lord of Oxford and Lord Seymour are fled out of England, and passed by Bruges to Brussels." It was in Brussels that the Earl of Westmorland, a leader of the Northern Rebellion of 1569, had established himself with his following upon the failure of the uprising; and it seems to have been thought that Oxford was going to join the attainted nobleman. His championship of Norfolk and later dealings with de Guaras, if they were what they seem, would have given grounds for such a fear. Indeed, it is hard to imagine why he would have made Brussels his objective except for the purpose of making common cause with the Queen's enemies. The rebels themselves evidently put this interpretation upon his action, and the prospect of gaining so stellar a recruit caused "a great triumph" among them, a correspondent of Burghley's wrote from Antwerp six weeks after the episode. He continued:

> In a council held at Louvain, it was concluded that the Earl of Westmorland
> should ride to Bruges to welcome him, and persuade him not to return. . . . It
> were a great pity such a valiant and noble young gentleman should communicate
> with such detestable men.

It would have been worse than a great pity if his headstrong nature could
have led him to such a reckless and unworthy extremity. But, as the correspondent noted, "the Earls did not meet." That Oxford ever intended to
meet Westmorland seems highly unlikely though it may have served his
purpose to have it thought he meant to.

The Queen for her part, upon learning of Edward's decampment for the
Continent, sent his friend Thomas Bedingfield to fetch him back. On July
6th Sir Francis Walsingham wrote to Burghley that "I made her Majesty
acquainted with my Lord of Oxford's arrival at Calais, who doth not interpret the same in any evil part. She conceiveth great hope of his return upon
some secret message sent him." If he was not, in fact, on a clandestine
mission for the Queen, it is quite possible that he had distanced himself from
the Court in a huff over a slight he had suffered at her hands, bluffing as to
her purpose; that Elizabeth's reaction was a half-exasperated, half-remorseful
"The impetuous young idiot!"; and that the secret message was to apologize
for affronting his touchy *amour propre* and to tell him not to be such an ass
and to come back lest she be really angry. Certainly the noble Earl of Sussex,
the pillar at Court of probity and selfless devotion to the Queen, pled
Oxford's cause, as we know from a letter Burghley wrote to thank him for
doing so. "My Lord," the Queen's chief councillor expounded, "howsoever
my Lord of Oxford be for his part [in] matters of thrift inconsiderate, I dare
avow him to be resolute in dutifulness to the Queen and his country." It is
a good illustration of Burghley's reverence for money: a man may be unthrifty
and yet stop short of treason.

Imprudence in money-matters, we see, was not only improvident but
verging on the criminal; and we have a further idea of the tutelary regime
under which Burghley's son-in-law must have ground his teeth when we learn
that the desire for travel was to be equated with immorality or depravity.
That comes out in a letter to Burghley from a trusted subordinate, Sir Walter
Mildmay, Chancellor of the Exchequer, who, obviously confident his view
would receive a concurring reception, wrote:

> Of my Lord of Oxford's return I am glad to hear. I trust the little journey will
> make him love home the better hereafter. It were a great pity he should not go
> straight, there be so many good things in him, to serve God and his Prince.

If Oxford saw the letter he must have hurled something across the room.

The letter does tell us that by July 27th, when it was dated, he was back
in England. We know, too, that Burghley and Lady Oxford had met the
errant, and surely unrepentant, son-in-law and husband in London and that

all three had repaired to Theobalds. There, within a few days, encouraging news arrived as to the Queen's attitude. On August 1st Walsingham wrote to Burghley from the Court, then at Woodstock, — and one speculates that he had escorted the Earl back across the Channel —

> I find her Majesty graciously enough inclined towards the Earl of Oxford, whose peace I think will be both easily and speedily made, for that Her Majesty doth conceive that his evidence in his return hath fully satisfied the contempt of his departure. And the rather through his honourable and dutiful carriage of himself towards the rebels and other undutiful subjects of Her Majesty in that country — an argument of his approved loyalty which, as opportunity shall serve, I shall not fail to lay before Her Majesty by acquainting her with your L. letters.

It is evident that his "L. letters" had served whatever purpose needed to be served, but Polonius-Burghley was not one lightly to conclude that any subject had benefitted sufficiently from his prolixity. Walsingham's reassurances prompted an immediate and lengthy response. Burghley wrote from Theobalds on August 3rd:

> Sir, Yesternight your letters came to Master Benigfeld [presumably Bedingfield] and me signifying Her Majesty's pleasure that my Lord of Oxford should come to Gloucester now at Her Majesty's being there. Whereof he being advertised by us was very ready to take the journey, showing in himself a mixture of contrary affections, although both reasonable and commendable. The one, fearful and doubtful in what sort he shall recover Her Majesty's favour because of his offence in departure as he did without licence; the other, glad and resolute to look for a speedy good end because he had in his abode so notoriusly rejected the attempts of Her Majesty's evil subjects, and in his return set apart all his own particular desires of foreign travel and come to present himself before Her Majesty, of whose goodness towards him he saith he cannot count. Hereupon he and Master Benigfeld departed this afternoon to London, where the Earl, as I perceive, will spend only two days or less to make him some apparel meet for the Court, although I would have had him forbear that new charge, considering his former apparel is very sufficient, and he not provided to increase a new charge.

There are times when one sympathizes with Burghley, too.

> I must be bold by this my letter to require you in my name most humbly to beseech Her Majesty that she will regard his loyalty and not his lightness in sudden joy over his confidence in her goodness and clemency, and not his boldness in attempting that which hath offended her.

The letter goes on to speak of Oxford's rejection of the "devices" by "Her Majesty's enemies . . . to stay him from returning" and of the comfort he has given his friends. It warns that

> If he shall not find comfort now in this amendment of his fault, I fear the malice of some discontented persons, wherewith the Court is overmuch sprinkled, [may] set to draw him to a repentence rather of his dutifulness in thus returning
> . . . .

Most surprisingly, we read:

> I cannot well end, neither will I end, without also praying you to remember Master Hatton to continue my Lord's friend, as he hath manifestly been, and as my Lord confesseth to me that he hopeth assuredly so to prove him. . . .

That my Lord confessed any such thing is not to be believed. Burghley cannot have imagined that the relationship between Oxford and Hatton could be other than antagonistic. The approach to be made to the Captain of the Queen's Body-Guard smacks altogether of sycophancy toward a favorite who enjoyed an intimacy with the Queen that had ever been beyond possibility for Burghley and was designed to advance not Oxford's interests but the writer's.

The letter would lend some justification to Hamlet's denomination of Polonius as an "intruding fool," but it displays, too, some understanding of Oxford, as where the writer says:

> I think it is sound counsel to be given to Her Majesty that this young nobleman, being of such a quality as he is for birth, office, and other notable valours of body and spirit, he may not be discomforted either by an extraordinary delay or by any outward sharp or unkind reproof. . . .

The counsel conforms with what I think we may take to be Oxford's own appreciation of the handling he requires. This comes in King Henry IV's advice to his son Thomas on the treatment most likely to be fruitful with the youth's older brother, Prince Hal:

> Blunt not his love,
> Nor lose the good advantage of his grace
> By seeming cold, or careless of his will;
> For he is gracious, if he be observ'd;
> He hath a tear for pity, and a hand
> Open as day for melting charity.
> Yet notwithstanding, being incens'd, he's flint;
> As humorous as winter, and as sudden
> As flaws [thaws?] congealed in the spring of day.
> His temper, therefore, must be well observ'd.
> Chide him for faults, and do it reverently,
> When you perceive his blood inclin'd to mirth;
> But being moody, give him line and scope
> Till that his passions, like a whale on ground,
> Confound themselves with working.

One may speculate on Oxford's reception by the Queen but must be content with guesswork. (I imagine she was glad to see him.) The upshot is, however, known to us from a letter, most likely by Walsingham:

> . . . I am sure you are not inadvertised how the Earl of Oxford is restored to Her Majesty's favour, in whose loyal behavior towards Her Majesty's rebels in the Low Country who sought conference with him, a thing he utterly refused, did very much qualify his contempt in departing without Her Majesty's leave.

534

> The desire of travel is not yet quenched in him, though he dare not make any motion unto Her Majesty that he may with her favour accomplish the said desire. By no means he can be drawn to follow the court, and yet there are many cunning devices used in that behalf of his stay. . . .

In fact, Oxford evidently accompanied the royal progress for forty days. Three days before his return to Theobalds his wife wrote to the Earl of Sussex asking that her allotment of two chambers at Hampton Court be increased to three in anticipation of the Queen's return to the palace "for the more commodious my lodging is the willinger I hope my Lord my husband will be to come thither" — a rather touching request made more so by her bethinking herself to add "thereby the oftener to attend her Majesty." (As Lord Chamberlain, Sussex was responsible for quarters.)

The purpose of the scheme was achieved; the couple spent October at Hampton Court. The signs are that Oxford found little in Anne to hold his interest and that he felt out of his element at Court. To B. M. Ward it is clear that the Earl "preferred his 'new country Muses' and his 'lewd friends,' as Burghley called his literary companions," and the preference, if such it was, was to grow upon him. Ward believes, too, that it was at this time that Oxford wrote *the Famous Victories of Henry the Fift,* having it ready for the Court theatrical season when it opened at Christmas. It may well have been. The historical dramas we know as Shakespeare's draw on Holinshed's *Chronicles* for their version of events, but *The Famous Victories* draws on Hall's, of 1548, indicating that Holinshed's, published in 1578, was not available when it was written. Ward proposes that Oxford wrote it to show his contrition about running away and as a promise of improved behavior in the future, on the model of Prince Hal's reformation. But I doubt that he intended to behave differently (he behaved worse) and I see nothing of contrition in the play. Rather, there is cocky bravado in the greatly exaggerated prominence given the 11th Earl of Oxford, who without foundation of fact is made Henry IV's principal adviser and the chief architect of the victory of Agincourt. That Edward de Vere at twenty-four, the truant presenting himself to the Queen's Majesty not in the sackcloth of the penitent but in new finery purchased out of a deflated purse, knew the meaning of the word contrition I very much doubt.

We get a glimpse of him at this time in testimony given against him some years later. His enemy Charles Arundel recounts in all seriousness, evidently seeing nothing funny in it, an outrageous yarn of exploits on the Continent Oxford would spin as the tale of his own adventures when the spirit of conviviality was upon him. As Arundel began the account:

> At his being in Flanders, the Duke of Alva, as he will constantly affirm, grew so much to affect him for the several parts he saw in him, as he made him his Lieutenant General over all the army then in the Low Countries.

Needless to say, Oxford would not conceivably have taken command of any part of the notorious Spaniard's army even if the Duke had gone mad and offered it, but that was immaterial. In fact, Alva had departed from the Low Countries the year before Oxford got there. (Suffering disastrous reverses and pleading ill health, he had been recalled in December 1573, and, returning home, had "made the infamous boast that during the course of six years, besides the multitudes destroyed in battle and massacred after victory, he had consigned 18,000 persons to the executioner.") Oxford could never have met Alva unless he had actually made that clandestine trip in 1571 in Norfolk's behalf.

Oxford's story as it actually unwound will never be known, but in Arundel's version, tailored to turn his judges against the original author, we have the Earl claiming that "so valiantly he behaved himself as he gained great love of all the soldiers, and no less admiration of his valour of all sorts." In his advance against the enemy, it goes on, he captured "divers bridges . . . with the loss of many a man's life . . . till at last he approached the place they went to besiege." After ten days' battering by his cannon he

> had made such a breach as by a general consent of all his captains he gave an assault, and to encourage his soldiers this valiant prince led them thereto, and through the force of his murdering arm many were sore wounded, but more killed . . .

Inadequately supported, the charge failed

> but determining to give a fresh and general assault the next day Master Beningefeld, as the devil would have it, came in upon his swift post-horse, and called him from this service by Her Majesty's letters, being the greatest disgrace any such general received. And now the question is whether this noble gentleman were more troubled with his calling home —

and here I can imagine Oxford setting down his empty tankard with a thump and speaking the very words given him —

> or Beningefeld more moved with pity and compassion to behold this slaughter

(now in my mind the narrator, in exaggerated actor-style, which he knew so well, with one brow raised, the other lowered, cocks an eye at an upper corner of the room)

> or the horse more afeared when he passed the bridges at sight of the dead bodies.

Arundel names ten persons of repute who he says will bear out his report, as will "divers other gentlemen" who have dined with Oxford. "And," he concludes in righteous disapprobation,

> if in his soberest moods he would allow this, it may easily be gathered what will pass him in his cups.

I dare say, but I should like to have heard it all the same.

That Oxford was no stranger to the cups is most probable. No teetotaler could have written Falstaff's eulogy of "a good sherris sack." It, he says,

> ascends me into the brain; dries me there all the foolish and dull and crudy vapours which environ it; makes it apprehensive, quick, forgetive [inventive, creative], full of nimble, fiery, and delectable shapes; which delivered o'er to the voice, the tongue, which is their birth, becomes excellent wit.

And

> Hereof comes it that Prince Harry is valiant; for the cold blood he did naturally inherit of his father, he hath, like lean, sterile, and bare land, manured, husbanded, and till'd with excellent endeavor of drinking good store of fertile sherris. . . .

What a testimonial, to have been the nurture and spark of Shakespeare's genius! "Come, give's some sack!"

27

"Why, Then, the World's Mine Oyster"

1575–1576: The argument for foreign travel in Two Gentlemen of Verona *as probably recapitulating Oxford's pleas. — The Queen's withdrawal of her objections and his departure for the Continent with his retinue. — His stay in Paris; his presentation to the King; the reports made on his behavior to Burghley, as to Polonius on his son's. — His glad reception of the news of his wife's pregnancy. — His stalling off of his creditors at home. — His journey to Strasbourg and conversations there with the Protestant leader and educator, Sturmius. — His crossing of the Alps into Italy and start on just such an itinerary as would be attributed to the author of Shakespeare's Italian plays, which afford quotations reflecting the successive stages of his travels. — His visits to Padua, Venice, Genoa, presumably Verona, then Venice again. — His injury, illness and temporary surfeit with Italy. — His return to Padua and request of Burghley that more of his lands be sold (vide Timon and Jaques) and thanks for the news of his wife's safe delivery. — His continued financial straits as he moved on to Florence. — His determination, evidently despite Burghley's wishes, to continue his travels in default of prospects in her Majesty's service. — The parody by a stock character in the Commedia dell' Arte of his participation in a mythical, glittering tournament, jousting with the "Countess of Edenburg." — His broadcast in Palermo of a challenge to all comers to a trial of arms. — The further wildly tall tales for which his Italian travels provide material. — His northward passage through Lyons en route to Paris after a two-month gap in the record. — The self-mockery in* All's Well *of the Italianate ways he is bringing back. — The gifts for the Queen he is also bringing back, along with something much more important.*

All this time, we may be sure, the young lord was consumed by thoughts of travel. He would have seen himself (as he would write in *Two Gentlemen of Verona*) as one decreed by his surrogate father

> to spend his youth at home,
> While other men of slender reputation
> Put forth their sons to seek preferment out;

(i.e., Philip Sidney's father); perhaps looked to Sussex to urge Burghley

> To let him spend his time no more at home,
> Which would be great impeachment at his age,
> In having known no travel in his youth;

and sought to insinuate into his father-in-law's mind how he should address the Queen:

I have considered well his loss of time,
And how he cannot be a perfect man,
Not being tried and tutor'd in the world.

At length, it being apparent that the young man's craving could no longer be gainsaid, the words or their equivalent must have been spoken by Burghley. The Queen's consent to the royal ward's Grand Tour was certainly obtained. Some time in 1575, presumably at the start of the year, Oxford entailed his estates

> for the preservation of the ancient "name of the Veers, whereof he is lineally descended, in alliance and kindred with most of the ancient nobility of this realm, and in the good will and good liking of the commonality of the same realm."

This meant that, upon Oxford's death, the de Vere holdings would remain under the family name, in the Earldom of Oxford, passing through a male heir of his grandfather's. Special provision appears to have been made for his cousins, Francis and Horace Vere, whom Oxford seems especially to have esteemed. Without the entail, the lands would have gone to the descendants of Edward's sister, Mary, and — so it would develop — into the Willoughby family, which fifty years hence would try to wrest the Earldom from Edward's heir. Other preparations for the trip included codification of the Earl's considerable debts and financial arrangements.

Oxford and his retinue set out from London on January 7th — on travels that would transform his outlook and (unless I am much misled) prove more consequential for literature than any since Odysseus hoisted sail. It is the gauge of his impatience that he must embark on the heaving waters of the Channel in the season of vilest weather — "On toward Calais, ho!" — and essay on horseback the strange and rutted roads of France in the rawest cold of the year when the days were two-thirds darkness. Still, it must have been a gay party, buoyant with the sense of adventure, fetching new and unpredictable scenes around every bend, warming up with mulled wine at a roadside hostelry, trying their French on the serving girls and probably carousing in the long evenings.

With him Oxford had — so Burghley noted for his records — "two gentlemen, two grooms, one payend, a harbinger, a housekeeper, and a trencherman." It strikes us as a veritable expedition, but for a nobleman to have traveled less well accompanied would have been not *de rigueur* as well as impractical and perhaps unsafe. Grooms were of course to care for the party's mounts. The payend was presumably the disburser and the trencherman a cook or caterer. The harbinger would have gone on ahead to arrange accommodations and the housekeeper have entered on his duties when the Earl took up fixed quarters for long enough to escape the discomforts of an inn. One of the members, according to John Aubrey, whose word we may take or leave, was Nicholas Hill, who "was so eminent for knowledge that he was the favorite of . . . the great earle of Oxford, who had him to accompany him in his travels (he was his steward). . . ." Hill, who wrote a work on philosophy, is indeed reported to have been a secretary to "the poetical and prodigal Earl of Oxford," as Anthony à Wood had it.

The gentlemen companions Oxford had with him evidently varied in the course of his travels. One with whom he started, a William Lewyn, was described by the English ambassador in Paris as "a Raphael, . . . both discreet and of good years, and one that my Lord [Oxford] doth respect."

Eva Turner Clark surmises that the travelers, proceeding south from Calais, would have picked a route through the ancient cities of Abbeville, Amiens and Beauvais, partly for their historic interest and partly for the amenities they offered compared with rural caravanserais. The 180 miles would probably have taken as much as ten days, as she says. That would most likely have put them in Paris by the end of the month, which would make their stay there at least six weeks.

Writing of the French capital in 1560, Michel de Castelnau praised the "splendor of its parlement" whose members "have reputation in all Christendom of being the best seen in human laws," as for "its faculty of theology and for the other tongues and sciences, which shine more in this town than in any other in the world, besides the mechanic arts and the marvellous traffic which render it very populous, rich and opulent." No doubt it exacted from the English visitors the same tribute of awe and enchantment it has on most of those who have followed them. The Louvre was then under construction. The reigning monarch, Henry III, whose two brothers had ruled successively from its expanding apartments, found Paris insalubrious under the sway of his Guise uncles and spent nearly all his time in Blois. There, probably, was where Oxford was presented to him and the Queen by the English ambassador, who reported to Burghley having done so on March 7th with the information that the royal couple "used him honourably." From this account we learn of the King's asking if Oxford were married and upon being assured that "he had a fair lady," remarking, "There, then, is a handsome (*beau*) couple." On March 12th the Venetian Ambassador reported to the Doge that

> . . . An English gentleman whose name is the Earl of Oxford has arrived in this city; he is a young man of about 20 or 22 [actually nearly 25]. It is said that he fled from England on account of his inclination to the Catholic religion; but having returned he received great favor from the Queen, who gave him full licence to travel and see the world when she ascertained that he had resolved to depart under any circumstances.

To learn what was being said is interesting.

By March 14th Oxford was ready to leave Paris. On that day the Ambassador wrote Burghley that he had "all passports and commissions for post-horses and letters . . . that he would require." Among these were letters from the Venetian Ambassador in Paris "both unto the State and unto the Ambassador's particular friends." And he inserts a comment indicating that Burghley has asked him to report on the Earl's conduct, as Polonius has his son's reported on in Paris: "indeed he was well liked of and governed himself very honorably while he was here." The better to set tongues to wagging about his son's behavior, Polonius instructs his spy to

> put on him
> What forgeries you please; marry, none so rank
> As may dishonour him — take heed of that;
> But, sir, such wanton, wild and usual slips
> As are companions noted and most known
> To youth and liberty.

Burghley had evidently been up to that game, for the Ambassador returned to the subject after the Earl's departure, protesting that

> I will assure your Lordship unfeignedly my Lord of Oxford used himself as orderly and moderately as might be desired, and with great commendation, neither is there any appearance of the likelihood of any other.

These were judgments that the Ambassador would never have thought to or have dared to volunteer or to have rendered without prompting from the highest level. Oxford must have had to exert self-control to avoid betraying contempt for his father-in-law.

Now came rousing news from that quarter: Lady Oxford was with child. Only it was not enough for Burghley to convey it; he must use it to try to euchre the husband into abandoning his pursuit of the treasures of Europe, on which his heart had long been fervently set and of which he had scarcely yet tasted, and come scurrying home. The father-to-be found in the event all the more reason to do the opposite. He replied on March 17th:

> My Lord, Your letters have made me a glad man, for these last have put me in assurance of that good fortune which you formerly mentioned doubtfully. I thank God therefore, with your Lordship, that it hath pleased Him to make me a father, where your Lordship is a grandfather; and if it be a boy I shall likewise be the partaker with you in a greater contentation. But thereby to take an occasion to return I am off from that opinion; for now it hath pleased God to give me a son of my own (as I hope it is) methinks I have the better occasion to travel, with whatsoever becometh of me I leave behind me one to supply my duty and service, either to my Prince or else my country.

It must say something of the marriage that Oxford received the tidings of his wife's pregnancy not from the lady but from her father. After thanking the latter for sending money, the writer continues:

> For fear of the inquisition I dare not pass by Milan, the bishop whereof exerciseth such tyranny; wherefor I take my way of Germany, where I mean to acquaint myself with Sturmius, with whom — after I have passed my journey which I now have in hand — I mean to pass some time.

After enlarging upon the connections that have been made for him in Venice, he says that

> if the Turks come — as they be looked for — upon the coasts of Italy or elsewhere, if I may I will see the service; if he cometh not, then perhaps I shall bestow two or three months to see Constantinople, and some part of Greece.

(In any case: "Father, and wife, and gentlemen, adieu; / I will to Venice," as Petruchio would exclaim.) Like Bertram in *All's Well,* Oxford left Paris in the hope of seeing military service in Italy. It was possible that he would. Since the defeat of the Turks at Lepanto in 1571 by a Spanish-Italian fleet (including also, it is believed, Sir Richard Grenville of Tennyson's *The Revenge*) four years earlier, the Grand Vizier had rebuilt the Ottoman navy, which was ravaging the coast of Sicily. Incidentally, Amurath III had only the year before ensured his succession to the Turkish throne by having his five brothers strangled, and in the play *King Henry the Fourth, Part Two,* the dramatist remembers and has Prince Hal dispel his brothers' fears of his succession with the lines

> This is the English, not the Turkish Court;
> Not Amurath an Amurath succeeds,
> But Harry Harry.

In his letter to Burghley Oxford transmits, persuasively, the English Ambassador's plea for deliverance from the financial straits into which his necessary expenses have driven him; the Earl ought to know! Then he turns to the problem of his own indebtedness. He would let

> my creditors bear with me a while, . . . [for] in a strange country, [I am] unknowing yet what need I may have of money myself. My revenue is appointed, with the profits of my lands, to pay them as I may; and if I cannot yet pay them as I would, yet as I can I will, but preferring my own necessity before theirs. And if at the end of my travels I shall have something left of my provision, they shall have it among them, but before I will not defurnish myself. Good my Lord, have an eye unto my men that I have put in trust. Thus making my commendations to your Lordship and my Lady, I commit you to God.

Johannes Sturm — Sturmius — was a German scholar then nearing seventy, the founder and for forty years the director of the Strasbourg Gymnasium, and a powerful influence on education in Europe. That Oxford would put himself out as he did for the sake of holding converse with him should lay to rest the picture of the Earl as a light-headed fop — though the image may be one he himself partly fostered in order to be let alone to pursue his serious interests.

The Alsatian capital lay almost 300 miles to the east. Probably the party, now reduced in number to the minimum, traveled mostly along the Marne, and doubtless as much as possible by boat. In any case the trip would have taken more than two weeks. But with spring stealing across the fields of Champagne and up the slopes of the Vosges it cannot have been all hardship. It is pleasant to think of Shakespeare's having made a pilgrimage to the supposed site of Gutenberg's invention of the printing-press; and the talks when he got there must have gone well, for the Earl remained in Strasbourg until April 26th. Lewyn later wrote to Sturm that Oxford "had a most high opinion of you, and had made the most honourable mention of you." Two years later Sturm remarked in a letter to Burghley, "As I write I think of the Earl of Oxford, and his Lady too understands Latin, I think." (That must be the language in which they conversed.) And the year before his death, when the Protestant North stood in dire peril from the Spanish legions and the German sage appealed to England for a commander to lead in its defense, Oxford would be his first choice.

Rather curiously, the Earl's path and Philip Sidney's, leading back to England, may have crossed in Strasbourg, for it seems to have been here that Oxford's retinue acquired Ralph Hopton, son of the Lieutenant of the Tower of London.

On April 26th, four days after Oxford's twenty-fifth birthday, the party left Strasbourg. The chances are it traveled southward up the Rhine by boat to Basel, where the river turns east, and perhaps was able to continue by boat most of the way to Lake Constance. There boats would have awaited the wayfarers again to spare them another two days in the saddle.

The necessity of avoiding the Duchy of Milan would have kept them continuing eastward along the northern border of Switzerland. They must have turned south to cross the Alps via the Reschen-Scheidek Pass or, going on to Innsbruck, by the better known Brenner Pass. Either way they may have had to battle snowstorms. Certainly they would have had snow-capped peaks rising around them — "the frozen ridges of the Alps." Here the future dramatist would have observed how white is the shroud of mountain snow, of which Ophelia would sing. He would have seen "far-off mountains turnèd into clouds" and others to make him think later of how it was to "stand firm as rocky mountains." He would have taken in with a poet's eye and heart how "jocund day / Stands on the misty mountain tops" and perhaps have felt "free as the mountain winds."

Whichever way the travelers essayed they would have descended the Adige River into Italy. I see them turning east from it at Trento for the Piave, which this time would not have "*murmuro, 'Non passa lo straniero!'*" but have welcomed the newcomers with the sight of orchards and vineyards and flowers blooming in the blessed sun. As E. T. Clark says, one can imagine Oxford spurring on his companions:

> And use thou all the endeavour of a man
> In speed for Padua.

And now the goal was at hand.

> . . . Since for the great desire I had
> To see fair Padua, nursery of the arts,
> I am arriv'd for fruitful Lombardy,
> The pleasant garden of great Italy;
> Here let us breathe, and haply institute
> A course of learning and ingenious studies.

Padua, in the Republic of Venice (which then extended across half of northern Italy), was famous for its university, founded by Frederick II, Holy Roman Emperor and perhaps the first modern man, in 1238, since when it had attracted not only Galileo but leading painters. Whether lectures were given in Latin or Italian, Oxford would have understood them, and undoubtedly he attended many. "For I have Pisa left," Lucentio in *The Taming of the Shrew* continues in the speech quoted above,

> And am to Padua come, as he that leaves
> A shallow plash to plunge him in the deep,
> And with satiety seeks to quench his thirst.

Probably it was the way Oxford felt in exchanging a lately barbaric England for the land from which Rome had ruled the world of antiquity, still in men's minds the supreme exemplar of civilization, and where a rediscovery of the potentialities of man's mind and spirit had carried the arts to new heights. The thirst for those deep waters, which he had long quaffed in imagination, he now would quench by drinking them to surfeit.

How long he remained in Padua we do not know. Uncertain information comes from William Lewyn, who had become detached from the Earl's party. In July, six months out of England, he wrote to Burghley that he did not know whether Lord Oxford had left for Greece or was still in Italy, but having heard of an English nobleman who was in Venice with a companion who had been with Philip Sidney, he thought they might be the Earl and Ralph Hopton. Oxford and his party had gone from Padua to Genoa, probably traveling up the valley of the Po, between Italy's two great mountain ranges

> . . . talking of the Alps and Apennines,
> The Pyrenean and the River Po.

Before summer's end they were on their way back. This may have been the time Oxford came to know the home of the *Two Gentlemen* and of the Montagues and Capulets.

> Verona, for a while I take my leave
> To see my friends in Padua.

On September 23rd a banker in Venice to whom funds for the Earl had been consigned, wrote a letter to Burghley about his son-in-law in which he said

> At this present your honour shall understand my Lord's better disposition, God be thanked, for now last coming from Genoa his Lordship found himself somewhat altered by the reason of the extreme heats; and before his Lordship hurt his knee in one of the Venetian galleys, but all is past without further harm.

Not to distress his powerful patron, the banker was evidently making light of the Earl's afflictions. Judging from a letter the victim himself wrote to his father-in-law the next day, September 24th, he had been severely stricken.

> My good Lord, Having looked for your Lordship's letters a great while, at length when I grew to despair of them, I received two packets from your Lordship. Three packets, which at sundry times I had sent this summer towards England returned back again, by reason of the plague being in the passages none were suffered to pass, but as they came were returned back; which I came not to the knowledge of till my return now to Venice, where I have been grieved with a fever; yet with the help of God now I have recovered the same, and am past the danger thereof, though brought very weak thereby, and hindered from a great deal of travel, which grieves me most seeing my time [is] not sufficient for my desire; for although I have seen so much as sufficeth me, yet would I fain have time to profit thereby.

He has seen enough in more than eight concentrated months but *would fain have time to profit thereby.* A writer will recognize the need to digest, order and assimilate a flood of impressions if they are to serve his ends. Moreover, he is travel-worn and seems to be suffering the revulsion known to all who have been on the go too long and been taken ill. The summer heat of Lombardy must have been prostrating to an Englishman who had never known its like, and the filth and smells pullulating in the inferno would have overpowered Shakespearean sensibilities.

> Your Lordship seems desirous to know how I like Italy, what is mine intention in travel, and when I mean to return. For my liking of Italy, my Lord, I am glad to have seen it, and I care not ever to see it any more, unless it be to serve my Prince and country. For mine intention to travel, I am desirous to see more of Germany, wherefore I shall desire your Lordship, with my Lord of Leicester, to procure me the next summer to continue my licence, at the end of which I mean undoubtedly to return. I thought to have seen Spain, but by Italy I guess the worst. . . . If this sickness had not happened unto me, which hath taken away this chiefest time of travel at this present, I should not have written for further leave, but to supply the which I doubt not Her Majesty will not deny me so small a favour.

So much for that. Now we come to the nub of the letter, as of so many from Oxford to Burghley.

> By reason of my great charges of travel and sickness have taken up of Master Baptista Nigrone 500 crowns, which I shall desire your Lordship to see them repaid, hoping by this time my money which is made of the sale of my land is all come in.

Rosalind in *As You Like It* will exclaim to Jaques, the melancholy side of Oxford:

> A traveller! By my faith, you have great reason to be sad. I fear you have sold
> your own lands to see other men's; then, to have seen much and to have nothing,
> is to have rich eyes and poor hands.

And Jaques will ruefully concur.

> Yes, I have gained my experience.

The "five hundred crowns" provided by Nigrone for Oxford's travels, by
the way, reminds us of the "five hundred crowns" provided by Adam for his
and Orlando's, also in *As You Like It*.

Oxford has one more thought. A lease-holder of his has joined the "Romish
Church" and been making "lewd speeches against the Queen's Majesty,"
also dealing "hardly" with the Earl's tenants; he asks that the lease be
reassigned to "my Lord of Bedford." Then he ends:

> Thus thanking your Lordship for the good news of my wife's delivery, I rec-
> ommend myself unto your favor. . . .

Was that his first and only acknowledgement of the word he had had from
Burghley of the Countess's having given birth to a daughter? If so, it would
show how far from his past and its connections at home his travels had taken
him, and how remote a place Anne occupied in his heart and thoughts.

That this is not necessarily the case there is some evidence in the form of
a poem said to have been copied from the flyleaf of a Greek Testament once
owned by Lady Oxford. Consisting of ten lines of Latin verse, it is addressed
"To the illustrious Lady Anne de Vere, Countess of Oxford, while her noble
husband, Edward Vere, Earl of Oxford, was occupied in foreign travel."
Ward says that the poem, which is mainly a series of puns on the words *Vere*
and *veritas,* may be translated as follows:

> Words of truth are fitting to a Vere; lies are foreign to the truth, and only
> true things stand fast, all else is fluctuating and comes to an end. Therefore,
> since thou, a Vere, art wife and mother of a Vere daughter, and seeing that thou
> mayest with good hope look forward to being mother of an heir of the Veres,
> may thy mind always glow with love of the truth, and may thy true motto be
> *Ever Lover of the Truth.* And that thou mayest the better attain to this, pray to
> the Author of all Truth that His Word may teach thee; that his spirit may
> nourish thy inner life. So that, thus alleviating the absent longing of thy dear
> husband, thou, a Vere, mayest be called the true glory of thy husband.

Even if the husband wrote the poem, however, its tone of admonition and
instruction can hardly have brought great comfort to the forsaken young
mother (which, however, bearing in mind how Ophelia lent herself to her
father's deceit, is not to say that she was not asking for a reminder of the
virtue of truth). We cannot say, however, that Oxford was not writing
affectionate letters to his wife all this time, only that none of any kind exists
today.

Chapter 27: Why, Then, the World's Mine Oyster

By November 24th the traveler was back in Padua, writing Burghley about the perennial problem:

> . . . Remembering my commendations to your good Lordship, these shall be to desire you to pardon the shortness of my letter, and to impute it at this present to the haste of the messenger's departure. And as concerning mine own matters, I shall desire your Lordship to make no stay of the sales of my land. . . .

Recalling that the needy young traveler had borrowed 500 crowns of *Baptista* Nigrone we are interested to learn that he now received a remittance through a Pasquino *Spinola*; for we are reminded that the rich gentleman of Padua whose daughter, Katherine, the Shrew, Petruchio will tame, is *Baptista Minola,* whose "crowns" are repeatedly mentioned. This is another of those connectives that a Stratfordian would be elated to discover between Shakspere and one of the plays.

On December 12th, says Ward, the day after receiving a remittance through Pasquino Spinola in Venice, Oxford was off for Florence.

> Towards Florence, is he? (*All's Well.*)

From Venice the trip over the Apennines would have taken eight or nine days, and more by the main route east through Verona.

> He's now in Florence. (*Othello.*)

He cannot have remained long at the seat of the Medicis, for by January 3rd he has ridden the 25 miles south to Siena and is writing a depressed letter to his father-in-law. Siena had lost a war to Florence twenty years before and thus been incorporated in the Grand Duchy of Tuscany; and the author of *All's Well* would remember the conflict when he had the King of France address his restless young courtiers:

> The Florentines and Senoys are by the ears; . . .
> Yet, for our gentlemen that mean to see
> The Tuscan service, freely have they leave
> To stand on either part.

That was the chivalric view of war, by the way. What mattered was how you fought, not which side you fought on.

When he sat down to unburden himself to Burghley, Oxford must have felt that, like Antonio in *The Merchant of Venice,* he was going to indite "the unpleasant'st words / That ever blotted paper"; and the words would in fact be of the same tenor as Antonio's confession that "my creditors grow cruel, my estate is very low."

> My Lord, I am sorry to hear how hard my fortune is in England, as I perceive by your Lordship's letters; but knowing how vain a thing it is to linger a necessary mischief — to know the worst of myself, and to let your Lordship understand wherein I would use your honourable friendship — in short, I have thus determined. That, whereas I understand the greatness of my debt and

> greediness of my creditors grows so dishonourable and troublesome to your Lordship, that that land of mine which in Cornwall I have appointed to be sold, according to that first order for mine expenses in this travel, be gone through and withal. And to stop my creditor's exclamations — or rather defamations I may call them — I shall desire your Lordship by virtue of this letter, which doth not err, as I take it, from any former purpose — which was that always upon my letter to authorize your Lordship to sell any portion of my land that you will sell more of my land where your Lordship shall think fittest, to disburden me of my debts to Her Majesty, my sister, or elsewhere I am exclaimed upon.

After some further requests of that nature, he continues:

> In doing these things your Lordship shall greatly pleasure me, in not doing them you shall as much hinder me; for although to part with land your Lordship hath advised to the contrary, and that your Lordship for the good affection you bear unto me could not wish it otherwise, yet you see I have no other remedies, I have no help but mine own, and mine is made to serve me and myself, not mine.

That was pretty cool. The consideration will be somewhat tempered when it recurs in *Timon of Athens*: "I must serve my turn / Out of mine own." His situation when he wrote Burghley from Siena and had no desire to be reminded of the advice not to sell his land a situation will come back to him elsewhere in the play.

> Immediate are my needs, and my relief
> Must not be toss'd and turn'd to me in words
> But find supply immediate.

Despite his financial embarrassments he is

> determined to continue my travel, the which thing in no wise I desire your Lordship to hinder, unless you have it thus: *ut nulla sit inter nos amicitia*. For having made an end of all hope to help myself by Her Majesty's service — considering that my youth is objected unto me, and for every step of mine a block is found to be laid in my way — I see it is but vain *calcitrare contra lit busse*; and the worst of things being known, they are the more easier to be provided for to bear and support them with patience.

We recall that Bertram's youth is objected unto him, too: "too young," he complains bitterly. And of course no one could have put his cause to the Queen more persuasively than her Lord Treasurer.

> That I am determined to hope for anything, I do not; but if anything do happen *preter spem*, I think before that time I must be [so] old [that] my son must give the thanks; and I am to content myself according to the English proverb that it is my hap to starve while the grass doth grow.

Hamlet will remember the proverb — which the dramatist would seem to recall having used ten years before — when Rosencranz reminds him of the advancement that will be his in time:

> As, Sir, but "while the grass grows" — the proverb is something musty.

The letter ends with a genuine-sounding sadness:

> Thus I leave your Lordship to the protection of Almighty God, whom I beseech to send you long and happy life, and better fortune to define your felicity in these your aged years than it hath pleased time to grant in my youth. But of a hard beginning we may expect a good and easy ending. Your Lordship's to command during life. The 3rd of January from Siena.
>
> Edward Oxeford.

Burghley, at fifty-four, must have appreciated the reference to his "aged years." He had nearly a quarter-century of active service to the Queen ahead of him.

That Oxford was acquainted with despondency even in his twenties is certain. But I think the prevailingly anxious and depressed tone of his letters to Burghley need not cause us to feel similarly on his account. If he were not enjoying himself he would not have protracted his travels at the risk of royal displeasure.[1] The two and only vignettes of him that have come down to us, both quite fortuitously, of his Italian days show him getting along famously, in both senses of the word.

The first was discovered by Julia Cooley Altrocchi in a book published in Naples in 1699, written by Andrea Perrucci and called *Dell' Arte Rappresentative Premeditata ed all' improviso (Dramatic Art by Rote and Extemporaneous)*. Mrs. Altrocchi writes:

> The extemporaneous portion treats, of course, of the *Commedia dell' Arte*. A long section of this is devoted to the stock character of Graziano, the talkative Bolognese doctor who tells long tales and never stops for breath. One of his famous recitals is the so-called Tirade of the Tournament (*Tirata della Giostra*) in which the actor rattles off the names of 20 or 30 knights and ladies, their titles and countries of origin, the color and trappings of their horses, the color and devices of their garments and shields and the events that befell each one on the field of tourney, for even the ladies took part in this hypothetical tournament. Perrucci proceeds to quote a typical Tirata: "I found myself ambassador of my illustrious country of Bologna at the court of the Emperor Polidor of Trebizond," spiels off the worthy doctor, "and attending the great tournament celebrating his marriage to Irene, Empress of Constantinople. Present were many great worthies, Basil, King of Zelconda, Doralba, Princess of Dacia, Arcont, vaivode of Moldavia, Arsileus, heir of Denmark, Isuf, pasha of Aleppo, Fatima, Sultan of Persia, Elmond, milord of Oxford," etc., etc.
>
> The horse of Milord of Oxford is faun-colored and goes by the name of Oltramarin (Beyond-the-Sea). Edward carries a large sword (*spadone*). His color of costume is violet. He carries for device a falcon with a motto taken from

---

[1] A report in the State Archives of Venice cited by Logan Pearsall Smith even has him setting a precedent for future generations of English writers by planning a second home in Italy. It is recorded that in 1627 Henry Wotton presented Henry de Vere the 18th Earl of Oxford to the Doge with the remark that the visitor's father "when he arrived in Venice, took no trouble to see the rest of the country, but stopped here, and even built himself a house." How much credence should be placed in this at least partially erroneous document it is difficult to say.

Terence: *Tendit in ardua virtus* (Valor proceeds to arduous undertakings).

In this Tirata, Milord of Oxford, amusingly enough, tilted against Alvida, countess of Edenburg, who was mounted on a dapple grey, was armed with a Frankish lance and was robed in lemon color. In the end, Edward and Alvida, alas, threw one another simultaneously, both landing face down in the dust!

Nevertheless, Emperor Polidor awarded to all the knights and amazons gifts out of the cupboard of antiquity. To Elmond — Edward — was given the horn of Astolf, paladin of Charlemagne, the magic horn to rout armies — a spear of sorts to shake, with enchanted consequences.

To Mrs. Altrocchi it signifies that Oxford

was well and very companionably known at the performances of the *Commedia dell' Arte* and that he was recognized as being not only so good a sportsman but so good a sport and possessed of so resilient a sense of humor that he could be introduced into a skit and, with impunity, described as meeting a woman in tilt and being unhorsed and rolled to the ground with her in the encounter! One can see him sitting in the performance-room at the Doge's Palace, or at the theatre, and hear him roaring during this recital of the Tirade of the Tournament, delivered hilariously in the stage-doctor's Bolognese dialect!

George Lyman Kittredge of Harvard says of *Love's Labour's Lost*:

The influence of the Italian *commedia dell' arte* is visible throughout the play. Several of the characters correspond to standard figures of the Italian convention: Armado to the bragging soldier (a lineal descendant of Pyrgopolynices of the *Miles Gloriosus* of Plautus); Moth to the zanni who regularly accompanies the braggart; Holofernes to the pedant; Nathaniel to the parasite; Costard to the rustic. Armado is styled "Braggart" and Holofernes "Pedant" in stage directions.

Richard David draws the same comparisons in the Arden Shakespeare, among them, Armado with Capitano Spavento del Vall' Inferno and Holofernes with "the pedant, Doctor Graziano" — the same Bolognese who recited the Tirade of the Tournament in which Oxford appeared.

The other vignette of Oxford in Italy has him in Palermo, in Sicily, and supplies the only information we have of his whereabouts during a period of three months. He could in that time have gone even farther, through the Straits of Messina and on to fulfill his hope of seeing Greece; the pagan magic of *A Midsummer-Night's Dream* could be the tribute of a remembrance.

To begin with, he may have gone from Siena down the Tiber to Rome — have seen "new-planted orchards / On this side Tiber" and upon a "gusty day / The troubled Tiber chafing with her shores." He would hardly have foregone the immortal city, in which tradition placed his ancestors, as George Chapman recognized in saying of Oxford that

> He had a face
> Like one of the most ancient honour'd Romans
> From whence his noble family was derived . . .

He may have stood before the ruins of the memorial to those who at Philippi wrought vengeance upon Caesar's murderers and, with the monuments of the Roman past around him, have found that Caesar was "mighty yet" and no more to be escaped by the dramatist he would become than Brutus by his spirit that "walks abroad."

Bound for Palermo from Rome, Oxford would most likely have elected to go by ship, and his ship would almost certainly have called at Naples. As Prospero tells his daughter, it was the King of Naples, "being an enemy / To me inveterate," who conspired with his wicked brother to have him cast adrift at sea and a "noble Neapolitan, Gonzalo," who rescued and provisioned him; the voyagers whose vessel Ariel has storm-driven to the magic island were bound "home for Naples," and in the end Prospero leaves it to the audience whether he "must be here confin'd by you, / Or sent to Naples." Citing Cowden-Clarke's statement that "The Neapolitans have a singularly drawling nasal twang in the utterance of their dialect," E. T. Clark comments that in *Othello* the dramatist has the Clown say to Cassio and the Musicians, "Why, masters, have your instruments been in Naples, that they speak i' th' nose thus?"

It was by great good fortune that a senior English army officer happened to be in Sicily at the time of Oxford's visit and should have published his recollections, as he did in 1590 in *The Travels of Edward Webbe.* In this he recalled the

> Many things I have omitted to speak of, which I have seen and noted in the time of my troublesome travel. One thing did greatly comfort me which I saw long since in Sicily, in the city of Palermo, a thing worthy of memory, where the Right Honourable the Earl of Oxford, a famous man of chivalry, at what time he travelled in foreign countries, being then personally present, made there a challenge against all manner of persons whatsoever, and at all manner of weapons, as Tournaments, Barriers with horse and armour, to fight a combat with any whatsoever in the defence of his Prince and Country. For which he was very highly commended, and yet no man durst be so hardy to encounter with him, so that all Italy over he is acknowledged the only Chevalier and Nobleman of England. This title they give unto him as worthily deserved.

E. T. Clark raises a provocative question: "Was this challenge intended for Don John who had, only a short time before [July 1574], won a famous tournament at Piacenza?" Don John of Austria, illegitimate son of Emperor Charles V, had been born only five years before Oxford and been only two years older than Oxford was in Sicily when he commanded the allied fleets that defeated the Turks at Lepanto, destroying all but 40 of their 237 galleys and freeing 10 to 15 thousand Christian slaves at the oars. Since then his name had been magic.

> He was indeed the glass
> Wherein the noble youth did dress themselves.
> . . . .
> In military rules, humours of blood,
> He was the mark and glass, copy and book,
> That fashion'd others.

That could well have been written of Don John. It is, however, a tribute paid in *Henry IV, Part Two,* to Hotspur, whom Prince Hal in *Part One* had defeated in single combat at the battle of Shrewsbury to redeem himself in his sovereign's and all England's eyes. (Though the historic Hotspur was killed at Shrewsbury, it is not known by whom.) If it was Oxford's purpose to bring him to the field, Don John — saving himself, perhaps, to deal with the Protestants in the Low Countries a few years later as he had dealt with the Turks in the Gulf of Petras — was having none of it. "Let hot Ætna cool in Sicily," he might have said with Titus Andronicus' brother. The tourney would have been one for the books, as the Army saying is, for, as he was to demonstrate six years later, Oxford had lost none of his prowess in the lists. Gervase Markham presumably knew about Oxford's challenge to all comers and perhaps about feats of arms he actually brought off when he wrote about the Earl half a century later, speaking of the "blessed peace" that in the days of Elizabeth,

> did so fold and embrace our Kingdom about, that every valiant arm for want of employment, lay as it were manacled and fettered from the use of weapons; yet this nobleman breaks off his gyves [shackles], and both in Italy and France and other nations, did more honour to this kingdom than all that have traveled since he took his journey to heaven.

Markham — who, let it be admitted, did not make a fetish of understatement — might have been speaking for and about Bertram in *All's Well.*

It shakes one to think that we know of Oxford's splendid gesture at Palermo only because the obscure Edward Webbe happened to witness it. Equally we owe our knowledge of a whole rich side of Oxford's character to the extraneous circumstance that the villainous Charles Arundel sought his undoing; for Italy gave rise to another of the Earl's tall stories, preserved through his enemy's malice. One can tell how the narrator piled upon one claim another still more preposterous while baffled indignation fretted the humorless Arundel. I quote his auditor's accusation here because it has Oxford speaking as, I think, one who has had a gay and zestful time on his travels. Said Arundel:

> I have heard him often tell that at his being in Italy, there fell discord and disunion in the city of Genoa between two families; whereupon it grew to wars, and great aid and assistance [was] given to either party. And that for the fame that ran throughout Italy of his service done in the Low Countries under the Duke of Alva, he was chosen and made General of 30,000 that the Pope sent to the aid of one party; and that in this action he showed so great discretion and government as by his wisdom the matters were compounded, and an accord made; being more for his glory than if he had fought the battle.

As if that were not enough, the Earl regaled his listeners about

> certain excellent orations he made, as namely to the state of Venice, at Padua, at Bologna, and divers other places in Italy, and one which pleased him above

the rest [was] to his army, when he marched toward Genoa; which, when he
had pronounced it, he left nothing to reply, but everyone to wonder at his
judgment, being reputed for his eloquence another Cicero, and for his conduct
a Caesar.

The wonder of it is, of course, that the returned traveler would show in
Henry the Fifth that he *could* address an army with a "judgment" that can
seldom have been equalled in military history and that in eloquence he would
prove himself in fact another Cicero, and more. Meanwhile, he would have
sublimated the fantasy of the army command in Genoa into the similar
distinction won by his embodiment, Bertram; to the untried young Count,
freshly escaped from the Court to which he was ward and from an unwelcome marriage, the Duke of Florence proclaims:

> The General of our Horse thou art; and we,
> Great in our hope, lay our best love and credence
> Upon thy promising fortune.

Before that particular speech, or that version of Bertram's appointment, was
written, it is more than likely Oxford would himself be named General of
the Horse in the Low Countries — only to find himself, in short order, back
at the Court in London.

Apart from Webbe's report of the challenge in Palermo, we hear nothing
of Oxford between January 3rd, when he wrote from Siena, and March
(1576), when, on his way back to Paris, he was in Lyon. Probably he had
shipped from Palermo or Naples to "Marseilles, to which place / we have
convenient convoy" (*All's Well*) and where his vessel could have been among
"an argosy / That now is lying in Marseilles' road" (*Taming of the Shrew*).
Those in Lyon might have said he "comes by post from Marseilles" (*All's
Well*). His route would have lain up the Rhône. On the way he would have
found himself in Tournon within a day's ride of the Castle of Rousillon, seat
of Bertram's family. On March 31st the English Ambassador reported his
arrival in Paris, and three days later the Venetian Ambassador informed the
Doge (or Duke, as Oxford insisted on calling him both in his letters and in
Othello) that

> The Earl of Oxford, an English gentlemen, has arrived here. He has come
> from Venice, and according to what has been said to me by the English Ambas-
> sador here resident speaks in great praise of the numerous courtesies which he
> has received in that city; and he reports that on his departure from Venice your
> Serenity had already elected an Ambassador to be sent to the Queen, and the
> English Ambassador expressed the greatest satisfaction at the intelligence.

In a few days Oxford would receive news that would send him home in a
dreadful state of mind; but before getting into that sorriest phase of his life,
we might observe that the succession of Shakespearean plays laid in Italy
testify to the rich and productive impression the country made upon him. I
think he came back with head swimming with Italy, his thoughts irradiated

with Italy, while bearing as well the outward stamp of his foreign adventures. *Speculum Tuscanismi,* the "Mirror of Tuscanism," Gabriel Harvey would entitle a poem manifestly about Oxford. "After practice of Italy in one year," the subject will be seen with

> . . . not a look but Tuscanish always.
> His cringeing side neck, eyes glancing, fisnamie smirking,
> With forefinger kiss, and brave embrace to the footward.
> Large-bellied Kodpeasd doublet, unkodpeasd half hose,
> Straight to the dock like a shirt, and close to the britch like a
> diveling.
> A little Apish flat couched fast to the pate like an oyster. . . .

And in *All's Well* the dramatist would make fun of himself and his Italianate ways in similar words when, after Bertram and his companions have returned from Tuscany, he has the Clown exclaim to the Countess:

> O madam! younder's my lord your son with a patch of velvet on's face. . . .
> Faith, there's a dozen of 'em, with delicate fine hats and most courteous feathers,
> which bow the head and nod at every man.

(But Harvey would recognize the contradictions in Oxford and in the same poem report that there was

> Not the like discourser for Tongue, and head to be found out,
> Not the like resolute man for great and serious affairs.)

Stow records in his *Annals* that

> Milliners or haberdashers had not any gloves embroidered or trimmed with gold or silk, neither gold nor embroidered girdles and hangers, neither could they make any costly wash or perfume; until about the 14th or 15th year of the Queen the right honourable Edward de Vere, Earl of Oxford, came from Italy, and brought with him gloves, sweet bags, a perfumed leather jerkin, and other pleasant things; and that year the Queen had a pair of perfumed gloves trimmed only with four tufts, or roses of coloured silk; the Queen took such pleasure in those gloves that she was pictured with those gloves upon her hands, and for many years after it was called the Earl of Oxford's perfume.

But what Oxford brought back from his travels was, I think, not just the trappings of Italy but the spirit of the Renaissance.

28

"Look So Strange upon Your Wife?"

1576: The poisoning of Oxford's good spirits in Paris, evidently by rumors at home, retailed by his receiver, Yorke, that Anne's child is not his. — Burghley's demand for his quick return. — His capture and release by pirates in the Channel. — His refusal to see his wife. — Burghley's distracted, rambling letter to Elizabeth on the rupture, to be parodied, seemingly, in a speech of Polonius's to the Queen. — Oxford's icily angry letter to Burghley delivering his wife over to her parents. — Burghley's vain renewal of his pleas for a reconciliation two months later. — The testimony of Anne's physician of more than a year earlier of her woeful doubt that her husband would accept the child. — Yorke's unsavory character and the likely role of Oxford's cousin, the treacherous Henry Howard. — Oxford's probable confusion of mind. — Anne's inadequacy as his wife and her evident primary allegiance to her parents. — The seeming separation in Two Gentlemen *and* Measure for Measure *of the two sides of the dramatist's nature in separate characters and the betrayal by the worser in both plays of the young woman who loves and has trusted him; the theme in* Cymbeline, Winter's Tale, *and* Othello *of the husband who rejects in murderous rage a chaste and devoted wife whom on the flimsiest grounds he has condemned for infidelity (with Yorke a credible Iago) and is brought to bitter repentance. — The near-unanimous censure of Oxford today for pretending a case against Anne in order to free himself from her. — The very different version of events to which a scrutiny of the record leads, with Oxford having grounds for believing himself not in fact the child's father. — The question of how Oxford was eventually brought to exonerate his wife and accept the child, and the story, possibly true, possibly floated by Burghley and accepted by Oxford, that he had been tricked into lying with his wife under the impression she was another woman, as Bertram in* All's Well *and Angelo in* Measure for Measure *would be tricked into lying with theirs; the other possibility that Oxford after years simply forgave a much-abused wife. — The final treatment of their relationship, as it would appear, in Hamlet's and Ophelia's.*

When Oxford returned to Paris on March 31st he was in good spirits, as far as we know. His mood permitted him to enlarge, evidently with enthusiasm, upon the courtesies he had received in Venice. This the Venetian Ambassador learned from his English colleague and reported on April 3rd. The next day, according to notes made by Burghley on April 25th, a change came over him, which would have drastic and long-lasting consequences. Burghley wrote:

> No unkindness known on his part at his departure. She [Anne] made him privy that she thought she was with child, whereof he said he was glad. When

> he was certified thereof at Paris he sent her his picture with kind letters and
> messages. He sent her two coach horses. When he heard she was delivered he
> gave me thanks by his letters for advising thereof. He never signified any mislik-
> ing of anything until the 4th of April in Paris, from whence he wrote somewhat
> that, by reason of a man of his, his receiver, he had conceived some unkindness,
> but he prayed me let pass the same for it did grow by the doubleness of servants.

The "receiver" was Rowland Yorke, who had accompanied the Earl during
the past several months, and of whom more later.

We should have much preferred it had Burghley saved Oxford's letter
rather than his own memorandum. This goes on to state that "I wrote to
Paris to him to hasten him homeward." No reason is given for that instruction. However, Oxford did hasten him homeward. On the way, during the
crossing of the Channel, his ship was set upon and captured by Dutch pirates,
and according to the French Ambassador, writing on April 21st, he was
stripped to his shirt and escaped with his life only because a Scotsman had
recognized him. (It would be Hamlet's fate, too, that while bound for England
"a pirate of very warlike appointment gave us chase" and captured him,
though "they dealt with me like thieves of mercy" because "they knew what
they did.") This transgression, coming on top of other provocations by
Dutchmen, moved the Queen to send a special envoy to the Prince of Orange
to demand satisfaction. Burghley declared that "anger leadeth my judgment,"
for in "the person" of "my Lord of Oxford . . . surely her Majesty and the
realm have taken disgrace" while he himself "in the person of the Earl of
Oxford [was] interested [sic] with this outrage."

Burghley's expressions of fury, which would not be assuaged merely by
"the hanging of v or vj such thieves," read rather strangely in the light of
the Prince's passing over the episode with a promise to content the Earl and
the arrest of a single culprit. He certainly, in assessing his son-in-law's attitude, makes no mention of the nearly fatal experience he had had, though it
could hardly have failed to affect the state of mind in which he disembarked.
What the Lord Treasurer does say is that his son Thomas at his behest
traveled to Dover to meet the returning traveler and arrived "within two
hours after my Lord [Henry] Howard and others, and . . . carried my
commendations and his wife's, and did not understand from him any point
of misliking." He advised his daughter not to go meet her husband "until
she should understand his contentation" — how well satisfied he was. But
she was too impatient to await Thomas's answer and so, with "Lady Mary"
— presumably Lady Mary Vere, her sister-in-law — who had asked to
accompany her, went down to Gravesend (about a third of the way from
London to Dover) to hasten the reunion. Burghley reiterates that "all this
while I knew of no misliking towards me or his wife." It is a curious
disclaimer since he had advised Anne not to meet her husband until she knew
how the land lay. Of the further course of events, he wrote as follows:

Chapter 28: Look So Strange upon Your Wife?

I sent letters to entreat him to take my house for his lodging, whereof I had no answer, and yet I wrote twice by two several messengers. But my son sent me word that he found him disposed to keep himself secretly two or three days in his own lodging and yet that Edward Yorke told him secretly that his Lordship would come first to my house, but he would nobody knew thereof. Whereupon I was very glad but his wife gladder. And the contrary I knew not until he was landed and then my son told me how he did suddenly leave the barge and took a wherry and only with Rowland Yorke landed about Yorke's house.

Hereupon I sent to welcome him and with request to take a lodging in my house, but thereto he answered that he meant to keep himself secret in his lodgings two or three days and then he would speak with me. And the messenger did come from his wife with request that if he should not come that night to her father's house she would come to him, for she desired to be one of the first that might see him. To it he answered neither yea nor nay, but said, "why, I have answered you," meaning that he would keep himself secret two or three days, as the messenger took it. Whereupon I thought it convenient she would forbear to go to him until we might see how others were suffered to come to him or he to resort to others. Within two hours I heard by them that had been with him how many had been with him without any his misliking . . . and that there was a coach preparing for my lady his sister to come to him, which, being heard by my daughter she very importunately required me she might go to him. And yet I required her to stay until I might send to my Lord Howard from whom I would know whether he knew that my Lord her husband would go to Court. . . . My Lord Howard sent me word that he as yet could not tell.

On April 23rd, two days before setting down the recapitulation for the record that we have just read, Burghley had written the Queen a letter that in its merciless, repetitious wordiness reads like the very effusion parodied in Polonius's speech in Act II, Scene 2, of *Hamlet* — the one beginning

My liege, and madam, to expostulate
What majesty should be, what duty is,
Why day is day, night night, and time is time,
Were nothing but to waste night, day, and time.
Therefore, since brevity is the soul of wit,
And tediousness the limbs and outward flourishes,
I will be brief. Your noble son is mad.
Mad, call I it; for, to define true madness,
What is't but to be nothing else but mad?

Burghley's letter rambles like some rivers, through continuous eddies:

Most sovereign lady, as I was accustomed to from the beginning of my service to your Majesty until of late by the permission of your goodness and by occasion of the place wherein I serve your Majesty, to be frequently an intercessor for others to your Majesty, and therein did find your Majesty always inclinable to give me gracious audience; so now do I find in the latter end of my years a necessary occasion to be an intercessor for another next to myself, in a cause godly, honest and just; and therefore, having had proof of your Majesty for most favours in causes not so important, I doubt not but to find the like influence of your grace in a cause so near touching myself as your Majesty will conceive it doth. . . .

> To enter to trouble your Majesty with the circumstances of my cause, I mean
> not for sundry respects but chiefly for two; the one is that I am very loth to be
> more cumbersome to your Majesty than need shall compel me; —

Burghley will be no more cumbersome than Polonius would be tedious.

> — the other is for that I hope in God's goodness, and for reverence borne to
> your Majesty, that success thereof may have a better end than the beginning
> threateneth. But your Majesty may think my suit will be very long where I am
> so long ere I begin it; and truly, most gracious sovereign lady, it is true that the
> nature of my cause is such as I have no pleasure to enter into it, but had rather
> seek means to shut it up for them to lay it open, not for lack of the soundness
> thereof on my part, but·for the wickedness of others from whom the ground
> work proceedeth.

The Queen would have known what led her counterpart in *Hamlet* to urge,
"More matter, with less art."

> My suit therefore shall be presently to your Majesty but in general sort, that
> whereas I am, by God's visitation with some infirmity and yet not great, stayed
> from coming to do my duty to your Majesty at this time, and my daughter, the
> Countess of Oxford, also occasioned to her great grief to be absent from your
> Majesty's Court, and that the occasion of her absence may be diversely reported
> to your Majesty — because the ground and working thereupon toucheth me as
> nearly as any wordly cause in my concept can do —

The sentence runs to no fewer than 248 words. The writer protests that "old
worn servant that he is" he compares with the best of the others "for loyalty
and devotion," while his daughter could challenge any "in fervent admiration
of your graces." Whether "the cause betwixt my Lord of Oxford and her"
arise from his "misliking of me or misdeeming of hers" he says he cannot
guess.

New Sentence. He cannot imagine that he has done "anything offensive
to him" and avows he has "been as diligent for his causes" as he has "been
for my own." He calls upon "God and his Angels" to witness that "I did
never see in her behaviour in word or deed . . . but that she hath always
used herself honestly, chastely, and lovingly towards him." Indeed, "No
young lover rooted or sotted in love . . . could more excessively show" how
desirous she was of his return, and she went to him "with assurance to be
well used by him" only to miss "of her expectation."

As the letter goes on and on, the sense is almost lost in its involutions.
Finally it comes to the writer's "humble request," which seems to be that if
he has "offered" himself with "dishonesty," he "may have your Majesty's
princely favour to seek my just defence for me and mine," whatever that
may mean. The interminable plea is clearly that of a wordy man distracted
by anxiety.

We learn from a letter he received from his son-in-law sent four days later
— the first since his return to England — that Burghley had been writing

him seeking a *rapprochement*. Oxford's haughty rejection of the overture follows:

> My Lord, Although I have forborne in some respect, which should [be] private to myself, either to write or come unto your Lordship, yet had I determined, as opportunity should have served me, to have accomplished the same in compass of a few days. But now, urged thereto by your letters, to satisfy you the sooner, I must let your Lordship understand this much: that is, until I can better satisfy or advertise myself of some mislikes, I am not determined, as touching my wife, to accompany her. What they are — because some are not to be spoken of or written upon as imperfections — I will not deal withal. Some that otherwise discontented me I will not blaze or publish until it please me. And last of all, I mean not to weary my life any more with such troubles and molestations as I have endured; nor will I, to please your Lordship only, discontent myself.
>
> Wherefore — as your Lordship very well writeth unto me — that you mean, if it standeth with my liking, to receive her into your house, these are likewise to let your Lordship understand that it doth very well content me; for there, as your daughter or her mother's, more than my wife, you may take comfort of her; and I, rid of the cumber thereby, shall remain well eased of many griefs. I do not doubt that she hath sufficient proportion for her being to live upon and to maintain herself.
>
> This might have been done through private conference before, and had not needed to have been the fable of the world if you would have had the patience to have understood me; but I do not know by whom, or whose advice it was to run that course so contrary to my will or meaning that made her so disgraced to the world [and] raised suspicions openly that, with private conference, might have been more silently handled, and hath given me more greater cause to mislike.
>
> Wherefore I desire your Lordship in these causes — now you shall understand me — not to urge me any further; and so I write unto your Lordship, as you have done unto me, this Friday, 27th April. Your Lordship's to be used in all things reasonable,
>
> Edward Oxeford

There is no mistaking the writer's icy rage, and his explanation of it is clear enough: Burghley's blabbering has raised open suspicions of his daughter and made her "disgraced to the world." As for what she is suspected of, we are left in the dark. Oxford's case against his parents-in-law, however, is put explicitly in his next letter to Burghley, written on the heels of the preceding. This is another of his that does not survive, thanks again, doubtless, to the forethought of the old fox of Theobalds, whose version alone, in the form of a memorandum for the record, is available to us. Ward summarizes it:

> The allegations against Lord Burghley are: not providing him with sufficient money; ill-treating his followers; purposely arousing the Queen's indignation against him; while Lady Burghley is accused of having declared she wished him dead; of undermining his wife's affection for him; and of slandering him. But as for Lady Oxford, Lord Burghley writes that the Earl 'meaneth not to discover

anything of the cause of his misliking' [which, as we shall see, was well enough known to Burghley]; and that "until he understand further of it," he "meaneth not to visit her."

Nearly a month and a half later, apparently without further exchange between them, Burghley wrote another memorandum headed "12th June, 1576. To be remembered." It began:

> The time now past almost two months without certainty whereupon to rest arguments of unkindness both towards my daughter, his wife, and me also.
> Rejecting of her from his company.
> Not regarding his child born of her.
> His absence from the Court in respect to avoid his offence, and her solitary lying.[1]

Says Ward:

> He goes on to declare that there is "no proof nor particularity advanced" by the Earl in his accusations against him. On the contrary, he calls to witness "my care to get him his money when his bankers had none; my endeavour to have his land sold to the truest advantage, or else not to be sold; my dealing with his creditors to stay their clamours for their debt; and my particular suits to her Majesty for his advancement to place of service, namely, to be Master of the Horse, as Her Majesty can testify."
> There was also the old question as to Lord Oxford's legitimacy, and Burghley points out that "I preferred his title to the Earldom, the Lord Windsor attempting to have made him illegitimate." He also points out that "I did my best to have the jury find the death of the poor man, whom he killed in my house, *se defendendo.*"

In conclusion, Burghley wrote:

> I desire that his Lordship will yield to her, being his wife, either that love that a loving and honest wife ought to have, or otherwise to be so used as all lewd and vain speeches may cease of his unkindness to her; and that with his favour and permission she may both come to his presence and be allowed to do her duty to her Majesty, if her Majesty therewith be content, and she shall bear as she may the lack of the rest.
> Or else his Lordship will notify some instant cause of her not deserving such favour and that she may be permitted to make her answer thereto before such as her Majesty may please to appoint.

If Burghley wrote a letter to his son-in-law incorporating any of the above, he evidently received no answer. On July 10th he wrote another memorandum. In this one he voices the belief that his son-in-law had been led by "the untrue reports of others" to "think unkindness in me towards him" and says that "these untruths are still continued in secret reports," causing some who

---

[1] He had at least taken part in a Court function three days before writing that coldly furious letter to his father-in-law, for Roy Strong reports that in a ceremony of the Order of the Garter on April 24th he had helped the Countess of Derby carry the Queen's train, having delegated the Earl of Hartford to bear the Sword of State.

"have no cause to speak amiss of me" to "think otherwise . . . than I deserve."
He proceeds "not only [to] avow the same to be untruths but the maintainers
and devisers of them to be liars and malicious backbiters." Undoubtedly,
beginning at the latest with Rowland Yorke in Paris, third parties had been
working to poison relations between Oxford and the family into which he
had married.

Burghley goes on to assert that far from depriving the Earl of money
rightly his during his travels he had advanced him over £2,000 of his own
when the Earl's sources ran dry.

On July 12th, two days after this memorandum was written, and a letter
of the same tenor very likely sent to Oxford, the two men met. The understanding they evidently reached on Oxford's terms was the subject of a letter
of his to his father-in-law written the next day.

> My very good Lord, Yesterday, at your Lordship's earnest request, I had some
> conference with you about your daughter. Wherein, for that Her Majesty had
> so often moved me, and that you dealt so earnestly with me, to content her as
> much as I could, I did agree that you could eft bring her to the Court, with
> condition that she should not come when I was present, nor at any time have
> speech with me, and further that your Lordship should not urge further in her
> cause. But now I understand that your Lordship means this day to bring her to
> the Court, and that you mean afterwards to prosecute the cause with further
> hope. Now if your Lordship shall do so, then shall you take more in hand than
> I have, or can, promise you; for always I have, and I will still, prefer mine own
> content before others. And observing that wherein I may temper or moderate
> for your sake, I will do [so] most willingly. Wherefore I shall desire your Lordship
> not to take advantage of my promise till you have given me your honourable
> assurance by letter or word of your performance of the condition; which being
> observed, I could yield, as it is my duty, to Her Majesty's request, and I will
> bear with your fatherly desire towards her. Otherwise all that is done can stand
> to no effect.
>
> From my lodging at Charing Cross this morning.
>
> Your Lordship's to employ,
Edward Oxeford.

Oxford turned over to his wife the house at Wivenhoe and their lodging
in the Savoy; live with her he would not. According to Burghley "he would
make the sons of the young uncle his heirs male if he could." These were his
cousins Francis and Horatio Vere, then aged sixteen and eleven respectively.
Of his antipathy toward Anne there could certainly be no question. How is
it to be accounted for?

Biographers seeking an answer begin with a letter written to Burghley by
Dr. Richard Masters, one of the Queen's physicians, reporting a meeting he
had had with the Queen, the letter being dated 7 March 1575, two months
to the day after Oxford had left the Court for the Continent. It is worth
quoting at length.

To the right honourable the Lord Burghley, the Lord Treasurer of England.

After my duty it may please your Lordship to understand that having Her Majesty this Monday morning in the chamber at the gallery and next to the Queen sitting alone, I said, "Seeing it hath pleased your Majesty oftentimes to inquire tenderly after my Lady of Oxford's health, it is now fallen out so (God be thanked) that she is with child evidently; and albeit it were but an indifferent thing for Her Majesty to hear of, yet it was more than indifferent for your Lordship to signify the same unto her." Herewithal she arose, or rather sprang up from the cushion, and said these words: "Indeed, it is a matter that concerneth my Lord's joy chiefly; yet I protest to God that next to them that have interest in it, there is nobody that can be more joyous of it than I am." Then I went forth and told her that your Lordship had a prior likelihood of it upon your coming from the court after Shrovetide [forty-odd days before Easter], but you had concealed it.

Her Majesty asked me how the young lady did bear the matter. I answered that she kept it secret four or five days from all persons and that her face was much fallen and thin with little colour, and that when she was counselled to be gladsome and so rejoice, she would cry: "Alas, alas, how should I rejoice seeing he that should rejoice with me is not here; and to say truth [I] stand in doubt whether he pass upon me and it or not"; and bemoaning her case would lament that after so long sickness of body she should enter a new grief and sorrow of mind. At this Her Majesty showed great compassion as your Lordship shall hear hereafter. And repeated my Lord of Oxford's answer to me, which he made openly in the presence chamber of Her Majesty, viz., that if she were with child it was not his. I answered that it was the common answer of lusty courtiers everywhere, so to say. . . . Then she asking and being answered of me [who] was in the next chamber, she called my Lord of Leicester and telleth him all. And here I told her that though your Lordship had concealed it awhile from her, yet you left it to her discretion either to reveal it or to keep it and lose. And here an end was made, taking advantage of my last words, that she would be with you for concealing it so long from her. And severally she showed herself unfeignedly to rejoice, and in great offence with my Lord of Oxford, repeating the same to my Lord of Leicester after he came to her. Thus much rather to show my goodwill than otherwise desiring your Lordship, that there may a note be taken from the day of the first quickening, for thereof somewhat may be known noteworthy. From Richmond the 7th of March, 1574 [1575 New Style].

By your Lordship's most bounden,
Richard Masters.

Our next fragment of information as to the state of affairs comes ten months later in a memorandum Burghley wrote to himself on 3 January 1576, after the child had been born, in which he said of his son-in-law that

He confessed to my Lord Howard that he lay not with his wife but at Hampton Court, and that then the child could not be his, because the child was born in July which was not the space of twelve months.

The figure of "twelve months" has naturally puzzled commentators.

Shortly thereafter, it would seem, Burghley wrote himself out a retrospective chronology of events relating to Oxford and his daughter, going back to July 1574. The last three items, beginning in mid-1575, are:

2nd July. The Countess delivered of a daughter.

24th September. The letter of the Earl by which he gives thanks for his wife's delivery. Mark well this letter.

3rd January. The Earl wrote to me.

Such are the facts as we know them. From them it has generally been inferred, no doubt correctly, that by the time of Oxford's return to Paris by the end of March 1576 the Court was abuzz with speculation as to the paternity of the Countess of Oxford's child and that Oxford's receiver, Rowland Yorke, probably abetted by Henry Howard, brought word to the Earl in Paris of the scandal attaching to his relations with his wife, moreover so worked upon him as to cause him to question her fidelity.

The trouble would appear to have gone back to the report given currency by Lord Howard of Oxford's confession prior to his departure that if his wife were with child it could not be by him since he had not lain with her since October. Henry Howard was the second son of the poetical Earl of Surrey, the elder having been Thomas, the ill-fated Duke of Norfolk. Thus he was Oxford's first cousin, and, as he was reputed one of the most learned noblemen of his day, it seems likely, as Ward believes, that the two cousins were drawn fairly close together by common intellectual interests.

A Catholic and secret supporter of Mary Queen of Scots, for which he was to spend many years in confinement, Howard was credited with "evil counsel which brought about his brother's ruin." A "dangerous, intelligenc-ing man, and no doubt a subtle papist inwardly," the sagacious Lady Anne Bacon, mother of Francis, called him in warning her son Anthony of him: "he, pretending courtesy, worketh mischief perilously" — a "subtle serpent." In the words of the French Ambassador he was "one of the greatest flatterers and calumniators that ever lived." Years later Oxford "affirmed to divers that the Howards were the most treacherous race under heaven . . . [and] my Lord Howard the worst villain that lived." But generous temperaments, honest temperaments, and artistic temperaments tend, I think, until disabused by experience, to be guileless and unsuspecting; and Oxford at twenty-six had a temperament that was all three.

Howard, for his part, had a strong motive for turning his cousin against his wife. To drive a wedge of mutual recrimination between the premier Earl of England and the powerful Lord Burghley, bulwark of English Protestant-ism, would be a major coup. A calumniator by taste, Howard strikes one, too, as a man capable of doing evil for its own sake, of "motiveless ma-lignity," as Coleridge said of Iago.

So does Rowland Yorke. A comrade in arms of George Gascoigne, Yorke had been in Oxford's household back in 1574. William Camden wrote of him:

> This York was a Londoner, a man of loose and dissolute behaviour, and desperately audacious, famous in his time amongst the common hacksters and

swaggerers, as being the first that, to the great admiration of many of his boldness, first brought into England that bold and dangerous way of foining with the rapier in duelling, whereas the English till that time used to fight with long swords and bucklers, striking with the edge, and thought it no part of a man, either to foin or strike beneath the girdle.

Arrested on a charge of felony in 1580, Yorke was unmasked in 1584 in a plot to betray Ghent to the Duke of Parma, under whom he later served in the siege of Antwerp; he, too, was a Roman Catholic. Having with the help of friends managed to get back to England, he ingratiated himself with Philip Sidney and wangled from Sidney's uncle, the Earl of Leicester, command of Zutphen sconce (a strategically located fortification), which, to pay back a grudge against the Earl, he surrendered to the Spanish. Obtaining a command of a troop of lancers in the Spanish service, he considered himself insufficiently rewarded, and his employers, anticipating double treachery, had him poisoned. We know him, I should guess, for his contribution to Parolles in *All's Well*, a braggart captain and follower of Bertram's whose baneful influence on the young Count is exorcised only when he is shown up as a coward and traitor.

One can imagine the kind of doubts that Yorke would have been able to incite in Oxford's mind. Why if his wife had conceived at Hampton Court in October — the last chance for Oxford to have been the father — did he not learn of it definitely until mid-March? Why if the child was born on July 2nd could Burghley not have got word of it to him until after mid-September? This is not the first time the receiver had come between Oxford and his wife. In a note to her father entitled "Notes of an Ill-used Wife," poor Anne would record how in January 1574 she had been kept out of her husband's chambers during a meal by "York and others within."

Yorke's insinuations must throw Oxford into terrible mental confusion. He does not know what to think. He cannot believe that docile and loving Anne would be led by lust to another man's embrace. Surely any such suspicions do her outrageous wrong. Hamlet will tell Ophelia "Be thou as chaste as ice, as pure as snow, thou shalt not escape calumny." Yet how are the facts alluded to by Yorke to be explained? And there is all that knowing talk at Court reported by Yorke. . . . On his return, we recall, Oxford would not rejoin his wife until satisfied as to certain "mislikes," these comprising the attitude of her parents and his father-in-law's having made his marital difficulties "the fable of the world." He pictures the Court making merry over the figure he cuts as a cuckold. He is still keeping away from it nearly two months after his return. That he should write Lord Burghley with insolently self-regarding hauteur is no surprise. He will finally brave it out at Court, but whatever the truth of the matter, he cannot bear the thought of Anne's company.

Chapter 28: Look So Strange upon Your Wife?

The suspicion has always attached to the Earl that his behavior at this time had something of the disingenuous and contrived about it. Hilda Amphlett, an Oxfordian scholar, writes: "In 1576 the break may have coincided with his dearer wishes; to be able to pursue his life according to his own tastes; to associate with the writers and actors for whom Burghley showed open scorn. His travels may have enfranchised his spirit, and he may have seen the chance to remove himself from Burghley's dominance." Percy Allen puts it baldly in speaking of "those slanders upon the Countess of Oxford, which became de Vere's excuse, if not his justification, for a long separation from his wife."

Without doubt the marriage of Edward de Vere and Anne Cecil had been a failure almost if not quite from the start. Edward Dowden illuminates one of the major difficulties when he refers to "Hamlet, with his piteous, foiled love for one who can give him no help or understanding sympathy." It would have been a rare wife with the intellect and wit to keep Oxford interested and yet with the unquestioning loyalty, compassion, and sufferance to support a creative genius in the trials he inevitably imposed on himself and endure those he imposed on others, herself included. (In general, I think, the harder we are on ourselves the harder we tend to be on others, the easier the easier; and creative geniuses are mercilessly exacting of themselves.) Gentle, sweet, submissive, and limited Anne was not that wife. Fatally, too, she seems to have remained primarily the daughter of her parents. I have called attention earlier to Ophelia's siding with her father in the crunch — how she denies to Hamlet her knowledge that her father is spying on them. Oxford was aware that in the inescapable division between him and her parents — her father who strove to bend him in ways antithetical to his nature, her disagreeable mother, whom he detested — Anne would ultimately not be his. "Receive her into your house," he told Burghley, "for there, as your daughter or her mother's, more than my wife, you may take comfort of her." One has it all in Westminster Abbey today where, in colorful effigies upon their joint tomb, Anne Cecil lies beside that severe dame her mother, Lady Burghley, in identical prayerful poses.

The necessity of resuming life with his wife at the end of his Continental travels, to be wordlessly and unremittingly reproached for his lack of affection by her constant and futile striving to please him, would have caused Oxford's heart to sink. It would be remarkable if the report that met him in Paris, reflecting upon her reputation, had not awakened in him, along with a sense of shame and fury at the thought of a sniggering Court, an incredulous relief at now having grounds for separating himself from Burghley's daughter and the whole self-righteous Burghley clan. This may even have tempered his anger at being required by Burghley, with the Queen's authority behind him, to return home at once from Paris, giving up another trip to Germany

— though that doubtless added to the truculent and rebellious spirit he brought back with him.

All that went into his state of mind Oxford would have been aware of, if not at the time, then later. The plays show that, if he could romanticize himself, he was capable also of pitiless self-appraisal, especially as concerned Anne. There is, for example, *Measure for Measure,* which Coleridge called Shakespeare's one painful play. As do Valentine and Proteus in *Two Gentlemen of Verona,* so the Duke and Angelo in this later comedy — if a play set in an atmosphere of such evil and corruption may be called a comedy — represent the two sides of the dramatist's character, the noble-benevolent and the false-malignant. (The name Angelo may, I think, be taken as Angel-O (for Oxford), "angel" in the Old English sense of a fallen spirit in rebellion against God — an apt, terse description of the villain.) Angelo is husband by pre-contract to Mariana of the moated grange (Married Anne of the moated grange of Theobalds?), which contract, he says,

> . . . was broke off,
> Partly for that her promised proportions
> Came short of composition, but in chief
> For that her reputation was disvalued
> In levity; since which time of five years
> I never spake with her . . .

It would be five years before Oxford went back to living with Anne. Angelo says he broke off the marriage contract with Mariana because "her reputation was disvalued in levity," just as Oxford had spoken of the cause of his alienation from Anne having been made "the fable of the world."

While Angelo cites the sullying of Mariana's reputation as the chief reason for his breaking off the marriage, we know that he is prevaricating. We have already had the truth of the matter from the personification of Oxford's better nature, the Duke. When Isabella, whose virtue Angelo has assaulted, as Proteus assaults Julia's in *Two Gentlemen,* commiserates over Mariana's fate and asks, "Did Angelo so leave her?" the Duke replies:

> Left her in tears and dried not one of them with his comfort; swallowed his vows whole, pretending in her discoveries of dishonour; in few, bestow'd her on her own lamentation, which she yet wears for his sake; and he, a marble to her tears, is washed with them but relents not.

Thus Oxford would seem, in a damning self-indictment, to admit that in holding Anne unworthy because of her alleged lapse from honor — the "dishonour" that Mariana had brought upon her name — he was "pretending" a reason for deserting her.

Both Proteus and Angelo are required upon the threat or near threat of death to marry the girl they had betrayed out of lust for another. That the dramatist would have such lovely young women of high quality welcome as husband such scoundrels and construe their doing so as a happy ending has disturbed many readers. Edward Dowden has to invoke the nature of "Renaissance literature" to explain, unconvincingly, that "Proteus is guilty of every baseness, . . . yet upon a repentance which is forced upon him almost at the edge of the sword, he is forgiven and received back by the wronged Julia." Of *Measure for Measure* he says the dramatist "perhaps . . . ought to have turned away from the subject, if it allowed no better denouement." Louis Auchincloss entitles a chapter of his book on Shakespeare "The Enigma of *Measure for Measure.*" Inevitably critics flounder when they do not recognize Shakespeare's plays as in very considerable measure the transmuted material of the dramatist's own life, this being what gives them the tantalizing indeterminacy of life itself and leaves them with the inconsistencies and loose ends of personal experience only partially reworked for the medium. (No deliberate craftsmen of plays would ever have Angelo, to justify his treatment of her, cite Mariana's having allowed her reputation to be disvalued in levity and give no hint of what she had done to expose herself to the charge — or, if the charge was baseless, fail to have Mariana utter a word in her defense.)

Anne took Edward back after he had forsaken her and betrayed her for a black-eyed enchantress who would evidently be Rosaline of *Love's Labour's Lost* and later the Dark Lady of the *Sonnets.* Thus Julia and Mariana take back the treacherous libertines who had forsaken *them.* Since it has all been gone through in real life, the reconciliation (which a deliberate playwright would sweat over through hundreds of lines to try to make plausible) can be effected in a few words. Proteus puts his sins behind him with a facile formula:

> O heaven, were man
> But constant, he were perfect! That one error
> Fills him with faults, makes him run through all th' sins.

And with an equally facile formula Mariana puts Angelo's behind him:

> They say best men are moulded out of faults,
> And, for the most, become much more the better
> For being a little bad.

If in most cases Oxford lets his worser self off lightly at the end it is only after stripping that worser self naked in terrible wrongdong. He does it in play after play. Proteus' callous and cruel treatment of Julia and Angelo's of Mariana is matched by Bertram's of Helena and Claudio's of Hero in *Much Ado,* while in three plays the male protagonist conceives a murderous animosity toward a loving wife by imagining her unfaithful to him on the flimsiest grounds, only to be later overwhelmed by remorse; and these three brutally condemned wives — Imogen in *Cymbeline,* Hermione in *The Win-*

ter's Tale and Desdemona in *Othello* — are generally adjudged the most saintly and faultless of Shakespeare's heroines.

Of Leontes in *The Winter's Tale,* Louis Auchincloss says that he needs "no evidence to inflame his jealousy. His fit is totally perverse. He is unable, despite the number of sycophants who habitually attach themselves to Shakespearean princes, to find a single courtier who is willing even to pretend to take his side. The enormity of his accusation appalls even the worst toadies. But Leontes clings to it. He *wants* to believe Hermione guilty, even though, on one level of consciousness, he must know she is innocent." This, of course, is just what is said of Oxford in his treatment of Anne. Reviewing a production of *The Winter's Tale* in 1980, T. E. Kalem in *Time* finds that "the chief problem is the arbitrary action of the drama; it springs from a motivational void." Though Hermione "acts no chummier with Polixenes than many wives do with other men at cocktail parties, . . . Leontes goes into a state of apoplectic jealousy." But the point is that the dramatist is not trying to make a case for Leontes's condemnation of Hermione. On the contrary, by making its baselessness plain he is expiating his condemnation of Anne; he is pleading *nolo contendere* to the worst charge he can bring against himself. And he is doing the same thing in *Othello.*

This tragedy, "perhaps the greatest work in the world," in Thomas Babington Macaulay's view (and one from which "we must descend," in Walter Savage Landor's, "whatever road we take") had its origin, like so many of the Shakespeare plays, in an existing, quite crude story. In this case, a tale in the *Hecatommithi* of Giraldi Cinthio, published in 1565, provided the bare bones of the plot and the *dramatis personae,* though of these only "Disdemona" is given a name. The dramatist's first intention, again as in many of the plays, seems to have been to write a parable of the times. The frame of reference may have been the menace of Philip II's Spain to Elizabeth and her England; the Spanish were sometimes called Moors by the English, and the early play *Titus Andronicus* had dealt with that theme in similar symbols, even including a dark, villainous Moor. E. T. Clark has argued ingeniously that Othello stood for the Duke of Alençon (whom Elizabeth called her "little Moor" and who rode into Antwerp on a Barbary horse, to which Othello was compared), Brabantio for the province of Brabant, and Desdemona partly for Antwerp (the fairest jewel of Brabant) and partly for Elizabeth; the period would have been that of Alençon's near engagement to Elizabeth and of his military assault upon Antwerp, known as the French Fury: 1581 to 1583. While the interpretation may seem far-fetched and be irritating, it is difficult to account for Brabantio's name otherwise. As an allegory, it would have been designed for political effect. We may be sure that it was hard for Oxford, as a de Vere and the 17th of his title, to give up the belief that he was destined to move great events in the world. Probably it was not until after the battle of the Armada, in which he took part, that he abandoned hope of military exploit and was finally committed to making words his sword. We recall again how Jaques declares:

> I must have liberty
> Withal, as large a charter as the wind,
> To blow on whom I please.
>   . . . .
> Invest me in my motley. Give me leave
> To speak my mind, and I will through and through
> Cleanse the foul body of th' infected world.

When the time was out of joint, it devolved upon him, as a prince of the realm, to set it right, unwelcome as the task might be in spells of despondency. By what means would he do so? The play was the thing. Only — and I realize I am repeating myself — it was impossible for him to keep his genius harnessed to predetermined, utilitarian ends. In one play after another his characters would come into a life of their own, performing not to point up topical issues but as robust, self-willed human beings of their kind would. They would take their personalities and their vitality from what every writer knows, or should know, was the only possible source: their creator himself and the men and women with whom he had been involved. They would behave as their counterparts had in real life. Every writer strives to bring his story to life, and the more he succeeds the more it will owe to his experience.

So Othello became Oxford, one who derived his "life and being / From men of royal siege"; Desdemona became Anne Cecil, who "was half the wooer"; her father Brabantio became Lord Burghley, "In his effect a voice potential / As double as the Duke"; and the villain of the drama became Oxford's receiver, Rowland Yorke, with Henry Howard added to him: "Iago" is almost a transliteration of "Y-orke." Oxford's sacrifice of Anne upon the rumors of her unchastity became Othello's murder of Desdemona upon his being tricked into believing in hers by Iago, that "Spartan dog, / More fell than anguish, hunger or the sea."

Now we move to a profounder level. Both Louis Auchincloss and the late Mark Van Doren astutely perceive the unity of Othello and Iago. To the novelist "Iago is evil; he is the evil in man and in Othello — not because Othello is peculiarly evil, but because Othello is a man." He continues: "To me the play reduces itself in the end to a picture of a man destroying his own happiness — perversely, madly, as men do." Professor Van Doren observes that the fatal by-play with the handkerchief — "a devilish jest" — "is such a jest as Othello's atmosphere might generate." And he declares that "Nothing that is in Iago is absent from Othello" and "it may be illuminating to point out that the response of one to the other is immediate, or if not immediate, sure." He says that "Othello is both the best and the worst of men," and that "the origin of everything . . . in the tragedy is in the character of the hero." Similarly, Harley Granville-Barker says of Hamlet that he "is the man whose tragedy is within him." As Professor Van Doren also says of Othello that "he is both superior to passion and its slave," so Edward Dowden of Hamlet that "he has passion and a distrust of passion."[2]

In other words, what Mark Van Doren and Louis Auchincloss alike perceive is the duality, the dichotomy, in Othello. While the noble and shameful are separated in Valentine and Proteus, the Duke and Angelo, Benedick and Claudio (of *Much Ado*) and Othello and Iago, we feel in each case that the former presupposes the latter, as one scale pan of a balance requires the other, representing, as surely they do, the opposing propensities that set the dramatist at odds with himself. The Moor is a man of "high integrity and noble character" (Auchincloss), "the noblest man of man's making" (Swinburne) and yet one whose color is the outward manifestation of his capacity for dark acts of barbaric violence. That, being the one, he can suffer so greatly the consequences of his being the other makes *Othello* the almost unbearably poignant play it is, to Wordsworth one of the three "most pathetic of human compositions."

When in *The Winter's Tale* Leontes has, as he believes, brought about his wife's death, as he has his son's, he mourns how

> Once a day I'll visit
> The chapel where they lie, and tears shed there
> Shall be my recreation.

Since the stricken King cannot mean that it will be his sport, he must intend re-creation in the literal sense of the "action of creating anew; a new creation" (*O.U.D.*). And to such an end it may be said that Oxford repeatedly revisited the injury he had done his wife; and when she died at thirty-two (their only son having lived but a few days) he may have felt he had more with which to accuse himself. He would expiate his sense of guilt and do penance in his plays. When Paulina, upon Hermione's seeming death, cries to Leontes

> O thou tyrant!
> Do not repent these things; for they are heavier
> Than all thy woes can stir. Therefore betake thee
> To nothing but despair . . .

and tells him that ten thousand years of self-scourging would not move the gods to look his way, he himself twists the knife she has thrust in him:

---

[2] I am not trying to say that Othello and Hamlet are the same character. What I suggest is that each is the author but seen, as it were, from a different angle, in a different aspect. It would have taken Hamlet in Othello's position about half a minute to see clear through Iago and Othello in Hamlet's little longer from his first meeting with the Ghost to reach Claudius's chamber and slice the regicide up into small pieces. But then in either case there would have been no play.

> Go on, go on.
> Thou canst not speak too much. I have deserv'd
> All tongues to talk their bitt'rest.

Othello outdoes him, and perhaps anyone else in literature, in self-revilement as he cries over the corpse of the wife he has slain:

> When we shall meet at compt,
> This look of thine will hurl my soul from Heav'n,
> And fiends will snatch at it.
> . . . .
> Whip me, ye devils,
> From the possession of this heavenly sight!
> Blow me about in winds! roast me in sulphur!
> Wash me in steep-down gulfs of liquid fire!

Literature's debt to Oxford's remorse is incalculable, but none would have accrued had Oxford not had the capacity to stand apart from his emotions and observe them with detachment, plotting their dramatization and contriving the verbal alchemy with which he would capture, reshape, and refine reality, milling human lives, most notably his own, to artistic ends with no more compunction than Iago in manipulating his victims to his inscrutable purposes.

If, as Deems Taylor said, Richard Wagner made "the women whose hearts he broke . . . deathless atonement with *Tristram and Isolde*," then surely Oxford did as much for Anne in *Romeo and Juliet* and in the gallery of unforgettable women he created to show us how faultless a woman's virtue could be, how enchanting the quick-silver of her nature, how worthy of a man's best her intellect.

To orthodox historians, seeing no connection between Oxford and the pangs of conscience revealed in Shakespeare's plays — pangs none the less real for being put to use by the writer residing in the penitent — the Earl was simply a monstrous egotist and a cad. In their book it goes without saying that Anne was guiltless of the charge against her. Even Oxfordians, or such as have written about it, are agreed upon that.[3] "The Earl's actions," says one of the most eminent, Charles W. Barrell, "must be set down as wrong-headed, misguided, not to say thoroughly reprehensible."

Anne's innocence is self-evident. But is it evident from the facts? Among these, if the truth is vital to us, we are now going to have to grub.

Recall the report Dr. Richard Masters made to Burghley on 7 March 1575 on his interview with the Queen, who had asked how Anne bore the matter of her being with child. Dr. Masters had replied that "her face was much fallen and thin with little colour, and that when she was comforted and counselled to be gladsome and so rejoice, she would cry: 'Alas, alas, how

---

[3] Except D. S. Ogburn, whose lead I shall now be following.

should I rejoice when he that should rejoice with me is not here; and to say truth [I] stand in doubt whether he pass upon me and it or not.'" The only reason I can credit why Oxford should not have acknowledged paternity was that he had not had sexual intercourse with her recently enough for the child to be his if she had become sure not earlier than the first of March that she was pregnant. And that she had not known it before then comes out in Dr. Masters's statement that "she kept it secret four or five days from all persons." The physician would have lost little time in communicating to Burghley the substance of so important an interview with the Queen. He had seen her "this Monday morning," and if my calculations are correct, Monday fell on March 7th in 1575, so he was writing the very day of the interview, when the news he had had from Anne was fresh. This takes us back to the questions with which we imagined Rowland Yorke arousing the Earl. If Oxford had not lain with his wife after October and she had not known she was pregnant before March it is no wonder that in anticipation of his reaction to her delivery the lady presented a sallow, thin, distraught countenance and was inconsolable.

When Dr. Masters told the Queen of the Countess's miserable apprehensions of her husband's attitude toward the child, Elizabeth repeated the remark she said Oxford made in her presence, "that if she were with child it was not his." The physician interpreted this — rather desperately, I fancy — as "the common answer of lusty courtiers." That, of course, is nonsense; a lusty courtier might claim as his a child that was not, but certainly he would not disavow one that was. The indication is, however, that Oxford spoke lightly. He was not charging his wife with infidelity but denying that she was with child. Since he was confident a child could not be his, he was confident there could be no child. Presumably his confidence on this score arose from his not having lain with his wife "but at Hampton Court" — in October — if we may believe that Oxford made this confession to Howard on the strength of his cousin's word as reported by Burghley. Again I picture the Earl speaking with offhand cheerfulness, only this time while experiencing that "property of your excellent sherris" which "is the warming of the blood." "So thou seest, Harry," I hear him adding, "she cannot be with child. I'm a whoreson rogue if I can account for that rumor"; for rumor there must have been. Burghley's record of the incident in his memorandum of 3 January 1576 is worth repeating, for it shows Burghley badly rattled, I think; by that date the reckoning with his son-in-law was approaching. He wrote:

> He confessed to my Lord Howard that he lay not with his wife but at Hampton Court, and that then the child could not be his, because the child was born in July which was not the space of twelve months.

No one has been able to make sense of that "not the space of twelve months." I think what was in Burghley's mind was this: "Lord Howard said that Oxford confessed to him that 'he lay not with his wife but at Hampton Court.' That would mean that a child born after the space of 12 months from their stay there could not be his. To be Oxford's the child would have to have been born in July." If only it had been, there would have been no reason for Burghley to be agitated or to marshal his thoughts on paper.

Dr. Masters, in informing Burghley of his interview with the Queen, had been aware of the potentialities for grave trouble in the matter of the date of the countess's conception. We see that from the advice he gave. This he volunteered "to show my goodwill [rather] than otherwise," he was careful to say, for the advice, implying a serious irregularity, might be taken much amiss. It was "that there may a note be taken from the first quickening, for thereof somewhat may be known noteworthy." In other words, the time of the conception was going to be important.

That Oxford had heard before his departure for Europe on 7 January 1575 that Anne might be expectant we know from what he wrote his father-in-law from Paris on March 17th: "Your letters have made me a glad man, for these last have put me in assurance of that good fortune which you formerly mentioned doubtfully, . . . that it hath pleased God to make me a father." He had, moreover, shown "no unkindness . . . at his departure," according to Burghley, writing a year later in his memorandum of 25 April 1576. Burghley added that Anne had "made him privy that she thought she was with child, whereof he was glad." Note, however, that it was from his father-in-law that Oxford said he had heard of his wife's possibly being with child, not from Anne, and the difference is a big one. On September 24th he thanked Burghley for the "good news of my wife's delivery."

So now it is shown that, as we inferred, when Oxford remarked that if Anne were with child it was not his he was not impugning her honor but dismissing the report. When he heard from her father that she might be pregnant after all he did not raise a storm as he would have if persuaded of her falsity. On the contrary, he welcomed the news as "good fortune." He had taken it for granted that a child would be his. Without any doubt Anne knew this. Why then, two months after his departure, *when for the first time she knew she was pregnant,* was she in an agony of uncertainty as to whether he would accept the child as his? Again we come back to that answer that I see as the only possible one: she knew the child was going to be born more than nine months after she had last lain with him — after, it would seem, "the space of twelve months." Oxford for his part, absolutely convinced as he was (like posterity) of his wife's virtue, had to believe that after all she had conceived at Hampton Court and, child as she was, had only three months later come to suspect that she had done so. Then when he heard shortly before September 24th that the child had been born on July 2nd, that would have been about right. With much else to occupy the mind, he let it go at that.

But in Paris, with Yorke to strike the scales from his eyes, it would have been a different story. The receiver could not only raise the question of why, if the child were born on July 2nd, the grandfather had been unable to get word to his son-in-law until past the middle of September. He could probably also report that the talk in Court was that it was not until September that the child had been born. For the husband there would have been a double torment. He had to picture his wife, of whose fidelity he had been sure and whose outward seeming had been the very garb of chastity, betaking her to lawless and lascivious sheets. With it he could hear his honor made the butt of the Court's amusement. Given his likely state of mind, his behavior after his disembarkation in England must seem not arbitrary and cruel but a model of restraint.

Burghley, for his part, must have been beside himself with anxiety. That he was so, indeed, comes out in his babbling and in spots almost incoherent Polonius-like letter to the Queen, in which, for all its length, he was never able to come to an intelligible point. His anxiety, too, must have dictated those memoranda to himself in which, it appears from our deductions, he was trying to accommodate the facts to a story that would hold up and satisfy posterity. One recalls especially the penultimate item in that chronology of which I have already quoted the last three: "24th Sept. The letter of the Earl by which he gives thanks for his wife's delivery. Mark well this letter." Mark well that sentence, we add. The next and last item is "3rd Jan. The Earl wrote to me." It was on the day the Earl wrote that letter, January 3rd, from Siena, that Burghley penned the distracted memorandum about Oxford's confession to Lord Howard.

That Burghley felt the need to write those memoranda is significant. *When* he felt that need is conclusive as to their importance. Both were written long before Oxford had betrayed any misgivings about his wife's pregnancy. Oxford's response to the news that his wife might be going to have a child and then that she had had one had been, as we have seen, altogether one of pleasure. I come back to the only basis I can find for Burghley's dreadful apprehensions and his daughter's: Anne had conceived the child after she had last lain with her husband.

How could such a thing have come about? Only two possible explanations suggest themselves. One is that Anne's appearance of devotion and loyalty to her marriage and of constancy of nature was deceptive. I strongly incline to the other: that her father was determined as far as humanly possible to ensure the continuation of the marriage and the status of his descendants as Earls of Oxford. Three years had passed since Anne's and Edward's wedding and still there was no sign of issue, while it had now become impossible any longer to deny his son-in-law a Continental trip from which, given the hazards of travel, he might not return. Thus, exploiting his daughter's uncommon filial submissiveness and the argument that a child would be the surest means of binding her husband to her, he overcame her compunctions and resistance and brought her to accept service by another male and one of proved fertility. (Who the other was is beside the point, but I imagine that if the choice had been Burghley's it was governed by two necessities. First, the absolute minimum number of persons must be in on the arrangements. Secondly, the offspring, since it could not resemble a de Vere, must on no account look like anyone but a Cecil. I leave it to the reader to take it from there.) If the child was born in September, the plan must have been carried out in the month before Oxford left for the Continent. Burghley would have started immediately the rumor of his daughter's pregnancy to have it antedate her husband's departure. I take it that Anne was either too embarrassed to confess to her father that her husband had been a stranger to her bed since October or counted — mistakenly — upon being able to bring him back to it before he got away. When Burghley learned how things stood in that department his heart must nearly have failed him.

We are left with a final mystery. How was Oxford brought to exonerate his wife in the face of the evidence? — and that the evidence was even more damning than we have seen, he would before long have discovered: the child had not been baptized until September 29th, which was practically three months after her alleged birth, an unconscionable delay in those days. How was he eventually brought to accept little Elizabeth Vere as his daughter, as Leontes eventually came to accept Perdita, the Lost One, as his?

This brings us to one of the most remarkable of all the congruences between Oxford's life and the plays of Shakespeare. In *The Histories of Essex*, of 1836, by Morant and Wright, J. T. Looney found a passage about the rupture between the Earl and Countess of Oxford in which he read to his astonishment that

> He forsook his lady's bed, [but] the father of Lady Anne by stratagem, contrived that her husband should unknowingly sleep with her, believing her to be another woman, and she bore a son to him in consequence of this meeting.

With quaint Victorian delicacy, Looney wrote that "We would willingly be spared the penning of such matter" but his scruples were overcome by "its importance as evidence." What he meant was as evidence of Oxford's authorship of *All's Well*, in which Bertram is brought to father a son by the same stratagem. It is of great interest that the B.B.C. in its 1980 production of *All's Well* cites the report about Oxford in *The Histories of Essex* in its "Perspective" on the program, which, as we have earlier noted, was photographed at Burghley House, presumably in recognition of the great Lord Treasurer's appearance in the play as the lord Lafeu. Indeed, several references are made to Oxford in "Perspective." In one the commentator dons showy Elizabethan costume and pronounces the Earl of Oxford to have been a fancy dresser, having been known as the "Italianate Englishman." The collapse of a dam — in this case, a barrier to any questioning of the Stratford theory — is sometimes preceded by just such trickles from its foundation.

In 1943, Charles W. Barrell discovered another and somewhat different version of the story of the substituted bed-partner from a source with a connection to the de Vere family. Francis Osborne (1593–1659) was Master of Horse to Philip Herbert, Earl of Montgomery, who was the husband of Oxford's youngest daughter. In his *Traditional Memoirs of the Reigns of Elizabeth and James I* he told of a quarrel between Montgomery and a hanger-on at Court named Ramsay, in which the Earl had been worsted and was left

> nothing to testify his manhood but a beard and children, by the daughter of that last great Earl of Oxford, whose lady was brought to his bed under the notion of his mistress and from such a virtuous deceit she (the Countess of Montgomery) is said to proceed.

Osborne refers to the story parenthetically, as one would to an accepted fact (and in the same way — which must give the orthodox historians some trouble — to Edward de Vere as the "great Earl of Oxford," as Aubrey did, too).

That the distraught but ever tricky Burghley launched the story to account for Elizabeth Vere's nativity is certainly a possibility. (It was the younger, Susan Vere, who became the Countess of Montgomery, but Osborne, who was born some years after the events in question, could well have slipped up on this particular, which in any case he cites as something only "said" to be.) It would argue that Oxford was occasionally so deep in his cups that Burghley could trust to his believing himself capable at such a time of having misidentified his partner in a tryst. But, if we are on the right track, did Burghley's fiction work? Was Oxford taken in? The evidence of the plays would be that he was.

In *All's Well*, as in the story of Boccaccio's on which it was based, and to which we may suppose the dramatist drawn because it paralleled his own, the ruse is not just a fiction that is given out but one that is actually employed: the young ladies are switched to bring Bertram to bed with his proper mate and produce a legitimate son and heir, effecting a reconciliation of the young Count with the long-suffering Helena. More notably, because here the dramatist introduced it on his own, the ruse is employed again in *Measure for Measure* to bring Angelo to consummate his marriage-by-pre-contract with Mariana. We are left, moreover, in no doubt that Postumus, Angelo, Leontes, and Othello are wholly culpable in condemning for infidelity a wife of transparent guiltlessness. Oxford, it would seem, was convinced both that he had impregnated Anne in the belief that she was another woman with whom he had an assignation and that his subsequent conduct had been faithless and detestable. Quite apart from the plays, he seems in time to have accepted little Elizabeth as his own.

Is that how it actually was? Years would pass before Oxford would surmount his aversion for Anne and be reconciled with her, and that he would ever love her again, if he had ever loved her at all, is most doubtful. Without being in the least persuaded that he had slept with her in December 1574 under the impression that she was another he may have come to feel that she was much more sinned against than sinning and that whatever she had done her fault lay in a too-trusting heart, in a forlorn hope and in a spirit made subservient by self-doubt. ("But yet the pity of it Iago, O Iago, the pity of it, Iago!") He may especially have felt that she had been driven to an extremity by despair at his coldness. For her long anguish and suffering he was to blame; and a woman's deep and never wholly assuageable hurt can make the man responsible forever unforgiving of himself. Oxford may have felt that he had destroyed Anne's life, helplessly, given what she was and what he was. It was this that he had to try to expiate. He could have writhed in self-reproach even while, exasperated by her limitations, he persisted in his aloofness from her, taking his guilt out on her as well as on himself.

Yet even in the throes of self-recrimination, we can imagine him obeying the writer that was in him, who was sizing it all up, turning the situation this way and that and perceiving all its dramatic possibilities — how a playwright could take a chaste and loving wife and a husband who is a self-centered young courtier such as he had been, anxious to escape domesticity and seek military adventures abroad . . . or a husband who is a malevolent libertine of an illicit lustfulness he could portray only too well . . . or a husband of a dual nature, as he had shown himself to possess, noble, yes, noble to the point of guilelessness, dark with a lurking capacity for destructive passion and violence, a great military captain such as he was — that was it, a great killer of Turks under the Venetian flag: did that coxcomb Don John of Austria, who could not be shamed to the field of honor at Palermo, think he was the only knight who could rout the Sultan's host? Maddened by a conviction of her infidelity, the husband could kill the doting wife and suffer pangs of remorse that would rack the language, or he could think he had killed her and call down the fires of repentance upon his head. Or he could cruelly put her from him and then be reconciled . . . and why not resolve their division by that device of substituting the wife, unbeknownst to him, for a young woman he lusts for? Thus the dramatic imagination at work.

The last time Oxford had recourse to his tragic relations with Anne for dramatic material would appear to have been in *Hamlet*. It is there, I think, that he showed his feelings most truly, in the give and take between the Prince and Ophelia. I cannot forget how after the first, all-revealing scene with the Ghost, Hamlet goes to Ophelia and, as she tells it

> . . . falls to such perusal of my face
> As he would draw it. Long stay'd he so.
> At last, a little shaking of mine arm,
> And thrice his head thus waving up and down,
> He rais'd a sigh so piteous and profound
> As it did seem to shatter all his bulk.

In what has preceded, however, there is nothing to account for such behavior on Hamlet's part. He has heard nothing about Ophelia to cause him any perturbation at what he might read in her face, let alone anguish of that order. It is one of those frequent passages in Shakespeare that have nothing to do with the business of the play such as occur in no other dramatic or narrative works I know of and to me, as I have said, are to be interpreted as intrusions of real life. Hamlet coming to Ophelia from an encounter in which the promptings of his "prophetic soul" have been confirmed is, as I see it, Oxford going to Anne, in imagination, and detecting in her eyes a confession of the terrible doubts he has had of her constancy. Later, upon Polonius's intrusion upon his reading, when he declares he wishes the elderly statesman were honest, he blurts out, "Conception is a blessing but not as your daughter may conceive." In his overwrought scene with Ophelia at the conclusion of the great soliloquy we have, as I see it, a revelation of Oxford's confusion and anguish of mind about Anne and about himself in relation to her. His near-demented state of mind is apparent from the start. In response to her solicitude for how his honor has been "for this many a day," he is "well, well, well." The "remembrances" she has had from him, which she returns, he denies ever having given her. Questioning her abruptly as to whether she is honest and fair, he unburdens himself of the thoughts that have been plaguing him. He tells her

> That if you be honest and fair, your honesty should admit no discourse to your beauty . . . for the power of beauty will sooner transform honesty from what it is to a bawd than the force of honesty can translate beauty into his likeness.

Admitting that he loved her once, he immediately denies it. He urges her to "Get thee to a nunnery" rather than be "a breeder of sinners," for he could

> accuse me of such things that it were better my mother had not borne me. . . . What should such fellows as I do, crawling between earth and heaven. We are arrant knaves all; believe none of us.

Chapter 28: Look So Strange upon Your Wife?

Suddenly he has a suspicion: "Where's your father?" Polonius and the King are in fact observing from hiding, having posted Ophelia as bait for the Prince. And Ophelia, caught unready, replies with a lie: "At home, my lord." For Hamlet, it is the end. Let him "play the fool nowhere but in's own house. Farewell." But he cannot so readily dismiss the tormenting conflict of his thoughts and he turns back to her.

> If thou dost marry, I'll give thee this plague for thy dowry; be thou as chaste as ice, as pure as snow, thou shalt not escape calumny.

But if he has veered to a belief that Anne has been calumniated, Oxford as quickly convicts her again.

> Or if thou wilt needs marry, marry a fool; for wise men know well enough what monsters you make of them. To a nunnery, go, and quickly too. Farewell.

But still he has more on his mind and cannot tear himself away. He pours out bitingly an indictment of the artificialities in his wife of her sex in general that, as I take it, have nettled him beyond endurance:

> I have heard of your paintings, too, well enough. God hath given you one face, and you make yourselves another. You jig, you amble, and you lisp; you nickname God's creatures and make your wantonness your ignorance. Go to, I'll no more on't! It hath made me mad. I say, we will have no moe marriages.

Two or three pages back I left an important question hanging. Was the deception of the switched women actually practiced upon Oxford? Did he, in reality, repair to the bed chamber of a lusted-after beauty for whom his wife had been substituted and proceed with his designs unaware of the difference, as Bertram and Angelo do? It would hardly seem that he could have been so deceived, unless he were seriously befuddled by drink. Moreover, if the substitution had actually been made and the child were his, would Anne and her father have been so distraught? An alternative is that Burghley, taking advantage of an occasion when the Earl had kept an assignation with an object of his desires when he had been drinking sufficiently to be confused, simply floated the story that the Lady Anne had been substituted for the occupant of the bed chamber.

If either of these postulations is correct the further question arises as to whether Oxford was actually deceived. As to that, my guess would be that he probably was. The final possibility is that neither was the switch practiced nor was the story floated by Burghley, that the explanation of the reports of Oxford's having been taken in by such a stratagem may be found in Bertram's having been so generally recognized in the inner circle of the Court as the dramatist himself that it came to be believed that the deception had been worked on Oxford himself. That is probably the view prevailing among Oxfordians, though the employment of the same device with Angelo reinforces my doubts that such was the case.

The question we are left with, as to the truth of the matter, may never be answered. Before leaving it to the reader's judgment, however, I should like to offer a final observation.

Diana, the name given to the maiden, left nameless by Boccaccio, to whose bedroom the covetous Bertram repairs, only to discover later that he had lain with his wife, is a name that, employed by any Elizabethan writer, meant only one person: Elizabeth; Diana in classical mythology was the embodiment of virgin purity.[4] Isabella, to whose bedroom the covetous Angelo repairs with analogous results, would in English be called Elizabeth; one name is simply a different form of the other. ("Isabella harps too much on her virginity," Louis Auchincloss complains, and as many at her Court must have felt Elizabeth did.) Why in both cases was a name representing Elizabeth chosen for the decoy by the dramatist? That is another question I cannot answer, but I am confident the choice was not mere coincidence.

---

[4] Among the scores of portraits of Elizabeth shown in Dr. Roy Strong's monograph on the subject is a Dutch engraving of 1584 or '85, circulated in England, depicting the Queen as a nude Diana presiding at the unveiling of Pope Gregory XIII in his iniquities.

29

"Phoebus Gins Arise"

1576–1578: The likely partial alienation of Oxford from his old life; the new direction given him by Italy; his inclination to the Church of Rome. — Construction in London of the first playhouse. — Presentation at Court of plays that seem likely to be early versions of Comedy of Errors, Timon of Athens *and* Titus Andronicus. — *"Shakespeare's" double nature, one sunny, gay, and high-minded, the other an addict of violence and horror. — The contrasting positions as poets of Oxford and Sidney, and Oxford's pointing to the future flowering of Elizabethan verse. — The betrothal of Lady Mary Vere and the Willoughbys' son Peregrine, who is destined for military fame, and Lady Willoughby's opposition to her son's marriage to a sister of Oxford's. — The future rocky course of the marriage and the good possibility that Peregrine and Mary are the originals of Petruchio and Katherina of* The Taming of the Shrew. — *Lady Willoughby's reconciliation to Oxford and her scheme to comply with a reported secret wish of his by springing his daughter upon him unexpectedly, the result perhaps to be seen in the father-and-daughter reunion scenes in* Pericles *and* Winter's Tale, *but not in any restoration of Oxford's marriage. — The possibility that Oxford is drawn to the story of* Pericles *by its similarity to his own and writes the first version of the play at this time. — Oxford's literary note revealed and the future pseudonym of "Shakespeare" suggested in an address to him before the Queen by Gabriel Harvey. — Oxford's anger at the Queen's slighting of his protector Sussex and refusal to dance before the French ambassador, to be echoed by Bertram. — Evidence of Oxford's hope to serve under arms; the dedication to him of a book on the military profession. — A grant of a manor to him by the Queen for good and faithful service and the possibility that the service is connected with the theatre.*

After returning home the traveler often has a feeling of letdown, and the thronging images of all he has experienced only make the present seem more futile. So it evidently was with Oxford. Jaques calls it

> . . . a melancholy of mine own, compounded of many simples, extracted from many objects, and indeed the sundry contemplation of my travels, which, by often rumination, wraps me in a most humorous sadness. ["A state of mind having no apparent ground or reason." (*O.U.D.*)]

To compound his discontent there was not only the crisis with his wife but the publication of *The Posies of George Gascoigne* in which some scores of poems he had written (if our deductions are correct) were appropriated by an inferior writer of malodorous reputation; and this had presumably been engineered by Christopher Hatton between intervals of dancing attendance upon and galliards for Elizabeth Regina, whose susceptibility to the shameless flattery of such a one would have gone down ill with a de Vere in the best of circumstances.

Seeing the Continent had widened the fissure between Oxford and conventional Court society, whether of the nobility to which he was born or of the rising class of mercantile origin into which he had married — or so I judge. He must have been more disposed to bohemian company. The local color of Italian cities woven through his plays shows how they had stirred his invention. Italy was classical antiquity, to which Europe still looked back for inspiration and instruction, and Italy was the Renaissance, which showed how far her children could go on the impetus of the rediscovery of antiquity. But something else was there. Italy was the solemn and gorgeous bastion of historical continuity and hierarchy, the Church of Rome, the Old Religion, to which the greatest of sculptors and painters did homage. This was the Church in which fifteen Earls of Oxford had been christened, married, and buried, and for the 17th not to have felt and responded to its undertow would have been remarkable. Soon after his return, according to the Catholic Record Society, he and several of his friends, including Lord Henry Howard, Charles Arundel, and Francis Southwell, made a secret profession of adherence to the Roman Catholic faith. At the same time a deeper-flowing current of Oxford's nature had evidently been set by his experience on the Continent to churning more purposefully.

Construction of the first playhouse in England was begun in Shoreditch a mile north of Vere House in Oxford Court by James Burbage, father of Richard, in 1576, the year of Oxford's return, and the coincidence makes one wonder if the Earl did not have something to do with it. Finished in the next year, it was called the Theatre, in the first recorded use of the word, which was derived from "amphitheatre"; many years later its timbers would be used in building the Globe. Another rose a few hundred yards away and almost as early on a plot of ground called The Curten, from which it took its name: the Curtain. These were to be followed by others. Together they gave the acting companies accommodations superior to the taverns for rehearsing plays before their performance at Court. The period of the Elizabethan theatre and that of Oxford's dramatic career would appear to have coincided down to the very year, at start and finish. Certainly this would be so if Eva Turner Clark is right in believing that some ten plays among those listed in the records of the Court Revels for the next few years after Oxford's return, given by companies with which he is thought to have been associated, were of Oxford's authorship.

The first was "The historie of Error," which was "shown at Hampton Court on New Year's Day at night, enacted by the Children of Paul's, in 1577. It seems highly likely that this was an early version of *The Comedy of Errors,* which, modeled on the *Menaechmi* of Plautus (but with twin servants added to twin masters) is certainly one of the earliest of the Shakespearean plays; its "doggerel verse" (Edward Dowden) and rhymes that "rattle like bleached bones" (Mark Van Doren) are almost a literary lifetime away from the verbal music of the *Sonnets.*[1] J. T. Looney was the first to remark on the resemblance between these lines in *The Comedy of Errors*:

> She is so hot because the meat is cold;
> The meat is cold because you come not home;
> You come not home because you have no stomach;
> You have no stomach, having broke your fast.

and these from a poem attributed to Oxford:

> What plague is greater than the grief of mind?
> The grief of mind that eats in every vein;
> In every vein that leaves such clots behind;
> Such clots behind as breed such bitter pain. . . .

It is the device of a versifier still apprentice to the art.

E. T. Clark calls attention to a joke in *Errors* of the kind with which Oxford liked to sprinkle the plays — caviar to the general but doubtless the meat of smothered guffaws to the insiders. At the tournament of 1571 at which Oxford received "the chief honour" and a tablet of diamonds from the Queen, Christopher Hatton's prize was a gold bell and chain. "An affected fribble," as Martin Hume calls him in *The Great Lord Burghley,* Hatton was probably prone to go tinkling about the Court in it. In Act II, Scene 1, there is an incessant repetition of "the chain," which Mark van Doren complains of as failing of effect; but the playwright's object, as I conceive it, was to prime the audience at Hampton Court for a jibe at the Captain of the Body-Guard in the form of a tie-in with a bell. And two scenes later it comes. On the flimsiest excuse Adriana exclaims

> A chain, a chain! Do you not hear it ring?

Whereupon her interlocutor asks

> What, the chain?

and receives the answer

> No, no, the bell!

It transpires that the clock has struck one.

A month and a half after *Errors* was put on at Hampton Court, *The Historie of the Solitarie Knight* was performed at another of the Queen's

---

[1] That Stratfordian writers of international reputation, like A. L. Rowse, are capable of dating the two within one to three years of each other or even, like Leslie Hotson, of having the *Sonnets* written before *The Comedy of Errors*; that a scholar of Sir E. K. Chambers's Olympian standing can write that "There is some disharmony between the tone of the *Sonnets* and that of the vivid comedies, which were contemporary with them" — this I shall have to leave to others to explain.

palaces, Whitehall, on the Thames, E. T. Clark believes it to have been an early version of *Timon of Athens,* which Oxford put more effort into later only to abandon it. (The general view is that this misanthropic play was completed by another writer in a spirit of some confusion before it appeared for the first time in the Folio of 1623, inserted there, mauled in the printer's haste, to fill a gap left by the temporary withdrawal of *Troilus and Cressida.*) Timon is a man of wealth on whom flatterers batten until their greed and his own profligate liberality bring him to ruin; whereupon, as he turns confidently to them for rescue, they abandon him. Timon might indeed be called a solitary knight as we see him both among his adulators, who care nothing for him, and when, in revulsion at humanity, he becomes a hermit and dies one, pronouncing a curse upon his fellows: "Graves only be men's works, and death their gain."

Mrs. Clark's idea is that *The Historie of the Solitarie Knight* was the product of Oxford's temporary eclipse upon his return from the Continent. The Queen was angry with him, and probably fair-weather friends sought more promising attachments. The Poet, the Painter, the Jeweler and the Merchant who prey on Timon's vanity doubtless helped bring Oxford, as they do Timon, to "an empty coffer." Indeed, Gervase Markham tells us — though we must make allowance for his habit of glowing hyperbole — that "It were infinite to speak of his [the Earl's] infinite expense, the infinite number of his attendants, or the infinite House he kept to feed all people." It sounds like Timon. Markham goes on to speak of "the alms he gave (which at this day [1624] would not only feed the poor, but the great man's family also)." We observed two chapters back how Oxford's decree in his letter to Burghley from Siena, "I have no other remedies, I have no other help but mine own, and mine is made to serve me and myself, not mine," seems to be echoed in Timon's

> I must serve my turn
> Out of mine own. . . . Immediate are my needs.

Oxford authorized his father-in-law "to sell any portion of my land," and Timon, bereft of it all, grandly proclaims, "Let all my land be sold." I rather think, though, that *Timon of Athens* as we know it owes more to the manifold adversities that overtook its author in the early 1580s, when the sale of thirty tracts of land in five years left him stripped near as bare as Timon, and may not have been begun before then.

If *Timon of Athens* seems an unconscionably bitter assessment of mankind, it is a bedtime story told by Polyanna beside *Titus Andronicus.* The attraction that cruelty, terror, and bloodshed had for the author of Shakespeare's plays must give us pause. It seems to me that, just as the dramatist was given to depicting himself in his noble-fair and sadistic-evil attributes in separate characters in the plays, so he could be one of two persons in writing them.

He not only wrote about the great-souled Othello and the inhuman Iago, he wrote *as* Othello and Iago, as Prospero and Caliban, by turns. I think it was only by giving vent to the black pessimism and horror that from time to time seized upon him that he was able to exorcise them.

A multitude of atrocities were to figure in future plays, none worse than the blinding of Gloucester in one of the last, *King Lear*; but never again would Oxford's Mr. Hyde have so free a hand over his Dr. Jekyll as in this, Hyde's first sally forth. Sir George Greenwood and others have refused to concede Shakespeare any part in *Titus*. Probably most scholars believe with Edward Dowden that he only "made corrections and additions" to the work of others, though those others were almost certainly the young Shakespeare himself, to which the much older made those corrections and additions.[2]

Accounts of the Court Revels show that a play called *The historye of Titus and Gisippus* was given at Whitehall two days after the showing of *Timon of Athens*. Mrs. Clark suggests that the copyist who kept the accounts, working from often illegible day-to-day slips of paper, could not decipher the name *Titus Andronicus,* which he had never heard before, and so wrote that of Boccaccio's story, being familiar with that. She also believes that the play represented Oxford's first use of drama for political ends and that the savageries enacted in it were meant to shock his fellow countrymen into a realization of the horrors committed wholesale by the Spanish in the rape of Antwerp. She may well be right on both counts. It would not be the last time evil would be evoked with a very disturbing vigor in the livery of an admirable cause — i.e., with redeeming social value.

By this time, Oxford had written probably almost all the poems openly linked with his name. Seven had been published, signed with the initials E. O. in *The Paradyse of Daintie Devises* of 1576, the initials appearing also as those of one of the eight contributors listed on the title-page; of these only one other, Lord Vaux, was a nobleman, and he was dead, as was *comme il faut* for one whose verse was published as admittedly his. When, three centuries later, Alexander B. Grosart made the first attempt to round up Oxford's poems he identified twenty-two as his. (Steven W. May of Georgetown College denies Oxford six of these and adds two others.) These he published in the *Fuller Worthies' Library* of 1872 with the perspicacious

---

[2] Having to date the play no earlier than the early 1590s, the Stratfordians are up against it. "I find it impossible to believe that at this date [1593] Shakespeare could have written such verse as appears in large tracts of *Titus,* or could then have produced so crude and unrelieved a melodrama of blood," says Dowden, while Sir E. K. Chambers is driven to nonsense: "He [Shakespeare] took his notions of plotting from Kyd, and outwent him in his use of realism, of horrors, of mystifications, of maniacal episodes; his notions of character-drawing from Marlowe and outwent him by representing Aaron as obsessed by a lust, not for power through conquest of gold, or knowledge, but for abstract villainy. [Like Iago, of whom Aaron was a forerunner in the person of a Moor like Othello.] He had learnt to write from Peele and others. . . ." How is it possible to get things so backward?

observation about their author that "An unlifted shadow lies across his memory." That they comprise only a small part of Oxford's output as known to his contemporaries is clear. J. T. Looney more than doubled their number with additions never attributed to Oxford but which he is convinced are his.

I have already quoted rather liberally from poems known to be Oxford's or believed by me to be his, a number to show a kinship with Shakespeare's. Before going on I might cite a few others.

The first stanza of Oxford's *The Meeting with Desire* would never be questioned as Shakespeare's, I think, if it appeared in one of the early comedies:

> The lively lark stretched forth her wing,
> 　The messenger of Morning bright;
> And with her cheerful voice did sing,
> 　The Day's approach, discharging Night;
> When that Aurora blushing red,
> 　Descried the guilt of Thetis' bed.

When to this we add two lines from another poem of Oxford's —

> When Phoebus from the bed
> 　Of Thetis doth arise, . . .

— we can hardly not be reminded of the song from *Cymbeline*:

> Hark, hark! the lark at heaven's gate sings,
> And Phoebus gins arise

Larks and dawn continually recur in Shakespeare.

Take Oxford's *What Cunning Can Express*, from which I quoted two lines above:

> What cunning can express
> 　The favour of her face?
> To whom in this distress,
> 　I do appeal for grace.
> A thousand Cupids fly
> About her gentle eye.
> 　　· · · ·
> 　The lily in the field,
> 　That glories in his white
> For pureness now must yield,
> 　And render up his right;
> Heaven pictured in her face,
> Doth promise joy and grace.
> 　　· · · ·
> 　With this there is a red,
> 　Exceeds the Damask-Rose;
> Which in her cheeks is spread,
> 　Whence every favour grows.
> In sky there is no star,
> But she surmounts it far.

The metaphor of roses and lilies for complexion is characteristic of Shake-speare. Compare these lines from Lucrece (37, 56, and 69):

> O how her fear did make her colour rise!
> First red as roses. . . .
> Her lily hand her rosy cheek lies under.

>   The colour in thy face,
> That even for anger makes the lily pale
> And the red rose blush at her own disgrace.

And these from Sonnets 98 and 130:

> Nor did I wonder at the lily's white,
> Nor praise the deep vermillion of the rose:
> They were but sweet, but figures of delight,
> Drawn after you. . . .

> I have seen roses damask'd, red and white,
> But no such roses see I in her cheeks.

Allowing for perhaps fifteen years' difference in time of composition and poetic experience, would we consider the following out of place as the ending of a sonnet of Shakespeare's?

> A mall-content yet seem I pleasèd still,
> Bragging of heaven yet feeling pains of hell.
> But Time shall frame a time unto my will,
> Whenas in sport this earnest will I tell;
>   Till then (sweet friend) abide these storms with me,
>   Which shall in joys of either fortunes be.

"Mall-content" is probably a word coined by Oxford, since for the first use of "malcontent" the *O.U.D.* gives 1581.

Consider these quatrains from Oxford's *Fond Desire*:

> What had'st thou then to drink?
>   Unfeignèd lover's tears.
> What cradle wert thou rockèd in?
>   In hope devoid of fears.

> What lulled thee to thy sleep?
>   Sweet thoughts that liked one best.
> And where is now thy dwelling place:
>   In gentle hearts I rest.
>   . . . .
>   Will ever age or death
> Bring thee unto decay?
> No, no, Desire both lives and dies
>   A thousand times a day.

Surely with these verses we are on the way to the song in *The Merchant of Venice*:

> Tell me, where is fancy bred,
> Or in the heart, or in the head:

How begot, how nourishèd?
　Reply, reply.

It is engender'd in the eyes,
With gazing fed; and fancy dies
In the cradle where it lies.

Five of Oxford's poems are written in the stanza of *Venus and Adonis* and *Lucrece,* which is the same as the final sestet of the Shakespearean sonnet. One is *Woman's Changeableness* (of which Professor May considers the attribution uncertain), from which I have already quoted, the other *Reason and Affection,* of which the last stanza is:

Then lofty Love thy sacred sails advance,
My sighing seas shall flow with stream of tears;
Amidst disdains drive forth thy doleful chance,
A valiant mind no deadly danger fears;
　Who loves aloft and sets his heart on high
　Deserves no pain, though he do pine and die.

There is no denying that Oxford the young versifier had a long way to go to become the Shakespeare of the *Sonnets* and of the great dramas, but I may repeat myself and suggest that he had little further to go than the Shakespeare who wrote the original parts of the early plays, some of which are so inferior that orthodoxy will not grant that he wrote them at all. It is worth recalling, too, that whatever the deficiency of Oxford's acknowledged verse, much of it, at least, was written at a time of life before the orthodox Shakespeare had been able to write any verse at all, or any that his inventors can produce. His partisans have, thus, no standing before the court if Oxford is to be tried on his early poems.

W. J. Courthope of Oxford University in his *History of English Poetry* tells us that de Vere and Philip Sidney were the leaders respectively of the two camps into which the court *littérateurs* were divided — de Vere, as he says, being not only "a great patron of literature but the author of verses "distinguished for their wit" and for "terse ingenuity," with a "studied concinnity of style [that is] remarkable." There was much to set the two men at odds with each other, as they notoriously were. In Sidney's "daily life," says Elizabeth Jenkins, "there was, perhaps, a slight sense of moral superiority which, it is easy to see, would at once exasperate the Earl of Oxford." Oxford's champion, Sussex, and Sidney's, his uncle Leicester, were virtually at daggers drawn. Oxford leaned, at least, to the Old Religion; Sidney, who had been in Paris during the massacre of St. Bartholomew's Day, was emphatically Protestant. Ms. Jenkins, who denies her readers any knowledge of the Earl's literary attainments, observes that "Unlike Oxford, who was attractive to those of his own age and looked upon by his elders with a mixture of admiration and disapproval, Sidney [though four and a half years the

Sir Philip Sidney at twenty-three

From a portrait by an unknown artist.

From *Thane's British Autography* by John Thane. Courtesy of Virginia State Library.

junior] was the darling of those older than himself." John Kenyon of the University of Hull, writes: "Philip Sidney was one of those young-hero figures who, though in the van of the latest thinking, typify the ideals of an age that was passing away. He was a brilliant Protestant soldier-poet-martyr whose death was in the tradition of medieval knighthood. Handsome and universally admired but curiously sexless; well-connected and well-loved; his career finds a curious echo in Rupert Brooke's. Like Brooke, he wrote poetry that was extravagantly admired, not just because it was melodious and accomplished, but because it did not go beyond the canons of fashionable acceptance."

Paradoxically, it was Oxford, the scion of ancient feudal lineage, who spoke for the future of English literature. As J. T. Looney has it:

> If . . . we compare his poetry with the work of Sidney we can only account for Sidney's being considered in any sense a rival by the fact that the feeble style of Sidney was in vogue at the time. What distinguishes Oxford's work from contemporary verse is its strength, reality, and true refinement. When Philip Sidney learnt to 'look into his heart and write' [as he said], he only showed that he had at last learnt a lesson that his rival had been teaching him. The reader may or may not be able to agree with the ideas and sentiments expressed by Oxford, but he will be unable to deny that every line written by the poet is a direct and real expression of himself in terms at once forceful and choice and no mere reflection of some fashionable pose. Even in these early years he was the pioneer of realism in English poetry.

589

In his *Life of Spenser,* Dean Church writes: "The ten years from 1580 to 1590 present . . . a picture of English poetry of which, though there are gleams of a better hope, . . . the general character is feebleness, fantastic absurdity, affection and bad taste. Who could suppose what was preparing under it all? But the dawn was at hand." During the next decade, 1590–1600, "there burst forth a new poetry, which with its reality, depth, sweetness, and nobleness took the world captive. The poetical aspirations of the Englishmen of the time had found at last adequate interpreters, and their own national and unrivalled expression." Of the more than two hundred English writers of poetry who published or gathered their works together, "forty have genius or talent," H. A. Taine declares. "An epoch of the mind came and passed away," — that "of instinctive and creative conception. These men had new senses, and not theories in their heads."

This new, more vigorous poetry, Dean Church says, superseded the preciousness of Sidney's *Defense of Poesie,* taking its vitality from the "rude play houses with their troupes of actors, most of them profligate and disreputable." Looney adds that "This vital change, then, was preparing in England between the time when Edward de Vere produced his early poetry" — providing those "gleams of a better hope" — "and the time when the Shakespearean dramas appeared." Of the poets of the three arid decades following the death of Surrey in 1547, we recall E. K. Chambers's summation, that the most hopeful was Edward de Vere — who would have been an aberrant unique in literature if, demonstrating such promise and excelling his peers as a poet, he "became mute in later life," as the great Shakespearean scholar supposed. In the years from about 1576 to 1586, the narrowly confined and self-centered court poet that Oxford had been, having had the portals of his mind thrown wide and his imagination set in ferment by the variety and vibrancy of Europe, by the Italian stage above all, haunted those rude playhouses, drank and sharpened wits with those disreputable actors, wrestled with the medium of the theatre, gaining in range, depth, and expression with every essay in stage-craft, to stand forth — unless I am grievously mistaken — as the ultimate poet and dramatist, the mysterious William Shakespeare. In just such words as might have been whispered at Court by those admiring but disapproving elders conjured up by Ms. Jenkins, Alan Gordon Smith writes in his *William Cecil; the Power Behind Elizabeth,* "Yet to the end, with but intervals of sulky compliance, Lord Oxford remained morose and defiant, writing plays and poetry in questionable retirement and perpetually associating with his disreputable actors and mountebanks" — other writers, the truth is. "An ungracious relative — though possibly, in his own way (as some conjecture) an even greater than the great Lord Burghley."

That was to come, however. The retirement would be later, when the metamorphosis from Court poet to shadowy dramatist embodying the "soul of the age" had been largely complete. A few months after the break with his wife he was spending part of his double life back in Court to stand for a few years at his zenith there, putting on the plays that would make him known as of all the playwrights among "the best for comedy." "The prince's fool," he would say of himself as Benedick in *Much Ado.* "Ha, it may be I go under that title because I am merry."

Morose and defiant he must have seemed to his father-in-law. Burghley wrote him that he could not "see the old year [1576] passed" without "assay by reasonable means to seek relief; specially for my daughter, whose grief is the greater and shall always be inasmuch as her love is most fervent and addicted to you, and because she cannot, or may not, without offence be suffered to come to your presence, as she desireth, to offer the sacrifice of her heart; nor can I find opportunity in open places, where we sometimes meet, to reveal my griefs. . . ." Since Oxford's reply, if any, is not preserved, we do not know what effect the pathetic appeal had on him; but probably it was not enhanced by the writer's inveterate way of paying out his suit through pages, like an endless rope. Asking to meet with the hostile husband, Burghley concludes with the significant assurance of "having made nobody privy with this my letter."

Burghley was not the only one whom Oxford was causing grief. There was also Katherine Bertie, Lady Willoughby d'Eresby and dowager Duchess of Suffolk, whose twenty-two-year-old son had engaged himself to marry Lady Mary Vere. She and her husband, Richard Bertie, a language scholar and fellow of Corpus Christi College, Oxford, were both ardent Protestants. As such they had had to flee the country in disguise during Queen Mary's reign, despite Katherine's advanced pregnancy. Their plight was such that when the wife's time came, catching them on the road, they had to take shelter in a church for the delivery. Their wanderings were commemorated when they christened the infant, a son, who thus acquired a name as priceless as any in English history, Peregrine Bertie. As Lord Willoughby d'Eresby, he would devote his life to the political and military service of his Queen, leading a diplomatic mission to establish friendly relations with the Danish King at Elsinore and commanding English forces in support of the Protestant cause in the Low Countries in 1587 to 1589 (when he was succeeded by Sir Francis Vere) and thereafter in France with Henry of Navarre. When in 1589, against a superior Spanish force under the Duke of Parma, he raised the siege of Bergen-op-Zoom, a popular ballad would relate how

> The news was brought to England
> With all the speed might be,
> And soon our gracious Queen was told
> Of this same victory
> "Oh, this is brave Lord Willoughby,
> My love who ever won;
> Of all my lords of honour
> 'Tis he great deeds has done."

Lady Mary Vere   Courtesy of Virginia State Library.

From *Thane's British Autography* by John Thane.

But that was a dozen years after 2 July 1577 when the Duchess of Suffolk, in her husband's absence, unburdened herself on the subject of her son's proposed match in a letter to her old friend Lord Burghley.

> It is very true that my wise son has gone very far with my Lady Mary Vere, I fear too far to turn. I must say to you in counsel what I have said to her plainly, that I had rather he had matched in any other place; and I told her the causes. Her friends made small account of me; her brother did what in him lay to deface my husband and son; besides, our religions agree not, and I cannot tell what more. If she should prove like her brother, if an empire follows her I should be sorry to match so. She said that she could not rule her brother's tongue, nor help the rest of his faults, but for herself she trusted so to use her as I should have no cause to mislike her. And seeing that it was so far forth between my son and her, she desired my good will and asked no more. "That is a seemly thing," quoth I, "for you to live on; for I fear that Master Bertie will so much mislike of these dealings that he will give little more than his good will, if he give that. Besides, if Her Majesty shall mislike of it, sure we turn him to the wide world." She told me how Lord Sussex and Master Hatton had promised to speak for her to the Queen, and that I would require you to do the like. I told her her brother used you and your daughter so evil that I could not require you to deal in it. Well, if I would write, she knew you would do it for my sake; and since there was no undoing it, she trusted I would, for my son's sake, help now.

Such from one of Lord Burghley's oldest friends.

Chapter 29: Phoebus Gins Arise

Oxford's opposition to the marriage could have had several explanations. The Berties were still strong Protestants; he was averse to another familial tie with the Cecil camp; he had well-founded doubts about his sister's prospects of happiness as Peregrine's wife. The Duchess for her part saw an opportunity for her son to marry an heiress "of a thousand marks land," as she told Burghley. Caught, moreover, between her son's obdurate attachment to Lady Mary and her husband's equally obdurate opposition to his marrying her, she again turned to Burghley for guidance two weeks later.

> My good Lord, I received this letter here enclosed yesterday from my husband wherein your Lordship may perceive his head is troubled, as I [can] not blame him. But if he knew as much as I of my good Lord of Oxford's dealings it would trouble him more. But the case standing as it doth I mean to keep it from him. . . . I cannot express how much this grieveth me, that my son, in the weightiest matter, hath so forgotten himself to the trouble and disquiet of his friends, and like enough to be his own undoing and the young lady's too. For if my Lord of Oxford's wilfulness come to my husband's ears I believe he would make his son but small marriage [settlement].

Unfortunately the agitated mother did not specify wherein the Earl's dealings and wilfulness had given offence. She continued:

> I wot not what to do therein. If I should stay for Her Majesty's good will in it, and my husband far off from it, you know he cannot take that well at my hand, that I should seek to bestow his son as it were against his will . . . and so I am dead at my wit's end. And yet I think if Her Majesty could be won to like it, I am sure my husband would be the easier won to it, if my Lord of Oxford's great uncourteousness do not too much trouble him.
> My good Lord, I cannot tell what to do or say in this; but as my good Lord and very friend I commit myself and the case to your good advice and counsel and help. . . .
> From Willoughby House, this 14th July,
>
> K. Suffoulk

But, as B. M. Ward comments, "if outside forces were trying to prevent the marriage the two persons most nearly concerned were equally determined on their union. In an affectionate letter to his fiancée Peregrine assures her that he 'makes more account of her than myself or life,' adding that he writes to let her know 'how uncourteously I am dealt with by my Lord your brother, who, as I hear, bandeth against me and sweareth my death.' The letter ends 'yours more than his own and so till death.'"

The young lover, it is clear, grossly exaggerated Oxford's ire, for the marriage took place before the end of the year, by which time the Duchess and Oxford were on amicable terms, as evidently Oxford and her son were to be in the future. The strains were not between Oxford and his new in-laws but between the young husband and wife. The marriage was evidently a troubled one, for before it was nine months old Sir Thomas Cecil was writing to his father of an "unkindness" that had grown up between them and anticipating that Lady Mary "will be beaten with that rod which heretofore she prepared for others." This arresting comment has naturally led to speculation that Peregrine and Mary were the originals of Petruchio and Katherina (sometimes Katherine, the name of Oxford's older half-sister), the principals in *The Taming of the Shrew*. They may well have been. In January 1579, a year after their wedding, there was shown at the palace at Richmond (a favorite of Elizabeth's) a play called *A Morrall of the marryage of Mynde and Measure,* enacted by the Children of Paul's. E. T. Clark believes this to have been the dramatist's start on *The Shrew,* written when Padua, its locale, was still fresh in his mind. She points out that Petruchio reiterates the *measures* he will take to subdue the wilful *mind* of Katherina, who in the final scene says to her friends, who have also been recently married, "My mind hath been as big as one of yours."

The Duchess of Suffolk by the time of her son's wedding was so far reconciled to having Oxford's sister for a daughter-in-law, and so well disposed toward Oxford, as to attempt to reconcile the Earl with his wife. She wrote Burghley that a young man visiting her house had told her daughter that he thought Oxford would be very glad to see his daughter (little Elizabeth Vere, then two and a half years old) but would not have his desire known. Her letter continued:

> On Thursday I went to see my Lady Mary Vere. After other talks she asked me what I would say to it if my Lord her brother would take his wife again. "Truly," quoth I, "nothing could comfort me more, for now I wish to your brother as much good as to my own son." "Indeed," quoth she, "he would very fain see the child, and is loth to send for her." "Then," quoth I, "an you will keep my counsel we will have sport with him. I will see if I can get the child hither to me, when you shall come hither; and whilst my Lord your brother is with you I will bring in the child as though it were some other child of my friend's, and we shall see how nature will work in him to like it, and tell him it is his own after." "Very well," quoth she; so we agreed hereon. Notwithstanding, I mean not to delay in it otherwise than it shall seem good to your Lordship, and in that sort that may best like you. I will do what I can either in that or anything else what may anyway lay in me. If it be clear about your house here in London I think if it may so please you it were good that both my Lady of Oxford and the child were there, and so the child might be quickly brought hither at my Lord's being there. I would wish speed that he might be taken in his good mood. I thank God I am at this present in his good favour. . . . Then I trust all things will follow to your desire. I hear he is about to buy a house here in London about Watling Street, and not to continue a Courtier as he hath done; but I pray you keep all these things secret or else you may undo those that do take pains to bring it to pass if my Lord's counsel should be betrayed before he list himself. And above all others my credit should be lost with him if he should know I dealt in anything without his consent; and therefore my good Lord I pray you keep it very secret, and write me two or three words what you would have me do in it.

And thus with my very hearty commendation I commit your Lordship to God, whom I pray to work all things to your comfort. From Willoughby House this 15th of December.

Your Lordship's very assured friend,
K. Suffoulk.

One wonders if Oxford was actuated by a wish to see whom the little girl resembled and what effect the meeting had on him. It did not lead to a restoration of the marriage.[3] However, it evidently touched his writer's imagination. In *Pericles, Prince of Tyre,* and later, as we have seen, in *The Winter's Tale,* the exquisite and enchanting, long-lost daughter of a mother believed dead is introduced to the presence of her unwitting grief-stricken royal father, to the subsequent joyful reunion of the three and the happy marriage of the young maiden to a deserving suitor.

Pericles, judging by the inferiority of much of the writing, must have been composed originally about the time we have reached in Oxford's life and have had the benefit of much later revisions.[4] The tale of the mythical Apollonius' driven journeyings among strange shores, through travail, storm at sea and shipwreck, encounter with pirates, knightly jousts, separation of hero from wife and daughter and alienation of his lands permeated European literature in the Middle Ages from an origin in a late Grecian romance. The immediate sources of the Shakespearean version, *Pericles,* were a narrative by John Gower, a friend of Chaucer's, and a novel drawn from the *Gesta Romanorum,* published in 1576. The tale may have appealed to Oxford as a parable of his own travels and vicissitudes. Why he changed the name of the hero from Apollonius to Pericles has remained a mystery.[5] E. T. Clark,

---

[3] Two reports in the "uncalendared" accounts at Hatfield House have it that, apparently at about this time, Lord and Lady Oxford came to Theobalds from London with "28 servants" or "28 persons." E. T. Clark suggests that Oxford had brought with them a troupe of actors to perform one or more of his plays for the extensive household. But there is nothing else to suggest that the Earl and his Countess were reunited for several years yet.

[4] In *Pericles,* as in *Timon* and *Titus,* orthodox scholars are faced with the problem of a Shakespearean play containing whole scenes, even acts, that in quality are altogether far below the work they recognize as Shakespeare's. What puts them in a bind is that their Shakespeare cannot have served an apprenticeship; there is no time for any such. Chronology requires that right from the start he be writing plays on the level of the *Henry the Sixes* and *Richard the Third.* Thus we have Edward Dowden ruling that "We may with confidence dismiss the notion entertained by Dryden and a few modern critics, that *Pericles* was an early play of Shakespeare['s]" and George Lyman Kittredge laying it down as "an obvious and undisputed fact" that "Pericles is not all Shakespeare's." From the denial of Shakespeare's sole authorship of initially early plays tangled ancillary problems arise to beset the orthodox. Another contributor or contributors must be scurried about for and when picked the question of which produced the original play and which added to it be wrestled with and the further question be resolved of how to assign the various parts, with little hope of agreement among the critics. To the truly awful question of why Shakespeare in the maturity of his surpassing genius should invest time and work in patching up a play woefully unworthy of him unless it were his own there is no answer at all.

[5] A good guess might be that Pericles, perhaps suggested by Perillie, the hero's name in a 15th century French version, is much more manageable than Apollonius in iambic meter, in which it has to be frequently spoken in the recurrent prologues in the play by "Gower."

however, has a plausible explanation of the change in the name of Pericles' lady from Tharsia to Thaisa: an Elizabethan would recognize the latter as combining the first three letters of Thalia, the Muse of lyric poetry and comedy, and the last three of Elissa, by which name the Queen was often referred to, especially in poetry.

If Oxford was drawn to the Prince of Tyre's story by resemblances to his own, one can only be disturbed by the episode that sets the hero on his wanderings. Pericles, as have many before him, has been resolved to wed the beauteous daughter of King Antiochus of Antioch, who, to keep so choice a prize for himself, has set a riddle which the suitor must solve or forfeit his life. The Prince is the first to grasp the meaning and is made "pale to read it"; the King has "provoked" the young woman to incest. Pericles, before he flees with his fatal knowledge to escape the monarch's wrath, declares in an aside:

> Fair glass of light, I lov'd you, and could still,
> Were not this glorious casket stor'd with ill.

Let us put down to an over-zealous imagination my notion that it may have been the susceptibility of this aspect of the play to scandalous inferences that kept *Pericles* out of the First Folio and the Second; though popular in earlier quarto editions, in which it was repeatedly described as "admired" and offered as by Shakespeare, the play took its place among its sister works only in the second edition of the Third Folio, in 1664, where it was entered along with half a dozen other plays not Shakespeare's.

The position to which Oxford had attained in letters was recognized in an address to him in July 1578 before the Queen by Gabriel Harvey, then a fellow at Trinity College, Cambridge. Harvey had matriculated at the University in 1566 and there had come to know the young de Vere, for as he was to recall later,

> In the prime of his [Lord Oxford's] gallantest youth he bestowed Angels [gold coins] upon me in Christ's College in Cambridge, and otherwise vouchsafed me many gracious favours at the affectionate commendation of my cousin, Master Thomas Smith, the son of Sir Thomas. . . .

Already, then, at sixteen, Edward had become a patron of other writers. Sir Thomas Smith had been briefly Edward's tutor in early boyhood. And it was to visit Sir Thomas that the Queen, bringing the whole Court with her, stopped off at Audley End in Essex — still an expansive, splendid mansion in a park-like setting — the scene of Harvey's address, during a Progress to Cambridge. Harvey had come down from the University for the occasion. After apostrophizing in turn the Queen, Burghley, and Leicester, he turned to Oxford.

> Thy splendid fame, demands even more than in the case of others the services of a poet possessing lofty eloquence. Thy merit doth not creep along the ground,

nor can it be confined within the limits of a song. It is a wonder which reaches as far as the heavenly orbs.

O great-hearted one, strong in thy mind and thy fiery will, thou wilt conquer thyself, thou wilt conquer others; thy glory will spread out in all directions beyond the Arctic Ocean; and England will put thee to the test and prove thee to be a native-born Achilles. Do thou but go forward boldly and without hesitation. Mars will obey thee, Hermes will be thy messenger, Pallas striking her shield with her spear shaft will attend thee. For a long time past Phoebus Apollo has cultivated thy mind in the arts. English poetical measures have been sung by thee long enough. Let that Courtly Epistle [to the reader of *The Courtier*] — more polished even than the writings of Castiglione himself — witness how greatly thou dost excel in letters. I have seen many Latin verses of thine, yea, even more English verses are extant; thou hast drunk deep draughts not only of the Muses of France and Italy, but hast learned the manners of many men, and the arts of foreign countries. It was not for nothing that Sturmius himself was visited by thee; neither in France, Italy, nor Germany are any such cultivated and polished men. O thou hero worthy of renown, throw away the insignificant pen, throw away bloodless books, and writings that serve no useful purpose; now must the sword be brought into play, now is the time for thee to sharpen the spear and to handle great engines of war. On all sides men are talking of camps and of deadly weapons; war and the Furies are everywhere, and Bellona reigns supreme. Now may all martial influences support thy eager mind, driving out the cares of Peace. Pull Hannibal up short at the gates of Britain. Defended though he be by a mighty host, let Don John of Austria come on only to be driven home again. Fate is unknown to man, nor are the counsels of the Thunderer fully determined. And what if suddenly a most powerful enemy should invade our borders? If the Turk should be arming his savage hosts against us? What though the terrible war trumpet is even now sounding its blast? Thou wilt see it all; even at this very moment thou art fiercely longing for the fray. I feel it. Our whole country knows it. In thy breast is noble blood, Courage animates thy brow, Mars lives in thy tongue, Minerva strengthens thy right hand, Bellona reigns in thy body, within thee burns the fire of Mars. Thine eyes flash fire, thy countenance shakes spears; who would not swear that Achilles had come to life again?

It is a remarkable address, worth careful attention for what it says of the figure Oxford presented to those around him. It marks him as one of such fame as to demand, *more than others,* the eulogy of a poet possessing lofty eloquence. It tells us that his writings were much more voluminous than those that have come down to us under his name, which include none of his Latin verses. It picks him out as one of the leading personages in the Court, great in merit. It insistently associates him with spears and spear-shaking, making it more natural that he should have taken the pseudoynm he did or indicating that already he was going about in the theatrical world under a *pro forma* incognito as Will Shakespeare. As for the exhortation that he put aside the bootless pen and take up weapons to oppose the enemies before whom England did indeed stand in peril, I cannot believe that Harvey would have presumed, on his own, to lecture the temperamental and touchy Earl. I take it as almost certain that the Earl, in his hankering for military exploit, had put him up to it. He *was* longing for the fray, and this was a way to reinforce his petitions to the Queen. I can see her flicking him with the gloves he had brought her from the Continent and telling him the decision was one for her to make.

That conjecture as to how the land lay finds some substantiation in a letter written by Bernardino de Mendoza, the Spanish Ambassador, about a minor brouhaha during the same Progress, one that throws a revealing light on all involved. The Queen, he wrote,

> has greatly feasted Alençon's Ambassador, and on one occasion when she was entertaining him at dinner she thought the sideboard was not so well furnished with pieces of plate as she would have liked the Frenchman to have seen it; she therefore called the Earl of Sussex, the Lord Steward, who had charge of these things, and asked him how it was there was so little plate. The Earl replied that he had, for many years, accompanied her and other Sovereigns of England in their Progresses, and he had never seen them take so much plate as she was carrying then. The Queen told him to hold his tongue, that he was a great rogue, and that the more good that was done to people like him the worse they got. She then turned to a certain [Baron] North [Leicester's brother-in-law], who was there in the room, and asked him whether he thought there was much or little plate on the sideboard, to which he replied there was very little, and threw the blame on Sussex. When North left the Queen's chamber Sussex told him that he had spoken wrongly and falsely in what he said to the Queen; whereupon North replied that if he (Sussex) did not belong to the Council he would prove what he said to his teeth. Sussex then went to Leicester and complained of the knavish behaviour of North, but Leicester told him the words he used should not be applied to such persons as North. Sussex answered that, whatever he might think of the words, North was a great knave; so that they remain offended with one another as they had been before on other matters. This may not be of importance, but I have thought well to relate it to you so that you may see how easily matters here may now be brought into discord, if care be taken on one side to ensure support against eventualities. The next day the Queen sent twice to tell the Earl of Oxford, who is a very gallant lad, to dance before the Ambassadors; whereupon he replied that he hoped Her Majesty would not order him to do so, as he did not wish to entertain Frenchmen. When the Lord Steward took him the message the second time he replied that he would not give pleasure to Frenchmen, nor listen to such a message, and with that he left the room.

Oxford was probably angry at the treatment of Sussex and also disgusted at being asked to dance while denied a military commission. (We recall again how Bertram railed at being kept "here the forehorse to a smock. . . . Till honour be bought up and no sword worn / But one to dance with.") Most of all, perhaps, he opposed the Queen's marriage to the Duke of Alençon, whom many expected her to accept.

Mendoza continued, reporting that Oxford

> is a lad who has a great following in the country, and has requested permission to go and serve His Highness [Don John of Austria], which the Queen refused, and asked him why he did not go and serve the Archduke Mathias, to which he replied that he would not go and serve another Sovereign than his own, unless it were a very great one, such as the King of Spain.

The characterization of Oxford as a lad with a great following was probably designed to give satisfaction in Madrid, where his religious leanings would be known. Still, it must have had some basis in truth. If only we could know what kind of following he had, and as what! One recalls that Hamlet was "lov'd of the distracted multitude." As for his serving with Don John (who was then attempting to subjugate the Low Countries with the further aim of invading England, marrying the Queen of Scots and establishing her on the English throne) or of serving King Philip himself, it is needless to say that Oxford, that "very gallant lad," would not for a moment have entertained such a notion, and if he had, the Queen was the last person to whom he would have confided it. What Mendoza had heard was a bit of banter between the two in which a sore-tried Oxford was ragging his sovereign to understand how serious he was about military service.

That Oxford's thoughts were bent on arms further evidence was found by Charles W. Barrell in the dedication written to him just before Christmas by Geffrey Gates of a book called *The Defence of Militarie profession, Wherein is . . . plainly prooved how necessary the exercise of armes is for this our age.* The author speaks of his book's coming "under the shield of your noble favour and judgment," and it may be supposed that the Earl encouraged and arranged for its publication. The copyright entry in the Stationers' Register was by John Harrison, who would put on sale in his bookshop "At the signe of the White Greyhound in Paules Churchyard" the first works bearing the name William Shakespeare.

I come back to the feeling that the Queen's refusal to grant a military commission to her ardent courtier, who in Palermo had for her honor challenged all comers to single combat, arose from a wise appraisal of the relative importance of the contributions to her reign he had it in him to make. That this was so may be indicated by the terms in which, in July 1578, she granted his suit for "the fee simple of Rysing, and as much of those lands in fee farm as shall make up the sum of £250." The manor had been among the Duke of Norfolk's possessions seized by the Crown. In acceding to the plea the Queen declared that

> We, as well in consideration of the good, true and faithful service done and given to Us before this time by Our most dear cousin Edward Earl of Oxford, Great Chamberlain of England, as for divers other causes and considerations moving Us by Our special grace, and out of Our certain knowledge and mere motion, We gave and granted, and by these presents for Us, Our heirs and successors do give and grant to the above named Edward Earl of Oxford, all that Our Lordship or Manor of Rysing. . . .

Unlike other recipients of such grants, Oxford had been appointed to no office under the Crown. It is possible that he had been carrying out some kind of secret political assignment for the Government, but nothing of the sort has ever come to light. A reasonable alternative is that his "good, true and faithful service" had been and was expected to continue to be in connection with the theatre. Though there is no way of knowing, I should not be surprised if the Queen, a devotee and champion of the drama, was one of the first to understand how much the entertainment the stage provided could do for the felicity of her subjects — a matter of prime importance to a monarch, even one by divine right — and how much the drama could affect their attitudes.

Portrait inscribed as of Edward de Vere, the 17th
Earl of Oxford

30

"Shall's Have a Play of This?"

1577–1579: Following Frobisher's unsuccessful search for a north-west passage through North America, the chartering of the Company of Cathay to exploit the supposed gold ore on Baffin Island, with the Queen leading the highly placed investors. — Oxford's purchase of shares in a later voyage, which puts him in bond for £3,000, as Antonio in The Merchant *would put himself in bond for 3,000 ducats in a trading venture. — Worthlessness of the rocks brought back by Frobisher, bankruptcy of the company, and metamorphosizing of Lok into Shylock. — The Duke of Alençon's proposal of marriage to Elizabeth; captivation of Elizabeth by his emissary, Simier; Simier's way of dealing with Leicester's opposition to the match. — Alençon's impassioned visit and courtship that for four years would preoccupy English foreign policy; division of public opinion over the match and the cutting off of an opponent's right hand. — Oxford's apparent commentary on it in the first* Cymbeline, *in which the wicked Queen stands for Catherine de' Medici, the uncouth Cloden for her son Alençon, Imogen for Elizabeth, and the kidnapped brothers for the outlawed young Seymour brothers, grandsons of Henry VIII; the case the play makes for defeat of Rome's temporal sway over Britain and preservation of bonds of sentiment as a parable for Elizabethan England. — Oxford's affair with Anne Vavasor; their joint poetical composition; Anne as Rosaline in* Love's Labour's Lost *and Beatrice in* Much Ado about Nothing *and her reappearance as the dark lady of the* Sonnets. — Evidence of first performance at this time of The Merchant of Venice, with Elizabeth as Portia, and of All's Well That Ends Well; the showing at Court of the play* Murderous Michael, *probably an initial version of* Arden of Feversham, *apparently with Oxford in the cast.*

In 1576 Sir Humphrey Gilbert, the soldier-navigator who was to begin the English colonization of North America, published a tract he had written ten years earlier embodying a dream of his. Entitled *A discourse of a discoverie for a new passage to Cataia,* it proclaimed that the new passage westward "were the only way for our princes to possess the wealth of all the East parts," thus setting a goal that would beckon English explorers for a century. There were other enthusiasts as well: Martin Frobisher, another seagoing soldier; Michael Lok, a London merchant with a Mediterranean business whose path de Vere may well have crossed in Venice or Genoa; Richard Hakluyt, geographer of Oxford University; and de Vere's old acquaintance John Dee, astrologer and mathematician, who, with newly achieved cartographic authority, pronounced the quest for a north-west passage sound. In June of that same year Frobisher took three small vessels as far as Baffin

Island, where he sailed up an inlet — now Frobisher Bay — which he thought a strait having Asia on the north and America on the south. After losing a ship to the rigors of the sea and a boat with five seamen to the Eskimos, the expedition picked up a bit of mineral on Hall's Island at the mouth of the Bay. This, on its return, was delivered to Lok and on the strength of conflicting assay reports declared to contain gold.

From the empty promise of a north-west passage interest now shifted to the empty promise of immediate riches from its shores. The "adventurers" in the voyage, who included Sussex, Leicester, Burghley, Walsingham, and Philip Sidney, had lost their investment, but this did not prevent the financing of a new expedition. The Company of Cathay was chartered in March 1577. The Queen herself became the leading "Cathaian," putting up £100 of the £4,500 required and contributing a ship; the Countess Olivia in *Twelfth Night* would be called a Cataian, evidently to establish a connection (and provoke a laugh at a Court performance), unless we believe Sir Toby was calling his lady a thief or scoundrel, as the epithet ordinarily means. Walsingham and Burghley, still hopeful, were good for £400 and £100 respectively. Oxford was one of a score who put up £25 each.

With a fleet of three again, Frobisher sailed down the Thames in May. In September he was back with 200 tons of ore. When this was assayed, the reports were once more conflicting. They were encouraging enough, however, for preparations to be made to smelt the ore at Deptford. Lok had said he expected a yield of £40 a ton and Dee signed a statement that he had obtained seven ounces of silver from 200 pounds of the ore. Before the smelters had produced more than samples — which were faked — a great new expedition was organized. Of fifteen vessels, it was intended to establish a permanent mining camp and bring back 2,000 tons of ore, after which 120 colonists would be sent out.

Against this vision of El Dorado, Oxford held out until four days before the fleet left — but no longer. Unlike others, however, he perceived that the truly important objective was discovering a way around North America to the Orient. He wrote as follows to his "very loving friends, . . . the Commissioners for the voyage to *Meta Incognita*":

> After my very hearty commendations: Understanding of the wise proceeding and orderly dealing for the continuing of the voyage for the discovery of Cathay by the north west (which this bearer, my friend Master Frobisher, hath already very honourably attempted and is now eftsoons to be employed for the better achieving thereof); and the rather induced, as well for the great liking Her Majesty hath to have the same passage discovered, as also for the special good favour I bear to Master Frobisher, to offer unto you to be an adventurer therein for the sum of £1000 or more, if you like to admit thereof; which sum or sums, upon your certificate of admittance, I will enter into bond, shall be paid for that

use unto you upon Michaelmas day next coming. Requesting your answers therein, I bid you heartily farewell. From the Court, the 21st of May 1578.

Your loving friend,
Edward Oxenford.

Inasmuch as this is the only known surviving letter written by Oxford after age thirteen except those composed, habitually under stress of deep incompatibility, to his disapproving Cecil in-laws (unless we count the letter to Bedingfield introducing his *Cardanus Comfort*), it is of peculiar interest; and one is struck by what distinguishes it from most business correspondence: its warm and affectionate tone, so little in keeping with the historians' characterizations of the sender.

It will be noticed that Oxford was now *in bond* for £1,000, just as Antonio in *The Merchant of Venice* is in bond for 3,000 ducats against the successful return of his vessels, with rich cargoes; and when Oxford bought up an additional £2,000 worth of stock from Lok, making him the biggest investor in the enterprise, he was then, like Antonio, in for 3,000. Antonio's friends at the start of the play whet his anxieties. One says,

> Believe me, sir, had I such venture forth,
> The better part of my affections would
> Be with my hopes abroad, I should be still
> Plucking the grass to know where sits the wind,
> Peering in maps for ports, and piers, and roads. . . .

Another takes over:

> My wind, cooling my broth,
> Would blow me to an ague when I thought
> What harm a wind too great might do at sea.
> I should not see the sandy hourglass run
> But I should think of shallows and of flats. . . .

Oxford was probably only too well acquainted with such apprehensions, and perhaps with such friends.

His investment was enormous. Its loss would be almost as staggering a blow as that befalling Antonio. And lose it he did. He knew he would even before the fleet returned in November. The ore from Hall's Island had already been found to be worthless. The new cargo would prove equally so. The Company collapsed to the tune of a £20,000 loss. Lok, whose credit had been heavily hypothecated, bore the brunt of the storm. Frobisher declared that he had been "a false accountant to the Company, a cozener to my Lord of Oxford, no venturer at all in the voyages, a bankrupt knave." It does look as if, in his readiness to part with £2,000 of his £5,000 investment to Oxford, he may have had prior knowledge of the likely value of the ore, as Frobisher charged.

Innocent, as he claimed to be, or guilty, Lok was imprisoned in the Fleet. And that was not all. When the scurrilous Lucio in *Measure for Measure* says "a sly fellow, the Duke," he is accusing that nobleman of dissembling the wickedness he practices; and Oxford would use the adjective in the same derogatory sense to make Shy-lock the personification of the ruthless creditor for as long as the English stage might last. (The American term "shyster" may preserve an old English usage.) The Shylock who wails about his daughter and his ducats, however, probably owes something to Burghley, too, as does the Shylock whose "craft" impresses Mark Van Doren, as does his contempt for music and merrymaking.

For Oxford, being granted the manor of Rysing at this juncture must have amounted to a rescue at Elizabeth's hands somewhat like Antonio's at Portia's. And as Portia was held a prize by noble foreign suitors, so too was Elizabeth, who was now the matrimonial desideratum of the third of Catherine de' Médicis' sons. It was in mid-summer of that year, 1578, shortly after the Court was at Audley End and its leading personages were being hailed in Latin Alexandrines by Harvey that the Queen received a formal proposal of marriage from the Duke of Alençon. It was, in fact, brought by the ambassador for whom Oxford refused to dance. At forty-five, Elizabeth could have been in no doubt that for marriage it was now or never, and Alençon would prove to be the most ardent of her princely suitors.

In January 1579 the Duke sent a personal emissary to urge his cause. Jehan de Simier is described by Lucy Aikin in *Memoirs of the Court of Queen Elizabeth* as "a person of great dexterity, who well knew how to ingratiate himself by a thousand amusing arts; by a sprightly style of conversation peculiarly suited to the taste of the queen; and by that ingenious flattery, the talent of his nation, which is seldom entirely thrown away even upon the sternest and most impenetrable natures." It was certainly not thrown away upon Elizabeth. Even in French eyes Simier was noted for *"une connaissance exquise des gaités d'amour."* The Queen seems to have been captivated, if not bowled over. She herself was far from lacking the power to charm. Edmund Bohun said of her that "Her skin was pure white, and her beauty lasted to her middle age." She had, besides, great élan, a keen mind, and a fencer's skill in repartée, all of which would have appealed to the Frenchman. Above all she had that for which no subject of Henri III's could have been prepared: an almost tangible aura and preternatural magnetism, which come only to a ruler fairly worshipped by the people. Soon the Queen and *le Singe,* as she called her Gallic gallant, were so habitually in each other's company, and sometimes in such compromising circumstances, as to send scandalous rumors through Europe. If these reached Alençon's ears, however, there was no sign of it.

Chapter 30: Shall's Have a Play of This?

It must be said for the Duke's agent that he never ceased to serve the object of his mission. He continued to press Alençon's suit. In this he quickly encountered vigorous opposition from Elizabeth's established favorite, the Earl of Leicester. Events put in his hands the means to deal with that, however. Some years after his wife Amy Robsart had fulfilled expectations by dying suddenly, Leicester, as the reader may recall, had gone through the motions of a marriage with the infatuated Lady Sheffield, four days before she presented him with a baby boy. (The Lady's husband had, upon discovering Leicester's philandering with his wife, died, also suddenly, before he could expose the adulterer.) That was in 1573. In 1576, having tired of his second consort and finding her indignantly opposed to removing herself for a cash settlement, the Earl had accomplished this end by informing her that the marriage had been invalid. This left him free to wed Lettice Knollys, the widowed Countess of Exeter. The young woman's father, knowing whom he was dealing with, insisted upon a second performance of the rites, before witnesses. Although many persons must thus have learned of it, Leicester succeeded in keeping it from the Queen, as he had his liaison with Lady Sheffield. Or he did until Simier got wind of it and spilled his information to his royal hostess.

Elizabeth's reaction gives us almost more insight into her character than we could ask for. Lucy Aikin tells it in the *Memoirs*:

> The rage of the queen on this disclosure transported her beyond all the bounds of justice, reason and decorum. It has been already remarked that she was habitually, or systematically, an open enemy to matrimony in general; and the higher any persons stood in her good graces and the more intimate their access to her, the greater was her resentment at detecting in them any aspirations after this state; because a kind of jealousy was in these cases superadded to her malignity; and it offended her pride that those who were honored with her favor should find themselves at leisure to covet another kind of happiness of which she was not the dispenser. But that Leicester, the dearest of her friends, the first of her favorites, after all the devotedness to her charms which he had so long professed and which she had requited by a preference so marked and benefits so signal, — that he, — her opinion unconsulted, her sanction unimplored, should have formed — and with her own near relation, — this indissoluble tie; and having formed it should have attempted to conceal the fact from her when known to so many others; — appeared to her the acme of ingratitude, perfidy and insult. She felt the injury like a weak disappointed woman; she resented it like a queen and a Tudor.
>
> She instantly ordered Leicester into confinement in a small fort then standing in Greenwich park; and she threw out the menace, nay actually entertained the design, of sending him to the Tower. But the lofty and honorable mind of the earl of Sussex revolted against proceedings so violent, so lawless and so disgraceful in every point of view to his royal kinswoman. He plainly represented to her, that it was contrary to all right and all decorum that any man should be punished for lawful matrimony; which was held in honor by all; and his known

hostility to the favorite giving weight to his remonstrance, the queen curbed her anger, gave up all thoughts of the Tower, and soon restored the earl to liberty. In no long time afterwards, he was readmitted to her presence; and so necessary had he made himself to her majesty, or so powerful in the state, that she found it expedient insensibly to restore him to the same place of trust and intimacy as before; though it is probable that he never entirely regained her affections; and his countess, for whom indeed she had never entertained any affection, remained the avowed object of her utter antipathy even after the death of Leicester; and in spite of all the intercessions in her behalf with which her son Essex, in the meridian of his favor, never ceased to importune his sovereign.

The Elizabeth-Simier-Alençon triangle was surely one of the oddest in history, not the least in the zeal with which the principals performed their parts, and evidently without rancor or qualms of conscience on any side. What made it the stranger was the double question of what a twenty-year-old boy with a royal duke's choice of the field could have seen in a woman the Queen's age or the Queen, accustomed to indulge a taste for handsome men with little constraint, in a figure of stunted, pock-marked homeliness. Yet, after the youth had impulsively crossed the Channel, arriving unannounced at Greenwich before the Queen had arisen (Simier had to restrain him from barging in upon her), mutual ardor for the match seemed to grow with acquaintance. (It may be granted that Alençon had done his cause no harm with the Tudor in Elizabeth by presenting her with a diamond ring worth perhaps a tenth of the entire national budget of England and distributing about the Court the rich jewels with which his mother had provided him.) The Queen seemed so determined upon marrying her *Grenouille,* her Frog, as she called her swain, that merely at the hesitancy of her Council in the matter she was to burst into tears of vexation. The Frog-Prince, for his part, upon being recalled to Paris after a mere fortnight, had written letters back to her on the way to Dover passionate enough, according to the French Ambassador, to set fire to water.

For four years, Conyers Read says, the French Duke would be the focal point of English foreign policy. "At Court everybody believed Elizabeth seriously contemplated marriage, and the Court circle was split in two on the subject, with Leicester leading the opposition to the match, Burghley and Sussex leading its supporters. To a considerable extent the country at large was divided, with the Puritans violently opposed, the Catholics, or crypto-Catholics, generally favorable." What moved Sussex was the fear that if Alençon were rejected, France and Spain would combine to work Elizabeth's overthrow. Burghley, in two detailed memoranda he wrote himself, carefully weighed the *pros* and *contras* of the marriage. That he came down on the pro side was primarily because he saw an urgent need for Elizabeth to produce an heir if domestic rebellion were not to be aroused in favor of Mary Queen of Scots and a disputed succession not to tempt foreign intervention. He believed the Queen still capable of bearing issue.[1] But whatever the reasons in favor of the match, the person of the suitor contributed little to them. Alençon was not only dwarfed and ugly but not very bright, though his adeptness at conversation tended to mislead others on this score.

Oxford is reported to have backed the marriage. He was hardly likely to oppose it openly, as did Leicester and Sidney, for which they were properly scorched by the Queen. Poor John Stubbs, who wrote a pamphlet arguing against it under a title invoking the Lord to let "Her Majesty see the sin and punishment thereof," suffered no mere royal disfavor. Though his admonition was kindly and avuncular, he had his right hand cut off by the hangman — whereupon, waving the bloody stump from the scaffold, he cried "Long live the Queen!" and fainted. "Such," says G. M. Trevelyan, "was the relation of that strange, subtle woman to her simple-hearted subjects." And such was the utter barbarity with which, whatever her actual intentions, she demonstrated that she was not going to have her seeming inclinations challenged by those she ruled.

If Oxford seemed on the Queen's side in her apparent decision, it was perhaps in deference to the Earl of Sussex. His actual views evidently came out on the stage, as usual, and, in this case, also in an extraordinary and wildly funny pantomime he put on from horseback in the Strand; a complex man, Edward de Vere.

The dramatic vehicle for his political statement was an early version of *Cymbeline,* unless I am altogether mistaken about it. Orthodoxy, ever unable to allow for an apprentice Shakespeare, makes the awkwardly plotted play one of the dramatist's latest, though as J. M. Robertson says, "it is so difficult to conceive Shakespeare in his last years planning *Cymbeline* as it stands, that even German conservatism has accepted Coleridge's theory of it as a play written by the Master in his youth and re-written in his last theatrical years." E. T. Clark thinks the early version was *An history of the cruelties of a Stepmother,* which was shown at the palace at Richmond on 28 December 1578. Certainly a cruel stepmother has a key role in the basic play. Cymbeline's unnamed Queen (whose counterpart we shall meet again as

---

[1] Conyers Read observes with warrant that "Burghley's discussion of Elizabeth's fruitfulness is the best thing we have on the subject. Coming from him, who was probably better informed than anyone else, and taken in connection with his persistent efforts to get her married in order that she might have children, it comes near to settling the perennial question of her ability to bear children." What Burghley wrote was:

> It cannot be denied but if her Majesty, when she was younger in years [had married] it had been better for her and the realm also; but considering the proportion of her body, having no impediment of smallness in stature, of largeness in body, nor no sickness, nor lack of natural functions in those things that properly belong to the procreation of children, but contrary wise, by judgment of physicians that know her estate in those things and by the opinion of women, being most acquainted with her Majesty's body in such things as properly appertain, to show probability of her aptness to have children, even at this day.

Regan in *King Lear*), she is seeking to marry her son by a previous marriage, the loutish Cloten, to Cymbeline's daughter, her own step-daughter, the heavenly Imogen, to whom Cloten pays avid court. In the interpretation I accept, Cymbeline (the historic King Cunobelin) represents a combination of England and Henry VIII and the Queen is Catherine de' Medici — Cymbeline's mate in that France was at this time England's ally — who is trying to wed her son d'Alençon (from the letters of which name the "Cloden" may be formed) to England-Henry's daughter Elizabeth, whom Alençon is ardently pursuing. As a Lord in Act II soliloquizes:

> That such a crafty devil as his mother
> Should yield the world this ass! a woman that
> Bears all down with her brain; and this her son
> Cannot take two from twenty, for his heart,
> And leave eighteen.

The Queen, her son Cloten, and Cymbeline's daughter Imogen are all added to the historical record by the dramatist — made up by him to make the cast of characters that of the years 1578 to 1581. The actual Cunobelin did have two sons, Guiderius and Arviragus, and these take significant parts in the play. The dramatist again departs drastically from history, however, in having had the two boys abducted from the Court in early childhood twenty years before the play begins by one Belarius, whom the King had banished; Belarius has brought the comely and noble youths up in ignorance of their identities in the wild Welsh mountains.

Here again the dramatist seems to be taking us into contemporary events, with Cymbeline's two "lost" heirs standing for two grandsons of Henry VIII, the young Seymour brothers. Their father, Edward Seymour, Earl of Hertford, had in 1560 secretly married Lady Catherine Grey, who (her sister Jane having been beheaded by Queen Mary) stood next in succession to Elizabeth under Henry VIII's will. Elizabeth was characteristically so incensed by the Seymour-Grey marriage when she learned of it that she had the couple imprisoned in the Tower and their marriage denied along with the legitimacy of their two sons. Of these the elder had been born in 1561. If, as I surmise, the basic *Cymbeline* was groomed to do chief service in 1581, when the Alençon affair reached its zenith (with Elizabeth's kissing the Duke full on the lips in public and telling the French Ambassador that he might report that she would marry him), then it would have been twenty years since Elizabeth had outlawed the Seymours and their sons just as it had been twenty years before the play opens that Cymbeline's two sons had been abducted. According to Leicester, Cecil had favored the elder Seymour boy as heir to the throne in the event of Elizabeth's dying childless and at one time had had the two brothers in his house. Oxford's companion when he left for France in 1574 had been "Lord Seymour," though which Seymour it was is not known.

In the play, upon Cymbeline's refusing to bow his neck to the yoke of Rome, the legions of Augustus Caesar invade his island kingdom, and it is the British King's two long-lost sons who, with Belarius, turn the tide of battle. After the victory they are reunited with their father, who exclaims:

> Ne'er mother
> Rejoic'd deliverance more. Blest pray you be,
> That after this strange starting from your orbs,
> You may reign in them now! O Imogen,
> Thou hast lost by this a kingdom.

But she protests that she has "got two worlds by't" — two brothers. By this time, happily, the Queen and her brutish son have met the ends they deserve.

Cymbeline as I have summarized it is to be regarded, I think, as Oxford's plea to Elizabeth to reject the Duke of Alençon and to welcome back the young Seymours, accepting the elder as her heir, and thus thwart the designs upon her kingdom of contemporary Roman power — that of the Continental Roman Catholic powers, primarily Spain. But here the dramatist seems to have something else important he wishes to convey in *Cymbeline*. The Britons would not be conquered by Rome and have repulsed the invading legions. Cymbeline had been trained by Augustus Caesar, however, and is well disposed toward Rome. At the end he declares:

> Although the victor, we submit to Caesar
> And to the Roman Empire, promising
> To pay our wonted tribute. . . .

While "the Roman eagle . . . in the beams o' th' sun" has "vanished," he proclaims:

> Let
> A Roman and a British ensign wave
> Friendly together.

In other words, while England must repel the Roman Catholic military forces it should voluntarily reaffirm its traditional affinity with the spiritual empire of Rome.

Readers familiar with *Cymbeline* will recognize that I have left out half of it — for the inexperienced dramatist undertook to splice into the story of the early British king an incongruous tale of 14th-century Italy from Boccaccio's *Decameron* of a young husband who wagers on his wife's fidelity and is tricked into believing that the other party to the wager has seduced her. As we have seen, this gave Oxford another opportunity to flagellate a husband who, too easily persuaded of her turpitude, cruelly mistreats a loyal and even saintly wife. It is, incidentally, a quite Othello-like story; the conscienceless villain is a shadow of Iago, indeed is called Iachimo; the wife — Imogen, who has a double role in the play — has, like Desdemona, been in her husband's eyes "as chaste as unsunn'd snow"; and the evidence that convicts her consists of intimate possessions that, like the fatal handkerchief in *Othello*, the betrayer has acquired by stealth. But we have, in place of a Moor in Venetian service, a Bertram-like young Briton travelling in Italy. Posthumus's illustrious paternity, noble virtue, martial aptitude, upbringing as a royal ward, impecunious marriage to his guardian's daughter against his guardian's wishes, and capacity for outrageous selfishness mark him as none other than Edward de Vere. When Oxford returned from the Continent he did so as an Italianate Englishman and more or less an adherent to the Roman Church. When Posthumus returns to England he does so in the ranks of the Romans. Soon, however, perceiving the threat to his country's freedom from the Roman legions, he declares:

> I am brought hither
> Among th' Italian gentry, and to fight
> Against my lady's kingdom. . . .
> Peace!
> I'll give no wound to thee. Therefore, good heavens,
> Hear patiently my purpose. I'll disrobe me
> Of these Italian weeds and suit myself
> As does a Britain peasant. So I'll fight
> Against the part I come with.

So it was with Oxford by 1581 — barring the bit about suiting himself as a peasant.

It is difficult to know when Oxford's self-accusations about Anne reached the pitch they register in the plays. We know, however, roughly when he acquired a reason for pangs of conscience about her of a different kind that may have added to the coals he heaped on his head in what he wrote. The cause would have been his evident infatuation with the third woman in his troubled emotional life. Her name was Anne Vavasor. According to Charles W. Barrell, who discovered the facts of the liaison, so far as we have them, she was born between about 1560 and 1562. Sir E. K. Chambers writes of her:

> She was the daughter of Henry Vavasour of Copmanthorpe in Yorkshire, by Margaret daughter of Sir Henry Knyvet, a cadet of the Knyvets of Buckenham in Norfolk. She had a brother Thomas Vavasour. . . . The Knyvets had played their parts in the royal household since the days of Henry the Eighth. Anne's uncle, Thomas Knyvet, was a Groom of the Privy Chamber. Her aunt, Katherine Knyvet, was a Maid of Honour, and afterwards Lady of the Bedchamber, to Elizabeth. . . . It was, no doubt, through the Knyvet influence that Anne Vavasor came to court, and was appointed in 1580 a Gentlewoman of the Bedchamber.

Barrell says that "The great Vavasor clan of Yorkshire was famous for its jurists, soldiers and beautiful women. Perhaps the outstanding Roman Catholic family of its day, the Vavasors had been given special permission by Henry VIII to retain their own parish chapel at the time of the dissolution of the Roman Church properties." He states that she was a young cousin of Lord Henry Howard's, another of whose cousins was Lord Oxford, and speculates that as between the two, Howard "played the part of the far-seeing pander in 1578 and 1579, hoping to wreck the Vere-Cecil alliance beyond all repair, by encouraging Oxford's liaison with the country cousin from Yorkshire. He is known to have done just this sort of thing in the notorious Somerset-Howard-Overbury case." She must have been an attractive young lady. Verses addressed to her (by Sir Walter Raleigh, it was said eighty years later) began:

> Many desire, but few or none deserve
> To win the Fort of thy most constant will:
> Therefore take heed, let fancy never swerve
> But unto him that will defend thee still.
>   For this be sure, the fort of fame once won,
>   Farewell the rest, thy happy days are done.

It cannot be said that *The Advice,* as the poem was called, sank in with Mistress Vavasor. Her fancy swerved, but she lived to confound the dire predictions of its doing so. It seems to be assumed that it was with the twenty-nine-year-old Edward de Vere that she first trod the path of dalliance, and this may very well have been so, though I know of no evidence that it was other than the apparent conviction of her relatives; and lines in *Love's Labour's Lost* that we shall come to cast doubt upon the charge. Where did the path lead her? Barrell asserts, though on what basis I again do not know, that she engaged in a "whole series of affairs," being "perhaps the most remarkable of all the aristocratic courtesans of the Elizabethan age." Anne may well have been "adored" by "many men" and have cut a rather wide swath during her career. Certainly she was to have three husbands, two of them at once — or so in 1618 the charge read under which she was to be convicted of bigamy and slapped with a heavy fine, later revoked. When Alice Vavasor in Anthony Trollope's *Can You Forgive Her?* ruefully observes that "We Vavasors don't seem to be good at marrying," she did not have this predecessor in mind. If Trollope considered the mere jilting of a fiancé of doubtful exculpability, Heaven knows what he would have reckoned Anne's prospects of redemption to be. But Anne would be able to laugh her virtuous contemporaries into limbo and most of their children as well, living — unregenerate to the last, one trusts — till past the age of ninety.

Anne's portraits show a woman of slim stature and narrow, perhaps calculating face with slightly aquiline nose, in youth with an ivory complexion and rosy cheeks, whether by nature or by art. And they show her of brunette coloring. All we know of her relations with Oxford is by their results: a son,

Anne Vavasor

From the portrait attributed to John
de Critz

By permission of The Paul Mellon Centre
for Studies in British Art, London, and the
Master and Wardens of the Armourers &
Brasiers' Company, London, owners of the
portrait.

murderous sword-play in the streets of London, and a poem. This last is linked with *Verses Made by the Earl of Oxford* (see page 393), which ends:

> From sighs and shedding amber tears into sweet song she brake,
> When thus the echo answered her to every word she spake:

Anne Vavasor's Echo (which requires giving "Vere" its original pronunciation of *vair*) follows:

> O heavens! who was the first that bred in me this f*ever*? Vere.
> Who was the first that gave the wound whose fear I wear for *ever*?
>   Vere.
> What tyrant, Cupid, to my harm usurps thy golden qui*ver*? Vere.
> What wight first caught this heart and can from bondage it deli*ver*?
>   Vere.
> Yet who doth most adore this wight, oh hollow caves tell true? You.
> What nymph deserves his liking best, yet doth in sorrow rue? You.
> What makes him not regard good will with some regard of ruth?
>   Youth.
> What makes him show besides his birth, such pride and such
>   untruth? Youth.
> May I his favour match with love, if he my love will try? Ay.
> May I requite his birth with faith? Then faithful will I die? Ay.
> And I that know this lady well,
> Said, Lord how great a miracle,
> To hear how Echo told the truth,
> As true as Phoebus' oracle.

As Anne Vavasor awakens the echo in the "hollow caves" to repeat the name of "Vere," so Juliet will "tear the cave where Echo lies . . . with repetition of my Romeo's name."

Such facts as we know of Anne together with those dark eyes and dark locks of hers are sufficient for Oxfordians to see in her the Rosaline of *Love's Labour's Lost* — that Rosaline of whom Berowne, mocking himself incredulously for having fallen in love with her — exclaims:

> A whitely wanton, with a velvet brow,
> With two pitch-balls stuck in her face for eyes;
> Ay, and, by heaven, one that will do the deed
> Though Argus were her eunuch and her guard!
> Am I to sigh for her! to watch for her!
> To pray for her!

Nothing in Rosaline's behavior in the play warrants these shocking slurs on her honor, which suggests that they were inspired by a real-life original of elastic morals. But the reader will have noticed something else about the passage: its expression of love that the poet-dramatist resists for a wanton whose dark features are emphasized. In this one can hardly help seeing a foreshadowing of the dark lady of the *Sonnets* and the feeling she inspires in the poet. Sir Sidney Lee observes that in Sonnets 127 and 132 "Shakespeare amiably notices the black complexion, hair, and eyes of his mistress" and "repeats almost verbatim his own lines in *Love's Labour's Lost* (iv.iii.241–247)" Berowne makes a virtue of what seems to bother him:

> Where is a book?
> That I may swear beauty doth beauty lack,
> If that she learn not of her eye to look:
> No face is fair that is not full so black.
> . . . .
> O! if in black my lady's brows be deck'd,
> It mourns that painting and usurping hair
> Should ravish doters with a false aspect;
> And therefore is she born to make black fair.

As Lee says, the same thoughts are expressed in the *Sonnets*:

> Therefore my mistress' brows are raven black,
> Her eyes so suited, and they mourners seem
> At such who, not born fair, no beauty lack,
> Sland'ring creation with a false esteem.
> Yet even so they mourn, becoming of their woe,
> That every tongue says beauty should look so.
> . . . .
> Then will I swear beauty herself is black
> And all they foul that thy complexion lack.

One would think that those parallels would at least raise in the orthodox mind the question of whether Berowne and Shakespeare were one, but evidently they do not.

The temptation to see in Anne Vavasor the model for Rosaline is one I mean not to resist. And if she was, she was also the model for Beatrice in *Much Ado,* and not only because of the similarities between the two young women. *Love's Labour's Lost* ends with Rosaline sentencing Berowne to "a twelve-month term" apart from her if she is "to be won, " while in *Much Ado,* Beatrice, speaking of Benedick's appeal to her heart, says, "marry, once before he won it of me with false dice": so there had been an amorous interlude between them in the past. I am persuaded that the latter play is the *Love's Labour's Won* listed by Francis Meres among Shakespeare's comedies and otherwise unknown. Love's labor is lost in one play, won in the sequel as the perennially sparring young lovers are brought to acknowledge their mutual affection and are wed, despite the prediction that "if they were but a week married they would talk themselves mad."

The high-spirited parry-and-thrust of wits between them in both plays, in which the young lady at least holds her own, may give an idea of how things were between Oxford and Anne Vavasor. As if to tell us so, Rosaline exclaims, "O that your face were not so full of O's!" But the point I started out to make is that if Anne was a Rosaline-Beatrice she was an exuberant, fetching, and tantalizing dish to set before an earl to which an earl like this one could hardly have been expected not to succumb, despite the arguments it would seem he mustered against his doing so. If she was also the dark lady of the *Sonnets,* as she would appear to have been, her hold on him, bitterly contested toward the end, with fulsome self-recrimination, spanned fifteen years, at least intermittently. Here, remembering that Anne lived to past ninety, we owe Oxford the tribute of recognizing his prescience in having another lady of the Princess's suite address Rosaline with the lines:

> Had she been light like you,
> Of such a merry, nimble, stirring spirit,
> She might 'a' been a grandam ere she died.
> And so may you; for a light heart lives long.

A first stepping-stone to *Love's Labour's Lost* may have been laid shortly before or after Anne Vavasor entered Oxford's life. On 11 January 1579 *A Double Mask* was "shown before her Majesty, the French Ambassador being present." It is recorded as *A Maske of Amasones and A Maske of Knights* and described as "an entertainment in imitation of a tournament between six ladies and a like number of gentlemen who surrendered to them." One thinks of the parody joust between Oxford and the Countess Alvilda in the "tournament" described by Graziano in the *Commedia dell' Arte* in which Oxford is unhorsed, and of the last act in *Love's Labour's* in which the King and his three attendant courtiers, garbed as Russians and masked, engage in amorous overtures with the visiting Princess and her suite of three ladies, also masked.

Later in that same year there appeared a book entitled *Schools of Abuse,* by Stephen Gosson, a graduate of Oxford and a satirist. Soon to take holy orders, Gosson wrote attacking poets and players as "caterpillars of the commonwealth" and deploring the effect of melodrama and vulgar comedy on the social life of London (anticipating the critics of television four centuries later). He made exceptions, however. "As some of the players are far from abuse, so some of their plays are without rebuke. . . ." Two of these were "the Jew and Ptolome, shown at the Bull," the former "representing the greediness of worldly chusers, and bloody minds of usurers." Including with them two other plays, one of his own writing, he says, "These plays are good plays and sweet plays, and most to be liked, worthy to be sung of the Muses." It appears likely that Gosson's "The Jew" and a play called *The history of Portio and demorantes* enacted at Whitehall on 2 February 1580 were the same, Gosson having seen it in the inn yard of the Bull tavern in a try-out before its presentation at Court, and that the play was a first version of *The Merchant of Venice;* "demorantes" could have been a mistranscription of "the merchants." In the year before, a letter from Edmund Spenser to Gabriel Harvey closed with the words, "He that is fast bound unto thee in more obligations than any merchant in Italy to any Jew there." The editor of Harvey's correspondence comments, "This is an evident allusion to the play *The Jew* . . . , then acting at the Bull Theatre, the precursor of Shakespeare's *Merchant of Venice* (see *Gosson's School of Abuse*)."

Oxford at this time was smarting from the loss of the £3,000 for which he had given bond to Michael Lok. As Gwynneth Bowen has shown, too, the matter of usury was at the same time one of pressing social and economic concern, having led to revival of a statute of Henry VIII's (repealed by his son) distinguishing between usury and interest and producing a spate of books on the subject.

Samuel Johnson in his notes on *The Merchant* wrote:

> I am always inclined to believe, that Shakespeare has more allusions to particular facts and persons than his readers commonly suppose. . . . Perhaps in this enumeration of Portia's suitors, there may be some covert allusion to those of Elizabeth.

It would certainly appear so. The foreign princes we see aspiring to Portia's hand put us in mind of those aspiring to Elizabeth's, ranging from "far-off Ivan the Terrible," Martin Hume says, "to the youngest of the Valois." And E. T. Clark suggests that Portia's ruminations on choosing a husband, beginning "If to do were as easy as to know what were good to do, chapels had been churches, and poor men's cottages princes' palaces," may be just such as Oxford had heard from Elizabeth. Specifically, the Queen would have had cause to lament as Portia does that

> I may neither choose whom I would nor refuse whom I dislike; so is the will of a living daughter curbed by the will of a dead father;

for Henry VIII had provided in his will that "our said daughter Elizabeth after our decease, shall not marry, nor take any person to be her husband without the assent and consent of the Privy-Councillors. . . ."

Portia, by the terms of her father's will, is to be won by the suitor who, given the choice of three caskets, picks the one that will be found to contain her picture. The Prince of Morocco chooses the one of gold, the Prince of Aragon the one of silver, and are both disappointed. Portia's fellow country-man, Bassanio, who loves her for herself, and whom she loves, is not moved by "the greed of worldly choosers," as Gosson put it. He opens the leaden casket to find the portrait within. It is painted, by the way, with hair like "a golden mesh to entrap the hearts of men"; the audience at Whitehall would have been in no doubt as to whom *that* referred. There was in this, I take it, a moral for Elizabeth, that her happiness and her subjects' rested in her being won not by a foreign prince, like Alençon, with an eye to material advantage, but by her own people, whose heart went out to her for herself alone. Bassanio in his success avows to Portia:

Chapter 30: Shall's Have a Play of This?

> . . . My blood speaks to you in my veins;
> And there is such confusion in my powers,
> As, after some oration fairly spoke
> By a beloved prince, there doth appear
> Among the buzzing pleasèd multitude;
> Where every something, being blent together,
> Turns to a wild of nothing, save of joy,
> Express'd and not express'd.

It is Elizabeth and her adoring people he is speaking of, I think — so intended and so understood.

The procession of solicitors for Elizabeth in marriage was necessarily ending with "the youngest of the Valois," Alençon, owing to the imminence of her "climacteric," as it was called then. The inception of the play would therefore, I believe, not be later than the time we have reached.

On Twelfth Night — January 6th — there had been shown at Richmond *The historie of the Rape of the second Helene.* This may have been the first go-around on *All's Well,* for in this play as we know it the connection is made between its heroine and Paris's fair captive when the Countess says "tell my gentlewoman I would speak with her; Helen, I mean," and the Clown sings:

> "Was this fair face the cause," quoth she
>> "Why the Grecians sackèd Troy?
> Fond done, done fond!
>> Was this King Priam's joy?"

Two months later, on 3 March 1579, "*The history of murderous mychael* [was] shown at Whitehall on Shrove Tuesday at night by the Lord Chamberlain's servants." Later Gilbert Talbot (whom we remember seven years earlier reporting that the Queen delighted more in Oxford than in any other) remarked in a letter to his father:

> At shrovetide, according, as it seemed, customary at the season, were shows presented at Court before her Majesty at night. The chiefest was a device presented by the persons of the Earl of Oxford, the Earl of Surrey, and the Lords Thomas and Windsor [husband of Oxford's elder sister]. But the device was prettier than it had hap to be performed; but the best of it, and I think the best liked, was two jewels, which were presented to her Majesty by the two Earls.

Of the actors in the "device," only Oxford had a reputation as a writer. Shrovetide comprises the three days before Ash Wednesday, so that there is a good chance that *Murderous Michael,* which was "shown on Shrove Tuesday" — *Mardi Gras* — was the one Talbot called the "chiefest" device. E. T. Clark observes, "The production of *Murderous Michael* at Court followed within a few months the printing of Holinshed's 'Chronicle' containing an account of the tragedy by which Arden of Feversham was cruelly murdered by his wife Alice, aided and abetted by her willing servant, Michael, who was unhesitatingly ready to kill anyone who interfered with his own plans or desires." It seems to me a fair surmise that the *Murderous Michael* of 1579 was a first attempt at the anonymous play *Arden of Feversham* of 1592, of which Swinburne wrote:

> There is more in it of the tragic humour and terrible or tender insight which were his [Shakespeare's] alone in the fullness and perfection of their power than will be found in the very greatest work of the very greatest of his followers and disciples: and to say this is to say much indeed: but less cannot and must not be said. And no poet of the time but Shakespeare and Webster has shown so noble an instinct for elevating and purifying the character of women or of men whom the chronicles they followed with close and meticulous fidelity had presented as merely debased and contemptible criminals: while the villain whose abject and savage egotism is the mainspring of the tragic action can hardly seem to any competent reader the creature of any hand then engaged in creation but Shakespeare's. Assuredly there is no other known to whom it could be plausibly or even possibly assigned. If it be not his, there was a greater than he in his youth at work for the tragic stage, whose very name has perished.

E. T. Clark cites almost 200 instances of language in Shakespeare akin to that in *Arden*, more than half of them from the trilogy formed by the second and third parts of *Henry the Sixth* and *Richard the Third*, which she believes written in original versions within a few years of *Murderous Michael*. There is to me a somewhat more sustained, unrelenting drive in *Arden* than in plays we know as Shakespeare's, but I must say about most of the writing in *Arden* that I could not be sure whether it was from a play of Shakespeare's if I did not know its source. It seems to me, for example, that from this passage in *Arden*

> Leave now to trouble me with worldly things,
> And let me meditate upon my Saviour Christ,
> Whose blood must save me from the blood I shed.

it is but a step to this in *Richard the Third*:

> I charge you, as you hope to have redemption
> By Christ's dear blood shed for our grievous sins,
> That you depart, and lay no hands on me.

31

"As the Style Shall Give Us Cause"

1579 et seq.: Tennis-court quarrel between Oxford and Leicester's nephew Philip Sidney; the bad name it gives Oxford; the parodying of Sidney as Sir Andrew Aguecheek. — Oxford as leader of the Euphuists, who seek to refine and enhance the language, in opposition to Sidney's less venturesome coterie. — Oxford and Sidney as the originals of Willie and Perigot in the rhyming match in Spenser's Shepheardes Calendar; *the rhyming matches in* Love's Labour's Lost, *with Oxford as Berowne and Sidney as Boyet; the sudden, scathing mockery of Boyet as, among other things, a plagiarist, which Sidney indeed was. — International associations of Euphuism; its English antecedent in the elaborate full title,* A Hundreth Sundry Flowres. — *Fruiting of the movement in John Lyly's* Euphues. — *Lyly as an employee of Oxford's. — Likely explanation of Lyly's supposed formative influence upon Shakespeare in his hand-in-glove relationship with Oxford, in which Lyly was the glove and Oxford the hand in bringing into being* Euphues *(the second step, after* The Adventures of Master F. I., *in the evolution of the English novel) and the courtly plays ascribed to Lyly, with their strongly Shakespearean lyrics, omitted from the published plays before 1632. — Literary feud between the Harveys (Gilbert and his two brothers) and the three playwrights Lyly, Nashe, and Greene. — Satirical, but invaluably informative, caricature of Oxford by Harvey in his* Mirror of Tuscanism; *the trouble it makes for Harvey; the reference by Nashe to a quarrel between "two great peers" and his charge that Harvey in his hatchet-job on Oxford was serving the "safe side," presumably Leicester.*

In September 1579 there occurred a set-to between Oxford and Philip Sidney that would help give the former a bad name. Unfortunately for him the quarrel was with one who would prove a darling of history and more unfortunately still, history would have to rely on what two great friends of Sidney's wrote about it. One was Fulke Greville, Lord Brooke, who so adored the martyred poet that he had himself described on his tomb as "servant to Queen Elizabeth, councillor to King James and friend to Philip Sidney."

Reading from Greville's *Life of the Renowned Sir Philip Sidney* (a "panegyric," the *Encyclopaedia Britannica* says), one gathers that Oxford came out upon a tennis-court upon which Sidney was playing and undertook to eject him that he might play himself, though this is not definitely stated and may not have happened. The facts tend to be lost in Greville's mouth-filling prose. The Earl himself is not named, being identified only as "a peer of this Realm, born great, greater by alliance, and superlative in the Prince's favor" — a characterization strikingly like the aphorism Greville would have known

619

from *Twelfth Night*, that "some are born great, some achieve greatness and some have greatness thrust upon them." As Greville relates it, "Sir Philip [who was not yet a Sir, by the way] answers that if his lordship had been pleased to express desire in milder characters perchance he might have led out those that he should now find would not be driven out with any scourge of fury. This answer (like a bellows) blowing up sparks of excess already kindled, made my Lord scornfully call Sir Philip by the name of 'puppy.'" Greville continues:

> The French Commissioners unfortunately had that day audience, in those private galleries, whose windows looked in to the Tennis-Court. They instantly drew all to this tumult: every sort of quarrels sorting well with their humors, especially this. Which Sir Philip perceiving, and rising with an inward strength by the prospect of a mighty faction against him; asked my lord, with a loud voice, that which he had heard clearly enough before. Who — like an echo, that still multiplies by reflexions — repeats this epithet of "Puppy" the second time. Sir Philip resolving in one answer to conclude both the attentive hearers and passionate actor, gave my lord a lie, impossible — as he averred — to be retorted; in respect all the world knows, puppies are gotten by dogs, and children by men.

My lord allowed this salvo of Sir Philip's wit to resound in a silence, "Thereupon, Sir Philip, tender of his Country's honour; with some words of sharp accent, led the way abruptly out of the Tennis-Court." With that "the great lord . . . continues his play," which we had not heard he had commenced. It would be interesting to know who his partner was and why nothing is heard of him.

As Greville tells it, the attitude of the French was that "true honour in both" demanded satisfaction and that this "stirred a resolution in his Lordship to send Sir Philip a Challenge." We learn, however, from an old friend of Sidney's, Hubert Languet, a French Huguenot diplomat and writer, that it was the other way around; and Languet had the facts fresh from Sidney in a letter written to him in Antwerp. In his reply of October 14th — which is not popular with historians though it was written directly after the event rather than many years later — Languet says:

> I am aware that by a habit inveterate in all Christendom, a nobleman is disgraced if he does not resent such an insult: still, I think you were unfortunate to be drawn into this contention, although I see that no blame is to be attached to you for it. You can derive no true honour from it, even if it gave you occasion to display to the world your constancy and courage. You want another stage for your character, and I wish you had chosen it in this part of the world.
>
> On the other hand be careful lest under the influence of swashbucklers you should overstep the bounds of your native modesty. In this very quarrel, sound as your position was, you have gone further than you ought to have done, for when you had flung back the insult thrown at you, you ought to have said no more; as a matter of fact, carried away by your quick temper, you sent him a challenge, and thus you have deprived yourself of the choice of weapons if at any time this controversy should have to be decided by a duel; for it is the

people who want to teach us how we should go mad by rule who have applied their own laws to duels, which of all things are the most unjust.

The consequence was, according to Greville, that

> the Queen, who saw that by loss or disgrace of either could gain nothing, presently undertakes Sir Philip, and (like an excellent Monarch) lays before him the difference in degree between Earls and Gentlemen, the respect inferiors owed to their superiors, and the necessity in Princes to maintain their own creations, as degrees descending between the people's licentiousness and the anointed sovereignty of Crowns; how the Gentleman's neglect of the Nobility taught the peasant to insult both.

With no word on the subject from Oxford surviving — naturally — it is impossible to know how blameworthy he may have been. Something not reported had provoked him, I imagine. The challenge, at least, he probably did not take seriously. In *Twelfth Night*, evidently written in the next year, he has Sir Andrew Aguecheek goaded by "swashbucklers" — such as Languet had warned Sidney of, notably Sir Toby Belch — into provoking the Duke's nobly born page (Viola disguised as a man) to a duel; and Sir Andrew's addle-pated challenge, as Percy Allen discovered, seems clearly modeled on a bellicose letter, similarly confused, sent by Sidney to his father's secretary, Molyneux, in May 1578, reading in part:

> *You have* play the very knave with me, and so I will make you know *if I have* good proof of it. But that for so much as is past. For that is to come. . . . I will thrust my dagger into you. And trust to it, for I speak in earnest. In the meantime farewell.

Even the incongruous "farewell" is imitated in Aguecheek's epistle.

Between Oxford and one whom he saw as Sir Andrew, there was hardly apt to be much spontaneous cordiality — and Sidney's Aguecheek leanings were evident enough even to be remarked by his friend Languet, who, pleading the freedom countenanced by friendship, wrote in 1578:

> . . . the habits of your court seemed to me somewhat less manly than I could have wished, and most of your noblemen appeared to me to seek for a reputation more by a kind of affected courtesy than by those virtues which are wholesome to the state, and which are most becoming to generous spirits and to men of high birth. I was sorry, therefore, and so were other friends of yours, to see you wasting the flower of your youth on such things. . . . If the arrogance and insolence of Oxford have roused you from your trance, he has done you less wrong than they who have hitherto been more indulgent to you.

Oxford's adherence to the Earl of Sussex and Sidney's to his uncle, the Earl of Leicester, would have set them at odds, too — and Oxford would have had unexceptionable grounds for detesting Leicester. There was cause for other differences between the two as well. "Philip Sidney and Edward Dyer, the recognized chiefs of the Leicester coterie," W. J. Courthope writes in *A History of English Poetry*, "were at this time [1578] amusing themselves with a proposed reform of English versification, based on the principles advocated at Cambridge by Gabriel Harvey." He quotes the poet Edmund Spenser as writing to Harvey that the two had

> proclaimed in their Areopagus a general surceasing and silence of bald rhymers, and also of the very best, too; instead whereof [i.e., instead of rhymes] they have by authority of their whole senate prescribed certain laws and rules of quantities of English syllables for English verse; having had thereof great practice and drawn me to their faction.

Courthope goes on to say that "At the head of the other literary party was Edward, Earl of Oxford," who "is unfortunate in being chiefly known to posterity as the antagonist of Sidney in the [tennis-court] quarrel . . . ; beyond this, little is known of him." He was, however, "a great favourer of the Euphuists, and himself a poet of some merit in the courtly Italian vein." Paying Oxford's verse the compliments cited in Chapter 30 and quoting three of his poems, Courthope says "He was not only witty in himself, but the cause of wit in others," curiously applying to Oxford the very words in which Falstaff describes himself. "Several of the courtiers set themselves to solve the problem proposed in his well-known epigram: —

> "Were I a king I might command content,
> Were I obscure unknown would be my cares,
> And were I dead no thought should me torment,
> Nor words, nor wrongs, nor love, nor hate, nor fears.
> A doubtful choice of three things one to crave,
> A kingdom or a cottage or a grave.

"Sir Philip Sidney declared that there could be no doubt as to the answer: —

> "Wert thou a king, yet not command content,
> Since empire none thy mind could yet suffice,
> Wert thou obscure, still cares would thee torment;
> But wert thou dead all care and sorrow dies.
> An easy choice of three things one to crave,
> No kingdom nor a cottage but a grave."

One gathers that the two versifiers made a game of poetical give-and-take between them. There is a rhyming match in Edmund Spenser's *The Shepheardes Calender* between Willie and Perigot, in which Willie is taken to be Oxford (partly on the strength of the evident reference to Oxford as Willie in the same poet's *Teares of the Muses* of 1590) and Perigot to be Sidney. It was to Sidney that the *Calender*, published in 1579, was dedicated. Various actual persons appear under pseudonyms in one or more of the twelve months into which it is divided, notably the author himself as Colin Clout and Gabriel Harvey as Hobbinol. (The Archbishop Grindall is made light of as Algrind under July, which so enraged Lord Burghley that Spenser was to suffer for it the rest of his life.) The friendly contest begins as follows:

> *Willie*: Tell me, Perigot, what shall be the game,
>   Wherefor with mine thou dare thy music match?
> Or been thy bagpipes run far out of frame?
>   Or hath the cramp thy joints benumbed with ache?
> *Perigot*: Ah! Willie, when the heart is ill assayed,
>   How can bagpipe or joints be well a-paid?

It continues through seven exchanges, these forming a succession of those six-line stanzas in iambic pentameter with an *a b a b c c* rhyme-scheme to which Oxford-Shakespeare was so partial. Then it moves into high gear:

> *Per.* It fell upon a holy even,
> *Wil.* Hey, ho, holiday!
> *Per.* When holy fathers were wont to shrieve;
> *Wil.* Now ginn*eth* this roundelay
> *Per.* Sitting upon a hill so high,
> *Wil.* Hey, ho the high hill!
> *Per.* The while my flock did feed thereby;
> *Wil.* The while the shepherd self did spill;
> *Per.* I saw the bouncing Bellibone,
> *Wil.* Hey, ho, Bonnibell!
> *Per.* Tripping over the dale alone;
> *Wil.* She can trip it very well.

This foolishness goes on for thirty more exchanges. One is reminded of Feste the Clown's song at the end of *Twelfth Night*, beginning:

> When that I was and a little tiny boy,
>   With hey, ho, the wind and the rain,
> A foolish thing was but a toy,
>   For the rain it raineth every day.

It may have come to Oxford in just such a match.

Contrapuntal rhyming, with — it seems evident — Sidney as Boyet and Oxford as Berowne, is prominent in *Love's Labour's*, which is another reason for tying the Perigot-Willie contest to these two. Pretty amateurish in quality, it takes up most of Act IV, Scene 1:

> *Costard*: I have a letter from Monsieur Berowne to one Lady
>   Rosaline.
> *Princess*: O, thy letter, thy letter! He's a good friend of mine
>   Stand aside, good bearer, Boyet, you can carve:
>   Break up this capon.
> *Boyet*:   I am bound to serve.
>   This letter is mistook; it importeth none here.
>   It is writ to Jaquenetta.
> *Princess*:   We will read it I swear.

In a few more lines the meter collects itself sufficiently for one to recognize it as that of *A Visit from St. Nicholas*.

> *Boyet*: I *am* much deceived but I remember the style.
> *Princess*: Else your memory is bad, going o'er it erewhile.
> *Boyet*: This Armado's a Spaniard that keeps here in court;
>   A phantasime, a Monarcho, and one that makes sport.

Contrapuntal jousting goes on for pages two scenes later. It proceeds in couplets until Berowne breaks the pace with one of those six-line *a b a b c c* stanzas. Thereafter it continues *a b a b c d c d e f e f* and so on, through a characteristic bit of Shakespearean naughtiness:

> *Berowne*: I'll prove her fair, or talk till doomsday here.
> *King*: No devil will fright thee then so much as she.
> *Dumain*: I never knew man hold vile stuff so dear.
> *Longaville*: Look, here's thy love; my foot and her face see.
>   [Shows his shoe.]
> *Berowne*: O, if the streets were paved with thine eyes,
>   Her feet were much too dainty for such tread!
> *Dumain*: O vile! Then, as she goes, what upward lies
>   The street should see as she walked overhead.

If all such early work of Shakespeare's were signed by Oxford, what a thankless task it would be to argue that its author wrote the *Sonnets, Othello,* and *Antony and Cleopatra*!

The dramatist treats Sidney quite amiably in *Love's Labour's Lost*, except for giving him a name meaning, "little boy," akin to the famous "puppy," until he reaches Act V, Scene 2, when Berowne lets him have it. He begins:

> This fellow pecks up wit as pigeons pease,
> And utters it again when God doth please.

Oxford was clearly irked at Sidney's borrowing from others' works. Sir Sidney Lee remarks that "Petrarch, Ronsard and Desportes inspired the majority of Sidney's efforts, and his addresses to abstractions like sleep, the moon, his muse, grief or lust are almost verbatim translations from the French." Sidney himself confessed that he "sought fit words" by "oft turning others' leaves." Sidney Lee comments that in his *Astrophel and Stella* "the 'beams' of the eyes of Sidney's mistress were 'wrapt in colour black' and wore 'this mourning weed,' so

> "That whereas black seems beauty's contrary,
> She even in black doth make all beauties flow."

Lee's purpose is to show how close these bits are to passages in *Love's Labour's Lost* and Shakespeare's *Sonnets* on the same subject, and we may dismiss the conclusion his orthodoxy reaches, that Sidney, being an earlier writer than Shakspere of Stratford, was the initiator, Shakespeare the copier.

While Oxford had other reasons for exasperation with Sidney, as we shall see, what evidently galled him especially was the extravagant praise given to Sidney as a poet. Berowne ends his mockery of Boyet with these lines, to which nothing in the play has led up:

> And consciences that will not die in debt
> Pay him the due of "honey-tongued Boyet."

Meanwhile Oxford has shown how scathing he could be:

> Why, this is he
> That kiss'd his hand away in courtesy.
> This is the ape of form, Monsieur the Nice
> That, when he plays at tables, chides the dice
> In honourable terms.

The speech has the earmarks of being a later interpolation in the play.

In calling Oxford the head of the literary party favoring Euphuism, Courthope explains that

> Euphuism was the form assumed in England by a linguistic movement which, at some particular stage of development, affected every literature in modern Europe. The process in all countries was the same, namely, to refine the vocabulary and syntax of the language by adapting the practice of early writers to the usage of modern conversation.

In France it had been a half-dozen poets called the Pléiade a generation earlier. "The object of this band was to bring the French language, in vocabulary, constructions and application on a level with the classical tongues by borrowing from the latter," says George Saintsbury, who might be talking about Shakespeare's object in England. And so he might also in speaking of their "best work," which, he tells us, was distinguished by "a racy mixture of scholarliness and natural beauty" with "magnificence of imagery": Shakespeare to a T. The most famous of the Pléiade was Pierre de Ronsard (1524–1585), like Oxford a product of the nobility and a favorite of the Court, as he was also of Queen Elizabeth. Oxford would have been familiar with his work and probably have met him in Paris — and there have had an earful from the "Prince of Poets" of the slander he had had to endure from the Huguenots as a protégé of the King's.

Interestingly, Courthope remarks that the approach of Euphuism was marked by the title of a book I have reasoned was chiefly Oxford's handiwork:

> A Hundreth sundrie Flowers bounde up in one small Poesie. Gathered partely (by translation) in the fyne outlandish Gardens of Euripedes, Ovid, Petrarke, Ariosto, and others: and partly by invention, out of our owne fruitefull Orchardes in Englande: Yielding sundrie sweet favours of Tragical, Comical, and Morall Discourses, both pleasaunt and profitable to the well smellyng noses of learned Readers.

Euphuism is associated by scholars above all with John Lyly (1553–1606) on the strength of his *Euphues: the Anatomy of Wyt,* which he said was "lying bound on the Stationers' stall at Christmas" 1578, and its sequel, *Euphues and his England,* which was entered in the Stationers' Register on 24 July 1579. Were it not for *The Adventures of Master F. I.* in *Flowres* it could be termed the first novel in English. R. Warwick Bond, Lyly's great biographer, calls it the "first considerable English romance of contemporary life" and says it "was hailed by the cultivated classes of society as a welcome change from the interminable adventures of wandering knights or classical heroes, and from a portraiture of the fair sex more chivalrous and conventional than lively or accurate." Tucker Brooke writes that one of the "allurements" of *Euphues* that the "fashionable public of the day found irresistible" was that "it was all transparently about themselves, the scene being London, the characters the highest circle of society. . . ." Reading the nearly static narrative today is to appreciate how starved those cultivated classes must have been for a novel. Euphues (the "well-natured"), an Athenian and "a young gentleman of great patrimony, and of so comely a personage, that it was doubted whether he were more bound to Nature for the lineaments of his person, or to fortune for the increase of his possessions," was welcomed to the highest circle, which, Professor Brooke says, would welcome his story. His conversations and ruminations were immediately all the rage. More than forty years later the publisher Edward Blount would recall of Lyly that

> our nation are in his debt for a new English which he taught them. *Euphues and his England* began first that language. All our ladies were then his scholars; and that beauty in Court who could not parley Euphuism was as little regarded as she which now there speaks not French.

Elizabeth herself became "one of the most ardent" practitioners.

That it was a style putting considerable demands on the speaker is indicated by a typical "salute" to his lady by Euphues:

> Mistress *Lucilla*, though my long absence might breed your just anger, (for that lovers desire nothing as much as often meeting) yet I hope my presence will dissolve your choler (for that lovers are soon pleased when of their wishes they be fully possessed.) My absence is the rather to be excused in that your father hath been always at home, whose frowns seemed to threaten my ill fortune, and my presence at this present the better to be accepted in that I have made such speedy repair to your presence.

Such language flowed continually in contrasting and balanced phrases, as in Lucilla's answering "gleek":

> Truly, *Euphues* you have missed the cushion, for I was neither angry with your long absence, neither am I well pleased at your presence, the one gave me rather a good hope hereafter never to see you, the other giveth me a greater occasion to abhor you.

Other samples would show it abounding in cadenced similes. It was a flowing, high-flown language and as such — though the vogue for it would not last a decade — destined to live on to the present in elegant, rhythmic English.

But what has it to do with this biography?

As early as 1573 the Earl of Oxford had two "tenements" in the Savoy, a Lancaster castle blown up and burned by Wat Tyler's followers and restored by Henry VII as a charitable foundation. Here deserving university students and writers could obtain lodging through an influential acquaintance. Lyly, by 1577 at the latest, was living at least part of the time at the Savoy, "probably," says R. W. Bond, "owing his residence there to Burghleigh's interest." For Burghley's interest I am confident that we can substitute his son-in-law's. While Lyly dedicated *Euphues: the Anatomy of Wyt* to Lord Delaware he dedicated its equally popular sequel, *Euphues and his England*, to Oxford. By that time he had become Oxford's secretary, as later he would become his theatrical manager. Lyly presents, like Arthur Golding, the case of a writer who, entering Oxford's *ambience*, glows with a refulgence unprecedented in his past and deserting him when once he is on his own again. We recall how he wrote of that "highest circle of society" as a familiar.

Lyly confessed to having written nothing before *Euphues*. For a first venture into letters the novel had a truly remarkable success. And so it becomes a matter of particular interest when we read in the dedication of the sequel to Oxford that of the "two children" he had brought into the world, he "was delivered" of the first "before my friends thought me conceived" — that is, before they thought he had it in him to write the book — and that he had "sent [it] to a Nobleman to nurse, who with great love brought him up for a year, so that wheresoever he wander he hath his Nurse's name in his forehead. . . ." That is, he would recognizably bear the nobleman's impress. It need not tax our imaginations to come up with the name of that nobleman. We have, moreover, Gabriel Harvey's reminding Lyly of "thy old acquaintance in the Savoy, when young Euphues hatched the eggs that his elder friends laid." What I conclude is that this "first considerable English romance" owed its origin to the conversations Lyly heard in Oxford's company and its finished form to its having been nursed and with great love brought up by Oxford for no lesser time than a year.

In 1593 Harvey had something more to say of note. He called Lyly "sometime the fiddlestick of Oxford, now the very bauble of London." Ostensibly he was speaking of Oxford the university, but since that would make the "sometime" of seventeen years' duration I rather think he meant Oxford the Earl, whose "minion secretary" Harvey had declared Lyly to be in 1589. I am the more persuaded to this view by Harvey's having in that passage also called Lyly "once the foil of Oxford, now the stale of London." A foil at that time was "an amalgam . . . placed behind the glass of a mirror, to produce a reflection," or "that which sets off another thing." (*O.U.D.*) If Harvey is saying what he seems to me to be saying, he is telling us that Lyly was the bow that Oxford manipulated to make music and Oxford's reflection, or the setting for Oxford's genius, as Shakespeare used the term: "A foil wherein thou art to set / The precious jewel. . . ." If such were the case, Oxford's regard for Sidney would hardly have been improved when Burghley's "darling Philip" took part of the scheme of his *Arcadia* from *Euphues*, or "possibly" did so, then "condemned the conceits of the euphuists" and on top of that was as "diffuse and artificial" and full of "tricks" of prose in the *Arcadia* as ever *Euphues* had been.

R. W. Bond, in his three-volume work, presents nine pages in small type of parallels in thought and language between *Euphues* and Shakespeare as examples of all that the former "fathered" in the latter, as he would have us believe, telling us *en passant* that "Jaques in *As You Like It* . . . is simply Euphues Redivivus." He calls Lyly

> the first regular English dramatist, the true inventor and introducer of dramatic style, conduct and dialogue.

And he says

> There is no play before Lyly. He wrote eight; and immediately thereafter England produced some hundreds — produced that marvel and pride of the greatest literature in the world, the Elizabethan Drama. What the long infancy of her stage had lacked was an example of form, of art: Lyly gave it.

He does not remark that, having written nothing before his association with Oxford, Lyly after its end wrote no more plays or anything else of the least merit though he desperately needed the kind of income his writing had brought. Dr. Bond does recognize that "From the Earl, probably, it was that Lyly first received the dramatic impulse"; but he misses the clue and asserts:

> In tragedy Shakespeare learned from Marlowe. . . . In comedy Lyly is Shakespeare's only model: the evidence of the latter's study and imitation of him is abundant.

Dr. Bond writes three compressed pages on similarities of characters, incidents, and language between the plays of the two writers. This he heads *What Shakespeare owes to Lyly*. He begins with the assertion that

> First of all he owes him very much for the example of intercourse between refined and well-bred folk, conducted with ease, grace, and naturalness; and especially of such among women, and of the flippant, tantalizing treatment of their lovers by women. As part of this he is his debtor for the example of a prose-dialogue, either brisk and witty or adorned with learning and fancy . . . [which] is yet as near the best talk of its day as was consistent with the literary heightening demanded for current effect and permanent vitality.

He could hardly do better, in my view, in epitomizing Lyly's debt to Oxford. Is not Dr. Bond inadvertently telling us that Lyly's plays, too, were nursed and brought up with great love by that nobleman?

Orthodoxy is of one mind with Dr. Bond in having the sun take its light from the moon. Dr. Sidney Lee, for one, is insistent upon deriving *Love's Labour's Lost, Much Ado,* and *A Midsummer-Night's Dream* in particular from Lyly. However, conceding that "The most attractive features [of his plays] are the lyrics, which were not published in the quartos but first appeared in Blount's collected edition of 1632," Lee acknowledges that "Some doubts have been expressed whether Lyly has shown sufficient capacity to make it altogether probable that he was the author of the lyrics which were not associated with his name in his lifetime." Dr. Bond is also uneasy. Crediting to Lyly's authorship "two or three of the most graceful songs our drama can boast — an authorship which, if still unsusceptible of positive proof, is equally so of disproof —" he judges that others "stamp him as negligent, uncritical, or else as inadequately practised in the art." (These, I should say, being those he did write.) The absence of the songs from the original editions of the plays — only their positions in the text being noted — he admits "has cast some doubt upon Lyly's authorship: but some of them seem too dainty to be written by an unknown hand." Of course, I believe the hand need not be unknown.

The edition of Lyly's plays brought out by Edward Blount (one of the printers of the First Folio of Shakespeare's plays) restored to them twenty-one of the songs. The nine still omitted, J. T. Looney surmises, "had already appeared elsewhere, probably in the pages of 'Shakespeare.'" He was the first but by no means the last to believe that the thirty-two lyrics in the plays were by Oxford. It is from these that all eleven selections ascribed to Lyly in the *Oxford Book of Sixteenth Century Verse* are chosen. I believe anyone would take the following two songs sung by fairies to be different parts of the same one:

> Pinch him, fairies, mutually;
> Pinch him for his villainy.
> Pinch him, and burn him, and turn him about,
> Till candles and starlight and moonshine be out.
> . . . .
> Pinch, pinch him, black and blue,
> Saucy mortals must not view
> What the Queen of Stars is doing,
> Nor pry into our fairy wooing.
> Pinch him blue
> And pinch him black,
> Let him not lack
> Sharp nails to pinch him blue and red
> Till sleep has rocked his addle head.

The first is from *Merry Wives*, the second from Lyly's *Endymion*.

About this time arose a literary feud that would range Gabriel Harvey and his two brothers against Lyly, Thomas Nashe, and Robert Greene, growing more bitter during the next dozen years. McKerrow says it seems to be an offshoot of the quarrel between Philip Sidney and Oxford, the Harveys being aligned with Sidney, the other three with the Earl. Thus, taking it a step further back, it derived from the enmity between the Earls of Leicester and Sussex. Gabriel Harvey seems to have introduced Edmund Spenser to Leicester's household, in which Spenser was to take up residence, there meeting his future patron, Sidney.

The spark that set off the literary feud may have been Gilbert Harvey's pique at Oxford's passing him by in choosing a secretary — if it be true that he wanted the post for himself — and his resultant jealousy and resentment of Lyly. It is certain that in mid-1580 Harvey vented his spleen to Spenser in a portrait of an Italianate Englishman, unmistakably Oxford, written "in a rattling bunch of English hexameters," as Nashe would call it.[1] In so doing he performed an invaluable service for posterity, for *Speculum Tuscanismi* — the "Mirror of Tuscanism" — derogatory as it is, taken together with its author's address to Oxford two years before at Audley End, gives us the best pictures we have of the man who would be Shakespeare, outside his own writings. I have quoted from the verses before, but here they are *in extenso* — and the reader will see that, while spiteful, they give the butt of the satire credit for a range of remarkable gifts, though what some of the lines mean I cannot say.

> Since Galatea came in, and Tuscanism gan usurp,
> Vanity above all; villainy next her, stateliness Empress.
> No man but a minion, stout, lout, plain, swain, quoth a Lording:
> No words but valorous, no works but womanish only.
> For life Magnificoes, not a beck but glorious in show,
> In deed most frivolous, not a look but Tuscanish always.
> His cringing side neck, eyes glancing, fisnamie smirking,
> With forefinger kiss, and brave embrace to the footward.
> Large-bellied Kodpeasd doublet, unkodpeasd half hose,
> Straight to the dock like a shirt, and close to the britch like a
>   diveling.
> A little Apish flat couched fast to the pate like an oyster,
> French Camarick ruffs, deep with a whiteness starched to the
>   purpose.
> Every one A per se A, his terms and braveries in print,
> Delicate in speech, quaint in array: conceited in all points,
> In Courtly guiles a passing singular odd man,
> For Gallants a brave Mirror, a Primrose of Honour,
> A Diamond for nonce, a fellow peerless in England.
> Not the like discourser for Tongue, and head to be found out,
> Not the like resolute man for great and serious affairs,
> Not the like Lynx to spy out secrets and privities of States,
> Eyed like to Argus, eared like to Midas, nos'd like to Naso,
> Wing'd like to Mercury, fittst of a thousand for to be employ'd;
> This, nay more than this, doth practise of Italy in one year.
> None do I name, but some do I know, that a piece of a twelve month
> Hath so perfited outly and inly both body, both soul,

---

[1] More fully, Nashe would say, "Needs must he cast up certain crude humours of English hexameter verses that lay upon his stomach; a Nobleman stood in his way, as he was vomiting, and from top to toe he all to beray'd him with *Tuscanisme*."

That none for sense and senses half matchable with them.
A vulture's smelling, Ape's tasting, sight of an Eagle,
A Spider's touching, Hart's hearing, might of a Lion.
Compounds of wisdom, wit, prowess, bounty, behaviour,
All gallant virtues, all qualities of body and soul:
O thrice ten hundred thousand times blessed and happy,
Blessed and happy travail, Travailer most blessed and happy. . . .

How the *Mirror,* together with three other letters its author had written Spenser, got published is unclear. Presumably Harvey was not responsible. As he would have known, liberties were not to be taken with the nobility in Tudor England. It was judged that Harvey "fell into the bowels of libeling," as it was phrased by Lyly, who said that the offender feared his ears would be clipped. Harvey himself admitted that "The sharpest part of those unlucky Letters was over-read at the Council Table." He blamed Lyly, who, he said

> would needs forsooth very courtly persuade the Earl of Oxford, that something in those Letters, and namely, the Mirror of Tuscanismo, was palpably intended against him: whose noble Lordship I protest I never meant to dishonour with the least prejudicial word of my tongue, or pen, but ever kept a mind full of many bounden duties toward the same. . . .

Harvey satisfied the Council with an apology.

That Oxford himself had brought charges is very unlikely. Harvey added to the above that "the noble Earl, not disposed to trouble his Jovial mind with such Saturnine paltry, but still continued his magnificent self." Nashe gloated that Harvey, whom he loathed, would have been "slashed . . . as small as chippings" had he not "hid himself eight weeks in that nobleman's house for whom with his pen he thus bladed." That was Leicester. The important disclosure Nashe makes in this blast is that Harvey had stepped in "on the safer side" in a quarrel between "two great Peers" who were "at jar" — a "quarrel that continued to bloodshed." The two peers between whom there was bloodshed must, it would seem, have been Leicester and Sussex or Oxford. And it was to serve Leicester, Nashe indicates, that Harvey undertook to "hew and slash" Oxford "with his hexameters" and had "bladed" him "with his pen" — knifed him. How one curses the paucity of the record!

32

"They Come Not Single Spies"

1580–1581: Oxford's prodigal sale of his estates. — His theatrical activities. — His probable composition at this time of Twelfth Night, *with Elizabeth as the Countess Olivia, Christopher Hatton as Malvolio, and himself as Feste the Clown, whose license as an "allowed fool" Oxford probably enjoyed. — Return of Francis Drake in* Golden Hind *with immense booty; the thrill to English pride; the Queen's defiance of Spanish anger; royal procession to Plymouth in which Oxford evokes the mirth of the crowd. — Bloody Spanish offensive in the Netherlands and the Jesuit invasion of England. — Oxford's denunciation of his erstwhile Catholic associates Henry Howard and Charles Arundel for treasonable conduct; the French ambassador's self-serving report of the episode; Howard's and Arundel's temporary retreat to the Spanish embassy. — The belying of Oxford's alleged disgrace by his entry and victory in a second great tournament. — Harsh measures against Roman Catholics that succeed Elizabeth's previous lenience. — The unnamed nobleman riding down the Strand in French frippery as probably Oxford in theatre costume deriding the looming Alençon match. — Venomous slandering of the Earl by the imprisoned and desperate Howard and Arundel, to the lasting prejudice of his reputation. — Oxford's own brief imprisonment. — Birth to Anne Vavasor of a child by Oxford and consignment of both parents to the Tower. — Possible composition at this time of* Richard the Third *and* Henry the Sixth, *Part Three, both celebrating earlier Earls of Oxford. — Oxford's release, but only to months-long house-arrest, despite Elizabeth's show of sympathy. — His wife's touching plea for a reconciliation. — Sword-fight between Oxford and Anne Vavasor's uncle, Thomas Knyvet, in which both are injured; the series of frays between Oxford's men and Knyvet's, as between Montagues and Capulets. — Burghley's protestation to the Queen of his son-in-law's innocence. — Parallels with* Romeo and Juliet: *Oxford as Romeo-Mercutio, Knyvet as Tybalt, Elizabeth as "fair Rosaline," whom Romeo is in love with before meeting Juliet, but then lashes out at with the dramatist's accumulated bitterness toward the original.*

The year 1580 got under way for Oxford to the great advantage of the Jeweler who helped bring Timon to his ruin. We read that his New Year's Day gift to the Queen was "a fair jewel of gold, being a ship garnished fully with diamonds and a mean pearl pendant." The great bulk of his sales of land took place between 1576, when his European trip had to be paid for, and 1584, and of these forty-seven transactions thirteen were concluded in the year 1580. In addition to that munificent present to the Queen, his affair with Anne Vavasor cannot have been cheap for a lover to whom a careful reckoning of expenses was an ignominy better left to tradesmen. But the principal drain on his finances is likely to have been the company of actors he acquired. I hardly doubt that, close as he was to the Earl of Sussex, who as Lord Chamberlain was primarily responsible for theatrical performances at Court, he had all along been active in managing the "Lord Chamberlain's servants." During the early months of 1580, however, he took over the Earl of Warwick's company. On Midsummer Day, June 21st, we find the Vice Chancellor of Oxford University responding to a communication from the Chancellor, Lord Burghley, whom it had "pleased" to "commend . . . my Lord of Oxford his players, that they might show their cunning in certain plays already practised by them before the Queen's Majesty." It was an interesting thing for Burghley to have done, given his chilled relations with his son-in-law, and argues for his understanding the value of the stage in forming public opinion; for whatever the differences between the two, they were as one in nationalism and devotion to the monarchy. But the Vice Chancellor, "hoping our most dear loving Chancellor will take our answer . . . in good part," perforce rejected the proposal because "the pestilence is not yet vanished," because "the commencement time" was "at hand which requireth rather diligence in study than dissoluteness in plays," because "of late we denied the like to the Right Honourable the Lord of Leicester his servants," and because "all assemblies in open places be expressly forbidden to this University and town, or within five miles compass by Her Majesty's Council's letter. . . ." Lord Burghley cannot often have been so snubbed as in being accused of favoring dissoluteness and of disregarding an order of his own Council. I rather imagine the Vice Chancellor's prospects of preferment were but little enhanced.

Oxford was not on the road with his company. Just at this time he was planting a bomb for himself on a nine-month fuse: he was getting Mistress Vavasor with child.

Probably toward the end of the year he was also, it seems likely, producing in its initial form one of the most beguiling of the Shakespearean comedies. That would appear to be the import of a passage in *Desiderata Curiosa* in which Francis Peck says he proposes to publish a manuscript called "a pleasant conceit of Vere, Earl of Oxford, discontented at the rising of a mean gentleman in the English Court, circa 1580." The one mean gentleman we know of whose rise may warrantably be judged to have irked the Earl of Oxford was Christopher Hatton, whom he was evidently to make fun of as Malvolio while in the same play having sport with Philip Sidney as Sir Andrew Aguecheek; thus one takes the "pleasant conceit" to have been *Twelfth Night.*

In that most engaging comedy we have apparently the same victim as in the jape contained in *A Hundreth Sundrie Flowres*: an infatuate suitor for a noblewoman's love who is made a fool of by a hoax in the form of a counterfeit screed in which he is made the object of the noblewoman's ardor, the two being signed with a similar "posy." Malvolio's undoing, it will be recalled, comes about when Maria composes a letter in her mistress Olivia's handwriting addressed to "The unknown beloved," in which the supposed writer confesses her passion for one "whom I may command where I adore" and adds "M. O. A. I. doth sway my life"; and the signature of the letter, which follows the sentence, "She that would alter services with thee," is "The Fortunate-Unhappy." In *Flowres* we have the love affair between the noblewoman and the supposed writer related in poems signed "F. I." and "Si fortunatus infoelix."

In a work on *Gabriel Harvey's Marginalia*, Ward discovered, an annotation made by Harvey in his copy of *The Posies of George Gascoigne*, beside "Fortunatus infoelix" reads "lately the posy of Sir Christopher Hatton." Moreover, Ward found that Harvey made the same link in the recitation he gave at Audley End in 1578 apostrophizing members of the Court. Addressing "The Honourable and brave knight Christopher Hatton . . . concerning his symbol Foelix infortunatus," he observed that "One man is happy, but unfortunate: another is fortunate but unhappy" and declared, "but . . . you actually are happy as well as fortunate." It seems to me fairly clear that just as the versifier in *Flowres* was pretending to be Hatton, so Malvolio was identified as Hatton in the subscription of the letter forged by Maria in *Twelfth Night*. Early in the play Malvolio is called a "rascally sheep-biter," not one who bites sheep, surely, but a sheep who bites, harking back to Hatton's letter assuring Elizabeth that "The Sheep hath no tooth to bite while the Boar's tusk doth both raze and tear." Malvolio — Mal-vol-io — lends itself to translation (so D. S. Ogburn has observed) as "Evil Will to E. O.," as Romeo's friend Benvolio becomes "Good Will to E. O."[1]

No more than that Mistress Elinor in *The Adventures of Master F. I.* in *Flowres* is Elizabeth can I prove that the Countess Olivia, in mourning for her "brother," as the English Court was at the time of *Twelfth Night* (if Oxfordians are right), for Admiral Coligny and the other victims of the anti-Protestant terror, was a reflection of Elizabeth, as Oxfordians have long held, but I believe she was. I cannot think of any reason why Olivia is called "a Cataian" other than that Elizabeth was a prime investor in the Cathay Company. Both ladies, by the way, were courted by a Duke, Alençon in one case, Orsino in the other, and became smitten by his emissary, Jehan de Simier in real life, Viola disguised as a youth in the play. Oxford was in this,

---

[1] A. L. Rowse says of *Twelfth Night*, "From the first the main interest of the play was seen to lie in the character of Malvolio," to which he adds firmly, "though no amount of conjecture can satisfy us that he had a recognizable original." Professor Rowse is well aware that for Shakspere to have ridiculed Christopher Hatton, the Queen's cherished companion, in a play would have been the last the stage would have heard of him.

I rather think, gently pulling Elizabeth's leg, if I may make familiar with the royal limb.

If *The Adventures of Master F. I.* was what I take it to have been it would of course have been recognized for what it was by the Court. Hatton would have been infuriated. The worst of it would have been that the venom he would have longed to spew at the perpetrator of the jape would have had to be swallowed smilingly, for any betrayal of resentment in public would only seem to give substance to the diabolical parable. But he would be less restrained with the Queen. Malvolio, even before his entrapment, is spiteful of Feste, the Clown, an intimate of Olivia's who recognizably serves as Oxford's *alter ego.* "I marvel," he grumbles loftily to the Countess, "your ladyship takes delight in such a barren rascal: I saw him put down the other day with an ordinary fool that has no more brain than a stone. . . . I protest, I take these wise men, that crow so at these set kind of fools, no better than the fools' zanies": to which Olivia replies, "O! you are sick of self-love Malvolio, and taste with a distempered appetite."[2] Then she utters a judgment that I think explains how Oxford got away with his outspokenness: "There is no slander in an allowed fool, though he do nothing but rail." This was the role, I imagine, that Elizabeth accorded her Turk, no doubt because his wit could carry it off; she must have wearied of solemn idolatry. However *The Adventures of Master F. I.* may have taxed her lenience, at least it preserved an outward decorum. She could be brazen enough, she knew, and it would have been like her to appreciate the drollery at Hatton's expense, solicitous as her affection was for the Captain of her Body-Guard; Olivia would not have harm come to Malvolio "for the half of my dowry."

There is some thought, I might add, that Maria in the play was suggested by Oxford's sister Mary and Sir Toby Belch by her husband Peregrine Bertie, Lord Willoughby. E. T. Clark observes: Ber*TIE*-Will*OUGHBY* equals T-OBY. And Willoughby seems to have been something of a toper.

What would have exacerbated Oxford's soreness of mind at this time with respect to Hatton (of whom the Queen was as solicitous as Olivia of Malvolio) was the stroke of enormous good fortune that had befallen the "mean gentleman." Oxford had cast his bread upon the waters and it had returned worthless rocks. The Captain of the Queen's Body-Guard had cast his upon the same waters and it had returned solid gold. With the Queen and Leicester he had invested in Francis Drake's expedition of 1577. The adventurers had reconciled themselves to the loss of all they had put up when on 23 September 1580 England was electrified by the news of Drake's return to Plymouth, after circumnavigation of the globe. Of the three vessels with which the sea-dog had sailed two years and ten months previously, one had sunk, one been

---

[2] We read that Hatton, being in the "high and undeserved station" of Lord Chancellor, "became proud and arrogant."

forced to return home, and the third, the *Pelican*, given up for lost. She very nearly was. But after passing through the Straits of Magellan and being renamed *Golden Hind* after Hatton's crest, she had come into her heyday on the coast of Peru. Raiding the Spanish coastal settlements and plundering Spanish ships, she had filled up with treasure. She refitted in a "fair and good bay," believed to be that of San Francisco, then set off across the Pacific. In the Moluccas, six tons of Portugal's equivalent of Peruvian gold — cloves — were loaded, though half had later to be jettisoned to float the vessel off a shoal.

The value of the treasure disembarked at Plymouth was immense, hardly to be reckoned. B. M. Ward quotes Sir Julian Corbett as estimating the Queen's share from an investment of a thousand crowns at £11,750 and Hatton's at £2,300, but Ward says the actual amounts may have been far greater. It added up to probably the most profitable piratical voyage in history, by far. And piracy it was, of course. Burghley held that the booty stored in the Tower should be returned, and he was not alone in that. He and Sussex both declined Drake's proffered gifts of gold. The Queen was torn between fear of war with Spain, which Mendoza, the Spanish Ambassador, threatened, and cupidity, in which Leicester, Walsingham, and Hatton abetted her. In the end she would don the crown of gold set with an array of diamonds and five huge emeralds that her heroic buccaneer had had made for her. But it was not acquisitiveness alone that prevailed. To have returned the spoils would have outraged a public wild with enthusiasm for the Devon lad who had carried the flag around the world and in so doing made mock of the most powerful empire since Rome. The national pride of Englishmen had been given a boost that would enable them to face up to the coming showdown with King Philip and to meet adversity with stouter spirits for centuries to come. It was an act of defiance of Spain for which the Queen had never been more popular than when on the deck of the *Golden Hind* she touched the kneeling mariner on the shoulder with his sword and bade him rise *Sir* Francis Drake.

It was one of those satisfying conjunctions of history that with the Queen in her Progress to Plymouth there should have been the man who would pour forth for the glory of her reign and the lasting enrichment of the nation a treasure eclipsing even that which Drake had brought. An anonymous witness of the Court's passage left an account of it in four stanzas of doggerel, of which the first two follow:

> Sir Francis, Sir Francis, Sir Francis is come;
> Sir Robert, and eke Sir William his son,
> And eke the good Earl of Huntington
> Marched gallantly on the road.

> Then came the Lord Chamberlain with his white staff,
> And all the people began to laugh;
> And then the Queen began to speak,
> "You're welcome home, Sir Francis Drake."

It would not have been at the Lord Chamberlain, the dignified and middle-aged Earl of Sussex, that the bystanders laughed. It would have been at the Lord Great Chamberlain, who carried the white staff his grandfather had held as Lord Great Chamberlain at the coronation dinner of Anne Boleyn. Why should Oxford have elicited a mirthful reception from the crowd? If Meres could rank him by name in later years as among the best for comedy it is quite possible that the theatre-going public recognized him as such at the time and was paying him the tribute of their open delight. It is also possible, given his addiction to the stage and the street performance he was evidently to put on in the next year, that the merry, madcap lord, having knocked back a couple, may have clowned it with a gesture or two — made himself "a motley to the view." Anyone who could turn the leaf of his nature from Hamlet to Falstaff was an uncommon amalgam — "a passing singular odd man," as Harvey had it.

Drake's exploits at Spain's expense brought nearer the day when Philip would decide that he could not finally bring the Low Countries to heel and have undisputed passage of the seas until England was decisively disposed of. All in all, it may be said that 1580 was the year that began to put the fat inextricably in the fire. Alexander Farnese, later Duke of Parma, had, after concluding a peace with the Catholic Flemish nobility, embarked upon the conquest of the Protestant Netherlands, and town after town was falling before him. Elizabeth Jenkins writes:

> The Spanish Fury, conducted by Parma, was raging in the Netherlands, and the tales of what was happening on the other side of the Channel to cities which opposed the forces of the Catholic King of Spain were overlaying even the memory of St. Bartholomew. The fall of Maestricht was but one agony among many, but every Englishman who heard of its garrison slaughtered with maniacal cruelty, of the women who had manned its defences torn to pieces in the streets and of Parma carried triumphantly in a litter over mutilated corpses and seas of blood, knew that when Philip had reduced the Netherlands to his will, England's turn would come next.

This — 1580 — was the year of the "Jesuit invasion." To number altogether a hundred, the Jesuits had been trained in France by the fanatical priest William Allen and in a similar college in Rome founded by Pope Gregory XIII, who had had a medal struck commemorating the massacre of St. Bartholomew's Day. While the prevailing purpose was doubtless the one given out, namely, to bring religious instruction to the English adherents of the Old Religion, too long suffering from its lapse, the Protestant half of the population took a different and agitated view of the incursion: Roman Catholicism meant first loyalty to the Pope and potential treason. That this fear — intensified by the Jesuits' attempt to operate a secret printing-press — was not altogether fanciful Allen himself would corroborate a few years hence in assuring the French and Spanish supporters of Mary Queen of Scots that his co-religionists in England would rise the moment a foreign army invading in her name touched English shores. The landing of a small, joint Papal-Spanish force in Smerwick, in Ireland — where it was defeated — showed that apprehension of an invasion was justified. But of far greater significance than that episode was Philip II's forceful annexation of Portugal, which would greatly strengthen Spain upon the seas and the danger to England. In December 1580, in response to a query by two English noblemen who asked to know if the assassination of Elizabeth would be a sin, the Cardinal Secretary at the Vatican wrote that "Since that guilty woman of England . . . is the cause of such injury to the Catholic faith and loss of so many millions of souls, there is no doubt that whosoever sends her out of the world with the pious intention of doing God service, not only does not sin, but gains merit. . . ."

In this same month Oxford evidently reached his limit with Rome. Probably alarmed by the mounting peril in which he saw England placed by the power of Roman Catholic Europe, and very likely to have received undercover intelligence brought from the Continent by his secretary, Anthony Munday (see Chapter 33), he came to a crucial decision and a few days before Christmas denounced his erstwhile associates, Henry Howard, Charles Arundel, and Francis Southwell. From subsequent developments it seems likely that he had got wind of the involvement of the first two at least in dangerous activities. The reader may be reminded that Lord Howard, fifteen years Oxford's senior, was the second son of the poetical Earl of Surrey, younger brother, therefore, of Thomas Howard, the 4th Duke of Norfolk, and a first cousin of Oxford's. The *Dictionary of National Biography* says of him that "Despite his lack of principle, he displayed a many-sided culture and was reputed the most learned nobleman of his time." Living and dying a Roman Catholic, he was generally reported, the *Dictionary* adds, "to have brought about his brother's ruin" in 1574. He himself had first been proposed as a husband for Mary. His relations with her "were undoubtedly close and mysterious" and he "supplied [her] for many years with political information," according to that same authority, which also states that one of Oxford's charges against him was further "treasonable correspondence with the Scottish Queen." His future would reveal him an inveterate traitor to his friends. One of these was the Queen's last favorite, the Earl of Essex, who "ought to have distrusted as well as despised" him, Lucy Aikin observes. Charles Arundel was even more unsavory. We shall find him a few years later fleeing England, taking up with the treasonous Charles Paget and with him seeking refuge in the Spanish Embassy in Paris, soon thereafter to be put on an allowance by King Philip. These are the two men whom Oxford appears to have incurred the displeasure of history by breaking with, and whose vicious testimony against him still colors his reputation.

So also does the record on which history depends for its version of the event. This is a report, obviously self-serving, made about three weeks later to his sovereign in Paris by the French Ambassador, Castelnau de Mauvissière. He wrote:

> A few days before Christmas the Earl of Oxford (who about four and a half years ago on his return from Italy made profession of the Catholic faith together with some of his relatives among the nobility and his best friends, and had sworn, as he says, and signed with them a declaration that they would do all they could for the advancement of the Catholic religion) accused his former friends to the Queen of England your good sister. For his own part he craved forgiveness for what he had done, saying that he now recognized that he had done wrong. He then proceeded to accuse his best friends who had supported him in his recent quarrels of having conspired against the State by having made profession of the Catholic faith, and he endeavored to do them all the harm he could. The Queen your good sister was very much upset about it, for she was very fond of most of those accused by the Earl; among whom were Lord Henry Howard, a brother of the late Duke of Norfolk, and Charles Arundel, who is very devoted to your Majesties and to Monseigneur your brother, both of them being strong advocates of the marriage. . . .
>
> It was to her great regret, as the Queen herself told me, that she was obliged to place them under restraint in the custody of some of her Councillors: Lord Henry under the charge of Sir Christopher Hatton, Captain of the Guard; and Francis Southwell under the charge of Sir Francis Walsingham.
>
> Having been questioned regarding the accusations preferred agaı t them by the Earl of Oxford, namely that they had conspired against the State, they were able to clear themselves very satisfactorily; and as concerns Catholicism, they are known to be well affected to it, as indeed is the case with most of the nobility of this kingdom. The Queen knew this perfectly well; and Lord Henry Howard, Arundel, and Southwell, although Catholics at heart, are nevertheless much esteemed and favored by her, seeing that both they and their friends have always been in favor of the marriage and of the French alliance. The Earl of Oxford thus found himself alone in his evidence and accusations. He has lost credit and honor, and has been abandoned by all his friends and by all the ladies of the Court. . . .

Let us strip this letter of its dissembling. What the Ambassador is desirous of doing, for his own satisfaction and that of his royal master, is to put Oxford in the worst kind of light for having made serious trouble for two important Roman Catholics who were both strong supporters of the Duke of Alençon's marital designs upon Elizabeth and the English throne. Oxford had not accused them "of having conspired against the State by having made profession of the Catholic faith." He accused Arundel of just what de Mauvissière boasted, his being "very devoted" to the French King and Queen

and both as being involved in criminal conspiracy. As for their having supported Oxford "in his recent quarrels," nothing is known of any such quarrels. Far from their having been "able to clear themselves very satisfactorily,"
Howard would spend at least the balance of the year under restraint and
Arundel apparently remained confined until 1583, when he would go altogether over to the Spanish side.

At this point in his letter the Ambassador becomes a little more candid.
The Queen had recently told him, he says

> that there were certainly plots being hatched, with their roots abroad; and that
> she very much regretted to find her own subjects implicated in them, especially
> those which were so well affected to France and so favorable to the marriage.
> She added that she would close her eyes to it as far as possible in view of their
> attitude towards the marriage. . . .

Evidently de Mauvissière did not understand the Queen's veiled method of
making a point. He passes on to theatrics, having Oxford repeatedly throwing
himself upon his knees before the Queen and begging him to confirm mean-
ingless or silly accusations about the Jesuits that he, the Ambassador, attributes to Oxford. A safe comment would be: fiddlesticks. A man less likely to
prostrate himself before a French official would be hard to find; Oxford's
faults lay in the other direction from public self-abasement. The truth is that
in a diplomatic memorandum of conversation the reporting officer is almost
always at pains to appear to great advantage himself, frustrating an opponent
and exposing his pitiable weaknesses. (I have read enough of such memoranda to know — have indeed written enough myself.) De Mauvissière's last
sentence is so characteristic of the *genre* as to be priceless:

> The effect of my reply was that the Earl was fairly put to confusion in the
> presence of his Mistress.

As for the Earl's having been brought low at this time and having "lost
all credit and honor," Oxford appears a month later, on 22 January 1581,
in another of the five great tournaments of Elizabeth's reign like that in which
he had starred ten years before. The occasion was to celebrate the succession
of Henry Howard's nephew, Philip Howard, to the Earldom of Arundel (not
to be associated with Charles Arundel). The new Earl was the challenger. To
help wash de Mauvissière's calumnies out of one's thoughts it is refreshing
to read that the prize was given to Oxford, one of the defendants. (In 1585,
Philip would be convicted of just such treasonable activities as Oxford had
charged his uncle Henry with committing and would spend the rest of his
life in prison.) Oxford's triumph must have brought no small glory with it,
for by this time, according to Roy Strong, the tilts "had been deliberately
developed into a gigantic public spectacle eclipsing every other form of court
festival."

To show how misinformed the French Ambassador was, or how badly he misinformed his king, there is a letter written by Mendoza, the Spanish Ambassador, on December 25th, within a few days of the event de Mauvissière would later report. In it he said:

> Milord Henry Howard, brother of the Duke of Norfolk, has for some years — as I know through some priests — been very Catholic. . . . He desired that the [French] match should take place; believing, like many other Catholics, that by this means they would be allowed to exercise their religion in freedom.
>
> On hearing that the Earl of Oxford had accused him, together with Charles [Arundel and Francis] Southwell of being reconciled to Rome, they did not dare to trust themselves to the French Ambassador; but, coming to my house at midnight, though I had never spoken to them, they told me the danger in which they found themselves of losing their lives, unless I would hide them. As they were Catholics I entertained them. . . . Milord Harry, in gratitude . . . has informed and continues to inform me of everything he hears. . . . To touch on the greatness of his affection with which he occupies himself in the service of your Majesty is impossible.

The two refugees must have ventured forth again very soon thereafter, for, as we have read, de Mauvissière spoke of their having been put under restraint by the Queen. Mendoza had reported their fate to King Philip two days earlier, on January 9th. He wrote:

> The Queen has recently ordered the arrest of Lord Howard brother of the Duke of Norfolk, and two other gentlemen, Charles Arundel and Southwell, who were formerly great favorites at the Court. The reason for this is partly religious . . . but it is suspected also that it may be attributed to their having been very intimate with the French Ambassador, with the apparent object of forwarding the Alençon match, together with some Court ladies of the same party who were favorites of the Queen's. What adds to the mystery of the matter is their having been taken to the Tower, and Leicester's having spread the rumor that they were plotting a massacre of the Protestants, beginning with the Queen. His object in this is to inflame the people against them and against the French, as well as against the Earl of Sussex who was their close friend.

Oxford may well have had something to do with the Queen's awakening to the possibilities of mischief in the influx of highly trained Jesuit agents. Camden in his *Annales*, referring to the activities of these agents, wrote:

> These and like things brought upon Papists new and sharper laws, made by Act of Parliament at Westminster in the month of January [1582], where all such were declared guilty of high treason, which dissuaded any of her Majesty's subjects from their obedience to their Prince, or from the religion now professed in England, or that should reconcile to the Church of Rome.

It is certain that the Queen, whose policy toward her Catholic subjects had been a lenient one, acquiesced in the new and harsh measures urged for some time by Lord Burghley and now by the Parliament of 1581 as well. "The government opened its counter-attack by securing greatly increased powers of repression," S. T. Bindoff writes. "The Act 'to retain the Queen's majesty's subjects in their due obedience' not only rounded off the earlier treason legislation, with an eye to the Jesuit and seminarist, but enormously increased the penalties on ordinary recusancy." The despair of the Roman Catholics lent impetus to the quest for a suitable place for colonization in North America where they could harbor. Jesuits were now mercilessly hunted down and from "1581 the executions multiplied," Bindoff says. There was much hysteria in this, but it was the hysteria of a people virtually under siege who found its worst apprehensions confirmed by every new report of the Spanish Fury across the Channel. Further confirmation would come when the priest Robert Parsons, one of the two heads of the Jesuit mission to England in 1580, escaped to the Continent to plot the Spanish invasion of England and openly speculate "what form or manner of Inquisition to bring in" when the invasion had succeeded. Commenting on the hangings, G. M. Trevelyan observes that "four Catholics suffered for every year of Elizabeth's reign, as against 56 Protestants for every year of Mary['s], and the charge was no longer heresy but treason."

Less than a fortnight after winning the prize at the tournament, Oxford put on another but different kind of public appearance on horseback, if Ward is right and a mounted figure seen early in February parading near Vere House in a costume parodying the French was his. It is not easy to see who else's it could have been, taking account of all the circumstances, including the sarcastic report we have of the figure from Barnable Riche, a soldier-writer and follower of Christopher Hatton's. Hatton, indeed, it probably was who instigated and paid for its publication. Riche wrote:

> It was my fortune at my last being at London to walk through the Strand towards Westminster, where I met one came riding towards me on a footcloth nag, apparelled in a French ruff, a French cloak, a French hose, and in his hand a great fan of feathers, bearing them up (very womanly) against the side of his face.

A "footcloth nag" would be a horse having a large, richly ornamented cloth hanging over its back to the ground, marking its rider as a nobleman.

> And for that I had never seen any man wear them before that day, I began to think it impossible that there might be a man be found so foolish as to make himself a scorn to the world to wear so womanish a toy; but rather thought it had been some shameless woman that had disguised herself like a man in our hose and our cloaks.

The writer, while mentioning the rider's beard, thinks it would be funny to pretend to mistake his sex — he was a real card — and asks one of his followers

> what gentlewoman his master was. But the fellow, not understanding my meaning, told me his master's name, and so departed.

Unfortunately for history, Riche lacked the courage to repeat the name. But I think there is little doubt that the performance he was witnessing and pretending not to understand was Oxford's mockery of the French nationality into which the Queen appeared disposed to marry, and that the show delighted the onlookers, most of whom would have shared his feelings about the proposed alliance.

It was not all merriment for the Earl, however. He prepared a series of interrogatories to draw out the men he had accused on the nature and extent of their covert activities. In this he was backing into a corner a pair who could be expected to strike back without restraint or scruple. They did. Denying all accusations against them as the emanations, in Arundel's words, "all of a giddy brain" which "must dissolve to nothing now," they weighed in with such slanders as would have brought Oxford to instant and permanent destruction had a tenth part of them been true. As it was, Arundel had cause to complain bitterly that while he was held a virtual prisoner his enemy was free to "graze in the pastures." Howard wrote:

> Touching mine accuser; if the botchie and deformities of his misshapen life suffice not to discredit and disgrace the warrant of his wreakful work: yet let his practices with some gentlemen to seek my life.

In his counter-charges, the desperate Howard gave himself free rein in the verbal excesses he imputed to Oxford. He accused the Earl of declaring

> That the Catholics were great Ave Maria coxcombs that they would not rebel against the Queen;
> My Lord of Norfolk worthy to lose his head for not following his [i.e., Oxford's] counsel at Litchfield to take arms;

And of

> Railing at my Lord of Arundel for putting his trust in the Queen;
> Railing at Francis Southwell for commending the Queen's singing one night at Hampton Court, and protesting by the blood of God that she had the worst voice and did everything with the worst grace that ever woman did, and that he was never [so] nonplussed but when he came to speak of her;
> Daily railing at the Queen, and falling out with Charles Arundel, Francis Southwell, and myself in defence of her.

No doubt Oxford was given to a certain reckless railing, though hardly to such lengths as Howard claimed. On Howard's charge sheet, beside the accusation that Oxford had railed at Francis Southwell for commending the Queen's singing and then lambasted it, Southwell himself had added the note, "I heard him, but he had been drinking." We are taken straight into a scene in *Henry the Fifth*, in which the monarch commands:

> Enlarge [free] the man committed yesterday
> That railed against our person. We consider
> It was excess of wine that set him on,
> And on his more advice, we pardon him.

That is probably a recapitulation of Elizabeth's reaction to the pillorying of
Oxford — for there is some evidence that he was committed and quickly
"enlarged" again. But the scene's re-enactment of the actual events, at least
as the dramatist would have them seen, does not stop with the monarch's
forgiveness of the railer's transgression. His lenience is protested by Cambridge, Scroop, and Grey — read Howard, Arundel, and Southwell — who
call for the railer's punishment. To their demands their sovereign replies:

> If little faults proceeding on distemper
> Shall not be winked at, how shall we stretch our eye
> When capital crimes, chew'd, swallow'd, and digested
> Appear before us?

He then presents the three with commissions, which they discover to be
indictments for treason unmasking their collaboration with the French.

Arundel's complaint that Oxford is "never restrained in this liberty of
railing" also reminds us of Olivia-Elizabeth's response in *Twelfth Night* to
Malvolio-Hatton's complaint of Feste-Oxford's license of speech: "There is
no slander in an allow'd fool, though he do nothing but rail," she says.
Those who felt its sting no doubt protested Oxford's freedom of speech,
especially, as Percy Allen says, when it chanced to amuse the Queen's Majesty.
That they themselves railed against the irrepressible Earl in accusing him of
railing we are told in John Davies's poem, published in 1610, *To Our English
Terence, Mr. Will. Shake-speare*, which defends him against the charge:

> Some others rail; but, rail as they see fit,
> Thou hast no railing, but, a reigning wit.

(What Stratfordians make of that, I have no idea.)

Arundel could hardly find words for his fulminations against Oxford:

> To record the vices of this monstrous earl were a labour without end; they
> are so many and so vile and so scandalous that it would be a shame to write
> them, and a loss of time to read them. . . . I will truly decipher him and lay all
> his villainies to open gaze, . . . his impertinent and senseless lies. . . . He hath
> perjured himself a hundred times and damned himself to the pit of hell. . . . He
> is a most notorious drunkard and very seldom sober; — in his drunken fits he
> is no man but a beast; — all acts of cruelty, injury and villainy, sparing no
> woman be she never so virtuous, nor any man, be he never so honourable. . . .
>
> To show that the world never brought forth such a villainous monster, and
> for a parting blow to give him his full payment, I will prove against him his
> most horrible and detestable blaspheme, in denial of the divinity of Christ our
> saviour, and terming the Trinity a fable. This heard my Lord Windsor, my Lord
> Harry, Rawlie, Southwell, and myself. And that Joseph was a wittold [a con-
> tended cuckold]. . . .
>
> *To conclude.* He is a beast in all respect, and in him no virtue to be found,
> and no vice wanting.

Among the monstrous crimes and villainies laid at Oxford's door is "the
detestable practice of hired murder," with Leicester and Sidney as the in-

tended victims, and, what was apparently worse, those "notable lies" about his adventures and exploits on the Continent. Of his tall tales, the outraged Arundel, summing up, cries, "Let these examples plead!"

> That the cobblers' wives of Milan are more richly dressed every working day than the Queen at Christmas.
> That St. Mark's Church is paved at Venice with diamonds and rubies.
> That a merchant at Genoa hath a mantle of a chimney of more price than all the treasure of the Tower.

There was one thing more, especially. Oxford was charged with homosexual activity. Some years ago A. L. Rowse reverted to the accusation in the *Times* of London, treating it as a matter of established fact and, with characteristic prurience, repeating the earthy details with which Arundel had sought to make his tale convincing. Rowse even accused "Miss" B. M. Ward of evading the issue, though Captain Ward had cited "unnatural crimes" among the charges against Oxford, which was about as far as one could go in 1928. Conyers Read concedes with what I suppose he considers exemplary fair-mindedness, that "Sodomy must be dismissed as unproved." The charge can have carried little weight at the time, coming as it did when Oxford brought the roof down on his head by excessive heterosexual zeal. His contemporaries cannot have failed to wonder, moreover, unlike subsequent historians, how Howard and Arundel could have been glad to count a loathesome monster of all depravities their friend as long as the monster reciprocated.

A Fugger news-letter of April 1st from Paris spoke of the fracas Oxford had touched off. (The Fuggers were a wealthy family of German merchants and bankers, strongly Roman Catholic, whose foreign agents reported in a form of communication from which newspapers were to evolve.) The correspondent wrote that:

> The English . . . declare that a plot has been formed by the Jesuits, Catholic nobles and other persons, whom the Queen has imprisoned. One important gentleman has fallen away, abjured the Roman faith and been set at liberty. The others are still in prison. In a word the English have a horror of the King of Spain and do not trust us here [i.e., the French] overmuch either.

That the "important gentleman" was Oxford is made clear in another Fugger news-letter, of April 29th, from London:

> Since amongst other things you ask for information about what has been done to the prisoners arrested four months ago, you should know that the brother of the last Duke of Norfolk and two knights are still in prison. This because they have again become reconciled to the Roman Church, having been led thereto by certain agents instigated for the purpose by the Pope. This is taken very ill in the country. There is a suspicion too that they have been plotting against the crown and realm of England. But, as hitherto nothing has been brought home to them, they remain in prison, simply because they are in bad odor. The Earl of Oxford [was] also arrested but soon set at liberty. . . .

Here we must break into the report and go back more than a month to a letter written by Sir Francis Walsingham on March 23rd:

> On Tuesday at night Anne Vavysor was brought to bed of a son in the maidens' chamber. The E. of Oxeford is avowed to be the father, who hath withdrawn himself with intent, as it is thought, to pass the seas. The ports are laid for him and therefore if he have any such determination it is not likely that he will escape. The gentlewoman the selfsame night she was delivered was conveyed out of the house and the next day committed to the Tower. Others that have found any ways party to the cause have also been committed. Her Majesty is greatly grieved with the accident, and therefore I hope there will be some order taken as the like inconvenience will be avoided.

Here was a bouleversement for fair. That the Earl had any idea of fleeing the country there is no indication. If he had had he would surely have had the wit "to have withdrawn himself" before Anne was actually brought to bed of the child. What Walsingham's letter chiefly reveals apart from the central fact of the birth is the Queen's vindictiveness toward any kind of sexual liaison, with or without benefit of clergy. Not only does she snatch the poor mother off the very night of her delivery, quite possibly endangering her life and the child's, but she commits her to the Tower and others who were in any way party to the affair, whoever they were and whatever they may have done.

The boy, we may say here, would be named Edward Vere, "undoubtedly," Barrell felt, "for the express purpose of keeping him in the forefront of his father's attention." As to how well this would succeed, there is no hint — unless we accept the theory, unconvincing to me, that many of the Sonnets were addressed to him. In default of this, we know absolutely nothing about Oxford's relations with the boy. There is a letter written by Edward Vere in the last year of Oxford's life from a battlefield in the Low Countries addressed to "Kind Father," whom it thanks for two letters, but whether his actual father was meant is not certain, though we may hope he was. (The son, as befitted a Vere, would distinguish himself in a military career and have a seat in Parliament as well.)

To resume with the interrupted Fugger news-letter of April 25th:

> ... The Earl of Oxford, also arrested (with the Howards) but soon set at liberty, is again in the Tower for forgetting himself with one of the Queen's Maids of Honor, who is in the Tower likewise. This in spite of his having a pretty wife, daughter of the Treasurer. But he will not live with her.

This time the reckless courtier-poet would taste the consequences of a transgression not allowed even "an allow'd fool" or one "superlative in the Prince's favour." For two and a half months, evidently, he would languish amid the silent echoes of innumerable ill-omened predecessors in the already ancient fortress. The Queen must have somewhat relented by June 8th, for on that date he was released. That we learn because the Yeoman Porter of

646

the Tower, upon demanding the prisoner's upper garments as a fee of his office, was turned down "for as much as his Lordship was not committed thither upon any cause of treason or any criminal cause."

Among the spectres that must have passed before the prisoner's eyes, like those which taunted Richard III on his last night, was probably that of the 13th Earl of Oxford's son, who died in the Tower while his father was in exile. Eva Turner Clark speculates that *Richard the Third*, with twenty-six references to the Tower, was written during Oxford's incarceration and would have served to remind the Queen of all the great 13th Earl of Oxford had done to put the first Tudor on the throne. I should certainly wager that the immediately preceding play, *Henry the Sixth, Part Three*, was written now, for it is in this that the Earl of Oxford is continually acclaimed. If I am right, the play was Edward de Vere's defiant boast while under royal displeasure, just as *The Famous Victories of Henry the Fift* had been seven years earlier. E. T. Clark remarks that the division of England between Lancastrians and Yorkists paralleled its current division between Protestants and Catholics, and the vacillation and indecisiveness of King Henry, which allowed the Yorkist Edward Earl of March to supplant him on the throne, would have conveyed a warning to an often irresolute Elizabeth, whose enemies were waiting to supplant her on the throne with Mary Queen of Scots.

The Queen, though releasing him from the Tower, was not prepared to give her erring courtier his liberty and kept him under house arrest. With the Duke of Alençon having returned to England on June 2nd, she may also have thought it best to keep the obstreperous Earl under wraps. Yet her heart was not altogether hardened against him, as a letter he sent Burghley at this time shows. He writes that one of his principal estate agents

> did yesterday tell me how honourably you had dealt with Her Majesty as touching my liberty, and that as this day she had made promises to your Lordship that it shall be. Unless your Lordship shall make some [motion] to put Her Majesty in [mind] thereof, I fear, in these other causes of the two Lords, she will forget me. For she is nothing of her own disposition, as I find, so ready to deliver as speedy to commit, and every little trifle gives her matter for a long delay.

He goes on to say that through Master Secretary Walsingham he has had a message

> which was to this effect: first, that she would have heard the matter again touching Henry Howard, Southwell and Arundel; then, that she understood that I meant to cut down all my woods especially about my house, which she did not so well like of as if I should sell some land else otherwise; and last, that she heard that I had been hardly used by some of my servants during this time of my committal, wherein she promised her aid so far as she could, with justice to redress the loss I had sustained thereby.

Referring to abusive reports of him made to his father-in-law by "certain of my men," he says he is sending "this bearer," who has also been abused,

> unto your Lordship at his most earnest desire, that your Lordship might so know him, as your evil opinion being conceived amiss by these lewd fellows may be revoked. And truly, my Lord, I hear of these things wherewith he is charged, and I can assure you wrongfully and slanderously. But the world is so cunning as of a shadow they can make a substance, and of a likelihood a truth. And these fellows, if they be those — as I suppose — I do not doubt but so to decipher them to the world as easily as your Lordship shall look into their lewdness and unfaithfulness.

Promising

> to revenge myself of such perverse and impudent dealing of servants, which I know have not wanted encouragement and setting on,

he concludes by acknowledging that he

> must not forget to give your Lordship those thanks which are due to you for this your honourable dealing to Her Majesty on my behalf, which I hope shall not be without effect. The which, attending from the Court, I will take my leave of your Lordship, and rest at your commandment at my house this morning.
>
> Your Lordship's assured,
Edward Oxenford.

On July 14th Walsingham reported to Burghley that he had "dealt very earnestly with the Queen touching the Earl of Oxford's liberty." He explained that

> The only stay groweth through the impertinent suit that is made for the delivery of the Lord Henry and Master Charles Arundel, whom, before their delivery, Her Majesty thinketh meet they should be confronted by the Earl, who hath made humble request to be set at liberty before he be brought to charge them, as he was at the time he first gave information against them.

He had to report, however, that the Queen "cannot as yet be brought to yield." The Earl remained under house arrest.

At this stage we find Burghley thanking Christopher Hatton for his "good and honourable dealing with Her Majesty in the case of my daughter of Oxford" but cautioning him not to give ground for the Earl to "suspect that I regard myself and my daughter more than he is regarded for his liberty." With both Burghley and Walsingham petitioning for Oxford's freedom the Queen might have been expected to grant it, unless a person close to her was putting his weight on the other side of the balance; and Ward comments that Hatton was at this time receiving long, obscure letters from Arundel, who, from prison, signed himself "your honour's fast and unfeigned friend."

Oxford has presumably not yet been freed when on October 1st we find Martin Frobisher writing the Earl of Leicester of his understanding that Leicester will put up £2,000 toward the £2,800 purchase price of a galleon with ordnance and furnishings but stating that he has not heard from certain others or "any of the rest but my L. of Oxford, who bears me in hand he will buy the Edward Bonaventure, and Mr. Bowland & I have offered 1500 pounds for her, but they hold her at 1800." Another expedition across the Atlantic was being prepared, worse luck for the ever-sanguine Oxford.

Two months later the Countess of Oxford sent a most touching appeal to her lord, from whom she had been separated for nearly five years. She wrote:

> My Lord, In what misery I may account myself to be, that neither can see any end thereof nor yet any hope to diminish it. And now of late having had some hope in my own conceit that your Lordship would have renewed some part of your favour that you began to show me this summer, when you made me assured of your good meaning, though you seemed fearful how to show it by open address. Now after long silence of hearing anything from you, at the length I am informed — but how truly I know not and yet how uncomfortably I do not seek it — that your Lordship is entered into for misliking of me without any cause in deed or thought. And therefore, my good Lord, I beseech you in the name of that God, which knoweth all my thoughts and love towards you, let me know the truth of your meaning towards me; upon what cause you are moved to continue me in this misery, and what you would have me do in my power to recover your constant favour, so as your Lordship may not be led still to detain me in calamity without some probable cause, whereof, I appeal to God, I am utterly innocent. From my father's house at Westminster, the 7th December 1581.

Her husband answered with scant delay. That his reply has disappeared brings me again to the point that every communication he ever made his wife in writing can hardly have vanished without someone's having exerted himself to that end. But if we were to be prevented from hearing Oxford's side, care was taken to preserve a record of Anne's. The foregoing and following letters of hers are both known to us from copies made for the files. The second was written on December 12th.

> My very good Lord, I most heartily thank you for your letter, and am most sorry to perceive how you are unquieted with the uncertainty of the world, whereof I myself am not without some taste. But seeing you will me to assure myself of anything that I may as your wife challenge of you, I will the more patient abide the adversity which otherwise I fear, and — if God would so permit it and that it might be good for you — I would leave the greater part of your adverse fortune, and make it my comfort to bear part with you. As for my father, I do assure you, whatsoever hath been reported of him, I know no man can wish better to you than he doth, and yet the practices in Court I fear do . . . seek to make contrary shows.

In response to his having warned her of certain associates, she said she had only been driven "for avoiding of malice and envy" and

> would not with my will do. Good my Lord, assure yourself it is you whom only I love and fear, and so am desirous above all the world to please you, wishing that I might hear oftener from you until better fortune will have us meet together.

Presumably the "adverse fortune" from which Oxford suffered was continued house arrest and the disfavor in which he stood at Court, where the "practices" against him were rife.

If this is all quite vague, the record is specific enough on the misfortune that befell him less than three months later. His separation from his Countess had been ended for more than two months when it happened. The diary of a clergyman for 3 March 1582 records that

> My Lord of Oxford fought with Master Knyvet about the quarrel of Bessie Bavisar, and was hurt, which grieved the Lord Treasurer the more for the Earl hath company with his wife since Christmas. But through this mishap and through the marriage of another daughter [Burghley's only other] to my Lord Wentworth on Shroveday, my Lord Treasurer was sick.

"Bessie Bavisar" was of course Anne Vavasor and Master Knyvet was her uncle Thomas, a relative of the Howards.

We learn a little more of the fight from a letter of March 17th written to Anthony Bacon.

> In England of late there hath been a fray between my Lord of Oxford and Master Thomas Knyvet of the Privy Chamber, who are both hurt, but my Lord of Oxford more dangerously. You know Master Knyvet is not meanly beloved in Court, and therefore he is not likely to speed ill whatsoever the quarrel may be.

In getting Mistress Vavasor in trouble, no matter how cooperative or even forward she had been in the brewing of it, Oxford had to expect to arouse her family. It was typical of his unluckiness, however, that the man who came charging forth was one whose star had risen high at Court while his own was at its nadir. Knyvet was not a little "beloved" there, and in addition to being a Gentleman of the Privy Chamber he had two months earlier been made Keeper of Westminster Palace. A greater misfortune was Oxford's dangerous wound. This may have been the cause of the lameness to which he adverts in the *Sonnets*. ("Speak of my lameness, and I straight will halt"; and "[I], decrepit, . . . made lame by fortune's dearest spite," yet, having the "comfort" of the young man's "worth and truth, . . . / So then I am not lame.")

The fight between Oxford and Knyvet is usually represented as a duel, though there is no evidence of its having been such. Gwynneth Bowen points out, "Knyvet was the injured party — and therefore more likely to resort to violence." And it would not be the last time — for several more set-tos between the two sides took place. Speaking of the combat between Lord Oxford and "a certain Thomas Knyvet," who "was allied with the Howards," Albert Feuillerat wrote in 1910, "This was the signal for war between the two houses. As at another time in Verona, the streets of London were filled with the quarrelling clamors (*clameurs querelleuses*) of these new Montagues and Capulets."

Ms. Bowen, who evidently alone has fully examined the documents of the feuds, writes:

> The "brabbles and frays," as Burghley called them, went on intermittently for about a year and several versions of the story are current, which differ considerably in detail. Historians almost unanimously lay the blame upon Oxford, but little is known of the facts and it seems that no-one has referred to the documents for about 50 years. . . . Yet Oxford's reputation for exceptional violence in an age of violence stems almost entirely from this episode, and in our time, this reputation for violence seems to be inseparable from any mention of his name, unless in "Oxfordian" books.

Despite the blame put on Oxford, he was not reported to have had a hand in any of the encounters except the first, in which, having no cause of contention, he may fairly be believed to have been set upon.

Our knowledge of the second fray begins with the Declaration of Roger Townsend, who was, on the one hand, secretary to Henry Howard's nephew, Philip Howard, Earl of Arundel, Knyvet's kinsman, and on the other a kinsman himself to Peregrine Bertie Lord Willoughby and a friend of Willoughby's brother-in-law, Lord Oxford. He was thus in the middle. (In this and in what follows I am drawing upon the information brought together by Miss Bowen.) Townsend had been invited to dine with a Mr. Jones on June 18th. As the Earl of Arundel was to be at the dinner, too, Townsend called for him at Arundel House. There, when they were on the point of departure, "my Lord Thomas Howard [Lord Arundel's brother] and Mr. Knyvet came in, and understood whither my Lord went [i.e., that Lord Arundel was going to Mr. Jones's] and did accompany him to the place where we dined."

After dinner — evidently the midday meal — one of Townsend's men came and informed him privately that he had been at Willoughby's house, where the owner and Lord Oxford were together (their differences evidently now a thing of the past) and there "had heard some speech that my Lord of Oxford's company meant to set upon Mr. Knyvet in the company of whomsoever they found him." Townsend, "thinking it was but some rash suspicion or speech of some ill disposed person," sent him back for further information. His skepticism also kept him from saying anything to Lord Arundel, whom, however, he undertook to persuade to go straight home from the dinner instead of attending to some business that would have taken him close to Willoughby House.

> And thereupon we went presently down the stairs to go to the Blackfriars [an old monastery just up from the Thames at today's Blackfriars Bridge converted to a private theatre]. And even at the door, my man came to me and told me that he had been at my Lord Willoughby's . . . and he did perceive that there was no such intent as was before spoken of. And so went to the Blackfriars; where Mr. Knyvet, going before us, was set upon. But who they were that did it I know not, for I was so far behind as I could not discern what they were.

Townsend offers further testimony on the course of events, but none that I can fit into what he has said so far or make much sense of. What stands out is, under the impression that Knyvet was set upon, Townsend and Lord Arundel make no attempt to ascertain his situation but take off in a boat.

But Knyvet was not set upon. He and his men were the aggressors. That is made plain in the statements of those who were at the site of the attack. There were several who chanced to be at Blackfriars Stairs — a landing on the river — and heard from the Thames watermen that, as two of them put it, "there would be a fray between my Lord of Oxford and Mr. Knyvet." They not only remained for the excitement but armed themselves with pike-staffs; "And shortly after," the recorder wrote, "Mr. Knyvet came and then the fray began. And he [the witness] seeing that they were but two of my Lord's men, and many men on the other side, he went in amongst them to keep the peace. He saw besides, 3 with staves, besides watermen with their hooks and staves." The three with staves were the others who happened to be on hand. One, seeming to speak for them all, said that, seeing "divers men assaulting two" of "my Lord of Oxford's men, he did help to rescue them, being then in some danger as he thought." The junior master of Caverley's fencing-school, which shared Blackfriars with the theatre, was able to name Oxford's two men as Gastrell and Horsleye. He had come upon the fray by chance; "And seeing swords drawn, and having only about him a single sword, he went in amongst them — only to keep the peace."

It is quite a picture of the times: Knyvet and his followers marching upon Blackfriars, where they knew Gastrell and Horsleye were to be found; word of their intent preceding them, to the delight of the watermen; the passersby picking up the excitement at second hand when the battle has been joined and enthusiastically wading in with what weapons are at hand. Of the issue of the combat and the extent of the mayhem there is nothing on the record. Presumably the authorities — the mayor or his deputies or both — arrived and the combatants, seeing them coming, melted away. That would hardly have been possible for Master Knyvet; but, as would soon be demonstrated, he was "not likely to speed ill whatsoever the quarrel may be."

Gastrell evidently did not take lightly his having been ganged up on. And certainly he was no coward. Ms. Bowen has blended the testimony of two witnesses to the next episode, which followed on June 22nd, only four days after the Blackfriars affair.

> "Upon Friday last, in the afternoon," they saw one called Gastrell and "maned" [named?] to be my Lord of Oxford's man draw his sword upon 3 or 4 of Mr. Knyvet's men. And one of Mr. Knyvet's men said twice or thrice: "Put up thy sword Gastrell, we will not deal with thee here, there is no place here," and desired the street to bear witness. Gastrell replied and said he *would* fight with them, and one Harvey, my Lord of Oxford's man, would have parted the fray and willed Gastrell to put up his sword, which he did accordingly. And then one of Mr. Knyvet's men said: "Gastrell, another time use thy discretion."

> Whereupon Gastrell drew again and ran upon one of Mr. Knyvet's men furiously; and they struck 5 or 6 blows, and Mr. Knyvet's man hurt Gastrell. The rest of Mr. Knyvet's men had their swords drawn but struck not at all. Harvey, my Lord of Oxford's man, with his sword drawn, would have parted the fray and was hurt by chance [according to one witness], by Gastrell, for he did not see any of Mr. Knyvet's men strike at him, or he at any of them.

It is another glimpse of things as they were in Elizabethan London.

The next flare-up of the feud was more serious. We know no more about it, however, than we are told in a secretary's notation in the margin of a letter of Christopher Hatton's of July 27th: "Mr. Knyvet had slain a man of the Earl of Oxford in fight." A Coroner's jury had returned a verdict of *se defendendo*. Hatton was writing in the Queen's name to warn the Lord Chancellor not to heed "the malice of his [i.e., Knyvet's] enemies," as the Queen put it, who "would have his trial at Newgate amongst common thieves," and to insist that the pardon to which the verdict entitled him be delivered more privately.

In the next year, 1583, on February 21st, according to the burial register of a church in Bishopsgate, Robert Brenings, another of Oxford's men, was slain. Presumably his death, too, could be laid to Knyvet's faction.

Then, later that month or early in the next Gastrell avenged the day at Blackfriars. He killed one of Knyvet's men called Long Tom. This comes out in a letter of March 12th from Burghley to Christopher Hatton.

Characteristically, the letter is long and wordy, but as it concerns Oxford it is much to the point and makes a moving appeal. Burghley thanks Hatton for interceding with the Queen to bring the troubles between Lord Oxford and Mr. Knyvet to an end, though he recognizes that so far this has been without result. Knyvet, who has access to the Queen, Burghley says, has complained to her "his men were evil used by my Lord of Oxford's men," one being killed "and no redress had." Observing that Leicester has been appointed by the Queen to examine the matter, Burghley doubts not that he will declare how "my Lord of Oxford resteth . . . unblotted, in any kind of matter objected by Master Knyvet." Long Tom, who had once served Oxford, was "a bad fellow" and Burghley says he is sending Hatton the records of the Coroner's inquest acquitting Gastrell, who, he adds, was not then Oxford's man, though Knyvet claimed he was. He doubts not that when the Queen has been informed of the truth by Leicester, her adverse opinion of Oxford will be mitigated.

Leicester will find, Burghley pursues, that Oxford is in nowise responsible "for the rest of those brabbles and frays." He maintains that the fights grew not from challenges by Oxford's men to Knyvet's but rather the other way around.

> My Lord of Oxford is neither heard nor hath presence either to complain or defend himself. And so long as he shall be subject to the disgrace of her Majesty

(from which God deliver him) I see it apparently that, innocent soever he shall be, the advantages will fall out with his adversaries; and so, I hear, they do prognosticate. . . .

However keenly Burghley must have suffered from Oxford's betrayal of his daughter with the young Vavasor woman, he sounds genuine in pleading for his son-in-law, though having little to say of his deserts and obviously being chiefly concerned by the ill consequences for his own house of the Queen's wrath at Oxford's having betrayed *her* with the black-eyed minx. He resumes:

> But I submit all these things to God's will, who knoweth best why it pleaseth Him to afflict my Lord of Oxford in this sort, who hath, I confess, forgotten his duty to God, and yet I hope he may be made a good servant to her Majesty, if it please her of her clemency to remit her displeasure; for his fall in her court, which is now twice yeared, and he punished as far [as] or farther than any like crime hath been, first by her Majesty, and then by the drab's friend in revenge to the peril of his life. . . . When our son-in-law was in prosperity, he was cause of our adversity by his unkind usage of us and ours; and now that he is ruined and in adversity, we only are partakers thereof, and by no means, no, not by bitter tears of my wife, can obtain a spark of favour for him, that hath satisfied his offence with punishment, and seeketh mercy by submission; but contrariwise, whilst we seek favour, all crosses are laid against him and by untruths sought to be kept in disgrace. . . .
>
> When I began to write, I neither meant nor thought I could have scribbled this much; but the matter hath ministered me the cause, for I take no pleasure therein.

That Burghley would call Anne Vavasor "the drab," the strumpet, in a letter to Hatton does not sound altogether as if she were regarded at Court as an innocent country maid corrupted by a wicked Lord. One other point: in speaking of Oxford as having "forgotten his duty to God," Burghley may be supposed to have referred to his backsliding into the Old Religion without having, upon renouncing it, returned to the new, as I judge was the case. And so, many years later, following the Essex rebellion, when it came out that the rebels had bribed the Lord Chamberlain's company to perform *King Richard the Second* because of the precedent it afforded for deposition of the monarch, Elizabeth would say, clearly speaking of the author of the play (Chapter 1), "He that will forget God will also forget his benefactor; this tragedy was played 40 times in open streets and houses." It would seem that Oxford's apostasy would not be forgotten.

> When in disgrace with fortune and men's eyes. . . .

So far as we know, Oxford never had more cause than now to "weep my outcast state." But he was mastering the means of turning the tables triumphantly upon adversity and those who took advantage of him. He had the drama. Albert Feuillerat was not the only one to be reminded by the quarrelling clamors in the London Streets of Verona and of the Montecchi and

Cappelletti. Long since, it seems, Oxford had bethought himself of the childish poem *Romeus and Juliet* and seen what might be made of it.

The commencement of the action in *The Tragedy of Romeo and Juliet* — of which the reader will certainly have been reminded by the scenes we have witnessed — is dated by the Nurse's remark that "'Tis since the earthquake now 11 years." She can hardly be referring to any other than the earthquake that struck in the neighborhood of Verona in 1570 and nearly destroyed Ferrara. In other words, the time is 1581. Oxford, as he often did, split in two for the play. His comic-fantastical side became Mercutio, his poetical-melancholy side Romeo, in whom Hamlet is already being born. The murderous swordsman Knyvet, Anne Vavasor's vengeful uncle, became the murderous swordsman Tybalt, the "Prince of Cats." (We might say that *ThOMas KnyvET* equals *Tom Ket* equals *Tomcat*.) I do not mean to equate Juliet with Anne Vavasor. She is probably to be regarded as the idealization of young girlhood abstracted from a number of models and perhaps made the age of Anne Cecil when she and Oxford were exchanging vows as an affectionate offering by Oxford to his wife upon their reconciliation, a gesture of amends. She does, however, recall Anne Vavasor of the *Echo Verses* when she cries:

> Bondage is hoarse and may not speak aloud;
> Else would I tear the cave where Echo lies,
> And make her airy tongue more hoarse than mine,
> With repetition of my Romeo's name,
> Romeo!

As in Anne Vavasor's poem, in which each line ends with *Vere*, the echo of the preceding word, so the echo of Juliet's repeated "Romeo!" would be *eo* or *E.O.*[3]

Elizabeth is plainly the "fair Rosaline" (not the dark Rosaline of *Much Ado*), the name perhaps signifying the Tudor rose. (I grant that at one point Romeo is said to have been "stabb'd with a white wench's black eye," meaning Rosaline's, but only, I think, because the dramatist was momentarily reverting to another cast of characters.) Rosaline does not appear in the play but at the beginning Romeo is "in love but out of favor" with her, and in what he says of her can be talking only of Elizabeth; for

> She hath Dian's wit,
> And, in strong proof of chastity well arm'd,
> From Love's weak childish bow she lives unharm'd.

---

[3] And bearing in mind that the only meanings of "roe" are a small species of deer and the egg mass of a (necessarily) female fish, the only sense anyone I know of has been able to make of the lines "Here comes Romeo, here comes Romeo / Without his roe, like a dried herring" is that "Romeo" without the *roe* is *meo*, or *Me, O*. Readers indignant at this seemingly far-fetched interpretation might hold their fire until reflecting upon the Elizabethan addiction to word-play of all kinds and upon Shakespeare's notorious weakness for puns.

She will not

> ope her lap to saint-seducing gold.
> O, she is rich in beauty; only poor
> That when she dies, with beauty dies her store.

For "she hath sworn that she will still live chaste"

> and in that sparing makes huge waste;
> For beauty, starv'd with her severity,
> Cuts beauty off from all posterity.
> She is too fair, too wise, wisely too fair,
> To merit bliss by making me despair.
> She has forsworn to love, and in that vow
> Do I live dead that live to tell it now.

These pretty compliments, going back to an earlier phase of Oxford's relations with Elizabeth (and sounding the note later heard in the *Sonnets* of beauty's death without an heir) would have pleased the Queen. They are, however, preparing the way for the dramatist's revenge for the wrongs he believes he has suffered at her hands. Romeo soliloquizes:

> But, soft, what light through yonder window breaks?
> It is the east, and Juliet is the sun!
> Arise, fair sun, and kill the envious moon,
> Who is already sick and pale with grief,
> That thou her maid are far more fair than she.
> Be not her maid, since she is envious.
> Her vestal livery is but sick and green,
> And none but fools do wear it; cast it off.

Percy Allen says, "The references here are unmistakable; for when it is remembered that the Tudor livery was green and white, the envious moon, or Diana as she was so frequently called, whose 'vestal livery is sick and green,' can be none other than Elizabeth"; the Queen was conventionally represented as the moon, Sidney Lee writes. To accuse the Vestal Moon of envy was a malicious cut at Elizabeth's notorious resentment toward the love affairs of those around her. In enjoining Juliet to "Be not her maid," Oxford could have been addressing either or both of his Annes, both of whom had been the Queen's Maids, "wearing her livery" — as was his second wife, too, for that matter.

Oxford's dangerous wound from Knyvet's weapon I take to be Mercutio's from Tybalt's, the wound "not so deep as a well, nor so wide as a church door." And doubtless Mercutio is speaking his creator's thoughts of Knyvet when he exclaims of his adversary, "Zounds, a dog, a rat, a mouse, a cat to scratch a man to death! a braggart, a rogue, a villain that fights by the book of arithmetic!"

In real life Knyvet went on to further honors, being knighted, then, having led the party that captured Guy Fawkes, made a baron; but the writer of fiction commands events. In the play, Oxford-Romeo has the exquisite satisfaction of dispatching Knyvet-Tybalt in a duel that the expert swordsmen of the Elizabethan stage would have fought with a fury and finesse holding breathless an audience of connoisseurs. The charm of authorship lies in ordering life to accord with what the writer decides it is trying to say and, when necessary, paying it back — even if that calls for dramatizing one's farewell to it in a romantic death-scene, which, of course, need not be the real thing either. As long as there was an English stage, Oxford had good reason to believe, he would carry the public with him in his triumph in Act III, Scene 2, and leave it with eyes streaming for the poignancy of his fate when he wrote finis to a story than which there never was one

> of more woe,
> Than this of Juliet and her Romeo.

But Oxford would pay dear for his satisfactions. If there was anything on which Elizabeth, Burghley and the other Cecils, Leicester and the other Dudleys, Christopher Hatton, the 3rd Earl of Southampton, and doubtless others who appeared in the plays and poems were agreed upon it was that the author must never, *never* be known for who he was, lest his characters be seen for who they were, if heaven and earth had to be moved to prevent it. And for all we know, the inheritors of their power well into the future would be aware of that necessity and be obedient to it.

33

"A Spirit Raised from Depth of Underground"

1581–1584: Alençon's last visit to England; his later disastrous attack upon the Dutch. — Allegory of his courtship of Elizabeth and final farewell in the play Sapho and Phao, *said to be by John Lyly, who would never have presumed so to trespass upon royalty's private lives. — Performance of a play identifiable as the first version of* Much Ado. *— Oxford's position as a literary arbiter suggested in a dedication by Thomas Watson, and the curious confusion of poems by the two. — Acquisition of Blackfriars Theatre by Oxford and its transfer to Lyly for rehearsing boy players for Court performance, notably of plays attributed to Lyly. — Needling in* Romeo and Juliet *of the Italian fencing-master who occupies a room in Blackfriars. — Failure of Fenton's trading expedition to the Spanish Main and loss of Oxford's investment. — Birth of a son to the Oxfords, his death, and the miserable Countess's poems on the loss. — The Earl's forgiveness by the Queen after bitter words between them. — Their joint heavy loss in the death of Sussex, whose rumored poisoning by Leicester suggests him as the model for Hamlet's father. — Oxford's gratitude to Burghley. — Exposure of another plot to put Mary on the throne; the complicity and eclipse of the Howards. — Restoration of Oxford's prospects as perhaps leading to the ebullient* Henry the Fourth, *Part One; Prince Hal's emergence from disreputable youth to greatness in* Henry the Fifth *as probably paralleling Oxford's view of his own life. — The Earl's financial setback in John Davis's failure to find a northwest passage and Hamlet's rueful allusion to it. — His purchase of the show-house called Fisher's Folly, perhaps as a headquarters for the literary circle forming around him. — Anthony Munday and Robert Greene as his protégés and the important disclosures they make about him in devoted dedications; their connecting him even more closely with Euphues. — Recent computer analysis making "Shakespeare" the author of the aborted play* Sir Thomas More, *of which the manuscript is mostly in Munday's hand. — Publication of an anthology by "John Soowthern," identified as a French employee of Oxford's, in which the Countess of Oxford's elegiac poems are printed together with one by Elizabeth and an ode to Oxford by Soowthern, who wrote the first in English. — Oxford's resentment of Burghley's attempt to suborn a man of his to spy upon him. — Performance of a clearly early version of* Troilus and Cressida. *— Exotic tournament on the anniversary of Elizabeth's accession and Oxford's participation.*

As long as he wrote, Oxford, like any novelist in verse or prose, would be revealing himself in his characters; but of this I think we have by now seen enough. Like others, too, he wrote on the whole with closest approximation to the circumstances and events of his life in his early works — and these we have already examined. *Hamlet*, as a play undertaken in mid-career, is an exception in bearing so closely upon its author's situation in life and upon the persons closest to him. It is the most autobiographical of all, the dramatist's considered and profoundest view of himself and his setting. But to this, too, I think we have given about as much attention as need be in preceding chapters. There remains much to be said of Oxford's poetry, attributed and otherwise, in its relation to that which we know as Shakespeare's, but this I had better leave to future scholarship. Accordingly, what I have left to say will mostly be about the external events in Oxford's life.

Through 1581 and 1582 Elizabeth was preoccupied with the question of her much-bruited marriage to the Duke of Alençon. Many, including perhaps Elizabeth herself, and certainly the Duke, believed she would go through with it. Not only was her beauty at last beginning to fade, the mid-point of her forties past, so that she knew if she were to wed at all it must be now, to her importunate Grenouille: polity, too, seemed to demand it. Good relations with France were vital in the face of the gathering Spanish menace. But however compelling the colors in which she presented the marriage to herself it seems clear that her inmost being balked absolutely. Alençon had been in England since October 1581 and had reached the point of declaring to Elizabeth, to her alarm, that if they were not to marry it were better they should both perish. By the end of the year she was eager to be rid of him. But Burghley made the decision inexpressibly difficult for her. Deeply concerned at the possibility of a Franco-Spanish alliance, he told her she must either wed the French Duke or make over a large sum of money to him, a sum far exceeding any precedent. She must have nearly fainted at the figure he had in mind. But she swallowed the dose. In February Alençon took his departure for the Continent with £10,000 in his pocket and a promise of £50,000 to come. En route to his ship the party escorting him detoured to Chatham to let him see the dockyards. Elizabeth Jenkins says, "They presented a spectacle that took the Frenchman's breath away. The masts of completed ships shaded the quays like groves, while in the yards vessels were building upon new and improved designs of which the world was presently to see the advantage." She goes on to say that the departed suitor "wrote letters to Elizabeth full of desolation at leaving her, and she exclaimed she would give a million pounds to have her frog swimming in the Thames again."

Several years earlier Alençon had accepted the title of "Defender of the Liberties of the Netherlands" at the urging of William of Orange, who was desperate for a counterpoise to the Spanish. Now, in the same month in which he left England, he was inaugurated as Duke of Brabant, with titles to other provinces to follow. Impatient at the restraints on his power, he came to the mad resolve in January 1583 to capture Antwerp and William himself with his French troops. But the citizens resisted the "French Fury" heroically and routed the attackers. His position in the Netherlands now impossible and himself probably broken in spirit, Elizabeth's Frog-Prince would die a year and a half later.

By the end of 1583 at the latest a play called *Sapho and Phao* had been written, ascribed to John Lyly and held to be his second, though first printed without an author's name, as were the other plays ascribed to him. In it, R. Warwick Bond writes, a

> medley of classical suggestion is made to serve the author's main purpose of flattering the Queen by an allegorical representation of the relations between herself and her suitor, the Duc d'Alençon. . . . It is to this underlying allegory, clearly alluded to in the Prologue at the Court and the Epilogue . . . that the changes made in the classical myth of Sappho are chiefly due. Hence the representation of her as a queen with a Court, and the suppression, surprisingly and needlessly thorough, of her poetic fame and functions; hence the striking beauty and majesty of person with which she is dowered: hence the invitation of Phao to her Court, her struggle against her passion and final conquest of it: while her secure assumption at the close of the prerogatives of Venus and the person of Cupid are in the happiest vein of courtly flattery. The distress and perplexities of Phao, and his departure from Sicily at the call of other destinies, are quite in keeping with the facts of Alençon's courtship; nor need the marked ugliness of the duke disqualify him for the part. Elizabeth had declared in 1579 that "she had never seen a man who pleased her so well, never one whom she could so willingly make her husband"; and the courtly poet saw and seized the opportunity in the tale that Love herself had made Phao beautiful.

Bond would hardly have stopped to think that in his "courtly poet" he was describing Lyly's employer more than Lyly. He does wonder, however, that "this classical tale, . . . manipulated with supreme address to serve the purposes of royal flattery, . . . though it deals with no less a matter than the proposed French match, . . . does not seem to have called down the veto of the Master of Revels nor the displeasure of the Queen" — as, he might have added, it certainly would have if presented by a man of Lyly's station. "How could one admit," Albert Feuillerat asks, "that a dramatist could be so audacious as to put on the stage the most intimate and secret sentiments of the Queen?" Only one close to her and of equal birth could have done so, surely. Lyly's part in it could hardly have been more than as "the fiddlestick of Oxford," whose guiding hand and sponsorship, I take it, *Sapho and Phao* enjoyed. It came as a graceful valedictory to the Alençon courtship, laying away its memories sentimentally like a girl's dance-program and pressed rose in a scented box after a ball. I should not be surprised if the Earl intended it as an overture to help restore him to the Queen's favor.

At about this time, on 12 February 1583, "*A historie of Ariodante and Genevora* was showed before her Majesty on Shrove Tuesday at night enacted by Mr. [Richard] Mulcaster's children," the boys of the Merchant Taylors

School. This is likely to have been the first version of *Much Ado About Nothing*, the main story of which comes from the tale of Ariodante and Ginevra in Ludovico Ariosto's epic *Orlando Furioso* (1532). One line in *Much Ado*, Don Pedro's "In time the savage bull doth bear the yoke," is quoted from Thomas Watson's *Hekatompathia, the Passionate Century of Love*.

Watson, an accomplished linguist, was considered the best poet in Latin of his day. His *Hekatompathia* was in English, however, a cycle of a hundred eighteen-line poems expressing "the Author's sufference in Love" and "his long farewell to love." It had been dedicated to Oxford on 31 March 1582. Recalling how Alexander the Great, by lingering over the paintings of Apelles, had created an insatiable demand for more of the same brush, Watson wrote that "many," having somehow heard that "your Honour had willingly vouchsafed the acceptance of this work, . . . have oftentimes and earnestly called upon me to put it to the press, that for their money they might but see what your Lordship with some liking had already perused." Plainly Oxford's word on literary matters carried weight. Among the good wishes with which the dedication closes, Watson includes, aptly, "the reconciliation of foes." Edward Arber, an authoritative critic of Elizabethan literature, writes of Watson's poems that "Whoever reads this remarkable work will wonder how it can have fallen into such oblivion." Calling attention to the short introductions that head the poems, he says, "They are most skilfully written. Who wrote them? May he have been the Earl of Oxford?" Watson himself, in an annotation to one of the poems, virtually identifies the dedicatee of the volume as a contributor to it. The literary relationship between Oxford and Watson was a curious one. As we have seen, parts of a poem in *A Hundreth Sundrie Flowres*, published when Watson was only sixteen, reappeared slightly altered in Watson's posthumous *Tears of Fancy* (1593), while Oxford's poem beginning "Who taught thee first to sigh, alas, my heart?" appeared as Watson's in the same collection.

The year 1583, E. K. Chambers says, was something of a turning-point in the history of the playing companies. The Queen's company was formed in that year and, to quote Chambers further, it "incorporated, in addition to Tarlton, . . . the leading members of the pre-existing companies," including "John Dutton from Oxford's." He recalls that "In 1580 the Duttons and the rest of the Earl of Warwick's men transferred to his service," as we have seen. Stow reported the turn of events:

> Comedians and stage players of former times were very poor and ignorant, in respect of these of this time, but being now grown very skilful and exquisite actors for all matters, they were entertained into the service of divers great Lords, out of which companies there were twelve of the best chosen . . . [and] sworn to the Queen's servants.

The Queen's Men would be the principal acting company until 1588, when the death of their "extemporal wit" and "wonder of his time," as Stow called Richard Tarlton, would cost it much of its vogue.

The loss of their star performers did not, however, mean that the companies of the "great Lords" went out of business. "Leicester's, Oxford's, and the Admiral's," Chambers writes, continued "setting up their bills side by side with those of the Queen's." Nor was that by any means all as far as Oxford was concerned. In the spring of 1583 he acquired the sublease of Blackfriars, the theatre established in the former monastery in 1576. Blackfriars was associated with the boy players. These had rather a long history. "In the earlier Tudor annals," Chambers says, "the great choirs of St. Paul's and the Chapel Royal had been at least as conspicuous as the professional companies." At this time, he believes, "the Paul's boys appear to have joined . . . a composite company, to which Lord Oxford's boys also contributed." Oxford transferred the lease of Blackfriars to his secretary, John Lyly, and at the same time probably gave him direct supervision of the new boys' company acting there. (Ten years later, Gabriel Harvey would write that Lyly "hath not played the Vice Master of Paul's, and the Fool Master of the Theatre for naughts.") M. C. Bradbook speculates that "Lyly was trying to amalgamate the children's troupes under Oxford's patronage. She writes, "in the spring of 1584 two plays [of Lyly's], *Campaspe* and *Sapho and Phao*, appeared as having been played before her Majesty by her Majesty's children and the children of Paul's." To this information, Chambers adds that "Harry Evans, who was also associated with this enterprise, took a play called *Agamemnon and Ulysses* on 27 December [1583]. On all three occasions the official patron of the company" — and much more, it seems likely — "was the Earl of Oxford." Moreover, R. W. Bond points out, all but one of Lyly's plays "are described on their title-pages as presented by these children" — that is, by the troupe in which Paul's and Oxford's boys were amalgamated, under Lyly as director and Oxford as patron.

In addition to his involvement in Court theatricals — and perhaps portentously — "in the 1583–1584 season," Samuel Schoenbaum says, "three troupes wearing the liveries of the earls of Oxford, Essex and Worcester, performed [in Stratford-upon-Avon] at Guild Hall and presumably also in the inn yards of Bridge Street."

In his *Shakespeare's Blackfriars Playhouse*, Irwin Smith writes: "Lord Oxford's prodigal gifts to Lyly had included not only the lease to the premises occupied by the playhouse, but also the lease to a room on the floor below," occupied by "a school of fence." This lease Lyly sold to the "master of fence, Rocco Bonetti," who "had come to England from Italy about 1569. . . . Bonetti was the most popular fencing master in Elizabethan England. George Silver, in his *Paradoxes of Defence*, 1599, says he was 'so excellent in his fight, that he would have hit any English man with a thrust, just upon any button in his doublet, and this was much spoken of.'" Professor Smith suggests that "it was he in all probability whom the dramatist [Shakespeare] had in mind when he characterized Tybalt as 'the very butcher of a silk button.'" It does indeed seem likely that, to lend Tybalt a local color of Italy, Knyvet is given an overlay of Bonetti in Mercutio's animadversions on the Veronese killer:

> He fights as you sing pricksong — keeps time, distance, and proportion; rests me his minim rest, one, two, and the third in your bosom! the very butcher of a silk button, a duellist, a duellist! A gentleman of the very first house, of the first and second cause. Ah, the immortal passado! the punto reverso! the hay!

Ward says Oxford seems to have had a quarrel with Bonetti, for unknown reasons, and this may have been the cause of Mercutio's exasperated addendum:

> The pox of such antic, lisping affecting fantasticoes — these new tuners of accenti! . . . these fashion-mongers, these pardona-mi's . . .

There is no longer any pretence that it is Mercutio speaking of a hot-blooded Capulet; what would an Italian have a fellow countryman say if not "pardona-mi"? It is an Englishman fulminating against a mincing, imported signore, specifically Signore Bonetti, the last line indicates:

> Oh, their bones, their bones!

It seems in tracing Oxford's life that from the time of his return from the Continent things generally went wrong for him, except in literature and the theatre. Very likely it was this that turned him — to the world's infinite gain — increasingly to those twin pursuits; as equally it could be argued that the more he gave himself to them the worse he was bound to fare in other spheres of his life.

As the spring of 1583 was an exciting time for him in the theatre, May was a particularly bad month outside it. Captain Edward Fenton, to whose trading expedition to the Spanish Main Oxford had apparently contributed *Edward Bonaventure*, returned empty-handed. The Spanish had thoroughly rebuffed him and attacked his little fleet, sinking the flagship. Again the Earl's investment had failed of a return.

Much worse was a burial recorded in the Parish Register of the church at Castle Hedingham — our first indication that the Earl and his Countess had resumed residence there:

> 1583. May 9th. The Earl of Oxenford's first son.

In the next year there was published in John Soowthern's *Pandora*

> *Four Epitaphs*
> made by the Countess of Oxenford
> upon the death of her young
> son, the Lord Bulbeck, & c.

It is perhaps no surprise that poor Anne should have sought to assuage her grief in verse, considering whom she was married to. The first of the *Epitaphs* begins:

> Had with morning the Gods left their wills undone,
> They had not so soon 'herited such a soul:
> Or if the mouth, time, did not glutton up all,
> Nor I, nor the world, were deprived of my son. . . .

Charles W. Barrell in an article on the *Epitaphs* draws attention to the Shakespearean images and terms that crop up in them. One notable example is in the foregoing lines. The *O.E.D.*, he observes, credits "Shake-speare" in the 1609 edition of the Sonnets with the first use of glutton or gluttoning as a transitive verb; yet here is the Countess of Oxford employing just such a usage a quarter-century earlier.

The *Epitaphs* sound as genuine in the grief they express as they are weak in poetical merit.

> My son is gone! and with it, death end my sorrow,
> But death makes me answer, "Madame, cease these moans:
> My force is but on bodies of blood and bones:
> And that of yours, is no more now, but a shadow."

Helena in *All's Well* is "but the shadow of a wife" — with less reason. The verse seems to me to speak genuinely of heartbreak, as does the following *Epitaph*, the best of them, which I quote in full to do the Countess justice:

> In doleful ways I spend the wealth of my time:
> Feeding on my heart, that ever comes again.
> Since the ordinance, of the *Destins*, hath been
> To end of the Seasons, of my years the prime.
> With my Son, my Gold, my Nightingale, and Rose,
> Is gone; for 'twas in him and no other where:
> And well though my eyes run down like fountains here,
> The stone will not speak yet, that doth it inclose.
> And *Destins* and Gods, you might rather have ta'en,
> My twenty years: than the two days of my son.
> And of this world what shall I hope, once I know,
> That in this respect, it can yield me but moss:
> Or what should I consume any more in woe,
> When *Destins*, God, and worlds, are all in my loss.

That loss included, of course, the hope she would have had that the heir to the title with which she was presenting her husband would finally bind him to her — a hope that lasted only the two days she tells us the infant lived.

Mr. Barrell makes the good point that "One outstanding feature of the Epitaphs is their complete lack of any allusion whatever to the consolations or sustaining hopes that the Christian religion might be supposed to offer a British mother of the 16th century who had lost her only son. The pagan imagery of Greek and Roman mythology predominates throughout . . ." —

indeed, makes up an entire *Epitaph*. In this she was much more like her husband than her father.

Four days after the burial, Walter Raleigh (who is said three years earlier to have attached himself to Oxford) wrote Lord Burghley of his intervention with the Queen on his son-in-law's behalf. Raleigh, already at thirty-one an experienced military captain and trans-Atlantic navigator — twice a duelist, too — had returned from a campaign in Ireland, where he had helped defeat and massacre the small Spanish-Papal force at Smerwick. An annuity, a profitable sinecure, and valuable properties came to him on his return — rewards out of proportion to the distinction of his service but not, in Elizabeth's eyes, in respect of his tall good looks, "caressive" manner, and agile wit. As it would turn out, his voice in Oxford's favor counted for much, doubtless to the Earl's shame that his star had fallen so low it could be elevated by a parvenu like Raleigh.

In his letter of May 13th Raleigh wrote that he had conveyed to the Queen how "grievously" Lord Burghley had taken her answer to his petition in Oxford's cause. Her Majesty, it appeared, "purposed to have a new repartition [whatever that may have meant] between the Lord Howard, Arundel and others, and the Earl; and said it was a matter not so slightly to be passed over." Raleigh had "answered that being assured Her Majesty would never permit anything to be prosecuted to the Earl's danger — if any such possibility were — . . . it were to small purpose, after [the Earl had suffered] so long absence and so many disgraces, to call his honour and name again in question." The Queen "confessed that she meant it only to give the Earl warning" — of what, the letter does not say. Raleigh "delivered her your Ladyship's letter" and intimated that it would be "honourable and profitable . . . for [Her] Majesty to have regard to your Lordship's health and quiet." He makes plain for whom he was doing all this:

> And the more to witness how desirous I am of your Lordship's favour and good opinion, I am content, for your sake, to lay the serpent before the fire as much as in me lieth; that, having recovered strength, myself may be most in danger of his poison and sting. . . .

What Raleigh had done to rouse the Earl's ire he does not say, and what kind of counter-strike he anticipated there is no knowing, unless he had in mind the job Oxford had done in *Twelfth Night* on Christopher Hatton. He had better have worried about Henry Howard's poison and sting, which he *would* experience. Howard would actually confess to Robert Cecil his intention, as opportunity arose, to turn King James against his rivals, Raleigh among them, by snaring them into questionable negotiations with Spain.

Elizabeth may have already felt that her determination to punish her former favorite had been partly satisfied by Burghley's account in March of the Earl's relative poverty; far from going about with "fifteen or sixteen pages in livery," as the Queen had heard, Burghley told her that he had but four servants altogether, of whom "one . . . waiteth upon his wife my daughter, another is in my house upon his daughter Bess [and] a third is a kind of tumbling boy." Even more, probably, would her heart have been softened toward her offending courtier by the death of his little son. He cannot have failed to have had her approbation in the theatrical entertainment he provided her Court, however scandalized she may have been by what she heard of his companions of the inn yards. But it was evidently Raleigh's intercession that was decisive. On June 2nd, Roger Manners wrote to his brother the Earl of Rutland, Oxford's old fellow ward:

> Her Majesty came yesterday to Greenwich from the Lord Treasurer's. . . . The day she came away, which was yesterday, the Earl of Oxford came to her presence, and after some bitter words and speeches, in the end all sins are forgiven, and he may repair to the Court at his pleasure. Master Raleigh was a great mean herein, whereat Pondus is angry for that he could not do so much.

(The name of the venerable councillor in *Hamlet* having been changed from Corambis — a play on Burghley's motto — in the first quarto to Polonius in the second, it is interesting to learn that Burghley evidently bore the nickname Pondus. "Can 'Polonius,'" E. K. Chambers asks, "have resembled some nickname of Burghley?"[1]

Oxford's satisfaction at his restoration to royal favor after twenty-six months would be offset eight days later by the death of the Earl of Sussex. For Elizabeth it was "a terrible loss," Elizabeth Jenkins says: "the quality of his loyalty was like no one else's." To Lucy Aikin, "Leicester lost the antagonist whom he most dreaded, and the nobility one of its principal ornaments." Sussex died with Leicester's dangerous malignance on his mind. In the presence of Leicester's ally, Hatton, he said: "Beware of the gypsy. He will betray you. You do not know the beast as well as I do." It has been suggested that Oxford had Sussex in mind in the character of John of Gaunt in *Richard the Second*, particularly as Gaunt, facing death, gives English patriotism its noblest expression in the speech "This royal throne of kings, this scepter'd isle. . . ." Sussex was twenty-five years older than Oxford, and, given their relationship of patron and protégé and the older man's childlessness, it is quite possible that Oxford looked upon him as upon a father; further, believing the rumor that he was poisoned by Leicester, Oxford may well have cast him in the role of the old King Hamlet, whose memory the young Prince so reveres. If so, then in holding up the two portraits,

---

[1] To "Pondus" may be added "Polus," which, as J. Valcour Miller points out in a striking study of the many analogies between Polonius and the Lord Treasurer, was thrice applied to Burghley by Gabriel Harvey in addressing him in his tribute at Audley End in 1578. The sobriquet, Miller explains, is from a Latin word for the pole around which the heavens turn and the axle of a wheel revolves.

Hamlet was asking the Queen to compare Sussex with Leicester. ("One of the most amazing things about this amazing woman," Conyers Read says of Elizabeth, "was her blind faith in Leicester.") It would be interesting indeed if Oxford felt called upon to avenge Sussex's death by slaying Leicester and castigated himself for his inability to bring himself to it. Did he at the first Court performance of *Hamlet* watch Leicester as narrowly as a cat a mouse, as Hamlet watches Claudius at the play within a play?

But back to fact. Within three weeks of his re-admission to Court, Oxford was writing to remind his father-in-law that he had "been an earnest suitor unto your Lordship for my Lord Lumley, that it would please you for my sake to stand his good Lord and friend" and to acknowledge that Lord Burghley's having done so was one "in a number of things more than I can reckon" for which he was "bound unto your Lordship." He recalls that Lord Lumley had "matched with a near kinswoman of mine [Elizabeth Darcy, his first cousin once removed], whose father [the second Lord Darcy] I was always beholden unto for his assured and kind disposition unto me." All the others of his blood, he says, "have embraced further alliances to leave their nearer consanguinity." He declared that for him his father-in-law comes "before anyone else in the world, both through match — whereby I count my greatest stay — and by your Lordship's friendly usage and sticking by me in this time wherein I am hedged with so many enemies." It is a remarkable acknowledgement. Craving pardon for troubling his father-in-law, who is already "troubled with many matters," he begs his help "in easing Lord Lumley's payment to Her Majesty, wherein we will all give your Lordship thanks." John Lumley, B. M. Ward writes, "once a member of the Privy Council, had been utterly ruined, and indeed had nearly lost his life, owing to the part he had played in the Ridolfi Plot in 1571. His political downfall had led him to devote the remainder of his life to scholarship and literature. For fifty years he was the High Steward of Oxford University; and he collected what must then have been the finest library of books and manuscripts in England. This library was later bought by King James I for his son Prince Henry and now forms the collection known as the 'Royal Library' in the British Museum."

A few months later another of those widely ramified plots against Elizabeth and Protestant England broke upon the public with the arrest of Francis Throckmorton. Throckmorton, who had come under Roman Catholic influence at Oxford, had helped hide the leaders of the Jesuit invasion in 1580, then later in that year had escaped to the Continent to conspire with exiled Papists. Returning in 1583, he came under the surveillance of the chief of Elizabeth's secret service. When Walsingham pounced in October, Throckmorton was engaged in enciphering a letter to Mary Queen of Scots. Before the constables could seize them he found time to pass a mass of incriminating papers to a maidservant for delivery to Mendoza, the Spanish Ambassador. Put on the rack, he stoutly denied the charges against him but when threatened with repetition he gave way and revealed what he knew. Obtained as it was, his confession would have meant little in itself, but documents acquired by Walsingham confirmed it. The plan thus exposed called for invasion of England by a French force under the Duke of Guise or by a Spanish and Italian force sent by Philip II, release of Mary Queen of Scots, and reestablishment of the Church of Rome. Mary had been apprised of it and Mendoza had been a prime mover in it — indeed had shortly before dissuaded the aging and weary Mary from coming to terms with Elizabeth and retiring to France. The Ambassador was called before the Privy Council and given fifteen days to quit the country, his furious demand that he first communicate with his sovereign being rejected. He would not be replaced. Instead of an ambassador, Spain would send the Armada.

The exposure of the Throckmorton plot sent a wave of apprehension and anger throughout England. The public outdid itself in homage to the Queen. Meanwhile, though there had been an exodus of conspirators from England, a number were arrested. Henry Howard was among them, and in December he was sent to the Fleet, whence, after many months, he was put on parole in the house of Sir Nicholas Bacon, never to regain Elizabeth's trust. His nephew, Philip Howard, Earl of Arundel, was put under house arrest and repeatedly interrogated about the Throckmorton plot. In the next year he would be received into the Roman Catholic Church, after appearing a last time in a tournament together with the Earl of Oxford. In the year after that, 1585, he would attempt to flee England only to be intercepted crossing the Channel, heavily fined, and imprisoned. (And in prison, convicted of high treason for sympathizing with the Spanish Armada, he would die ten years later.)

With both the Howards in detention and Charles Arundel a fugitive on the Continent, the year 1583 had made a clean sweep of Oxford's Catholic enemies. Probably exhilarated by the turn in his fortunes, he may during the next year have written one of the two most spirited of his plays, *Henry the Fourth, Part One*, in which Prince Hal provokes and enjoys the company of the immortal comic creation originally called Sir John Oldcastle — "alias the Jockey" in *The Famous Victories of Henry the Fift* — and Sir John Falstaff in the final version, when (to repeat) "Shake-speare" had become a "Fallstaff." At least 1584 is the date assigned to the play by Eva Turner Clark, who argues that the rebels in the play — the Percys and Worcester — do double duty, representing both the rebellious earls in the northern uprising of 1569 and the Howards in 1583; the objective of the northern rebellion and that of the Throckmorton plot differed but little. It is certain that *Henry the Fourth* begins with the monarch asking Prince Hal with grieving and angry contempt what Elizabeth might have demanded of Oxford in respect of his bohemian ways: how

> Could such inordinate and low desires,
> Such poor, such bare, such lewd, such mean attempts,
> Such barren pleasures, rude society,
> As thou art match'd withal and grafted to,
> Accompany the greatness of thy blood,
> And hold their level with thy princely heart?

To which the Prince protests

> . . . God forgive them that so much hath sway'd
> Your Majesty's good thoughts away from me,

promising such vengeance upon his kingly father's enemies as

> . . . may salve
> The long-grown wounds of my intemperance —

This vow he carries out by defeating the renowned warrior Henry Percy, called Hotspur, thus saving his father's throne, as Oxford is likely to have thought he helped save Elizabeth's by exposing the Howards. His having won the prize in the tournament of 1581, in which Philip had been on the other side, would have given a little more congruence to the analogy.

The main point is that in the trilogy of the two *Henry the Fourths* and *Henry the Fifth* (the three plays into which *The Famous Victories* divided) Prince Hal's undisciplined and unseemly youth, his resort to the taverns, his low company, his impudence, recklessness, and affronts to respectability, all so unworthy of his blood, turn out to be the hotbed of the most manly and noble virtues and attainments. It is a point that I believe was of great importance to Oxford as being a theme of his own life.

> The breath no sooner left his father's body,

says the Archbishop of Canterbury in the opening scene of *Henry the Fifth*

> But that his wildness, mortified in him,
> Seem'd to die too;
>   . . . .
>   Never was such a sudden scholar made;
> Never came reformation in a flood,
> With such a heady currance, scouring faults.

"You'll see," the dramatist seems to be promising Elizabeth. The Bishop of Ely declares

> We are blessed in the change.

Canterbury then warms to his theme, and his wonder at the multi-faceted character of Henry's genius is not far from ours of Shakespeare's:

> Hear him but reason in divinity,
> And all-admiring with an inward wish

> You would desire the king were made a prelate:
> Hear him debate of commonwealth affairs,
> You would say it hath been all in all his study:
> List his discourse of war, and you shall hear
> A fearful battle rendered you in music:
> Turn him to any cause of policy,
> The Gordian knot of it he will unloose,
> Familiar as his garter: that, when he speaks
> The air, a charter'd libertine, is still,
> And the mute wonder lurketh in men's ears,
> To steal his sweet and honey'd sentences; . . .

(What a writer, to promise so much of a character, and then live up to the promise!)

> So that the art and practic part of life
> Must be the mistress of this theoric:
> Which is a wonder how his grace should glean it,
> Since his addiction was to courses vain,
> His companies unletter'd rude and shallow,
> His hours fill'd up with riots, banquets, sports. . . .

Ely has the answer:

> The strawberry grows underneath the nettle,
> And wholesome berries thrive and ripen best
> Neighbour'd by fruit of baser quality.

When the Dauphin's ambassador taunts him with savoring too much of his youth and sneers that dukedoms cannot be won by nimbleness in dance and revelry, the response by the new King Henry might be Oxford's to Howard's and Arundel's charges:

> And we understand him well,
> How he comes o'er us with our wilder days,
> Not measuring what use we made of them.

The use that Oxford made of them is measured in the poems and plays of Shakespeare.

But in *King Henry the Fifth* we are looking a few years ahead.

Oxford's euphoria at this time, if such it was, bore less happy fruit than the zest of *Henry the Fourth, Part One*. The siren voice of the sea-route westward sang for him again — for the fourth time. Quite probably it did so with the tongue of his old acquaintance John Dee. Sir Humphrey Gilbert had assigned to Dee all his rights in all lands north of the 15th parallel, which cuts through northern Newfoundland. "This may have been for services rendered," David B. Quinn writes, "since Dee was busy constructing maps (he gave one to Gilbert in 1582) which confidently showed passages through and around America both in Arctic and temperate latitudes, and was also engaged in conducting seances to summon up supernatural guidance on the discovery of a passage." Shortly after this, of course, we have the magician-warrior Owen Glendower announcing that he "can call spirits from the vasty deep" — and in Hotspur's ironic retort, "But do they come when you do call for them?" probably a reflection of Oxford's experiences with the astrologer's divinations. At this time Dee went off to the Continent in the company of a Polish nobleman and fellow necromancer. The application for a patent authorizing a search for the Northwest Passage, which Dee was to have made, now fell to Humphrey Gilbert's brother Adrian. The latter, with his half-brother Walter Raleigh (who soon dropped out) organized The Colleagues of the Fellowship for the Discovery of the North West Passage. With the Earls of Leicester and Bedford, Oxford became a shareholder in the new company. A first-rate seaman and navigator was engaged in the person of John Davis. With *Sunshine* and *Moonshine* Davis would up anchors in June 1585 to return in September, having made Baffin Island north of Frobisher's explorations and sailed up Cumberland Sound. This he would of course take for the strait he was seeking and bring back renewed hope of finding the all-important Passage — but nothing else to recompense the stockholders. Hamlet had reason the next year to lament wryly "I am but mad north northwest." But the worldly misfortunes of writers tend to be the profit of their art, and it may be to Oxford's interest in exploration of the North American littoral that we owe *The Tempest.*

Oxford to the end would be pursuing schemes for raising money — a necessity forced on most artists by their unhandiness in its management and acquisition. To the charge that his object was to feed an addiction to extravagant tastes the answer is that even while selling most of his lands he was living a life that was spartan compared with the lives of those he rubbed shoulders with at Court. (Hatton was building a rival to Theobalds.) One seeming indulgence in costly luxury in the period we have reached is likely to have had serious purposes. This was the purchase of a huge house, called Fisher's Folly, occupying the present site of Devonshire Square, which, as Barrell says, "Oxford, with characteristic disregard of his own financial uncertainty, appears to have taken over about 1584," though "his city residence was still maintained at Oxford Court [Vere House] by London Stone."

We read in an account of 1598 that on the high street from Bishopgate and Hound's ditch,

> There is there a fair house of late builded by John Powlet. Next to that, a far more large and beautiful house with gardens of pleasure, bowling alleys and such like, builded by Jasper Fisher, free of the Goldsmiths, late one of the six clarks of the Chauncerie, and a Justice of the Peace. It hath since for a time been the Earle of Oxford's place. The Queen's Majesty Elizabeth hath lodged there. . . . This house being so large and sumptuously builded by a man of no greater calling, possessions or wealth (for he was indebted to many) was mockingly called Fisher's Folly, and rhyme was made upon it.

This report that Elizabeth lodged here with Oxford (where perhaps the owner would "challenge her to bowl," as Costard advises a suitor in *Love's Labour's Lost*) provides our only knowledge of how far he had been restored to her favor.

Mr. Barrell's idea is that Oxford acquired the mansion "as headquarters for the school of poets and dramatists who openly acknowledged his patronage and leadership." He may equally have sought a dwelling suitable for visits by the Queen.

The circle of writers began to form around Oxford when he was in the forefront of the euphuist movement. With John Lyly there was Anthony Munday, who in 1579 had dedicated *The Mirrour of Mutabilitie* to Oxford with a euphuistic opening wishing the Earl "after this life a crown of everlasting felicity in the eternal hierarchy." He goes on to say

> After that I had delivered (Right Honourable) unto your courteous and gentle perusing my book entitled *Galien of France*, wherein, having not so fully comprised such pithiness of style as one of a more riper invention could cunningly have carved, I rest, Right Honourable, on your clemency, to amend my errors committed so unskilfully.

In the next year Munday dedicated to Oxford his *Zelauto* and to two gentlemen "attendant upon the Earl of Oxford" his *A View of Sundry Examples*, of events "strange and monstrous."[2] In the first, the author pays tribute to "the rare virtues of your noble mind" and "the heroical qualities of your prudent person" and refers to abler writers who have dedicated works to Oxford, or, as he puts it, "such commendable writers, as prefer to your seemly self works worthy of eternal memory." Then he says:

> Yet this much I am to assure your Honour, that among all them which owe you dutiful service, and among all the brave books which have been bestowed, these my little labours contain so much faithful zeal to your welfare as others whatsoever, I speak without any exception. But lest your honour should deem I forge my tale on flattery, and that I utter with my mouth my heart thinketh not, I wish for the trial of my trustiness what reasonable affairs your Honour can best devise, so shall your mind be delivered from doubt, and myself rid of any such reproach.

That he feels Oxford might be in need of service is suggested by his observation that "the puissantest Prince is not void of enemies, the gallantest champion free from foes, and the honest liver without some backbiters." Let us bear in mind that this was written back in 1580 when Oxford's position seemed impregnable.

---

[2] George Lyman Kittredge, in his introduction to *The Merchant of Venice*, says that "Anthony Munday combines the bond story with the winning of the usurer's daughter in Part III of his *Zelauto*. . . ."

Chapter 33: A Spirit Raised from Depth of Underground

There may be more in Munday's apostrophes to Oxford than has been perceived. He ends *The Mirror of Mutability* with a quatrain in Latin translated by Ward as:

> My noble master, farewell. May your desires which are dear to us all prevail. Earnestly do I pray for your welfare and success in the struggle. To the guardianship of Christ I commit you and yours, till the day when as conquerors we may peacefully resume our literary discussions.

What kind of talk is this? In what struggle is he praying for his patron's welfare and success? In 1578 Munday had cropped up in Rome. He says in the dedication of *The Mirror* that after writing *Galien of France* (apparently also dedicated to Oxford) he had set off as a traveller "to attain to some understanding in the languages" and because "my wild oats required to be furrowed in a foreign ground"; but, we read, "he must be regarded, if not as a spy sent to report on the English Jesuit College in Rome, as a journalist who meant to make literary capital out of the designs of the English Catholics resident in France and Italy."

It strikes me that Munday, addressing Oxford in 1579 with talk of their being able to resume their literary discussions after emerging as conquerors from a mysterious struggle, may have brought the Earl alarming reports of the Jesuits' designs upon England in the year before their invasion and urged the need for counter-measures. If so, he may have had much to do with Oxford's break with Rome and, if the information he brought back were of such a kind, with his denunciation of Howard, Arundel, and Southwell. That Munday felt the Jesuit invasion called for counter-action is certain. In 1581, while Oxford was under detention, he "turned from the stage" — he had been an actor — "to the more congenial work of exposing in five tracts 'the horrible and unnatural treasons' of the Catholics." (*Dictionary of National Biography*.) He was one of the chief witnesses against Edmund Campion, the most prominent leader of the incursion whom the Queen herself tried to win over to observance of Anglican forms to clear himself of the capital charge of treason.

But Munday is important to our inquiry for other reasons. What did he mean by the following dedication, already mentioned?

> Zelauto. The Fountain of Fame. Erected in an Orchard of Amorous Adventures. Containing a Delicate Disputation, gallantly discoursed between two noble gentlemen of Italy. Given for a friendly entertainment to Euphues, at his late arrival in England. By A. M. Servant to the Right Honourable the Earle of Oxenforde, 1580.

Am I right in believing that in giving to Euphues for a friendly entertainment a book he is dedicating — that is, giving — to Oxford, Munday is coming as close as discretion permitted to saying that Oxford (who had also come to England from Italy) is Euphues? I hardly see what else he could mean, particularly in view of the other circumstances linking Euphues and Oxford. If such is the case, it is of special interest that Euphues is made a foppish native of Athens, birthplace of Western drama, and in the end returns to Athens, to which "serious and weighty affairs of his own" — Tucker Brooke says, "hitherto quite unsuspected" — recall him. That the reference would have been to Oxford's dramatic activities is an appealing conjecture.

The provocative figure of Euphues, whom we recall today in the language we speak and in our taste for novels, stalks forth again with the next adherent to Oxford's circle. This was Robert Greene, who took his place with Lyly, Munday, and Thomas Watson at about the time Oxford was acquiring Fisher's Folly.

The twenty-four-year-old had for four years as a sizar at Cambridge "consumed the flower of his youth," as he put it, "among wags as lewd as himself." Between 1578 and 1583 he had travelled widely in Europe. Back in London, he launched himself on a meteoric career as "an author of plays and a penner of love-pamphlets, so that I soon grew famous in that quality that who for that trade grown so ordinary about London as Robin Greene?" He became not only ordinary but by his own account — probably exaggerated — disgracefully debauched. In one of his spells of reform he married, but after spending his wife's marriage portion and becoming a father, he deserted the child's mother, because, he said, she tried to "persuade him from his wilful wickedness." She did not succeed. "He continued his wild career of carouse and revelry with consistent weakness, giving hereby to his numerous literary adversaries a powerful weapon against him," the shocked Grosart recounts. "Intemperance, licentiousness, and irreverence for religion . . . were the sins with which he was charged by his enemies, and to which he pleaded guilty." When Lord Burghley decried his son-in-law's "lewd" associates, he must have closed his eyes and shuddered at the thought of the red-bearded Robert Greene declaiming "What talk you of hell to me? I know if I once come there, I shall have the company of better men than myself, I shall also meet with some mad knaves in that place and so long as I shall not sit there alone, my care is the less." But, said Thomas Nashe, who would follow his friend into Oxford's fellowship, "Glad was that printer that might be so blessed to pay him dear for the very dregs of his wit." He was prolific and adaptable, and with his "bright fancy, ingenuity and wit" he "anticipated . . . the development of the English novel." (*Encyclopaedia Britannica*.) The English novel's line of descent is clear: from *The Adventures of Master F. I.*, through *Euphues* (which followed *The Adventures*, R. W. Bond says, "in its subject-matter, its love-making, its letters, the coquetry of its heroine, and its general aspect as a picture of polite society"), through the romances of Greene. Of these last, two, the *Encyclopaedia Britannica* points out, announced themselves by their very titles as a kind of sequel to *Euphues*, while the first, *Mamillia*, "is closely modelled on 'Euphues,'" according to the *Dictionary of National Biography*, which adds that "all his [Greene's] love-pamphlets bear traces of Lyly's [*sic*] influence." Gabriel Harvey, let us notice, called Greene "The Ape of Euphues."

There we have it, if the evidence is as unmistakable as it seems. Central to the genesis of the English novel was — Oxford.

One of Greene's novels, *Pandosta*, of 1588, would tell the same story as *The Winter's Tale*.

Four years earlier, Greene had dedicated one of his first books, *Greene's Card of Fancy*, to Oxford. The opening of the dedication cites distinguished figures of antiquity who had been indulgent toward the well-meaning when these had been only indifferently successful. The last part reads:

> Wheresoever Mæcenas lodgeth, thither no doubt will scholars flock. And your Honour being a worthy favourer and fosterer of learning hath forced many through your excellent virtue to offer the first-fruits of their study at the shrine of your Lordship's courtesy. But though they have waded far and found mines, and I gadded abroad to get nothing but mites, yet this I assure myself, that they never presented unto your Honour their treasure with a more willing mind than I do this simple trash, which I hope your Lordship will so accept. Resting therefore upon your Honour's wonted clemency, I commit your Lordship to the Almighty.
>
> Your Lordship's most dutifully to command,
> Robert Greene

Between the two parts Greene makes the highly significant statement:

> All that courted Atalanta were hunters, and none sued to Sapho but poets.

In other words, it was not only as a friend and munificent patron of literary men that Oxford drew writers to his circle — and Nashe would also call him a Mæcenas — but a writer himself pre-eminent among writers. Greene, like Munday, goes as far as discretion allows.

Like Greene, Munday contributed much to the newly popular prose fiction and reaped much advantage from it. "Labours which mainly commended Munday to his generation," says the *Dictionary of National Biography*, "were doubtless his voluminous translations of popular romances." At least fifteen of these were in a cycle called *The Romances of Chivalry*, from French, Italian, and Spanish originals, according to B. M. Ward, published between 1583 and 1618. The first editions of at least five, he says, bore dedications to Oxford. In the only one of these surviving, one of 1588, Munday speaks of Oxford's "special knowledge" of the "other languages" from which he has made a "bad translation." Recalling that "among the Spartans . . . nothing was accounted more odious than the forgetfulness of the servant towards the master," he declares

> For if this vice were so despised among such famous persons, what reproach
> would it be to so poor an abject as myself, being once so happy as to serve a
> master so noble, to forget his precious virtues, which makes him generally
> beloved, but chiefly mine own duty, which nothing but death can discharge.

I have the impression that Oxford was indeed beloved among the writers he
took under his wing.

In the original draft of this book, I took leave of Munday with some
observations of Sidney Lee's, to wit, that "In his versatility the epitome of
his age," few but the greatest Elizabethans "contributed more largely to
public information and entertainment"; that of the eighteen plays he had a
hand in, "several were highly successful"; and that these began in 1584 with
one "written . . . for the Earl of Oxford's company." Now, however, comes
Thomas Merriam of Basingstoke, England, with evidence that would show
Munday to have been a link directly associating Oxford with the composition
of Shakespeare's plays.

The evidence arises from that much mulled-over play, *The Book of Sir
Thomas More*. This we took up in Chapter 8 in connection with orthodoxy's
claim that "Shakespeare" wrote one of the scenes. (That he was its author
seemed quite possible, but that it was penned by him in the manuscript we
have was quite unconvincing.) The reader may remember that although the
manuscript of the play (which was not published until 1844) contains revisions or interpolations in five different hands, "the original matter is written
throughout in a single hand," as is vouchsafed by E. K. Chambers, who, as
do other scholars, identifies "the original hand with Anthony Munday's."

Armed with a microprocessor using "41 non-positional tests" re-inforced
by "an adaptation of Dr. Eliot Slater's rare-word-link method," Mr. Merriam
compared the stylistic characteristics of *Sir Thomas More* with those of *Julius
Caesar*, *Titus Andronicus*, and *Pericles* and found that *More* was altogether
by Shakespeare, "although the third act had a few eccentricities." Of course
it is hardly conceivable that a play written by the conventional Shakespeare
would be found in Munday's handwriting. Orthodoxy could have none of
such an idea. The editors of two British scholarly journals refused to publish
Merriam's exposition of his findings, but *The Observer* printed a tabulation
of them. Replying for the Stratfordians, Professor Muriel Bradbrook of
Cambridge University, a leading Elizabethan specialist, did the best she could.
She threw the case out of court, according to a report in the *New York Times*
by R. W. Apple, Jr., of 10 July 1980, on the grounds that the attribution of
Pericles and *Titus Andronicus* is questionable while the text of *Julius Caesar*
is probably corrupt.

Merriam explains that he picked those three plays because the Reverend
Andrew Q. Morton of Edinburgh University had used them for stylistic tests
— which, incidentally, Merriam says are compatible with his own in outcome.

To meet objections, he substituted *King Lear* for *Pericles* and "found no difference in the result." Next, as he writes, "a professor who was visiting Oxford" objected that he "had used tests that would not distinguish Elizabethan plays by different authors," for example, "a Marlowe play . . . from *Julius Caesar*." Mr. Merriam "then proceeded to test Munday's *John a Kent and John a Cumber* against *King Lear*, *Julius Caesar* and *Titus Andronicus*, using the same 41 non-positional tests." Measured against "a composite value for Shakespeare, . . . for *More* the final probability was .26. For *Lear* it was .40. For *Caesar* it was .45. For *Pericles* it was .35 and for *John a Kent and John a Cumber* it was .000000163." And Merriam reminds us that the handwriting in *John a Kent* is the same as Munday's in *More*, while the two manuscripts are bound in a similar material.

Merriam's report was printed in the February 1981 issue of Louis Marder's *Shakespeare Newsletter*, from which I have been quoting. In the April issue Dr. Marder hailed a "brilliant analysis of Dr. Carol Chillington, University of Warwick," purporting to rebut Mr. Merriam's findings by "the usual methods of scholarly investigation" — the same methods that made a global figure of an obscure Stratfordian — and "solid literary intuition based on historical and literary analysis." As Gordon C. Cyr shows in the September 1981 issue of the *Newsletter*, however, Dr. Chillington lacks historical data for her case and presents a weak argument, while as for "literary intuition," he not unreasonably prefers statistics to an educated hunch. Unless a much better basis can be found for refuting it, Thomas Merriam's finding that Shakespeare was the original and virtually sole author of *Sir Thomas More* will stand. To it, we need only add that the identification of Oxford as Shakespeare makes it quite unremarkable that the manuscript of the play should be in the hand of his secretary, Anthony Munday. To judge by its quality, my guess would be that Oxford wrote the original version of the play around 1580 and that the much more recognizably Shakespearean scene was added much later.

. . . .

It was in 1584 that John Soowthern's *Pandora* came out, with the Countess of Oxford's *Epitaphs*, followed, most surprisingly, by an *Epitaph, made by the Queenes Maiestie, at the death of the Princesse of Espinoye*. The volume also contained the first odes in English, by Soowthern himself. Of these, the principal celebrates the Earl of Oxford. It invokes the Muses:

> Come Nymphs while I have a desire,
> To strike on a well-sounding lyre,
> *Dever*, that hath given him in part:
> The love, the war, honour and art,
> And with them an eternal fame.

. . . .

> Among our well renowned men,
> *Dever* merits a silver pen
> Eternally to write his honour,
> And I in a well-polished verse,
> Can set up in our universe
> A fame to *en*dure for *ever*.   [My stresses.]

The poet asks rhetorically "who marketh better than he, / The seven turning flames of the sky [the planets in astrology] / Or hath read more of the antique," who has greater knowledge of languages, or understanding of music or "a fairer grace," vaulting onto his courser, than he, "half-horse, half-man." Indeed,

> . . . it pleases me to say too,
> (with a loving I protest true)
> That in England we cannot see,
> Anything like *Dever*, but he.
> Only himself he must resemble,
> Virtues so much in him assemble.

The poet avows that

> I shall never sing,
> A man so much honoured as thee,
> And both of the Muses and [of] me.

From Spenser, too, we shall hear that Oxford was "most beloved" of the Muses.

There being no other appearance of a John Soowthern, the name (modernized as Southern) has always been recognized as a pseudonym. C. W. Barrell recalls that in the 18th century, George Steevens deduced from the poet's quirks of language that he was a Frenchman — which would explain his plagiarizing the verse of Ronsard — and that he had been admitted "into the family of the Earl of Oxford," where "he might easily have obtained confidential transcripts of the Epitaphs written by the wife of his Patron and Queen Elizabeth." Barrell persuades us that he was none other than "Deny the Frenchman" who took part in the Gads Hill holdup of 1573, who was clearly the "Denys the Frenchman that Francis Vere said was a retainer of Oxford's accompanying him to Paris in his youth a few years later and who in 1585 would go with Oxford to the wars in the Low Countries, where he would become the respected Captain Morrys Denys.

The Oxford of 1584, the dramatist and keeper of players, the friend, counselor, and patron of writers, whom he depleted his means to support and whose company — imaginative, talkative, probably often boisterous and inebriate — he preferred to any other, himself the Atalanta and Sappho of writers meriting a silver pen, a reckless investor far more interested in creating the English novel than in managing his finances, . . . such a man would have been the bafflement and despair of Anne Cecil and incomprehensible to her father. Burghley, for whom the realm had fewer secrets than for any other subject or the Queen herself, would, I think, have found it intolerably provoking that, when so little else escaped him, his son-in-law should do so. It was not enough that Oxford should declare himself bound to him before anyone else in the world. He must have his daughter's husband in his possession, as he had his daughter and so much else. Clandestine surveillance would have automatically suggested itself. (A few years earlier, Drake had detected a spy of Burghley's, Thomas Doughty, aboard *Pelican* and on the coast of Patagonia hanged him with his own hands.) Thus he made short work of his son-in-law's gratitude by attempting to suborn his servants. Little could have been calculated more to enrage the Earl than such underhandedness, so inconceivable for a gentleman to stoop to. His shock comes out in a letter of 30 October 1584 he wrote to Lord Burghley:

> My Lord, This other day your man, Stainner, told me that you sent for Amis, my man, and if he were absent that Lyly should come unto you. I sent Amis, for he was in the way. And I think [it] very strange that your Lordship should enter into that course towards me; whereby I must learn that which I knew not before, both of your opinion and good will towards me. But I pray, my Lord, leave that course, for I mean not to be your ward nor your child. I serve Her Majesty, and I am that I am; and by alliance near to your Lordship, but free; and scorn to be offered that injury to think I am so weak of government as to be ruled by servants, or not able to govern myself. If your Lordship take and follow this course you deceive yourself, and make me take another course that I have not yet thought of.
>
> Wherefore these shall be to desire your Lordship, if that I may make account of your friendship, that you will leave that course as hurtful to us both.

There are several tangential points of interest in the letter. The phrase "I am that I am" we shall meet again in Sonnet 121; Oxford would have got it from his Geneva Bible (*Exodus* 3:14), in which it stands out in capital letters. In the only-too-human threat of a weaponless man "to take another course that I have not yet thought of," Oxford is anticipating the helpless Lear who, when his heartless daughter forbids him his retainers, cries

> I will do such things —
> What they are yet, I know not; but they shall be
> The terrors of the earth!

Then there is the reminder, "I serve Her Majesty." The only capacity in which he is known to have been doing so was in connection with the theatre, providing entertainment with his acting company and with his boy players who, under Lyly's direction, whetted their skills in Blackfriars to perform at Court. The inference to be drawn is that his theatrical services — I should say most of all as a writer of plays — had an official if undeclared status.

We see him, it appears likely, in both capacities — as writer and producer — in one of the last plays shown at Court in 1584. "The history of Agamemnon and Ulisses [was] presented and enacted before her majesty by the

Earl of Oxenford his boys on St. John's Day [December 27th] at night at Greenwich." It seems to me at least a fair bet that J. T. Looney is right in taking the play to be one "forming the original ground-work for the 'Shakespeare' play of *Troilus and Cressida*"; for in the latter, as he points out, "Agamemnon, as the king, holds precedence and leads off with his thirty lines of blank verse, and Ulysses has by far the lion['s] share of orating throughout the scene." He suspects that *Agamemnon and Ulisses* represented "the Elizabethan drama in an early simple stage of its evolution, with few speakers and long speeches" before its author had achieved "command over the resources of true dramatic dialogue and a multitude of dramatis personae." The evidence is in the long speeches remaining in *Troilus and Cressida*, which Mark Van Doren says that "in any school of rhetoric would be a model for students of the amplifying art."

In the previous month Oxford's superlative riding had restored him in the public eye to the place of honour he had once held. This was at an event witnessed by Lupold von Wedel of Pomerania and described by him with such an appreciative eye for the theatrical and spirited procedures — what a vital age it was! — that I am reluctant to leave out anything he wrote. Here is his account:

> The 17th of November (the anniversary of the day on which Elizabeth was proclaimed Queen), the date on which the tournament is annually held having arrived, the Queen at twelve o'clock seated herself with her ladies at the windows of a long room facing Whitehall near Westminster. A broad staircase before the tilt-yard leads up to this room. Round the yard are erected wooden stands. Every one who wishes to look on and have a seat on the stands must pay eighteen pence. As however one penny is of pure silver, it is worth as much as in our country a groschen. On the stand were very many thousands of men, women and girls, to say nothing of those who were in the tilt-yard and had nothing to pay. The tournament began with two knights, who were desirous of contending with one another, riding simultaneously into the lists to the loud blare of trumpets and other music. And this mode of procedure was observed throughout the tournament. Every knight taking part in the tournament had dressed himself and his attendants in particular colours, although none of the underlings rode into the lists with the knights, but walked beside them on either side. Some of the knights had bedizened themselves and their train like savages; some like the natives of Ireland with their hair streaming like a woman's down to their girdles. Some had crescent moons upon their heads; some came into the lists with their horses caparisoned like elephants; some came driving, their carriages drawn by people most oddly attired. Some of the carriages seemed to be drawn along without traction. All of these carriages were oddly and peculiarly fitted up, but all the knights had their horses with them, and being ready accoutred for the fight mounted their steeds. Some of them however were dressed like horsemen and bravely decked out. If any failed to take part in the tournament it cost him some thousands of crowns, willynilly.
>
> Now when a knight entered the lists with his following, he rode or drove up to the staircase that led up to the room in which the Queen was. Then one of his followers ascended the staircase into the Queen's presence. This servant wore

a very fine livery in the colours of his master. He then addressed the Queen at length in rhymes that he had learnt by rote and at the same time quaintly and decorously cut merry capers. This evoked laughter from the Queen and those around her. When the man had finished his speech, he in the name of his master handed the Queen a beautiful present which she accepted and then gave the donor permission to take part in the tournament. Now the knights jousted and broke lances in the lists two at a time. On this day there were to be seen many fine horses and beautiful women, not only amongst the ladies of the Queen, but also amongst those of the gentry, nobility and burghers. This tournament lasted until five o'clock. Then my Lord Lester, the Queen's Master of the Horse, bade the knights cease from combat. The Queen then presented the prizes to the Earl of Oxenfort and to the Earl of Arrendel, the eldest son of the Duke of Norfolk whom the Queen had beheaded on Catharine Place where the scaffold still stands. Although the Duke's son had for his father's sake been so long in disfavour, he is now again in the Queen's good graces, and she permitted him to take part in the tournament. Lastly each knight who had acquitted himself well and nobly received a gift, and so this tourney closed.

It was the third and last of Oxford's appearances in tournaments of which we know, all of them victorious.

34

"For Fair England's Sake!"

1584–1588: Sturmius's appeal for English military help against Spain in the Low Countries under such a commander as Oxford. — Siege of Antwerp and dispatch of an English army, Oxford with it; his appointment to command of horse; his unexplained departure for England; capture of his ship, like Hamlet's, by pirates; his replacement in command by Sidney, like Othello's by the resented Cassio. — Insulting letter from one of the Vavasors challenging him to a duel. — Singling out of Oxford in two works on English poetry as the best among the poets of the Court. — Angel Day's acclamation of him as one whose life from infancy has been "sacred to the Muses." — Extraordinary grant to Oxford by the Queen of the immense sum of £1,000 a year exempt from accounting to the Exchequer and the difficulty of explaining it except as a subsidy of his dramatic activities. — Appeal to English nationalism of the Shakespearean historical plays as the showdown with Spain looms. — Shakespeare's Fluellen as originating in Oxford's follower Roger Williams. — Philip II's anger at his treatment in English plays. — Marlowe's Tamburlaine as aimed at Philip and Oxford as the likely lord for whose players Marlowe would be said to have written. — Varied evidence of the first Hamlet's having been written at this time and also Love's Labour's Lost largely as we know it. — The Babington plot to put Mary Queen of Scots on the throne; her arrest and trial before a commission of which Oxford is a member; the skill and histrionic effectiveness of her self-defense; Portia's speech on mercy as Oxford's appeal to Elizabeth's tortured inability to order Mary's death sentence executed; the near ruin of Burghley when he and other councillors take it upon themselves to do so. — Death of the Countess of Oxford and her father's tasteless self-promotion on her tomb in Westminster. — Coming of the Armada and the English attack, with Oxford commanding his own ship; its presumed crippling and friction between him and Leicester over his next service. — Harassment, defeat, and costly retreat of the Armada; foreshadowing of an accommodation between religion and patriotism such as Oxford evidently stood for.

For the Protestants in the Low Countries, it required all their religious conviction to persist in the terrible struggle against the Spanish, driven by an equally unquestioning faith in their cause. On 15 March 1584, after the failure of the French intervention under the Duke of Alençon, Jakob Sturm — Sturmius — the leader of Protestant thought in the Rhineland — appealed to Queen Elizabeth for an English force to come to the aid of his desperate co-religionists, and to command the force he urged "some faithful and zealous personage such as the Earl of Oxford, the Earl of Leicester, or Philip Sidney." Though English volunteer companies had been serving in the Low Countries since 1572, Elizabeth was infinitely cautious when it came to involving the nation in hostilities — not to say procrastinating. Moreover, on 10 July 1584, in the month after Alençon's death, a Catholic fanatic fired point blank at Prince William the Silent of Orange, fatally wounding him and leaving authority in the Netherlands ill defined. Farnese's advance continued. In his path was poor Antwerp, which had suffered the Spanish Fury eight years before, having 6,000 of its citizens massacred and 800 of its houses burned down, and had had to repel the French Fury two years before. By May 1585 it was under siege again.

Oxford had evidently been given to believe that a command in the coming conflict would be his. On June 25th he wrote his father-in-law that

> being now almost at a point to taste that good which Her Majesty shall determine, yet am I as one that hath long besieged a fort and not able to compass the end or reap the fruit of his travail, being forced to levy his siege for want of munition. Being thus disfurnished and unprovided to follow Her Majesty, as I perceive she will look for, I most earnestly desire your Lordship you will lend me £200 till Her Majesty performeth her promise, out of which I shall make payment, if it please you, with the rest that your Lordship hath at sundry times, to my great furtherance and help in my causes, sent me. . . .

He prays his Lordship to bear with him, explaining that had not some unidentified "tedious suit" kept him away from the Queen he would have found means "to have served my turn" — a favorite phrase, occurring at least thirteen times in the Shakespearean plays — "till Her Majesty had despatched me."

And of course he had his theatrical concerns. Gwynneth Bowen has shown that he is likely at this time to have taken over the Earl of Worcester's players.

With Antwerp's position growing more desperate, Elizabeth had come to realize that Farnese must be stopped. The city's fall on August 19th led her to summon Leicester and Burghley to help her decide upon a course. Only five days later under a treaty previously concluded with the Netherlands, Colonel John Norris left for Holland as Commander of a Field Army to comprise 4,000 foot and 400 horse. Three days later, English ships arrived off Flushing and on the next day "the Guard of the Earl of Oxford" disembarked. On August 29th Oxford himself left to join it. When the news reached Paris, Mendoza wrote King Philip from there, on September 11th, that "about 2000 Englishmen had gone to Zeeland under Colonel Norris, about 4000 more were to follow. The latter force was being raised and it was said that the leader of it would be the Earl of Oxford.

The terms of the agreement with the Dutch were that the towns of Flushing and Brill were to be held by the English as security until the £4,500 monthly the Queen had undertaken to put up in their cause had been repaid; Elizabeth was not lax at the bargaining-table. But, as Gilbert Talbot wrote his father,

"It is thought that her Majesty shall be forced of very necessity to send some great person with great forces presently for the defence of Holland and Zeeland, or else they will, out of hand, follow Antwerp." The Dutch urged that Leicester be appointed to the command and his nephew Philip Sidney to the governorship of Flushing; later they would ask for Thomas Cecil as governor of Brill. Elizabeth blew hot and cold on Leicester. Sidney, apparently believing that Burghley's influence now outweighed his uncle's and that Flushing would be given to another, "greatly to his disgrace," as Walsingham said, took off for Plymouth to join Francis Drake in an expedition to harry the Spanish. But Elizabeth, having made up her mind to give Leicester overall command in the Low Countries, sent for his nephew to return to London post haste. This he did on September 21st and peace was restored between them — with Flushing to be his. On the 27th Walsingham pointedly informed Leicester that he "would be glad to understand whether your Lordship hath had Sir Thomas Cecil in mind." Knowing what was good for him, Leicester hath had. He first thought "a charge of horsemen will like him best," but later Sir Thomas received, as first proposed, the governorship of Brill. Meanwhile, a Spanish agent in London reported on September 19th, "Five or six thousand English soldiers" had "arrived in Flanders with the Earl of Oxford and Colonel Norris."

Leicester would depart for the Netherlands in December after an extraordinary exchange with Burghley of mutual assurances of common purpose. That he was averse to having Oxford in an important position in his theatre of operations may be taken for granted. If he did not fear to have Sussex's death avenged upon him, he would not have cared to have the "lynx-eyed" Earl observing and reporting on his performance. Certainly, too, he would have wished to promote Sidney's fortunes at Oxford's expense. Burghley's complaisance, I should guess, was bought by the appointment of his problem-son Thomas to a post of power and honor. In any event, having received from Burghley a letter informing him that he had been placed in command of the Horse, Oxford was on his way back to England by October 21st. So much we learn from a report of that date by Elizabeth's principal political agent in the Netherlands, William Davison, that "the Earl of Oxford had returned this night into England, upon what humor I know not." B. M. Ward says he had been recalled, and this must be the assumption. A week earlier it had been reported to Leicester that a ship taking Oxford's "money, apparel, wine and venison . . . to England" had been "captured off Dunkirk by the Spaniards." Among his belongings, according to the report, was the letter referred to above telling him of the command given him. How a correspondent of Leicester's came into that information, and so quickly, it would be interesting to know.

Chapter 34: For Fair England's Sake!

Although the record has been stripped of any word from Oxford on these events, I think there can be but little doubt about "what humour" the Earl was in, especially after he heard that Sidney was to replace him in command of the Horse. It can hardly have been other than bitter disappointment, his feeling less regretful than those Othello would voice, perhaps within a year:

> Farewell the plumed troop and the big wars
> That make ambition virtue! O, farewell,
> Farewell the neighing steed and the shrill trump,
> The spirit-stirring drum, the ear-piercing fife,
> The royal banner and all quality,
> Pride, pomp and circumstance of glorious war!

Othello, too, was replaced in command by one he resented: Cassio.

Within a year of Oxford's departure from Holland, Sidney would die of a wound in the thigh he suffered twenty-five days earlier. And it may well be that Elizabeth's fear of Oxford's suffering such a fate had as much to do with his recall as Leicester's animosity. Repeatedly we are led to suspect that her reluctance to have her poet-dramatist exposed to the dangers of "glorious war" stood in the way of the military preferment he sought. It would be only eight months after his return that she would make him, in effect, a national institution. Most curious is the total silence of Burghley's copious files respecting his son-in-law's connection with the expeditionary force in the Low Countries.

Oxford can have found no pleasure in Sidney's death, though he may have felt that the triviality of its occasion was in character. (Because a fellow officer was setting off for battle without his leg-armor, Sidney quixotically doffed his, which would have protected him from the fatal bullet.) But he must have smiled at seeing Leicester come a cropper. He accepted "the sovereignty of the States [-General], as he has intended to from the first," and assumed the title of Governor General, against the Queen's express wish. Whereupon "the rage of Elizabeth knew no bounds. This would make her infamous, she said, to all the world." Proving, it is said, so inferior to the Dutch in political skills and to Farnese in military, he would be withdrawn, a failure, in November 1587.

But the army Leicester had taken to the Netherlands would remain, and thereafter, S. T. Bindhoff writes, "there were never less than 6,000 troops there, besides those in the pay of the Dutch Republic." These, G. M. Trevelyan says, "led by 'the fighting Veres' helped to defeat . . . the infantry of Spain, till then unconquerable in the open field." Other "famous captains" named by Bindhoff as fighting alongside the Veres are Willoughby, Oxford's brother-in-law, and Roger Williams, a "follower" of Oxford's. "They helped the young Prince Maurice of Orange to parry [Farnese, now the Duke of]

Parma's final thrust in 1589" and "Maurice quickly proved one of the great commanders of the age." Those "Englishmen in that foreign service," in Trevelyan's view, "have some claim to be regarded as the founders of the military traditions of their native land." Of them all, none was more renowned than "the fighting Veres," Oxford's cousins, Francis and Horatio. Of the former, it is written that "He gave early proof of a warlike genius and undaunted courage," and: "Applying himself early to the art of war, he became one of the most famous generals of his time." Similarly, Horace Vere, Baron of Tilbury, "took to a military life from his youth, and accompanied his brother, Sir Francis, in his most signal exploits, being in courage equal and in hazards undaunted." The effect on Oxford of the frustration of his own martial ambitions, for whatever reason, while his relatives achieved such distinction in the field for him to measure himself and be measured against, may be imagined.

· · · ·

In the Landsdown manuscript collection is a document of 19 January 1585 endorsed "A lewd letter from Vavasor to the Earl of Oxford." The signatory, evidently a brother of Anne Vavasor's, jumped in without preliminaries:

> If thy body had been as deformed as thy mind is dishonourable, my house had been yet unspotted, and thyself remained with thy cowardice unknown. I speak this that I fear thou art so much wedded to that shadow of thine, that nothing can force to awake thy base and sleepy spirits. Is not the revenge taken of thy victims sufficient, but wilt thou yet use unworthy instruments to provoke my unwilling mind? Or dost thou fear thyself, and therefore has sent thy forlorn kindred, whom as thou has left nothing to inherit so thou dost thrust them violently into thy shameful quarrels? If it be so (as I too much doubt) then stay at home thyself and send my abuses; but if there be yet any spark of honour left in thee, or iota of regard of thy decayed reputation, use not thy birth for an excuse, for I am a gentleman, but meet me thyself alone and thy lackey to hold thy horse. For the weapons I leave them to thy choice for that I challenge, and the place to be appointed by us both at our meeting, which I think may conveniently be at Nunnington or elsewhere. Thyself shall send me word by this bearer, by whom I expect an answer.
>
> Tho. Vavasor.

What led up to the fiery letter so long after Oxford's clash with Knyvet and with Howard and Arundel — evidently referred to in the letter as "thy victims" — is as impossible to know as what its outcome was. It is doubtful that Oxford would have responded to such intemperate insults, especially when he had already satisfied honor by risking and nearly losing his life over his having "spotted" the Vavasor family. The challenger, moreover, was probably very young; E. K. Chambers suspected that he "was only a boy at the time of his sister's dishonor." But if the letter failed to provoke its target, it is provocative to us today, with its accusation that Oxford was too "much wedded to that shadow of thine." What can the writer have meant? What shadow did Oxford have to which he was wedded, to which even the slanderous Thomas Vavasor held back from giving definition? May it not have been his literary-theatrical *alter ego*, which in the next decade would acquire the identity of a mysterious William Shakespeare?

"To 'live by verses' was a disgrace," Phoebe A. B. Sheavyn writes in *The Literary Profession in the Elizabethan Age*. "The gentleman regarded it as degrading to sell the products of one's labour." Although "poetry was a major art necessary to Courtly culture," she goes on, "the leading Court poets genuinely avoided print: Sidney, Dyer, Raleigh, the Earl of Oxford, Wotten." She recalls Ben Jonson's protest: "Thou call'st me *Poet*, as term of shame." Moreover, "if possible, the dramatist was in even worse case than [the] poet." That literary works of Oxford's quite beyond a mere sprinkling of poems signed E. O. were known to contemporaries of his, and known to be of his pen, is plain. In 1586, William Webbe wrote in *A Discourse of English Poetry*:

> I may not omit the deserved commendations of many honourable and noble Lords and Gentlemen in Her Majesty's Court, which, in the rare devices of poetry, have been and yet are most skilful; among whom the right honourable Earl of Oxford may challenge to himself the title of most excellent among the rest.

This was eight years after Gabriel Harvey spoke of the "many Latin verses" of Oxford's he had seen and "the even more English verses."

Three years later in *The Arte of English Poesie* (1589), generally attributed to George Puttenham, almost the identical tribute would be paid to Oxford, preceded by a reminder of the reason noblemen kept their names off their literary works. "The credit and esteem" in which poets were held, the author states, was formerly

> not small. But in these days (although some learned princes may take delight in them) yet universally it is not so. For as well poets as poesie are despised & the name become of honourable infamous, subject to scorn and derision, and rather a reproach than a praise to any that useth it. . . . Among the nobility or gentry as may be very well seen in many laudable sciences and especially in making poesie, it is so come to pass that they have no courage to write & if they have are loath to be known of their skill. So as I know very many notable gentlemen in the Court that have written commendably, and suppressed it again, or else suffered it to be published without their own names to it: as if it were a discredit for a gentlemen, to seem learned.

Notice that Puttenham says their *own* names. After reviewing notable English writers of the past, he reverts to the theme:

> And in her Majesty's time that now is are sprung up another crew of Courtly makers [poets], Noblemen and Gentlemen of Her Majesty's own servants, who have written excellently well as it would appear if their doings could be found

out and made public with the rest, of which number is first that noble gentleman Edward Earl of Oxford.[1]

In 1586, the year of Webbe's tribute, a writer with the quaint name of Angel Day dedicated his first, and very successful work, *The English Secretary*, to Oxford, "whose infancy from the beginning," he states arrestingly, "was ever sacred to the Muses." He avows that:

> the exceeding bounty wherewith your good Lordship hath ever wonted to entertain the deserts of all men, and very appearance of nobility herself, well known to have reposed her delights in the worthiness of your stately mind, warranteth me almost that I need not blush to recommend unto your courteous view the first-fruits of these my foremost labours, and to honour this present discourse with the memory of your everlasting worthiness.

It would be difficult to find two persons more unlike than the Oxford of Howard's, Arundel's, and Thomas Vavasor's diatribes, or, for that matter, Burghley's affronted view, and the Oxford whom literary figures knew.

The year 1586 may be taken as the divide in Oxford's life, to which his progress so far had led, from which the balance of his life would take its course. The event, if it has been rightly judged, committed him to the drama, and from this nothing in the future, except briefly the defense of England's shores, would long deflect him. On June 26th the Queen signed a Privy Seal Warrant as follows:

> Elizabeth, etc., to the Treasurer and Chamberlains of our Exchequer, Greeting. We will and command you of Our treasure being and remaining from time to time within the receipt of Our Exchequer, to deliver and pay, or cause to be delivered and paid, unto Our right trusty and well beloved Cousin the Earl of Oxford or to his assigns sufficiently authorized by him, the sum of One Thousand Pounds good and lawful money of England. The same to be yearly delivered and paid unto Our said Cousin at four terms of the year by even portions: and so to be continued unto him during Our pleasure, or until such time as he shall be by Us otherwise provided for to be in some manner relieved; at what time Our pleasure is that this payment of One Thousand Pounds yearly to Our said Cousin in manner above specified shall cease. And for the same or any part thereof, Our further will and commandment is that neither the said Earl nor his assigns nor his or their executors nor any of them shall by way of account, imprest, or any other way whatsoever be charged towards Us, our heirs or successors. And these Our letters shall be your sufficient warrant and discharge in that behalf.

What the last two sentences mean is that no accounting for expenditures under the grant is to be required by the Exchequer. "This," says B. M. Ward, "is the usual formula made use of in the case of secret service money." As he points out, however, the evidence is all against Oxford's having had an

---

[1] A. L. Rowse, asserting in his *Raleigh and the Throckmortons* that, among the men the Queen "delighted to favour," Sir Walter Raleigh "was alone in being able to recommend himself in verse that had the principle of life in it," quotes the foregoing passage on page 150, but, not to have it known that Puttenham puts Oxford first, cuts it short with "the rest."

assignment calling for such funds; for one thing, he never left the country after receiving the grant. The more one looks into the circumstances — as Ward, the discoverer of the Warrant, did — the more apparent its singularity becomes. As Ward observes, Elizabeth's customary method of rewarding men like Leicester, Hatton, Raleigh, and Essex for their faithful service was by gifts of land or monopolies. Moreover, "the grant was continued as a matter of routine after the accession of King James, until payment was regularized by a new Privy Seal Warrant issued by the King." And during the entire term of the grant — that is, for eighteen years, until Oxford's death — the Earl had no known official office other than as a member of the Privy Council. (That the Queen appointed him to this body counters the derogation, indulged in by his detractors today, of the Earl as a light-weight.) The purpose was not simply support for a worthy and impecunious nobleman; Oxford's successor in the Earldom, his son Henry, would receive such an annuity, Percy Allen reports, but it amounted to only £200. There would be no reduction in Oxford's grant when his wife died, and the expense of his children's upkeep was borne by his father-in-law.

It is the grant's magnitude that is its truly astonishing feature. Ward made up a table of the principal gratuities, salaries, and annuities paid from the Exchequer during the period and found that apart from the large grants made for political reasons to the King of Scots, the grant to Oxford is larger than any of the other grants and annuities with the exception of one of £1,200 annually given to the Master of the Posts for maintaining all the country's ordinary postal services. The Earl of Huntingdon received £1,000 a year as Lord President of the North, but the post was one of great responsibility and demanding duties and the grant had to cover the "diets and stipends" of his Council.

The only mention of the grant to Oxford that I have found earlier than B. M. Ward's report of 1928 — and it is one that seems to have been overlooked by everyone — is in Edmund Bohun's *Queen Elizabeth* of 1693, which relates that

> The Earl of Oxford was one of the most ancient houses amongst the nobility, but by the excessive bounty and splendor of the former Earl was reduced to a very low and mean condition, so that the family was no longer able to maintain its dignity and grandeur: And the Queen allowed that house one thousand pound the year out of her Exchequer that one of the most illustrious houses in her kingdom might not suffer want.

As we have heard argued, however, it is scarcely credible that the Queen would have so extravagantly subsidized the dignity and grandeur even of a de Vere. For at least the last fifteen years of the grant there is no sign of any heavy expenditure on Oxford's part; the Earl was largely retired from the public eye. Certainly he made no display of excessive splendor.

Lord Effingham, Earl of Nottingham, it is true, received an annuity just the size of Oxford's in 1619, but he had devoted a lifetime to the service of the Crown. He had commanded the English fleet in the victory over the Armada, and it is said that "no important commission seems to have been considered complete unless Nottingham was a member of it." Moreover, it was King James who authorized his pension.

What makes the size of Oxford's grant — equivalent to probably more than three times the Prime Minister's salary today — most remarkable is that, an authority says, Elizabeth's "parsimony was phenomenal." She might endow her favorites with expropriated estates, for they cost her nothing, though as the same authority remarks, "It may be doubted whether any of those who enjoyed her greatest favor (with the single exception of Leicester) were at all the richer for their devotion to her person." Elizabeth Jenkins writes, "She had acquired a name for close-fistedness and avarice, all, all, that she might remain solvent." Why would Oxford be treated with such signal generosity, and not with sequestered lands but with cold cash out of the Exchequer, which was quite a different matter?

The reader will not have forgotten the Reverend John Ward's diary-entry of 1662, that "Mr. Shakespeare . . . had an allowance so large, that he spent at the rate of £1000 a year, as I have heard." It seems to me reasonable to believe that Oxford received the grant as Shakespeare, to finance his activities in the theatre. It is significant, I think, that the all-knowing and voluble Burghley never mentions this stunning event in the life of his son-in-law and one critical to his finances. Today's denigrators of Oxford as Shakespeare seldom mention it either — except that A. L. Rowse does cozen us with the statement that Oxford "ended up as a pensioner of the Crown." Some pension, and some period during which to have "ended up": from thirty-six years of age to fifty-four![2] Though he would, of course, have had to earn his stipend, it must have come as a godsend. Yet characteristically he appears to have contrived to find it a source of dissatisfaction and shame, I suppose on the grounds that a de Vere had been hired like a common artisan. That, at least, is the only interpretation that occurs to me of his chiding Fortune in Sonnet 111,

---

[2] For Stratfordians, the facts are of course acutely distasteful. "Mr. Ogburn cites [the Rev. John] Ward on the question of Shakespeare's income, which he thereupon transfers to Oxford," Gwynne Evans and Harry Levin complain, misrepresenting the case. "But how could Ward," they continue, "have become acquainted with the minutiae of Oxford's finances?" Well, when a man is subsidized from public funds on the scale that Oxford was, some word of it is almost certain to leak out. But the point is not *how* Ward would have heard what he did, but that he *did* hear that "Shakespeare" had an allowance of £1,000 a year, which certainly the Stratford man had not. It is this which awaits the professors' explanation. (I find myself wondering, too, by what standards they class under "minutiae" an item of income sufficient today to pay for winters in Acapulco and summers in Bar Harbor.)

Chapter 34: For Fair England's Sake!

> The guilty goddess of my harmful deeds
> That did not better for my life provide
> Than public means which public manners breeds.

We need not, however, grieve greatly for him on that account.
George Bernard Shaw wrote:

> The theatre is literally making the minds of our urban population today. It is a huge factory of sentiment, of character, of points of honor, of conceptions of conduct, of everything that finally determines the destiny of a nation. And yet it is openly said that the theatre is only a place of amusement. It is nothing of the kind; a theatre is a place of culture, a place where people learn how to think, act, and feel; more important than all the schools in Christendom.

It is likely that Elizabeth made a similar appraisal of the theatre; she would hardly have regularly paid the large sum of £10 for a performance at Court unless she attached great importance to the drama. Bohun reports that her

> care was to restrain the license of the theatre, and she prohibited all exercises and plays but what were manly, and tended to be fitting of her subjects for war by making their bodies more hardy and active, and their souls more valiant.

She would have been especially solicitous on this score in 1586, when the showdown with Spain was approaching. By every means the energies and resolution of the nation had to be rallied. This may have had a bearing on Oxford's recall from the Netherlands. Elizabeth had (I judge) heard him bring England's past to life on the stage with riveting eloquence, appalling audiences with the bloody costs of national disunity, and it is easy to see how she would have wanted more of the drama's powerful medicine infused into her cause. One has only to listen to Winston Churchill, who concludes his chapter on the Spanish Armada in *A History of the English-Speaking Peoples* with the final words of Shakespeare's *King John* that "struck into the hearts of his audiences":

> Come the three corners of the world in arms,
> And we shall shock them. Nought shall make us rue
> If England to itself do rest but true.

J. Enoch Powell, M.P., declares of the Shakespearean historical plays,

> Athwart this mainstream of pride and power there runs in all of them the cross-current of English patriotism: it is heard through the humiliations of John, defeated on the Continent and at home; it is heard through the French wars of Henry VI; it is heard out loud in *Richard II*'s dying Gaunt and faintly in the vanquishing of Richard III; but it reaches its climax with Henry V.

That the last-named was initially produced when invasion from Spain was imminent, I venture, with others, to believe, as in World War II it was given its greatest production ever when British nerves were strained in a mortal contest with another ruthless continental Empire.[3] That the Welsh Fluellen in *Henry the Fifth* was — incidentally — a stage-version of Sir Roger Williams, a follower of Oxford's, as we have heard from Sir Francis Vere, Charles W. Barrell leaves virtually no doubt. (We read that "In 1587, the town of Sluys being besieged by the Prince of Parma, . . . Mr. Vere with Sir Roger Williams, and a garrison of English and Walloons, bravely defended it.") Both captains were of Monmouthshire. Of the original, the *Dictionary of National Biography* says: "He rapidly acquired a wide reputation for exceptional courage and daring. Like Shakespeare's Fluellen, he was constitutionally of a choleric temper and blunt of speech, but the defects of judgment with which he is commonly credited seem exaggerated." Mr. Barrell remarks that "Many of the speeches that the author of *Henry the Fifth* puts in the mouth of the argumentative Fluellen are merely poetical paraphrases of Sir Roger's own arguments and 'instances' in his posthumous book, *The Actions of the Lowe Countries*. Both Williams and his stage double are extravagant admirers of Edward III and his military exploits. . . . Both men refer quaintly to Alexander the Great, speak boastfully of their native soil and evince reverence for 'the literature of the wars.' Williams is a firm advocate of military discipline, which he expatiates upon endlessly. . . . The same insistence upon 'discipline' becomes a catchword with Fluellen: 'the disciplines of the wars,' 'the disciplines of the pristine wars of the Romans,' 'the true disciplines of the wars, . . .'" How Shakspere of Stratford would have acquired a familiar acquaintance with the renowned warrior has not been explained. How Oxford would have, with both the man and the manuscript of his book, does not need to be.

Less than a month after the grant was made to Oxford, the Venetian ambassador in Spain was reporting to the Signory:

> But what has enraged him [King Philip II] much more than all else, and has caused him to show a resentment such as he has never displayed in all his life, is the account of the masquerades and comedies which the Queen of England orders to be acted at his expense.

Those are strong words: "enraged him more than all else . . . resentment such as he has never displayed in all his life." Thus the playwrights got

---

[3] Philip Henslowe's *Diary* shows performances of a *harey of cornwall* alternating at The Rose with those of *harey the vj* in the spring of 1592, and because the latter, accepted as *King Henry the Sixth, Part One*, is marked "ne," meaning new, the presumption is that the former, not so marked, was old. And there is also a presumption that *harey of cornwall*, otherwise unknown as a play, was the term employed by the quaint, only semi-literate Henslowe for *King Henry the Fifth*, in which the King, disguised, identifies himself as "Harry LeRoy," and Pistol observes, "Le Roy, a Cornish man. . . ." Another point: Professor A. F. Pollard points out that the line in the play "Then brook abridgment, and your eyes advance" is a pun on Brook's *Abridgement*, the most famous legal textbook before the days of Coke. The pun would have been timely and funny in 1586 or shortly thereafter, when the *Abridgement* was reprinted after ten years, but would have had no point in 1598, when orthodoxy has *Henry the Fifth* first appearing.

through to Philip even more infuriatingly than that "Master Thief of the unknown world," as the Spanish called Sir Francis Drake. It appears to be probable that the Queen had put Oxford to work directly upon his return from the Low Countries, nine months earlier, promoting the composition and production of the plays that would hold her mortal foe up to scorn.

If *Othello* had been presented at Court by this time, as is likely, it would have been outstanding as a "masquerade" enraging Philip, for the reports of it reaching him could have given a very different impression of the play from ours. "Moor," it may be repeated, was an English term of contempt for a Spaniard, and Othello, slayer of Brabantio's daughter, could have seemed to Philip a scurrilous composite of his half-brother, John of Austria, and himself. Don John had, like Othello, won great fame defending Venice from the Turks, then become the murderer — in English eyes — of Brabantia's daughter-city, Antwerp, while Philip, quite apart from the carnage of war he had waged, was rumored to have arranged the murders of Elizabeth of Valois (his third wife) and of the Princess of Eboli, said to have been his mistress.

In the next year, 1587, the young Christopher Marlowe's *Tamburlaine* would probably have put Philip further out of countenance. Eva T. Clark observes how the tyrant beholds himself as master not only of the lands but of the seas, boasting that

> Even from Persepolis to Mexico
> And thence unto the Straits of Jubalter,
> Where they shall meet and join their force in one,
> Keeping in awe the Bay of Portingale,
> And all the ocean by the British shore;
> And by this means I'll win the world at last.

"The passage," she says, "seems more applicable to the Spanish King than to Tamburlaine and Dr. [Frederick S.] Boas comments upon it as follows: 'The last lines seem to be almost an ironic anticipation of the proud aims with which Philip of Spain was so soon after the production of the play to send the Invincible Armada to its doom.'" Audiences at the Rose would have been quick to make the connection when the Prologue told them they would hear

> Tamburlaine
> Threatening the world with high astounding terms
> And scourging kingdoms with his conquering sword.

And when the brooding Scythian emperor, closing upon Damascus, proclaims

> Were in that city all the world contain'd
> Not one should scape, but perish by our swords;

then, demanding of a captain

> What, have your horsemen shown the virgins death?

is informed

> They have, my lord, and on Damascus's walls
> Have hoisted up their slaughtered carcasses!

Cries from the pit of "Antwerp!" and "Spanish murderers" (if I am not imagining too much) would have reached the ears of that other brooding emperor planning, in the Escorial, the invasion of "the ocean by the British shore."

In May 1593 — and I am looking ahead in this — when the Star Chamber took action upon certain "lewd libels" and "blasphemies" of Marlowe's and papers of Thomas Kyd's were found among them, Kyd as well as Marlowe was arrested. Testifying under torture to Marlowe's atheism, he protested that "My first acquaintance with this Marlowe, rose upon his bearing name to serve my Lord, although his Lordship never knew his service, but in writing for his players." Dr. Boas comments: "It is one of the most tantalizing problems in Marlovian biography that Kyd omits to give a clue to the identification of this lord of whose household he had been a member in some capacity for nearly six years." That would put the enlistment of Kyd in the mysterious lord's service back to the end of 1587. *The Spanish Tragedy*, attributed to Kyd on the strength of a single reference many years later, is believed to have been produced, according to Edmund Gosse, "between 1584 and 1586." That is interesting, since *Hamlet*, to which it bears curious similarities, was being written probably in 1585; and, as Gosse says, "John Lyly had a more marked influence on his [Kyd's] manner than any of his contemporaries": Lyly again! It all seems to tie together, and I think future investigation will bear out E. T. Clark's opinion that the mysterious, unnamable lord of whose household Kyd was a part for six years, and for whose players Marlowe wrote, was Oxford. It was about the time of Oxford's grant and of Philip's rage over the plays shown at his expense, Ms. Clark points out, "that we begin to hear about the University Wits"; and the inference she draws is that "in order to keep a heavy program going, Lord Oxford appealed to recent graduates of Oxford and Cambridge, and even to those on the point of graduation, who gave promise of dramatic ability, to assist in this important work of stage propaganda." And she suggests that it was he who discovered Marlowe's dramatic ability and brought out Tamburlaine to teach the people what might be expected of a ruthless conqueror like Philip. Certainly no great part of the £1,000 he was receiving annually went for conspicuous personal consumption; by the third year he would be pressed for funds.

The relationship between the two playwrights at this time may be taken to account for the similarities in Shakespeare's early historical dramas to *Edward the Second*, printed in 1594 as Marlowe's, which orthodoxy always cites as proof of the greater author's "debt" to the lesser, if not of his plagiarism. The supposition would be that the play was an early one of Oxford's that the Earl turned over in draft to Marlowe to make what he would of it.[4] The combination of Shakespearean conceptions and recurrent Shakespearean language in *Arden of Feversham* and of un-Shakespearean pace and drive, and the evidence of Marlowe's hand that Professor Bronson Feldman finds in it, may be explicable on the same basis.

Writing of plays based on "the English Chronicles," John Payne Collier says (1831): "It is very certain . . . that anterior to 1588 such pieces had been written, and acted, before public audiences." (He comments in a footnote that "Tarleton . . . obtained great celebrity by his performance . . . in the old historical play of 'The Famous Victories of Henry the Fifth.'") Among those "engaged in these representations," he mentioned Oxford's company. He goes on to report that

> A person who calls himself "a soldier," writing to Secretary Walsingham in January, 1586, tells him that "every day in the week the players' bills are set up in sundry places in the city," and after mentioning the actors of the Queen, the Earl of Leicester, the Earl of Oxford, and the Lord Admiral, he goes on to state that not fewer than two hundred persons, thus retained and employed, strutted in their silks about the streets. . . .
> The manner in which, about this time, the players were bribed away from Oxford is curious, and one of the items in the account expressly applies to the Earl of Leicester's servants.

Thereby must hang a tale indeed, and thereby must have arisen another score against Leicester-Claudius to be settled in *Hamlet*.

In 1589 Thomas Nashe wrote of "English Seneca," who, "read by candlelight, yields many good sentences" and "will afford you whole *Hamlets*, I should say handfuls, of tragical speeches." The passage was "quite clearly directed against Kyd, among others," says A. S. Cairncross, who deduces that *Hamlet* as we have it was written at the end of 1588 or 1589. Students of Oxford date the play several years earlier. Dr. Cairncross calls attention to Marcellus's query in the first scene:

> Why such impress of shipwrights, whose sore task
> Does not divide the Sunday from the week?
> Why this same strict and most observant watch
> So nightly toils the subject of the land;
> And why such daily cast of brazen cannon. . . ?

He considers the lines a reflection of the naval preparations for the Spanish assault, but by mid-1588 these would have been too late; and we have heard how staggered the Duke of Alençon was by the work of the shipwrights in

---

[4] D. S. Ogburn writes of the "evidence that *Edward the Second* is a direct forerunner of 2 and 3 *Henry the Sixth* (1 *Henry the Sixth* having come later) and of *Richard the Second* and is by the same hand, created out of the same consciousness: it is not plagiarized from someone else. There are innumerable correspondences between *Edward the Second* and these dramas, not only in locutions, imagery and mannerisms, but also in point of view."

1583. Dr. Cairncross recognizes in Osric's mincing language a ridicule of euphuism, but the affectations would not have been worth ridiculing much after 1586. It had been in 1582 that Oxford's brother-in-law, Lord Willoughby, had returned from a diplomatic mission to Denmark (on which he had embarked a month after we found him in Oxford's company just before an outbreak of the Knyvet feud) with a "relation" describing the feasting at Elsinore to the accompaniment of "a whole volley of all the great shot of the castle discharged" — surely the origin of King Claudius's vow that

> No jocund health that Denmark drinks today,
> But the great cannon to the clouds shall tell. . . .

Oxford would probably also have had a first-hand description from Willoughby of the floor-to-ceiling silken tapestry dividing the great hall at the palace bearing the portraits of the Kings of Denmark, suggesting Hamlet's command to his mother to contrast the last two royal visages — "Look here upon this picture and on this" — and providing the arras for Polonius to hide behind as they spoke.

In 1585, E. K. Chambers states, "the chief rivals of the Queen's men at Court were . . . the boy players." And the rivalry is touched on when Hamlet asks if the actors "grow rusty" and Rosencranz replies that "endeavor keeps them in the wonted pace" against the threat of "an eyrie of children, little eyases," prompting Hamlet to wonder whether "the boys" upon growing up will "exclaim against their own succession." Then, as E. T. Clark has brought out, Polonius's categorizing of plays in the lines:

> The best actors in the world, either for tragedy, comedy, history, pastoral, pastoral-comical, historical-pastoral, tragical-historical, tragical-comical-historical-pastoral. . . .

is unmistakably a parody of a passage in Sidney's *Apologie for Poetrie*:

> The most notable [poets] be the Heroic, Lyric, Tragic, Comic,
> Satiric, Iambic, Elegiac, Pastoral. . . . It is to be noted that some
> Poesies have coupled together two or three kinds, as Tragical
> and Comical, whereupon is risen, the Tragi-comical. Some in like
> manner have mingled Prose and Verse. . . . Some have mingled
> matters Heroical and Pastoral. . . .

But, as she says, to have made fun of Sidney after the mortal wound he received in battle would have been unthinkable. Hence *Hamlet* must have been introduced by September 1586.

Finally, it was in 1584 that the sensational and scandalous *Leicester's Commonwealth* was circulated. Of anonymous authorship and stunning public effect, it depicted the Earl of Leicester as a force of consummate wickedness, catering to his sexuality with aphrodisiacs and gaining his ends through a crew of bawds, abortionists, and poisoners. Among his victims it cited the Earl of Sussex as the latest — and one wonders if Oxford on reading that charge exclaimed with Hamlet, "My prophetic soul!" Thus disposing by poison of the one figure whose nobility and character and long and close relationship with the Queen imposed a bar to his designs, Leicester is shown as arrogantly claiming virtual possession of a frail and intimidated Elizabeth. It was possibly the *Commonwealth* that first gave Oxford the idea of Leicester as King Claudius.

Leicester had, says Elizabeth Jenkins, "the reputation of a lecher who would expend fantastic sums to gratify himself." And Hamlet cries out against Claudius as "Treacherous, lecherous, kindless villain." Actually Claudius is not shown ever to have committed a lecherous deed or had a lecherous thought in his life; ambition would have accounted for his designs on Gertrude. Presumably the dramatist's mind was so full of Leicester's lechery that he unconsciously more or less took it for granted that Claudius's lechery would be self-evident. That is how it goes when reality is carried straight over into art.

How much the early *Hamlet* resembled the play we know is impossible to say; the dramatist would apparently keep going back to it almost as long as he lived, putting more and more of himself into it, having the Prince age many years in a supposed few months. In the play as we have it "the total length of Hamlet's speeches far exceeds that of those allotted by Shakespeare to any others of his characters," Sidney Lee remarks.

I shall avoid spending much more time on the dating of the plays, but this consideration, always important, is especially so for another peculiarly autobiographical play that would appear to have received a going-over at about the time of the initial essay of *Hamlet*.

The reasons for believing that *Love's Labour's Lost* goes back to the period of Oxford's first infatuation with Anne Vavasor I have already suggested. Of its framework, Kittredge writes that "a hint for the visit of the Princess and her ladies has been detected in a picturesque incident of 1578 — the visit of Queen Catherine of France and Marguerite de Valois to the court of Navarre." (The occasion of the play is the visit of "the Princess of France" to the King of Navarre.) And regarding Boyet's description of the visiting fantastic, Armado, as "A phantisime, a Monarcho," he says that "The real Monarcho was an Italian, a harmless and amusing madman who frequented the English court and was dead by 1580." (Whether it would have occurred to Shakspere of Stratford to have reached back over a decade for such a comparison or whether he would ever even have heard of Monarcho, the professor does not consider.) *Love's Labour's Lost* is generally recognized as being what Kittredge calls "a pleasant parody of Euphuism." Berowne-Oxford himself gives a colorful characterization of the Euphuistic style in forswearing it:

Taffeta phrases, silken terms precise,
Three-pil'd hyperboles, spruce affectation,
Figures pedantical; these summer flies
Have blown me full of maggot ostentation.

and he ought to know, as the evident inventor and certainly early champion of the style. That he had now turned away from Euphuism indicates to me that he revised and added to the play around 1586. (That was long before he enriched it with the brilliant speeches of the mature Shakespeare as it was printed in 1598, "Newly corrected and augmented by W. Shakespeare.")[5]

In October 1586 Oxford was called upon to perform a duty he doubtless would more than willingly have escaped. As listed by Camden, he is ranked only by the Marquess of Winchester among the forty-two commissioners who sat under Burghley's leadership in trial upon Mary Queen of Scots.

Mary had involved herself in one too many plots to gain the ends she had set herself on returning to Scotland from France a quarter-century earlier. Correspondence in cipher with her agents abroad in 1585, intercepted by Walsingham, had encouraged revival of the plan for a Spanish invasion of England, this time by Farnese, now Duke of Parma. But these schemes, Algernon Charles Swinburne says, "to reconsign the kingdom to the keeping of the inquisition . . . were superseded by the attraction of a conspiracy against the throne and life of Elizabeth." The chief agent this time was Anthony Babington, who had fallen under Mary's potent charm as a child in the castle of her internment. He willingly lent himself to a plan hatched by English Catholic priests in France in collaboration with Lord Thomas Paget, whom we last saw in Paris in the company of Charles Arundel. Walsingham knew of the plan but allowed it to mature. In August he sprung the trap. Babington and his several fellows confessed, evidently in the vain

---

[5] As a parody of Euphuism in 1594 and 1595, when Professor Kittredge thinks it was written, *Love's Labour's Lost* would have been even more outmoded, of course, than the burlesque of its mannerisms in Osric's speech had this been first offered in 1589. Moreover — to repeat — most of the writing in the play is painfully inferior to that of later Shakespearean plays. Hence thoughtful Stratfordians date it as early as they dare. Edward Dowden puts it in 1589 and 1590, Leslie Hotson in 1588 and 1589, recognizing that this calls for a "serious revision" of orthodox chronology. How Dowden believes the son of a failed glover, newly out of his native, near-bookless Warwickshire village, could have composed "a satirical extravaganza," as he calls it, "embodying" a "criticism upon contemporary fashions and foibles in speech, manners and literature," a play with, as Kittredge acknowledges, "the influence of the Italian *commedia dell' arte* . . . visible throughout" is a mystery. Georg Brandes finds "throughout the play the over-luxuriant and farfetched method of expression, universally characteristic of the age, which Shakespeare himself has as yet by no means succeeded in shaking off"; dating the play "in its original form" to 1589, he must imagine that Shakspere's Warwickshire dialect flowered into the full bloom of super-cultivated Euphuist periods immediately upon his arrival in London. We should know by now, however, that all things were possible to the Stratfordian. *Love's Labour's Lost*, Marchette Chute tells us, "was written by a man who . . . could enter into the aristocratic life of the city with the same ease as he could enter into Plautus or the court of Henry VI."

As indeed it was.

hope of saving their skins. (With revolting but routine savagery they would be hanged, cut down still alive, then disemboweled before a crowd craning for a better view.) While Mary was detained on a hunt her quarters were searched and papers seized. These were sufficiently incriminating. Now Elizabeth's torment of indecision about Mary set in. It proved difficult for her councillors even to bring her to settle on a place for the trial. Fotheringham Castle, 75 miles from London, was at length selected, and it was there, after more vacillations over forms and procedures, that the trial was held on October 14th and 15th.

"Mary conducted the whole of her own defense with courage incomparable and unsurpassable ability," Swinburne writes. "Pathos and indignation, subtlety and simplicity, personal appeal and political reasoning, were the alternate weapons with which she fought against all odds of evidence or inference, and disputed every inch of debatable ground." To Lord Burghley, "her intention was, by long artificial speeches, to lay all blame upon the Queen's Majesty, or rather upon the Council. . . ." The Commissioners met again in the Star Chamber on the 25th and reviewed the evidence, and "albeit some of them," as Walsingham wrote, "stood well affected to her" — including Oxford's friend Lord John Lumley — "considering the plainness and evidence of the proofs, every one of them after this gave his sentence upon her, finding her not only accessory and privy to the conspiracy but also an imaginer and compasser of her Majesty's destruction." Burghley was within sight of attaining a goal of fifteen years' standing.

He was not there yet, however. Elizabeth had to be reconciled to bringing an anointed Queen to the block, and for her this was an agony. For Oxford, too, the prospect would have been abhorrent; his Bolingbroke, Henry IV, never forgave himself the death of Richard II.

Quoting Martin Hume's observation that "In her argument with Burghley she [Mary] reached a point of touching eloquence which might have moved the hearts though it did not convince the intellects, of her august judges," J. Thomas Looney cites "the terms of Portia's speech on 'Mercy,' all turning upon conceptions of royal power, with its symbols of crown and sceptre." He asks the reader "whether this speech is not vastly more appropriate to Mary Queen of Scots pleading her own cause . . . than to an Italian lady pleading to an old Jew for the life of a merchant she had never seen before." I think he is right, but not in his inference that it is Oxford's "poetical rendering of Mary's speeches." My guess is that the passage is entirely his own, interpolated in *The Merchant* for a new performance of the play at Court or at Fisher's Folly to persuade the Queen to spare Mary's life. And how better to win her over than to have the appeal voiced by a character she would have recognized pleasurably as representing herself? Whatever the reader may think of that proposition, he can hardly doubt that the entreaty, which would puzzle and astonish a vengeful money-lender, a scorner of Portia's religion, if addressed to him, is more appropriate to royal ears, invoking an authority to which even monarchs are answerable. "The quality of mercy," Portia urges, is

> mightiest in the mighty.   It becomes
> The throned monarch better than his crown.
> His sceptre shows the force of temporal power,
> The attribute to awe and majesty,
> Wherein doth sit the dread and fear of kings;
> But mercy is above this sceptred sway;
> It is enthroned in the hearts of kings,
> It is an attribute to God himself;
> And earthly power doth then show likest God's
> When mercy seasons justice.

Could the speech be any more explicitly an admonishment to a monarch?

In Elizabeth's resistance to proceeding with the sentence demanded, with Oxford probably working on her qualms in opposition to his father-in-law, it was the Duke of Norfolk all over again, but worse. French envoys interceded for Mary's life, as of course did Mary's son, King James of Scotland, but to lend the Queen resolution Burghley and his colleagues persuaded her to convene Parliament. Hatton denounced Mary in the Commons, Burghley in the Lords, where Oxford would not have forgotten his demanding Norfolk's head. The two Houses petitioned the Queen to proceed against Mary. In her inner turmoil she even attempted to suborn an agent of hers, to his horror, to do away quietly with her dangerous cousin. (In *King John* the dramatist embroiders on history to have a functionary of the monarch's refuse with sickening heart to carry out his sovereign's desire to have young Arthur, whose claim to the throne is a strong one, eliminated by an act of sadistic violence.) From France and Scotland the word was that there, too, an assassination was considered preferable to a public decapitation.

It fell to Burghley to draw up the warrant for Mary's death. On 1 February 1587 it was presented to the Queen, who put her name to it. "Her long, delicate-fingered, jewelled hand had drawn the elaborate signature," Ms. Jenkins writes, "and she had let it go from her with a sarcastic word, an eerie smile, and no hint that the ordeal was threatening to unseat her reason."

But she still could not be counted upon to take the final step of having the warrant executed. Her councillors knew it and ten of them, feeling protected by their numbers, took the matter into their own hands. The fatal day came: February 8th. The condemned woman's demand to see a priest was rejected with inexcusable cruelty. She confronted the executioner in scarlet raiment with the pride of a queen and of a religious martyr. Elizabeth's reaction when she heard of it was an outburst of weeping in private, then one of rage vented upon her councillors. Conyers Read believes that had Burghley "not acted as he did, Mary would have been spared to plague Protestant England as long as she lived," but that his decision "seems to have come as close as anything he ever did to accomplishing his downfall."

Writing of Mary, Swinburne says, "Elizabeth, so shamefully her inferior in personal loyalty, fidelity and gratitude, was as clearly her superior on the one all-important point of patriotism. The saving salt of Elizabeth's character, with all its wellnigh incredible mixture of heroism and egotism, meanness and magnificence, was simply this, that however much she loved herself, she did yet love England better." In the next year, bracing the kingdom for the blow from Spain, she would give that love expression in unforgettable words at the camp of Tilbury.

In the relations between Oxford and his wife and her father, the year 1587 seems to have dragged itself out in friction and bitterness. The reader is cautioned that once again we have only Burghley's words for any of what passed, and no one had ever better appreciated the value of a favorable record than the Lord Treasurer.

In May, three months after the beheading of the Scots Queen had probably left Oxford shaken, Burghley complains in a letter to Walsingham of the Earl's having reduced his daughter to "dolour and weeping" by his "reproach of me" and bewails her affliction "great with child" as she is, "to behold the misery of her husband and his children, to whom he will not leave a farthing of land" — because, the implication is, there will be no land to leave. Asking Walsingham's help in speeding the delivery to Oxford of an estate promised him by the Queen, he concludes:

> No enemy I have can envy me this match; for thereby neither honour nor land nor goods shall come to their children; for whom, being three already to be kept and a fourth like to follow, I am only at charge even with sundry families in sundry places for their sustenance. But if their father was of that good nature as to be thankful for the same I would be less grieved with the burden.

Walsingham's intercession with the Queen is successful, and a week after his first letter Burghley is writing to thank him "for your care of my Lord of Oxford's cause: wishing his own case was like to convert Her Majesty's goodness to his own benefit, and in some part for his children": what exactly that means I do not know. To explain why he would ask a subordinate's help with the Queen, he writes: "For anything directed by me is sure of his lewd friends, who still rule him by flatteries." (The language is again obscure, but "lewd friends" are recognizable as the writers Oxford was maintaining, at a cost that kept him financially strapped.) But there is another explanation. Burghley is still having to suffer the Queen's resentment, which allegedly is being nursed by Leicester with the aim of putting him in the Tower. On June 1st one of Walsingham's informers reports to him that "Not many days past, Her Majesty entered into marvellous cruel speeches with the Lord Treasurer, calling him traitor, false dissembler and wicked wretch, commending him to avoid her presence, and all about the death of the Queen of Scotland." By the end of the month, however, the storm had passed, the Queen is again visiting at Theobalds, and once again her host is her most trusted counsellor.

Six months later Oxford is evidently seeking some kind of "preferment" at Court, though what, it is impossible to guess. On December 15th Burghley writes to him that "You seem to infer that the lack of your preferment cometh of me." He tells his son-in-law that "you mistaketh my power" and "secondly," that he could

> make it manifest, by testimony of Councillors, how often I have propounded ways to prefer your service. But why these could not take place, I must not particularly set them down in writing, lest either I discover the hinderers or offend yourself, in showing the allegations to impeach your Lordship from such preferments.

Apparently Oxford had enemies even beyond those he was aware of. But one wishes we could know what the allegations against him were.

Although we have no word of Oxford's side in these disharmonies, we can deduce that his genius and what it cost him, and the besetting current of his nature, were outside his father-in-law's comprehension. Again one is struck by how fully the mischievous fates were in character in bonding these two wilful men, each almost the last to have understood the other.

But the bond, after twenty-four years, was to be weakened. In September, Frances Vere, an elder but still young daughter of the ill-matched Earl and Countess of Oxford, had died, and in June 1588 she was followed by her unfortunate mother. Perhaps Anne was better off dead. I doubt, however, that that was what the elegist meant who wrote upon her passing a recitation of her virtues, exclaiming

> And happy father of so good a child,
> And happy husband of so true a wife,
> And happy earth for such a virtuous wight,
> But happy she thus happily to die.

It was not because of what she was escaping in this world, but rather

> . . . as she live'd an Angel on the earth,
> So like an Angel doth she sit on high.

If her husband had much to reproach himself for on her account, so also had her father, who had sacrificed her to his own preferment. Her funeral was attended by "many persons of great quality and honour," including Oxford's sister Lady Mary, John Vere (brother of Francis and Horace Vere) and the most notable Cecils.

In the next year the bereaved father would have occasion to erect a common tomb for his daughter and her mother, in the chapel of St. Nicholas in Westminster Abbey. There the sepulchre may be seen today, the scarlet-clad figures of the Countess of Oxford and Lady Mildred Burghley, alike in the pose of death but with hands pressed together above their breasts in prayer — alike, too, in the prominent, sharp, Cooke nose, which suggests that Anne may not have been as docile as generally made out. Facing them at their heads but behind them, in blue, are the three living young Ladies Oxford, kneeling with hands also in prayer. Sentiments attributed to the three girls on the occasion are engraved on the tomb and reveal their author, Lord Burghley, as a self-promoter devoid of taste. Oxford must have squirmed as he read them, beginning with

> Lady Elizabeth Vere, daughter of the most noble Edward Earl of Oxford and Anne his wife, daughter of Lord Burghley, born 2nd July 1575. She is 14 years old and grieves bitterly and not without cause for the loss of her grandmother and mother, but she feels happier because her most gracious Majesty has taken her into service as a Maid of Honour.

Lady Elizabeth is followed by Lady Bridget, born 6th April 1584,

> hardly more than four years old . . . yet it was not without tears that she recognized that her mother had been taken away from her and shortly afterward her grandmother as well. It is not true to say that she was left an orphan seeing that her father is living and a most affectionate grandfather who acts as her painstaking guardian.

Last is Lady Susan, born 26th May 1587, who was too young

> to recognize either her mother or her grandmother

But

> is beginning to recognize her most loving grand-father, who has the care of all these children, so that they may not be deprived either of a pious education or of a suitable upbringing.

This on a tomb! One comes to appreciate what the son-in-law had to contend with and to suspect that if Lord Burghley was "at charge" for the children the reason their father was not "of that good nature to be thankful for the same" was that he had it continually thrown up to him.

Oxford is not mentioned among those listed as accompanying Anne's body to its interment, either because his attendance was taken for granted, or, contrariwise, because (as I have heard) husbands in Elizabethan times were considered unequal to the ordeal of a last farewell to their wives. Whichever it may have been, the Earl had another powerful claim on his attention at this time. In June 1588 the Armada had already been a month assembled in Spain and he had to make ready the vessel he meant to take into battle against it. Presumably this was the *Edward Bonaventure*, which he had purchased and contributed to Edward Fenton's expedition of 1582.

Even in this he would incur the slurs of history. Lucy Aikin in her *Memoirs of the Court of Queen Elizabeth* (1819), evidently harking back to the bad name given him in the Knyvet fray, would have it that

> The earl of Oxford, in expiation perhaps of some of those violences of temper and irregularities of conduct by which he was perpetually offending the queen and obstructing his own advancement in the state; equipped on this occasion a vessel which he commanded.

Even Leicester would do better by the Earl than that. Writing to Burghley as commander of the English land forces from the camp at Tilbury on July 27th, when Oxford had already been in action, he said, "I trust he be free to go to the enemy, for he seems most willing to hazard his life in this quarrel."

Oxford would have been no more eager than anyone else to end in "the fatal bowels of the deep" among those things "the profound sea hides in unknown fathoms," but he knew that England's fate for generations and perhaps forever hung in the balance of that sea-fight.

The Invincible Armada had been meant to sail in 1587, but Sir Francis Drake had upset plans by his "singeing of the King of Spain's beard." He had dashed into the harbor of Cadiz in April, destroying thirty ships and making off with great treasure, then had stormed a castle guarding the approach to Lisbon, which he blockaded for a critical month before turning upon the Azores to capture a carrack with a cargo that defrayed the cost of the expedition twice over; a stout fellow, Sir Francis. Striking a telling blow at haughty Spain's self-confidence, he had won his nation a year's reprieve during which the capable Admiral Santa Cruz died. His replacement, the Duke of Sidonia Medina, had no naval experience outside the Mediterranean and so little belief in himself he had to be peremptorily ordered by the King to take command of the fleet. This had assembled at Lisbon in time to sail on the 20th May 1588. With 132 ships and nearly 30,000 men, it could well expect to accomplish its mission: to sweep the Channel of opposition and permit the Duke of Parma to cross with an army to subjugate the impudent English. Less than half the fleet was of fighting ships, however, and the seamen numbered only 8,000, the balance being soldiers intended for boarding. To meet the invader, the English mustered 197 vessels, but the great majority were privately owned and very small. Only thirty-four were the Queen's ships. These, however, embodied the new designs that Sir John Hawkins, Drake's cousin, had been working out during the quarter-century he had been freebooting in the Spanish Main. Lower silhouettes and deeper keels increased speed and seaworthiness, and heavier, long-range guns were mounted with which to batter an enemy at a distance and frustrate his boarding-parties. About 16,000 men, the great majority seamen, manned the English fleet.

On June 10th the Armada was mauled by a storm off the northwestern cape of Spain and had to put into port to refit. Not until July 12th was it able to take to sea again. On the 19th it was sighted off the Lizard, the

southern cape of England's western tip. The story is that Drake received the
news while he was playing at bowls and insisted on finishing his game before
leaving to join Admiral Howard and his fellow captains, Hawkins and Frobisher. An awesome sight awaited them. When, Camden wrote,

> the English came within ken of the Spanish Armada, built high like towers and
> castles, rallied into the form of a crescent, whose horns were at least seven miles
> distant, coming slowly on. . . . Although under full sails, . . . though the winds
> labored, and the ocean sighed under the burthen of it, the English purposely
> suffered them to pass by them, that they might pursue them with a favoring gale
> of wind.

Toward evening the Armada hove to off Plymouth; and the sun that went
down upon it went down, too, upon an outworn age on the seas, in a last
stupendous pageant. That day, Stow tells us,

> The 19th July, the English Admiral . . . sends a special summons unto all the
> English fleet. . . . The Queen forthwith commands more ships to the sea,
> whereupon, yet in voluntary manner, the Earls of Oxford, Northumberland and
> Cumberland, Sir Thomas Cecil, Sir Robert Cecil, Sir Walter Rawleigh . . . and
> many other honorable personages, were suddenly embarked, committing them-
> selves unto the present chance of war.

At 2 A.M. on the 20th the main English fleet appeared astern the Spanish,
and from the beginning the ships of the future, fast, manoeuvrable, throwing
their punches from afar, proved their merit. The Spanish were defeated in
all their efforts to board. Among the ships they lost at the start was the
flagship of the squadron of Andalucia, *Nuestra Señora del Rosario.*

And now, back to Camden, reporting under date of July 26th:

> So far was the title of invincible or their terrible aspect unable to affright our
> English shores; that the youth of England . . . with ships hired at their own
> charges, joined themselves in great numbers with the fleet [before Calais], with
> generous alacrity, and incredible courage; and amongst others, the Earls of
> Oxford, Northumberland . . .

and the others we have heard named.

> The Admiral with Lion on his crest,
> Like to Alcides on the strand of Troy,
> Armèd at assay to battle is addressed;
> The sea that saw his powers waxt calm and coy,
>   As when that Neptune with three-forkèd mace
>   For Trojans' sake did keep the winds in chase.
>
> De Vere, whose fame and loyalty hath pierced
> The Tuscan clime, and through the Belgike lands
> By wingèd Fame for valour is rehearsed,
> Like warlike Mars upon the hatches stands.
>   His tuskèd Boar 'gan foam for inward ire,
>   While Pallas filled his breast with warlike fire.

The two stanzas are from a poem on the battle published in the next year by I. L., almost surely John Lyly, there being still no capital J in English. One has the impression that Oxford's theatrical manager was himself on board to behold the Earl standing on the hatch-cover breathing fire instilled in him by Pallas, the Spear-shaker. (Incidentally, anyone who compares the well-meaning but labored and awkward poem with the mellifluous lyrics from "Lyly's" plays will abandon any idea of their having the same author, if, in fact, I. L. was Ihon Lyllie, as our Lyly signed himself.

On July 27th, as we have learned from Leicester, Oxford had left the fleet and come to Tilbury, a village on the Thames two-thirds of the way from London to the sea. No reason is reported. Had his ship been disabled? In any case, he had gone directly for his armor, according to Leicester. "The hated, the disgraced, the incapable," as Lucy Aikin calls him, Leicester had nonetheless been appointed by the Queen "to the station of highest honor, danger and importance, that of commander in chief of the army at Tilbury." One can imagine how galling it was to Oxford to receive his next commission from such hands. That the aversion was mutual is evident from a letter of Leicester's of August 1st to Walsingham, in which he reported that he

> did, as Her Majesty liked well, deliver to my Lord of Oxford her gracious consent of his willingness to serve her; and for that he was content to serve her among the foremost as he seemed. She was well pleased that he should have the government of Harwich, and all those that are appointed to attend the place — which should be two thousand men — a place of great trust and of great danger. My Lord seemed at the first to like well of it. Afterward he came to me and told me he thought the place of no service or credit; and therefore he would to the Court and understand Her Majesty's further pleasure.

Leicester went on to say that "Her Majesty would make him know that it was good grace to appoint that place to him, having no more experience than he hath" — Leicester having got his command after flubbing the only comparable one he had ever had — and that he "would be gladder to be rid him than to have him."

If any trust may be placed in this report, it would appear that Oxford had decided that Harwich, a two-days' ride away on a peninsula east of Colchester, offered scant prospect of action, whatever might have been said of it a week earlier. What the sequel was we cannot tell; no more would be heard of him for four months. But before he could have got back into the fight the decisive battle had been fought. The Spanish, their decks raked with such deadly fury by the English guns that blood could be seen trailing from their scuppers, took shelter in the Calais roads on the afternoon of July 27th, the day Oxford reached Tilbury. It was a fatal mistake. The detachment of the English fleet, thirty-five ships strong, which had been supporting the Dutch naval blockade of Parma's army now joined the main force. On the evening of the 28th Admiral Howard decided to attack. At midnight eight

150-ton vessels loaded with explosives were set afire and sent among the great hulks huddled in the roads. As they started to blow sky high, showering burning timbers everywhere, they spread terror. Most of the Spanish slipped their cables and beat pell mell for open water, many colliding with one another on the way, while others weighed anchor and followed in better order. One of the largest galleys went aground.

As best he could, Admiral Medina made for an expected rendezvous with Parma's transports. Lack of a favorable tide, however, had kept these in their berths. And now the reinforced English fleet came up. For eight hours the battle raged at close quarters off Gravelines, the English seeking to pin their foes against the grim sandbanks, the Spanish battling for seaway. A hard northwesterly threatened to send the whole beleaguered fleet to its doom on the lee shore, but by the morning of the 30th the wind had backed and the Spanish were able to reach deeper water. By now, however, they had been thoroughly disheartened by the superior English gunnery and manoeuvrability and the losses they had suffered, and Medina's only thought was for escape back to Spain. On their side the English were discouraged in that exhaustion of their ammunition permitted the Armada as a whole to survive. Word was sent back to the Government that "Howard in fight spoiled a great number of the Spaniards, sank three and drove four or five on the banks." The Admiral himself wrote, "Their force is wonderful great and strong, yet we pluck their feathers by little and little."

The powerful Armada was in fact still mainly intact. The English, certainly those ashore, had no way of knowing the peril had been lifted. On August 8th Queen Elizabeth repaired to her army at Tilbury, in the belief shared by all that a battle-hardened and ruthless military force was poised against her kingdom but a few hours distant. A stunning sight Gloriana must have made, "like a second Boadicea," says Lucy Aikin:

> Mounted on a noble charger, with a general's truncheon in her hand; a corselet of polished steel laced over her magnificent apparel; and a page in attendance bearing her white-plumed helmet; she rode bareheaded from rank to rank with a courageous deportment and smiling countenance, . . . amid the affectionate plaudits and shouts of military ardor which burst from the animated and admiring soldiery. . . .

Her dauntless address to her troops, which was written down and read out to them by their officers, was positively Shakespearean in elevation, simple nobility, and power. (Indeed, the odd expression "foul scorn" occurs both in the address and in Shakespeare, "hearts and goodwill" in one and "heart and goodwill" in the other.)

To have retraced their wakes back down the Channel, the Spanish would have had to brook headwinds and the embattled English. They turned north and through mountainous seas made a passage past the coast of Norway.

Beating a homeward course, they were forced by lack of water to make for Ireland. Autumn winds of unprecedented violence destroyed nineteen ships, and crews put ashore that fell into the hands of English officers were annihilated; 5,000 failed to get away. It was remarkable, all things considered, that half the undermanned Armada was brought by sick and starving sailors into port in Iberia, though without perhaps two-thirds of those who had sailed in it.

The English sea-captains, who incredibly had not lost a ship, were dissatisfied at the showing; but — though the war with Spain would continue for another fifteen years — the English people blinked in the light of their deliverance from the Invincible Armada as at a miracle. What cannot have been the least of Elizabeth's satisfactions was the loyalty given her by the mass of English Catholics. Certainly that was a bitter cup for Philip to have to quaff, with added gall in the news that even some of the young English students at the Jesuit College in Rome had cheered their country's victory. The presage was clear: the time was mercifully coming when religion would no longer be a cause of war, precluding any genuine peace. It was, I believe, an order of things to which Oxford had aspired for his country, whereby an Englishman could practice the Old Religion or regard it with affection (as Shakespeare does his friars) yet with patriotism unquestioned serve in the forefront of the nation's defenders against any enemy.

35

"For That Have I Laid by My Majesty . . ."

1588–1592: Procession of thanksgiving for the defeat of the Armada, in which Oxford helps bear the canopy over the Queen. — His sale of Fisher's Folly (in secret to foil Burghley's claim on the proceeds) to William Cornwallis, one of whose family, Anne, makes a handwritten collection of poems, one by Oxford and one attributed to Shakespeare hitherto unpublished. — Sale also of Vere House in Oxford Court and disappearance of Oxford's players. — The Earl's permanent retirement from public view and the presumption that from now on he is giving final form to the Shakespearean plays. — His association with Bilton and Billesley in the Avon valley near the Forest of Arden, where he would be in the setting and mood of As You Like It. — Anonymous Puritan Martin Marprelate's attacks on the Episcopacy in hard-hitting vernacular and the secret commissioning, quite possibly through Oxford, of Lyly, Nashe, and Greene to reply in kind. — Burghley's hope of marrying Elizabeth Vere to his ward Henry Wriothesley, 3rd Earl of Southampton, which the youngsters successfully resist, though at immense cost to the boy Earl. — Publication of Spenser's Faerie Queene; the poetical tributes to Spenser at the beginning, one very likely to be by Oxford on which Jonson will draw in the First Folio, followed by sonnets to illustrious persons by Spenser, the one to Oxford outstanding in the love it voices and in praise of its subject as ever beloved of the Muses. — Publication of Spenser's Teares of the Muses, which laments the withdrawal of "pleasant Willie," who is lauded in terms befitting Shakespeare and, like the Willie of The Shepheardes Calender, may be taken to be Oxford. — Dedication to Oxford as one who loves the science of music of a book on counterpoint by John Farmer, organist and choirmaster. — Oxford's futile schemes for raising money and his alienation of Castle Hedingham to Burghley in trust for his daughters and the parallel with King Lear. — His marriage to one of the Queen's Maids of Honor, Elizabeth Trentham, most surprisingly with the Queen's apparent blessing.

On 24 November 1588 the victory over the Armada was celebrated by a royal procession to St. Paul's for a thanksgiving service. Three months earlier, three weeks after her arrival at Tilbury, Elizabeth had been stricken as at the loss of a long-beloved husband by Leicester's death, which there were few if any others to mourn. She showed the ravages of her grief, but must have been buoyed in spirit by the outpouring of popular emotion as well, no doubt, as by the presence beside her of the auburn-haired, twenty-one-year-old Earl of Essex, who would be the last great emotional attachment of her life. *A joyful ballad of the Royal Entrance of Queen Elizabeth into the City of London* on the occasion gives a picture of the procession:

An hundreth knights and gentlemen did first before her ride,
On gallant fair and stately steeds their servants by their side;
The Aldermen in scarlet gowns did after take their place;
Then rode her Highness' trumpeters sounding before her Grace.

. . . .

The noble Lord High Chancellor nigh gravely rode in place;
The Archbishop of Canterbury before her Royal Grace.
The Lord Ambassador of France and all his gentlemen
In velvet black among the Lords did take his place as then.

. . . .

The Lord Marquess of Winchester bare-headed there was seen,
Who bare the sword in comely sort before our noble Queen;
The noble Earl of Oxford then High Chamberlain of England
Rode right before Her Majesty his bonnet in his hand.

Then all her Grace's pensioners on foot did take their place
With their weapons in their hands to guard her Royal Grace;
The Earl of Essex after her did ride the next indeed
Which by a costly silken rein did lead her Grace's steed.

. . . .

And after by two noblemen along the Church was led,
With a golden canopy carried o'er her head.
The clergy with procession brought her Grace into the choir;
Whereas her Majesty was set the service for to hear.

And afterwards unto Paul's cross she did directly pass,
There by the Bishop of Salisbury a sermon preached was.
The Earl of Oxford opening then the windows for her Grace
The Children of the Hospital she saw before her face.

The reference to the "golden canopy carried o'er her head" recalls the opening line of Sonnet 125, "Were't aught to me I bore the canopy." B. M. Ward cites in this connection "the List or Roll of all Estates that were in this Princely Proceeding," which shows immediately leading "the Queen's Majesty in her Chariot" six dignitaries in two ranks, the second composed of the three leading peers of the realm, one being "The Lord Great Chamberlain of England," the Earl of Oxford. The strong presumption is that these six had the honor of bearing the "rich canopy" under which, Stow reports, the Queen was "brought through the long West aisle to her travers in the quire."[1]

Despite the large sums coming to him quarterly from the Exchequer, Oxford appears now to have come to the end of his financial resources. Probably he had paid dearly to equip his ship for battle with the Spanish. Within a month of the thanksgiving procession he sold Fisher's Folly. This he did hurriedly and evidently surreptitiously. The reason lay in his indebt-

---

[1] A. L. Rowse explains that the poet in the sonnet addressed to Southampton means "Were it anything to me that I bore the canopy over you," leaving it uncertain whether it was Shakespeare, in Rowse's view, or Rowse himself who entertained the notion that a canopy would be borne over an earl.

edness to the Court of Wards, of which Burghley was Master. As Professor Joel Hurstfield puts it in *The Queen's Wards*:

> The Earl had entered into obligations to purchase his marriage from the Court of Wards, a necessary procedure before he could be free to marry Anne Cecil. The full price of his marriage had never been paid and this, and other debts, had long hung over him in the Court of Wards. Then early in 1589, shortly after the death of Anne, Burghley instituted procedures against the Earl for his debt, and some of his lands were seized and held for payment.

That, being in debt for the right to marry Burghley's daughter, Oxford managed to keep his father-in-law from getting his hands on the proceeds of the sale of the Folly to William Cornwallis need not distress us unduly. The prospect of being on the wrong side of the Lord Treasurer, however, frightened the purchaser's father, Sir Thomas Cornwallis, who protested to the great man himself

> that I never saw nor heard any part of the assurance which hath passed between the Earl and my son. . . . And, good my Lord, . . . think me not so doting and foolish in my age that for the attaining of Fisher's Folly, I would once put in adventure to lose the goodwill and favor which I have ever found towards me. . . .

Later he wrote that his son denied "any intent or knowledge to defeat any purpose of your Lordship" and "for the hasty conclusion" of the transaction, "he layeth it wholly upon my Lord of Oxford."

What makes the episode of special interest is the following concatenation of circumstances:

§ In 1852 a small volume of poems copied out by hand by Anne Cornwallis was discovered by J. O. Halliwell-Phillipps, who identified the transcriber as the daughter of William Cornwallis, purchaser of Fisher's Folly and descendant of the 11th Earl of Oxford.

§ Among the poems in *Anne Cornwaleys her booke* are the *Verses Made by the Earl of Oxforde* and *Anne Vavasor's Echo*. Also there is a poem that appeared as number XIX in a pirated collection published by W. Jaggard in 1599 as *The Passionate Pilgrim* with the name "W. Shakespeare" on the title-page. This book contained two of Shakespeare's *Sonnets*, the only ones published before 1609.

§ Halliwell-Phillipps's original estimate was that Anne's collection was written down by 1590, and though he extended this to 1595 (which would bring it more within Shakspere's time-span), Charles W. Barrell cites reasons for holding to the original date.

§ Anne's version of poem XIX, Barrell observes, is superior textually to the one published piratically by Jaggard. He states, incidentally, that as far as he has been able to discover, Anne's is the only handwritten copy of a poem attributed to Shakespeare dating from the 16th century.

Barrell speculates that Anne may have found the verses in question in an overlooked corner of Oxford's library at Fisher's Folly when the Cornwallises moved in early in 1589.

At about the time the Earl parted with the Folly, Vere House in Oxford Place went too. His financial distress must have been acute. Gwynneth Bowen says, "Oxford was certainly in no position at this time to maintain a London company of players, and a company traveling under his name is last heard of at Maidstone in 1589–90." It would be at least six or seven years later before another would be known as his.

From now on Oxford will be out of the public eye, as far as the record shows; his whereabouts and movements remain generally unknown to us. These last fifteen years we may suppose he spent active in the theatre and in writing or, as in most cases, revising, the poems and plays we know as Shakespeare's. "That never am less idle, lo!" he had written, "Than when I am alone." Where did he go in 1589? There is some thought that he spent part of his time at the old manor house of Stoke Newington, which would be his temporary home after his second marriage. It is also possible that he repaired to the valley of the Avon.

There is in Billesley Hall, three and a quarter miles from Stratford, a room long known as the Shakespeare room. Billesley in the 1580s had been owned for more than 400 years by the Trussel family, of which Oxford was an offshoot through his maternal grandmother, Elizabeth Trussel, who had married the 15th Earl.[2] It is asserted, I do not know on what basis, that Billesley was part of her inheritance as an heiress of the wealthy Edward Trussel, and by some, evidently in error, that it passed to Edward de Vere. In any event, it was in the possession of Thomas Trussel in the early 1580s. (Shakspere was evidently also derived on his mother's side from a Trussel family, leading to speculation that he and Oxford were related.) According to a local rumor, *As You Like It* was written in Billesley Hall, a rumor most easily accounted for as having originated in fact.

It would perhaps not be surprising if Thomas Trussel had offered the hospitality of his home to his illustrious kinsman or that Oxford had found in it at times a welcome escape from the Court and its demands and intrigues. The owner, however, "made conveyances of the manor in 1585," which may or may not have included the Hall, and "on 6 August of that year . . . committed robbery and felony on the highway at Bromley, Kent, and was in 1588 attainted and sentenced to death," according to the *Victoria History*

---

[2] Percy Allen states that Elizabeth had as her family crest a "trussel," or candle-holder, and that Romeo refers to it when, in declining to take part in the Capulets' ball, he explains:

. . . I am proverb'd with a grandsire phrase;
I'll be a candle-holder and look on.

of the County of Warwickshire (1951), which further states that "Billesley manor passed to the Crown and was granted in 1590 to John Willes and others"; for the two-year interregnum it might again have been available to Oxford.

It would appear that the sentence of death cannot have been executed, for the *Dictionary of National Biography,* which does not mention the indiscretion at Bromley, has Thomas living until 1625, having sold Billesley "before 1619" and written *The Souldier pleading his own cause,* of which a "second impression, much enlarged with Military Instructions" appeared in 1619. The subject would have given him a bond with Oxford, as, for that matter, would the hold-up on the highway.

One property in the neighborhood of the Avon that definitely belonged to Elizabeth Trussel and passed from her to her grandson Edward was Bilton Manor, situated on the outskirts of Rugby on a tableland rising from the south bank. Bilton Hall, as far as I know, is the only one of Oxford's houses that he may have occupied, not counting the keep at Hedingham, which is standing today. It is a long, low building predominantly of muted red brick

Bilton Hall

(The extension at right dates from 1623.)

Photograph by the author.

beneath a high, sloping roof, the chimneys much higher still, with three-story, gabled extensions. Closing your eyes to the lofty annex dated 1623 that overshadows it now, you see it probably much as it would have appeared to Oxford and enter through a shallow-arched doorway through which he would have passed.

We read of Bilton manor in *The Victoria History* that "In 1574, Edward, Earl of Oxford, leased it to John, Lord Darcye and in 1580 he sold it to John Shuckburgh, who immediately leased it to Edward Cordell." For the first report, a record of 16 Elizabeth is cited and for the second one of 22 Elizabeth. What was leased and sold is not, however, entirely clear. It was not until 1600, according to the *O.U.D.*, that "manor" came to denote "the mansion of a lord with the land belonging to it; a landed possession." Before then it signified "A unit of English territorial organization, orig. of the nature of a feudal lordship." The difference could conceivably account for the discrepancy between *The Victoria History* and Sir William Dugdale's *Antiquities of Warwickshire,* which states of Bilton that "by Edward, Earl of Oxford, towards the latter end of Qu. Eliz. reign was it sold unto John Shugborough, Esq., then one of six Clerks in Chancery, which John dyed seized thereof in 42 Eliz." That would have made it one of the last of his properties that Oxford relinquished. In 1711, Bilton would be purchased by another literary figure, Joseph Addison.

Oxford would have found near Billesley and Bilton still sizable remnants of the once vast Forest of Arden. And this of course brings us again to *As You Like It,* which takes place mostly in a woodland of that name. A sunny evocation of the charm of the simple life in dappled glades, the comedy is nominally laid in France and therefore the forest is that of Ardennes, as we should render it, but I think no one doubts that it was the English woodland the dramatist was thinking of. *As You Like It* is really two plays. "Probably Shakespeare revised, and in part rewrote, an earlier play of his own," Kittredge judges. The original is in the style of the early comedies, Edward Dowden says, and was probably written about 1581. It provided the story on which Thomas Lodge based his novel *Rosalynde,* composed during a sea-voyage, "when every line was wet with surge," and published in 1590 — a novel "intensely Euphuistic in style," Kittredge says. The later, finer parts, "written in a manner which we hardly find in Shakespeare before the production of *Hamlet,*" to quote Dowden again, could have been inspired by the dramatist's stay in Billesley or Bilton. These parts include the half-dozen characters not appearing in Lodge, notably Jaques and Touchstone, the two sides of Oxford. The sanctuary the troubled spirits of the play find in the Forest of Arden could well be the refuge that Oxford found there. His mood would have been expressed by Duke Senior in the speech beginning Act II, which could scarcely have come from a dramatist not himself a nobleman and courtier. I venture to quote it again, more fully:

> Now, my co-mates and brothers in exile,
> Hath not old custom made this life more sweet
> Than that of painted pomp? Are not these woods
> More free from peril than the envious court?
> Here we feel but the penalty of Adam,
> The seasons' difference; as the icy fang
> And churlish chiding of the winter's wind,
> Which, when it bites and blows upon my body,
> Even till I shrink with cold, I smile and say
> "This is no flattery: these are counsellors
> That feelingly persuade me what I am."
> Sweet are the uses of adversity;
> Which, like the toad, ugly and venomous,
> Wears yet a precious jewel in his head:
> And this our life exempt from public haunt
> Finds tongues in trees, books in the running brooks,
> Sermons in stones and good in everything.
> I would not change it.

An indication of the date of the second layer of *As You Like It* is in the clergyman Sir Oliver Martext. He is obviously an afterthought since there was already an Oliver in the play. No less obviously he is given his fleeting appearance for the sake of a topical jest of the kind that was the dramatist's weakness. As he is leaving, Touchstone sings

> O sweet Oliver
> O sweet Oliver
> Leave me not behind thee.

E. T. Clark brings out, "there was entered in the Stationers' Register, August 6, 1584, the ballad 'O swete Olyver, altered to ye scriptures.'" Olyver was evidently the Puritan minister Oliver Pigge who had written a treatise on the First Epistle of St. Peter. But beyond Oliver Pigge, Touchstone's slurs upon Oliver *Mar*text are likely to have been a flick at a much more serious target: *Mar*tin *Mar*prelate.

For thirty years an Ecclesiastical Court of High Commission had had the power of censorship over the press to deal with offenses against the status of the Anglican Church. The combination of bishop and censor was a goad to the Puritans. To counter it they set up a clandestine press in mid-1588 to bring out tracts of a kind forbidden by the authorities. In November, month of the great thanksgiving service at St. Paul's, appeared the first of these promoting the Puritan cause and attacking the Episcopacy, signed Martin Marprelate. An official reply was long-winded and tedious. By contrast, Martin's "sturdy and youthful invective," Winston Churchill says, "shows a robust and relishing consciousness of the possibilities of English prose." The ecclesiastical authorities, R. B. McKerrow writes, saw that "the only way to silence Martin was to have him attacked in his own railing style, and accordingly certain writers of ready wit, among them John Lyly, Thomas Nashe and Robert Greene, were secretly commissioned to answer the pamphlets." This they did in other pamphlets and plays (now lost). All three writers were satellites of Oxford's, and perhaps someday it will be possible to discover if it were through the Earl that the secret commissioning took place; it would be hard to think of anyone better circumstanced to handle the matter. The one pamphlet Lyly contributed to the war, *Pappe with a Hatchett,* was "such tinkerly stuff," Gabriel Harvey declared, "so oddly huddled and bungled together, in so madbrain a sort" that, R. W. Bond acknowledges, its "authenticity" as "an emanation from the pen that wrote *Euphues*" has "been questioned," as "is not surprising." The difference, I should think, is between Oxford's guiding hand in *Euphues* and Lyly's unaided in *Pappe.*) The itinerant press was captured in August by agents of the 4th Earl of Derby, whose son would marry Oxford's daughter, and by the end of 1589 the Marprelate Controversy had run its course. It had, however, sounded the themes that would lead to the outbreak of civil war in 1642 and so aroused the Puritans against the stage that Paul's boys, who had performed an anti-Martinist play, had to cease operations.

In mid-July 1590 we hear the first of Burghley's design to marry the fifteen-year-old Elizabeth Vere to his royal ward, Henry Wriothesley, the 3rd Earl of Southampton, then going on seventeen. According to Charlotte C. Stopes, "he really liked his brilliant young ward, he trusted him, he approved of his property and the dwellings he would have to live in on his coming of age. . . . There is no allusion at any time to the inclinations of the young lady. . . :" Indeed, there is no evidence that anyone shared the Lord Treasurer's enthusiasm for the match. G. P. V. Akrigg remarks, "Southampton resolutely refused to marry the girl, despite the prospect of his paying a heavy forfeit if he held out, which the law allowed, since he was Burghley's ward, and even though Burghley, he feared, would neglect to maintain his estate." Nevertheless, if it was Burghley's promotion of the match that brought the proposed groom and the proposed bride's father together, the consequences for Oxford's life and for literature were to be immense. In the end, as we may recall, Southampton was reported in a letter by an English Jesuit to have had to pay what Akrigg calls the "staggering sum" of £5,000 for declining to marry as Burghley had ordained. Akrigg believes the report credible, citing "that love of money for which Burghley was notorious." This is the man that Oxford incurs the opprobrium of history for sometimes having antagonized.

Incompatible as the two men were by nature, Anne's removal from the scene yet appears to have eliminated the chief source of discord between them, and for the remaining eight years of Burghley's life their relations, at least on the surface, were amicable. At this very time, however, in August 1590, we are reminded by a letter of Oxford's to the Lord Treasurer that the latter exercised a surely galling veto over the disposition of his property. Writing of his wish to sell a lease, he says that "I therefore most earnestly desire your Lordship to signify your liking to me in writing, to dispose of the said lease at my pleasure; otherwise there is not any will deal with me for the same nor for any part thereof." Evidently the ruckus that Burghley had raised over the sale of Fisher's Folly behind his back had taught everyone a lesson. Oxford explained in his letter that he needed money for his "present wants" and £300 "to redeem certain leases at Hedingham, which were gotten from me very unreasonably. . . ." In a letter on legal matters in September, he speaks of having found his father-in-law "in all my causes . . . mine honourable good Lord, and to deal more fatherly than friendly with me, for the which I do acknowledge — and ever will — myself in most especial wise bound."

The drain on his purse from his patronage of men of letters was doubtless a constant one. His authorization of Thomas Churchyard at this time to take quarters at his expense was probably typical. Churchyard, it may be recalled, had twenty years earlier gone on an intelligence mission to the Low Countries while technically in the seventeen-year-old Earl's employment. Evidently the subsequent division between them had been healed. Early in 1591 we find Churchyard writing to his landlady, one Juliana Penn, a relative of Burghley's secretary's, that

> I have lovingly and truly dealt with you for the Earl of Oxford, a nobleman of such worth as I will employ all I have to honour his worthiness. So touching what bargain I made, and order taken from his Lordship's own mouth for taking some rooms in your house. . . . I stand to that bargain, knowing my good Lord so noble — and of such great consideration — that he will perform what I promised. . . . I absolutely here, for the love and honour I owe to my lord, bind myself and all I have in the world unto you, for the satisfying of you for the first quarter's rent of the rooms my Lord did take. And further for the coals, billets, faggots, beer, wine, and any other thing spent by his honourable means, I bind myself to answer. . . .

Evidently Oxford was remiss in making good on his word, for Mistress Penn writes him somewhat hysterically, reproaching him for her "grief and sorrow" over his "unkind dealing with me," which had made her "believe you bereft of all honour and virtue." Those would seem pretty strong words for a renter of rooms to address to the first Earl of the realm, and evidently the letter-writer thought so too. She assures him that she would have been glad to do "a thousand times more" for "you or your men." She would "be loth to offend your honour in anything that is in it...." Apparently the Earl's favor was shown, for nothing more is heard of his delinquency.

In 1590 Edmund Spenser published his *Faerie Queene*. The work, filling a hefty volume, was preceded by half a dozen tributes in verse from other poets. Most are signed with initials — two W.R., for Walter Raleigh. One is signed Hobynoll, for Gabriel Harvey. The last is by Ignoto. It is the most direct and straightforward of the lot and sounds like Oxford-Shakespeare. The authorship is important because of the third of the four stanzas, which are in the iambic-pentameter-*a b a b c c* form we have seen so much of. It reads:

> Thus then, to show my judgment to be such
> As can discern of colours black and white
> As else to free my mind from envy's touch,
> That never gives to any man his rights;
>   I here pronounce this workmanship is such
>   As that no pen can set it forth too much.

There can be but little question that Ben Jonson was harking back to those lines when he began his eulogy in the First Folio:

> To draw no envy (Shakespeare) on thy name,
>   Am I thus ample to thy Book and Fame;
> While I confess thy writings to be such,
>   As neither Man, nor Muse, can praise too much.

These tributary poems are followed by sonnets addressed by Spenser to sixteen of the leading figures around the Queen, with a seventeenth "To All the Gracious and Beautiful Ladies in the Court." The third is to Oxford and in its terms makes it very likely that the Earl would have offered one of the tributes to the poet and was hence Ignoto.

> ... the love which thou dost bear
> To th' Heliconian imps, and they to thee; —

The Heliconian imps are the Muses —

> They unto thee, and thou to them, most dear.

Had the lines been addressed to Shakspere of Stratford, it would be taken for granted that they called him the favorite of the Muses, hence the leading writer of the day. All the sonnets are highly laudatory, but with a few exceptions are impersonal, as to a worthy whom Spenser had not necessarily met. The one to Oxford not only makes him first in love of the Muses and in their love but sets him very much apart by the warmth of feeling it expresses for him. It tells him that

> Dear as thou art unto thyself, so love
> That loves and honours thee; as doth behove.

In other words, "As dear as you are to yourself, so are you to me, who loves and honours you, as it behooves me to."

The *Faerie Queene* was followed at the end of that same year, 1590, by the entry in the Stationers' Register of another poem of Spenser's. This was his *Teares of the Muses,* in which each of the nine sister-goddesses in turn bemoans in extreme terms the sad condition to which the art assigned to her patronage has fallen — this in the blooming of a golden age! Thalia's lament differs from the rest in having a specific topicality and in speaking of a person who practices the art, an actual individual. The Muse of Comedy, she begins by asking

> Where be the sweet delight of Learning's treasure
> That wont with comic sock to beautify
> The painted theatres, and fill with pleasure
> The listeners' eyes and ears with melody. . . ?

"O! all is gone," she wails, and instead "sits ugly Barbarism and brutish Ignorance." The sixth and eighth stanzas have attracted the attention of all students of Elizabethan drama and embarrassed the orthodox.

> And he, the man whom nature self had made
> To mock her self, and truth to imitate,
> With kindly counter under mimic shade,
> Our pleasant Willy, ah! is dead of late;
> With whom all joy and jolly merriment
> Is also deaded, and in dolour rent.
>
>   . . . .
>
>   But that same gentle spirit, from whose pen
> Large streams of honey and sweet nectar flow,
> Scorning the boldness of such base-born men,
> Which dare their follies forth so rashly throw;
> Doth rather choose to sit in idle cell,
> Than so himself to mockery to sell.

A pleasant Willy created by nature "to hold as 'twere the mirror up to nature," to reproduce truth itself, a playwright of gentle spirit from whose pen sweet nectar flowed: who would he be but Shakespeare? — for, Nicholas Rowe pointed out in 1709, "It is plain that Mr. Spencer does not mean that he was then really dead, but only that he had withdrawn from the public." Rowe also observed that "The character is not applicable to any man of the time but himself [Shakespeare]." In this, Rowe was following Dryden. Collier wrote, "We should be convinced that by 'our pleasant Willy' Spenser meant William Shakespeare, by the fact that such a character as he gives could belong to no other dramatist of the time." To Sir Henry Irving, the terms in which Willy are praised "indisputably applied with most felicitous exactness to the works he [Shakespeare] has left behind him." I hardly see how these critics can be gainsaid.

But if Willy was Shakespeare he certainly was not Shakspere. In 1590 the Stratfordian surely could not have been "dead of late" when he had so far given no sign of life in Spenser's sense or have sat "in idle cell," when so far he had given no evidence of activity. E. K. Chambers sees this. "If Shakespeare had written any comedies by 1590, of which there is no proof and little probability, he was at the beginning of his career and not, in a literary sense, 'dead.'" He could not, in Rowe's words, have "withdrawn from the public" when he had never been before it. Incidentally, for the Warwickshire villager to scorn "base-born men" would have been more than a bit thick.

The peril to Stratfordian theory is plain. How is it to be circumvented? To Chambers, "the passage as a whole seems most appropriate to Lyly, whose series of plays for Paul's terminated about 1590." Lyly again! — and if our deductions as to Lyly's relations with his noble employer are warranted, Chambers comes closer to being right than he could have been witting of. Orthodoxy, however, has not grasped the straw thus held out to it. Its desperation comes out in Schoenbaum's overruling of Rowe: "it would remain for twentieth-century scholarship to associate Willy, more plausibly, with" — Guess who, reader. Who was the glowing, golden exception to the sorry state of the arts in 1590? — "Richard Wills or Willey, the learned author of *De Re Poetica,* who died around 1579"!

We may, I think, safely return to the identification of Willy as Shakespeare and, in my view, be satisfied that the Willy from whose pen sweet nectar flowed, who brought joy and merriment to the comic state, who, rather than stoop to the follies base-born men put forth, withdrew to himself, taking with him the sweet delights of learning and the melody that filled the listeners' ears with pleasure, was the same Willie who had engaged in a rhyming contest with Perigot in Spenser's *The Shepheardes Calendar* of 1579 and was that same man to whom the muses were most dear and was most dear to them; and this "pleasant Willy," we must note, exercised the arts of Thalia from "*under mimic shade,*" just as Sir John Davies's "sweet companion" of 1596 (companion = *comes* = count = earl) "which of a shadow, under a shadow, sing[s]." Even if we cannot on the strength of Spenser's testimony alone declare Oxford to have been Shakespeare, I am content to believe it tells us much about him, including his having been known as Willy.

If in retreat at this time, and on the Avon, Oxford was not forgotten by his protégés. In 1591 John Farmer, at one time organist and master of the children of the choir at Christ Church Cathedral in Dublin, dedicated the first of his two books to Oxford, as he would the second as well. Both were works of a pioneer composer of madrigals and explorer of counterpoint. In presenting *Divers and sundry Waies of Two Parts in One, to the Number of Fortie, upon one Playn Song* to the Earl, Farmer was "emboldened for your Lordship's great affection to the noble science" of music and assured him that "all that is in me is dedicated to your Lordship's service."

Chapter 35: For That Have I Laid by My Majesty . . .

Withdrawal from the world, if such it was, did nothing to enhance Oxford's grasp of finances. On May 18th he made a harebrained proposal that his father-in-law intercede with the Queen to have his £1,000 annuity cancelled in favor of an immediate payment of £5,000 to enable him to buy a property with a yearly rent of £230. Alternatively he would have the Queen advance the sum against his hereditary claim to the Forest of Essex. He "would be glad to be sure of something that were mine own" and "to have an equal care with your Lordship over my children," to which, if his proposal is accepted, he would devote "some £500 or £600 a year." He concludes:

> So shall my children be provided for, myself at length settled in quiet, and I hope your Lordship contented, remaining no cause for you to think me an evil father, nor any doubt in me but that I may enjoy that friendship from your Lordship that so near a match, and not fruitless, may lawfully expect. Good my Lord, think of this, and let me have both your furtherance and counsel in this cause. For to tell the truth, I am weary of an unsettled life, which is the very pestilence that happens unto Courtiers, that propound unto themselves no end of their time therein bestowed.

Burghley probably threw up his hands in despair before he got halfway through the epistle. Apparently he simply filed the request. The £1,000 annuity continued.

Hedingham was one of the properties that by Oxford's reckoning was to produce the £500 to 600 for his daughters' upkeep, and though the plan he put forward came to naught, Hedingham was to serve that purpose none the less. In December 1591 the Earl made it over to Burghley in trust for his daughters. At the same time he authorized the dismantling of part of the castle and many outbuildings, which may be assumed to have fallen into the decay of long desuetude — doubtless the source of L. Majendie's report of 200 years later that he ordered the destruction to spite his father-in-law.[3] The parallel with King Lear, whose intention was to give up his kingdom and castle to his three daughters, was no doubt present in Oxford's mind when he picked the story of the play from Geoffrey of Monmouth and Holinshed; that Hedingham was in his thoughts seems to be indicated by the Fool's chiding the homeless monarch with the observation that "a snail has a house . . . to put's *head in,* not to give away to his daughters," and that "He that has a house to put's *head in* had a good *head*piece." *Head in,* which is rather dragged in, does suggest *Hedin*'ham. I think, however, what was causing Oxford to suffer as Lear suffers was not his surrender of Hedingham but the necessity, perhaps put to him in terms of what was owing his offspring, of renouncing all claim to the authorship of the poetical and dramatic masterpieces he had brought into being. Those were his kingdom.

---

[3] Mr. Majendie may also have taken too literally the report in Camden's *Annales* for 1562 that "This year John Vere, the Earle of Oxford, died the fifteenth [*sic*] of that illustrious house who . . . by his second wife Margaret Goulding [had] Edw. Earle of Oxford, who overthrew and wasted his patrimony, and Mary. . . ."

Schemes for repairing his finances, as we have gathered, were never long out of Oxford's mind. In 1592 he had another one — to obtain from the Queen the monopoly in the sale of oils, wool, and fruit. It was by granting monopolies that the Queen circumvented Parliament's parsimony in providing revenues for the state's essential expenses. The increment in the price of goods covered by the monopoly, divided between the monopoly-holder and the Exchequer, was a tax. Usually a monopoly was granted as payment for services rendered. Oxford sought to buy his. He would still be pressing his suit in October 1593 — but in vain.

To do him justice we have to recognize that he had some legitimate grievances in property matters. When he sought the Queen's leave to try his title to the Forest at Essex at law, he reported to Burghley that instead "of receiving that ordinary favour which is of course granted to the meanest subject, I was browbeaten and had many bitter speeches given me." Yet King James in the first year of his reign would accept the validity of Oxford's hereditary claim to the Forest, which suggests that it had been improperly withheld from him for thirty-two years. That the close-fisted Queen, who had from her point of view provided munificently for Oxford's needs, would lose patience when those needs proved everlasting, is understandable. From Oxford's point of view he was spending the annuity in her service and having to sell his remaining estates into the bargain.

In 1591 or 1592, moreover, Oxford had a solid reason for needing ready money, as he called it. In the latter half of the one year or early in the next he married again. His bride was Elizabeth Trentham, about whom little is known other than that Oxford must have been acquainted with her for ten years or more. B. M. Ward found that she was the daughter of Sir Thomas Trentham, a Staffordshire landowner, and one of the Queen's Maids of Honour about whom it was said in a gossipy letter nine years earlier that

> Mistress Trentham is as fair, Mistress Edgecumbe as modest, Mistress Radcliff as comely and Mistress Garrat jolly as ever. . . .

This was the second time Oxford had married a Maid of Honour, and what is most extraordinary is that neither marriage met with royal opposition, let alone rage. Elizabeth had probably helped arrange the match with Anne Cecil for selfish reasons. If she did not actively encourage the second marriage, Ward believes that the equanimity with which she accepted it showed a notable concern for Oxford's welfare and happiness. It may well be so. The new couple settled in Stoke Newington just north of Shoreditch, where the Theatre and the Curtain were located.

36

"... And Plodded Like a Man for Working Days"

1592–1597: Beginning of recorded performances of "Shakespeare's" plays. — Death of Greene and Harvey's vicious attack upon him; Chettle's forgery of Greenes Groats-worth of Wit. — Nashe's reply to Harvey in Strange News, *recalling Harvey's libel of Oxford and divulging the presence of "Will Monox," surely Oxford, at the banquet Harvey had said had proved fatal to Greene; the dedication of* Strange News *to a Master Apis Lapis, an "infinite Maecenas," almost necessarily Oxford, whom Nashe addresses with jocularity mingled with grateful respect and sketches in revealing strokes. — The fatal dinner attended by Greene, Nashe, "Will Monox," and probably Marlowe seen as having given Chettle the idea for "Greene's" famous warning to his fellow playwrights. — Dissolution of Oxford's literary circle. — Birth to the Oxfords of an heir to the Earldom. — Publication of* Venus and Adonis *and* Lucrece *and growing warmth the latter attests of the poet's affection for Southampton. — Beginning of the sonnet-record of Oxford's conflicting infatuations with Southampton and Anne Vavasor, if the indications are what they seem. — Elizabeth Vere's marriage to the 6th Earl of Derby. — Formation from the late 5th Earl of Derby's players of the famous acting company (said to be Shakespeare's) under the Lord Chamberlain. — The evidence that this best-managed and most-successful company from 1594 to 1604 was actually under the direction of the Lord Great Chamberlain, Oxford. — Possibility that Southampton was the "Shake-scene" vilified in* Groats-worth. *— First known reference to Shakespeare, in* Willobie His Avisa, *which recounts in verse the repulse by a chaste wife, transparently Elizabeth, of five would-be seducers and seems to prove that the signatory of* Lucrece *had been recognized as a highly placed courtier. — Return to England of Henry May, who, on a trading voyage in which a ship formerly and perhaps still belonging to Oxford had taken part, had been shipwrecked on Bermuda, from which he brings back any information required for* The Tempest. *— The French King's request for Oxford's intercession with Elizabeth. — Move by the Earl and his Countess to King's Place in Hackney and a modern reader's hope that with his new wife and little heir and the companionship of his musically inclined and dramatically inclined son-in-law, Oxford achieves a long-sought tranquillity.*

We are now in the period of better information on plays given public presentation and with it in that of familiar "Shakespearean" history. Thomas Nashe had already referred to *Hamlet* in 1589 and in August 1592 he wrote of the reaction of "ten thousand spectators at least" to seeing Lord Talbot "triumph again on the stage." That was a plain reference to *Henry the Sixth, Part One*, which Henslowe had produced as new — to him — on March

3rd. Philip Henslowe had been connected with the theatre since 1584, when, having married a rich widow, he bought the land on which stood the Little Rose playhouse, which he rebuilt as the Rose, but the invaluable diary he kept of performances he put on does not begin until 1592. In orthodoxy, Shakespeare's London biography begins in this same year with a misreading of a forged last testament foisted upon the deceased Robert Greene.

Greene had died in the house of a poor shoemaker near Dowgate on the 3rd September 1592, after penning his *Repentence,* in which he cried "Cursed be the day wherein I was born, and hapless be the breasts that gave me suck," and leaving a note to his long-suffering Doll:

> Sweet wife, as ever there was any good will or friendship between thee and me, see this bearer (my host) satisfied of his debt: I owe him ten pound, and but for him I had perished in the streets. Forget and forgive my wrongs done unto thee, and Almighty God have mercy on my soul. Farewell till we meet in heaven, for on earth thou shalt never see me more.
> This 2nd September 1592. Written by thy dying husband. Robert Greene.

The contrast with the leisurely, long-winded, and fancy writing of the *Groats-worth of Wit,* so soon to be planted upon the dead man, could hardly be greater.

In the Marprelate Controversy, the three Harvey brothers had injected themselves against the anti-Martinist writers Lyly, Nashe, and Greene and stinging exchanges between the two factions had taken place. Now, with Greene buried, Gabriel Harvey lost no time in pouring abuse on Greene in one of his *Foure Letters,* wishing "that Grace might finally abound, where wickedness did overflow" and, sinking his teeth in his victim in a revolting account of the circumstances in which he died, declared, "The dead bite not: and I am none of those, that bite the dead." Six years later, Francis Meres would write in his *Palladis Tamia:*

> As Achilles tortured the dead body of Hector, and as Antonius and his wife Fulvia tormented the lifeless corpse of Cicero; so Gabriel Harvey hath showed the same inhumanity to Greene that lies full low in his grave.

Poor Greene! By September 20th, only sixteen days after his funeral, Henry Chettle had finished forging the *Groats-worth,* in which Greene is made to view "his poems, pamphlets, plays and triumphs," in Alexander Grosart's words, as "utterly vain and frivolous." Though the spuriousness of the publication was indicated by Greene's friend Nashe, who castigated it as "that scald trivial lying pamphlet called Greens groats-worth of wit," scholarship would take it at face value and orthodoxy, two centuries after its publication, conceive the notion that with its denunciation of a "shake-scene" and its parody of a line from *Henry the Sixth, Part Three,* it concerned William Shakspere; thus would literary history be set off on a false scent, with epic consequences. But having heard in Chapter 8 the story of Chettle's handiwork and the construction put upon it, the reader will not need to have it repeated. We can go on to what comes out about Oxford as a result of Harvey's attack on Greene.

Harvey had said in his *Foure Letters* that on inquiring of Greene, he had heard that the "famous author" was sick "of a surfeit of pickle herring and Rhenish wine. . . ." Nashe replied to Harvey in defense of Greene: "A good fellow he was, and would have drunk with thee for more angels than the Lord thou libeldst gave thee in Christ's College." The Lord Harvey had libeled — in *Speculum* — and who had given him the gold angels in Cambridge was of course Oxford. Nashe goes on: "I and one of my fellows, Will. Monox (Hast thou never heard of him and his great dagger?) were in company with him a month before he died, at that fatal banquet of Rhenish wine and pickled herring (if thou wilt needs have it so) and then the inventory of his apparel came to more than three shillings (though thou sayst the contrary)." (That Greene was in funds at the fatal dinner may have given a misleading impression of his circumstances. It would speak ill indeed of Oxford had he knowingly let Greene die in dire want.) I do not see how it can be doubted that Nashe's Will. Monox was Oxford, his "great dagger" perhaps the Sword of State he guarded as Lord Great Chamberlain, or that, as Spenser indicated, the Earl was known to his literary companions by a name that would expunge distinctions of class between them — the same "Will" he would call himself in the *Sonnets.*

The quotations from Nashe are from his *Strange News,* which was entered in the Stationers' Register on the 12th January 1593, with a long *Epistle Dedicatorie*

> To the most copious Carminist of our time, and famous persecutor of Priscian, his verie friend Master Apis Lapis: Tho. Nashe wisheth new strings to his old tawnie Purse. . . .

Apis Lapis long puzzled scholars — still does the orthodox. An explanation that holds up and is highly enlightening was, however, offered by Gerald W. Phillips. He proposed that the term was a punning reference to the Earl of Oxford on the basis that *Apis* refers to the sacred bull of Egypt, which appears in Greek and Roman writers, and that *Apis Lapis,* literally "Bull Stone," signifies — indelicately — stoned or castrated bull — ox or Oxe, as the Earl was familiarly called. "Apex," incidentally, is Latin for boar, another de Vere symbol. "*Verie* friend" becomes another pun, playing on "Vere" and the Latin "*vero,*" meaning "truth" and appearing in the motto of the de Veres: *Nihil Vero Verius.* Reading tawny and Oxford blue were the colors of the de Veres. Nashe, in wishing new strings to Master Apis Lapis's tawny purse is, by this token, hoping that the Earl may recover some of his lost estate. Later in the *Epistle,* Nashe exclaims, "Shall I presume to dilate of the gravity of your round cap and your dudgeon dagger?" Here we have the dagger again, identifying Apis Lapis with Will. Monox. ("Dudgeon dagger" is a kind with a wooden hilt.) The plain round cap was worn by persons of authority in Elizabethan days. In the portrait inscribed as that of the 17th Earl of Oxford and assigned to Gheeraedts the subject is shown wearing just such a plain, round, black cap.

If we take Apis Lapis to be Oxford, what does the Epistle tell us of him? He showed "a high countenance . . . unto scholars" and a generosity to poets: "a famous pottle-pot Patron . . . to old Poets." He was "an infinite Maecenas" — a comparison we may remember Greene's having made, too — "to learned men," none of whom "but have tasted the cool streams of your liberality." In the second edition, this is amplified with a reference to Oxford's gratitude for the most modest books presented to him: "there is not that morsel of meat they can carve you, but you will eat for their sakes, and accept very thankfully." (The statement in the first edition that "you kept three maids together in your house a long time" is changed in the second to "three decayed students you kept attending upon you a long time." One trusts that the maids and the students got along well together.) Oxford was a "copious Carminist," *carmens* (a term taken from Horace) are analogous to cantos, divisions of a long poem; this seconds Harvey's allusions to the many poems in Latin and English that Oxford had written — clearly far in excess of the two dozen or fewer conventionally attributed to him. That Oxford was something of a trencherman is indicated ironically: "Think not, though under correction of your boon companionship, I am disposed to be a little pleasant, I condemn you of any immoderation either in eating or drinking for" — and here there seems to be a reference to the Earl's proper demeanor as Lord Great Chamberlain — "I know your government and carriage to be in every way Canonical."

The picture is of the double life Oxford lived. As Falstaff may salute Prince Hal with "How now, lad?" and tell him "Thou art essentially mad without seeming so,"[1] Nashe can address the Earl (whom they all call Will) with flippant impudence, joking that "Thou art a good fellow, I know, and hadst rather spend jests than money" — having usually it seems, spent all he had. Being Spenser's Willie and Shakespeare's Berowne, Oxford naturally went in for rhyming contests, and Nashe twits him for being not above doing so for a meal; he cannot "acquit" Apis Lapis of being a "verser, . . . for M[aster] Vaux of Lambeth [a vintner, C. W. Barrell discovered] brings in sore evidence of a breakfast you won of him one morning at an unlawful game called rhyming." At the same time he does not forget who Oxford is. As a "patron" of "scholars," he could not let "a thread-bare cloak sooner peep forth, but you strait press it to be an outbrother of your bounty." As a nobleman of rank, Oxford could prove a powerful friend, and Nashe, while beseeching

[1] Having a knight so address a prince and future king we may be sure, I think, would have struck a tradesman's son from Stratford as unheard-of presumption and never have occurred to him.

him to "give me nothing for the dedication of my pamphlet," adjures him to "Let it be the task of thy best terms, to safeconduct this book through the enemy's country." And however "merrily" he might write, Nashe vows that "I love and admire thy pleasant witty humor, which no care or cross can make unconversable" and is "Thine entirely."

So much, evidently, does the *Epistle Dedicatorie* tell about Oxford that not surprisingly (according to R. B. McKerrow, editor of Nashe's works) in the editions following the first it was printed in especially small type, making it difficult to read, or was dropped altogether. But Nashe has more to say of interest. Professor McKerrow writes:

> We have two references to a "Lord" who was apparently Nashe's patron in the autumn of 1592: the first in *Pierce Pennilesse*, where Nashe mentions that "the feare of infection detained me with my Lord in the country." The other, in *Strange News*, written in the winter of 1592–1593, where, replying to charges brought by Harvey, he says, "For the order of my life, it is as ciuil as a ciuil orenge; I lurke in no corners, but converse in a house of credit, as well gouerned as any Colledge where there be more rare qualified men and selected good Schollers than in any Nobleman's house that I know in England."

I should guess that the "Lord" who was Nashe's patron was Oxford, and if so that it was at Bilton or Billesley that Nashe was "with my Lord in the country."

To revert to, and conclude with, *Greenes Groats-worth of Wit,* I think we now know enough to make informed guesses as to the identity of the three playwrights addressed by "R.G." in the famous letter warning of the upstart Crow. The principal one I should say was Oxford-Shakespeare. Another I take to be Nashe, this being at the time when he seems likely to have been in the Earl's household. It was during the time also when Marlowe "bore name to serve my Lord," and so I think the chances were good that he was the third. We know that "Will. Monox" and Nashe were with Greene at that fatal dinner of Rhenish wine and pickled herrings, and it may well be that this dinner, with Marlowe as a fourth, gave Chettle the idea for an address by Greene to three fellow playwrights. The words he put in Greene's mouth were, I suspect, designed to profit Chettle by creating a scandal and provoking Marlowe and especially the man of the dudgeon dagger; and maybe "dudgeon" was another of Nashe's plays on words. That Chettle subsequently met Will. Monox and, finding him "no less civil than /. . . excellent in the quality he professes," regretted having given him offense I can believe. After all, Chettle had found that "divers of worship . . . reported his uprightness of dealing, which argues his honesty, and his facetious grace in writing, that approves [displays] his Art." That leaves the question of who the upstart Crow was — who, that is, Chettle meant him to be taken for when he had "R.G." vilifying him. As to that, I shall venture a tentative suggestion presently.

It is natural to us that Oxford continued to rejoice in the company of his "lewd friends" and not beyond our comprehension that he found in good Rhenish and sherris sack alleviation of the heartache and weariness of spirit that the lonely struggle with the daemon of his creative genius cost him and may have overdone the therapy. How the new Countess of Oxford may have felt about the irregularities in his life is of course another matter and beyond our guessing. The plays, so illuminating about his past life, throw no light on his second marriage, so far as one can see, though some of the sonnets may be found to refer to this second Elizabeth. It would be no surprise if, after the Court, it came as a shock to her to have all those "rare qualified men and selected good scholars" making free of her house, enlivening it till cock's-crow with a prairie-fire of talk and heaven knows what all.

Within a year of the marriage, however, the stalwarts began to fall away. Robert Greene had died in September 1592 and Marlowe was murdered in the next May. The man whom Kyd had called "my Lord" evidently parted company with him after he had virtually consigned Marlowe to the faggots to save himself, though he had done so only under torture; that, I surmise, reduced Oxford's household by a third playwright. By then Lyly must have gone too. It was in 1589 that Harvey had called him Oxford's "minion secretary" and he was probably still in Oxford's employment when the children's company of Paul's was finally suppressed in 1591, but 1592 marks the end of his career as a successful playwright. (A. L. Rowse asserts that "Life in the proximity of the Earl of Oxford was far from smooth, and in the end Lyly left his service — sooner or later one always quarrelled with Edward de Vere." There is not a shred of evidence that Lyly quarrelled with Oxford. On the contrary, we find him in July 1582 pleading with Lord Burghley to intercede for him with Oxford, since "It hath pleased my Lord upon what colour I cannot tell, certain I am upon no cause, to be displeased with me, the grief whereof is more than the loss can be." He closes with the assurance that "I know my Lord to be most honorable." Summarizing Lyly's career, R. W. Bond says, "We see him making enemies in the household of Lord Oxford. . . ." There is that which, gnawing at Professor Rowse, can be assuaged only by slander of Oxford and Oxfordians, whose disbelief in the Stratford theory he calls "crackpot nonsense" and "sheer lunacy.")

A decided change would surely have come over Oxford's household when on the 24th February 1593 the Countess was delivered of a son. At last, in the father's forty-third year, an heir to the Earldom had been born who would survive. On March 31st the infant was christened Henry at the Parish Church in Stoke Newington. The name was a new one, as Edward had been, in a family of Roberts and Johns. Oxfordians are persuaded that it was chosen as a compliment to Henry Wriothesley, Earl of Southampton.

Only eighteen days after the christening the narrative poem *Venus and Adonis* with its courtly dedication to the nineteen-year-old youth signed William Shakespeare was entered in the Stationers' Register to Richard Field "under the hands of the Archbishop of Canterbury and Master Warden Stirrop." (Orthodox writers, I may repeat, make a great point over Field's having been a native of Stratford-on-Avon, which would have made it natural for Shakspere to have taken him his manuscript. Field had, however, been apprenticed to a printer who had published three of Arthur Golding's books, and took over the business of John Harrison, who had brought out a book by Geoffrey Gates dedicated to Oxford, publication of which had probably been arranged by Oxford himself. *Lucrece* came out as published "by Richard Field for John Harrison," and probably the earlier work was too.) The much greater poetical maturity of the *Sonnets,* which Oxford would be beginning at about this time, leaves little doubt that *Venus and Adonis* and its successor, *Lucrece,* were works of a much earlier date that the author refurbished for publication as witnesses of the sway that the beautiful young Earl had gained over him. (Samuel Taylor Coleridge declares that these were "works which give at once strong promises of the strength, and yet obvious proofs of the immaturity, of his genius.")

This was, of course, the first time we find the name William Shakespeare in print, and the question naturally arises as to how Oxford came to select it. His crest as Viscount Bulbeck was a lion brandishing a broken spear and he was himself a champion with that weapon. What is likely to have had more to do with it is that Pallas Athena, *hasti-vibrans,* the spear-shaker, was the patron goddess of the Athenians, who created the drama as we know it. Incidentally, we might observe that the poet-dramatist never, as far as we can tell, affixed the name William Shakespeare to any other work. For all we know to the contrary it was always others who made that attribution.

Venus and Adonis was an immediate hit and was to go through nine printings by the end of 1602. On the 9th May 1594 *Lucrece* was entered in the Stationers' Register, being the "graver labour" promised in the dedication of its predecessor. ("It is a greater poem" says Edward Dowden, but with "faults" that are "partly the errors of immaturity.") This second long narrative poem, with its much more intimate dedication to Southampton, would go through six printings by 1616, when, in the year of Shakspere's death, the name William Shakespeare would appear for the first time on the title-page and the title be expanded to *The Rape of Lucrece.* In an edition of *Venus and Adonis* of 1630 in the Bodleian Library, the name is still confined to the dedication.

In the year's interval between publication of the two poems, Oxford's relationship with Southampton had grown much closer, if we may judge by the second dedication. In this "The love I dedicate to your Lordship is without end. . . . What I have done is yours, what I have to do is yours, being part in all I have, devoted yours." Speaking of these "expressions of affection," Professor D. Nichol Smith of Oxford writes in *Shakespeare's England*, "There is no other dedication like this in Elizabethan literature."

We are now well into the period of the *Sonnets*, which would last until near if not quite to the end of the author's life. It is a period of heartfelt preoccupation with Southampton (if we may accept him as the young friend of the sequence), especially at the beginning; the human frame could hardly sustain for very long the intensity of obsession the *Sonnets* make us so painfully aware of in the first few years. It is a period, too, the *Sonnets* tell us, of destructive infatuation, bitterly resisted, with the dark lady, though we may trust this was short-lived. The indications that this *femme fatale* was Anne Vavasor — Rosaline-Beatrice — I have already brought out. If so, it is of interest to know that Anne, Gwynneth Bowen writes, "after a succession of illicit love affairs, had married a sea captain named John Finche, but left him about 1589 for the redoubtable Queen's Champion, Sir Henry Lee, then nearly 60 years old and on the point of retiring. Nevertheless, with Sir Henry Lee she continued to live, steadfastly if not faithfully, to his dying day, 21 years later. Their son, Thomas Vavasor (later known as Thomas Freeman), was born in 1589 when his half-brother, Edward Vere, was eight years old, but no one knows where Edward was during these turbulent years." (It is curious that Anne bore sons to both the stellar performers of the tournament of 1571.) That the dark lady was married to a man in his middle sixties during the flare-up of her intimacy with Oxford would conform quite well with what the *Sonnets* say of the liaison.

In Chapter 16 I extracted from the *Sonnets* to the best of my ability and that of others on whom I relied what they appear to tell us of the principals and their responses to and interactions upon one another. Only two additional points seem to me to need making.

First, the poet is so self-abnegating with respect to his young friend, so self-accusative with respect to the woman, and withal so tortured by his betrayal at their joint hands that I think he may have given us an inadequate idea of the regard in which his "two loves" must have held him. I imagine both found him fascinating with inexhaustible riches of personality, a dazzling enlarger of the world they lived in. And who would not be proud and flattered to be singled out for impassioned attention by a man who was bringing forth the works of Shakespeare and receiving the devoted admiration of other creative minds? Again, the unknown quantity is the party who made this strange, emotion-racked triangle a quadrangle: the Countess of Oxford. One can only hope her suffering was not too keen. It could hardly have been greater than her distracted Lord's and may have been mitigated by her perception of his.

The second point I should make is that the impression we receive from the *Sonnets* of the poet's being driven almost out of his mind by the exaltation and despair that flowered in this deathless verse must be a misleading one. No one could have written those 2,445 lines of intensely demanding poetry without a degree of detachment. It is the artist's saving grace, where it is not his curse, to be able to stand aside from himself and observe his most excruciating symptoms with a calculating thoughtfulness. Besides that, the author's energies were otherwise sorely taxed. Apart from the *Sonnets* themselves, there was the great body of his dramatic work to be wrought into shape. Nor was that all. The Lord Chamberlain's company came into being at this time — as a formal organization differing from the *ad hoc* group of players who had performed at Court in the past under the Lord Chamberlain's authority.

One of the acting companies had since 1576 been under the patronage of Fernando Stanley, Lord Strange, who became the 5th Earl of Derby in September 1593. Among his players by this time were the famous actors Edward Alleyn and Will Kempe. Perhaps because of them, the company had begun to play at Court in the winter of 1591 and 1592. In 1592 they were also performing plays of Shakespeare's for Philip Henslowe at the Rose. On the 16th April 1594 the new Earl of Derby died.

Here I must interrupt theatrical history to remark that less than a month later, on May 9th, a "motion of marriage" was reported between William Stanley, younger brother of the late Fernando, the 5th Earl of Derby, and Oxford's oldest daughter Elizabeth. The Countess of Derby had been pregnant at the time of the Earl's death and the engaged couple waited to marry until the baby was born. It was a girl, and accordingly the title passed to William and the condition on which Burghley would give his consent to the match was met. The marriage took place on 26th January 1595 "with great solemnity and triumph" in the presence of the Queen and the Court, and one tradition has it that *A Midsummer-Night's Dream* was performed for the occasion. Oxford acquired a son-in-law only eleven years his junior to whom he would apparently be close, one of tastes so similar to his own that, as we saw in Chapter 9, a case can be made out for the 6th Earl of Derby's himself having been Shakespeare.

To return to the acting company that the 5th Earl of Derby had left to the dowager Countess: by June 5th, E. K. Chambers says, "the patronage of the Lord Chamberlain, Henry Lord Hunsdon, must have been obtained," for this was the company that, beginning on that date, Henslowe called the Lord Chamberlain's men in recording it as taking part in joint performances with

Lady Elizabeth Vere Countess of Derby

Artist unknown

By permission of the Duke of Atholl and the National Galleries of Scotland, holders of copyright. Photo by Tom Scott, Edinburgh.

the Lord Admiral's men in plays that included *Titus Andronicus, Hamlet,* and *Taming of the Shrew*. Soon thereafter, however, the combination broke up. "On October 8," Chambers resumes, "Lord Hunsdon was negotiating with the Lord Mayor for the use of 'my nowe companie' of the Cross Keys Inn for the winter season." The members of the new company included Richard Burbage, Will Kempe, Thomas Pope, John Heminge, Augustine Phillips, and George Bryan. Alleyn had dropped out, and perhaps for that reason, Chambers speculates, the Lord Chamberlain's company as a business organization had to make a new start with new financing. "In some way," he continues, "all those ['books'] for Shakespeare's earlier plays, including any which had been performed by Pembroke's or Sussex's, seem to have passed into the hands of the Chamberlain's." The history of the company "is continuous throughout Shakespeare's career, and there is nothing to show that he ever wrote for any other company. It became dominant at court, giving 32 performances during Elizabeth's reign to 20 by the Admiral's and

13 by other companies. And during this period its run of prosperity seems to have been substantially unbroken."

But which Lord Chamberlain was it who was patron of the company? To orthodoxy there are no two ways about it. It was *the Lord Chamberlain.* Nominally that was certainly so. From the founding of the company until 1603 the title was held by the Lords Hunsdon in succession — Henry Carey and his son George — with an eight-month interregnum when Lord Cobham was Lord Chamberlain. But Charles W. Barrell has raised a serious question as to whether these men had much to do with the company and whether it was not another Lord Chamberlain who managed its affairs so splendidly, after seeing to it that "in some way . . . Shakespeare's earlier plays . . . passed into the hands of the Chamberlain's." Henry, the first Lord Hunsdon, held the important posts of Warden of the East Marches Toward Scotland and Governor of Berwick until his death in 1596 at about age seventy-two, we read in the *Dictionary of National Biography.* Although the Queen appointed him her Lord Chamberlain in 1583, his "frequent absence from Berwick" caused her in the next year to threaten "in a torrent of passion" to "'set him by his feet' and send another in his place," despite his being her first cousin. He must have got the idea, for, the *Dictionary* tells us, "his office in the north did not allow him to reside regularly at court." His career was a long series of military and political offices, among which during his last years was service as a commissioner in four treason trials, two at the time the Lord Chamberlain's company was being formed. Even had his demanding duties given him time for the affairs of an acting troupe, his inclination can hardly have been in that direction, for "he lacked most of the literary culture of his class."

The 1st Lord Hunsdon's successor held the office of Lord Chamberlain but briefly. The aged Court politician, Lord Cobham, "appears in the chronicles as a choleric and domineering baron of the old school," says Barrell, "with Puritan affiliations" and, apparently, "no liking for the acting profession."

George Carey, the 2nd Lord Hunsdon, appointed Lord Chamberlain in March 1596, was as preoccupied as his father had been with military and diplomatic duties, being highly praised for his fortification of the Isle of Wight. Of his attachment to the theatre in general and the Lord Chamberlain's men in particular there must be extreme doubt. In 1596, when James Burbage sought to open a new playhouse at Blackfriars, where Lord Oxford had once held a lease, "curiously enough," Chambers relates, "one of the protestants was the new Lord Hunsdon." Although "the new house [was one] which James Burbage may be presumed to have planned for the use of his son [Richard] and his son's fellows," of whom Hunsdon "was now the patron"! Hunsdon's name was in fact second on the list of those opposing this new opportunity for the Lord Chamberlain's men! By 1601, Barrell says, Elizabeth was persuaded of Hunsdon's incapacitation and had to appoint two successive Vice Chamberlains.

The Lord Chamberlain's was the best-organized and most-favored and successful acting company in England from the time of its organization in 1594. Marchette Chute astutely observes that "Although such a record was almost inconceivable in Elizabethan London, no members of the Chamberlain's company seem to have been sent to prison." For a troupe that enjoyed so exemplary a standing to have had the benefit of no more sustained and able direction or interested source of support than the Hunsdons and Cobham would have provided seems to me hardly to be believed.

That the company's halcyon days ended when they did, shortly after the troupe received the patronage of James I and became the King's men, is also significant. Sir Henry Irving writes in his edition of Shakespeare's works:

> No sooner had our great dramatist ceased to take part in the public performances of the King's players, than the company appears to have thrown off the restraint by which it had been unusually controlled ever since its formation and to have produced plays which were objectionable to the court, as well as offensive to private persons. Shakespeare, from his abilities, station and experience, must have possessed great influence with the body at large, and due deference, we may readily believe, was shown to his knowledge and judgment in the selection and acceptance of plays. . . . We suppose Shakespeare to have ceased to act in the summer of 1604.

John Payne Collier had earlier written:

> We suppose Shakespeare to have ceased to act in the summer of 1604, and in the winter of that very year we find the King's players giving offense to "some great counsellors."

It was in June 1604 that Edward de Vere died.

It seems to me, in other words, reasonable to infer from the facts that the Lord Chamberlain under whom the company so prospered was the Lord Great Chamberlain, whose title was sometimes shortened by the omission of the "Great." This, I suspect, is the explanation for the hard-pressed Countess of Southampton's record of a payment to "Shakespeare," *inter alia,* for performances by the Lord Chamberlain's men.

The Earl of Oxford was a keen devotee of the theatre, could draw upon a generous annual allowance for, we may believe, just such purposes as maintaining a first-rate company to perform before the Queen and public, and (unless I am woefully in error) was the author who provided the company with the peerless dramas that made its name immortal. It is significant, as Professor Bronson Feldman brings out, that Robert Armin remarked in his *Quips upon Questions* of 1600, by which time he had become chief jester with the Lord Chamberlain's Men ("Shakespeare's jester," Professor T. W. Baldwin calls him), that he would "take my journey (to wait on the right Honourable good Lord my Master whom I serve) to Hackney." Almost of necessity, Feldman shows, this was Oxford.

In his supervision of the company it is easy to imagine Oxford's having had eager collaboration by his theatrically minded son-in-law, William Stanley, Earl of Derby, whose elder brother had been patron of the predecessor company for eighteen years. Southampton would surely have been irresistibly drawn to the enterprise. It was said of him, Charlotte C. Stopes writes, that he went to the theatre every day, first to see a play, then to hear a play, and then to study the art of the actor. In 1599 it would be recorded that he and his friend Lord Rutland "come not to Court" but "pass away the time merely in going to plays every day." Conceivably he was such a shadow of Oxford-Shakespeare's in the society of the Lord Chamberlain's men as to become known as a second, young "Will," a nickname by which the young friend of the *Sonnets* seems to be known in numbers 134 and 135. Moreover, with Oxford surreptitiously playing "kingly parts in sport," it is possible that Southampton also sneaked onto the stage incognito in a few roles. As we have it on Mrs. Stopes's word that "He was in the habit of giving good advice about their business to all the players, . . ." we might imagine that he went about speaking on matters theatrical with the authority of a protégé and favorite of Oxford-Shakespeare's, a know-it-all. If so, could he have been the Johannes Factotum of "R.G.'s" outburst, the upstart Crow "beautified" with an actor's "feathers" and "in his own conceit the only Shake-scene in a country"? I am not by any means suggesting that he would have fitted the part well enough for Greene to have vilified him as such. What we have, remember, is not the playwright Greene speaking in this but the outsider and imposter Henry Chettle shooting probably much in the dark on the basis of rumor to exploit a possible scandal and sell his "scald, lying pamphlet." This is all conjectural, however, in the extreme. Orthodoxy, for its part, has never ventured to say who the upstart Crow might have been if he were not Shakespeare, as we may be sure he was not.

Whatever the truth of the matter, it would seem that Southampton's addiction to the drama was such as to call forth a warning from his older friend:

> For I am sham'd by that which I bring forth,
> And so should you, to love things nothing worth.

But the warning must have been hard to take seriously if you heard Oxford addressing the players with such care for their craft as moves Hamlet when he does likewise.

In the month after the Lord Chamberlain's company was formed, in July

1594, Oxford wrote a letter to Burghley destined to tantalize future readers with two references to his "office." In this office "both Her Majesty and I were greatly hindered" by "sundry abuses," which he hoped "that it might please your Lordship that I might find such favour from you that I might have the same redressed." In connection with some unspecified legal cause of his he goes on to say that his Lordship, "to whom my estate is so well known," knew too how important it was for him "not to neglect, as heretofore, such occasions . . . to amend the same as may arise from mine office." It was a hope held out to Burghley that Oxford must have been well aware was vain.

In September 1594 came an historic event. This was the first reference to Shakespeare known to us, and it came in the introductory verses to a mysterious publication of undisclosed authorship. *Willobie His Avisa* is clearly as significant for our inquiries as it is awkward for orthodoxy, and that is saying a great deal. The first of the two stanzas sounding the theme of the work speaks of a "constant dame" in Rome who "lost the garland of her rarest fame," though the faith she inspired is matched in England — by, as it will turn out, the faith investing the lady Avisa, of whom we are told that in virtue "This Brytan Bird outflies them all." The second stanza makes clear that the constant Roman dame was Lucrece, whose husband, Collatine, had found what "most in vain have sought" — "a fair and constant wife" —

> Yet Tarquin plucks his glistering grape,
> And Shake-speare paints poor Lucrece rape.

In this first surviving reference to Shakespeare, the insertion of the hyphen leaves no doubt in my mind that the name signed to the dedications of *Venus and Adonis* and *Lucrece* had been recognized as a pseudonym.

Willobie His Avisa is composed of hundreds of six-line stanzas, fast-paced, smooth, and professional, making up a running dialogue. The speakers are, in turn, five would-be seducers of Avisa who are cryptically identified, and Avisa herself, who, as a virtuous wife, repels and rebukes them all. Plainly it had the appeal of a titillating *roman à clef*, for it went through five editions in fifteen years, despite the authorities' efforts to "call it in." G. B. Harrison writes, "The initials of Avisa's suitors covered, or rather revealed to contemporaries, persons of great importance; so great, in fact, that the scandals about them were still commercially worth retailing forty years later." As he says, there was "doubtless good reason why, in June 1599, *Willobie His Avisa* should have been included in the category of books to be burned."

Who were these V.I.P.s? The author says, "Concerning the name Avisa, I think it be a feigned name," and, "I would not have Avisa be thought a polite fiction, nor a truthless invention." When Avisa has occasion to reply in writing to attempts on her virtue, she signs herself *Always the same Avisa,* and, to call attention to its importance, the subscription is rendered in the largest type in the book. Professor G. P. V. Akrigg observes that "'Always the same' translated into Latin becomes *Semper Eadem,* the motto of Elizabeth I. Significantly the later editions of *Avisa* include an 'Apologie' which goes to great lengths to emphasize that the poet had no original for Avisa. . . . This disingenuous disclaimer was drafted only a few weeks after the banning of *Avisa* in 1599." Another Canadian professor, Barbara N. DeLuna of the University of Alberta, cites half a dozen attributes of Elizabeth shared by Avisa. To the objection that the Queen was not a wife, she recalls that Elizabeth had declared in 1559, "I have already joined myself in marriage to an husband, namely the Kingdome of England." She adds that Avisa's husband "is not a man of flesh and blood at all . . . but a disembodied presence: England."

As to the lovers, Professor DeLuna argues, ably, that the first four are Thomas Seymour, Philip II, the Duke of Alençon, and Christopher Hatton. The fifth, "H.W.," is evidently to be identified with the alleged author, "Henrico Willobego. Italo-Hispanensis."

When *Willobie* appeared, no one familiar with the Court would have taken an H.W. close to the Queen to be anyone other than the twenty-one-year-old Henry Wriothesley, particularly because H.W. is set forth as young: "If years I want, . . ." he says; and "I love, that never loved before." Akrigg, the young nobleman's biographer, states, "The H.W. who was seeking Avisa's favour in 1594 can only have been Henry Wriothesley, Earl of Southampton." Much to the point, he says, undeniably, "The unriddling of *Avisa* has a particular interest for Shakespeareans because of the passage presenting H.W. to the book's readers." This begins:

> H. W. being suddenly infected with the contagion of a fantastical fit, at the first sight of *A,* pineth a while in secret grief, at length not able any longer to endure the burning heat of so fervent a humour, bewrayeth the secrecy of his disease unto his familiar friend W. S. who not long before had tried the courtesy of the passion, and was now newly recovered of the like infection. . . .

Who is W.S.? Among scholars today I think there is but little question as to that. "Remembering that *Willobie His Avisa* treats of important persons," G. B. Harrison writes, "there is strong probability that H. W. is to be identified with Henry Wriothesley, Earl of Southampton, and W. S. with William Shakespeare." Recalling that John Collier had first pointed out this link, Schoenbaum includes the perception among his "valid contributions to knowledge." E. K. Chambers bases on "the apparent testimony of *Willobie His Avisa*" his judgment that Shakespeare "in or shortly before 1594" had "an unsuccessful love affair." Akrigg accepts W.S. as Shakespeare outright. William Jaggard, the outstanding Shakespearean bibliographer, even calls the depiction of W.S. "the most convincing version of his [Shakespeare's] personality known throughout all literature." Let us see where this identification takes us.

H.W., finding himself "at length not able any longer to endure the burning heat" of his passion for "A," loses no time, it would seem, in carrying out his decision to take "his familiar friend W.S." into his confidence. He cries:

> But yonder comes my faithful friend,
> That like assaults hath often tried,
> On his advice I will depend,
> Where I shall win, or be denied. . . .

Upon hearing from H.W. how

> The smothered flame, too closely pent,
> Burns more extreme for want of vent,

W.S. is ready with advice to proffer "friend Harry" on winning Avisa over:

> Apply her still with divers things,
> (For gifts the wisest will deceive)
> Sometimes with gold, sometimes with rings,
> No time nor fit occasion leave. . . .
>   . . . .
>   You must commend her loving face,
> For women joy in beauty's praise
> You must admire her sober grace,
> Her wisdom and her virtuous ways,
>   Say, t'was her wit and modest show,
>   That made you like and love her so.

At this juncture in the groves of Academe, I have to say, ultimate bewilderment sets in with me. Are we actually to believe that Southampton would make a "familiar friend" of a common player of Shakspere's background and submit to being called "friend Harry" by him? That the aristocratic, spoiled young Earl would make a confidant of such a one and seek his advice on how to prevail with the Queen of England, whose hand future kings had tried by every means to gain? Are we to imagine that the untutored commoner — even supposing that his experience permitted him to expound with self-assurance on the efficacy of gifts of rings and gold in deceiving the wisest — would presume to declare of the near divinity on the English throne:

> Well, say no more; I know thy grief,
> And face from whence these flames arise,
> It is not hard to find relief,
> If thou wilt follow good advice:
>   She is no Saint, She is no Nun,
>   I think in time she may be won.

All that rules out Shakspere as the W.S. of the poem is to me readily acceptable as applying to Shakespeare-Oxford, if taken as inspired by gossip;

and I dare say Charlotte Stopes is right when she comments on *Willobie* that "Such a translation of the friendship which resulted in the writing of the Sonnets . . . could only have been made by the enemies of both [men]."

Let me resume where I left off in quoting the introduction to H.W. We recall that W.S. "was now newly recovered of a like infection;"

> yet finding his friend let blood in the same vein, he took pleasure for a time to see him bleed, & instead of stopping the issue, he enlargeth the wound, with the sharp razor of a willing conceit, persuading him that he thought it a matter very easy to be compassed, & no doubt with pain, diligence & some cost in time to be obtained. Thus the miserable comforter comforting his friend with an impossibility, either for that he now would secretly laugh at his friend's folly, that had given occasion not long before unto others to laugh at his own, or because he would see whether another could play his part better than himself, & in viewing afar off the course of this loving comedy, he determined to see whether it would sort to a happier end for this new actor, than it did for the old player.

It seems to me unmistakable from what we have read that the lady "A," who has awakened "so fervent a humour" in H.W., is the same with whom W.S. "like assaults hath often tried." I venture to think that even those Stratfordians able to picture the obscure Will Shakspere as moving familiarly in the august company presented in *Willobie His Avisa* stop short of having him credited with repeated attempts to seduce the Queen of England. But can it be believed that Southampton had conceived a burning desire for a woman forty years his senior? Hardly, I should say. Where, then, does this leave us? Remembering that H.W. was identified by the phrase "Italo-Hispanensis," and bearing in mind that the young Southampton was noted for having had the writer Giovanni Florio as his tutor for some years at Titchfield and that Essex won his spurs in battle with Spain, let us consider what Sir Sidney tells us of Southampton:

> According to Florio the earl quickly acquired a thorough knowledge of Italian. About 1590, when he was hardly more than seventeen, he was presented to Queen Elizabeth, who showed him kindly notice and her favorite, the Earl of Essex, thenceforth displayed in his welfare a brotherly interest.

It seems to me likely that H.W. is an amalgam of Southampton and Essex, whom Professor DeLuna considers predominant in the character. If, however, H.W. in his ardor for Elizabeth is primarily Essex, I share the suspicion of others, acknowledged by Ms. Stopes, that the triangle of W.S., H.W., and Avisa owes something to the triangle in the *Sonnets,* as the author of *Willobie* construed it; indeed, in the context of the triangle, Avisa as combining Elizabeth and A. Vavasor would work out quite well. We must not forget that this *succès de scandale* may be no more than merest guesswork based on rumor and spiced with malicious fancy. If it be no more than that, it still tells us what kind of purported disclosures about Elizabeth and her suitors and courtiers found an avid and continuing market. More to the point: accepting W.S. as the "Shake-speare" of the introductory verses, we have in *Willobie* seemingly conclusive evidence that the name was recognized from the start as the *nom de plume* of a courtier close to the Queen, of a station immeasurably far beyond hope of attainment by the Stratford man, who

Susan Vere, Countess of Montgomery, as Thomyris in "The Masque of Queenes" by Inigo Jones.

From *Shakespeare's England*.

By permission of the Oxford University Press.

even several years later was so little known as to be untraceable by the tax-collectors.

A month before the publication of *Willobie* one Henry May arrived at Falmouth from a sea-faring expedition that had departed more than three years before for Africa and the East Indies. One of the three vessels taking part was *Edward Bonaventure*. May would write an account of the voyage for the 1600 edition of Hakluyt telling of the return home via the West Indies and of his shipwreck on the isle of Bermuda, in which only twenty-six in the crew of fifty were saved. Whether Oxford retained an investment in *Edward Bonaventure* is not known.[2] In any case, May's adventures may have interested him, and because May and his fellows had had to spend five months in Bermuda before being able to set forth for Newfoundland in a bark they had built, he could certainly have found out from the mariner almost everything there was to know about the island for the needs, if any, of *The Tempest*.

A year later we find Oxford having just left the house in Cannon Row to which the Earl of Derby had brought his Countess after their wedding eight months earlier. In a letter to his father-in-law of the 7th August 1595, he reports that

> On my coming to Byfleet from Cannon Row the Earl of Derby was very earnest that he might assure £1000 a year for my daughter, and marvelled that Sir Robert Cecil her uncle, and I her father were so slack to call upon it; so I desire something may be done therein.

The Queen had said that the Stanleys were the richest family in England, which would help account for the enormous size of the annuity, matching that of the Countess's father's, which the present head of the family purposed to settle upon his wife.

In the next month the French ambassador brought Oxford a note that came to light in 1972 when Craig Huston, an attorney of Philadelphia, found a copy of it in the British Museum. Addressed to Le Grand Chambellan d'Angleterre, it reads in Mr. Huston's translation:

> Lord Great Chamberlain, I am having this note brought to you by Loménie whom I send before the Queen my good sister with respect to the matters which concern the well being of her affairs and mine, in order to inform you of the satisfaction I feel for the good offices you have performed on my behalf in her presence, which I beg you to continue and believe that I will always consider it a great pleasure to reciprocate in whatever might bring about your personal satisfaction, as I have charged the said Loménie to tell you, whom I pray you to believe as myself, who prays God to keep you, Lord Great Chamberlain, in his care. This 5th of October at Paris. Signed Henri.

[2] The indexes of ships in the National Maritime Museum of London disclose only one reference to the history of the *Edward Bonaventure*. This describes her as a merchant vessel sailing with the Turkey Company; then in November 1585 engaging with Spanish off Pantalaria; involved against the Spanish Armada, 1588; and in 1591/3 making the first successful British voyage to India and back. Either in 1585 or 1588 her captain was James Lancaster.

Antoine de Loménie's successor as ambassador from Paris would say that the fault of "the French is never to have well understood how to treat with the Lord Treasurer." Probably it was to get around Burghley that Henri IV sought Oxford's services in his continuing quest for more help in his war with Spain, about which Burghley was inclined to be niggardly. But it is surprising to find the French King and the Earl on such good terms and the latter engaged in affairs of state at this time.

It is almost the last we hear of what he was doing. In the next year, 1596, he moved with his Countess into a house she had bought in Hackney, and the obscurity that would surround his life here, where he would remain as long as he lived, is almost impenetrable, B. M. Ward says.

Hackney, lying to the north of London, was one of the city's first suburbs of any consequence. When the Oxfords settled there it was considered the "Court end of town"; Queen Elizabeth had a house only a mile and a half to the east, in Canonbury. The Oxfords' house was known as King's Place, later as Brooke House. (See opposite.) Its history can be traced back to the 1470s. It was described as "a large mansion" and "a fair house, all of brick, with a fair hall and parlour, a large gallery, a proper chapel, and a proper library to lay books in." It stood until 1955, when, having been badly damaged by bombs in the war, it was most unfortunately torn down. The Shakespeare Authorship Society of London pleaded for its preservation, but their pleas were rendered futile by the tenacity of the Stratford legend. Visitors to the site today will find Brooke School occupying it.

My belief, or rather my hope, is that the settled tranquility Oxford had sought now came to him: that the Countess Elizabeth proved a more understanding wife than Anne had been, with no division of her loyalties; that the turbulence of the two infatuations that make the *Sonnets* painful reading had subsided; that the overexcitations and irregularities of life with highly charged bohemians had diminished; that the company of his son-in-law brought the rewards of shared theatrical and musical interests in an easy familial setting. We do know that the Oxfords and the Derbys were visitors in each others' homes. In September 1596 we find Oxford again staying with his son-in-law in Cannon Row. There is a question, however, as to his health. A year later, on the 8th September 1597, we read in a letter to Burghley of his regretting that he cannot attend her Majesty at Theobalds as "I have not an able body."

The occasion of his writing was the perseverance of Lord and Lady Pembroke in promoting a marriage between their son and Oxford's second daughter. Judging the young man to be "fair conditioned" and "of many good parts" the Earl says the proposal "doth greatly content me for Bridget's sake, whom I always wished a good husband," and as "being a thing agreeable to your Lordship's fatherly care and love to my daughter" and to "all

Brooke House — earlier King's
Place — Hackney in 1761.

From *The History and Antiquities of the
Parish of Hackney in the County of
Middlesex* by William Robinson.

Courtesy of Virginia State Library.

parties." The marriage fell through, however; Bridget in 1599 would marry
Francis Norris, who in the next year would succeed to the Barony of Rycote.
Nevertheless, the young man, William Herbert, would play an important
role in Oxford's history, as the Earl of Pembroke. It would be he, as it would
appear, who would be largely instrumental in bringing about publication of
the First Folio, which would be dedicated to him and his brother, the Earl
of Montgomery, the husband of Oxford's youngest daughter, Susan.

37

"For It Is Parting from Us"

1598–1604 et seq.: The death of Burghley. — The end, signalized by publication of Meres's Palladis Tamia, of any prospect of the Shakespearean plays' being credited to their author and Oxford's probable terrible inner conflict in the matter. — Marston's anticipation that the "unvalu'd worth" of, seemingly, Edward de Vere, "shall mount fair place when Apes are turnèd forth." — Salting of the Shakespearean plays with references to Shakspere's role in the deception as to their authorship: his appearance as Christopher Sly in The Shrew, *as William Vizor in* Henry the Fourth, Part Two, *as William the Clown in* As You Like It. *— Oxford addressed with respectful affection by his nephew with an enigmatic reference to his "most serious affairs." — Uncertainty of his relations with his son by Anne Vavasor. — Dedication of John Farmer's madrigals to Oxford as one who could have gone further in music than most professionals. — Derby as playwright and patron of an acting company. — Reappearance of Oxford's players and their assignment to the Boar's Head. — His unsuccessful efforts to win further sources of income with the help of Robert Cecil. — Rebellion, after a checkered career, of Elizabeth's last favorite, the Earl of Essex, supported by the Earl of Southampton; plan to elicit public support for a move against the monarch by a performance of* Richard the Second; *arrest, trial, and condemnation to death of the two earls and their allies; commutation of Southampton's sentence to imprisonment. — The Queen's tormented indecision over Essex's fate; his death; her receipt of the news at the virginals and Oxford's historical bitter pun aimed at Raleigh for his part in Essex's destruction. — Oxford's effort, again vain, to obtain forfeited estates promised him by the Queen. — Elizabeth's death, hastened by anguish over Essex. — Chettle's reproach of Shakespeare for not joining in the elegiac chorus of poets. — Oxford's grief and feeling that his loss is greatest of anyone's. — His inability to go meet the approaching new King owing to his "infirmity." — James's favor shown in the renewal of his £1,000 annual grant and the return of ancestral holdings. — Sonnet 107 as describing the happy events of the time, including James's immediate release of Southampton, but anticipating the poet's death. — Oxford's farewell in* The Tempest *(with a last fling at Shakspere) and in Hamlet's dying speech. — His death and interment in Hackney Church; performance of seven Shakespearean plays at Court. — Subsequent death of his wife and her burial beside him. — Later report that he "lieth at Westminster." — Final tributes. — A valedictory across the years.*

The year 1598 was to bring two landmark events in Elizabeth's reign.

One was the death of Lord Burghley at seventy-eight. His last major effort was to achieve peace with Spain, in which he was opposed by the Earl of Essex, who stood firm for the defense of Protestantism and in his mistrust of the Spanish. Burghley did not live to win his peace, which, indeed, would have to wait upon the death of Elizabeth. In July he was failing rapidly. On

744

the 10th he wrote his son Robert the last letter he would manage in his own hand, in which he said of the Queen that, "though she would not be a mother, yet she showed herself by feeding me, with her own princely hand, as a careful nurse." He closed the letter with a postscript: "Serve God by serving the Queen, for all other service is indeed bondage to the devil." As the end drew near he lamented "Oh, what a heart I have that will not die." But die it did on August 4th. According to Arthur Collins he left an enormous estate: £11,000 in money and £15,000 in plate and jewelry, with lands worth £4,000 a year. Of these, Francis Peck lists 298 separate properties. Most of the estate was willed to his son Robert and his grand-daughters, Bridget and Susan, who became Robert's wards. Already Principal Minister, Robert, future Earl of Salisbury, would become Lord Treasurer in 1608.

A month after Burghley died a kind of death was visited upon Oxford. On 7th September 1598, Francis Meres's *Palladis Tamia: Wits Treasury,* was entered in the Stationers' Register. With its eulogy of "Shakespeare" as a poet and as a playwright supreme, it was clearly designed to fix upon that mysterious "Shakespeare" the authorship of the dramas heretofore anonymous. Although even by orthodox reckoning fifteen or sixteen of these had already been produced, of which Meres goes out of his way to list twelve, and though Shakspere had been in London for ten years, we are assured, the reader will recall that the record fails to show that the name Shakespeare had ever been heard as that of a playwright. The inference must be — and I am still repeating — that the Queen, Burghley, and his son Robert had decided that to prevent the pseudonym "William Shakespeare" from being exposed as such there would have to be an actual person to go with it, officially, and though others of similar name were probably available, picked William Shakspere. He had the advantage of having lived in London, as the dramatist must have, of writing only with difficulty, which would prevent his leaving attestations of third-rate literary skill behind him, and of being readily transportable back to an out-of-the-way village to protect the fiction. The tradition, we recall, as reported by Nicholas Rowe a century later, was that Southampton gave him £1,000; that was a lot of money, but it probably took a lot to ensure his return to that dreary community and to his wife and children. As for what connection there may have been between Oxford and Shakspere either in Warwickshire or London the record is mute. Such a connection there evidently was between their antecedents, on Oxford's side through his grandmother, Elizabeth Trussell (from whom Bilton came to him) — even a blood relationship, it has been asserted. Speaking of Shakspere's grandfather and great-grandfather in a Warwickshire history, Mary Dorner Harris writes, "When in 1501, the Ardens, father and son, chose to associate themselves with a Thomas Trussel for assuring the descent of certain property, they were choosing, as trustee, not necessarily a relation but a just neighbor of respected character and established position." In any case, as we shall see, the plays indicate that the Earl knew of the Shakspere family in Stratford, and I should certainly suppose that he became acquainted with William in London.

A more compelling question to me is what Oxford's feelings were about the sentence passed upon him of divorcement from his life's work. Even if his better judgment called for protection of the de Vere name, for the sake of his heirs, from a taint of association with the authorship of plays for the public theatre, the denial of recognition could well, I should think, have reduced him to such despair as Lear voices when he cries out to the elements, "let fall / Your horrible pleasure," and at the end, "Never, never, never, never, never."

It is almost unbearable to suppose that the dramatist went to his grave believing that the marvellous creations into which he had poured his life and soul would forever be held the artifices of the kind of man Shakspere was. Perhaps because the enormity is so unthinkable I venture to doubt that Oxford did believe it, that he credited posterity with so little sense that it would allow such sleazy wool to be pulled over its eyes. One poet, at least, I judge, willed that it not be so. It was in 1598, the very year of Meres's *Palladis Tamia,* that John Marston (Chapter 19) addressed him "whose silent name / One letter bounds" — surely *Edward de VerE* — and who was "most, most of me beloved," foreseeing that "thy unvalu'd worth / Shall mount fair place when Apes are turnèd forth."

Ben Jonson himself may have supplied us with a tip-off. In *Every Man Out of His Humour* (III i 2022–2028), the knight Puntarvolo (conjectured to represent Oxford) elicits from the character Sogliardo, recognizably Shakspere (Chapter 3) the information that his new-bought coat-of-arms has for its crest "your boar without a head rampant," to which a third character adds, "ramping to gentility." Needless to add, the de Vere crest was a boar.

Oxford must have felt that his hand in the plays was betrayed in instance after instance, but in addition he salted them with references to the role the Stratford man played in the charade. I am not sure whether he wished to or simply could not help himself. In any case, the end served was that the Ape would be turnèd forth, for all who could read. He was boldest in *The Taming of the Shrew.*

In the Induction, or preamble, to the play, a skit of two scenes having nothing to do with the play itself, an unnamed lord and his hunting party discover a beggar asleep on the road. The lord, disgusted by the "loathsome" spectacle, proposes as an experiment to have him

> . . . convey'd to bed,
> Wrapped in sweet clothes, rings put upon his fingers,
> A most delicious banquet by his bed,
> And brave attendants near him when he wakes,

and in all ways to treat him as if he were the lord himself: "Would not the beggar then forget himself?"

The beggar, who says he is Christopher Sly, describes himself as "old Sly's son, of Burton-heath" and says "Ask Marian Hacket, the fat ale-wife of Wincot, if she know me not." Barton-in-the-Heath was where Shakspere's uncle and aunt, the Lamberts, lived, and Shakspere's mother was Mary Arden of Wilmcote, probably pronounced much like Wincot. If these details are not supplied to identify Christopher Sly (the sly fellow who bore the Lord?) with Shakspere, why are we given them? The oaf declares that "the Slys . . . came in with Richard Conqueror" — probably a cut at the pretension of the Shaksperes to gentility through the Ardens — and says that among other things he is "by education a card-maker," as young Will probably was, being taught to make cards used in combing wool by dealers like his father. It sounds as if Oxford were quite well acquainted with the Shaksperes of Stratford, less than 20 miles down the Avon from Bilton, three from Billesley. . . . Answering the question the lord had raised, Sly does of course forget himself and imagines himself the lord. Certainly we are not to suppose that Shakspere imagined himself the dramatist, but it is quite possible that during the 1590s, when it was whispered that the author of the works of genius appearing on the London boards was the William Shakespeare of the dedications of *Venus and Adonis* and *Lucrece,* the Stratfordian was not above allowing the ignorant and credulous to believe him the man. If he was the subject of Ben Jonson's *On Poor Poet-Ape* (see page 193) he traded on the name (he "would be thought our chief") in his business, which was play-brokerage and robbery of others' wares. The cream of the jest is that *The Taming of the Shrew* proper is presented for the entertainment of Christopher Sly as the lord, who is found nodding by the end of the first scene. Roused by his "wife," he exclaims "'Tis a very excellent piece of work, madam lady. Would 'twere done!" I shall readily abandon this interpretation of the Induction if someone will account more reasonably for its features.

Two Williams are brought briefly and quite strikingly into the Shakespearean plays, by the hair of their heads in a manner of speaking, for neither has any connection with the plot.

In Act V, Scene I of *Henry the Fourth, Part Two,* Davy says to his master, Justice Shallow, "I beseech you, sir, to countenance William Visor of Woncot. . . ." Shallow replies, "There is many complaints, Davy, against that Visor. That Visor is an arrant knave, on my knowledge"; but on Davy's stipulation that "The knave is mine honest friend," agrees that "he shall have no wrong." "Woncot" takes us back to Wincot and Wilmcote; and although I do not wish to make a mountain out of a molehill to support my case, I cannot imagine what the meaning of the gratuitous exchange is unless it concerns William of Stratford as a vizor. For the purpose of the colloquy

Davy may be conceived of, I rather imagine, as Robert Cecil asking his father, Lord Burghley, whose understudy he was, to accept Shakspere — an arrant knave but one who could be trusted — as Oxford's mask.

The other William is a country fellow in *As You Like It*. He exists only as Touchstone's butt near the end of the play. Touchstone, the ex-courtier, says, as Oxford might have said at Bilton, that he is in the Forest of Arden with "goats, as the most capricious poet, honest Ovid, was among the Goths." He then reveals he is more particularly in Oxford's shoes by declaring apropos of nothing, as we remember, "When a man's verses cannot be understood, nor a man's good wit seconded with the forward child under-standing, it strikes a man more dead than a great reckoning in a little room": when a man's works are not understood to be his he is struck as dead as the murdered Marlowe was. When William appears, Touchstone quickly draws out of him that he has "a pretty wit" but is "not learned," just as the Reverend Dr. Ward heard at Stratford that "Shakespeare" was "a natural wit, without any art at all"). Then, again out of a clear sky, Touchstone declares that "drink, being pour'd out of a cup into a glass, by filling the one doth empty the other; for all your writers do consent that *ipse* is he. Now, you are not *ipse*, for I am he." The remark makes absolutely no sense in reference to the William in the play, whose reaction must have been, "What the devil does he mean, filling a glass, and *ipse*, and all my writers?" It makes no sense in reference to anything else in the play. To the dramatist, it must have been important for him to have departed from the story to insert it. It will be important to us if we recognize what he evidently is talking about. *Ipse* is, and was then, familiar in the phrase *ipse dixit,* which the O.U.D. translates as "he himself (the master) has said it." The remark, I take it, has Touchstone / Oxford saying to William (Shakspere) "Now you are not the master, for I am he." This, it would seem, is the proposition to which — whatever the public in general may think — the writers of the time all consent. The metaphor of the drink would be in keeping with this hy-pothesis: as Shakspere is filled with credit for the plays, Oxford is emptied of it. This interpretation, I recognize, sounds far-fetched. Schoenbaum has treated it (for I am not its originator) with particular scorn. I am left to rely upon it, however, by his having ignored the inviting opportunity to explain what the dramatist *really* meant by the scene and why Shakespeare — the professor's Shakespeare — should have given his name, William, to the unlearned country wit who is brought in only to be condescendingly sent packing. My impression is that writers do not give characters their own name unless the circumstances are exceptional. Although there are no Edwards in Shakespeare apart from historical personages, three non-historical Williams figure in the plays, each briefly and with no connection to the story, and each as a subordinate. A fourth, incidentally, is mentioned just before the discussion of William Visor, a William Cook, to permit Davy to ask of Justice Shallow if he means "to stop any of William's wages about the sack he lost the other day at Hinkley Fair." Hinkley is only two or three miles from Warwickshire, while the lost sack recalls the indication of the original Stratford monument that Shakspere was a dealer in sacked goods.

Having inserted in the plays not just a word to the wise but a number of such words — unless I am imagining things — Oxford would have had reason to expect the plays to be openly recognized as his when the danger of their being so had passed — or, rather, when those endangered would have departed this life. Yet the pointers were not so flagrant as to prevent his telling himself, contrariwise, that, faithful to his dearest canon ("The purest treasure mortal times afford / Is spotless reputation. . . . / Mine honour is my life."), he was preserving the de Vere name from the dishonor of open acknowledgement of his connection with the stage. That, anyhow, is the rationalization I impute to him, perhaps quite wrongly. I should like to think, at least, that, having it both ways, he enjoyed some peace of mind on the score of the authorship, as there is some excuse for believing he did in other departments of life.

To show that he inspired more family warmth than would ever be guessed from the documents allowed to survive, there is a letter written to him in French on 3rd March 1599 by his sister Lady Mary Willoughby's son, Robert Bertie, expressing deep affection and respect. The seventeen-year-old, traveling on the Continent, speaks of the eternal service he has vowed "to you and all your house" and of his readiness "to receive your commands with such devotion that I shall all my life be your very humble servant and nephew." Most interestingly he says that he has not written earlier because he had not found a "*subject assez digne de vous divertir de vos plus serieux affaires.*" If only he could have said just a few words more about those "most serious affairs"!

Did Oxford, at this time, also enjoy a warm relationship with his son by Anne Vavasor, Edward Vere? The boy, C. W. Barrell discovered, had been sent to the University of Leyden and thence had taken service under his first cousins once removed, Francis and Horatio Vere, in their campaigning in the Low Countries; by 1600, at age nineteen, he had become a captain and by 1607 would be knighted. The only possible clue to his relations with his father is offered by a letter he wrote on the 14th August 1603 from the camp at Heoghstraet dealing in detail with military matters. The letter is today in the Sidney papers classified "Sir Edward Vere to Sir William Browne." It begins, however, "Kind Father" and is signed "Yours most affectionately." Why he should address Browne as Father or whether the letter was addressed to his actual father and became misplaced and misconstrued are questions at present impossible to answer. So too is the further question of whether, if the letter *was* meant for Sir William, the remark at its end, "You write nothing of our Lord, of which we would gladly hear something," is an inquiry about the young man's actual father. This it could well be, for the "our" and "we" would associate his relatives, the two Vere brothers, with the unnamed Lord and attribute to them an interest in having news of him, which would be natural.

That the Oxfords in 1599 were visiting and being visited in turn by the Derbys would seem to argue a degree of domestic felicity on their part. The two Earls must have enjoyed each other's company. Derby's proficiency in music is attested by his "Pavin, made for the Opharion," published in a book of madrigals and pastorals in 1624 and Oxford's by the dedication to him of the organist John Farmer's second book, *The First Set of English Madrigals,* published in 1599. In this the composer declares that "it cometh not within the compass of my power to express all the duty I owe, nor to pay the least part. . . . I have presumed to tender these Madrigals only as remembrances of my service and witness of your Lordship's liberal hand, by which I have so long lived, and from your honourable mind that so much have all liberal sciences." Appealing for the protection that "your greatness" could give and that "your judgment in music . . . may," Farmer adds that "For without flattery be it spoke, those that know your Lordship know this, that using this science as a recreation, your Lordship have overgone most of them that make it a profession." *The Earl of Oxford's March* and *The Earl of Oxford's Galliard,* the latter now lost, may or may not be of Oxford's composition.

Music was an avocation the two Earls shared. The theatre was more. It was at about this time the Jesuit George Fanner reported in an intercepted letter to his superiors that "The Earl of Derby is busied only in penning comedies for the common players." Sir E. K. Chambers suggests that the comedies were being performed by Derby's own players. How much these meant to him comes out in an undated letter quoted by Chambers in which his wife entreats her uncle, Robert Cecil, that the company

> may not be barred from their accustomed playing, in maintenance whereof they have consumed the better part of their substance. If so vain a matter shall not seem troublesome to you, I could desire that your furtherance might be a mean to uphold them; for that my Lord taking delight in them, it will keep him from more prodigal courses.

None knew better than Oxford's eldest daughter just where "prodigal courses" in connection with the theatre could lead. One can imagine her wailing, "Not my husband, too!"

At the same time her father once again probably had his own servants. Muriel C. Bradbrook writes: "The boys' private theatres were reopened and by 1602 the Earl of Oxford had persuaded the Queen to tolerate a third men's troupe, his own men combined with Worcester's. The Council therefore assigned them to the Boar's Head to prevent their 'changing their place at their own discretion.'" — the Council having found that "the Boar's Head is the place they have especially used and do best like of." As Gwynneth Bowen observes, the London companies had been officially limited to two, the Chamberlain's and the Admiral's, but toleration was granted to a third by September 1599, which she believes was the company allowed "at the suit of the Earl of Oxford" and that "if so we have succeeded in tracing the company back almost to the year 1596."[1]

The expenses went on. There were those of the theatre, whether "prodigal courses" or not, and his "Lordship's liberal hand," by which many "have so long lived." In June 1600 we find Oxford entreating his brother-in-law's help in obtaining for him the Governorship of the Isle of Jersey, which presumably he could have exercised from London. The letter makes, withal, sad reading:

> Although my bad success in former suits to Her Majesty have given me cause to bury my hopes in the deep abyss and bottom of despair ["in the deep bosom of the ocean buried," as Richard of Gloucester says], rather than now to attempt, after so many trials made in vain and so many opportunities escaped, the effect of fair words or fruits of golden promises ["I can . . . fill his aged ears / With golden promises," Tamora boasts of Titus]; yet for that I cannot believe but that there hath been always a true correspondence of word and intention in Her Majesty, so I do conjecture that with a little help that which of itself hath brought forth so fair blossoms will also yield fruit.

He believes his brother-in-law can supply that little help, "for I know Her Majesty doth give you good ear."

But the office he sought is given to Sir Walter Raleigh. In January 1601 he tries his luck at another, the Presidency of Wales, though certainly he had no more intention of living in Wales than in Jersey. In appealing again for Robert Cecil's help, he asks, in a sentence that says much, that Her Majesty have

> regard of my youth, time, and fortune spent in her Court, and her favours and promises which drew me on without any mistrust the more to presume in mine own expenses. . . .

If Oxford had not, in fact, exhausted his resources in the Queen's behalf it is highly unlikely he would have said so to Robert Cecil. In March he evidently received a favorable "message" in response to his appeal, for he writes of it that

> What for the old love I have borne you — which I assure you was very great — what for the alliance which is between us, which is tied so fast by my children

---

[1] Several inns had names like Boar's Head, but the site of the one we are interested in, according to C. J. Sisson's exhaustive study, "is commemorated in the street-name Boar's Head yard, leading off Whitechapel Street on its north side between Middlesex Street (Petticoat Lane) and Goulston Street."

Sir Robert Cecil   Courtesy of Virginia State Library.

From *Thane's British Autography* by John
Thane.

of your own sister; what for my own disposition to yourself, which hath been
rooted by long and many familiarities of a more youthful time, there could have
been nothing so dearly welcome unto me. . . . I do assure you that you shall
have no faster friend or well-wisher to you than myself. . . .

Ill-wishers seem still, however, to be seeking to divide Cecil from Vere:

I protest you shall do me wrong and yourself greater, if either through fables,
which are mischievous, or conceit, which is dangerous, you think otherwise of
me than humanity or consanguinity require.

Since he "cannot so well urge mine own business to her Majesty," he hopes
his brother-in-law will think of his suit "when these troublesome times give
opportunity."

"Troublesome" is not overstating the condition of the times. Between
Oxford's two letters, on the 7th February, Robert Devereux, 2nd Earl of
Essex, led what he expected would be an uprising in the streets of London.

Essex, whose widowed mother, Lettice Knollys, had married Leicester
(rumored to have made her a widow with his poison phial) was a courageous,
chivalrous, magnetic, and very impulsive man, pulled in opposing directions
by his craving for foreign adventure and exploit and his opportunities at
Court. He was the last of those courtiers whose charm, manner, vitality, and
grace of person captivated the Queen. Elizabeth even forgave him — in time

— his secret marriage to Sir Philip Sidney's widow, which had sent her into an unbridled fury. Essex took a valiant if not always brilliant part in naval and military campaigns. The most successful, in which he had partial command, was an expedition in 1596 in which the Spanish fleet was defeated, Cadiz pillaged, and fifty-three merchant vessels destroyed. The next, in which he shared command with Sir Walter Raleigh, nearly having him court-martialed before the end, was against the Azores in 1597 and failed in the objective of capturing the treasure fleet. The Earl of Southampton, ominously for him, had found Essex a kindred spirit since youth and had taken part in both forays, distinguishing himself in the latter; his absences are one reason for believing that Oxford found his relations with his young idol more manageable after 1595. Back from the Azores, both Southampton and Essex came to a crisis with the Queen. The former hastily married Elizabeth Vernon, whom he had got with child, and the Queen in her anger threw them both in the Fleet prison. Essex, in a painful interview in which an important office was denied him by Elizabeth and some taunting words cast at him, responded in a way that was utterly unimaginable. He turned his back upon the Queen in a manner expressive of contempt. Elizabeth fetched him a blow on the side of the head as she once had his mother, and at that the Earl capped his previous insubordination by clapping his hand to the hilt of his sword, which evidently he would have drawn had he not been prevented, then strode off swearing he would not have taken such an insult even from Henry VIII — who, of course, would have had his head before nightfall.

Essex was thirty-three years younger than Elizabeth, and their relations remind one to some extent of those of an attractive, spoiled, wilful, but promising son and his doting, indulgent mother whose love for him was unstinting, within the limits of the possible for a Queen whose people held first place in her heart. Even after his unthinkable display of temper before the Queen's Majesty, Essex was made Governor General of Ireland in 1599 with a force under his command (almost the equal of that assembled at Tilbury) to put down the Earl of Tyrone. In this he failed after frittering away his army and squandering an immense treasure. Coming to a truce with the rebellious lord in disobedience of orders, he quit his post to return hell-for-leather at the head of an armed detachment. His object was to put his case before the Queen, into whose bed-chamber he burst even as a cosmetic paste was being applied to the poor sixty-seven-year-old face by the women in waiting. He had the audience he sought later and his chance to justify himself to his sovereign whose mind, he had declared, had been poisoned against him by his enemies; and surely if it had not been it was not for want of their trying. The Earl was, however, referred to the Council, and there he was stripped of his honors. He fell ill. Prayers were offered for him in all the churches, and execrations of Robert Cecil, who was blamed for his fall, were scrawled on walls, even those of Whitehall. He recovered but his hope of recouping his position was dashed by withdrawal of his trading monopoly. Outraged and despairing, he resolved to arouse the populace in his cause, then to "surprise the Court and the Queen's person" and put his foes on trial for their lives. Southampton, who had been with him in the Irish campaign, stood by him, as did a number of other men of rank, the young Earl explaining that he did so simply out of love for Essex and with no thought that any harm should come to the Queen.

Southampton assisted in arranging for the Lord Chamberlain's men to enact the "old play" *Richard the Second* on the eve of the insurrection "in the hope that the play-scene of the deposition of a king might excite the citizens of London to countenance their rebellious design," Sir Sidney Lee says, commenting: "It seems that the fascination that the drama had for Southampton and his friends led them to exaggerate the influence it was capable of exerting on the emotions of the multitude." The performance, however, seems not to have been given. (Nevertheless the scheme to bring it about would play an important part in the trial of the plotters, though as the reader may recall, the name of its author resounded through the proceedings by never being mentioned.) The next day Essex marched through London at the head of 300 swordsmen, calling out that Lord Cobham and Sir Walter Raleigh would have murdered him and shouting "For the Queen! A plot is laid for my life!" But the populace, instead of rallying to his cause, had "scarcely any other feelings," it is said, "than mild perplexity and wonder." The Earl and his followers were forced to retreat to Essex house. There, after a brief defense, they surrendered and were arrested, Southampton appealing to the Queen to "blame them that are the most blameworthy, those atheists and caterpillars, I mean, that laid plots to bereave us of our lives."

Oxford was compelled to serve at the trial as the senior nobleman of the twenty-five who made up the tribunal — and if the trial of Mary Queen of Scots was an ordeal for him, this one must have been an agony. The case for the Crown was marked by the excessive and unnecessary bitterness with which Francis Bacon attacked the Earl of Essex, who had been his benefactor and closest friend. The verdict was inevitable: guilty of treason. Essex and Southampton were condemned to death. It may be imagined with what pleas Oxford joined those of the two Countesses of Southampton. The younger Earl's sentence was commuted to imprisonment for life, credit being given to Robert Cecil for the mercy shown him. With respect to Essex, the Queen went through the same vacillations that had followed the sentencing of Norfolk and Mary of Scots, but these were more abbreviated.

The sentence was carried out upon the Earl on February 25th. The Queen was in the Privy Chamber playing the virginals when the news was brought to her. With what must have been extraordinary self-command she continued to play. Oxford, who rather unexpectedly was among the listeners, observed in a bitter pun destined to enter history, "When Jacks start up, heads go down." "Jack" was a term both for "a man of the common people" (*O.U.D.*), as in "When every Jack became a gentleman" (*Richard the Third*), and for the mechanism in the virginals that leaps up to pluck the string when the key is struck.[2] Oxford may not have known of a vicious letter Raleigh had written Robert Cecil a year earlier subtly but unmistakably advising him that Essex be done away with, as other noblemen had been (whom he named), so that he might not "be able to harm you and yours." But he had doubtless read Raleigh's heart well enough.

B. M. Ward comments that Oxford attended the sessions of the House of Lords only intermittently, but the only one he forewent entirely was the ninth under Elizabeth of 1601. To this he appointed his friend Admiral Lord Charles Howard of Effingham to sit in his place and exercise his proxy. Maybe he had lost heart for such things. We do know that on November 22nd he was asking Robert Cecil to excuse him for not having answered his letter since "by reason of my sickness I have not been able to write."

The correspondence arose from the Queen's undertaking to grant Oxford the large estate of Sir Charles Danvers, who had gone to the block for his complicity in the Essex plot. On October 7th the Earl had written to Cecil from Hackney of being advised how something might be accomplished "if a warrant may be procured to my cousin Bacon" — his only known reference to Sir Francis.

In the reply to Cecil delayed by his sickness he says

> For the rest of your letter, although it be some discouragement to me, yet I cannot alter the opinion I have conceived of your constancy.

But the strain on his faith in his brother-in-law grows. On December 4th he writes:

> I cannot conceive in so short a time in so small an absence how so great a change is happened to you. For in the beginning of my suit to her Majesty I was doubtful to enter thereunto both for the want I had of friends and the doubt I

---

[2] In Sonnet 128, employing the imagery of the virginals throughout, the poet exlaims

How oft, when thou, my music, music play'st,

    . . . .

Do I envy those jacks that nimble leap
To kiss the tender inward of thy hand.

Of this, the *O.U.D.* says under "Jack" that Shakespeare applied the term "erroneously to the key." It is the *O.U.D.* and others that have ventured this criticism that are in error. The keys of the virginals do not "nimble leap." To use the metaphor at all, the poet had to speak of the jacks nimbly leaping, and the poetic license is minor — if any, for he does not say the jacks *do* "kiss the tender inward of thy hand." Later in the sonnet he *does* refer to the keys when he speaks of

    . . . those dancing chips
O'er whom thy fingers walk with gentle gait.

Henry de Vere, the 18th Earl of Oxford

In a portrait by an unknown artist.

By permission of the National Portrait Gallery, London.

had of the Careys [the Queen's cousins, Robert and George, Lord Hunsdon]. But I was encouraged by you, who did not only assure me to be an assured friend unto me, but further did undertake to move it to her; which you so well performed that her Majesty was contented.

But "the other party" had received greater favor so

that what might have been done in one month is now almost a year deferred. . . . What good words you gave me and what assurance of your constancy to me, if you have forgotten, it is vain for me to remember.

However,

I have written to her Majesty, and received a most gracious answer to do me good in all that she can, and that she will speak with you about it. Now therefore, it is in your power alone, *I know it,* that if you will deal for me, as I have cause to believe, that it may have an end according to my expectation.

In the next month, January 1602, he writes to Cecil of the "many inventions of delay" the matter has received, having "been heard before all the Judges both unlawful and lawful" whose report will be put off

whereby all my hopes will end in smoke. . . . Now, in this conjuncture, I find myself destitute of friends, having relied on her Majesty. Another confidence I had in yourself, in whom, without offence let me speak it, I am to cast some doubt.

756

By March 2nd, as he writes, "It is now a year since her Majesty granted her interest in Danvers escheat." He has "twice moved her Majesty" to grant him a deed, "whereof there are hundreds of examples," so that "I may upon ground seek and try her Majesty's right." After this he evidently gave up in discouragement. His brother-in-law had plainly declined to help. His hopes, as he had feared on the basis of so much past experience, had proved to "end in smoke."

It is gratifying to find the Countess of Oxford, later in the year, shouldering the burden of one of her husband's affairs, as it is hardly imaginable that his girl-wife Anne would have done. She writes on his behalf to a judge of the High Court for help in recovering the lease or obtaining the rent from "an insolent tenant, that for the space of many years hath neither paid any rent nor will show his lease for my Lord's satisfaction." She must have felt it was high time to do something.

It is difficult to know what Oxford's relations were with the Queen, or what the reasons were if there was an estrangement over the years. Damage caused by the Anne Vavasor affair may have been irreparable, and discord over Southampton may have entered into it, especially after his sentencing. If either brought to the other in their last years the consolation of an intimacy originating thirty years back there is no evidence of it; and by late 1601 Oxford's health may have prevented his attendance at Court. Elizabeth, there is little doubt, was desperately lonely. Sussex, Leicester, and Burghley had known her since girlhood, and in the mirror of their eyes she had been able to see herself as still young. One by one they had died. And now she had killed the man who for a decade had been closest to her heart.

"O, you must wear your rue with a difference," says the unbalanced Ophelia in the Queen's presence; and it has been said that an Elizabethan audience, always on the look-out for word-play in an odd sentence like that would quickly have converted "rue with a difference" to *divers-rue,* or Devereux — Robert Devereux, Earl of Essex. It may be. Ophelia sings:

> For bonny sweet Robin is all my joy.

The *Hamlet* we know was printed in 1604 (with "*Head-title,* under ornament with royal arms," Sir E. K. Chambers says, without undertaking to explain this extraordinary circumstance).

Essex proved fatal to Elizabeth as she to him. Of her final illness, Bohun wrote: "Yet after all, her mind was more afflicted than her body; she was night and day troubled with a sorrowful remembrance of the late executed Earl of Essex." And Lucy Aikin: "The prevalent opinion, even at the time, appears to have been, that the grief or compunction for the death of Essex, with which she had long maintained a secret struggle, broke forth in the end superior to control. . . . She lost the power of speech." When questioned as to her successor — a subject heretofore treasonable to raise — she replied

Letter from the Earl of Oxford to
Sir Robert Cecil,

in which the writer refers to "my cosen
Bacon."

By permission of the Marquess of Salisbury.
Photograph by Basil D. King, St. Albans.

758

by a gesture interpeted as her acquiescence in James VI of Scotland. She died on the 24th March 1603.

The poets, with a conspicuous exception. sang her praises and her dirge. The mischief-making Henry Chettle, forger of *Greenes Groatsworth,* took "Shakespeare" to task for his silence:

> Nor doth the silver-tongued Melicert
> Drop from his honeyed muse one sable tear,
> To mourn her death that graced his desert
> And to his lays opened her royal ear.
> Shepherd, remember our Elizabeth,
> And sing her Rape, done by that Tarquin, Death.

But, as Chettle probably well knew, the man who was Shakespeare was not going to write a eulogy of the Queen for attribution to that man who was now officially Shakespeare, that William Visor, the arrant, if honest, knave, otherwise Christopher Sly, otherwise Ben Jonson's impudent, unlettered country fellow Sogliardo. After all these years since he had last been represented as a poet himself, Oxford was not going to write a eulogy, and one of Shakespearean quality, for his own signature. After the sentences meted out to Essex and Southampton, moreover, he may not have been in a mood to extol Elizabeth publicly. Why Shakspere would not have done so, being as prominent and as familiar with the Court as orthodoxy says, his backers do not tell us.

Shakspere's silence is not all of significance that Chettle brings out. He reveals to us that the Queen was an audience for Shakespeare's lyrics and "graced his desert." There is no report of her having recognized any deserts of Shakspere's, for all the combing of the record, but Oxford-Shakespeare's she surely graced handsomely with that generous annuity.

Oxford's feelings upon Elizabeth's death are expressed some weeks later in a letter to Cecil.

> I cannot but find great grief in myself to remember the Mistress which we have lost, under whom both you and myself from our greenest years have been in a manner brought up; and although it hath pleased God after an earthly kingdom to take her up into a more permanent and heavenly state, wherein I do not doubt but she is crowned with glory; and to give us a Prince wise, learned, and enriched with all virtues, yet the long time which we spent in her service, we cannot look for so much left of our days as to bestow upon another, neither the long acquaintance and kind familiarities wherewith she did use us, we are not ever to expect from another Prince as denied by the infirmity of age and common course of reason. In this common shipwreck mine is above all the rest, who least regarded though often comforted of all her followers, she hath left to try my fortune among the alterations of time and chance, either without sail whereby to take advantage of any prosperous gale, or with anchor to ride till the storm be overpast. There is nothing therefore left to my comfort but the excellent virtues and deep wisdom wherewith God hath endured our new Master

and Sovereign Lord, who doth not come amongst us as a stranger but as a
natural Prince, succeeding by right of blood and inheritance, not as a conqueror
but as the true Shepherd of Christ's flock to cherish and comfort them.

The letter is not without its politic aspect, Cecil having been in illicit correspondence with James respecting his succession while Elizabeth was still alive.
But Oxford's hopes of Queen Mary of Scotland's son would prove not
misplaced.

The letter was written just before the new King, James I of England, making
a leisurely Progress from one great house to another on his way southward
from Edinburgh, was about to reach Theobalds, to be received by the late
Queen's Principal Secretary. The occasion of Oxford's writing was the need
for him to know "what course is devised by you of the Council and the rest
of the Lords concerning our duties to the King's Majesty . . . and what order
is resolved on amongst you either for the attending or meeting of His Majesty;
for by reasons of mine infirmity I cannot come amongst you as often as I
wish."

The new royal family's partiality to the stage and the King's respect for
Oxford were matters left not long in doubt. James himself took over the
patronage of the Lord Chamberlain's players, who became the King's Men,
Queen Anne that of the combined company of Oxford's and Worcester's
players, and Prince Henry that of the Admiral's. Oxford had nothing to fear
of "shipwreck." In the first month after his coronation on the 25th July 1603
James renewed the annuity of £1,000 in the same words in which it had
been granted seventeen years earlier. He reappointed Oxford to the Royal
Privy Council. Even before his coronation the King had granted the Earl's
petition for custody of the Forest of Essex and the Keepership of Havering
House. Of these Oxford had submitted that

> Till the 12th of Henry VIII, mine ancestors have possessed the same, almost
> since the time of William Conqueror, and at that time — which was the 12th
> year of Henry VIII — the King took it for term of his life from my grandfather;
> since which time, what by the alterations of Princes and Wardships, I have been
> kept from my rightful possession; yet from time to time both my father and
> myself have, as opportunities fell out, not neglected our claim. Twice in my time
> it had passage by law and judgment was to have been passed on my side;
> whereof Her Majesty the late Queen, being advertised, with assured promises
> and words of a Prince to restore it herself unto me, caused me to let fall the
> suit. But so it was she was not so ready to perform her word, as I was too ready
> to believe it.

It is possible, too, that James had Oxford's comfort partly in mind in
making the freeing of Southampton his first act as King of England. (In
addition he virtually adopted the Earl of Essex's son on his arrival in London,
restoring his title in the next year.) It was the primary inspiration of Sonnet
107, which is worth taking note of again. "The mortal moon hath her eclipse
endur'd": Elizabeth had died; "Cynthia (i.e., the moon)," Sidney Lee says,

"was the Queen's recognized appellation." "And the sad augurs mock their own presage": the prophets of disorders to follow her death have had to eat their words. Moreover, "Incertainties now crown themselves assur'd, / And peace proclaims olives of endless age": James, Gervase Markham put it, came "with a whole forest of olives round about him, for he brought not peace to this kingdom alone" but to all Europe. Most of all, though "Suppos'd as forfeit to a confin'd doom," "with the drops of this most balmy time / My love looks fresh"; as Lee explains, "James came to England in a springtide of rarely rivalled clemency" and "on April 10, 1603," Southampton's "prison gates were opened." Alas, however, "Death to me subscribes." (Lee, in painstakingly analyzing the sonnet, discreetly passes over that crucial piece of information.) But Death cannot triumph over such a poet as he, and he knows it:

> . . . Spite of him, I'll live in this poor rhyme
> While he insults o'er dull and speechless tribes;
>   And thou in this shall find thy monument
>   When tyrants' crests and tombs of brass are spent.

One is glad that in Oxford's last known letter he has occasion to offer his brother-in-law his "simple yet hearty thanks" for his help in the matter of the Forest of Essex and to say

> I do well perceive how your Lordship doth travail for me in this cause of an especial grace and favour, notwithstanding the burden of more importunate and general affairs. . . .

Of his last year there is not a word on the record until almost the end. I suppose he devoted his strength to making final revisions in the plays and to writing his last, *The Tempest.* Bartholomew Gosnold had returned in summer 1602 from his exploratory voyage along the island-coast of Massachusetts, having named Cape Cod and Martha's Vineyard and landed on Cuttyhunk-Nashawena — then a single isle — and called it Elizabeth, the name by which the whole little archipelago is now known. That his reports (added perhaps to May's of Bermuda) provided the dramatist with descriptive material seems likely, and may have provided the idea for the play. Whether Oxford had time to finish *The Tempest* or left a considerable amount for another hand to fill in, very likely Derby's, is debatable.

What the play tells us as it bears upon our story seems, however, not difficult of discernment. That Prospero is the author himself I think there is little dispute. With the magic he commands he is the ruler of the island, a place of haunting illusions, even to the brutish Caliban one of

> Sounds and sweet airs that give delight and hurt not
>   . . . and sometimes voices
> That, if I then had wak'd after long sleep,
> Will make me sleep again.

The island, in other words, is the theatre, in which "strange shapes" may enter "bringing in a banquet, and dance about it," which then "with a quaint device, . . . vanishes." Indeed, to demonstrate his powers, Prospero has a play put on by spirits representing Ceres, Iris, and Juno. The dramatist, exercising his craft through his genius, the ethereal spirit Ariel, holds Caliban, representing in this context the uncouth multitude, captive in the theatre through his enchantments, endeavoring to educate and elevate the monster but in the end failing; such, I think, is at least one of the meanings. Among the party in the storm-tossed vessel brought to a mooring at the island by Ariel is the drunken lout Stephano, and it soon comes to us that he is Christopher Sly making another appearance. This time he is not put in the lord's place, in the lord's garments, to imagine himself master of the lord's estate. He un-

The church at Hackney where the Earl and Countess of Oxford were buried.

Photograph by the author.

dertakes to accomplish this end himself and by dispossessing and killing Prospero to make himself "king o' the isle" with the idolatrous aid of Caliban; a point is made of Stephano's donning attire from Prospero's wardrobe. But he is exposed by Ariel and foiled, and Caliban has his eyes opened, declaring

> what a thrice-double ass
> Was I to take this drunkard for a god
> And worship this dull fool!

Prospero's recovery of his Dukedom, which he had lost to a usurper owing to his having neglected "wordly ends" to make "the liberal arts . . . all my study," perhaps corresponded in Oxford's mind with his having recovered finally his ancient holdings of the Forest of Essex and of Havering, and, beyond that, his wishful anticipation of having possession of his plays and poems restored to him. But above all in *The Tempest,* the dramatist recognizes that the time has come when he must make an end. Prospero foreswears his magic and releases Ariel. In the Epilogue that he delivers the dramatist addresses his audience for the last time.

> Now my charms are all o'erthrown,
> And what strength I have's mine own,
> Which is most faint.
>   . . . .
>   . . . release me from my bands
> With the help of your good hands.
> Gentle breath of yours my sails
> Must fill, or else my project fails,
> Which was to please. Now I want
> Spirits to enforce, art to enchant;
> And my ending is despair
> Unless I be reliev'd by prayer,
> Which pierces so that it assaults
> Mercy itself and frees all faults.
> As you from crimes would pardon'd be,
> Let your indulgence set me free.

In *Hamlet,* on which I suspect he was working almost to the last, Oxford takes another kind of leave of us, more as his human self. Anticipating, correctly, a harsh verdict on his life from the uncomprehending, he turns to his cousin to

> Report me and my cause aright
> To the unsatisfied.

As the report has come down to us of Horatio Vere that "it was true of him what is said of the Caspian Sea, that it doth never ebb nor flow, observing a constant tenor neither elated nor depressed," so Hamlet exclaims to his beloved companion, Horatio:

Horace Vere of Tilbury, Baron

In a portrait attributed to J. J. van
Miereveldt

By permission of the National Portrait
Gallery, London.

> For thou has been
> As one, in suff'ring all, that suffers nothing;
> A man that Fortune's buffets and rewards
> Hast ta'en with equal thanks; and blest are those
> Whose blood and judgment are so well commingled
> That they are not a pipe for Fortune's finger
> To sound what stop she please.

To his fellow who is not passion's slave, whom he wears in his heart's core,
Hamlet-Oxford makes his final plea:

> O good Horatio, what a wounded name
> (Things standing thus unknown) shall live behind me!
> If thou didst ever hold me in thy heart,
> Absent thee from felicity awhile,
> And in this harsh world draw thy breath in pain,
> To tell my story.

Sir Horatio Vere would perhaps feel the obligation was fulfilled as well as it
could be (if my conjecture has a basis in fact) in the immediate publication
of *Hamlet* under the royal coat-of-arms, from the author's manuscript, and
in the later publication of the First Folio containing thirty-six of Shakespeare's

764

plays, which would tell the story for all who would not close their eyes to it.

Just before the end, Oxford arranged for his son-in-law, Francis Lord Norris, and Sir Francis Vere, who had just returned from twenty years' continuous campaigning in the Low Countries, to share custody of the Forest of Essex, and made the latter his son Henry's guardian.

On 24 June 1604 he died, leaving no will, as far as is known. An entry in the old Register of the Church of St. Augustine in Hackney reads: "Edward de Vere, Erle of Oxenford, was buried the 6th day of July, anno 1604." In the margin of the page is the annotation "The plague." Perhaps, already weakened in health, he was one of its victims. No grave marker has ever been found. Visitors to the site today will conceive scant hope that one ever will be. The Tudor church was destroyed in 1798, having fallen into irremediable disrepair, and replaced by a larger near by. Of the old one, however, there remains the imposing tower. In the adjacent park-like churchyard the ancient gravestones, defaced by time, are stacked against a wall half a dozen deep.

When the Countess of Oxford made her will (bequeathing an unspecified sum to be paid quarterly "to my dombe man," we might remind ourselves) on the 25th November 1612, six weeks before her death, she wrote:

> I joyfully commit my body to the earth from whence it was taken, desiring to be buried in the Church of Hackney, within the County of Middlesex, as near unto the body of my said dear and noble Lord and husband as may be, and that to be done as privately and with as little pomp and ceremony as possible may be. Only I will that there be in the said Church erected for us a tomb fitting our degree, and of such charge as shall seem good to mine executors.

A description a century later of "an ancient Table Monument with a fair grey marble" could well have been of the Oxford tomb. On this subject, however, Percy Allen made a striking discovery. In a book by Percival Golding, Arthur Golding's youngest son and Oxford's first cousin, entitled *The Armes, Honours, Matches and Issues of the Ancient and Illustrious family of Veer,* he found on page 51 this paragraph:

> Edward de Veer, only son of John, born the Twelfth day of April A° 1550, Earle of Oxenforde, high Chamberlain, Lord Bolebec, Sandford and Badelesmere, Steward of the Forest in Essex, and of the Privy Council to the King's Majesty that now is: Of whom I will only speak what all men's voices confirm; he was a man in mind and body absolutely accomplished with honourable endowments: he died at his house at Hackney in the month of June Anno 1604 and lieth buried at Westminster.

Golding was certainly in a position to know the facts. There is, however, no mention of the 17th Earl of Oxford in the burial records of the Abbey. When Francis Vere died in 1609 his widow had a magnificent tomb of striking statuary built for him in the north transept of the Abbey. Oxford's son Henry, the 18th Earl, when he died at only age thirty-two from wounds received while fighting under Horatio Vere in the Low Countries, was interred in the tomb, as was Horatio Vere, then Lord Vere of Tilbury, when he died in 1635. Here, Edward de Vere would presumably also have been buried.[3] But the final resting place of the greatest of Elizabethans, who "distinguished himself both as a man of valour and of genius," as a *History of Hackney* of 1842 has it, may never be known and the final word remain his own: "The earth can yield me but a common grave." His epitaph must remain unknown, except as it is written in the tributes of those who spoke of what they knew. He was one who

> from the beginning was ever sacred to the Muses: They unto him, and him unto them, most dear — a fellow peerless in England.

I owe to G. P. V. Akrigg my knowledge of a letter written by James to Robert Cecil late in 1604, Professor Akrigg believes, in which, reporting Lord Sheffield's feeling that the pension of £1,000 he had been offered was insufficient, the King writes:

> . . . as I had already told him, never greater gift of that nature was given in England. Great Oxford when his state was whole ruined got no more of the late Queen.[4]

In his entire life, while he had sat on the Royal Privy Council, to which James had re-appointed him, Oxford had held not a single public office, with the exception, for a matter of days, of the command of the horse in the Netherlands, and had performed not a single overt service for the state apart from his brief participation in the Battle of the Armada. Why, then, "Great Oxford"? On the strength of his family name? I doubt it. Had his whole service to the de Vere name been to bankrupt the de Vere estate, the nobility of the name would have redounded only to his more particular discredit. In his recent study of de Vere's poetry, Steven W. May, though certainly no friend to de Vere, calls him "a nobleman with extraordinary intellectual interests and commitments" and with "a lifelong devotion to learning." He goes on to say that "The range of Oxford's patronage is as remarkable as its substance," as attested by "the thirty-three works dedicated to the Earl." That the King would call him "great" on that account, however, is highly unlikely. "The Second Earl of Essex," Professor May points out, "was a much greater patron." (What sets Oxford apart, he makes clear, is the

---

[3] There has been some thought that an unmarked stone coffin beneath the floor at the foot of the tomb might be his, but the librarian of the Abbey tells me that it long antedates the tomb and could not contain a body of the 17th century unless emptied of earlier contents.

[4] It should be remarked that in 1603, Lord Sheffield had been appointed Lord-lieutenant of Yorkshire and President of the Council of the North, the latter post having paid £1,000 a year even under Elizabeth, though granted that then its responsibilities were greater.

uniquely high proportion of literary works dedicated to him.) My belief of course is that the King had in mind an achievement for which Oxford's greatness should long ago have been proclaimed by his heirs.

I find some substantiation for that belief in the King's having during the Christmas season of 1604–1605 — the first the plague had allowed the royal couple to spend in London — had seven of the Shakespearean plays presented at Court, one of them twice. (In reporting this fact, Ms. Clark raises the question, for which I believe orthodoxy has no answer, of why if he were the poet-dramatist the Stratfordian failed to take any advantage of this extraordinary mark of favor and why, amid the chorus of poets lauding the new King and in 1612 lamenting the untimely death of the immensely popular young Prince of Wales the name conspicuously missing is Shakespeare's.) Incidentally, the Earl of Southampton, within a year of his release from the Tower, entertained Queen Anne of Denmark with a performance by the King's Men at his house on the Strand of the "old" play of *Love's Labour's Lost* in the expectation that its "wit and mirth would please her Majesty exceedingly."

In 1619 Anthony Munday, dedicating all three parts of a new edition of his *Primaleon of Greece* to Henry, 18th Earl of Oxford, spoke of "having served that most noble Earl your father of famous and desertful memory" and later in the dedication of "your honourable father's matchless virtues."

Three years later Henry Peacham published a 250-page work on education as it was in his day and as it should be. In a chapter on Poetry he calls the reign of Elizabeth "a golden age (for such a world of refined wits and excellent spirits it produced whose like are hardly to be hoped for in any succeeding age)," then lists by rank those "who honoured poesie with their pens and practice" as follows:

> Edward Earl of Oxford, the Lord Buckhurst, Henry Lord Paget, our phoenix, the noble Sir Philip Sidney, M. Edward Dyer, M. Edmund Spenser, Master Samuel Daniel, with sundry others whom (together with those admirable wits yet living and so well known) not out of envy, but to avoid tediousness, I overpass.

Inasmuch as it would have been quite unthinkable to deny Shakespeare, the greatest of all, an express place among the poets who had made Elizabeth's a golden age (and orthodoxy's "Shakespeare" in 1622 could not, like Ben Jonson, George Chapman, and Michael Drayton, be excluded as among "those admirable wits yet living"), it can only be that his name was subsumed in another's.

The 18th Earl having died childless, the title passed to his cousin Robert. Of his son, Macaulay wrote, "The noblest subject in England, and indeed, as Englishman loved to say, the noblest subject in Europe, was Aubrey de Vere, twentieth, and last of the old Earls of Oxford," with whose death in

1702 there "closed the longest and most illustrious line of nobles that England has seen." It is in this passage, reciting the distinctions of the de Veres from the battle of Hastings to the fall of the 18th Earl "for the Protestant religion and for the liberties of Europe under the walls of Maestricht" that Macaulay declared that "The seventeenth earl had shone at the court of Elizabeth, and had won for himself an honourable place among the early masters of English poetry." If only Macaulay had known the facts as we have them, what a peroration his would have been!

Having Shakespeare's sad prophecy indelibly in mind, that "I, once gone, to all the world must die," one longs to call across the void to the man he was, "It is not so!" and turn upon him the words he sent ringing down the ages and earned more than anyone else has ever earned such a tribute with a pen:

Not marble nor the gilded monuments
Of princes shall outlive this pow'rful rhyme;
But you shall shine more bright in these contents
Than unswept stone, besmear'd with sluttish time.
When wasteful war shall statues overturn,
And broils root out the work of masonry,
Nor Mars his sword nor war's quick fire shall burn
The living record of your memory.
'Gainst death and all-oblivious enmity
Shall you pace forth; your praise shall still find room
Even in the eyes of all posterity
That wear this world out to the ending doom.

Shine forth, thou star of poets!

END

Chronology Appendix Citations Bibliography Index

Chronology of the Principals in the Case of William Shakespeare

	Related Events	Edward de Vere	"William Shakespeare"	William Shakspere
1550		Apr 22: Born at Castle Hedingham, Essex, of John de Vere, 16th Earl of Oxford, and Margaret Golding.		
1551				His father fined for having a dunghill in front of his house in Stratford-on-Avon, indicating that he has moved there from Snittersfield.
1553	Queen Mary crowned, ...	with his father officiating as Lord Great Chamberlain but subsequently withdrawing for safety to country.		
1554		? His sister Mary born		
1556				His father buys two houses in Henley Street.
1557				His father marries Mary Arden of Wilmcote.
1559	Queen Elizabeth crowned,	with his father officiating, having come out of retirement to escort Elizabeth from Hatfield to London. His mother appointed Maid of Honour.		
	Son of the King of Sweden visits England, ...	with his father attending him.		
		Matriculates at St. John's College, Cambridge.		
1561	The Queen visits Castle Hedingham for four days,	when he would have come to know her.		His father is elected a chamberlain of the borough.
1562		Sep: His father dies, his mother later marrying Charles Tyrrell. As the 17th Earl of Oxford he leaves Hedingham to reside in William Cecil's household in London as a royal ward.		
	Romeus and Juliet published:	of his authorship?		

Chronology of the Principals in the Case of William Shakespeare

	Related Events	Edward de Vere	"William Shakespeare"	William Shakspere
1563		His title challenged by his half-brother-in-law.		
1564	May: *The histories of Trogus Pompeius* by Arthur Golding published,	with dedication to him. Aug: Receives degree from Cambridge University.		Baptized April 26 at Stratford-on-Avon.
1566		Befriends Gabriel Harvey at Cambridge. Receives degree of Master of Arts from Oxford.		Oct: His brother Gilbert baptized.
1567	Arthur Golding's translation of Ovid's *Metamorphoses* published, ...	being largely of his authorship? Admitted to Gray's Inn. Cecil's under-cook dies on the point of his sword in unknown circumstances. Sends Thomas Churchyard to Low Countries on mission to Prince William.		His father acquires prefix of "Mr." in official records.
1568				His father named bailiff.
1569	*Aethiopian Historie* by Thomas Underdowne published, ...	with dedication to him. His mother dies.		Apr: His sister Jean baptized.
	Northern rebellion launched.			
1570	Rebels in the north defeated.	Apr: Enlists under the Earl of Sussex in the campaign in Scotland. Is in correspondence with Dr. Dee.		
1571	William Cecil created Baron Burghley.	Is victor in tournament at Westminster and is reported the leading luminary at Court. Allegedly plans the escape of his cousin the Duke of Norfolk to save his life. Dec: He and Anne Cecil wed.		His father is chief alderman Sep: His sister Ann baptized (and dies in 1579). To collect a debt of £50, his father takes legal action against Richard Quiney, son of an old friend.
1572	Bartholomew Clerke's Latin Translation of *Il Cortegiano* published .... Jan: Duke of Norfolk brought to trial and sentenced to death. Sentence executed in June.	with a preface by him in Latin. Evidently pleads powerfully with Queen for Norfolk's life; her indecision long and agonizing. Aug: Takes leading part in royal entertainment at Warwick Castle.		His father's part in municipal affairs begins to decline.

Chronology of the Principals in the Case of William Shakespeare

	Related Events	Edward de Vere	"William Shakespeare"	William Shakspere
		His position with the Queen schemed against by Christopher Hatton.		
1573	*Calvin's version of the Psalms of David* by Arthur Golding published,	with a dedication to him.		His father is sued for £30 and a warrant issued for his arrest.
		By now possesses two apartments in the Savoy, abode of writers.		
	Breviary of Britain by Thomas Twyne published,	with dedication to him.		
		May: His men accused of holding up travelers on Gravesend–Rochester Road.		
	Translation of *Cardanus Comfort* by Thomas Bedingfield published, ...	under his sponsorship and with a preface by him.		
	A Hundreth Sundrie Flowres published, ...	having been edited and largely written by him?		
	Oct: Henry Wriothesley, future 3rd Earl of Southampton and almost surely young friend of *Sonnets*, born	Original version of *Merry Wives* written during this period, and by him?		
1574	Campaign by the Duke of Alva in the Low Countries in full tide.	Jan: Cited by Ralph Lane as being involved with Spanish agent de Guaras.		Mar: A brother, Richard, baptized.
		Mar: Accompanies Queen on visit to Archbishop of Canterbury.		
		Mid-year: Escapes to the Continent without permission and is brought back.		
		Famous Victories of Henry the Fift written by him at this time?		
1575		Jan: Sets out for travels on the Continent, with authorization.		His father buys two houses in Stratford.
		Mar.–Apr: Is in France, mostly Paris.		
		Apr: Visits Sturmius in Strasbourg.		
		May–Dec: Is in Italy, visiting cities between Venice and Genoa and reported in Palermo, where he issues a challenge to all comers to joust with any weapon for honor of their prince.		
		Mid-Sep: Hears that his wife was delivered of a daughter, Elizabeth, in July.		

773

Chronology of the Principals in the Case of William Shakespeare

	Related Events	Edward de Vere	"William Shakespeare"	William Shakspere
1576	*Flowres* "sanitized" and republished as *The Posies of George Gascoigne.* The Theatre, first playhouse in England, constructed and followed this same year by The Curtain, both in Shoreditch.	Jan–Mar: His whereabouts unknown. Mar–Apr: Is back in France. Apr: Evidently in grip of suspicions that child Elizabeth not his, returns post haste to England (being stripped of possessions by pirates en route), to separate himself from his wife Anne for five years. Apr: Although self-exiled from Court, helps carry Queen's train at ceremony. Seven (?) of his poems published in *The Paradyse of Daintie Devices.* Sells five estates.		His father contributes 12d to the beadle's salary.
1577	Jan: *The historie of Error* performed at Court, ... Feb: *The historye of Titus and Gisippus* performed at Court, ... *The Staffe of Christian Faith* by John Brooke published, ... , John Lyly now living at the Savoy, ...	being an early version of *The Comedy of Errors,* of his authorship? being actually *Titus Andronicus,* of his authorship? May: Invests in Frobisher's voyage. with dedication to him. in quarters provided by him? Original version of *Pericles* written by him about this time? Sells three estates.		His father falls lastingly on hard times and discontinues attending the meetings of the town council. The property inherited by his wife is mortgaged and not subsequently redeemed.
1578	July: Gabriel Harvey in Queen's presence eulogizes the chief figures at Court, . Dec: *Euphues: the Anatomy of Wyt* by John Lyly appears on sale, ... Dec: *An history of the cruelties of A Stepmother* performed at Court, ...	May: Invests heavily in Frobisher's second and larger expedition. singling him out for special praise as prolific poet and one whose "countenance shakes spears." Is considered head of Euphuist faction of poets. with a confession that it had been reared for a year by a nobleman. being an early version of *Cymbeline,* of his authorship? Sells two estates.		

Related Events	Edward de Vere	"William Shakespeare"	William Shakspere
	For "good, true and faithful service," is granted Manor of Rysing by Queen.		
1579 Jan: *The historie of the second Helene* performed at Court, ...	being an early version of *All's Well*, and of his authorship?		His father is unable to pay town levies.
Jan: *A Morrall of the marryage of Mynde and Measure* performed at Court, ...	being an early version of *The Taming of the Shrew,* and of his authorship?		
Jan: *A Maske of Amazones and a Maske of Knights* performed at Court, ...	being an early version of *Love's Labour's Lost,* and of his authorship?		
Mar: *The history of murderous Michael* performed at Court	being an early version of *Arden of Feversham,* and of his authorship? He acts in a play at Court at same time *Murderous Michael* is given.		
July: Lyly's *Euphues and his England* registered . . .	with dedication to him. Lyly is now his secretary.		
The Jew performed, ...	With Spenser-Harvey exchange indicating this an early version of *The Merchant of Venice.* Of his authorship?		
Mirrour of Mutabilitie by Anthony Munday published, ...	with dedication to him promising their becoming "conquerors."		
Shepheardes Calender by Edmund Spenser published, ...	with rhyming match in which he appears as Willie?		
	Sep: Quarrels with Philip Sydney at the tennis-court.		
	Sells five estates.		
1580 Feb: *The history of Portio and demorantes* performed at Court, with "demorantes" very likely an error for "the Merchants"	"A pleasant conceit . . . by de Vere" mentioned: an early version of *Twelfth Night?*		May: Another brother, Edmund, baptized. His father bound over for breach of the peace and fined £20.
	and the play thus the same as *The Jew,* and of his authorship?		His father fails to repay debt of £40 to his brother-in-law and his wife thus loses her property in Wilmcote.
Munday's *Zelauto* published, ...	with dedication to him evidently identifying him as Euphues.		
	Early in year takes over Earl of Warwick's company.		

Chronology of the Principals in the Case of William Shakespeare

Related Events	Edward de Vere	"William Shakespeare"	William Shakspere
Mid-year: Harvey's *Speculum Tuscanismi* published,	in which he is caricatured as an Italianate Englishman, but also highly praised as "peerless in England" and without like as "discourser for tongue."		
Sir Thomas More written probably about now ..... The Duke of Alençon's courtship of Elizabeth in full swing, with most of Protestant England opposed to match.	in handwriting of his secretary, Munday, and almost certainly by author of Shakespeare's plays.		
	Arouses merriment of crowd in Royal Progress to Plymouth.		
	Dec: Denounces his erstwhile Catholic associates, Howard, Arundel and Southwell, as enemies of state and in turn is vilified by first two.		
	Sells thirteen estates.		
1581	Jan: Wins prize in second tournament.		
	Mocks the French on a footcloth nag?		
	Mar: His son born to Anne Vavasor, with whom he is sent to Tower, to be released in June but to remain under house arrest.		
	Oct: Evidently purchases ship *Edward Bonaventure*.		
	Romeo and Juliet begun about now.		
	Henry Sixth, Pt. 3, and *Richard Third* possibly written now.		
	Dec: Resumes living with wife.		
1582	Mar: Wounded in fight with Thomas Knyvet, starting frays in which Knyvet and followers of both take part sporadically for about a year.		Nov 27: License for marriage of "Willelmum Shaxpere" to Anne Whately of Temple Grafton issued.
Thomas Watson's *Hekatompathia* published, ...	with dedication to him and indication he may have contributed to it.		Nov 28: Marriage bond names "William Shagspere" and Anne Hathwey of Stratford.
	His brother-in-law returns from a mission to Elsinore.		
	Love's Labour's Lost probably revised and augmented about now.		
	Sells four estates.		

Chronology of the Principals in the Case of William Shakespeare

	Related Events	Edward de Vere	"William Shakespeare"	William Shakspere
1583	Feb: *A historie of Ariod-ante and Genevora* performed at Court, ...	being the first version of *Much Ado,* of his authorship?		May 26: A daughter, Susanna, baptized.
		May 9: His newly-born son buried.		
		Spring: Acquires sub-lease of Blackfriars Theatre and transfers it to Lyly.		
		His and his wife's relative poverty, with only three servants, reported by Burghley to Queen.		
	Queen's company of players formed, ...	to which one of his actors is transferred.		
		Apparently contributes *Edward Bonaventure* to Fenton's unsuccessful expedition to Spanish Main, for purposes of trade.		
	Dec: *Agamemnon and Ulysses* performed at Court, ...	under his patronage, being first version of *Troilus and Cressida,* of his authorship?		
		'83–'84: His company of actors performs during season at Stratford.		
1584	Towns in the Low Countries falling before the Duke of Parma.	Mar: Sturmius asks that he be sent with an English force to aid Protestants on the Continent.		
	Apr: *Sapho and Phao,* allegorizing the courtship of Elizabeth by Alençon (now well past), performed at Court and later printed, ascribed to Lyly, ..	who probably acts as a front for his employer.		
		Apr: His daughter Bridget born.		
	Spring: *Campaspe,* ascribed to Lyly, performed at Court, ...	by company of which he is the official patron and probably with his having taken part in the writing of the play.		
		Takes over the Earl of Worcester's company about this time.		
	Greene's Card of Fancy, by Robert Greene, published	with dedication to him evidently as to a pre-eminent writer as well as to a "Mæcenas."		
		Acquires Fisher's Folly about this time.		

Chronology of the Principals in the Case of William Shakespeare

	Related Events	Edward de Vere	"William Shakespeare"	William Shakspere
	John Soowthern's *Pandora* published, ...	containing his wife Anne's *Epitaphes*, verse by the Queen and an ode celebrating him.		
	Queen finally agrees to an English expeditionary force to Low Countries to rescue the Protestant cause, with Earl of Leicester in command.	*Henry Fourth, Pt. 1*, perhaps written about this time.		
		Aug 29: Leaves for Continent to take command of English horse.		
		Oct 21: Is by now on way back to England, reason unknown, his ship being again captured by pirates, which Burghley protests to Dutch.		
		Oct 30: Protests Burghley's spying upon him.		
		Nov 17: Wins prize — his third — in tournament on anniversary of Elizabeth's		
	Dec: *The history of Agamemnon and Ulysses* performed at Court	coronation.		
		by his "boys" — again, probably an early version of *Troilus and Cressida* of his authorship.		
		Sells seven estates, acquires two.		
1585	July: "Masquerades and comedies which the Queen orders enacted" reportedly enrage King Philip of Spain.	Becomes a shareholder in Fellowship for Discovery of Northwest Passage.		Feb. 2: His twins, Hamnet and Judeth, baptized.
		Is challenged to a duel by a brother (?) of Anne Vavasor's.		
1586		June 26: Granted an extraordinary annuity of £1000 by Queen with no accounting to be required by Exchequer.		
	The English Secretary by Angel Day published, ...	with dedication to him as one who from "infancy" was "ever sacred to the Muses."		
		Called by William Webbe "most excellent" among Court poets.		
		Hamlet probably written now, *Henry Fifth* probably also about now.		
	Oct: Mary Queen of Scots tried and sentenced to death	by tribunal on which he serves, perhaps pleading for mercy for her in speech given by Portia.		

Chronology of the Principals in the Case of William Shakespeare

	Related Events	Edward de Vere	"William Shakespeare"	William Shakspere
1587	Christopher Marlowe's *Tamburlaine* produced.	May: His daughter Susan born. Thomas Kyd now evidently a member of his household. Marlowe apparently begins writing for his players about now. Sep: His daughter Frances dies, in childhood. Sells two estates, acquires one.	(Note: Dates of works ascribed to "Shakespeare" are those assigned by orthodox scholars, specifically by E. K. Chambers except where otherwise noted.) '87–'90: *Sonnets* written (Hotson, Highet).	His father's entanglement in the affairs of his brother Henry adds to his financial embarrassment. For not coming to town council meetings he is replaced as alderman.
1588	July 19: Spanish Armada sighted off the Lizard. English engage it on 20th. Munday's *Palmerin d'Oliva* published, ... Nov: First of Martin Marprelate's tracts issued; Lyly, Nashe and Greene marshalled to reply to them.	June: His wife Anne dies. July 19: Sets forth in command of his own ship, presumably *Edward Bonaventure,* to battle Armada. July 27: Out of action, is offered and declines governorship of Harwich. with dedication to him, as are at least four others of Munday's "Romances of Chivalry." Nov 24: Plays prominent part in thanksgiving celebration of victory over Armada. Dec: Sells Fisher's Folly, probably also Vere House about this time. Probably revamps *As You Like It* about now.		
1589	Thomas Nashe refers in Epistle to Greene's *Menaphon* to "whole *Hamlets* of tragical speeches."	Is sued by Burghley for balance of marriage fee. indicating he has written first version of *Hamlet.* Lyly called his "minion secretary" by Harvey. Called by George Puttenham first among nobleman-poets who would be seen to have written "excellently well" if their doings could be made public.	*Hamlet* written by summer or autumn (Cairncross). *Love's Labour's Lost* written by now (Hotson, Brandes). *Henry Fourth, Pts. 1* and *2, Henry Fifth, Comedy of Errors, Titus Andronicus* and *Julius Caesar* written by now (Cairncross).	Is named in legal proceedings with his father aimed at recovering his mother's property in Wilmcote, on which his father had failed to lift mortgage.
1590	*Rosalynde* by Thomas Lodge published, ...	having basic story of *As You Like It.* Marriage between his (?) daughter Elizabeth and Southampton promoted by Burghley, unsuccessfully.	*King John* evidently written by now (F. P. Wilson). No proof that *Two Gentlemen of Verona, Comedy of Errors, Taming of Shrew* and *All's Well* not written before now (Knight, Elze).	Nothing known of whereabouts or activities.

779

Chronology of the Principals in the Case of William Shakespeare

	Related Events	Edward de Vere	"William Shakespeare"	William Shakspere
	Publication of Edmund Spenser's *Faerie Queene*, . .	His acting company evidently disbanded. to which he contributed a laudatory poem (?) and in which he is hailed as "most dear" to the Muses, as to the poet.	*Love's Labour's Lost* written by now (Dowden). '90–'91: *Henry Sixth, Pts. 2 and 3* written.	
	Publication of Spenser's *Teares of the Muses*, ...	in which he appears as "our pleasant Willy" (?) who "is dead of late," as is therefore "all joy":		
		Autumn: Authorizes Churchyard to take lodgings at his expense.	poem could clearly apply only to "Shakespeare" . . .	and not possibly to Shakspere.
1591	*Troublesome Raigne of John King of England* published, ...	. . . . Dec: Makes Hedingham over to Burghley in trust for daughters. Later this year or next: Marries Elizabeth Trentham.	Evidently corrupt version of *King John* (Cairncross). *Hamlet* evidently produced in Germany (Cairncross). *Othello, Macbeth* and *King Lear* written by now and *Romeo and Juliet* and *Taming of Shrew* perhaps so (Cairncross).	Nothing known of whereabouts or activities.
	John Farmer's book on *Playn Song* published, . . .	with dedication to him. (Note: From now on he will be largely out of public eye; conjectured that he will be revising plays we know as Shakespeare's and writing others.)	'91–'92: *Henry Sixth Pt. 1* written. '91–'95: *Sonnets* written (Rowse).	
1592	"*harey of Cornwall*" produced by Henslowe:	. . . .	Actually *Henry Fifth*?	Nothing known of whereabouts or activities.
	Lyly's career as a successful playwright at an end. *Arden of Feversham* published, ... Sep 3: Robert Greene dies.	Unsuccessfully seeks a trading monopoly. being a recast of *Murderous Michael* (1579) written by him and turned over to Marlowe to complete?	*Sonnets* written on different occasions from now to 1609 (Kittredge).	
	Sep 20: *Greenes groatsworth of wit* published by, and now known to have been written by, Henry Chettle, ...	Aug: Present at banquet with Nashe and Greene allegedly fatal to latter?		
	Dec 8: Registration of *Kind-Harts Dreame*, wherein Chettle regrets not having "spared" one of playwrights figuring in *Groats-worth*.	. . . .	with parody of a line from *Henry Sixth, Pt. 3* and denigration of a "Shakescene," an actor, ... *Twelfth Night* written (Cairncross). Plays later ascribed to him being performed by Lord Strange's company for Henslowe at the Rose.	(Taken by orthodoxy with Chettle's apology to identify Shakspere as now actor and playwright but on basis of misreading of texts and misapprehension as to identity of author of *Groats-worth*. Nothing associates Shakspere with proceedings.)

Chronology of the Principals in the Case of William Shakespeare

	Related Events	Edward de Vere	"William Shakespeare"	William Shakspere
1593	Jan: Nashe's *Strange News* published, ... May: Christopher Marlowe murdered.	with "Epistle Dedicatorie" to Apis Lapis — almost surely he — who is called a Mæcenas to scholars and a copious poet. First seventeen of series of sonnets addressed to young friend written by February? Feb 24: His son and heir to title, Henry, born.	Apr: *Venus and Adonis* registered and published later in year with dedication to 3rd Earl of Southampton signed "William Shakespeare." '93–'94: *Titus Andronicus* and *Taming of Shrew* written. '93–'96: *Sonnets* written, with additions "more sparsely to '99 or thereabouts."	Nothing known of whereabouts or activities.
1594	Apr: *King Leare* registered and produced two days later by Henslowe: ...... *Hamlet* produced by Henslowe .... June 5: Lord Strange's company, with Burbage and Kempe, has become Lord Chamberlain's men, nominally under 1st Lord Hunsdon. *The Taming of a Shrew* published with author unnamed: .... *A Wynters nightes pastime* registered. .... *Edward Second,* later ascribed to Marlowe, published: .... Henry May, after shipwreck on Bermuda, returns from expedition to India, ... Sep: *Willobie His Avisa* published with author unnamed, ...	Surely his .... Writing of *Sonnets* evidently proceeding apace. Surely his .... As Lord Great Chamberlain with long and close theatrical connections, he is probably in actual charge of Lord Chamberlain's men until death. Surely an early version of *The Taming of the Shrew* and his. Surely *The Winter's Tale*, and his. An early play of his which he had turned over to Marlowe to complete? of which his ship *Edward Bonaventure* a part. in which figure of "W. S." can hardly be other than his	Accepted by some (Cairncross, Alexander) but not most orthodoxists as Shakespeare's. Accepted as Shakespeare's by at least one orthodoxist (Cairncross) but called *Ur-Hamlet* of unknown authorship by others. *Macbeth* written (Alexander). "Books" for his earlier plays acquired by Lord Chamberlain's men, the company for which he is to write from now on. *Henry Sixth, Pt. 2,* and *Titus Andronicus* published, with author unnamed. '94–'95: *Two Gentlemen of Verona, Love's Labour's Lost* and *Romeo and Juliet* written. May: *The Rape of Lucrece* registered and published later in year with intimate dedication to Southampton signed "William Shakespeare." and which contains first known reference to "Shake-speare," as author of *Lucrece*; also with much about "W. S.," making clear he is an intimate of the Queen's and of "H. W.'s," generally recognized as Henry Wriothesley — Southampton.	Nothing known of whereabouts or activities.

781

Chronology of the Principals in the Case of William Shakespeare

	Related Events	Edward de Vere	"William Shakespeare"	William Shakspere
1595		Jan: His (?) daughter Elizabeth married to 6th Earl of Derby. Sep: The French King thanks him for his good offices with Queen Elizabeth. Rate of writing *Sonnets* probably still undiminished, with pace perhaps slackening the next year.	Mar: "Will Shakespeare" is named with Burbage and Kempe as receiving payments for performances before the Queen of preceding December in much later statement by Dowager Countess of Southampton to make up for discrepancy in accounts: . . . . *Henry Sixth, Pt. 3* published, with author unnamed. '95–'96: *Richard Second* and *Midsummer Night's Dream* written.	Nothing known of whereabouts or activities. (Taken by orthodoxy to refer to him and to show him a prominent member of Lord Chamberlain's men, but circumstances are all against this. Nothing associates him with the proceedings.)
1596	Henry Carey, 1st Lord Hunsdon, dies, and after office is held briefly by Lord Cobham, his son George Carey, 2nd Lord Hunsdon, appointed Lord Chamberlain in his place.	Settles with his Countess, Elizabeth, in King's Place, Hackney, for the rest of his life. His turmoil over the young friend of the *Sonnets* perhaps eased by Southampton's enlistment in Essex's expedition against Cadiz and later campaign in Ireland.	'96–'97: *King John* and *Merchant of Venice* written.	Aug: His son Hamnet buried. Grant of coat of arms evidently made to his father after initial rejection. Late in year, London: William Wayte craves sureties of peace against "William Shakspare" and three others.
1597		Lord and Lady Pembroke seek his daughter Bridget's hand for their son. Writes to Burghley that he has not "an able body."	*Richard Third, Romeo and Juliet* and *Richard Second* published, all with author unnamed. '97–'98: *Henry Fourth, Pts 1* and 2 written.	May: "Willielmum Shakespeare" buys New Place, second largest house in Stratford. Nov: "William Shakspere" cited in Bishopsgate, London, as having disappeared, making collection of tax on him impossible.
1598	*Scourge of Villanie* by John Marston published, Sep 7: *Palladis Tamia* by Francis Meres registered	evidently speaking of him as "most of me beloved" who will "mount fair place when Apes are turned forth." in which he is named as among those "best for comedy."	and in which Shakespeare (without first name) is mentioned for first time as a playwright and called best for both tragedy and comedy and extolled as poet. *Love's Labour's Lost,* "Newly corrected and augmented by W. Shakespeare," and *Henry Fourth, Pt. 1,* published. *Merchant of Venice* registered.	Jan: Letter written from Stratford says "Mr. Shakspere" may be moved to deal in matter of tithes. Feb: "Wm Shackspere" listed in Stratford among those holding grain during famine. Oct: "William Shakespeare" listed again as a tax delinquent in London, in St. Helen's parish. Oct: Richard Quiney writes letter, evidently not sent, to "Mr. Wm. Shackspere" asking for loan to pay debts in London. Town of Stratford pays "Mr. Shaxpere" for a load of stone.

782

Chronology of the Principals in the Case of William Shakespeare

	Related Events	Edward de Vere	"William Shakespeare"	William Shakspere
			'98–'99: *Much Ado About Nothing* and *Henry Fifth* written.	
1599	June: *Willobie His Avisa* included in category of books to be burned. The Globe, constructed of timbers from The Theatre, opened. John Farmer's *Set of English Madrigals* published, Queen permits a third company of actors, ...	Mar: Receives devoted letter from nephew referring to "your most serious affairs." He and Countess exchanging visits with Derbys. About now Derby is reported to be penning plays for the common players. with dedication to him as one who in music has "overgone" most professionals. which evidently is his.	"W. Shakespeare" credited with authorship of *The Passionate Pilgrim,* published by Jaggard. Sep: Performance of *Julius Caesar* witnessed. '99–'oo: *As You Like It* and *Twelfth Night* written.	As of February, "William Shakespere" is reported twenty years later by Heminge and Condell to hold ten-per-cent interest in the Globe. May: Reported among those occupying a new house in St. Saviour parish. Oct: Reported as tax delinquent of St. Helen's parish who had moved to Sussex. Is derided in play by Jonson as Sogliardo, a rustic clown who buys the name of gentleman and coat of arms and "comes up every term to take tobacco and see new motions."
1600	This or preceding or following year Cambridge students put on *Pilgrimage to Parnassus,*	June: Seeks Robert Cecil's help in obtaining Governorship of Jersey, without result. His natural son Edward Vere made captain.	Aug: Publication of *As You Like It* stayed in Stationers' Register and play not published until 1623. *Henry Fifth* and *Much Ado* also stayed but both published later in month, former without author's name, latter with. 'oo–'o1: *Hamlet* and *Merry Wives* written. with speech by "Kempe" clearly composed to show that only an ignoramus could believe that Shakespeare is a fellow of a stage-clown and without college education or classical reference in writings.	Oct: Tax owed by "Willelmus Shakspere" referred for collection to Bishop of Worcester. Passage from *Pilgrimage to Parnassus* is first and, for 15 years, only indication (apart from suggestion in Marsden's *Scourge of Villanie* of 1598) that plays of Shakespeare's are being attributed to such a fellow as he evidently was.
1601	Feb 7: Essex leads aborted revolt with support of Southampton, for which both are condemned to death, with latter's sentence commuted.	Jan: Seeks Cecil's help in obtaining Presidency of Wales, without result. Feb: Serves on tribunal trying the plotters.	Early Feb: Conspirators in Essex revolt seek to have *Richard Second,* "an old play," performed to prepare populace for action against Queen. 'o1–'o2: *Troilus and Cressida* written.	
1602		His players and Worcester's combined in third allowed company, authorized to perform at the Boar's Head.	*Hamlet* and *Merry Wives* registered, with latter thereupon published as by "William Shakespeare." 'o2–'o3: *All's Well* written.	May: "William Shakespeare," described as "of Stratford upon Avon," pays enormous sum of £320 for land near town, deed "sealed and delivered to Gilbert Shakspere," his brother.

Chronology of the Principals in the Case of William Shakespeare

	Related Events	Edward de Vere	"William Shakespeare"	William Shakspere
				Sep: "Shackespere" buys a cottage across from New Place. Later: In legal action in Stratford is described for first time as "generosus," gentleman.
1603	Mar 24: Queen Elizabeth dies and is succeeded by James I. Apr 10: Southampton released from the Tower. Sponsorship of Lord Chamberlain's men taken over by James and they become King's men. Reversion of Mastership of Revels given to a resident of Castle Hedingham, later to George Buck, ...	Writes to Cecil of his "great grief" at Queen's death and of his "shipwreck" as "above all the rest." May: Refers to "mine infirmity." Sponsorship of his and Worcester's joint company taken over by Queen Anne. a friend of his. July: His annuity of £1000 renewed by the King. Aug: His son Edward Vere writes letter either addressed to or inquiring of him.	Is reproached by Chettle for his silence upon the Queen's death in verse revealing that Queen had given ear to his "lays" and "graced his desert." *Troilus and Cressida* registered. *The Tempest,* last of his plays, written this year or soon thereafter (Cairncross). *Hamlet* published as by "William Shake-speare." In Sonnet 107, clearly of this year, he writes that "Death to me subscribes." With Buck as Master of Revels, publication of hitherto unprinted plays of his ceases for nineteen years except for three in 1608–'09.	May: "Willm Shakespeare" named among King's men authorized to perform in plays.
1604	Mid-summer: King's men, having led charmed lives for past twenty years, now begin to get into trouble with authorities.	His petition for custody of Forest of Essex and Keepership of Havering granted by King and he is reappointed to Royal Privy Council. June 24: He dies, reportedly of the plague, and is buried in the church at Hackney on July 6.	*The Tempest* written (Elze). *Love's Labour's Lost* put on by Southampton for Queen Anne. *Hamlet* published in most nearly full version, evidently from author's MS, under royal coat of arms. Christmas season: King has seven plays of his performed, including *Measure for Measure* and *Othello*.	As one of King's men, "William Shakespeare" heads list of those to receive red cloth in preparation for Royal Progress through London. Sometime this year lodging with Mountjoy, maker of women's headdresses. Last indication of his being domiciled in London. July: "Willielmus Shexpere" brings action against Stratford apothecary to collect loan made in March.
1605	Philip Herbert is made Earl of Montgomery, ...	marrying de Vere's daughter Susan.	Death of author of *Die Schöne Sidea,* which, in absence of discoverable common source, must be taken as based on *The Tempest.*	May: Augustine Phillipps of King's men makes a will leaving £5 to be divided among "hired men" of company, "my fellow William Shakespeare" leading list. July: "William Shakespear" purchases tithes in Stratford parish for enormous sum of £440.

784

Chronology of the Principals in the Case of William Shakespeare

Related Events	Edward de Vere	"William Shakespeare"	William Shakspere
1606		*Macbeth* written. Dec: *King Lear* performed at Court. '06–'07: *Antony and Cleopatra* written.	
1607	His son Edward Vere knighted.	Nov: *King Lear* registered as by Master William Shakespeare.	June 5: Marriage of "John Hall gentleman and Susanna Shaxpere" recorded.
1608	Countess of Oxford sells King's Place, Hackney, confusion perhaps enabling pirates to get hands on MSS of *Sonnets* and only three unpublished Shakespearean plays printed between 1603 and 1622.	*King Lear* printed as by "Mr. William Shakspeare," corrected in later edition to "Shake-speare." *Pericles* registered; also *Antony and Cleopatra*, unheard of again until 1623.	Feb 21: A daughter, Elizabeth, born to the Halls. Aug: According to testimony of 1619, Shakespeare was now one of seven lessors of Blackfriars Theatre. In 1635, he was said to have been one of "men Players . . . placed" on purchase of lease. Dec: "Shackspeare" begins proceedings for collection of debt against fellow townsman, then against his surety.
1609		*Troilus and Cressida*, having made "escape" from "grand possessors," and *Pericles* published, both as by "William Shake-speare." *Shake-speares Sonnets* published with plain indications that their author dead. '09–'10: *Cymbeline* written.	
1610		'10–'11: *Winter's Tale* written.	"Shakespere" involved in legal action in Stratford, perhaps buying more land.
1611		*Winter's Tale* performed in public and at Court and *Tempest* at latter.	"Mr. William Shackspere" added to names of citizens contributing to highway fund.
1612	Nov 25: Countess of Oxford dies, willing x number of pounds to "my dumb man,"	'12–'13: *Henry Eighth* and *Two Noble Kinsman* written.	Jan: John Combe draws up his will leaving "Mr William Shackspere" £5. who is very likely he. May: Makes deposition in suit brought against his one-time landlord in London, Mountjoy, signing it "Willn Shakp." His daughter Susanna accused of immorality with two men of village and brings action for defamation of character.

Chronology of the Principals in the Case of William Shakespeare

	Related Events	Edward de Vere	"William Shakespeare"	William Shakspere
1613	Mar: Payment to a "Mr. Shakspeare" by Earl of Rutland's steward "about my Lord's impreso," which Burbage was to paint, was certainly not to the Stratfordian Shakspere.		June: *Henry Eighth* performed, suggesting this a revision of play in early 1590s cited by Alleyn as calling for Henry VIII's and Cardinal's costumes.	Mar: "William Shakespeare of Stratford upon Avon . . . gentleman" buys a house in Blackfriars near theatre and mortgages it back to owner. Signs one instrument "William Shakspē," the other "Wᵐ Shakspē."
1614				Collects from town for two quarts of wine served a preacher. Fall: As "Shakspeare" and "Schackespeare" is involved as either participant or neutral in enclosure of village common lands.
1615	William Herbert, Earl of Pembroke and brother-in-law of de Vere's daughter Susan, wins appointment as Lord Chamberlain after several years' effort. With Buck as Master of Revels, control of public theatre and publication of plays is in hands of de Vere's friends			
1616	*The Workes of Ben Jonson* published by the author	. . . . , . . .	naming "Will. Shakespeare" at head of cast of *Every Man in His Humour* as enacted in 1598 and "Will. Shake-Speare" in cast of *Sejanus* as enacted in 1603, ...	Feb 10: His daughter Judith marries Thomas Quiney without special license required and they are excommunicated. (but hardly supports attribution of stage career to the Stratfordian: ulterior motives are to be suspected in this long-*ex-post-facto* listing, and "Shakespeare" and its variants was *never* hyphenated as a bona fide surname.) Mar 15: Margaret Wheeler, whom Quiney had got with child, is buried together with the infant. Mar 25: "Wᵐʲ Schackspeare" makes his will, leaving bulk of estate to Susanna Apr 25: The burial register of Trinity Church reads: "Will. Shakspere gent."

Chronology of the Principals in the Case of William Shakespeare

	Related Events	Edward de Vere	"William Shakespeare"	William Shakspere
1619		In a dedication to the 18th Earl of Oxford, Munday speaks of his father's "famous and desertful memory" and "matchless virtues."		
1621	Oct 5: Buck found to have lost his mind, ... Reversion of his office is obtained for Ben Jonson.	. . . .	and *Othello* is registered on Oct. 6.	
1622	July: Mastership of Revels leased by Pembroke's young kinsman, Sir Henry Herbert. Henry Peacham in a list of poets who made Elizabeth's "a golden age" names Edward de Vere . .		*Othello* published as by "William Shakespeare." but makes no mention of a Shakespeare.	About this time a monument is erected in the wall of Trinity Church to "Shakspeare" with bust of man with his hands on a sack and a wordy English inscription making no mention of the subject's having been a poet, playwright or actor.
1623			Dedicated to the Earls of Pembroke and Montgomery, who doubtless bore the great costs involved, and with a strikingly ambiguous treatment of the authorship, *Mr. William Shakespeares Comedies, Histories & Tragedies* are published in a folio volume (the First Folio) containing thirty-six plays of Shakespeare's, twenty never before published.	Aug 8: The burial register of Trinity Church reads "Mrs. Shakspeare."

Appendix. Adventures in the Quest for the Shakespeare Manuscripts

Pursuing an interest in the authorship of Shakespeare's works is likely to make you aware of much in those works that would otherwise have escaped you. It is likely also to afford you some insights into the mind of society, if I may so call it, that you otherwise might have been spared. In nothing has it been so instructive to me on that subject as in my coming upon a possible clue to the disposition of the vanished Shakespeare manuscripts. In an article that the editors of *Harper's Magazine* were courageous enough to publish in the issue of June 1972, I wrote:

> That recovering the manuscripts would be worth almost any effort is without question. Last year, in connection with speculation about a signature in a law book seeming to read "Wm Shakspere," dealers were quoted as estimating that if it were authenticated, it would be worth a million dollars. That's just for a signature. The monetary value of a body of Shakespeare's manuscripts would be almost incalculable. Beyond that would be the satisfaction of possessing the words as they actually came from the dramatist's hand. Depending on how many of the manuscripts were found, we would for the first time have the dramas exactly as they were intended, not just the best approximations that scholar-detectives have been able to arrive at working with faulty texts.
>
> Is there any possibility that manuscripts of Shakespeare have survived? "The greatest battery of organized research that has ever been directed upon a single person," as Professor Hugh R. Trevor-Roper calls it, conducted by "armies of scholars," has come up with nothing generally accepted to be in the illustrious Stratfordian's hand except six very awkwardly executed signatures. But here I am reminded of "The Purloined Letter": in the Poe story an incriminating missive known to be in a certain house is overlooked by the experts of the Parisian police in the course of the most meticulous search. How? By having been placed conspicuously in a card rack, where, instantly advertised to all eyes, it registers on none.
>
> If a theory of mine about the disposition of the Shakespeare manuscripts is correct, we are confronted with a similar situation and could have the manuscripts within our grasp. The instructions for finding the lost manuscripts may have been staring the world in the face for three and a half centuries, waiting for someone to read three simple lines and ask what they mean. . . .
>
> Orthodox scholars resist recognizing that anything about Shakespeare raises unanswered questions. They hold that his manuscripts were destroyed early on, as the British would say, and as a matter of course. "Plays were not regarded as 'literature' at all," Louis B. Wright, the former director of the Folger Shakespeare Library, explains. "Once a printer had used a manuscript play, he threw out the dead copy and was glad to get rid of the rubbish." But this explanation, neat as it is, hardly stands up.

Appendix. Adventures in the Quest for the Shakespeare Manuscripts

The first known reference to Shakespeare as a dramatist, where he was described as best among the English for both tragedy and comedy, compared him with Plautus and Seneca. Shakespeare's contemporaries published a collection of his plays (the First Folio of 1623) and bought up the entire printing of a thousand copies for what would today be about 70 dollars each. Shakespeare was the only dramatist they so honored. In a poem at the front of the volume, Ben Jonson called up the greatest writers of other times and places to witness Shakespeare's dramatic genius and cried, "Triumph, my Britaine . . . !" Shakespeare's dramas were assuredly regarded as literature by his contemporaries; the Elizabethans were not fools.

Wright's second assertion also falls afoul of the facts. The manuscripts of most, if not all, of Shakespeare's plays never reached the printer. The editors of the First Folio refer to previous editions of the plays — the quartos, in which 16 of the plays had been printed — as "maimed, and deformed" by the "impostors" who published them. But the First Folio, in which 20 of the 36 plays were printed for the first time, was itself a mélange of errors. "The text alike of the First Folio and the quartos," the preface to the Oxford edition of Shakespeare tells us, "was doubtless supplied by playhouse copies which often embodied the ill-conditioned interpolations and alterations of actors and theatrical managers."

In the article I went on to observe that

To account for the foregoing facts of publication within the framework of orthodoxy you have to accept the Yale scholar Charles Tyler Prouty's contention in the Yale facsimile of the First Folio that "there is no reason to believe that he [Shakespeare] or anyone else was interested in preserving definitive texts of the plays he had written," and Anthony Burgess's that the author "didn't much care" whether the plays survived.

And as in the body of the present book, I proceed to invite attention to the irrationality of those beliefs and to show how they are contradicted by what Shakespeare and his contemporaries wrote on the subject. The article continued to the end as follows:

The alternative to the untenable orthodox view is that the manuscripts were a "hot" property and not to be shown, even to a printer. Presumably this was because of the light they would throw on the authorship; no other reason suggests itself. The safest thing, of course, would have been for those who held them to destroy them. Perhaps they were destroyed. But could any person likely to have acquired them — and the evidence of the preface to a 1609 edition of *Troilus and Cressida* is that they were held by certain "grand possessors" from whom it would require a "new English Inquisition" to spring them — have brought himself to destroy them, knowing no other authentic texts existed? It is hard to believe. But to hide them so that they would never be found would be tantamount to destroying them. So what to do? Could they be disposed of so that they would not be found until the existing authorities had passed from the scene? If my theory holds, that is what was done, and with consummate shrewdness. Only one thing went wrong. Posterity, when in due course it came to take an interest in the place of concealment, refused to take note of the instructions.

What happened in my case?

I was reading an adversary's comments on the book to which I had contributed. The book had made the point that Ben Jonson, when he wrote in the First

Folio, "Thou art a monument without a tomb," could hardly have had the Stratford man in mind as Shakespeare the dramatist, since if there was one thing the former was not without in 1623 it was a tomb — the one with the famous curse on it. My critic countered that Jonson was speaking metaphorically or figuratively. His argument was, however, invalid; Jonson was replying to a proposal that Shakespeare be buried in Westminster Abbey. He could not be, Jonson was saying, because he had no tomb — no body. As I reflected on this there came to my mind a line from the letter of dedication in the First Folio to the Earls of Pembroke and Montgomery: "we most humbly consecrate to your H. H. these remains of your servant Shakespeare."

Shakespeare's remains were his works. Shakespeare had no body. "Thou art a monument."

Suddenly my blood seemed to turn to ice. I had remembered the mysterious line in the inscription on the monument in Trinity Church, Stratford: WHOM ENVIOVS DEATH HATH PLAST [PLACED] WITH IN THIS MONVMENT SHAKSPEARE. The reputed Shakespeare is buried under the floor. The monument, placed in the wall, obviously — being too small — contains nobody at all. No body, that is. But if Shakespeare's body were his works . . .

My electrification was complete as I remembered all of the heretofore inexplicable first three lines of the English inscription:

> STAY PASSENGER, WHY GOEST THOV BY SO FAST / READ IF THOV CANST
> WHOM ENVIOVS DEATH HATH PLAST / WITH IN THIS MONVMENT SHAKSPEARE

If all were above board in the Shakespeare authorship, requiring us to take these lines at face value, the inscription would be preposterous. Could its author, having as challenging an opportunity as has ever been offered an epitaphist, find no better use for the space than to warn the visitor not to hurry by without taking in what he was seeing? Why should it have been anticipated that the passerby would not realize who was entombed in this particular monument (supposing that anyone could have been)? If there were such a danger, why not engrave "William Shakespeare" in bold letters in a conspicuous place on the monument instead of burying simply the last name in the body of the inscription? Why would the viewer be challenged to read if he could who had been placed within the monument? Why was he asked to believe the impossible — that Shakespeare was within the monument? In terms of orthodox theory these questions are unanswerable.

But, if Shakespeare were not a person but a body of works, the matter is altogether different. In that case, everything makes brilliant sense. The epitaphist, with reason, implores the visitor not to hurry by without taking in what he is seeing. Read this, he urges. You know it cannot be Shakespeare's literal corpse that is within the monument. So what is it? . . . Can't you read?

I then remembered, with a sense that everything was suddenly falling into place, the first reference to the memorial known to us. It is in the poem by Leonard Digges in the introductory material in the First Folio — that most curious assemblage — and it calls up a future "when that stone is rent, / And Time dissolves thy Stratford Moniment. . . ." That seemed suggestive, to say the least, especially in the light of a further statement of Digges's ". . . ev'ry line, each verse / Here shall revive, redeeme thee from thy Herse." Would the conventionally accepted Shakespeare have required redemption from an ironbound, toothed frame of timber — as a man in an oubliette would?

Then there was the monument itself, two features of which I now saw as noteworthy. The first was the two naked children that adorn it, one on either side, supposedly modeled on similar but much smaller and insignificant figures representing Labor and Rest on the 5th Earl of Rutland's tomb. Regardless of the derivation, I found it striking that the Stratford monument should be surmounted by these figures, each on a mound of earth, one holding a spade, the other a torch. If the architects had wished to direct us to dig into and search within the monument, well . . .

The other feature is a jawless skull at the top of the monument. It reminds us of what placed "Shakespeare" within the monument: it was envious death — envy being from the Latin *invidere*, "to look upon with malice." And this in turn recalls Ben Jonson's little-noted reference in the First Folio to the "crafty Malice" that sought "to ruine" his "beloved, the author." Could the interment of the too-revealing manuscripts be considered the death imposed on that author, his silencing (a jawless skull) by that same crafty malice?

One final observation: it is in the Stratford monument that we find the first suggestion that the man christened Gulielmus Shaksper (or Shakspere) in Stratford-upon-Avon was the author William Shakespeare. To employ the monument as the repository of the documents that would prove the author someone else and disclose his identity — would this not have been ironical and mischievous in a way that would appeal to the gusto of pre-Puritan Englishmen?

Perhaps there is only one chance in ten that the apparent clues mean what to me they appear to. But if there is any chance at all, should they not be followed up? No desecration, as of a tomb, would be involved. At worst, nothing would be lost but a few hundred dollars to pay a competent mason. Would it not, in the circumstances, be little short of criminal to neglect the possibility, however slight, of recovering the Shakespeare manuscripts, the originals of the greatest literary works of our civilization?

The Shakespeare Birthplace Trust of Stratford has refused to entertain any suggestion that the monument be opened. While inquiries have left me with little hope of support from orthodox scholars, I cannot believe its decision will prove final.

I did not and do not pretend to be any better judge than anyone else of the merits of my hypothesis. It has, however, seemed to me consistent with the known facts and, at last, to make sense of the inscription on the monument — which, if it does not mean what I have conjectured it to mean, apparently remains, after three and a half centuries, beyond anyone's ability to explain. When the idea came to me and I set it forth in writing, in 1962, I felt sure of at least one thing. The world would discover if it was sound. Given its plausibility, public interest would allow little time to be lost in putting it to the test by an examination of the conjectured repository.

Little did I know! It would be ten years before the world would even hear of my theory — in the *Harper's* article.

To begin with, I gave a copy of the exposition I had written to Francis T. Carmody, a New York lawyer and then president of the Shakespeare-Oxford Society. This he sent to his friend David E. K. Bruce, our ambassador in London at the time. Seven weeks later he received a reply:

> I certainly share your interest in the Shakespeare mystery, and I enjoyed reading your letter and Ogburn's article. I regret, however, to say that an inquiry

> to the Director of the Shakespeare Birthplace Trust has convinced me that any
> further action on my part would not only be fruitless but inappropriate.
>
> As you can imagine, the Trust is extremely sensitive on this subject, and it
> appears doubtful that even a recommendation by the highest church or political
> authorities here would bring about an opening of the wall.

That the Trust's opposition could be overcome by public opinion I had no
doubt.

I asked Louis Marder, to whom I sent a copy of my exposition, if he would
not be willing to support its objective by stating publicly that although he
had absolute confidence in the Stratfordian's authorship he felt that no chance
of finding the manuscripts, however slight it might be, should be neglected.
Professor Marder, who makes a point of affording a hearing to anti-Stratfordian views, would do nothing of the kind. He responded by printing a
note on my theory in his *Shakespeare Newsletter* followed by a mocking,
sarcastic comment he had elicited from the director of the Shakespeare
Birthplace Trust, Levi Fox.

I next sent a copy of my proposal to Eustace Seligman of the noted law
firm of Sullivan & Cromwell, chairman of the Folger Library Committee of
the Trustees of Amherst College, writing him that I thought the Folger's
support of a demand to look where the signs suggested the manuscripts might
be cached would be decisive and hoped it would be given. Mr. Seligman
replied:

> The Trustees of the Folger Shakespeare Library have steadfastly refrained
> from in any way participating in the discussions as to the identity of the author
> of the plays credited to William Shakespeare. To comply with your request
> would, in my judgment, constitute a departure from this position, and it will,
> therefore, not be possible for them to comply with your request.

(Some time later, having called the attention of the president of Amherst,
Calvin H. Plimpton, to the methods practiced by Louis B. Wright to make
honest, open discussion of the issue of the Shakespeare authorship impossible
— methods combining defamation of the dissenters and refusal to debate
with an ability to get away with it accruing from his position as director of
the Folger Library — I received from President Plimpton the reply that

> What is needed, it seems to me, is not so much a public debate as fresh evidence.

Those who spoke for the Folger thus rejected public debate on the authorship
on the grounds that what was needed was fresh evidence and refused to offer
indispensable support for a promising quest for invaluable new evidence on
the grounds that their doing so would involve them in the question of the
authorship! Add to this the denial to the dissenters of the opportunity to
present evidence, new or old, in support of their point of view in the Folger's
Shakespeare Quarterly or from its lecture platform and you have the troublesome elements pretty well under control.

Not until O. B. Hardison replaced Dr. Wright and instilled a welcome new atmosphere at the Folger was any approval expressed at the Library for following up my proposal. This came from Dr. Hardison's lively and talented assistant, Richmond Crinkley, who said he would favor an examination of the monument and sent congratulations on the *Harper's* article.

Meanwhile, beginning back in 1962, I had been seeing with growing clarity that I was going to have to look to the press rather than to the academic world. Francis Carr, the British Baconian, published extracts of my article in his small, short-lived magazine, *Past and Future,* in November 1962. The results were nil. Well, as I had known what was needed was publication of the full exposition in a vehicle that commanded wide attention. That there could be any difficulty about this seemed to me at first impossible.

I soon discovered otherwise. No one, it seemed, was interested in the possibility of discovering, with negligible effort, a treasure worth untold millions of dollars and of a cultural importance far transcending its monetary value. Actually, I doubt that any editor asked himself whether the article might lead to the manuscripts. The question was: "How shall we look if we publish this, and do we wish to be 'involved'?" I tried magazines to which I had previously contributed. Had I had greater detachment I would have been amused to see how some of the editors shifted from foot to foot trying to think of a reason for rejecting the offering. One wrote: "You know, if we ran this story, people would expect us to run similar things every month." None would touch it. I made two efforts, several years apart, with the *Washington Post,* which had always been well disposed toward me. Alfred Friendly, the managing editor, turned it down as being too long and too complicated for the *Post's* readers, whose reaction in any case would be: why not look in the monument instead of writing about it? I was somewhat consoled when I discovered that Mr. Friendly was a trustee of the Folger Library. I fared no better, however, with Harold Kneeland, editor of one of the Sunday supplements. He wrote that "Frankly I lack the courage to open the Shakespeare argument once again." Letting Louis B. Wright fulminate against his opponents in the *Washington Post* did not constitute opening the Shakespeare argument because where one side only is heard it cannot be called an argument.

In July 1971 I sent a rewritten version of the article to John Fischer, former editor of *Harper's Magazine,* who fourteen years earlier had given me my chance to become a full-time writer. Having rather tried his patience in the past on the subject of the Shakespeare authorship I had been reluctant to tax it further. But it was owing to his good will and interest and the courage of his successor at *Harper's,* Robert Schnayerson, that the article was accepted. Mr. Fischer had some changes to recommend and thought we ought to approach the director of the Birthplace Trust one more time. This I did in a letter identifying myself and my purpose, which, I wrote, was to suggest that I send you my analysis, which, if correct in its facts and reasonable inferences, leads inescapably to the conclusion that the chances of the manuscripts' having been originally placed in the monument are at least good. My thought is that if you perceived critical flaws in the argument it would, of course, have to be scrapped and the mystery of the manuscripts' disappearance be reconsidered from scratch. On the other hand, I should hope that you would allow the expectation that if you did not perceive such flaws the Trust would make no objection in principle to an examination of the monument.

Levi Fox's reply, dated July 27th, was as brief and to the point as I had foreseen:

> I have your letter of the 17th July and I know that you will be disappointed when I tell you that there is no likelihood of my being able to accede to your request.

"Shakespeare's Missing Manuscripts: An Answer to an Old Riddle" appeared, albeit somewhat cut, in the June 1972 issue of *Harper's*. It brought many letters of interest and support, a few printed in *Harper's* for August. If the argument broke down at any point, no one showed where. Yet in all the faculties of English literature not one voice was raised to propose putting the theory to the test. To achieve such conformity of behavior must, I thought, be the dream of every dictatorship. Evidently there was not a single professor of English who, rather than concede any possibility of error in academia's identification of Shakespeare, would not rather take a chance of the manuscripts' rotting away unseen.

With no prospect of any build-up in public opinion to force a change in Levi Fox's position, I cast about for leads to an electronic device that could detect a cavity within a stone structure. Though I had the help of William B. Michael, a physicist, at the University of California at Berkeley, such a device seemed to be unavailable.

In this impasse I had a telephone call from a writer for the *Daily Telegraph* in London, Byron Rogers, who told me what steps to take if I were really interested in pressing my search for the manuscripts. Dr. Fox, it appeared, had no authority in the matter. I should submit to the Diocesan Registrar at Coventry a Petition for Faculty, as it was called, signed by a resident of Stratford, on which would be set forth my aims with respect to the monument. A Consistory Court would then be called to hear those who wished to speak on the application and render a decision. If I were willing to go ahead with this, Mr. Rogers would write an article on my quest for the *Daily Telegraph Sunday Magazine*. It sounded like a large order, but I said I would do my best.

The article came out on 23 January 1973, under the apt and amusing title of "Bard Thou Never Wert?" It gave the gist of my *Harper's* article and the background and, apart from identifying J. T. Looney as an American, was ably done. The writer had interviewed the Diocesan Registrar, S. L. Penn, who had recalled the Petition for Faculty to open both the monument and the tomb submitted in 1964 by the Shakespeare Action Committee, headed by Francis Carr (who had published extracts of my article). "I thought we were really for it this time," Mr. Penn had declared. "I was looking forward to it. It would have been a job for silk. It would have been bitterly opposed, you see. But then suddenly everything just drifted away." "The difficulty was," Mr. Rogers explained, "that the Action Committee had failed to get a Stratford resident to sign their application." Mr. Rogers had even sounded out a local monumental mason about the problem of removing the panel bearing the inscription, behind which "there could be a depth of two or three feet." The mason's opinion was that "you'd have more trouble with the authorities than with actually getting something out."

Two eminent orthodox writers whom Mr. Rogers had consulted were of course derisive. Peter Quennell described the quest as "the sort of dotty thing Americans come up with from time to time." Ivor Brown said shortly, "I think it's nonsense," and added rather lamely, "There's no other example of this, is there?" I wrote both men expressing disappointment that they had evaded the issue posed by the inscription and offering to send them the full account of my reasoning in the *Harper's* article to find fault with if they could. Each having invested time and reputation in successful orthodox Shakespearean biographies, however, they were having no part of that. I received no reply from either.

"Bard Thou Never Wert?" was reprinted in newspapers all over, from at least as far as Athens and Durban, South Africa, to Boston, Chicago, and Cleveland. The silence of the English professors and literary luminaries remained as profound as that of Shakspere's tomb.

I had obtained, meanwhile, the form for Petition for Faculty from the Diocesan Registrar. How I was to persuade a resident of Stratford to sign it where Mr. Carr had failed remained to be seen. Lawrence Hughes, president of William Morrow & Co., had generously offered to pay for my going to England and doing what I could to arrange the necessaries. It was not to come to that, however. In correspondence with S. L. Penn I learned that the costs of the Consistory Court, which he allowed could be "considerable" in view of the "National and indeed International interest" and of the numbers of those who would probably wish to speak — "'high powered' adversaries," including "scholars and literary giants, . . . certainly lawyers representing interested parties" — could be awarded at the Court's discretion. I could see the Court assessing an intruding, bumptious American for the entire amount, after turning him down: thousands of dollars. Mr. Hughes could hardly be expected to assume an open-ended obligation, and it was certain I could not afford to.

There the matter rested until September 24th, when Reuters carried the following dispatch, datelined Washington, D.C.:

Appendix. Adventures in the Quest for the Shakespeare Manuscripts

> A student of Shakespeare believes he has stumbled across a clue to the location of the Bard's manuscripts: behind the monument at the church where he lies buried. John Louther, a journalist with the Mutual Broadcasting System, outlined his discovery at a press conference. The clue consists of a relatively simple "cipher rhyme-scheme" which he claims was Shakespeare's last creation and a guide for posterity someday to retrieve his handwritten works. . . . Louther acknowledges that authorities on Shakespeare have for years speculated that the monument might hide the written works. But his finding the cipher rhyme scheme, he adds, could help them remove any doubts.

A week later, on Thursday, October 4th, Mr. Louther's press conference had startling consequences, widely but not very prominently reported. Here is the *Daily Telegraph's* account:

> A gang searching for Shakespeare's manuscripts broke into Stratford-on-Avon parish church on Tuesday night, it was discovered yesterday. The poet is buried in the chancel, and above the grave is a monument which it has been claimed may contain hidden scrolls.
> Police Supt. George Jackson, head of Stratford police, said: "The intruders found nothing and they ignored valuables that ordinary thieves would have taken. They were tidy and considerate."
> He said the men lifted a 3 cwt [400 pounds, according to other accounts] bust of Shakespeare from the wall and attacked a stone plinth in which they thought documents might be hidden. He requested information from anyone who saw men in the churchyard between 9:15 P.M. on Tuesday and 7:30 A.M. yesterday.

I thought it interesting that Superintendent Jackson knew what the intruders were after and knew that they had found nothing.

In another report, Levi Fox was quoted as saying that "The intruders used an altar table as a stand to get up to the monument, and something like an iron bar to prise it [the bust] off. There was superficial damage to the bust itself and more serious damage to the mounting. It was a very ugly and frightening sight." A police spokesman said, "They took extreme care. They took down the bust — it is so heavy that three large detectives had to pick it up again, and they had a deal of difficulty — and removed part of the plinth to see if it was hollow. It was not."

John Louther, with whom I was soon in correspondence, wrote me: "This is a very frustrating situation. And it gets more so as new questions keep popping up." He remarked that on October 4th Levi Fox had told reporters that "It's going to be a tricky, intricate and expensive job to put the monument back," while on October 7th the Chief of Police, George Jackson, told him during a trans-Atlantic telephone conversation that "There is very little damage to the plinth or to the bust. It has been replaced and is back in position now." He said a cavity had been chipped away under the bust to a depth of about four inches." The next day Levi Fox told him on the telephone that until the Vicar of the church, Peter Barnes, returned from a holiday, "no firm decisions about restoration will be made." He contended that the hole chiseled in the plinth was deeper than four inches. While he agreed with the Police Chief that no other part of the monument had been touched, he asserted that "Now, there is absolutely no cache or hiding place or hollow at all."

The case presents some odd features. The Vicar had told Byron Rogers that "The church we daren't leave unoccupied because of souvenir hunters." Yet sometime during a space of ten hours — the police cannot be more specific — a party of at least three husky men enters the church. They busy themselves in it for some time. They are not only undetected as they wrench a 400-pound bust from its niche but they do not fear detection; as the Police Chief points out, they are tidy-minded and considerate and sweep up before they leave! No reporters, as far as is said, are called in when the outrage is discovered. The newspaper reports seem to be based exclusively on what Dr. Fox and the Chief of Police give out. If any photographs are taken showing what has been done they are not produced. Dr. Fox knows that Francis Carr, with the greatest interest in the contents of the monument, is only two hours away, yet he does not notify him and invite him to come see for himself that "there is absolutely no cache or hiding place." No one seems to suggest that desecration of the nation's most notable memorial is worth the attention of Scotland Yard. The local police express no determination to apprehend the miscreants and apparently no steps are taken to pick up their trails. Indeed, the "gang" seems to have been forgotten from the start.

To these peculiar elements I add as a catalyst two bits from Byron Rogers's article. One is Dr. Fox's "scathing" appraisal of "the doubters." The other is Mr. Rogers's observation that "If anything sensational were discovered the loss to Stratford would be incalculable. An index to just what this small Warwickshire town owes to tourism is the fact that a Stratford Hilton is at present being built. A *Stratford Hilton*! Last year 964,545 people visited the five Shakespeare properties." And what precipitates out of the mixture is a question. Did the "intruders" excavate deeply enough into the monument to satisfy themselves that it contained no manuscripts? Or were their probings superficial, intended merely to ensure that a Consistory Court could follow its bent with a clear conscience and find that the question of a possible repository in the monument had been settled, as Dr. Fox was quoted as stating was the case?

About a year after the break-in, the president of the Shakespeare-Oxford Society, the late Richard C. Horne, Jr., visited Stratford and managed to obtain an interview with the Chief of Police. The frosty and uncommunicative reception he received did little to allay his wonderment, and mine, at the circumstances of the case.

Some months earlier, in July 1973, I had been approached by Central Virginia Educational Television to make an appearance on WCVE-TV in connection with the *Harper's* article. I had gone to Richmond and discussions had proceeded encouragingly. The Folger Library under its new head, Dr. Hardison, had been going to cooperate and Richmond Crinkley — ever a good fellow — was interested and would go to Richmond (the city) to be taped. The break-in at Stratford, however, seemed rather to put a damper on the project and this was further set back by Dr. Crinkley's transfer to a job demanding all his time at the Kennedy Center for the Performing Arts. It was finally shelved by, I gather, lack of financing and of a Stratfordian academic to appear on the program. Knowing how difficult it would be to persuade any such to do so in the company of a dissenter, I considered Louis Marder of the University of Illinois the most likely prospect. I received no reply from him to my letter proposing his taking part, however.

Shortly before this Dr. Marder had telephoned me to obtain what information I could supply for his *Shakespeare Newsletter* on the Stratford break-in — a matter I bring up for the further light it throws on academic *mores*. Experience with Dr. Marder should have put me on my guard. Allowing myself to be reassured by his disarming manner, however, I passed on to him in writing what I knew of the events and even ventured one or two off-the-record observations, as to a fellow worker in the vineyard. My foolish trust resulted in my being held up to scorn in the next issue of his newsletter. I suppose I deserved it for being so simple-minded, but I did not like it the better for that. A remark I had made in confidence, viz., that "The suspicion that the invasion of the church was undertaken not without the knowledge of influential persons is hard to avoid" was published in quotation marks and made the occasion for denouncing me: "the extreme audacity of Mr. Ogburn's position is almost libelous." Dr. Marder declared, however, that audacious near-libel was "not unusual for those who not only suspect competent scholars of concealing evidence of the authorship of the plays, but who also think that everyone contemporary with Shakespeare was implicated in a gigantic plot to conceal the true author." He went on to assert that "What espousers of the Oxford authorship never seem to remember is that Edward de Vere, the 17th Earl of Oxford, was born on April 12, 1550, and died on June 24, 1604, before some of the greatest plays were written." They were guilty, he wrote, of "attempts to redate all the plays back to the 1570's," and these attempts, he said, "have been considered just as absurd as the agitation to dismember the monument." That every one of the charges he brought against me and those who shared my views was of course a falsehood no doubt attested to a deep sense of insecurity on his part as to his position, and perhaps in recognizing this fact I should have been reconciled to being characterized as wholly irrational, but I cannot say that the consideration mollified me, particularly because there was more to come. Recalling that he had telephoned me in the previous March, Dr. Marder said, "I asked him whether he would give up his Oxfordian position if nothing were found within the monument." Inasmuch as the "Oxfordian position," as he well knew, was not in the smallest degree dependent on the contents of the monument, if any, I naturally said I should not. This answer, he claimed, without giving any hint as to what it was, "bore out what a psychiatrist once quoted in SNL [Dr. Marder's *Shakespeare Newsletter*] said of Shakespearean heretics in general: such people will never give up their position because they operate on emotion rather than reason." While conceding magnanimously that "letters and conversations with Mr. Louther and Mr. Ogburn convince me that neither of them is directly responsible for what happened in early October" — i.e., a criminal assault on a cherished public monument — he accused us of having by our "opinions and public statements inspired the incident which Mr. Fox said could only have shocked thousands of people throughout the English-speaking world." Dr. Marder obviously believed that one who found evidence of the Shakespeare manuscripts' concealment in the Stratford monument was to be censured if he did not keep the evidence to himself.

Of course I wrote Dr. Marder a letter for publication in his newsletter to correct the misrepresentation of my views, but as I might have expected the letter was not published or even acknowledged, while the acting dean of his college, Richard M. Johnson, similarly declined to reply to a letter I subsequently sent him detailing Dr. Marder's transgressions against common honesty. . . . In brief: if one looks to academia for respect for truth and intellectual decency one had better not count on finding it there.

For several years nothing much happened on the monument front, apart from my having the following interesting passage from James Joyce's *Ulysses* brought to my attention:

> — Dowden believes there is some mystery in *Hamlet* but will say no more. Herr Bleibtreu, the man Piper met in Berlin, who is working up that Rutland theory, believes that the secret is hidden in the Stratford monument.

Then I received the following letter on the stationery of SRI International of Menlo Park, California, dated 23 March 1978:

> Dear Mr. Ogburn,
>
> I recently reread your article "Shakespeare's Missing Manuscripts," together with the discussion that followed in the August 1972 number of *Harper's*; I wonder what, if anything, has developed in the years between.
>
> My organization and associates are interested in the application of high technology methods of archeology, and we feel that the Shakespearean manuscripts are worthy of a substantial effort. One of our teams is currently in Egypt exploring the Sphinx and a reported boat pit near one of the pyramids.
>
> Please let me know how we might support you in this important project.

The letter was signed by W. A. Edson, Staff Assistant, Radio Physics Laboratory.

To reply to the writer's question as to what, if anything, had happened in the years since the publication of the article took me more than three pages, single spaced. In conclusion I wrote:

> Your letter has awakened a new and exciting hope that the theory I put forward in the *Harper's* article nearly six years ago may now be put to the test. . . . I do not see how any difficulty could be made about an examination that did not involve any sort of dismantling of the monument.

I did not hear again from Dr. Edson for nearly three months. Then came a letter dated June 6th transmitting a technical statement of the problem and equipment needed, together with questions about the construction of the monument to which answers were required. This was signed by Lambert Dolphin, whose absence in Egypt had delayed the communication. Dr. Edson in his covering letter made the ominous remark that "As usual, our principal problem is funding," but added that "We do have the needed technology, interest and recognition in the world of exploration and archaeology."

I wrote that I planned to go to England in September and while there would try to obtain precise answers to the questions Dr. Dolphin had raised and I said that I awaited the estimate of costs in some trepidation. This proved amply justified. Dr. Edson forwarded to me "with some misgiving" a memorandum from Dr. Dolphin calling for "Funding of the order of $10,000 minimum," which he acknowledged to be "arbitrary to some extent in that processing smaller proposals causes internal problems." These I felt would surely be very small, I wrote Dr. Edson, compared with the internal problems that raising $10,000 would cause me. I sent Dr. Edson my own itemized estimate of $2,500. Even that, I wrote, "is a fair amount of money for a private individual [a writer, anyhow]. But on top of that I have to reckon on the cost of a trial at the Consistory Court if the acoustic sounder produces positive readings." If it did, the Court's permission would of course still be required to open the monument. Later I began to wonder why the costs should devolve upon me. I had put thousands of dollars worth of time into the venture as it was.

A note from the Reverend Canon D. P. K. Barnes, Rector of Holy Trinity Church in Stratford, agreeing to my calling upon him, awaited me when my wife and I arrived in England. The night before the day set we spent in Oxford. There our departure was unavoidably delayed, and I am sure my wife will not forget our ride to Stratford on what was to me still the wrong side of the road as I strove to reach our destination before the Rector had to leave on other business. By running several blocks after parking the car I caught him in the nick of time. He was at once to be perceived as a fine gentleman with an unsullied integrity transparent in his candid blue eyes.

Dr. Barnes said that the interlopers had gained access to his church by taking advantage of the practice session a group of singers held one evening a week, their custom being to leave the door unlocked behind them. After hiding until the singers had departed, they would have had a clear field for their operations. I do not recall how he said they would have got out of the church, assuming that the singers had locked the door on departing; the interview was rather hurried. He did not consider it remarkable that the intruders were not heard at their work, though I should have thought the clang of hammer-blows on a cold chisel biting into stone would have aroused the neighborhood. For the rest, as I reported to Dr. Edson:

> I learned that it would not be necessary to have the permission of the Consistory Court to take electronic soundings of the monument; Dr. Barnes would simply have to consult with his superiors. He said that soundings would detect cavities anywhere in the church walls since these consist of an inner and an outer shell, separated, and more or less filled with rubble. He also maintains that the outer shell behind the monument would have been removed when the charnel house was razed a century or more ago and that this would have revealed any cache behind the stone on which the bust rests. He was out of town when the intruders chiseled into this stone but saw their handiwork. He says that after removing the bust they went in two or three inches and evidently convinced themselves there was nothing but solid stone behind the inscription plate. He thinks we are on a wild goose chase but cannot suggest what the inscription means if it does not mean what I think it does. Right now I feel rather baffled by the whole thing.

That was in 1978. At present, as at the beginning, I should assess the odds as to my theory's being correct — that is, that the monument was designed to house the manuscripts — at fifty-fifty. For the rest, I take it to begin with that the manuscripts were not available to the Herbert brothers — the Earls of Pembroke and Montgomery — who, I believe, had the First Folio printed, when the edition was compiled; this would seem to follow from the multitudinous errors in the text. The inference would be, then, that (1) the Herberts had been relieved of them by a higher authority seeking to prevent publication of the plays and some disposition made of them which we cannot guess, or (2) the manuscripts had been placed in the monument before compilation of the Folio began, either by the Herberts (to save them from threatened seizure) or some other "grand possessors." In the latter case, they (1) were removed from the monument at some time in the past, I should think early in the game, or (2) are still there, in some part of the monument or below it. In any case, I find it as hard as ever to believe that the manuscripts would have been destroyed to the last page when no other version of most of the plays as the author conceived them existed; the mind balks at the thought of such vandalism. If mischance did not claim the entire lot with an unlikely extreme thoroughness, it seems to me probable that they still survive.

It was reassuring to hear from Dr. Edson that

> . . . My faith in your conjecture has not dimmed.
> I will continue to seek a workable nondestructive technique for exploring the contents of the monument and of reducing the cost of making the test.

Appendix. Adventures in the Quest for the Shakespeare Manuscripts

I wrote him that I should like to proceed by first finishing a book I was working on which would present evidence sufficient, I should think, to topple the Stratford man several times over from his artificial pedestal and, with that done, the difficulties in the way of the quest for the manuscripts should mostly melt away.

The chief impression that quest has left with me is of the enormous power of conventional belief. As I wrote in a letter in *Harper's*, speaking about men of standing in fields of scholarship and letters:

> So far, none of them has come forward to show where my theory breaks down. Their failure to do so would, it seems to me, be tantamount to an admission that they cannot, and this in turn to their admitting that there is at least a possibility, however slim, of the manuscripts' being in the monument. If, then, they do not demand that this possibility be followed up — and I am speaking particularly of the Shakespearean specialists — the inference would appear to be inescapable that they are disinclined to have anything further learned about the writer known to us as William Shakespeare.

Apart from Richmond Crinkley, not one Stratfordian academic — and this goes for Louis Marder, too, on whose attention I forced the passage — ever had a word to say in response.

Citations

Note: Sources of quotations are indicated by the author's name and, where called for, the name of the publication in which they appear. The author's name alone is cited where only one of his publications is listed in the Bibliography or where one is predominantly drawn upon and is listed first in the Bibliography. For example, "Chambers, II, 147," refers to Sir E. K. Chambers's *William Shakespeare: A Study of Facts and Problems*, volume II. A quotation from another of his listed books will be cited as, say, "Chambers, *Sir Henry Lee*, 95."

xi "With This Acknowledgment": *Henry Fifth*, IV viii.

xv "If Thou Read This": *Julius Caesar*, II iii.

xv Pepys on performances of Shakespeare: Ingleby, 316–323.

xviii Documents in IBM case: Gerhart, 21–22.

Book One. "The Cause and Question Now in Hand": *Troilus and Cressida*, II ii.

---

3 Chapter 1. "A Mystery? Ay, Sir, a Mystery": *Measure for Measure*, IV ii.

3–4 Statements about Shakespeare in *Palladis Tamia*: Meres, *Ancient Critical Essays*, II, 152–153; Ingleby, 21–23; Chambers, II, 193–195.

4 De Quincey on those to whom Shakespeare's works are primal necessities: (*Encyclopaedia Britannica*, 7th ed., 1838), *Shakespeare Criticism*, 337.

4 Carlyle on the sacredness of Shakespeare's being sent into this Earth: "The Hero as Poet" (1840), Ibid., 368.

4–5 Heine on Shakespeare: Seldon, 29.

5 "There is one book . . . written or spoken upon earth": Swinburne, v.

5 Shakespeare in foreign languages and libraries: Marder, 29.

5 Shakespeare in paperback editions: R. H. Smith, quoted by Eve Auchincloss, "Book World," *Washington Post*, 7 March 1976.

6 Verse by John Davies: From *Scourge of Folly: To Our English Terence Mr. Will Shake-speare*: Ingleby, 94; Chambers, II, 214.

6 "The drift of his plays . . . impress of that genius": Ingleby, xii–xiii.

7 ". . . the bard of our admiration . . . exemplar of his species": Ibid., xi.

7 Publication of poems and plays while Shakespeare was alive: Marder, 8.

7 Shakespeare as in hearts of the people: Knight, *Studies*, 504.

7 Shakespeare as a showman unknown to his men: Ingleby, xii.

7 Popularity of Shakespeare's plays and characters: Ibid. Lucy Toulmin Smith, Preface to 2nd ed., xx.

7 Eulogies of Shakespeare by early 17th century: Marder, 9.

7 "Absence of contemporary panegyric": Emerson, *English Traits*, 237.

Citations

8–9 Manningham's anecdote of Burbage and Shakespeare: Ingleby, 45; Chambers, II, 212.

9 Manningham on *Twelfth Night*: Ingleby, 45; Chambers, II, 327–328.

9 Epigram "To Mr. William Shake-spear": *Witts Recreations*, no. 25.

10 Elizabeth and Lambarde on *Richard the Second*: Nichols, III, 562.

11 Absence of commendatory verses to Shakespeare: Fleay, 73–74.

11 The life of Shakespeare as a "fine mystery": Dickens, Letter to William Sandys, 13 June 1847, *Complete Writings*, XXXVII, 206.

11 "Just within the possibility of authorship": Emerson, "Representative Men," *Complete Works*, IV, 212.

---

12 **Chapter 2.** "Cry Out Thus upon No Trail": *Merry Wives*, IV ii.

14 Shakespeare's bringing fame to Stratford: McManaway, 23.

14–15 Hammond on the Stratford monument and verses to Combe: Chambers, II, 242.

14–15 Verses ascribed to "Shakespear": Aubrey, II, 226; Chambers, II, 252–253.

15 Biographical sketch of "Shakespear": Aubrey, II, 225–227; Chambers, II, 252–253.

15 Beeston as knowing most from Lacy: Aubrey, I, 97.

15–17 First serious attempt at a biography of "Shakespeare": Rowe—early years, ii–vi; acquaintance with Jonson, xii–xiii; retirement, xxxv–xxxvi. Rowe's version of "Shakespeare's" epitaph to Combe reads:
Ten in the hundred lies here ingrav'd,
'Tis a hundred to ten, his soul is not sav'd:
If any man ask, who lies in this tomb?
Oh! Oh! quoth the Devil, 'tis my John-a-Combe.

18 Characterization of Aubrey: *Encyclopaedia Britannica*, I, 891a.

18 Ward's testimony as "unimpeachable": McManaway, 24.

18–19 Ward's notes on "Shakespeare": Ingleby, 317; Chambers, II, 249–250.

19–20 Fuller's observations on "Shakespeare": Ingleby, 246–247; Chambers, II, 244.

20 "Beyond a similarity . . . to conceal his authorship": M. Johnson, Letter to Professor Gwynne Blakemore Evans of Harvard, 20 February 1975.

20 "In no case . . . questioned his authorship": McManaway, 31.

21 Interrogation: Deposition of Giles E. Dawson, 6 October 1949, U.S. District Court for the District of Columbia, Civil Action No. 2698–48, p. 17.

21 "Of some fifty . . . authorship of the plays": *Washington Post*, 26 April 1964.

22 "Sweetest Shakespeare, fancy's child": Milton, *L'Allegro*, lines 133–134.

22 Shakespeare as having "largest and most comprehensive soul": Dryden, "An Essay of Dramatic Poesy," *Works*, XV, 344.

22 Quotation on quadricentennial festivities: Isaacs, 685.

---

23 **Chapter 3.** "Such a Deadly Life": *Twelfth Night*, I v.

23 McManaway on Stonley's purchase of *Venus and Adonis*: Jean M. White, "Twelve Pence for the Bard," *Washington Post*, 23 April 1973, B 1.

23 "We know more . . . a longer life": Rowse, *Shakespeare the Man*, 1.

Citations

23 "For a playwright . . . well documented": McManaway, 1.

24 Whitman on the blankness of Shakspere's record: Traubel, 136.

24 "The last time . . . a young apprentice": Isaacs, 685.

24 "One hundredth . . . a respectable biography": Trevor-Roper, MS of an article cited in Bibliography.

24 Shakespeare Birthplace Trust as not carrying on a trade: Arthur Osman, London, *Times*, 2 October 1964.

24-5 The Stratford frauds: B. Levin, London, *Daily Mail*, 18 February and 30 November 1966.

25 The innate snobbishness of doubts about Shakspere: Watts, "Two on the Aisle," *New York Post*, undated clipping, April 1964.

25 Ardens as superior folk: Rowse, *Shakespeare the Man*, 7.

25 Ardens as lordly people: I. Brown, *Shakespeare*, Time edition, 23.

25 Sources of the statements in paragraph on John Shakspere are cited in Chambers, I, 11–15.

26 Shakspere's marriage license and bond of sureties: Chambers, II, 41; G. E. Bentley, 29–31.

26 Anne Hathaway's marriage to Wilson: Hunter, I, 48.

26 Christening of Susanna: Chambers, II, 1; G. E. Bentley, 32.

26 Christening of Hamnet and Judith: Chambers, II, 3; G. E. Bentley, 33.

26 Proceedings to recover property of Mary Arden: Chambers II, 35.

26 Shakespeare's "happy and copious industry": Webster, Epistle to *The White Devil*, 1612; Chambers, II, 218.

26-7 Shakespeare's having perhaps traveled in Europe: I. Brown, *Shakespeare in His Time*, 15.

27 Postulations of Shakspere's activities during "lost years": Bénézet, "The Stratford Defendant Compromised by His Own Advocates," *Shake. Fellow. Quar.*, V, no. 3, July 1944; VI, no. 1, January, no. 2, April, and no. 3, July 1945.

27 Quotations from Arthur Gray and Frances Yates: Schoenbaum, 727, 736.

27 "Who shall say . . . may have brought him": Chambers, I, 26.

27 Shakspere's taking the road to London: Rowse, *Shakespeare the Man*, 38.

28 Payment to Kemp, Shakespeare, and Burbage: G. E. Bentley, 99–100.

28 Burial of Hamnet: Chambers, II, 4; G. E. Bentley, 33.

28 Paragraph on Shakspere's coat-of-arms: Information from Chambers, II, 24; Scott-Giles, 29–31.

28-9 Sureties of peace sought against "Shakspare": G. E. Bentley, 74.

29 Shakspere's purchase of New Place: Chambers, II, 103; G. E. Bentley, 36.

29 Failure to collect tax owed by "Shackspere": Chambers, II, 87; G. E. Bentley, 71–72.

29 Sturley's letter about "Shaksper" and the tithes: Chambers, II, 103; G. E. Bentley, 37–38.

29 "Shackespere" as holding x quarters of grain: Chambers, II, 99–101; G. E. Bentley (who omits any mention of resentment of hoarders), 37.

29 "Shakespeare" again a tax-delinquent: Chambers, II, 87; G. E. Bentley, 72–73.

29 Quiney's letter to "Shackespere," his father's letter about "Mr. Sha.," and Sturley's letter to Quiney: Chambers, II, 101–103; G. E. Bentley, 38–39.

Citations

29 Payment to "Shaxpere" for load of stone: Chambers, II, 96; omitted by Bentley.

29–30 "Shakespere" as a shareholder in the Globe: Chambers, II, 52–57; G. E. Bentley, 102–104.

30 "Shakspere" among "deserving men" in building the Globe: Chambers, II, 65–69; G. E. Bentley, 106–107.

30 "Shakespeare" as one of occupants of house in St. Saviour: G. E. Bentley, 105.

30 "Shakespeare" as tax-delinquent moved to Sussex: Chambers, II, 88; G. E. Bentley, 73.

30 Tax owed by "Shakspeare" referred to Bishop of Worcester for collection: Ibid.

30 "Shakespeare" buys land from the Combes: Chambers, II, 107; G. E. Bentley, 42–43.

30 "Shakespeare" in legal action described as "generosum": Chambers, II, 96; G. E. Bentley, 42, neglects to point out that this record of 1602 is the first in which the Stratfordian is described as "gentleman."

30 Lease on barn east of New Place: Chambers, II, 96.

30 "Shakespeare" listed among actors licensed to perform: Chambers, II, 72; G. E. Bentley, 93–94.

30 "Shakespeare" listed among members of King's Company to receive cloth: Chambers, II, 73; G. E. Bentley, 111–112.

30–31 Deposition by "Shakespeare" in the Belott-Mountjoy case: Chambers, II, 94; G. E. Bentley, 76–80.

31 "Shexpere" seeks to collect debt for malt from Rogers: Chambers, II, 113; G. E. Bentley, 47.

31 Phillipps names "Shakespeare" among beneficiaries in his will: Chambers, II, 73; G. E. Bentley, 114–115.

31 "Shakespear's" purchase of tithes: Chambers, II, 119–120; G. E. Bentley, 43–44.

31 Marriage of "Susanna Shaxpere" and John Hall: Chambers, II, 4; G. E. Bentley, 32, 46.

31 "Shakespeare" among seven men leasing Blackfriars: Chambers, II, 58; G. E. Bentley, 115–116.

31 "Shakspeare" named among "men players" in connection with Blackfriars: Chambers, II, 65–66; G. E. Bentley, 116.

31 "Shackspeare" proceeds against debtor: Chambers, II, 114; G. E. Bentley, 47.

31 "Shackspeare" proceeds against the debtor's surety: Chambers, II, 115. Chambers leaves this unsavory record in Latin and Bentley omits it altogether. See Greenwood, 185.

31 "Shakespeare" in legal action about New Place: Chambers, II, 109; G. E. Bentley, 47–48.

31–32 "Shackspeare" and the non-payment of rents by fellow leaseholders: Chambers, II, 114.

32 "Shackspere" among those contributing to highway fund: Chambers, II, 152–153; G. E. Bentley, 48–49.

32 "Shackspere" named in Combe's will: Chambers, II, 127; G. E. Bentley, 49.

32   A "Mr. Shakspeare" paid for work on the Earl of Rutland's impreso: Chambers, II, 153; G. E. Bentley, 82.

32   Suggestion that a John Shakespeare meant: Stopes, *Burbage and Shakespeare's Stage*, 109.

32   "Shakespeare" buys a house in Blackfriars and mortgages it: Chambers, II, 157; G. E. Bentley, 83–86.

32   Shakspere duns town for claret given to preacher: Chambers, II, 153. G. E. Bentley passes over the record.

32–3 The Welcombe enclosure and Shakspere's remark to Greene: Chambers, II, 141–144; G. E. Bentley, 51–56. Bentley is an apologist of enclosure as representing modernization.

33   Shakspere's indemnifying himself against injury: Chambers, II, 148.

33   Shakspere sides with Combe: S. Lee, *Life of William Shakespeare*, 279–280.

33   Suit to clear up ownership of Blackfriars properties: G. E. Bentley, 86.

33   Judith's marriage to Quiney and Quiney's betrayal of Margaret Wheeler: Isaacs, 685–686.

33–5 Shakspere's will: Chambers, II, 169–174; G. E. Bentley, 57–61.

34   Bequest to the three actors: Chambers, II, 172; G. E. Bentley, 62.

34   The second-best bed: Chambers, II, 173; G. E. Bentley, 63.

34   Lurid tales consequent to the slighting bequest: G. E. Bentley, 63.

34   Mrs. Shakspere's dower rights: Chambers, II, 176–177; G. E. Bentley, 63.

34   Lack of personal feeling in Shakspere's will: Chute, 320.

34–5 Lack of mention of theatrical shares in will: Chambers, II, 179.

35   Bénézet on contrasting wills of Heminge and Condell: *Shake. Fellow. Newsletter*, IV, no. 6, October 1943, p. 78.

35   Inclusion of books with personal belongings: I. Brown, *Shakespeare*, Collins, 320.

35   Lack of evidence of Shakspere's ever owning a book: Baldwin, II, 666.

35   Manuscripts as property of the company: G. E. Bentley, 62.

35   Inclusion of "early drafts" with "household stuff": G. E. Bentley, ibid.

36   Alleyn's affectionate letters to wife: Chute, 106.

37   Respect shown Dr. Hall: G. E. Bentley, 68.

---

38   **Chapter 4. "A Case of Lives":** *Henry the Fifth*, III ii.

38   Hall on Drayton as "excellent poet": Chambers, II, 11.

39   Crudity of epitaph passed off as mischievous: *A Walk Round Holy Trinity Church, Stratford-upon-Avon*, undated.

39   The original epitaph: S. Johnson (with Steevens, *Prefaces*), 144.

39   Dowdall on the epitaph: Chambers, II, 259.

39   Hall's explanation of the crudity of the epitaph: Chambers, II, 260.

39   The "obvious purpose" of the "rude doggerel": Dawson, 15.

40   The baker's epitaph: Chambers, II, 181.

40   Basse's quatrain: Chambers, II, 226.

40   Shakspere's taking no part in affairs of the town: Chute, 299.

Citations

42 Shakspere's obscurity: Twain, 371–2.

42 Richardson on our lack of knowledge of Shakespeare: I. Brown, *Shakespeare*, Time Edition, xi.

42 Shakspere's having no history. Twain, 372.

42 Our knowing much about Shakespeare: Rowse, *Shakespeare the Man*, 1.

42 Shakespeare's life as well documented: McManaway, 1.

42–3 "More records . . . except Ben Jonson": G. E. Bentley, 3, 5.

43 Less known about others than about Shakespeare: Wright, *Folger Shakespeare*, xxx.

43 More on record about Shakespeare than about others: Wright, *Shakespeare for Everyman*, 106.

43 Greatest Elizabethan dramatist the best documented: Chute, 179.

43 "We know more . . . one of the best known citizens. . . .": Bergen Evans, "Good Friend for Iesus Sake Forebeare." *Saturday Review of Literature*, 7 May 1949, 8.

43 Lyly at the university: Bond, 1, 6.

43 Writes to Lord Burghley: *Ibid.* 12, 13.

43 Sent to the country to nurse: *Ibid.*, 13.

43 Harvey on Lyly at Oxford: "Pierces Supererogation," 1593, Harvey, *Works*, II, 28.

43 Lodging at the Savoy: Bond, 17.

43 Lyly's resentment of Harvey's slur: *Ibid.*, 8.

44 Encouraged by and dedicates work to Oxford: *Ibid.*, 24.

44 Alludes to love affair in letter to Watson: Ibid., 25, 26.

44 Harvey in trouble for a satire on Oxford: Ibid., 30, 31.

44 Lyly encouraged to aim at Mastership of Revels: Ibid., 63, 64.

44 Suggests retiring to thatched cottage: Ibid., 33, 70–71.

44 Made vice-master, St. Paul's: Ibid., 33, 44.

44 Complains of lack of advancement by Queen: Ibid., 33, 68–69.

45 Elected to Parliament: Ibid., 55.

45 Associated with Nashe in Marprelate battle: Ibid., 51, 60.

45 Reader for Bishop of London: Ibid., 44.

45 As represented by Jonson in play: Ibid., 61.

45 Eclipsed as writer: Ibid., 78.

45 Final poverty and death: Ibid., 76.

45 Rediscovery during increasing study of Shakspeare: Ibid., 81.

46 Orgal on how much is known about Shakespeare: "William Shakespeare: Scenes from his Daily Life," "Book World," *Washington Post*, 17 May 1981, 4.

46 Spenser's origins and paternity: *Works*, Oxford ed., vii; *Encyclopaedia Britannica*, XXV, 639b.

46 His education at Merchant Taylors school: *Works*, Oxford ed., vii–viii.

46 His first poems: *Works*, Oxford ed., viii; *Encyclopaedia Britannica*, XXV, 639b.

46–7 Spenser at Cambridge: *Works*, Hazard ed., 6; *Works*, Oxford ed., viii.

Citations

47   Association with Harvey: *Works*, Oxford ed., ix–x.

47   Sojourn in the north, relations with Rosalind: *Works*, Hazard ed., 7; *Works*, Oxford ed., xi.

47   Return to London, introduction to Sidney, employment in Leicester's household: *Works*, Hazard ed., 8–9; *Works*, Oxford ed., xii.

47   As seen in correspondence with Harvey: *Encyclopaedia Britannica*, XXV, 640b.

48   Warned by Harvey of another "Rosalindula": *Works*, Oxford ed., xii.

48   Burghley's hostility provoked: *Works*, Hazard ed., 8; *Works*, Oxford ed., xii; Brooke (quoted), 488.

48   With Sidney and Dyer in the *Areopagus*: Brooke, 473; *Works*, Oxford ed., xxi.

48   His view of poetry as not a gentleman's profession: Ibid., xxi.

48   Belief in striking while the iron hot: Ibid.

48   Service as Secretary to Lord Grey de Wilton: Ibid., xxiii.

48–9   De Selincourt on Spenser in Ireland: Ibid., xxiv–xxv.

49   Spenser's life on the forfeited Desmond estates, popularity with the English colony of Dublin, and exegesis of *Faerie Queene*: Ibid., xxv–xxvii; *Works*, Hazard ed., 9.

49–50   Relations with Raleigh: *Works*, Hazard ed., 5, 8; *Works*, Oxford ed., xxvii–xxviii.

50   Publication of *Faerie Queene* with commendatory and dedicatory poems: *Works*, Hazard ed., 3–8; *Works*, Oxford ed., xxviii, 405–413.

50   Success of *Faerie Queene*, Spenser's courtly connections, presentation to Queen, and pension: *Works*, Hazard ed., 10; *Works*, Oxford ed., xxix.

50   His return to Kilcolman, marriage to Elizabeth Boyle, boundary dispute: *Works*, Oxford ed., xxx–xxxi, xxxv.

50   Return to London with second part of *Faerie Queene*; *Fowre Hymnes*; registration of *Veue of the Present State of Ireland*: Ibid., xxxvi–xxxvii.

50–1   Return to Kilcolman; appointment as Sheriff of Cork; burning of Kilcolman with possibility that last part of *Faerie Queene* destroyed; de Selincourt on Spenser's return to London with dispatches: *Works*, Hazard ed., 19; *Works*, Oxford ed., xxxviii–xxxix.

51   Spenser's death after rejection of £20 from Essex: *Encyclopaedia Britannica*, XXV, 643a; *Works*, Oxford ed., xxxix.

51   Minimization of information about Spenser: McManaway, 4.

52   Denial of letters to or from Spenser: Ibid.

52   Spenser's holographs: W. W. Greg, Part II, *Poets*, XXXIX and XL.

53   Elegiac tributes by fellow poets: *Works*, Hazard ed., 19.

53   Monument to Spenser in Westminster: Ibid.

---

55   **Chapter 5.** "The Baseless Fabric": *The Tempest*, IV i.

55   Biographies as showing how little known of Shakespeare: Review of Rowse's *Shakespeare the Man*, *Publishers Weekly*, 23 April 1973.

55–6   Tributes to Burbage and Shakespeare: Rowse, *Shakespeare the Man*, 132.

Citations

56 First certainty of Shakespeare in London in Greene's attack: Chambers, I, 22.

56 Facts established by Greene's attack: Chute, 85.

56–7 "R. G.'s" attack on the "upstart Crow": Greene, *Works*, XII, 141, 143–144; Chambers, II, 188–189.

56 Shakespeare seen as both player and maker of plays: Ibid., I, 59.

56 "Most important thing . . . Stratford in 1585": Chute, 85.

57 Shown as rival to University Wits: G. E. Bentley, 95.

58 Actors now with writer of their own: Chambers, I, 58.

58 Chettle's *Kind-Harts Dreame*: Chambers, II, 189.

58 Schoenbaum as "the foremost living Shakespearean scholar": Folger Educational Catalogue, 1981.

58–9 Shakespeare's presentation of testimonials to Chettle: Schoenbaum, 52.

59 Chettle's handsome apology: Rowse, *Shakespeare the Man*, 61–62.

59 Shakespeare not one of those who took offense: Fleay, 111.

60 Castle on inability of a whole succession of Stratfordian scholars to read *Groatsworth* correctly: Greenwood, 316.

60 Assertions based on omission of vital parts of *Groatsworth*: by Marchette Chute, 83, and by Rowse, *Shakespeare the Man*, 61.

60 Categorical identification of upstart Crow as Shakespeare: by McManaway, 15, and by Wright, *Shakespeare for Everyman*, 129.

60 Historical scholar superior to lawyer in analysis of evidence: Wright, Ibid., 97.

60 Lawyers as not interested in evidence: Wright, Report from Folger Library, IX, no. 1, 20 May 1960, p. 5.

60 Leach on identity of jurist quoted by Wright: *Shakespeare Cross-Examination*, 121–122.

60–1 Lawyers as trained to win cases regardless of evidence: Wright, *Shakespeare for Everyman*, 97.

61–2 "Looseness in Chettle's language": Chambers, I, 59.

62–3 Greene "savagely attacked his rival . . . who presumed to write plays": McManaway, *Washington Post*, B1, 23 April 1973.

63 Hardison on Greene as warning of the playwright Shakespeare: "Shakespeare: Was He Shakespeare?" "Outlook," *Washington Post*, 8 December 1974.

63 Ogburn as baffled by Groatsworth: Evans-Levin, 41–42.

63 *Riverside Shakespeare* and Harvard literary scholarship: Professor Walter Kaiser of Harvard in letter to John Bethell of 22 November 1974.

63 Levin on Greene's "truculent outburst": *Riverside Shakespeare*, 2.

63–4 Dismissal of Professor Austin's "Hypothesis": Schoenbaum, *Documentary Life*, 156.

64 "Desperate shaft directed against Shakespeare": Ibid., 115.

64 "The swan sings . . . youth's pleasures": Greene, "Groatsworth," *Works*, XII, 101.

64 "Cursed be the day . . . gave me suck": Greene, "Repentence," *Works*, II, 166.

64 Entry of GREENES *Groatsworth*: Register of the Company of Stationers, II, 292b.

Citations

64 Nashe disavows any part in Groatsworth: "Pierce Penilesse His Suplication to the Divell," Nashe, *Works*, I, 154.

65 On vital information in Treasurer's Accounts: I. Brown, *Shakespeare*, Collins, 164.

65 Payments to Kempe, Shakespeare, and Burbage: G. E. Bentley, 99–100.

65 On Shakespeare's appearing in fifteen new plays a year: Chute, 196.

65 Lord Chamberlain's called "Shakespeare's company": Harrison, *Introducing Shakespeare*, heading of Chap. IV.

65 Shakespeare as with Lord Chamberlain's company from the start: Dawson, 8.

65 Lord Chamberlain's company as playing at Gray's Inn on December 28: Chambers, II, 319.

65–6 The gap in the Treasurer's accounts, the deficit, and the Queen's demand that the widow make it up: Stopes, *Shakespeare's Industry*, 221–222.

66 Prominence of Kempe and Burbage: G. E. Bentley, 100.

---

68 **Chapter 6. "How Much Art Thou Shrunk!"** *1 Henry the Fourth*, V iv.

68 Review of Harbage's *Conceptions of Shakespeare*: O. J. Campbell, *New York Times Book Review*, 16 October 1966.

68 Void at the center of biographies of Shakespeare: E. Jones, 1.

69 Russell on the emptiness of biographies of Shakespeare: "Week in Review," *New York Times*, 18 June 1981.

69 Lack of good biographies of Shakespeare: Harrison, "Book Week," *Washington Post*, 5 July 1964, 5.

69–70 Exasperating dearth of information about Shakespeare: Trevor-Roper, 41.

70 On how little of what counts we know of Shakespeare: Hallam, II, 275–276.

70 On unsatisfactory record of Shakespeare: Trevor-Roper, 41.

70 How Shakespeare made commonplace by commentators: F. Harris, xi.

71 Quinn's assertion that facts of his life have little to do with his plays: "How to Know Everything about Shakespeare," "Book World," *Washington Post*, 21 June 1970.

71 "Shakespeare" as complete man of theatre, good actor, good company, with mobile, sexy features: Rowse, *Shakespeare the Man*, 40.

71–2 Shakspere "had already become interested . . . librarian, prompter and producer": O. J. Campbell, 178.

72 Ms. Buckmaster sees anti-Stratfordians feeding voluptuously: *Chicago Tribune*, 5 June 1963.

72 "Inevitable drawbacks" of Ms. Buckmaster's novel: P. Albert Duhamel, *New York Times*, 11 November 1962.

72 Review of *You, My Brother*: Ogburn, *Washington Post*, B10, 19 October 1973.

72 Ned wonders what in Will's soul could produce Hamlet: *You, My Brother*, New York: Random House, 1973.

72 Shakespeare as "relaxed and happy man": Chute, 134.

72 Shakespeare as "prudent, discreet man" of "good business sense": Rowse, *Shakespeare the Man*, 230.

811

Citations

72 Busy Shakespeare "knocking off an *Othello*": I. Brown, "Speaking of Books," *New York Times Book Review*, 2 October 1960.

72–3 "How did he reach the wit . . . answer there is none": Sampson, 259.

73 Mystery of how Shakespeare came to write Hamlet: *Riverside Shakespeare*, 1135.

73 Anti-Stratfordians as band of zealots: Evans-Levin, 39.

73 As "cranks . . . ignorant . . . morbid . . .": Sampson, 256.

73 "Mr. Fox . . . does not trouble himself to answer": "Debate on the Authorship Question," *Shake. Auth. Review*, no. 10, Autumn 1963, p. 9.

73–4 Gainsborough's confession of inability to portray Shakespeare: Hartman, 12, 13.

74 Stratfordian as a Shylock: Greenwood, 185.

74 Shakspere's effort to elevate himself with coat-of-arms; noblemen as seeking the acquaintance of actors: J. Q. Adams, 243, 240.

74 Jonson's cut at Shakspere's gentility: Harrison, *Shakespeare at Work*, 202.

74–5 Making fun of the Heralds and paying to be Gentlemen: Rowse, *Shakespeare the Man*, 181.

75 Not a "portrait" of Shakespeare: Chambers, II, 202.

75 Never let go of Stratford: Ibid., I, 74.

75 No wife and family in London: Chute, 54.

75 Responsible member of society: Rowse, *Shakespeare the Man*, 148.

75 "Normal family man": Ibid., 66.

75 Anne Shakspere's unpaid debt to Whittington: S. Lee, 194.

75 A commentary on Shakspere, that he left his wife unprovided for: Greenwood, 182.

76 Shakespeare's aim to please an illiterate audience: Halliwell-Phillipps, 7th ed., I, 117.

76 Shakespeare as more concerned with gentility than fate of plays: London, *Times Literary Supplement*, 19 September 1968.

76 Shakespeare's aim to make money and become a gentleman: Burgess, *Urgent Copy*, 159–160.

76 "What point of morals . . . rudeness of his behavior": Emerson, "Representative Men," *Works*, IV, 209–210.

76 "An ordinary man . . . who took the money and ran": Burgess, London, *Times*, 6 August 1973.

76 On writing as a trade that grows harder: Burgess, "The Genesis of *Earthly Powers*," "Book World," *Washington Post*, 23 November 1980.

76–7 The vulgar error that Shakespeare wrote for gain; his aim to make *Hamlet* worthy: Swinburne, *Complete Works*, 117.

78 On Shakespeare's viewing plays as not worth mentioning: Chute, 114.

78 English drama as born to the purple, delighting monarch and court: London, *Times Literary Supplement*, 19 September 1968.

78 London theatre regarded as glory of nation: Rowse, *Shakespeare the Man*, 49.

78–9 Plays not considered literature: McManaway, 16.

79 The supreme achievements of Shakespeare in poetry and human insights: Swinburne, xxxvi.

Citations

79   Shakespeare as greatest writer who will ever live: Steiner, "'Why, He Doth Bestride the Narrow World Like a Colossus,'" *New York Times Book Review*, 19 April 1964, 43.

80   Shakespeare's being unable to make a living writing plays: Chute, 130.

80   The "dark lady" as a black whore: Burgess interviewed by Bill Moyers on WETA, Arlington, Va., 17 February 1981; film from WGBH, Boston.

80–1   Shakespeare as careless of future fame and fate of his works: S. Johnson, 40.

81   Shakespeare's not bothering to preserve his texts: I. Brown, London, *Observer*, 26 April 1953.

81   Shakespeare as astonished at longevity of the *Merchant*: I. Brown, "Is England Shakespeare Crazy?" New York *Herald Tribune*, 26 April 1953.

82   Shakespeare's prophetic insight: Levin, *Riverside Shakespeare*, 1.

82   Superiority of the *Sonnets* to the narrative poems: Dowden, *Histories and Poems*, 1053.

82–3   "One of the problems . . . their appearance in print": Collier, xxiv.

83   Shakespeare as interested only in play on the stage: Rowse, *Shakespeare the Man*, 130.

83   "A working dramatist . . . on the stage": Harrison, *The Genius of Shakespeare*, 15.

83   "Shakespeare's proper context . . . the London commercial theatres": G. E. Bentley, *Shakespeare Survey*, 168.

83   His plays as written for worthy audiences: Richard Levin, London, *Times Literary Supplement*, 25 January 1974, 81.

83   Shakespeare as man of the theatre: Auchincloss, 30.

83–4   "Never wrote merely for the stage . . . same additions in our own": Swinburne, *Complete Works*, 119.

84   Running-time of Elizabethan plays: A. Hart, *Shakespeare and the Homilies*, 96.

84   Playing time set at two hours: Chute, 157.

84   Length of Shakespeare's plays: A. Hart, 88.

84–5   Uncut *Hamlet* as racing by, "a thrilling entity": J. M. Brown, *Broadway in Review*, New York: Norton, 1940, 43.

85   Shakespeare as no more intelligible in his day than now: Coleridge, *Shakespeare Criticism*, 271.

85   "Shakespeare . . . contemptuous of stage-craft": Harris, 332.

85–6   *Antony and Cleopatra's* unfitness for the stage: Dowden, *Tragedies*, 949, 950.

86   Cibber's *King Richard the Third* as theatrically effective: Ibid., *Histories and Poems*, 736.

86   As more effective on the stage than Shakespeare's arrangement: Shaw, "Barry Sullivan, Shakespeare and Shaw," London, *Strand*, October 1947, 23.

86   *Henry the Fifth* as liberated by Olivier's film: *Time*, 8 April 1946.

86–7   Inferiority of *Henry the Fourth* on the stage to the film of *Henry the Fifth*: J. M. Brown, "The Old Vic and *Henry V*," *Saturday Review*, 25 May 1946, 24.

87   The inadequacy of any actor to represent Lear: Lamb, "On the Tragedies of Shakespeare," *Shakespeare Criticism*, 205.

87   Plays of Shakespeare not calculated for the stage: Ibid., 193.

Citations

87–8   Dislike of seeing Shakespeare's plays acted, with *Midsummer Night's Dream* as dull pantomime: Hazlitt, Ibid., 291, 299.

88   "Shakespeare was not a scholar . . . to these trades at the end": Wilson, review of *Fortunes of Falstaff* by John Dover Wilson, *The New Yorker,* 29 April 1944.

88–9   On "expertise": Laski, *The Limitations of the Expert,* Fabian Tract 235, Fabian Society, London, 1931.

89   Elizabeth and Shakespeare as brother and sister, with plays as conquests for an expanding England: Sinsheimer, 22, 25, 26.

90   Marlborough's history from Shakespeare, a "National Epic": Carlyle, "The Hero as Poet," *Shakespeare Criticism,* 366.

90   Shakespeare as taking up Homer and Dante: Swinburne, xii.

---

91   **Chapter 7.** "And Thereupon These Errors Are Arose": *Comedy of Errors,* V i.

91–2   Justice Wilberforce's and Trevor-Roper's opinions on the authorship: *All England Law Reports,* 1964, III, summarized in *Shake. Auth. Review,* no. 18, Autumn 1967, 14–18.

92   Ogburn accused of slurring Trevor-Roper: Evans-Levin, 40.

92–3   The rendering of Shakspere's name in Stratford: Chambers, II, App. E, no. iii, 373.

93   John's name as Shaxpeyr: Ibid.

93   Roche's spelling it Shaxbere: Greenwood, *Is There a Shakespeare Problem?* 339–340.

94   Quotation from Ovid on title-page of *Venus and Adonis* translated: Greenwood, 58.

94   "Grand gentlemanly manner" of dedication of *Venus and Adonis:* Rowse, *William Shakespeare,* 149.

95   "Joyed brave Talbot . . . ten thousand spectators": "Pierce Penilesse His Supplication to the Divell," Nashe, *Works,* I, 212.

95   Shakespeare as rushing for money and advancement: Burgess, *Urgent Copy,* 160.

96   A parallel poem to *Venus and Adonis,* with a parodying dedication: J. Q. Adams, *Oenone and Paris,* by T. H.

97   "The spear of Pallas shake": "Achilles his concealment of his sex in the court of Lycomedes," *Poems Written by Wil. Shake-Speare,* no page no.

97   Epigram to Brayne-Hardie: *Works of Jonson,* VIII, 32.

97   Hyphenation of Shake-speare as meaning nothing: Marder, "Debate on the Authorship Question," *Shake. Auth. Review,* no. 10, Autumn 1963, 5.

98   Hyphens called "occasionally misplaced": Evans-Levin, 42.

98–9   Shakespeare's name on *Love's Labour's Lost:* Ibid., 42.

99   Shakespeare with actor's capacity to enter into minds of others: Ibid., 40.

99   Henslowe's records of theatrical receipts and payments: Bénézet, "Look in the Chronicles," *Shake. Fellow. Newsletter,* IV, no. 3, April 1943, 25.

100   Ogburn's vain search in Henslowe's and Alleyn's records: Evans-Levin, 42.

100   Analogy with president of General Motors: McManaway, 36.

Citations

100   Shakspere as actor and playwright by late 1580s: Ibid., 15.

100   Shakspere's supposed early successes with company performing for Henslowe: J. Q. Adams, *Life of William Shakespeare*, 189.

100   The Rose as scene of Shakspere's first successes: S. Lee, 38.

101   "Sir William Davenant . . . to play Prince Hamlet": McManaway, 9.

101   Downes on Betterton's having instructed Davenant: Chambers, II, 263.

101   Shakspere's having acted the part of a decrepit old man: Wm. Oldys, quoted by Chambers, II, 278.

101–2   Shakspere as the Ghost in his own Hamlet: Rowe, vi.

102   Dowdall on the clerk who showed him the Stratford Church: Chambers, II, 259.

102   "His father was a butcher . . . make a speech": Aubrey, II, 226; Chambers, II, 253.

103   "Shakespeare" as "the great jester": Graves, II, 233.

103   Shakespeare in lists of actors in Folio: Evans-Levin, 42.

104   Davies's poem to "M. Will. Shake-speare": *The Scourge of Folly, Epigram 159*; Chambers, II, 214.

104   Derivation of "honesty": Partridge, 123.

105   "Companion for a King" as cryptic: Chambers, II, 214.

105   "Tradition" of Shakspere's having "played 'kingly' parts": Rowse, *Shakespeare the Man*, 40.

105   "Poem quoted and misquoted": Evans-Levin, 41.

105   Davies's verses initialed "W.S.R.B.": Respectively from *Microcosmos* and *The Civile Warres of Death and Fortune*, Chambers, II, 213–214.

105   Davies's verses to "sweet Companion": *Orchestra, or a Poem of Dancing, The Oxford Book of Sixteenth Century verse*, 772.

106   Shakespeare as saluted in *Parnassus* plays: Evans-Levin, 42.

106   Speech by Kempe on "our fellow Shakspeare": *Three Parnassus Plays*, 337.

106   Burbage and Kemp as an illiterate pair: Ibid.

106   *Pilgrimage to Parnassus*, character dragging a clown: Ibid., 129.

107   Derivation of *Venus and Adonis* and *Lucrece* from Ovid: Dowden, *Histories and Poems*, 946, 989.

107   Ovid as "Shakespeare's favorite classical poet": Schoenbaum, *The Globe and the World*, 29.

107–8   Kempe's boast of acting for making money and of himself and Burbage; actors despised as "leaden spouts": *Three Paranssus Plays*, 339, 344–345.

108   Respectful treatment of "Mr. Shakespeare" by Gullio and Ingenoso: Ibid., 183, 184, 185, 192.

108–9   "F.B.'s" poetical letter to Ben Jonson as usually read: Chambers, II, 224.

109–10   Shakespeare said to be revealed by Beaumont as having gone far by the dim light of nature: Martin, 30.

109   Part of "F.B.'s" letter habitually overlooked: Chambers, II, 224.

109   The plan to have Shakespeare appear uneducated: Charlton Ogburn, Jr., *Shakespeare and the Man of Stratford*, New York: Shakespeare-Oxford Society, 1964, 29.

110   Ogburn found straining evidence: Martin, 140–142.

Citations

110 Ogburn accused of misstating view of Stratford man held by his contemporaries: Evans-Levin, 42.

110 Shakespeare's contemporaries as having no doubt of his authorship: London, *Times Literary Supplement*, 27 July 1962.

110 Shakespeare's authorship as not doubted by contemporaries and for century and a half: "Topics," *New York Times*, 21 April 1963.

111 Shakespeare as "greatest of intellects": Carlyle, "The Hero as Poet," *Shakespeare Criticism*, 364.

112 Lack of outpouring of homage: Schoenbaum, 56.

112 Observances of Drayton's death: Drayton, *Works*, V, xxx.

112 Lamentations on Burbage's death: Stopes, *Burbage and Shakespeare's Stage*, 116–117.

112 Shakespeare among "most pregnant wits of these our times": Camden, "Epigrams," *Remaines*, 344.

112 Omission of Shakespeare from description of Stratford: Camden, *Britannia*, 502–503.

113 Shakspere's achievement of a place in *Britannia* of 1695: Ibid., 512.

113 Burbage's death recorded: Camden's *Remaines*, 541; *Dictionary of National Biography*, III, 288a.

113 Malone's report of "Shakespeare's" response to the drunken blacksmith: Chambers, II, 273–274.

113 Shakspere's killing a calf in high style and his equal in wit: Aubrey, II, 225; Chambers, II, 253.

113 "Shakspere's" inclusion among "deserving men": Chambers, II, 65–66.

114–5 An author's rights in his works in Elizabethan times: Greenwood, 303–306.

116 Writers likely and unlikely to be pirated: Pollard, 34.

116 Tribute to Pollard: Schoenbaum, 696, 704.

---

117 **Chapter 8. "Are They Not Lamely Writ?":** *Two Gentlemen of Verona*, II i.

117 Shakspere's parents as illiterate: Halliwell-Phillipps, 2nd ed. (1882), 24.

117 John's use of a mark on most solemn documents: Greenwood, *The Shakespeare Problem Restated*, 7.

117 "John would have written his name if he could have": Marder, "Debate on Authorship Question," *Shake. Author. Review*, no. 10, Autumn 1963, 3.

117 "Judith . . . couldn't write": Rowse, *William Shakespeare*, 451.

117 Judith's illiteracy as cancelled by Susanna's literacy: Marder, "Debate on the Authorship Question," *Shake. Auth. Review*, no. 10, Autumn 1963, 3.

117 Susanna as denying that her husband's writing was his: Halliwell-Phillipps, I, 272.

118 ". . . & if invited to writ: he was in pain": Chambers, II, 252.

118 Insertion of comma after "to": Schoenbaum, 106.

118 Insertion of comma after both "and" and "to": I. Brown, *Shakespeare*, Collins, 315.

118 Citation of Beeston and insertion of comma after "to" and of "[that]" after "wrote": McManaway, 9.

Citations

119 Ogburn found ignorant of secretary hand: Evans-Levin, 41.

119 Tributes to Chambers: Schoenbaum, 705, 718.

119 Shakspere's London signatures and their incompleteness unexplained: Chambers, I, 540–545.

119 Signatures on will deciphered and Thompson's opinion: Ibid., I, 505.

119 Harrison's analysis of the signatures and finding that Shakspere in decline: Report Reference 78-10-27 to Professor Gordon C. Cyr, Shakespéare-Oxford Society, Baltimore, Md.

121–2 English's finding that Shakspere not used to writing his name: Laboratory Report, 14 October 1977 to Professor Gordon C. Cyr, as above.

122 Acceptance of *Sir Thomas More* in Shakespeare canon: Evans-Levin, 41.

122 Question of whether "Shakespeare's" hand identifiable in MS of *Sir Thomas More*: Chambers, I, 507–508.

122 Harrison finds no "family resemblance" between the two hands: Report Reference 78-10-27, as above.

123 The plays as proof of Shakspere's literacy: Evans, *Saturday Review*, 7 May 1949.

123 The disappearance of Lord Chamberlain's books during the years of Shakespearean history: Stopes, *Burbage and Shakespeare's Stage*, 257.

123–4 Disappearance of the books of the Masters of the Revels: Barrell, *Shake. Fellow. Quar.*, VII, no. 2, April 1946, 22b.

124 Disappearance of Burbage's papers: Rowse, *Shakespeare the Man*, 141.

---

125 **Chapter 9.** "Look Here, on this Picture, and on This": *Hamlet*, III 4.

125–6 "Shakespear's" theft of his gifts: Lawrence, 145–149.

126 How "Shakespeare" had been "fathered" with dramas actually written by *Transmigratus: Learned Pig*, 36–39.

129 Doubts about Shakespeare voiced by Lord Cadurcis: Disraeli, 437.

129 The setting up of "Shakespeare" as author of "neglected plays": J. C. Hart, 208.

129 On "Shakspear's" becoming a professional thief: Quoted from Abel Lefranc, R. C. Churchill, 31.

129 Offensive language in Shakespeare: J. C. Hart, 228.

129–30 The "unaccountable mystery" of "Shakespeare's private life": Ibid., 212.

130 The contrast between Shakespeare's work and life: Emerson, "Representative Men," *Works*, IV, 218.

130–1 Article on "Who Wrote Shakspere?": *Chambers's Edinburgh Journal*, 7 August 1852, 87–89.

131–2 Delia Bacon's view of Shakespeare's plays as intended to instruct masses and not comprehensible if assigned to an illiterate: *Putnam's Monthly*, January 1856, quoted by Martin Pares, in *Shakespeare Cross-Examination*, 90–91.

132 Hawthorne on Miss Bacon: D. Bacon, Preface, xii, xiv.

132 Miss Bacon's "paranoia": Schoenbaum, 539.

133 Lack of connection between Shakespeare and his works: W. H. Smith, 3.

133 Mysterious vagueness of Jonson's laudatory verses: Ibid., 29.

Citations

133 Bacon compared with Greece and Rome: Ibid., 35; Jonson, *Discoveries*, 48.

133 Bacon's faculties such as those exhibited in plays: W. H. Smith, 18.

133 Lack of mention of plays by Shakespeare, of Shakespeare by Bacon: Ibid., 90.

134 Tribute to Bacon's *Essays*: Emerson, MS Lecture on Bacon; quoted by Comdr. Martin Pares, R.N., in *Shakespeare Cross-Examination*, 88.

134 Jonson on Bacon as one of greatest men: *Discoveries*, 49.

134 The MS associating Bacon's name with Shakespeare's and two "Rychards": Chambers, II, 196, which includes a facsimile of the Northumberland MS and a transcript — the original being in the secretary hand.

134 Ms. Bowen's explanation of manuscript: *Shake. Auth. Review*, no. 21, Spring 1969, 12–15.

135–6 The *Arena* articles cited are in vols. 7–9 (Library of Congress microfilm 34824). The quotation from A. B. Brown is from vol. 8, p. 738, that from A. E. Dolbear from vol. 9, pp. 369–370.

136 James on Shakespeare as a "Personal Poet" and "Nothing Else": Edel, *Henry James; the Master*, 145.

136 Shakespeare's "great soul"; Bacon as of "earth material": Carlyle, "The Hero as Poet," *Shakespeare Criticism*, 360–361.

137 Bacon's balanced judgment of Richard III: *The Life and Reign of King Henry VII: A Complete History of England*, London, 1706, p. 578.

137 Contrast between Bacon's care and abounding errors of the Folio: Brandes, 88.

137 Poor showing of "Shakespeare" in books on authorship: Ibid., 87.

137 Bacon as condoning and recommending torture: Jardine, I, 18–19.

138 Marlowe's associates, place in poetry, service to Shakespeare: Swinburne, *Encyclopaedia Britannica*, XVII, 741a and b, 743b.

139 Marlowe's acknowledged influence on Shakespeare: Schoenbaum, 624.

140 Dr. Schreiber's testimony: Bentley, *Shakespeare Cross-Examination*, 11.

141 Marlowe's diminishing vocabulary: A. Hart, *Stolne and Surreptitious Copies*, 459, 451.

141 Shakespeare as the originator: Coleridge, "Table Talk," 15 March 1834, *Shakespeare Criticism*, 271.

141–2 Shakespeare as innovator in tragedy and comedy, character and dialogue: S. Johnson, Preface to *Prefaces*, 34.

142 Derby as penning plays: Reported by George Fanner, Ward, 321.

143 Lefranc's research: Georges Lambin, "Professor Abel Lefranc (1863–1952)," *Shake. Auth. Review*, no. 8, Autumn 1962, 10–12.

143–4 Lambin's discoveries about Shakespeare in France and Italy: Review by Sir John Russell, ibid., no. 9, Spring 1963, 11–14.

144 Vilification of Lefranc: Ibid., second citation above.

144 Facts about Greenwood: Elsie Greenwood, "Sir George Greenwood (1850–1928)," ibid., no. 8, Autumn 1962, 6–7.

144–5 Reviews of *The Shakespeare Problem Restated*: Last pages of Greenwood's *Is There a Shakespeare Problem?*

145 Looney's "unfortunate name": Hamblin, 72b.

145 Facts about Looney: Professor the Reverend V. A. Demant, "John Thomas Looney (1870–1944)," *Shake. Auth. Review*, no. 8, Autumn 1962, 8–9.

Citations

146 Burgess's tribute to *"Shakespeare" Identified*: Letter of 19 May 1920, quoted by R. L. Miller in Looney, 3rd rev. ed., II, jacket.

146 Called "best detective story" by Galsworthy: Ibid., I, 648.

146 Freud a follower of Looney's: Letter from Freud to Looney, June 1938, ibid., II, 273.

146 Björkman's tribute to Looney: *The Bookman*, LI, no. 6, August 1920, 679–681.

147 *"Shakespeare" Identified* welcomed on behalf of libraries: *Library Journal*, New York: R. R. Bowker, 15 October 1949.

147 Looney compared with Darwin: McFee, Introduction, *"Shakespeare" Identified*, 2nd ed., xix.

149 Oxford as the strongest 20th-century candidate: *Encyclopaedia Britannica*, 15th ed., 1981, *Micropaedia*, VII, 647b–c.

149 The question of who had the qualifications to write Shakespeare's plays: McManaway, 30–31.

149 Disagreement on "rival candidates": Evans-Levin, 40.

150 Immateriality of who wrote Shakespeare: Editorial, *Wall Street Journal*, 11 February 1953.

150 Brown on author's deserving to be known, and the excitement of the mystery: R. C. Churchill, Preface, xi.

150 How much it matters who wrote Shakespeare, who deserves to be revered: Hamblin, 76.

---

151 **Chapter 10. "To Defend the City from the Rebels"** 2 *Henry the Sixth*, IV v.

151 Galland's bibliography of Shakespearean dissent: Schoenbaum, 267.

151 Palmerston's joy in "the explosion of the Shakespearian illusions": Diary of Mount-Stewart E. Grant, Durning-Lawrence, 178.

151 Walt Whitman as "firm against Shaksper": Traubel, 136.

151 Whittier as believing that Shakspere neither did nor could write the plays: Durning-Lawrence, 179.

151–2 James on "the divine William" as a successful fraud: Lubbock, I, 424.

152 Furness's inability to bring Shakspere's life and the plays into proximity: Letter to Nathaniel Holmes, 29 October 1866, Durning-Lawrence, 179–180.

152 Certainty that the Stratfordian did not write the plays: Twain, 324.

152 Bright on a believer in the Stratfordian as a fool: Greenwood, 203.

152 "I hardly think it was the Stratford boy": Chaplin, 364.

152 De Gaulle as skeptical of "Shakespeare's" existence: Rex North, undated U.P. clipping.

153 Denunciation of anti-Stratfordians as imbecile, half-educated: Brandes, 87.

153 Lee's fulminations and Baildon's warning of agnosticism quoted: Greenwood, xiii, xiv.

154 Poetic genius as overleaping space and time: McManaway, 34.

154 Anti-Stratfordians flayed as neurotic, gloomy sectarians: Wright, *The Anti-Shakespeare Industry*, 290–291.

154–5 "The Jack Rubys . . . Washington or the Angel Gabriel": Murphy, 4–11.

155 "Anti-Stratfordians hate Shakespeare . . . involved in real life": Ibid., 11.

Citations

155   Dr. Lockwood on "right" and "wrong," etc.: Letter to the author, 4 March 1965.

155   President Lockwood's explanation of quotation marks: Letter to author, 20 April 1981.

156   "He reveals in the *Sonnets* . . . takes his choice": Murphy, 7.

156   "Anti-Stratfordians . . . hysterical fury": Thorpe, "Portfolio 2," *Sunday (Washington) Star,* 3 December 1972.

156   Lack of vested interest in the Stratfordian: Wright, *Shakespeare for Everyman,* 98.

157   Discrediting of the Stratfordian as improving Stratford's business: Wright, *The Anti-Shakespeare Industry,* 294.

157   Threat to Stratford if Shakspere found not to be author: Guthrie, "Threat of Newness to Olde Stratford," *New York Times Magazine,* 22 April 1962, 12.

157   Doris Dawson's apprehensions: London, *Daily Mirror,* 21 September 1962.

157   Budget of Stratford Birthplace Trust: B. Rogers, 10.

158   "In academic debates . . . total ruthlessness": Alsop, "A Cautionary Tale," *Washington Post,* 7 March 1977.

158   "I am a professor . . . and conceited": Weisberger, "Book World," *Washington Post,* 7 April 1974.

158   Intolerance of dissent and "religious zeal" in academy: Greeley, "Some Professors Bent on Remaking Man," *Washington Post,* 8 November 1970, 85.

159–60   Geologists and the theory of continental movement: Calder, 44b, 46b, 42b.

159   Conventional geological principles reaffirmed: *The Crust of the Earth: An Introduction to Geology,* ed. by Samuel Rapport and Helen Wright, New York: Signet Science Library Book, The New American Library, 1955. The two quotations are respectively from Samuel J. Shand (p. 117) and W. D. Hotchkiss (p. 11).

161   Anti-Stratfordians as "naive" and guilty of "snobbery": Wright, *Folger Library Shakespeare,* xviii.

162   Rowse's claims for his biographical methods: *Shakespeare the Man,* x.

162   "No flesh-and-blood figure" stalking out of *Shakespeare the Man: Publishers Weekly,* 23 April 1973.

162   Orthodox Shakespeare scholarship at dead end: Rowse, *Shakespeare the Man,* xi.

162   The dispirited old geology: Calder, 21a.

163   **Chapter 11.** "I Will Hereupon Confess": *Love's Labour's Lost,* I ii.

163   "Anti-Shakespeare business" and publishers: Wright, *The Anti-Shakespeare Industry,* 289–290.

166   Freud on the man of Stratford and Oxford: Repeats quotation on page 146.

166   Frohman's enthusiasm for *"Shakespeare" Identified*: Rutherford, "Daniel Frohman Introduces the Great Unknown," *Shake. Fellow. Quar.,* VII, no. 1, January 1946, 1.

167–8   Misrepresentations of *This Star of England*: Murphy, 10.

169   Dissenters as "tiresome" and prone to "snobbery": Wright, "Years of Drollery Amid Shakespeare," *National Observer,* 29 April 1968, 1.

Citations

169   Scholars as unwilling to discuss "Shakespeare controversy": Wright, Letter to Joseph Borkin, Washington, D.C., 27 June 1968.

170   Thorpe's article on the Shakespeare controversy: "New Shakespeare Controversy," *Washington Star Magazine*, 26 August 1962.

170   Reference to attitude of *Times* is to "Speaking of Books" by J. C. Furnas, *New York Times*, 2 September 1962.

170   Review in *American Bar Association Journal*: Chicago, November 1962, 1070.

171   Review in *Life*: "Fresh Troops Join the Battle of the Bard," 7 September 1962, 4.

171   Notices in *Library Journal*: First by Burton A. Robie, issue of 15 June 1962, 2381; second, issue of 15 November 1962, 4295.

171   Brinton's comments on *The Man Behind the Name*: Letter of 1 May 1962 to John T. Lawrence, President, William Morrow & Co.

171   G. B. Harrison's review of *The Man Behind the Name*: "Shakespeare, or a Man Named Shakespeare," in "Books," *New York Herald-Tribune*, 26 August 1962, 6.

174   On submitting pamphlet to Kiosk Committee: Letter to author, 20 December 1978.

177   Evans on the *Harvard* article as "half-baked guff": Letter to Bethell, 25 November 1974.

177   Kaiser on the article as "giving idiocies a Harvard accent": Letter, 22 November 1974, to Bethell and Professors H. Baker, R. Brower, Evans, and Levin.

177–78   Levin on the article as opening "a Pandora's box" and the author as a "crackpot": Letter, 25 November 1974, to Bethell, President Derek Bok, Dean Henry Rosovsky, and Professor Kaiser.

178–9   *Harvard* article in *Outlook*: Issue of 24 November 1974.

179   Hardison's reply in *Outlook*: Issue of 8 December 1974.

179   Fisher's disgust at the "stale spinach of the Oxford lunacy": Letters section, *Harvard Magazine*, 77, no. 5, January 1975.

179   Wirth finds Ogburn "a fool and a snob": Ibid.

179   Dickinson on Evans's and Levin's "paranoid" and "hysterical defense": Ibid., 77, no. 8, April 1975.

179   Hinton on persisting doubts: Ibid.

179   Ogburn's proposal of a trial and Weld's offer to finance it: Ibid.

179–80   Letter to Levin, 31 August 1975.

180   Evans's attack on Ogburn's article: Letter to Morse Johnson, 28 February 1975.

180   Full quotation from James on "the divine William" as a "successful fraud": Lubbock, I, 424.

180   On the plays not squaring with the facts of "the lout from Stratford": Edel, 145.

180   The Stratford attribution as a foolish delusion: Greenwood, *Shakespeare, Lee and a Tertium Quid*, 20.

---

182   **Chapter 12.** "My Name Be Buried Where My Body Is": Sonnet 72.

182   The Oxford case as assuming a conspiracy: *Life*, 7 September 1962.

183   The danger of writing modern history: Raleigh (Died 1618), Preface, lxiii.

Citations

184–5 Punishment for slander of Lord Treasurer: Stow, *Annales* (1614), 812.

185 Pollard's highlights of Cecil's career: *Encyclopaedia Britannica*, IV, 816b–817a.

186 Pollard on Cecil and the Court of Wards: Ibid., 817a.

186 Burghley as a middle-class heretic: Trevelyan, II, 84.

186 "The most hopeful of them was Edward de Vere": Chambers, *Sixteenth Century Verse*, vi–vii.

186 Oxford called "the best for comedy in his time": Wood, I, 355.

187 De Vere's uneasy relationship with Cecil: Edwards, "The Earl of Oxford's Escape Plot," *Shake. Auth. Review*, no. 26, Summer 1972, 12.

188 Hubler quoted on middle-class origin of great English writers: Atkinson, "Critic at Large," *New York Times*, 12 July 1963.

188 Byron as speaking in the voice of Calliope: Van Doren, *The Noble Voice*, xi.

188 Pride of family in Scott: William Minto, *Encyclopaedia Britannica*, XXIV, 469a.

189 Imputation of writing Shakespeare's plays as an insult to Oxford: R. C. Churchill, 129.

190 "Shakespeare's love of good blood": Harris, 272.

191–2 The author of *Lear* as having passed through mental illness: Slater, *Shake. Auth. Review*, no. 23, Spring 1970, 21–22.

192fn. Ward on "Shakespear's" fatal "merry meeting": Ingleby 317; Chambers, II, 250.

193 *On Poet-Ape*: Jonson, "Epigrammes," *Works*, VIII, 44–45.

193 Hints that "Shakespeare" was a "poet-ape": I. Brown, *Shakespeare*, Time edition, 337.

194 Southampton's reported gift to Shakespeare of £1,000: Rowe, viii.

194 The size of Burbage's estate: Stopes, *Burbage and Shakespeare's Stage*, 116.

194 Henrietta Maria's stay at New Place: G. E. Bentley, 36–37.

195fn. Jonson's inclusion of Shakespeare in casts of two plays: Evans-Levin, 42–43.

195 Meres's tributes to Shakespeare and listing of Oxford among best for comedy: *Ancient Critical Essays*, II, 152–153; Ingleby, 21–23; Chambers, II, 193–195.

195 Meres as establishing separate identity of Oxford and Shakespeare: Campbell, 172.

196 Meres's singling out Shakespeare for extended comment: Chute, 179.

196 Meres as not believing Oxford the author of the plays: Schoenbaum, 601.

197fn Early version of the epitaph to Combe: Chambers, II, 138–139. According to Chambers, this version appeared in *A Happy Husband* in 1619, not credited to Shakspere — who, we may judge, was not then of sufficient note to be fathered with the doggerel, legitimately or not.

200 Elizabeth as sending for Burghley: D. Cecil, 2.

201 Oxford's request of Burghley to sell lands to pay debts: Hatfield MSS, Cal. II.

201 Camden's instructions to write history from memorials "opened up" by Burghley: Camden, "The Author to the Reader," *Annales*.

201–2 How for fifty years England ruled by Cecils: Edwards, *Shake. Auth. Review*, no. 25, Autumn 1971, 17.

202 Burghley on the eyes, ears, and arms of princes: Peck, Liber I, p. 61, no. 15.

Citations

204 Propagandistic aims of Burghley's writings: Read, 508.

205 Preface to *Troilus and Cressida*: Chambers, II, 216–217.

206 Shakespeare's "song was worthy merit": Barkstead, *Myrrha*, Ingleby, 76; Chambers, II, 216.

206 "Ever-living" as never applied to a living person: Ferguson, "The Sonnets of Shakespeare," *Shake. Auth. Review*, no. 13, Spring 1965, 12.

206 Preface as by publisher, not author: G. E. Bentley, 170.

208 **Chapter 13. "A Very Ancient and Fish-Like Smell":** *The Tempest*, II ii.

212 The stupid air of the bust as wronging the dead poet: Wilson, 5.

212 Certainty the bust not the original: Greenwood, 245.

213 Evidence that Dugdale frequently misrepresents: Marder, "Debate on the Authorship Question," *Shake. Auth. Review*, no. 10, Autumn 1963, 8.

213 Dugdale supported: Carr, ibid., 9.

213 The Stratford monument in the 1709 edition of Shakespeare: Rowe, 37.

214 Shakespeare as an English Ovid: Rowse, *Shakespeare the Man*, 26.

216 Montgomery as a favorite of James's: *Encyclopaedia Britannica*, XXI, 80a.

216–18 Sir George Buck, the Herberts, and Ben Jonson and the publication of Shakespeare's plays: Bowen, "The Incomparable Pair and 'The Works of William Shakespeare,'" *Shake. Auth. Review*, no. 6, Autumn 1961, 3–8.

218 Shakespeare as failing to see plays through the press: Bentley, 183–184.

218 Uncertainty as to whether he ever saw or collected copies: Ibid.

219–20 "Censure of English poets": Jonson, *Conversations*, 5.

219 Shakespeare's "Shipwreck in Bohemia": Ibid., 20.

220 Jonson as lover of himself and scorner of others: Ibid., 56.

220 Jonson's reminiscences: Ibid., 26–27.

220 Epigram to one who desired not to be named: Jonson, *Epigrammes, Works*, Routledge ed., no. LXXVII, 671.

220–1 *De Shakespeare nostrati*: Jonson, *Timber*, 35–36.

221 Jonson's quotation from *Julius Caesar* as making sense: Ingleby, 175.

221 Jonson's "evil eye" for a competitor: Rowe, xiii.

221 Fuller on "wits-combats" between the two dramatists: Ingleby, 246–247; Chambers, II, 244.

221–2 Jonson, the Herberts, and Oxford's daughters: R. L. Miller, "Oxfordian Vistas," Looney, 3rd ed., 7–8.

222 Gainsborough on the stupidity of the Droeshout engraving: Sir John Russell, *Shake. Auth. Review*, no. 14, Autumn 1965, 16.

222 Engraving compared to "puddin'-headed" effigy: I. Brown, *Amazing Monument*, 38–39.

222 Obvious falsity of Droeshout's "pudding-faced effigy": Wilson, 6.

222–4 Abnormalities of the Droeshout engraving: Schoenbaum, 11.

224 Droeshout's subject as thinking too much and over-fastidious: Payne, xiv.

224 Brain on subject's two right eyes: London, *Observer*, 15 February 1964.

224 *Gentlemen's Tailor* on the harlequin appearance of Droeshout's representation: *Ibid.*

Citations

227 Errors in Folio *Richard Second*: Pollard, "Shakespeare's Text," *Companion to Shakespeare Studies*, 278.

227 Folio editors called "lying rascals": Swinburne, xi.

227 Textual sources of the First Folio: Prouty, Yale facsimile, xxiii.

227–8 "The inevitable absence of his autograph MSS": Lee, *Facsimile*, xix.

229 Verse prefacing *Faerie Queene*, by Ignoto: Spenser, *Works*, Oxford ed., 410.

232 On Shakespeare's "small Latin and less Greek": Johnson, Preface to *Prefaces*, 32.

232–3 Explication of "small Latin and less Greek" passage: Ingleby, 151–152.

236 List of actors in printed plays as unprecedented: G. E. Bentley, 188.

237 Spray of olive as adorning conqueror's crown at ovation: *Encyclopaedia Britannica*, XX, 86b.

238 Athena's gift of the olive tree to Attica: Ibid., 86a.

238 "The spear of Pallas shake": "Achilles his concealment of his sex in the court of Lycomedes," *Poems Written by Wil. Shake-speare*.

238 Folio as greatest secular work in English: McManaway, review of Norton facsimile, *New York Times Book Review*, 8 December 1968, 4.

---

240 **Chapter 14. "Most Like a Noble Lord":** *Cymbeline*, V v.

241 Shakespeare's sense of the "inviolability of the Crown": Auchincloss, 107.

241 His belief in good blood's "wondrous efficacy": Harris, 272.

241 "Social snobbery" of anti-Stratfordians": Evans-Levin, 40.

241 Need of people to know their place and do their duty: Rowse, *Shakespeare the Man*, 223.

243 Shakespeare's "snobbishness . . . flunkeyism": Harris, 235.

245 Shakespeare's lack of "smallest acquaintance" with royalty: Auchincloss, 106.

246 "Arcady and England" in *As You Like It*: Dowden, *Comedies*, 667.

249 Coriolanus as ruined by haughty egoism: Ibid., 112.

251 Tempo of Royal Shakespeare Company's *Coriolanus*: *Time*, 4 December 1978, 108.

251–2 Shakespeare as an unquestioning aristocrat to whom popular leaders are vulgar demagogues: Trevor-Roper, 42.

253 Shakespeare and Castiglione compared: Evans-Levin, 41.

254 Non-noble characters held worthy of Shakespeare's genius: Ibid., 40.

254fn. Shakespeare's taking side of the oppressed in Shylock: Sinsheimer, 101.

254 Shakespeare an aristocrat whose lower orders are food for farce: Harris, 235.

254–5 Shakespeare as a cultured aristocrat contemptuous of sub-noble world: Trevor-Roper, 42.

255 Shakespeare's "low-characters" as "foils to the aristocracy": Whitman, 408.

255 Shakespeare's and Jonson's treatment of noble and middle-class characters: Bénézet, "Shakespeare and Ben Jonson," *Shake. Fellow. News-Letter*, I, no. 4, June 1940, 5.

255 Need of writer to know a subject that is near at home: Knapp, "Shakespeare and Mark Twain," *Shake. Fellow. News-Letter*, II, no. 2, February 1941, 22b.

256 Rebuttal of crackpot theories of authorship held waste of time: Auchincloss, 105.

Citations

256 Shakespeare found a "hick" in portrayals of royalty: Ibid., 107.

256 Total regality of Lear and Cleopatra: Ibid., 112–113.

257 Dislike of Shakespearean themes of honor and unlikelihood that humble beginnings were behind them: Chaplin, 364.

257 How Terence charmed the "high Roman circle": Evans-Levin, 41.

257 Terence's advantages and possibly having been a mask for another authorship: *Encyclopaedia Britannica*, XXVI, 639b, 640b.

257 Scipio as source of "pure fine talk" of Roman nobility in Terence: Ascham, 247.

257–8 How Shakespeare took his material on kings from popular histories: Wright, *The Anti-Shakespeare Industry*, 297.

258 Shakespeare as tavern guest of noblemen: J. Q. Adams, 241.

258 Shakespeare's ease in meeting kings and queens: Payne, xiv.

258 Shakespeare's intimate friends among aristocrats: Phelps, "Notes on Shakespeare," *Proceedings of the American Philosophical Society*, Philadelphia, 25 September 1939.

258 Shakespeare's acquaintance with upper-class life from performing at court: Rowse, London, *Times*, 23 August 1974.

258 Shakespeare's seeing Queen in person: Auchincloss, 109.

258 Shakespeare's regular court performances: Evans-Levin, 40.

259 Advantage in Shakespeare's friendship with Southampton: Rowse, London, *Times*, 23 April 1974.

259 "His fellow townsmen . . . grand London associations": Rowse, *Shakespeare the Man*, 158.

259 Jonson as only playwright conversant in courts: Dryden, "Defense of the Epilogue; or, the Dramatic Poetry of the Last Age," *Works*, IV, 240.

260 The *mythos* in the Shakespeare question and the historical plays as conceived out of the heat of feudalism by a wolfish earl: W. Whitman, II, 404.

260 Irreconcilability of the Stratford legend and the dramatist's aristocratic attitude: Chaplin, 364.

260 Shakespeare's gaffes and lack of book learning: Wright, *The Anti-Shakespeare Industry*, 295, 296.

260 Shakespeare's disregard of grammar: Chaplin, 364.

260 Shakespeare's royal exploitation of grammar: Gordon, 255–256.

260–1 Bismarck on Shakespeare's experience of affairs of state, unlikelihood of retirement to Stratford: S. Whitman, 135–136.

261 James's disbelief that Shakespeare could have applied an extinguisher to his radiant faculty: Edel, *Henry James; the Master*, 148.

261–2 Shakespeare's first-hand acquaintance with political behavior at summit of power: Powell, Address to the Shakespeare Club, 8, 10–11.

262 Contempt for money in Shakespeare: Harris, 193.

263 Shakespeare as among best sportsmen: *Shakespeare's England*, II, 350.

264 Shakespeare's fixation on hunting: Rowse, *Shakespeare the Man*, 33.

264 Fortescue's elucidation of hunting passages: *Shakespeare's England*, II, 348–349.

264–5 How an acute mind can pick up technical matters: Neilson and Thorndike, 50.

Citations

265 Shakespeare's acquaintance with hunting contrasted with Jonson's: *Shakespeare's England*, II, 342–343.

265 Shakespeare's subconscious introduction of fishing metaphors: Huhner, 45, 49.

265 Sieveking on Shakespeare's knowledge of fish: *Shakespeare's England*, II, 372.

266 Shakespeare on faults in hunting dogs, by Fortescue: Ibid., II, 348.

266 Sieveking on technicalities of greyhound hunting in Shakespeare: Ibid., II, 368.

266 Allocation of falcons by rank: *Encyclopaedia Britannica*, X, 141b.

269 "Sweet mercy . . . badge": *Titus Andronicus*, I ii.

269 Fortescue on hare-hunting summed up in *Venus and Adonis*: *Shakespeare's England*, II, 347.

270 Shakespeare's love of animals and fondness for bowls: Spurgeon, 204, 27.

270 His sensitivity, courage, and fastidiousness: Ibid., 206, 121, 79.

270 The house-slops and offal characterizing Stratford: Halliwell-Phillipps, 24.

270 "Ever managed . . . smells of Elizabethan England": Spurgeon, 205.

270–1 Shakespeare's delicacy, sensitivity, sympathy for animals in the rough Elizabethan age: Trevor-Roper, 43.

Chapter 15. Myriad-Minded Man of the Renaissance — 1.

273 Shakespeare's "university of life": Rowse, *Shakespeare the Man*, 23.

273 Experience of life as best school for a writer: Wright, *The Anti-Shakespeare Industry*, 296–297.

273 Stratford as a metropolis: Campbell, 175.

273–4 Population of Stratford: Fox, 13–14; Knight, 15.

274 Bretchgirdle's "large library": I. Brown, *Shakespeare*, Collins, 47.

274 Bretchgirdle's library scattered: Baldwin, II, 490–491.

274 Repressive medieval character of Stratford: Chute, 2, 3.

274 Processions of the bailiff and serjeants: Rowse, *Shakespeare the Man*, 20.

274–5 Unpopularity of corporation offices: Eccles, 43, 44, 47, 49, 58.

275 Prevailing illiteracy of officials: Knight, 15.

275 "Sad to think . . . to be had for nothing": Greenwood, 41.

275 McCabe on the Stratford school syllabus, the proof of "Shakespeare's" authorship and the skeptics: "big lie": "Talk of the Town," *The New Yorker*, 20 June 1959.

275–6 Corporal punishment in Elizabethan schools: I. Brown, *Shakespeare in His Time*, 39, 41.

276 How the angry schoolmaster beats the scholar: Ascham, III, 97.

276 "The master . . . being as ignorant as the child": Ibid., III, 89.

276 Poor quality of teaching: Peacham, 33.

276 The Stratford school as one of the best: Campbell, 175; Wright, *Folger Shakespeare Library Report*, 1 March 1956.

276 High salary paid Stratford schoolmaster: I. Brown, *Shakespeare in His Time*, 38; Marder, "Debate on the Authorship Question," *Shake. Auth. Review*, no. 10, Autumn 1963, 2.

Citations

276 Expenses the Stratford schoolmaster had to defray: Schoenbaum, *Documentary Life*, 52.

276 "Stratford Grammar School . . . if not going to school?": Evans-Levin, 41.

277 Public as "gross and dark"; literacy valued for its rarity: Johnson, Preface to *Prefaces*, 27–28.

277 Ignorance of common people; lack of books: Goadby, 116.

277 Safety in not reading: Knight, 17.

277 How Shakspere should have learned to read from someone: Baldwin, I, 468.

277 Baldwin recommended: Evans-Levin, 41.

277 Shakespeare's "small Latin and less Greek": Baldwin, II, 677.

278 "Grammar-school . . . converse in Latin": Rowse, *Shakespeare the Man*, 22, 24.

278 "Latin . . . still more Latin": Chute, 15.

278 "Boys would have read Terence . . . Seneca": G. E. Bentley, 27–28.

278 Shakespeare's lack of knowledge of ancient poets: Rowe, vi.

278–9 Superiority in Latin of Stratford school to American college; inapplicability of "small Latin" to Oxford: O. J. Campbell, 176.

279 "Not a scholar": Wilson, Review of J. Dover Wilson's *Fortunes of Falstaff*, *The New Yorker*, 29 April 1944.

279 "If Shakespeare . . . to be a parson": Wright, *The Anti-Shakespeare Industry*, 297.

279 "Like their dentists": Ibid., 296.

279 "Even learned Ben . . . stepfather's trade": Ibid.

279 "He provided . . . good education": *Encyclopaedia Brittanica*, XV, 502a.

280 Jonson on indebtedness to Camden: Jonson, "Epigrammes," *Works*, VIII, 31.

280 Mulcaster's faith in capacities of English: Joseph, 5.

280 "Sterility . . . university education": Wright, *Anti-Shakespeare Industry*, 297.

280 The breadth of education tutors could provide: Curtis, 107.

280–1 Poetry and plays by students: Notestein, 143.

281 Play of Pope as Anti-Christ: Bradbrook, 31.

281 "Mongst russet coats . . . nectar to my soul": *Three Parnassus Plays*, 141.

281 Transformation of boy from "mean" background: Notestein, 144–145.

281 Subsidizing of bright students: Ibid., 124.

281 "The greatest intellect . . . of literature": Carlyle, "The Hero as Poet," *Shakespeare Criticism*, 359.

282 "In the wonder of his genius . . .": Nicoll, 68.

282 Genius as explaining nothing: Arnold Wilson, oral observation, confirmed in communication to author of 10 September 1981.

282 "Nature gives no man . . . only what he had learned": Johnson, *Preface to Shakespeare*, 105.

282 Shakespeare's knowledge as habitual through patient study: Coleridge, *Shakespeare Criticism*, 219.

283 "If we are forced . . . mark of literary culture": J. Q. Adams, 96.

283 Shakespeare's education as requiring a belief in miracles or disbelief in the Stratford man: Wilson, 41–42.

Citations

283   The unanswerable question of how Shakespeare reached his wit and humor: Sampson, 256.

283–4   Shakespeare's grounding in Latin culture through teaching: J. Q. Adams, 96.

284   Young Will as singing boy for Catholic nobleman: Wilson, 41.

284   The report of Shakespeare a schoolmaster: Aubrey, II, 227; Chambers, II, 254.

284   The "tradition" of Shakespeare as a schoolmaster: O. J. Campbell; Schoenbaum, 731; Evans-Levin, 41.

284   Beeston as source of the report: Aubrey, II, 227; Chambers, II, 254.

284   Aubrey "a shiftless person . . ." who "confused everything": *Encyclopaedia Britannica*, I, 891a.

284fn.   Wood as having "weathered less well" than Aubrey: Evans-Levin, 43.

284fn.   Aubrey as foolish and detestable gossip: Halliwell-Phillipps, 6th ed., x.

284fn.   *Brief Lives* as "wildly inaccurate": Freedman, "Book World," *Washington Post*, 5 September 1971.

284fn.   Aubrey's report that Jonson killed Marlowe: Aubrey, II, 13.

285   Ovid as love of Shakespeare's life: Rowse, *Shakespeare the Man*, 25.

285   Shakspere's bondsmen two illiterate husbandmen: Hunter, I, 50.

285   Shakespeare as of "enormous erudition": Barnett, 139.

285   Shakespeare an accomplished Grecian and Latinist: Powell, Letter, *Books and Bookmen*, January 1977, 4.

285   Shakespeare as a *lusus naturae* to the Harvard professors: Evans-Levin, 41.

285   Shakespeare as no *lusus naturae*, no wild genius; "does God choose idiots . . . ?": Coleridge, "Shakespeare's Judgment," *Shakespeare Criticism*, 226–227, 232–233.

285–6   Shakespeare as no mere "child of nature" but of assured familiarity with wide learning: Trevor-Roper, 42.

286   Shakespeare as parading his learning: Nicoll, 71, 72.

286   Shakespeare as faker of knowledge: Harbage, *Conceptions of Shakespeare*, 24.

286   Information in the plays as not having been "looked up": Harbage, *Shakespeare and the Professions*, 13–14.

286   Shakespeare's complete assimilation of source material: Dwyer, *Shake. Fellow. News-Letter*, I, no. 5, August 1940, 7a.

286–7   Jonson's Greek and Latin "padding": Wilson, *The New Yorker*, 6 November 1948, 124.

287   Collins on Shakespeare's familiarity with Latin classics and deduction that he must have been saturated with them: Greenwood, 93–94.

287–8   The numerous parallels between Shakespeare's works and the Greek classics, the dramatist's use of Attic rhetorical devices, his Grecian ethic, his reading of Greek: Ibid., 96–100.

288   Evidence of Shakespeare's knowledge of Greek tragedies in the original language, specifically *Ajax: Annotations by Samuel Johnson and George Steevens upon Titus Andronicus*, Act I, lines 383–386.

288   "If Shakespeare had not read the *Ajax* . . . haunt his dramas: Collins, 63.

288   On similarities between Shakespeare and Æschylus: Highet, *The Classical Tradition*, 201.

Citations

288–9 Socrates' references to "some garden of Adonis": *The Dialogues of Plato*, I, 279.

289 Shakespeare's readings in Italian and French: Prouty, "Shakespeare's Sources," *Times Literary Supplement*, 14 September 1951.

289 French and Italian writers known to Shakespeare: Neilson and Thorndike, 57.

289 Shakespeare's reading of *Orlando Furioso* in Italian: Cairncross, *Shakespeare Quarterly*, Autumn 1977, 421, 475.

289 Echoes of Dante in Shakespeare: Dwyer, "Had Shakespeare Read Dante?" *Shake. Fellow. News-Letter*, I, no. 5, August 1940, 7–11, and II, no. 4, 51–52.

289–90 Shakespeare's wide reading in Latin, French, Italian, and English: Nicoll, 69.

290 A Spanish romance as the source of *Two Gentlemen*: Dowden, *Comedies*, 70–71.

290 Shakespeare's extensive preparatory reading: Nicoll, 69.

290 Shakespeare's many English sources and knowledge of the Bible: Neilson and Thorndike, 64.

290–1 Shakespeare's use of Bible as equaling that of other writers combined: C. Wordsworth, 345, 9.

291 Shakespeare's rapid reading: Rowse, *Shakespeare the Man*, 28, 235.

291 Shakespeare's "verbal riches": A. Hart, 28.

291 Shakespeare's superlative vocabulary: Müller, 278.

291 Shakespeare with vocabulary of 17,677 words: A. Hart, *Stolne and Surreptitious Copies*, 21.

292 Shakespeare's use of words as compared with King James Bible: Marder, 25.

292 Shakespeare as owing more to nature than to art: Evans-Levin, 41.

292 "Sweetest Shakespeare, fancy's child": Milton, *L'Allegro*, lines 133–134.

292 Words peculiar to a single Shakespeare play: A. Hart, *Stolne and Surreptitious Copies*, 22, 451.

292 *Oxford English Dictionary* on words Shakespeare first to use: Ibid., 28.

292 Shakespeare's "effusion of Latin words made into English": Theobald, *Eighteenth Century Essays on Shakespeare*, 21.

292 Revelation of Shakespeare's mastery of rhetoric: Van Doren, New York *Herald Tribune*, 4 July 1948.

292–3 Shakespeare's use of whole body of rhetoric: Joseph, 13.

293 Tudor figures as approximating 200: Ibid., 4.

293 Exemplification in Shakespeare of whole theory of composition: Ibid., 37.

293 Shakespeare's supremacy in logic and rhetoric: Ibid., 4.

293 Sophistication of Shakespeare's art: Ibid., 79.

293 Nature as the basis of art: Ibid., 43.

293 Shakespeare's surpassing contribution to phraseology: Weekley, 53.

293 Shakespeare's service to English as vehicle for ideas: Dwyer, *Shake. Fellow. News-Letter*, I, no. 5, August 1940, 7a.

293 English as greatest symbol system: Mitchell, *Time*, 29 January 1979.

Chapter 16. Myriad-Minded Man of the Renaissance — 2.

296 Underhill's deprecation of Shakespeare's law: *Shakespeare's England,* I, 381.

296 The Shakesperes' experience of litigation: Ibid.

296 Shakespeare's failure to mention real estate law: Ibid., 403–404.

296–8 Greenwood on Shakespeare's knowledge of the law, with quotations from other experts: *The Shakespeare Problem Restated,* 371–375.

298 Greenwood's disavowal of "Baconian heresy": *Is There a Shakespeare Problem?* 2.

298 Robertson on lawyers' differing views: R. C. Churchill, 162.

298fn. Topcliffe's investigation into the authorship of *Richard the Second:* Ibid., 186–187.

298fn. Brown's and Wright's testimonials to Churchill's fairness: Ibid., ix, *Shakespeare for Everyman,* 93.

298–9 Schoenbaum's commentary on Greenwood: 594.

298fn. Schoenbaum and Harbage on Mark Twain: Ibid., 572.

299 Parallel between Lincoln and Shakespeare: Clary, "The Case for the Defense: De Vere et al. v. Shakespeare," *Shakespeare Cross-Examination,* 27–28.

300 Debt to Shakespeare of King James Bible: C. Wordsworth, 9.

300 Citations of Shakespeare's informed use of law from plays: Ogburn, "A Mystery Solved: The True Identity of Shakespeare," *Shakespeare Cross-Examination,* 17–20.

300 Superior use of law by other Elizabethan playwrights: Hauser, "The Shakespearean Controversy: A Stratfordian Rejoinder," Ibid., 36–38.

300–1 Testimony to Shakespeare's "remarkable legal attainments" and Greenwood's refutation of Allen: R. Bentley, "Elizabethan Whodunit: Supplementary Notes," Ibid., 62–64.

301 Shakespeare's familiarity with law as exceeding that possible to Shakspere: Greenwood, 395.

301 The law as part of Shakespeare: I. Brown, *Shakespeare,* Collins, 90.

301 Necessity of Shakspere's having had experience in an attorney's office: Fripp, 145.

301 Ruling out of such experience by Campbell and Penzance: Greenwood, 376.

302 Evidence of Shakespeare's having been in Italy in 1592–1594: Chambers, I, 61.

302 Shakespeare's extraordinary knowledge of Italy and topography of Venice: Trevor-Roper, 42.

302 Grillo's support of the above: *Shake. Author. Review,* no. 6, Autumn 1961, 12.

302 Rebora on Shakespeare's knowledge of Italian language and culture: Quoted in Amphlett, 36.

302 *The Merchant* and *Othello* as transferring us to Venice: Elze, 271.

303 The poetic imagination as no substitute for knowledge: Ibid., 278.

303 The Venetian merchants' residences as the prototype of Belmont: Ibid.

303 Shakespeare's knowledge of the traghetto and of the Rialtos and the Gobbo: Ibid., 280.

Citations

303 How Shakespeare transfers us into an Italian atmosphere; the moonlight scene at Belmont: Ibid., 272.

304 The contrast with Jonson's "bookworm" learning: Ibid., 272.

304 The Italy evoked by Shakespeare: Perowne, London, *Times*, 6 June 1964.

304–5 Shakespeare's ignorance of art: Isaacs, 685.

305 Shakespeare's use of art terms and evident acquaintance with Italian paintings: Cust, "Painting, Sculpture and Engraving," *Shakespeare's England*, II 9–10.

305 Shakespeare's not knowing that Giulio was not a sculptor: Isaacs, 685.

305 Vasari's record of Giulio's epitaph and the conclusion that the dramatist must either have studied Vasari or seen the artist's work: Elze, 287–289.

308 Amusement of professionals at fictional counterparts: Swerdlow, book review, *Washington Post*, 25 August 1978.

308–9 Shakespeare's knowledge of medicine and insanity: Brandes, 93.

309 Shakespeare's knowledge as that of an Elizabethan M.D.: Dodek quoted in *Washington Post*, 20 July 1965.

309 Dazzling array of medical references in Shakespeare; his remarkable knowledge of Renaissance medicine: Miller, *Medicine in Shakespeare*, MS supplied the author, 1979.

309 Shakespeare's understanding of senescence and physiology: Talk by Dr. Vest, St. Louis congress, 9–14 September 1951.

309 "Shakespeare" as "greatest analyst" and "front-man": Schneider, New York *Herald Tribune*, 8 October 1950.

310 Shakespeare's intellectual society and high culture: Brandes, 95.

310fn. Shakespeare as not having "got beyond the Ptolemaic system": Ibid.

310 Shakespeare as "a devoted gardener": Trevor-Roper, 42.

310–11 The 150 varieties of flowers in Shakespeare: Schoenbaum, *The Globe and the World*, 29–32.

312 Shakespeare's love of country and vision of man as part of nature: Trevor-Roper, 42.

312 "System of civil and economical prudence": Johnson, Preface to *Prefaces*, 5.

313 Shakespeare's 500 passages about music: Schonberg, *New York Times*, 23 March 1964.

313 His use of 100 musical terms: Marder, *His Exits and His Entrances*, 24.

314 Shakespeare's "protecting talisman" in war: Hemingway, 6.

314–5 Falconer's *Shakespeare and the Sea* and Vice Admiral McGeoch's comments: *Shake. Author. Review*, no. 14, Autumn 1965, 11.

316 Brown on Shakespeare's "marine contacts" and his conviction that he "did have voyages": *A Word in Your Ear*, 135; *Shakespeare*, Time edition, 74.

316 Exaggeration of claims of Shakespeare's proficiencies: Harbage, *Conceptions of Shakespeare*, 23–24.

316 Physicians praised for the restraint of their testimony: Harbage, *Shakespeare and the Professions*, 12.

316–7 Contrast between Shakespeare's enlightened prescription and that of Dr. Hall: Ibid., 22–23.

317 A "coterie" of authors as required to account for the special fields of knowledge ascribed to Shakespeare: McManaway, 33.

Citations

319   **Chapter 17.** "As the Very True Sonnet Is . . .": *Twelfth Night*, III iv.

319   *Sonnets* as the greatest puzzle in English literature: Rowse, *Shakespeare's Sonnets*, vii.

319–20   *Sonnets* as only hint of the poet's autobiography: Auchincloss, 139, 143.

320   *Sonnets* as "mere poetical exercises": Schoenbaum, 439.

320   Question of why, if so, author did not publish them with an explanation: Dowden, *Histories and Poems*, 1053–1054.

320   Regret that the *Sonnets* were ever written: Hallam, III, 264.

320   *Sonnets* as key unlocking Shakespeare's heart: William Wordsworth, Essay Supplementary to the Preface, *Poems*, 1815.

320–1   "If so, the less Shakespeare he!": "House," *Poems of Robert Browning, From the Author's Revised Text of 1889*, New York: Crowell, 1896, 440.

321   "Doubt it not . . . struggling for his life": Carlyle, "The Hero as Poet," *Shakespeare Criticism*, 365.

321   "The intensity" of the Sonnets' "quiet personal appeal . . ."; "the force of their reality": Raleigh (1861–1922), 87–88.

321   The *Sonnets* as mainly literary exercises: Lee, 113; J. Q. Adams, 167–168.

321   How the *Sonnets'* story "tells us next to nothing": Sampson, 272.

321   How little can be said about them: Chute, 343.

322   Thorpe as from "humblest ranks": Lee, 409.

322   Shakespeare's dissociation from publication of the *Sonnets*: G. E. Bentley, 153.

322   Description of the *Sonnets* by groups: Dowden, *Histories and Poems*, 1052–1053.

324   Time as "the single great subject of the sonnets": Van Doren, 13.

325   The story of the *Sonnets* as unparalleled: Dowden, *Histories and Poems*, 1053.

328   *Sonnets* as "covered thick in fingerprints": Durrell, *Times Literary Supplement*, London, 5 January 1951.

329   The confident devotion and "certain lordliness" of the dedication of *Lucrece*: Rowse, *Shakespeare's Southampton*, 88–89.

329   Its "rank impertinence" if by "a prentice player": Rendall, *Shake. Auth. Review*, no. 11, Spring 1964, 4.

329   Whitgift's license of *Venus and Adonis*: Akrigg, 197.

329   Dignity and restraint of dedication of *Venus and Adonis*: Rowse, *Shakespeare's Southampton*, 134.

331   Characterization of Southampton, weaknesses and virtues: Akrigg, 282–285.

331fn.   Lack of evidence as to meeting of Shakespeare and Southampton: Ibid., 193.

332fn.   Scenario of Southampton's and Shakespeare's beginning acquaintance: Stopes, *Third Earl of Southampton*, 40–41.

332fn.   Schoenbaum's estimate of Stopes's biography: *Shakespeare's Lives*, 644.

332   "Begetter" as "either the author or the inspirer": Dowden, *Histories and Poems*, 1055.

332–3   Disqualification of William Herbert as "W.H.": Barrell, "'Shakespeare's' Own Secret Drama," *Shake. Fellow. News-Letter*, III, no. 2, April 1942, 28.

333   Rendering of Nicholas Ling as "L.N.": *Englands Helicon*, ed. by Hugh Macdonald, Harvard University Press, 1950, xviii–xix.

Citations

335fn.   Dating of Sonnet 107: Auchincloss, 142.

335fn.   Robert Cecil's reference to the "moon" and its possible "eclipse": Stopes, *Third Earl of Southampton*, 94.

335   Comments on groups of and individual sonnets: Auchincloss, 144–145.

337   The poet as "middle-aging": Rowse, *Shakespeare the Man*, 94.

337   The comparative worth of the *Sonnets* and the narrative poems: Dowden, *Histories and Poems*, 1053.

338   The ravages of "swift-footed, terrible Time" in the *Sonnets*: Van Doren, 13.

338   Shakespeare's calling himself old protested: Rowse, *Shakespeare's Sonnets*, 129.

338   "Straight talk" and "tutorial attitude": Ibid., 141, 197.

338   *Sonnets* as never before studied by an historian: Ibid., viii.

339   As not written for publication: Ibid., xxxiv.

340   On the poet's bearing the canopy: Ibid., 259.

342   Possibility of Southampton's having had homosexual phases: Akrigg, 182.

343   Probabilities against his homosexuality: E. Hubler, 15.

343   Hillyer on enthusiasm as evoking passionate terms: *A New Variorum Edition of Shakespeare: The Sonnets*, review by H. E. Rollins, *New York Times Book Review*.

343   Rowse's "absurd claims" and "slipshod methods": B. Levin, London, *Observer*, 29 April, 1973.

343   "Quasi-parental element" in poet's attitude to young friend: Rowse, *Shakespeare the Man*, 85.

345   Terms appropriate to princes in address to young friend: Hotson, *Mr. W. H.*, London: Rupert Hart-Davis, 1964.

346   Sonnet 130 as making fun of Spenser: Disher, "The Trend of Shakespeare's Thought," London, *Times Literary Supplement*, 20 and 27 October and 3 November 1950.

347   Young friend as necessarily called Will: Dowden, *Histories and Poems*, 1056.

347fn.   Rendering of Sonnets 135 and 136 obscene by converting "Will" to "will": Rowse, *Shakespeare's Sonnets*, 280–281.

348   Southampton's "good advice" to players: Stopes, *Third Earl of Southampton*, 40.

---

350   **Chapter 18.** "Have Writ Your Annals True": *Coriolanus*, V v.

350   Approval of quotation from France on talking only of ourselves: Conrad, *A Personal Record*, Garden City, N.Y.: Doubleday, Doran, 1928, 95.

350   "Every man's work" as "always a portrait of himself": Butler, *The Way of All Flesh*, New York: Dutton, 1916, 70.

350-1   A man's work as necessarily autobiographical: Wallace quoted by Carlos Baker, *New York Times Book Review*, 20 August 1967.

351   "Every artist writes his own autobiography": Ellis, *The New Spirit, Tolstoi II*, quoted in *Oxford Dictionary of Quotations*, 2nd ed., 1955, 198b.

351   A playwright's source material as the people he knows: Albee, quoted in *Washington Post*, confirmed by card from Albee to author.

833

Citations

351   Drama as traditionally objective: Evans-Levin, 40.

351   On Shaw's having put himself in his every character: Coe, *Washington Post*, 13 February 1976.

351   All characters as representing an aspect of the author: Atkinson, *New York Times*, 16 March 1965.

351   O'Neill's plays as autobiographical: Gelb, *New York Times*, 3 March 1973.

352   Chekhov's characters as borrowed from the provincial society he knew: Gillès, 65–66.

352   The principals of *The Sea Gull* as taken from Chekhov's intimates: Ibid., 217.

353   Jonson's characters as mere fragments of himself: Wilson, *The New Yorker*, 6 November 1948, 124.

353   Writer seen as exposed in his many guises in his stories: Gallico, *Further Confessions of a Story Writer*, New York: Doubleday, 1961.

353   "All a novelist's characters are himself": Auchincloss, *A Writer's Capital*.

353   "Greatest creative personalities" as "interpenetrated" by their art: Lord, *New York Times*, 17 December 1967.

353   Andersen's fairy tales as "transfigurations of his own life": Pritchett, *The New Yorker*, 17 May 1976.

353   An artist's work as bound up with his life: Quennell, "Speaking of Books," *New York Times Book Review*, 1 September 1968.

354   Writers who reveal their lives in their works called second-rate: Wain, "Fiction and Fact," *New York Times Book Review*, 24 January 1965.

354fn.   Joyce as self-revelatory: Wain, *Washington Post*, July 1971.

354   Fry on Shakespeare as without a private personality: E. Hubler, 46.

354   Artist's self-revelation as measure of his genius: F. Harris, 4–5.

355   Novelist as writing himself into his novels: P. H. Johnson, *Important to Me*, New York: Scribner, 1975.

355   Shakespeare's vision as his own, undistorted by others: S. Johnson, Preface to *Prefaces*, 37–38.

355   Attribution to Shakespeare of "impersonality" and "chameleonic empathy": Evans-Levin, 40.

355   Shakespeare as exhibited in his creatures: Taine, II, 425.

355   Artist as seeing things as he is: Quoted by Philip Hamburger, *The New Yorker*, 13 June 1977.

355   Reflection of the "deer-stealing incident" in the plays: Evans-Levin, 43.

357   "Shakespeare's" theft of venison and his whipping: Chambers, II, 257.

357   Insufficiency of grounds for denying the legend: G. E. Bentley, 34.

357   The eddies under Clopton Bridge and those in *Lucrece*: Evans-Levin, 43.

357   The "slow-gliding waters" of the Avon: Fox, 2.

358fn.   Shakespeare's dialogue as seeming to arise from common conversations: S. Johnson, Preface to *Prefaces*, 25.

359   Hamlet as being what we all are: France, *La Vie Littéraire*, I, 7–8, quoted *in extenso* in Introduction to *Hamlet*, Cambridge ed., lxvi–lxvii.

359   Hamlet as truly existing and as a credible genius: Van Doren, 196.

360   The autobiographical nature of Hamlet as shown by his recurrence in other characters: F. Harris, 7, 8, 10.

Citations

360 Romeo as Hamlet's younger brother: Ibid., 10, 12–13.

360–1 Hamlet as a combination of Romeo and Jaques: Ibid., 14–15.

361 Richard II as a despot murdering in "cold hatred": W. Churchill, 385, 387.

361 Hamlet's take-over of the character of Richard: F. Harris, 68, 70.

361–2 Macbeth as a second Hamlet: Ibid.,

362 Charge that Harris brackets Macbeth with Hamlet as a kindly aesthete: Schoenbaum, 671.

362–3 "Makbeth's" good qualities; his and his wife's ambitions: Holinshed, *Scottish Chronicles*, I, 334, 340–341.

363 Harris called "liar," "scoundrel," "literary charlatan": Schoenbaum, 666, 670, 675.

363 Bennett's praise of *The Man Shakespeare*: Ibid., 669.

363 Brandes as a "royalist" for seeing Shakespeare's experience in Hamlet's: Ibid., 502, 503.

364 Shakespeare as objective, not given to inserting autobiography: Chute, 294.

364 *Sonnets* as useless to biographer: Ibid., 344.

364 Hamlet as a product of *fin de siècle* glooming and of pathology: Ibid., 228.

364 Ms. Chute's biography as "admirably sane": Schoenbaum, 759.

365–6 The light thrown on the dramatist's character and circumstances of his life by Hamlet's: Halle, 110, 111, 112, 114–115.

366–7 Life-like character of *Hamlet* with "no set purpose" or "straining": Hazlitt, *Shakespeare Criticism*, 288–289.

368 Polonius and Laertes as reflections of Burghley and his sons: Chambers, I, 418.

369 Polonius made to look ancient to be "spit image" of Burghley: Taylor, 137–138.

369 Burghley's birth during Diet of Worms: G. W. Phillips, 144.

369 Burghley's making Wednesday a meatless day: Read, *Mr. Secretary Cecil and Queen Elizabeth*, 271–274.

370 Shakespeare's postulated knowledge of MS of *Preceptes*: Chambers, I, 418.

370 Burghley's *Certaine Preceptes*: Peck, 47–49.

370 *Hamlet* as the prototype of autobiographical fiction: Brophy et al., *Fifty Works of English Literature the World Could Do Without*, New York: Stein & Day, as quoted in "Book World," *Washington Post*, 11 February 1968.

370 Ogburn's inability to make up his mind as to the prototype of Gertrude: Evans-Levin, 40.

371 De Vere's having "in a manner been brought up" by Elizabeth: Ward, 342.

371 *Hamlet* as of esoteric origins and not a "letter in code": Evans-Levin, 43.

372 1604 *Hamlet* as possibly from author's MS: Chambers, I, 412.

373 **Chapter 19.** "See, Where Oxford Comes!": *3 Henry Sixth*, V i.

374 Delayed appreciation and adequate criticism of Shakespeare: Looney, 101–102.

374 Convergence of currents leading to identification of "Shakespeare": Ibid., 20–21.

Citations

375 Looney's method described as "irrational" and based on "exploded assumption": Evans-Levin, 40.

375 "Common-sense method of searching for an unknown man": Looney, 104.

375 Ogburn as confounding the meaning of the epigrammatist's key words: Evans-Levin, 42.

376 Looney as motivated by snobbery: Schoenbaum, 598.

376 As "covetous of priority": Ibid.

376–7 Derivation of Manx family of Looney: Looney, letter of 6 January 1937, reproduced in *"Shakespeare" Identified* as edited by Ruth Loyd Miller, xxx.

377 "Looney" as "adding risibility to derision": Schoenbaum, 610.

377 On the tax-collectors' unsuccessful search for Shakspere: Looney, 57–58.

377 "In an unconsciously . . . to his door": Schoenbaum, 598.

377 "The American lady in the Lake Country" invoked: Ibid., 602.

377 The "rough beast" that "slouched towards Stratford": Ibid., 529.

378 Joseph C. Hart attacked and accused of mental derangement: Ibid., 547–549.

378 Schoenbaum's book lauded and anti-Stratfordian record found one of "fatuity, madness, meanness,": DeMott, *Saturday Review*, 7 November 1970, 35.

378–80 Postulations about "Shakespeare's" life, relationships, and characteristics: Looney, 109, 118–119, 131.

380–1 *Venus and Adonis* and de Vere's *Women*: Ibid., 136, 138.

381 De Vere as "among the early masters of English poetry": Macaulay, 448–449.

381 Silence of histories with respect to Oxford: Looney, 139.

382 Oxford's death before Shakespeare's best plays said to have been written: Evans-Levin, 43.

382 Ten plays as appearing after Oxford's death: Schoenbaum, 601.

382–3 Post-1590 plays seen as improvements by a mature man on earlier work: Looney, 100.

383 Disappearance of plays of the 1580s: F. P. Wilson, 106.

383 Performance of plays in public prior to Court showings and in houses of the nobility": Sisson, "The Theatres and Companies," *Companion to Shakespeare Studies*, 17, 18.

383 Shakespeare as writing old-fashioned plays under James: Chute, 146.

383 Shakespeare called "a magpie" and "most generous borrower": Rowse, *William Shakespeare*, 81–82, 93.

383 "Shakespeare was the Homer . . .": Dryden, "Essay of Dramatic Poesy," *Works*, XV, 347–348.

384 Shakespeare as basing *King John* upon an older play: Dowden, *Histories and Poems*, 2.

384 Shakespeare as having "the old book before him" in writing *King John*: Chambers, I, 367.

384 *2* and *3 Henry Sixth* as recasts of earlier dramas: Dowden, *Histories and Poems*, 535.

384 *Henry the Fifth* as based on *The Famous Victories*: Ibid., 358.

384 *The Famous Victories* as a piracy and three Shakespeare histories as written by 1588: Cairncross, 144.

384 Earlier dating of Shakespeare's plays as requiring revision of ideas about his relationship with contemporaries: F. P. Wilson, 108.

Citations

384–5   Shakespeare's "fairly obvious use" of an older play in *Lear*: Chambers, I, 469.

385   Shakespeare's *Lear* as written first, and ten years earlier than supposed: Cairncross, 157.

385   Peter Alexander's concurrence: *Shakespeare*, Home University Library, Oxford University Press, 81.

385fn.   Relationship of *King Lear*, Harsnett, the "booke of Miracles" and Oxford: Bowen, *Hackney, Harsnett and the Devils in King Lear*, *Shake. Auth. Review*, no. 14, Autumn 1965, 2–7.

385   Dating of Shakespeare's early comic drama earlier than orthodoxy allows by part played in them by euphuism: E. T. Clark, *Shake. Fellow. News-Letter*, III, no. 3, April 1942, 41b.

385–6   Dating of *Love's Labour's Lost* (1589 or 1590); its basis in Italian comedy; Pater's recognition of its fashionable foppery: Dowden, *Comedies*, 438, 440–441.

386   Knight's five Shakespearean comedies that could have been written before 1590: Elze, "The Date of *The Tempest*," *Essays*, 19, quoting Knight's *Wm. Shakespeare: A Biography*, 347 ff.

386   Topical allusions in *Twelfth Night* and its identification with "a pleasant conceit of Vere" as dating it about 1580: E. T. Clark, "Topicalities in the Plays," *Shake. Fellow. News-Letter*, I, no. 6, October 1940, 9, and II, no. 3, April 1941, 34–35.

386   Identification of "new map" in *Twelfth Night* with one of 1592 and dating its performance in January 1593: Cairncross, xviii.

386   Reference to a play called *The Jew*: Gosson, 30.

386   Reference to "any marchant in Italy" and "any Jew there": Harvey, *Letter Book of*, 78.

386   *Winter's Tale* as play entered in Stationer's Register in 1594: Charles W. Barrell, "A Literary Pirate's Attempt to Publish *The Winter's Tale* in 1594," *Shake. Fellow. Quar.*, III, no. 2, April 1946, 20 ff.

386–7   Collier on costumes presumably used in *Henry the Eighth*: Louis P. Bénézet, "False Shakspearean Chronology," *Shake. Fellow. Quar.*, VII, no. 3, July 1946, 43.

387   Whether the original *Hamlet* by Kyd: Chambers, I, 424.

387–8   Relationship of *Hamlet* and *The Spanish Tragedy* and the evidence dating the former to 1588 and making it the play referred to by Nashe in 1589; its evident production in Germany in 1591: Cairncross, 103–106, 125.

388   Strachey's report of 1610 cited as source of *The Tempest*: Chambers, I, 491–492.

388–9   Differences between Strachey's account of the wreck and the wreck in *The Tempest*: Kittredge, 3–4.

389   Similarities between Gosnold's description of Cuttyhunk and the island in *The Tempest*: J. D. Adams, "Speaking of Books," *New York Times Book Review*, undated clipping.

389   Interpolation in plays of references to later events: I. Brown, *Shakespeare*, Collins, 166.

389   Composition of *The Tempest* in 1604: Elze, "The Date of *The Tempest*," *Essays*, 18.

389–90   Similarities between *The Tempest* and pre-1605 German play ascribed to possible common source: Chambers, I, 493.

837

Citations

390   Chronology of the plays with earlier dates than orthodoxy assigns: Cairncross, 179, 182–183.

390   Plays found written "in much more rapid succession": Cairncross, 179.

390   Oxford's way with language as that of a court wit: Evans-Levin, 43.

392   Lack of character-studies in *Love's Labour's Lost*: Dowden, *Comedies*, 438.

392   Rattling rhymes, stiff speeches, dull fooling in *Comedy of Errors*: Van Doren, 45.

392fn.   On viewing the *Wives* as genially as we are able: Dowden, *Comedies*, 139.

392   The *Wives* as one of Shakespeare's "heartless farces": Van Doren, 139–140.

392fn.   Elizabeth's desire to see Falstaff in love: Rowe, viii–ix.

392   The *Shrew* as "a hasty revision . . . of an older play": Dowden, *Comedies*, 745.

392   Shakespeare's having a "collaborator" in the *Shrew*: Chambers, I, 324.

393–6   Bénézet's pot-pourri of Oxford's and Shakespeare's poetry; the reactions of Phelps and Kittredge: "Shakspere, Shakespeare and de Vere," *Shake. Fellow. News-Letter*, III, no. 5, August 1942, 67–68.

396–7   May's views on poems by and not by Oxford: See Bibliography.

397   De Vere as "a frightful headache": Rowse, *William Shakespeare*, 122.

398   Faulkner on the amorality of the artist: Malcolm Cowley, — *And I Worked at the Writer's Trade*, New York: Viking Press, 1978, 259.

398fn.   Esther Singleton's transformation into an Oxfordian: *Shake. Fellow. News-Letter*, I, no. 4, June-July 1940, pp. 10–11.

399   Lady Cavendish on how one would think Shakespeare had been all his characters: Ingleby, 332.

400   Lack of humor in Oxford's poems and letters: Campbell, "To Be or Not to Be," *New York Times Book Review*, 8 February, 1953, 7.

401   Oxford as among courtly poets who "have written excellently well": George Puttenham, "The Arte of English Poesie," *Ancient Critical Essays*, I, 49.

401   Verses on Oxford "coming from Italy, in Germany": Chapman, *Revenge of Bussy d'Ambois*, ed. by Frederick S. Boas, Boston: Heath, 1905, 237.

401   "Far fly thy fame . . . when Apes are turned forth": Marston, "Here's a toy to mocke an Ape indeed," *Satyre IX*.

403   Defining Shakespeare's personality and rescuing him from abstraction: Lewis, 20.

403   Shakespeare as semi-mythical figure: Eliot, "Observations," London, *The Egoist*, May 1918, 69.

Book Two. "Is Not Oxford Here Another Anchor?": *3 Henry VI*, V iv.

---

407   **Chapter 20.** "What's Past Is Prologue": *The Tempest*, II iv.

407   Elizabeth's "capacity for inspiring devotion": W. Churchill, *The New World*, 103.

408   Her mind as free of female weakness: Jenkins, 34.

408   The beauty of her handwriting: Ibid., 19.

Citations

408 Elizabeth a "paragon of the new learning": W. Churchill, *The New World*, 104.

408 Elizabeth's boast of being "mere English": Trevelyan, II, 85.

408 The 16th Earl of Oxford meets and entertains the Swedish prince: Stow's *Annales*, 697a–b.

410 Earls Colne and Colmekill in *Macbeth*: Patience, *Shake. Author. Review*, no. 20, Autumn 1968, 11.

413 The "sad remnants" of the "monumental effigies" of the de Veres: Innes-Smith, "The Chapel-Barn of St. Stephen, Bures."

414 Majendie's story that the 17th Earl had the buildings at Hedingham destroyed: Ward, 386.

414–5 Crewe's exordium: "The Resolution delivered by Crew Chief Justice in Parliament, concerning the Earldom of Oxford," *Anno Primo Caroli Regis*, W. Jones, 101.

415–6 The inspiration that flowed through Wyatt and Surrey: Brooke, 339.

416 Surrey's posthumous publication: *Dictionary of National Biography*, X, 27a.

416 Grace and natural beauty in Surrey's work; his resemblance to Byron: Brooke, 342–343.

416 Players of Oxford and others rewarded by Henry VII: Bradbrook, 27, 28.

416fn. Performance by 16th Earl's players during a dirge for Henry VIII: Chambers, *Elizabethan Stage*, II, 99.

417 "Our Veres" as the "most glorious sun . . . the imitation to all the Princes of the world": Markham, 10.

417 Descent of the de Veres: Allen, 3; Innes-Smith, "The Earls of Oxford."

418 Functions of the Lord Great Chamberlain: *Encyclopaedia Britannica*, XVII, 2b–3a.

418 Alighting of the white scar on Albry's standard: Ward, 4.

419 Whether Prince Hal paralleled the young Stratfordian: Dowden, *Histories and Poems*, 261.

419 Description of the third Aubrey: Allen, 6–7.

419 "Restless energy . . . pitch of instability": W. Churchill, *The Birth of Britain*, 242.

419 The loyalty of "Alberike de Veere": Holinshed, II, 304.

419–20 King John's capture of "Hidingham": Ibid., II, 329.

422 Friendship of the 9th Earl and Richard II as "fatal to both": *Dictionary of National Biography*, XX, 244a.

422 Accounts of the 9th Earl of Oxford: Holinshed, II, 774, 789–790.

422–3 The misery to which Duke Robert reduced: Ibid., II, 821.

423 The King honors Robert's corpse: Ibid., II, 830.

425 The build-up of the medieval Oxford as serving the cause of Edward de Vere: Pitcher, 185–194.

427 Oxford's seizure of St. Michael's Mount and exile to Hammes: *Encyclopaedia Britannica*, XX, 403a.

427 "Richard was no monster born": Trevelyan, I, 349.

428 The support of Richmond by Oxford and others; the slaughter of King Richard: W. Churchill, *The Birth of Britain*, 493–494, 499.

Citations

429 Further martial successes of the 13th Earl: *Encyclopaedia Britannica*, XX, 403a.

429 The Duchess of Cleveland's account of the imposition of a fine upon the 13th Earl by Henry VII: Duchess of Cleveland, *Battle Abbey Roll*, London: John Murray, 1889, III, 210.

429 Fine as start of de Veres' financial decline: E. T. Clark, "The Red Rose," *Shake. Fel. News-Letter*, III, no. 3, April 1942, 53.

429 The 15th Earl of Oxford at the siege of Boulogne: *Biographia Britannica*, 403I.

429–30 The Oxfords at Anne Boleyn's coronation: Stow, *Annales*, ed. 1631, 567.

430 Crumwell's indebtedness to Oxford for his pleasure at the hunt: Allen, 16.

430 The 16th Earl as a good landlord and sportsman: *Dictionary of National Biography*, XX, 242.

430 The 16th Earl and the boar-hunt: Markham, 14–16.

430–1 The 16th Earl's liaison with Dorothy and the challenge to Edward de Vere's legitimacy: Ward, 7–8.

431 De Vere's *Loss of Good Name*: Looney, *Poems of Edward de Vere*, 22.

432 The 16th Earl's attendance on the Swedish prince; as "the good earl": *Dictionary of National Biography*, XX, 242.

432 The Earl at Oxford House: Stow, *Survey*, Oxford ed., 316.

432 The Earl's procession into London: Stow, *Survey*, 89–90.

434 *Hamlet* as embodying the relationships of Elizabeth, Leicester, and Oxford; Leicester's succession to the de Vere lands: Bowen, "What Happened at Hedingham and Earls Colne?" *Shake. Auth. Review*, no. 24, Spring 1971, 9–10.

434 Edmund Dudley as an extortioner of Henry VII: *Encyclopaedia Britannica*, VIII, 636b.

---

435 **Chapter 21.** "Learning and Ingenious Studies": *Taming of the Shrew*, I i.

435 Funeral of the 16th Earl: Ward, 14.

436 Burghley's Wards: Read, 125.

437 Oxford's arrival in London with seven score horses: Ward, 15.

437 Description of Cecil House: Ward, 16.

437–8 Burghley's delight in gardens and fountains: Read. 123.

438 Elizabeth's and Burghley's forty-year collaboration: W. Churchill, *The New World*, 105.

438–9 Inspiration for Polonius' maxims in Burghley's *Certaine Preceptes*: Chambers, I, 418.

440 Edward's schedule of studies: Ward, 20.

440 His distinction as student and classical scholar, talent as poet, interest in drama: Read, 125.

440–1 Nowell's instruction not much longer to be required: Ward, 20.

442 Edward at Cambridge, the award of degrees to him and Manners, Manners's future eminence, Brooke's testimony to Edward's devotion to learning: Ward, 22–23; Read, 125.

442 Elizabeth at Cambridge, as "a product of the Renaissance": Jenkins, 106.

Citations

442 The award of M.A. degrees to de Vere and Manners at Oxford; the collapse of the wall: Ward, 27; Jenkins, 125.

442–3 The dedication to Edward of Arthur Golding's *The Abridgement*: Ward, 23–24.

443 Shakespeare as "an English Ovid": Rowse, *Shakespeare the Man*, 26.

443 Shakespeare's habitual echoing of Ovid and certain familiarity with the Golding translation: Nims, xx.

443–4 The oddity of collaboration between the scandalous Ovid and the convinced Puritan: Nims, xiv.

444 The strangeness of Ovid's being translated by the author of *Discourse*: *Encyclopaedia Britannica*, XII, 212b.

444 Wordiness, parade of adjectives, inversion in the Golding translation: Nims, xxi–xxiv.

444 Pound's view of Golding's work as the most beautiful book in the language and belief that Shakespeare shared it: Nims, xxi.

444 "Still more enjoyable, more plain fun . . .": Nims, xxi.

445 The racy gusto of the Golding work; the "Englishing" of the stories; its greatest merit is description; the zest of the boar hunt; the book's near-best in Ceres' search for her daughter; the spicy evocation of the old country couple; the Lewis-Carroll words: Nims, xxxi–xxxv.

---

457 **Chapter 22.** "Amongst the Infinite Doings of the World": *Winter's Tale*, I ii.

457 Oxford's prominence at Court in boyhood: *Dictionary of National Biography*, XX, 226a.

458–9 The magnificence of Elizabeth's palaces, the jewels, carpets, statues": Bohun, 341–342.

459 "A court so decent, so learned . . .": Aikin, II, 508.

459–60 The Earl of Oxford as "an excellent poet and comedian": Wood, *Fasti Oxonienses*, I, 727.

460 The addiction of the courtiers to the theatre: Bohun, 345.

460 Elizabeth's insistence that da Silva watch a comedy: Jenkins, 105.

460 "The cry of hounds for Theseus" in the play: Jenkins, 125.

462 The "new type of Privy Councillor": Trevelyan, II, 22.

464 Mary's "lust for power" and "incapacity for ruling": Jenkins, 92.

464 "Played at being queen . . . men who were Mary's undoing": Bindhoff, 206.

464 Darnley's scant qualifications: Ibid.

464 Elizabeth's response to Mary's bearing a son: Jenkins, 124.

465 Mary's promise to de Spes to be Queen of England with Spanish help: Jenkins, 147.

465 Mary as a "politique": Edwards, "Oxford and the Duke of Norfolk," *Shake. Auth. Review*, no. 28, Summer 1973, 12.

466 Oxford's appeal to Cecil for service to "Prince and country": Ward, 39–40.

467 Elizabeth's directive sparing the lives of the wealthy: Jenkins, 154.

467 Her "callous savagery" in reprisals: *Dictionary of National Biography*, VI, 631b.

Citations

468   The memory Sussex speaks of leaving in Scotland: Ward, 48.

468   Cecil's letter on the Queen's sending Oxford to the north: Ibid., 40.

468   The Queen's letter to Sussex praising him for his conduct: Ibid., 46–47.

469   Sussex as a great noble, diplomat, patron of literature: *Encyclopaedia Britannica*, XXVI, 165a.

469   Oxford as supporter of Sussex, as Sidney of Leicester: Ward, 48; Jenkins, 202.

469   Oxford as bad-tempered, selfish, poor, ruthless, but attractive to Maids: Jenkins, 166.

469   As an "unwhipped cub": Read, 135.

469   Oxford shown as "hard, cold, calculating" in the Welbeck portrait: Read, 133.

470   Strong's opinions of the Hilliard and Gheeraedts portraits; Letters to the author of 6 May 1981 and 3 December 1981.

470   Gibson's opinion of the Gheeraedts portrait: Letter to the author of 27 March 1980.

472   Chapman's encomium to Oxford discounted: Read, 135.

472   King Henri's compliment to Oxford's appearance: Ward, 101.

472   Scholastic resistance to change: Hardison, 62.

473   Underdowne's dedication of *An aethiopian Historie* to Oxford: R. L. Miller, "Notes on Cymbeline," 3rd ed.; E. T. Clark, *Hidden Allusions*, 99.

473   Golding's dedication to Oxford of Calvin's *Psalms of David*: Ward, 77–78.

473–4   Twyne's dedication to Oxford of a *Breviary of Britain*: Ward, 84–85.

474   Oxford's relations with Churchyard: Ward, 28–30.

474   Churchyard's proposed dedications to Oxford: May, 9 fn.

474   Dee's relations with Elizabeth: *Encyclopaedia Britannica*, VII, 920b.

474   Dee's letters from Oxford: Ward, 50.

475   Bedingfield's letter to Oxford accompanying *Cardanus Comfort*: Ward, 86.

476fn.   Shakespeare as standing for the sceptres of the past: Whitman, 407.

476   How Parliament besought Elizabeth to marry: Camden, quoted, Jenkins, 123.

476   Expectation of Elizabeth's husband to be more than that: Bindhoff, 204.

476   Value of match as weapon against European combination: W. Churchill, *The New World*, 108.

477   Catherine's ambitions for "her goblin brood": Jenkins, 122.

477   Calvinism as a force to shatter English church and state: W. Churchill, *The New World*, 114.

478   Segar on the conduct of a tournament: Ward, 57–59.

479   The Tournament of May 1571 and Oxford's victory: Ward, 59–60; Stow, *Annales*, 1141.

479   Oxford's as the highest score at the tilt: Chambers, *Sir Henry Lee*, 134.

479   Oxford's as "an amazing performance": Read, 126.

479   Lee as "flower of chivalry": Strong, *Portraits of Queen Elizabeth*, 28.

479   Fletcher's tribute to Oxford's horsemanship and valor: Ward, 60.

480   Delves on Oxford as at the zenith of the Court: Ibid.

480   Oxford as seeming to have everything but lacking enthusiasm for the courtier's game: Read, 127.

Citations

481 Burghley as secure in position and wealthy; his imposing building: Ibid., 17.

481 The costly construction of Theobalds: Ibid., 122.

482 A German visitor's description of Theobalds: Nicols, III, 241.

---

483 **Chapter 23.** "And Summon Him to Marriage": *Merchant of Venice*, III ii.

483 St. John's letter on Oxford's getting him a wife: Ward, 61–62.

483–4 Burghley's letter to Rutland on the projected marriage: Ward, 62–63.

484 Burghley's expressions of affection for Sidney; the promotion of a match between Philip and Anne; Leicester's and Burghley's proposed financial contributions to the two partners respectively: *Dictionary of National Biography*, XVIII, 220b.

485 Burghley's indifference to his children's views on marriages: Read, 128.

485 Local color of Windsor in *Merry Wives*: Dowden, *Comedies*, 139.

486 Fenton as recognizably Oxford to any courtier: Quoted by R. L. Miller, Looney, 3rd ed., II, 176.

486 Slender as "arm-in-arm" with Aguecheek: Dowden, *Comedies*, 139.

487 The "fit" between the marriage arrangement of Anne Page and Slender and that of Anne Cecil and Sidney: "The Earl of Oxford as Shakespeare," *The Golden Hind*, I–II, nos. 1–8, October 1922 to July 1924; reproduced in Looney, 3rd ed., 168–176.

488 Fenton's dedication to the Countess of Oxford: Tenison, II, 177.

Style of *All's Well* as combining that of *Hamlet* and of early comedies: Dowden, *Comedies*, 827.

488 Quotations from the *Decameron* are from the edition of Chatto and Windus, London, 1924.

488 The "struggle" with "obstinate material": Dowden, *Comedies*, 829.

488 The padding of a "dry skeleton": Van Doren, 210.

489 Bertram's supremacy in "caddishness": Auchincloss, 89.

489 Bertram's attractions, and his shortcomings seen as normal: Ibid., 92.

490 Roussillon, Hélène of Tournon and Oxford's travels: Wainewright, summary of lecture, *Shake. Auth. Review*, no. 24, Spring 1971, 19–21.

491 The French Ambassador's report of Oxford's marriage as arranged to counter Norfolk's influence: Tenison, II, 175.

491 Fitz-Williams's report of plan for Edward-Anne wedding in September: Ward, 63.

492 Oxford as "an entire friend" of Norfolk's: Dugdale, *Baronage*, I, 199.

492–3 Fénélon's report of Lane's reference to "certain proposal" by Oxford: Ward, 66.

493 The "poor woman's" report of Oxford's provision of a ship for the rescue of Norfolk: Ward, 66–67.

---

494 **Chapter 24.** "Of Courts, of Princes, of the Tricks . . .": *Cymbeline*, III, iii.

494 De Spes's report of the loss to the Catholics of two families: Ward, 68.

495 Demands for forfeit of Norfolk's life: Jenkins, 180.

Citations

495 Norfolk's indignant repudiation of charges against him: Rev. Francis Edwards, S.J., "Oxford and the Duke of Norfolk," *Shake. Auth. Review*, no. 28, Summer 1973, 11.

495 Burghley on Elizabeth's agonized vacillations over Norfolk's sentence: Jenkins, 180; Read, 47.

495 Walsingham's "marvellous agony": Read, 48.

496 The "person . . . whom no law can touch": Jenkins, 181–182.

496 Agent's report of Oxford's friendship for Norfolk and "great displeasure" with Burghley: Ward, 68.

496 The report as "idle gossip" and good relationship between Oxford and Burghley within year: Read, 129.

496 Allegation that Oxford sold his inheritance to ruin Burghley's daughter: Dugdale, *Baronage*, I, 199.

496 Oxford's sales of estates: Ward, 354.

496 Oxford's alleged vow to "ruin the Lord Treasurer's daughter": Jenkins, 192. Norfolk's death as Burghley's triumph, strengthening his hold on the Queen: A. G. Smith, 171.

497 The Court of Urbino as purest and most elevated: *Encyclopaedia Britannica*, VI, 474b.

498–9 Oxford's prefatory letter to Clerke's translation of *The Courtier*: Ward, 80–83.

499 Hamlet as the exemplar of *The Courtier*, "*the* Prince," and Shakespeare himself as following Castiglione: W. B. Drayton Henderson, Introduction, *The Book of the Courtier*, New York: Dutton, 1928, xiv, xvi.

501 Elizabeth's discrimination between "the sexual act" and naked display; the trauma of her past as deterrent to the act: Jenkins, 100.

501 Elizabeth as reviving her father: Jenkins, 94.

502 The scandal of Elizabeth's relations with Hatton: Jenkins, 166.

502–3 Oxford as dazzling the Queen: Jenkins, 166.

503 Dyer's recommended strategy for Hatton to follow to circumvent "Crm" or "Chm" or "Oxen": Letter reproduced *in extenso* in Sargent, 24–25.

504 Oxford as scion of Norman nobility: Sargent, 24.

504 Hatton's ardent letter to the Queen, warning of the "boar's tusk": Ward, 75.

504–5 The royal entertainment at Warwick Castle and Oxford's starring role: Ward, 70–71.

504fn. The eleven-year-old Will Shakspere at the Kenilworth festivities: Rowse, *Shakespeare the Man*, 5.

506 Oxford's letter on the murder of the French Huguenot nobles, expressing his solicitude for Burghley: Ward, 71–72.

507 Oxford's letter to Burghley asking for service abroad or at sea: Ward, 71–73.

508 The Queen's visit to Havering-in-the-Bowerie: Morant's *Essex*, I, 59; cited by Nichols, I, 387.

508 Oxford's letter appealing for Burghley's good opinion against reports of "backfriends": Ward, 76.

844

Citations

510 **Chapter 25. "Entertainment to My Princely Queen":** 2 *Henry the Sixth*, I, i.

510–11 Talbot on the Queen's delight in Oxford and Lady Burghley's jealousy: Nichols, I, 328–329.

511 Elizabeth's visit to, and Morant's description of Havering: Nichols, III, 70–71, 241.

511 Elizabeth's second and subsequent visits to Havering: Nichols, I, 387.

512 Self-abandonment and self-pity in *Sonnets*: Harris, 203.

513 Elizabeth's and Cleopatra's similarities: E. T. Clark, *Hidden Allusions*, drawing especially on Plutarch and Lytton Strachey, 204–206.

514 Black and white as Elizabeth's colors: Jenkins, 105.

514ff For the text of *A Hundreth Sundrie Flowres* I have relied chiefly upon B. M. Ward's edition of 1926. Page-numbers of the quotations that I introduce will not be cited because these differ between Ward's and the two extant editions of the anthology (see Bibliography) and between them also.

514 *Flowres* as "richest collection . . .": Brooke, 394.

514 Hazlitt on curiosity and literary value of *Flowres*: Ward, *Flowres*, vii.

515 *The Adventures of Master F. I.* as "drawn from life": Brooke, 417.

515 *Fortunatus Infoelix* as the posy of Hatton: Harvey, *Marginalia*, 166.

516 The closing of a door by Gascoigne's *Posies*: Brooke, 394.

516 "Gascoigne responsible for whole": S. Lee, *Dictionary of National Biography*, VII, 916b.

518 Shakespeare's interest in medieval tale of Troilus: Kittredge, 879.

519 Unburdening of Shakespeare's heart in *Troilus and Cressida*: Dowden, *Tragedies*, 9.

519 Shakespeare's bitterness in *Troilus and Cressida* and Cressida and Elizabeth as having same model: Harris, 300, 302.

519 *Troilus and Cressida* as one of three unsuccessful comedies: Van Doren, 202.

520fn. "The golden world," the gentlemen and ladies of Shakespeare's comedies: Ibid., 54.

521 Oxford's gift of gloves to Elizabeth: *Biographia Britannica*, 4031.

522 The "reconciliation" in "which no one believes": Van Doren, 56.

522 The "stumbling-block" of Valentine's surrender of Silvia and the strangeness of Silvia's silence: Dowden, *Comedies*, 73.

523 Elizabeth's ability to bear ten children: Jenkins, 123.

523 The Earl's "well wishes" toward the marriage of Norfolk and Mary of Scots: Dugdale, from Stopes, *Third Earl of Southampton*, 5.

523 The Earl writes of his wife's delivery of a "goodly boy": Ibid., 1–2.

523 Stopes on the birth of the boy rumored to be the second son: Ibid., 2.

523 The strange lack of a record of Henry's baptism and of godparents: Ibid.

524 On the Countess's sending her son to her husband: Ibid., 4.

525 **Chapter 26. "To Me It Is a Prison":** *Hamlet*, II ii.

526 Cardano on the aim of *De Consolatione* and Shakespeare's addiction to the conception: Barrell, *Shake. Fellow. Quar.*, VII, no. 3, July 1946, 37.

Citations

526–7 Oxford's letter may be found in its entirety in Ward, 87–89, and in facsimile in Looney, 3rd ed., I, 133.

527 Parallels between Oxford's letter to Bedingfield and Shakespeare's plays: Barrell, *Shake. Fellow, Quar.*, VII, no. 4, October 1946; reprinted in Looney, 3rd ed., I, 574–579.

527 Parallels between the letter and the *Sonnets*: P. Allen, 46–47; G. Bowen, *Shake. Auth. Review*, no. 17, Spring 1967, 6–12.

528 Liking to believe that Hamlet reading Cardan while baiting Polonius: L. B. Campbell, note 3, 133–134.

528–9 The waylaying of two of Oxford's former men on the road from Gravesend to Rochester: Ward, 90–92.

529–30 Lane's letter on Oxford's involvement with de Guaras: Ward, *A Hundreth Sundrie Flowres*, 2nd ed., 330.

530 "Matter is puzzling . . . desperately for action": Read, 130.

530 Oxford's longing for foreign parts and abortive financial arrangements therefor: Ward, 92.

531 Sidney's gift to the Queen of a cambric smock: *Dictionary of National Biography*, XVIII, 273b.

531–2 Oxford's flight to the Continent; the report of Burghley's correspondent in Antwerp; the dispatch of Bedingfield to bring the Earl back; Oxford's return; Burghley's thanks to Sussex for his intercession: Ward, 93–94.

532 Mildmay's letter to Burghley: Ibid., 94.

533 Walsingham's report of the Queen's favorable inclination to Oxford: Ibid., 95.

533–4 Burghley's letter to Walsingham on Oxford's making his peace with the Queen, with an appraisal of Oxford's character: Ibid., 95–96.

534–5 Letter reporting Oxford restored to royal favor but still restless; his wife's request of Sussex for larger quarters; Ward's belief he was chiefly interested in "country Muses" and "lewd friends": Ibid., 97–98.

535 Ward's dating *Famous Victories* of this time: E. T. Clark, Hidden Allusions, 13.

535 *The Famous Victories'* reliance on Edward Hall's *The Union of the Noble and Illustre Famelies of Lancastre and York*: Pitcher, 199–225.

535–6 Oxford's tall story of serving Alva: Ward, 99–100.

---

538 **Chapter 27.** "Why, Then, the World's Mine Oyster": *Merry Wives*, II ii.

539 The entail in 1575 of Oxford's properties: *Dictionary of National Biography*, XX, 219b.

539–53 Oxford's itinerary on the Continent and texts of his correspondence with Burghley may be found in Ward, 100–113. His travels are described, with citations to references in Shakespeare's plays to cities the Earl visited, by E. T. Clark in *Shake. Fellow. Quar.*, VI, no. 1, January 1945, 3–10.

539–40 Hill as a companion of Oxford's travels: Aubrey, I, 319.

540 Hill as secretary to Oxford: *Dictionary of National Biography*, IX, 855b–856a.

540 De Castelnau on Paris in 1560: *Encyclopaedia Britannica*, XX, 817b–818a.

Citations

540   Venetian ambassador's report to Doge of Oxford's arrival in Paris: Letter, Lisa Sergio, citing file no. 9, Register no. 79, 1575–1576; Series, Dispatches from Ambassadors, sub-series, France; Senato secreta; State Archives of the Republic of Venice.

540–1   English ambassador's letters to Burghley of March 1575: Ward, 101.

542–3   Oxford and Sturmius: Ward, 104–105, 250.

544   Lewyn's report of Oxford's being possibly in Venice: Ibid., 106.

546   Inscription on the flyleaf of Lady Oxford's Greek Testament: Ibid., 108–109.

547   Oxford and the Bankers Baptista Nigrone and Pasquino Spinola: Ibid., 108, 109.

549fn.   Report of Oxford's building a house in Venice: Logan Pearsall Smith, *Life and Letters of Sir Henry Wotton*, Oxford: Clarendon Press, 1907, II, 113, note 3.

549–50   Oxford and the *Commedia dell' Arte*: J. C. Altrocchi, *Shake. Auth. Rev.*, No. 2, Autumn, 1959, reprinted E. T. Clark's *Hidden Allusions*, 3rd ed., 134–135.

550   Influence of the *Commedia dell' Arte* on *Love's Labour's Lost*: Kittredge, 194.

550   Holofernes compared with Doctor Graziano: David, xxxvi.

551   The nasal twang of Naples and the jibe in *Othello*: E. T. Clark, *Shake. Fellow. Quar.*, VI, no. 1, January 1945, 8b.

551   Webbe's report of Oxford's challenge to all comers at Palermo: Edward Webbe, *His Travailes*, ed. by Edward Arber, London: Alex Murray & Son, 1869, 32.

551   Oxford's challenge at Palermo as meant for Don John: E. T. Clark, as in the second item above, 9a.

552   The honor Oxford did to England in his travels: Markham, 16.

552–3   Arundel's report of Oxford's tall stories of exploits in Italy: Ward, 128–129.

553   Venetian ambassador's report of Oxford's arrival in Paris: Ibid., 113.

554   *Speculum Tuscanismi* mocking Oxford's new Italianate ways: Harvey, *Works*, II, 83–86.

554   Oxford's gifts to Elizabeth: Stow, *Annales*, 868b.

---

555   **Chapter 28. "Look So Strange upon Your Wife?"** *All's Well*, V iii.

555–6   Burghley's notes of April 25th recounting at length Oxford's behavior on his return from Paris: Read, 134–135.

556–7   Interception of Oxford's ship by pirates: Read, 133, 174–175.

557–8   Burghley's verbose, rambling letter to the Queen of April 23rd: Ibid., 135–136.

559   Oxford's letter to Burghley of April 27 announcing his decision not to accompany his wife until he has satisfied himself of some mistakes and objecting that the issue has been made "the fable of the world": Ward, 121–122.

559–60   Oxford's allegations against Burghley summarized: Ward, 123.

560   Burghley's memorandum of June 12th particularizing Oxford's offenses and calling for his return to his wife: Ward, 123–124; Read, 137.

560fn.   Oxford's carrying the train: Strong, *Cult of Elizabeth*, 168.

560–1   Burghley's memorandum of July 10 blaming Oxford's "unkindness" on "untrue reports of others": Ward, 124–125.

Citations

561 Oxford's letter of July 12th agreeing to wife's return to Court: Ibid., 125–126.

561 Oxford's provision for wife and choice of heirs: Ibid., 126.

561–2 Dr. Masters's letter to Burghley: Ibid., 114–115.

562–3 Burghley's memorandum on Oxford's last lying with his wife and reception of the news of her delivery: Ward, 115, 117.

563 Henry Howard's learning, Roman Catholicism, involvement with Mary of Scots, treason, repeated jailing: *Dictionary of National Biography*, X, 32a, 31b, 29a–b.

563 Lady Bacon and the French ambassador on Howard's dangerous nature: Amphlett, 96–97.

563–4 Yorke's dissolute, audacious behavior, introduction of rapier: Camden, *True and Royal History*, 397.

564 Yorke's treacheries: *Dictionary of National Biography*, XXI, 1252a–b.

564 Lady Oxford reports being kept out of husband's chamber by Yorke: R. L. Miller in E. T. Clark's *Hidden Allusions*, 3rd ed., 147.

565 Oxford suspected of wish to be free of wife to associate with actors and writers: Amphlett, 98–99.

565 Hamlet's "foiled love" for an inadequate Ophelia: Dowden, *Tragedies*, 92.

567 Proteus' forgiveness explained by nature of Renaissance literature: Dowden, *Comedies*, 72.

567 *Measure for Measure* condemned on basis of denouement: Dowden, *Comedies*, 219.

568 The perversity of Leontes's accusation: Auchincloss, 133–134.

568 "Motivational void" in *Winter's Tale*: Kalen, *Time*, 13 March 1980.

568 Macaulay's and Landor's encomiums to *Othello*: Quoted by Dowden, *Tragedies*, 844.

568 Othello as an allegory of Alençon, Elizabeth, and the French assault on Antwerp: E. T. Clark, *Hidden Allusions*, 388, 392.

569 Iago as the evil in man and in Othello, who perversely destroys his own happiness: Auchincloss, 11.

569–70 "Nothing in Iago absent in Othello" and "everything in the tragedy in the character of hero" who is "superior to passion and its slave": Van Doren, 225, 228, 229.

570 Hamlet as a "man whose tragedy is within him": Granville-Barker, 30.

570 Passion and distrust of passion in Hamlet: Dowden, *Tragedies*, 626.

570 "High integrity and noble character" of Othello: Auchincloss, 5.

570 Othello as "the noblest man of man's making," whose tragedy is one of "most pathetic of human compositions": Swinburne and Wordsworth quoted by Dowden, *Tragedies*, 844.

571 Wagner's atonement to women: Taylor, *Talks*, C.B.S., New York, January 1937.

571 "Earl's actions . . . reprehensible": Barrell, *Shake. Fellow. News Let.*, III, no. 6, 71a.

575 Report that "father of Lady Anne . . . contrived that her husband should unknowingly sleep with her": Looney, 1st ed., 280–281.

576   Report that Oxford's "lady was brought to his bed under the notion of his mistress": Barrell, *Shake. Fellow. News-Letter*, IV, no. 2, February 1943, 14a.

580   "Isabella harps too much on her virginity": Auchincloss, 100.

580fn.   Engraving of Elizabeth as Diana: Strong, *Portraits of Queen Elizabeth I*, 109, 112.

581   **Chapter 29.** "Phoebus Gins Arise": *Cymbeline*, II iii.

582   Oxford's alleged profession of Roman Catholic faith: Ward, 206–207.

582   Listing of ten plays possibly of Oxford's by Court Revels in latter 1570s: E. T. Clark, *Shake. Fellow. News-Letter*, III, no. 2, 40b–41a.

582   "The historie of Error . . . shown at Hampton Court": E. T. Clark, *Hidden Allusions*, 19.

583   "Doggerel verse" in *Comedy of Errors*: Dowden, *Comedies*, 300.

583   Rhymes that "rattle like bleached bones": Van Doren, 45.

583   Jibe at Hatton's gold bell and chain: E. T. Clark, *Hidden Allusions*, 22–23.

583   Hatton as "an affected fribble": Hume,

583   Incessant reference to chain as failing in effect: Van Doren, 16.

583–4   The performance of *The Historie of the Solitary Knight* at Whitehall and speculation that it was an early version of *Timon of Athens* reflecting Oxford's troubles: E. T. Clark, *Hidden Allusions*, 26–38.

584   Oxford's "infinite expense" and the alms he gave: Markham, 16, 17.

585   Shakespeare's authorship of large parts of *Titus* disputed: Dowden, *Tragedies*, 217, 220, 221.

585fn.   Shakespeare as drawing upon Kyd, Marlowe, Peele, and others for *Titus*: Chambers, I, 318.

585   Performance of *Titus and Gisippus* at Whitehall and speculation that it was *Titus Andronicus* and Oxford's political use of drama: E. T. Clark, *Shake. Fellow. News-Letter*, III, no. 2, 41a; *Hidden Allusions*, 43.

585   *The Paradyse of Daintie Devises* is interestingly discussed in Brooke, 384, where it is called one of two books that "had most effect in shaping Shakespeare's first notion of lyric."

585   Denial of Oxford's authorship of six poems ascribed to the Earl by Grosart: May, 11.

588   Oxford and Sidney as heads of opposing literary camps: Courthope, II, 211.

588–9   Differences between Oxford and Sidney: Jenkins, 202–203.

589   Sidney as young-hero figure echoed by Rupert Brooke: Kenyon, "Book World," *Washington Post*, 16 July 1972.

589–90   Spenser's "feebleness" contrasted with Oxford's "strength, reality," and Dean Church quoted on revolution in English poetry between 1580s and 1590s: Looney, 160–161.

590   Of English poets, forty as having genius and "new senses": Taine, 205–206.

590   Oxford "writing plays and poetry" and possibly "an even greater than Lord Burghley": A. G. Smith, 178–179.

591   Burghley's letter to Oxford at end of 1576 trying "by reasonable means to seek relief" for his daughter, who "may not come to your presence": Ward, 147–148.

Citations

591   Ballad of *The Brave Lord Willoughby*: T. Percy, 238–241.

592–3   The Duchess of Suffolk's letters to Burghley asking his help in the proposed marriage of her son Peregrine to Lady Mary Vere, which she and her husband bitterly oppose: Ward, 152–153.

593   Peregrine's fear that Oxford intends his death; the marriage; the "unkindness" between the partners; the prospect of Mary's being beaten with her own rod: Ibid., 153–154.

594   Enactment of *A Morrall of the marryage of Mynde and Measure*; the indications that it might have been inspired by the marriage of the Willoughbys: E. T. Clark, *Hidden Allusions*, 94–101.

594–5   The Duchess of Suffolk's letter to Burghley of her plan to bring Oxford and his little daughter together: Ward, 154–156.

595fn.   Reports of Lord and Lady Oxford visiting Theobalds with retinue of twenty-eight, with speculation that these were players: E. T. Clark, *Hidden Allusions*, 59.

595fn.   Dismissal of notion that *Pericles* an early play of Shakespeare's: Dowden, *Tragedies*, 1158.

595fn.   Assertion that "*Pericles* is not all Shakespeare's": Kittredge, 1377.

595fn.   *Perille* as origin of the name *Pericles*: Chambers, I, 527, quoting A. H. Smith, *Shakespeare's Pericles and Apollonius of Tyre* (1898).

595–6   Theory of the change of *Tharsia* to *Thaisa*: E. T. Clark, *Hidden Allusions*, 56–57.

596   Oxford's bestowal of angels upon Harvey in Christ's College: Harvey "Foure letters," *Works*, 183–184.

596–7   Harvey's address to Oxford before Queen at Audley End: Ward, 157–158; reprinted by R. L. Miller in Ward, *A Hundreth Sundrie Flowres*, 2nd ed., 65–66.

598–9   Mendoza's account of the Queen's reprimand of Sussex during Progress: Sussex's spat with North and Leicester; Oxford's refusal to dance before the French, his "great following," and his reference to serving the King of Spain: Ward, 160–162.

599   Dedication to Oxford of Gates's *The Defense of Militarie profession*: Barrell, *Shake. Fellow. Quar.*, VI, no. 2, April 1945, 31.

599   The Queen's grant to Oxford of the Manor of Rysing: Ward, 149.

---

601   **Chapter 30. "Shall's Have a Play of This?":** *Cymbeline*, V v.

601–2   Gilbert's tract on *a new passage to Cataia*; Hakluyt and Dee's endorsement of the quest; Lok and Frobisher as subscribers; Frobisher's expedition to Baffin Island of 1576: Quinn, 371–372; Ward, 237; *Encyclopaedia Britannica*, XI, 237b.

602   Company of Cathay chartered with Queen as leading subscriber; Frobisher's second expedition and return with 200 tons of ore: Quinn, 373; Ward, 237–238.

602–3   Frobisher's third expedition, of 1578, with fifteen ships; Oxford's letter to the Commissioners and his pledge of £3,000; the worthlessness of the ore brought back; and the collapse of the company: Quinn, 373–374; Ward, 238–239; E. T. Clark, *Hidden Allusions*, 195.

604   Shylock's craft, contempt for music, merrymaking: Van Doren, 103.

604   Simier's arts of ingratiating himself: Aikin, II, 67.

604   Simier's *connaissance . . . d'amour*: Jenkins, 218.

604   Bohun on the Queen's lasting beauty: Ibid.

605–6   The Queen's rage at Leicester's secret marriage, Sussex's intercession, and Leicester's recouping: Aikin, 68–70.

606   Alençon as the four-year focal-point of English foreign policy, with the anticipated marriage dividing the country: Read, 206.

607fn.   Burghley's memoranda on the marriage and analysis of the Queen's childbearing prospects: Ibid., 208–211.

607   Stubb's suffrance of his fate: Trevelyan, II, 123.

607   *Cymbeline* as written in author's youth and later rewritten: Robertson, 218.

607–8   *Cruelties of a Stepmother* as perhaps an early version of *Cymbeline*: E. T. Clark, *Hidden Allusions*, 75.

608   The young Seymour brothers; imprisonment by Elizabeth; Burghley's reported favoring the elder's succession: Allen, 51, 92; Jenkins, 89, 98, 101–102; Read, note 7 to p. 19, 549.

610–11   Descent of Anne Vavasor and *The Advice*: Chambers, *Sir Henry Lee*, 151.

611   Anne Vavasor, her background and entry into Court: Barrell, *Shake. Fellow. News-Letter*, III, no. 3, April 1942, 28b–29a.

611   Later career of Anne Vavasor: Gwynneth Bowen, "Sir Edward Vere and His Mother, Anne Vavasor," *Shake. Auth. Review*, no. 15, Spring 1966, 5–6.

611   Vavasors not very good at marrying: Trollope, *Can You Forgive Her?* London: Oxford University Press, 1973, 297.

613–4   Lines from Sonnets 127 and 132 on black features of the poet's mistress as repeated in *Love's Labour's Lost*: S. Lee, 122–123.

615   Performance of *A Double Maske* before Queen on 11 January 1579 and indications that it was a partial early version of *Love's Labour's Lost*: E. T. Clark, *Hidden Allusions*, 107.

615   "The Jew and Ptolome" called "good plays and sweet plays": Gosson, 30.

615   Performance of *The history of Portio and demorantes* on 2 February 1580 and probability it was *The Merchant of Venice*: E. T. Clark, *Hidden Allusions*, 191.

615–6   "He that is fast . . . any Jew there": Harvey, *Letter-Book*, 78; Editor's comment, xiii.

616   Distinction between usury and interest as of pressing concern at that time in England: Gwynneth Bowen, "The Merchant and the Jew," *Shake. Auth. Review*, no. 14, Autumn 1965, 12–13.

616   Covert allusions to Queen Elizabeth in Portia: S. Johnson, quoted by R. L. Miller in E. T. Clark, *Hidden Allusions*, 3rd rev. ed., 342.

616   Range of Elizabeth's suitors: Hume, *Courtships of Queen Elizabeth*, 33.

616   Limitation on choice of husband placed on Elizabeth and Portia by their fathers: E. T. Clark, *Hidden Allusions*, 194.

617   Performance of *The second Helene* and the possibility of its having been a first version of *All's Well*: Ibid., 102.

617   Talbot's letter on the device presented at Shrovetide by Oxford and others: Ward, 163–164.

Citations

617–8   Performance of *The history of murderous mychael* as following by a few months Holinshed's account of the murder of Arden: E. T. Clark, *Hidden Allusions*, 116–117.

618   Swinburne on qualities of *Arden* comparable to Shakespeare's: Dowden, General Introduction, *Comedies*, ix.

618   Kinship of language in Arden to that in three Shakespeare plays: E. T. Clark, *Hidden Allusions*, 121–161.

---

619   **Chapter 31.** "As the Style Shall Give Us Cause": *Love's Labour's Lost*, I i.

619–20   The tennis-court quarrel between Oxford and Sidney: Greville, 66–68.

620–1   Languet's admonition of Sidney: Ward, 171–172.
The Queen's reproof of Sidney: Greville, 69.

621   Sidney's bellicose letter to Molyneux: Allen, 142–143.

621   Languet's disappointment in Sidney at Court: *Correspondence of Sidney and Languet*, 185.

621–2   Sidney and Oxford as heads of opposing literary factions, the Areopagus, character of Oxford's poetry, his epigram, and Sidney's reply: Courthope, II, 311–313.

622–3   Rhyming contest between Willie and Perigot: Spenser, Oxford ed., 448–449.

624   Sidney's imitation of Petrarch and of Ronsard and other French writers: Sidney Lee, quoted in Looney, 299.

624   His search for words in "others' leaves": *Encyclopaedia Britannica*, XXV, 44a.

624   Approximation by Sidney in *Astrophel and Stella* of lines in Shakespeare's *Sonnets* of the blackness of his mistress's features: Lee, 123.

625   Euphuism as a linguistic movement affecting all modern European languages: Courthope, II, 312.

625   Promotion of the French version of euphuism by the Pléiade, most prominently by Ronsard: Saintsbury, *Encyclopaedia Britannica*, XI, 122b.

625–6   Appearance of the two *Euphues* books and the welcome accorded them as romances of contemporary life: Bond, I, 19–20.

626   Irresistibility of *Euphues* to highest society as being about itself: Brooke, 419.

626   Introduction to the young Athenian, Euphues: Lyly, I, 184.

626   Blount on the new English begun by *Euphues* that the Court beauty must "parlay," with the Queen as a devotee: *Encyclopaedia Britannica*, IX, 899a.

626   Extracts from *Euphues: The Anatomy of Wyt*: Lyly, I, 237.

626–7   Oxford's tenements in the Savoy: Bond, I, 17.

627   Lyly's residence at the Savoy through Burghley's interest: Bond, I, 18.

627   The author's being delivered of the first *Euphues* before his friends thought him conceived and of his sending it to a noble man to nurse: Lyly, II, 4.

627   Young Euphues as having hatched eggs his elder friends laid: Harvey, "Pierces Supererogation," *Works*, II, 124.

627   Lyly as "the fiddlestick of Oxford": Harvey, II, 212.

627   Lyly as Oxford's "minion secretary" and his "foil": Harvey, II, 132.

627–8   Sidney's condemnation and outdoing of euphuism: *Dictionary of National Biography*, XVIII, 231a–b.

Citations

628 Parallels between *Euphues* and Shakespeare: Bond, I, 165–175.

628 Lyly as the inventor of the dramatic style who introduced the great Elizabethan drama: Ibid., vi.

628 Lyly as Shakespeare's only model for comedy: Ibid., 243.

628 "What Shakespeare owes to Lyly": Ibid., 296–299.

628 Insistence upon the derivation of three of Shakespeare's comedies from Lyly: S. Lee, 64–65.

628–9 Sidney Lee's acknowledgement of doubts about Lyly's authorship of songs in his plays: *Dictionary of National Biography*, XII, 331b.

629 Lyly credited with some of "most graceful songs our drama can boast" of unproved authorship and in contrast to other inferior work: Bond, I, vii.

629 Doubt cast on Lyly's authorship of songs by their omission from original editions of his plays: Ibid., II, 265.

629 Pre-publication as Shakespeare's of songs omitted in Blount's edition of Lyly's plays surmised: Looney, 331.

629 Fairies' song from *Endymion*: Lyly, III, 59–60.

629–30 Harvey-Nashe feud as offshoot of Sidney-Oxford quarrel: Nashe, V, 73.

630fn. Harvey as having vomited Tuscanisme over a nobleman: Nashe, I, 295.

630–1 *Speculum Tuscanismi*, lampooning Oxford: Harvey, I, 83–86.

631 Harvey as having fallen "into the bowels of libeling": Lyly, III, 400.

631 Lyly blamed for having got him into trouble with Oxford: Harvey, II, 183.

631 "The noble Earl, not disposed to trouble his jovial mind": Harvey, I, 184.

631 How Harvey would have been slashed into "chippings" had he not hidden in the house of the nobleman for whom he had slashed Oxford: Nashe, III, 78.

---

632 **Chapter 32. "They Come Not Single Spies":** *Hamlet*, IV v.

632 Oxford's gift to the Queen of a jeweled ship: Cooper, II, 360.

632 Oxford's sales of estates between 1576 and 1584: Ward, 353.

633 Oxford takes over the Earl of Warwick's players: Ward, 267.

633 The Vice Chancellor of Oxford rejects Burghley's request for permission for Oxford's players to perform at the University: Ibid., 268.

633 "A pleasant conceit of Vere": Peck, ed. of 1779 (London), I, 270.

634fn. Unrecognizability of Malvolio: Rowse, *Shakespeare the Man*, 192.

635fn. Hatton as "proud and arrogant": Bohun, 360.

635 Toby Belch as Bertie Willoughby: E. T. Clark, *Hidden Allusions*, 224.

636 Estimate of the value of Drake's booty: Ward, 240. City Entertainments of Plymouth, preparing a celebration of the 400th anniversary of Drake's return, did not reply to my request for a current estimate.

636–7 Verses on the Court's passage to Plymouth, including Lord Chamberlain with his white staff: Ault, 104.

The Spanish Fury in the Netherlands, with England's turn to come next: Jenkins, 243.

638 The Cardinal's assurance that a pious assassin of Elizabeth would gain merit: Jenkins, 240–241.

638 Character of Henry Howard; connivance with Mary of Scots: *Dictionary of National Biography*, X, 29a–b, 32a.

Citations

638 Cause for Essex to distrust and despise Howard: Aikin, II, 466.

639 Castelnau's report to Paris of Oxford's accusation of his friends, whom the Queen puts under restraint, and of Oxford's alleged loss of credit and honor: Ward, 207–209.

640 Oxford's victory in another tournament: Ibid., 57.

640 The gigantic spectacle of the tilt: Strong, *Cult of Elizabeth*, 133.

641 The Spanish Ambassador Mendoza's report of Howard's taking refuge in his house and of his service to "your Majesty": Ward, 209–210.

641 Mendoza's further letter reporting the arrest of Howard, Arundel, and Southwell and of Leicester's spreading rumor of their plot against the Queen: Ibid., 215.

641 Speculation that Oxford "opened the Queen's eyes" and led to sterner measures against Roman Catholics reported by Stow: Ibid., 214.

641–2 The new and harsher penalties against Jesuits and recusants, the multiplication of executions: Bindhoff, 238–239.

642 Parson's plan to bring the Inquisition to England: Trevelyan, 131.

642 Elizabeth's lesser severity toward Catholics than Mary's toward Protestants: Ibid.

642 Riche's report of the unnamed nobleman in French costume on a foot-cloth nag: Ward, 193–194.

643 Arundel's complaint of being held prisoner while Oxford at large: Ibid., 211.

643 Howard's counter-charges against Oxford: Ibid., 212–213; Allen, 157, 159, 160; both from State Papers Domestic for 1581.

643 Southwell's note that Oxford had been drinking: Ward, 213.

645 Oxford charged by Arundel with attributing fabulous riches to Italy: Ibid., 128–129.

645 Resurrection of charge of homosexuality against Oxford: Rowse, London, *Times*, 24 April 1971.

645 Sodomy as unproved: Read, 129.

645 Fugger news-letter of April 1 reports imprisonment of Catholic nobles, one of whom has "fallen away": Fugger, 53.

645 News-letter of April 29 reports Norfolk's brother and two knights still in prison as Catholics, while Oxford arrested but released: Ibid., 55.

646 Walsingham's report of Anne Vavasor's delivery, with Oxford avowed to be the father: Barrell, *Shake. Fellow. News-Letter*, III, no. 3, April 1942, 28a–29b.

646–7 Denial of Oxford's garments to the Porter of the Tower: Ward, 211.

647 Speculation that *Richard the Third* written during Oxford's imprisonment: E. T. Clark, *Hidden Allusions*, 257–259.

647 Parallels between situations of Elizabeth and Henry VI: Ibid., 234–240.

647–8 Oxford's long letter to Burghley thanking him for dealing honorably for him with the Queen, reporting the Queen's solicitude, as ascribed to "lewd fellows"; Burghley's "evil opinion" of certain of his men: Ward: 223–224.

648 Walsingham on the Queen's desire that Lord Henry and Arundel be confronted by Oxford: Ibid., 224.

648 Burghley's thanks to Hatton; latter's correspondence with Arundel: Ibid., 225.

648–9 Frobisher on Oxford's intention to buy *Edward Bonaventure*: Ibid., 240–241.

Citations

649 Lady Oxford's touching appeal to her husband and assurance of her father's good will and her own love, of late 1581: Ibid., 226–227.

650 Fight between Oxford and Knyvet recorded by Rev. Richard Madox: Ibid., 227–228.

650 Report to Anthony Bacon that both men wounded in the fray, but Oxford the more seriously: Ibid., 227.

650 "The quarreling clamors of these new Montagues and Capulets": Feuillerat, 126.

651 The history of the feud between Oxford's men and Knyvet is condensed from two articles by Gwynneth Bowen in *Shake. Auth. Review*, no. 18, Autumn 1967, 1–7, and no. 20, Autumn 1968, 4–10, and the latter reproducing in full Burghley's letter to Leicester exonerating Oxford of blame in the feud over "the drab" and grieving over the injustice done him and therefore the writer and his daughter. Both articles are reprinted in their entirety by R. L. Miller in Looney, 3rd rev. ed. II, 85–94.

655 The earthquake in Verona of 1570: Reports cited by E. T. Clark, *Shake. Author. News-Letter*, II, no. 2, February 1941, 20.

656 Romeo's sideswipes at Elizabeth as the moon and in Tudor livery: Allen, 192.

656 Conventional representation of Elizabeth as the moon: S. Lee, 152.

---

658 **Chapter 33. "A Spirit Raised from Depth of Underground":** 2 *Henry Sixth*, I ii.

659 Alençon's amazement at ship-building and exchange of letters with Elizabeth: Jenkins, 249.

660 *Sapho and Phao* as an allegory of Elizabeth and Alençon: Bond, II, 367.

660 The play's remarkable escape from official censure: Ibid., I, 31.

660 Feuillerat on the dramatist's audacity: Ward, 277.

660–1 Performance of *Ariodante and Genevora* and likelihood of its having been first version of *Much Ado*: E. T. Clark, *Hidden Allusions*, 372 ff.

661 Derivation of *Much Ado* from tale of *Ariodante and Ginevra*: Kittredge, 159–60; Dowden, *Comedies*, 359.

661 Repetition in *Much Ado* of a line of Watson's: E. T. Clark, 377.

661 Dedication of Watson's *Hekatompathia* to Oxford; relationship of the two writers; Arber's speculation that latter contributed introductions to Watson's poems: Ward, 195–196.

661 Formation of the Queen's company incorporating a player of Oxford's; continuation of Oxford's company: Chambers, *Elizabethan Stage*, II, 5.

661–2 Elevation of the status of actors; selection of the best for the Queen's servants; Tarlton as "the wonder": Stow, *Annales*, 697a–b.

662 Oxford's acquisition of Blackfriars' and its transfer to Lyly: Bradbrook, 299; Ward 270.

662 Combination of Paul's and Oxford's boys; Oxford as patron of their Court appearances: Chambers, *Elizabethan Stage*, II, 17.

662 Lyly as "Vice Master of Paul's": Harvey, I, 212.

662 Performance of Lyly's plays at Court by amalgamated troupes: Bradbrook, 229.

662 Presentation of all Lyly's plays but one by "these children": Bond, I, 36.

Citations

662 Oxford's troupe among others performing at Guild Hall: Schoenbaum, *Documentary Life*, 89.

662–3 Irwin Smith on Bonetti's tenancy of Blackfriars and his suggesting character of Tybalt: Quoted by R. L. Miller in *Oxfordian Vistas*, 138–139.

663 Oxford's supposed quarrel with Bonetti: Ward, 269.

663 Failure of Fenton's expedition to the Spanish Main: Ibid., 242; R. L. Miller in *Oxfordian Vistas* quotes Fenton's letter to Burghley reporting his ill success, 449.

663 Death of the Oxfords' infant son: Ward, 232.

663–4 Lady Oxford's four epitaphs in verse: Barrell, *Shake. Fellow. News-Letter*, IV, no. 2, February 1943, 16–20.

665 Raleigh's letter to Burghley of the Queen's purpose to have a new "repartition" between Oxford and the accused-accusers: Ward, 245–246.

665 Howard's effort to snare Raleigh into negotiations with Spain: *Dictionary of National Biography*, X, 30b.

665–6 Burghley's report of Oxford's relative poverty and Manners's of his forgiveness by the Queen: Ward, 232–233.

666 "Can 'Polonius' . . . nickname of Burghley?" Chambers, I, 418.

666fn. Harvey's address to Burghley as "Polus": R. L. Miller, *Oxfordian Vistas* in Looney, 3rd ed., II, 432.

666 Sussex's death, his nobility and loyalty, his warning of Leicester as "the gypsy": Jenkins, 252; Aikin, II, 121.

667 Elizabeth's "blind faith in Leicester": Read, 435.

667 Oxford's plea for Burghley's help for Lumley and declaration that Burghley comes "before anyone else in the world": Ward, 245–246.

667 Lumley's career: Ibid., 245.

667–8 The Throckmorton plot; Mendoza's and Mary's part in it: Read, 287; Jenkins, 253.

668 The fate of Howard and the Earl of Arundel: E. T. Clark, *Hidden Allusions*, 493, 496–497.

668 *1 Henry Fourth* as paralleling the Northern rebellion and the Throckmorton plot: Ibid., 491 ff.; Allen, 215–218.

670–1 Dee's interest in the Northwest passage; formation of the Fellowship for its discovery; Oxford's participation; the engagement of John Davis; the lack of tangible return: Ward, 243; Quinn, 376–7.

671 Oxford's purchase of Fisher's Folly, perhaps as headquarters for his literary protégés: Barrell, *Shake. Fellow. Quar.*, VI, no. 2, April 1945, 25b.

671–2 Description of Fisher's Folly; Oxford as host to Elizabeth there: Stow, *Survey*, 167.

672–3 Munday's dedication to Oxford of *Mirrour of Mutabilitie* and *Zelauto* and to his attendants of *Sunday Examples*: Ward, 184–188.

672fn. Parallels between *Zelauto* and *The Merchant*: Kittredge, 258.

673 Munday's investigations of English Catholics on the Continent: *Encyclopaedia Britannica*, XIX, 3a.

673 Munday's turning from the stage to expose the Catholics' "unnatural treasons": *Dictionary of National Biography*, XII, 1188b.

674 Euphues' recall to Athens by heretofore unsuspected affairs: Brooke, 419.

Citations

674 Greene's education, life in London, literary success, contribution to the English novel: *Encyclopaedia Britannica*, XII, 539a–540b.

674 "An author of plays and a penner of love-pamphlets": Greene, *Works*, XII, 166.

674 "His wild career of carouse . . . pleaded guilty": Ibid., I, 34.

674 "What talk you of hell? . . . care is the less": Ibid., XII, 172–173.

674 *Master F. I.* as a precursor of *Euphues*: Bond, I, 159.

675 Influence of *Euphues* on Greene: *Dictionary of National Biography*, VII, 570b.

675 "The Ape of Euphues": Harvey, I, 183.
    Dedication of *Greene's Card of Fancy* to Oxford: Ward, 197–198.

675 Popularity of Munday's translations of romances: *Dictionary of National Biography*, XIII, 1190b.

675–6 Munday's dedications to Oxford of *The Romances of Chivalry*: Ward, 200–201.

676 Munday's versatility, contribution to public information; plays, including one for Oxford's company: *Dictionary of National Biography*: XIII, 1191a.

676 Original of *More* as written in Munday's hand: Chambers, I, 502, 503.

678 Identification of Soowthern as "Deny the Frenchman" and his connections with Oxford: Barrell, *Shake. Fellow. News-Letter*, IV, no. 6, October 1946, 71 ff.

679 Drake's hanging of Burghley's spy: Hume, 346–347.

679 Oxford's letter to Burghley complaining of his father-in-law's effort to suborn a servant; reference to his serving her Majesty: Ward, 247–248.

679–80 Showing of *Agamemnon and Ulisses* and speculation that it was an early version of *Troilus and Cressida*: Looney, 312–314; E. T. Clark, *Hidden Allusions*, 449 ff.

680 "School of rhetoric . . . amplifying art": Van Doren, 204.

680–1 The tournament honoring the anniversary of Elizabeth's coronation: Lupold von Wedel, 330–332.

---

682 **Chapter 34.** "For Fair England's Sake!": *Richard Third*, V iii.

682–4 Military developments in the Low Countries, 1584–1585; Sturm's request for a zealous commander like Oxford; Oxford's request of Burghley for financial help; his dispatch to Netherlands in command of troops; governorships in Flanders given to Sidney and Thomas Cecil; Oxford's return and capture by pirates: *Encyclopaedia Britannica*, XIII, 596b; Ward, 250–254.

685 Elizabeth's rage at Leicester's assuming the sovereignty of the States: Hume, 399.

685–6 The English force in the Low Countries under their "famous captains" and their help in Maurice's defeat of Parma: Bindhoff, 277.

685–6 The "fighting Veres," the defeat of the Spanish infantry, and the founding of England's military tradition: Trevelyan, 120–121.

686 The military zeal of Francis and Horatio Vere: *Biographia Britannica*, VI, 3998, 4006.

686 The "lewd letter" from Vavasor to Oxford: Ward, 229.

686 Thomas Vavasor a boy: Chambers, *Sir Henry Lee*, 158.

Citations

687 Inhibition of the gentleman-poet from publishing and the even greater stigma incurred by the dramatist: Sheavyn, 162–163, 168.

687 Oxford as "most excellent" of the Court in poetry: Webbe, II, 34.

687 Suppression of commendable writing by notable gentlemen owing to the scorn and derision in which poetry held: Puttenham, "The Arte of English Poesie," *Ancient Critical Essays*, I, 13.

687–8 Oxford as first among Courtly poets whose excellence would be known if their doings could be made public and as deserving of highest praise for comedy and interlude: Ibid., I, 49, 51, 63.

688 Angel Day's dedication to Oxford: Ward, 199.

688 The grant to Oxford of £1,000 by Privy Seal Warrant: Ibid., 257.

689 The singularity of a grant of such magnitude from the Exchequer: Ibid., 257–258.

689 The grant as compared in size with others: Ibid., 258–260, 355–358.

689 The 18th Earl's £200 pension: Allen, 234.

689 The grant to Oxford as making up for the former Earl's excessive splendor: Bohun, 330.

690 Elizabeth's "name for close-fistedness and avarice": Jenkins, 154.

690 Elizabeth's parsimony and the failure of her favorites to grow rich: *Dictionary of National Biography*, VI, 648a, 644b.

690 Nottingham's pension and service on all important commissions: *Dictionary of National Biography*, X, 4b, 5a.

690 Oxford's ending as "a pensioner of the Crown": Rowse, *Wm. Shakespeare: A Biography*, 122.

690fn. Question of Ward's acquaintance with Oxford's finances: Evans and Levin, 43.

691 Shaw on the theatre's determining a nation's destiny: Henderson, 153.

691 Elizabeth's support of plays fitting her subjects for war: Bohun, 297.

691 "Cross-current of English patriotism in Shakespeare's plays": Powell, Address to Shakespeare Club, 11.

692fn. Showing of "harey of cornwall" by Henslowe: Barrell, *Shake. Fellow. Quar.*, VII, no. 4, October 1946, 51b–52a, 53a.

692fn. Brook's Abridgement and *Henry the Fifth*: E. T. Clark, *Shake. Fellow. News-Letter*, I, no. 6, October 1940, 10.

692 Francis Vere and Roger Williams in joint defense of Sluys: *Biographia Britannica*, VI, 3998.

692 Roger Williams compared with Fluellen in temper and bluntness: *Dictionary of National Biography*, XXI, 441b.

692 Parallels between Fluellen and Roger Williams: Barrell, *Shake. Fellow. News-Letter*, II, no. 5, August 1941, 59–61.

692 Philip's rage at plays acted at his expense: Allen, 227–229.

693 *Tamburlane* as directed against Philip: E. T. Clark, *Shake. Fellow. News-Letter*, II, no. 4, June 1941, 47b–48a; Allen, 227–229.

694 Kyd's testimony on Marlowe's serving "my Lord" and regret of lack of clue to lord's identity: Boas, 241.

694 Gosse on date of Kyd's *Tragedy* and Lyly's influence: *Encyclopaedia Britannica*, XV, 958b.

Citations

694 Speculation that lord with whom Kyd and Marlowe were associated was Oxford, who had gathered University Wits around him: E. T. Clark, *Shake. Fellow. News-Letter*, II, no. 4, June 1941, 47b–50a.

695fn. Evidence that *Edward the Second* by the same hand as early Shakespearean historical plays: D. S. Ogburn, *Shake. Auth. Review* no. 18, Autumn 1967, 8–11.

695 Marlowe's hand hypothesized in *Arden*: Feldman, "A Preface to *Arden of Feversham*," *The Bard* (London), no. 3, 1979, 100–109.

695 Performance of plays from English Chronicle before 1588; the posting of playbills and strutting of actors in the streets; the bribing-away of Oxford's players: Collier, xiiib.

695 "English Seneca . . . will afford you whole Hamlets": Nashe, Preface to Green's *Menaphon*, *Works*, III, 315.

695 "Quite clearly directed against Kyd": Cairncross, 51.

Nashe, "impress of shipwrights" and Osric's euphuism as dating *Hamlet*: Cairncross, 82, 81.

695–6 "Volley of all the great shot": Ward, 235.

696 Willoughby's mission to Denmark and the tapestry dividing the hall: Allen, 205.

696 Boy players as chief rivals to Queen's in 1585: Chambers, I, 32.

696 Polonius' categorizing of plays and Sidney's of poetry: E. T. Clark, *Hidden Allusions*, 3rd rev. ed., 678.

696–7 *Leicester's Commonwealth*, depicting the subject as a depraved sensualist and murderer and naming Sussex as a victim: Jenkins, 257.

697 Leicester's reputation as a lecher: Jenkins, 188.

697 The exceeding length of Hamlet's speeches: S. Lee, 233.

697 Catherine's visit to court of Navarre: the real Monarcho: Kittredge, 193, 194.

698fn. *Love's Labour's Lost* dated 1589–1590: Dowden, *Comedies*, 438.

698fn. Dated 1588–1589, requiring "serious revision" of chronology: Hotson, *Shake.-Oxford Soc. Newsletter*, September 1964.

698fn. *Love's Labour's* as an "extravaganza" on "fashions and foibles in speech": Dowden, *Shakespere, His Mind and Art*, 62–63.

698fn. Influence of the *commedia dell' arte* throughout *Love's Labour's*: Kittredge, 194.

698fn. "Over-luxuriant and far-fetched method of expression" of *Love's Labour's*; its original composition in 1589: Brandes, 44, 38.

698fn. Author of *Love's Labour's* as able to "enter into aristocratic life . . . or the court of Henry VI": Chute, 103.

698 Oxford named commissioner in trial of Mary: Camden, *Annales*, Booke 6, 14.

698 "To reconsign the kingdom . . . life of Elizabeth": Swinburne, *Encyclopaedia Britannica*, XVII, 822a.

699 Mary's able defense: Ibid., 822b.

699 Walsingham's report on the unanimity of the commissioners on Mary's guilt as "compasser" of the Queen's destruction: Read, 361–362.

699 Portia's speech as appropriate to Mary's pleading her cause: Looney, 358–359.

Citations

700   The call for Mary's execution by Hatton in the Commons, Burghley in the Lords: Read, 361–362.

700   Elizabeth's effort to have her agent do away with Mary and the preference in France and Scotland for this course: Read, 378–8; Jenkins, II, 278.

700   "Her long, delicate-fingered . . . unseat her reason": Jenkins, 279.

700–1   Had Burghley "not acted as he did . . . accomplishing his downfall": Read, 370.

701   Elizabeth's inferiority to Mary in loyalty and gratitude, superiority in patriotism: Swinburne, *Encyclopaedia Britannica*, XVII, 823b–824a.

701   Burghley's report to Walsingham of his anguish at his daughter's dolour over her husband's misery and subsequent thanks to Walsingham for his care of Oxford's cause, with mention of his "lewd friends": Ward, 285–286.

701–2   Report to Walsingham of the Queen's railing against Burghley for death of Mary; healing of breach with Queen's visit to Theobalds: Read, 378, 379.

702   Burghley's letter speaking of "hinderers" of Oxford: Ward, 286–287.

702   Lady Anne, Countess of Oxford, dies; her virtues eulogized; her funeral attended by the nobility: Ward, 287–288.

703–4   Oxford's equipping a vessel in expiation of his "violences": Aikin, II, 221.

704   Leicester on Oxford's willingness to hazard his life: Ward, 289–290.

704–8   Battle of the Armada: See especially Churchill's *The New World*, 123–131.

705   The Armada, like towers and castles, in a crescent: Camden, *Annales*, Booke 3, 267–268.

705   The English fleet summoned; the embarkation of Oxford, Northumberland, et al. as the Queen commands: Stow, *Annales* (1614), 746a.

705   How unaffrighted the youth of England join their ships to the fleet, amongst them, Oxford, Northumberland, et al.: Camden, *Annales*, Booke 3, 277.

705   Verses celebrating the Lord Admiral and Oxford in battle: Ward, 291.

706   The appointment of "the disgraced, the incapable" Leicester to command of the army at Tilbury: Aikin, II, 227.

706   Leicester's report to Walsingham of Oxford's rejection of government of Harwich: Ward, 292.

707   "Howard in fight . . ."; "We pluck their feathers . . .": Churchill, *The New World*, 130.

708   Elizabeth at Tilbury "like a second Boadicea" before the "admiring soldiery": Aikin, II, 228.

---

709   **Chapter 35.** "For That Have I Laid by My Majesty . . .": *Henry Fifth*, I ii.

709–10   The celebration of the victory over the Armada and the ballad of the procession: Ward, 293–295.

710fn.   The notion that Shakespeare bore the canopy over Southampton: Rowse, *Shakespeare's Sonnets*, 259.

711   Burghley's seizure of Oxford's lands in lieu of payment for right to marry his daughter: Joel Hurstfield, *The Queen's Wards*, London: Frank Cass, 1973, 253.

711   Oxford's sale of Fisher's Folly; Cornwallis's anxiety: Barrell, *Shake. Fellow. Quar.*, VI, no. 2, April 1945, 25.

Citations

711–12   *Anne Cornwalyes her booke*, containing verses of Oxford's: Ibid., 22–25a.

712–13   Thos. Trussel's ownership of Billesley and robbery: *The Victoria History*, III, 60.

713   Trussel's survival and authorship of *Souldier: Dictionary of National Biography*, XIX, 1196a.

714   Owners of Bilton: *The Victoria History*, VI, 32;

714   Oxford's retention of Bilton: Dugdale, 196.

714   Shakespeare's revision of an earlier play in *As You Like It*: the related *Rosalynde* as euphuistic: Kittredge, 290.

715   References in Stationers' Register to "swete Olyver": E. T. Clark, *Shake. Fellow. News-Letter*, I, no. 6, October 1940, 9.

716   Martin's "sturdy . . . English prose": Churchill, *The New World*, 116.

716   Having Martin attacked in own style by Lyly, Nashe, Greene: McKerrow, *Encyclopaedia Britannica*, XVII, 750a.

716   Harvey on *Pappe* and doubt of its derivation from pen of *Euphues*: Bond, I, 56–57.

716   "Liked his brilliant young ward . . . of the young lady": Stopes, *Third Earl of Southampton*: 34.

716   Southampton's refusal to marry the girl despite heavy forfeit; report that this was "staggering sum" of £5,000: Akrigg, 32, 39.

717   Oxford's request for Burghley's permission to sell lease; his need of £300; his having found Burghley "mine honourable good Lord": Ward, 304.

717   Churchyard's letter on Oxford's delinquency in rent; Mistress Penn's complaint of the Earl's "unkind dealing": Ibid., 301–303.

718   Tribute to the *Faerie Queene* by Ignoto: Spenser, *Works*, Oxford ed., 410.

718   Sonnet to Oxford: Ibid.

719   Thalia's lament, finding Willy "dead of late" and "in idle cell": Ibid., 482.

719   Applicability of "Willy" to no one but Shakespeare, who Spenser does not mean was really dead: Rowe, xii.

719   Impossibility of character given Willy belonging to any other dramatist but Shakespeare: Collier, xxxiv.

719   Spenser's lines as applying with felicitous exactitude to Shakespeare's works: Irving, xxiv.

720   Shakespeare as at beginning of career in 1590; appropriateness of passage to Lyly: Chambers, II, 186.

720   Association of Willy with Richard Wills: Schoenbaum, 133.

720   John Farmer and his dedication to Oxford of *Divers and Sundry Waies . . . upon one Playn Song: New Grove Dictionary of Music and Musicians*, ed. by Stanley Sadie, London, Washington, D.C.: Macmillan, 1975; Barrell, *Shake. Fellow, News-Letter*, II, no. 4, June 1941, 39b–40a.

721   Oxford's proposal to Burghley to convert his annuity to lump sum to provide for children and gain settled life: Ward, 305.

721   Oxford makes Hedingham over to Burghley in trust for daughters, orders probably decayed buildings dismantled: Ibid., 306.

722   Oxford seeks monopoly on sale of oils, wood, and fruit and Queen's leave to try his title to Forest of Essex: complaint that he was browbeated: Ibid., 308–312.

Citations

722 Sale of last of Oxford's inherited lands: Barrell, *Shake. Fellow. News-Letter*, IV, no. 1, December 1942, 4a.

722 Oxford's marriage to Elizabeth Trentham: Ward, 307.

---

723 **Chapter 36.** "... And Plodded Like a Man for Working Days": *Henry Fifth*, I ii.

723 Lord Talbot's triumph on the stage: Nashe, "Pierce Penilesse," *Works*, I, 212.

724 Quotation from *Repentence*: Greene, *Works*, XII, 166.

724 Farewell letter to wife: Greene, ibid., XII, 185–186.

724 "Where wickedness did overflow"; "The dead bite not ...": Harvey, "Foure Letters," *Works*, I, 171–172.

724 Meres on Harvey's showing same inhumanity to Greene as Achilles to Hector: *Ancient Critical Essays*, II, 157.

724 Grosart on Greene's repudiation of his works in *Groatsworth*: Greene, I, 149–150.

724 "Scald, trivial, lying pamphlet": Nashe, "Pierce Penilesse," *Works*, I, 154.

725 "A surfeit of pickle herring ...": Harvey, I, 162.

725 "A good fellow ... in Christ's College"; "I and one of my fellows, Will. Monox. ...": Nashe, "Strange News," *Works*, I, 287.

725–7 *"Epistle Dedicatorie"* to "Strange News": Nashe, *Works*, I, 256 ff.

725 Identification of Apis Lapis as Sacred Ox: Phillips, 62.

726 Identification of Vaux of Lambeth: Barrell in a long analysis (pp. 55–66) of Nashe's "Epistle," *Shake. Fellow. Quar.*, V, no. 4, October 1944, 64a.

727 References to "Lord" who was Nashe's patron: Nashe, *Works*, V, 19–20.

728 Lyly as having left the service of Oxford, with whom "one always quarrelled": Rowse, *William Shakespeare*, 122.

728 Lyly reports Oxford's displeasure to Burghley: Bond, I, 28–29.

728 Lyly as having made enemies in Oxford's household: Ibid., 77.

728 Disbelief in the Stratford theory called nonsense and lunacy: Rowse, *The Spectator*, 2 June 1973.

728 Birth of a son to the Oxfords; his christening: Ward, 313.

729 Immaturity of the narrative poems: Coleridge, "A critical analysis of Shakespeare's *Venus and Adonis* and *Lucrece*," *Shakespeare Criticism*, 213.

729 *Lucrece* as the greater but with faults of immaturity: Dowden, *Histories and Poems*, 990.

730 Dedication to *Lucrece* as unique in Elizabethan literature: D. N. Smith, "Authors and Patrons," *Shakespeare's England*, II, 201.

730 Anne Vavasor's affairs, marriage, offspring: G. Bowen, "Sir Edward Vere and His Mother, Anne Vavasor," *Shake. Auth. Review*, no. 15, Spring 1966, 5–6.

731 The marriage of Elizabeth Vere and 6th Earl of Derby: Ward, 316–318.

731–3 Formation of Lord Chamberlain's company from the 5th Earl of Derby's; its membership, acquisition of Shakespeare's plays, and dominance it acquires at Court: Chambers, I, 63–64; Ward, 322.

733–4 Evidence that the Lords Chamberlain were only nominal patrons of the company and that it was under the supervision of the Lord Great Chamberlain,

Oxford, who was sometimes called Lord Chamberlain: Barrell, *Shake. Fellow. Quar.*, V, no. 3, July 1944, 33–40; recapitulated by R. L. Miller, Looney, 3rd rev. ed., II, 128–138.

733–4 Preoccupations of the 1st and 2nd Lords Hunsdon: *Dictionary of National Biography*, III, 978, 974b–975.

733–4 Hunsdon's anomalous position *re* opening of new Blackfriars playhouse: Chambers, I, 64.

734 "Inconceivable" freedom of Lord Chamberlain's players from arrest: Chute, 246.

734 Irregularities in behavior of Lord Chamberlain's men after 1604: Irving, xxxixb; Collier, liv.

734–5 Armin's serving a lord at Hackney: Feldman, *Shake. Fellow. Quar.*, VIII, no. 3, Autumn 1947.

735 Southampton's daily visits to the theatre: Stopes, *Third Earl of Southampton*, 40.

735 Report that Southampton and Rutland pass time in going to theatre daily: Ibid., 173.

735 Southampton as giving advice to the players: Ibid., 40.

Oxford's letter to Burghley with two references to his "office": Ward, 312–313.

736 Introductory verses to *Willobie*, Shake-speare and Lucrece, the "Brytan Bird": *Willobie*, 19, 20.

736 Avisa's suitors as "persons of great importance"; reason for *Willobie* among books to be burned: Harrison, ibid., 186.

736 Avisa's name "feigned"; Avisa not a "fiction" or "invention": Ibid., 6, 9.

737 "Always the same" as Elizabeth's motto; the "disingenuous disclaimer": Akrigg, 216–217.

737 Common attributes of Avisa and Elizabeth: De Luna, 3–4.

737 Elizabeth's husband as the Kingdom of England: Ibid., 5.

737 Lovers of Avisa-Elizabeth identified: Ibid., 47, 54.

737 Self-declared youth of H.W.: *Willobie*, 205.

737 H.W. as necessarily H. Wriothesley; the unriddling as of interest to Shakespeareans: Akrigg, 218–219.

737 Passage presenting H.W.: *Willobie*, 115–116.

737 Probability of H.W. as H. Wriothesley, W.S. as Shakespeare: Harrison, ibid., 214.

737 Collier's contribution to knowledge: Schoenbaum, 346–347.

737 Evidence of Shakespeare's love affair in about 1594: Chambers, I, 62.

737–8 W.S. as convincing vision of Shakespeare: Jaggard, 691.

738 Verses in which H.W. hails his friend and W.S. advises on how "*A*" may be won: *Willobie*, 119–123.

738 "Well, say no more . . . may be won": Ibid., 121.

739 "Such a translation . . . enemies of both": Stopes, *Third Earl of Southampton*, 68.

739 Lee on Southampton's knowledge of Italian and Essex's interest in him: *Dictionary of National Biography*, XXI, 1056a.

Citations

739 Essex as predominant in H.W.: De Luna, 82–94.

741 Henry May's expedition; his shipwreck on Bermuda: Hakluyt, 196–203. These pages are reproduced by R. L. Miller in Looney, 3rd rev. ed., I, 453–454.

741fn. History of *Edward Bonaventure*: Letter to author of 12 January 1981 from R. A. Morriss, National Maritime Museum.

741 Oxford's letter to Burghley on Derby's assurance of £1,000 for his daughter: Ward, 319.

741 Letter to Oxford from the French king thanking him for his "good offices" with Elizabeth: R. L. Miller in E. T. Clark, *Hidden Allusions*, 3rd rev. ed., 131–132.

742 The French . . . treat with the Lord Treasurer": Read, 538–539.

742 The Oxfords' removal to Hackney and the obscurity of the Earl's life there: Ward, 319, 348.

742 Description of King's Place, later Brooke House: William Robinson, *History of Hackney*, John Bowyer Nichol & Son, Piccadilly and Hackney, 1842.

742–3 Oxford's favor of a marriage between his daughter Bridget and the Pembrokes' son; "I have not an able body": Ward, 320.

---

744 **Chapter 37. "For It Is Parting from Us":** *Troilus and Cressida*, IV iv.

745 Burghley's statements as his end nears, and his death: Read, 545–546.

745 List of Burghley's tracts of land: Peck, 184–197.

745 Collins on Burghley's estate: Ward, 332.

745 Relationship of Trussels and Ardens: M. D. Harris, 20.

749 Affectionate letter to Oxford from Robert Bertie: Ward, 333.

749–50 What is known about Edward Vere is reproduced by R. L. Miller in *Oxfordian Vistas* 94–106 (though I do not agree that the sonnet quoted is addressed to the boy), with the full text of the letter.

750 Dedication to Oxford of Farmer's *English Madrigals*: Ward, 203–204.

750 Report that Derby penning comedies: Ward, 321.

750 Countess of Derby's entreaty to Cecil that her husband's players not be barred from their place of acting: Chambers, *Elizabethan Stage*, II, 127.

750–1 Queen's acceptance of a troupe combining Oxford's and Worcester's men and their assignment to Boar's Head: Bradbrook, 61.

751 Suggestion that third company allowed at Oxford's suit and implication that his company thus traced back almost to 1596: G. Bowen, *Shake. Auth. Review*, no. 28, Summer 1973, 5–6.

751fn. Identification of location of Boar's Head Inn: Ibid., no. 27, Winter 1972, 21.

751 Oxford's solicitation of Cecil's help in obtaining Governorship of Jersey: Ward, 333–334.

751 Oxford's appeals to Cecil for help in obtaining presidency of Wales: Ibid., 334–336.

754 Southampton's fascination with the drama as leading to over-expectation from *Richard the Second*: S. Lee, 399.

754 Essex's exhortations in streets; the mild perplexity of the public: *Encyclopaedia Britannica*, IX, 783a; Stopes, *Third Earl of Southampton*, 190.

Citations

754 "Those atheists and caterpillars . . . of our lives: Stopes, *Third Earl of Southampton*, 192.

755 "When Jacks start up, heads go down": Wood, II, 236 fn., from *Fragm Regalia*, &c, London: Sir R. Naunton, 1650, p. 57.

755 Raleigh's advice to Cecil that Essex be done away with: Wallace, 164.

755 Oxford's deputizing Effingham to sit in Parliament in his place: Ward, 352.

755 Oxford's sickness and his correspondence with Cecil on the Danvers estate: R. Ridgill Trout, *Shake. Auth. Review*, no. 17, Spring 1967, 13–16; Ward, 337.

757 The Countess of Oxford's appeal to the High Court: Ward, 337–338.

757 Printing of *Hamlet* with royal arms: Chambers, I, 408.

757 Death of Elizabeth under burden of grief for Essex: Bohun, 369; Aikin, II, 497, 494.

759 Chettle's reproach of Melicert for not dropping "one sable tear": Chambers, II, 189.

759–60 Oxford's letter to Cecil on death of Elizabeth: Ward, 340–341.

760 Renewal of Oxford's grant by James: Ibid., 355.

760 Oxford's letter on the Forest of Essex and Havering House and James's grant to him of their custody: Ward, 342, 344.

760–1 Sidney Lee's interpretation of Sonnet 107: S. Lee, 151–153.

761 Oxford's last letter, expressing gratitude to Cecil: Ward, 343–354.

763 Horatio Vere compared in equability to the Caspian Sea: *Dictionary of National Biography*, XX, 238b.

765 Oxford's final arrangements, death, and burial: Ibid., 347.

765 The Countess of Oxford's directions for her burial, her death: Ibid.

765 Percival Golding's work on the Vere family and his tribute to Oxford, with the statement that he is buried in Westminster: Phyllis Carrington, *Shake. Fellow. News-Letter*, IV, no. 4, June 1943, 42–43.

765–6 Death and interment of Oxford's cousins and son: Ibid.

766 James's letter referring to "Great Oxford": Letter to the author from G. P. V. Akrigg, 8 October 1981, citing the Historical Manuscript Commission's *Calendar of Manuscripts in the Possession of the Marquess of Salisbury*.

766 Lord Sheffield's posts: *Dictionary of National Biography*, XVIII, 116a–b.

766 Oxford's "extraordinary intellectual interests" and patronage: May, 8–9.

767 Performance of seven Shakespearean plays for James's Court; significant absence of "Shakespeare" from the scene: E. T. Clark, *Shake. Fellow. Quar.*, VII, no. 4, October 1946, 55–57.

767 Performance of *Love's Labour's Lost* for Anne of Denmark: S. Lee, 400.

767 Munday's tribute to the "most noble Earl" in dedication to his son: Ward, 201–202.

767 Poets who made Elizabeth's reign "a golden age": Peacham, 108.

767–8 Macaulay's apostrophe of the Veres; "the seventeenth earl had shone at the court of Elizabeth": Macaulay, 448–449.

Bibliography

Note: Quotations from the works of William Shakespeare are taken from the Oxford University Press edition (London: Humphrey Milford) of 1912 to 1935, prepared by W. J. Craig.

Adams, Joseph Quincy. *A Life of William Shakespeare.* Boston: Houghton Mifflin, 1923.

————. *Oenone and Paris, by T. H.* Washington, D.C.: Folger Shakespeare Library, 1943.

Aikin, Lucy. *Memoirs of the Court of Queen Elizabeth,* 4th ed. London: Longman, Hurst, Rees, Orme and Brown, 1819.

Akrigg, George Philip V. *Shakespeare and the Earl of Southampton.* London: Hamish Hamilton, 1968.

Allen, Percy. *The Life Story of Edward de Vere as "William Shakespeare."* London: Cecil Palmer, 1932.

Amphlett, Hilda. *Who Was Shakespeare?* London: Heinemann, 1955.

Ancient Critical Essays upon English Poets and Poesy. Ed. by Joseph Haslewood. London: Robert Triphook, 1811.

Ascham, Roger, *The Whole Works of Roger Ascham.* Collected by Rev. Dr. Giles. London: John Russell Smith, 1864.

Aubrey, John. *Aubrey's Brief Lives.* Ed. by Andrew A. Clark. Oxford: Clarendon Press, 1898.

Auchincloss, Louis. *Motiveless Malignity.* Boston: Houghton Mifflin, 1969.

————. *A Writer's Capital.* Minneapolis: University of Minnesota Press, 1974.

Ault, Norman. *Elizabethan Lyrics.* London: Longman's, Green, 1925.

Baldwin, T. W. *Shakspere's Small Latine and Lesse Greek.* Urbana: University of Illinois Press, 1944.

Barnett, Lincoln. *The Treasure of Our Tongue.* New York: Knopf, 1964.

Bentley, Gerald Eades. *Shakespeare: A Biographical Handbook.* New Haven: Yale University Press, 1961.

————. *Shakespeare Survey for 1948.* Ed. by Allardyce Nicoll. London: Cambridge University Press, 1948.

Bindhoff, S. T. *Tudor England.* Harmondsworth, Middlesex: Penguin Books, 1950.

Biographia Britannica. London: J. Walthoe, 1763.

Boas, Frederick S. *Christopher Marlowe.* Oxford: Clarendon Press, 1940.

Bohun, Edmund. *The Character of Queen Elizabeth.* London: Printed for R. Chiswell, 1693.

Bond, W. Warwick. *Life, Essays, Notes in The Complete Works of John Lyly.* Oxford: Clarendon Press, 1902.

Bradbrook, Muriel C. *The Rise of the Common Player.* London: Chatto and Windus, 1962.

Brandes, Georg. *William Shakespeare: A Critical Study.* New York: Macmillan, 1909.

Brooke, Tucker, "The Renaissance," in *A Literary History of England.* Ed. by Albert C. Baugh. New York: Appleton-Century, 1948.

Brown, Ivor. *Shakespeare.* London: Collins, 1949.

————. *Shakespeare.* Time Reading Program edition, 1962.

————. *Shakespeare in His Time.* Edinburgh: Thomas Nelson, 1960.

————. *Amazing Monument.* London: Heinemann, 1939.

Bibliography

————. *A Word in Your Ear.* New York: Dutton, 1945.

Brown, John Mason. *Broadway in Review.* New York: Norton, 1940.

Burgess, Anthony. *Urgent Copy: Literary Studies in Search of Shakespeare the Man.* New York: Norton, 1968.

Cairncross, Alfred S. *The Problem of Hamlet: A Solution.* London: Macmillan, 1936.

Calder, Nigel. *The Restless Earth.* New York: Viking, 1972.

Camden, William. *Annales: The True and Royal History of the famous Empresse Elizabeth, Queene of England, France and Ireland.* London: Printed for Benjamin Fisher, 1625.

————. *Remaines Concerning Britain* (1674). London: John Russell Smith, 1870.

————. *Britannia.* New Translated in English: With large additions and improvements. Pub. by Edmund Gibson of Queen's College in Oxford. London: A. S. Walle, 1695.

Campbell, Lily B. *Shakespeare's Tragic Heroes.* Cambridge University Press, 1930.

Campbell, Oscar James. "Shakespeare Himself." *Harper's Magazine,* October 1940.

Cecil, Lord David. *Hatfield House.* London: St. George's Press, 1973.

Chambers, Sir Edmund K. *William Shakespeare: A Study of Facts and Problems.* Oxford: Clarendon Press, 1930.

————. *Elizabethan Stage.* Oxford: Clarendon Press, 1923.

————. *The Oxford Book of Sixteenth Century Verse.* Oxford: Clarendon Press, 1932, 1961.

————. *Sir Henry Lee.* Oxford: Clarendon Press, 1936.

Chaplin, Sir Charles Spencer. *My Autobiography.* New York: Simon & Schuster, 1964.

Churchill, R. C. *Shakespeare and His Betters: A History and a Criticism of the Authorship Question.* Bloomington: University of Indiana Press, 1958.

Churchill, Sir Winston. *A History of the English-Speaking People.* New York: Dodd, Mead, 1956.

Chute, Marchette. *Shakespeare of London.* New York: Dutton, 1949.

Clark, Eva Turner. *Hidden Allusions in Shakespeare's Plays,* 3rd revised ed. New York: William Farquhar Payson, 1930. Ed. by Ruth Loyd Miller. Port Jefferson, N.Y.: Kennikat Press, 1974.

Collier, John Payne. "History of the English Drama and Stage to the Time of Shakespeare." *The Works of William Shakespeare.* New York: Redfield, 1856.

Collins, John Churton. *Studies in Shakespeare.* Westminster: Archibald Constable, 1904.

A Companion to Shakespeare Studies. Ed. by H. Granville-Barker and G. B. Harrison. Cambridge University Press, 1949.

Cooper, Charles H. *Athenæ Cantabrigienses.* Cambridge: Deighton Bell, 1861(?).

Correspondence of Philip Sidney and Hubert Languet. Ed. by William Aspenwall Bradley. Boston: Merrymount Press, 1912.

Courthope, W. J. *A History of English Poetry.* London: Macmillan, 1920.

Curtis, Mark H. *Oxford and Cambridge in Transition, 1558–1642.* Oxford: Clarendon Press, 1959.

David, Richard W. Introduction, *Love's Labour's Lost,* Arden Edition of Shakespeare's Works. London: Methuen, 1951.

Dawson, Giles E. *The Life of William Shakespeare.* Folger Booklet. Washington, D.C.: Folger Shakespeare Library, 1958.

De Luna, Barbara N. *The Queen Declined: An Interpretation of Willobie His Avisa.* Oxford: Clarendon Press, 1970.

Dickens, Charles. *Complete Writings of Charles Dickens.* Ed. "by his sister-in-law." Boston: Charles E. Lauriat, 1923.

Disraeli, Benjamin, Lord Beaconsfield. *Venetia.* New York: George Routledge, 1837.

Bibliography

Dowden, Edward. "Introductory Studies of the Several Plays," in *Comedies, Tragedies* and *Histories and Poems of Shakespeare*. 3 vols. London: Oxford University Press, 1911.

Drayton, Michael. *Works of Michael Drayton*. Ed. by J. William Hebel. Oxford: Shakespeare Head, 1941.

Dryden, John. *The Works of John Dryden*. Notes and Life by Sir Walter Scott. Revised by George Saintsbury. Edinburgh: William Patterson, 1882–1883.

Dugdale, Sir William. *Antiquities of Warwickshire*. London: Thomas Warren, 1656.

———. *Baronage of England*. London: Abel Roper, John Martin and Henry Herringman, 1675–1677.

Durning-Lawrence, Sir Edwin. *Bacon Is Shakespeare*. London: Gay and Hancock, 1910.

Eccles, Mark. *Shakespeare in Warwickshire*. Madison: University of Wisconsin Press, 1961.

Edel, Leon. *Henry James; The Master: 1901–1916*. New York: Lippincott, 1972.

Elze, Karl. *Essays on Shakespeare*. Trans. by L. Dora Schmitz. London: Macmillan, 1874.

Emerson, Ralph Waldo. *English Traits*. New York: Houghton Mifflin, 1903.

———. *Complete Works*, Centenary Edition. Boston: Houghton Mifflin, 1903.

Evans, Gwynne Blakemore, and Harry Levin. "Shakespeare as Shakespeare." *Harvard Magazine*. Vol. 77, no. 6, February 1974.

Feuillerat, Albert. *John Lyly: Contribution à l'Histoire de la Renaissance en Angleterre*. Cambridge: The University Press, 1910.

Fleay, Frederick G. *Life and Works of William Shakespeare*. London: John C. Nimmo, 1886.

Fox, Levi. *Stratford-upon-Avon*. Bristol: Garland Press for Corporation of Stratford-upon-Avon, 1951.

Fripp, Edgar I. *Shakespeare, Man and Artist*. London: Oxford University Press, Humphrey, 1938.

Fugger News-Letters, 2nd series. Ed. by Victor von Klarwill, trans. by L. S. R. Byrne. New York: Putnam, 1926.

Gerhart, Peter M. *Report of the National Commission for the Review of Anti-Trust Laws and Procedure,* Vol. II. *Reports of Case Studies Project and Advisory Panels*. Washington, D.C.: U.S. Government Printing Office, 15 January 1979.

Gillés, Daniel. *Chekhov: Observer Without Illusions*. Trans. by Charles Lom Markmann. New York: Funk and Wagnalls, 1967.

Goadby, Edwin. *The England of Shakespeare*. London: Cassell, 1981.

Golding, Louis Thorn. *An Elizabethan Portrait: Arthur Golding*. New York: Richard D. Smith, 1937.

Gordon, George Stuart. *Shakespeare's English*. Oxford: Clarendon Press, 1928.

Gosson, Stephen. *Schoole of Abuse*. (Licensed 1577, Published 1579.) Reprinted for the Shakespeare Society, London, 1841.

Granville-Barker, Harley. *Prefaces to Shakespeare*. Princeton University Press, 1946.

Graves, Richard. *The Spiritual Quixote: or, the Summer's Ramble of Mr. Geoffrey Wildgoose. A comic romance*. 1773; reprinted London: Crosby, 1803.

Greene, Robert. *Life and Works of Robert Greene*. Ed. with notes by Alexander B. Grosart. London and Aylesbury: Huth Library; printed for private circulation, 1881–1886.

Greenwood, Sir [G.] George. *The Shakespeare Problem Restated*. London: John Lane The Bodley Head, 1908.

———. *Is There a Shakespeare Problem?* London: John Lane The Bodley Head, 1916.

———. *Shakespeare, Lee and a Tertium Quid*. London: Cecil Palmer, 1923.

Greg, Walter W. *English Literary Autographs, 1550–1650*. Oxford University Press, 1932.

868

Bibliography

Hakluyt, Richard. *Third and Last Volume of the Voyages, Navigations, etc.* London: Bishop, Newberie and Barker, 1600.

Hallam, Henry. *Introduction to the Literature of Europe in the Fifteenth, Sixteenth and Seventeenth Centuries.* London: J. Murray, 1882.

Halle, Louis J. "Hamlet and the World," in *The Search for an Eternal Norm.* Washington, D.C.: University Press of America, 1981.

Halliwell-Phillipps, James O. *Outline of the Life of Shakespeare.* London: Longman's, 6th ed., 1886; 7th ed., 1887.

Hamblin, Dora Jane. "History's Biggest Literary Whodunit." *Life.* Vol. 56, no. 17, 24 April 1964.

Harbage, Alfred. *Conceptions of Shakespeare.* Harvard University Press, 1966.

———. *Shakespeare and the Professions.* Fred S. Tupper Memorial Lecture. Washington, D.C.: George Washington University Press, 2 April 1965.

Hardison, O. B. *Entering the Maze.* New York: Oxford University Press, 1981.

Hardy, Thomas. *To Shakespeare After Three Hundred Years.* London: Chitwick Press (50 copies), 1916.

Harris, Frank. *The Man Shakespeare and His Tragic Life-Story.* London: Frank Palmer, 1911.

Harris, Mary Dorner. *Some Manors, Churches and Villages of Warwickshire.* The Coventry City Guild, 1937.

Harrison, George B. *Introduction to Shakespeare.* England: Penguin, 1939.

———. *The Genius of Shakespeare.* New York: Harper, 1927.

Hart, Alfred. *Shakespeare and the Homilies.* Melbourne (Australia) University Press, 1934.

———. *Stolen and Surreptitious Copies.* Melbourne University Press, 1942.

Hart, Joseph C. *The Romance of Yachting.* New York: Harper, 1848.

Hartman, Sadakichi. *Shakespeare in Art.* Boston: L. C. Page, 1901.

Harvey, Gabriel. *Works of Gabriel Harvey.* Collected and with introduction and notes by Alexander Grosart. London: Printed for private circulation, 1884.

———. *Letter-Book of Gabriel Harvey, 1573–1580.* Vol. 33. Ed. with notes by Edward John Long Scott. Westminster: Nichols and Sons for the Camden Society, 1884.

———. *Gabriel Harvey's Marginalia.* Collected and ed. by G. C. Moore Smith. Stratford-upon-Avon: Shakespeare Head Press, 1913.

Hemingway, Ernest. *Men at War.* New York: Crown, 1942.

Henderson, Archibald. *George Bernard Shaw: Man of the Century.* New York: Appleton-Century, 1956.

Holinshed, Raphael. *Chronicles of England, Scotland and Ireland* (1957). London: J. Johnson et al., 1807.

———. *The Scottish Chronicles, or a Complete History and Description of Scotland.* Printed by J. Findlay, 1805.

Highet, Gilbert. *The Classical Tradition.* New York: Oxford University Press, 1949.

———. *The Powers of Poetry.* New York: Oxford University Press, 1966.

Hoffman, Calvin. *The Murder of the Man Who Was Shakespeare.* New York: J. Messner, 1955.

Hubler, Edward. *The Riddle of Shakespeare's Sonnets.* New York: Basic Books, 1962. Includes *How True a Twain* by Northrop Frye.

Huhner, Max. *Shakespeare Studies.* New York: Farrar, Straus and Young, 1952.

Hume, Martin A. S. *The Great Lord Burghley: A Study in Elizabethan Statecraft.* London: J. Nisbet, 1898.

———. *The Courtships of Queen Elizabeth.* London: E. Nashe, 1906.

Hunter, Joseph. *New Illustrations of the Life, Studies and Writing of Shakespeare.* London: J. B. Nichols and Son, 1845.

Bibliography

Ingleby, C. M. *Shakespeare's Centurie of Prayse,* 2nd ed. London: Published for the New Shakspere Society by N. Trübner, 1879.

Innes-Smith, Robert. "The Chapel-Barn of St. Stephen, Bures, and the de Vere Monuments" and "The Earls of Oxford." Combined undated and unpaginated reprint from *East Anglia Life.*

Irving, Sir Henry. *Works of William Shakespeare.* New York: Literary Digest, Funk and Wagnalls, 1927.

Isaacs, J. "Shakespeare after 400 Years." *The Listener and BBC-Television News.* London, 10 November 1966.

Jaggard, William. *Shakespeare Bibliography.* Stratford: Shakespeare Press, 1911.

Jardine, David. *Criminal Trials During the Reigns of Queen Elizabeth and James I.* London: M. A. Nattali, 1847.

Jenkins, Elizabeth. *Elizabeth the Great.* New York: Coward-McCann, 1959.

Johnson, Samuel. Preface to *Prefaces by Different Editors, with an Account of the Life and Writings of Shakespeare.* London: Johnson and Steevens, 1785, 1788.

———. *Annotations by Samuel Johnson and George Steevens and the various commentators upon Titus Andronicus.* London: John Bell, British Library, 1787.

Jones, Emrys. *The Origins of Shakespeare.* London: Oxford University Press, 1977.

Jonson, Ben. *Timber: or Discoveries; Made upon Men and Matter.* Intro. and notes by Maurice Castelain. Paris and London: Librairie Hachette, 1906.

———. *Ben Jonson's Conversations with William Drummond of Hawthornden.* Ed. with intro. and notes by R. F. Petterson. London: Blackie and Son, 1923.

———. *Works of Ben Jonson.* Ed. by C. H. Herford and Percy and Evelyn Simpson. Oxford: Clarendon Press, 1947.

Joseph, Sister Miriam, C.S.C. *Shakespeare's Use of the Arts of Language.* New York: Columbia University Press, 1947.

Kittredge, George Lyman. *The Complete Works of Shakespeare.* Boston: Ginn, 1936.

Knight, Charles. *William Shakespeare: A Biography.* London: C. Knight & Co., 1843. Revised and augmented. New York: G. Routledge, 1865. *Studies of Shakespeare.* London: C. Knight & Co., 1849.

Lawrence, Herbert. *The Life and Adventures of Common Sense: An Historical Allegory.* London: Montague Lawrence, 1769.

Learned Pig, The Story of the. by an Officer of the Royal Navy. London: R. Jameson, 1786.

Lee, Sir Sidney. *A Life of William Shakespeare.* New York: Macmillan, 1909.

———. *Shakespeare's Comedies, Histories and Tragedies. 1623 Facsimile.* Oxford: Clarendon Press, 1902.

Lewis, Wyndham. *The Lion and the Fox.* New York: Harper, undated.

Looney, J. Thomas. *"Shakespeare" Identified as Edward de Vere, the 17th Earl of Oxford.* London: Cecil Palmer, 1920. 2nd ed. Foreword by William McFee. New York: Duell, Sloan and Pearce, 1949. 3rd ed. Ed. and augmented by Ruth Loyd Miller. Port Washington, N.Y.: Kennikat Press, 1975.

———. *The Poems of Edward de Vere.* London: Cecil Palmer, 1921. (Reprinted Looney, "Shakespeare Identified," 3rd ed., Vol. II, Appendix III.)

Lubbock, Percy, ed. *The Letters of Henry James.* New York: Scribner, 1920.

Lyly, John. *Complete Works of John Lyly.* Ed. with Life, Bibliography, Essays and Notes by R. Warwick Bond. Oxford: Clarendon Press, 1902.

Macaulay, Thomas Babington, Lord. *Miscellaneous Writings.* London: Longman, Green, Longman and Roberts, 1860.

McManaway, James G. *The Authorship of Shakespeare.* Folger Booklet. Washington, D.C.: Folger Shakespeare Library, 1962.

Bibliography

Madden, D. H. *The Diary of Master William Silence*. London: Longman's, 1907.

Marder, Louis. *His Exits and His Entrances: The Story of Shakespeare's Reputation*. Philadelphia: Lippincott, 1963.

Markham, Gervase. *Honour in His Perfection*. London: Benjamin Fisher, 1624.

Marston, John. *The Scourge of Villanie, Three Bookes of Satyres*. No author named. London: John Buzbie, 1598.

Martin, Milward W. *Was Shakespeare Shakespeare? A Lawyer Reviews the Evidence*. New York: Cooper Square Publishers, 1965.

May, Stephen W. *The Poems of Edward de Vere, Seventeenth Earl of Oxford, and of Robert Devereux, Second Earl of Essex. Studies in Philology*. Chapel Hill: University of North Carolina Press. Vol. XXVII, no. 5, Early Winter, 1980.

Meres, Francis. *Palladis Tamia. Wits Treasury* (1598). *Ancient Critical Essays upon English Poets and Poësy*. Ed. by Joseph Haslewood. London: Robert Triphook, 1815.

Miller, Ruth Loyd. *Oxfordian Vistas*. Forms Vol. II of Looney, 3rd ed.

Müller, (Friederich) Max. *The Science of Language*. Delhi: Munchi Ram Manhar Lal. ca., 1861.

Murphy, William M. "Thirty-six Plays in Search of an Author." Schenectady, N.Y.: Union College Quarterly, *Symposium*. Vol. 3, no. 3, Summer 1964.

Nashe, Thomas. *Works of Thomas Nashe*. Ed. by Ronald B. McKerrow, rev. by F. P. Wilson. Oxford: Basil Blackwell, 1958.

Neilson, William Allen, and Ashley Horace Thorndike. *Facts About Shakespere*. New York: Macmillan (1913), 1937.

Nichols, John. *Progresses and Public Processions of Queen Elizabeth*. 3 vols. London: J. Nichols and Son, 1823.

Nicoll, Allardyce. *Shakespeare*. London: Methuen, 1952.

Nims, John Frederick. Introduction to "Arthur Golding's translation" of Ovid's *Metamorphoses* of 1567. New York: Macmillan, 1965.

Noble, Richmond S. H. *Shakespeare's Biblical Knowledge*. London: Society for Promoting Christian Knowledge, 1935.

Notestein, Wallace. *The English People on the Eve of Colonization*. New York: Harper, 1954.

Ogburn, Dorothy, and Charlton Ogburn. *This Star of England*. New York: Coward-McCann, 1952.

Ogburn, Dorothy, and Charlton Ogburn, Jr. *Shake-speare: The Man Behind the Name*. New York: William Morrow, 1962.

Ovid (Publius Ovidius Naso). *Metamorphoses*. Trans. by "Arthur Golding." Ed. with intro. and notes by John Frederick Nims. New York: Macmillan, 1965.

Oxford Book of Sixteenth Century Verse. Chosen by E. K. Chambers. Oxford: Clarendon Press (1932), 1961.

Payne, Robert. *By Me, William Shakespeare*. New York: Everest House, 1980.

Peacham, Henry. *The Complete Gentleman* (1622). Ithaca, N.Y.: Cornell University Press, for Folger Shakespeare Library, 1962.

Peck, Francis. *Desiderata Curiosa*. London (no pub. named), 1732–1735.

Percy, Thomas. *Reliques of Ancient English Poetry*. London: Bickers & Son, 1876.

Phillips, Gerald W. *Lord Burghley in Shakespeare*. London: Thornton Butterworth, 1936.

Pitcher, Seymour M. *The Case for Shakespeare's Authorship of "The Famous Victories."* London: Alvin Redman, 1962.

Plato. *The Dialogues of Plato. Phaedrus*. Trans. by B. Jowett. 2 vols. New York: Random House, 1937.

Poems Written by Wil. Shake-speare, Gent. London: Tho. Cotes, and are to be sold by Iohn Benson, 1640.

Pollard, Alfred W. *Shakespeare's Fight with the Pirates.* London: Alexander Moring, 1917.

Powell, J. Enoch, M.P. Address to the Shakespeare Club, Stratford on Avon. *Shake. Auth. Rev.* No. 25, Autumn 1971. Reprinted in E. T. Clark, *Hidden Allusions,* 2nd ed., 1974, by R. L. Miller, 722–728.

———. Letter, *Books and Bookmen,* London, January 1977.

Prouty, Charles Tyler. *Introduction.* Facsimile ed. of First Folio prepared by Helge Kökeritz. New Haven: Yale University Press, 1954.

———. George Gascoigne's "A Hundreth Sundrie Flowres." Columbia: University of Missouri Press, 1942.

? Puttenham, George or Richard. *The Arte of English Poesie* (1589). *Ancient Critical Essays.* Ed. by Joseph Haslewood. London: Robert Triphook, 1811.

Quinn, David B. *North America from Earliest Discovery to First Settlements: The Norse Voyages to 1612.* New York: Harper & Row, 1977.

Raleigh, Sir Walter (d. 1618). *The History of the World. The Works of Sir Walter Raleigh.* London: Oxford University Press, 1929.

Raleigh, Sir Walter (d. 1922). *Shakespeare.* New York: Macmillan, 1907.

Read, Conyers. *Lord Burghley and Queen Elizabeth.* New York: Knopf, 1960.

———. *Mr. Secretary Cecil and Queen Elizabeth.* London: Jonathan Cape, 1955.

Register of the Company of Stationers, A Transcript of, 1554–1640. Ed. by Edward Arber. London: Privately printed, 1875.

Riverside Shakespeare. The Complete Works. Intro. by Harry Levin. Textual ed., Gwynne Blakemore Evans. Boston: Houghton Mifflin, 1974.

Robertson, John M. *Shakespeare and Chapman.* London: Unwin, 1917.

Rogers, Byron. "Bard Thou Never Wert?" *Sunday Telegraph Magazine.* London, 26 January 1973.

Rowe, Nicholas. "Some Account of the Life, &c, of Mr. William Shakespeare." *The Works of Mr. William Shakespeare in Six Volumes.* London: Jacob Tonson, 1709.

Rowse, Alfred L. *William Shakespeare: A Biography.* New York: Harper & Row, 1963.

———. *Shakespeare's Sonnets.* New York: Harper & Row, 1964.

———. *Shakespeare's Southampton.* London: Macmillan, 1965.

———. *Shakespeare the Man.* London: Macmillan, 1973.

Sampson, George. *The Concise Cambridge History of English Literature,* 2nd ed. Cambridge: The University Press, 1961.

Sargent, Ralph M. *At the Court of Queen Elizabeth: The Life and Lyrics of Sir Edward Dyer.* London: Oxford University Press, 1938.

Schoenbaum, Samuel. *Shakespeare's Lives.* New York: Oxford University Press, 1970.

———. *William Shakespeare: A Documentary Life.* Oxford: Clarendon Press, 1975.

———. *Shakespeare: The Globe and the World.* Folger Shakespeare Library. New York: Oxford University Press, 1979.

Scott, Giles O. W. *Shakespeare's Heraldry.* London: Dent, 1950.

Seldon, Camille. *Derniers Jours de Henri Heine.* Paris: Calmann-Lévy, 1884.

Shakespeare, William. *Comedies, Histories & Tragedies.* Facsimiles of First Folio (1623). (1) Prepared by Helge Kökeritz, Intro. by Charles Tyler Prouty. New Haven: Yale University Press, 1954. (2) Prepared by Charlton Hinman. New York: Norton, 1968.

———. *The Comedies of, The Tragedies of, The Histories and the Poems of William Shakespeare.* (Separate vols.) Prepared by W. J. Craig, with Introductory Studies of the several Plays by Edward Dowden. London: Oxford University Press, Humphrey Milford (1912), 1935.

Bibliography

————. *Poems Written by Wil. Shake-speare, Gent.* London: Tho. Cotes, and are to be sold by Iohn Benson, 1640.

Shakespeare Criticism: A Selection, 1623–1840. London: Oxford University Press, Ed. of 1968.

Shakespeare Cross-Examination. Ed. by Richard Bentley. Composed of articles and letters on various candidates for Shakespeare's place originally published in the *American Bar Association Journal.* Chicago: Cuneo Press, 1961.

Shakespeare Survey (Annual). Ed. by Allardyce Nicoll. Cambridge University Press, 1948.

Shakespeare's England: An Account of the Life & Manners of his Age. Oxford: Clarendon Press, 1916.

Sheavyn, Phoebe A. B. *The Literary Profession in the Elizabethan Age.* Manchester University Press, 1967.

Sinsheimer, Hermann. *Shylock: The History of a Character.* London: Gollancz, 1947.

Smith, Alan Gordon. *William Cecil: The Power Behind Elizabeth.* London: Kegan Paul, Trench Trübner, 1934.

Smith, Roger H. *Paperback Parnassus.* Boulder, Colo.: Westview Press, 1976.

Smith, William Henry. *Bacon and Shakespeare: An Inquiry Touching Players, Playhouses, and Play-Writers in the Days of Elizabeth.* London: John Russell Smith, 1857.

Soowthern, John. *Pandora.* Reproduced from the Original Edition, 1584, by Columbia University Press as Publication No. 43 of the Facsimile Text Society, 1938.

Spenser, Edmund. *The Works of Edmund Spenser. With Observations on his Life and Writings,* by J. C. Philadelphia: Willis P. Hazard, 1857.

————. *Poetical Works of Edmund Spenser.* Ed. and with notes by J. C. Smith and E. de Selincourt and Introduction by de Selincourt. London: Oxford University Press (1912), 1950.

Spurgeon, Caroline. *Shakespeare's Imagery and What It Tells Us.* Cambridge: The University Press, 1935.

Steevens, George. *Prefaces by Different Editors; with an account of the Life and Writings of Shakespear As Prefaced by [Samuel] Johnson and Steevens to their Edition of his works.* London, 1788.

Stopes, Charlotte C. *Burbage and Shakespeare's Stage.* London: Alexander Moring, the De La More Press, 1913.

————. *The Life of Henry, Third Earl of Southampton, Shakespeare's Patron.* Cambridge: The University Press, 1922.

Stow, John. *A Survey of London.* (Written in 1598, printed 1603.) Introduction and notes by Charles Lethbridge Kingsford. Oxford: Clarendon Press, 1971.

————. *The Annales of England.* London: Ralfe Newberry, 1592.

————. *The Annales, or Grand Chronology of England.* London: Thomas Adams, 1614.

Strong, Roy. *Portraits of Queen Elizabeth.* Oxford: Clarendon Press, 1963.

————. *Cult of Elizabeth.* London: Thomas and Hudson, 1977.

Swinburne, Algernon Charles. General Introduction to the Works of Shakespeare, preceding *The Comedies of Shakespeare.* London: Oxford University Press, 1911.

————. *Complete Works of Algernon Charles Swinburne.* Vol. XI. *Prose Works.* Bonchurch Edition. Ed. by Sir Edmund Gosse and Thomas James Wise. London: Heinemann, 1926.

Taine, Hippolyte Adolphe. *History of English Literature.* Trans. by Henri van Laun. New York: A. L. Burt, undated.

Taylor, Elizabeth. *In a Summer Season.* New York: *Viking,* 1961.

Theobald, Lewis. Preface to *The Works of Shakespeare* (1733). *Eighteenth Century Essays on Shakespeare.* Ed. by D. Nichol Smith. Oxford: Clarendon Press, 1963.

Tenison, Eva Mabel. *Elizabethan England.* Royal Leamington Spa, County of Warwick: At the Sign of The Dove and the Griffin, 1933.

Bibliography

Thorpe, Day. "Does the Folger Want the Truth About Shakespeare?" Washington, D.C.: *The Sunday Star and Daily News*, 3 December 1972.

The Three Parnassus Plays. Ed. and with Introduction and Commentary by James B. Leishman. London: Ivor Nicholson & Watson, 1949.

Traubel, Horace. *With Walt Whitman in Camden*. Boston: Small, Maynard, 1906.

Trevelyan, George Macauley. *History of England*. Garden City, N.Y.: Doubleday, 1953.

Trevor-Roper, Hugh R., The Lord Dacre of Glanton. "What's in a Name?" Paris: *Réalités* (English-language ed.), November 1962.

Turberville, George. *Epitaphes, Epigrams, Songs and Sonets*. London: Henry Denham, 1567. Reprinted with intro. by Richard J. Panefsky in Scholars' Facsimiles and Reprints. Delmar, N.Y., 1977.

Twain, Mark. "Is Shakespeare Dead?" *My Autobiography*. New York: Harper, 1909.

Van Doren, Mark. *Shakespeare*. New York: Holt, 1939.

———. *The Noble Voice*. New York: Henry Holt, 1946.

Victoria History of Warwick County, The. Ed. by L. F. Salzman. London: Oxford University Press, 1951.

Wallace, Willard M. *Sir Walter Raleigh*. Princeton University Press, 1959.

Ward, Bernard M., Capt. *The Seventeenth Earl of Oxford (1550–1604), from Contemporary Documents*. London: John Murray, 1928.

———. *A Hundreth Sundrie Flowres*. From the Original Edition. London: Frederick Etchells and Hugh Macdonald, 1926. 2nd ed., ed. and with notes by Ruth Loyd Miller. Port Washington, N.Y.: Kennikat Press, 1975.

Webbe, William. *A Discourse of English Poetry* (1586). *Ancient Critical Essays*. Ed. by Joseph Haslewood. London: Robert Triphook, 1815.

Wedel, Lupold Von. "A Knight Errant," in *Queen Elizabeth and Some Foreigners*. Ed. by Victor von Klarwill, trans. by T. H. Nash. London: John Lane, the Bodley Head, 1928.

Weekley, Ernest. *The English Language*. New York: Jonathan Cape & Harrison Smith, 1929.

Whitman, Sidney. *Personal Reminiscences of Prince Bismarck*. London: John Murray, 1902.

Whitman, Walt. "November Boughs," in *Complete Poetry and Prose of Walt Whitman, as prepared by him for the Death bed Edition*. New York: Pelligrini and Cudahy, 1948.

Willobie his Avisa (1594). With essay by G. B. Harrison. London: John Lane; New York: Dutton, 1926.

Wilson, Frank Percy. *Marlowe and the Early Shakespeare*. Oxford: Clarendon Press, 1953.

Wilson, John Dover. *The Essential Shakespeare*. Cambridge University Press, 1932.

Witts Recreations Selected from the Finest Fancies of Modern Muses. London: Humphrey Blanden, 1640.

Wood, Anthony à. *Athenæ Oxonienses* (1691–1692). Hildesheim, Germany: Georg Olms, 1969.

Wordsworth, Charles, Bishop. *Shakespeare's Knowledge and Use of the Bible*, 4th ed., rev. London: Eden, Remington, 1892.

Wright, Louis Booker. "The Anti-Shakespeare Industry and the Growth of Cults." Charlottesville: *Virginia Quarterly Review*, Vol. 35, no. 2, Spring 1959.

———. *Shakespeare for Everyman*. New York: Washington Square Press, Simon & Schuster, 1964.

———. *The Folger Library General Reader's Shakespeare*. (With Virginia A. La Mar.) New York: Washington Square Press, Simon & Schuster, 1960.

Bibliography

Reference Works

Encyclopaedia Britannica, 11th ed. New York: Encyclopaedia Britannica, Inc., 1910–1911.

Dictionary of National Biography. Ed. by Sir Leslie Stephen and Sir Sidney Lee. London: Oxford University Press, 1921–1922.

Origins: A Short Etymological Dictionary of Modern English. By Eric Partridge. New York: Macmillan, 1963.

Oxford Universal Dictionary on Historical Principles, 3rd ed. Prepared by William Little, H. W. Fowler, and J. Coulson. Rev. and ed. by C. T. Onions. Oxford: Clarendon Press (1933), 1955.

Special Periodicals

The Shakespeare Fellowship News-Letter, later *Quarterly.* New York.

The Shakespeare-Oxford Society Newsletter. Successor to the above. Currently Baltimore.

The Shakespearean Authorship Review. London.

The Shakespeare Newsletter. Pub. and ed., Louis Marder. Currently Evanston, Ill.

General Index

Index

Index

Index

Index

Index

Index

Index

Index

Index

and Sidney, 545, 588, 619–25, 629
and Spenser, 401, 622–3, 718–20 (?)
and Lyly, 43–44, 626–29, 660, 662, 674
and Harvey, 44, 498, 596–97, 627
and Nashe, 630fn., 631, 725, (725–26?)
and Marlowe, 138
and Greene, 674–75
as Euphues, 673–74
as Will Monox, 727
and *Groats-worth*, 727
acts at Court, 617
as having forgotten God, 654
death of first son, 663
Membership in Royal Privy Council, 760, 766
his command in Low Countries, 683–85, 691
his £1,000 annuity, 402, 688, 721, 759, 760
and trial of Mary Queen of Scots, 698
and the Armada, 703–06, 710
  and his bearing the canopy at celebration, 710
residences on the Avon, 712–13
and Marprelate, 716
addiction to music, 720, 750
marries Elizabeth Trentham, 722,
  and birth of their son, 728
makes Hedingham over to Burghley, 721
in charge of Lord Chamberlain's men (?), 66–67, 734,735
charged with destroying buildings at Hedingham, 414, 721
is thanked for good offices by French king, 741
identified as Shakespeare by Looney, 145–47, 164–65
as strongest candidate for Shakespeare's honors, 148–49, 317–18, 341–42, 373
objections to his identification as Shakespeare:
  his dates, 382–390
  quality of his verse, 390–397
  his character, 397–402
his lack of disqualification as Shakespeare, 318, 373
similarities of his writing to Shakespeare's, 201, 381, 391, 393–396, 498, 518, 527–28, 583, 586–88, 679, 683, 751
reasons for concealment of his authorship, 189–91, 524, 657, 687
reasons for his selection of name "Shakespeare," 597, 729
extolling of his ancestors in plays, 420, 425–26
official decision to deny him credit for plays, 194, 745
his feeling about enforced anonymity, 190–92, 525–26, 746
his likely acquaintance with Shakspere and treatment of in plays, 746, 747–49
his ultimate triumph foreseen (?), 401, 746
his later ill health, 742, 755, 760
devoted letter from nephew, 749
asks Robert Cecil's help with Queen, 751–52, 755
and trial of Essex and Southampton, 754

puns on Raleigh's part in Essex's death, 755, 756, 761
letters from, 201, 506, 507, 508, 541–42, 545–49, 559, 561, 602, 647–48, 667, 679, 683, 717, 721, 735–36, 742, 751–52, 755–56, 760, 761
  and selective destruction of, 399–400
death and burial of
self-depictions of in Shakespeare: *See All's Well, As You Like It, Cymbeline, Hamlet, Henry Fourth Pt. 1, Henry Fourth Pt. 2, Henry Fifth, King John, King Lear, Love's Labour's Lost, Measure for Measure, Merchant of Venice, Merry Wives, Much Ado, Othello, Romeo and Juliet, The Tempest, Troilus and Cressida, Twelfth Night, Winter's Tale.*
Oxford, Henry de Vere, 18th Earl of, 470, 728, 765, 766, 767–68
Oxford, John de Vere, 7th Earl of, 411
Oxford, John de Vere, 12th Earl of, 426
Oxford, John de Vere, 13th Earl of, 412, 426–29
Oxford, John de Vere, 14th Earl of, 429
Oxford, John de Vere, 15th Earl of, 412, 429–30, 432
Oxford, John de Vere, 16th Earl of, 408, 416, 430, 432, 433, 435, 455
Oxford, Richard de Vere, 11th Earl of, 411, 425
Oxford, Robert de Vere, 3rd Earl of, 413, 419–20
Oxford, Robert de Vere, 5th Earl of, 411, 421
Oxford, Robert de Vere, 6th Earl of, 421–22
Oxford, Robert de Vere, 9th Earl of, 422–23
Oxford, Robert de Vere, 19th Earl of, 767
Oxford House, 492, 712

Paget, Charles, 639, 698
Pallas Athena, 97, 238, 729
Palmerston, H. J. T., 3rd Viscount, 151
Paperback Parnassus, 5
Parma, Alexander Farnese, Duke of, 564, 637, 683, 685–86, 706
Parsons, Robert, 642
Pater, Walter, 386
Patience, Harold, 410–11
Paul's Boys, 388, 716
Pavier, Thomas, 62fn., 218
Payne, Robert, 224, 258
Peacham, Henry, 306, 767
Peck, Francis, 386, 633, 745
Peele, George, 60, 61
Pembroke, Mary Sidney, Countess of, 50, 216
Pembroke, William Herbert, 3rd Earl of, 12, 113, 216, 220, 221, 225, 742–43, 801
  as "W. H." of *Sonnets*, 332–33
Penn, Julia, 717–18
Penn, S. L., 794–95
Penzance, James Plaisted Wilde, Baron, 297–98, 301
Pepys, Samuel, xvi
Percy, Henry, called "Hotspur," 467
Perowne, Stewart, 304
Phelps, William Lyon, 258, 394
Philip II, 476, 492, 637, 708
  his anger at stage-plays, 692

885

Index

Index

First Folio, 12–13, 79, 82, 103, 218–19,
 272, 789, 790, 801
 shortcomings of, 238–39
 characterization of by Stratfordians, 70–72,
  74, 76, 80, 83, 88, 95, 316, 327, 383
 payment to, for performances, 65–66, 734
 his name, first appearances of, 3, 6, 729
  as a pseudonym, 93–99, 736, 740
  and hyphenation of, 97–98
  and variants of, 97
 first reference to, 736
 poems, edition of 1640, 236–38
 poems copied by Anne Cornwallis, 711
 his alleged blunders, 219, 221, 306–08
  as revealed in his works, 352, 357–363,
   365–72
 his plays as topical, 368, 371, 461, 504fn.,
  616
 as "imitative," 383, 449
 and Ovid, 94, 96, 106–07, 195, 214
 his alleged debt to Lyly, 628
 and Golding, 443, 447–48
 and Castiglione, 498–99
 and the Pléiade, 625
 and *Sir Thomas More*, 122, 676–77
 as Spenser's Willy, 719
 and *Willobie*, 736–40
 disappearance of his MSS, 239
  and disposition of (?), 789–91
 failure to mourn Queen's death, 759
 death of, 11, 112, 206, 261, 334–36
 vocabulary, grammar, and rhetoric, 242fn.,
  291–93
 knowledge of Continent, 143–44
  and of Italy, 302–04
 as spokesman of the Renaissance, 458, 459
 his political conservatism and nobleman's
  outlook, 90–91, 240–71
 his contempt for money, 262–63
 need to redeem realm expressed by, 189,
  462, 569
 frame of reference of, 272, 291
 knowledge of hunting, 263–66
  and sympathy for quarry, 269–70
 knowledge of sports of nobility, 263–69
  of falconry, 266–69
 knowledge of politics, 261–62
 knowledge of fishing, 265
 education of, 285, 291, 310, 312
 feeling for flowers and nature, 310–12, 438,
  439
 love and knowledge of music, 313
 acquaintance with art, 304–06
 experience of war and the sea, 313–16, 387,
  388fn.
 and English patriotism, 666, 691
 knowledge of the classics and classical languages, 242fn., 285, 287–89, 300
 knowledge of modern languages and literature, 389–91
 knowledge of Bible, 290–91, 447, 679
  and contribution to King James translation, 300
 knowledge of law, 296–98
 knowledge of medicine, 308–10, 316–17
 acquaintaince with geology and physics, 300

Shakespeare Authorship Society, 147, 742
Shakespeare Birthplace Trust, 24, 157, 792,
 793
Shakespeare Quarterly, 5, 174–75
Shakespeare-Oxford Society (orig. Shakespeare
 Fellowship), 121, 147, 178, 181, 797
Shakespeare's England, 263–64, 295–96, 305,
 730
Shakspere, Anne, 25, 26, 34, 75
Shakspere, John, 16, 24, 25, 26, 28, 92, 274
Shakspere, William:
 case for as Shakespeare, xvi, 13, 41
 appeal of legend of, 160–61
  and profitability to Stratford, 156, 797
  and extent of disbelief in, xvii, 137fn.,
   151–52
 life of, 14, 15–17, 24–37, 102, 113, 212
  and marriage of, 14, 26
 his offspring, 26, 31, 33–34, 36
 his education, 42, 272–279
 as a teacher, 27, 283–85
 his removal to London, 27
 as an actor, 13, 16, 28, 30, 31, 42, 65–66,
  98–105, 195fn., 209
 as theatrical shareholder, 29–30, 34, 194,
  197, 209
 experiences attributed to him, 26–27, 149,
  285–84
 question of how he grew rich, 80
 his wit, 15, 16, 19, 103, 215, 748
 supernatural power of his "genius," 154,
  282, 294
 his signatures and doubtful literacy, 30–1,
  32, 36–37, 42, 117, 277
 his parents' and daughters' illiteracy, 117
 his lack of intellectual interests, 42, 111
 his name as not Shakespeare, 14fn., 20, 92–
  93
 irreconcilability of his authorship with *Sonnets*, 337, 341
 his lack of connection with Shakespeare's
  works, 35, 42, 71, 72–73, 114, 130,
  354
 his disregard of plays' fate, 35–36, 76, 77,
  81, 217, 789
 his lack of standing in Stratford, 38–39, 42,
  101–03, 113, 128
 his disqualifications summarized, 17, 20,
  111–14
 unattractive character of, 28, 74–76
 deer-stealing by, 16, 357
 as thieving play-broker (?), 193
 his coat of arms, 28, 74, 75
 disappearance of documents relating to,
  123
 conjectured acquaintance with Southampton,
  258, 259, 331–32
 failure to capitalize on favor shown plays by
  James, 767
 failure to eulogize Queen on her death, 759
 his part in dissimulation of authorship (?),
  192–94, 197, 745, 765
 last years, 31–33
 his will, 33–35
 death of, 37, 112
 his burial and tombstone, 37, 38–39

887

Index

Index

Index of Literary Works

Index

Index